5OOO FACTS AND FANCIES

A CYCLOPÆDIA OF IMPORTANT, CURIOUS, QUAINT, AND
UNIQUE INFORMATION

IN

HISTORY, LITERATURE, SCIENCE, ART, AND NATURE

INCLUDING NOTEWORTHY HISTORICAL EVENTS ; CIVIL, MILITARY, AND RELIGIOUS IN-
STITUTIONS ; SCIENTIFIC FACTS AND THEORIES ; NATURAL CURIOSITIES ; FAMOUS
BUILDINGS, MONUMENTS, STATUES, PAINTINGS, AND OTHER WORKS OF ART
AND UTILITY ; CELEBRATED LITERARY PRODUCTIONS ; SOBRIQUETS
AND NICKNAMES ; LITERARY PSEUDONYMS ; MYTHOLOGICAL AND
IMAGINARY CHARACTERS ; POLITICAL AND SLANG TERMS ;
DERIVATIONS OF PECULIAR WORDS AND PHRASES ;
ETC., ETC.

BY

WILLIAM HENRY P. PHYFE

AUTHOR OF " 12,000 WORDS OFTEN MISPRONOUNCED "
" HOW SHOULD I PRONOUNCE? " ETC.

REVISED AND CORRECTED EDITION

Trifles make perfection, but perfection is no trifle.—*Michael Angelo.*

I have here made a nosegay of culled flowers, and have brought nothing of my own
but the string that ties them.—*Montaigne.*

G. P. PUTNAM'S SONS
NEW YORK AND LONDON
The Knickerbocker Press

REPUBLISHED BY GALE RESEARCH COMPANY, BOOK TOWER, DETROIT, 1966

Library of Congress Catalog Card Number 66-24369

PAPER USED IN THIS EDITION IS
A FINE ACID FREE PERMANENT/DURABLE PAPER
COMMONLY REFERRED TO AS "300-YEAR" PAPER

The Knickerbocker Press, New York

TO THE
MEMORY OF MY MOTHER

PREFACE

IT is a well-known fact that, although works of reference abound, the majority of them are limited to some special field of inquiry and frequently fail to furnish the desired information : in consequence, people are continually confronted, in their conversation and reading, with queries that they are unable to answer, owing to the lack of suitable books. It is indeed true that the answers to these queries may generally be found in works of reference, but the vast number of volumes that must needs be consulted, renders them practically unavailable for the average inquirer, while the full series of such volumes is rarely found even in well-equipped libraries.

In the present work the effort has accordingly been made to bring together such a selection of '' Facts and Fancies '' as will fairly represent the needs of the ordinary reader. In this task the author trusts he has succeeded, and desires to call attention to the following points :

(1) The articles—over 5000 in number—have been carefully selected from a very wide range of topics, and represent much that is important, curious, quaint, and unique in history, literature, science, art, and nature.

(2) In order to secure space for a large number of articles, they have generally been made concise,—thus affording room for many that must otherwise have been excluded.

(3) The topics included comprise noteworthy historical events ; civil, military, and religious institutions ; scientific facts and theories ; natural curiosities ; famous buildings, monuments, statues, paintings, and other works of art and utility ; celebrated literary productions ; sobriquets and nicknames ; literary pseudonyms ; mythological and imaginary characters ; political and slang terms ; derivations of peculiar words and phrases; etc.

(4) The list of authorities consulted is too large to be given. It may

be said, however, that more than 200 works of reference have been made use of in the preparation of this cyclopædia, and that this labor has been supplemented by a large amount of original investigation.

(5) On disputed points in dates, statistics, etc. (which are much more numerous than the reader might suppose), the author has followed what appeared to be the most reliable authority.

(6) The number of cross-references will be found unusually large,—thus facilitating the use of the book.

(7) The dates in parentheses, following the names of rulers, include the years during which they exercised authority ; in the case of other individuals these dates indicate the years of birth and death.

(8) Pronunciations of proper names have not been given, since these may generally be found in the author's handbook—*12,000 Words Often Mispronounced.*

In conclusion, the author sincerely hopes that this collection of " 5000 Facts and Fancies " will be found to provide the reader with the peculiar kind of information sought.

W. H. P. P.

August 25th, 1901.

Revised April 23, 1913.

LIST OF ABBREVIATIONS.

The following abbreviations are made use of in this book :

A.D. = Anno Domini.

Ar. = Arabic.

b. = born.

B.C. = Before Christ.

d. = died.

fl. = flourished.

Fr. = French.

Ger. = German.

Gr. = Greek.

Heb. = Hebrew.

It. = Italian.

Lat. = Latin.

pl. = plural.

prop. = properly.

Span. = Spanish.

Turk. = Turkish.

Five Thousand Facts and Fancies

A

A1. A symbol used in *Lloyd's Register of British and Foreign Shipping* and in the *Record of American and Foreign Shipping* in rating vessels for insurance. The condition of the ship's hull is indicated by *letters*, and that of its anchors, cables, etc., by *figures*. Thus, A1 signifies hull first-rate, furniture ditto ; A2, hull first-rate, furniture second-rate. The expression A1 has come into general use to denote anything first-class.

Aaron's Breastplate. A piece of embroidery highly wrought, and worn by the Jewish high-priest upon his breast. The front was set with 12 precious stones, on each of which was engraved the name of one of the tribes of Israel. These stones were arranged in 4 rows, and were probably placed in the following order :

First row.	Zebulun.	Issachar.	Judah.
	Carbuncle.	*Topaz.*	*Sardius.*
Second row.	Gad.	Simeon.	Reuben.
	Diamond.	*Sapphire.*	*Emerald.*
Third row.	Benjamin.	Manasseh.	Ephraim.
	Amethyst.	*Agate.*	*Ligure.*
Fourth row.	Naphthali.	Asher.	Dan.
	Jasper.	*Onyx.*	*Beryl.*

Abacus. An instrument for calculation, consisting of a frame crossed by stiff wires, on which balls or beads are strung. The word is said to owe its derivation to the Hebrew *abak* (*dust*), because the Orientals used tables covered with dust for computations and diagrams. The multiplication-table, invented by Pythagoras, is termed *Abacus Pythagoricus.*

The word *abacus* often refers to the uppermost part of the capital of a column,—the part between the cushion of the capital and the architrave.

Abaddon. The angel of the bottomless pit, mentioned in *Revelation* ix, 11 : " And they had a king over them, which is the angel of the bottomless pit, whose name in the Hebrew tongue is Abaddon, but in the Greek tongue hath his name Apollyon.'' Milton also refers to Abaddon in *Paradise Regained*, iv, 624. The word is derived from the Hebrew *abad* (*lost*), and means *the lost one.* Abaddon must not be confounded with the two angels mentioned by Klopstock in *The Messiah :*—one of which is Obaddon, the angel of death, and the other Abbadona, the repentant devil. See *Apollyon.*

Abattoirs (*Fr. Slaughter-Houses*). First established in 1810 by Napoleon I, who decreed that five abattoirs should be erected near Paris. These were opened in 1818. Edinburgh established them in 1851, London in 1855, and the United States in 1866.

Abbassides. A family of Arab caliphs that ruled at Bagdad from 750 to 1258 A.D. They were 37 in number, and traced their descent from Abbas ben Abd-al-Motalleb, the paternal uncle of the prophet Mohammed. Among their number was the famous Haroun al-Raschid, who reigned from 786 to 809. Under the rule of this enlightened dynasty, literature and the arts were sedulously cultivated and Bagdad became the Oxford of her time. The Abbassides succeeded the Ommiades, whom they overthrew. See *Ommiades.*

Abbaye, L'. A military prison in Paris, built in 1522 and demolished in 1854. In 1789, the French Guards that had refused to fire on the populace were confined there, but were afterwards released by the mob. In September, 1792, 164 persons imprisoned in L'Abbaye were murdered by the infuriated Republicans, led by Maillard. At this time (September 2-5, 1792), at least 1200 persons were massacred in Paris, — among them the lovely Princess de Lamballe. These atrocities are known as the "September Massacres." "À l'Abbaye !" was a famous rallying-cry during the French Revolution. See *September Massacres*.

Abbotsford. The name given by Sir Walter Scott (1771–1832) to his residence on the banks of the Tweed, from a tradition that the abbots of Melrose forded the river there, in olden times. The house was begun in 1817, and completed in 1824. It is chiefly interesting as the home of the poet and novelist, and contains several valuable relics. Scott had lived at Abbotsford about a year when reverses overtook him through the failure of his publisher. Although liable for about $600,000, the great author asked only for time ; and in five years realized for his creditors the sum of nearly $400,-ooo. To accomplish this herculean task, he labored 10, 12, and sometimes 14 hours a day. Scott died at Abbotsford in 1832, and by 1847 the property was entirely disencumbered of debt.

A. B. C. Club. The name of a Parisian club of Republican enthusiasts, who professed to relieve the *abaissés*, or depressed. Their insurrection on the 5th of June, 1832, was suppressed with bloodshed on the following day. A narrative of these events is found in Victor Hugo's *Les Misérables* (1862).

Abderian Laughter. Scoffing laughter, — so named from Abdera, the Thracian seaport, and birthplace of Democritus, the scoffing or laughing philosopher. See *Abderite, The*.

Abderite, The. A sobriquet conferred upon Democritus (470 ?–362 ? B.C.), the laughing philosopher, who

was born at Abdera in Thrace. See *Abderian Laughter*.

Abdications. The following are the most important abdications of rulers in history :

(1) *Voluntary.*

Sulla, Roman Dictator..........	B.C.	79
Diocletian, Roman Emperor	A.D.	305
Charles V., Emperor of Germany,	"	1555
James II of England *..........	"	1688
Philip V of Spain	"	1724
Victor Amadeus of Sardinia......	"	1730
Charles of the Two Sicilies......	"	1759
Amadeus of Spain..............	"	1873
Milan I of Servia...............	"	1889

(2) *Compulsory.*

John Balliol of Scotland........	A.D.	1296
Stanislaus II of Poland.........	"	1795
Francis II of Germany..........	"	1804
Charles IV of Spain.............	"	1808
Gustavus IV of Sweden.........	"	1809
Louis Bonaparte of Holland.	"	1810
Napoleon I of France	"	1814
Napoleon I of France	"	1815
Charles X. of France...........	"	1830
Louis Philippe of France........	"	1848
Ferdinand of Austria...........	"	1848
Pedro II of Brazil	"	1889

Abdiel. The faithful seraph who alone, among the hierarchy of angels, opposed Satan, and preserved his allegiance to his Maker. Milton, in *Paradise Lost*, v, 896–903, thus describes him :

——" the Seraph Abdiel, faithful found
Among the faithless, faithful only he ;
Among innumerable false, unmoved,
Unshaken, unseduced, unterrified,
His loyalty he kept, his love, his zeal ;
Nor numbers, nor example, with him
        wrought
To swerve from truth, or change his con-
        stant mind,
Though single."

Abecedarian Hymns or Psalms. Hymns or psalms, the verses of which commence with the consecutive letters of the alphabet. The 119th Psalm is a notable example of this. It was a custom of the early Church to compose

* His flight was declared an abdication by Lords and Commons.

hymns and psalms of this kind,—each part having its proper letter at the head of it. The Christian Church probably borrowed this custom from the Hebrew service, and used it as a device to aid the memory.

Abecedarians. An Anabaptist sect of the 16th century, — founded by Storch, a disciple of Luther. They taught that all *human* knowledge was a hindrance since it prevented men from heeding God's voice inwardly instructing them ; and that the only means of obviating this was to learn nothing,—not even the alphabet. With them, to learn was to risk salvation. See *Anabaptists.*

Abélard and Héloïse. The romance of Abélard and Héloïse is, in its passion and subsequent misfortunes, one of the most famous in history. Abélard was a man of extensive learning, and the father of the so-called scholastic theology. He established a school of divinity in Paris, of which Guizot says: "In this celebrated school were trained one pope (Celestine II), 19 cardinals, more than 50 bishops and archbishops, French, English, and German ; and a much larger number of those men with whom popes, bishops, and cardinals had often to contend, such men as Arnold of Brescia, and many others. The number of pupils who used at that time to assemble round Abélard has been estimated at upward of 5000." When about 35 years of age (1118), Abélard formed the acquaintance of Héloïse, a niece of Fulbert, a canon in the Cathedral of Paris. Her age, at this time, is variously estimated at from 17 to 20. The issue of the *liaison* between them was a son, named Peter Astrolabus. Abélard afterwards married Héloïse—some say, under compulsion. Some time after, he retired to the monastery of St. Denis, and persuaded Héloïse to withdraw to Argenteuil, near Paris. Her relatives became enraged at this ; and, charging Abélard with deception, re-

venged themselves by performing upon him a nameless mutilation. Abélard, from that time, devoted himself to theology ; and, in 1142, died of grief at St. Marcel, whither he had retired for his health. Héloïse begged his body, and buried it in the convent of the Paraclete, of which she was the abbess. In 1164 she was buried by his side. In 1800, the remains of Abélard and Héloïse were taken to the Museum of French Monuments, and later were transferred to the Cemetery of Père-Lachaise, where they now rest. See *Paraclete ; Tomb of Abélard and Héloïse.*

Abernethy Biscuits. These biscuits were not named after the famous Scotch surgeon, Abernethy. It is stated that when the surgeon was told by a patient that he ate his biscuits every morning for breakfast, Abernethy replied : "*My* biscuits ! I 've nothing to do with them ! They were called after the baker that introduced them, whose name was *Abernethy.*"

Abigail. A name familiarly given to a lady's maid, in allusion to Abigail, the handmaiden that introduced herself to David.

"And when Abigail saw David, she hasted and lighted off the ass, and fell before David on her face, and bowed herself to the ground," 1 *Samuel* xxv, 23.

Abiogenesis (*Gr. ἀ, without, βίος, life, γένεσις, origin*). A name given to the doctrine of the origin of living from non-living matter. It was first used by Professor Huxley, in his *Address before the British Association* in 1870, in lieu of the less accurate expression, "spontaneous generation." The doctrine of *abiogenesis* is not generally accepted by scientists. See *Biogenesis.*

Abolitionists. The name given to a band of political agitators, in the Northern states of the American Union, who demanded the immediate and total abolition of human slavery in the United States. Their views were at first deemed extreme, and little heed was paid to them ; but, after 1820, their influence rapidly increased. It was through the labors of the Abolitionists that the North was finally awakened to a realization of the iniquity of negro-slavery. The Civil War (1861–1865) put an end to slavery in the United States, and thus the ends of the Abolitionists were attained. See *Anti-Slavery Society, American.*

Abou Hassan. A rich young merchant of Bagdad, who is miraculously transported to the palace of Haroun al-Raschid. By a stratagem of the monarch, Abou Hassan is treated with every courtesy, and is twice made to believe himself the caliph. He finally becomes the caliph's friend and companion. A similar trick is played upon Christopher Sly, the tinker, in the Induction to the *Taming of the Shrew.*

Aboukir, Battle of. (1) A desperate battle fought on July 25th, 1799, at Aboukir, Egypt,—13 miles northeast of Alexandria,—between 5000 French soldiers commanded by Napoleon Bonaparte, and 15,000 Turks under Mustapha. The French attacked the Turks in their intrenched camp, and, after a desperate struggle, routed them with great slaughter. The Turkish army was annihilated, and the survivors threw themselves headlong into the sea, in the vain hope of escaping destruction by swimming to their ships. The brilliant charge of the French cavalry, commanded by Murat, greatly contributed to the success of the day.

(2) On March 8th, 1801, Sir Ralph Abercromby's expedition to Egypt landed at Aboukir, in the face of the French forces, and defeated them in the battle that ensued. Abercromby died of the wounds received in this action, on March 28th, 1801. This engagement is sometimes called the Battle of Aboukir.

(3) The Battle of the Nile—a famous naval contest fought on August 1st, 1798 — is also known as the Battle of Aboukir, because fought in the bay of that name. See *Nile, Battle of the.*

Abracadabra. A mystical word, constructed out of certain letters of the alphabet, and supposed to be an antidote against ague and fevers. The word was generally arranged in the form of an equilateral triangle inverted,— each line being shorter than the preceding one by the omission of the final letter, and the letter *a* alone remaining as the apex. It was written on parchment, and suspended around the neck by a linen thread. It was worn as an amulet for nine days ; and was finally thrown backward, before sunrise, into a stream running towards the east. The following arrangement of the letters is the one generally seen:

Abraham, Heights (or Plains) of. An eminence near the city of Quebec, where, on September 13th, 1759, was fought a desperate battle between the English under General Wolfe, and the French under the Marquis de Montcalm. Both commanders fell in the contest, but the victory remained with the English. A monument to the memory of General Wolfe has been erected on the field,—marking the spot where he fell.

Absalom and Achitophel. A political satire written by John Dryden (1631–1700), in defence of Charles II, the " David" of the poem, and against the Whig party. "Absalom " was the Duke of Monmouth, the natural son of Charles II, and " Achitophel " was the Earl of Shaftesbury. The

Duke of Buckingham was satirized as
"Zimri." It is considered by many
the most vigorous, elastic, and finished
satire in the English language.

Abstinence. Among the most famous cases of abstinence on record are
the following. The first five are generally considered mythical.

(1) St. Anthony lived to the age of
105, on 12 ounces of bread and water
daily.

(2) James the Hermit lived to the
age of 104.

(3) St. Epiphanius lived to the age
of 115.

(4) Simeon the Stylite lived to the
age of 112.

(5) Kentigern, commonly called St.
Mungo, lived to the age of 185.

(6) Cicely de Ridgway (1347) is said
to have fasted 40 days to avoid plead-
ing, when accused of murdering her
husband. She was discharged as miraculously saved.

(7) Dr. Tanner of New York City
fasted 40 days,— from June 28th to
August 7th, 1880. His weight was
reduced from 157½ lbs. to 121½ lbs.

(8) Louise Latteau, said to have
lived 12 years without food. Died,
August, 1883, at the age of 33.

(9) Giovanni Succi fasted at the
Westminster Aquarium, London, for
40 days, ending April 26th, 1890. He
lost about 20 lbs. Drank water and
smoked. On the 20th of December,
1890, Succi ended a fast of 45 days,
and lost somewhat less than a pound
per day. Drank water. At the Westminster Aquarium, London, he commenced a fast of 52 days, but stopped
January 29th, 1892, after completing
43 days.

The following are well authenticated
impostures.

(1) Ann Moore, "the Fasting Woman of Tutbury," claimed to have
lived 20 months without food. Exposed in 1808.

(2) Cavanagh, an Irishman, claimed
to have lived two years without food.
Was exposed and imprisoned in 1841.

(3) Sarah Jacobs, a Welsh girl, said
to have lived more than a year without
food. Died from exhaustion, 1869.
Her parents were sentenced to imprisonment for fraud, July 15th, 1870.

Abydos, Tablet of. A genealogical
tablet, in hieroglyphics, of the ancestors of Rameses II (fl. 2300 B.C.), and
dedicated to them. It was discovered
in 1818, in the ruined temple of Osiris,
at Abydos, an ancient city of Upper
Egypt, on the left bank of the Nile.
It was purchased for the British Museum in 1837. A similar tablet, but
more complete, was discovered in 1865
by Mariette, the famous French Egyptologist. It is now in Paris.

Academic School of Philosophy.
A school of philosophy founded by
Plato the Athenian (B.C. 429-347),
and so named because his lectures
were delivered in the "Academy" or
groves of Academus, near Athens. It
comprised the *Old Academy*, which
consisted of Plato and his immediate
disciples ; the *Second* or *Middle Academy*, led by Arcesilaus ; and the *New
Academy*, or sceptical school of Carne-
ades. Platonic doctrines, as taught
by Philo and Antiochus respectively,
are often spoken of as the *Fourth* and
Fifth Academies. See *Academy*.

Academy. A pleasure-ground situated a mile northwest of Athens, and
adorned with beautiful trees, statues, and altars. It was said to have
been presented to the city for gymnas-
tic exercises by the mythical hero
Academus,— hence the name. Other
authorities state that Cimon, the son of
Miltiades, adorned it and presented it
to the city. Lewes, in his *Biographical History of Philosophy*, says that it
"was planted with lofty plane-trees,
and adorned with temples and statues;
a gentle stream rolled through it, with

' A sound as of a hidden brook
  In the leafy month of June,
 Which to the sleeping woods all night
 Singeth a quiet tune.'

It was a delicious retreat, ' for contemplation framed.' The longing thoughts of posterity have often hovered round it as the centre of myriad associations. Poets have sung of it. Philosophers have sighed for it." The word " academy " has come, in later times, to mean a place of instruction, or an association of learned men for the promotion of literature, science, or art. See *Academic School of Philosophy.*

Academy, French (*Fr. L'Académie Française*). The most important and best known of the five academies composing the French Institute, the other four being L'Académie des Inscriptions et Belles-Lettres, L'Académie des Sciences, L'Académie des Beaux-Arts, and L'Académie des Sciences Morales et Politiques. It was founded by Cardinal Richelieu in 1635, and consists of 40 members,—popularly known as " The Forty Immortals." Its objects are to prepare a dictionary of the French language, and to render the Gallic tongue pure and capable of treating the arts and sciences. The first edition of the dictionary appeared in 1694 ; it reached its 7th edition in 1878. It has been severely criticised, and is by many considered inferior to the great work of Littré. Owing to its extremely conservative tendencies, the Academy has frequently chosen its members from among men whose careers were practically ended. Hence its humorous designation — the *Hôtel des Invalides of Literature.* Many well-known men of letters have failed of election to the French Academy, and the term " the forty-first chair " has come to designate a man of note whose scholarship entitled him to membership in that body. See *Forty Immortals ; Institute of France.*

Acadia. The original and, at present, the poetic name of Nova Scotia and New Brunswick. It was given to that region by the French, who settled there in 1604. The word is said to be derived from *Shubencadia,* the name of one of the rivers of Nova Scotia. The

English claimed the country by right of discovery, and, after years of contest, it was finally ceded to them in 1713. In 1755, the French inhabitants of Acadia numbered between 14,000 and 15,000. Being deemed a dangerous element in the community, many of them were kidnapped, transported, and dispersed among the inhabitants of the Atlantic coast. More than 1000 were carried to Massachusetts alone. This barbarous and inhuman deed forms the subject of Longfellow's *Evangeline.*

Acanthus. A genus of plants, of the order *Acanthaceæ,* whose foliage is said to have suggested to Callimachus, in 540 B.C., the design of the Corinthian capital. It is related of him that, on the death of his daughter, he placed a basket of flowers on her grave, and covered it with a tile to prevent the wind from blowing it away. When next he visited the spot, an acanthus had grown around the basket, and had assumed a form so pleasing to the architect that he forthwith introduced the design into his compositions. See *Architecture, Orders of.*

Accadians. A people of Turanian or non-Aryan origin, said to have come from the north of Europe and Asia, and to have settled in Mesopotamia long before the advent of the Assyrians and Babylonians. From them, these last mentioned nations derived much of their early culture, and to them is attributed the earliest form of cuneiform writing. They had libraries 17 centuries before the Christian era. In *Genesis* x, 10, we find the city of " Accad " mentioned as one of four cities in the land of Shinar,— the others being Babel, Erech, and Calneh.

" According to Gunter." A phrase, in common use, to describe anything that has been correctly and properly done. Gunter was an English mathematician of eminence, who died in 1626. He was the inventor of a chain and a scale, known respectively as *Gunter's Chain* and *Gunter's Scale*.

" The expression ' according to Hoyle ' is also common ; and an old fellow who never played a game of whist in his life, always said ' according to *Hodge*.' "—Bartlett's *Dictionary of Americanisms*.

Aceldama. A field, south of Jerusalem, purchased by the priests with the " thirty pieces of silver " returned to them by Judas, and used as a "potter's field " or burial-place for strangers. Its reputed site is on a hillside, opposite the Pool of Siloam. It is no longer used as a place of interment. The word means, in Chaldee, " field of blood."

Acetylene. A luminous hydrocarbon gas ($C_2 H_2$), with a disagreeable odor. It is found in coal-gas. It was discovered by Berthelot, and made known in 1862. Sometimes called *ethine*.

Achæan League. A confederation of 13 cities of the northern part of the Peloponnesus, established about 80 years after the close of the Trojan war. It exercised little influence upon Grecian affairs till the time of Alexander's successors. The Achæan League was revived in the year 280 B.C. by the four cities Dyme, Patræ, Tritæa, and Pharæ, and was subsequently joined by other towns. It afterwards extended itself through Greece, gaining in power and influence till 146 B.C., when Greece came under the power and dominion of Rome. It was not till the 3rd century B.C. that the confederation was known as the Achæan League. See *Ætolian League*.

Acheron. The river of " Eternal Woe," and one of the five rivers of the infernal regions, — the others being Cocytus, Lethe, Phlegethon, and Styx. The word " Acheron " is often used by later writers to designate *all* of the lower world.

"Sad *Acheron* of sorrow, black and deep."
Paradise Lost, II, 578.

Achilles of England. A sobriquet conferred upon Arthur Wellesley (1769-1852), Duke of Wellington.

Achilles's Tendon. The name given to the tendon that attaches the soleus and the gastrocnemius muscles of the calf of the leg to the heel-bone. It can resist a tension straining of 1000 pounds' weight ; and yet, as in the case of a sudden strain, it may be easily ruptured. It is so called from the fable of Achilles, whose mother held him by the heel when she dipped him in the Styx.

Acrocorinthus. A solitary and steep mountain—1900 feet in height—rising from the Corinthian plain. The city of Corinth was built upon its northern slope, and its summit served as the citadel of the town for 3000 years. The site of Corinth is indicated by the ruins of a few Doric columns,— the only remains of the ancient city.

" Stranger, wilt thou follow now,
And sit with me on *Acro-Corinth's* brow?"
Byron.

Acropolis of Athens. The ancient citadel of Athens— sometimes called Cecropia, from its reputed founder, the mythical Cecrops – was built upon a rock, 500 feet above the Attic plain. This eminence was 1150 feet in length from east to west, and 500 feet in width from north to south; and was accessible on the west side only,— through the Propylæa or " Entrances," built by Pericles. Upon its summit were the world-famous Parthenon,— sacred to Minerva, — the Temple of Wingless Victory, the Erechtheum, and other structures. Between the Parthenon and the Erechtheum stood the colossal figure of Minerva,— the protectress of the city, — 70 feet in height. See *Erechtheum ; Nike-Apteros, Temple of ; Parthenon ; Propylæa*.

Acta Diurna (*Lat. Daily Doings*). A newspaper or gazette published daily at Rome, under the Republic and Empire. Its origin is attributed by some to Julius Cæsar (100–44 B.C.) ; by others to Servius Tullius (550 B.C.). Haydn's *Dictionary of Dates* gives 691 B.C. as the time of its first appearance. It contained the daily proceedings of the senate and the people, as well as records of births, deaths, marriages, divorces, edicts, executions, etc.

Acta Eruditorum (*Lat. Doings of the Learned*). A literary journal,— the first of its kind that appeared in Germany. It lasted 100 years (1682–1782). Its best years were previous to 1754. It was in this journal that Leibnitz, the eminent scientist and philosopher, first enunciated his theory of the Infinitesimal Calculus.

Acta Sanctorum (*Lat. Doings of the Saints*). A title given to any collection of narratives of the lives of ancient martyrs and saints of the Greek and Roman Catholic Churches. Also more specifically, the name of a work commenced by one John Bolland of Antwerp, a Jesuit, in 1643, and continued by certain Jesuit divines, known as "Bollandists." In 1794, the work comprised 54 volumes. Six additional volumes have appeared since that year. In the narrative, the "lives" follow the order of the calendar. The volumes contain the lives of at least 30,000 saints, and have enlisted the services of 33 collaborators. The work contains about 50,000 folio pages, and is valued at $650.

Actium, Battle of. A naval battle fought off the promontory of Actium on the west coast of Greece, between the fleet of Octavius Cæsar and those of Mark Antony and Cleopatra, on September 2nd, 31 B.C. In the early part of the engagement — while the result of the contest was still in doubt — Cleopatra abandoned the struggle, and fled with her 60 galleys. Antony recklessly followed her, and gave the victory to Octavius. The abandoned fleet fought desperately for some time after, but was finally vanquished. The land-forces, after waiting in vain for seven days for the return of Mark Antony, surrendered to Octavius. Antony thereupon fell upon his sword, and Cleopatra — failing to win the regard of Octavius — also committed suicide.

Actresses. Actresses were unknown in ancient times,— the female parts in plays being assumed by men and eunuchs. Charles II (1660–1685) is said to have first encouraged women to appear on the stage in England, in 1662. Queen Anne, wife of James I, had previously appeared at a theatre at court. In 1656, Mrs. Colman performed the part of *Ianthe*, in Davenant's *Siege of Rhodes* before a select audience. Mrs. Davenport as *Roxalana*, and Mrs. Saunderson (afterwards Mrs. Betterton) as *Ianthe*, were the first bona-fide English actresses. They first appeared in 1661.

Acts of Merit. The following are the " acts of merit " recognized by the Roman Catholic Church. They are five in number :

(1) Almsgiving.
(2) Confession.
(3) Penance.
(4) Vows.
(5) Communion.

Adamites. A Gnostic sect first heard of in Africa about 130 A.D. They abstained from all carnal indulgences,— hoping thus to reach the state of man's innocence before the fall. They rejected marriage, and appeared quite naked at their religious assemblies. Their chief was Prodicus. A similar sect called *Picards*, from the name of its founder, appeared in Bohemia about 1421, but was almost totally destroyed by Ziska. See *Gnostics ; Pre-Adamites.*

Adam's Profession. A phrase applied to agriculture and gardening. According to *Genesis*, Adam, in his state of innocence, was directed to dress and keep the garden of Eden, and, after his fall, was driven out to till the soil by the sweat of his brow.

Shakespeare makes reference to this fact in *Hamlet*, v, 1:

"There is no ancient gentlemen but gardeners, ditchers, and gravemakers ; they hold up *Adam's profession*."

Addison of the North. A sobriquet conferred upon Henry Mackenzie (1745–1831), on account of the purity and finish of his literary style.

Addison's Disease. A serious disease of the supra-renal capsules, so called because described at length by its discoverer, Dr. Thomas Addison, of Guy's Hospital, London, in 1855. One of its symptoms is a bronzing of the skin, which increases until the patient assumes the appearance of a mulatto. The disease occurs much more frequently in males than in females ; and is rarely met with in patients under 10 or over 50 years of age.

Adersbach Rocks. A remarkable sandstone formation near the village of Adersbach, in Bohemia. It occupies a tract 5 or 6 miles in length, and 3 in breadth. It has not been produced by any violent convulsion of nature, but is simply the result of the rain, frost, and other atmospheric agencies, which have worn and carved the soft sandstone into thousands of fantastic shapes. There are hundreds of tall pinnacles,— two of which, the " Praying Monk " and the " Sugarloaf," are especially noticeable. It is a perfect labyrinth of tortuous passages, and the explorer without a guide is liable to lose his way.

Admirable Crichton (written also *Creighton*). James Crichton, surnamed the " Admirable," was born in Scotland in 1560. He was educated at St. Salvator's College, St. Andrew's, where he was graduated master of arts, at the age of 14. According to the generally received account, he was a classical scholar, a poet, a musician, a sculptor, a painter, an actor, a horseman, and a fencer; and excelled in all.

During the two years following his graduation he was in France, where he seems to have served in the army. He drifted thence to Venice, and in 1581 went to Padua, where he overcame all the scholars at the university, in public disputations. He is said to have been fatally stabbed by a gang of desperadoes led by his own pupil, Vincenzo Gonzaga, son of the Duke of Mantua. The date of his death is uncertain, —somewhere between the years 1585– 1591. His great reputation for versatility has been much questioned. Early in his brief career he dedicated a Latin poem to Aldus Manutius, a grandson of the founder of the famous " Aldine Press." Aldus was in the habit of praising, in extravagant terms, promising young strangers at the Italian universities, and doubtless extolled Crichton's accomplishments unduly. His faculty of memory, however, was marvellous ; and his skill as a fencer, remarkable. See *Aldine Editions*.

Admirable Doctor. An epithet bestowed upon Roger Bacon (1214–1292), an English monk of the Franciscan order. He was, incontestably, the greatest philosopher of his time. His great work — the *Opus Majus* — was written about 1265, and first printed in 1733. It treats of nearly all the sciences. He was accused of practicing the art of magic ; and, in 1278, a council of the Franciscans, jealous of his superiority, condemned his writings and committed him to prison in Paris, where he remained for ten years. He died at Oxford about 1292. See *Opus Majus*.

Adonais. The name of the elegy on Keats, written by Shelley. The word was coined by Shelley to call attention to the similarity between the untimely death of Keats and that of Adonis. See *Adonis*.

Adonis. A beautiful young boy, beloved by Venus and Proserpine. They quarreled about his possession, but the dispute was settled by Jupiter, who decreed that Adonis should annually spend eight months with Venus in the upper world and four months with Proserpine in the lower world. Adonis was fatally wounded by a wild boar, during the chase, and was changed by Venus into an anemone. She yearly mourned him on the anniversary of his death. Shakespeare has commemorated the love of Venus for Adonis in a long descriptive poem, entitled *Venus and Adonis*.

Adrian's Wall. See *Hadrian's Wall*.

Adriatic Sea Wedded to the Doge. This custom was instituted by Pope Alexander III (1159-1181), who, in 1174, drew a gold ring from his finger and gave it to the Doge of Venice in token of the victory of the Venetian fleet at Istria, over Frederick Barbarossa. The Doge was requested to drop a similar ring into the Adriatic on Ascension Day of each year, in honor of the event. This, accordingly, became the annual custom at Venice ; and, in consequence, a consecrated ring was each year thrown into the sea by the Doge, in the presence of his nobles, with the declaration : " We wed thee, O sea, in sign of true and perpetual dominion." The Bucentaur or state-galley was not used on these occasions until some centuries later. See *Bucentaur*.

Adullam, Cave of. See *Cave of Adullam*.

Adullamites. The attempt, by the ministry of Lord John Russell and Mr. Gladstone, to extend the franchise in 1866, led many of the Liberals to secede from their party and vote with the Conservatives. The term *Adullamites* was applied to them in consequence of a remark of John Bright, wherein he compared these recalcitrant members to the outlaws that had fled with David to the cave of Adullam. See *Cave of Adullam*.

Advancement of Learning. The

title of a philosophic treatise by Lord Bacon (1561-1626). It was published in 1605; afterwards enlarged and translated into Latin, and published in 1623, under the title, *De Augmentis Scientiarum*. It is the introductory book of the *Instauratio Magna*, and lays down the first principles of Bacon's system of philosophy. See *Instauratio Magna*.

Advent. A season of preparation for Christmas, as Lent is for Easter. It includes the four Sundays previous to Christmas,—the first being the nearest Sunday to St. Andrew's Day (November 30th), before or after. Since the 6th century, this season has been recognized as the beginning of the church year. In the Greek Church, the Advent season comprises forty days, and, in England, in the early days of Christianity, it was of the same duration.

Adventists. A religious sect in the United States, originally followers of William Miller (1781-1849). They teach the speedy second coming of Christ, and practise adult baptism. They predicted the end of the world in October, 1843. Despite their many mistakes in prophecy, they have continued to increase ; and in 1900, according to the *World Almanac*, their numbers amounted to 89,482 communicants and 1491 ministers. The Adventists were formerly known as *Millerites*. See *Millennium*.

Ae Fond Kiss. The title of a song written by Robert Burns (1759-1796). It is supposed to refer to his parting with Clarinda. In it occur the familiar lines :

" But to see her was to love her ;
Love but her and love forever.
Had we never lov'd sae kindly,
Had we never lov'd sae blindly,
Never met—or never parted,
We had ne'er been broken-hearted."

Sir Walter Scott says : " These exquisitely affecting stanzas contain the essence of a thousand love-tales."

Æginetan Marbles. A collection of sculptures that decorated the pediment of the temple of Pallas Athene, at Ægina,— an island off the western coast of Attica. They were discovered in 1811, and excavated by a party of Germans, Danes, and English. They were purchased by Ludwig, Crown-Prince of Bavaria, for the Glyptothek at Munich. One group represents a combat between Greeks and Trojans for the body of Achilles. These " Marbles " were probably produced about 50 years before the time of Phidias (fl. 450 B.C.) and mark the transition period in Greek sculpture from the old to the new style.

A E I. (*Gr. ἀεί, always*). A word frequently used as a motto for jewelry. It signifies " for ever and for aye."

A E I O U. The initial letters of the Latin words composing the motto of Frederick III (1440–1493), Emperor of Germany. The following is the motto in full—" Austriae Est Imperare Orbi Universi " (Austria Is To Rule All The World). In German, the words are *Alle Erde Ist Oesterreichs Unterthan*. A strange motto, surely, for one who was surnamed the " Pacific," and manifested weakness and incapacity as a ruler.

Ælia Lælia Crispis. The name of an inscription preserved at Bologna, Italy,— perhaps the most famous of all enigmas. It has puzzled the wisest heads, and has been finally given up as incapable of solution. Some, indeed, consider it a mere hoax. It is as follows :

ÆLIA LÆLIA CRISPIS.

Nec vir, nec mulier, nec androgyna ;
Nec puella, nec juvenis, nec anus ;
    Nec meretrix, nec pudica ;
        Sed omnia :
Sublata neque famo, nec ferro, neque veneno;
        Sed omnibus :
Nec cœlo, nec aquis, nec terris ;
        Sed ubique jacet.
    Lucius Agatho Priscus,
Nec maritus, nec amator, nec necessarius ;

Neque mœrens, neque gaudens, neque flens ;
        Sed omnia :
Hanc neque molem, neque pyramidum, neque sepulchrum,
    Scit et nescit quid poserit.
Hoc est sepulchrum intus cadaver non habens ;
Hoc est cadaver sepulchrum extra non habens ;
    Sed cadaver idem est, et sepulchrum sibi.

It has been rendered into English, as follows :

ÆLIA LÆLIA CRISPIS.

Neither man, nor woman, nor hermaphrodite ;
Neither girl, nor boy, nor old woman ;
    Neither harlot nor virgin ;
        But all of these :
Destroyed neither by hunger, nor sword, nor poison ;
        But by all of them :
Lies neither in heaven, nor in the water, nor in the ground ;
        But everywhere.
    Lucius Agatho Priscus,
Neither husband, nor lover, nor kinsman ;
Neither sad, nor glad, nor weeping ;
        But all together ;
This, neither funeral pile, nor pyramid, nor tomb,
    He knows and knows not what he has erected.
This is a tomb having no corpse within it ;
This is a corpse having no tomb without it ;
    But corpse and tomb are one and the same.

The following are some of the discarded explanations of this enigma :
    (1) Rain Water.
    (2) The so-called Materia Prima.
    (3) The Philosopher's Stone.
    (4) A Shadow.
    (5) An Embryo.
    (6) Love.
    (7) A Dissected Person.
    (8) Hemp.

Æneid. The name of the great Latin epic poem, written by Virgil (70–19 B.C.). It is in twelve books, and records the wanderings of Æneas, one of the Trojan heroes. It was commenced in 30 B.C. and, at Virgil's death, was left in an unfinished condition. The first six books are modelled after Homer's Iliad and the last six after the Odyssey. The Æneid embodies the traditions of ancient Rome, and traces the descent of the Emperor Augustus from Æneas. It was first printed in Rome, in 1469.

Æolus. The god and ruler of the winds. He resided in the islands of the Tyrrhenian Sea, called from him the Æolian Islands, — now the Lipari group. He was given by Jupiter dominion over the winds, and kept them confined in a cave in the mountain. Juno applied to him when she wished to destroy the fleet of the Trojans.

There was another Æolus, ruler of Thessaly and mythical founder of the Æolic branch of the Hellenic race.

Æsculapius. The god of the healing art. In the Homeric poems he is known as "the blameless physician"; but in later legends he has been deified. He is said to have been killed by Jupiter with a thunderbolt, for raising the dead to life. He was worshipped all over Greece. His temples were generally built outside of towns, and near wells that were believed to have remedial powers. Cocks or goats were offered in sacrifice by those that had been cured of their diseases, and tablets were often erected, recording the name, disease, and manner of cure.

Æsop, Fables of. A collection of fables, bearing this name, were popular at Athens during its palmiest days. Æsop, the reputed author of them, was born about 619 B.C. He is said to have been a native of Phrygia, and a slave. On gaining his freedom, he visited the court of Crœsus, King of Lydia, and won the favor of that monarch. He was employed on several missions of importance, in one of which, at Delphi, he was thrown over the precipice by the priests, who became enraged at his witticisms. The Athenians erected a statue in his honor. In the collections of fables that pass under the name of Æsop, many doubtless are spurious, and all have been more or less modified

by the compilers. The close likeness between the fables of Æsop and those of the Eastern fabulist Lokman (who is by some made a contemporary of the psalmist David) suggests that all these fables have a common Chinese or Indian origin. See *Lokman, Fables of ; Pilpay, Fables of.*

Æsop of Arabia. An appellation conferred upon Lokman, the reputed author of Arabic fables. He is of remote and uncertain date. See *Lokman, Fables of.*

Æsop of England. A title conferred upon John Say (1688–1732), the English poet and dramatist.

Æsop of France. An appellation bestowed upon Jean de La Fontaine (1621–1695), the famous French fabulist.

Æsop of Germany. A title conferred upon Gotthold Ephraim Lessing (1729–1781), the German dramatist and critic.

Ætolian League. A confederacy which, at one time, included not only Ætolia proper, but also Acarnania, part of Thessaly, Locris, and the island of Cephallenia. It first came into prominence about 323 B.C., and became an important rival of the Achæan League. Its annual assembly, called the *Panætolicon*, was held in the autumn. Together with the Romans, it opposed the Achæan League ; but later it espoused the cause of Antiochus III of Syria against the Romans, who subjugated it in 189 B.C. In 146 B.C., the countries comprising it were included in the Roman province of Achaia. See *Achæan League.*

African Roscius. A sobriquet conferred upon Ira Aldridge, the famous negro tragedian. He appeared with Edmund Kean in several plays, and rose to distinction in his profession. Honors were conferred upon him by the emperor of Austria and the kings of Prussia and Sweden. He died in 1867.

"**After us the Deluge**" (*Fr. Après nous le Déluge*). This is really a saying of Madame de Pompadour (1721–1764), the most famous of the mistresses of Louis XV. By some it is attributed to the King himself ; and by others, to Metternich.

Agapæ. Love-Feasts or Feasts of Charity. They were held by the early Christians, and are referred to in *Jude* 12. The wealthy members of the Church furnished the repast, and invited their poorer brethren. Prayers were offered, hymns sung, and the meetings terminated with the " holy kiss." In the 3rd and 4th centuries after Christ, these meetings had degenerated into ordinary banquets which, in later years, became occasions of debauchery. They were finally forbidden by the Church. In recent times, certain Protestant denominations have revived them in the form of tea-meetings, with prayer, praise, and song.

Agate. This precious stone derives its name, according to Pliny, from the river Achates in Sicily, near which it was first found.

Age of Reason. A treatise advocating deism, written by Thomas Paine (1737–1809). Paine, having incurred the displeasure of the Robespierre faction during the French Revolution, was imprisoned in Paris for the greater part of the year 1794; and it was while he was thus confined that he completed the second part of the work. This was published after his release, in 1795. A portion of the third part appeared in 1807. The book, owing to its pronounced doctrines, alienated many of Paine's personal friends.

Ages, Archæologic. Anthropologists have commonly divided the history of man into the following three ages :
(1) The Stone Age.
(2) The Bronze Age.
(3) The Iron Age.
In the *Stone Age*, man was in a state of savagism, and used stone implements and weapons. This age is further subdivided into the Palæolithic or *Old* Stone Age (called also the Age of *Rough* Stone Implements), and the Neolithic or *New* Stone Age (called also the Age of *Polished* Stone Implements).

In the *Bronze Age*, man first learned the uses of the metals. Copper mingled with tin — forming bronze — took the place of stone, and by its superior adaptability to man's needs raised him to the state of barbarism.

In the *Iron Age*, man discovered the manifold uses of iron, and, in consequence, made enormous strides in development. It has been truly said that without iron man would have remained in a state of barbarism.

Some historians have added to these three "Ages," two others : the *Age of Printing*, and the *Age of Steam*, while others are inclined to append a third — the *Age of Electricity*. No satisfactory estimate of the length of these ages has been made. It has been conjectured that the Stone Age lasted 90,000 years ; the Bronze Age, 8000 years ; the Iron Age, 2000 years ; the Press Age, 320 years ; and the Steam Age, 125 years. According to this subdivision, man is now in the Electric Age.

Ages, Mythologic. According to Hesiod, the Greek poet, the history of mankind was divided into the following five ages :—
(1) The Golden Age.
(2) The Silver Age.
(3) The Brazen Age.
(4) The Heroic Age.
(5) The Iron Age.
In the *Golden Age*, the earth brought forth its fruits of its own accord; pain and sickness were unknown, and men passed away in a gentle sleep.

In the *Silver Age*, men lapsed from their state of goodness, refused to worship the gods, and, for their impiety, were buried in the earth.

In the *Brazen Age*, men were warlike, cruel, and vindictive. It was the "Age of Violence."

In the *Heroic Age*, men fought nobly ; and, as a reward after death, were permitted, three times a year, to reap the free produce of the soil.

In the *Iron Age*, men were sunk in degradation and vice, and cruelty reigned supreme.

Ages of Famous Old People. See *Famous Old People, Ages of.*

Agglutinative Languages. Languages in which the roots are not kept separated as in the Chinese, nor blended as in the Aryan languages ; but are *glued together*, so that the links and joints are clearly seen. They are by far the most numerous class of languages, but generally belong to peoples in a low state of civilization. See *Inflected Languages; Monosyllabic Languages.*

Agincourt, Battle of. (Sometimes written *Azincourt*.) The internal dissensions in France, under the rule of the imbecile king, Charles VI (1380–1422), encouraged Henry V (1413–1422) of England to renew the ancient claim of his dynasty to the French crown. He accordingly landed at Harfleur, and marched to Calais to take up his winter quarters there. While on his way, he was intercepted by a French army of 50,000 men, commanded by the Constable d'Albret. The English army, amounting to about 14,000, was weakened in numbers and suffering from want of provisions, but in the battle that ensued on October 25th, 1415, the French were signally defeated; 10,000 Frenchmen were slain, including the commander-in-chief, 3 dukes, and 90 barons ; 14,000 prisoners were taken. Soon after this battle, Henry reduced all Normandy, was declared regent of France, and acknowledged heir to the crown.

Agnosticism. A theory that neither asserts nor denies, but simply professes ignorance. More especially, the doctrine that asserts that man cannot have any real knowledge of anything, and must be content simply with a knowledge of appearances or phenomena. As a result, all fundamental realities, such as matter, motion, force, etc., must, in their ultimate essence, remain forever unknowable. The word "agnostic" is said to have been suggested by the late Professor Huxley, in 1869.

"Agnostics are not atheists, because they believe the question of God's existence unfathomable, and the question of his non-existence equally so. Man, they say, has no means of knowing either the one or the other. Human knowledge cannot go beyond human observation and experience."—Brewer's *Historic Note-Book.*

"Most of my colleagues [in the Metaphysical Society] were 'ists,' . . . and I, the man without a rag of a label, . . . took thought and invented what I conceived to be the appropriate title of '*Agnostic.*' It came into my head as suggestively antithetic to 'gnostic' of church history, who professed to know so much about the very things of which I was ignorant."—Huxley's *Essays upon Some Controverted Questions.* See *Gnostics.*

Agnus Dei (*Lat. Lamb of God*). A cake of wax or dough — sometimes a disk of silver or gold — stamped with the figure of a lamb supporting the banner of the Cross. It is blessed by the Pope, and distributed, on the Sunday after Easter, among the faithful, as an amulet. Christ is often called the "Lamb of God." These words are also applied to a prayer, so called because its opening words are "Agnus Dei, qui tollit peccata mundi" (*Lat., O Lamb of God, that takest away the sins of the world*). This symbol — a lamb bearing the banner of the Cross — is frequently used to typify Christ.

Ahriman or Ahrimanes. In the Zoroastrian religion, Ahriman is the deity that personifies the principle of evil. He is in perpetual conflict with

Ormuzd, the principle of good. Ahriman will eventually perish, but Ormuzd is eternal. See *Ormuzd, or Oromasdes*.

Akbar's Palace. A famous palace at Agra in Hindostan, built by Akbar (1554–1605), the renowned Mogul emperor. The substructure is of sandstone, but the corridors and pavilions are of marble,—beautifully carved, and inlaid with jasper, agate, lapis-lazuli, and other precious stones. The building is, as Bayard Taylor declares, in a far better state of preservation than the Alhambra. The palace and the famous Pearl Mosque are both within the Fortress of Agra. See *Pearl Mosque*.

Alabama. A steam-vessel built by the Messrs. Laird of Birkenhead, near Liverpool, for the Confederate States of America. She was launched on May 15th, 1862. On July 28th of the same year, she sailed quietly from the Mersey, and later, under the command of Captain Raphael Semmes, inflicted great damage on American commerce. She is said to have captured over 60 vessels, and to have destroyed about 45 others. On June 19th, 1864, she was sunk by the United States war-ship *Kearsarge*, off Cherbourg, France, after an engagement of one hour. See *Alabama Claims; Kearsarge*.

Alabama Claims. In consequence of the connivance of the English government at the ravages inflicted by the *Alabama*, compensation was demanded from Great Britain by the United States government. A commission met at Washington in 1871; and, by a treaty concluded there, it was decided to refer the matter to a tribunal composed of five arbitrators, of whom the Queen of England, the King of Italy, the President of the Swiss Confederation, the Emperor of Brazil, and the President of the United States were each to appoint one. These met at Geneva, Switzerland, in December, 1871. As a result of their deliberations, the sum of $15,500,000, with in-

terest, was ordered to be paid to the United States by Great Britain. This amount was duly paid, and a surplus of $8,000,000 remained in the hands of the United States government, after meeting all just claims. The arbitrators chosen were : Sir Alexander E. Cockburn, by the Queen of England ; Count Edward Sclopis, by the King of Italy; Mr. Jacob Staempfli, by the President of the Swiss Confederation ; Viscount d'Itajuba, by the Emperor of Brazil ; and Mr. Charles Francis Adams, by the President of the United States. See *Alabama; Geneva Award*.

Alabama Letter. A letter on the annexation of Texas, written in 1844 by Henry Clay (1775–1852) to a friend in Alabama. Mr. Clay was the Whig candidate for the presidency at the time, and is said to have owed his defeat to this letter, which, as his adversaries asserted, revealed a complete change of policy on his part.

Aladdin's Lamp. A phrase sometimes used to denote the source of wealth and good fortune. The allusion is, of course, to the marvellous lamp possessed by Aladdin, and by means of which he obtained wealth, rank, and influence. The story of *Aladdin; or, The Wonderful Lamp*, is, perhaps, the most famous of all the tales of the *Arabian Nights' Entertainments*.

Alaric's Grave. Alaric, the chief of the Visigoths, is said to have been buried in the bed of the river Busento in Italy, in 410 A.D. The stream was turned, for the time, from its natural channel, and the captives that assisted at the burial were afterwards put to death to conceal all knowledge of the event from the Romans.

Alaska. This extensive territory, formerly known as Russian America, was purchased — together with a great number of islands, principally in the Pacific Ocean — by the United States of America from Russia, by treaty of

March 13th, 1867, for the sum of $7,-250,000. This amount was paid August 1st, 1868. It is now a Territory of the United States, with Sitka for its capital. Its land area is estimated at 570,000 square miles,— about as large as Great Britain, Ireland, France, and Spain combined. The present population is about 31,000.

"The territory of Alaska received its name from Charles Sumner in a speech addressed to the Senate in favor of the purchase of the territory. It is a corruption of an Aleut word referring to the continent as distinguished from the Aleutian islands." — Baedeker's *United States.*

Albany. The capital of the State of New York was so named in honor of James, Duke of York and Albany (afterwards James II of England), to whom Charles II gave a grant of the colony. The city was founded by the Dutch in 1614, and ceded to the English in 1664. It received its charter in 1686, and is the oldest chartered city in the United States.

Albany Regency. A name given to a cabal of Democratic politicians, whose headquarters were at Albany, New York. They controlled the politics of the State for a number of years (1820–1854), and thus exerted much influence in national politics.

Albatross. A web-footed bird of the genus *Diomedea*, several species of which are known. It is the largest of sea-birds, measuring 4 feet in length, and weighing 20 pounds or more. It abounds in the southern seas, and is called by the sailors the "Cape Sheep," because it frequents the Cape of Good Hope. Sailors say it is fatal to shoot an albatross ; and on this superstition is based Coleridge's poem of *The Ancient Mariner.* See *Ancient Mariner, Rime of the.*

"'God save thee, ancient Mariner !
    From the fiends, that plague thee thus !—
    Why look'st thou so ?'—'With my cross-bow
I shot the *Albatross !* '"
                Ancient Mariner, Rime of the.

Albert Embankment. A superb granite structure extending along the south bank of the Thames at London, from Westminster Bridge to Vauxhall Bridge, a distance of nearly one mile. It has a roadway 60 feet in width. Completed in 1869, at a cost exceeding £1,000,000. See *Victoria Embankment.*

Albert Memorial. This magnificent monument to the memory of the Prince Consort, husband of the late Queen Victoria, was erected at a cost of $600,000, one half of which amount was defrayed by voluntary contributions. It was designed by Gilbert G. Scott. The monument is in the form of a gorgeously decorated Gothic canopy,— surmounted by a spire that reaches to a height of 175 feet. The whole is surmounted by an Eleanor Cross. Beneath the canopy is a colossal gilded bronze statue of the Prince, 15 feet in height. This entire structure rests upon a spacious platform or pedestal, at the four corners of which are colossal groups of statuary,—each representing one of the four great divisions of the globe,— Asia, Africa, Europe, and America. The four sides of this pedestal are exquisitely carved in relief, and contain 169 figures of the world's greatest men in letters, art, and history.

Albert Nyanza, Lake. A fresh-water lake in eastern equatorial Africa, discovered by Captains Speke and Grant in 1862, and visited by Sir Samuel Baker in 1864. It is situated 80 miles northwest of Lake Victoria Nyanza, and is 140 miles long and 40 miles broad. Lake Albert Nyanza lies about 2700 feet above sea-level. It was long confounded with Lake Albert Edward Nyanza, discovered by Stanley in 1887, and named in 1889. See *Victoria Nyanza, Lake.*

Albertus Magnus. A title conferred upon Albertus, Count of Bollstadt (1200 ?–1280), the great scholar of the 13th century. His name has become a synonym for universal knowledge, and to him more than to any other man is due the credit of having brought about that union of theology and Aristotelianism, which forms the basis of the scholastic philosophy. Like Roger Bacon, his studies in alchemy exposed him to the charge of sorcery; but, fortunately, he escaped imprisonment.

Albigenses. A religious community formerly living at Albi in Languedoc and also at Toulouse, who, about 1200, dissented from the doctrines and practices of the Church of Rome. They were accused of being Manichæans, and a crusade against them was proclaimed by Pope Innocent III (1198–1216) in 1204. At Minerba, 150 Albigenses were burned alive by Simon de Montfort, the leader of the expedition. During the crusade, fully 30,000 persons—Roman Catholics as well as heretics—were massacred. The Albigenses were first heard of about 1000 A.D., and disappeared about 1250 A.D. See *Waldenses.*

Albino (*Lat. albus, white*). A name first given by the Portuguese to negroes that were dappled with white spots. It has since been shown that this peculiarity exists in individuals of all races, and is owing to the absence of coloring matter in the skin, eyes, and hair. It occurs not only in human beings, but also in animals and plants.

Albion. The ancient name of Great Britain,—first found in the work *De Mundo,* ascribed to Aristotle (384–322 B.C.). According to many authorities, however, the word is derived from the Latin *albus* (*white*), and was first used by Julius Cæsar (100–44 B.C.) on beholding the white chalk cliffs of England. The most probable origin of the word is from the Keltic *alb, alp* (*high*). Albion is now used as a poetic designation for England. See *Albyn ; Perfidious Albion.*

Al Borak. A marvellous animal of surpassing swiftness, on which Mohammed is said to have made a nocturnal journey from the temple at Mecca to Jerusalem and thence to the seventh heaven, under the guidance of the angel Gabriel. Its eyes were like stars, and its body was resplendent with precious stones. It had the wings of an eagle, and a human face with the cheeks of a horse. See *Animals Admitted into Heaven.*

Albyn. The ancient name of Scotland, and now a poetic term for that country. Before the time of Julius Cæsar (100–44 B.C.), the word was applied to the island of Great Britain. Its origin is believed to be the same as that of Albion. See *Albion.*

" But woe to his kindred and woe to his cause,
When *Albyn* her claymore indignantly draws."
Thomas Campbell.

Alchemy. A pseudo-science and the forerunner of modern chemistry. Its objects were two in number:
(1) To discover the " Philosopher's Stone," by means of which all the baser metals might be transmuted into gold and silver.
(2) To produce the " Elixir Vitæ " (Elixir of Life), by means of which human life might be indefinitely prolonged. Paracelsus (1493–1541) was the most famous alchemist. See *Elixir of Life ; Philosopher's Stone.*

Alciphron ; or, The Minute Philosopher. The title of a philosophic work written by Bishop Berkeley (1684–1753). It is also termed *An Apology for the Christian Religion,* and is designed " to expose the weakness of infidelity." *Alciphron* is also the name given to a poem by Thomas Moore (1779–1852).

Alcohol, Percentage of, in Wines, Liquors, etc.

Beer	4.0	Hock	11.6
Porter	4.5	Champagne	12.2
Ale	7.4	Claret	13.3
Cider	8.6	Burgundy	13.6
Tokay	10.2	Sherry	19.0
Rhine Wine	11.0	Vermouth	19.0

Madeira	21.0	Rum	53.7
Port	23.2	Whisky, Irish	53.9
Curaçoa	27.0	Whisky,	
Aniseed	33.0	Bourbon	54.0
Maraschino	34.0	Whisky, Rye	54.0
Chartreuse	43.0	Whisky,	
Gin	51.6	Scotch	54.3
Brandy	53.4		

"Spirits are said to be 'proof' when they contain 57 per cent. The maximum amount of alcohol, says Parkes, that a man takes daily without injury to his health is that contained in 2 oz. brandy, ¼ pint of sherry, ½ pint of claret, or 1 pint of beer." — Mulhall's *Dictionary of Statistics.*

Alderney Cows. In Edwards's *Words, Facts, and Phrases,* we find the following amusing item : "There are certainly not a hundred cows approaching the pure Alderney breed in the entire island of Alderney ; yet one dealer advertises in the 'Times' that he annually imports 'from the island' upwards of 1000 cows! He does not tell us by what process they are produced."

Aldershot Camp. A permanent camp for military exercises, situated 35 miles southwest of London, and 19 miles south of Windsor. It was established in 1855, after the Crimean War. About 3 square miles of land were secured, and more than £1,250,000 were expended during the first 5 years. The number of troops at the camp averages from 10,000 to 15,000. Regular troops are generally quartered at "Aldershot Camp" during the two years preceding their departure for India.

Aldiborontesphoscophornio. A nickname conferred by Sir Walter Scott on the publisher, John Ballantyne, in allusion to his pomposity and dignity of manner. "Aldiborontesphoscophornio" is a pompous individual in the burlesque of *Chrononhotonthologus.* See *Chrononhotonthologus.*

Aldine Editions. The name given to editions, chiefly of the Greek and Latin classics, issued from the Venetian press of Aldus Manutius during the 15th and 16th centuries. The house was founded in 1490, and remained in existence until 1597. Aldus (or, more properly, his engraver, Francesco of Bologna) invented the kind of type now called italic, but originally known as *aldine.* It was first used in an edition of Virgil that appeared in 1501. This volume was also notable as being the first octavo ever issued. The "Aldine Press" printed more than 900 books, consisting of "first editions" of the classics, corrected texts of Dante, Petrarch, and Boccaccio, and works on grammar and philology. Aldus revolutionized the art of printing and bookmaking, and his trade-mark — consisting of a dolphin and an anchor intertwined, and bearing the motto, *festina lente* or *sudarit et alsit*—became famous throughout Europe. See *Elzevir Editions.*

Aldobrandini Marriage. A famous ancient fresco, discovered in 1606 among the ruins of the Baths of Titus at Rome, and now in the Vatican gallery. It is supposed by some to represent the marriage of Peleus and Thetis, and derives its name from Cardinal Aldobrandini, by whom it was purchased soon after its discovery. Said to have been executed during the reign of the Emperor Augustus Cæsar (27 B.C.–14 A.D.). See *Baths of Titus.*

Alexander Column. The greatest monolith of modern times. It stands in the Admiralty Square in St. Petersburg, and faces the Winter Palace. It consists of a single shaft of red granite, 80 feet in height, and weighs nearly 400 tons. This rests upon a pedestal of the same material, about 25 feet square. The column is surmounted by a capital formed of a Turkish cannon, above which are the statue of an angel 14 feet high, and a cross 7 feet high. The whole structure is 150 feet in altitude. It was erected in memory of the Czar Alexander I, and commemorates the Russian War of 1812.

Alexander, Mrs. A pseudonym adopted by Mrs. Annie F. Hector, the popular novelist (b. 1825).

Alexander of the North. A title conferred upon Charles XII (1697–1718) of Sweden, whose military talents and exploits bore a considerable resemblance to those of Alexander of Macedon. He was signally defeated by Peter the Great at the battle of Pultowa (1709). See *Pultowa, Battle of.*

Alexander the Corrector. A name assumed by Alexander Cruden (1700–1770), the compiler of the famous *Concordance to the Bible.* During his life, he was twice confined in a lunatic asylum, where he seems to have been cruelly treated. He imagined himself divinely commissioned to rectify all manner of abuses, and in consequence assumed the title above mentioned. He carried about with him a sponge, with which he effaced all inscriptions that seemed in any way objectionable. His *bête-noire* was John Wilkes.

Alexandrian Codex. A Greek manuscript of the *Old* and *New Testaments*, written on parchment in uncial letters, without accents and without spaces between the words. Its probable date is about 450. The *Old Testament* is in the translation of the Septuagint. This famous manuscript belonged in 1098 to the Patriarch of Alexandria. In 1621, it was taken to Constantinople by Cyrillus Lucaris, the patriarch ; and in 1628 was presented by him to Charles I of England. It was first placed in the Royal Library; and in 1753 was transferred to the British Museum. See *Ephraem Codex ; Sinaitic Codex ; Vatican Codex.*

Alexandrian Library. This most famous library of antiquity was founded at Alexandria, Egypt, by Ptolemy Soter (323–283 B.C.). His successor, Ptolemy Philadelphus, made large additions to it, and at his death it numbered about 100,000 volumes. According to some authorities, it contained during its most flourishing period 490,000 volumes ; according to others, 700,000. The larger part of the library was contained in the famous Museum, and the remaining part in the Serapeum, or Temple of Jupiter Serapis. During the siege of Alexandria by Julius Cæsar, the part contained in the Museum was destroyed by fire. This was afterwards replaced by the collection of Pergamos, which was presented to Cleopatra by Mark Antony. During the reign of Theodosius the Great (379–395), that emperor permitted the destruction of all the heathen temples throughout the empire ; and the Temple of Jupiter Serapis was not spared. In 391, a mob of fanatic Christians, under the leadership of one Archbishop Theophilus, destroyed this temple, with most of its literary treasures. The destruction of the library by Omar in 641 was simply a *completion* of the work begun by Theophilus, and the statement that the Moslems used the volumes of the famous library to heat the 4000 baths of the city for 6 months is doubtless an exaggeration. See *Museum ; Serapeum.*

Alexandrian School of Philosophy. Founded at Alexandria, Egypt, about 323 B.C. It was under the patronage of the Ptolemies, and under their wise guidance rose to great distinction. The city of Alexandria soon after became the intellectual centre of the time, and scholars from every part of the ancient world resorted there for study and instruction. The history of the school is divided into two periods : *first*, the period from 323 to 30 B.C. ; and, *second*, the period from 30 B.C. to 640 A.D., when Alexandria fell into the hands of the Saracens. During the first period, its leading teachers and philosophers were Euclid, Archimedes, Apollonius, Aristarchus, Eratosthenes, Hero, and Hipparchus. This was the period of its greatest influence. During the second period, Ptolemy the astronomer and Galen the physician were the most famous names. The introduction of Christianity into the Roman Empire gave rise, at Alexandria, to Neo-Platonism, a system of philosophy formed from a blending of some of the doctrines of Plato with certain ones of the Christian religion. Plotinus was its most noted teacher. Gnosticism also flourished there ; and the dogmas of the Trinity and the Logos are, by many, ascribed to Alexandrian influence. See *Neo-Platonism*.

Alexandrines. Verses of 12 or 13 syllables, with a division into two parts between the 6th and 7th syllables. According to some authorities, these verses were so called because first used in an old French poem on Alexander the Great ; according to others, because Alexander of Paris first employed them, about 1164 A.D.

In Pope's *Essay on Criticism*, we find the following familiar couplet, which gives an excellent illustration of an Alexandrine verse :

"A needless Alexandrine ends the song
    That, like a wounded snake, | drags its
        slow length along."

Algebra. Although the origin of the science of algebra is in doubt, the credit of its invention is generally given to Diophantus of Alexandria, who lived during the 4th century after Christ. His treatise on the subject comprises 13 volumes, of which 6 only are extant. To the Arabs is due the introduction of algebra into Spain, about 900 A.D.; it is thought by many that they derived their knowledge of the science from India. Leonardo Bonaccio of Pisa, an Italian merchant, acquired a knowledge of algebra while travelling in the East, and on his return, about 1200 A.D., introduced its study among his countrymen. Francis Vieta, a French mathematician, proposed the use of symbols for the expression of quantities, and thus greatly extended the scope of the science. Descartes, in 1657, first applied algebra to geometry ; and Newton, in 1668, discovered the Binomial Theorem.

This last discovery laid the foundation of Newton's Theory of Fluxions. Algebra is now used extensively in the higher mathematics, and even in formal logic.

Alhambra (*Ar. The Red Castle*). This famous palace-fortress of the ancient Moorish kings is situated upon an elevation near the city of Granada, Spain, and commands a superb view of the plain below, comprising an area of 56 square miles. It was commenced by Ibn-1-Ahmar in 1248, and completed by his grandson, Mohammed III, in 1314. It surrendered to the Christians in 1496. Within the palace are two oblong courts, — world-renowned for their beauty, — the Court of Lions and the Court of the Myrtles. They consist of porticos, fountains, gardens, and pavements of mosaic. There also is one of the most beautiful apartments in Europe, — the Hall of the Abencerrages. Charles V demolished a large part of the palace to make way for a new one, but the work was not completed. In later times, the Alhambra suffered much from neglect. Although the French, when they occupied the Alhambra, did much to preserve it from decay, yet when they abandoned the fortress, they blew up 8 of the towers, and tried to destroy the whole structure. It afterwards suffered a severe earthquake shock. Queen Isabella partially restored the palace in 1862. See *Court of Lions*.

Alien and Sedition Laws. In 1798, war seemed imminent between France and the United States. There were at that time in the United States 30,000 Frenchmen, organized in political clubs, and 50,000 naturalized Englishmen who sympathized with France. Fearing danger, Congress passed several acts, authorizing the President, at his discretion, to banish alien enemies during the next two years. These laws were never actively enforced; but, owing to their extreme unpopularity, they were among the chief causes in dislodging the Federal party from power. Kentucky and Virginia both passed resolutions declaring the "Alien and Sedition Laws" to be unconstitutional. Kentucky even asserted the right of any State to nullify any act of Congress that it deemed unconstitutional. This was probably the first declaration of the doctrine of States' Rights in our history. The Kentucky Resolutions were drawn by Jefferson, and those of Virginia by Madison. See *State Rights.*

Alkali Desert. An extensive tract of land in Wyoming, Nebraska, and Montana,—characterized by the presence of extensive alkaline deposits in the soil and on its surface.

"And now we entered upon one of that species of deserts whose concentrated hideousness shames the diffused and diluted horrors of Sahara, — an *alkali desert.* For sixty-eight miles there was but one break in it. The *alkali dust* cut through our lips, it persecuted our eyes, it ate through the delicate membranes and made our noses bleed and kept them bleeding." — *Roughing It* (Mark Twain).

Alloway Kirk. A ruined church on the banks of the Doon, near Ayr, Scotland. It was through the windows of this church that Tam o' Shanter peered at the witches' dance. It is said that the old bell of the church still hangs in the ruin, although little more than the four walls are now standing. See *Burns's Cottage.*

All Saints' Day. A festival common to the Roman Catholic, Anglican, and Lutheran Churches. It falls on November 1st. It was introduced by Pope Boniface IV (607–614) in 607, and established by Pope Gregory IV (827–844) about 830, in memory of those saints to whom no special day had been assigned. It is known in Old English as All-Hallows, All-Hallowmass, or simply Hallowmass. The eve of "All Saints' Day" (October 31st) is known as Halloween. The

festival of "All Saints' Day" originally occurred on May 1st ; but was changed in 834 to the present date. See *All Souls' Day ; Halloween.*

All Souls' Day. A festival of the Roman Catholic Church. It falls on November 2nd,— the day following "All Saints' Day." It was instituted about 993 by Odilo, abbot of Cluny, to alleviate, by prayers and almsgivings, the sufferings of the souls in purgatory.

It is related that a pilgrim, when returning from the Holy Land, was wrecked on an island between Sicily and Thessalonica. While there, he fell in with a hermit, who told him that, among the cliffs of the island, might be found a great opening through which ascended huge flames, as well as the groans of the tormented ones. The hermit further declared that he had often heard the devils complain of the souls snatched from them by the prayers and alms of the pious. They were especially incensed against the monks of Cluny. The pilgrim communicated these facts (?) to the worthy abbot, who straightway instituted this festival in his monastery. See *All Saints' Day.*

"All this for a Song." A saying uttered by Lord Burleigh, when commanded by Queen Elizabeth (1558–1603) to present Edmund Spenser, the poet, with the sum of £100, as a token of her appreciation.

Almack's. The name of a noted suite of assembly-rooms in King Street, London. They were opened in 1765, by a Scotchman named Macall, who, it is said, transposed the two syllables of his name — making it Almack or Allmack — to conceal his identity. The rooms became famous for the balls given there under the direction of a committee of ladies of high rank ; and to be allowed the privilege of attending one was a social distinction to be envied. The rooms were a fashionable resort till about 1840, when their importance gradually declined. Their name was changed to " Willis's Rooms " in 1863. They are still used for dinners, balls, and concerts. "Almack's " is the name also of a famous club in London, founded in 1764. It was noted as a gambling-resort, and among its members were Gibbon and Fox.

Almagest. The name given by the Arabian translators to the *Syntaxis* of Ptolemy Claudius, the Alexandrian astronomer. The word is derived from the Arabic *al* (*the*), and the Greek μεγίστη (*greatest*). See *Syntaxis.*

"We find in the *Almagest* a clear exposition of the system of the world, of the arrangement of the celestial bodies and their revolutions, a complete treatise of rectilinear and spherical trigonometry, and all the phenomena of diurnal motion explained and calculated with remarkable precision."—*Delambre.*

Alma Mater (*Lat. Fostering Mother*). A phrase applied, especially in modern times, to the college or university where one has been graduated.

Almanach de Gotha. Published annually at Gotha since 1764. It was originally printed in the German language, and so continued until Napoleon I became emperor, when it was printed in French. Since the Franco-German War, it has appeared in both languages. At present, the "Almanach " is a small volume of over 1100 pages and contains a vast amount of statistical information, a complete summary of historical events, obituary notices of prominent persons, and names of the sovereigns and royal families of every civilized country.

Almighty Dollar. A phrase that originated with Washington Irving (1783-1859), and was intended to personify the prevailing passion for gain in America.

"The *Almighty Dollar*, that great object of universal devotion throughout our land,

seems to have no genuine devotees in these peculiar villages."—*Wolfert's Roost* (Irving).

Almighty Nose. A sobriquet conferred upon Oliver Cromwell (1599-1658) by Marchamont Needham, in his journal, *Mercurius Pragmaticus.*

Alonzo Sees Cross. According to the legend, Alonzo, Duke of Portugal, while drawing up his army for battle against the Moors, beheld in the eastern sky the figure of a cross with Christ suspended upon it. The Savior promised Alonzo a complete victory over the Infidels ; and in token of his gratitude the conqueror assumed, for the royal device, an emblem suggesting the five wounds of Christ. See *Constantine Sees Cross.*

Alpha and Omega. The names of the first and last letters of the Greek alphabet. In ecclesiastical symbolism, these words are used to signify the " beginning " and the "end," and are therefore suggestive of God. The tombs of the early Christians were engraved with these letters to distinguish them from the tombs of the heathens.

"I am *Alpha and Omega*, the first and the last : "—*Revelation* i, 11.

Alphonsine Tables. Astronomical tables, so called because compiled by Spanish and Arabian astronomers, under the patronage of Alphonso X (1252-1284) of Leon and Castile. They were designed to correct the planetary tables in Ptolemy's *Almagest.* For this work 50 of the most celebrated astronomers of the age were assembled at Toledo, and in 1252 the "Alphonsine Tables " were completed at a cost of 40,000 ducats. The Spanish government ordered the work of Alphonso to be reprinted from the most accurate MSS., and the work was commenced in 1863.

Alps Melted with Vinegar. According to Livy, Hannibal, in his passage of the Alps, melted the rocks with hot vinegar. Polybius, the Greek historian, pertinently asks where Hannibal obtained the vinegar, and how he heated it, as there was not a tree to be found for fire-wood. The whole notion is manifestly absurd.

Alsace-Lorraine (*Ger. Elsass-Lothringen*). A state or " imperial territory " of the German Empire, since 1871. From the 10th century, it formed part of the German Empire ; but, in 1648, a considerable portion was ceded to France by the Peace of Westphalia ; and, in 1681, Louis XIV seized the remaining part in time of peace. This aggression was ratified by the Peace of Ryswick, in 1697. After the fall of Napoleon I in 1814, Germany demanded the restitution of the province ; but, as Russia objected, the matter remained in abeyance till the Franco-German War of 1870, when, by the Treaty of Frankfort, the province was incorporated into the new German Empire. The majority of the population was violently opposed to the change ; but, although 160,000 voted to be French citizens, only 50,000 went into voluntary exile. Since then, the sentiment against Germany has steadily increased, and the conquered province remains a standing menace to the peace of Europe.

Al Sirat. An imaginary bridge between this world and the next. It extends over the abyss of hell, and must be passed by all that would reach the Mohammedan paradise. It is very narrow, and has been likened by some writers to the thread of a famished spider, and by others to the edge of a razor-blade. In crossing, one's speed is proportioned to one's virtue. Some pass with the rapidity of lightning ; others, more slowly ; while the wicked, on account of the weight of their sins, are precipitated into the gulf below.

Alter Ego (*Lat. The other I*). One's double, or other self. More specifically, it applied to the Spanish viceroys when they exercised royal power. The term was also used to designate a substitute appointed by the King of the Two Sicilies to administer the affairs of the kingdom, during the insurrection of 1820.

Alter Ego of Richelieu. A name given to François Leclerc du Tremblay (1577–1638), better known as "Father Joseph." He was the agent and confidant of Richelieu in his negotiations and intrigues, and always remained his firm friend. See *Cardinal's Right Arm*.

Aluminium. A metal of extreme lightness, somewhat resembling silver, but possessing a bluish tint that reminds one of zinc. It was discovered by Wöhler in 1828, and possesses many qualities that fit it for general use. It does not oxidize, while sulphuretted hydrogen — the gas that so readily tarnishes silver—has no effect upon it. It is about one-fourth as heavy as silver, is very sonorous, and is an excellent conductor of heat and electricity ; while its strength and extreme lightness render it suitable for the manufacture of many articles. Yet it has failed, in spite of these advantages, to take the market. Its cost of production is steadily decreasing.

Amadis de Gaul (*Span. Amadis de Gaula*). A Portuguese romance, said to have been written by Vasco de Labeira about 1342. It was translated into Spanish by Montalvo, about 1485. A French version by Herberay was published about 1555, under the title of *Amadis des Gaules*, meaning France. Gaula is Wales in the original ; and the subject, scenes, and characters are British.

Amaranth. A leading genus of the order *Amaranthaceæ*,—famous from early times as a symbol of immortality, because the red bracts that surround the flowers retain their freshness long after they have been gathered. The word "amaranth" is from the Greek and means "everlasting." Clement of Alexandria said : " Amarantus flos symbolum est immortalitatis." (*Lat.* *The amaranth flower is the symbol of immortality*).

Amaryllis. The name of a country-girl in the *Idyls* of Theocritus and the *Eclogues* of Virgil. The word has come into use, in modern pastoral poetry, to designate a sweetheart or mistress.

"To sport with *Amaryllis* in the shade."
Milton.

Amaryllis is also the name of a genus of plants and the title of a musical composition attributed to Louis XIII (1610–1643) of France.

Amazon. The name of the largest, but not the longest river on the globe, —the Nile being of equal length, and the Mississippi, with the Missouri, much longer. Its actual length is not known, but is supposed to be about 3000 miles. It is 60 miles wide at its mouth, 4 miles wide at a distance of 1000 miles from the sea, and more than 1 mile wide at a distance of 2000 miles from the sea. The river drains an area of 2,500,000 square miles, which equals about one third of the area of Europe. The main stream and its tributaries are said to afford over 25,000 miles of waterway for steam-navigation. With all its side-channels navigable for smaller craft, the Amazon probably furnishes 50,000 miles of navigable waters. The river was discovered by Vicente Yañez Pinzon in 1500, and was explored by Orellana, one of Pizarro's officers, in 1541. Observing, as he supposed, armed women on the banks as he sailed down the river from Peru to the ocean, he fancied them to be "Amazons," and thus the river obtained its name. These people were simply the native Indians. They parted their hair in the middle, and wore long tunics. Thus to the imagination of the Spaniards they seemed to be the fabled women-warriors of antiquity. See *Amazons*.

Amazons. A race of warlike women that suffered no man to dwell among them. They were ruled by a queen, and marched to battle under her command. Their husbands having been slain in war, they resolved to form a female state, and declared marriage to be a painful servitude. That they might the better use the bow and javelin, they burned off their right breasts. From this custom it is said that they received the name of Amazons, or "breastless ones." Others derive the name from the Circassian word *Maza*, signifying the moon, as if this myth had taken its origin from the worship of the moon.

Three nations of Amazons are mentioned by the ancients,—the Asiatic, the Scythian, and the African. The Asiatic Amazons, from whom the others branched off, dwelt on the shores of the Black Sea and among the Caucasus Mountains. They were said to have founded the cities of Ephesus, Smyrna, and Cumæ ; and were famous for their three queens: Hippolyta, who was conquered by Hercules ; Penthesilea, who was slain by Achilles while aiding the Trojans; and Thalestris, who visited Alexander the Great, with 300 maidens in her train.

This myth of the "Amazons" has always been a fertile one with Greek artists, and even as late as the Middle Ages Amazons were said to dwell in Africa and America. See *Amazon*.

Amber. A fossilized vegetable resin, found in great abundance on the shores of the Baltic Sea, especially between Königsberg and Memel. In all probability, it is derived from extinct coniferous trees. It becomes negatively electric when rubbed, and manifests this property in a marked degree. The word "electricity" is derived from *elektron*, the Greek word for amber.

According to an ancient fable, amber is the tears of the sisters of Phæthon, who, after his death, were turned into poplars. By some, amber is said to be a concretion of birds' tears ; and this fancy finds expression in the following lines from *The Fire Worshippers*, by Thomas Moore :

"Around thee shall glisten the loveliest
    amber
That ever the sorrowing sea - bird hath
    wept."

Ambrosia (*Gr. αμβρόσιος, immortal*). According to classical mythology, the food of the Olympian gods. It was brought by doves to Jupiter, and was sometimes bestowed by him upon such mortals as were his special favorites. To those that ate it, were given immortal youth and beauty. The goddesses also employed it as a salve to heighten their charms, and even Jove himself did not disdain to anoint his locks with it. See *Nectar*.

Ambrosian Chant. A method of singing introduced from the Eastern into the Western Church by St. Ambrose (333–397 A.D.), a Church Father, and Bishop of Milan. It was the first effort to systematize the traditional music of the Church, and was used till superseded by the Gregorian Chant (590). St. Ambrose was the author of many hymns. The *Te Deum Laudamus* is by many considered to have been partly composed by him. See *Gregorian Chant ; Te Deum.*

Amende Honorable. A form of punishment that originated in France, in the 9th century. It was inflicted upon murderers, traitors, and sacrilegious persons. The culprit was delivered into the hands of the hangman ; his shirt was stripped from his back ; a halter was placed around his neck, and a lighted taper in his hand. In this condition, he was brought into court, and there made to ask pardon of God, the king, and the country. Death or banishment sometimes followed. As the phrase is now used, it refers to any apology or reparation made to an injured person.

America. The name of the great Western Continent is, without doubt, derived from Amerigo Vespucci (1451–1512), a Florentine merchant. He accompanied Ojeda in his expedition to the eastern coast of America in 1499, one year after Columbus had discovered the mainland. He wrote letters home to his friends in Italy, and is charged with presumptuously inserting the words "Tierra de Amerigo" in the maps drawn by himself. Humboldt, however, is of the opinion that the word "America" was first used by one Hylacomylus (or Waldsemüller), a German geographer,— without the knowledge of Vespucci,—in 1507.

America, When Discovered. 500 years before the time of Columbus, there were Norse colonies, not only in Greenland, but farther south as well. These, however, had perished or been abandoned, and were forgotten in his day. It is certain that the Norsemen or Vikings visited America in the 10th or 11th centuries after Christ. In 1000, Leif, the son of Eric the Red, sailed in search of the New World, and touched at Labrador. He stopped near Boston for the winter, and returned home in the spring of 1001. All of these efforts, however, were of a transient character ; and it is with Columbus that the era of *permanent* discovery begins. To him is due the honor of having first *really* discovered land on the other side of the ocean, and of having made America an actual fact. On October 12th, 1492, he discovered the island of Guanahani, one of the Bahamas, and named it San Salvador. On June 24th, 1497, John Cabot, who had been sent on a voyage of exploration by Henry VII (1485–1509) of England, sighted the coast of Labrador. On August 1st, 1498, Columbus, while on his *third* voyage, discovered the continent of South America.

American Epic Poem. *The Vision of Columbus* — afterwards enlarged and called *The Columbiad* — is, perhaps, the only poem that aspires to the dignity of an American epic. It was written by Joel Barlow (1755–1812), and consists of ten books. After an invocation to Freedom and a description of Columbus in prison, Hesperus, the guardian angel of America, takes the great explorer up on the Mount of Vision, and from one of its loftiest pinnacles unfolds to him a prophetic panorama of American history. The seven succeeding books furnish an account of the conquest of Mexico and Peru, and deal with the early affairs of Massachusetts and Virginia, the colonial days, and the American Revolution. In the two concluding books of the poem, Atlas, the guardian angel of Africa, denounces the crime of human slavery to Hesperus. A prophetic forecast of America's progress in science and the arts is then given, and this progress is compared with the history of ancient times. The poem concludes with the hope that the federal system of government may be extended over the whole earth. *The Columbiad* has been severely criticised, and has never been generally accepted as the representative American epic. By many, Longfellow's *Hiawatha* is called the Indian epic of America. See *Hiawatha, Song of.*

American Fabius. A title conferred upon George Washington (1732–1799) by the American newspapers of 1775–1785, in allusion to his military policy during the Revolution, which, by declining to meet the enemy in open battle, bore a striking resemblance to that of Fabius, the Roman general, in his contest with Hannibal. See *Cunctator ; Fabian Policy.*

American Flag. See *Flag, United States.*

American Montaigne. A name frequently applied to Ralph Waldo Emerson (1803–1882), the American essayist and poet.

American Museum of Natural History. Situated at Manhattan Square and 77th Street, New York City, and incorporated in 1869 by the legislature, for the purpose of establishing and maintaining in that city a museum and library of natural history. The corner-stone was laid by President Grant on June 2nd, 1874, and the building was formally opened by President Hayes on December 22nd, 1877. Several wings have been added since, as the structure was so designed as to permit of indefinite extension. The collections of mammals, birds, insects, rocks, minerals, shells, and implements of aboriginal man in America are especially noteworthy. Some of the more notable exhibits are the collections of woods and building-stones of the United States, presented by Morris K. Jesup ; the American gems and gem-minerals exhibited by Tiffany & Company at the Paris Exposition of 1889; the Spang collection of minerals; and the Jay collection of shells. The Museum contains, in addition, a valuable library of works on natural history, and a fine lecture-hall.

American Socrates. A sobriquet conferred upon Benjamin Franklin (1706–1790), the philosopher-statesman, by Sir James Mackintosh.

In independence of thought, preference for the useful over the merely ornamental, and homeliness of illustration, Franklin bears a striking likeness to his illustrious prototype.

American Tupper. A sobriquet conferred upon Josiah G. Holland (1819–1881), the American author and editor, on account of the aphoristic style of his writings.

American War of Independence. The first engagement occurred at Lexington and Concord on April 19th, 1775. The war was terminated on September 3rd, 1783, by the Peace of Versailles, signed at Paris. During the war, there were fought 17 important battles, of which the Americans won 8 and the British 5, while 4 were doubtful in their issue. The fighting lasted eight years to a day. On April 19, 1775, hostilities commenced at

Lexington, and on April 19th, 1783, Washington proclaimed the cessation of hostilities with Great Britain.

Amethyst. This precious stone— believed by the ancients to be a remedy for drunkenness — derives its name from the Greek αμέθυστος (*not drunken*).

Ami du Peuple (*Fr. Friend of the People*). An appellation bestowed upon Jean Paul Marat (1744-1793), the French revolutionist. It was also the name of an infamous democratic journal, conducted by Marat himself. The tone of its articles was most bitter ; and none, save the dregs of the people, were deemed unworthy of its attacks. Marat is the most repulsive figure in the French Revolution. Cruel, filthy, and loathsome, he typifies its vilest aspects.

Amiens, Peace of. The preliminary articles of this peace between Great Britain, France, Spain, and Holland were signed in London on October 1st, 1801 ; and on March 27th, 1802, the treaty was definitively signed at Amiens by the Marquis of Cornwallis for England, Joseph Bonaparte for France, Azara for Spain, and Schimmelpennick for Holland. According to Lord Grenville, " England gave up everything, and France nothing." War broke out again in 1803.

Ammonia. This pungent, suffocating, colorless gas received its name from the temple of Jupiter Ammon in Libya, near which sal-ammoniac, one of its compounds, was once manufactured. It was formerly called hartshorn, because in England it was made from the horns of the hart. It is obtained at the present day chiefly by the dry distillation of organic bodies containing nitrogen, such as bones, coal, etc.

Among the Gods. See *Gods, Among the.*

Ampère's Law. See *Avogadro's Law.*

Ampersand. A word used to describe the character &. It is a corruption of *and*, per se *and* (*i.e.*, & by itself [makes] *and*).

" Any odd shape folks understand
To mean my Protean *Amperzand !* "
London Punch.

Amphictyonic Council (*Gr. ἀμφικτίονες, dwellers round about*). A politico-religious council of ancient Greece, composed of twelve of the northern tribes of the country, and traditionally said to have been founded by Amphictyon, son of Deucalion. It existed from 1498 to 31 B.C. Each tribe was represented by two deputies, and two meetings were held annually,— one during the spring in the temple of Apollo at Delphi, and one during the autumn at Anthela, near Thermopylæ. At the time of Demosthenes (382-322 B.C.) the glory of the Amphictyonic Council had departed.

Amphion. A Theban prince, the son of Jupiter and Antiope. He received from Mercury a golden lyre, and became so skilled in its use that when he built the walls of Thebes the stones arranged themselves, of their own accord, in their proper places, at the sound of his music. The meaning of this fable doubtless is that Amphion, by his eloquence, persuaded the hitherto barbarous citizens of Thebes to build the walls around their city. Pope, in the *Temple of Fame*, says :

" Amphion there the loud creating lyre
Strikes, and behold a sudden Thebes
aspire."

Amphitheatres. Buildings of a round or oval shape, designed, in ancient times, for combats between gladiators and wild beasts. The first amphitheatres are said to have been built by Curio in 76 B.C., and by Julius Cæsar in 46 B.C. The first stone amphitheatre was built by Statilius for the Emperor Augustus Cæsar. The most famous of the amphitheatres at Rome was that of Vespasian, generally known as the "Coliseum." It was commenced by Vespasian, and completed by his son Titus in 80 A.D. It held 87,000 people.

The following are the names of the famous amphitheatres of ancient times, with their dimensions, according to Mulhall :

Coliseum............	615 x 510 feet.
Verona.............	513 x 410 "
Vienne.............	508 x 436 "
Pozzuoli............	480 x 382 "
Arles...............	460 x 338 "
Limoges............	450 x 378 "
Nîmes	437 x 332 "
Pompeii............	430 x 335 "

See *Coliseum ; Nîmes, Arena of ; Verona, Arena of.*

Amphrysian Prophetess. The Cumæan Sibyl, so named from the Amphrysus, a small river of Thessaly, on the banks of which Apollo fed the herds of Admetus. Hence "Amphrysian" and "Apollonian" are interchangeable terms.

Amyclæan Silence (*Dangerous Silence*). The city of Amyclæ was situated in Laconia, 20 miles southeast of Sparta. According to the story, the Amyclæans had been so often alarmed by false reports of the arrival of the Spartans, that a law was passed forbidding anyone to speak of the enemy. Accordingly, when the Spartans *did* come, no one dared to raise the alarm, and so Amyclæ was taken. Hence have arisen the proverbs : "Amyclæ perished through silence," and "Amyclis ipsis taciturnior" (Lat. *More silent than the Amyclæans themselves.* See *Silent City.*

Anabaptists (*Gr. ἀνά, again, βαπτίζω, I baptize*). An epithet applied to a religious sect that did not recognize the validity of *infant* baptism, but believed that the rite should be administered only to adults that had made public confession of faith. The name was first given to Thomas Münzer, Storck, and other fanatics, who preached in Saxony in 1521 and incited insurrections in various parts of Germany. They were quelled with bloodshed in 1525. The word "Anabaptist," in recent times, has fallen into disuse. See *Abecedarians ; Pædobaptists.*

Anabasis (*Gr. ἀνάβασις, going up*). The name of a book written by Xenophon [445 (?)–355 (?)] the Athenian, narrating the history of the expedition of Cyrus the Younger against his elder brother Artaxerxes, King of Persia. At the battle of Cunaxa (401 B.C.), Cyrus was slain; and Xenophon, being elected one of the generals, took the principal part in leading the 10,000 Greek mercenaries in safety back to their homes. See *Retreat of the Ten Thousand.*

Anacharsis Clootz. A name assumed by Baron Jean Baptiste Clootz, an eccentric individual, born at Cleves in Prussia in 1755. Having inherited a large fortune, he conceived the idea of reforming the human race, and, for that purpose, traveled through England and the Continent, denouncing all kings and rulers, and even the Deity Himself. Having assumed the title of "The Orator of the Human Race," he appeared at the bar of the French National Assembly in 1790, as the pretended head of a deputation from foreign nations. He was elected a member of the Assembly in 1792, but was proscribed by Robespierre, and guillotined in 1794. Clootz called himself *Anacharsis*, in allusion to the Scythian prince and philosopher of that name, who traveled widely in search of knowledge, and visited Athens in the time of Solon. See *Orator of the Human Race.*

Anathema. A solemn curse or denunciation pronounced, in the early Church, against those that were debarred from its privileges. In the 9th century, a distinction was made between "excommunication" and "anathema"—the latter being the more extreme form of denunciation. In 325 A.D., the Council of Nice anathematized those that embraced the Arian heresy. In 1 *Corinthians* xvi, 22, we find the words: " If any man love not the Lord Jesus Christ, let him be Anathema, Maran atha." It has been thought by many that the expression "Anathema Maran atha" means a more fearful kind of denunciation ; but, according to the best authorities, the Syriac words *Maran athâ (Our Lord cometh)* should be read as a separate sentence. It is so given in the " Revised Version " of the *New Testament.*

Anatomist of Humanity. An appellation sometimes bestowed upon the French dramatist Molière (1622–1673), whose real name was Jean Baptiste Poquelin. He excelled as a deep and penetrating analyst of human nature, and exposed, with keen satire, the follies of his day.

Anatomy. The following interesting facts of human anatomy and physiology have been gathered from Mulhall's *Dictionary of Statistics :*

(1) *Blood.* An adult has ordinarily 28 lbs. of blood, and, at each pulsation of the heart, 10 lbs. are sent through the arteries and veins. The pulsations average 120 per minute in infancy, 80 in manhood, and 60 in old age, and are rather more rapid in women than in men.

(2) *Temperature of the Human Blood.*

Good Health...........	98.6 (Fahrenheit).
Fever.................	101.3 "
Strong Fever (morning).	102.2 "
" " (evening).	104.0 "

(3) *Brain.* According to Bastian and others, the following brain-weights are given :

Scotch.....	50.0 oz.	Pawnees ...	47.1 oz.
Germans...	49.6 "	Italians....	46.9 "
English....	49.5 "	Hindoos ...	45.1 "
French.....	47.9 "	Gypsies....	44.8 "
Zulus	47.5 "	Bushmen...	44.6 "
Chinese....	47.2 "	Esquimaux.	43.9 "

(4) *Capacity of Brain-Case.*

Anglo-Saxon	105	cubic inches.	
German..................	105	"	"
Negro...................	96	"	"
Ancient Egyptian........	93	"	"
Hottentot..	58	"	"
Australian Natives	58	"	"

In all races, the male brain is about 10 per cent. heavier than the female. After the age of 50, the brain loses an ounce in weight every 10 years. Cuvier's brain weighed 64 ounces ; Byron's, 79 ounces ; and Cromwell's, 90 ounces; but this last was diseased. Post-mortem examinations of the brains of criminals in France give an average of 55 to 60 ounces for those of the worst class.

(5) *Hair.* The number of hairs on an adult's head averages from 129,000 to 150,000.

(6) *Respiration.* The quantity of carbonic acid gas exhaled in 24 hours is as follows :

Person.	Age.	Ounces exhaled.
Girl	10	9
Boy............	10	10
Woman........	19	12
Boy	16	16
Man...........	28	17

(7) *Weight.* The following scale of normal weights for height is given by Banting :

Inches.	Lbs.	Inches.	Lbs.
61..............	120	67..............	148
62..............	126	68..............	155
63..............	133	69..............	162
64..............	136	70..............	169
65..............	142	71..............	174
66..............	145	72..............	178

See *Brain, Human.*

Anatomy of Melancholy. The name of a famous book, written by Robert Burton (1576–1640). Its full title is as follows : " Anatomy of Melancholy: what it is, with all the kinds, causes, symtomes, prognosticks, and severall cures of it. In three maine partitions, with their severall sections, members, and subsections. Philosophically, medicinally, historically opened and cut up. By Democritus Junior."

Burton is said to have written the work to banish melancholy, and Dr. Johnson declared it to be the only book that ever caused him to get out of bed two hours earlier than he wished.

Anchorites. A famous class of hermits that lived in solitary cells, from which they rarely, if ever, emerged. They were most numerous in the East, and are first met with in the 4th century after Christ. Paul, Anthony, and Pachomius were among the most celebrated. These hermits of early times must not be confounded with the anchorites of the 12th, 13th, and 14th centuries. The former were confined in solitary cells ; the latter were allowed to go abroad freely.

Ancient Mariner, Rime of the. The title of a famous poem by Samuel Taylor Coleridge (1772–1834). The "Ancient Mariner," while at sea, has shot an albatross (a bird of good-omen to sailors) ; in consequence, he is doomed to fearful sufferings in expiation of his crime, and is forced to wander over the earth and relate his experiences as a warning to others. See *Albatross.*

Ancients, Council of. The upper chamber of the French legislature, during the rule of the Directory. It consisted of 250 members, each of whom was at least 40 years of age. It was instituted at Paris, November 1st, 1795, and dissolved by Napoleon Bonaparte, November 9th, 1799. Bonaparte, Ducos, and Sieyès were immediately declared "Consuls Provisoires." See *Five Hundred, Council of.*

Andalusia. A name formerly applied to the southern part of Spain, and still retaining much of its significance. The word is a corruption of *Vandalitia* or *Vandalusia*, from the Vandals, who overran the country from 409 to 429 A.D. In Phœnician times, this region was known as Tartessus, probably the "Tarshish" of the Bible. See *Tarshish ; Vandals.*

Andaman Islands. A group of islands in the eastern part of the Bay of Bengal. A penal settlement was established there by Great Britain in 1858. The native inhabitants are dwarfs, and rank among the very lowest in the stage of civilization. They are between 4 and 5 feet in height ; have no settled habitations, but pass freely from island to island ; and subsist on fish, small animals, and fruit. Their number does not exceed 3000, and is rapidly diminishing. Since their first intercourse with Europeans they have suffered moral deterioration.

Andersonville. A village in Georgia, which, during the Civil War, was famous as the seat of a Confederate military prison. This consisted of an open pen in a field,—1540 feet long by 750 feet broad,— surrounded by a stockade. The spot became notorious for its unwholesomeness, as well as for the cruelties inflicted upon the prisoners. It is stated that of 44,882 prisoners received in one year, 12,996 died of starvation and neglect. Henry Wirz, the superintendent, was tried for cruelty, and hanged November 10th, 1865. The trenches where the prisoners were buried were converted into a national cemetery containing over 13,000 graves.

Angelic Doctor. An appellation bestowed upon Thomas Aquinas, or St. Thomas of Aquino (1227–1274). It is said that he was so called because he discussed the question of "how many angels can dance on the point of a needle," or, more strictly speaking, "if an angel passes from one point to another, does he pass over the intervening space ? " The Doctor's answer was "No."

He belonged to the Dominican Order, and was canonized by Pope John XXII (1316–1334) in 1323, and declared by Pope Pius V (1566–1572) in 1567 to be the "Fifth Doctor of the Church,"—the other four being Ambrose, Augustine, Jerome, and Gregory. Aquinas was a Nominalist. His great opponent was Duns Scotus, a Realist, of the Franciscan Order. From this fact, the Nominalists were often called "Thomists," and the Realists, "Scotists." Among other titles given to Thomas Aquinas were "The Angel of the Schools," "The Eagle of Divines," and "The Universal Doctor."

Angelus. The name given to a prayer to the Virgin Mary, instituted by Pope Urban II (1088–1099). It begins with the words, "Angelus Domini nuntiavit Mariæ" (*Lat. The angel of the Lord announced to Mary*): this is followed by the words, "Ave Maria," etc., — the salutation of the angel Gabriel. The prayer consists of three verses, and each verse ends with the salutation.

The word "Angelus" is also used to mean the bell that is rung three times daily to call the faithful to recite this prayer. This custom was instituted, in 1316, by Pope John XXII (1316–1334). Louis XI (1461–1483) of France commanded the "Angelus" to be rung every day at noon.

Animals Admitted into Heaven. According to the Mohammedan faith, certain animals are admitted into Heaven. They are as follows :

(1) The dog Kratim, of the Seven Sleepers of Ephesus.

(2) Balaam's Ass, which reproved the Prophet.

(3) Solomon's Ant, which reproved the sluggard.

(4) Jonah's Whale, which swallowed him.

(5) The Ram of Israel, offered in sacrifice by Abraham, in place of Isaac.

(6) The Camel of Saleh.

(7) The Cuckoo of Belkis.

(8) The Ox of Moses.

(9) Al Borak, which conveyed Mohammed to Heaven.

(10) The Ass on which our Savior rode into Jerusalem.

The following is sometimes added or substituted : The Ass on which the Queen of Sheba rode, on her visit to Solomon. See *Al Borak.*

Animals, Cruelty to. The first Society for the Prevention of Cruelty to Animals was founded in England in 1824 by Mr. Martin, M.P. The Scottish society was founded in 1839. In 1879, the "Fellowship of Animals' Friends" was organized, with the Earl of Shaftesbury as president. The

"American Society for the Prevention of Cruelty to Animals" was organized in New York City in 1865. It was chartered by the State of New York in 1866, and Henry Bergh was elected president. Between 1866 and 1881 more than 30 branches were founded in the United States, and the movement was extended into France and Germany. Nearly all the States of the American Union have passed laws punishing cruelty to animals with fine and imprisonment. The "Dogs' Home" in London was founded in 1861. Ellen M. Gifford established the "Sheltering Home of Animals" at Brighton, Mass., where homeless and injured cats and dogs are sheltered and protected.

Animals, Facts Concerning.

Duration of Life.

Whales	500 years.
Alligators	300 "
Eagles	200 "
Elephants	100 "

Camels can travel 12 or 14 days without water, going 40 miles a day. They are ready for work at 5 years of age, remain in their prime until 25, and live about 40 years. The Tartars have herds of 1000 or more. Job had 3000. Napoleon, while in Egypt, conveyed 1500 infantry on camels across the desert from Cairo to St. Jean d'Acre.

The number of *cats* in Great Britain and Ireland is about 7,000,000. They came into England before 1066 A.D. Southey says that the first settlers in Brazil paid £300 for a cat, and for kittens their weight in gold-dust. £500 was offered for a Persian cat at the Sydenham cat-show in 1869. The offer was declined.

The number of *dogs* in Great Britain and Ireland is at least 2,000,000, and their value is estimated at £800,000. Hydrophobia is much more prevalent among male dogs than among female dogs, — 100 of the former going mad, as compared with 14 of the latter. A dog accidentally confined at Metz passed 39 days without food, and recovered.

The tusks of an ordinary *elephant* weigh 120 lbs. and are worth £60. It requires 12,000 elephants to supply 650 tons of ivory to the English market. Sheffield takes one-third.

There are 4,000,000 *llamas* in Peru. They are the camels of South America.

25,000,000 *squirrels* are killed annually in Russia for their skins.

A large *turtle* gives 80 lbs. of tortoise-shell.

(I am indebted to Mulhall's *Dictionary of Statistics* for the above facts.)

Animism. The name of a theory originally propounded by Stahl, about 1707. It asserts that the soul is the vital principle and only cause of life, and that the functions of plant and animal life depend upon this principle of vitality, and not upon mere mechanical and chemical action. As the word "animism" is now used, it denotes the general doctrine of spiritual beings. It is not itself a religion, but a sort of primitive philosophy. The term was first so used by Dr. E. B. Tylor, in 1869.

Anne Hathaway's Cottage. A charming little cottage in the village of Shottery, near Stratford-on-Avon, England. There Anne Hathaway is said to have lived before she became the wife of Shakespeare. The house is built of wood and plaster; the parlor has a high oaken wainscot; and in one of the principal rooms may be seen a large and heavily carved bedstead. It was doubtless a comfortable home for a prosperous yeoman of the days of Queen Elizabeth.

Anne's Fan, Queen. The name given to a gesture made by putting the thumb to the nose and spreading the other fingers of the hand.

Annie Laurie. The title of a famous song, composed about 1700, by Mr. Douglass Finland, in honor of Annie Laurie, of whom he was deeply enamored. She was the daughter of Sir Robert Laurie, and became the most beautiful girl of the day. She did not return the affection of her devoted admirer, but married his rival, Alexander Furgusson.

> " Her brow is like the snowdrift,
>   Her throat is like the swan,
> Her face it is the fairest
>   That e'er the sun shone on,
> That e'er the sun shone on,
>   And dark blue is her eye,
> And for bonnie *Annie Laurie*
>   I 'd lay me down and die."

Annus Mirabilis (*Lat. Wonderful Year*). The year 1666, memorable for the "Great Fire of London," and for the English victories over the Dutch. Dryden has commemorated both of these events by a poem entitled *Annus Mirabilis*.

Antediluvians. A name applied to the people that are said to have lived before the Flood, during the patriarchal ages between Adam and Noah. In accordance with Archbishop Usher's chronology, the Deluge occurred 1656 years after the Creation. According to the tables of Mr. Whiston, the population of the globe in the year of the world 1482 was 549,755,000,000. Burnet's estimate is much more moderate, — 10,733,418,240. It is needless to say that both these estimates are utterly absurd. The present population of the globe is estimated at about 1,400,-000,000. See *Population of the World*.

Anthony's Nose. A high peak on the Hudson River, situated on the east bank, about 45 miles from New York. It is about 1500 feet in height, and forms, with Dunderberg Mountain on the opposite bank, the southern gate of the Highlands. It derives its name, according to some, from St. Anthony, the founder of monasticism. Others, however, with more show of reason, say that the mountain was so named by Peter Stuyvesant, in honor of the lusty nose of his trumpeter, Anthony Van Corlear.

Anthropomorphism. The ascription to the Deity, of qualities that belong to human beings. Thus, we speak of the anger, the jealousy, or the love of God. This tendency is a necessary one, since, in its highest abstractions of the Deity, the mind must depend upon human analogies. Feuerbach regards this tendency of the human mind as the source of all religions. Fichte rejects the anthropomorphic nature of the Deity, and regards God simply as the moral order of the universe.

Anthropophagi (*Gr. Man-Eaters.*) A name given by the Greeks to the cannibals of ancient times. It is used by Homer and Herodotus. Cannibalism still exists in some of the South Sea Islands. Shakespeare, in *Othello*, 1, 4, writes as follows :

" And of the Cannibals that each other eat,
The *Anthropophagi*, and men whose heads
Do grow beneath their shoulders."

Antichrist. Any opponent or enemy of Christ. The word occurs in the *New Testament* in the following places : — 1 *John* ii, 18, 22, iv. 3 ; 2 *John* 7. The " Man of Sin," whose coming is foretold by St. Paul in 2 *Thessalonians* ii, is supposed by many to refer to the same. In *Revelation* xii, xiii, emblematic references are made to Antichrist. Theologians have puzzled their wits to identify this archenemy of Christianity. Roman Catholics see him incarnated in heresy, while Protestants declare the Pope to be Antichrist. Nero, Mohammed, the Grand Turk, Napoleon I, and Napoleon III have all in turn been distinguished with this appellation. It is declared that Antichrist will appear before the coming of Christ in his glory.

Antietam, Battle of. A bloody battle fought on the banks of Antietam Creek, near Sharpsburg, Maryland, on September 17th, 1862, between the Union forces under General McClellan and the Confederates under General Lee. About 100,000 men were engaged. The battle lasted from five o'clock in the morning until night, when the Confederates retreated with a loss of about 14,000 men. The Union loss was about 12,000.

Antinous. A youth of surpassing beauty. He was the page and favorite of the Emperor Hadrian (117–138 A.D.), and his companion on all his journeys. Antinous was born at Claudiopolis in Bithynia, and was drowned in the Nile, 122 A.D. His death has been, by many, ascribed to suicide, either because of weariness engendered by his mode of life, or because he deemed that his voluntary death would avert disaster from the Emperor. Hadrian's grief at the loss of his favorite knew no bounds. Antinous was deified, and the city of Antinopolis was founded in his honor. See *Antinous of the Capitol ; Antinous of the Vatican.*

Antinous of the Capitol. A famous statue of Antinous, the favorite of the Emperor Hadrian. It was found at Hadrian's Villa, in 1730. See *Antinous ; Hadrian's Villa.*

" This exquisite statue has commanded the admiration of all critics by its exceeding beauty."—*Murray.*

Antinous of the Vatican. A famous colossal statue of Antinous, the favorite of the Emperor Hadrian. It was found at Palestrina, in 1773. The figure has a pensive attitude, with the left foot slightly raised.

Lübke says it is " characterized by an expression of thoughtful melancholy in the drooping head, by brows overshadowed by clustering curls, and by a suggestion of sadness in the curve of the voluptuous mouth." See *Antinous.*

Antipopes. Roman Catholic pontiffs, elected in opposition to those canonically chosen. The first antipope was Felix II (355–358), and the last, Felix V (1439–1449).

Anti-Slavery Society, American. Was founded in Philadelphia on December 6th, 1833. William Lloyd

Garrison was soon after elected president. In May, 1865, Garrison resigned, and Wendell Phillips was chosen president. In April, 1870, after a commemorative meeting in New York City, the Society adjourned *sine die*. See *Abolitionists*.

Antonine Column. A column standing on the Piazza Colonna at Rome. It was erected by the Roman Senate, 174 A.D., in honor of the victories of the Emperor Marcus Aurelius Antoninus (161–180 A.D.) over the Marcomanni and other Germanic tribes. Bas-reliefs, arranged spirally on the shaft of the column, represent the triumphs of the Roman armies. The column was originally surmounted by a statue of the Emperor. Pope Sixtus V (1585–1590) removed this, and substituted for it a gilded statue of St. Paul holding a Latin cross.

Aphrodite. The Greek name for Venus, the goddess of love and beauty. She was the wife of Hephæstus, but was not especially noted for conjugal fidelity. Among her amours were those with Ares and Dionysos among the gods, and with Adonis and Anchises among mortals. By Anchises, she became the mother of Æneas, and was accordingly regarded by the Romans as their progenitor. She is said to have sprung from the foam of the sea, whence the name *Aphrodite* (*Gr. ἀφρός, foam*).

Apis. In Egyptian mythology, the bull sacred to the god Osiris, the husband of Isis and the chief divinity of Egypt. He lived in an enclosure in the Temple of Ptah at Memphis, and was attended by a retinue of priests, who sacrificed red oxen to him. His movements, changes of position, and variations of appetite were carefully recorded and studied as oracles. He was never allowed to live more than 25 years,—at the end of which period he was secretly put to death and buried in a sacred well. If, however, he died a natural death, he was solemnly interred in the Temple of Sera-

pis at Memphis, after which a suitable successor was sought; when found, he was installed with bacchanalian rites. It is thought that the worship of the "Golden Calf" by the Israelites in the wilderness, and, later, the adoration of golden calves as symbols of the Deity by Jeroboam, were derived from the Egyptian worship of Apis. See *Osiris*.

Apocalypse. The last book of the *New Testament*, commonly known as the *Revelation of St. John the Divine*. Its authorship is generally ascribed to St. John, who is said to have written it during his banishment to the island of Patmos, 95 A.D. Some, however, declare Cerinthus, the heretic, to have been the author; and others, John, the presbyter of Ephesus. During the early centuries of Christianity, many churches disowned it. The Council of Laodicea excluded it from the sacred canon in the 4th century; but it was finally included in the list of canonical writings by the Council of Trent in 1546. Luther, Michaelis, and others rejected it.

Apocrypha. A name given by the early Christian Church to certain books that were said to be inspired, but were not admitted to the sacred canon. When the word "Apocrypha" is used, it generally refers to the apocryphal books of the *Old Testament*. These books are found in the Septuagint Version of the *Old Testament*, but not in the Hebrew canon. They were rejected by the Council of Laodicea in 366, but were accepted by the Roman Catholic Church at the Council of Trent in 1546. The Protestant denominations do not accept them as canonical. They are 14 in number, and are as follows:

(1) First Esdras.
(2) Second Esdras.
(3) Tobit.
(4) Judith.
(5) Esther.
(6) Wisdom of Solomon.
(7) Ecclesiasticus.
(8) Baruch.

(9) Song of the Three Children.
(10) History of Susannah.
(11) Bel and the Dragon.
(12) Prayer of Manasses.
(13) First Maccabees.
(14) Second Maccabees.

The Apocryphal books of the *New Testament* have never been accepted as canonical. They consist of spurious gospels and epistles.

Apollo Belvedere. A famous statue of Apollo, discovered in 1495 among the ruins of ancient Antium (the modern Porto d'Anzio), and purchased by Pope Julius II (1503–1513), when cardinal. It was placed by him in the "Belvedere" of the Vatican palace at Rome, whence its name. The Apollo Belvedere is more than seven feet in height, and is probably the work of Calamis, the Greek sculptor, who flourished during the 5th century before Christ. When the statue was discovered, the left hand and the right forearm were wanting. These were restored by Montosorli, a pupil of Michael Angelo. The Apollo Belvedere is thought to be a copy of a bronze statue erected at Delphi, representing the god in the act of defending his shrine from an attack of the Gauls.

"There are, doubtless, finer statues in the world than the Apollo,—works proceeding from a deeper vein of sentiment, and breathing a more simple grandeur,—but there are none more fascinating. In this statue, more than in any other work in marble, we recognize the grace and animation of a living form ; a sympathetic charm which every one can feel."—*Six Months in Italy* (Hillard).

Apollo of Portugal. A sobriquet conferred upon Luis de Camoëns (1524–1580), the author of *The Lusiad*, in allusion to the charm and stateliness of his verse. See *Homer of Portugal*.

Apollyon. The Greek name of the angel of the bottomless pit. In Hebrew, the name is Abaddon. Bunyan, in his *Pilgrim's Progress*, introduces Apollyon. He engages Christian in conflict, but is worsted in the encounter. See *Abaddon*.

Apologia pro Vitâ Suâ (*Lat. Apology for His Life*). The title of the autobiography of John Henry Newman (1801–1890), cardinal of the Roman Catholic Church in England. It was published in 1864, and afterwards slightly recast as *A History of My Religious Opinions*. Newman was originally a clergyman of the Established Church of England ; but in 1845 he was received into the Roman Catholic communion.

Apostate. A surname applied to Julianus Flavius Claudius (361–363 A.D.), the Roman Emperor, familiarly known as "Julian the Apostate." On his accession to the throne, he renounced Christianity and embraced paganism. He proclaimed liberty of conscience to all, commanded the pagan temples to be reopened, and even attempted to rebuild the Temple at Jerusalem. It is said that sulphurous flames, issuing from the ground, forced the workmen to desist from their labors. He was killed in a war undertaken against the Persians.

Apostle of Andalusia. An appellation bestowed upon Juan de Ovila (1500–1569), an eloquent and indefatigable Spanish preacher, who labored for 20 years with great success as a home-missionary in the south of Spain. Among his converts were St. Francisco Borgia and St. Teresa de Jesus.

Apostle of Free-Trade. A title conferred upon Richard Cobden (1804–1865) in allusion to his efforts and triumphs in the cause of free-trade.

Apostle of Germany. A title bestowed upon St. Boniface (680–755 A.D.), who, for over 30 years, labored among the Germans and converted many of them to Christianity. He was born in Devonshire, England. In 732, he was appointed by Pope Gregory III (731–741) archbishop and primate of Germany. He was assassinated by an armed band of pagans.

Apostle of Infidelity. An appellation given to Voltaire (1694–1778), in consequence of his satirical and bitter attacks upon the Christian religion.

It is only just to the memory of Voltaire to say that he was in no sense an atheist, and that there are to be found in his works some of the most beautiful and admirable arguments ever presented in favor of the existence of a God.

Apostle of Ireland. An appellation conferred upon St. Patrick (372–493 A.D.), a native of Scotland, who is supposed to have introduced Christianity into Ireland. He labored for twenty years among the Irish people, and, according to some of his biographers, founded 365 churches, baptized with his own hands 12,000 persons, and consecrated 450 bishops. The Irish observe the 17th of March in his honor.

Apostle of Liberty. A nickname given to Henry Clay (1777–1852), who, by his eloquence in Congress, urged the country to declare war against England in 1812, and advocated the recognition of the independence of the states of Spanish America. This title has been applied also to Thomas Jefferson (1743–1826), the third president of the United States.

Apostle of Temperance. A title bestowed upon Father Mathew (1790–1856), a native of Ireland. In 1838 he became president of a temperance society in Cork, and, through his instrumentality, 150,000 persons in that city alone were induced to sign the pledge. He afterwards visited different parts of Ireland, England, and the United States. In recognition of his services to the cause of temperance and good morals, Queen Victoria granted him an annuity of £500. See *Sinner's Friend.*

Apostle of the English. A title conferred upon St. Augustine or Austin (d. 604 A.D.), first archbishop of Canterbury. In 596 he was sent, with 40 other monks, by Pope Gregory I (590–604) to convert the Anglo-Saxons to Christianity. It is recorded that in one day he baptized 10,000 persons in the river Swale. He must not be confounded with the great St. Augustine, Bishop of Hippo in Numidia.

Apostle of the French. A title bestowed upon St. Denis (d. 272 or 290 A.D.), first bishop of Paris, and patron-saint of France. He was sent from Rome, about 250, to preach the gospel to the Gauls. He proceeded as far as Paris (*Lat. Lutetia Parisiorum*), where he suffered martyrdom by order of the Roman governor. The words "Montjoie St. Denis!" have been for many years a French rallying-cry in battle.

Apostle of the Gauls. A name given to St. Irenæus (130–208 A.D.). He was a pupil of the famous Polycarp of Smyrna, and became bishop of Lyons, France, about 177 A.D. He labored among the churches of Gaul with zeal and discretion.

Apostle of the Gentiles. This well-known appellation was bestowed upon St. Paul, owing to his fervor and zeal in preaching Christianity to all mankind, without distinction of any sort whatsoever.

Apostle of the Highlanders. A name given to St. Columba (521–597 A.D.), a native of Ireland, who visited Scotland in 565, and is believed to have been the first to preach Christianity there. He also founded an abbey and a college in Iona, one of the Hebrides. It is an interesting fact that it was an Irishman who introduced Christianity into Scotland, and a Scotchman [St. Patrick] who first preached the Christian religion in Ireland.

Apostle of the Indians. A title bestowed upon Bartolomé de las Casas (1474–1566) and upon John Eliot (1604–1690), for their labors in the prosecution of missionary work among the North American Indians. During the years 1661-1663, John Eliot translated the Bible into the Indian language.

Apostle of the Picts. A sobriquet conferred upon St. Ninian, a British bishop, who converted the Picts living south of the Grampian Hills, during the 5th century.

Apostle of the Sword. An epithet conferred upon Mohammed (570-632 A.D.), because he enforced the religion of Islam at the point of the sword.

Apostle to the Indies. A name given to St. Francis Xavier (1506-1552 A.D.), a celebrated Jesuit missionary, who spent ten years in endeavoring to introduce Christianity into the East. In Travancore, he is said to have baptized 10,000 idolaters within nine months. After laboring in India, he desired to penetrate into China and carry the gospel thither ; but ere he could reach this new field of labor, he died on the island of Sancian, near China. He was canonized in 1622.

Apostles' Creed. Probably the earliest form of Christian creed that exists. Not only has it been attributed to the apostles directly, but, according to a legend, each one of the twelve clauses has been contributed by one of the apostles. This account of its origin was given by Rufinus early in the 4th century; but other and more reliable authorities regard the story as unworthy of credence. The "Apostles' Creed" is doubtless the formula of belief that existed in all the early Latin churches. It was made a part of the public worship of the Greek Church at Antioch, and was introduced into the Roman Catholic Church in the 11th century. It thus found its way into the Church of England. See *Athanasian Creed; Nicene Creed ; Twelve Articles of the Symbol.*

Apostles, Twelve. According to the *New Testament* and Church tradition, the following are the names of the twelve apostles : Simon Peter, Andrew, John and James (the sons of Zebedee), Philip, Bartholomew, Thomas, Matthew or Levi, James the Less, Jude or Thaddeus, Simon, and Judas Iscariot. Matthias was subsequently chosen in place of Judas Iscariot. Early tradition says that all of the apostles, except John, suffered martyrdom.

Apostolic Council. The name given to the first convention of the Christian Church, held at Jerusalem in 47 A.D. This general meeting of the apostles and elders of the early Church was held for the purpose of deciding whether converts from paganism should be admitted into the Christian communion, without first submitting to the rite of circumcision and to other observances of the Mosaic ceremonial. After Peter's experience with Cornelius had been recounted, as well as the labors of Paul and Barnabas among the Gentiles, James, as president of the Council, declared that all converts from Gentilism to Christianity should be admitted into the Church without any requirement whatever.

Apostolic Fathers. A name given to certain Christian writers that were contemporaries or immediate successors of the apostles : *i. e.*, that lived and wrote before 120 A.D. Those generally mentioned are Barnabas, Clement of Rome, Ignatius of Antioch, Hermas, and Polycarp. Irenæus adds Papias of Hierapolis, but this is probably an error. Their writings are deemed far inferior to the apostolic epistles, although in form and spirit they may be considered a continuation of them. Their main purpose is to exhort believers to faith and goodness before the second coming of Christ. The following works are generally attributed to these writers:

(1) The Epistle of Barnabas.

(2) Two Epistles of Clement, bishop of Rome, to the Corinthians.

(3) Several Epistles of Ignatius, bishop of Antioch.

(4) Epistle of Polycarp, bishop of Smyrna, to the Philippians.

(5) Book entitled Pastor Hermas.

Some fragments of Papias are generally included among the writings of the Apostolic Fathers.

Apostolic Succession. A doctrine held by the Roman Catholic Church and by most Episcopalians. It teaches:

1st. That there has been an uninterrupted line of clerical ordination from the days of the apostles to the present time.

2nd. That the bishops of the Church alone have the right to ordain, as being the representatives, in an unbroken line, of the apostles themselves, who, in their turn, were the representatives of Christ.

3rd. That all that have not been thus ordained are excluded from the ministry.

4th. That Christ conferred this power of ordination upon the apostles for the proper guidance and government of the Church, and that it has been handed down unbroken to the present day.

Apotheosis of Augustus. The largest cameo in the world. It is of Roman workmanship, and is carved on a sardonyx, nearly a foot in height. There are 26 figures, and among them are those of Augustus, Æneas, Julius Cæsar, Drusus, Tiberius, Livia, Germanicus, Agrippina, and Caligula. The cameo was brought to France in 1224, and sold to Louis IX, who presented it to La Sainte Chapelle. It passed thence to the Cabinet of Medals and Antiques in the Bibliothèque Nationale at Paris, where it now is. It was originally supposed to represent a triumphal procession of Joseph in Egypt.

Appalachian Mountains. The name given to an extensive mountain-system in North America, extending nearly parallel with the Atlantic coast from the Gulf of St. Lawrence to the State of Alabama. It is geologically older than the western or Rocky Mountain system, but nowhere attains so great an altitude. Its highest peak is Mount Mitchell in North Carolina (6711 feet); Mount Washington in New Hampshire (perhaps the most noted) is 6293 feet. Locally, the range has various names : in New Hampshire, it is known as the White Mountains; in Vermont, as the Green Mountains ; in Massachusetts, as the Hoosac and Taghanic ranges; in New York, as the Catskills and the Highlands ; in Pennsylvania, as the Alleghanies; in Virginia, as the Blue Ridge; in North Carolina, as the Smoky ; in Tennessee and Alabama, as the Cumberland ; and in Georgia, as the Sand, Lookout, etc. The word "Appalachian" is derived from a tribe of Indians, the Appalachees, formerly living in Florida, near the Appalachicola River.

Appeal to Cæsar. According to the famous "Porcian Law," no Roman citizen could be bound, scourged, or put to death without a hearing. He could always appeal to a trial before the "Centuries," but, during the Empire, Cæsar represented the "Centuries." The "Appeal to Cæsar" was much like the right of "habeas corpus," which insures to all accused persons a fair trial. See *Habeas Corpus.*

Appian Way. The oldest and most famous of the Roman military roads. It was commenced by Appius Claudius Cæcus, while censor, in 312 B.C., and originally extended from the Porta Capena at Rome to Capua, a distance of 120 miles. In 30 B.C., the "Appian Way" was continued to Brundisium, 320 miles from Rome. By means of its branches, it connected Rome with all of Southern Italy. During the rule of Pope Pius IX (1846–1878), a portion of this road — extending about 11 miles out of Rome — was laid bare. It is remarkable for its pavement, which consists of large hexagonal blocks of basalt; but more especially for the ruins of the once magnificent tombs that line its sides. The central portion of the roadway — 16 feet wide — was designed for the passage of infantry, while the two side-passages — each, also, 16 feet wide—were used for horsemen and vehicles. The Romans called the Appian Way *Regina Viarum* (*Queen of Roads*). See *Roman Roads*.

Apple of Discord. At the marriage of Peleus and Thetis, all the gods and goddesses — except Eris, or Discord, —were present. Angry at not being invited, she threw among them a golden apple, bearing the inscription " To the most beautiful." Juno, Minerva, and Venus each claimed the prize, and Zeus referred them for a decision to Paris, a shepherd on Mount Ida. Venus, having promised to Paris the most beautiful woman in the world for his wife, was awarded the apple. By so doing, Paris incurred the enmity of Juno and Minerva, who, by their spite, brought on the Trojan War.

Apple-Pie Bed. A bed in which the sheets are so folded that a person cannot get down into it. Some have thought that the expression is derived from the French *plier* (*to fold*).

Apple-Pie Order. Primness and neatness of arrangement, extending to the most trifling detail.

Apples of Sodom. Imaginary fruit, said by the ancients to grow near the Dead Sea. They were beautiful to behold, but turned to ashes on the lips. Sometimes called "Dead-Sea Fruit." See *Dead-Sea Fruit ; Sodom, Vine of.*

" There are apple-trees on the sides of the Dead Sea which bear lovely fruit, but within are full of ashes."—*Thevenot.*

" Like to the apples on the Dead Sea's shore, All ashes to the taste."

Childe Harold, III, 34.

Appomattox Court-House. A village in Virginia, 20 miles east of Lynchburg. There on April 9th, 1865, General Lee surrendered to General Grant the Army of Northern Virginia, consisting of 27,805 men. This event practically ended the Civil War.

Apsley House. Once the residence of the Duke of Wellington (1769–1852). It is situated on Piccadilly, London, and immediately adjoins Hyde Park. It was built about 1785 for Charles Bathurst, Lord Apsley, and in 1820 was purchased by the government, and presented to the Duke of Wellington as a reward for his distinguished services. At present it contains a picture-gallery, and numerous portraits and statues.

Apteryx (*Gr. ἄπτερος, without wings*). A bird first brought to England from New Zealand in 1813. It is usually about the size of a large hen ; and, although incapable of flight, is not in reality wingless. Fossil remains of an extinct species were discovered by Walter Mantell in New Zealand in 1843. It is named *Dinornis*, and has been much studied by Professor Richard Owen.

Aqua Claudia. A famous aqueduct of ancient Rome, commenced by Caligula, and completed by Claudius in 50 A.D. It was 46 miles long, and had an altitude of over 200 feet. It crossed the Campagna upon a series of arches for a distance of 10 miles ; 6 miles of these arches are still standing, and form the grandest ruin outside of the city of Rome.

Aqua-Regia (*Lat. Royal Water*). A liquid composed of hydrochloric and nitric acids. It is so called because it dissolves gold, the " king of the metals." In the chemical reaction that ensues, chlorine gas is set free ; this attacks the gold and combines with it.

Aquarians. A Christian sect, during the third century, that used consecrated water instead of wine at the Eucharist. The name was also given to certain persons in Africa, who, in times of persecution, used water instead of wine at the celebration of the Lord's Supper in the morning, lest the odor should betray them.

Aquinian Sage. An epithet bestowed upon Juvenal (40–125 A.D.), the Roman poet, whose birthplace and home were at Aquinum, a town of the Volscians.

Arabesques. A fantastic kind of ornamentation,—either sculptured or painted,—said to have been introduced into modern Europe by the Spanish Moors. As the Mohammedan religion forbade the use of figures of animals for decorative purposes, the Moorish arabesques were composed of vines, leaves, flowers, and fruit, curiously intertwined. The most beautiful are to be found in the palace of the Alhambra, at Granada. The Moors are supposed to have derived their notions of this form of art from the Egyptians. Animals, and even human figures, are now introduced into arabesque decorations. The most famous and beautiful of modern times are those with which Raphael adorned the galleries of the Vatican.

Arabia Felix. Arabia is commonly divided into three parts :—Arabia Felix, Arabia Petræa, and Arabia Deserta. Arabia Felix borders on the Indian Ocean, the Persian Gulf, and the south part of the Red Sea. The meaning of the word " Felix " is a matter of dispute. Many claim that the word means " happy " or " blessed," and was applied to this part of the peninsula by the British merchants that bought the produce of India that came by way of Arabia, thinking it was the product of the latter country. Others assert that the word signifies " the land lying to the right," i. e., to the south of Mecca. With the Orientals, the cardinal point is east, not north. See *Arabia Petræa.*

Arabian Nights' Entertainments. A collection of tales of Indian, Persian, and Arabic origin. They are also called *The Thousand and One Nights,* from the number of nights supposed to have been spent in their recital. They were discovered in Syria, in the latter part of the 17th century, and introduced into Europe by Antoine Galland, the French Orientalist, who travelled extensively in the East, under the patronage of Colbert. Galland afterwards translated them, and published them in Paris in twelve volumes, in 1708–1712. Their authenticity was doubted for many years; but it is now admitted that they were composed some time during the 16th century. The best English translation is that of E. W. Lane, published in 1839, with notes and illustrations.

Arabia Petræa. The correct translation of this phrase is not *Stony Arabia,* but *Arabia of the city of Petra.* The adjective "Petræa" is not formed from the Greek πέτρος (*rock*) ; but from Petra, a city in the northwest of Arabia. See *Arabia Felix.*

Aramaic Language. A branch of the Semitic family of languages. It is divided into two forms or dialects,—the Syriac or West Aramaic and the Chaldee or East Aramaic. The Syriac or West Aramaic dialect is the form spoken by the Jews at the beginning of the Christian era, and is probably the one used by Jesus Christ.

Arbela, Battle of. The third and final battle between Alexander the Great (336–323 B.C.) and Darius Codomanus (336–330 B.C.) was fought on a plain in Assyria, between the towns of Arbela and Gaugamela, on October 1st, 331 B.C. It resulted in a decisive victory for Alexander, and put an end to the Persian Empire. The army of Darius consisted of 1,000,000 infantry and 40,000 cavalry ; while that of Alexander numbered only 40,000 foot-soldiers and 7000 horsemen. Before the battle was ended, Darius fled from the field, leaving 300,000 dead. He escaped into Media, and afterwards into Bactria, where he was assassinated by Bessus, the satrap of the province. The entire Persian Empire soon after submitted to the conqueror. As the result of his victory, Alexander secured 30,000,000 sterling, in gold and silver, from the cities of Susa, Persepolis, and Babylon ; while the treasures obtained from the spoils of Darius sufficed to load 20,000 mules and 5000 camels.

Arbiter Elegantiæ (*Lat. Umpire of Taste*). A title conferred upon Caius Petronius by Tacitus, the Roman historian. He was placed in charge of the pleasures and amusements at the court of Nero, and nothing was deemed in good taste unless stamped with his approval. Falling into disgrace with the Emperor, he committed suicide in 66 A.D. He is supposed to be identical with Petronius, a licentious Roman author during the time of Nero, who wrote the satirical novel *Satyricon*, describing the vices of the day. Fragments of this work are still extant. See *Satyricon*.

Arbor Day. A day set apart in the United States and Canada for the planting of shade-trees, shrubs, etc. It is chiefly observed by the children of the public schools. This idea, it is said, was first suggested by Governor Morton of Nebraska, for the purpose of protecting the land from the fierce western and southern winds. The notion proved to be a popular one, and spread rapidly to the other States of the Union. Different days have been chosen in the different States. The custom has been in vogue about ten years, and during that time millions of trees have been planted.

Arcadia. The central state of the ancient Peloponnesus, Greece. It derived its name from Arcas, the son of Callisto. The inhabitants considered themselves the most ancient in Greece; they lived in a state of peace and innocence, and hence the word "Arcadia" has come to denote rustic simplicity and content.

"Arcadia" is also the name of a pastoral romance by Sir Philip Sidney (1554–1586) ; an Italian pastoral fable by Jacopo Sannazaro (1458–1530); and a pastoral heroic poem by Lope de Vega Carpio (1562–1635). See *Arcady*.

Arcady. A poetic name for Arcadia, a country of ancient Greece. See *Arcadia*.

"And round us all the thicket rang
To many a flute of *Arcady*."
In Memoriam, xxiii (Tennyson).

Arcana (*Lat. Secrets*). A word meaning either the great secrets sought by the alchemists, such as the "philosopher's stone," the "elixir of life," etc., or their most valued preparations, such as the double arcanum (*sulphate of potash*), the coral arcanum (*deutoxide of red mercury, prepared with nitric acid*), and the jovial arcanum (*a mixture of the deutoxide of tin and the nitrate of mercury*).

Arcana Cœlestia (*Lat. Heavenly Secrets*). The title of Swedenborg's (1688–1772) first theological work. It comprised eight quarto volumes,—the first appearing in 1749, and the last in 1758. It is an exposition of the books of *Genesis* and *Exodus*, with additional chapters describing the wonders of the world to come. See *Swedenborgians*.

Arc de Triomphe de l'Étoile. The largest triumphal arch of modern times, — standing on the Place de l'Étoile in Paris, at the west end of the Avenue des Champs Elysées, about two miles from the Louvre. It was dedicated by Napoleon I, in commemoration of the campaigns of the Grande Armée. The corner-stone was laid on August 15th, 1806. On the downfall of Napoleon, work was suspended, and the structure was not completed until 1836, under Louis Philippe. It is 152 feet high, 138 feet wide, and 68 feet deep. The foundations extend 25 feet below the level of the ground. The first architect was Chalgrin. The arch is elaborately carved with colossal figures in high relief, and upon it are inscribed the names of 96 of Napoleon's victories and of 384 of his generals. The structure cost $2,000,000. When the Germans entered Paris as conquerors in 1871, they passed under this arch.

Arc du Carrousel. A triumphal arch in the Place du Carrousel, Paris, erected in 1806 by Napoleon I. It is a modified copy of the arch of Septimius Severus at Rome. The structure is 45 feet high, 60 feet wide, and 21 feet deep, and is surmounted by a *quadriga* or four-horse chariot of Victory. When the arch was completed, the gilt bronze horses (known as *Les Chevaux de Co-rinthe*) that Napoleon took from the Cathedral of St. Mark in Venice were placed upon it. In 1815, the allies insisted that Venice should have her property restored to her. The present group was modelled after the former one, and was placed on the top of the arch in 1828. The arch is unfortunately placed, being dwarfed by the tall buildings that surround it, and does not command the attention it deserves. See *Arch of Septimius Severus; Bronze Horses ; Place du Carrousel.*

Arch. According to Wilkinson, the Egyptians and Assyrians were acquainted with the principles of the arch, and used it in their buildings. The Greeks also must have had a knowledge of it, although it occurs in none of their structures. The Romans probably derived their acquaintance with it from the Etruscans, and it is to the former that the nations of modern Europe are indebted for this form of construction. The oldest arch in the world is probably in the Cloaca Maxima at Rome, built about 600 B.C. The Chinese bridges, which are structures of great antiquity, are built with arches. Triumphal arches were a prominent feature in Roman architecture. Among them may be mentioned the Arch of Titus, the Arch of Constantine, the Arch of Septimius Severus, and the Arch of Trajan.

Archbishop. An ecclesiastical title first bestowed in the 4th and 5th centuries after Christ, and conferred upon the bishops of the leading cities,—such as Jerusalem, Antioch, Ephesus, Alexandria, Constantinople, and Rome. Athanasius (296–373) first used the word in his *Apology* against the Arians. In the 6th century after Christ, the title of Pope was claimed ex-

clusively by the Archbishop of Rome. In the Established Church of England there are two archbishops, one of whom has his seat at Canterbury, and the other at York. The Archbishop of Canterbury is styled "Primate of All England," and to him belongs the honor of placing the crown upon the sovereign's head at the coronation. The Roman Catholic Church has but one archiepiscopal see in England,—that of Westminster ; in the United States there are 14 ecclesiastic provinces, each under an archbishop. There are no Protestant archbishops in this country.

Archdeacon. In an episcopal diocese, the name of an ecclesiastical dignitary, occupying a position subordinate to that of a bishop. Originally, archdeacons were simply the first or senior deacons. They assisted the bishop in the church services, in managing the revenues, and in directing the deacons in the performance of their duties. After the Council of Nice (325 A.D.), the function of archdeacon became a dignity above that of priest. In the 13th century, their powers were curtailed by the establishment of episcopal courts. The office of archdeacon has been introduced into some of the Protestant Episcopal dioceses of the United States.

Archimago. The name of an arch-hypocrite, in Spenser's *Faerie Queene.* He deceived Una and the Red Cross Knight, and was cast into a dungeon. Later he escaped from captivity and induced Braggaccio to attack the Red Cross Knight. See *Faerie Queene.*

Archimedes's Screw. The name of a machine for raising water, said to have been invented by Archimedes (287–212 B.C.), while he was in Egypt. It was used for draining and irrigating the land. It consists of a tube bent spirally around a cylinder, and placed in an inclined position, with the mouth below the surface of the liquid to be raised. As the cylinder is turned, the tube is gradually filled with water, which it discharges at a higher level.

Architecture, Orders of. There are five great orders of architecture, — the Doric, the Ionic, the Corinthian, the Tuscan, and the Composite. The first three are of Greek origin. The Doric Order is characterized by extreme simplicity : its column is without a base, and is seen at its best in the ruins of the Temple of Minerva, or the Parthenon, at Athens. The column of the Ionic Order has a base, while the shaft is lighter and more graceful than the Doric. The curves of its capital are said to have been suggested by the curls on each side of the human face. The Corinthian Order is the most ornate of the three. It is said to have been invented by Callimachus, a sculptor of the time of Pericles. The other orders of architecture—the Tuscan and the Composite—were introduced by the Romans. The Tuscan Order was formed by adding a base to the Doric column, and otherwise altering it. The Composite Order is a blending of the Ionic and Corinthian Orders. The Corinthian Order was the one most used by the Romans in the construction of their public buildings. See *Acanthus.*

Arch of Constantine. A famous triumphal arch in Rome, standing over the Via Triumphalis, near the Coliseum. It was erected by Constantine (306–337 A.D.), in 311, in commemoration of his victory over Maxentius. The structure, although a ruin, is in a fine state of preservation, and is, by many, considered the most imposing monument of ancient Rome. The ornamentations consist largely of bas-reliefs and medallions taken from the Arch of Trajan. Some writers, indeed, consider the Arch of Constantine as simply a transformation of the Arch of Trajan.

Arch of Septimius Severus. A noted monument in Rome, erected in 205 A.D., by the Senate in honor of the Emperor Septimius Severus (193–211 A.D.) and his sons Caracalla and Geta. It is built of marble, and stands at the northwest angle of the Forum. It was originally surmounted by a car containing statues of the emperor and his two sons, drawn by six horses abreast. The inscription on the arch, relating to Geta, was erased after his death, at his brother's command.

Arch of Titus. This magnificent triumphal arch stands on the Via Sacra at Rome, between the Forum and the Coliseum. It was erected in 81 A.D., by the Roman Senate in honor of Titus (79–81 A.D.), to commemorate his conquest of the Jews, ending with the destruction of Jerusalem. It contains, in bas-relief, a representation of the spoils brought from the temple at Jerusalem, among which were the golden candlestick, the silver trumpets, and the table of shewbread. It is said that the Jews, to this day, never pass under this arch, associated as it is with the downfall of their nation and the desecration of their temple.

Arcola, Battle of. This famous battle, between the French under Bonaparte and the Austrians commanded by Alvinzi, was fought on November 14th–17th, 1796, at Arcola in Lombardy. The Austrians were totally defeated, with a loss of 18,000 men — killed, wounded, and taken prisoners, — 4 flags, and 18 guns. The French lost 15,000 men, but became masters of Italy.

Arctic. The name of a steamship of the "Collins Transatlantic Line." In the autumn of 1854, she sank off the banks of Newfoundland, in consequence of a collision with the *Vesta*, during a dense fog. Many lives were lost, and the catastrophe proved a deathblow to the popularity of the line.

Arctic Explorations. During the 16th and 17th centuries, the English made many attempts to find a northern passage to India and China, since the southern routes, by way of the Cape of Good Hope and the Straits of Magellan, were closely guarded by the Portuguese and Spaniards. A northeast passage along the coast of Asia was finally proved to exist—though useless to commerce—by Behring (1728–1741), and this was at length actually traversed by Professor Nordenskiöld of Stockholm in 1879. In 1850, McClure had the good fortune to discover the "Northwest Passage." Conditions having changed, and the southern routes having become accessible to all, the original purpose of Arctic Explorations was abandoned, and the object of recent ones has been simply to reach the North Pole. Among these may be mentioned the German expeditions of Koldewey (1868–1869); the Austrian expedition of Payer and Weyprecht (1872); the British expedition of Nares (1875–1876); and the United States expedition of Greely (1881–1884). This last reached 83° 24′ north latitude (460 statute miles from the North Pole). Baron Nordenskiöld, in 1883, made a journey over the inland ice of Greenland, and in 1888, Dr. Nansen crossed Greenland from sea to sea. Later still (1894) an expedition to Greenland, under Lieutenant Peary, set out from the United States. In April, 1900, the expedition of the Prince Luigi, Duke of the Abruzzi, of Italy, reached a point 86° 33′ north latitude—239 statute miles distant from the North Pole. Robert E. Peary, U. S. N., reached the North Pole on April 6, 1909.

Arda Viraf Namak (*The Book of Arda Viraf*). A religious book among the Parsees, written in Pehlevi. The author and the date of the production are unknown ; but the book belongs, without doubt, to Sassanian times (226–651 A.D.). It gives an account of the visit of Arda Viraf to the land of the dead, in search of knowledge as to the truth of the Zoroastrian religion. He was guided on his expedition through heaven and hell by Sraosha, " the angel of obedience " and Ataro Yazad, " the angel of the fire." The book contains a minute account of the joys of heaven and the pains of hell. See *Parsees.*

Arden, Forest of. A forest in England, formerly existing, and lying between the Avon and the Severn. It is the scene of the Duke's banishment in Shakespeare's comedy of *As You Like It.* See *Ardennes, Forest of.*

Ardennes, Forest of. A forest of great extent, formerly existing in Belgium and the north of France. The wood of Soignies, south of Brussels, is supposed to be a remnant of the Forest of Ardennes. Byron, in *Childe Harold*, speaking of the march of the British soldiers through the wood of Soignies, before the battle of Waterloo, says :

"And *Ardennes* waves above them her green leaves,
Dewy with nature's tear-drops as they pass."

See *Arden, Forest of.*

Areopagus. A Greek tribunal, or council of elders, established at Athens about 1507 B.C.; its origin was also attributed to Cecrops about 1550 B.C. The Areopagus is said to have held its sessions in darkness, so that its judges might be blind to everything save facts. Its powers were extended by Solon about 594 B.C., and curtailed by Pericles in 461 B.C. This tribunal met on the *Areios Pagos*, or "Hill of Mars," between the Pnyx and the Acropolis, from which circumstance it derived its name. According to tradition, the first person tried before the Areopagus was the god Mars, who was accused of the murder of Halirrhotius, the ravisher of his daughter Alcippe.

Arethusa, Fountain of. See *Fountain of Arethusa.*

Argenteus Codex. A MS. of part of the *New Testament*, so called from the silver letters in which it is written. It contains fragments of the four gospels (arranged in the *Latin* order, Matthew, John, Luke, Mark). It is preserved in the University of Upsala, and is a copy from the Gothic version of Bishop Ulphilas (311–381 A.D.). It was discovered in the Benedictine Abbey, at Werden, Westphalia, in 1597.

Argo. The name of the 50-oared ship in which Jason and his 50 companions sailed in their voyage to Colchis, in search of the " Golden Fleece." Some authorities derive the word *Argo* from the Greek word *argos* (*swift*); others, from the name of the builder, Argus, the son of Phrixus. See *Argonauts; Golden Fleece.*

Argon. A gaseous constituent of the atmosphere, discovered in 1894, at Oxford, England, by Lord Rayleigh and Professor Ramsay. It is chiefly remarkable for its chemical inertness. The facts thus far obtained do not warrant a final decision as to its elemental nature. In March, 1895, Lord Rayleigh received the Faraday medal of the Chemical Society, and in August of the same year Lord Rayleigh and Professor Ramsay were awarded by the Smithsonian Institution at Washington, D. C., the first Hodgkins prize of $10,000, for their discovery of argon.

Argonauts. In the legendary history of Greece, an expedition undertaken by Jason, to avenge the death of his kinsman Phrixus and to recover the treasure stolen by his murderer, Æëtes, King of Colchis. The date of the enterprise is variously given as 1263, 1225, and 1169 B.C. The ship in which Phrixus sailed was adorned with the figure of a dragon, and this led to the belief that the journey was undertaken to recover a golden fleece. According to the legend, Jason, accompanied by 50 of the heroes and demigods of Greece,— among them Theseus, Castor and Pollux, Orpheus, and Æsculapius,— sailed in the ship *Argo* from Tolchos in Thessaly, to Æa in Colchis, on the eastern shore of the Black Sea. According to

some accounts, it was a genuine golden fleece that was sought. This hung upon a tree, in a grove sacred to Mars, and was guarded by a dragon that never slept. Through the aid of Medea, the daughter of Æëtes, the fleece was recovered. See *Argo; Golden Fleece.*

" We have no means of settling even the preliminary question whether the voyage was actual or legendary from the beginning."— *Grote.*

Argonauts of '49. A name given to the early settlers in California, who went there in large numbers in 1849, owing to the discovery of gold. They are sometimes called " Forty-Niners."

Argus. An imaginary being of prodigious strength, and possessed of 100 eyes,— of which two only were closed in sleep at any one time. He was surnamed Panoptes, or the " All-Seeing One." Having been appointed by Juno to watch over Io, he was killed by Mercury at the command of Jupiter. Juno thereupon placed his 100 eyes in the tail of the peacock, her favorite bird.

Ariadne on the Panther. The masterpiece of Dannecker (1758–1841), in the Ariadneum, or Bethmann's Museum, Frankfort-on-the-Main, Germany. It is considered one of the loveliest pieces of modern sculpture. The conception seems, however, to have been borrowed from the figure of a woman seated on a lynx, in the Lateran Museum at Rome.

Ariadne, Sleeping. A famous statue in the Vatican at Rome. The figure is of colossal size, and represents Ariadne, sleeping on the island of Naxos, at the time of her desertion by Theseus. It is famous as the only marble statue with eyelashes. The drapery is without a parallel in any known statue. Found in 1503.

Arians. The followers of Arius, a presbyter of the church at Alexandria, and author of the greatest schism that ever divided the Christian world. He maintained : *1st*, that the Father and Son are distinct beings ; *2nd*, that the Son, though divine, is not equal to the Father ; *3rd*, that the Son had existed previous to his appearance on earth, but not from all eternity; *4th*, that Christ, when on earth, was not a real man, but a spiritual being in the flesh.

Arius preached these doctrines about 315, and died in 336. They were condemned as heretical by the Council of Nice (325). Arian teachings, however, long prevailed in the Church, and were favored by Constantius II, in 341. In 1551, Servetus published his treatise against the Trinity, and was burnt in 1553. After the death of Arius, his followers rallied around Eusebius, Bishop of Constantinople, from whom they were called *Eusebians.*

Ariel. A spirit of the air, in Shakespeare's *Tempest.* He was imprisoned for twelve years, in the rift of a cloven pine-tree, by the foul witch Sycorax, for failing to perform some impossible task. On the death of Sycorax, he became the slave of the monster Caliban, by whom he was cruelly tortured. Being liberated from the pine-tree by Prospero, the grateful Ariel served him faithfully for 16 years, at the end of which time he regained his freedom. He was able to assume any shape, and even to render himself invisible. See *Caliban.*

Arion. The name of a famous Greek poet and musician, who lived about 625 B.C. The following curious fable is related of him by Herodotus: On one occasion, while on a voyage from Italy to Corinth, laden with presents,—the trophies of a musical contest in which he had engaged,— the sailors attempted to murder him in order to secure the treasure. Being forewarned of their intention, Arion placed himself on the prow of the ship and, after invoking the gods in inspired strains, threw himself into the sea ; whereupon, one of the song-loving dolphins that had gathered around the ship took him upon his back and bore him in safety to land.

Aristotelian Categories. A name given by Aristotle (384–322 B.C.), in his *Logic,* to the several classes, or genera, under which the various forms of thought and being may be included and to which they may all be reduced. They are ten in number, and are as follows :

(1) Substance.
(2) Quantity.
(3) Quality.
(4) Relation.
(5) Action.
(6) Passion.
(7) The Where.
(8) The When.
(9) Position in Space.
(10) Possession.

These categories were afterwards reduced to eight.

Aristotelian Philosophy. The system of philosophy formulated by Aristotle (384–322 B.C.). It is one of the most comprehensive systems ever devised by man. Aristotle divided philosophy into metaphysics and logic, physics, and ethics. Under physics, he included psychology. Probably no other system of philosophy has ever exercised so vast a sway over the minds of men, and for 2000 years it was without a rival. It was unduly exalted by the Schoolmen during the Middle Ages, but after the Reformation (1517) it fell into undeserved neglect.

Ark of Noah. The vessel in which Noah and his family are said to have been preserved during the Deluge; which event, according to biblical chronology, occurred in 2348 B.C. The ark was 300 cubits long, 50 cubits wide, and 30 cubits high. It consisted of three floors,—the first for beasts; the second for provisions ; and the third for birds and for Noah's family. It was built of gopher-wood, and made waterproof with bitumen.

Ark of the Covenant. The sacred chest, or coffer, in which the two "Tables of the Law" were deposited by Moses in 1491 B.C. It was made of shittimwood and was covered within and without with plates of gold. The lid of the ark was called the "Mercy Seat"; it was made of gold, and upon its opposite ends were two kneeling cherubim—also of gold—facing each other. According to the Scriptures, the blossoming rod of Aaron, a golden vase of manna gathered in the wilderness, and a copy of the books of the Law were deposited within the ark. It appears to have been destroyed during the captivity of the Jews at Babylon (606–536 B.C.).

Arkansas Toothpick. A name given to a peculiar kind of bowie-knife, the blade of which closes into the handle.

Arlington House. A famous old Virginia mansion, situated on Arlington Heights, opposite Washington, overlooking the Potomac and the picturesque region of the District of Columbia. The entire estate consists of over 1100 acres. The property was originally owned by Martha Washington, and was inherited by her grandson, George Washington Parke Custis. The mansion was built and occupied by him until his death in 1857. It then passed into the hands of his daughter, the wife of General Robert E. Lee, who resided there until 1861. During the War the estate was confiscated by the United States Government; but, subsequently, a suit of ejectment was brought by George Washington Custis Lee and a judgment was rendered in his favor. A compromise was afterwards effected, by the terms of which he received the sum of $150,000. "Arlington House" is now held as a national possession. It is the site of the Union soldiers' cemetery, and the mansion is occupied by the superintendent.

Armada, Invincible. A famous naval armament, organized and equipped by Philip II (1555–1598), King of Spain, for the subjugation of England. It was placed under the command of the Duke of Medina Sidonia, and consisted of 130 ships, more than 3000 cannon, 8000 sailors, and 20,000 soldiers. The Armada arrived in the English Channel on the 19th of July, 1588, where it was opposed by a squadron of English ships,—80 in number,—commanded by Howard, Drake, Frobisher, and others. In spite of the disparity in numbers, the Spanish fleet was defeated in the first engagement, with a loss of several ships and 4000 men. Fearing to risk another battle, the Spanish commanders resolved to return home; but, being prevented by adverse winds from escaping through the English Channel, an attempt was made to sail around the Orkneys. It proved disastrous. The ships were wrecked among the rocks and shallows of the Scottish and Irish coasts, and of the entire Armada only 53 vessels and one-third of the army reached Spain; 5000 men were either drowned, killed, or taken prisoners on the retreat. The English lost only one ship.

Armed Soldier of Democracy. A sobriquet frequently conferred upon Napoleon Bonaparte (1769–1821).

Armida. The name of a beautiful sorceress in Tasso's *Jerusalem Delivered*. She was employed by Satan to seduce Rinaldo and other Crusaders. In her society he forgot all of his vows, and was only liberated from his voluptuous bondage by two messengers from the Christian army—Carlo and Ubaldo, —who brought with them so potent a talisman that the witchery of Armida was destroyed. Rinaldo thereupon escaped, and Armida, not being able to lure him back, set fire to her palace, rushed into the combat, and was slain.

When war was declared between France and Prussia, in 1806, Queen Louise, the young wife of Frederick William III of Prussia, rode among the troops in military costume, to arouse their ardor. Napoleon I, when told of this, declared : " She is *Armida*, in her distraction setting fire to her own palace."

Armillary Sphere. An astronomical instrument commonly made of brass, and so constructed as to show the greater and lesser circles of the sphere in their natural position and motion. It is said to have been invented by Eratosthenes in 255 B.C. Ptolemy and Hipparchus used it in many of their observations, and even Tycho Brahé employed it in his astronomical work. It is now used only as an aid to instruction in astronomy, and, even in this office, has been supplanted by the celestial globe.

Arminians. Followers of James Arminius, or Harmensen (1560–1609), a celebrated Dutch theologian. In 1610, they presented a "Remonstrance" to the States-General, and hence are frequently called *Remonstrants*. Arminianism was a recoil from the Augustinian doctrine of unconditional predestination, as revived and extended by Calvin and others during the Reformation. The following five salient points of Arminianism are taken from Brewer's *Historic Note-Book :*

(1) God wills that all should be saved, and His predestination is only the effect of His foreknowledge.

(2) Christ died for all, and God will bestow eternal life on all who repent and believe on Christ.

(3) Man is of himself incapable of true faith, and hence the necessity of being born again by the Holy Ghost.

(4) All good works are to be attributed to the Holy Ghost, but the Holy Ghost forces no one against his own inclination.

(5) God gives to the true believer the means of continuing in grace.

These " points " were condemned by the Synod of Dort in 1618. See *Five Points of Calvinism.*

Armstrong Gun. The name applied to a form of cannon, invented by William George Armstrong (1810–

1900) in 1854. Its essential feature— whether rifled or smooth-bore, muzzle-loading or breech-loading—is that the barrel is built up by the coiling of one wrought-iron tube over another, until a sufficient thickness is obtained. This is welded around a mandrel into a highly tenacious and homogeneous mass. Armstrong extended this principle to guns of all sizes, from the 6-pounder to the 600-pounder weighing 20 tons. The result is a gun of great durability and extreme lightness, with great extent of range and accuracy of aim. Ordinary 32-pounders weigh 57 cwt., and require 10 lbs. of powder for a charge ; Armstrong's 32-pounders weigh 32 cwt., and require 5 lbs. of powder for a charge. The former would send a shot or shell 3000 yards ; the latter, more than 9000 yards. The Armstrong gun has been extensively adopted by foreign governments. In 1887, Armstrong was raised to the peerage with the title of baron.

Army of Women. During the Tae-Ping Rebellion in China, which broke out in 1850, women as well as men rendered military service. In 1853, in the city of Nanking, an army of 500,000 women — recruited from various parts of the Chinese Empire—was organized and divided into brigades of 13,000 each, under female officers. Ten thousand of these were specially selected for garrison-duty in the city. The rest performed the drudgery of the ordinary soldier's life—digging trenches, throwing up earthworks, and planting batteries. The Tae-Ping Rebellion was not finally suppressed until 1864.

Arnold von Winkelried. A brave Swiss patriot who, at the battle of Sempach against the Austrians, in 1386, broke through the Austrian phalanx and gave the victory to his countrymen. He accomplished this by gathering as many spears as he could within his arms, and bearing them to the ground. Although he fell pierced with many wounds, the

Swiss effected a passage over his body, and, in the battle that ensued, put the Austrians to flight.

Ars Amatoria (*Lat. The Art of Love*). A famous poem — sometimes termed *De Arte Amandi* — written by Ovid (43 B.C.–18 A.D.). He was banished from Rome by Augustus in 8 A.D., and the reason assigned for this act was the publication of his immodest poem, *The Art of Love*. This was not probably the real cause, as the poem was published ten years earlier. Ovid himself speaks, in his later writings, of some offence for which he justly suffers ; but the nature of it he carefully conceals.

Arsenal of Venice. This famous structure dates from the early part of the 12th century after Christ, and, within 100 years of its foundation, it had attained its present dimensions. It is built upon several small islands, which are united by a wall two miles in circuit. For a long period, it was the most complete and extensive establishment of the kind in the world. In the height of Venice's prosperity, 16,000 laborers are said to have been employed at the Arsenal. It contains a curious collection of weapons and armor, and many mementos of the power and naval supremacy of Venice.

Artemis. The Greek name of the goddess Diana. She was the daughter of Jupiter and Latona, and sister of Apollo. She was born on the island of Delos, and hence is often called *Delia*. Artemis was also goddess of the moon, in which character she was known as *Phœbe* and *Cynthia*. She was also the patroness of hunting, chastity, and marriage. Her temple at Ephesus was considered one of the wonders of the world. See *Ephesus, Temple at.*

Artesian Wells. A name given to perpendicular borings into the ground through which water rises from various depths. They are formed by boring through the upper soil to strata containing water that has percolated from a higher level and rises in the boring-tube to that level. They derive their name from the province of Artois (formerly *Artesia*), in France, where the oldest one known in Europe was sunk in 1126 A.D. The most famous artesian well, perhaps, is that of Grenelle, near Paris. It was bored in 1833–1841, and its water is brought from a depth of 1792 feet. It yields 516 gallons of water per minute, and rises 32 feet above the surface. At St Louis, Missouri, there are two artesian wells of great depth,—being 2197 and 3843½ feet deep, respectively. The Chinese and Egyptians were acquainted with artesian wells, and they have been in use for many centuries in Austria, particularly in the neighborhood of Vienna. At present they are very numerous in the United States.

Artful Dodger. A sobriquet given to John Dawkins, a character in Charles Dickens's novel of *Oliver Twist* (1837). He is a young thief and an adept in every kind of villainy.

Arthur, King. A semi-legendary king of Britain, supposed to have lived during the early part of the 6th century after Christ. He is represented as having united the British tribes in resisting pagan invaders, and as having been the champion of Christianity. He was, according to tradition, victorious over Cerdic the Saxon, and died at Gastonbury in 542, from wounds received at Camlan, in a battle against Modred, his rebellious nephew. His true history has been so overlaid with fiction that by many he has been erroneously deemed a mythical character. It was long a popular belief that Arthur had not died of his wounds, but that he had been transported to fairy-land to be healed of them, and would some day return to avenge his countrymen and rule over them. His life and imaginary exploits have been a favorite theme with poets and romancers.

Arthur's Seat. A hill, in the vicinity of Edinburgh, Scotland, 820 feet in height. It derives its name from King Arthur. *St. Anthony's Chapel*, on the way up the hill, is associated with incidents in Scott's *Heart of Midlothian*.

Articles, Thirty-Nine. See *Thirty-Nine Articles*.

Artificial Teeth. Although the use of artificial teeth is of comparatively modern date, yet allusion is made to them by the Latin epigrammatic poet Martial, in the 1st century after Christ, as follows :

" You use, without a blush, *false teeth* and hair :
But, Lælia, your squint is past repair."

In *The Silent Woman* (1609), by Ben Jonson, reference is also made to artificial teeth.

Arundelian Marbles. Part of a collection of ancient sculptures secured by Mr. (afterwards Sir William) Petty and John Evelyn, who were commissioned by the Earl of Arundel to collect marbles, books, and other curiosities in Italy, Greece, and Asia Minor. They were brought to England in 1610, and originally consisted of 37 statues, 128 busts, and 250 inscribed marbles, besides altars, sarcophagi, and gems. The collection was seriously injured during the reign of Charles I (1625–1649), but what remained was presented to the University of Oxford by Henry Howard (afterwards Duke of Norfolk), the grandson of the Earl of Arundel. On this account, they are often called the " Oxford Marbles." The gem of the collection is the " Parian Inscription," —consisting of fragments of a marble inscription,— so called because it is supposed to have been made in the island of Paros, about 263 B.C. In its perfect state, it gave Greek dates from 1582 to 264 B.C. The chronicle for the last 90 years is lost, and the remaining part is much defaced. The characters of the inscriptions are Greek. A vari-

orum edition of the inscriptions by Maittaire appeared in 1732, and one by Chandler in 1763. Translations appeared,—by Selden in 1628 and by Prideaux in 1676. See *Arundel Society; Elgin Marbles*.

Arundel Society. The name given to a society, organized in 1848, to promote the cultivation of art. It takes its name from Thomas Howard, Earl of Arundel, one of the earliest lovers of art in England, and noted in modern literature as the " Mæcenas of All Politer Arts." Its object is to publish engravings of rare and important objects, not within reach of the general public. Henry Layard, whose researches have done so much to reveal the hidden treasures of Nineveh and Babylon, was one of the most enthusiastic workers in behalf of the society. See *Arundelian Marbles*.

Aryan Languages. The name of a great family of related tongues, to which our own belongs. These are supposed to have one common source, and bear a strong family likeness to one another. The Aryan family is sometimes known as the Indo-European, Indo-Germanic, Sanskritic, or Japhetic. It is composed of seven great branches : the Indian, the Iranian or Persian, the Greek, the Italic, the Celtic, the Slavonic or Slavo-Lettic, and the Germanic or Teutonic. See *Hamitic Languages ; Semitic Languages*.

Aryans. One of the three great families of the White or Caucasian race, — the others being the Semites and Hamites. They lived originally, it is conjectured, somewhere in Asia,—probably in Bactria. They were in the pastoral stage of civilization ; and, though they seem to have known gold, silver, and copper, they were unacquainted with the use of iron. They worshipped the Sun, the Dawn, Fire, the Winds, and the Clouds. At a period not later than 3000 B.C., the Aryans began to migrate in search of new dwelling-places. Some of the tribes spread themselves over the tablelands of Iran and the plains of India, and became the progenitors of the Medes, the Persians, and the Hindus. Others spread to the westward and entered Europe in successive migrations, known as the Graeco-Italic, the Celtic, the Teutonic, and the Slavonic. All of the Europeans, except the Basques, Hungarians, Turks, Lapps, and Finns, are of Aryan descent, and manifest, in their religions, laws, manners, customs, and languages, many evidences of a common ancestry. The theory that the Aryan stock was originally not Asiatic, but European, is supported by many eminent German and English scholars. See *Hamites; Semites.*

"The conclusion may be accepted that the Aryan people originated in Western Europe, and migrated eastward."—*Races and Peoples* (Brinton).

Ascanius. A son of Æneas and Creusa. He accompanied his father in his wanderings after the fall of Troy, and succeeded him in the kingdom of Latinus. He built the city of Alba Longa. Some writers declare that Ascanius was also called Ilus or Iulus. The *Gens Julia* at Rome traced its origin from Iulus, or Ascanius.

Ascraean Poet. A sobriquet conferred upon Hesiod (fl. 800 B.C.), the Greek poet, whose birthplace was at Ascra in Boeotia.

Ashburton Treaty. A treaty between Great Britain and the United States, framed by Lord Ashburton (Alexander Baring, head of the house of Baring Brothers), commissioner for Great Britain, and Daniel Webster, Secretary of State under President Tyler. It was signed at Washington on August 9th, 1842; ratified on the 20th of the same month; and proclaimed on the 10th of November. It provided for the extradition of criminals, and settled the long-disputed boundary-line between Canada and the State of Maine.

Ashtavakra. The hero of a story in the *Mahábhárata.* Because, though yet unborn, he rebuked Kahoda, his father, for neglecting his wife, Ashtavakra incurred the displeasure of his sire, who decreed that he should be born crooked, whence the name, from *ashtan* (*eight*), and *vakra* (*crooked*). When Kahoda was worsted in argument at the court of Janaka and was drowned in accordance with the terms of the contest, Ashtavakra set out to avenge his father, and overcame the sage. Kahoda was then restored to life. He ordered Ashtavakra to bathe in the Samanga River, whereupon he became perfect in form. See *Mahábhárata.*

Ash-Wednesday. The first day of Lent originally fell on what is now known as the first Sunday in Lent. In 487, Pope Felix III (483–492) is said to have added the four days now preceding the old Lent Sunday, in order to raise the number of fasting-days to 40. Pope Gregory the Great (590–604) introduced the custom of sprinkling ashes on the first of these four additional days. Hence the words, *Dies Cinerum* (*Lat. Days of Ashes*).

Asmodeus. In Jewish devil-lore, the demon of vanity and dress, whom some have identified with Beelzebub and Azrael. He is called, in the *Talmud,* "the king of devils." In the book of *Tobit,* he is in love with Sarah, the daughter of Raguel, and destroys her seven husbands in succession, —each on his wedding-night. When Sarah married Tobit, Asmodeus was driven by a charm into Egypt.

Asmodeus has been given a lasting place in literature in Le Sage's novel, *Le Diable Boiteux; or, The Devil on Two Sticks.* He is the companion of Don Cleofas, and transports him at night through the air, until they alight upon the steeple of San Salvador in Madrid. From that elevated point, Asmodeus removes the roofs from the houses below them; and, notwithstanding the darkness, their interiors become plainly visible. See *Azrael; Devil upon Two Sticks; Diable Boiteux, Le.*

Aspern, Battle of. The name given to a series of desperate and sanguinary conflicts that took place on May 21st–22nd, 1809, between the French and Austrians, in the villages of Aspern and Essling, on the left bank of the Danube, opposite Vienna. The Austrians were commanded by the Archduke Charles, and the French by Napoleon I, who received there the first serious check in his career. The French, on the second day, were driven back with a loss of 30,000 men ; their bridge over the Danube was destroyed, and their communications were threatened. The Austrians lost 20,000 men, but failed to reap the fruits of their success.

Assassins or Assassinians. A band of Mohammedan fanatics, under the leadership of Hassan-ben-Sabah. They settled in Persia in 1090, and possessed a large tract of land in Syria, among the mountains of Lebanon. Their chief was called the " Ancient of the Mountain," and the " Old Man of the Mountain," because he made Mount Lebanon his stronghold. The "Assassins" murdered the Marquis of Montferrat in 1192, Lewis of Bavaria in 1213, and the Khan of Tartary in 1254. They were the terror of the world for two centuries, and were extirpated in Persia about 1258, and in Syria about 1272. From them is derived our word *assassin.*

Assembly, National. See *National Assembly of France.*

Asses' Bridge (*Lat. Pons Asinorum*). A term humorously applied to the fifth proposition of the First Book of Euclid: " *The angles at the base of an isosceles triangle are equal to each other.*" It is so named because of the difficulty that many beginners in geometry find with its demonstration. This phrase is also applied, but less correctly, to the famous Pythagorean proposition — the

47th of the First Book of Euclid: " *The square described on the hypothenuse of a plane right-angled triangle is equivalent to the sum of the squares described on the other two sides.*" See *Pythagorean Theorem.*

Assignats. French government notes issued by the National Assembly to support the public credit during the Revolution. They were first issued in April, 1790, to the amount of 400,-000,000 francs. The church-lands, which the government had confiscated but was unable to sell, were made security for repayment, and the notes were termed *assignats,* because they represented land *assigned* to the holder. They were negotiable, like ordinary bank-notes, and were generally issued for 100 francs each. Repeated issues raised the amount of paper-money in circulation to the sum of 8,000,000,000 francs; and in March, 1796, a sovereign would have brought 7200 francs of assignats. They were then bought in by the government at one-thirtieth of their nominal value, and were superseded by a new kind of paper-money, called *mandats.* These notes soon fell to one-seventieth of their nominal value. This disastrous system of paper-currency came to an end in 1797.

Assizes of Jerusalem. A code of feudal laws for the kingdom of Jerusalem, compiled in 1099 A.D. by an assembly of the Latin barons and of the clergy and laity, under the direction of Godfrey of Bouillon, the Defender and Baron of the Holy Sepulchre. It is a most valuable compilation, and is called by Gibbon " a precious monument of feudatory jurisprudence."

Assumption, Feast of the. A festival annually observed on the 15th of August, by the Greek and Roman Catholic Churches, in honor of the Virgin Mary, who is said to have miraculously ascended into heaven on that day, 45 A.D., in her 75th year. The festival was instituted in the 7th century, and enjoined by the Council of Mentz, in 813.

Assumption of the Virgin. A famous painting by Titian (1477–1576), in the Academy of Fine Arts at Venice. It is one of the best examples of the work of this renowned colorist, and is generally considered to be his masterpiece.

"Venetian art centres in this work, and perhaps reaches its climax."—*Taine.*

Astley's. A famous place of entertainment on Westminster Bridge Road, London,—so called from Philip Astley (1742–1814), the builder of 19 theatres. It was built, in 1805, of the wood of an old man-of-war; was burned down in 1841; and re-erected in 1850. It was originally designed for equestrian performances, spectacles, and farces.

"There is no place which recalls so strongly our recollections of childhood as *Astley's.*"—*Charles Dickens.*

Astor Library. A famous library in New York City, founded by virtue of a codicil of John Jacob Astor's will, which bequeathed $400,000 for the purpose. It was incorporated on January 1st, 1849, and opened to the public in 1854. In 1864, the books numbered 100,000. William B. Astor, son of the founder, added a second hall to the library in 1859, and gave, in all, $550,000. In 1881, John Jacob Astor, grandson of the founder, added the third hall. His gifts exceeded $800,000. The library contains, at present, over 250,000 books and 15,000 pamphlets. It has, yearly, more than 50,000 readers,— reading nearly 200,000 books,—besides 8000 visitors to the alcoves. The Astor Library has, within recent years, been united with the Lenox and Tilden "Foundations," and a new building has been erected for these libraries on the site of the old reservoir at Fifth Avenue, 40th and 42nd Streets, New York City.

Astor Place Riot. Occurred on May 9th, 1849, while Macready, the English actor, was performing *Macbeth* at the Astor Place Opera-House, in New York City. A mob of 20,000 people attacked the theatre, broke the windows with paving-stones, and scattered the police-force of 300 men. The Seventh Regiment was called out, and, after a pitched battle, dispersed the mob and restored order ; 141 of the regiment were injured, 34 of the mob were killed, and many wounded. The riot grew out of a feud between Edwin Forrest, the American actor, and Macready, the English actor. It is sometimes known as the *Forrest-Macready Riot.*

Astral Spirits. The Oriental religions taught that each star had its special spirit, termed " soul " or " vital principle." This doctrine passed into the religions of the Greeks and Jews, and even into that of the Christian world. During the Middle Ages, these astral spirits were conceived of sometimes as fallen angels, sometimes as souls of departed men, and sometimes as spirits originating in fire. Paracelsus (1493–1541 A.D.) taught that every person had his guardian-star, which presided over his destiny from his birth, and at his death received him into its keeping till the resurrection-day.

Astrology. A term originally applied to the science of the heavenly bodies and their supposed influence over human affairs. At the present day, however, the word is limited, in its meaning, to the doctrine of the influence of the stars over the destinies of men. Astrology is one of the oldest of superstitions, and has been sedulously cultivated by the Egyptians, Chaldæans, Hindus, Chinese, and Etruscans. The Arabs also pursued the study with great zeal from the 7th to the 13th century, and it was in great vogue in Italy and France during the 16th century. In England it was cultivated by Bede (673–745) and Roger Bacon (1214–1292). Queen Elizabeth (1558–1603) was a dupe of the astrologer Dee, and Lord Burleigh is said to have calculated the nativity of the "Virgin Queen." Sir William Lilly was frequently consulted by Charles I (1625–1649). Nostradamus was the great astrologer of the 16th century, after which time this pseudo-science failed to attract superior minds. The discoveries of Copernicus, Kepler, and Galileo were death-blows to astrology, which, however, continues to exist, even at the present day. Astrological almanacs are still published, and fortune-tellers still drive a thriving trade among the ignorant and superstitious.

Astronomer-Royal. The name applied to the astronomer-in-chief at the Royal Observatory at Greenwich, England. This structure was built by Charles II (1660–1685) at the solicitation of Sir Jonas Moore and Sir Christopher Wren, in 1675, on the summit of Flamsteed Hill, so called from the name of the first astronomer-royal. See *Greenwich Observatory.*

The following is a list of the names of the astronomers-royal and the dates of their appointment, from the founding of the Observatory to the present day:

John Flamsteed....................1675
Edmund Halley....................1719
James Bradley....................1742
Nathaniel Bliss....................1762
Nevil Maskelyne....................1765
John Pond....................1811
Sir George Biddell Airy...........1835
William Henry Mahoney Christie..1881

Astrophel. A name given to Sir Philip Sidney, in Edmund Spenser's pastoral elegy entitled *Astrophel.* It is compounded of Phil. Sid., a contraction of Philos Sidus. On changing the Latin *sidus* (*star*) to the Greek *astron* (*star*), and inverting the order of the words, we get *astron-philos* (*lover of a star*). The "star" beloved by Sidney was Penelope Devereux, daughter of the Earl of Essex. She was called "Stella" by Sir Philip, and was betrothed to him. He has celebrated her virtues in a poem entitled *Astrophel and Stella: wherein the excellence of Sweet Poesie is concluded.*

Athanasian Creed. One of the three great creeds of Christendom,— the two others being the *Apostles' Creed* and the *Nicene Creed.* It derives its name from Athanasius (296–373 A.D.), the opponent of Arius and champion of orthodoxy, by whom it was formerly supposed to have been written. It is the most rigid of the three creeds mentioned, and was the standard of orthodoxy during the Middle Ages. It is famous for its so-called "damnatory clauses." By many it is thought to have been written by St. Hilary of Arles, about 450; some argue for a later date, between 700 and 800; while others pronounce it a forgery. See *Apostles' Creed; Nicene Creed.*

Athenæum. A temple in ancient Athens,— sacred to Pallas-Athene,— where the poets and philosophers were accustomed to declaim and recite their compositions. There was also an Athenæum at Rome (a structure of great beauty), erected by the Emperor Hadrian in 125 A.D. It was founded for the study of poetry and rhetoric, had a regular staff of professors, and existed as the *Schola Romana* until the 5th century. Similar institutions existed at Constantinople, Lyons, and Nîmes. The word "athenæum" has been applied in later times to any association or building devoted to literary or artistic purposes.

Athenæum, Boston. Situated on Beacon Street. It originated in a literary club called the *Anthology Club*, formed in 1804. In 1806, a reading-room was established by the association, and a year later the society was incorporated as the "Boston Athenæum." It contains a library of nearly 200,000 volumes, and, until recently, a fine collection of paintings and statuary. The greater part of these works of art is now in the "Museum of Fine Arts" in Boston. One of the most interesting collections is the library of George Washington, purchased in 1848 for $5000. In the vestibule is a marble statue of Washington, a copy of the original by Houdon in the Capitol at Richmond, Virginia.

Athenæum Club. A famous club in London, situated in Pall-Mall, and composed of individuals distinguished for their literary and scientific attainments, or as patrons of learning. It was organized in 1823, and the present building erected in 1829–1830, on the site of the old Carlton Palace. It is of Grecian architecture, and is famous for its frieze, which is an exact copy of the Panathenaic procession, which formed the frieze of the Parthenon. It has the finest club-library in Europe.

The name *Athenæum* is also given to an English weekly literary journal. It was first published in 1828.

Athenian Bee. A title bestowed upon Plato (429–347 B.C.), the Athenian philosopher, owing to the sweetness of his style. It is said that while he was an infant lying in his cradle, a bee settled upon his mouth, thus foretelling that words of honeyed sweetness would flow from his lips and pen. See *Attic Bee.*

Athens of America. A name often given to Boston, Massachusetts, not only on account of the high intellectual attainments of its citizens, but also because of its many famous literary, scientific, and educational institutions.

Athens of Ireland. An appellation conferred upon the city of Cork, Ireland, in allusion to the high degree of culture that characterizes many of its inhabitants.

Athens of the North. A title frequently conferred upon the city of Edinburgh, Scotland, not only on account of its striking resemblance to ancient Athens, but also because of the high literary and scientific attainments of its inhabitants.

Athos, Mount. The name given by the ancients to a mountain, 6780 feet

in height, at the extremity of the peninsula called Acte, which projects from Chalcide in Macedonia into the Ægean Sea. This promontory was considered so dangerous by mariners that Xerxes cut a canal through the isthmus that connects the peninsula with the mainland, to afford safe passage for his fleet. Distinct traces of this canal still remain. The mountain is at present known as Monte Santo, owing to the numerous monasteries and chapels in the vicinity. The libraries of these religious institutions contain many MSS., especially of the *Old* and *New Testaments*, of great antiquity. See *Sacred Isle* (4).

Atkins, Tommy. See *Tommy Atkins.*

Atlantic Cables. The following are the names of the companies operating cables between the Old and the New Worlds :

(1) The Anglo-American Telegraph Co.

(2) The Commercial Cable Co.

(3) The Direct United States Cable Co.

(4) The Western Union Telegraph Co.

(5) La Compagnie Française des Câbles Télégraphiques.

(6) The Brazilian Submarine Telegraph Co.

Atlantis. The name of an imaginary island of vast extent, lying in the Atlantic Ocean off the Pillars of Hercules. It is said that an Egyptian priest first told Solon of its existence. It is mentioned for the first time by Plato, in the *Timæus* and *Critias.* He gives a glowing account of the land, and enriches it with a fabulous history. About 9000 years before his time, the island is said to have been submerged by an earthquake, sent as a punishment for the wickedness of the people. Some authorities have identified the Canary Islands with the lost Atlantis, while others declare the entire story to be fabulous. See *Pillars of Hercules.*

Atlantis, New. The title of an unfinished allegory by Lord Bacon (1561–1626), and the name of an imaginary island in the southern Atlantic. According to the story, this island is the seat of an ideal community, and Bacon represents himself as shipwrecked upon it. He finds there a society called "Solomon's House," organized for the study of nature and the cultivation of the arts and sciences. *The New Atlantis* is supposed by many to be the modern Australia. Plato's *Republic*, Sir Thomas More's *Utopia*, and Sir Philip Sidney's *Arcadia* are other well-known descriptions of ideal communities.

Atlas. Son of Iapetus and Clymene, and brother of Prometheus and Epimetheus. He was one of the Titans, and the father of the Pleiades and Hyades. Having attempted to scale the battlements of heaven, he was condemned by Jupiter to bear upon his head and hands the celestial vault. A volume of maps bound together with letterpress is called an *atlas*, probably from the representation of the Titan "Atlas" supporting the globe, — with which the title-pages of such collections were formerly adorned. See *Pillars of Heaven*.

Atmosphere. The name applied to the gaseous envelope that surrounds the globe. It consists of a mechanical union of nitrogen and oxygen, in the ratio of 4 to 1, together with a relatively small amount of carbonic acid gas and a little watery vapor. Its thickness is about 50 miles, although it probably extends, in an attenuated form, as far as 500 miles. This is inferred from the observation of luminous meteors. It exerts a pressure of 15 lbs. to the square inch at the earth's surface, and weighs over $11\frac{1}{2}$ trillions of lbs. Each adult inhales one gallon of air per minute, and consumes 30 ounces of oxygen daily. An ordinary gas-jet consumes as much oxygen as five persons.

Atomic Theory. This theory, which lies at the basis of modern chemistry, was first formulated by John Dalton, in his *Chemical Philosophy*, in 1808. It assumes : —

(1) That each element is composed of indivisible atoms that are exactly equal to one another in size and weight.

(2) That the relative weights of the atoms of various kinds are represented by the atomic weights.

(3) That the atoms of different kinds unite to form compounds in the proportion of their atomic weights, or multiples of them.

(4) That the molecular weight of a compound is equal to the atomic weights of its elements.

In his standard of atomic weights, Dalton takes hydrogen as 1. Berzelius, as the result of researches in 1848, takes oxygen as 100. The first standard is used in England ; the second in Continental countries.

Broadly speaking, the atomic theory asserts that all chemical combinations between atoms take place in definite proportions.

Atropos. See *Fates*.

Attic Bee. A title bestowed upon Sophocles (495–405 B.C.), the tragic poet. He was a native of Colonus, near Athens, and was famed for the sweetness of his literary style. The phrase "Attic Bee" is also applied to Plato. See *Athenian Bee*.

Attic Muse. A name given to Xenophon (445–355 B.C.), the historian, and pupil of Socrates. He was a native of Athens, and was famous for his style, which combined purity, simplicity, and elegance. He is sometimes called *The Muse of Greece*.

Attic Salt. A poignant, delicate wit, peculiar to the Athenians. In Latin and Greek, the word "salt" was frequently used for wit, when delicately and gracefully expressed. Cicero says: "Scipio omnes sale superabat" (*Lat. Scipio excelled all in wit*). See *Attic Wit.*

Attic Story. A phrase sometimes applied to the head,—the body being compared to a house. The head is the highest part, and is accordingly regarded as the top or attic story. Brewer, in his *Dictionary of Phrase and Fable*, says: "Professor Goldstücker refers the word 'attic' in this sense to the Sanskrit *attaka*, a room on the top of the house."

Attic Wit. The inhabitants of Attica were celebrated for their clever sayings; hence, the phrase "Attic wit" was used to denote any keen or clever observation. The expression "Attic salt" has the same meaning. See *Attic Salt.*

Auburn. The name of the hamlet described in the poem of *The Deserted Village*, by Oliver Goldsmith (1728–1774.) Its location has been a matter of much dispute,—some identifying it with Lissoy or Lishoy, in County Westmeath, Ireland; while others say that the village of Auburn or Albourne in Wiltshire, England, is meant. The probability is that Goldsmith had no particular spot in mind when he wrote *The Deserted Village*, but simply drew upon his imagination in selecting a scene for his poem.

"Sweet *Auburn!* loveliest village of the
  plain,
Where health and plenty cheered the
  laboring swain,—"

A. U. C. An abbreviation, consisting of the initial letters of the Latin words, *Anno Urbis Conditæ* (in the year of the founding of the city). The city here referred to is Rome, and the date of its founding is 753 B.C.

Audiphone. An instrument to assist the hearing of those partially deaf, whose auditory nerve has not been entirely destroyed. It was invented in 1879 by Mr. R. G. Rhodes of Chicago, and modified in 1880 by M. Colladon of Geneva, Switzerland. It consists of a thin sheet of hard ebonite rubber, in shape and size resembling a palm-leaf fan. This is slightly convex and has a handle and strings to bend it into a curved shape. The audiphone is pressed against the upper front teeth, with the convex side turned outward, and the vibrations of sound are communicated by the teeth and bones of the head to the organs of hearing. The audiphone must be focused to different sounds by different degrees of convexity.

Augean Stables. The stables of Augeas, King of the Epeans, in Elis, contained a herd of 3000 oxen, and had not been cleansed for 30 years. Eurystheus imposed upon Hercules the labor of cleansing the stalls in one day. This he accomplished by leading the rivers Alpheus and Peneus through the stables. As a reward, the hero was to receive a tenth part of the oxen; but when he had accomplished his task Augeas refused to keep his promise. Hercules thereupon killed the King and all of his sons, with the exception of Phyleus, who succeeded his father. The phrase "Augean stables" generally refers to a state of corruption almost beyond the power of man to remedy.

Augian Manuscript. A Greek and Latin MS. of the Epistles of St. Paul. It is supposed to have been written during the latter part of the 9th century, and derives its name from *Augia Major*, a monastery at Rheinau, where it was discovered. In 1718, after passing through several hands, it was purchased by Dr. Bentley for 250 Dutch florins, and is now in the library of Trinity College, Cambridge, England. It is defective in parts. The Greek text is very valuable; but the Latin, although a pure form of the *Vulgate*, is in a style of character known as Anglo-Saxon. On this account it is supposed to have been written in the west of Europe, where that form of letter was in common use, between the 7th and 12th centuries.

August. "Augustus Cæsar gave his name to this month, which had been previously known in Rome as *sextilis.* In Gallia, however, and in other remote parts of the empire, the ancient name for this month was *Eaust,* or *Aust, i. e.,* harvest ; and this similarity, as in the case of July, . . . no doubt suggested the change. It is curious that the French have never adopted the Roman *August,* either in spelling or pronunciation. They continued to use the ancient name, altering the spelling first to *Aoust,* and then to its present form, *Août.* The Dutch word for harvest is *Oegst,* or *Oogst.*"—Edwards's *Words, Facts, and Phrases.* See *July.*

August 10th. See *Tenth of August, Massacre of the.*

Augustan Age. A name applied to the period during which Augustus Cæsar was emperor of Rome (27 B.C.–14 A.D.). It was famous for its splendid achievements in arms and arts, and especially in literature. Those were the days of Virgil, Horace, Ovid, Livy, Sallust, Lucretius, and Catullus. Augustus added greatly to the architectural beauty of Rome, and boasted that he had found it a city of brick, and would leave it a city of marble.

Augustan Age of England. An appellation bestowed upon the reign of Queen Elizabeth (1558–1603). During her long reign of 45 years, England rose from the rank of a second-rate power to a prominent position among the leading states of Europe, and attained a higher degree of prosperity in agriculture, commerce, arts, and literature than she had ever before known. In literature, this was the age of Sidney, Beaumont and Fletcher, Hooker, Spenser, Shakespeare, and Bacon. By many, the reign of Queen Anne (1702–1714) is called the "Augustan Age of England."

Augustan Age of France. A title frequently given to the reign of Louis XIV (1643–1715). It was the longest and most brilliant in the history of France, and was pre-eminently distinguished for the famous men of letters that shed lustre upon it. Among these may be mentioned Bourdaloue, Bossuet, Fénelon, and Massillon, among divines; Molière, Corneille, Racine, and La Fontaine among poets ; and Descartes and Pascal among philosophers. Architecture was represented by Mansard and Perrault ; sculpture by Puget and Giraudon ; and painting by Le Brun, Poussin, and Claude Lorraine.

Augustan History (*Lat. Historia Augusta*). The name of a collection of biographies of the Roman emperors from Hadrian (117–138 A.D.) to Numerianus (284 A.D.), bearing the names of Ælius Spartianus, Julius Capitolinus, Vulcacius Gallicanus, Trebellius Pollio, Ælius Lampridius, and Flavius Vopiscus. This last author is regarded by some critics as the ablest of the writers of the *Historia Augusta.*

Auld Lang Syne. The name of a famous Scotch song of unknown authorship, but generally attributed to Robert Burns (1759–1796). The first two lines are as follows :

" Should auld acquaintance be forgot,
    And never brought to min' ? "

Burns, in a letter to Mrs. Dunlop, wrote as follows, concerning this song: " Is not the Scotch phrase ' Auld Lang Syne ' exceedingly expressive ? There is an old song and tune which has often thrilled through my soul. . . . Light be the turf on the breast of the heaven-inspired poet who composed this glorious fragment."

Auld Reekie. An epithet formerly applied to the city of Edinburgh, either on account of its smoky aspect as viewed from a distance, or because of the extreme uncleanliness of its public thoroughfares.

Aulic Council. One of the two highest courts of the Holy Roman

Empire. It was established in 1501 by Maximilian I (1493–1519), and consisted of a president, a vice-chancellor, and 18 councillors. It always followed the imperial court, and hence was termed *aulic* (*Lat. aula, the court*). The "Aulic Council" was suppressed in 1806, when the empire was reconstructed. Its co-ordinate branch — called the Imperial Chamber — was instituted at Worms in 1495. These two courts heard appeals, in special cases, from the courts of the German states. See *Holy Roman Empire*.

Aurora. A famous fresco by Guido Reni (1575–1642), painted on the ceiling of the summer-house of the Rospiglioni Palace in Rome. It is considered to be the artist's masterpiece ; and, as Byron said, it is " worth a journey to Rome to see." It represents Phœbus, the God of Day, seated in a chariot drawn by prancing steeds, and surrounded by the " Hours." Aurora is represented as scattering flowers in advance of the procession ; while, above the horses, Cupid floats gracefully as the Morning Star.

"Certainly, taking all in all, the most perfect painting in the last 200 years."—*Burckhardt.*

Aurora Borealis. (*Lat. Northern Light*). The name given to a luminous phenomenon occasionally seen in the north temperate zone, and frequently in the polar regions. It is said to be due to the passage of electricity through the rarefied air of the arctic zone. The name " aurora borealis " was first used by Gassendi, who, in 1621, observed one in France, and wrote a description of it. The " aurora " is periodic in its manifestations, —the finest displays being at intervals of 60 years, and less marked ones at intervals of 10 or 11 years. It is also asserted that these greater and lesser displays correspond with the increase and decrease of spots on the sun. This phenomenon is generally manifested in the following way: A dim light appears on the horizon shortly after twilight, and gradually assumes the shape of an arch having a pale yellow color, with its concave side turned earthward. From this arch streams of light shoot forth, passing from yellow to green, and then to brilliant violet. The name *Aurora Australis* (*Lat. Southern Light*) is applied to a similar phenomenon visible in the vicinity of the South Pole.

Ausonia. An ancient and, at present, a poetic name for Italy, so called from Auson, son of Ulysses and Calypso or Circe. It was originally applied to the land of the Ausones on the western coast, now known as Campania.

Campbell says, in *Gertrude of Wyoming :*

". . . romantic Spain,—
Gay lilied fields of France, or, more refined,
The soft *Ausonia's* monumental reign."

Auster. The name, among the Romans, of the south wind, or, more properly, the southwest wind. It was called *Notus* by the Greeks. It frequently brought with it fogs and rainy weather ; but at other times it was dry and sultry, and was then known as *Plumbeus Auster,* — the *Sirocco* of modern Italy. Auster was personified as the god of the southwest wind, and son of Astræus and Eos (Aurora).

Austerlitz, Battle of. The most famous of Napoleon's victories. It was fought at Austerlitz, a town in Moravia, on December 2nd, 1805, between the French commanded by Napoleon I, and the allied Russian and Austrian armies under Kutusoff. Owing to the presence of Alexander of Russia, Francis of Austria, and Napoleon of France, this contest is sometimes called the " Battle of the Three Emperors." The allies were signally defeated, with a loss of over 30,000 men in killed and wounded. The French captured 40 standards, 150 cannon, and thousands of prisoners, and lost 12,000 men. This decisive victory led to the Treaty of Presburg, signed on December 26th, 1805. See *Battle of the Three Emperors.*

Australia. This name of the great island-continent,—meaning the "southern land,"—was suggested by Captain Flinders, and adopted by the colony in 1817. It is said that the word was used as early as 1625, in *Purchas his Pilgrimes.* Australia was visited by the Dutch in 1606, and named New Holland by the Dutch government in 1664.

Australian Federation. A federation comprising the Australian provinces of New South Wales, Victoria, South Australia, Queensland, Westralia (formerly known as West Australia), and Tasmania. Although the question of federation had been considered as early as 1852, it was not until 1886 that definite action was taken; in that year a deliberative body, known as the Federal Council, met at Hobart. A plan of federation, resembling that of the United States of America, was drafted by Sir Henry Parkes, the Australian statesman, in 1891, but failed to meet with popular favor. Another scheme, submitted in 1895, shared a similar fate. In 1900, however, a federation measure, drafted by a conference held at Melbourne in 1898, passed the Imperial Parliament, and was finally enacted into law; and on January 1st, 1901, the "Confederation of Australia" (which is the title agreed upon by the people of the Australian Federation) was inaugurated. The government is in the hands of a Governor-General, appointed by the British Cabinet to represent the sovereign. The legislative power is vested in a parliament, consisting of two chambers, —a Senate of 36 members (6 from each state), and a Representative Chamber of 75 members. The population of the Confederation of Australia is estimated at about 4,800,000,—200,000 of whom are blacks.

Austria. This word is derived from *Oesterreich*, the name given to the East-

ern Empire to distinguish it from the Western Empire founded by Charlemagne (768–814 A.D.) in 800.

Austrian, The. A term of contempt bestowed upon Marie Antoinette, Queen of France, during the French Revolution. Marie Antoinette (1755–1793) was the daughter of Francis I and Maria Theresa of Germany.

Austrian Lip. A term applied to the thick, protruding under-lip and heavy under-jaw, characteristic of the House of Hapsburg, the present reigning dynasty of Austria. It is also called the "Cimburgis Under-Lip," because it was inherited from Cimburgis, a Polish princess, mother of the Emperor Frederick III, and grandmother of Maximilian I.

Authentic Doctor. An appellation conferred upon Gregory of Rimini (d. 1357), the noted scholar.

Authorized Version of 1611. A term applied to the English translation of the Bible, authorized by James I of England. It is often called the "King James's Bible," or the "King's Bible," and is based upon the "Bishops' Bible," which appeared in 1572. The decision to revise the Holy Scriptures was reached as the result of a conference held at Hampton Court palace by James I in 1604, to reconcile opposing factions in the Church of England. Five months elapsed before the revisers were selected and their work assigned them. Then 54 persons—divided into five committees—were appointed by the King. Among them were many of the most eminent scholars in England. Seven of those appointed died or resigned before the translation was commenced, so that 47 men performed the work. This was commenced in 1604 and completed in 1611. So thoroughly was the labor performed, that parts of the translation passed through the committees' hands 17 times. Since 1611, this version has been in use throughout the English-speaking world, and millions of copies have been printed. See *Revised Version of the Bible.*

Autocrat. A title conferred upon Oliver Wendell Holmes (1809–1894), the author of *The Autocrat of the Breakfast Table.*

Auto da Fé (*Span. Act of Faith*). A term applied, in Spain and Portugal, to the burning of heretics condemned by the Inquisition. Owing to the fact that the Church was forbidden to shed blood, the victims were either strangled or burned. The "Inquisition" was established in 1210–1215, and flourished especially in Spain and Italy. The first *auto da fé* was held at Seville in 1481, and the most splendid one at Madrid in 1680, under Charles II. Even as late as 1826, a Jew and a deistic schoolmaster were, the one hanged and the other burned at Valencia, under an *auto da fé*. It is said that more than 100,000 victims have perished by fire in this way. The day chosen was generally a Sunday between Whitsunday and Advent,—often All Saints' Day. See *Inquisition.*

Avalon. The poetic name of Glastonbury, a town in the county of Somerset, England. It occupies a peninsula, —known in ancient days as the island of Avalon or Apples,—and is the burial-place of the famous King Arthur, whose remains were found there many centuries ago. Avalon contains the ruins of a superb abbey, founded in 605 ; this occupies the site of a British church, which is said to have owed its origin to Joseph of Arimathea, whose "miraculous thorn" blossomed there yearly on Christmas Day. The shrine of St. Dunstan—located there—used to attract thousands of pilgrims during the Middle Ages.

Ave Maria (*Lat. Hail Mary !*). The first two words of an invocation to the Virgin Mary, addressed to her by the Roman Catholic Church. They are taken from the salutation of the angel Gabriel to the Virgin Mary

(*Luke* i, 28). This invocation was at first said by the priests, during mass, on the fourth Sunday after Advent ; but afterwards became a lay-prayer of equal use with the"Pater-Noster." In 1326, Pope John XXII (1316–1334) ordained that every Catholic should, morning, noon, and night, repeat three "aves." The "aves" are reckoned by the *small* beads of the rosary, and the "pater-nosters" by the *large* ones. See *Pater-Noster.*

Avernus, Lake. A small lake in Campania, Italy, situated between Cumæ, Puteoli, and Baiæ. It is about a mile and a half in circumference ; very deep ; and surrounded by high banks, which, in ancient times, were covered with a dense forest, sacred to Hecate. It is said that, in olden days, sulphurous vapors arose from its waters and caused the death of birds that flew across the surface ; whence arose, according to some, the Greek appellation *Aornos* (*birdless*). In ancient mythology, Lake Avernus was the place of descent to the lower world. The Cimmerians dwelt upon its shores in deep caverns, without ever seeing the light of day ; and near the lake was the cave of the Cumæan Sibyl, through which Æneas descended to the lower regions. There also were placed the Elysian Fields. On the eastern shore are the ruins of a temple of Apollo, and on the southern side is shown the so-called Grotto of the Sibyl. See *Cimmerians ; Sibyl, Cumæan ; Elysian Fields.*

Avesta. The name given to a collection of documents containing the sacred writings of the religion of Zoroaster. In its present fragmentary form the *Avesta* consists of the *Yaçna*, the *Vispered,* the *Vendidad,* and the *Khordah-Avesta.* Although popularly attributed to Zoroaster, the *Avesta* is, at least in greater part, of later date. It was first made known to Europe by a Frenchman named Anquetil-Duperron, who, in 1771, published the result of his labors. It is erroneously termed the *Zend-Avesta*, and on this point the late Professor W. D. Whitney says :

"The whole body of canonical scriptures is called by the Pârsîs the *Avesta :* the origin of this appellation, and its proper signification, are not certainly known. . . . The *Avesta* is written in a language to which, by an unfortunate blunder, the name of *Zend* has been given, and now, by long usage, become so firmly attached that it is perhaps in vain to hope that they will ever be separated."

According to a legend, the *Avesta* is said to have been written by Zoroaster in letters of gold on 12,000 skins of parchment, and to have been deposited by Darius Hystaspes in the Castle of Persepolis, about 500 B.C.

Avignon Captivity. The name given to the period during which the popes resided at Avignon, a city in the southeast of France. It lasted about 70 years (1309-1377), and is hence often called the "Babylonian Captivity." In 1309, Clement V (1305-1314), a Frenchman, having been chosen pope through the influence of Philip IV of France, transferred the seat of the papacy to Avignon; seven popes ruled there,—all under the control of France. The papal court became luxurious and venal; the church revenues fell off; and Pope Gregory XI (1370-1378)—fearing to lose all authority in Italy—restored the papal seat to Rome in 1378. From that year until 1418, Avignon was the residence of the French antipopes. See *Babylonian Captivity ; Captivity of the Popes.*

Avogadro's Law. The name given to a famous generalization of modern chemistry. It was first stated by Amadeo Avogadro, an Italian physicist, in 1811, and afterward by Ampère, a French scientist, in 1814: hence it is often called *Ampère's Law.* It may be enunciated as follows :

Equal volumes of all substances, when in the gaseous state and under like conditions, contain the same number of molecules. From this it follows :

(1) That the molecules of all bodies, when in the gaseous state, are of equal size.

(2) That the weight of any molecule —compared with that of hydrogen—is proportional to the weight of any given volume—also compared with the same volume of hydrogen.

"If one liter of oxygen—which weighs 16 times as much as a liter of hydrogen—contains the same number of molecules, then it is obvious that each molecule of oxygen must be 16 times as heavy as a molecule of hydrogen. If the density of nitrogen be 14, a molecule of nitrogen must be 14 times heavier than a molecule of hydrogen."—Barker's *College Chemistry.*

Ayrshire Poet. A sobriquet conferred upon Robert Burns (1759-1796), the Scottish poet, in allusion to the county of Ayrshire, in which he was born.

Azote (*Gr. ἀ, without, ζωή, life*). A name given by the French chemist Lavoisier (1743-1794) to the gas nitrogen, because it is not capable of sustaining life. It is still the accepted chemical term in France. See *Nitrogen.*

Azrael. In Moslem mythology, one of the four archangels that surround the throne of God. Azrael is called the angel of death, and is commissioned to watch over the dying and to separate the soul from the body at the time of dissolution. It is said that he will be the last to die, but that he is doomed to expire at the sound of the trump of the second archangel. Mohammed asserted that Azrael's eyes were 70,000 days' journey apart. See *Asmodeus ; Seven Archangels.*

Aztecs. A race of people that invaded Mexico from the north, about the close of the 12th century A.D., and, after various wanderings, founded the city of Tenochtitlan, or Mexico, about 1325. Two and a half centuries later, they had become the ruling class of the country. Unlike the Toltecs, whom they succeeded, the Aztecs were a cruel and ferocious people, having a gloomy religion, and delighting in human sacrifices,—20,000 of which are said to have been offered annually. At the time of the conquest of Mexico by Cortez in 1521, the Aztecs did not exceed 250,000 in number. See *Toltecs*.

B

Baal. The chief male deity of the Phœnician and Canaanite nations. He was also worshipped by the Israelites, even during their wanderings in the desert, as recorded in the book of *Numbers*. During the reign of Ahab (915–895 B.C.) and his Syrian wife, Jezebel, the worship of Baal spread throughout the kingdom of Israel, in spite of the remonstrances of the prophet Elijah. This idolatrous worship was finally banished from Israel by Jehu, in 884 B.C. Ashtoreth was the corresponding female divinity. Baal was probably worshipped as the god of the sun.

Baalbek. A famous city of Syria, situated about 35 miles northwest of Damascus, and noted for its stupendous ruins. The name Baalbek signifies the "City of Baal," the sun-god; but, during the rule of the Seleucidæ, this was changed to Heliopolis (the city of the sun). The most famous ruin is that of the Great Temple, built by Antoninus Pius (138–161 A.D.). The natives at present ascribe its origin to Solomon. This building was rectangular in shape—290 feet long by 162 feet wide,—with a peristyle of 54 Corinthian columns, 19 at each side and 10 at each end of the structure ; 6 only of these columns remain standing. The circumference of each column is 22 feet, and the length of the shaft 54 feet. With the pedestal, capital, and entablature, it measures 88 feet. With the exception of these 6 columns, little of the temple remains. South of the Great Temple are the ruins of a smaller one—228 feet long by 124 feet wide—called the Temple of Jupiter. It is similar in shape, and remains in a better state of preservation. At a distance of about 1000 feet from these stupendous structures stands a circular building supported by 6 granite columns. As late as the 18th century, it was used as a Greek church. Baalbek was sacked by the Arabs in 748 A.D., and utterly ruined by Timur Beg in 1400. In 1759 a terrific earthquake completed the work of destruction, and the proud "city of the sun " is to-day a wretched Syrian village. See *Heliopolis (I)*.

Babel, Tower of. According to the account given in *Genesis* xi, the descendants of Noah journeyed eastward, after the flood, to the plain of Shinar, and there attempted to erect a tower whose top should reach to heaven,— hoping thereby to prevent their dispersion. Jehovah, in His anger, confounded the language of the builders, and scattered them over the face of the earth. On this account, the tower was called *Babel* or " confusion." The structure was built of burned bricks and slime or bitumen. The site of the Tower of Babel has always been a matter of dispute. It is generally identified with the great pile of Birs Nimroud at Borsippa, a suburb of Babylon, about 8 miles distant. This was dedicated to Nebo, and called the " Temple of the Seven Lights." Its ruins still attain an elevation of 153 feet above the plain. According to Sir Henry Rawlinson, this mound consists of seven courses of brickwork on an earthen platform. According, however, to other authorities, the site of the Tower of Babel was within the city of Babylon itself, at a spot known as the ruins of Amran. There may be seen a mound 3300 feet in length and 2400 feet in breadth.

Babylonian Captivity. A term applied to the period of time during which the Jews were held in captivity in Babylon. This period is generally estimated at 70 years,— from 606 B.C., when Nebuchadnezzar invaded Judea and carried many of its inhabitants into captivity, till 536 B.C., when Cyrus overthrew the Babylonian Empire and allowed the Jews to return to their own country. During the period of their captivity, the Jews were, in general, kindly treated ; many of them acquired wealth and were even called to high offices in the state. They were allowed the free exercise of their religion, and it was during this period that Ezekiel and Daniel flourished as prophets of the Jewish people. When Cyrus allowed the Jews to return to their native land, about 42,000 are said to have accepted the offer. The number deported from Judea to Babylon is unknown. The term " Babylonian Captivity " is frequently applied to the period (1309–1377) during which the papal court was held at Avignon, France. See *Avignon Captivity*.

Bachelors. From time immemorial, penalties have been imposed by the state upon male celibates, on the ground that every citizen is bound to rear legitimate children for the service of the nation. In Greece and Rome, various fines and penalties were imposed on bachelors. It is said that, in Sparta, the women at certain festivals laid violent hands on the old bachelors, and dragged them around their altars, while inflicting upon them marks of disgrace and ignominy. In England, there are numerous instances of additional taxes imposed on bachelors and widowers. As late as 1785, Pitt imposed higher taxes on the servants of bachelors. These taxes were continued for a considerable time.

Back-Bay District. A portion of the city of Boston, formed by filling in an expansion of the Charles River—the main stream of which flows into Boston harbor. On this newly made land are located some of the finest streets and buildings of the city. It forms the aristocratic part of the metropolis.

Backgammon. A game of great antiquity, said to have been invented by Palamedes of Greece about 1224 B.C.

Others assign its invention to the Welsh, during the period preceding the Norman Conquest. Until the 17th century, it was known in England by the name of " the tables." The French call it *tric-trac*.

Baconian Philosophy. A system of philosophy propounded by Lord Francis Bacon (1561–1626), in his work, the *Novum Organum*, published in 1620. It is generally known as the Inductive System of Philosophy. Bacon abandoned the Deductive or Aristotelian System of Philosophy, wherein preconceived theories were constructed without reference to actual facts, and were so arranged as to lead to conclusions unverified by observation and experiment. His philosophy consists in the accumulation and systematic arrangement of facts obtained by observation and experiment. From these facts alone are any conclusions to be drawn. Although the inductive method of inquiry had been applied long before Bacon's time, he was the first to present this method in its philosophic form and to call attention to its merits. See *Inductive Philosophy ; Novum Organum*.

Bacon of Theology. A sobriquet conferred upon Bishop Joseph Butler (1692–1752), the author of *The Analogy of Religion*.

Badger State. A name popularly given to the State of Wisconsin, owing to the number of badgers that once infested its forests. A representation of this animal appears upon the coat-of-arms of the State.

Badinguet. A nickname sometimes applied to Napoleon III (1852–1870). Badinguet (afterwards called Radot) was a Moor, in whose disguise Prince Louis Napoleon (afterwards Napoleon III) escaped from the fortress of Ham in 1846. Badinguet died in 1883.

Bad Lands. A term applied to certain portions of the northwestern United States, noted for an almost total absence of vegetation. The soft strata of these regions have been fantastically carved by nature into an infinite variety of forms, which, at a little distance, appear like fields of desolate ruins. The French term "mauvaises terres" was first applied to a Miocene formation found in the Black Hills in South Dakota.

Bad Old Man. A nickname given by the Confederate soldiers to General Jubal Anderson Early (1816–1894), during the Civil War.

Baker's Dozen. A phrase meaning 13 for 12. When heavy penalties were imposed for short weight or measure, bakers used to add an extra loaf to every dozen, to avoid the risk of incurring a fine. The thirteenth loaf was called the "vantage loaf." "To give a man a baker's dozen" is to inflict upon him a sound drubbing, i. e., all he merits and one more.

Balance of Power. An expression used to denote a principle, in European politics, that forbids any one nation to have such a preponderance of power as may endanger the independence of the rest. This is not, however, a modern idea, but was held as a principle even in the days of Athens, Sparta, and Thebes,—the rival states of Greece. Although it still has considerable influence in European affairs, it does not play the part it did during the 18th century and the first half of the 19th.

Balance of Trade. An expression used by political economists to indicate the difference between the money-value of the exports and that of the imports of a country. This theory of the balance of trade grew out of the Mercantile theory. According to the Mercantile theory, which considers the possession of gold to be the grand object of trade, there naturally grew up the belief that a nation increases its wealth to the extent that the *money value* of its exports exceeds that of its imports. Hence this "balance" is said

to be in favor of a country or against it, according as the money-value of its exports or of its imports is in excess. See *Mercantile System*.

Baldacchino of St. Peter's. An imposing bronze canopy in St. Peter's Church at Rome. It is supported by four gilded spiral columns, and was erected by Pope Urban VIII (1623–1644), from designs by Bernini. The metal used in its construction was taken from the Pantheon. Its height—including the cross—is 95 feet, and its weight 93 tons. The high altar—consecrated in 1594—is immediately under the canopy. The structure stands directly over the reputed tomb of St. Peter. See *St. Peter's Church*.

Balearic Isles. A group of islands in the Mediterranean Sea, lying off the coast of Spain. The principal ones are Majorca, Minorca, and Iviza. The name "Balearic" is derived from the Greek word $\beta\alpha'\lambda\lambda\omega$ (*to throw*),—and was given in ancient times to these islands because the inhabitants were noted slingers. Balearic slingers frequently served as mercenaries in the armies of antiquity. Cyrus the Younger employed them in his disastrous expedition against his brother Artaxerxes.

Balloon Post. During the siege of Paris, in 1870-1871, balloons were frequently used to convey letters from the invested city; 54 balloons are said to have been despatched, carrying 2,500,000 letters weighing 10 tons. Gambetta left the city in this way. There was no attempt to return by balloon,—carrier-pigeons being used for return messages. The first balloon left Paris on September 23rd, 1870; the last on January 20th, 1871. A balloon, named the *Ville d'Orléans*, that left Paris on November 21st, 1870, landed 15 hours later near Christiania, in Norway. One that was sent up on November 30th, 1870, was never heard from afterwards, and was doubtless lost at sea.

Balloons. Although Cavendish, by his discovery of hydrogen gas in 1766, and Professor Black, by his suggestion, in 1767, that a light envelope containing this gas would rise of itself, laid the foundation of the science of aëronautics, yet the invention of the balloon is justly ascribed to the brothers Stephen and Joseph Montgolfier, papermakers at Annonay in France. These men, after repeated attempts, finally succeeded in raising a balloon, 35 feet in diameter, to a height of 1500 feet. This was in June, 1783. In August of the same year, Professor Charles raised a balloon filled with hydrogen; it ascended, in the presence of 300,000 spectators, — half the population of the city of Paris. The introduction of coal-gas, instead of hydrogen, by Mr. Green, about 1830, was one of the most important eras in ballooning. Balloons have been much used for scientific purposes. In 1804, Gay-Lussac rose to the altitude of 23,000 feet. Scientific ascents were also made by Humboldt in America. Between 1862 and 1866, important ascents in the interest of science were made by Mr. Glaisher. Out of 28 ascents made by him, 11 were in behalf of the "British Association." The highest ascent on record was made from Wolverhampton on September 5th, 1862, by Messrs. Glaisher and Coxwell. They reached a height of fully seven miles, or 37,000 feet. The cold, at this altitude, was 12 degrees below zero, Fahrenheit. Glaisher became insensible and Coxwell's hands were frozen ; but, by the aid of his teeth, he was enabled to open the valve and descend in safety. As regards the possibility of steering balloons and thus directing their course, Glaisher and Coxwell have declared it to be impossible; while Dr. W. Pole and Sir F. Bramwell take a more optimistic view.

Balmoral Castle. A castle in Scotland on the river Dee, about 50 miles west of Aberdeen. It was one of the favorite residences of the late Queen Victoria. The property consists of 10,000 acres, and belonged originally to the Earl of Fife. It was purchased by the Prince Consort in 1852, for the sum of $160,000. The castle, which is built of Scotch granite, was erected by the Prince Consort in 1853–1855, at a cost of $500,000. More than 100 persons can be comfortably entertained, at one time, at Balmoral. The surrounding country is of surpassing beauty, and the summit of the tower of the castle commands an enchanting view.

Balthazar ("Lord of Treasures"). The name of one of the three "kings," "magi," or "wise men," led to the manger at Bethlehem by the Star in the East. According to the tradition, Balthazar offered myrrh in token of death. It is claimed that the bones of the three "wise men" are deposited in the cathedral at Cologne, and these persons are, accordingly, often spoken of as the "Three Kings of Cologne." See *City of the Three Kings ; Cologne, Three Kings of ; Gaspar ; Melchior ; Star in the East.*

Baltic Sea. The word "Baltic" is derived from the Swedish *bält* (*strait*), and denotes a sea abounding in belts or straits.

Bambino Santissimo (*It. Most Holy Babe*). A wooden figure of the infant Jesus, in the Church of Ara Cœli at Rome. According to the legend, it was carved out of a piece of wood from Mount Olivet, by a Franciscan pilgrim, and was painted by St. Luke while the artist was asleep over his work. The image is said to effect miraculous cures, and receives more fees than any physician in Rome. The festival of the "Bambino" occurs at the Epiphany. At that time, this painted image of wood, in swaddling clothes and covered with jewels, is exhibited to the people.

Banbury Cross. Banbury is a small town in Oxfordshire, about 80 miles northwest of London. It was always noted—especially during the Civil War—for the puritanic zeal of its inhabitants; and, in Ben Jonson's time, for its cakes and ale, for which it is still famous. During the latter part of the 16th century, an attempt was made to restore at Banbury some of the pageants of the Roman Catholic Church. When the high cross was reached, a collision took place between the Roman Catholics and the Puritans, in which the former were worsted. The high cross was cut down and hacked to pieces, and later the church itself suffered a like fate. See *Banbury Man*.

Banbury Man. A term often applied to a Puritan, in England, especially during the 16th and 17th centuries. The town of Banbury in Oxfordshire was noted, at that time, for the rigid notions and ideas entertained by its inhabitants. Swift speaks of a " Banbury Saint,"—meaning an extremely rigid and even hypocritical Puritan. It is a tradition of the place that cats that killed mice on Sunday were hanged on Monday. See *Banbury Cross*.

Bank Holidays. In 1871, an act of Parliament was passed, declaring certain days to be legal or bank holidays. For England and Ireland these are Easter - Monday, Whit - Monday, the first Monday in August, and December 26th. In Scotland, the bank holidays are New Year's Day, Christmas Day (if either falls on Sunday, the day following is taken), Good Friday, and the first Mondays in May and August. Bank holidays are frequently called "St. Lubbock's days," because it was mainly through the efforts of Sir John Lubbock that the acts of Parliament establishing these holidays were passed.

Bank of England. This institution —familiarly known as the "Old Lady of Threadneedle Street "—was projected by a Scotchman named William Paterson, and established in the City of London in 1694. Though a public institution, it is in itself a private corporation. Its capital is about $75,-000,000, and its bullion is valued at over $125,000,000. It is managed by a governor, deputy-governor, 24 directors, and 900 clerks. The South Sea Bubble (1720) and the Jacobite Rebellion (1745) seriously affected the Bank. See *South Sea Bubble*.

Bank of France. Situated in the Rue de la Vrillière in Paris. It was established by Napoleon Bonaparte in 1803, by the fusion of three local firms, and has the sole privilege in France of issuing notes. Its capital is over 180,000,-000 francs, and the bullion in its vaults averages about 300,000,000 francs. It is directed jointly by representatives of the state and of the proprietors, and its executive force consists of a governor, 2 assistant-governors, 15 regents, and 3 censors. The "Bank of France " has branch houses in all the principal towns in the departments of France.

Bank of the United States. The first Bank of the United States—often known as " Hamilton's Bank "—was chartered in 1791, and, after varying fortunes, went out of existence in 1811. In 1816, a second Bank was established with a capital of $35,000,000, and began business on January 1st of the following year. As the charter was to expire in 1836, the Bank applied to Congress in 1832 for a renewal. This application was granted, but President Jackson interposed his veto, and the bill failed to become a law. The President then determined to remove the government deposits and give them to the State banks ; and, after much opposition from Congress, succeeded in doing so. These deposits—amounting to $9,800,-000—were in October, 1833, distributed among 89 " pet banks " in the different States. By this act, the " Bank of the United States," as a national institution, received its death-blow ; and although it accepted a charter from the State of Pennsylvania in 1836, it went down in the financial panic of 1837-1841, and suspended payment on February 5th, 1841.

Banker-Poet. A sobriquet applied

to Samuel Rogers (1763–1855), and later to Edmund Clarence Stedman (1833–1908).

Banks of Rivers. The right and left bank of a river are those that lie on the right- and left-hand side, respectively, when sailing down a stream, or facing its mouth.

Bannockburn, Battle of. A famous battle fought on June 24th, 1314, between Robert Bruce (1306–1329) of Scotland and Edward II (1307–1327) of England. The contest occurred at the village of Bannockburn, three miles S. E. of Stirling in Scotland, and resulted in a complete victory for Bruce, who thereby established his claim to the throne of Scotland and secured the complete independence of the country. The Scotch forces amounted to 30,000 men, and the English to over 100,000. The Scotch are said to have lost 8000 men, and the English more than 30,000. In the rout that ensued, the English king narrowly escaped capture. On an eminence near by is still to be seen the famous "Bore Stone," on which Bruce erected the royal standard on the day of the battle. Near this is a flag-staff 120 feet high, erected in 1870.

Baptistery of Florence. A celebrated structure — octagonal in shape — measuring about 100 feet in diameter. It was erected upon the site of a pagan temple, in the 6th century. In 1293, the walls—which are of brick—were encased with white and black marble, and in 1550 the dome was surmounted by a lantern. The Baptistery is especially famous for its bronze doors or gates, with their beautiful bas-reliefs. The most celebrated of these gates were executed by Lorenzo Ghiberti (1378–1455). They consist of ten scenes, in relief, from the *Old Testament*, and, in some respects, have never been surpassed. Michael Angelo thought them worthy to be the gates of Paradise. It is said that Ghiberti spent 40 years upon this work. The Baptistery of Florence is often called the Church of St. John the Baptist.

Baptistery of Pisa. A structure of circular shape, having a diameter of more than 100 feet and a height of 190 feet. It is built of marble, and is of great architectural beauty. It contains the baptismal font, and the celebrated pulpit of Nicolo Pisano (fl. 1260). This work of art is hexagonal in shape, and rests upon seven pillars of various materials. There are five bas-reliefs upon as many sides of the pulpit,—the 6th side being occupied by the doorway. These bas-reliefs represent scenes from the *New Testament.* This pulpit was held in such high esteem that it was placed under the special protection of the law ; and, during Holy Week, it was guarded by an officer detailed for the purpose.

Barataria. The name of an island city, mentioned in Cervantes's romance of *Don Quixote*, whose government was entrusted to Sancho Panza. In this famous romance, we read as follows: "Sancho, then, with all his attendants, arrived at a town containing about a thousand inhabitants, which was one of the largest and best the duke had. They gave him to understand that it was called the island of Barataria, either because Barataria was really the name of the place, or because he obtained the government of it at so cheap a rate. On his arrival near the gates of the town, which was walled about, the municipal officers came out to receive him. . . . Presently after, with certain ridiculous ceremonies, they presented him the keys of the town, and constituted him perpetual governor of the island of Barataria."

Barbarossa (*"The Red Beard"*). A nickname given to Frederick I (1152–1190), Emperor of Germany, owing to the color of his beard. Frederick Barbarossa was one of the three leaders of the Third Crusade,— the other two leaders being Richard I of England and Philip Augustus of

France. Barbarossa was a prince of consummate valor, and was endowed with great strength of character. He was drowned while bathing in a little stream in Cilicia, in Asia Minor, in 1190. According to a legend, it is said that Frederick Barbarossa never died, but that he is sleeping with six of his knights in Thuringia. At the appointed time he will come forth and lead Germany to the foremost place among the nations of the world.

Barberini Vase. The name by which the famous Portland vase was known, before it came into the possession of the Duchess of Portland. During two centuries it was the chief ornament of the Barberini Palace, in Rome. See *Portland Vase*.

Barbers. The tonsorial art is one of high antiquity, and is referred to in *Ezekiel* v, 1. Barbers flourished in Greece in the 5th century B.C., and in Rome in the 2nd century B.C. In England in former times, the surgeon often combined with his art that of the barber, and was denominated a surgeon-barber. In all parts of the world the barber has been famed for his garrulity, and the barber-shops of Rome were the fashionable haunts of idlers and scandal-mongers. To Horace is attributed the saying : "Omnibus notum tonsoribus " (*Lat. A thing known to all barbers*). See *Barber's Pole*.

Barber's Pole. In former times, when the barber united with his art that of surgery, or at least of blood-letting, the barber's-pole had a real significance. The gilt ball at the top represented the brass basin used for lathering the customers; the pole represented the staff held by persons during venesection; while the two spiral ribbons painted on the pole represented, —the one, the bandage twisted round the arm previous to blood-letting, and the other, the bandage used for binding up the arm afterwards. Now that the barber's art has fallen from its once

high estate, the barber's-pole has only a historic significance. See *Barbers*.

Barca. A word meaning "lightning," and a sobriquet conferred upon Hamilcar (d. 229 B.C.), the Carthaginian leader and general, because of the rapidity of his attacks. Hamilcar Barca was the father of the famous Hannibal.

Barclay and Perkins's Brewery. One of the largest and most famous breweries in the city of London. It was founded by one Thrale, a friend of Dr. Johnson; and occupies, in part, the site of the Globe Theatre of Shakespeare's time. It covers an area of over 12 acres, and forms a miniature town in itself. More than 200,000 quarters of malt are annually consumed there, and the yearly duty paid to the government exceeds $900,000. The stables connected with the brewery contain more than 150 horses, mainly bred in Yorkshire. See *Heidelberg Tun*.

Bard of Avon. A title often given to William Shakespeare (1564–1616), who was born and buried at Stratford-upon-Avon. See *Swan of Avon, Sweet*.

Bard of Ayrshire. A title frequently bestowed upon the Scottish poet, Robert Burns (1759–1796), who was born and lived in the county of Ayr.

Bard of Rydal Mount. An appellation sometimes given to William Wordsworth (1770–1850), who resided at Rydal Mount on Lake Windermere for nearly 40 years. He is also called the "Poet of the Excursion," from his principal poem.

Barebone's Parliament. A parliament convened by Cromwell, July 4th, 1653, and so named from Praise-God Barebone or Barbon — a fanatical leather-dealer, who controlled its deliberations. It was also called the " Little Parliament." It consisted of 133 members, and lasted until December 13th, 1653, when it was suddenly dissolved, and Cromwell made Lord Protector. See *Praise-God Barebone.*

Barleycorn, Sir John. A personification of malt-liquor, whether in the form of ale or beer. The expression is chiefly used in England and Scotland. "Sir John Barleycorn" is also the subject of an old ballad of the same name. According to Brewer's *Reader's Hand-Book,* although this song is ascribed to Robert Burns, all he did was to slightly alter parts of it.

Barmecide's Feast. An imaginary feast, whose description occurs in the *Story of the Barber's Sixth Brother,* in the *Arabian Nights' Entertainments.* According to the story, Barmecide, a rich man, invited Shacabac, a famished beggar, to dine with him. At the dinner, which existed only in imagination, Barmecide pretended to eat and urged Shacabac to do the same. The poor wretch entered into the spirit of the joke with so much zest and good sense that Barmecide was delighted. He afterwards placed before Shacabac a genuine banquet, which the beggar enjoyed to his heart's content. The term "Barmecide's Feast" has come to mean any pleasure existing only in one's imagination.

Barnburners. A name given to the extreme or radical wing of the Democratic party in the State of New York in 1844-1848. It was also called the "Young Democracy." The Barnburners were opposed to the formation of all corporations,—fearing the reestablishment of the United States Bank. The conservative wing of the Democratic party was called "Old Hunkers." When the slavery question came to the front, the Barnburners joined the Free-Soil party of 1848, while the Hunkers maintained their usual conservative attitude. The origin of the word "Barnburners" is in doubt. According to Thurlow Weed, in a letter to George William Curtis, written in 1873, the expression started during "Dorr's Rebellion," when

Dorr's followers were called "robbers," "rioters," "incendiaries," and "barn-burners." According to another version, the word is derived from the story of the farmer that burned his barn to destroy the rats that infested it. See *Dorr's Rebellion; Hunkers.*

Barometer. The weight of the atmosphere at normal pressure will sustain a column of mercury at a height of 30 inches. This is the principle of the barometer, which was discovered by Torricelli, a pupil of Galileo, about 1643. Barometers were made soon after, and in 1649 Pascal first made use of the instrument in measuring the heights of mountains. Wheel-barometers were invented in 1668; pendent-barometers in 1695; marine-barometers in 1700. The aneroid barometer was devised by Vidi, and attracted much attention in 1848-1849. No mercury is used in its construction,—the atmospheric pressure being exerted on a metallic disk connected with a spring. Glycerine-barometers have been made, in which one inch is expanded to nearly 11 inches. See *Thermometer.*

Bartholdi's Statue. Auguste Bartholdi's "Liberty Enlightening the World" is the tallest statue of ancient or modern times. It was presented by France to the United States in commemoration of the traditional good-will existing between the two countries, and is situated on Liberty Island in New York harbor. The figure is of repoussé copper—151 feet in height,—is crowned with a diadem, and holds in its extended right hand a torch, while the left arm clasps close to the body a tablet, bearing the inscription: "July 4, 1776." The statue weighs 25 tons, and cost $200,000, defrayed by popular subscription in France. The pedestal is 155 feet in height, and is constructed of granite and concrete. It cost $250,-000, and was paid for by popular subscription in the United States. The statue was unveiled in October, 1886. Some of its dimensions will prove interesting. The nose is 4 feet long ; the right forefinger, 8 feet long and 5 feet in circumference; and the head, 14 feet high. As many as 1500 birds have killed themselves in a single night by flying against the lighted torch of the statue.

Bartholomew Fair. A famous fair held annually from 1133 to 1855, at West Smithfield, London, on the festival of St. Bartholomew (August 24th). The charter was granted by Henry I (1100-1135) to a monk named Rahere, who had been the King's jester, and later had founded the priory of St. Bartholomew. In its early days, Bartholomew Fair was one of the chief markets of the nation for cloths, leather, pewter, and live stock. In 1685, the fair began to show signs of decay as a place of trade. In 1840, it was removed to Islington; in 1850, the last proclamation by the lord mayor was issued ; and in 1855 the fair held its last annual meeting.

Base-Ball. A game played by 18 persons, — 9 on each side. It is generally known as the " American National Game," and is supposed to be an evolution from the American games of " One Old Cat " and " Two Old Cat." Others derive its origin from the English game of " Rounders." The first permanent organization for base-ball was formed in 1845, and was called the " Knickerbocker Club of New York." It played regularly at the Elysian Fields in Hoboken. In 1857, a uniform set of rules was adopted by a convention of clubs; and in 1858 " The National Association of Base-Ball Players " was organized. The " National League of Professional Base-Ball Clubs " was formed in 1876, and the " American Association " in 1882. From 1884 to 1890 inclusive, the winners of the respective pennants of the " National League " and the " American Association " played a series of post-season games for the championship of America. Owing to a disagreement between these two bod-

ies, this series was omitted in 1891 ; and in December of the same year the " American Association " was merged into the " National League." The " Intercollegiate League "—organized in 1880 — has varied in membership almost every year since its organization.

Bashan. A hilly region east of the Jordan, between the mountains of Hermon on the north, and those of Gilead and Ammon on the south. The country is frequently mentioned in the Bible, and was famous for its cattle, its stately oaks, and its rich pasture-lands. " The strong bulls of Bashan " long retained their proverbial fame. The region is said to take its name from its soft and sandy soil.

Basilica. The name of a code of laws of the Byzantine Empire. It includes the *Institutes of Justinian*, the *Pandects*, etc., and was commenced by order of the Emperor Basil I (866–886 A.D.) of Macedonia, and completed by his son Leo VI (886–911 A.D.), surnamed " The Philosopher." *The Basilica* was an adaptation, to altered circumstances, of the *Code of Justinian*, and was first published in 887, in 60 volumes. The name *Basilica* is by some supposed to be a shortened form of *basilika nomina* (*imperial constitutions*) ; while others derive it from Basil, the name of the emperor that first ordered the compilation. See *Code of Justinian*.

Basilicas. A name given, in ancient Rome, to buildings used as places of meeting for business men, and as courts of justice. A basilica consisted of a long central hall or nave, with aisles,—the aisles being separated from the nave by pillars supporting the roof. At the end of the nave, opposite the entrance, was a raised platform, or dais, with seats for the judges. To give additional space there was sometimes added at this farther end a semicircular structure, called an apse. After the introduction of Christianity, basilicas were very generally converted into churches, and thus it is that the form of the modern cathedral is derived from the ancient Roman basilica.

Basilicon Doron (*Gr. Royal Gift*). The name of a book containing advice and instruction in the art of government. It was written by James I (1603–1625) of England (then James VI of Scotland) in 1599, for the use of his eldest son, Prince Henry. It expounds James's views on the principle of the divine right of kings.

Basque Language. A peculiar language, spoken by about 500,000 persons, — three-fourths of whom belong to Spain, and the remaining one-fourth to France. The origin of the Basque language is involved in obscurity. According to certain philologists, it is a language akin to that of the ancient Iberians, who, before the arrival of the Aryans, occupied the entire peninsula. This theory cannot, however, be considered as established; and in the present state of linguistic knowledge, the origin of the Basque language is a matter for conjecture. It belongs to the agglutinative group of languages, as distinguished from the monosyllabic and inflected groups. See *Agglutinative Languages; Basques.*

Basques. A peculiar people, supposed to be the descendants of the ancient Iberians, who occupied the Spanish peninsula before the advent of the Aryans. At present, they occupy the Spanish provinces of Biscaya, Guipuzcoa, and Olava, together with about one-third part of the department of Basses Pyrénées in France. They were called Vascones by the Romans, and successfully resisted them. The Goths conquered them about 580, and in the 13th and 14th centuries they were united to Castile. They retain, at the present time, many of their ancient manners and customs. See *Basque Language.*

Bastard of Orleans. A title conferred upon Jean Dunois (1402–1468),

natural son of Louis, Duke of Orleans, and nephew of Charles VI of France. As a reward for his brilliant victories during the "Hundred Years' War," he was created a prince of the blood, under the title of Count of Orleans, by Charles VII. See *Hundred Years' War.*

Bastille. A famous castle and fortress in Paris, built by Charles V (1364–1380) of France, to defend the city against the English. It was begun in 1369, and completed in 1383. Louis XI (1461–1483) first used it as a state-prison, and in this capacity it afterwards became famous. "The Man with the Iron Mask" was imprisoned there, and died in 1703. The Bastille was an oblong stone building, with eight semi-engaged towers. On July 14th–15th, 1789, the building was attacked and destroyed by a mob of 50,000 persons, assisted by the Gardes Françaises. The governor, Delaunay, and his small garrison surrendered after a feeble resistance. Only seven prisoners were found in the Bastille. See *Iron Mask, Man with the.*

Batavia. The ancient Roman name for Holland,—now used only in a poetic sense. Julius Cæsar, in his *Commentaries on the Gallic War*, speaks of the "island of the Batavians" (*insulam Batavorum*). Batavia is also the capital of the island of Java, founded by the Dutch in 1619. See *Batavian Republic.*

Batavian Republic. A title assumed by the seven united provinces of the Netherlands at the time of their organization as a republic, May 16th, 1795. They retained this title until 1806, when the form of government was changed, and the provinces were converted into the Kingdom of Holland, under Louis Bonaparte as king. The title is derived from Batavia, the Latin name for Holland and the Netherlands. See *Batavia.*

Baths of Caracalla. Situated on the Via di San Sebastiano in Rome.

They form the largest mass of ruins in the city, except the Coliseum. These baths were commenced 212 A.D. by Caracalla (212–217 A.D.), and completed under Alexander Severus (222–235 A.D.). The entire structure was nearly a mile in circuit, and covered an area of 2,625,000 square yards. The part devoted to the baths was supplied with water from the Antonine Aqueduct, and could accommodate 1600 persons at one time. Among the ruins have been found many treasures of sculpture,—now in the galleries of Rome and Naples. The "Farnese Hercules"—now in Naples—was discovered there. The Baths of Caracalla were a favorite resort of the poet Shelley, and it was there that he wrote his *Prometheus Unbound*. See *Farnese Hercules*.

Baths of Diocletian. A collection of ruins, of vast extent, in the city of Rome. These baths were begun about 302 A.D., under the Emperors Diocletian and Maximian, and, when completed, covered a space of 440,000 square yards. It is said that 40,000 Christians were employed in their construction. They could accommodate over 3000 bathers at one time, and, with the adjoining buildings, enclosed an area about a mile in circumference.

Baths of Titus. A mass of ruins, situated on the Esquiline Hill near the Coliseum, in Rome. They were built by the Emperor Titus about 80 A.D., and covered an area of about 108,000 square yards. The marble group of the "Laocoön" was discovered in 1506, among the ruins; and there also was found, in 1606, the celebrated fresco-painting entitled "The Aldobrandini Marriage." Both of these treasures of art are now in the Vatican. See *Aldobrandini Marriage ; Laocoön*.

Bathybius Haeckelii. The name of a shiny or gelatinous substance, found at the bottom of the sea, to which attention was first directed during the laying of the Atlantic cable in 1857. It was at first supposed to be a low form of animal life, and was so considered by Professor Huxley, who, in 1868, named it *Bathybius Haeckelii*, in honor of Professor Haeckel, the German scientist. Later investigations, however, caused Huxley to retract his earlier statements; but Haeckel refused to abandon his namesake, and held firmly to his belief in its organic nature. The word *bathybius* is from two Greek words, meaning " deep life."

Batrachomyomachia. The name of a mock-heroic poem, sometimes ascribed to Homer, but with greater reason to Pigres, the Halicarnassian tyrant, and brother of Artemisia. Müller, however, says that "everything tends to show that the *Batrachomyomachia* is a production of the close of this [the Homeric] era." The poem describes a battle of frogs and mice (whence its name), and thus satirizes the Trojan War and the action of the gods in that contest.

Battery. A public park, of about 21 acres, in the city of New York. It occupies the extreme southern point of Manhattan Island, and derives its name from the fortifications erected there by the early Dutch settlers. During colonial days and for some time after, the Battery was the aristocratic quarter of the town, and was surrounded by the homes of the wealthy and fashionable set. The park is well kept, and is delightfully cool in midsummer. Castle Garden— now the Aquarium — and the United States Revenue Barge Office are within its limits ; and the terminus of all the elevated roads is on its eastern side. See *Castle Garden*.

Battle-Hymn of the Republic. A majestic war-lyric, written by Julia Ward Howe (b. 1819), beginning with the words:

" Mine eyes have seen the glory of the coming of the Lord."

Battle Monument. A monument erected in Baltimore, in 1815, in memory of the soldiers that fell in the defense of the city against the British, in the previous year. It is 72 feet in height, and has inscribed upon it the names of those whose patriotic deeds it serves to commemorate. It is surmounted by a female figure in marble, emblematic of the city of Baltimore.

Battle of the Amazons. A famous painting by Peter Paul Rubens (1577–1640), in the Old Pinakothek at Munich. It represents the victory of Theseus over the Amazons. The main struggle is on a bridge, from which the Greeks are driving the Amazons, while horses and riders,—dead and wounded,—are falling in confusion into the stream. See *Pinakothek.*

Battle of the Brothers. A title often applied to the battle of Fontenaille or Fontenay, fought June 25th, 841, between the three sons of Louis le Débonnaire. The title of emperor had fallen to Lothaire, the eldest son, but his brothers, Charles the Bald and Louis the German, refused submission to him and totally defeated him in the battle that ensued; 100,000 men are said to have perished in this sanguinary contest. The empire of Charlemagne was thereupon divided,— Lothaire retaining the title of emperor, and receiving as his portion Italy, together with a strip of territory extending across Europe to the North Sea. To Louis was given the territory east of the Rhine, and to Charles all of ancient Gaul. Thus were established the three monarchies of Italy, Germany, and France. This battle is sometimes called "The Judgment of God."

Battle of the Herrings. A name given by historians to a battle fought near Orléans, France, on February 12th, 1429, between the French under the Duke of Bourbon, and the English commanded by Sir John Fastolfe. The contest is so called from an unsuccessful attempt on the part of the French to intercept and capture a convoy of salted herrings, on its way from Paris to the English forces besieging Orléans.

Battle of the Kegs. The title and subject of a mock-heroic poem by Francis Hopkinson (1737 – 1791), founded upon a real incident. During the Revolutionary War, the patriots, hoping to destroy the British fleet at Philadelphia, set afloat a number of explosive machines shaped like kegs. The danger being discovered, the British assembled on the ships and wharves, and fired indiscriminately at everything that floated by them on the ebb-tide.

Battle of the Nations. A name frequently given to the battle of Leipsic, in allusion to the various nationalities —French, Russian, Austrian, Prussian, etc.—engaged. It was fought on October 16th–19th, 1813, between Napoleon I and the allies, and resulted in a crushing defeat for the former, who was, in consequence, driven out of Germany. See *Leipsic, Battle of (I).*

Battle of the Spurs. (1) A name given to the battle of Courtrai, fought in Flanders on July 11th, 1302, between the French and the Flemings. The French were practically annihilated ; and, after the battle, 4000— some authorities say 7000 — gilt spurs were picked up on the field, and hung up in the church of Notre Dâme de Courtrai.

(2) A name given to the battle of Guinegate, fought near Calais, France, in which the English, under Henry VIII (1509–1547), defeated the French on August 18th, 1513. The allusion is to the good use of their spurs made by the French cavalry in their ignominious flight from the field.

Battle of the Three Emperors. An appellation often bestowed upon the battle of Austerlitz, because of the presence on the field of the Emperors Napoleon of France, Alexander of Russia, and Francis of Austria. It was fought on December 2nd, 1805, between the French and the Austro-Russian armies, and resulted in a signal victory for Napoleon. See *Austerlitz, Battle of.*

Baubee. A copper coin, of the value of a half-penny, issued in the reign of James VI (1567–1625) of Scotland. The word is sometimes used to denote a marriage-portion, but more commonly to suggest a mere trifle.

Bautzen, Battle of. A sanguinary battle fought near Bautzen, Saxony, on May 20th–22nd, 1813, between the French (150,000 in number), commanded by Napoleon I, and the Russians and Prussians (numbering 160,000), under the Emperor of Russia and the King of Prussia. The contest resulted in a victory for Napoleon, which was, however, barren of results. The allies retreated in good order,— losing few prisoners and not a single gun. The French lost, in killed, from 15,000 to 18,000 men, and the allied forces an equal number. "What!" exclaimed Napoleon, "no results after such a butchery! no guns, no prisoners? These people will not leave me so much as a nail!"

Bayardo. The name of the famous steed of Rinaldo. It once belonged to Amadis of Gaul ; and was found, together with the sword Fusberta, by Malagigi, in a grotto. Malagigi gave them to his cousin Rinaldo.

Bayeux Tapestry. A famous piece of tapestry discovered in the cathedral at Bayeux, near Cannes, in 1748. It is traditionally claimed to be the work of Matilda, wife of William the Conqueror, and the ladies of her court. It is 214 feet long and 20 inches wide, and is divided into 72 sections,—each representing some scene in the life of Harold, the Saxon King, from the time of his visit to the Norman Court until his death at the battle of Hastings, in 1066. When Napoleon contemplated the invasion of England in 1803,

he removed this tapestry to Paris, and caused it to be exhibited in the National Museum. It was returned to Bayeux in 1804, and placed in the public library in 1842. The tapestry contains 1522 figures.

Bayonet. A short sword fastened to the end of a musket or rifle, said to have been invented about 1650 by Puséygur of Bayonne,— whence the name. Other authorities, with less reason, derive the word *bayonet* from Bayona, in Toledo, famous for the temper of its steel. Bayonets were used at Killiecrankie in 1689, and at Marsaglia, by the French, in 1693.

Bayonne Decree. A decree issued at Bayonne by Napoleon I, April 17th, 1808, ordering the seizure of all foreign vessels then in the ports of France.

Bayou State. A name sometimes given to the State of Mississippi, owing to the great number of bayous or creeks that indent its river shores.

Bay Psalm-Book. The name of the first Psalter prepared for use in public worship in New England, and the first important book printed in this country. It was begun in 1639, and published at Cambridge, Massachusetts, in 1640. It continued in general use in New England during the entire colonial period, and in 1750 had passed through 27 editions. It was also reprinted several times in England and Scotland, and much used in those countries by dissenting congregations.

"In comparison with the 'Bay Psalm-Book,' that dullest of Middle-English poems, the 'Ormulum' is a masterpiece of genius and a model of metrical skill."—*American Literature* (Richardson).

Bayreuth Festival. A musical festival, held at the *National Theatre* in Bayreuth, Bavaria, built for the performance of Wagner's works. The foundation-stone of this structure was laid in 1872, and in 1876 the theatre was opened by Wagner himself, with a grand presentation of the *Nibelungen*

Trilogy. In July, 1882, the first performance of *Parsifal* was given there under the direction of the great composer.

Bay State. An appellation often given to the State of Massachusetts. Before the adoption of the Federal Constitution it was called the "Colony of Massachusetts Bay."

" When first the Pilgrims landed on the *Bay State's* iron shore,
The word went forth that slavery should one day be no more."
James Russell Lowell.

Beacon Hill. An eminence in the city of Boston,— north of the "Common,"— at present covered with streets and houses. The State-House occupies a commanding site upon its highest point. It derives its name from the fact that in early days a torch was placed upon its summit, to warn the inhabitants of the surrounding country in case of an attack by the Indians.

Beagle, Voyage of. An expedition undertaken for the scientific survey of South American waters, by H. M. Ship *Beagle*, under Captain Fitzroy, R. N. The voyage occupied nearly five years, from December 27th, 1831, to October 2nd, 1836. Darwin accompanied this expedition as naturalist, and it was during these long years that he obtained that intimate knowledge of nature that was afterwards used by him, with such brilliant results, in his theory of "Natural Selection."

Beans, Black and White. Black and white beans were often used by the ancient Greeks and Romans for voting at trials,—a white bean signifying acquittal, and a black one, conviction.

Bear, Great. A famous constellation in the northern heavens, known also to the shepherds of Chaldea and the Iroquois Indians of North America by the same name. It contains 138 stars visible to the naked eye, among them a noticeable cluster of seven stars

familiarly termed the "Dipper." This cluster consists of six stars of the second magnitude and one of the fourth magnitude. The "Dipper" is known in England as *Charles's Wain*, from a fancied resemblance to a wagon drawn by three horses tandem. Two of the stars composing the "Dipper" are called "pointers," because they serve to point out the polar star. See *Charles's Wain; Pole-Star.*

Bear, Little. A constellation in the northern heavens, containing 24 stars, — seven of which form a cluster called the "Little Dipper." Polaris, at the extremity of the handle, is the famous North Polar star. The ancients called it *Cynosure.* It is estimated by astronomers that the light from Polaris requires 50 years to reach the earth. If this be so, we see the pole-star at the present day as it appeared 50 years ago. See *Pole-Star.*

Bears of Berne. From time immemorial the natives of Berne have worshipped bears, as the natives of Constantinople do pigeons, and the ancient Egyptians did cats. The word "Berne" signifies bear; and this animal is the armorial device of the city, and a favorite effigy. For many centuries, numerous bears have been kept at the expense of the city, and a fund is devoted to that purpose. In 1798, Napoleon Bonaparte removed the bears of Berne to Paris, where, for some years, they held their court at the *Jardin des Plantes ;* after his fall, however, they were restored to their rightful owners.

Bear State. A name sometimes applied to the State of Arkansas, on account of the great number of bears that once infested its forests.

Beatrice Cenci, Portrait of. A famous portrait in the Barberini palace at Rome, commonly considered to be the work of Guido Reni (1575-1642). According to one account, it was painted on the night before her execution ; according to another, it was executed from memory by Guido, after he had seen her on the scaffold. Later research has, however, revealed the fact that Guido never painted in Rome until nine years after Beatrice's death.

Hawthorne declares it to be " the very saddest picture ever painted or conceived; it involves an unfathomable depth of sorrow, the sense of which comes to the observer by a sort of intuition." See *Beautiful Parricide*.

Beatrice Portinari. An Italian lady of rare beauty and loveliness of character, immortalized by Dante in his *Divine Comedy*. In his *Vita Nuova*, the poet tells us how he first set eyes on " the glorious lady of his heart, Beatrice,"—he being at the time nine years of age, and she a few months younger. There is no evidence that his love was ever returned. Beatrice, at an early age, married Simone de' Bardi ; but neither this nor the poet's subsequent marriage ever interfered with his pure and exalted love for her. This love even became intensified after her death, which occurred June 9th, 1290. Dante's marriage to Gemma Donati is said to have resulted disastrously; but for this statement there is not sufficient evidence. See *Divine Comedy ; Vita Nuova*.

Beau Brummel. A nickname given to George Bryan Brummel, the arbiter of dress and fashion, and first of English fops. He was born in London in 1778, inherited a moderate fortune, and studied at Oxford, where he developed a talent for Latin verse. He became a friend and favorite of the Prince of Wales (afterwards George IV), lived in splendid style, and associated with the nobility on equal terms. He was long a leader of fashion and an oracle in questions of dress and etiquette. Having incurred the displeasure of the Prince, he fell into disgrace, and, his fortune being dissipated, he retired, in 1815, to France, where he died in poverty, in 1840.

Beauclerc. A sobriquet — meaning *good scholar* — applied to Henry I

(1100–1135) of England, because he possessed a better scholastic education than was at that time common,—even among princes.

Beau Nash. A sobriquet bestowed upon Richard Nash, a fashionable personage of the 18th century. He was born in Wales in 1674, and studied law, but had an unconquerable aversion to study. Later he became a gambler, in which occupation his skill yielded him an ample revenue. In 1704, he transformed Bath from a vulgar and neglected watering-place into a gay and fashionable resort. The city of Bath, in gratitude for his services, placed his statue between those of Newton and Pope. He lived until the advanced age of 87 ; but his last years were spent in poverty, owing to the act of Parliament that suppressed gambling. See *King of Bath*.

Beau of Princes. A nickname bestowed upon George IV (1820–1830) of England, while he was Prince of Wales and Prince Regent. This title fits him better than that of "The First Gentleman of Europe," by which he is generally known.

Beau Sabreur. A title — meaning the *Handsome Swordsman* — bestowed upon Joachim Murat (1771–1815), in allusion to his handsome person and distinguished appearance. He was universally considered to be the first cavalry officer in Europe.

Beautiful Parricide. A name given to Beatrice Cenci, a Roman lady of great beauty and high birth. In company with her step-mother and brother, she is said to have planned the murder of her father, who had violently defiled her person. Although she protested her innocence to the last, she was condemned, and beheaded on September 10th, 1599. Shelley has written a powerful tragedy on this subject, entitled *The Cenci*. See *Beatrice Cenci, Portrait of*.

Becket's Murder. Thomas à Becket

was born in London in 1117. According to the received account, his father was an Englishman, and his mother a Saracen. He became Archdeacon of Canterbury in 1154, and Chancellor of England in 1158. Through the influence of Henry II (1154–1189), he was made Archbishop of Canterbury in 1162. From that time he steadily opposed the efforts of Henry to diminish the power of the Church, and, after a spirited contest with the King concerning the "Constitutions of Clarendon," Becket fled to France in 1164. There he appealed to the Pope, and, obtaining his support, excommunicated Henry's ministers and behaved with the utmost obstinacy. He was allowed to return to England in 1170, but not long after — in December of the same year — he was cruelly murdered by four barons, servants of the King, before the altar in Canterbury Cathedral. The King was absolved of any complicity in the affair, and made a pilgrimage to the tomb in 1174. Becket was the first Saxon archbishop after the Norman Conquest, and was regarded by thousands of Saxons as the champion of their race against the Norman oppression. He was canonized by the Pope in 1172, and his shrine became in after years the resort of thousands of pilgrims. See *Shrine of St. Thomas à Becket.*

Bedlam. A corruption of *Bethlem* or *Bethlehem*, the name of a religious house in London, founded in 1246, and converted into a lunatic asylum in 1546 or 1547, under Henry VIII (1509–1547). It is believed to be the oldest insane asylum in Europe, with the possible exception of one in Spain. Until 1770, it was one of the sights of the city. Previous to 1815, the patients were kept chained to the walls of their cells. In 1676, Bedlam was transferred to Moorfields; and, in 1815, to its present site in St. George's Fields, Lambeth. The present establishment can accommodate over 400 patients, and is fitted up with every convenience.

Bed of Justice (*Fr. Lit de Justice*). The name given to the ceremony by which the kings of France compelled the registration of their edicts by the parliament of Paris. On such occasions the King attended parliament in person, and commanded the registration to be made. It was held that this personal interference of the sovereign suspended, for the time being, the functions of all inferior magistrates. At such times the King sat in a canopied chair termed a "bed." The last "Bed of Justice" was held at Versailles, by Louis XVI (1774–1789), on November 19th, 1787. Resistance to this step led to the assembling of the States-General. See *States-General.*

Beecher's Bibles. During the struggle over the admission of Kansas into the Union (1854–1860), Henry Ward Beecher declared that, for the slaveholder of Kansas, the Sharpe rifle would be a more potent moral influence than the Bible. In consequence of this remark, Sharpe's rifles were frequently called "Beecher's Bibles."

Beef-Eaters. A name applied to the Yeomen of the Guard,—a company organized by King Henry VII (1485–1509) for his own protection, on the day of his coronation, October 30th, 1485. They have, ever since that time, served as a bodyguard to the sovereign. Some derive the word "Beef-Eaters" from the French *buffetiers;* while others contend that the Yeomen of the Guard never had charge of the royal buffet or sideboard. The wardens of the Tower of London — though an entirely different body of men — are, owing to their dress, popularly called "Beef-Eaters."

Beelzebub. The title of a heathen deity, to whom the Jews ascribed the sovereignty of the evil spirits,—calling him the "prince of the devils" (*Matthew* xii, 24). Beelzebub — or more correctly Beelzebul — is the name by which the god Baal was worshipped by the Ekronites. The word means "lord of flies," it being the office of this deity to protect his worshippers from the flies and gnats with which Ekron was infested. As the Jews regarded all heathen deities as devils, the name "Beelzebub" was applied by them to the chief of the demons. Milton, however, in his *Paradise Lost*, makes Beelzebub second in power to Satan. See *Asmodeus ; Baal.*

Bee-Mouthed. A term applied to Plato (429–347 B.C.), the Greek philosopher. According to the story, a swarm of bees alighted on the lips of Plato, while he was sleeping in his cradle, to signify that words of honeyed eloquence would, in future years, drop from his lips. The expression " bee-mouthed " was also applied to Sophocles, the Greek tragic poet, and to St. Ambrose, one of the Latin Fathers, and similar legends account for their words of sweetness.

Beggar Boy. The name of a famous painting by Velasquez (1599–1660), in the Louvre, in Paris. A second picture on the same subject by the same artist, is in the Pinakothek, at Munich.

Beggar's Opera. The title of an operatic play by John Gay (1688–1732), in which the leading characters are thieves and highwaymen. The play had a run of 62 nights in London, and became the rage of the town. Its success had the effect also of giving rise to the English opera — a form of light comedy, enlivened by songs and music,— which, for a time, supplanted the Italian opera. According to Sir John Fielding, this play was never acted " without creating an additional number of thieves." The title, " Orpheus of Highwaymen," was given to Gay, on account of the great success of his play.

Behistun Inscription. A famous inscription at Behistun, the site of an ancient Persian city, 22 miles east of the city of Kirmanshahan, in Khurdistan. It is engraved upon the per-

pendicular face of a rock, 300 feet above the ground, and is in three forms of cuneiform writing, — Persian, Babylonian, and Median. The inscription recites the genealogy of Darius Hystaspis (521–485 B.C.), King of Persia, through eight generations, enumerates the provinces of his empire, and recounts his victories over his rebellious subjects during the early years of his reign. Rawlinson fixes the date of this sculpture at about 516–515 B.C.

Bel and the Dragon. An apocryphal book of the *Old Testament*, originally appended to the book of *Daniel*. Although it appears in the Septuagint version, it was never accepted as canonical by the Jews, and is extant neither in Hebrew nor in Chaldee. Jerome calls it the " fable " of Bel and the Dragon. It is considered inspired by the Roman Catholic Church,— having been declared canonical by the Council of Trent (1546). Its aim is to render idolatry ridiculous. The Protestants generally reject it as spurious. See *Apocrypha.*

Belial. In Milton's *Paradise Lost*, one of the chief princes of darkness. He is characterized as timorous and slothful, " though his tongue dropt manna, and could make the worse appear the better reason." In Hebrew, the word *belial* means " moral worthlessness," and, in the *Old Testament*, " sons of Belial " were " worthless fellows." In the *New Testament*, the word *Belial* is used as an appellative of Satan ; or, in Bengel's opinion, as a name for Antichrist. See *Antichrist.*

Belisarius. A famous soldier — heroic and loyal — who served under the Emperor Justinian I (527–565 A.D.), and whose military exploits were the chief glory of his reign. In his old age, Belisarius was accused of conspiracy against the Emperor, and cast into prison. He was, however, released after an imprisonment of six months, and all his property and honors were restored to him. Out of this was woven the legend that his eyes were put out and that he was obliged to beg his bread in the streets of Constantinople. It is furthermore said that he fastened a bag outside his hut, and exclaimed to those that passed by : " Give an obolus to Belisarius, who rose by merit and was cast down by envy." This fiction of Belisarius, blind and begging for bread, supplied the painter Gérard with a subject for an effective picture.

Bell, Acton. A pseudonym adopted by Anne Brontë (1820–1849), the English novelist. She was a sister of Charlotte Brontë, and the author of *Agnes Grey* and *The Tenant of Wildfield Hall.*

Bell, Currer. A pseudonym adopted by Charlotte Brontë (1816–1855), the famous English novelist, and author of *Jane Eyre, Shirley,* and *Villette.*

Bell, Ellis. A pseudonym adopted by Emily Brontë (1819–1848), an English novelist, and sister of Charlotte Brontë. She wrote *Wuthering Heights,* a novel of considerable but very unequal power.

Bell, Book, and Candle. The name given to the ancient form of excommunication practised in the Roman Catholic Church. Its origin is ascribed to the eighth century. After reading the formula of excommunication, the bell is rung, the book is closed, and the candle is extinguished,—to signify that the excommunicated person is excluded from the society of the faithful, from divine worship, and from participation in the sacraments. The following are the closing words of the formula used on that occasion :

"Cursed be they from the crown of the head to the sole of the foot. Out be they taken from the book of life, and as this candle is cast from the sight of men, so be their souls cast from the sight of God into the deepest pit of hell. Amen."

Belle Alliance. The name of a farm-house still standing on the field of Waterloo, where Napoleon spent the day during the battle. This modest structure occupied the centre of the French line during the conflict of that eventful day. By the Prussians the battle of Waterloo is known as the battle of La Belle Alliance. See *Waterloo, Battle of.*

Belle Indienne. A sobriquet conferred upon Madame de Maintenon (1635–1719), who, although a native of France, spent part of her early life in the island of Martinique in the West Indies.

Belle Jardinière. The name of a famous Madonna by Raphael (1483–1520), now in the Louvre, in Paris. It was painted in 1507, and belongs to Raphael's Florentine or earlier period. The Virgin is represented as sitting in a garden, with the infant Christ at her knee, while the youthful John kneels in adoration. Pure maternal joy — a favorite motive in Raphael's Madonnas —is wonderfully portrayed in the face of the Virgin. The original drawings for this work were bequeathed to the Louvre some years ago.

Belle Joconde (*It. La Gioconda*). A famous portrait of Mona Lisa, wife of Francesco del Giocondo, by Leonardo da Vinci (1452–1519), now in the Louvre, in Paris. Leonardo is said to have worked at this picture for four years.

"This picture attracts me, it fascinates and absorbs me : I go to it in spite of myself, as the bird is drawn to the serpent."—*Michelet.*

Bellerophon. An English line-of-battle ship, in which Napoleon I was conveyed from Rochefort to Plymouth, July 15th–26th, 1815. On August 7th, he was transferred to the *Northumberland,* and conveyed to St. Helena. After Napoleon's second abdication, he fled to Rochefort, hoping to obtain means to escape to America. Finding the harbor closely watched by British cruisers, he surrendered himself to Captain Maitland of the *Bellerophon,* saying, in a letter to the Prince Regent of England, that he claimed an asylum, " like Themistocles, among the most powerful, the most constant, and the most generous of his enemies."

Bellevue Avenue. A famous broad roadway at Newport, Rhode Island, two miles in length, and lined with palatial residences. It is connected with Ocean Avenue, 10 miles in length and 80 feet in width. The two avenues form a superb driveway, and, during the season, at fashionable hours, are crowded with elegant equipages. Ocean Avenue affords an unobstructed view of the ocean, for nearly the entire length of the drive.

Bell of Moscow. The largest bell in the world is the "Great Bell of Moscow," known also as the "Monarch" or "Czar Bell." It is 19 feet in height, measures 60 feet around the rim, and weighs 198 tons. It was cast in 1653; but, being cracked before it left the foundry, was never hung. In 1837, it was placed upon a granite base, and converted into a little chapel, — the broken part forming a doorway. The largest bell in use is also in Moscow, and weighs 128 tons. According to one account, the alloy composing the " Great Bell of Moscow " consists of gold, silver, and copper, and is valued at $150,000. According to Mulhall, the weight of this bell is 202 tons. See *Bells*.

Bellona. The Roman goddess of war. She was probably a Sabine divinity, and was described by the poets as the companion, wife, or sister of Mars. She prepared his chariot for war, and appeared in the strife, armed with a bloody scourge, with which she roused her votaries to resistless enthusiasm in battle. The priests of the goddess were called *Bellonarii*, and, at the festival of the " day of blood," used to gash their arms and shoulders, —thus offering their own blood.

Bells. Mulhall, in his *Dictionary of Statistics*, gives the following list of the largest bells in the world, with their weight in tons.

	Tons.		Tons.
Moscow	202	Vienna	18
Burmah	117	St. Paul's	16
Pekin	53	Westminster	14
Novgorod	31	Montreal	12
Nôtre Dame	18	Cologne	11
Rouen	18	Oxford	8
Olmutz	18	St. Peter's	8

Bell-the-Cat. A sobriquet conferred upon Archibald Douglas, Earl of Angus, owing to an incident that occurred at Lauder, Scotland, where the great nobles had assembled in council. James III (1460–1488) of Scotland, who had always shown great partiality to men of lowly birth, had capped the climax by elevating to the peerage one Cochrane, an architect. This so enraged the nobles that they met at Lauder to consider how they might rid themselves of such parvenus. In the debate that followed, Lord Gray asked, " Who will bell the cat ? " " I will," said Douglas ; and as the story goes he put to death this unworthy upstart in the King's presence.

Bell-Time on Shipboard.

"*Time*, A.M.	*Time*, A.M.	*Time*, A.M.
1 Bell...12.30	1 Bell... 4.30	1 Bell... 8.30
2 Bells.. 1.00	2 Bells.. 5.00	2 Bells.. 9.00
3 " .. 1.30	3 " .. 5.30	3 " .. 9.30
4 " .. 2.00	4 " .. 6.00	4 " .10.00
5 " .. 2.30	5 " .. 6.30	5 " .10.30
6 " .. 3.00	6 " .. 7.00	6 " .11.00
7 " .. 3.30	7 " .. 7.30	7 " .11.30
8 " .. 4.00	8 " .. 8.00	8 " Noon

Time, P.M.	*Time*, P.M	*Time*, P.M.
1 Bell...12.30	1 Bell... 4.30	1 Bell... 8.30
2 Bells.. 1.00	2 Bells.. 5.00	2 Bells.. 9.00
3 " .. 1.30	3 " .. 5.30	3 " .. 9.30
4 " .. 2.00	4 " .. 6.00	4 " .10.00
5 " .. 2.30	1 Bell... 6.30	5 " .10.30
6 " .. 3.00	2 Bells.. 7.00	6 " .11.00
7 " .. 3.30	3 " .. 7.30	7 " .11.30
8 " .. 4.00	4 " .. 8.00	8 " Midn't

" On shipboard, for purpose of discipline and to divide the watch fairly, the crew is mustered in two divisions, the Starboard (right side, looking toward the head) and the Port (left). The day commences at noon, and is thus divided : Afternoon Watch, noon to 4 P.M.; First Dog Watch, 4 P.M. to 6 P.M.; Second Dog Watch, 6 P.M. to 8 P.M.; First Watch, 8 P. M. to Midnight ; Middle Watch, 12 A.M. to 4 A.M.; Morning Watch, 4 A.M.

to 8 A.M.; Foreuoou Watch, 8 A.M. to noon. This makes seven WATCHES, which enables the crew to keep them alternately, as the Watch which comes on duty at noon one day has the afternoon next day, and the men who have only four hours' rest one night have eight hours the next. This is the reason for having Dog Watches, which are made by dividing the hours between 4 P.M. and 8 P.M. into two Watches. Time is kept by means of 'Bells,' although sometimes there is but one Bell on the ship.—*Whitaker.*" *World Almanac* for 1901.

Belmont. The name of a famous mansion in the vicinity of Philadelphia, afterwards included within the limits of Fairmount Park. It was erected about 1745, and was occupied by Richard Peters, the famous jurist, patriot, and poet, during many years of his long life. Belmont was famous for the brilliant assemblages that gathered within its walls. Washington was a frequent visitor there, as well as Franklin, Jefferson, Robert Morris, and Lafayette. Talleyrand and Louis Philippe both visited the place. A memento of Lafayette's visit still remains in the form of a white-walnut tree, planted by him in 1824. In later years, this historic mansion degenerated into a restaurant.

Belmont, Battle of. A battle fought at Belmont, Missouri, on November 7th, 1861, between the Union forces — numbering about 2500 men — under General Grant, and the Confederates, commanded by General Pillow. The Union forces were at first successful, but were finally driven back and compelled to withdraw. Belmont was General Grant's first battle during the Civil War.

Beloved Disciple. A title often bestowed upon John, the evangelist and apostle, on account of the peculiar distinction he enjoyed of being the chosen friend and beloved one of our Lord.

Beloved Physician. An appellation frequently bestowed upon Luke, the evangelist. He was first so called by Paul, in his *Epistle to the Colossians,* iv, 14 :

"Luke the *beloved physician*, and Demas, greet you."

Benedicite. A canticle appointed by the rubric of the Protestant Episcopal Church to be said or sung at the morning service, instead of the hymn *Te Deum,* when the minister may see fit. In the *Book of Common Prayer,* published under sanction of Edward VI (1547-1553), the *Te Deum* was ordered to be said every day during the year, except in Lent, when the *Benedicite* was to be used. At that time the minister had no alternative ; but, in the subsequent revision of the Prayer-Book, the choice was left to him. This canticle is as old as the 3rd century, and Chrysostom speaks of it as being sung in all places throughout the Christian world.

Benedick. A young lord of Padua, — wild, witty, and light-hearted,— in Shakespeare's play of *Much Ado about Nothing.* Though vowed to celibacy, he meets and falls in love with Beatrice, whom he marries, after a courtship which is a contest of wit and raillery. The word " Benedict " — meaning a newly married man—is by some considered to be a corruption of *Benedick,* while others derive it from the Latin *benedictus* (*blessed*). Still others find its origin in a skit on the "Order of St. Benedict," celebrated for its ascetic habits, and, in consequence, bound to celibacy.

Benefit of Clergy. A privilege, once enjoyed by the clergy of England, whereby they were exempted from civil punishment. The origin of this exemption is unknown, but the custom was probably based on the text : " Touch not mine anointed, and do my prophets no harm." 1 *Chronicles* xvi, 22 ; *Psalms* cv, 15. Edward I (1272-1307), in 1274, extended this privilege to all laymen that could read. Such a criminal could not be put to death, but was to be branded on the left hand. The first verse of Psalm li. was chosen as the reading-test, and hence was known as the " neck-verse." In 1691, this privilege was extended to women. After various restrictions of the privileges of " Benefit of Clergy," it was finally abolished in 1827, during the reign of George IV (1820–1830). Long before this, however, it had become a dead letter. See *Neck-Verse.*

Benicia Boy. A sobriquet bestowed upon John C. Heenan, the famous American prize-fighter, who lived for a time at Benicia, California. In 1860, he fought with Tom Sayers, the champion of England. After a two hours' contest, the fight was stopped by the interference of the police, or, as some say, by the incursion of the spectators into the ring.

Ben Nevis. A mountain of Inverness-shire, Scotland, seven miles southeast of Fort William. It is the tallest mountain in Great Britain, being 4406 feet in height. The base of the mountain consists of granite and gneiss, and the upper part of porphyry. Upon the northeast side, there is a tremendous precipice, 1500 feet high. In 1883, a meteorological observatory was erected on the summit.

Beowulf. The name of an Anglo-Saxon poem of epic character, consisting of about 6000 short alliterative lines. Its author is unknown. It relates the heroic deeds of Beowulf, Prince of the Geatas,— especially his struggles with Grendel, a grisly monster, and, long afterwards, with a dragon. His victory over the latter cost him his life. The poem, in its present form, may be assigned, with a fair degree of certainty, to the early part of the 8th century; but it cannot be determined whether it was originally brought by our forefathers from the continent, and afterwards rewritten by some Anglo-Saxon editor, or was entirely due to the creative genius of some native Anglo-Saxon poet.

The only known manuscript of the poem is now in the British Museum. It once belonged to Sir Robert Cotton, and was almost totally destroyed by the fire in the Cottonian Library, in 1731. See *Cottonian Library.*

Beresina. The name of a river in Russia, memorable for the disastrous passage of the French army, during its retreat from Moscow in November, 1812. Of two bridges hastily constructed by the French, one broke, and the other becoming choked, multitudes were forced into the stream, while the Russian cannon played upon the struggling masses. A considerable number of sick and wounded soldiers, women, and children still remained upon the other side, until preparations to burn the bridge were completed by the Russians. Then, in their wild efforts to escape, these unfortunates either threw themselves in desperation into the flames, or sought refuge in the river. The Russians took 16,000 prisoners and 25 pieces of cannon. When the ice melted, 12,000 dead bodies were found on the shores of the river. The Russians have a proverb : " Every streamlet shall prove a new Beresina."

Berlin, Congress of. A congress held at Berlin in 1878, composed of representatives of Great Britain, France, Germany, Russia, Austria, Italy, and Turkey. Prince Bismarck was president of the congress, and the Earl of Beaconsfield and the Marquis of Salisbury were the English plenipotentiaries. The primary object was to revise the preliminary Treaty of San Stefano, concluded by Russia and Turkey, after the war of 1877–1878. The principal result of the congress— as embodied in the Treaty of Berlin— was to force Turkey to surrender a vast extent of territory and to grant religious toleration to her subjects. Bulgaria was made an autonomous principality, tributary to the Sultan ; eastern Rumelia was made a province, partly autonomous; Bosnia and Herzegovina were occupied and administered by Austro-Hungary ; and Montenegro, Servia, and Rumania were made independent states. The first meeting of the congress was held on June 13th, 1878, and the twentieth and last on July 13th of the same year. The Treaty of Berlin was signed on July 13th, 1878, and ratified on August 3rd, 1878.

Berlin Decree. A decree issued by Napoleon I from Berlin, on November 21st, 1806. It declared the British Isles to be in a state of blockade, and prohibited all commerce or correspondence with them. It also excluded all British vessels and products from France and from countries under French dominion. All merchandise, belonging to Englishmen, became lawful prize; and no ship coming from Great Britain or from a British colony was allowed to enter any continental port. The "Berlin Decree" furthermore declared that all Englishmen found in countries occupied by French troops should be treated as prisoners of war. See *Continental System; Milan Decree; Orders in Council.*

Bernardo del Carpio. A celebrated semi-mythical Spanish hero of the 9th century, who signalized himself by his deeds of daring in the wars against the Moors. He is a favorite hero in the old Spanish ballads and romances, and his exploits form the subject of several dramas by Lope de Vega. According to tradition, he defeated the famous Roland at Roncesvalles. Finding him invulnerable, Bernardo lifted him in his arms and squeezed him to death, as Hercules did the giant Antæus.

Bernese Oberland. A mountainous region in the southern part of the canton of Berne, Switzerland, famous for the beauty of its valleys, the chief of which are the Simmenthal, Lauterbrunnen, Grindelwald, and Hasli. It contains a number of tourist-centres, such as Interlaken, Grindelwald, and Meiringen, together with the lofty peaks of the Jungfrau, Finster-aar-Horn, Schreckhorn, and Mönch.

Bess, Good Queen. See *Good Queen Bess.*

Bethlehem. A village of great antiquity, situated six miles south of Jerusalem, and mentioned in *Genesis* xlviii, 7, under the name of Ephrath. It is memorable as the birthplace of David (1085 B.C.), and later (according to the evangelists Matthew, Luke, and John) as the birthplace of Jesus Christ. The village contains a large convent, built by the Empress Helena in 327 A.D.; this was destroyed by the Moslems in 1236, and supposedly restored by the Crusaders. Within this structure is the Church of the Nativity — jointly controlled by the Latin, Greek, and Armenian Christians. The church is built in the form of a cross; at the head of this cross is a carved marble star, which the Bethlehemites say marks the central spot of the earth. Thence, a long, winding passage leads to the crypt where the Virgin Mary is said to have given birth to the infant Jesus. A silver star marks the spot, with the accompanying words, *Hic de virgine Maria Jesus Christus natus est* (*Lat.* Here Jesus Christ was born of the Virgin Mary). Bethlehem also contains a square-domed building, marking the reputed site of Rachel's tomb. It is now a village of about 3000 inhabitants, and is much visited by pilgrims. See *Church of the Nativity.*

Beulah, Land of. The name given, in Bunyan's immortal allegory, *The Pilgrim's Progress*, to a region of peace and quiet, lying on this side of the river of Death. There the pilgrims tarried after their journey was over, till summoned to cross the river and enter upon the joys of the Celestial City. The Land of Beulah symbolizes the Christian's peace of mind, after his struggles and temptations are at an end. The word "Beulah" occurs in *Isaiah* lxii, 4.

Bhagavad-Gîtâ (*The Song of the Adorable*). An ancient Sanskrit poem, forming part of the *Mahábhá-rata*. It has been incorporated in the great Indian epic, but is clearly of later date than the rest of that work, having probably been composed during the first or second century of the Christian era. Its central theme is the exaltation of Vishnu in his human form or avatâr of Krishna. See *Mahábhá-rata*.

"The poem is divided into three sections, each containing six chapters, called *upanishads* ('secret doctrine'), a name which shows the mystical character of the work. In the *first* section, the duties and observances of caste are directly inculcated, and asserted to be entirely in harmony with the principles of the Yoga philosophy — viz., asceticism and meditation, by which absorption in the Deity, the highest object of humanity, is obtained. In the *second*, the pantheistic doctrines of the Vedânta philosophy are expounded and taught. In the *third*, the pantheism of the Vedânta is interwoven with the dualism of the Sânkhya philosophy."—*Chambers's Encyclopædia*.

Bible Societies. The *British and Foreign Bible Society* was founded in 1804, and has distributed, up to the present time, over 150,000,000 Bibles and portions of the Bible, in about 330 languages and dialects. The expenditure of the Society in 1895–1896 was nearly $1,000,000. The *American Bible Society* was established in 1816. During the years 1896–1897, it issued over 1,500,000 Bibles and Testaments ; and during the eighty-one years of its existence, over 63,000,000 copies. This includes the Bible in many foreign tongues, and in the languages of several American Indian tribes. The *Prussian Central Bible Society* at Berlin was founded in 1814, and distributes annually 80,000 Bibles and Testaments. A large number of Bibles is annually supplied to the people of Germany by the agents of the *British and Foreign Bible Society*. In 1886, these amounted to more than 360,000 copies. Bible Societies were prohibited by the Austrian government in 1817. The *Russian Bible Society* was founded in 1813, at St.

Petersburg, under the patronage of the Emperor Alexander I (1801–1825); but its operations were suspended, on the accession of the Emperor Nicholas in 1826. The *British and Foreign Bible Society*, however, carries on an important work in Russia. In 1886, the issues were more than 450,000 copies.

Bible Statistics. In Horne's *Introduction to the Study of the Scriptures* may be found the following facts concerning the "King James Version of the Bible." Their compilation is said to have required more than three years.

	Old Testament.	New Testament.	Total.	Apocrypha.
Books......	39	27	66	14
Chapters..	929	260	1,189	183
Verses.....	33,214	7,959	41,173	6,031
Words.....	593,493	181,253	774,746	125,185
Letters....	2,728,100	838,380	3,566,480	1,063,876

The following additional facts concerning the Bible are here added :

The middle line is 2 *Chronicles* iv, 16.

The middle chapter is *Psalm* cxvii.

The shortest chapter is *Psalm* cxvii.

The middle verse is the 8th verse of *Psalm* cxviii.

Ezra vii, 21, contains all the letters of the alphabet except j.

Isaiah xxxvii and 2 *Kings* xix are alike.

Esther viii, 9, is the longest verse.

John xi, 35, is the shortest verse.

Verses 8, 15, 21, 31 of *Psalm* cvii are alike.

All the verses of *Psalm* cxxxvi end alike.

The Bible contains no words of more than six syllables.

Biblia Pauperum (*Lat. Bible of the Poor*). A mediæval picture-book, printed for the use of those that could not read. It consisted of about 40 or 50 pages, each containing, together with an appropriate Latin text, a picture of some leading event in the scheme of salvation through Jesus Christ, as found in the *Old* and *New Testaments*. These books were much used by the Mendicant Friars in their work among the poor, whence the name. The work is said to have been compiled by Bonaventura, general of the Franciscans, about 1260. The printing of it is attributed to Laurens Koster of Germany, about 1415. It is one of the earliest specimens of " block books," printed before the introduction of movable type. A similar work also existed, entitled *Speculum Humanæ Salvationis* (*Lat. The Mirror of Human Salvation*): it was more extended in scope, and had the texts in rhyme. These two books were the principal ones used by the monks in preaching, before the Reformation (1517).

Bibliothèque Nationale. A public library in Paris, probably the most extensive collection of books in the world. In 1350, King John (1350–1364), is said to have possessed about eight or ten volumes, probably the nucleus of the present library. Charles V (1364–1380) added to it until it numbered over 900 volumes. These books were deposited in the Louvre, and free access to them at all times was granted. In the time of Louis XIII (1610–1643), this collection numbered over 16,000 volumes, and at the death of his successor, Louis XIV (1643–1715), about 70,000. In 1721, the library was placed in the Hôtel Mazarin, a building occupying the site of the present one in the Rue de Richelieu. The number of volumes is now considerably over 3,000,000, of which 450,000 are exclusively devoted to French history. The Bibliothèque Nationale is said to contain 2,400,000 engravings, 300,-000 pamphlets, 175,000 MSS., 300,000 maps and charts, 150,000 coins and medals, and 100,000 portraits. The annual grant for binding and purchases is $40,000. In the Salle des Globes are two copper globes, nearly 21 feet in diameter. Among the MSS. may be found letters of Henry IV, Louis XIV, etc., the original of Fénelon's *Télémaque*, and some writings of Galileo. The library has been variously known as La Bibliothèque du Roi, La Bibliothèque Royale, La Bibliothèque Nationale, and La Bibliothèque Impériale, according to the form of government in power.

Bicêtre. A celebrated hospital, situated on an eminence in the southern vicinity of Paris, commanding a fine view of the city and the Seine. It was founded by Louis IX (1226–1270) as a Carthusian monastery, and destroyed in 1632, because it had become the hiding-place of thieves. It was restored by Louis XIII (1610–1643), and made a hospital for old soldiers and insane people. Afterwards, it was used as a prison for criminals, and is now a retreat for indigent old men and hopeless lunatics. The word " Bicêtre " is said to be a corruption of Winchester—John, Bishop of Winchester, having lived there in 1290. It is often used in French to express a notion of folly or nonsense. " To escape from Bicêtre " is to give one's self up to foolishness. Bicêtre is also the name of one of the detached forts that defend the approaches to Paris.

Bidëford Postman. A sobriquet conferred upon Edward Capern, the English poet, who, at one period of his life, was a letter-carrier in the town of Bidëford, Devonshire.

Bien Aimé. A sobriquet bestowed upon Louis XV (1715–1774), King of France.

Big Ben. A name popularly given to the great bell in the clock-tower of the Houses of Parliament, London. It is named after Sir Benjamin Hall, Chief Commissioner of Works at the time of its erection, and is the largest bell in England. It was cast in 1857, is slightly cracked, and weighs 13 tons. By filing the crack open, the tone of the bell was made quite clear. In calm weather, " Big Ben " may be heard over the greater part of London.

Biglow Papers. A series of humorous, satirical poems, in the Yankee dialect, written by James Russell Lowell (1819–1891). They were mainly directed against the Mexican War, the evils of slavery, and the War of the Rebellion.

"Apart from their special impulse and influence, the *Biglow Papers* were essentially and purely American. They could have been written nowhere else but in Yankee New England by a New England Yankee. With *Uncle Tom's Cabin*, they are the chief literary memorial of the contest,—a memorial which, as literature, and for their own delight, our children's children will read, as we read to-day the satires that scourge the long-vanished Rome which Juvenal knew, and the orations of Burke that discuss long-perished politics." — *Address on Lowell* (G. W. Curtis).

Big Trees of California. The name popularly given to certain gigantic evergreen trees (genus *Sequoia*) growing in groves along the Sierra Nevada, from 6000 to 7000 feet above the sea-level. With the exception of the Australian eucalyptus, they are the tallest trees known. The best-known grove is in Calaveras County. A similar one is found in Mariposa County. It covers about 2500 acres, is 6500 feet above the sea, and has been reserved as the *Sequoia National Park*. It contains more than 300 big trees, somewhat marred by fire, but wonderfully impressive. See *Calaveras Pines*.

Billingsgate. A famous fish-market in London, long noted for the coarse language indulged in by the fish-venders,—especially the female ones. It stands on the left bank of the Thames, a little below London Bridge ; and, according to Geoffrey of Monmouth, derives its name from Belin, King of the Britons, who built there the first water-gate, in 400 B.C. Customs were paid there under Ethelred II in 979 ; and in 1699 Billingsgate was made a free market. It was destroyed by fire in 1715, and rebuilt. A new one was erected in 1852, and still another was completed in 1876. The word "Billingsgate" has long been used to denote foul or coarse language of any sort.

Bill of Rights. An important statutory declaration of popular rights, made by the Lords and Commons of Great Britain on the accession of William and Mary to the throne (February 13th, 1689). It distinctly specified the rights and liberties of the subject, and regulated the succession of the crown. The phrase "Bill of Rights" is also applied to a similar declaration of rights and privileges drawn up by the Commons, and granted by Charles I (1625–1649) on June 26th, 1628. See *Glorious Revolution ; Petition of Right.*

Bi-Metallism. The name given to a monetary system in which gold and silver are on exactly the same footing as regards mintage and legal-tender. This theory has been much advocated by Cernuschi and Laveleye since 1867. In 1803, a bi-metallic currency was established in France, and was recommended for Germany in 1879. The question was further discussed at a monetary conference held at Paris in 1881. An international conference on bi-metallism was held at Brussels in 1892, but the views and proposals of the representatives of the various countries were so divergent that no satisfactory agreement could be reached, and the conference adjourned till May, 1893. The general result of the conference was regarded as unfavorable to the cause of bi-metallism. This question has been agitated for many years in the United States, and formed the leading issue in the presidential campaign of 1896, and again in that of 1900. Although the victory in both elections rested with the advocates of the single standard, it is generally admitted that the question has not been finally and definitively settled.

Biogenesis (*Gr. βίος, life, γένεσις, origin*). A name used by Professor Huxley for the theory that living matter always arises through the agency of pre-existing living matter. It is opposed to the doctrine of *abiogenesis*. Biogenesis is, at present, the theory most generally accepted by scientific men. See *Abiogenesis.*

Birds of America. The name of a famous work on ornithology, prepared by John James Audubon (1780–1851). It required ten years for its preparation and is said to have cost $100,000. In its completed form, it consisted of 448 plates representing 1065 species of birds,— life-size and beautifully colored. These illustrations appeared in five volumes, folio, and were accompanied by five volumes of letter-press. Cuvier expressed the opinion that the *Birds of America* "is the most magnificent monument that art has ever erected to ornithology." The work was published in England (1830–1839) by subscription, at $1000 per copy.

Birnam Hill. A hill in Perthshire, Scotland, 1324 feet high, near Dunkeld, commanding a lovely view of the valley of the Tay. It was once part of a royal forest immortalized as *Birnam Wood* by Shakespeare in his tragedy of *Macbeth.*

" Macbeth shall never vanquished be, until
  Great *Birnam wood* to high Dunsinane hill
  Shall come against him."
                                Act iv, Sc. 1.

Birthplace of Napoleon III. Although it is universally said that Napoleon III was born in the palace of the Tuileries, Mr. Bertrand Payne, the author of the *Index of Biography*, declares this statement to be inaccurate. He says: " A friend of mine submitted a proof to the illustrious original, who then and there made three slight corrections in it with his own hand, one of which was to expunge the word ' Tuileries,' and to substitute ' Rue Ceruti (now Lafitte).' "

Birthyears of Dramatic and Musical Celebrities.

Adams, Maude	1872
Albani, Emma	1851
Anderson, Mary	1859
Barnabee, H. C.	1833
Barrett, Wilson	1846
Barrymore, Maurice	1847
Bellew, Kyrle	1845
Bernhardt, Sarah	1844
Booth, Agnes	1843
Calvé, Emma	1864
Cayvan, Georgia	1858
Claxton, Kate	1848
Cody, William F.	1845
Coghlan, Rose	1853
Coquelin, Benoît C	1841
Crabtree, Lotta	1847
Crane, William H.	1845
De Reszke, Édouard	1855
De Reszke, Jean	1852
Dickinson, Anna	1842
Drew, John	1853
Duse, Eleanora	1861
Eames, Emma	1868
Gilbert, Mrs. G. H.	1820
Hading, Jane	1861
Hopper, De Wolf	1862
Irving, Henry	1838
Janauschek, Francesca	1830
Jefferson, Joseph	1829
Langtry, Lily	1852
Mansfield, Richard	1857
Marlowe, Julia	1865
Melba, Nellie	1866
Mitchell, Maggie	1832
Modjeska, Helena	1844
Morris, Clara	1846
Mounet-Sully	1841
Nilsson, Christine	1843
Nordica, Lillian	1858
Paderewski, I. J.	1860
Patti, Adelina	1843
Rehan, Ada	1860
Russell, Lillian	1860
Salvini, Tommaso	1830
Sothern, E. H.	1864
Stoddart, J. H.	1827
Terry, Ellen	1848
Toole, John L.	1833
Willard, E. S.	1853
Wilson, Francis	1865

Bishop of Sodor and Man. A title held by the Bishop of the Isle of Man. This bishopric is said to have been founded by St. Patrick in 447, and had, originally, jurisdiction over the Hebrides as well. The word Sodor is an abbreviation of Sudoreys (South), and was used by the Norwegians to distinguish the Hebrides or Southern Islands off the coast of Scotland from the Orkney or Northern Islands. Hence the expression "Sodor and Man" originally meant "Hebrides or Southern Islands and Man." The Hebrides are now included in the ecclesiastical system of Scotland, and the true Bishop of Sodor is the Scotch Bishop of the Isles. But the full title is still retained by the Bishop of the Isle of Man. The Bishop of Sodor and Man, not being counted as one of the English bishops, has no seat in the House of Lords.

Bishops' Bible. An English revision of the Holy Scriptures, published in folio, in 1568. It was executed with great care by about 15 learned men, 8 of whom were bishops: hence the name — "Bishops' Bible." The revision was made under the direction of Archbishop Parker ; and is, in consequence, often called "Parker's Bible." This edition is adorned with 143 engravings, together with maps and portraits. It was the version authorized to be read in the parish churches ; but in private use it never displaced the Geneva version. In 1569, the "Bishops' Bible" was published in octavo, the chapters being divided into verses, as in the Geneva Bible.

Black Agnes. A nickname conferred upon the Countess of Dunbar and March, on account of her swarthy complexion. This brave and intrepid woman completedly foiled the Earl of Salisbury in his attempt to capture Dunbar Castle in 1337.

Black Box. A box supposed to contain the marriage-contract of Charles II and Lucy Barlow [or Walters], the mother of the Duke of Monmouth, and said to have been stolen from her. If these papers had been found, they would have secured to Monmouth the right of succession to the throne of England, to the exclusion of the hated Duke of York, the brother of the king. The "Black Box" is referred to in *Lorna Doone* and is twice mentioned by Macaulay. The story never had the slightest basis of truth, but was readily believed by the masses,— always fond of romantic adventure.

Black Death. The name given to the fearful epidemic that devastated Asia and Europe in the 14th century of the Christian era. It was so called from the black spots that appeared upon the skin at the time of death, and was probably a highly malignant form of typhus fever. It ravaged China in 1333–1347, and carried off 13,000,000 of its inhabitants, and 24,-000,000 in the rest of Asia. The Black Death first appeared in Europe in 1342, but it was not until August, 1348, that it reached England, and began to rage with unparalleled fury. In London 100,000 persons died of it, and in Norwich over 60,000. It is estimated that the victims of this one visitation numbered from one-third to one-half of the entire population of England, which, at that time amounted to about 5,000,-000 souls. The Black Death reappeared in Europe in 1360, 1373, and 1382. It is said to have carried off, in all its visitations, over 30,000,000 Europeans.

Black Eagle. A Prussian order instituted January 17th, 1701, by Frederick, Elector of Brandenburg, on his accession to the throne as first king of Prussia. There are thirty knights in the order, besides those belonging to the royal family. Their vows are justice and chastity, and protection to widows and children. An orange ribbon and a Maltese cross, with the legend *Cuique Suum*, are the insignia of the order.

Blackfriars Bridge. A famous bridge across the Thames at London. The original structure was built by Robert Mylne in 1760–1769. Owing to its piers giving way, it was replaced by an iron structure, resting on granite piers. It is 1272 feet long and 80 feet broad; was built by Cubitt, and completed in 1869. The bridge derives its name from an ancient monastery of the Black Friars, which once stood on the bank of the river, close at hand. It dated from 1276, and was the scene of several parliaments. It was there also that Cardinals Wolsey and Campeggio pronounced sentence of divorce against Queen Catherine of Aragon, June 21st, 1529. In 1599, Shakespeare acted in a theatre that occupied part of the site of the ancient monastery.

Black Friday.

(1) December 6th, 1745. On that day news reached London that the army of Prince Charles (the " Young Pretender ") had reached Derby, on its victorious march. London was in a perfect panic ; there was a run on the Bank of England ; all business was suspended and the shops were closed. The king himself (George II) is said to have ordered his yachts to the Tower stairs, and to have embarked many of his valuables. The panic, however, was of short duration, as the invaders retreated on the following day.

(2) May 11th, 1866. A disastrous day in London, owing to the suspension of the banking house of Overend, Gurney & Company. The panic was terrible, but fortunately of brief duration.

(3) September 24th, 1869. A day of fierce excitement in New York, occasioned by a clique of speculators, who suddenly advanced the price of gold to 162½, and thus caused a disastrous panic,— sweeping hundreds of firms and individuals into bankruptcy.

Black Hawk War.

A war between the United States and the North American Indian tribes of Sacs and Foxes, under the leadership of one of their chiefs, Black Hawk. It occurred in 1832, and was waged for the recovery of certain lands originally ceded by the Indians to the whites. Although the trouble commenced in 1831, the decisive battle of Bad Axe River, Wisconsin, was not fought till August 1st-2nd, 1832. This resulted in the utter defeat of the Indian tribes. Black Hawk was captured soon after by a party of friendly Indians, and taken to the principal cities of the United States, to impress him with the greatness of the nation. He died in 1838.

Black Hole of Calcutta.

The name given to a small dungeon or cell in Fort William, Calcutta, the scene of one of the most tragic events in the history of British India. When Calcutta was taken by Suraja Dowlah, on June 18th, 1756, he imprisoned, overnight, in this confined place, the British garrison of 146 men. The apartment was only 18 feet square, and was poorly ventilated, having only two small windows, obstructed by a verandah. In the morning 23 only were found to be alive, the remaining 123 having perished from lack of air, heat, thirst, and pressure. The " Black Hole " was afterwards used as a warehouse. One of the survivors, Mr. Holwell, published, in 1758, a narrative of his experiences.

Black Hussar of Literature.

A title conferred upon Sir Walter Scott (1771–1832) by his son-in-law, Lockhart.

Black Jack.

A nickname bestowed by his soldiers during the Civil War upon General John A. Logan (1826–1886), on account of his long, black hair and swarthy complexion. The term " Black Jack " is also used by miners to denote blende or sulphide of zinc.

Black-Letter Days.

Unlucky days were marked by the Romans with a piece of charcoal, and lucky ones with a piece of white chalk. Hence the expression —" Black-Letter Days "— came to mean, with them, days of misfortune. In the Anglican calendar, the Black-Letter Saints' Days were so named because they were printed in black or ordinary letters, while the more important feasts were usually printed in red, and hence were called Red-Letter Days. See *Red-Letter Days.*

Black Maria. An appellation popularly given to the closed van that conveys prisoners to and from the prison and the court-house. It is generally painted black, and has several small openings for light and ventilation. The term " Black Maria " is said to have originated in Philadelphia, in 1838.

Black Monday.

(1) April 14th, 1360 (Easter Monday). On this day, while Edward III (1327–1377) of England lay encamped before Paris, the darkness was so intense and the cold so bitter that many of the men and horses perished. Hence the Monday after Easter is frequently called, in England, Black Monday, in memory of this disastrous affair. In the *Merchant of Venice*, Act ii, Scene 5, Launcelot says :

" —it was not for nothing that my nose fell a bleeding on *Black-Monday* last, at six o'clock i' the morning. . . ."

(2) February 27th, 1865. On this day (Monday), a terrible sirocco swept over Victoria, Australia, and did fearful damage from Sandhurst to Castlemaine.

Black Prince. A sobriquet bestowed upon Edward, Prince of Wales, and son of Edward III. There is great difference of opinion as to the origin of this appellation. Froissart says that he was styled black " by terror of his arms," while Strutt states that he was surnamed the " Black " for his warlike prowess. The commonly received notion is that he was called the "Black Prince " owing to the color of his armor ; but Meyrick and Shaw both assert that his armor was anything but black.

Black Republic. A name bestowed upon Hayti, whose citizens are almost all negroes.

Black Republicans. A term of reproach bestowed by pro-slavery men upon the members of the Republican party at the time of its formation

(1856), and for some years after. The Republican party was organized to prevent the extension of slavery into any new State or Territory, and to confine it within those States in which it had a recognized legal existence.

Black Rod, Gentleman-Usher of. An officer of the House of Lords, appointed by letters-patent. He derives his title from his wand-of-office, which consists of a black rod surmounted by a gold lion. He is chief gentleman-usher to the sovereign, and usher of the Order of the Garter,—as well as doorkeeper at the meetings of the chapter. He maintains order in the House of Lords ; takes into custody any peer guilty of a breach of privilege ; and — either personally or by deputy—summons the House of Commons to the House of Lords whenever its presence is required. He is a member of the Order of the Garter.

Black Rood of Scotland. A piece of wood — said to be a part of the true cross—set in an ebony figure of Christ. This was enclosed in a casket of gold, elaborately wrought and shaped like a cross. It was brought to Scotland by Margaret, wife of Malcolm, king of that country, about 1270, and became the most venerated relic in the kingdom. Holyrood Abbey at Edinburgh was dedicated to the " Holy Rood." In 1291, it was delivered to Edward I (1272–1307) of England, and in 1328 was restored to Scotland. When David II invaded England in 1346, the " Holy Rood " was carried before the army, but fell into the hands of the English at the battle of Neville's Cross. It was then placed in the shrine of St. Cuthbert in Durham Cathedral, where it remained till the time of the Reformation (1517), when it disappeared. Since then, all traces of the " Holy Rood " have been lost.

Black Sea. This inland sea, connected with the Mediterranean by the Bosporus, the Sea of Marmora, and the Dardanelles, is said to owe its designation to the black rocks with which it abounds.

Blacksmith of Antwerp. A nickname conferred upon Quentin Matsys (1460-1529), the Flemish painter, in allusion to his original occupation.

Black Stone of Mecca. A dark-colored stone — apparently a meteorite —contained in the temple of the Caaba, at Mecca. It is about nine inches long, and is built into the southeast corner of the building at the proper height for kissing. The Mohammedans claim that it was given to Abraham by an angel. Pilgrims to Mecca circumambulate the Caaba seven times, and kiss the Black Stone. The Caaba was the temple of Mecca for ages before the time of Mohammed, and attracted pagan pilgrims in those days, just as now it draws thousands of Moslems. It is a legend that the "Black Stone" was at one time white; but turned black, owing to the sins of men. See *Caaba.*

Black Vomit. A term often applied to yellow-fever, owing to the dark matter, of the color of coffee-grounds, vomited during the last stages of the disease.

Blackwell's Island. A long, narrow island in the East River, included within the limits of the Borough of Manhattan, New York City. It has an area of about 120 acres, and was purchased by the city for $50,000, in 1828. It contains many of the reformatory and charitable institutions of the city,—among others, the Charity Hospital, the Hospital for Incurables, the Insane Asylum, Almshouse, Penitentiary, and Workhouse. The old Blackwell homestead—130 years old— is still standing, and is used by the warden of the Almshouse as his residence. The population of the island is about 7000. It is reached from foot of East 26th Street, New York, by ferry.

Bladensburg. A village of Maryland, about six miles northeast of Washington, memorable as the scene of a battle between the British and American forces, August 24th, 1814. The British army consisted of about 5000 men, under the command of General Ross and Admiral Cockburn ; the American forces, of militia hastily gathered, under General Winder. The battle resulted in a defeat for the Americans, after a brief contest, with small losses on both sides. The British soon after captured Washington, and burned the Capitol and several of the other public buildings. Bladensburg was famous, in more recent times, as a duelling-ground. There was fought, March 22nd, 1820, the famous duel between Barron and Decatur, in which the former was severely, and the latter fatally, wounded.

Blarney Stone. A famous stone, among the ruins of Blarney Castle, Ireland, supposed to possess the power of imparting persuasive, but not over-honest, eloquence to every one that kisses it. The position of the stone is a matter of much dispute. Some claim that it is inserted in the wall of the castle, about twenty feet from the top, and that the person wishing to kiss it must be suspended by his heels. According to others, the stone is lying in fragments on the ground ; while still others affirm that it is on the summit of the square tower, originally forming the donjon or keep of the castle. The village of Blarney is about four miles from Cork. The castle, situated in the midst of beautiful groves, was built in the 15th century. Its walls are 18 feet thick. According to a legend, the "Blarney Stone" originally belonged to the inhabitants of Tyre and Carthage, to whom its miraculous powers were well known. Some Carthaginian adventurers, having carried away the stone to the island of Minorca by stealth, were afterwards driven into Cork harbor. Thereupon they hid their treasure amid "the groves of Blarney," whence it was removed for use in building the castle.

Blenheim. The residence of the Duke of Marlborough, situated at Woodstock, about nine miles from the city of Oxford, England. It was erected at public expense, during the reign of Queen Anne (1702–1714), and presented by the British Parliament to the hero of Blenheim, in recognition of his distinguished services to the nation. The building was designed by Sir John Vanbrugh, and has a frontage of 348 feet. Its interior is magnificent, and originally contained a priceless collection of paintings—principally by Rubens—and a valuable library; these, however, were sold at auction between the years 1875–1886. Eleven of the paintings were offered to the nation for £350,000. Among these, the "Ansidei Madonna," by Raphael, was purchased for the National Gallery for £70,000. Blenheim Park consists of nearly 3000 acres, and contains a triumphal arch, and a column 130 feet high, surmounted by a statue of the great Duke. The total cost of the entire estate is said to have been nearly £600,000. See *Blenheim, Battle of ; Most Costly Painting in the World.*

Blenheim, Battle of. A battle fought near Blenheim, a village in Bavaria, on August 13th, 1704, between the allies, commanded by the Duke of Marlborough and Prince Eugene, and the French and Bavarians under Tallard, Marsin, and the Elector of Bavaria. The French and Bavarians were utterly routed, losing from 30,000 to 40,000 men, killed, wounded, and taken prisoners, besides 120 pieces of cannon and 130 standards. The allied loss was about 5000 killed and 8000 wounded. See *Blenheim.*

Blennerhassett's Island. An island in the Ohio River, near Parkersburg, West Virginia, famous as the residence of Harman Blennerhassett (1770–1831), a wealthy Irishman. The island was purchased by him in 1798, and a spacious mansion was erected upon it. In 1805, he was visited by Aaron Burr, and induced to assist him in his treasonable scheme of founding an empire in the West. Blennerhassett was arrested as one of Burr's accomplices, but was finally discharged without a trial. His house and grounds were ruined by an infuriated mob. The remainder of his life was spent in an unavailing attempt to retrieve his fortunes. See *Burr's Conspiracy.*

Blind Harry. A sobriquet applied to Henry the Minstrel, a wandering Scotch bard who lived during the 15th century. He is said to have been blind from his infancy. He was the author of a poem, entitled *Sir William Wallace,* in twelve books, containing about 12,000 lines. This poem, in its modernized form, still enjoys considerable popularity.

Blind Old Man of Scio's Rocky Isle. An appellation bestowed upon Homer by Byron in *The Bride of Abydos,* ii, 2. Although seven cities claimed the honor of being the birthplace of the poet, he is generally supposed to have been born at Smyrna or at Chios (Scio). Byron, from his allusion to Homer in the poem above mentioned, evidently gives the preference to the latter. The following are the names of the seven cities that are said to have disputed for the honor of having given birth to Homer: Smyrna, Chios, Colophon, Ithaca, Pylos, Argos, and Athens. Some writers substitute Salamis for Ithaca.

" Seven cities warred for Homer being dead ;
  Who living had no roofe to shrowd his head."
                              Thomas Heywood.

Blind Preacher. A sobriquet conferred upon William Henry Milburn, a blind Methodist minister, born in Philadelphia in 1823. He was for several years chaplain of the House of Representatives, at Washington, D. C., and has served the Senate in the same capacity since 1893.

Blocks of Five. An expression that became famous throughout the United States, during the presidential campaign of 1888. A letter alleged to have been written by W. W. Dudley, Treasurer of the Republican National Committee, was circulated broadcast by the managers of the Democratic party. In it occurred the recommendation to secure " floaters in blocks of five." This was interpreted to mean the purchase of the floating vote in large quantities. Dudley disavowed the letter, and brought suits for libel ; but these were abandoned after the election.

Blondel de Nesle. A famous French minstrel, born at Nesle in Picardy, in the 12th century. He was a favorite of Richard Cœur-de-Lion (1189–1199), and accompanied him on his expedition to Palestine. While Richard was returning from the Holy Land — attended by his minstrel — he was seized by Leopold, Duke of Austria, and imprisoned in the castle of Durrenstein. As the story goes, Blondel travelled through Germany, seeking his master, till he reached Durrenstein, where he learned that an illustrious captive was imprisoned. The minstrel thereupon placed himself at the foot of the tower, and commenced to sing a love-song that the king and he had composed together. He had barely finished the first stanza, when the king's voice, singing the second stanza, was heard within the walls of the prison. Blondel is said, thereupon, to have hastened to England, and to have been the means of having the king ransomed and restored to his subjects.

Blood, Circulation of the. The circulation of the blood was hinted at by Aristotle, Nemesius, Mondino, and Berenger. Michael Servetus (1509–1553) first taught the pulmonary circulation, or the passage of the blood through the lungs for purposes of aëration. In 1569, Cæsalpinus published a general notion of the circulation. Paul of Venia (or, as others claim, Fabricius Aquapendente) discovered the valves in the veins. To William Harvey (1578–1657), however, is due the distinguished honor of fully explaining the matter. He first announced his discovery in 1619, and published his first book upon it in 1628.

Blood-Heat. The normal temperature of the human body is about 98½ degrees, Fahrenheit. This is known as blood - heat, and is maintained, within one or two degrees, whether in the arctic or the tropical regions. Any deviation from the average is injurious ; and, if it be great or long-continued, is likely to prove fatal. In the animal kingdom, mammals have about the same temperature as man ; birds are warmer than man by 8 or 10 degrees ; while reptiles, fishes, and all invertebrates differ only slightly from the temperature of the medium in which they live.

Blood of St. Januarius. St. Januarius, or San Gennaro, was Bishop of Benevento, and suffered martyrdom at Pozzuoli, near Naples, in 305 A.D. His body is preserved in the cathedral at Naples, and in the chapel of the same church are preserved the martyr's head and two vials said to contain about an ounce of his blood. This blood, it is claimed, was caught by a woman, at the time of the saint's decapitation. Three times a year,— on the first Sunday evening in May, on September 19th (the anniversary of the saint's martyrdom), and on December 16th,—the head and the two vials are borne, in solemn procession, to the high altar of the cathedral. After prayer, the vials are brought into contact with the head, and the blood contained in them is, thereupon, believed to liquefy. It is then shown to the congregation, alike for the edification of the believer and the conviction of the skeptic. If the miracle is slow in taking place, the excitement of the congregation is raised to the highest pitch ; if it fails entirely, the direst distress prevails.   This same ceremony is performed on occasions of public danger or calamity.

Bloody Assizes.   A term applied to the judicial cruelties inflicted in 1685, after the defeat of the Duke of Monmouth, by the infamous Judge Jeffreys, while on a circuit through the western counties of England.   More than 300 persons were executed, many were whipped, fined, and imprisoned, and over 1000 were transported, as slaves, to plantations in America.

Bloody Butcher.   A name given to the Duke of Cumberland (1721–1765), second son of George II of England, on account of his merciless and cruel slaughter of the adherents of the Young Pretender, after the battle of Culloden (1746).   On his return to England, the Duke of Cumberland was hailed as the savior of his country, and an annual pension of £25,000 was settled upon him and his heirs. See *Butcher of Culloden ; Culloden, Battle of.*

Bloody Mary.   A sobriquet applied to Mary (1553–1558), Queen of England, and daughter of Henry VIII and Catherine of Aragon.   As a result of her attempt to restore the Roman Catholic religion in England, it is estimated that, during a period of four years, nearly 300 persons were burned at the stake, in addition to many that were punished by imprisonments, fines, and confiscations.   Among those that suffered death by fire for the principles of the reformed religion were Archbishop Cranmer, and Bishops Hooper, Ridley, and Latimer.   In justice, however, to Mary, it should be said that the religious persecutions during her reign were fully equalled by those inflicted during the reign of her successor, Elizabeth, and fell far short of those that occurred during the reign of Henry VIII.

Bloody Shirt.   " To wave the bloody shirt " is an expression meaning to keep up, by appeals to passion, the sectional animosities engendered by the Civil War in the United States.   It was a common political phrase during the ten years following the Rebellion of 1861–1865. Some derive the saying from an ancient Corsican custom, — nearly or quite obsolete, — according to which, before the burial of a murdered man, his blood-stained shirt was hung above his head, and his firearms were placed near his hand.   During the " wake " that followed, his friends and relatives, in loud and excited tones, declared their love for the dead man and called down curses upon his enemies.

Senator Conkling, in a speech delivered in 1880, declared that the origin of the expression—" the bloody shirt "—could be traced to an event that happened in Scotland three centuries before.   After a massacre at Glenfruin, 220 widows, riding on white palfreys, and bearing aloft—each on her spear—the bloody shirt of her husband, appeared at Stirling Tower, and so roused the people that they inflicted terrible revenge upon their enemies, and made the name of Glenfruin one of terror for several generations.

Bloody Tower.   One of the twelve towers of the Inner Ward in the Tower of London.   It is so called, because of the tradition that Edward V and his brother, the Duke of York (sons of Edward IV), were imprisoned and afterwards murdered there by order of their uncle, Richard III, in 1483. Some years later, a chest filled with bones — supposed to be those of the unfortunate princes — was found at the foot of a staircase in the Tower. These bones were removed to Westminster Abbey and buried there, in the Chapel of Henry VII.   The Bloody Tower was called the Garden Tower in the reign of Henry VII.   See *Tower of London.*

Bloody Wedding.   A term applied to the marriage of Henry of Navarre, afterwards Henry IV (1589-1610) of France, with Margaret of Valois, because it was solemnized a few days before the Massacre of St. Bartholomew, in which so many Huguenots were slain. See *St. Bartholomew, Massacre of.*

Bloomer Costume. A style of dress for women, — approximating male attire. It was introduced into America in 1849, by Mrs. Amelia Jenks Bloomer (1818–1894); but never became popular, and was soon totally discarded. The costume consisted of a jacket, with open front and closely fitting sleeves; a skirt falling a little below the knee; and a pair of trousers, like those worn by the Turks, but gathered in at the ankles. Since the days of "Bloomerism," reforms of a less radical type have been advocated, and the "divided skirt" still has its champions.

Bluebacks. A term applied to the paper-money of the Confederate States of America, to distinguish it from the paper-money of the North, known as "greenbacks." When the paper-money of the South became worthless, it was known as "shucks." See *Greenbacks.*

Blue-Beard. The hero of a well-known nursery-tale, so named from the color of his beard. The story is widely known throughout western Europe, but the form in which it is familiar in England is a translation from a tale in Charles Perrault's *Contes du Temps.* Some persons have thought to find the original of the story in one Giles de Laval, Seigneur de Retz, born in 1396. He was accused of murdering six of his seven wives, and was finally burned at the stake at Nantes, in 1440, by order of the Duc de Bretagne. Others profess to find in Henry VIII of England the prototype of Blue-Beard, owing to that monarch's numerous matrimonial ventures. The story of "Blue-Beard" is found, however, in so many different languages,

that it seems idle to attempt to identify its hero with any historic personage.

Bluebellies. A name given by the Confederates, during the Civil War, to the Federal soldiers, on account of the light blue overcoats and cloaks worn by them. The Confederates, owing to their gray uniforms, were often called "Graybacks" by the Federals.

Blue-Books. A name popularly given to the reports and other proceedings printed by the British Parliament, because they are usually bound in blue paper wrappers. The practice of printing, and to some extent of publishing, the proceedings of the House of Commons was begun in 1681 ; in 1836, Parliament adopted the practice of selling these published reports at a low price. The official books of other governments are also designated by the color of their covers. Thus, France has a Yellow-Book; Germany, a White-Book ; Italy, a Green-Book ; Spain, a Red-Book ; and Portugal, a White-Book.

In the United States, the name "Blue-Book" is given to a volume containing the names of all persons holding office, under the Federal Government, in the civil, military, and naval service, with their salaries, places of birth, etc. It corresponds to the "Red-Books" of Great Britain and of Canada. See *Red-Book.*

Blue-Grass Region. The name given to a high, undulating plateau in the north-central part of Kentucky. It covers about 10,000 square miles, and is remarkable for the extreme fertility of the soil. The rock underlying this region for 150 feet is a blue fossiliferous limestone, rich in phosphate of lime. This rock crumbles on exposure to the air, and thus constantly enriches the soil with the best constituents. Tobacco and hemp — two crops that rapidly exhaust the soil—grow there to a prodigious height. The native orchard-grass still grows in shady places, but elsewhere it has been run out by the smooth-stalked meadow-grass, supposed to have been introduced from England. This last has a small blue flower ; but there is no real blue-grass, and the origin of the term is unknown. This meadow-grass seems to grow continually, and, even in winter pushes itself up through the snow, thus furnishing winter pasturage. The "Blue Grass Region" is one of the most beautiful spots in the world, and is specially famous for its trotting-horses. For many years it has been the American centre for blooded stock of all kinds. Lexington is in the midst of the Blue-Grass Region.

Blue Grotto. A famous cavern on the island of Capri, near Naples. It is about 170 feet in length, 100 feet in breadth, and 40 feet in height, and is reached from the sea by a narrow arch in the limestone cliff, about a yard high. The water within resembles a liquid sapphire, and shimmers and sparkles with a pale blue light. The walls and roof of the grotto are of a superb ultra-marine color ; while any object, immersed in the water, sparkles like phosphorescent silver. This blue color is supposedly produced by the refraction of the sun's rays in passing through the water in the cave. The opening of the grotto being extremely small, practically all the light that reaches the cavern must first pass through the water and thus be refracted before entering the cave. It is necessary to remain at least twenty minutes in the grotto, to accustom the eye to the color. See *Green Grotto*.

Blue Hen's Chickens. An appellation sometimes bestowed upon the inhabitants of the State of Delaware. The expression is said to have arisen in connection with a certain Captain Caldwell, who was, for a time, an officer in the first Delaware regiment during the Revolution, and was much addicted to the sport of cock-fighting. His regiment reached a high degree of

efficiency,—chiefly through his exertions,—and whenever its officers were sent out on recruiting-expeditions it was said that they had gone in search of Caldwell's game-cocks. The captain, however, having declared that no cock could be "game" unless its mother was a blue hen, it naturally came about that the expression "Blue Hen's Chickens" was used instead of game-cocks.

Blue Laws of Connecticut. A term applied, in derision, to certain rules and regulations, said to have existed in the early government of New Haven Plantation. They were adopted by the settlers as early as 1639–1642, and imposed the death-penalty for the following offenses :
(1) Worshipping any God but the God of the Bible.
(2) Speaking disrespectfully of sacred things.
(3) Witchcraft, adultery, theft, perjury, disobedience to parents.
They are declared to have been compiled by the Rev. Samuel Peters, but are generally believed to be apocryphal. The chapter entitled "Capitall Lawes" in the Code of 1650 is an almost exact rendering of the Mosaic Law. The term "blue" was an epithet applied to the Puritans, in England, after the Restoration, and was given to all those that regarded with disfavor the licentiousness of the times. It was therefore natural that this term of reproach should find its way to the colonists on this side of the Atlantic, and should be applied not only to persons, but also to all laws, customs, and institutions tinged with the spirit of Puritanism.

Blue-Lights. An American political expression, applied to the Federalists during the War of 1812 and afterwards. In the summer and autumn of 1813, Commodore Decatur, with several vessels, was blockaded in the harbor of New London, Connecticut, by Sir Thomas Hardy with two

7

frigates and other smaller vessels. On the night of December 2nd, Decatur prepared to run the blockade; all preparations were made, when, just as the ships were about to weigh anchor, blue lights were seen burning on both shores. These were interpreted by Decatur as signals to the British, and the attempt was abandoned,—the ships remaining imprisoned during the rest of the war. As the Federalists were opposed to the War of 1812, they were accused of the deed ; but the charge was an unjust one, as no American was ever detected in, or even suspected of, the act.

"*Blue-lights*, meaning treason on the part of Connecticut Federalists during the war, is a standard word in the flash dictionary of Democracy. Even to this day, Connecticut *Blue-Lights* are the grizzly monsters with which the nursing fathers and mothers of Democracy frighten their children into obedience — just before elections."—*Goodrich*.

Blue-Noses. A nickname popularly given to the inhabitants of Nova Scotia and New Brunswick, owing to the effect produced upon the nose and other parts of the face by the coldness of the climate. Others say that this term was first applied to a particular kind of potato, cultivated extensively by the inhabitants, and that the expression was afterwards transferred to the inhabitants themselves. Others, again, declare that this sobriquet is derived from the custom, among certain aboriginal tribes, of painting blue the nose of any person guilty of the crime against chastity.

Blue-Skins. A term applied to the Presbyterians in England, after the restoration of Charles II (1660–1685), on account of their serious and grave demeanor. In the reaction that followed the days of the Commonwealth, wellnigh everything savoring of that dreary period was called, in derision, "blue," and Presbyterianism shared a similar fate.

Blue-Stocking. A name given, in good-natured derision, to any learned or literary woman that displays her knowledge in a pedantic manner, to the neglect of her womanly duties. The term was often made use of, during the latter part of the 18th century and the beginning of the 19th, but, since then, has fallen into disuse. The origin of the expression is in dispute. According to some authorities, it is derived from the attire of Mr. Benjamin Stillingfleet, who appeared at one of Mrs. Montague's literary reunions in London, in 1750, wearing a pair of blue worsted stockings, in place of silk ones. His conversation, however, was such an acquisition to the club that, in his absence, it was frequently remarked : "We can do nothing without the blue-stockings." From this saying, the literary reunions of the time were called Blue-Stocking Clubs. Others, however, affirm that the phrase arose in the following manner : At the literary receptions held in London by Mrs, Vesey, about 1750, dress was considered of so little consequence that a foreigner who was, on one occasion, invited to be present, was informed that he might attend, if he so desired, in blue stockings. This he interpreted literally, and afterwards spoke of the affair, in French, as a Bas-Bleu meeting. According to a third authority, as early as 1400 a society of ladies and gentlemen was formed at Venice. They were distinguished by the blue color of their stockings, and were addicted to literary pursuits. See *Blue-Stocking Clubs*.

Blue-Stocking Clubs. A name given to assemblies held in London, about 1750, at the houses of Mrs. Montague, Mrs. Vesey, and other ladies,—at which literary conversation and other intellectual pastimes were substituted for cards and gossip. These reunions were further characterized by plainness of dress on the part of some of the guests. See *Blue-Stocking*.

Bluff King Hal. A sobriquet bestowed upon Henry VIII (1509–1547) of England, on account of his bluff and hearty manner. It is said that the king delighted in being so called, and that hence the phrase became his most popular designation. See *Burly King Harry*.

Boanerges. A surname—signifying "Sons of Thunder"—conferred by Jesus Christ upon his disciples James and John, the sons of Zebedee,—probably on account of their fervid zeal and impetuous spirit.

"And James the son of Zebedee, and John the brother of James ; and he surnamed them *Boanerges*, which is, The sons of thunder."
—*Mark* iii, 17.

Bobadil. An ignorant and cowardly braggart, but regarded by his dupes as a great hero. Captain Bobadil is one of the characters in Ben Jonson's comedy, *Every Man in his Humor*. The name is supposed to have been suggested by Bobadilla, first governor of Cuba, who, on some trifling charge, sent Columbus to Spain in chains.

"As he [Lowell] would not accept a vulgar caricature of the New Englander as a Yankee, so he spurned Captain *Bobadil* as a type of the American, for he knew that a nation may be as well-bred among nations as a gentleman among gentlemen, and that to bully weakness or to cringe to strength are equally cowardly, and therefore not truly American."—*Address on Lowell* (G. W. Curtis).

Boboli Gardens. A beautiful and well-known pleasure-ground, adjoining the Pitti Palace, in Florence, Italy. The gardens are so named from the Boboli family, who once had a mansion there. They were laid out in a formal manner by Il Triboli, and are adorned with beautiful statues. Tennyson says :

"At Florence, too, what golden hours
In those long galleries were ours ;
What drives about the fresh Cascine,
Or walks in *Boboli's* ducal bowers."

Bock Beer. A strong variety of German beer, so called, not because its use causes the drinker to caper like a *bock*, or goat, but because of its association with Eimbock—now Einbeck— a town in Prussia, at one time famous for its beer.

Bode's Law. The name given to the arithmetical relation subsisting between the distances of the planets from the sun. Although this law was first discovered by Kepler, it was named *Bode's Law*, in honor of the German astronomer, to whom the credit for its discovery is universally given. If we take the numbers 0, 3, 6, 12, 24, 48, 96, 192, 384 (each of which, after the second, is double the preceding one), and add 4 to each of them, we get the following new series : 4, 7, 10, 16, 28, 52, 100, 196, 388.

When this law was discovered, the numbers above given represented approximately the relative distances from the sun of the planets then known,— taking the earth's distance as 10,—except that there was a blank opposite 28. On the first of January, 1801, however, Piazzi discovered the asteroid Ceres at almost the precise distance necessary to fill this gap. Other asteroids were soon after discovered ; and it is estimated at the present day that there are hundreds of thousands of these small bodies.

Bodleian Library. The public library of the University of Oxford, England. It is called the Bodleian Library, owing to its restoration by Sir Thomas Bodley in 1598,—his first act having been the presentation of a large collection of books purchased on the Continent at an expense of £10,000. It occupies the site of the old University Library, which was despoiled of its contents during the reign of Edward VI (1547–1553). The Bodleian Library contains over 400,000 printed volumes, in addition to 20,000 or 30,000 volumes in MS. It receives, by copyright-law, a copy of every volume published in the United Kingdom. The library has been, from time to time, enriched by valuable donations of books and MSS.

In the matter of rare books and MSS. it is second only to the library of the Vatican, at Rome.

Bœotian Confederacy. A league of the fourteen greater cities of Bœotia, with Thebes at the head. The chief magistrates of the league were called Bœotarchs, and were elected annually, —two for Thebes and one for each of the subordinate cities. The number of these chief magistrates varied, since the number of cities composing the league was not constant ; but fifteen may be roughly estimated as the average. The league continued, in a shadowy form, till the time of the Roman Empire.

Bœotian Ears. An expression meaning ears incapable of appreciating music or poetry. This phrase had its origin among the ancient Athenians, who considered their neighbors, the Bœotians, stupid, illiterate, and uninfluenced by the refinements of life. See *Bœotians*.

Bœotians. The inhabitants of a division of ancient Greece, having Thebes for its capital. The Athenians regarded the Bœotians with contempt, as lacking appreciation for the culture and refinement of Attica. The Bœotians were devoted to agriculture and pastoral pursuits, and, in the opinion of the Athenians, they were as thick and dull as their own atmosphere. Nevertheless, Bœotia produced Hesiod, Pindar, Plutarch, Epaminondas, and Pelopidas. During the days of Epaminondas, Thebes was the leading city of Greece. See *Bœotian Ears*.

Boers. The name of the Dutch settlers in South Africa, who at present occupy the Transvaal, the Orange Free State, and the republic of Zululand. Their first settlement was made at the Cape of Good Hope in the 16th century ; and although, since then, they have been reinforced by Huguenots from France, they have always retained their distinguishing traits of character. When the Cape of Good Hope was finally ceded to England in 1614, the Boers, disliking the change of government, began to seek other regions, and finally, in 1836, great numbers *trekked*, or emigrated, northwards, and began to settle in the territory at present occupied by them, —seizing upon the lands of the natives as pasture-ground, and reducing the inhabitants to a form of slavery. The Boers are sober and industrious, good horsemen and marksmen, and remarkable for their love of freedom and for courage. In 1899, the Transvaal or South African Republic adopted laws regarding the franchise which were not acceptable to the government of Great Britain. Both countries made immediate preparations for war, which broke out on October 12th of the same year. In this contest, the Transvaal had the support of the Orange Free State. War ended May 31, 1902.

Bohemia. A slang word used to denote certain sections in the leading cities of Europe and America frequented by roving adventurers in art or letters, who are without settled occupation. They are further characterized by unconventional habits, questionable tastes, and free morals. Bohemia was long supposed to be the original home of gypsies. See *Gypsies*.

Bohemian Brigade. A term sometimes applied to newspaper reporters because, like the gypsies of Bohemia, they live by their wits, and roam from place to place, without fixed habitation or abode.

Bohn's Libraries. The name given to a series of " libraries " or collections of books on various subjects, originally published by Henry G. Bohn. The first series—known as " The Standard Library "—was begun in 1846, and was followed by collections of classical, scientific, antiquarian, and illustrated books, amounting in all to more than 600 volumes. On Bohn's retirement from business in 1864, these collections were purchased by Messrs. Bell and Daldy, and many other volumes were added to them. It is impossible to estimate too highly the services rendered to the reading community by Bohn, in reprinting in cheap form so great a number of important works in the leading departments of knowledge.

Bois de Boulogne. A beautiful park in the outskirts of Paris, covering an area of 2250 acres, so named from the town of Boulogne in its immediate vicinity. It is a fragment of the extensive old *Forêt de Rouvray*, but the park, as we now see it, was commenced by Napoleon I, who laid out new walks and planted many trees. Previous to his time, it was a neglected spot — the resort of duellists, suicides, and robbers. In 1852, under the rule of Napoleon III, the property was transferred from the state to the municipality of Paris, on condition that 2,000,000 francs should be expended on it within four years ; the city furthermore was held responsible for its well-being. In 1853, two lakes were dug ; and, in 1855, the boundaries of the " Bois " were much extended, and the park greatly beautified. On account of its straight roads and level stretches, the Bois de Boulogne presents a formal and monotonous aspect, in spite of the efforts that have been made to introduce the element of variety. It suffered severely from loss of trees during the siege of Paris in 1870–1871, but these ravages have been almost entirely repaired of late years.

Bolivia. The name given by the inhabitants to Upper Peru, in 1825, when it became a republic. It was so named in honor of General Simon Bolivar (1783–1830), the liberator of South America from the Spanish yoke.

Bomba, King. An epithet applied to Ferdinand II (1830–1859), King of the Two Sicilies, on account of his cruel bombardment of Messina, in 1848. The expressions *Bombalino (It.*

Little Bomba) and *Bomba II* were bestowed upon his son, Francis II, for his bombardment of Palermo, in 1860. Other authorities say that the title, *King Bomba*, means the "Liar King," —the word *bomba* denoting, in Italy, the puffed and distended cheek, expressive of disbelief,—and was applied to Ferdinand II owing to his reputation for mendacity.

Bond Street. The name of a street in London,—famous in years gone by, — forming, after Regent Street, the main artery between Oxford Street and Piccadilly. In the days of Beau Brummel (1778–1840), it was the fashionable street, *par excellence*, of London ; but, since that time, it has been eclipsed by its younger rival, Regent Street. It still has many attractive shops, and is famous for its exhibitions and art galleries,— among these the Grosvenor Gallery, erected by Sir Coutts Lindsay. See *Beau Brummel.*

Bones of St. Mark. According to tradition, the bones of Mark, the evangelist, rest in the Cathedral of St. Mark, in Venice. St. Mark is said to have been sent by St. Peter to preach the gospel in Egypt, and to have suffered martyrdom at Alexandria in 68 A.D. For many centuries, the Christians guarded his remains in that city, but in 815 A.D. they were carried off by stealth by two Venetian merchants trading at Alexandria, and conveyed by them to Venice, lest they should fall into the hands of the Caliph of Egypt, who was at that time building a new palace at Alexandria, and adorning it with the spoils of Christian churches. These relics were received with great rejoicing in Venice ; the Church of St. Mark was built to receive them ; and St. Mark was made the patron-saint of the city, in place of St. Theodore, its former guardian. The original Church of St. Mark was destroyed by fire in 976, and the remains of the evangelist doubtless perished at the same time. Still, in 1085, more than a century later, it was announced that the bones of St. Mark had been miraculously recovered. This, Ruskin says, was "one of the most successful impostures ever attempted by the Romish Church." The day of their rediscovery was celebrated for several years with much religious ceremony.

Boney. A diminutive of Bonaparte, often used, in a depreciatory sense, by English writers and speakers, in the early part of the last century.

Bon Homme Richard. The name of a famous war-ship, originally a merchantman called the *Duras*, and rechristened the *Bon Homme Richard* by Paul Jones, in honor of Benjamin Franklin. She mounted 42 guns, and, while cruising in the English Channel (September, 1779), encountered the British frigate *Serapis*, carrying 50 guns. A terrible contest ensued, lasting nearly three hours, and terminating in the surrender of the English vessel. During the entire engagement, the ships were in close proximity, and, towards the end of the conflict, in actual contact. Jones was afterwards received in France with great honor, the king presenting him with a sword and the cross of the Order of Military Merit. The American Congress gave him a vote of thanks, and caused a gold medal to be struck and presented to him.

Bon Marché. A noted department-store in Paris, founded by Aristide Boucicaut.

"All his genius lay in a few principles—to suppress bargaining by a fixed price, to sell at retail for almost the same price as at wholesale and make up the difference by the quantity of the sales ; finally, to interest the employés in the business by a commission. Seventeen years later his house had swallowed up all the immense space between the Rues de Sèvres, Valpeau, du Bac, and de Babylone. Lately it has crossed this last street and begun to spread out on the other side, and the business it does every year amounts to over a hundred millions of francs. . . . It is governed by a triumvirate of directors chosen from its own members, who have mounted successively every round of the ladder for a term of three years, and are ineligible for reëlection. Every employé receives not only a salary, but a percentage of the yearly profits. The house has a restaurant on the top floor, where its employés are fed ; it has comfortable dormitories where they live."—De Forest's *Paris As It Is.*

Bonnet Rouge. The red cap of liberty, worn during the French Revolution. It is supposed to be an imitation of the Phrygian cap which, among the Romans, was the emblem of liberty, and was assumed by slaves when manumitted. The term *Bonnet Rouge* is often applied to a red or radical Republican.

Bonsecours Market. A famous market in Montreal, Canada, facing the St. Lawrence River. It is built of stone, in the Doric order of architecture, and is admirably suited to its purpose. From the dome surmounting the building may be obtained a beautiful view of the river and the surrounding country.

Bookkeeping. Although from certain passages in Cicero and Pliny the ancient Romans seem to have had some knowledge of accounts, still bookkeeping, as an art, appears to have originated in the great Italian mercantile cities during the 15th century. From there the principles of the Italian or "double-entry" system spread over Europe. The earliest treatise on the subject may be found in an algebraic work, published in Venice, by Luca di Borgo, in 1495. The great work of Edward Thomas Jones, first published in 1795, is the standard on bookkeeping in England. It is entitled *Jones's English System of Bookkeeping*, and is a simplified form of the Italian or "double-entry" method, with various rules and suggestions.

Book of Martyrs. The popular name of a celebrated book, written by John Fox or Foxe (1517-1587), the martyrologist, and entitled *History of the Acts and Monuments of these Latter* *and Perilous Days, Touching Matters of the Church.* The first part originally appeared in Latin, and was published at Strasburg in 1554. The first English edition appeared in one volume, folio, in 1563. The book received the official sanction of the archbishops of the Church of England, and was ordered to be placed in every parish-church and in the hall of every episcopal palace in England. It has had an enormous circulation, although no longer so generally and devoutly read as formerly. It is a fine specimen of English style, but its statements cannot in every case be accepted as trustworthy.

Book of Mormon. The sacred book of the Mormons or "Latter-Day Saints," which Joseph Smith the founder of the sect, declared to be a divine revelation. According to Smith's account, an angel from heaven appeared to him in 1827, and informed him where this book—the Bible of the Western Continent and supplement to the *New Testament*—lay hidden. On the spot designated, Smith found, in a box hidden in the earth, a volume composed of thin gold plates, covered with writing in the Reformed Egyptian tongue. By the side of these plates was found a pair of magic spectacles, which Smith called his Urim and Thummim, and which, he claimed, were miraculously given him to decipher the sacred records. These were translated by Smith, dictated to his private secretary Oliver Cowdery, and published in 1830,—together with testimonials from eleven persons who had seen the plates before they miraculously (?) disappeared. It was afterwards conclusively shown that this so-called sacred *Book of Mormon* was simply a plagiarism of a historic romance by one Solomon Spalding, a Presbyterian minister, who, at the time of his death, left the MS. of a strange production purporting to be the history of the Ten Tribes of Israel after their dispersion, and maintaining the hypothesis that the North American Indians are descended from them. Smith, in some way, obtained this MS., and published it, with sundry alterations and additions, under the name of the *Book of Mormon.* See *Latter-Day Saints; Mormons.*

Book of the Dead. The name of the most famous book of the ancient Egyptians,—more properly called the *Book of the Manifestation to Light.* It dates from the 4th dynasty (3733–3566 B.C.), and is written in Egyptian hieroglyphics. It contains prayers and exorcisms for the benefit of the soul on its long and perilous journeys in the lower world, as well as minute instructions by which it may vanquish the frightful monsters that will assail it before reaching the first gate of heaven. The following sentences, in the soul's defense before Osiris, are interesting, as throwing light on Egyptian morals : " I have not been idle ; I have not been intoxicated ; I have not told secrets; I have not told falsehoods ; I have not defrauded ; I have not slandered; I have not caused tears; I have given food to the hungry, drink to the thirsty, and clothes to the naked." The text of the *Book of the Dead*, carefully revised after much labor, with illustrations, was published by M. Édouard Naville, in 1886. Translations in several European languages have also appeared.

Booth's Conspiracy. The name given to a conspiracy formed at the close of the American Civil War, having for its purpose the assassination of the President and Vice-President of the United States, the Secretary of State, and the General-in-chief of the army. The leader of the conspiracy was John Wilkes Booth, and with him were associated the following persons: George A. Atzerodt, Lewis Payne (Powell), Michael O'Laughlin, David E. Herold, John H. Surratt, Mary E. Surratt (his mother), Edward Spangler Samuel Arnold, and Dr. Samuel A, Mudd. President Lincoln, while at

Ford's Theatre in Washington, was shot and fatally wounded by Booth, on the evening of April 14th, 1865. At about the same hour the Secretary of State, William H. Seward, was dangerously wounded by Payne; but the other intended victims suffered no injury. Booth was shot and killed, while attempting to escape, a few days afterwards, and the remaining conspirators, with the exception of John H. Surratt, were captured and tried before a military commission in Washington. Herold, Atzerodt, Payne, and Mary E. Surratt were hanged on July 7th, 1865; O'Laughlin, Arnold, and Dr. Mudd were imprisoned for life; and Edward Spangler was imprisoned for six years. Dr. Mudd, Arnold, and Spangler were afterwards pardoned. John H. Surratt was apprehended in Egypt, and brought to this country; but after several futile attempts to bring him to justice he was finally set at liberty. See *Ford's Theatre.*

Booth's Theatre. A superb place of amusement — formerly existing in the city of New York — erected by Edwin Booth, and opened by him on February 3rd, 1869, with the tragedy of *Romeo and Juliet.* It was built of Concord granite, in the Renaissance style of architecture, and seated 1800 persons, with standing-room for 300 more. The enterprise proved to be a financial failure, and the theatre passed out of Booth's hands in 1873. After varying fortunes at the hands of different managers, the house was finally closed, April 30th, 1883; soon after it was demolished, and a business building was erected upon the site.

Border. A name popularly given to the boundary line between England and Scotland. From the latter part of the 10th century until the beginning of the 18th, it was the scene not only of innumerable wars between the two countries, but also of incessant feuds and quarrels between clans and families. Elizabeth (1558–

1603) and James I (1603–1625) made great efforts to quell these disturbances, but it was not until 1707 — when the union of England and Scotland took place — that these troubles finally ceased. Border warfare was temporarily revived during the Jacobite rebellion of 1745.

Border Minstrel. A sobriquet frequently bestowed upon Sir Walter Scott (1771–1832), the famous poet and novelist, who traced his descent from a powerful Border family, now represented by the Dukes of Buccleugh. See *Minstrel of the Border.*

"When last along its banks I wandered,
  Through groves that had begun to shed
Their golden leaves upon the pathways,
  My steps the *Border Minstrel* led."
          Yarrow Revisited (Wordsworth).

Border States. A name given, previous to the War of the Rebellion in the United States of America, to those slave States that bordered on the line of the free States. They were Delaware, Maryland, Virginia, Kentucky, and Missouri. After slavery was abolished, the term "Border States" lost its significance.

Borghese Gladiator. A famous statue now in the Louvre in Paris. It was found at Antium, near Rome, in one of the imperial palaces, and is attributed to Agasias, son of Dositheos of Ephesus, whose name is inscribed on the statue. He seems to have lived during the closing years of the Republic or the early days of the Empire. The statue represents a hero contending; and from the attitude of the combatant it has been inferred that the statue did not originally stand alone, but was placed opposite some antagonist — possibly, an Amazon on horseback. Otherwise the attitude of the figure seems meaningless.

Borghese Palace. A magnificent private palace, of immense size, in Rome. It was commenced in 1590, and completed by Pope Paul V (1605–1621), one of the Borghese family. It formerly contained a gallery of paintings—800 in number—which were removed to the Villa Borghese in 1891. The court of the palace is surrounded by a portico of 96 columns. See *Villa Borghese.*

Borghese Villa. See *Villa Borghese.*

Borneo. This word is derived from the Sanskrit *bhurni (land).*

Borodino, Battle of. The name of one of the most sanguinary battles of modern times. It was fought on September 7th, 1812, between the French under Napoleon I, and the Russians under Kutusoff,—about 260,000 men being engaged. The losses, in killed and wounded, were about 80,000, and were shared about equally between the contestants. Each side claimed the victory, but as the Russians retreated and left the road to Moscow open, the honor certainly belongs to the French. The village of Borodino, which gives its name to the battle, is 70 miles west of Moscow. It is situated on the river Moskwa, and the French accordingly call this conflict the battle of the Moskwa.

Borromean Islands. A group of four small islands in the Bay of Tosca, which forms the western arm of Lago Maggiore, in northern Italy. These islands are named after the Borromeo family, who have been their owners since the 13th century. They are as follows : Isola San Giovanni, Isola Madre, Isola Superiore or dei Pescatori, and Isola Bella. In 1671, Vitaliano, Count Borromeo, caused soil to be conveyed to these islands, and converted them into beautiful gardens. The most celebrated is Isola Bella. On its west side, the grounds rise above the water in ten terraces, and are crowned by a palace filled with rare paintings and statues, while the gardens contain fine specimens of tropical plants. Isola Madre (the largest of the group) is covered with orange- and

citron-trees ; it is laid out in terraces, like Isola Bella, and is crowned by a dilapidated palace. Isola Superiore or dei Pescatori is inhabited by fishermen, and contains a small church. Isola San Giovanni is the most northern of the group, and is laid out in gardens. See *Isola Bella.*

Boscobel. The name of a manor-house near Donington, Shropshire, England, where Charles II (after his defeat at Worcester, September 3rd, 1651) remained concealed for several days. For greater security, the King hid himself for 24 hours among the leaves of an oak-tree near by, and narrowly escaped capture. This tree—afterwards known as the "Royal Oak"—was for many years regarded by the inhabitants of the neighborhood with great veneration. Near Boscobel, there exists at the present time an oak-tree said to have sprung from an acorn of the original tree. The name Boscobel (*It. bosco bello, fair wood*) was given to the place by its first owner, Mr. Giffard. When Charles II took refuge there, the place was occupied by one Penderell, a farmer. See *Royal Oak.*

Bosporus (*less correctly written Bosphorus*). A narrow passage, which connects the Sea of Marmora with the Black Sea, and separates Europe from Asia. It is about 17 miles long, and varies in width from half a mile to 1¼ miles. The word "Bosporus" is said to be derived from the two Greek words βοῦς, *an ox*, and πόρος, *a ford*, and means literally an ox-ford or cow-ford. It was so called because, according to the legend, Io, in the form of a cow, forded or swam across this strait.

Boston Athenæum. See *Athenæum, Boston.*

Boston Fire. The name given to a disastrous conflagration that occurred in the city of Boston, Massachusetts, November 9th–11th, 1872. Owing to a strong northwest wind that prevailed at the time, the fire spread with amazing rapidity. Nearly 800 buildings were destroyed,—709 of these being of brick or stone,—covering an area of 65 acres. About 60 dwelling-houses were burned. The fire occurred in the wholesale district, and the loss fell chiefly on the shoe, leather, and wool interests. Only 14 lives are known to have been lost. The total loss was estimated at about $80,000,000. See *Chicago Fire*.

Boston Latin School. A famous public school in Boston, Massachusetts, founded in 1634. It is the oldest educational institution in the country, —antedating Harvard University by nearly two years. The school-building originally stood on School Street; but the present structure, facing on Warren Avenue, was dedicated in 1881. Among the honored names enrolled as pupils at the Boston Latin School may be mentioned those of Cotton Mather, Benjamin Franklin, Samuel Adams, John Hancock, Robert Treat Paine, Charles Sumner, Ralph Waldo Emerson, Henry Ward Beecher, Wendell Phillips, Edward Everett Hale, and Phillips Brooks.

Boston Massacre. The name popularly given to a street affray that occurred in Boston, Massachusetts, on March 5th, 1770, between the British soldiery and the citizens. The garrison, being annoyed by several hundred of the populace, who were pelting them with snow-balls and otherwise embarrassing them, fired upon the crowd, with the result of killing three and wounding several others. Among those killed was the leader of the townspeople, a colored man named Crispus Attucks. The affair created intense excitement, and doubtless hastened the breaking out of hostilities. Until the beginning of the Revolution, five years later, the anniversary of the day was celebrated, and the incidents of the occasion were made the subject of oratory.

Boston Museum of Fine Arts. A superb structure, in the Italo-Gothic style of architecture, situated on Copley Square, Boston, Massachusetts. It was founded in 1870, and first occupied in 1876. The Museum contains many hundreds of rare and valuable paintings, as well as splendid collections of statuary, tapestries, embroideries, porcelains, pottery, wood and ivory carvings, prints and drawings, coins and bronzes, weapons and armor. Art schools — attended by students from all parts of the country—are connected with the Museum.

"It is entitled to respect among the museums of the world, as it certainly stands first among the museums of our own country."—*Clarence Cook*.

Boston Public Library. A magnificent building, in the style of the Italian Renaissance, situated on Copley Square, Boston, Massachusetts. It was completed in 1895, at a cost of over $2,500,-000. The library contains about 700,000 volumes and has 1300 periodicals in the reading-room. It is the largest in the world for free circulation, and loans 1,200,000 books annually for home reading. This popular and useful institution was projected in 1841 and opened in 1852, chiefly through the efforts of George Ticknor, Edward Everett, and others. A yearly grant of about $120,000 is made to the library by the municipality of Boston. The interior of the building is adorned with Abbey's series of paintings of *The Search for the Holy Grail* and Sargent's paintings of *The Growth of Religion*.

Boston Tea - Party. The name facetiously given to a group of citizens of Boston, Massachusetts, who, on December 16th, 1773, in the disguise of Indians, boarded three ships that had recently entered the harbor, and hurriedly threw overboard several hundred chests of tea with which these vessels were laden. This was done as a protest against the English plan of taxing the American colonies without granting them representation in Parliament. As a consequence of this act, the British closed the port of Boston, by way of retaliation.

Bosworth Field, Battle of. The name of a sanguinary contest between Richard III (1483-1485) of England and the Earl of Richmond (afterwards Henry VII). It was fought near Leicester, England, August 22nd, 1485, and resulted in the defeat and death of Richard, who was slain on the field. The fate of this battle, which terminated the *Wars of the Roses*, was decided by the action of the Earl of Stanley, who, at a critical moment, transferred his forces to the Earl of Richmond, and gave him the victory. A well is still shown where Richard is said to have drunk during the battle, and also an eminence called Crownhill, where Lord Stanley placed the crown on the head of the Earl of Richmond. See *Roses, Wars of the.*

Botany Bay. A shallow inlet on the coast of New South Wales, Australia, about five miles south of Sydney. It was discovered by the navigator, Captain Cook, on April 28th, 1770, and was so named by him on account of the great variety of unknown plants found growing there. The first penal settlement made by the English in Australia was established there in 1787; in the following year, the settlement was removed to Port Jackson, about 13 miles farther north. The name "Botany Bay," however, still remains not only the popular designation of this penal colony, but also the general term for Australian convict-settlements. The spot where Cook landed is now marked by a monument. The expression "Botany Bay of American Colleges" was formerly applied to Union College, Schenectady, because of the tradition that students that had failed to graduate from other institutions were frequently allowed to complete their studies there.

Boulevards. A name originally given in French cities to broad avenues planted with rows of trees; but more especially applied to certain wide and magnificent streets in Paris. The most famous of these are the *Old* or *Inner Boulevards*, which are divided by the Seine into a northern and a southern half. They derive their name from having been constructed, during the reign of Louis XIV (1643-1715), on the site of the ancient "bulwarks" or fortifications of the city. The northern half—known as the *Great Boulevards*—extends in a semicircle from the Church of the Madeleine to the Place de la Bastille, a distance of nearly three miles. They are never less than 100 feet in width, are beautifully shaded with trees, and reflect at all hours the life and gayety of the metropolis. The southern half is continued on the left bank of the Seine, under the name of the *Boulevard St. Germain*. The northern Boulevards were originally promenades, and were afterwards converted into streets.

Since the time of Louis XIV, many other new and beautiful streets, called "boulevards," have been opened in Paris. Among them may be mentioned the *New Boulevards*, laid out by Napoleon III, and with these may be ranked numerous other avenues, such as the *Avenue de l'Opéra*, the *Avenue des Champs Elysées*, the *Avenue de Friedland*, etc. Of late years the word "boulevard" has been generally applied to any broad and handsome avenue devoted to pleasure.

Boulogne Flotilla. A naval armament that was assembled at Boulogne-sur-Mer, in 1804, by Napoleon I, for the purpose of invading England. It consisted of 2400 transports and 17,000 sailors and marines. The army of invasion—known as the Army of England—amounted to 180,000 men and 10,000 horses, and was so trained in embarking and disembarking, that within a single tide the entire flotilla could be made ready for sea. As a result of Nelson's victory at Trafalgar in 1805, the expedition was abandoned and the flotilla disbanded. As a memorial of this projected enterprise, a tall marble column was erected on the high ground near Boulogne, and in 1841 this was surmounted by a colossal statue of Napoleon. See *Column of the Grand Army.*

Bounty. A famous vessel that sailed from England in 1787, for the Society Islands in the South Pacific Ocean. As the result of a mutiny that occurred on board, Captain Bligh, with 19 of his men, was set adrift near Annamooka, one of the Friendly Islands, in an open boat,—being furnished with 140 pounds of bread, some meat, and a small amount of water. After being at sea for 46 days, the little band reached New Holland (Australia), having vainly attempted to land at Otaheite. Captain Bligh, on his return to England, published an account of the mutiny. Some of the mutineers were captured and tried : of these, six were condemned to death and three executed. Eight others colonized Pitcairn's Island in 1789, and remained there, unknown to the world, until 1814, when they were accidentally discovered. See *Pitcairn's Island.*

Bounty-Jumper. A term applied, during the Civil War in the United States, to any person who, after receiving a bounty for enlisting in the army, fled to another State, and enlisted a second time. Instances were known, during the Civil War, of men that received several bounties in this way.

Bourbon, House of. The name given to the royal family that, for several generations, occupied the thrones of France, Naples, and Spain, and still reigns in the last - named country. The house of Bourbon was founded about 900 A.D., by Adhemar, lord of Bourbon, who traced his descent to Charles Martel. The first French sovereign of that line was Henry of Navarre, who, in 1589, became king, with the title of Henry

IV. The Bourbon family retained the throne of France until the French Revolution, when it was deposed in the person of Louis XVI. In 1814, after the fall of Napoleon I, it was restored to power and held the sovereignty until 1830, when it was superseded by the house of Orleans, a younger branch of the Bourbon family. See *Legitimists ; Orleanists.*

Bourgeoisie. A term applied to the great middle class of the French people,—consisting of the merchants, manufacturers, and upper tradesmen. Previous to the 13th century, they were included among the serfs, and, for long after, were forbidden the use of certain ornaments and stuffs reserved exclusively for the nobility. Owing to the favor shown them by Philip Augustus (1180–1223), their social position was much improved. As late as 1614, the president of the *States-General,* speaking of the bourgeoisie, said : " It is a great insolence to wish to establish any sort of equality between us and them ; they are only to us as the valet to his master." The nobles further demanded that " the common people be forbidden to carry pistols, to wear velvet or satin, or to own any but hamstrung dogs."

Boustrapa. A nickname applied to Napoleon III (1852–1870). It consists of the first syllables of the words *Bou*-logne, *Stra*-sburg, and *Pa*-ris, and refers to his two unsuccessful attempts to obtain the throne — at Boulogne in 1840, and at Strasburg in 1836,— as well as to his successful effort at Paris, in 1851, while president of the French Republic.

Boustrophedon. A name applied to a method of writing, among the ancient Greeks, in which the words were written alternately from right to left and from left to right, after the fashion of ploughing. In the Phœnician and other Semitic languages the direction of writing was, and still is, from right to left. When the Greeks borrowed the Phœnician alphabet, they adopted this method of writing ; but, afterwards, they effected a compromise,—writing the lines alternately from right to left and from left to right. Finally they adopted the method of writing only from left to right, which is the style in vogue among all civilized nations at the present time. The word *boustrophedon* is derived from the two Greek words, βοῦς, *an ox*, and στρέφω, *I turn ;* and refers to the line traced by a plough in ploughing a field.

Bow-Bells. The name given to a famous chime of bells in the belfry of the church of St. Mary-le-Bow—or simply Bow Church,—Cheapside, London. It is a tradition in the city that any person born within the sound of the Bow-Bells is a true cockney or genuine Londoner. These bells are mentioned in the legend of Sir Richard Whittington, as cheering him with the words :

"Turn again, Whittington,
Thrice Lord Mayor of London."

See *Cheapside ; Cockney ; Whittington Stone.*

Bower of Bliss.

(1) A garden of surpassing loveliness, mentioned by Tasso, in his *Jerusalem Delivered*, as belonging to the beautiful Armida. There Rinaldo passed the hours under the spell of the enchantress, until, being at last found by the two knights Carlo and Ubaldo, who were sent to rescue him, he broke with Armida and returned to the war.

(2) The home of Acrasia, the beautiful witch in Spenser's *Faerie Queene*. She was intemperance personified, and lived on a floating island called the Wandering Island, which contained everything calculated to charm the senses. See *Armida ; Faerie Queene ; Gerusalemme Liberata.*

Bowery. A famous street in New York City, extending in a line nearly

parallel with Broadway, from Chatham Square to the junction of Third and Fourth Avenues. In the Dutch and early colonial periods the Bowery was a lane passing between the farms or " bouweries " of the worthy Dutch burghers,— hence the name. At present the street is largely given over to cheap shops, lodging-houses, theatres, concert-halls, and dime-museums. The "Bowery boy"—once the terror of the neighborhood—is now happily a thing of the past. Germans and Hebrews, form a large part of the residents of the street at the present day.

Bowie-Knife. A long, stout knife, having a blade about 10 or 15 inches in length, and 2 inches in width. It was originally carried by hunters in the western and southwestern parts of the United States, and derives its name from Col. Jim Bowie, a notorious character, born in Logan Co., Kentucky. Other authorities say that the first bowie-knife was made by R. P. Bowie about 1820. Its blade was about $9\frac{1}{2}$ inches in length and $1\frac{1}{4}$ inches in width, and was made for hunting purposes.

Bowling Green. A small oval park in New York City, situated at the beginning of Broadway, and just north of the Battery. During the Dutch and colonial times it was the aristocratic quarter of the city, and was surrounded by the homes of the wealthiest and most influential citizens. South of Bowling Green is the site of Fort Amsterdam, erected in 1626. This was a capacious structure,—containing a church, the governor's residence, and quarters for a garrison of 300 men. During pre-Revolutionary days, there stood in Bowling Green a leaden equestrian statue of George III. On the evening when the Declaration of Independence was read to the soldiers, this statue was overthrown and destroyed. The lead was afterwards converted into bullets by the family of Governor Wolcott of Connecticut.

Bowling Green has been recently selected as the site for a new Custom House, now in process of erection by the United States government.

Bow of Ulysses. A famous bow belonging to Ulysses, King of Ithaca. He alone could draw it, and with it he is said to have shot an arrow through 12 rings. On his return home from his wanderings after the Trojan War, Ulysses slew all of Penelope's suitors with this bow, and thus made himself known to his wife.

Boxing Day. The name formerly given to the 26th of December, because on that day the alms-boxes in the churches were opened and their contents distributed among the poor by the clergy.

Boyle's Law. The name given to a famous principle in pneumatics, known as the law of the compressibility of gases. It was first discovered by Boyle in 1662, and afterwards independently by Mariotte in 1679. Hence, in England, it is popularly known as Boyle's Law, and on the Continent as Mariotte's Law. It is as follows : *The temperature remaining the same, the volume of a given quantity of gas is inversely as the pressure which it bears ;* in other words, when a given volume of any gas or vapor is compressed, so as to occupy a smaller space, its elastic force is increased; on the contrary, when the volume is increased, its elastic force is diminished. See *Mariotte's Law.*

Boyle Lectures. The name given to a series of eight sermons annually preached to prove the truth of the Christian religion. They are so named in honor of the Hon. Robert Boyle (1626–1691), the English scientist, who, by the terms of his will, stipulated that the sum of £50 should be paid yearly to the person selected for this purpose. The office of lecturer or preacher may be held for three years. The first series was delivered in 1692,

and was entitled *A Confutation of Atheism.* The sermons are at present delivered in the Chapel Royal, Whitehall. Among the eminent scholars that have delivered the *Boyle Lectures,* in recent years, may be named F. D. Maurice, Merivale, Prof. Plumptre, and Dr. Maclear.

Boy Popes. A title given to two youthful incumbents of the papal chair —John XII (956–963), and Benedict IX (1033–1044). John XII became pope at the age of 18, and died at the age of 25,—having occupied the pontifical chair for seven years. Benedict IX was raised to the papal see at the age of 10, and expelled at the age of 21, —having been pope for eleven years. Both of these popes were dissolute, tyrannical, and extravagant. One of the mistresses of John XII, named Joan, exercised great influence at Rome during his pontificate, and it is thought by many that this circumstance may have given rise to the story of Pope Joan. See *Pope Joan.*

Boz. A pseudonym under which Charles Dickens contributed, to the London *Morning Chronicle,* a series of *Sketches of Life and Character,*— familiarly known as *Sketches by Boz.*

"*Boz,* my signature in the *Morning Chronicle* . . . was the nickname of a pet child, a younger brother, whom I had dubbed Moses, in honor of the *Vicar of Wakefield,* which, being facetiously pronounced through the nose, became *Boses,* and being shortened, *Boz. Boz* was a very familiar household word to me long before I was an author, and so I came to adopt it." —*Charles Dickens.*

Bozzy. A diminutive of the surname of James Boswell, the biographer of Dr. Samuel Johnson. It is said that this nickname was given to Boswell by the great lexicographer himself.

Braganza Diamond. The name of the largest diamond in existence. It was discovered in Brazil in 1741, and is now among the crown-jewels of Portugal. It is the size of a hen's egg, is uncut, and weighs 1680 carats. It is valued at £58,350,000. This diamond is by many thought to be a white topaz ; if this is the case, the diamond of the Rajah of Mattan, Borneo, is the largest known—weighing as cut, $367\frac{9}{10}$ carats. See *Diamonds, Famous.*

Brahma. The chief god of the Hindus,—usually represented as having four heads and four arms. He is considered the creator of the universe, and constitutes, with Vishnu the preserver, and Siva the destroyer, the "Trimúrti," or Trinity, of the Brahminical religion. Brahma is said to have descended to earth nine times, in various forms, already ; and is to appear, for the tenth and last time, in the figure of a warrior upon a white horse, to punish the refractory and incorrigible. Brahma (neuter) is not a personality, but designates the universal spirit and cause of all existence ; Brahma (masculine) is the supreme being of creation. See *Siva ; Vishnu.*

Brain, Human. The average weight of the human brain, as given by Quain, is 49½ ounces avoirdupois for males, and 44 ounces for females. This general result was obtained by comparing and combining the tables prepared by Sims, Clendinning, Tiedemann, and Reid. The number of male brains weighed was 278, and of female brains, 191. In males, the minimum weight was 34 ounces, and the maximum, 65 ounces. In females, the minimum weight was 31 ounces, and the maximum, 56 ounces. In newborn infants, the brain weighs about 11.65 ounces for the male, and 10 ounces for the female.

In both sexes, "the weight of the brain generally increases rapidly up to the seventh year, then more slowly to between sixteen and twenty, and again more slowly to between thirty-one and forty, at which time it reaches its maximum point. Beyond that period, there appears a slow but progressive diminution in weight of about one ounce during each subsequent decennial period ; thus con-

firming the opinion that the brain diminishes in advanced life."—*Quain.*

The following table has been prepared from a much longer one found in Flint's *Text-Book of Human Physiology.*

Table of Weights of the Human Encephalon, in ounces avoirdupois, in Individuals, in some of whom the Degree of Intelligence is more or less accurately known.

Cromwell, aged 59 (not accepted by physiologists)	82.29 oz.
Byron, aged 36 (not accepted by physiologists)	79.00 "
Bricklayer, aged 38 ; fair intelligence, but could neither read nor write (reported by Dr. James Morris)	67.00 "
Cuvier, aged 63 (*Archives générales de médecine*, 1832)	64.33 "
Abercrombie, aged 63 (reported by Dr. Adam Hunter)	63.00 "
Congenital epileptic idiot (reported by Dr. Tuke)	60.00 "
Ruloff, aged 53 ; above medium stature ; executed for murder in 1871 ; well versed in languages, imagining that he had discovered new and important principles in philology (reported by Dr. George Burr)	59.00 "
James Fisk, Jr., aged 37 ; killed in New York, in 1872 ; illiterate, but said to possess great executive ability; notorious for colossal and unscrupulous financial speculations (reported by Dr. Marsh)	58.00 "
Spurzheim (*Medico - Chirurgical Review*, 1836)	55.06 "
Adult man ; an idiot since two years of age (Wagner)	54.95 "
Daniel Webster, aged 70 (reported by Dr. John Jeffries)	53.50 "
Executed criminal, aged 45 ; medium stature ; of less than ordinary intelligence, and uncultivated (Lélut)	53.12 "
Dupuytren, aged 58 (Cruveilhier, Husson, and Bouillaud)	49.68 "
Day-laborer, aged 49 (Wagner)	48.85 "
Celebrated philologist, aged 54 ; 5 feet 7½ inches tall (Wagner)	47.90 "
Executed criminal, aged 34 ; small stature ; intelligence developed and cultivated (Lélut)	47.79 "
Celebrated mineralogist, aged 77 ; above medium stature (Wagner)	43.24 "
Man, 44 years of age ; idiocy very profound ; a little below medium stature (Lélut)	34.39 "

" A careful study of the weights given in

this table shows the impossibility of applying to individuals an absolute rule that the greatest brain-power is connected with the greatest amount of brain-substance." — Flint's *Text-Book of Human Physiology.*
See *Anatomy.*

Brandenburg Gate. A famous historic archway in Berlin, situated at the western terminus of the Unter den Linden. It was erected in 1789, in imitation of the Propylæa at Athens, at a cost of $370,000 ; and is considered the finest gateway in Europe, after the Arc de Triomphe at Paris. It is 65 feet high and 205 feet in width, and is pierced by five passageways,—the central one being reserved for the carriages of royalty. Upon the summit is the famous quadriga or four-horse car of Victory, by Schadow. When Napoleon I passed under this gate as conqueror, after the battle of Jena, in 1806, he ordered the triumphal chariot taken to Paris, to adorn that city. It remained there until 1814—the year of Napoleon's downfall,— when the Prussians, with great rejoicing, restored the chariot to its original position, and named the open square, facing the Brandenburg Gate, the Place of Paris. Beyond this gate is the "Thiergarten," a famous park of Berlin. See *Unter den Linden.*

Brandy. This word is an abbreviated form of *brand-wine*, meaning literally burnt or distilled wine.

Brandy Nan. A nickname given to Queen Anne (1702–1714) of England by the London populace, on account of her fondness for ardent spirits. Upon the statue of Queen Anne, in front of St. Paul's Cathedral, a wit once wrote the following words :

"*Brandy Nan, Brandy Nan*, left in the lurch,
Her face to the gin-shop, her back to the church."

Brandywine, Battle of the. The name of a battle fought on the banks of Brandywine Creek, Pennsylvania, on September 11th, 1777, between 13,-000 Americans under General Washington, and 18,000 British under Lord Howe. The Americans were defeated with a loss of about 1200 men, the British losing about 800. General Lafayette was wounded in this battle. As a result of their victory, the British occupied Philadelphia on September 26th. Washington attempted to dislodge the British, and attacked Germantown ; he was, however, forced to retreat, and retired to winter-quarters at Valley Forge, 20 miles northwest of Philadelphia. See *Valley Forge.*

Bravest Man in England. The Rev. Mr. Narcross of Framlingham having willed the sum of £500 to the bravest man in England, the executors of the estate requested the Duke of Wellington to decide upon the person to whom this amount should be awarded. The Duke replied that, since the battle of Waterloo was one of the greatest battles ever fought by the English, and since its success, in his opinion, turned upon closing the gates of Hougomont at the proper moment, the money was rightfully due to the man that had closed them in the nick of time. This man proved to be Sir James Macdonnel. When Macdonnel was informed of the decision, he requested that he might share the legacy with his sergeant, John Graham, who had rushed forward and assisted him at the critical moment. The request was granted.

Bravest of the Brave. An appellation conferred upon Marshal Ney (1769–1815) by Napoleon I, during the Russian campaign of 1812. He commanded the centre during the terrible battle of Borodino, or the Moskwa, from which he derived his title of Prince. In the retreat from Moscow, Ney commanded the rear-guard, and maintained his courage amid the greatest disasters. When, in November, 1812, he was summoned to capitulate, he replied : "A marshal of France never surrenders."

According to some authorities, the title "Bravest of the Brave" was conferred upon Marshal Ney by the soldiers, on account of his fearless bravery during the battle of Friedland, June 14th, 1807.

Brazen Age. See *Ages, Mythologic.*

Brazen Bull. An instrument of torture, said to have been devised by Perillus, at Athens, for Phalaris, tyrant of Agrigentum in Sicily, who began to rule about 570 B.C. The victims were admitted to the interior through an opening in the side, while a fire, kindled underneath, roasted them to death. According to tradition, Phalaris caused Perillus, the inventor, to become the first victim. The inhabitants of Agrigentum afterwards revolted against the inhumanities of the tyrant, tore out his tongue, and roasted him in the brazen bull (549 B.C.). Pindar (522-442 B.C.) speaks of the cruelties of Phalaris; but more recent writers give him a better character, even declaring him to have been kind and humane.

Bread Street. A street in London, famous as being the birthplace of John Milton. The poet was born there on December 9th, 1608, and was baptized on December 20th of the same year, at the church of All Hallows, which once stood on the corner of Bread Street and Watling Street. Bread Street was so named from a market in which bread was formerly sold. In 1302, according to Stow, the bakers of London were forbidden to sell bread anywhere except in this market.

Break. A large four-wheeled vehicle, so called because used for breaking horses.

Breda, Declaration of. A famous document issued at Breda in the Netherlands, by Charles II (1660-1685) of England, on April 14, 1660, just before the Restoration. It declared a general amnesty; offered liberty of conscience; assured the soldiers of all their arrears; and promised them, in the future, the same pay as they then enjoyed. The document was received with wild enthusiasm by the Convention Parliament—so called because it had not been regularly summoned—on May 1st ; and by a unanimous vote a committee was appointed to frame an appropriate answer. It was further voted that the declaration should be immediately published.

Breeches Bible. A name popularly applied to a version of the Scriptures, properly called the "Geneva Bible," printed in 1560. It was given on account of the use of the word *breeches*, instead of *aprons*, in *Genesis* iii, 7 :

"The eyes of them both were opened . . . and they sewed figge-tree leaves together and made themselves *breeches*."
See *Geneva Bible.*

Breed's Hill. An eminence in Charlestown (now a part of Boston), Massachusetts. It is crowned by the Bunker Hill Monument, and is popularly known as Bunker Hill. In point of fact, Bunker Hill is somewhat to the north, and is the place to which the Americans retreated after their defeat. It was the original intention to throw up intrenchments on Bunker Hill, but Breed's Hill was afterwards chosen as being nearer the city of Boston. The battle of Bunker Hill is sometimes spoken of as the battle of Breed's Hill. See *Bunker Hill, Battle of.*

Brentford, Two Kings of. Two characters in *The Rehearsal,*—a farce composed by George Villiers (1627-1688), Duke of Buckingham, with the aid of Butler, Sprat, and others. It was written in ridicule of the heroic plays of Dryden, which are in rhyming verse and deal entirely with the deeds of exalted personages. As a result of this parody, Dryden made his plays more natural and wrote them in blank verse.

Brera, La. A famous palace in

8

Milan, Italy, devoted to science and art. It was erected in 1618, and presumably derives its name from the Latin *prædium* (*meadow*). La Brera contains a gallery of paintings by such masters as Raphael, Da Vinci, Titian, and Vandyck ; an academy of art ; a national library containing 162,000 volumes and 3650 MSS.; an archæological museum ; and an observatory. In the centre of the court is a fine bronze statue of Napoleon I, by Canova. He is robed as a Roman emperor ; in his right hand he holds a statue of Victory, and in his left a long staff. Around the walls of the court are the statues of eminent civilians and scholars.

Brewer of Ghent. An appellation bestowed upon Jacob van Artevelde, a wealthy brewer of Ghent, who became a famous popular leader during the first half of the 14th century. In 1335, while war was raging between England and France, van Artevelde sided with the former power ; he compelled the Count of Flanders, who supported France, to take refuge in that country, and finally concluded a treaty with Edward III (1327–1377). Thereupon he was chosen governor of Flanders, and ruled with almost absolute power for nine years. In 1345, he proposed that the Black Prince (son of Edward III) should be elected Count of Flanders. This so enraged the people that they rose in insurrection, and in the tumult that ensued van Artevelde was killed, July 24th, 1345.

Briareus. In Greek mythology, a giant with 100 arms and 50 heads. He was the son of Uranus and Gæa, and had two brothers,— Gyges and Cottus,— giants also. According to the most ancient tradition, Briareus and his brothers conquered the Titans when they made war upon the gods, and secured the victory to Jupiter, who, thereupon, thrust the Titans into Tartarus and appointed Briareus and his brothers to guard them. Other legends

say that Briareus was one of the giants that attacked Olympus; he was buried alive under Mount Ætna, as a punishment. According to Homer, this giant was called Briareus by the gods, and Ægeon by men. See *Titans*.

Briareus of Languages. A title conferred upon Mezzofanti (1774–1849), the famous Italian linguist, by Lord Byron, who declared him to be "a walking polyglot, a master of languages, a Briareus of parts of speech," and asserted that he should have lived in the times of the Tower of Babel, to serve as a universal interpreter. Mezzofanti is said to have spoken 58 different languages, and to have been thoroughly versed in the idioms and provincialisms peculiar to each.

" Brick, He is a." An expression said, according to Plutarch, to have originated with Lycurgus, the lawgiver of Sparta. As the story goes, an ambassador from Epirus to the city of Sparta was much impressed with what he saw, but wondered greatly that the city possessed no walls nor any other defensive works, and so expressed himself. "Wait till morning," said Lycurgus ; "you cannot have looked carefully !" Early on the following day, the lawgiver conducted the ambassador to the field-of-exercise outside the city, and, pointing proudly to the army drawn up in array of battle, exclaimed, "There thou beholdest the walls of Sparta, and every man is a brick."

Bricklayer. A nickname given to Ben Jonson (1574–1637), by his contemporaries. His father died a month previous to his birth, and his mother subsequently married a master-bricklayer. Jonson entered the University of Cambridge in his 16th year, but, on account of straitened circumstances, was obliged to leave college and assist his stepfather for a time, as mason and bricklayer. It is said that he worked at the building of Lincoln's

Inn with a trowel in his hand and a book in his pocket.

Bridal Veil. The name of a noted waterfall in the Yosemite Valley, California, having a total height of 900 feet. The water, on entering the valley, falls in a vertical sheet of 600 feet, then strikes a mass of débris, and rushes on in a series of cascades for 300 feet more. When the stream is at the proper height, the falling water vibrates with the varying force of the wind, producing a graceful, swaying motion, which has given to the fall its poetic name. The Indians called it "Pohono," a term referring to the chilliness experienced near the fall and under the overhanging cliff. See *Yosemite Valley.*

Bride of Abydos. The title of a Turkish tale, by Lord Byron (1788–1824). Brewer, in his *Dictionary of Phrase and Fable*, says : " As she was never wed, she should be called the affianced or betrothed."

Bride of Lammermoor. The title of a novel by Sir Walter Scott (1771–1832). It was published in 1819, and forms, with the *Legend of Montrose*, the third series of the *Tales of my Landlord.* Donizetti has written an opera, entitled *Lucia di Lammermoor*, which has the same plot as the novel.

Bride of the Sea. A poetic term bestowed upon Venice, in allusion to the ancient annual custom of the Doge, who, on Ascension Day, in the presence of his courtiers, dropped a ring into the Adriatic, uttering the following words: " We wed thee, O sea, in sign of a true and perpetual dominion." See *Adriatic Sea Wedded to the Doge.*

Bridge of Alcantara (*Span. Puente de Alcantara*). A famous and impressive Roman ruin in the town of Alcantara, Spain. The bridge spans the river Tagus, and was erected 105 A.D., during the reign of the Emperor Trajan (98–117 A.D.). The structure is 670 feet in length, and 210 feet in height. It consists of six arches,—the central span being 110 feet,—and is constructed of immense granite blocks, laid without cement. Although this bridge has been twice partially destroyed in time of war, the larger part is still intact. Alcantara, in Arabic, means " the bridge."

Bridge of Asses. See *Asses' Bridge.*

Bridge of Lodi. A bridge over the river Adda at Lodi, Italy, famous as the scene of a terrible contest between the French under Bonaparte, and the Austrians under Beaulieu, May 10th, 1796. The Austrians were strongly intrenched on the opposite bank of the Adda and their formidable artillery swept the bridge, but Bonaparte — charging at the head of his grenadiers —bayoneted the cannoneers at their guns and drove the defeated Austrians into the mountains of the Tyrol. As a result of this victory, Milan capitulated to Bonaparte a few days later. This battle is frequently spoken of as the " Terrible Passage of the Bridge of Lodi." It was Bonaparte's first important victory over the Austrians, and, as he afterwards declared, kindled the first spark of his ambition.

Bridge of Sighs (*It. Ponte dei Sospiri*). A covered stone bridge over the Rio Canal, connecting the Doge's palace with the state-prisons of Venice. Prisoners of state were conveyed across this bridge from the Judgment-Hall to the place of execution. This, at least, is the tradition, although Ruskin says :

" No prisoner whose name is worth remembering, or whose sorrows deserved sympathy, ever crossed that *Bridge of Sighs*, which is the centre of the Byronic ideal of Venice."

" The *Bridge of Sighs* was not built till the end of the sixteenth century, and no romantic episode of political imprisonment and punishment (except that of Antonio Foscarini) occurs in Venetian history later than that period."—*W. D. Howells.*

Bridgewater Canal. The oldest

canal in England, constructed by the Duke of Bridgewater, after plans by James Brindley, the famous civil-engineer. This canal was commenced in 1759, and opened on July 17th, 1761. It is 42 miles long, and unites Worsley with Manchester and Runcorn-on-the-Mersey, near Liverpool. At Barton Ridge, the canal crosses the river Irwell on an aqueduct 39 feet high and 600 feet long. The Bridgewater Canal was sold, in 1887, to the "Manchester Ship-Canal Co." for £1,710,000. See *Manchester Ship-Canal.*

Bridgewater Treatises. The name given to eight famous treatises, written by eight eminent men, on *The Power, Wisdom, and Goodness of God, as Manifested in the Creation.* Their titles are as follows :

(1) *The Adaptation of External Nature to the Moral and Intellectual Constitution of Man*, by Thomas Chalmers (1833).

(2) *Chemistry, Meteorology, and Digestion*, by William Proutt, M.D. (1834).

(3) *History, Habits, and Instincts of Animals*, by Kirby (1835).

(4) *Geology and Mineralogy*, by Dean Buckland (1837).

(5) *The Hand, as Evincing Design*, by Sir Charles Bell (1837).

(6) *The Adaptation of External Nature to the Physical Condition of Man*, by J. Kidd, M.D. (1837).

(7) *Astronomy and General Physics*, by Whewell (1839).

(8) *Animal and Vegetable Physiology*, by P. M. Roget, M.D. (1840).

Francis Henry Egerton, eighth and last Earl of Bridgewater, left at his death, in 1829, the sum of £8000, to be paid to the author of the best treatise on *The Power, Wisdom, and Goodness of God, as Manifested in the Creation.* The committee, to whom the decision was entrusted, resolved to distribute the money to the eight persons above mentioned. Their productions accordingly became known as the "Bridgewater Treatises." Charles Babbage

published, in 1837, a *Ninth Bridgewater Treatise*, so called.

Bright's Disease. A disease of the kidneys, so called after Dr. Richard Bright (1789–1858), an English physician, who first carefully investigated its nature. In 1827, he published an important work, entitled *Original Researches into the Pathology of Diseases of the Kidney.*

Brilliant Madman. A nickname given to Charles XII (1682–1718) of Sweden, both on account of his eccentricities of behavior and his phenomenal successes in war. See *Madman of the North.*

Britannia Bridge. A famous iron tubular bridge, spanning the Menai Strait and connecting the island of Anglesea with Carnarvon, Wales. It was built by Robert Stephenson, and opened for traffic in March, 1850. The bridge consists of two independent, continuous wrought-iron tubes, 1510 feet in length, weighing 4680 tons each. These tubes rest on three stone piers and two stone abutments, at a height of 100 feet above high-water. The central pier—called the Britannia Tower—is 230 feet high, and rests on a rock in the middle of the strait. The tubes sometimes expand as much as 2½ inches, vertically or horizontally, when the sun shines upon them. See *Menai Suspension Bridge.*

British Empire. A term collectively applied to the United Kingdom of Great Britain and Ireland, with its colonies and dependencies. The following statistics are taken from the *Century Cyclopædia of Names :* Area of the United Kingdom, India, and colonies, 9,180,700 square miles ; population, 345,282,960. Area of protectorates and spheres of influence, 2,240,400 square miles ; population, 36,122,000. Grand total of British Empire: Area, 11,421,100 square miles; population, 381,404,960.

"The East Indian possessions extend over a territory larger than the continent of

Europe without Russia; but the North American possessions are greater still, and, inclusive of Hudson's Bay and the great lakes, have a larger area than the whole of Europe."—*World Almanac.*

British Museum. A famous institution in London, founded in 1753, when the government, by act of parliament, purchased for £20,000 (two-fifths of the original cost) Sir Hans Sloane's extensive collection of curiosities of natural history, works of art, books, and manuscripts. This collection — together with the Harleian MSS. and the Cottonian Library—was deposited in Montague House, which was bought for the purpose, and opened as the British Museum, in 1759. The present buildings were erected during the years 1823–1857. The Museum was originally divided into three departments, viz.: (1) Printed Books ; (2) Manuscripts; and (3) Natural History. At present the contents are arranged in seven sections, as follows: (1) Printed Books (Maps and Plans); (2) Manuscripts; (3) Prints and Drawings; (4) Oriental Antiquities ; (5) British and Mediæval Antiquities and Ethnography; (6) Greek and Roman Antiquities; and (7) Coins and Medals. The sections of Zoölogy, Botany, Mineralogy, and Geology are now at the South Kensington Museum. The library consists of about 1,800,000 volumes, and receives a copy of every book published in the United Kingdom. It increases at the rate of about 46,000 volumes annually. The Elgin Marbles, the Egyptian antiquities, and the Assyrian antiquities collected by Layard are among the most famous curiosities in the Museum. See *Cottonian Library.*

British Solomon. A title conferred upon James I (1603–1625) of England, on account of his literary proclivities. He was the author of *Basilicon Doron ; The Essays of a Prentice in the Divine Art of Poesy ; The True Law of Free Monarchies ; Dæmonology ;* and *A Counterblast to Tobacco.* Sully called him " the most learned " (not the wisest) " fool in Christendom." See *Solomon of England.*

Broad=Arrow. An official mark used by the British government, and stamped, cut, or in some way fixed on all solid materials in dockyards, and on ordnance of all kinds, to prevent embezzlement. Its use by private persons is prohibited by law. The origin of this mark is unknown. Pepys thought it represented the anchor introduced as a crown mark in 1627. Others have said that it was suggested by the three nails of the cross. A commonly received explanation is that it is the device of Viscount Sydney, Earl of Romney, master-general of the ordnance in 1693–1702.

Broadcloth. The name given to a smooth-faced woolen cloth for men's garments, usually of double width (*i. e.,* a yard and a half). It is so called to distinguish it from woolens having a width of three quarters of a yard.

Brobdingnag. An imaginary country, described in *Gulliver's Travels*—a satirical romance by Jonathan Swift (1667–1745). Brobdingnag was a land peopled by giants, as tall as church-steeples, to whom Gulliver was but a pigmy. Everything else in this strange region was proportionately large.

Brocade. This word is derived from the Low Latin *brocare* (*to stitch, to figure, to emboss*).

Brocken, Spectre of the. A striking optical phenomenon, seen under peculiar atmospheric conditions, at sunrise or sunset, from the summit of the Brocken or Blocksberg, the highest of the Harz Mountains, in Saxony. It consists of a gigantic figure of the observer, projected on the mists that rise out of the valley, on the side of the mountain opposite to the sun. This phenomenon is seen about eight or nine times every year, and was formerly the cause of many popular superstitions.

Bronze Door of Capitol at Washington. A work of art, forming the entrance to the Rotunda from the eastern portico of the Capitol. It was designed by Randolph Rogers, an American sculptor; cast by Von Müller at Munich; and cost $30,000. It weighs 20,000 lbs., is 17 feet high and 9 feet wide, and contains eight panels in *alto-rilievo*, comemorating scenes in the life of Columbus and the discovery of America. There are also bronze doors at the entrance to the senate-wing of the Capitol,—designed by Crawford, and completed (after his death) by Rhinehart, of Baltimore.

Bronze Horses. Four famous figures of horses, of gilded bronze, standing over the principal entrance of the Cathedral of St. Mark, in Venice. They are five feet in height, and weigh more than 1900 lbs. each. It is supposed that they came originally from the island of Chios; but all that seems certain is that they were taken from Alexandria to Rome by the Emperor Augustus and placed on a triumphal arch, and were afterwards transferred to triumphal arches of their own construction by Nero, Domitian, Trajan, and Constantine. When "Blind Old Dandolo," the Doge of Venice, captured Constantinople in 1204, he brought these "Bronze Horses" to Venice, and placed them over the vestibule portal of St. Mark's Cathedral. There they remained until 1797, when Napoleon Bonaparte removed them to Paris to adorn the summit of the Arc du Carrousel, erected in 1806. After Napoleon's fall in 1814, the " Bronze Horses " were restored to Venice by the Emperor Francis of Austria. Owing to their many journeys, they are frequently referred to as the "Traveled Horses." See *Arc du Carrousel; St. Mark's Cathedral; Traveled Horses.*

Brook Farm. A famous socialistic community, organized for agricultural and educational purposes by George Ripley and others, in 1841; located near West Roxbury, Massachusetts. It was, to a great extent, an outcome of the Transcendental movement of the time. There, on an estate of 200 acres, a company of educated men and women settled down to a communistic experiment, in which each member was to perform his share of necessary manual labor. The enterprise proved to be an utter failure, and was abandoned in 1846. Among the persons, eminent in literature, that were connected with Brook Farm, may be mentioned George Ripley, Charles A. Dana, Ralph Waldo Emerson, Nathaniel Hawthorne, George William Curtis, Theodore Parker, Margaret Fuller, and Dr. Channing. Brook Farm is said to have suggested Hawthorne's *Blithedale Romance.*

Brooklyn Bridge. See *East River Bridge.*

Brooks's. A famous Whig Club in London, founded in 1764. It was originally called Almack's Club. In 1778, the club-house on St. James's Street was opened. Brooks's Club was the resort of the most noted men in London in the 18th century. Among these may be mentioned Sir Joshua Reynolds, Burke, Hume, Garrick, Gibbon, Horace Walpole, Sheridan, and Wilberforce. See *Almack's; White's.*

Brother Jonathan. A popular nickname of the people of the United States of America. It was originally applied, in a humorous way, by General Washington, during the War of the Revolution, to Jonathan Trumbull of Connecticut, and afterwards became a popular designation of the American nation. When Washington went to Massachusetts to organize the Revolutionary Army, he found it sadly in need of ammunition and other means of defense. On one occasion during that critical period, a council of officers was held to remedy this state of affairs, but no means were devised to supply the deficiency; whereupon Washington exclaimed: "We must consult Brother Jonathan on the subject," meaning Jonathan Trumbull, who was then Governor of Connecticut. The General did so, and so successful was the Governor in supplying the needs of the army that, whenever difficulties afterwards arose, it became the custom among the soldiers to say: "We must consult Brother Jonathan." The origin of the term was soon lost sight of, but the expression has remained in use until the present day. See *Uncle Sam.*

Brown, Jones, and Robinson. The names of three imaginary Englishmen of the middle class, who traveled together in Europe. Their adventures —amusingly caricatured by Richard Doyle—appeared in *Punch*, and formed an excellent satire on the snobbishness, vulgarity, and narrow-mindedness of the average British tourist.

Brown's Insurrection. An attempt made by John Brown (1800–1859), a fanatic on the question of slavery, to rouse the negroes of the South to assert their freedom by force of arms. John Brown, accompanied by 16 white and 6 colored men, entered Harper's Ferry, Virginia, on the evening of October 16th, 1859, seized the railroad bridge and government arsenal, and soon had the entire town under his control. On the following day, many of the townspeople were arrested, and held as hostages. The citizens, however, quickly obtained arms, and, with the assistance of 90 United States marines and two pieces of artillery, dislodged Brown and his party from the arsenal where they had taken refuge; 10 of Brown's party were killed at Harper's Ferry, 6 escaped, and the 7 remaining ones — including John Brown himself — were tried at Charlestown, Virginia, and hanged. This affair at Harper's Ferry caused great excitement both North and South, and was one of the most potent causes in hastening the Civil War.

Brown-Study. An expression applied to an absent-minded state, as manifested in deep thought and abstract meditation. Brewer seems to derive the word "brown" from the French *brun*, meaning *sad, gloomy, dull.*

Reddall, in his *Fact, Fancy, and Fable*, says: "It is more probably one of the group of similar phrases in which colors are employed to designate characteristics or temper; as 'black melancholy,' 'blue-devils,' 'green-eyed monster,' 'yellow-stockings,' 'blue-stockings,' 'white feather,' etc."

Others declare the expression to mean *brow*-study.

Brut. An old English metrical chronicle, by Layamon, more fully entitled *Brutus of England.* It is a narrative of British affairs from the arrival of Brutus, an imaginary son of Æneas of Troy, to the death of King Cadwalader, 689 A.D. The date of its composition is not later, probably, than the year 1205. Layamon's chronicle, *Brutus of England*, is a translation, with many additions, of the French *Brut d' Angleterre* by Wace, a Norman-French poet, who took the story from Geoffrey of Monmouth.

Buccaneers. A celebrated band of piratical adventurers, — French, English, and Dutch, — called also "Brethren of the Sea," who, during almost two centuries (1525–1700 A.D.), maintained themselves in the Caribbean Sea, and waged ceaseless war against the Spaniards in the West Indies. The word "Buccaneer" means a seller of smoke-dried meat, and was first applied to the French settlers in Hayti, who hunted animals for their skins, and smoke-dried and sold the flesh—chiefly to the Dutch. The most famous commanders of the Buccaneers were Montbars, surnamed "The Exterminator," Lolonois, Basco, and Morgan. In 1685, when their fleet defied the Spanish power in the Bay of Panama, their glory was at its height. After this time, the Buccaneers began steadily to decline; and, after the Peace of Ryswick (1697), they finally disappeared, to make way for a race of mere cutthroats and vulgar desperadoes. The last famous event in their history was the capture of Carthagena in 1697, where the spoils were enormous.

Bucentaur. The name of the state-galley in which the Doge of Venice—surrounded by his nobles—sailed out annually on Ascension Day, to wed the Adriatic. The word "Bucentaur" is said to be a corruption of the Latin *ducentorum* (*of two hundred* [*oars*]), or of *bucintoro* or *buzino d'oro* (*golden bark*). There have been only three Bucentaurs. The first was built in 1520; the second (a more magnificent one) was constructed in the following century; the third and last was completed in 1725, and destroyed by the French in 1797. It is said that the gilding alone of the latter cost $40,000. The ceremony of the wedding of the Adriatic is of greater antiquity than the construction of the first Bucentaur. See *Adriatic Sea Wedded to the Doge.*

Bucephalus. The famous war-horse of Alexander the Great (336–323 B.C.), bought by his father, Philip of Macedon, for 13 talents ($17,500). He was so wild and refractory that no one was able to mount him; but Alexander finally broke him in,—thus fulfilling the condition of the oracle necessary to secure the Macedonian crown. Bucephalus carried Alexander through all of his Asiatic campaigns, and lived to the age of 30 years. He died in northern India in 327 B.C.; and on the site of his burial-place Alexander founded the city of Bucephala.

Buckeye State. A name popularly applied to the State of Ohio, on account of the great number of buckeye-trees that flourish within its borders.

Buckingham Palace. The London residence of the late Queen Victoria (1837–1901), situated at the west end of St. James's Park. It occupies the site of Buckingham House, erected by John Sheffield, Duke of Buckingham, in 1703. That building was purchased by George III in 1761, and was occasionally occupied by him. It was demolished in 1825, and the present palace commenced on its site. This was completed after an expense of nearly £1,000,000, and first occupied by Queen Victoria on July 13th, 1837. From that time it was used by her as a town residence until her death. At one period it was used *exclusively* for that purpose — all "drawing-rooms" and "levees" being held at St. James's Palace; but during later years, owing to the crush, these entertainments were transferred to the larger rooms of Buckingham Palace. The palace contains some good paintings, but no regular collection. Buckingham Palace is now the town residence of the present sovereign, George V. See *St. James's Palace.*

Buddha. A title conferred upon Siddartha (624 (?)–543 (?) B.C.), the reputed founder of Buddhism. The word means the "Awakened" or the "Enlightened," and was applied to the great teacher in his state of perfection. It is derived from the root *budh* (*to awake* or *to know*); and means, in this connection, "he who is liberated from existence by the knowledge of the truth." See *Gautama.*

Bug Bible. A name popularly applied to a version of the Scriptures, properly called *Mathew's Bible*, printed in 1561. The title was given on account of the use of the word *bugges*, in *Psalms* xci, 5: "So thou shalt not nede to be afraid for any *bugges* by nighte, nor for the arrow that flyeth by day." Bug was originally identical with *bogie*, and has virtually the same meaning as "terror," the word substituted in the Authorized Version (1611).

Buggy. This word is said to be a corruption of *bourgeois*, the French name of a vehicle in use among the middle classes.

Bull. This word—meaning a blunder—is said to be derived from one Obadiah Bull, an Irish lawyer, who resided in London during the reign of Henry VII (1485–1509), and whose blunders were notorious. The *Standard Dictionary* denies this, and says : " No foundation appears for the guess that the word originated in ' a contemptuous allusion to papal edicts,' nor for the assertion of the ' British Apollo ' . . . ' that it became a Proverb from the repeated Blunders of one Obadiah Bull, a Lawyer of London, who liv'd in the Reign of K. Henry the Seventh.' "

Chaucer (1328–1400) uses the word *bole* in our modern sense of a verbal mistake. See *Golden Bull*.

Bull, Young. A famous painting by Paul Potter (1625–1654), the Dutch painter, in the Royal Museum of The Hague. It is frequently called " Paul Potter's Bull," and represents a young bull standing in a field, while close at hand are a cow reposing, a sheep, and a shepherd. These figures are life-size, and remarkably realistic in treatment. According to some critics, the legs of the bull and the bent foreleg of the cow are somewhat stiff in treatment.

Bullion State. A popular appellation of the State of Missouri, given on account of the exertions of its senator, Thomas H. Benton (1782–1858), in favor of gold and silver currency, in opposition to paper-money. Benton himself received the sobriquet of *Old Bullion*. See *Old Bullion*.

Bull Run, Battle of.

(1) The first important battle of the American Civil War, fought on July 21st, 1861, betweeen 28,455 Federals commanded by General McDowell, and 32,072 Confederates under Generals Beauregard and Johnston. The Federals were defeated and fled panic-

stricken to Washington, having lost 481 killed, 1011 wounded, and 1216 missing. The Confederate loss was 387 killed and 1582 wounded.

(2) A battle during the American Civil War, fought on August 30th, 1862, between the Federals under General Pope and the Confederates commanded by Generals Lee and " Stonewall " Jackson. The Federals were defeated after a fierce struggle, and were forced to retire.

Bully Boy. An expression commonly thought to be indigenous to America. It is, however, an old English saying, as the following quotation from *Deuteromelia, etc.*, published in London in 1609, will show :

" We be three poore mariners,
 Newly come from the seas,
We spend oure liues in ieopordy
 Whiles others liue at ease ;
Shall we goe daunce the round, the round,
 And shall we goe daunce the round,
And he that is a *bully-boy*,
 Come pledge me on the ground."

Bulwer-Clayton Treaty. A treaty between Great Britain and the United States of America, concluded on April 19th, 1850, and ratified on July 4th of the same year. It was negotiated by Sir Henry Lytton Bulwer for the British, and John Middleton Clayton for the United States government, and guaranteed the neutrality of lines of interoceanic communication across Nicaragua or elsewhere, declaring that neither nation should obtain exclusive control over the proposed ship-canal through Central America, or should erect any fortification in any part of that country. Also called the *Clayton-Bulwer Treaty*. See *Nicaragua Canal ; Mosquito Coast*.

Bulwig. A nickname originally applied to Bulwer (1805–1873), in *Frazer's Magazine*, in 1830. Thackeray afterwards made use of the same expression in *Frazer* and *Punch*, while directing his sneers at Bulwer and his novel *Pelham*. In Thackeray's collected magazine-articles, published years after, he declared that he was unacquainted with Bulwer in the days when he spoke disparagingly of him ; nevertheless he allowed the word *Bulwig* to remain in his collected works, and thus perpetuated the sneer.

Bummer. This word—meaning an idle, worthless fellow, without visible means of support — is generally supposed to be an Americanism. It is, however, simply a descendant of the old English word *bummaree*, which may be found in the *English Market By-Laws* of more than 200 years ago. The word meant a person that peddled fish outside the regular market, and that was accordingly looked down upon and regarded as a cheat by the established dealers. The word *bummaree* accordingly came to mean a worthless person of irregular habits. *Bummer* was first used in the United States about 1850, in California ; during the Civil War, it came into more general use,— meaning a camp-follower or straggler, especially one connected with Sherman's famous march to the sea. See *Sherman's March*.

Bumper. The origin of the word *bumper*—meaning a glass filled to the brim—has been variously accounted for. According to some authorities, when the Roman Catholics were in the ascendant in England it was their custom to drink the health of the Pope —*au bon père*—in a full glass, immediately after dinner ; hence, the word *bumper*. Others, however, say that the Pope was never known as *bon père*, but as *saint père ;* and that the word *bumper* refers to a glass so filled that if a small piece of cork be dropped upon the centre it will take a permanent position there,— standing well up above the level of the brim. If the glass contains a few drops less, the bit of cork will float to the edge and remain there. This last is called a *brimmer.* Murray thinks that the word *bumper* is perhaps derived from *bump*, with the notion of *bumping*, *i. e.*, large, swelling.

Buncombe or Bunkum. This word — meaning inflated or bombastic speechmaking, simply for effect — is said to have originated in the following way : During the famous debate on the Missouri Compromise, in the XVIth Congress, Felix Walker, an old mountaineer of North Carolina, who represented *Buncombe* County as part of his district, rose to speak. The House, however, was clamoring for the "question," and several members gathered about the Carolinian, begging him to desist, while others left the hall. The old man, however, persisted,—saying that the people of his district expected him to speak, and that he was, in consequence, bound to make a speech for *Buncombe*. Hence the meaning of the word : to speak for mere show or popularity. See *Missouri Compromise*.

Bundesrath. The name given to the Federal Council of the German Empire, the members of which are annually chosen by the governments of the various States. It deliberates upon the proposals to be submitted to the Reichstag, and upon the resolutions received from it. In addition to its legislative functions, it constitutes an advisory and administrative board, under the direction of the Imperial Chancellor. See *Reichstag*.

Bunker Hill, Battle of. The name of a famous battle during the American Revolutionary War, fought near Boston on June 17th, 1775, between 3000 British commanded by Lord Howe and 1200 Americans under Prescott and Putnam. It resulted in a defeat for the Americans, with a loss of 453 in killed and wounded. The British loss was about 1050. The latter were the attacking party, while the Americans fought behind a redoubt, hastily thrown up on the summit of Breed's Hill. Twice the British advanced to carry the rampart and twice they were driven back with great loss of life. At the third charge the Americans yielded, owing to lack of ammunition. The battle was regarded as a great triumph for the American cause, since it proved that raw and untrained militia could stand successfully against the veteran soldiers of England. See *Breed's Hill; Bunker Hill Monument.*

Bunker Hill Monument. A tall obelisk of Quincy granite, on Breed's Hill (now called Bunker Hill), in Charlestown, a part of the city of Boston. It is 221 feet in height, 30 feet square at the base, and 15 feet square at the apex. A spiral flight of 295 steps (inside this shaft) leads to a chamber, 11 feet square, immediately under the apex. The corner-stone was laid on June 17th, 1825 — the 50th anniversary of the battle — by Lafayette, while on a visit to this country, and the oration was delivered by Daniel Webster. The monument was completed on July 23rd, 1842, at a cost of about $100,000, raised by voluntary contributions. It was dedicated, with imposing ceremonies, on June 17th, 1843, in the presence of President Tyler and his Cabinet. Daniel Webster delivered the oration before an assemblage of 50,000 persons, on this notable occasion. See *Bunker Hill, Battle of.*

Buonarroti Papers. A name given to the archives of the famous Buonarroti family of Florence. They cover a period of about 600 years (1250–1860), and contain information of great historic value. When Count Buonarroti died in 1860, he bequeathed these papers to the city of Florence, on condition that their contents should never be made known. Fortunately, however, for the world, a part of them came, by purchase, into the possession of the British Museum. Among these have been found 150 letters of Michael Angelo, in his own handwriting. It is said that 200 additional letters of his remain in the original collection in Florence.

Burgos, Laws of. A set of laws for the regulation of Indian labor in America, promulgated at Burgos, Spain, on December 27th, 1512.

"The Dominicans of Hispaniola had represented that the Indians were very badly treated : the colonists opposed the monks, and the junta appointed to consider the question framed these laws. They provided that the Indian laborers should have houses, ground for culture, and religious instruction, with a peso of gold annually to buy clothes : those in the mines to work only five consecutive months, and to have official inspectors. The laws caused much dissatisfaction."
—*Century Cyclopædia of Names.*

Burly King Harry. A nickname given to Henry VIII (1509–1547) of England, on account of his swaggering, burly manner. See *Bluff King Hal.*

Burns's Cottage. A humble house about two miles from the town of Ayr, in Ayrshire, Scotland, where Robert Burns was born on January 25th, 1759. The house, which was originally a structure of the simplest kind, was rebuilt by the poet's father. It is said that the little bedstead in which the poet once slept was bought by a stable-boy for a trifle, and was afterwards sold by him for £20. The Burns Cottage is now a public-house, and is visited by more than 30,000 strangers every year. The region thereabout is called the "Land of Burns," and abounds in memorials of the poet. See *Alloway Kirk.*

Burr's Conspiracy. A wild attempt, made by Aaron Burr in 1805–1806,—after the ruin of his political fortunes,—to take Mexico from Spain, unite it to some of the Western or Southwestern States, and establish an empire with himself as dictator. By this means he hoped to gain sufficient power to overthrow the United States government. In this scheme Burr was aided by Harman Blennerhassett, who advanced large sums of money, and was, in consequence, ruined financially and socially. Burr was arrested in Kentucky, but the grand jury on November 25th, 1806, failed to find a true bill against him. On the 27th of the same month, President Jefferson issued a proclamation against the supposed conspiracy, and warned all citizens against engaging in it. Burr was arrested a second time, on July 19th, 1807. He was taken to Richmond on horseback, indicted in the district of Virginia for treason, and brought to trial; but this resulted in his acquittal, on account of lack of evidence showing that he had actually raised an army in the State where the trial was held. It was felt by many, however, that the acquittal was a partisan act, and Chief-Justice Marshall, who presided at the trial, was accused of having favored Burr on political grounds. See *Blennerhassett's Island.*

Burying Alive. A method of capital punishment in vogue in Bœotia, where Creon ordered Antigone, the sister of Polynices, to be buried alive. The unchaste Roman vestals, Minutia (337 B.C.), Sextilla (274 B.C.), and Cornelia (92 A.D.), were buried alive. Lord Bacon gives instances of the resurrection of persons that had been buried alive,—the famous Duns Scotus being of the number. It is said that unchaste nuns were thus punished, in earlier days, by the Roman Catholic Church. The two assassins of Capo d'Istria, President of Greece, were sentenced to be immured in brick walls, up to their chins, and to be supplied with food till they died. This was in October, 1831.

Burying at Crossroads. In the Middle Ages, the bodies of persons that had committed suicide could not be buried with the rites of the Church, nor in consecrated ground. They were, accordingly, interred at the junction of four crossroads, where crosses were generally erected. These spots were considered self-consecrated, and next in sanctity to hallowed ground.

Burying on the South Side of Churches. This custom is said to date back to the time of sun-worship. Whether this is the true explanation or not, it is certain that early burial-places in Switzerland and other continental countries are on the southern slopes of hills.

Burying the Hatchet. This expression, meaning "let bygones be bygones," is derived from a custom once in vogue among the North American Indians. According to a command of the "Great Spirit," they were obliged, when they smoked the calumet or pipe-of-peace, to bury in the ground their tomahawks, scalping-knives, and war-clubs, in token that all enmity was at an end.

Longfellow says, in *Hiawatha:*

"Buried was the bloody hatchet;
 Buried was the dreadful war-club;
 Buried were all warlike weapons,
 And the war-cry was forgotten:
 There was peace among the nations."

Buskin. The tragic actors of ancient Greece and Rome used to wear a sandal, two or three inches in thickness, to which was attached a strong protecting covering for the foot and part of the leg, called a buskin. The whole was known as a *cothurnus*, and was worn to give an appearance of elevation to the stature and thus impart dignity to it. Hence, the word *buskin* has become symbolic of the tragic drama, and is often so used. See *Sock.*

Dryden says:

"Great Fletcher never treads in *buskins* here,
 No greater Jonson dares in socks appear."

Butcher of Culloden. An epithet bestowed upon William Augustus (1721–1765), Duke of Cumberland, in allusion to the shocking and needless cruelties inflicted by him on the inhabitants of Scotland, after the battle of Culloden (April 16th, 1746). See *Bloody Butcher; Culloden, Battle of.*

By-Law. The expression *by-law* is used at present by civic societies to denote a law less important than a general law and subsidiary to it; and, in this sense, has probably been influenced by *by*, meaning *secondary* or *aside*.

"*By* is an old Danish word signifying town, burg, or borough. It is still retained in many names of places, as Grimsby, Derby, Whitby, all of which towns were renamed by the Danes. The term *bye-law* is therefore 'the law of the *by* or town.' "—Edwards's *Words, Facts, and Phrases*.

Byzantine Empire. A name given to the eastern division of the Roman Empire. It dates from 395 A.D., when the Emperor Theodosius the Great died, having divided the Roman Empire between his two sons, Arcadius and Honorius,—giving to the former the eastern half and to the latter the western. The Byzantine Empire took its name from Byzantium, the ancient title of its capital, which, after 330 A.D., was called Constantinople or New Rome. It originally included Syria, Asia Minor, and Pontus, stretching along the shores of the Black Sea in Asia ; Egypt in Africa ; Thrace, Moesia, Macedonia, Greece, and Crete in Europe. After a period of prosperity lasting nearly 700 years, the Eastern Empire began to decline (1057–1204). In 1204–1261 it was occupied by the French and Venetians, and during the years 1261–1453 it gradually succumbed to the Turks. The Empire thus lasted more than 1000 years, and was ruled over by about 90 emperors, none of whom was of any account. On May 29th, 1453, Mohammed II captured Constantinople, and the Byzantine Empire ceased to exist. The Christians were granted personal security and the free exercise of their religion.

C

Caaba (*also written Kaaba*). The temple of Mecca, said to occupy the exact spot of the tabernacle that was let down from heaven at the prayer of repentant Adam, after his wanderings of 200 years. According to tradition, it was built by Ishmael, assisted by his father, Abraham, and contains the famous "Black Stone of Mecca." The temple has been twice rebuilt within historical times, but still retains its original shape. It is in the form of a cube, 50 x 30 feet, and about 40 feet in height. It is richly decorated, and is annually re-covered with handsome brocaded hangings presented by the Sultan of Turkey. The interior is finished in marble and silver-gilt plating, and contains beautiful silk hangings, but is devoid of objects of genuine interest. See *Black Stone of Mecca*.

Cabal Ministry. The name given to an intriguing and unprincipled ministry, under Charles II (1660–1685) of England. It existed during the years 1667-1674, and was so called because the initials of the names of its five principal members formed the word " cabal." These members were *Clifford, Ashley, Buckingham, Arlington*, and *Lauderdale*. The word " cabal " originally meant simply a secret council or committee ; but, since the days of the " Merry Monarch," it has been used, in politics, to designate a secret and dangerous association.

Cabala. A system of philosophy or theosophy in vogue among the Jewish rabbis and certain mediæval Christians. It treats of the nature of God and the mystery of human existence, and assumes that every word, number, and accent of Scripture contains some hidden meaning, which it is the province of the Cabala to interpret. By this means, the Cabalists professed to expound the Scriptures, and to foretell future events. According to some of the rabbis, the Cabala was given to Adam by the angel Raziel, to Shem by the angel Japhiel, and to Abraham by the angel Zedekiel. The more common belief, however, is that God instructed Moses in its mysteries ; Moses, his brother Aaron : and so on, from age to age. It is said that the Cabala was lost by the Jews during the Babylonian Captivity, but was revealed a second time to Ezra.

Cabinet, Kitchen. A name given to a group of political advisers in the confidence of President Jackson,— so called because they occupied no official position but were consulted by the President simply as private citizens. The principal members of this "cabinet" were Amos Kendall, William B. Lewis, Isaac Hill, Duff Green, and Francis P. Blair. It is said that the Whigs gave these men this appellation, because it was their custom, whenever they called upon the President, to go in by the back or kitchen-door, to avoid observation.

Cabinet, United States. A body of men—nine in number—constituting the official advisers of the President of the United States, and charged with the administration of the executive departments of the government. They are appointed by the President, by and with the advice and consent of the Senate, and may be removed at the will of the President alone. The following are the titles of the Cabinet officers, as arranged in the order of their possible succession to the presidency :

(1) Secretary of State, established in 1789.

(2) Secretary of the Treasury, established in 1789.

(3) Secretary of War, established in 1789.

(4) Attorney-General, established in 1789.

(Although the office of attorney-general was created in 1789, the attorney-general did not become a member of the Cabinet until 1814.)

(5) Postmaster-General, established in 1829.

(6) Secretary of the Navy, established in 1798.

(7) Secretary of the Interior, established in 1849.

(8) Secretary of Agriculture, established in 1889.*

Each department has its official seal for public documents. The salary of each member of the Cabinet is $12,000 per year.

*(9) Secretary of Commerce and Labor, established in 1903.

Cabs. The word cab is an abbreviation of *cabriolet ;* twelve of these vehicles were introduced into London in 1822; in 1831, the number had increased to 165 ; and, in 1862, the number exceeded 6000. According to Mulhall (1891), there are 11.000 cabs in London, and 6000 in Paris. The London cabs average 80,000 passengers daily, and the Paris cabs 50,000. The earnings in London per cab are 19 shillings daily during the season, and 9 shillings during the rest of the year, or 12 shillings the year round. Of all males that die in England, one in 260 is killed by a cab or other vehicle ; and of all females, one in 2550. The value of articles found in London cabs, and handed over to the police at Scotland Yard, averages £21,000 annually. See *Scotland Yard.*

Cachet, Lettres de. A name given, in France, to warrants sealed with the king's seal, ordering persons to be thrown into prison or exiled. They came into use about 1670. It is said that 9000 lettres de cachet were issued during the reign of Louis XIV (1643–1715), and 80,000 during the administration of Cardinal Fleury, prime minister of Louis XV (1715–1774),— the majority of the latter having been directed against the Jansenists. In many cases these terrible documents were sold as a source of revenue. They were frequently signed in blank, and any person holding them might fill in any names he chose. In the reigns of Louis XIV and Louis XV, during the contentions of the Mirabeau family, 59 were issued on the demand of one or other of that family. The National Assembly abolished this iniquitous privilege on November 1st, 1789.

Cad. According to Brewer, this word is an abbreviation of *cadaver* (*Lat., dead body*), and is properly used to designate a non-member of a university. In university parlance, men are divided into two groups,— those that are members of the university, and those that are not. Those that are members being men, it follows that the others are not men ; but since they bear the human form, they are human bodies (*cad*-avers), but not human beings (men).

Others say that the word " cad " is probably derived from *cadet*, a younger son. Among the nobility, the younger sons were undoubtedly looked upon with something akin to scorn by their elder and richer brothers ; hence the expression " He 's only a *cad*," *i. e.*, a cadet, possessing no property, and unworthy of notice. When omnibuses were first introduced into London, the conductors were known as cads. The word is often used in this sense in Dickens's earlier works. At present the word " cad " means simply a vulgar, ill-bred fellow.

Cade's Insurrection. In 1450,— during the reign of Henry VI (1422– 1461),—Jack or John Cade, an Irishman, assumed the name of Mortimer and headed a band of 20,000 Kentish men, armed to punish ministers and redress grievances. Sir Humphrey Stafford opposed Cade with a small force, and was defeated and killed near Sevenoke, on June 27th ; whereupon Cade advanced toward London, and encamped on Blackheath. A few days later, he entered the city, and beheaded several persons of consequence. For a time Cade maintained strict order among his followers, but finally they broke into and plundered a rich man's house ; whereupon the citizens of London rose up against the rebels, drove them from the city, and, shortly afterward, repulsed them with great slaughter. A pardon was soon after offered to the insurgents, and being accepted by them, Cade was deserted by his followers and obliged to flee. A reward was offered for his apprehension ; but, on refusing to surrender, he was killed by Alexander Iden, sheriff of Kent, on July 11th. Many of his followers suffered capital punishment afterwards.

Cadi. An Arabic word signifying a judge, or a person learned in the law. It is the title of an inferior judge among the Mohammedan nations. Since all Moslem law is founded on the *Koran*, the Cadi, like the Mollah or superior judge, must be chosen from the upper ranks of the priesthood.

Cadmean Letters. A term applied to the old Greek alphabet of 16 letters, because it was said to have been invented by Cadmus, or perhaps simply introduced by him into Greece from Egypt and Phœnicia. These letters are as follows : $\alpha\ \beta\ \gamma\ \delta\ \varepsilon\ \iota\ \varkappa\ \lambda\ \mu\ \nu\ o\ \pi\ \rho\ \sigma\ \tau\ \upsilon$. The 8 additional letters— $\zeta\ \eta\ \theta\ \xi\ \phi\ \chi\ \psi\ \omega$—were called Ionic letters. Cadmus, according to Greek mythology, was the son of Agenor and Telephassa, and the founder of the city of Thebes in Bœotia.

Cadmean Victory. An appellation given to any triumph in which the victors suffer as much as the vanquished. This expression was originally applied to the victory of the Cadmeans (known later as the Thebans) over the famous "Seven," which was afterwards terribly avenged by the Epigoni, the descendants of the conquered. Others say that the expression " Cadmean victory " refers to the fratricidal war between Eteocles and Polyneikes, sons of Œdipus.

Caduceus. The name given, in classical mythology, to the wand or staff of Mercury. It consists of a winged rod, with serpents twined about it. The poets declared that, by means of the caduceus, Mercury could give sleep to whomsoever he chose ; hence Milton, in *Paradise Lost*, speaks of " the pastoral reed of Hermes, or his opiate rod."

Cæsar. A title borne by the first twelve emperors of Rome — hence known as the *Twelve Cæsars*—in honor of Julius Cæsar, the first of the line. After the death of Domitian, the last of the Twelve, in 96 A.D., the word

Cæsar dropped out of use, and was not revived until the reign of Hadrian (117–138), who conferred the title upon the heir-presumptive. In the reign of Diocletian (284–305), the emperors of Constantinople and Rome were styled *Augustus*, and the viceroys of Gaul and Illyricum were called *Cæsar*. This arrangement, however, ceased with the death of the emperor. The titles *Kaiser* (borne by the emperors of Germany and Austria) and *Czar* (belonging to the emperor of Russia) are modified forms of the word *Cæsar*. See *Cæsarean Operation; Cæsars, Twelve; Czar; Kaiser.*

Cæsarean Operation. The name of a surgical operation, which consists in the removal of a child from its mother, by making an incision in the abdomen. Pliny alludes to it in his *Natural History*, and says that Julius Cæsar was so called from being thus taken from his mother—such persons being called *cæsones*. In the case of Julius Cæsar, however, this statement must be regarded as extremely doubtful. The operation was successfully performed, in 1738, upon the wife of a poor farmer by an illiterate Irish midwife. In 1847, the same operation was performed in St. Bartholomew's Hospital, London, upon a young woman under the influence of ether; she died on the following day. The operation has been more frequently and more successfully performed on the Continent than in England.

Cæsars, Twelve. A name given to the first twelve emperors of Rome, by which title they are generally known. The *Twelve Cæsars* are as follows:

	b.	Became Emperor. *d.*	
(1) Julius Cæsar.	100 B.C.	45 B.C.	44 B.C.
(2) Augustus....	63 "	27 "	14 A.D.
(3) Tiberius.....	42 "	14 A.D.	37 "
(4) Caligula.....	12 A.D.	37 "	41 "
(5) Claudius....	10 B.C.	41 "	54 "
(6) Nero........	37 A.D.	54 "	68 "
(7) Galba.......	4 B.C.	68 "	69 "
(8) Otho	31 A.D.	69 "	69 "
(9) Vitellius	15 "	69 "	69 "
(10) Vespasian...	10 "	69 "	79 "

	b.	Became Emperor. *d.*	
(11) Titus........	40 A.D.	79 A.D.	81 A.D.
(12) Domitian....	51 "	81 "	96 "

With Nero ended the line of the *Julii*. Vespasian, Titus, and Domitian are also known as the Flavian emperors. See *Cæsar.*

Cagliostro, Count. A famous charlatan and impostor, whose real name was Giuseppe Balsamo (1743–1795). Under the assumed title of "count," he traveled in many countries, professing alchemy and free-masonry, practising medicine and divination, and raising money by various forms of imposture. His handsome wife, Seraphina, who was also a free-mason, accompanied him on these journeys. Cagliostro reached the acme of his fame and fortune in 1783, when he made a dupe of the Prince Cardinal de Rohan, in the "Affair of the Diamond Necklace." For this he was arrested in 1785, and confined for nine months in the Bastille. After his release, he was ordered to leave France; whereupon he sought refuge in England, and afterwards in Rome. There he was arrested and condemned to death for free-masonry; the sentence was, however, commuted to imprisonment for life, and Cagliostro was confined in the fortress of San Leone, where, in spite of his "elixir of immortal youth," he died at the age of 52 years.

Carlyle calls him "the quack of quacks, the most perfect scoundrel that, in these latter ages, has marked the world's history." See *Diamond Necklace.*

Cain of America. A term of opprobrium bestowed upon Chevalier de Villegagnon (1510–1571), a French admiral, on account of his alleged treachery towards a colony of French Protestants that had settled on Coligny Island in Brazil, in 1555–1557. The colony was not a success, and Villegagnon returned to France, where he was censured for his mismanagement of the enterprise.

Cain's Hill. The name given to an eminence about four miles from Damascus in Syria, where Cain is said to have killed his brother Abel. This statement is made by Henry Maundrell (1650–1710), an English traveler, who visited Palestine in 1697, and published in 1698 his *Journey from Aleppo to Jerusalem.*

"Ca Ira." A French optimistic expression, nearly equivalent to the English "It will come all right in the end," said to have originated with Benjamin Franklin, while he was United States Minister to France, at the time of the American Revolution. It was during the darkest days of our struggle for freedom,— the days of Valley Forge,— when the friends of the colonies began to despair of success, that Franklin uttered these cheering words and reanimated their drooping spirits. Afterwards, during the French Revolution, the words were remembered, and formed the refrain of a popular song, sung to the tune of *Le Carillon National*, as follows :

"Ah! ça ira, ça ira, ça ira! Malgré les
     mutins, tout réussira."
(It will go! In spite of the mutineers, all
     will succeed.)

The words, "Les aristocrates à la lanterne!" (Hang the aristocrats!), were added afterwards. The author of the song is unknown. It was heard in Paris for the first time on October 5th, 1789 ; and, until the appearance of the *Marseillaise Hymn*, was without a rival in the public estimation. See *Carmagnole ; Marseillaise Hymn.*

Calaveras Pines. A noted grove of gigantic pine-trees in Calaveras County, California. It includes nearly 100 specimens, several of which are over 300 feet in height and 30 feet in diameter. One of them required the labor of five men for 22 days to cut it down, and its stump now forms the floor of a pavilion, 22 x 24 feet in area. These trees have been visited by thousands of tourists since their discovery in 1852. See *Big Trees of California.*

Caledonia. An ancient Roman name for that part of Scotland lying north of the Wall of Antoninus, which extended between the Firths of Forth and Clyde. The word is perhaps derived from *Gael, Gaelmen,* or *Gadeldoine*, corrupted by the Romans into *Caledonia ;* others say that it is a corruption of *Cetyddon*, a Celtic word meaning "a dweller in woods and forests." The word first appeared in Lucan and Tacitus during the 1st century after Christ, and remained in use until about the middle of the 3rd century. At that time the country was invaded by the Scoti, from the north of Ireland, who drove the Picts northwards and settled in the Lowlands, giving their name eventually to the entire country. In more recent times, the word *Caledonia* has been used by Scott and others as a poetical designation of the entire country.

"O *Caledonia*, stern and wild,
     Meet nurse for a poetic child."
                                   Sir Walter Scott.

See *Scotia.*

Caledonian Canal. A famous ship-canal in Scotland, consisting of a chain of natural lakes connected by artificial canals, and extending in a southwesterly direction from the North Sea to the Atlantic Ocean. It was built to facilitate navigation between the ports of western England and Ireland and those of the Baltic and North Seas, and lessens the distance in some instances 800, and in others 1000 miles. The canal was commenced in 1803, under Telford, and was opened for navigation in 1823. It is 60 miles in length, from 17 to 20 feet in depth, and 120 feet in width, and contains 28 locks. Up to 1849, the total cost had been £1,311,270. The canal has never been a financial success. The scenery along the route is romantic in the extreme, and annually attracts large numbers of tourists. See *Neptune's Staircase*.

Caledonian Forest. The name of an extensive forest that once existed in the south of Scotland, and covered the entire country from sea to sea. In the grounds of Hamilton Palace, the seat of the Duke of Hamilton, may be seen some of the largest oaks in Great Britain. These trees are said to be a remnant of the once famous Caledonian Forest.

Calf's Head. This phrase—meaning the head of a calf — is often erroneously written *calves' head*. Unless one head is common to two or more calves, the expression is manifestly absurd. More ridiculous still is the phrase *half a calves' head*.

Caliban. In Shakespeare's *Tempest*, a savage, deformed slave—half beast, half man—in the service of Prospero, the magician. He was the offspring of Sycorax, a foul hag banished from Argier (or Algiers) to the enchanted island, afterwards inhabited by Prospero. The word *Caliban* is sometimes used to denote anything new or strange. The allusion is, of course, to Caliban, in the *Tempest*, a character in which Shakespeare has blended qualities both hideous and repulsive. See *Ariel*.

Calico. A cotton fabric named from Calicut, a city in southwestern Hindustan, where calico-printing was once extensively carried on. Calicut was first visited by the Portuguese in 1498, and calico was first brought to England by the East India Company in 1631. The first calico print-works in England were established near Richmond, in 1676, by a Frenchman. Calicoes were prohibited to be printed or worn in 1700, and in 1721 a penalty of £5 was laid on the wearer, and £20 on the seller, of calico. Manchester first commenced to manufacture them in 1771. Since 1834, numerous improvements in machinery and dyes have greatly increased the amount of calico produced. It is said that the United States uses more calico than any other nation.

California Column. The name given to a body of troops raised in 1862 by James Henry Carleton (1814–1873), a brigadier-general of volunteers. With these men, he marched across the Yuma and Gila deserts to Mesilla on the Rio Grande.

Califs. The name given to the successors of Mohammed in temporal and spiritual power. For a short time, the Saracen Empire—which exceeded that of Rome in extent—was ruled by one calif, whose will was obeyed from the Indus to the Pyrenees. Dissensions, however, soon arose, and the empire was divided in 753 A.D., between the Ommiades of Spain,— descendants of Omar,— who reigned at Cordova, and the Abbassides,— descendants of Mohammed's uncle, Abbâs, — who ruled at Bagdad. In 970 A.D., there were three reigning califs, an additional one having arisen at Cairo. In 1031, the califate of Cordova ceased to exist, and gave place to the Moorish Empire. In 1258, Mustasem, the last calif of Bagdad, was put to death by Hulagu, the grandson of Genghis Khân. In 1517, the Turks conquered Egypt, and in 1538 the Sultan of Turkey assumed the title of calif. It is little recognized, except by his own subjects. See *Abbassides; Ommiades*.

Calliope. One of the nine Muses. She presided over eloquence and epic poetry, and is represented with a tablet and stylus—sometimes with a roll of paper. Calliope was the mother of Orpheus, and chief of the nine Muses. See *Muses*.

Callithumpians. The name given to groups of people that were accustomed to parade the streets in New York City and elsewhere, dressed in fantastic costumes and provided with tin horns, tin pans, bells, rattles, and other discordant instruments. Their purpose was to make as much noise as possible, or, sometimes, to manifest ill-feeling towards some one. This custom has, fortunately, fallen into disuse; but a remnant of it may be found in New York, at present, in the crowds of small boys, dressed in ridiculous attire, who solicit alms on Thanksgiving and Christmas Day. The word "Callithumpian" is also applied to any burlesque serenade,— especially when given to unpopular persons soon after marriage.

Caloric Engine. The name given to any engine in which heated air is used as the motive power, in place of steam. The advantages claimed for it are (1) that it will render an explosion impossible, or at least harmless, and (2) that a boiler may be entirely dispensed with. Sir John Cayley invented a caloric engine in 1807, and Mr. Stirling used it in raising water in 1818; but it was not until 1852 that such an engine was made practically available. In that year, John Ericsson built a ship in which this kind of a motor was used as the propelling power; and, in the following year, this vessel sailed successfully from New York to Alexandria on the Potomac, and back, in very stormy weather. This achievement astonished the scientific world, but the speed attained was not sufficiently great to lead to any practical result. In 1858, Ericsson patented a caloric engine, which has proved eminently useful for all purposes requiring moderate power, and has been extensively used in the United States, Cuba, Canada, and in many parts of South America and Europe as well.

Calton Hill. An eminence in the city of Edinburgh, Scotland, adorned with monuments to Robert Burns, Dugald Stewart, Melville, and Lord Nelson. Near Nelson's Monument is the famous National Monument, erected to the memory of the heroes of Water-loo. It was intended as an imitation of the Parthenon; but was never finished, owing to lack of funds. In Calton churchyard is a tower erected to the memory of David Hume, the historian.

Calumet. The name of the peace-pipe used by the North American Indians. It consisted of a tobacco-pipe, having a large bowl—usually of highly polished red marble or soapstone—and a stem of reed or painted wood, decorated with feathers, about $2\frac{1}{2}$ feet long. After a treaty had been signed, the Indians used to fill the pipe with the best tobacco and present it to the representatives of the party with which they had entered into an alliance,— themselves smoking it afterwards. The Indians also presented the calumet to strangers as a mark of hospitality, and to refuse it was deemed tantamount to an act of hostility. The word "calumet" is not of Indian origin, but is simply the Norman name for a shepherd's pipe, and was given by the early French settlers to the Indian pipe-of-peace from its general resemblance to that pastoral instrument.

"Wash the war-paint from your faces,
Wash the blood-stains from your fingers,
Bury your war-clubs and your weapons,
Break the red-stone from this quarry,
Mould and make it into Peace-Pipes,
Take the reeds that grow beside you,
Deck them with your brightest feathers,
Smoke the *calumet* together,
And as brothers live henceforward."
Longfellow's *Hiawatha*.

Calvary. The name of a rock in the Church of the Holy Sepulchre at Jerusalem, said to be the site of the crucifixion of Jesus Christ. It is 30 feet long, 15 feet high, and as many broad. The summit is reached by two flights of steps,—one used exclusively by the Greek, and the other by the Latin, Christians. On the top is the Chapel of the Elevation of the Cross, the floor of which is paved with marble and the walls draped with velvet. At the eastern end, directly in front of the altar, is a hole in the rock, 2 feet deep by 1½ feet square, in which the foot of the cross is said to have rested. On both sides of this are holes for the crosses of the two thieves, and near by is a rent in the rock, said to have been caused by the earthquake at the time of Christ's death. It is considered by many that the Mosque of Omar occupies the true site of the crucifixion. See *Church of the Holy Sepulchre ; Golgotha ; Mosque of Omar.*

Calypso. In Homer's *Odyssey*, the name of a nymph that dwelt on the island of Ogygia, on which Ulysses was shipwrecked during his wanderings after the Trojan War. Calypso received him with kindness, and offered to marry him,—promising immortality and eternal youth, if he would consent. Ulysses refused, and Calypso, after detaining him for seven years, was commanded by the gods to release him. This she did, and taught him how to build a raft, on which he left the island and continued his journey. See *Calypso's Isle.*

Calypso's Isle. Gozo or Gozzo,— an island near Malta,—said to be the Ogygia of Homer's *Odyssey*, the home of the nymph Calypso. According to many, however, the location or the existence, even, of Ogygia is a matter of doubt. See *Calypso.*

Cam and Isis. A popular designation of the sister universities of Cambridge and Oxford, England, in allusion to the rivers on which they are situated,—Cambridge being on the Cam, and Oxford on the Isis.

Cambrai, League of. The name given to a compact made on December 10th, 1508, between Pope Julius II (1503–1513), Louis XII (1498–1515) of France, Maximilian I (1493–1519) of Germany, and Ferdinand V (1461–1519) of Spain. Its object was to dismember the republic of Venice, and blot it out from the map of Europe. Louis descended into Italy and defeated the Venetians at the battle of Agnadello, May 14th, 1509. The Venetians, however, succeeded in bribing the Pope, and securing his promise to break up the league. Julius II thereupon made a compact with the Swiss to drive the French out of Lombardy, and on October 9th, 1510, announced the formation of the " Holy League " between himself, Spain, Switzerland, and Venice, for the ostensible purpose of maintaining the see of Rome against the schismatical Council of Pisa, but really with the object of expelling the French from Italy. This was finally accomplished, and Pope Julius expired on February 24th, 1513, having had the rare gratification of witnessing, before his death, the complete and signal triumph of the " Holy League." See *Holy League* (1).

Cambria. The ancient Latin name of Wales, often used by modern poets. So called on account of the Cymri or Kimri, who peopled it.

Wheeler, in his *Dictionary of Noted Names of Fiction*, says: " It [Cambria] is derived from *Camber*, the son of Brutus, a legendary king of Britain. Brutus at his death left the isle to his three sons, one of whom, Camber, received the western part."

Cambridge University. One of the two famous English universities. It is situated at Cambridge, 48 miles northeast of London. The early history of the university is traditional until the 12th century. Sigebert, king of the East Angles, is said to have established a school at Cambridge about 630 A.D. The university received its first charter from Henry III (1216–1272) in 1231, was incorporated by Elizabeth (1558–1603) in 1571, and sent two members to Parliament in 1603,—a privilege which it has enjoyed ever since. It consists of 17 colleges and 4 halls, and has an average attendance of about 3300 students. The university possesses a library of more than 200,000 volumes, exclusive of MSS.;

an observatory ; a museum ; a botanical garden ; a biological collection ; and a divinity school. Mathematics forms an important branch of study at Cambridge. Newton, Bacon, and many of the greatest scholars and poets of England have shed lustre on this institution. See *Oxford University*.

Camel-Driver of Mecca. An appellation bestowed upon Mohammed (571–632 A.D.), the famous religious teacher and founder of Mohammedanism.

Camellia. This flower is so named in honor of Georg Josef Camelli (b. 1690), the German botanist and missionary, who introduced it into Europe from the East.

Camelot. A legendary city in Britain, famous in the time of King Arthur. Brewer, in his *Reader's Handbook*, says that there are two Camelots,—the one referred to in *King Lear* being in Cornwall, and the one of Arthurian renown in Winchester, where visitors are still shown certain large intrenchments once belonging to King Arthur's palace.

"In some places, even in Arthurian romance, *Camelot* seems the city on the Camel, in Cornwall. Thus, when sir Tristram left Tintagil to go to Ireland, a tempest 'drove him back to Camelot.'"—Brewer's *Reader's Handbook*.

Camera Obscura (*Lat. dark chamber*). An instrument invented by Battista Porta (1540–1615 A.D.), an eminent Italian physicist, about 1560 A.D. It consists of a rectangular box, with a lens whose focal length is equal to the length and depth of the box. On the side of the box opposite to the lens is placed a plane reflector at an angle of 45°. By this means, the image of any object towards which the lens may be directed is thrown upon a piece of ground glass on the top of the box, in an upright position. By this instrument, objects may be viewed or sketched from, as in nature.

Newton remodeled the camera obscura, and a new interest was taken in it when, by the invention of Daguerre in 1839, the pictures became " fixed." See *Daguerreotype*.

Cameronians. The name of a religious body in Scotland, so called from Richard Cameron, one of their ministers, who was killed in a skirmish in 1680. They are officially known as Reformed Presbyterians. They resisted the attempts of Charles II (1660–1685) to revive episcopacy in Scotland in 1661, and in the revolt that occurred in 1666 many of them were slain in battle or died on the scaffold, after suffering cruel tortures. Their 200th anniversary was held in 1880. They have at present about 30 or 40 congregations in Scotland, but are steadily declining in numbers and influence.

Camille. The name of a well-known play and novel. These are English versions of a French play and novel, entitled *La Dame aux Camélias*, by Alexandre Dumas, fils. In the French works the name of the heroine is Marguerite Gautier ; but in the English version it is Camille.

Camisards. A name given to the French Huguenots that inhabited the Cévennes, a mountainous region in the south of France. The word *Camisard* is said to be derived from *camise*, a species of blouse worn by the peasants, to enable them to recognize one another in nocturnal battles. The Camisards were subjected to much persecution after the revocation of the Edict of Nantes, October 12th, 1685 ; and in July, 1702, they took up arms to avenge the cruelties inflicted on some of their number. In 1703, Marshal Montrevel was sent against them at the head of 60,000 men. Large numbers of Camisards were shot down or executed, and 436 villages were destroyed. In 1704, Marshal Montrevel was succeeded by Marshal Villars, and the rebellion was finally suppressed by him in 1705. The contest terminated in the desolation of the entire province, and the execution or banishment of a large number of the inhabitants.

Camorra. The name of a secret society, formerly existing in Naples and the vicinity, the members of which were called *Camorristi*. For many years it terrorized the country, plundering the inhabitants and extorting money from all trades and occupations. It also transported smuggled goods, and contracted for the commission of desperate crimes. The *Camorristi* were long tolerated for political reasons, and rendered efficient aid to the cause of Garibaldi in the expulsion of the Bourbons; but, some years after, they proved so annoying to the newly established government of Italy that, in 1874, 200 of their number were banished. See *Mafia*.

Campagna. This word — meaning *country*, in Italian — is applied to the undulating plain that extends around Rome in all directions. It includes the larger part of ancient Latium, and was once densely filled with populous villages, and adorned with Roman villas and gardens. Pliny speaks of the salubrity of the Campagna, during the days of the Empire ; but it is now a desolate, uninhabited region, of volcanic formation, subject to malarial influences. It is about 90 miles long and 25 miles wide. Pope Pius VI (1775-1799) drained a part of the Campagna ; and in 1878 draining and planting were authorized by the Italian senate, but little has been done in that direction.

Charles Dickens speaks of the Campagna as " the aptest and fittest burial-ground for the Dead City."

Campania. A province on the western coast of ancient Italy, lying between Latium, Samnium, and Lucania. It was occupied by Hannibal in 216 B.C., and several of its cities— including Capua — declared in his

favor. It was, however, reconquered by the Romans in 211 B.C. Campania was one of the most fertile regions in the world,— yielding in abundance corn and wine, —and was famous for its soft and genial climate, and the beauty of its scenery. The Romans called it *regio felix*, dotted it with splendid villas and gardens, and made Baiæ the centre of their fashionable world.

Campo Formio, Treaty of. A treaty of peace, concluded between Austria and the French Republic, October 17th, 1797. By the terms of this humiliating treaty, Austria ceded to France the Netherlands, the Ionian Islands, part of Venetia, and its possessions in Albania ; while Milan, Modena, and Mantua were given to the Cisalpine Republic. Austria received, in compensation, Istria, Dalmatia, and the left bank of the Adige, with the capital, Venice ; furthermore, she recognized the Alps and the long-coveted left bank of the Rhine, as the natural boundaries of France.

Campo Santo of Dissenters. A name given by Southey to the Bunhill Fields Cemetery in London, once the principal burial-place for Nonconformists, but now disused. Among those buried there are John Bunyan, author of *Pilgrim's Progress ;* George Fox, founder of the Society of Friends; Daniel Defoe, author of *Robinson Crusoe ;* Dr. Thomas Goodwin, who attended Cromwell during his last hours ; Dr. John Owen, who preached the first sermon before Parliament, after the execution of Charles I ; Susannah Wesley, the mother of John and Charles Wesley; Dr. Isaac Watts ; William Blake ; and Horne Tooke, author of *Diversions of Purley*.

Campo Santo of Pisa. A famous cemetery at Pisa, Italy, near the Cathedral and Baptistery. The cemetery proper consists of soil brought in 53 vessels from Mount Calvary in Jerusalem, about 1200 A.D., by Archbishop Ubaldo de' Lanfranchi, upon the retreat of the Crusaders, after their expulsion from the Holy Land by Saladin. In 1278–1283, this ground was enclosed within two sets of walls, designed and built by Giovanni Pisano. The outer walls are without windows, and have only two doors. These face the cathedral, and thus the frescoes, with which the inner surfaces of the walls are covered, are preserved, as much as possible, from the salt and damp sea-air. These frescoes are in 24 compartments, and give the *Old Testament* history from the time of Adam to that of Solomon. They are by Giotto, Orcagna, Benozzo Gozzoli, and others. The inner walls, which are pierced by Gothic windows, giving a view of the cemetery, are separated from the outer ones by a broad arcade, paved with marble, and lined with a fine collection of monuments and with fragments of ancient sculpture. The name Campo Santo (meaning a *holy field*) was originally applied to this burying-ground, and afterwards given to all similarly constructed Italian cemeteries.

Campus Martius. A vast, irregular plain situated in the suburbs of ancient Rome, and surrounded by the Pincian, Quirinal, Viminal, and Capitoline Hills. It contained a temple of Mars, and was used for assemblies of the people, for the election of magistrates, and for athletic sports. In the latter days of the republic, the Campus Martius was adorned with spacious porticoes, superb triumphal arches, and beautiful public monuments. Of these the Pantheon and a few fragments of other buildings are all that remain of its ancient splendor. Although the Campus Martius now includes a considerable part of modern Rome, it was outside the walls of the ancient city.

Canard. This word — meaning an extravagant or absurd newspaper report or story — is said to have come into use in the following way : Nor-

bert Cornelissen declared in the newspapers that he had twenty ducks, one of which he cut up and threw to the remaining nineteen, which immediately devoured it. He thereupon cut up a second, then a third, and so on, until nineteen were thus disposed of. As the nineteenth was eaten by the surviving duck, it logically followed that it had eaten its nineteen companions in an incredibly brief period of time. This ridiculous story went the round of the newspapers in France and elsewhere, and furnished the word *canard* (*duck*) in the sense of hoax, —first to the French language, and afterwards to the languages of other nations.

Candlemas Day. A festival in the Roman Catholic Church in honor of the purification of the Virgin Mary, when she presented the infant Jesus in the Temple. It is held on the second of February, the fortieth day after Christmas. The name "Candlemas" came into use at a later period, after the introduction of candles into the service of this procession in honor of the Virgin. On this day, the Roman Catholics consecrate all the candles and tapers used in the churches during the coming year. At Rome, the Pope himself performs this ceremony, and afterwards distributes the candles to the cardinals, who carry them in solemn procession through the great hall of the Pope's palace. In many Lutheran churches, this festival is still celebrated, but in the Church of England it was discontinued in the second year of the reign of Edward VI (1547–1553). The feast of expiation and purification (*Lat. Februa*) was held in ancient Rome on the 15th of February; and this is thought by some to be the origin of the Christian festival. There is a tradition all over Christendom that a fair Candlemas Day portends a severe spring ; in Scotland, this notion is expressed in the following couplet :

" If *Candlemas* is fair and clear,
    There 'll be twa winters in the year."

Cannæ, Battle of. A sanguinary battle fought in 216 B.C., during the Second Punic War, in which Hannibal with 50,000 Africans, Gauls, and Spaniards defeated the Roman army of 88,000 men, commanded by the consuls Paulus Æmilius and Terentius Varro. The Romans lost their consul Æmilius and his chief officers, more than 80 senators, and 40,000 men. It is said that Hannibal sent home to Carthage, as trophies of his great victory, three bushels of gold rings taken from Roman knights on the field. See *Capua.*

Cannon First Used. The exact date at which cannon were first used is not known, but they were employed, under the name of "crakys of war," by Edward III (1327–1377) of England against the Scots in 1327 ; by the French at the siege of Puy Guillaume in 1338; and by Edward III at Cressy in 1346.

Haydn says : "The first piece was a small one contrived by Swartz, a German cordelier, soon after the invention of gunpowder in 1330." Shakespeare speaks of cannons and "bullets wrapp'd in fire," in *King John ;* but here his chronology was at fault, since King John died in 1216, before cannon were invented.

Canon Laws. A set of laws and ordinances used for the regulation of the Church of Rome. These laws originated in ecclesiastical decrees promulgated from the 4th to the 12th century, inclusive ; they treated of benefices, the mode of life of the clergy, marriage, divorce, and other affairs within the province of church discipline. Canon law is still in force in Roman Catholic countries, although it has been greatly modified by modern legislation and by "concordats" or agreements with the Pope. The canon law of the Church of England is still used in the ecclesiastical courts and in the courts of the universities of Oxford and Cambridge. See *English Law.*

Canon of Scripture. According to Brewer's *Dictionary of Miracles*, the canon of Scripture was completed in 494 A.D. The Council of Laodicea (360–364 A.D.) determined the canon of the *New Testament* Scriptures, but rejected the *Apocalypse.* The *Apocalypse* was admitted in 494 A.D. The *Old Testament*, in its present form, was not completed until 130 B.C. ; there was, however, a compilation in existence as early as 285 B.C. The Apocryphal books were declared uncanonical in the 5th century after Christ. The expression "Canon of Scripture" has reference to those books of the *Old* and *New Testaments* contained in the ordinary Bible, and regarded by the Protestant denominations as inspired, in contradistinction to the Apocryphal books.

Cañon of the Colorado. A wonderful chasm cut by the Colorado River, in its passage through the territory of Arizona. It extends from the Colorado Chiquito to the desert at the Grand Wash, and has a length of 220 miles, with walls from 5000 to 6500 feet in height—very precipitous and in many places perpendicular. The river, in its passage through this cañon, descends 3000 feet, and forms a series of rapid and roaring cataracts. The walls of the chasm are fantastically sculptured and brilliantly tinted in deep red and yellow, brown and gray, purple and black. The Cañon of the Colorado is only one of a series of stupendous chasms through which the Colorado River and its tributaries make their foaming way. Among the others may be mentioned the Glen Cañon and the Marble Cañon.

Cañon of the Yellowstone. A deep gorge cut by the Yellowstone River, in its passage through the Yellowstone National Park. It has a length of 24 miles and a depth of from 600 to 1200 feet, while its width at the top varies from 300 to 1500 yards.

"The upper part of the cañon, where it is at its deepest and narrowest, is also the scene of its most gorgeous coloring, the tints of the enclosing cliffs including the most brilliant shades of red, orange, yellow, and purple, 'as if a rainbow had fallen from the sky and been shattered on the rocks.' The formation of the crags and cliffs is exceedingly bold and picturesque. Far below flows the river, a thread of the most exquisite blue. The margins of the cañon are fringed with dark green pines."—Baedeker's *United States*.

Canossa. The name of a ruined castle in Modena, where Henry IV (1056–1105) of Germany, having been excommunicated by Pope Gregory VII (1073–1080), was forced to do penance by standing for three entire days (January 25th–28th, 1077), shivering, bareheaded, and barefooted, in the open courtyard of the palace. At the expiration of that time he was admitted to the presence of the arrogant pontiff, who granted him absolution and removed the ban of excommunication. This event gave rise to the famous expression, uttered by Bismarck during his controversy with the Roman Catholics : "We shall not go to *Canossa*."

Canter. This word is said to be an abbreviation of the expression "Canterbury gallop," and refers to the easy, ambling pace adopted by the pilgrims to the shrine of Thomas à Becket at Canterbury.

Canterbury Tales. A poem by Geoffrey Chaucer (1328–1400), consisting of eighteen tales, purporting to have been told by a party of equestrian pilgrims, going from Tabard Inn, Southwark, on a pilgrimage to the shrine of Thomas à Becket at Canterbury. The party, consisting of twenty-nine pilgrims, agreed to tell one tale each — both on going and returning, with the understanding that the person that should tell the best tale should be treated by the rest to a supper at the Tabard Inn, on their return journey. Out of a possible fifty-eight, only eighteen tales were told, and not one on the homeward route. *The Canter-*

bury Tales were written about 1364, and were first printed by Caxton about 1475. They are at present little read, on account of the great number of obsolete words which they contain ; but their merit places Chaucer in the front rank of English poets. See *Tabard Inn*.

Cape Cod Turkeys. A name given to codfish in the State of Massachusetts, especially in the vicinity of Cape Cod. See *Marblehead Turkeys*.

Capet. A surname given to Hugues, the founder of the French monarchy and ancestor of thirty-two French kings. The origin of this surname is in doubt. Some say that it is derived from *capetus* (*Lat. clothed with a capote* or *monk's hood*), because Hugues used the crown only at his coronation, and continued to wear, throughout life, the cape of an abbot. Others say that the word means "a jester"; yet others, "big-headed"; and so on. Capet was considered the family-name of the French kings from the accession of Hugues Capet in 987 ; hence, when Louis XVI was arraigned at the bar of the National Convention, he was addressed as Louis Capet. See *Capetian Dynasty*.

Capetian Dynasty. The third dynasty of French kings, founded in 987 by Hugues Capet, Count of Paris and Orleans, one of the great feudal lords of the time. At the death of Louis V (986–987), surnamed the Indolent, Hugues Capet was elected king, on account of his military valor and public virtues, to the exclusion of Charles of Lorraine, the rightful heir. Capet's ascension to the throne may be considered the real beginning of French history ; Paris became the capital, and French was made the language of the court. The Capetian dynasty ruled in France from 987 to 1328,—a period of 341 years,—when it was succeeded by the House of Valois. See *Capet*.

Capital Punishment in the United States.

"The States in which the death penalty is forbidden by law are Colorado, Rhode Island, Maine, Michigan, and Wisconsin. It was abolished in Iowa in 1872 and restored in 1878. In Rhode Island the only alternative is imprisonment for life. In Kansas the signature of the Governor is necessary to an execution. The death penalty is inflicted in all the States for murder, except the five above named; and in addition, in Louisiana, for rape, assault with intent to kill, administering poison, arson, and burglary; in Delaware and North Carolina, for rape, arson, and burglary; in Alabama, for rape, arson, robbery, treason, immoral relations with female under ten years of age, or married woman by falsely personating her husband; in Georgia, for rape, mayhem, and arson : in Missouri, for perjury and rape ; in Virginia, West Virginia, South Carolina, and Mississippi, for rape and arson ; in Florida, Kentucky, Tennessee, Texas, and Arkansas, for rape ; in Montana, for arson of dwelling by night ; in Maryland, for any variety of arson; in Texas, for perjury to a material fact in a capital case; in Connecticut, for causing death by putting obstructions on railroad. In some of these instances the court may, in its discretion, substitute imprisonment. States in which the judge may substitute life imprisonment for the death penalty on the recommendation of the jury are : Alabama, Arizona, California, South Dakota, Georgia, Illinois, Indiana, Iowa, Kentucky, Mississippi, Nebraska, Ohio, Oklahoma, and South Carolina, and those in which a like discretion is given to the trial court are : Minnesota, New Mexico, North Dakota, and Texas. In Utah the court may exercise the discretion if the jury so recommends. In New York and Ohio the death penalty is now inflicted by the means of electricity."—*World Almanac* (1901).

Capitol. The state-fortress and great national temple of ancient Rome, occupying the summit of the Capitoline Hill. It is said to have been so called from a bloody head (*Lat. caput*) found while excavating for the foundations of the Temple of Jupiter. The foundation of the Capitol was laid by Tarquinius Priscus in 616 B.C., and the building was completed by Tarquinius Superbus, but not dedicated until 507 B.C., under the consul Horatius. It covered eight acres, and was reached from the Forum by an ascent of 100 steps. The Capitol was burned during the Civil Wars (83 B.C.) ; was rebuilt by Sulla ; was burned a second time by the soldiers of Vitellius (69 A.D.); was rebuilt by Vespasian ; was burned a third time during the reign of Titus (81 A.D.) ; and was restored by Domitian (82 A.D.). This splendid restoration by Domitian lasted until a late period of the Empire, although the building was sacked by Genseric in 455 A.D. The Roman consuls made large gifts to the Capitol, and the Emperor Augustus is said to have bestowed upon it, on one occasion, 2000 lbs., in weight, of gold, of which metal the roof was composed. The thresholds were of brass, and the interior was decorated with shields of solid silver. The famous "Sibylline Books" were kept in the Capitol, and there the consuls went to offer sacrifices, and to make vows before entering upon their duties of office. There, also, the victorious general was borne in triumph to render thanks to Jupiter. Upon the site of the ancient Capitol, Michael Angelo built the modern structure. It is used, at the present time, principally as a museum of art. See *Sibylline Books*.

Capitol of New York. An imposing structure in the city of Albany, New York, situated 150 feet above the level of the Hudson River. The cornerstone was laid, with appropriate ceremonies, June 24th, 1871. The building is constructed of Maine granite, in the Renaissance style of architecture ; covers an area of three acres ; and measures 300 feet north and south and 400 feet east and west. It contains the Senate and Assembly chambers for the use of the Legislature, the Executive chamber, the Court of Appeals, and the State library, together with other rooms devoted to the administration of State affairs. Although the building has been in course of erection since 1869, it is not yet completed, and has already cost the State considerably more than $15,000,000.

Capitol of Texas. Situated at Austin, the capital of the State ; and said to be the largest State building in the United States, and the seventh in size among the buildings of the world. It is in the form of a vast Greek cross, with a central rotunda surmounted by a dome 311 feet in height. The building is built of red Texas granite, and cost about $3,500,000. It was commenced in 1881 and finished in 1888 ; and was paid for with 3,000,000 acres of land,—deeded by the State to the capitalists that did the work.

Capitol of the United States. A superb and majestic structure at Washington, D. C., devoted to the uses of the American Congress. It is probably the most magnificent public edifice in the world, and occupies the crown of Capitol Hill, 90 feet above the Potomac. The original building was founded by Washington in 1793, but was destroyed by the British in 1814. The central part of the present structure was built in 1817–1827, and the extensions were begun in 1851. The present building is 751 feet in length and covers an area of 3½ acres. The central portion is of light yellow freestone painted white, but the extensions are of pure white marble. The main front faces the east, and is adorned with three grand porticoes of Corinthian columns. The Capitol is in the classic style of architecture, and has probably cost, with its furnishings, over $30,000,000. It consists of a central part,—containing the Rotunda, the National Hall of Statuary, and the Supreme Court ; a north wing for the Senate Chamber ; and a south wing for the Hall of Representatives. The Rotunda is 96 feet in diameter, and 180 feet in height, and is adorned with eight large paintings representing events in American history. Above this rotunda rises the dome, 307½ feet in height, and 135 feet in diameter. It is of iron, painted white, and is the fifth largest dome in the world,—being exceeded in size only by the domes of St. Peter's,

St. Paul's, the Invalides, and St. Isaac's. It contains 4000 tons of iron, and is surmounted by a peristyled lantern, above which stands Crawford's majestic bronze statue of Liberty, 19½ feet high. The Capitol contains, in addition, the President's Room, the most richly decorated in America ; the Vice-President's Room ; the Marble Room ; the famous marble staircases in the legislative wings, besides many beautiful paintings and other works of art. The grounds surrounding the Capitol are beautifully cultivated ; they are adorned with fountains and statuary, and comprise about fifty acres.

Capitol Saved. In 390 B.C., the Gauls, under Brennus, invaded Italy, defeated the Romans in battle, and sacked and burned a large part of the city of Rome. The Capitol, however, remained in possession of the Romans, and this the enemy attempted to seize. While the guards slept, a chosen party of Gauls cautiously ascended the Capitoline Hill, under the cover of night, and had almost reached the summit, when, suddenly, some geese kept in the Temple of Juno, hard by, began to cackle and flap their wings. This roused the garrison, the invaders were repelled, and the Capitol saved. The goose was ever after held in high esteem in Rome.

Capitoline Hill. One of the original seven hills upon which ancient Rome was built, and, at present, included within the confines of the modern city. It is the smallest, but also the most famous of them all, and is about three-quarters of a mile in circumference at the base, —terminating, at its southern extremity, in a precipice eighty feet in height, known as the Tarpeian Rock. A depression called the " Intermontium " divides the summit into two elevations, upon one of which stood the Temple of Jupiter Capitolinus, and upon the other the "Arx," or Citadel of Rome. The Church of Ara Cœli is thought to occupy the site of the Temple of Jupiter Capitolinus. See *Capitol; Tarpeian Rock.*

Capri. This word, meaning the "island of goats," is derived from the Latin *caper* (*he-goat*).

Captivity of the Popes. An expression applied to the period (1309-1377) during which the popes resided and held their court at Avignon, in the south of France. See *Avignon Captivity.*

Capua. A city of ancient Italy, which opened its gates to Hannibal after the battle of Cannæ, 216 B.C., and where his army went into winter quarters. Capua was the most luxurious city in Italy, and Hannibal's army was greatly enervated as a result of its residence there. When the Romans regained possession of Capua, 211 B.C., they scourged and beheaded the surviving senators,—many of them having poisoned themselves before the surrender of the city. Only two persons, it is said, escaped : one, a woman who had prayed for the success of the Roman arms, and the other, a woman who had succored two prisoners. The word "Capua" has become a synonym for luxury and self-indulgence. See *Cannæ, Battle of.*

Capuchins. A branch of the order of Franciscans, so called from the *capuche* or cowl worn by them as a head-dress. The order was founded by Matthew Baschi about 1525, and established by Pope Clement VII (1523-1534) in 1529. See *Cordeliers.*

Capulets and Montagues. The English spelling of the names of *Cappelletti* and *Montecchi*, two noble families of northern Italy, belonging to the Ghibelline faction. Their feuds and enmities form the subject of Shakespeare's tragedy of *Romeo and Juliet.* Juliet belonged to the house of Capulet, and Romeo to that of Montague. The expression, "the tomb of all the Capulets," does not occur in Shakespeare, but is found in a letter from Burke to Matthew Smith, in which he says : "I would rather sleep in the corner of a little country churchyard than in *the tomb of all the Capulets.*"

Caput Mortuum (*Lat. head of the dead*). An expression, made use of by the old chemists in a distillation or sublimation, to designate the solid residuum after the volatile substances had escaped. The phrase is still used, metaphorically, to denote any thing or institution which has lost its real usefulness,—the *form* only remaining, — hence, any worthless residue.

Carabas, Marquis of. A name first found in Perrault's nursery-tale, entitled *Puss in Boots*, and afterwards adopted by Béranger (1780-1857) as the title of one of his songs. The expression is used to denote any pompous or purse-proud individual. Owen Meredith thus employs it in his poem entitled *Aux Italiens :*

"I have not a doubt she was thinking then
Of her former lord, good soul that he was,
Who died the richest and roundest of men,
The *Marquis of Carabas.*"

See *Puss in Boots.*

Carbon. An elementary substance widely diffused throughout nature. It occurs uncombined in two distinct forms or allotropic conditions,—viz., graphite or black-lead, and the diamond, which is pure *crystallized* carbon. It is, however, more commonly found in combination with other elementary substances than in the free state. United with oxygen, it occurs as carbonic-acid gas (CO_2), and exists in the atmosphere, in natural waters, in limestone, dolomite, and ironstone. In combination with hydrogen, it forms the extensive series of chemical compounds known as hydrocarbons. It is also an important constituent of wood, starch, sugar, gum, oil, bone, and flesh. No other element is so characteristic of the plant and animal world as carbon. In 1788, Lavoisier showed it to be an independent element. He furthermore proved the diamond to be the purest form of carbon, and, by combustion, converted it into carbonic-acid gas.

Carbonari (*It. charcoal - burners*). The name given to certain secret societies that flourished in Italy during the early part of the 19th century. They had for their objects the expulsion of foreigners from the peninsula, and the establishment of civil and religious freedom. In 1818 the Carbonari spread into France, and attempted to overthrow the restored Bourbon dynasty. Their membership in Italy alone, in 1820, was variously estimated at from 300,000 to 700,000. In 1831, the more active of this revolutionary party were absorbed by the "Young Italy" movement, headed by Mazzini. Since 1848, the Carbonari have gradually disappeared. The name is said to have originated with the Guelphs, who, in order to elude the Ghibellines, used to meet in the huts of charcoal-burners in the forests of Italy. See *Young Italy*.

Cardiff Giant. A famous imposture, in the shape of a man, disinterred near the village of Cardiff, Onondaga County, New York, in October, 1869. The figure was of gypsum, 10½ feet in height, and was declared to be either a piece of ancient sculpture, or, more probably, a fossil man of prehistoric times. It was publicly exhibited in all the principal cities of the United States, and was accepted as genuine by many of the leading archæologists and men of science in America. The imposture was finally detected, and the fact became known that the figure had been carved in Chicago, from gypsum sent from Iowa for that special purpose, and had been secretly buried near Cardiff, where it was soon afterwards accidentally (?) discovered.

Cardinals. The highest dignitaries in the Roman Catholic Church, next to the Pope, who is chosen from among them. They constitute the Sacred College or Conclave, and were originally the principal bishops, priests, and deacons in the diocese of Rome. In 1179, they claimed the exclusive privilege of electing the Pope. They first wore the red hat, as a reminder that they should be willing to shed their blood in defense of the Church, and were declared princes of the Church by Innocent IV (1243–1254) in 1243 or 1245. They received the scarlet habit from Paul II (1464–1471) in 1464, and the title of "Eminence" from Urban VIII (1623–1644) in 1623 or 1630. After many fluctuations, the number of cardinals was fixed by Sixtus V (1585–1590) in 1586 at 70, as follows: 6 cardinal-bishops, 50 cardinal-priests, and 14 cardinal - deacons. There are generally vacancies ; and, in 1902, the number of cardinals was 64. The cardinals are appointed by the Pope, after consultation with the Sacred College. At their head is the dean, who is usually bishop of Ostia, and senior cardinal-bishop. Three cardinals have been created in the United States : John McCloskey, appointed March 15th, 1875, died October 10th, 1885 ; James Gibbons of Baltimore, appointed June 7th, 1886 ; and Martinelli, who took the oath of office May 2nd, 1901.

Cardinal's Right Arm. An appellation bestowed by Cardinal Richelieu upon his confidant and familiar, François Leclerc du Tremblay (1577–1638), better known as *Father Joseph*. See *Alter Ego of Richelieu*.

Cardinal Virtues. The chief virtues of the ancients, as far back as Socrates, were Justice, Prudence, Temperance, and Fortitude. They were called cardinal virtues (from the Latin *cardo, a hinge*), because human virtue turned, or "hinged," upon them. The Roman Catholic Church called them the moral virtues, to distinguish them from the theological virtues— faith, hope, and charity. Such an enumeration is by no means exhaustive; as Whewell says, it omits entirely the fundamental virtue of benevolence.

Cards, Playing-. The origin of playing-cards is uncertain, although it is probable that they appeared independently in Europe about 1350. It is claimed, however, that the Arabs, Saracens, or Moors introduced them into Europe by way of Spain. They are said to have been brought (according to Covelluzzo) from the country of the Saracens to Viterbo in Italy, in 1379. The earliest known mention of European cards occurs in 1392, at which time an entry was made in the Treasury-books of France of "fifty sols of France paid to Jacquemin Gringonneur for three packs of cards for the amusement of the King" (Charles VI), who had lost his reason. Early in the 15th century, the use of playing-cards spread all over Europe. A duty was first placed on playing-cards in England in 1615. It is estimated that from 14,000,000 to 15,000,000 packs are annually manufactured in the United States.

Caribbean Sea. This sea — situated between the Antilles and the South and Central American mainland —derives its name from the Caribs,— meaning cruel men,—a warlike Indian tribe formerly inhabiting its shores and islands. The Caribs were addicted to cannibalism, and the word *cannibal* is probably a corruption of the name.

Carinæ. Women hired by the Romans to weep at funerals. They were so called from Caria in Asia Minor, whence most of them came.

Carisbrooke Castle. A ruined castle in the Isle of Wight, said to have been founded by the Romans in 45 A.D., and to have been completed by the Saxons and Danes, in after years. The outworks date from the time of the Spanish Armada panic in the 16th century. Charles I (1625–1649) of England was imprisoned at Carisbrooke Castle from November,

1647, to November, 1648, as were also his children, Prince Henry and the Princess Elizabeth, — the latter of whom died there, presumably of a broken heart, on September 8th, 1650. Within the castle is a well—200 feet deep—the water of which is raised by a donkey inside a wheel.

Carlo Borromeo, Statue of. A colossal bronze statue, erected to the memory of St. Charles Borromeo, in 1697. It is situated on the western shore of Lake Maggiore, near Arona (the place of his birth). The statue, including the pedestal, is 106 feet in height.

Carlovingian Dynasty. The second dynasty of French kings—founded by Pepin le Bref, son of Charles Martel, in 752 A.D. Pepin, who, as mayor of the palace, wielded supreme power, imprisoned Childéric III in a monastery, and, with the consent of the Pope, was proclaimed king,—being lifted on a shield, after the Frankish custom. The Carlovingian dynasty lasted from 752 to 987 A.D. (a period of 235 years), when it was succeeded by the Capetian line of kings. According to some authorities, the Carlovingian dynasty received its name from Charles Martel, the father of Pepin le Bref ; according to others, from Charlemagne, the son of Pepin. See *Merovingian Dynasty.*

Carlsbad (*Ger. Charles's bath*). A famous watering-place in Bohemia, widely celebrated for its hot mineral springs, the temperature of which varies from 117° to 167° Fahrenheit. Said to have been discovered by the Emperor Charles IV (1346–1378) of Germany in 1347. Carlsbad is visited during the season—April to October— by more than 30,000 persons. The principal spring is the *Sprudel.* The daily flow of all the springs at Carlsbad is estimated at 2,000,000 gallons. The principal ingredient is sulphate of soda.

Carlton House. A famous mansion

in London, which formerly stood in Waterloo Place, near Pall Mall. It was erected in 1709 by Lord Carlton, and was afterwards the residence, successively, of Frederick, Prince of Wales (father of George III), and of George IV when Prince of Wales. The building was removed in 1826. Carlton Club—the famous Conservative club—was founded by the Duke of Wellington, in 1831. It occupies a position near the site of Carlton House, whence the name.

Carmagnole. A famous song and dance, popular during the French Revolution. Each verse ended with the refrain :

"Dansons la *Carmagnole*— vive le son du canon"!

The origin of the word is in doubt. Littré says that this name was given to the song because it was sung by persons wearing the carmagnole—a dress in fashion during the French Revolution,—consisting of a blouse, a red cap, and a tricolored girdle. Others refer the origin of the word to Carmagnola in Piedmont—the home of the Savoyards, a people noted for streetsinging and dancing. The *Carmagnole* rivalled in popularity the *Ça Ira* and the *Marseillaise Hymn*. It was suppressed by Napoleon Bonaparte when he became First Consul, as smacking too much of republican fervor. The word "carmagnole" is sometimes applied in France to red republicans, and sometimes to wild and fantastic reports of French successes in the field. See *Ça Ira ; Marseillaise Hymn*.

Carmelites. A monastic order founded on Mount Carmel in Syria, by Berthold, a pilgrim or crusader from Calabria, about 1156. Tradition, however, assigns the foundation of this order to the prophet Elijah; while, according to another story, the Virgin Mary was a Carmelite nun. The Carmelites were driven out of Syria by the Saracens, and settled first in Cyprus in 1238, and afterwards in different parts of western and southern Europe. They became established in England in 1240, and in France in 1252. Pope Innocent IV (1243–1254), in 1247, changed the Carmelites into a mendicant order. In 1880, 176 Carmelites were banished from France.

Carnation. This name is derived from the Latin *caro* (*flesh*), and is applied to the flower on account of its pink, flesh-like color.

Carnival. A word derived from the Italian *carnovale*, which comes in turn from the Late Latin *carnelevamen*, meaning *a solace of the flesh*. "Carnival" is sometimes incorrectly derived from the two Latin words *caro* (*flesh*) and *vale* (*farewell*), and its origin is thus explained by Byron, in his poem of *Beppo : A Venetian Story :*

"This feast is named the *Carnival*, which being
Interpreted, implies 'farewell to flesh.'"

The word *Carnival* was originally applied to a festival lasting from the day after the Feast of the Epiphany till midnight on Shrove-Tuesday. In later times, however, the period was limited to three or eight days before Ash-Wednesday, and is now generally restricted to the Tuesday preceding the beginning of Lent. Venice was once famed for its Carnival, but that of Rome is at present the one best known. See *Mardi-Gras*.

Carolina. The name originally given to the territory extending from the Atlantic to the Pacific Ocean—between latitude 31° and 36° north. It was granted by Charles II (1660–1685) of England in 1663 to the Earl of Clarendon and seven others, and was named *Carolina*—from *Carolus* (*Latin for Charles*)—in honor of the king. According to other authorities, when Jean Ribault, at the head of a small band of French Protestants, landed at Port Royal in 1562, he founded a settlement there and named the country *Carolina*, in honor of Charles (or *Carolus*) IX (1560–1574), then king of

France. The colony, however, did not flourish, and the surviving Frenchmen soon after returned to France.

Caroline Islands. This group of islands in the western Pacific Ocean was so named by Lopez de Villalobos in 1543, in honor of Charles V, emperor of Germany and king of Spain.

Carpet-Baggers. A name given, in reproach, to a set of Northern political adventurers that invaded the Southern States soon after the Civil War, and for ten years (1866–1876), by the aid of the negro vote, got themselves elected to all the chief offices, plundered the people, piled up huge debts, and stole the proceeds. When, in 1877, President Hayes refused Federal protection to the carpet-baggers, their system fell to pieces, and the whites regained control of the government.

According to the New York *World:* "The *carpet-bag* Governments of the Southern States, under the protection of Grant's bayonets, have rolled up an aggregate debt in the nine cotton States of $194,000,000."

Of course, the term "carpet-bagger" implied a person whose genuine interest in the region he visited was limited to the contents of his own carpet-bag. See *White League.*

Carpet Knight. The name given to a person knighted for other than military achievements, in allusion to the carpet on which all civilians kneel when the honor of knighthood is conferred upon them. The expression is used at present in a derisive sense, to denote a person that has gained distinction without earning it.

"*Carpet Knights* are men who are, by the prince's grace and favour, made knights at home and in the time of peace, by the imposition or laying on of the king's sword, having, by some special service done to the commonwealth, deserved this title and dignity. They are called 'Carpet Knights' because they receive their honour in the court,

and upon carpets [and not on the battlefield]."—Francis Markham, *Booke of Honour* (1625).

Carrara. A town in northern Italy near Leghorn, famous for its quarries of marble. These are situated on the side of the mountains—a branch of the Apennines,—at heights ranging from 500 to 3500 feet ; they are over 400 in number, and give employment to 5000 men. The quarries have been worked for over 2000 years, and fortunately are practically inexhaustible. About 150,000 tons are annually exported, but it is estimated that to produce this amount fully 500,000 tons are annually quarried,—the difference being wasted on account of the imperfect methods employed. Carrara marble is a white saccharoid limestone, and is of value to the sculptor on account of its purity and fineness of texture. Only a few of the quarries, however, furnish the finer grades of marble.

Carrier-Pigeons. A method of transportation in use among the ancients. At the siege of Modena, Brutus and Hirtius are said to have corresponded by means of carrier-pigeons. Persian pigeons were used by the califs of Bagdad to carry messages between that city and Cairo, and are hence often called Bagdad pigeons. The Prince of Orange used carrier-pigeons at the siege of Leyden, in 1574. During the siege of Paris (1870–1871), it is estimated that 150,000 official despatches and 1,000,000 private ones were sent out of the city in this way. If printed in ordinary type, they would have filled 500 volumes. Carrier-pigeons will fly 30 miles per hour ; some have been known to fly 60 or even 90 miles per hour.

Carroccio. The car of state of the Lombard Republic. It was constructed about 1035 A.D., and consisted of a massive four-wheeled car, painted red and drawn by eight milk-white oxen with scarlet trappings. From a tall pole or mast in the centre of the car floated the banner of the republic, and beneath this was an image of the crucified Savior. The *Carroccio* always went into battle, and formed the centre of the Lombard army. Three hundred of the most distinguished soldiers—known as the "Cohort of the Three Hundred"—were appointed to guard it in battle; while next in point of rank came nine hundred chosen men, called the "Cohort of Death." According to some authorities, the *Carroccio* was an imitation of the Jewish Ark of the Covenant; certain it is that feelings of religion and military glory were associated with it.

Cartaphilus. The name of the "Wandering Jew," according to the commonly received account. Tradition makes him a porter in the service of Pontius Pilate. As he led Christ from the judgment-hall, he struck him, saying: "Get on faster, Jesus!" whereupon the Savior answered: "I am going fast, Cartaphilus, but tarry thou till I come again." After Christ's crucifixion, Cartaphilus was baptized, and received the name of Joseph. He is said to fall asleep at the close of each century, and to awaken, after a short time, as a young man of about 30 years. See *Wandering Jew.*

Cartes-de-visite. The name given to small photographic portraits, said to have been first taken by M. Ferrier at Nice, in 1857. The Duke of Parma, to gratify a whim, placed one of these pictures of himself upon his visiting-card, and this notion soon became the fashion in London and Paris. The term " cartes-de-visite," although no longer appropriate, has become the name for these small pictures, the world over.

Cartesian Philosophy. A term applied to the doctrines taught by René Descartes (1596–1650), the famous French philosopher. Descartes's speculations manifest an original and daring genius, endowed with great

force and subtlety of thought. He performed the same service in the world of metaphysics that Bacon did in the world of natural science. Descartes found the basis of all knowledge in self-consciousness, as expressed in the famous enthymeme—*Cogito ; ergo sum (Lat. I think ; therefore I am).* From this, he inferred that whatever thinks must necessarily exist: therefore, God exists. Yet for all this Descartes was called an atheist, and his *Meditations* were condemned by the College of Cardinals at Rome.

Carthaginian Lion. A title conferred upon Hannibal (247–183 B.C.), in allusion to his great courage, energy, and determination.

Carthusians. A monastic order (springing from the Benedictines), founded in 1086 by St. Bruno of Cologne, who, with six companions, retired to the solitude of La Chartreuse in Dauphiné, France, and there built hermitages, wore coarse garments, and lived upon food of the simplest and coarsest kind. The Carthusians were extremely rigid in their mode of life—living in unbroken silence (save on rare occasions), and devoting themselves to hospitality and to deeds of charity. In 1176, the order received the approbation of the Pope, and spread rapidly. It appeared in England in 1180, and established a monastery on the site of the present Charterhouse in London, in 1371. The Carthusians were principally found in France, Italy, and Switzerland. The word Charterhouse is a corruption of Chartreuse-house. See *Charterhouse ; Chartreuse, Grande.*

Cartoons of Raphael. A collection of seven large drawings by Raphael (1483–1520), in the South Kensington Museum, London. They are original designs on cardboard (*It. cartone*), for tapestries to adorn the lower walls of the Sistine Chapel in the Vatican at Rome, and were executed by order of

10

Pope Leo X (1513–1522) in 1515–1516. These cartoons are 12 feet in height by 14 to 18 feet in length, and are drawn with chalk, tinted in distemper. The weavers, for greater convenience, cut them into strips, and threw them away after the tapestries were completed. They were, however, picked up and stored away in boxes, but lay neglected until 1630, when Charles I (1625–1649) of England, at the suggestion of Rubens, purchased them and had them sent to England. Of the original ten, Nos. 1, 8, and 10 are lost. After the Restoration, they were sold by Charles II (1660–1685) to the French ambassador, but Lord Danby interfered and prevented their removal from England. In the time of William III (1689–1702), the strips were pasted upon canvas, and the cartoons, thus restored, were placed in Hampton Court Palace, where they remained until 1865, when they were removed to South Kensington. Three sets of tapestry have been made from Raphael's cartoons—those at Rome, Berlin, and Dresden. The subjects of the seven existing cartoons are as follows:

(1) The Miraculous Draught of Fishes.

(2) The Charge to Peter.

(3) Peter and John Healing the Lame at the Gate of the Temple.

(4) The Death of Ananias.

(5) Elymas the Sorcerer Stricken with Blindness.

(6) The Sacrifice to Paul and Barnabas at Lystra.

(7) Paul Preaching at Athens.

See *Tapestries of the Vatican.*

Caryatides (*Gr. Women of Caryæ*). A name given, in Greek architecture, to figures of women, when used in place of columns to support an entablature. According to tradition, the city of Caryæ in Arcadia sided with the Persians after the battle of Thermopylæ (480 B.C.); whereupon the Greeks destroyed the place, slew the men, and made the women captives. To perpetuate this disgrace, Praxiteles and other Athenian sculptors employed figures of the women of Caryæ (*Caryatides*), and of Persian men (*Atlantes*), in place of columns.

Casa de Pilatos (*Span. House of Pilate*). A Moorish house in the city of Seville, Spain, said, according to tradition, to be the original palace of Pilate at Jerusalem, and to have been transported to Spain by the angels. The building was probably erected in 1533, in imitation of Pilate's house, by Fredrique Enriquez de Ribera, to commemorate his successful pilgrimage to the Holy Land in 1519. According to other authorities, the *Casa de Pilatos* was built by Moorish slaves in the service of a duke of Medina Cœli.

Casa Guidi. A house in Florence, Italy, of interest to English-speaking people as the residence, for a number of years, of Elizabeth Barrett Browning (1807–1861). It was there that she wrote the poem entitled *Casa Guidi Windows,*—describing her impressions of certain events in Tuscany, of which she had been an eye-witness. There is a tablet on the house to the memory of the poetess.

Casella. A musician and old friend of Dante,—famed for the sweetness of his voice, and immortalized by the poet in his *Divine Comedy.* Dante meets him on his arrival in Purgatory, and requests of him a song ; whereupon Casella sings, with surpassing sweetness, the words of Dante's second canzone.

Cash. This word, meaning ready money, is derived from the French word *caisse,* a chest or box in which money is kept.

"Originally, 'cash' meant that which was *encaissé, i. e.,* put into chest or till. Strictly speaking, it should consist of actual specie, and the word is used in some English banks to include only coin of the realm. But I find that bank cashiers use it with every shade of meaning. Some take Bank of England notes to be *cash.* Others go so far as to include checks upon other banks of the same town, and even country notes."—*W. Stanley Jevons.*

Casket Homer. A famous edition of Homer—with notes by Aristotle—highly esteemed by Alexander the Great, and kept by him in a beautiful casket encrusted with gems. After the battle of Arbela, which resulted in a victory for Alexander over Darius, this casket was found in the tent of the Persian king. Alexander, being asked to what use it should be put, replied that there was only one thing in the world worthy of so costly a depository, and placed therein his copy of Homer, which, on this account, received the title of the "Casket Homer."

Caspian Sea. This inland sea or salt lake — the largest in the world — has an area of about 170,000 square miles. It was known to the Greeks and Romans, and derives its name, according to Strabo, from the *Caspii*, a tribe that inhabited its western shores. In later times, the western portion only was known as the Caspian Sea, the eastern part being called the Hyrcanian Sea.

Cassandra. According to the Homeric legend, Cassandra was the daughter of Priam and Hecuba, and twin-sister of Helenus. Apollo, having fallen in love with her, conferred upon her the gift of prophecy on receiving her promise to comply with his desires; but when she became possessed of the prophetic art, she refused to fulfil her promise. Thereupon the god, in anger, laid upon her the curse that her prophecies should never be believed. During the siege of Troy, Cassandra foretold the destruction of the city and the treachery of the Trojan horse, but her words were considered to be the mere ravings of a mad woman. On the fall of Troy, she fell to the lot of Agamemnon, and was taken by him to Mycenæ. There she was murdered by Clytemnestra.

"Those who foresee and predict the down-fall, meet with the fate of *Cassandra*."—*London Times.*

Cassation, Court of. The name of a supreme court of appeal in France, established in 1790, by the National Assembly, whose function it is to quash or annul the decisions of other and inferior courts. The Court of Cassation simply decides whether the view taken of the law and of the proper methods of administering it by the lower court has been the right one : hence it is less of a court, in the ordinary sense, than of a department of the government, to which is assigned the function of inspecting the administration of justice. The judges are appointed by the president of the republic, and their decisions are irrevocable. The court is divided into three sections, viz., the *Chambre des Requêtes*, the *Chambre Civile*, and the *Chambre Criminelle*. The word "cassation" is derived from the French *casser* (*to break or annul*).

Castalian Spring. A celebrated fountain on the slope of Mount Parnassus, sacred to Apollo and the Muses, who were hence called *Castalides*. All those that visited the temple at Delphi were accustomed to bathe their hair in the water of this fountain, while those that needed purification from the sin of murder immersed the entire body. Its waters were said to give poetic inspiration to those that drank of them. The name *Castalian* is derived from Castalia, daughter of Achelous, who threw herself into the spring when pursued by Apollo. It is said that, during the earthquake of 1870, a piece of rock, falling from the cliff above, crushed the basin and buried the water out of sight.

Caste. A term specially applied to separate and distinct classes of society in India, to each of which certain pursuits were limited by the Laws of Manu, 900 B.C. These classes were as follows :

(1) *The Sacerdotal Class*, called

Brahmans, whose proper business is religion and philosophy.

(2) *The Military Class,* called *Kshatriyas,* devoted to war and government.

(3) *The Agricultural and Mercantile Class,* called *Vaisyas,* concerned with agriculture and trade.

(4) *The Servile Class,* called *Sûdras,* composed of the artisans and laborers of the community. Below these were the *Chandalas* and *Pariahs:* they performed the most menial services, and were regarded as the dregs of society. Caste in India, at the present day, is very different from what it was in the time of Manu; indeed, with the exception of the Brahmans, pure caste has disappeared. According to the *Rig-Veda,* the Brahmans sprang from the mouth of Brahma ; the Kshatriyas from his arm ; the Vaisyas from his thigh ; and the Sûdras from his foot.

Casting Shoe after Bride. An old custom in England and Scotland,— symbolizing the fact that the parents gave up all control over their daughter, after her marriage. This practice— still semi-humorously indulged in at weddings—is said to have originated in the custom, among the ancient Israelites, of delivering a shoe as a testimony in the transference of a possession.

In *Psalms* lx, 8, we read the words : " Over Edom will I cast out my shoe," where reference is made to the custom of throwing a shoe on land as a token of new ownership.

Castle Garden. A circular building, situated on the Battery, at the southern extremity of New York City. It was erected as a fortress by the general government, in 1807, and received the name of Castle Clinton. At that time its site was about 300 yards from the mainland, but this intervening space has since been filled in. In 1822, the structure, having outgrown its usefulness as a means of defense, was ceded to the city, and soon after

was converted into a concert-hall, with accommodations for 10,000 persons. It was there that Jenny Lind first appeared in America, under the management of P. T. Barnum, on September 11th, 1850. In 1855, the building was turned into a depot for the reception of immigrants, and was used for that purpose until the spring of 1890. During 1897, it was converted into an aquarium, under the control of the Department of Public Parks, and is still so used. See *Battery.*

Castle of St. Angelo. Originally, the mausoleum of Hadrian, by whom it was erected in 130 A.D. The remains of the Emperors Hadrian, Lucius Verus, the Antonines, Commodus, and Septimius Severus were buried there. The tomb was converted into a fortress in 423 ; in 537 it was besieged, and its statues and other architectural adornments were hurled down upon the besiegers. From the 9th century to the 13th, the Castle of St. Angelo became the stronghold of the Popes. It is said that, during these years, a subterranean passage connected the fortress with the Vatican. Beatrice Cenci was confined there for a year before her execution. See *Hadrian's Mausoleum.*

Castro, Inez de. A queen of Portugal, to whom was accorded the unique distinction of being crowned after her death. She was originally a maid-of-honor at the court of Alfonso IV of Portugal, and in 1347 was secretly married to Don Pedro, heir to the throne. Alfonso, having contracted Don Pedro in marriage to a Spanish princess, was incensed at this clandestine union, and three years afterwards caused Inez de Castro to be assassinated. The grief and wrath of Don Pedro knew no bounds, and it was with difficulty that he was restrained from murdering his father. When he ascended the throne as Don Pedro I in 1357, he caused the body of his wife to be taken from her grave and dressed in robes of royalty. She was then placed upon a magnificent throne and crowned queen of Portugal, in presence of the entire court, who were then compelled to do homage to her as to a living queen. On the night after the coronation, her remains—escorted by a procession many miles in length—were conveyed to the royal abbey of Alcobaça, where they were interred with great ceremony. Her monument and that of Don Pedro may still be seen there. A political reason has been assigned for this posthumous coronation, since the marriage was thereby made legal, and the offspring were declared legitimate. Camoens has introduced the story of Inez de Castro into his poem *The Lusiads*, and several dramatists have made it the subject of tragedies. See *Lusiads, The.*

Casus Belli. A term applied to any act or series of acts, on the part of one nation towards another, deemed sufficient to cause a declaration of war. It is impossible to reduce these reasons to any definite code ; and many of the most sanguinary wars of history have resulted from the most trifling causes.

Catacombs of Alexandria. Extensive subterranean galleries and tombs near Alexandria, Egypt. They are hollowed out of the solid rock, and occupy the site of the ancient Necropolis, west of the city.

"The extent of these catacombs is remarkable ; but the principal inducement to visit them is the elegance and symmetry of the architecture in one of the chambers, having a Doric entablature and mouldings, in good Greek taste, which is not to be met with in any other part of Egypt."—*Murray.*

Catacombs of Paris. These catacombs were formerly subterranean quarries, worked as far back as the time of the Romans, and yield a soft kind of limestone, which hardens on exposure to the air. They underlie a large part of the city, and much of the stone used for building purposes has been taken from them. In 1784, several of the streets in the southern part of Paris having shown symptoms of sinking, steps were taken by the government to avert the danger by constructing piers and buttresses where the upper surface was insufficiently supported. At about the same time, the Council of State ordered the removal of the remains from the Cemetery of the Innocents, which, for 700 years, had received the dead bodies of all the neighboring parishes. Accordingly, in 1786, these quarries were converted into a vast subterranean burying-ground, and called the *Catacombs.* During the Revolution and the Reign of Terror, vast numbers of bodies and human bones were collected from all quarters and thrown into these cavities. In 1810, the Catacombs were much improved, the passages being widened and adorned with appropriate inscriptions. The galleries and compartments are lined with human bones and skulls, carefully arranged. The number of bodies in this subterranean charnel-house is said to be over 3,000,-000. According to another authority, the bones of 20,000,000 people are estimated to rest there. Each subterranean gallery in the Catacombs corresponds to a street above ground.

Catacombs of Rome. The name given to vast subterranean cemeteries —consisting of innumerable passages —lying outside the walls of the city of Rome. They formed the burial-places of the early Christians, and continued to be so used until the capture and sack of Rome by Alaric, in 410 A.D. These catacombs also served as places of worship, and as hiding-places for the early Christians during times of persecution. They were about 60 in number ; and, according to one estimate, contained 6,000,000 bodies. The most famous are the Catacombs of St. Agnes, St. Calixtus, St. Sebastian, and St. Priscilla.

Catch a Tartar. This expression, meaning to be outdone or outwitted, is said to have originated in the following manner : In a battle between the Russians and the Turks, a Russian soldier called to his captain that he had caught a Tartar. " Bring him along, then," said the superior officer. " But he won't come," replied the soldier. " Then come yourself," was the further command. " But he won't let me," cried the struggling private. According to another account, the soldier that thought he had made a capture was not a Russian, but an Irishman in the Russian army.

Cat Hoax. A joke perpetrated by some wag in the city of Chester, England, in 1815, just previous to the departure of Napoleon I for the island of St. Helena. Handbills were distributed—saying that the island was overrun with rats, and that 16s. would be paid for every full-grown tom-cat, 10s. for every full-grown tabby, and 2s. 6d. for every kitten that could feed itself. On the day appointed, the city was filled with men, women, and children carrying cats. A riot ensued, and the cats escaped in the *mêlée;* 500 of them were killed and many others were drowned, while the remainder infested the neighboring houses and barns for weeks afterwards.

Catechumens. A name given, in the early Christian Church, to those converted Jews and heathens that had not yet been baptized, but were undergoing a course of training and instruction preparatory thereto. They occupied a special place in the congregation, but were not permitted to be present at the celebration of the Lord's Supper. In later times the term "Catechumens" was applied to young Christians that were receiving instruction preparatory to confirmation. The word is still used in this sense.

Cathay. An old name for China, said to have been introduced into Europe by Marco Polo (1252–1324), the Venetian traveler. The word is a corruption of Khitaï, derived from the

Khitan, the earliest of the northern races known to have conquered China. They disappeared about the beginning of the 12th century. In more recent times, the word " Cathay " has been used as a poetic term for China.

" Better fifty years of Europe than a cycle of *Cathay.*"

                 Locksley Hall.

Cathedral, The. The title of a poem by James Russell Lowell (1819–1891). It appeared in 1870.

Catholic Epistles. The name given to certain epistles in the *New Testament,*— seven in number,— not addressed to particular churches or individuals, but to Christians in general. They are as follows : The Epistle of James, the two Epistles of Peter, the three Epistles of John, and the Epistle of Jude. Originally only the first Epistle of Peter and the first Epistle of John were called Catholic Epistles ; but as early as the 3rd century the other five were included in this designation, although their genuineness was not universally acknowledged.

Catholic Summer-School. A summer-school,— sometimes known as the "Champlain Assembly,"—situated at Cliff Haven, near Plattsburg, New York, on Lake Champlain. It was first opened at New London, Connecticut, in 1892, under the auspices of prominent clergymen and laymen of the Roman Catholic Church, and held meetings during the summer of that year. Afterwards, the association secured property near Plattsburg ; there suitable buildings have been erected, and a summer-school—similar to that at Chautauqua—is held during the months of July and August. During the rest of the year, the work of instruction is carried on by means of reading-circles and study-clubs. See *Chautauqua System of Education.*

Catiline's Conspiracy. Lucius Sergius Catiline (108–62 B.C.), a dissolute Roman patrician, having failed to attain the consulship, conspired with many other illustrious Romans, in 63 B.C., to overthrow the government, murder the consuls, plunder the treasury, and fire the city. This plot, however, was fortunately discovered by Cicero, who was then consul. Catiline, having dared to appear in the senate after his guilt had become known, was driven from the city by Cicero's eloquence, and took refuge with his army in Etruria. The conspirators that remained in Rome — among them Lentulus and Cethegus — were put to death. In 62 B.C., the army of the senate overtook Catiline's forces near Pistoia, in Etruria, and in the battle that ensued Catiline was slain with about 3000 of his partisans. As a reward for his preservation of the state from this conspiracy, Cicero received unbounded honors; he was saluted as the father of his country by Catulus and Cato, and hailed as the savior of Rome by the people.

"Roma Patrem Patriæ Ciceronem libera dixit."

Juvenal (*Satire viii*).

Cato-Street Conspiracy. A plot formed in London, in 1820, for the murder of Lord Castlereagh and other Cabinet ministers. It was headed by one Arthur Thistlewood, and was so called from the place of meeting of the conspirators in Cato Street, near Edgeware Road. The plot was revealed by one of their number, and the entire gang was captured by the police, after a short struggle, on February 23rd, 1820. On May 1st of the same year, Thistlewood and four of his companions were hanged, and five others were transported for life.

Caucus. A term used in American politics to denote a private meeting of the leading members of a party to decide upon the plans to be pursued in an approaching election, or session of a legislative body. The conclusions arrived at are usually considered binding on the members during the succeeding public meetings. The origin of the word *caucus* is in doubt. Ac-

cording to the generally accepted explanation, the word is referred to a political club founded in Boston in 1724 by Henry Adams (father of Samuel Adams) and his friends, most of whom were sea-captains, shipwrights, and persons identified with shipping interests. On this account, the organization was known as the "Calkers' Club." Since the object of the organization was the advancement of its members to places of political power, the word *caucus* may well be a corruption of its name.

Similar meetings are occasionally held in London by Liberals and Conservatives.

A less obvious derivation is suggested by Dr. Trumbull of Hartford, who says, "Its origin is the Indian *cau-cau-as'u*," which he defines or translates as "one who advises, urges, encourages, etc." (*American Philological Association Transactions* for 1872.)

Caudine Forks. Two narrow, fork-shaped mountain gorges in the valley of Caudium, in ancient Samnium, on the borders of Campania. There, during the Second Samnite War (321 B.C.), four legions of the Roman army were entrapped and obliged to surrender, and afterwards to " pass under the yoke." The terms of surrender made by the Roman consuls were repudiated by the Senate, and the consuls were sent back as prisoners to Caius Pontius, the Samnite general. He, however, refused to accept them.

Caudle Lectures. A series of humorous papers originally contributed to London *Punch* by Douglas Jerrold (1803–1857), under the title of *Mrs. Caudle's Curtain Lectures.* They are represented as having been delivered nightly by Mrs. Caudle to Job Caudle, her long-suffering spouse, during a period of thirty years. See *Curtain-Lecture.*

Causeries du Lundi. A series of able critiques by Charles Augustin

Sainte-Beuve (1804–1869). They first appeared in the *Constitutionnel*, and were afterwards collected into thirteen volumes (1851–1857).

Cautionary Towns. A name given to four towns in Holland,—the Briel, Flushing, Rammerkins, and Walcheren,—so called because they were placed in possession of Queen Elizabeth (1558–1603) of England in 1585, as security for payment of the troops furnished by England to the Netherlands during the war with Spain. In 1616, during the reign of James I, these towns were restored to the republic of Holland, although only one-third of the sum advanced by England had been refunded.

Cavaliers and Roundheads. During the Civil War in England (1642–1649), the partisans of Charles I were known as Cavaliers, while those that espoused the cause of Parliament were termed Roundheads. These nicknames were first bestowed in 1641, as terms of reproach ; but afterwards they came to be adopted as titles of honor. The Cavaliers wore long hair falling in ringlets over their shoulders; while the Roundheads wore their hair cropped short, and affected extreme simplicity in dress. See *Roundheads*.

Cave Canem, House of the. A disinterred private residence at Pompeii, Italy, known also as the *House of Homer* and the *House of the Tragic Poet*. It is famous not only for the beautiful paintings that adorn its walls, but also for a mosaic formerly on the threshold of the building—representing a chained watch-dog, with the words *Cave Canem* (*Lat. Beware of the Dog*); from which circumstance the house derives one of its names. This mosaic is now in the National Museum at Naples.

Cavendish. The *nom-de-plume* of Henry Jones, a well known authority on whist and other games.

Cavendish Experiment. An ingenious device of Henry Cavendish (1731–1810), the famous scientist, for estimating the mean density of the earth by comparing the force of terrestrial attraction with that of leaden balls of known size and density, by means of the torsion balance. According to Cavendish, the weight of the earth is 5.48 times the weight of an equal volume of water, or 6,000,-000,000,000,000,000,000 (six sextillion) tons. This experiment was described by Cavendish in 1798.

Cave of Adullam. A cave to which David fled to escape from the persecution of Saul. Its location is uncertain. Tradition places it in the hill-country of Judea, about six miles southeast of Bethlehem. There may be found a vast cavern, capable of holding several thousand people. The year 1062 B.C. is given as the date of David's flight. See 1 *Samuel* xxii, 1, 2.

Cave of Jeremiah. An interesting cave near Jerusalem, access to which is gained through a doorway cut in the hillside. The interior consists of a series of caverns, resembling chapels and crypts, separated from one another by natural pillars. In some of these rocky recesses, mass is performed at times by monks of the Roman Catholic Church.

Cave of Machpelah. The burial-place in Hebron, which Abraham bought of Ephron the Hittite, for a family sepulchre. There, according to the account given in the book of *Genesis*, the patriarchs Abraham, Isaac, and Jacob were buried, together with their wives Sarah, Rebekah, and Leah. The site of the cave is now occupied by a small Mohammedan mosque, which Christians are not permitted to. enter under any pretence whatever. Tradition asserts that the embalmed remains of the patriarchs and their wives are still lying there, and there is no intrinsic improbability in this supposition. The Moslems even are not permitted to descend into the cavern.

Cave of the Nativity. A cave or grotto in Bethlehem, Judea, said to have been the residence of the Virgin Mary and the birthplace of Jesus Christ. Over it is the Church of the Nativity, erected by the Empress Helena. The grotto or cave of the Nativity is about twenty feet below the level of the church, and is reached by two spiral staircases. It is lined with Italian marbles, and lighted with numerous lamps. A silver star, encircled with the inscription, in Latin, " Here Jesus Christ was born of the Virgin Mary," marks the exact spot where Christ is said to have been born. Sixteen silver lamps shed a soft light upon this shrine, while from golden censers incense continually rises. The place of the manger is also shown, as well as the spot where the Magi made their offerings. See *Church of the Nativity.*

Cave of the Winds. A spacious cavern behind the Centre or Luna Fall, at Niagara. One side of it is formed by the cliff, and the other side by the solid mass of water that falls from the height above. The cave is much visited by tourists, who, if clothed in waterproof garments and accompanied by competent guides, can make the trip without danger. The " Cave of the Winds " is famous for its beautiful rainbow effects, perfect circles—two or three at a time being sometimes seen.

Cawnpore, Massacre of. During the Sepoy Mutiny in 1857 a party of 1000 Europeans—560 of whom were women—intrenched themselves in the city of Cawnpore, and made a desperate resistance, — surrendering only after half their number had been killed, and Nana Sahib, the rebel leader, had promised them safe-conduct to Allahabad. No sooner, however, had they embarked in boats on the Ganges than a murderous fire was opened upon them, and only four men escaped. The women and children were reserved as prisoners of war, and taken back to Cawnpore. Nana Sahib, hearing that General Havelock was within two days' march of the city, advanced to meet him ; but, having been driven back, gave orders for the instant massacre of all the prisoners, who, dead and dying, were cast into a well. A memorial church occupies the site of the intrenchment, while the scene of the massacre has been converted into a memorial garden. Over the well a mound has been erected, and its summit has been crowned by an octagonal Gothic structure, with Marochetti's white marble angel in the centre. See *Indian Mutiny.*

Cecrops or Kekrops. A hero of the Pelasgic race, who, according to ancient legends, was the first king and lawgiver of Attica. He is said to have founded Athens (the citadel of which was named Cecropia, in his honor) ; to have instituted marriage; abolished bloody sacrifices ; and taught his subjects to worship the gods. He is described in classic mythology as an autochthon,—the upper part of whose body was human, and the lower part that of a dragon. The people of Attica were sometimes called *Cecropidæ*.

Cedar Creek, Battle of. A battle of the American Civil War, fought on October 19th, 1864, between the Union forces under General Sheridan and the Confederates commanded by General Early. In the early morning, the Federals were surprised and driven back with a loss of 24 guns and 1500 prisoners, but by three o'clock in the afternoon they re-formed their line and drove the Confederates from the field in utter confusion. It was Sheridan's timely return from Washington that turned the tide of battle on that eventful day ; and on that incident in his career is based the stirring poem by Thomas Buchanan Reade, entitled *Sheridan's Ride.*

Cedars of Lebanon. A grove of trees situated at the head of the Kedisha valley, on the central ridge of Lebanon in northern Palestine, at an elevation of about 6000 feet. In 1875, the grove consisted of 377 trees, of which five only were of gigantic size. A few only of these trees are of great antiquity, although it is impossible to determine their exact age. They are highly venerated by Arabs of all creeds, while Maronites, Greeks, and Armenians annually celebrate mass at their base. The cedar of Lebanon has been celebrated from very early times for its beauty and longevity, as well as for the extreme durability of its timber. It supplied the wood for Solomon's Temple, and has always been a favorite symbol of prosperity and strength in *Old Testament* poetry.

Celestial City. The name given by Bunyan, in the *Pilgrim's Progress*, to the city towards which Christian and Hopeful were journeying, and which they finally reached after passing through the river of Death.

Celestial Empire. A title frequently bestowed upon China. According to S. Wells Williams, this expression is derived from the Chinese words Tien Chan, *i. e.*, the Heavenly Dynasty,— meaning the kingdom which the heaven-appointed dynasty rules over. Tradition says that the first emperors of China were all celestial deities, and reigned for a period of 300,000 years previous to To-hi, whose accession to the throne is placed at 2953 B.C. From the expression " Celestial Empire " has arisen the epithet " Celestials," contemptuously applied to the Chinese by the Europeans.

Cell Theory. Propounded by Schleiden and Schwann in 1839–1840. It asserts that the ultimate units of all plants and animals are minute cells, and that the lowest forms of vegetal and animal life, such as the *protococcus* and the *protamœba*, are monocellular,

i. e., consist of a single cell. This generalization is no longer held simply as a theory, but as an established fact.

Cemeteries, National. The government of the United States has established cemeteries in various parts of the country for the burial of men that have died in the military and naval service. There are 82 of these burial - places scattered throughout 21 States of the Union, principally in the South. The total number of graves is, according to Harper's *Book of Facts*, 322,851 ; of which 9438 are those of Confederates. Eleven of these cemeteries contain over 10,000 graves each. The Gettysburg Cemetery, although one of the smallest, is famous as having been dedicated by President Lincoln in 1863. About 3500 soldiers are buried there. In 1872, it passed under the control of the United States government.

Cemetery Hill. A hill near Gettysburg, Pennsylvania, famous in connection with the terrible battle fought there on July 1st, 2nd, and 3rd, 1863. It formed the centre of the Union line, and was the objective point of Pickett's famous charge of 18,000 men, on the afternoon of July 3rd. This charge was repulsed by the Union forces, and the battle of Gettysburg was won. The hill has been converted into a national cemetery, and an imposing memorial has been erected there. See *Gettysburg, Battle of ; Seminary Ridge.*

Cenci Palace. A private palace of vast extent, in Rome, on or near the site of the theatre of Balbus. It was formerly the residence of the Cenci family; but, after the Cenci tragedy, was deserted for many years.

Censor of the Age. A title sometimes bestowed upon Thomas Carlyle (1795–1881), on account of the critical and fault-finding spirit manifested in some of his writings.

Centennial Exposition. An exposition held in Philadelphia in 1876, to commemorate the one hundredth anniversary of American independence; 33 foreign countries participated, and sent representative productions. The total number of buildings erected was 199. The five principal buildings covered 75 acres, while the main building alone had an area of 21 acres. The total number of persons that attended the Exposition was 9,-910,966 ; and the largest number admitted in any one day was 274,919. It was opened by President Grant on May 19th, 1876, and closed on November 10th of the same year.

Centre of Population. The centre of population in the United States of America in 1910 was estimated to be in the city of Bloomington, Indiana. In 1790—one hundred and twenty years before—the centre of population was 23 miles east of Baltimore, Maryland.

"This centre, by the way, has moved about in a rather interesting fashion. In 1790 it was some 23 miles east of Baltimore. Between then and 1800 it moved 41 miles almost due west, to a point about 18 miles west of Baltimore. By 1810 it had moved 36 miles, westward and slightly southward, to a point about 40 miles northwest by west from Washington, the southward movement appearing to have been due to the annexation of the Louisiana territory, and the migration induced thereby. By 1820 it had moved 50 miles, westward and slightly southward, to a point about 16 miles north of Woodstock, Va., this second southward tendency being due to the settlements in Mississippi, Alabama, and Georgia. Between 1820 and 1830 it moved 39 miles, westward and southward, to a point about 19 miles southwest of Moorefield, now in West Virginia—the most decided southward movement during any census period, and attributable in a great measure to the building up of the southwest, in Louisiana, Mississippi, and Arkansas especially. By 1840 it had swung a little north of westward, and travelled 55 miles, to a spot about 16 miles south of Clarksburg, W. Va., the northward movement being the result of the settlement of the prairie states of the Mississippi Valley. Another drop to a southerly course occurred in the next ten years, during which Texas had been annexed, the centre again travelling 55 miles, and settling at a point 23 miles southwest of Parkersburg, W. Va. By 1860 it had taken a northward turn once more, and stopped about 20 miles from Chillicothe, Ohio, 81 miles from its latest location. In 1870 there were some errors of enumeration, which probably threw it somewhat too sharply northward, carrying it 42 miles and leaving it 48 miles east by north of Cincinnati. Another ten years found it 58 miles further on, and once more on almost the same parallel as in 1860. Between 1880 and 1890 the migration from the North southward, which followed the civil war, was corrected, and the movement was 48 miles west by north, to a place in southern Indiana, on nearly the same parallel as in 1870.

Thus, in the first century of census-taking, the centre of population moved 505 miles in a generally westerly direction, from Maryland to Indiana, varying less than a half-degree, north and south. Some of the newspaper prophets are now guessing that the census of 1900 will show the centre to have moved somewhat to the east, reversing the uniform trend from the foundation of the republic. These calculations, of course, ignore anything west of our Pacific Coast proper, and may be found to have other marked shortcomings."—*New York Evening Post.*

Central Park. A beautiful pleasure-ground in the city of New York. It is in the form of a parallelogram, 2½ miles long and half a mile wide, and comprises 840 acres,—400 of which consist of wooded ground. The park has 9 miles of carriage-roads, 6 miles of bridle-paths, and 30 miles of foot-paths. It was begun in 1857, under the mayoralty of Fernando Wood, and has cost $16,500,000, exclusive of the amount of $300,000 which has been yearly expended upon it. It is not unusual for 150,000 persons to visit Central Park in a single pleasant day in summer, and as many as 15,000,000 visit it every year. It is about twice the size of Hyde Park or Regent's Park in London, and far surpasses them in beauty.

Cerberus. The name of the famous dog that guarded the entrance of Hades. According to Hesiod, he was the offspring of Typhaon and Echidna, and had fifty heads. Later writers describe him as a monster with only three heads, and with a tail and mane composed of serpents. Orpheus charmed him with the music of his lyre, and Hercules overcame him by sheer strength and dragged him to the upper world.

Cesnola Collection. A remarkable collection of Egyptian, Phœnician, and Grecian antiquities, gathered by the Count di Cesnola, an Italian nobleman, while United States consul at Cyprus (1865–1877). It is now the property of the Metropolitan Museum of Art in New York City, and consists of stone sculptures, sarcophagi, inscriptions, coins, ivories, lamps, pottery, bronzes, gems, etc. See *Metropolitan Museum of Art.*

Cestui que trust. A legal term derived from the Norman-French, meaning a person for whose benefit property — either real or personal — is held in trust. The expression means, in the English law and also in the law of the United States, precisely what " beneficiary " means in Scots law.

Ceylon. This word is part of the original Sanskrit *Sinhala-dwipa* (*Island of Lions*).

Challenger, Voyage of. An expedition undertaken for the scientific exploration of the open sea by the British ship *Challenger*, under Captain Nares. The voyage occupied about three and a half years,—from December 7th, 1872, to May 24th, 1876. During this time, the *Challenger* cruised over 68,000 nautical miles, and made investigations at 362 stations, at each of which the depth of channel, currents, fauna, and atmospheric and meteorologic conditions were carefully observed. The deepest sounding (4575 fathoms) was made on March 23rd, 1875, between the Admiralty Islands and Japan. This is the deepest sounding on record, with the exception of two. See *Depth of the Ocean.*

Châlons, Battle of. One of the most sanguinary battles recorded in history,— fought in June, 451 A.D., near Châlons-sur-Marne, France, between the allied Romans and Gauls under Ætius, and the Huns commanded by their king, the dreaded Attila. The slaughter was so prodigious and the confusion so great that when night fell it was impossible to determine which side was victorious. The next morning, however, Attila remained inactive in his camp and thus confessed himself vanquished. It is estimated that 162,000 men (some authorities say 400,000) perished in this battle. Attila soon after evacuated Gaul and carried devastation into northern Italy,—advancing almost to the gates of Rome.

Cham. The sovereign prince of Tartary,—now usually written *Khan.* The word is said to be a corruption of *Chan* or *Khan* (*lord or prince*).

" Fetch you a hair off the great *Cham's* beard."
         Much Ado about Nothing, ii, 1.

Champagne. An ancient province in the northeastern part of France, once a portion of the kingdom of Burgundy. It now forms the departments of Marne, Haute Marne, Aube, and Ardennes, and part also of Yonne, Aisne, Seine-et-Marne, and Meuse. The effervescing wine called champagne, so named because first made in this province, became popular in the latter part of the 18th century.

Champ de Mai. A festival held on the Champ de Mars in Paris, by Napoleon I, on June 1st, 1815, during the *Hundred Days.* On that occasion, in the presence of the electors of the departments, representatives of the people, and deputations from the army, the emperor proclaimed the new constitution entitled *L'Acte Additionel aux Constitutions de l'Empire*, and swore allegiance to it. See *Champ de Mars ; Hundred Days.*

Champ de Mars. A large open space in the city of Paris—1100 yards in length and 550 yards in breadth,—extending from the *École Militaire* nearly to the banks of the Seine. Until 1861, it was enclosed by embankments—15 to 20 feet high—upon which were placed seats from which thousands of spectators could witness the scenes enacted below. These embankments were erected by the Parisians themselves in 1790. On July 14th of the same year (the anniversary of the capture of the Bastille), occurred the *Fête de la Fédération*, on which occasion Louis XVI (1774–1789), the National Assembly, and the representatives of the army and the provinces swore allegiance to the new constitution, before the "Altar of the Country," in the presence of hundreds of thousands of spectators. There in 1830, Louis Philippe (1830–1848) presented the colors to the National Guard, and there also, in 1852, Napoleon III (1852–1870) distributed the imperial eagles to the army. The "Expositions Universelles" of 1867, 1878, and 1889 were held on the Champ de Mars. It is said that the ancient Franks held their annual assemblies there in the month of March,—whence the name. According to other authorities, the expression *Champ de Mars* is derived from *Campus Martius*, a similar open space in ancient Rome. See *Campus Martius ; Champ de Mai.*

Champs Elysées. A beautiful avenue and pleasure-ground in Paris, extending for a mile and a quarter, from the Place de la Concorde to the Arc de Triomphe. It was originally laid out in 1616 by Marie de Médicis, the widow of Henry IV, and called the *Cours de la Reine*. The Champs Elysées are adorned with beautiful trees and flower-gardens, fountains and statuary, and constitute one of the most fashionable promenades in Paris. Cafés-chantants, restaurants, and shows of all kinds abound ; and the avenue, especially in the evening, presents a brilliant and animated appearance.

Chamuel. In Christian and Jewish tradition, one of the seven archangels, —the other six being Michael, Raphael, Gabriel, Uriel, Zadkiel, and Zophiel.

Chancellor of the Exchequer. The name given, in modern times, to the first finance-minister of the Crown in England. This position is sometimes held by the Prime-Minister, when he is a member of the House of Commons; in that case he receives only one-half the salary of the office. The Chancellor of the Exchequer was originally appointed as under-treasurer, — to check the proceedings of the Lord High Treasurer.

Chancellor of England, Lord High. The first lay-subject in England, after the princes of the blood royal. If a baron, he takes precedence of every temporal lord not a member of the royal family, and of all bishops except the Archbishop of Canterbury. He is the keeper of the great seal, which it is his duty to impress on all documents issued in the name of the sovereign, and is head of the Court of Chancery. He appoints all justices of the peace, is a privy councillor, and, *ex officio*, the Speaker of the House of Lords. He is also the protector of infants, idiots, and lunatics, and has the general superintendence of all charitable foundations throughout the kingdom. He appoints all the judges of the county and superior courts, except the Chief-Justice, who is appointed by the Prime-Minister. The salary of the Lord Chancellor is £10,-000 per annum, with an annuity of £5000, on retiring from office. In 1813, the office of Vice-Chancellor was established. The Lord Chancellor is now a Cabinet officer, and resigns his office with the party to which he is attached. Cardinal Wolsey (1515), Sir Thomas More (1529), and Sir Francis Bacon (1617) were Lord Chancellors ; and in recent times the office has been held by Erskine (1806),

Lyndhurst (1827, 1834, 1841), and Brougham (1830).

Chancellorsville, Battle of. A sanguinary battle during the Civil War, fought near Chancellorsville, Va., on May 2nd, 3rd, and 4th, 1863. The Union forces—numbering 120,000 men (of whom about 90,000 were engaged)—were commanded by General Hooker and the Confederate forces—numbering 62,000 men—by General Lee. The battle resulted in a signal defeat for the Union forces, with a loss of over 17,000 men. The Confederates lost about 13,000, together with their able lieutenant, " Stonewall " Jackson, who was accidentally shot by his own men.

Channel Islands. The name applied to a group of small islands in the English Channel, lying off the north-west coast of France. Their total area is about 75 square miles, and their population numbers somewhat over 92,000. The principal islands are Jersey, Guernsey, Alderney, and Sark. Jersey, Alderney, and Guernsey are famous for their cattle. The "Channel Islands " were anciently an appanage of the Duchy of Normandy, and have belonged to England since the Conquest. The inhabitants speak the old Norman-French language.

Channel-Tunnel Scheme. In 1869 it was proposed to construct a tunnel —measuring 23 miles, including land-approaches—under the narrow strait between Dover and Calais. Experimental boring was commenced in France in 1876, and in England in 1882. About 2200 yards have been bored under the sea on the English side, and an equal distance has been reached on the French side. Thus about one-tenth of the entire distance has been successfully experimented. The original estimated cost was £10,-000,000, but this has since been reduced to £4,000,000. The tunnel was disapproved of by Sir Garnett Wolseley and other officers, British and foreign, in

March, 1882, mainly for military reasons; and work upon it was stopped by the British government on July 6th, 1882. Since then, several bills for experimental work in the tunnel have been opposed by the government, and rejected in the House of Commons. The Prince Consort, Lords Derby and Beaconsfield, Mr. Cobden, and Mr. Gladstone were all warm supporters of the channel-tunnel scheme.

Chanson de Roland. Attributed to Théroulde, a Norman trouvère. It is the earliest poem of the *Charlemagne Cycle of Romances*, and is doubtless the work of more than one person. It was sung by the minstrel Taillefer during the battle of Hastings (1066), and was probably composed during the eleventh century.

Chapelle Expiatoire. A structure, erected in 1820–1826, to the memory of Louis XVI and Marie Antoinette, the martyr king and queen of France. It occupies the site of the old cemetery of the Madeleine, where their bodies rested from 1793 to 1815, when they were removed to the royal vault at St. Denis. The interior contains two groups in marble,— one representing the king sustained by an angel, and the other the queen supported by Religion. Steps on each side of the altar lead to the crypt, which occupies the place where Louis was originally buried.

Chapultepec, Battle of. A battle fought on September 13th, 1847, between the Mexicans and the Americans under General Scott. It resulted in a victory for the American forces, who, on the following day, entered the City of Mexico in triumph. Chapultepec was a strongly fortified castle, on a hill 150 feet high, and constituted the last stronghold of the Mexicans between Vera Cruz and the capital.

Charge of the Light Brigade. Owing to some confusion in the orders at the battle of Balaklava, September

26th, 1854, a brigade of 670 British light cavalry, under Lord Cardigan, charged the Russian army of 12,000 men ; got possession of their artillery ; and cut their way back through a body of cavalry. Of the 670 British horsemen, only 198 returned. Tennyson has commemorated this useless sacrifice of life in his noble poem entitled *The Charge of the Light Brigade.*

Charing Cross. A large area on the south side of Trafalgar Square, London, between the Strand and Whitehall. It probably derives its name from the village of *Cheringe*, which stood there in the thirteenth century. A fanciful tradition, however, assigns the origin of the name to the stone cross erected there by Edward I (1272–1307), in memory of his beloved wife, Eleanor, *la chère reine (the dear queen).* According to other authorities, this word is said to be derived from the Saxon *charan (to bend)*,—both river and road making a bend there. The cross erected there by Edward I was pulled down by the Long Parliament in 1647. A modern cross, designed as a reproduction of the original one, has been recently erected in front of the Charing Cross Railway Station. The Regicides were put to death there in 1660.

Charities of American Civil War. The amounts contributed by the people of the loyal States for philanthropic purposes, during the Civil War, are as follows :

(1) Contributions from States, counties, and towns, for the aid and relief of soldiers, $187,209,608.62.

(2) Contributions from associations and individuals for the aid and relief of soldiers, $24,044,865.96.

(3) Contributions for sufferers abroad, $380,040.74.

(4) Contributions for sufferers by the July riots, for freedmen, and white refugees, $639,633.13.

These amounts make a grand total of $212,274,248.45, exclusive of expenditures of the government.

Charivari. A burlesque or mocking serenade, produced by the beating of pans and kettles, mingled with groans and hisses, and expressive of displeasure toward those against whom it is directed. In France, during the Middle Ages, persons contracting second nuptials were thus assailed. The origin of the word is in doubt. The Germans translate it by *Katzenmusik*, to which *Cats'-concert* corresponds in English. The name *Charivari* was given to a French satirical journal, established in Paris in 1831 and still in existence. London *Punch* is the English *Charivari.*

Charlemagne Asleep. According to the legend, Charlemagne is not dead, but has simply fallen asleep. Crowned and armed, he waits in Odenberg or Untersberg, near Saltzburg, till the coming of Antichrist, when he will arise and overcome his adversary, and thus prepare Christendom for the second advent and personal reign on earth of Jesus Christ.

Charles's Wain. A name frequently given in England to a group of seven stars — familiarly known as the *Dipper*—in the constellation of the Great Bear. The name is sometimes applied to the entire constellation, and is probably a corruption of *Ceorles Wain (Churl's Wagon).* See *Bear, Great.*

Charlottenburg. A town in Prussia, about three miles west of Berlin, famous for the *Mausoleum*, containing the remains of Frederick William III (1797–1840) of Prussia, his queen, Louise, and their son, William I (1871–1888), emperor of Germany. The temple — designed by Schinkel, at the request of Frederick—is in the Doric style of architecture, and contains recumbent marble figures of the dead king and queen. These are the work of the sculptor Rauch, and are regarded as masterpieces.* At the foot of the statues is the heart of Frederick William IV. (who died in 1861), enclosed in a marble casket.

* "The recumbent marble figures of the Emperor William I and the Empress Augusta are by Encke."

Charon. In classic mythology, the son of Erebus and Nox, whose duty it was to convey the shades of the buried dead across the rivers of the lower world. For this service he exacted an obolus; and, accordingly, a coin of this value was always placed in the dead person's mouth. To neglect this rite was to doom the unhappy shade to wander restlessly along the shores of Acheron, since Charon refused to ferry any one that did not pay the fee. Charon is generally represented as an old man, with unkempt beard and filthy clothes.

Charterhouse. A celebrated hospital and school in London, instituted in 1611 by Thomas Sutton. The site had been originally occupied by a Carthusian monastery, founded in 1371 by Sir Walter de Manny; but, on the suppression of monasteries under Henry VIII (1509–1547), the building underwent various alterations, and was finally converted into an asylum for poor brethren and a school for boys. The poor brethren are eighty in number. To be eligible, they must be fifty years of age, bachelors, and members of the Church of England. Some of the most eminent men of England have been educated at Charterhouse school. The word *Charterhouse* is a corruption of Chartreuse-house. See *Carthusians; Chartreuse, Grande.*

Charter Oak. A tree, famous in American history, which formerly stood in Hartford, Connecticut, and derived its name from the following circumstance: In 1687, Sir Edmund Andros, the royal governor, appeared at Hartford and demanded the charter of the colony, in the name of James II of England. While the Assembly, in session at Hartford, was considering the governor's request, the lights were suddenly extinguished; and, in the darkness and confusion that ensued, the charter was snatched from the table by a patriot, Captain William Wadsworth, and secreted in the hollow of an oak tree. This tree, which was ever after known as the Charter Oak, was carefully preserved until 1856, when it was destroyed by a violent storm. The charter was renewed when William and Mary ascended the throne in 1689.

Chartists. The name given to a political party that arose in England about 1838, in consequence of the disappointment of the working-classes with the Reform Bill of 1832. Their demands were embodied in the *People's Charter*, and consisted of the following six points:

(1) Universal Suffrage.
(2) Vote by Ballot.
(3) Yearly Parliaments.
(4) Payment of Members.
(5) Abolition of Property Qualification.
(6) Equal Electoral Districts.

In June, 1839, a petition in favor of the Charter, signed by 1,280,000 persons, was presented to the House of Commons. The House declined to appoint a day for its consideration, and several riots occurred in consequence. The Chartists announced a gigantic meeting for the 10th of April, 1848, on which occasion half a million men were to carry to the House of Commons a petition for reform signed by 6,000,000 persons. Only 50,000 persons appeared, however, and no demonstration occurred. Chartism gradually died out after 1848.

Chartreuse, Grande. The original monastery of the Carthusians, founded in 1084. It is situated among the mountains in the French department of Isère, about fourteen miles northeast of Grenoble, and is famous for an aromatic cordial made by the monks, the secret of which they have long possessed. The monastery was despoiled during the French Revolution, and the inmates exiled from 1796 to 1816. They returned after the restoration of Louis XVIII (1814), but never recovered their former wealth and influence. Now at Tarragona, Spain. See *Carthusians, Charterhouse.*

Charybdis. A celebrated whirlpool in the Strait of Messina, off the coast of Sicily, opposite to a rock, called Scylla, on the Italian coast. It is caused by the meeting of currents, and is seldom dangerous, but was much dreaded by the ancients. According to Homer, Charybdis proved fatal to a part of the fleet of Ulysses. See *Scylla.*

Chassepot-Rifle. A breech-loading firearm of the needle-gun type, invented by Antoine Alphonse Chassepot (b. 1833), and adopted by the French government in 1866. It was extensively used by the army during the Franco-Prussian War, and was considered a success. " The range of the chassepot being 1800 paces, and that of the needle-gun only between 600 and 700, the Germans in all their charges had to traverse 1200 paces before their arms could be used to purpose." After the battle of Sedan, September 2nd, 1870, many of the Prussians were armed with the chassepot-rifle. See *Needle-Gun.*

Châteaux en Espagne (*Fr. Castles in Spain*). An expression, used originally by the French, to denote any visionary project or baseless scheme. It is said that the term had its origin in the fact that no castles exist in Spain. For a like reason, the expression *châteaux en Asie* (*castles in Asia*) was also used.

Chatsworth. The residence of the Duke of Devonshire, situated in Derbyshire, about 25 miles northwest of Derby, and considered one of the finest private mansions in England. The present edifice was begun in 1687 by the first Duke of Devonshire, and the north wing was added in 1820. The building is almost a perfect square, with an inner quadrangle, and a façade of 720 feet. It is famous for its library ; and contains, in addition, a very valuable collection of paintings and sculptures. The park and gardens — ten miles in extent — were laid out by Loudon and Paxton, and are celebrated for their trees, fountains, and deer. The conservatory covers nearly an acre, and has 70,000 square feet of glass. It served as a model for the original Crystal Palace.

Chattanooga, Battle of. A battle of the American Civil War, fought on November 25th, 1863, between 65,000 Federals under General Grant and 45,000 Confederates under General Bragg. It resulted in a decisive victory for the Federals, who lost between 5000 and 6000 men. The Confederate loss was estimated at more than 9000 killed, wounded, and taken prisoners, 40 pieces of artillery, and 7000 stands of small-arms.

Chautauqua System of Education. *The Chautauqua Assembly* was organized in 1874, by Lewis Miller and John H. Vincent. Annual sessions are held at Chautauqua, New York, during July and August, and instruction is given in language and literature, science and the arts. Lectures, concerts, musicales, and various other forms of recreation are also provided.

The Chautauqua Literary and Scientific Circle was organized in 1878, for the purpose of continuing the work of the *Assembly* throughout the year, in all parts of the country. Up to the present time, more than 350,000 persons have become members. The object of this organization is to promote habits of reading and study, and to give, not the essentials of a college course, but what may be termed " the college outlook " on the world and life. The course of reading covers four years, although each year's course is complete in itself. The time required is about one-half hour daily for nine months. Certificates are granted to all persons that complete the course. The annual fee is 50 cents. See *Catholic Summer-School.*

11

Chauvinism. An expression originally used to denote an intense admiration for the first Napoleon and his régime, but latterly employed to mean an absurd patriotism and pride in one's own country. In this last sense, it is the French equivalent of *Jingoism*. The word is derived from *Chauvin*, the principal character in Scribe's *Le Soldat Laboureur*. He is represented as a veteran soldier of the First Empire and a passionate admirer of the Emperor. See *Jingoes*.

Cheapside. A noted street in London, and, with the exception of London Bridge, the busiest thoroughfare in the world. It is still famous for its jewelers' and linen-drapers' shops, although its importance as a place of trade has steadily declined. Cheapside Cross—erected by Edward I (1272–1307) to the memory of Queen Eleanor—stood on this street, until destroyed by the Puritans in 1647. Bow Church, with its projecting clock and famous chime of bells, is one of the relics of the Cheapside of the past. The word *Cheapside* is derived from the Saxon *chepe* (*market*); according to other authorities, from the Saxon *cyppan* (*to buy or bargain*). See *Bow-Bells; Cockney.*

Cheeryble Brothers. Twin brothers famous for their warm, sunny natures, no less than for their many acts of kindness. They figure as characters in Charles Dickens's *Nicholas Nickleby*, and are said to have been drawn from the Manchester firm of William Grant & Brothers.

Chelsea Hospital. A royal hospital for aged and disabled soldiers at Chelsea, London. It was built from designs by Sir Christopher Wren, and cost £150,000. The foundation-stone was laid by Charles II (1660–1685) in 1682, and the building was opened in 1692. The hospital is known locally as Chelsea College, — having been erected on the site of a theological institution founded by James I (1603–1625) in 1609. In 1888, there were 87,703 out-pensioners, and about 550 in-pensioners or inmates. The remains of the Duke of Wellington lay in state at Chelsea Hospital in November, 1852.

Chelsea Philosopher. A sobriquet conferred upon Thomas Carlyle (1795–1881), the noted English writer, because of his long residence in Chelsea, a suburb of London.

Chemical Composition of Man.

"Huxley's table on the 'Chemical composition of man of the average weight of 154 pounds' was for years the standard, but it has recently been superseded by a new one compiled by the French Academy of Sciences. The table is appended:

Elements.	Pounds.	Ounces.	Grains.
Oxygen	111	8	0
Hydrogen	21	6	0
Carbon	21	0	0
Nitrogen	3	10	0
Phosphorus	1	2	88
Calcium	2	0	0
Sulphur	0	0	219
Chlorine	0	2	47
Sodium (salt)	0	2	116
Iron	0	0	100
Potassium	0	0	290
Magnesium	0	0	12
Silica	0	0	2 "

World Almanac.

Chesapeake. A United States frigate, carrying about 50 guns and 300 men, commanded by Captain James Lawrence. On June 1st, 1813, after a desperate engagement outside Boston harbor with the British frigate *Shannon*, the *Chesapeake* was disabled and captured, with a loss of 48 killed and 98 wounded, among the latter being Captain Lawrence. The *Chesapeake* was conveyed to Halifax, and there Lawrence died on June 5th. His remains were removed to New York and buried in the churchyard of Trinity Church, where a handsome monument was erected to his memory. Lawrence's dying words, "Don't give up the ship!" became a household expression in the United States. See *Shannon.*

Chess. A game of great antiquity, whose origin, according to Hyde and Sir William Jones, is attributed to the Hindus. From Hindustan it passed into Persia, and thence into Arabia. The Arabs introduced it into Spain in the eighth century, and thence it spread throughout western Europe. Others assign its origin to Palamedes, a Greek hero in the Trojan War, about 1180 B.C. It is said that the word *chess* is derived from the Persian *shah* (*king*), and checkmate from *shahmat*, meaning *king overcome.*

Chester. A city situated on the river Dee, sixteen miles southeast of Liverpool, England. It was an important camp (*Lat. castrum*) and military post of the Romans during their occupation of Britain, and derives its name from this circumstance. The " walls," originally built by the Romans, still remain. They enclose the central part of the town, and are about two miles in circumference, forming a delightful promenade. Chester was the last city in England to yield to William the Conqueror (1066-1087), and was taken by the Parliamentary forces in 1645. Along the principal street, called Watergate, the shops are upon the second floor. A covered gallery, sixteen feet in width, extends in front of them, and is reached by stairways from the street below. Chester contains, in addition, a castle, first built in the time of William the Conqueror, and a cathedral dating from the 12th century.

Chestnut Street. The principal thoroughfare — at once business and fashionable — in the city of Philadelphia. It is considered to have the handsomest display of shop-fronts in the United States.

Chevy Chase. The name of an early English ballad—the authorship of which is unknown — based on the story of the battle of Otterburn (August, 1388). The earlier version is supposed, according to *Percy's Rel-*

iques, to have been written in the time of Henry VI (1422-1461), while the more modern one cannot be of earlier date than the time of Elizabeth (1558-1603). Its original title was the *Hunting a' the Cheviat.* The oldest MS. of the ballad is in the Bodleian Library at Oxford, with the name attached of Richard Sheale, a ballad-singer or reciter during the reigns of Mary and Elizabeth. Sir Philip Sidney declared that the ballad of *Chevy Chase* stirred him like the sound of a trumpet.

Chicago Fire. The most disastrous conflagration of the nineteenth century occurred in the city of Chicago, Illinois, October 8th-11th, 1871, and destroyed 17,450 buildings; 250 persons perished, while 98,500 were rendered homeless and destitute. The area burned over covered 1⅓ square miles, and contained 73 miles of streets. The total loss was estimated at $290,000,000. Of the $96,500,000 of insurance upon the property destroyed, only $38,000,000 was ever paid,— 68 companies, with $24,000,000. liabilities, being completely wiped out, while many others paid but a small percentage of their losses. Contributions to the amount of over $7,100,000 poured in from all quarters ; and within two years from the date of the Great Fire, very few traces of it remained. See *Boston Fire.*

Chickamauga, Battle of. A battle of the American Civil War, fought on September 19th-20th, 1863, between the Federals under General Rosecrans and the Confederates under General Bragg. Although the Federal right and centre were routed during the battle, the left, under General Thomas, held firm and enabled Rosecrans to fall back to Chattanooga, which he fortified. The Union loss was placed at 16,000, and the Confederate loss at 18,000.

Childe Harold. The hero of Lord Byron's famous poem in four cantos, entitled *Childe Harold's Pilgrimage*. He has always been considered to be the poet himself; although Byron, in the preface, declares the character to be fictitious. Childe Harold is represented as a man of high birth and fine intelligence, who, having exhausted all the pleasures of early life, resolves to travel in the hope of dissipating his ennui. But although he wanders through some of the loveliest parts of the world he fails to attain the object of his journey.

Childermas Day. A festival in the Roman Catholic, Anglican, Greek, and various Oriental churches. It occurs on December 28th (in the East on the 29th), and commemorates the slaughter of the Innocents by Herod. It was long considered an unlucky day on which to begin any work or to marry, and in Fenn's *Letters* we read that the coronation of Edward IV (1461–1483) was postponed until Monday, because the preceding Sunday was Childermas Day. Childermas Day is more commonly known at present as Innocents' Day. See *Innocents, Massacre of the.*

Child of Fortune. An epithet conferred upon Masséna (1758–1817) by Napoleon Bonaparte, after the battle of Rivoli, January 14th–15th, 1797. When the Empire was established, Masséna was created a marshal of France and Duke of Rivoli.

Children's Crusade. In August, 1212, an army of unarmed children— 30,000 in number—set out from Marseilles, France, under the leadership of Stephen, a peasant-boy, to rescue the Holy Land from the Infidels. In the same year, a similar army of German children — 20,000 in number,— under the guidance of a peasant-boy named Nicholas, crossed the Alps at Mont Cenis ; while a second German army of 20,000 children crossed the Alps at a more westerly point and reached the sea at Brindisi. Part of the French contingent perished by shipwreck, and the rest were sold as slaves to the Mohammedans. Of the German chil-

dren, 5000 reached Genoa and were persuaded to remain there, while the others sailed for Palestine from Brindisi, and were soon forgotten.

Chillon, Castle of. A famous castle and prison at the eastern extremity of the Lake of Geneva in Switzerland, six miles southeast of Vevay. It stands on an isolated rock—22 yards from the shore—and is almost surrounded by deep water. The castle probably dates from the eighth century, but was rebuilt by Amadeus IV of Savoy in 1238. It was long used as a state prison. Bonnivard, on account of his efforts to liberate the Genevese, was imprisoned there for six years (1530– 1536); and this fact doubtless gave rise to Byron's famous poem of *The Prisoner of Chillon.* The castle contains several gloomy dungeons, and is much visited by tourists. It is now used as an arsenal for military stores. See *Prisoner of Chillon.*

Chiltern Hundreds, Steward of. An officer of the English Crown, originally appointed to protect the people of Bucks from the robbers that infested the Chiltern Hills. The office is now a sinecure, but is conferred upon a member of the House of Commons wishing to resign his seat, since, owing to an English custom, no member is allowed to do so unless disqualified either by the acceptance of some place of honor and profit under the Crown, or for some other reason. As soon as the office has been secured, it is immediately vacated. In case the stewardship of Chiltern Hundreds is not vacant, the same end is attained by the stewardships of East Hendred, Northshead, and Hempholme. This custom originated about 1750, and the gift lies with the Chancellor of the Exchequer. The strict legality of the practice has been questioned.

Chimborazo. A famous conical peak of the Andes, situated in Ecuador. It is perpetually covered with snow, and rises to a height of 21,420 feet above the sea-level, although only 11,000 feet above the city of Quito. Chimborazo was ascended by Alexander von Humboldt, to the height of 19,286 feet, on June 23rd, 1802. The summit was twice reached in 1880 by Edward Whymper.

China, Great Wall of. A celebrated line of fortifications in China, extending for a distance of over 1700 miles across the northern boundary of the Chinese Empire. It was built by the Emperor Chi-hoang-ti, about 200 B.C., to protect his dominions against the incursions of the Tartars, Kalmucks, and other northern tribes; but proved utterly useless. It was from 25 to 30 feet high and 20 feet thick at the base, but tapered to a thickness of 15 feet at the top. It was surmounted by towers 35 to 40 feet in height, at intervals of 200 or 300 yards. The "Great Wall" is said to have required ten years to build, and to have caused the death of tens of thousands of workmen. It is now, for the most part, a heap of rubbish.

Chinaman, John. A cant or popular surname bestowed upon the Chinese. According to Wheeler's *Dictionary of the Noted Names of Fiction*, the earliest known instance of the use of *John Chinaman* is in *A Letter to the Committee of Management of Drury-Lane Theatre*, London, 1819, p. 64.

Chinese Gordon. A sobriquet conferred upon Charles George Gordon (1833-1885), the English officer, in allusion to his career in China in 1863-1864, where he aided in suppressing the Tae-Ping Rebellion.

Chiselhurst. A village in Kent, eleven miles southeast of London, famous as the place of retreat of the Emperor Napoleon III after his deposition in 1870, and later as the scene of his death and burial. The remains of the Emperor and those of his son, the Prince Imperial, were originally buried in the chapel at Camden Place, the residence of the imperial family at Chiselhurst; but, in 1888, they were removed to the mausoleum at Farnborough Hill, the home of the Empress Eugénie.

Chivalry. A mediæval institution, which arose out of the feudal system in the eighth century, and perished with it. It was at its height from the twelfth to the fifteenth century, and did much to refine the manners of western Europe during the Middle Ages. It also elevated the position of woman, and spread abroad a spirit of courtesy and kindliness, which had a powerful and salutary effect upon modern society. The word chivalry is derived from *chevalier (knight)*, and this from *caballarius (an equipped feudal tenant on horseback)*.

Choragic Monuments. The name given, in ancient Greece, to monuments erected by private individuals, as memorials of their triumphs in public musical contests. The word *choragic* is derived from *choragus (chorus-leader)*. The reward of victory was usually a tripod, and the monument erected was either a column designed for its support, or perhaps some more elaborate substructure. The most beautiful choragic monument in Athens was erected by Lysicrates, in honor of a victory won by him in 334 B.C. The "Street of the Tripods" was a name given to an avenue in Athens lined with monuments of this description. See *Lantern of Diogenes*.

Chouans. The name given to bands of Brittany peasants, that espoused the royal cause during the French Revolution, and organized a reactionary movement in 1792. Their first leader, Jean Cottereau, was killed in 1794. Later, the insurrection, under Cadoudal and Charette, assumed vast proportions, and for a time imperilled the safety of the French Republic. It was, however, stamped out by La Hoche, and its leaders forced to lay down their arms. Another attempt at insurrection was made in 1799, but this also was mercilessly crushed. Chouannerie again made its appearance in 1814–1815, and was finally wiped out in 1830, through the efforts of Thiers. The word *Chouans* is said to be a corruption of *chat-huant* (*Fr. screech-owl*), and to have been given, either on account of the nocturnal habits of the band, or because of some special call of recognition in use among them. Others trace the origin of the word to Cottereau, the first leader.

Chrism. The name given to the oil consecrated by the bishop on Holy Thursday in the Roman Catholic and Greek Churches, and used in baptism, confirmation, ordination, and extreme unction. There are two kinds of chrism: the one, a mixture of oil and balsam, used in baptism, confirmation, and ordination ; the other, a pure oil, used only in extreme unction.

Christ, Birth of. The birth of Jesus Christ is now generally considered to have occurred about four years before the period from which we reckon our years in the Christian era. The following table, taken from Brewer's *Historic Note-Book*, gives a list of several dates to which Christ's birth has been assigned, together with the authority for each date.

December,	B.C.	7	Idler.
25	"	5	Petavius and Usher.
"	"	4	Bengel.
March,	"	4	Anger and Winer.
October,	"	3	Scaliger.
25 December,	"	3	St. Jerome.
6 January,	"	2	Eusebius.

According to Irenæus, Jesus Christ was born about fifteen years before the time commonly assigned, and lived to be about fifty years of age. Banage, in his *Histoire des Juifs*, places the birth of the Savior about one hundred years earlier than A.D. 1.

The custom of dating from the birth of Christ was introduced by Dionysius "Exiguus" in 526 A.D. See *Christmas*.

Christ, Likeness of. In 1702, the Rev. H. Rowlands, while engaged in antiquarian research near Aberfraw, Wales, found a beautiful brass medal of Jesus Christ, in a fine state of preservation, which he immediately forwarded to the Rev. E. Llwyd, at the time curator of the Asmolean Library at Oxford. The medal has, on the obverse side, the figure of a head of Christ exactly corresponding to a description of him given by Publius Lentulus, in a letter sent by him to the Emperor Tiberius and the Roman Senate. On the reverse side are found the following words in Hebrew—" This is Jesus the Mediator " or " Jesus the great Messias." It is possible that this medal, having been found among the ruins of the chief Druids, may have belonged to some Christian connected with Bran the Blessed, who was one of the hostages of Caractacus at Rome from 52 to 59 A.D. Two years later (61 A.D.), the Roman general Suetonius drove all the Druids out of the island of Great Britain.

Christabel. The name of an unfinished poem by Samuel Taylor Coleridge (1772–1834). It is a romantic, supernatural tale, filled with wild imagery and characterized by remarkable modulation of verse.

Christian Commission, United States. An organization established in the loyal States of the Union during the Civil War, not only to aid and co-operate with the Sanitary Commission, but also to minister to the spiritual wants of the soldiers in the field. It originated in a call for assistance from the Young Men's Christian Association of New York City, in 1861. The Commission was unsectarian in its methods, and accomplished a vast amount of valuable work. See *Sanitary Commission, United States.*

Christians. The followers of Jesus Christ were first called " Christians " at Antioch, Syria, during the year 43 A.D., spent there by Paul and Barnabas in preaching the gospel.

" And the disciples were called *Christians* first in Antioch."—*Acts* xi, 26.

Christian Science. A system of moral and spiritual instruction, combined with a method of treating diseases mentally. Rev. Mary Baker G. Eddy, the founder and so-called discoverer of " Christian Science," says, in her *Science and Health*, that "Christian Science is based on teachings of Scripture which it interprets, giving the Christ Principle and rule in Divine metaphysics which heals the sick and sinner. It explains all cause and effect as mental, and shows the scientific relation of man to God." The number of Christian Scientists in the United States amounts to hundreds of thousands; and, according to their estimates, fully 1,000,000 hopeless cases have been cured by their methods. " There are 1306 organized churches, 134 places where regular Sunday services are held, but without a church organization, and 75 dispensaries for the healing of patients and the free distribution of Christian Science literature." The *Christian Science Journal*, published in Boston, is the official organ of the Christian Scientists.

" Christian Science is demonstrable Christianity. Through the spiritual understanding of the teachings of Christ Jesus, its followers are enabled to obey His command to 'heal the sick' and do the works He and His disciples did. The omnipotence, omnipresence, and omniscience of God are proved to be true. Christian Science is not mind-cure, as that is popularly understood, because it recognizes but one mind, God. It is not faith-cure, because it does not perform its wonderful works through blind faith in a personal god, but through the understanding of man's relation to God. It is not mesmerism or hypnotism, because it denies absolutely the power of the human mind and human will, and claims no will but God's. Through recognizing the one mind, and man as the reflection of that mind, it forever establishes the brotherhood of man. It is the perfect salvation from sin, disease, and death Christ Jesus came to bring. In 'Rudimental Divine Science,' Mrs. Eddy defines Christian Science as 'the law of God, the law of good, interpreting and demonstrating the principle and rule of eternal harmony.'"—*World Almanac.*

Christian Venus. A term sometimes applied to Raphael's famous painting, the *Madonna della Sedia*, in the gallery of the Pitti Palace in Florence. See *Madonna della Sedia*.

Hawthorne says: "The most beautiful picture in the world, I am convinced, is Raphael's *Madonna della Sedia*."

Christmas. A festival of the Christian Church, annually celebrated in honor of the birth of Jesus Christ, the exact date of which event is unknown. It is said to have been observed as early as 98. According to the forged *Isidorian Decretals*, Christmas was ordered to be held as a church-festival by Pope Telesphorus (127–139), about 137 ; but the first certain traces of its observance are found during the reign of the Emperor Commodus (138–161). Among the early Christians, some celebrated it in May, others in April, and still others in June. It could not have occurred in December, since this is the rainy season in Judea, when shepherds would scarcely be found watching their flocks by night on the plains. By the fifth century it was generally observed on the 25th of December. Whether this change was the result of some ancient tradition, or sprang from the desire, on the part of the Church, to supplant certain heathen festivals held at this season of the year, is unknown. The Puritans abolished Christmas, and made the decoration of churches and houses a seditious act. The use of mistletoe and holly at Christmas are remains of the religious customs of the Druids. See *Christ, Birth of*.

Christ's Hospital. A famous public school in London, on the site of the old Greyfriars' monastery,—founded by Edward VI (1547–1553) in 1553, for the maintenance of poor orphans. It is usually known as the " Blue Coat

School," on account of the old-fashioned costume of the boys,—consisting of long blue gowns, yellow stockings, and knee-breeches. No head-covering is worn, even in winter. About 1100 boys and 90 girls attend this institution. The present net income is about £58,000 per year. Many distinguished Englishmen have been educated at Christ's Hospital ; among these may be mentioned Coleridge, Leigh Hunt, Charles Lamb, and Richardson, the novelist.

Chromosphere. The name given to a layer of incandescent vapors in the sun, enveloping the entire photosphere. Its depth varies at different times and in different parts, and ranges from 6000 to 9000 miles. The chromosphere consists chiefly of hydrogen, and an element known as helium, while heavier vapors, such as those of iron, calcium, titanium, magnesium, etc., are sometimes projected into it from the photosphere. The so-called "prominences" are due to projections of hydrogen that are shot up to enormous altitudes, with velocities exceeding 149 miles per second. The name chromosphere (*Gr. color-sphere*) is given to this solar envelope, on account of its beautiful rosy hue. It is visible only during total eclipses of the sun, or by the aid of the spectroscope ; and is said to have been first noticed by Father Secchi (1818–1878) during an eclipse. See *Helium ; Photosphere.*

Chrononhotonthologos. A pompous character in a burlesque tragedy of the same name, written by Henry Carey (1663–1743). This appellation was also given as a nickname to General Burgoyne, on account of a pompous address delivered by him to the American Indians during the War of the Revolution. See *Aldiborontesphoscophornio.*

Chrysanthemum. This word means literally a golden flower, and is derived from the Greek χρυσός (*gold*), and ἄνθεμον (*flower*).

Church Fathers. The name given to a set of ecclesiastical teachers that flourished from the time of the apostles to about the seventh century,—the most of whom left writings relating to the doctrines of the early Church. According to Brewer's *Dictionary of Miracles*, the Fathers of the Greek and Latin Churches, arranged in chronological order, are as follows:

(1) Justin (103–167).

(2) Irenæus, bishop of Lyons (b. 130, 177–200).

(3) Athenagoras (*flourished* 177).

(4) Clement, or Clemens of Alexandria (*died* 220).

(5) Tertullian, a Latin Father (160–240).

(6) Origen, a Greek Father (185–253).

(7) Cyprian, bishop of Carthage (b. 200, 248–258).

(8) Lactantius (*died* 325).

(9) Hilary of Poitiers (*bishop* 350–367).

(10) Athanasius, bishop of Alexandria (b. 296, 326–373).

(11) Basil *the Great*, bishop of Cæsarea (b. 329, 371–379).

(12) Cyril of Jerusalem (b. 315, 348–386).

(13) Gregory Nazianzen, bishop of Carthage (b. 329, 380–390).

(14) Gregory, bishop of Nyssa (332–396).

(15) Ambrose, bishop of Milan (b. 340, 374–397).

(16) John Chrysostom (347–407).

(17) Jerome (345–420).

(18) Augustine, bishop of Hippo (b. 354, 395–430).

(19) Cyril, bishop of Alexandria (*bishop* 412–444).

(20) Theodoret, bishop of Tyre (387–458).

(21) Pope Leo I *the Great* (b. 390, 440–461).

(22) Pope Gregory I *the Great* (b. 544, 590–604).

See *Doctors of the Church.*

Church of the Ascension. A church, formerly standing on the summit of the Mount of Olives, near Jerusalem, erected by the Empress Helena to mark the traditional spot of the ascension of Christ. This basilica gave way, in after years, to the round church of Modestus, open to the sky "because of the passage of the Lord's body." The second edifice has long since disappeared, and the site is at present occupied by a Mohammedan mosque, near which is a small domed building, covering a rock on which is the supposed impress of the Savior's foot where he last touched the earth. See *Mount of Olives.*

Church of the Holy Sepulchre. A church in Jerusalem, erected by the Empress Helena, the mother of Constantine the Great, and said to enclose the site of the sepulchre of Jesus Christ. It is a Byzantine structure, and consists of a nave 300 feet in length and a transept 180 feet in width, with chapels for Latin, Greek, and Armenian Christians. In the centre of the rotunda of the church stands a small temple — 10 feet broad, 10 feet high, and 20 feet long, — containing the reputed sepulchre. The interior is divided into two small chapels; the first is where the angel was seen, and contains the throne on which he sat, while the second contains the sepulchre itself. The tomb is incased with marble, and is three feet above the floor; 42 gold lamps burn continually before the tomb, and incense from a golden censer rises as a perpetual offering. The visitor to the Church of the Holy Sepulchre is also shown the rock of Calvary, the pillar of Flagellation ; the place of the Cross ; the chapel of the Apparition, where Christ appeared to Mary ; the tombs of Adam, Nicodemus, and Joseph of Arimathea ; and the stone of Unction, on which the body of Christ was anointed for burial. See *Calvary.*

Church of the Nativity. A magnificent basilica at Bethlehem, erected by the Empress Helena in 327 A.D. It is the oldest monument of Christian architecture in the world, and marks the traditional birthplace of the infant Jesus. The Greeks, Latins, and Armenians hold joint possession of the church, and, adjoining it, are the monasteries for the use and entertainment of the respective orders. Owing, however, to the mutual jealousies of these rival sects, the building has been suffered to fall into decay, and presents a dilapidated appearance. According to tradition, the 48 columns in the interior were taken from the porches of the Temple at Jerusalem. See *Bethlehem ; Cave of the Nativity.*

Church, States of the. A group of states in central Italy, formerly united under the Pope as temporal sovereign, but now forming part of the kingdom of Italy. The temporal power of the Popes had its origin in the gift of the exarchate of Ravenna by Pepin Le Bref (752–768), to Pope Stephen II (752–757) in 754, and rose to its greatest height under Pope Innocent III (1198–1216). In 1859, the area of the papal dominions amounted to 15,774 square miles, with a population of over 3,000,000. The war of 1859 reduced this territory to an area of 4493 square miles, with a population of 700,000. When, in 1870, the French troops were withdrawn from Rome, the Papal States were united to the kingdom of Italy, and the temporal power of the Popes came to an end.

Cicero of France. A sobriquet conferred upon Jean Baptiste Massillon (1663–1742), the noted French pulpit orator.

Cicero of the British Senate. An appellation conferred upon George Canning (1770–1827), the English orator and statesman, in allusion to his eloquence.

Cicero's Mouth. A sobriquet conferred upon Philippe Pot (1428–1494), prime-minister to Louis XI of France, in allusion to his eloquence.

Cid, Chronicle of the. An epic poem of unknown authorship, probably written during the latter part of the twelfth century, and doubtless the oldest production in the Spanish language. It consists of about 11,000 lines, and celebrates the redoubtable deeds of the Spanish hero, Cid El Campeador. It is chiefly valuable as presenting an accurate account of the manners and customs of the eleventh century. See *Cid El Campeador.*

Cid El Campeador. A name, or rather names, given to Rodrigo or Ruy Diaz, a renowned Spanish warrior of the eleventh century, famous for his victories over the Moors. He was born at Burgos, or at Bivar near it, about 1040, and was a Castilian of noble birth. It is said that, after defeating two large armies sent against him by the Almoravides, then in possession of central and southern Spain, the Cid established himself in Valencia, and reigned there until his death in 1099. His deeds are, however, so mixed with fable that it is well-nigh impossible to learn what he actually did. He was such a terror to the Moors that they called him *El Seid* (Arabic for *The Lord*) ; they also called him *El Campeador* (Spanish for *The Champion*). Finally, he was almost always known as *Cid Campeador* (*Lord Champion*). See *Cid, Chronicle of the.*

Cimmerian Darkness. An expression often used to denote profound darkness, in allusion to the Cimmerians, a fabulous people who are said to have lived, in ancient times, in perpetual darkness. See *Cimmerians.*

Cimmerians. A people mentioned in Homer's *Odyssey*, as dwelling " beyond the ocean-stream, where the sun never shines, and perpetual darkness reigns." According to Pliny's *Natural History*, Cimmeria was near Lake Avernus in Italy, " where the sun never penetrates." The inhabitants lived in dark caverns, worked metals, but never came to the light of day. The historic Cimmerians are said to have been the ancient inhabitants of the Crimea. See *Avernus, Lake ; Cimmerian Darkness.*

Cinchona (*properly chinchona*). A genus of evergreen trees, of the order *Rubiaceæ*, growing naturally in the tropical valleys of the Andes, and yielding a bark of great medicinal value, known as Peruvian bark, Jesuits' bark, Cinchona bark, etc. It is so named from the Countess of Chinchon (commonly, but incorrectly written Cinchon), vice-queen of Peru, who, by the use of this bark, was cured of intermittent fever. After her return to Spain, in 1632, she made known the value of this remedy. To perpetuate the memory of her important service to mankind, Linnæus named this plant *cinchona*. It was also sometimes called *Countess's Bark* and *Countess's Powder.*

Cincinnati Oysters. An expression sometimes used in the United States to denote pigs' feet.

Cincinnati, Society of the. A patriotic and historic order founded in May, 1783, by the American and French officers, at the close of the Revolutionary War, " to perpetuate their friendship, and to raise a fund for relieving the widows and orphans of those fallen during the war." It was so named because it contained many patriots who, like Cincinnatus, had abandoned rural occupations to serve their country. The first general meeting was held at Philadelphia, in May, 1784. At the second general meeting, held three years later, Washington was elected president-general, and was re-elected at each subsequent triennial meeting until his death. He was succeeded by Alexander Hamilton. The society was charged with attempting to establish a hereditary military aristocracy; and, in consequence of this, the State societies of New Hampshire, Connecticut, Delaware, Virginia, and Georgia were dissolved in 1804. The number of living members in June 1911 (including those of the newly readmitted Virginia Society), was 981. The next triennial meeting will be held in Baltimore, Maryland, in May, 1914. The badge of the society consists of a bald eagle having on its breast a figure of Cincinnatus receiving the military ensigns from the Roman senators; around this are the words, *Omnia reliquit servare rempublicam* (*Lat. He forsook all to serve the republic*).

Cincinnatus of the Americans. A title bestowed upon George Washington (1732–1799), because of his resemblance to Lucius Quintus Cincinnatus (fl. 456 B.C.), a hero of the Roman Republic and a pattern of virtue and probity. Byron, in his *Ode to Napoleon*, calls Washington the "Cincinnatus of the West."

Cinderella and the Glass Slipper. " This pretty tale of a ' little cinder girl ' comes to us from the French ; but the translator made a curious mistake, which has been so long current in English that it seems like sacrilege to disturb it. In the original the slipper is described as *pantoufle en vair*, that is, a slipper made of fur (*vair*). The translator, being more familiar with the sound than the sense, read this as if it were *verre*, that is, glass ; and the *glass* slipper, we suppose, will remain for ever a part of the story."— Edwards's *Dictionary of Words, Facts, and Phrases*.

Cinque-Cento. A name applied to the style of art and literature that arose in Italy about the year 1500 A.D., and prevailed during the sixteenth century. It is frequently used in the same sense as the word *renaissance*, and denotes the period characterized by the revival of classical taste. Among the great Italian artists and writers of the sixteenth century (known as *Cinquecentisti*) may be mentioned Leonardo da Vinci, Michael Angelo, Raphael, Correggio, Titian, Benvenuto Cellini, Ariosto, Tasso, Giovanni Rucellai, and Macchiavelli.

The expression *cinque-cento* is the Italian for " five hundred " ; in reality, it is a contraction for " one thousand five hundred."

Cinq-Mars, Conspiracy of. A conspiracy entered into in 1642 by Cinq-Mars, a brilliant young noble and favorite of Louis XIII (1610–1643) of France, the Duke of Orleans (brother of the king), and several other ambitious nobles, for the purpose of murdering Cardinal Richelieu. United with this was a larger plot with Spain, to overcome the cardinal by force of arms. It is said that the King secretly encouraged the conspiracy,— being anxious to rid himself of his imperious minister. The plot, however, was discovered, and Cinq-Mars, with his friend de Thou, was beheaded at Lyons. The infamous Duke of Orleans turned king's evidence ; his life was spared, but he was commanded to retire from court. Alfred de Vigny (1799–1863) has woven this story into the well-known historical romance, *Cinq-Mars*.

Cinque Ports. The name originally given to five seaport towns on the south coast of England (in Sussex and Kent). They are Hastings, Romney, Hythe, Dover, and Sandwich. Winchelsea and Rye were added afterwards. The original Cinque Ports were created by William the Conqueror (1066–1087), and special privileges were granted to them in consideration of their providing a certain number of ships-of-war, when required. Their control was placed in the hands of certain barons, called " wardens." The governor was entitled Lord-Warden. This, however, is at present only an honorary dignity, its peculiar jurisdiction having been abolished in 1855.

Cipango (*written also Zipangi, Zipangri*). The name of a marvelous island in the eastern seas, described by Marco Polo (1252-1324 A.D.), the Venetian traveler, and sought for in vain by Christopher Columbus and other early navigators. Wild and fantastic tales were told of its wealth and beauty. By many it is supposed to be the same as Japan.

Cipher Despatches. The result of the presidential election of 1876 was long in doubt, and depended upon the electoral votes of four States,—South Carolina, Florida, Louisiana, and Oregon. This entire number was needed by Mr. Hayes, the Republican candidate, while one vote only was necessary to secure the election of Mr. Tilden, the Democratic candidate. While awaiting the result, many despatches in cipher passed between Tilden and his friends, relative to the States in dispute. These were translated and printed by the New York *Tribune* in 1877, and suggested attempted bribery. The charges were investigated by a committee of Congress, which declared that Mr. Tilden was not implicated in the affair. On October 16th, 1878, Tilden published a card in which he publicly disclaimed all knowledge of the despatches.

Circe. In classic mythology, the daughter of Helios (the Sun) and Perse. She was a famous sorceress, and lived in the island of Ææa,—surrounded by numbers of people whom she had changed, by her incantations, into animal forms. When Ulysses, in the course of his wanderings after the fall of Troy, reached this island, the enchantress turned 22 of his companions into swine ; but Ulysses, through the influence of an herb given him by Mercury, sought out the sorceress, remained unharmed by her spells, and forced her to restore his comrades to their original condition.

Circe of the Revolution. An appellation bestowed upon Madame Roland (1754-1793), on account of her fascinating manners. She was one of the leaders of the Girondists, and was called the "inspiring soul" of the party. She suffered death by the guillotine, November 9th, 1793, and her last words, according to the popular statement, were : "O Liberty ! what crimes are committed in thy name !"

Circumnavigation of Globe. On August 10th, 1519, Ferdinand Magellan, a Portuguese navigator in the service of Spain, set sail from Seville with five ships, carrying 237 men, for the purpose of reaching the Moluccas or Spice Islands by sailing to the west. On November 28th, 1520, after a year and a quarter of anxious search, he passed through the strait that now bears his name, and entered the Pacific Ocean, across which he sailed for 12,-000 miles without seeing inhabited land. Magellan was killed in a conflict in the Philippine Islands on April 17th, 1521, but his lieutenant, Sebastian del Cano, reached San Lucar, near Seville, in the *Vittoria*, the only remaining ship of the five, on September 7th, 1522. The *Vittoria* was the first vessel to circumnavigate the globe, and accomplished the journey in a trifle over three years. Draper in his *History of the Intellectual Development of Europe*, regards this act of circumnavigation as the grandest achievement in the history of the human race. See *Drake's Circumnavigation of Globe*.

"Of all armorial bearings ever granted for the accomplishment of a great and daring deed, his [del Cano's] were the proudest and noblest—the globe of the earth belted with the inscription : 'Primus circumdedisti me !' "—Draper's *History of the Intellectual Development of Europe*.

Circus Maximus. A famous circus in ancient Rome—now a heap of ruins —situated between the Palatine and Aventine Hills. It was erected by Tarquin the Elder in 605 B.C. ; enlarged by Julius Cæsar, so as to accommodate 150,000 persons ; and rebuilt by Augustus. During the reign of Vespasian (69–79 A.D.), it was again rebuilt with a capacity sufficient for 400,000 spectators. It was surrounded by a canal ten feet wide and ten feet deep, and could easily be flooded for naval exhibitions.

Cirque, Le (*Fr. The Circus*).—A superb natural curiosity near Gavernie, a frontier village of France, in the department of Hautes-Pyrénées. It consists of an immense semicircular rock-formation, having lofty precipitous sides, the centre being filled with débris from the neighboring cliffs.

Cisalpine Republic. Founded by the French in May, 1797. It was formed from the Cispadane and Transpadane republics, and comprised the territories of Milan, Mantua, Modena, Bergamo, Ferrara, Bologna, Ravenna, etc., in northern Italy. The republic had a territory of over 16,000 square miles and a population of 3½ millions, and was acknowledged by the Emperor of Germany in the treaty of Campo Formio. In 1798, it received a new constitution, and, in 1802, took the name of the Italian Republic and chose Napoleon Bonaparte for president. In March, 1805, a deputation from the republic conferred upon the Emperor Napoleon I the title of king ; after which the Italian republic formed the kingdom of Italy. In 1814, after the fall of Napoleon, it was ceded to Austria by the Congress of Vienna. See *Cispadane Republic.*

Cispadane Republic. A republic, south of the Po, formed by Napoleon Bonaparte, in 1796. In the following year (1797), it was united with the Transpadane Republic to form the Cisalpine Republic. See *Cisalpine Republic; Transpadane Republic.*

Cities of Refuge. The name given to six cities appointed by the Mosaic law as places of refuge for those guilty of unintentional manslaughter. These cities were Kedesh, Shechem, and Hebron on the west side of the Jordan, and Bezer, Ramoth-Gilead, and Golan on the east side. Within the walls of each of these cities or for 1000 yards around it, the homicide was safe from his enemy, but he was not released from banishment until the death of the high-priest.

Cities of the Plain. The name given to Sodom and Gomorrah and other cities in the plain of the Jordan, which, on account of their wickedness, are said to have been destroyed by fire and brimstone from heaven. According to the commonly received account, their sites were overwhelmed by the waters of the Dead Sea. See *Dead Sea.*

Citizen King. A name given to Louis Philippe (1830–1848), who was chosen by the people as constitutional ruler of France. He was called to the throne, not as " King of France," but as " King of the French," to show that he ruled, not by divine right, but by the will of the people. See *King of the French.*

City Destroyed by Silence. See *Amyclæan Silence.*

City of Brotherly Love (*Gr. φιλα-δελφία, brotherly love*). The city of Philadelphia is often so called, with reference to the literal meaning of the word.

City of Churches. A name popularly given to the Borough of Brooklyn, New York City, on account of the unusually large number of churches that it contains in proportion to its population. It is claimed, however, that Cincinnati holds the first place in this respect, at present,—Brooklyn being relegated to the fifth.

City of David. A name given to the city of Jerusalem by King David (1055–1015 B.C.), who, in 1049 B.C., wrested it from the Jebusites, and made it the religious and political centre of his kingdom. The expression " city of David," found in *Luke* ii, 11, refers to Bethlehem in Judea, the reputed birthplace of David.

City of Destruction. In Bunyan's *Pilgrim's Progress*, the name given to the city where Christian dwelt, and whence he started on his pilgrimage to the Celestial City. It typifies the worldly and unconverted state of man.

City of Elms. A popular appellation bestowed upon the city of New Haven, Connecticut, on account of the noble elms with which many of its principal streets are shaded. See *Elm City*.

City of God. The name of a famous religious treatise by St. Augustine (354-430 A.D.), entitled in Latin, *De Civitate Dei*. It was written, after the sack of Rome by Alaric, to refute the assertion that the disasters that had befallen the Empire were due to the abandonment of the national deities and the adoption of the Christian religion. The book was commenced in 413 and completed in 426, and is generally considered to be St. Augustine's greatest work.

City of Homes. A surname given to the city of Philadelphia, Pa., on account of the relatively large number of private dwellings it contains.

City of Intelligence. A title conferred upon the city of Berlin, Prussia, in allusion to the high degree of culture possessed by its inhabitants.

City of Magnificent Distances. A name given to Washington, D. C., the capital of the United States, in allusion to the vast scale on which it was laid out by the French military engineer, L'Enfant, in anticipation of its becoming a great metropolis. The plan of the city covers an area 4½ miles long by 2½ miles broad, embracing nearly 9½ square miles. A relatively small portion of this is, as yet, built upon. The city is traversed by two sets of streets, from 70 to 100 feet in width, at right angles to one another. Across

their geometric regularity run 21 diagonal avenues, from 120 to 160 feet in width. Washington is sometimes spoken of as " the city of Philadelphia griddled across the city of Versailles."

City of Masts. A title frequently bestowed upon London, England, on account of the vast extent of its commerce.

City of Notions. A name by which Boston, the capital of Massachusetts, is sometimes known.

City of Palaces. A name given to Genoa, Italy, in allusion to the many palaces with which the city is adorned. As Genoa is built upon rising ground, these structures present an imposing appearance when seen from the harbor.

The term *City of Palaces* has also been applied to ancient Rome, Calcutta, modern Paris, and Edinburgh.

" 'The Superb' and the ' City of Palaces ' are names which Genoa has held for centuries. She is full of palaces, certainly, and the palaces are sumptuous inside, but they are very rusty without, and make no pretensions to architectural magnificence."—*Innocents Abroad* (Mark Twain).

City of Peace. An appellation bestowed upon the city of Jerusalem, the most ancient name of which was Salem, meaning *peace*. The term *City of Peace* has also been applied to Bagdad, the capital of the Abbasside dynasty.

City of Rocks. An appellation conferred upon the city of Nashville, Tennessee.

City of Smoke. A name sometimes given to the city of London, England, in allusion to its grimy, smoky atmosphere.

City of Spindles. A term popularly applied to the city of Lowell, Massachusetts. It runs a million spindles in its cotton mills, making 145,000 miles of cotton cloth annually, and employing for this purpose over 25,000 operatives.

City of the Golden Gate. A popular designation of the city of San Francisco, California,— so named because of its proximity to the Golden Gate, a narrow strait connecting the bay of San Francisco·with the Pacific Ocean.

City of the Great King. The city of Jerusalem is so called in the *Old* and *New Testaments.* See *Psalms* xlviii, 2 ; *Matthew* v, 35.

City of the Prophet. A name often given to the city of Medina in Arabia, where Mohammed took refuge after his flight from Mecca, on September 13th, 622 A.D. This " flight " is known in history as the *Hegira*, and constitutes an important epoch in chronology. The tomb of Mohammed is at Medina. See *Hegira ; Tomb of Mohammed.*

City of the Sea. A name frequently given to the city of Venice, for reasons too obvious to require specification.

City of the Seven Hills. Rome is frequently so called on account of the seven hills upon and around which the ancient city was built, and which were enclosed within the line of fortifications erected by Servius Tullius. The names of these hills are as follows : Palatinus, Capitolinus, Quirinalis, Cælius, Aventinus, Viminalis, and Esquilinus. The title *City of the Seven Hills* is also given to Constantinople, for a similar reason.

City of the Straits. An appellation given to Detroit, Michigan, from its situation on the strait, or river, connecting Lake Erie with Lake St. Clair.

City of the Sun.
(1) An appellation often bestowed upon the city of Baalbek in Syria,— now a heap of ruins. The word Baalbek means the " City of Baal," the sun-god. See *Baalbek.*
(2) The name of a philosophic romance by Tomasso Campanella (1568–1639), an Italian philosopher and Dominican monk. It describes a city placed in an ideal republic, and is similar to the *Republic* of Plato, the *Utopia* of Sir Thomas More, and the *Atlantis* of Francis Bacon.

City of the Three Kings. A name given to the city of Cologne, Germany, as being the reputed burial-place of the " Three Kings," " Magi," or " Wise Men," who came to Bethlehem to offer gifts to the infant Jesus. According to the legend, their bones were brought from Milan to Cologne by the Emperor Frederick Barbarossa in 1162, and presented to the Archbishop of Cologne. The skulls of these " Magi," crowned with diamonds, with their names inscribed in rubies, are shown to visitors to the cathedral. See *Balthazar ; Cologne, Three Kings of.*

City of the Violated Treaty. A sobriquet bestowed upon the city of Limerick, Ireland, in allusion to the repeated violations of a treaty signed October, 1691,— the first article of which stipulated that the Roman Catholics of the city of Limerick should be granted such freedom in the exercise of their religion as they had enjoyed in the reign of Charles II (1660–1685). This provision was adhered to by William III (1689–1702), but was disregarded by Queen Anne (1702–1714).

City of the Violet Crown. An appellation bestowed upon the city of Athens by the ancient Athenians. The origin of the term is in dispute, and is variously explained. According to some authorities, the violet was the favorite flower of the Athenians, and thus became the symbol of the city. Aristophanes, in his *Equites* and *Acharnians*, speaks of Athens as the " Violet - Crowned." According to others, Ion (the Greek for *violet*) was a king of Athens, and Athens was, in consequence, Ion's city, the violet city, the city of King Ion, or the city of King Violet. The statement that the expression—" City of the Violet Crown "—is derived from the fact that Athens was the principal city in Europe of the *Ion*-ian race is too absurd to merit serious consideration.

City of the West. A name given to the city of Glasgow, Scotland, in allusion to its situation near the western coast.

City of Victory. A title conferred upon the city of Cairo, Egypt. Its Arabic name, *El Kahira*, means *The Victorious*.

Civil List. A term applied to the annual sum settled on the English Crown by Parliament, in lieu of the ancient income derived from the possessions of the sovereign. This grant originated in the reign of William and Mary (1689–1702), and included the entire expenses of the government, exclusive of the army and navy and the interest on the national debt. The Civil List, at present, includes only the household expenses of the Crown, and was fixed in 1837 at £385,000, on the accession of Queen Victoria (1837–1901), who, in consideration of this yearly sum, together with £1200 annually for pensions " to those who have just claims on the royal bounty," surrendered the hereditary revenues of the Crown. The entire revenue of Elizabeth (1558–1603) did not exceed £600,000, while that of Charles I (1625–1649) was about £800,000. In 1689, the Civil List revenue of William and Mary amounted to £700,000. The Civil List of George II (1727–1760) was increased to £800,000, while that of George III (1760–1820), in 1815, reached the sum of £1,030,000.

Civil-Service Reform. The first definite steps towards a reform of the Civil Service of the United States were taken by President Grant, who, in 1870, asked assistance from Congress for that purpose. An act passed by Congress on March 3rd, 1871, enabled the President on January 1st, 1872, to appoint a Civil-Service Commission, which instituted competitive examinations for appointments and promotions in certain departments of the service. The reform was opposed by politicians generally ; and Congress, in 1873, refused to appropriate the sum of $25,000 necessary to carry on the work. In 1877, President Hayes appointed the Jay Commission, whose report led to the removal of Collector Arthur and Naval Officer Cornell of the port of New York. The Pendleton Bill—the principal feature of which was open competitive examinations—was passed by Congress, and received the President's signature on January 16th, 1883. The total number of persons in the classified Civil Service is at present about 84,000. The name of George William Curtis will always be held in fond remembrance by the friends of Civil-Service Reform in the United States.

Clan-na-Gael (*Brotherhood of Gaels*). An Irish Fenian society founded in Philadelphia in 1881, and known in secret as the " United Brotherhood." It belonged to the Irish National League in the United States, of which it was the extreme radical wing, and had for its object the liberation of Ireland from the rule of Great Britain. See *Fenians*.

Clans of Scotland. Said to have arisen in Scotland about 1008 A.D., during the reign of Malcolm II (1003–1033). In 1747, as a result of the Rebellion of 1745, the legal power of the chiefs was abolished, and liberty was granted to the clansmen. In addition to his badge, each chief of a clan wears two eagle's feathers in his bonnet.

The following list of all the known clans of Scotland, together with the badge worn by each clan, is taken from Haydn's *Dictionary of Dates*:

Name.	*Badge.*
Buchanan	Birch.
Cameron	Oak.

Name.	Badge.
Campbell	Myrtle.
Chisholm	Alder.
Colquhoun	Hazel.
Cumming	Common Sallow.
Drummond	Holly.
Farquharson	Purple Foxglove.
Ferguson	Poplar.
Forbes	Broom.
Frazer	Yew.
Gordon	Ivy.
Graham	Laurel.
Grant	Cranberry heath.
Gun	Rosewort.
Lamont	Crab-apple tree.
McAlister	Five-leaved heath.
McDonald	Bell heath.
McDonnell	Mountain heath.
McDougall	Cypress.
McFarlane	Cloudberry bush.
McGregor	Pine.
McIntosh	Boxwood.
McKay	Bulrush.
McKenzie	Deer-grass.
McKinnon	St. John's-wort.
McLachlan	Mountain-ash.
McLean	Blackberry heath.
McLeod	Red whortleberries.
McNab	Rose blackberries.
McNeil	Seaware.
McPherson	Variegated boxwood.
McQuarrie	Blackthorn.
McRae	Fir-club moss.
Menzies	Ash.
Munro	Eagle's feathers.
Murray	Juniper.
Ogilvie	Hawthorn.
Oliphant	Great Maple.
Robertson	Fern or brechans.
Rose	Briar-rose.
Ross	Bearberries.
Sinclair	Clover.
Stewart	Thistle.
Sutherland	Cat's-tail grass.

Clarence. The name given to a single- or double-seated four-wheeled carriage, usually having a glass front and a driver's seat outside. It was so called, in honor of the Duke of Clarence [afterwards William IV (1830–1837)], with whom it was a favorite vehicle.

Clarendon, Constitutions of. A series of laws enacted by a general council of the nobles and prelates of England, at Clarendon in Wiltshire, on January 25th, 1164, during the reign of Henry II (1154–1189). They were sixteen in number, and sought to limit the power of the clergy as well as to bring clerical offenders under secular jurisdiction. These "Constitutions" were unanimously adopted, and were signed, although reluctantly, by Becket, Archbishop of Canterbury. Pope Alexander III (1159–1181) having refused to ratify them, Becket withdrew his consent, and thus paved the way to the memorable quarrel between himself and the King. The Constitutions of Clarendon were annulled by the Pope, and finally ignored by the King in 1174.

Clarendon Press. The name formerly given to the press of the University of Oxford. The original building was erected by Sir John Vanbrugh in 1711–1713, the expense having been defrayed by the profits derived from the sale of Lord Clarendon's *History of the Rebellion*. A new printing-office was built in 1825–1830. Since 1830, the Clarendon Press has been known as the University Press.

Claret. The red wine, so called, does not derive its name from its color, but owes its designation to the French word *clair* (*clear*) given to it because it is a clarified wine. The term is now used in England and America as a general name for the red wines of Bordeaux; but, in this sense, it is unknown in France.

Classics. Servius Tullius, in 573 B.C., divided the citizens of Rome into six classes, the first and most influential of which were called *Classici*. The word was afterwards figuratively applied to authors of the first rank, as early as the second century after Christ. The term "classics," as now used, refers to productions in art or literature, in ancient or modern times, that are regarded as models worthy of imitation. In a narrower sense, the term refers to the most famous writers of Greece and Rome, and as thus used is almost synonymous with the word "ancient."

Claude Lorraine. The name given to Claude Gelée (1600–1682), the famous French landscape painter, who was born at the Château-de-Chamage in Lorraine.

Thomas, in his *Dictionary of Biography and Mythology*, writes the name Claude Lorrain, and says : "The last part of this name is often incorrectly written *Lorraine*. It should be remembered that it is an *adjective*, agreeing with Claude, in the masculine gender, which is always without the final *e*. The whole name signifies 'Claude the Lorrainer.' In case we should say Claude of Lorraine, it should then be written with the *e*, as reference is made to the province of Lorraine, which is feminine."

Clayton-Bulwer Treaty. See *Bulwer-Clayton Treaty*.

Clementines and Urbanists. The respective names given to the followers of Clement VII, pope in Avignon, and Urban VI, pope in Rome. In 1378, Pope Gregory XI (1370–1378) restored the papal seat from Avignon to Rome, and died almost immediately afterwards. Urban VI was thereupon elected ; but the French cardinals, supported by the king of France and the Angevin queen of Naples, rebelled and chose Clement VII. France, Spain, and Scotland adhered to Clement, and Rome, Italy, and England to Urban. The schism was terminated in 1447 by the election of Pope Alexander V, and the resignation of his rival, Felix V, two years later.

Cleopatra and the Pearl. It is related that, at a banquet given by Cleopatra in honor of Mark Antony, the triumvir was so overcome by the magnificence of the occasion, that he could not refrain from expressing his surprise ; whereupon the Egyptian queen, taking a pearl of great value, dissolved it in acid and drank to the health of the Roman, saying as she did so : "My draught to Antony shall far exceed it." It is difficult, however, to imagine an acid sufficiently powerful to dissolve a pearl, and yet sufficiently harmless to form a beverage.

Brewer, in his *Dictionary of Phrase and Fable*, thus ingeniously disposes of the difficulty : " . . . the pearl was sold to some merchant whose name was synonymous with a strong acid, and the money given to Antony as a present by the fond queen. The pearl melted, and Cleopatra drank to the health of Antony as she handed him the money."

Cleopatra's Needles. A name improperly given to two famous obelisks erected by Thothmes III at On (Heliopolis) about 1500 B.C., and brought to Alexandria by Augustus about 23 B.C., to add to the beauty of the city. One of these granite monoliths now stands on the Victoria Embankment in London, while the other occupies a commanding position in Central Park, New York. See *Obelisk in London ; Obelisk in New York ; Victoria Embankment.*

Clerks of the Revels. The name given to an incorporated society that once existed in Paris, and was charged with the duty of regulating the public amusements. As the society known as the "Fraternity of the Passion" had obtained the royal privilege to produce the *Mysteries*, the Clerks of the Revels were obliged to invent a new series of plays, termed the *Moralities*, in which the *dramatis personæ* were personifications of the virtues and vices. According to some authorities, modern comedy owes its origin to the Clerks of the Revels. See *Moralities ; Mysteries.*

Clermont. The name of the first successful vessel in the world, propelled by steam. She was designed by the inventor, Robert Fulton (1765–1815), and launched in September, 1807. The *Clermont* made the trip from New York to Albany—a distance of about 150 miles — in 32 hours ; but the time, owing to improvements in the machinery, was reduced, in 1817, to 18 hours. Although the idea of steam navigation had been previously conceived by others, Fulton is generally admitted to have been the first to successfully realize it. See *Fulton's Folly*.

Clichy. The name of a debtors' prison that once existed in Paris, and was situated in the Rue de Clichy. It is now demolished, and with it has passed away imprisonment for debt.

Climacteric Years. The name given to certain years, in a man's life, that were long believed to be of peculiar significance to him, as turning-points in his health and fortune. These are the mystic number 7 and its multiples with odd numbers (*e. g.*, 21, 35, 49, 63). The most important of all was the 63rd year, which was considered fatal to most men. It consists of three times three multiplied by seven — all sacred numbers,—and is known as the " Grand Climacteric." See *Grand Climacteric*.

Clinton's Ditch. An expression formerly applied, in derision, to the Erie Canal, which connects the Hudson River with the Great Lakes, on account of the zeal manifested in its construction by De Witt Clinton, then Governor of New York, in the face of a determined opposition. See *Erie Canal*.

Clio. In classic mythology, one of the nine Muses. She presided over history. See *Muses*.

Clio. A sobriquet bestowed upon Joseph Addison (1672–1719) by his admirers, because his most delightful papers to the *Spectator* were signed by one or other of the letters forming this word. These letters are supposed by many to refer to the places where the essays were written, namely, Chelsea, London, Islington, and the Office ; but the notion that Addison meant to adopt the name of the Muse of History is the one that has generally prevailed.

Cliquot. A nickname given by the London *Punch* to Frederick William IV (1840–1861) of Prussia, on account of his fondness for champagne of that brand.

Cloaca Maxima. A famous sewer of ancient Rome, leading from the lower part of the Forum to the Tiber. It was built by Tarquinius Priscus and his successors about 600 B.C., and is still in a perfect state of preservation, although 2500 years old. The Cloaca Maxima was originally 12 feet high and 11 feet wide ; but one-third is at present choked with mud. Strabo (60 B.C.–24 A.D.) said that it was large enough to admit a wagon loaded with hay, and Pliny (23–79 A.D.) declared that it had existed for 700 years.

Clock-Tower of Berne. A tower in the city of Berne, Switzerland, famous for its mechanical clock, which, at the striking of the hours, presents an interesting pantomimic display. Three minutes before the hour, a cock crows and flaps its wings ; several bears march around a seated figure of Time, which thereupon reverses an hourglass, raises its sceptre, and opens its mouth as often as the clock strikes; while the bear on the right inclines its head. The cock once more crows and flaps its wings, and the performance is at an end. This clock-tower was originally a watch-tower, and stood at the eastern extremity of the city ; but is now in the centre of the town.

Clotho. See *Fates*.

Clouds. The name of a famous comedy by Aristophanes (444–380 B.C.). It is a powerful satire against the Sophists, and was written in 423 B.C.

" In this play he [Aristophanes] ridiculed and misrepresented Socrates, whom he unjustly confounded with the Sophists. Plato, in his ' Apology,' identifies Aristophanes with the accusers of Socrates, and with those who excited the popular prejudice against him as a sceptic and a corrupter of the youth."—Lippincott's *Biographical Dictionary*.

Clovis in Battle. It is related by Gregory of Tours, in his *Historia Francorum*, that as Clovis, King of the Franks, was setting forth to battle against Alaric II the Arian, King of the Visigoths, in 507 A.D., he was met by St. Hilary, who had been dead nearly 150 years. The pontiff was still a relentless adversary of the Arians, and cried aloud, " Up, Clovis, and delay not, for as captain of the Lord's hosts am I come to thee this day, and the God of battles will deliver the foe into thy hands." Clovis, confident of victory, advanced against the Visigoths, slew Alaric, and won a signal triumph.

Cnidian Venus. See *Venus of Cnidus.*

Coal-Area of the World. The following table gives the area of the world's coal-fields in square miles:

China and Japan	200,000
United States	194,000
India	35,000
Russia	27,000
Great Britain	9,000
Germany	3,600
France	1,800
Belgium, Spain, etc.	1,400

"The coal-fields of China, Japan, Great Britain, Germany, Russia, and India contain apparently 303,080,000,000 tons, which is enough for 700 years at present rate of consumption. If to the above be added the coal-fields of the United States, Canada, and other countries, the supply will be found ample for 1000 years. Improved machinery has greatly increased the yield per miner, and thus produced a fall in price to the advantage of all industries."—*World Almanac.*

Coalitions against France. The term applied to the various unions effected by the nations of Europe to restrain the excesses of the French Revolution and limit the gigantic power of Napoleon Bonaparte. These coalitions were as follows:

(1) First Coalition, between Austria, Prussia, and Great Britain 1793
(2) Second Coalition, between Great Britain, Germany, Russia, Naples, Portugal, and Turkey...... 1799

(3) Third Coalition, between Great Britain, Russia, Austria, and Naples........................ 1805
(4) Fourth Coalition, between Great Britain, Russia, Prussia, and Saxony........................ 1806
(5) Fifth Coalition, between Great Britain and Austria................ 1809
(6) Sixth Coalition, between Russia and Prussia........................ 1813

Coast-Survey of the United States. A complete survey of the entire coast of the United States was first proposed by Professor Patterson in 1806. Albert Gallatin, Secretary of the Treasury, encouraged the project, and after consultation with various learned men, adopted the plans of Mr. F. R. Hassler, first superintendent of the Coast-Survey. In 1817, work was commenced on a small scale, and was carried on intermittently until 1844. Since this last date, work has been carried on much more systematically under Professor Bache and his successor, Professor Pierce. Nine States on the Atlantic seaboard were reached by the Coast-Survey in 1844 ; 13 States in 1845 ; 15 in 1846 ; and 18 in 1847. Since then, this work has been extended to the Pacific coast, to Alaska, and through the Great Lakes. The entire work is under the control of the Treasury Department.

Cobden Club. Founded in England about 1866, to promulgate the free-trade doctrines of Richard Cobden (1804–1865). It consists of about 1000 members. The first dinner was held on July 21st, 1866, with Right Honorable William Ewart Gladstone in the chair. Several American statesmen and students of economics are honorary members of the club.

Cock-and-Bull Story. This expression—as applied to a highly exaggerated account of a trifling affair—is probably derived from the custom, in the old fables, of endowing cocks, bulls, and other animals with the power of speech. According to another version, the papal bulls were so named on account of the *bulla* or seal attached to them. This seal bore the impression of St. Peter accompanied by the cock. Accordingly, after the Reformation, any tale that was considered of little moment was placed on a par with a papal bull, and became known as a " cock-and-bull story."

Cockerel Church. A Methodist Episcopal church on Hanover Street, Boston, Massachusetts. It was so named from having a rooster for a vane on its spire. The opening lines of the dedicatory hymn, written for this church by N. P. Willis, are as follows :

> " The perfect world by Adam trod,
> Was the first temple, built by God ;
> His fiat laid the corner-stone,
> And heaved its pillars, one by one."

Cock-Eye. A nickname bestowed upon General Benjamin F. Butler (1818–1893) by his soldiers during the Civil War, on account of one of his eyes being afflicted with strabismus.

Cock Lane Ghost. The name given to a hoax perpetrated in London in 1762, by one William Parsons, his wife, and daughter, at their house, 33 Cock Lane. According to the account, a luminous figure resembling Mrs. Kemt, a deceased lady that once resided in the house, was seen, while certain knockings and scratchings were heard every night in the room formerly occupied by her. Suspicions as to Mr. Kemt having murdered his wife were at once aroused and were confirmed by the ghost, which, on being interrogated, replied in the affirmative by knockings, as is the way with spirits at the present day. The Duke of York, Dr. Johnson, Horace Walpole, and others visited the house and investigated the affair. An examination proved it to be a conspiracy on the part of Parsons and his wife, for the purpose of extorting money from Mr. Kemt. They were tried for imposture and defamation of character, and were condemned to the pillory and imprisonment on July 10th, 1762.

Cockney. A familiar name for a Londoner. It is as old as the twelfth century, being found in some verses attributed to Hugh Bagot, Earl of Norfolk, in the reign of Henry II (1154–1189). The origin of the word is in dispute. Wedgwood, in his *Dictionary of Etymology*, says that " the original meaning of cockney is a child too delicately nurtured—one kept in the house and not hardened by out-door life ; hence applied to citizens as opposed to the hardier inhabitants of the country, and in modern times confined to the citizens of London." According to Camden, the river Thames was once known as the Cockney, and hence a cockney means simply one born on the banks of the Thames. The French, at an early period, called the English *cocagne* men, *i. e., bon-vivants*, beef-and-pudding men.

According to a commonly received definition, a cockney is a person born within sound of Bow-Bells, *i. e.*, the bells of St. Mary-le-Bow, Cheapside. See *Bow-Bells ; Cheapside.*

Cockpit of Europe. A name given to Belgium, because it has been the scene of a greater number of important battles than any other country in Europe. Among these may be mentioned Oudenarde, Ramillies, Fontenoy, Fleurus, Jemappes, Ligny, Quatre-Bras, and Waterloo.

Cocksure. Said by some to be a corruption of the French phrase *à coup sûr*, meaning *certainly, without doubt*. Others declare it to be an abbreviation of *cocky sure* (*sure in a cock-like way*), *i. e.*, in the manner of a barnyard fowl.

Cocytus. In classic mythology, one of the five rivers of the lower regions,—the other four being Acheron, Lethe, Phlegethon, and Styx. Homer makes the Cocytus a tributary of the Styx ; Virgil represents the Acheron as flowing into the Cocytus. Cocytus means the " river of weeping," because " into this river fall the tears of the wicked."

"*Cocytus*, named of lamentation loud,
Heard on the rueful stream."
Paradise Lost, ii, 579.

Code Napoléon. The name given to a great body of law—civil, criminal, and commercial—prepared by order of Napoleon I, and promulgated between 1804 and 1810. It superseded the ancient laws of France, and remains the legal code until this day. The *Code Napoléon* consists of five parts, as follows: (1) the *Code Civil*; (2) the *Code de Procédure Civile*; (3) the *Code de Commerce*; (4) the *Code d'Instruction Criminelle*; and (5) the *Code Pénal*. These parts were independent of one another, although prepared on the same general plan. The *Code Napoléon* has become a model for a large number of continental codes, viz., for those of Belgium, Italy, and Greece. The provinces of the Rhine, upon which this code was originally imposed by force, still use it as the basis of legislation. Napoleon considered the Code his most enduring monument, and declared that he should go down to posterity with it in his hand. Previous to the Revolution, each province in France had its own set of laws,—a condition of affairs which drew from Voltaire the witty remark that in traveling through France a person changed laws oftener than horses. The *Code Napoléon* has been rechristened, under the Republic, the *Code Civil*.

Code of Justinian. The name of a famous code of laws — the most celebrated of ancient times—prepared during the reign of the Emperor Justinian (527–565 A.D.), and so named in his honor. This code was completed in fourteen months by the learned Tribonian, assisted by a commission of ten persons, and was promulgated in 529. It incorporated the earlier codes of Gregorianus, Hermogenianus, and Theodosius. A revised edition of this work, with a number of new enactments of Justinian himself, was promulgated in 534, under the name of the *Codex Repe-

titæ Prælectionis. This is now known to us as the *Codex Justinianus*, and consists of twelve books. See *Basilica;* *Pandects of Justinian.*

Codex Alexandrinus. See *Alexandrian Codex.*

Codex Ephraemi. See *Ephraem Codex.*

Codex Sinaiticus. See *Sinaitic Codex.*

Codex Vaticanus. See *Vatican Codex.*

Codfish Aristocracy. A term originally applied to certain Massachusetts families that had grown wealthy from the cod fisheries. At present, the expression is used to denote people that make a vulgar display of recently acquired wealth, and are lacking in intelligence and refinement.

Coffins. According to Thucydides, the coffins of the Athenians were made of cedar, on account of its aromatic and incorruptible qualities. The Romans frequently used coffins of marble and stone, sometimes of a peculiar kind of stone brought from Assos, in Troas, which was said to consume the entire body—the teeth excepted—in forty days, and was hence called *sarcophagus* (*flesh-eater*). In ancient Rome, it was the custom to bury the dead; but during the Empire and before the growth of Christianity, burning the dead became the fashion. Alexander the Great is said to have been buried in a golden coffin. The earliest mentioned wooden coffin in England was that of King Arthur, who, in 542, was buried in an entire trunk of oak, hollowed out. Patent coffins were invented in 1796, and airtight metallic coffins were introduced in 1861.

Cogito; ergo sum (*Lat. I think; therefore I am*). A famous axiom of Descartes, and the starting-point and first principle of his philosophy. See *Cartesian Philosophy.*

Cognac. A superior quality of French brandy, so called from the town of Cognac, France, where it was first distilled.

Cold Harbor, Battle of. A sanguinary contest during the Civil War (June 3rd, 1864), between the Union army under General Grant, and the Confederate forces under General Lee. The battle was fought a few miles from Richmond, Virginia, and resulted in a loss to the Union forces of nearly 15,000 men,—12,000 of whom are said to have been killed in half an hour. The Confederate loss was 1700. Although repulsed, Grant advanced his line somewhat, and held his new position. On the night of June 12th, the Union army fell back in the direction of the James River.

Colenso Controversy. John William Colenso (1814–1883), first bishop of Natal, published in 1862 the first part of his work on *The Pentateuch and the Book of Joshua Critically Examined,* in which he called in question the historical accuracy and the Mosaic authorship of the books cited. The second part of the work appeared in 1863. As a result he was censured by the bishops in convocation, and deposed by his metropolitan, Bishop Gray of Capetown. Colenso appealed from this judgment in 1865, whereupon the Privy Council declared the deposition to be " null and void in law." The bishops—constituting the council of the Colonial Bishoprics Fund —refused to pay Colenso his income, upon which he appealed to the Court of Chancery. That tribunal also declared in his favor, and ordered the bishop's income with all arrears to be paid, unless his accusers should bring him to trial for heresy. This they declined to do. Colenso continued to perform the duties of his office until his death in 1883.

Coliseum (*more properly, Colosseum*). The most famous amphitheatre of ancient Rome,— now a ruin. The Coliseum was commenced by Vespasian (69–79 A.D.) about 72 A.D., and completed by Titus (79–81 A.D.) in 80. It was elliptical in shape, covered about 5 acres, and had seats for 87,-000 spectators. Its greatest length was 615 feet and its greatest breadth 510 feet. The exterior of the Coliseum is 160 feet in height, and consists of four stories,—the first and second being respectively Doric and Ionic, and the two upper, Corinthian. For nearly 400 years the Coliseum was the scene of gladiatorial combats ; but in 405 these were abolished by the Emperor Honorius (395-423 A.D.). In 1750, Pope Benedict XIV (1740–1758) consecrated the Coliseum to the blood of the martyrs that had perished there. In the Middle Ages it served as a fortress, and for several centuries afterwards was used as a quarry from which stone was obtained for new buildings. It was originally called the *Flavian Amphitheatre* and received the name *Coliseum* either from its colossal size or from the Colossus of Nero, which stood in the square before the entrance. St. Ignatius was martyred there during the reign of Trajan (98-117 A.D.). It is said that, when the Coliseum was dedicated, 5000 wild beasts were slain in the arena—the games lasting for 100 days. See *Amphitheatres.*

Colleen Bawn. A term of endearment given to Eily O'Connor, the heroine of *The Collegians* (a novel by Gerald Griffin), and of *The Colleen Bawn* (a play by Dion Boucicault). The word " colleen " means *girl,* and " bawn," *blonde.* Hence the *Colleen Bawn* is the *blonde girl.*

College-Cheers. The following is a list of the college-cheers of some of the leading educational institutions in the United States :
Amherst.—" Rah! Rah! Rah! Rah! Rah ! Rah ! Amherst ! ''

Bowdoin. — " B-o-w-d-o-i-n, Rah, Rah, Rah ! "

Brown University.—" Rah ! Rah!— Rah ! Rah ! — Rah ! Rah ! — Brown, Brown, Brown — KIYI, KIYI, KIYI — Hicki, Hicki, Hoorah!'' (three times).

Colgate University.—" Hip-Hu-rah! (twice), Colgate ! Colgate ! Rah-Rah-Rah ! Colgate ! "

College of the City of New York.— " 'Rah, 'Rah 'Rah ! C. C. N. Y."

Columbia University.—" 'Ray, 'Ray, 'Ray, C-o-l-u-m-b-i-a ! "

Cornell University. — " Cornell ! I Yell, Yell, Yell ! Cornell ! "

Dartmouth.—" Wah hoo wah! wah hoo wah ! da-da-da, Dartmouth ! wah hoo wah ! T-i-g-e-r ! "

Hamilton. — " Rah ! rah ! rah ! Ham-il-ton ! Zip ! rah ! boom ! "

Harvard University.—" Rāh, rāh, rāh ! rāh, rāh, rāh ! rāh, rāh, rāh !— Harvard ! "

Hobart.—" Hip, Ho-bart! Hip, Ho-bart ! Hip, Ho ! Hip, Ho ! Hip, Ho-bart ! "

Johns Hopkins University.—" Hullaballoo, Kanuck, Kanuck! Hullaballoo, Kanuck, Kanuck! Hoorah! J. H. U!''

Lafayette. — " Rah ! Rah ! Rah ! Lafayette ! "

Lehigh University.—" Hoo-rah-ray! Hoo-rah-ray! Ray, ray, ray, Lehigh, Lehigh, Lehigh ! "

Leland Stanford, Jr., University.— " Rah-Rah-Rah! (twice). Rah ! Rah! —Stanford ! "

New York University.—"Rah! Rah! Rah ! N. Y. U., Siss ! Boom ! Ah ! New York ! New York ! New York ! "

Oberlin.— " Hi, O!— Hi, O!— Hi! O! Hi! Hi! O! Hi, O-ber-lin! "

Princeton University. — " Hooray ! Hooray ! Hooray ! Tiger ! Siss ! Boom ! Ah ! Princeton ! "

Rutgers.—" Rah ! rah ! rah ! bow-wow-wow ! Rutgers ! "

Trinity.—" Trinity ! Trinity ! boom-rah ! boom-rah ! Trinity ! "

Union.—" Rah ! Rah ! Rah ! U-N-I-O-N Hikah ! Hikah ! Hikah ! "

University of Chicago.— " Chicago, Chicago, Chicago, go ! Go it, Chica-go it, Chica-go it, Chi-ca-go."

University of Michigan.—" U. of M, Hurrah ! Hurrah ! Hōō-ráh ! Hōō-ráh ! Michigan ! Michigan ! Michigan ! ráh ! ráh ! ráh ! "

University of Pennsylvania.—" Hoo-rah! Hoo-rah! Hoo-rah ! Penn-syl-va-ni-a ! "

U. S. Military Academy.—" Rah ! Rah! Ray! Rah! Rah! Ray! West Point ! West Point ! Armay! "

Wesleyan University.—" Rah ! Rah! Rah ! Rah ! Wes-ley-an-a ! Rah ! Rah ! Rah ! Rah ! Rah ! "

Yale University.—" Rah, Rah, Rah! Rah, Rah, Rah ! Rah, Rah, Rah ! Yale ! "

College-Colors.

Amherst.—Purple and white.

Bowdoin.—White.

Brown University. — Brown and white.

Colgate University. — Maroon and orange.

College of the City of New York.— Lavender.

Columbia University. — Light-blue and white.

Cornell University.—Carnelian and white.

Dartmouth.—Dark-green.

Hamilton. — Continental blue and buff.

Harvard University.—Crimson.

Johns Hopkins University. — Black and old-gold.

Lafayette.—Maroon and white.

Lehigh University. — Brown and white.

Leland Stanford, Jr., University.— Cardinal.

New York University.—Violet.

Oberlin.—Crimson and gold.

Princeton University.— Orange and black.

Rutgers.— Scarlet.

Trinity.—Dark-blue and old-gold.

Union.—Garnet.

University of Chicago.—Maroon.

University of Michigan.—Maize and blue.

University of Pennsylvania.— Red and blue.

U. S. Military Academy.—Black and gray.

Wesleyan University.—Cardinal and black.

Williams College.—Royal purple.

Yale University.—Dark-blue.

Colleges in the United States. There are in the United States nearly 450 institutions of learning either for males or for both sexes, and 200 for females alone. A list of 50 would include the principal ones. The oldest college is Harvard,— founded in 1636. It had its beginning at Newtown, Massachusetts, and was afterwards removed to Cambridge. Yale College was founded at Saybrook, Connecticut, in 1701, and removed to New Haven in 1717.

College Fraternities. There are, at present, 28 Greek-letter college societies in the United States, having about 1000 chapters and a membership of 100,000. These societies own 70 halls or houses in various college towns and cities. The oldest college fraternity is the *Kappa Alpha*, founded at Union College, Schenectady, in 1825. There are 11 women's college fraternities, the oldest — the *Kappa Alpha Theta*—having been founded in 1870. There are also 16 professional fraternities founded by professional schools attached to colleges. These fraternities have 50 active chapters and 3500 members. Local fraternities also exist.

College of Cardinals. See *Cardinals.*

Cologne Cathedral. One of the finest specimens of Gothic architecture in Europe, and by many considered to be the grandest ecclesiastical structure outside of Italy. The present edifice was founded in 1248, and the choir—the first part completed—was consecrated in 1322. The work progressed slowly until 1509, when it was suspended, and, during the subsequent centuries, the building was not kept in proper repair. The work of renovation was commenced in 1823; and in 1848 — 600 years after its foundation—the nave, aisles, and transepts of the church were finished. The cathedral, exclusive of the western spires, was completed in 1863. These last were finished in 1880, and on October 15th of the same year the completion of the great cathedral was celebrated with imposing ceremonies, in the presence of the Emperor William I (1871–1888). The church is 440 feet in length and 240 feet in width ; the height of the nave is 150 feet, while the spires attain an elevation of 515 feet above the pavement of the nave. The bell weighs 25 tons, and was cast from cannon taken from the French in 1870. It is estimated that $5,000,-000 have been expended on the building since 1823, and that the total cost has been $10,000,000.

Cologne, Three Kings of. A name sometimes given to the "Three Kings," " Magi," or " Wise Men," who came to Bethlehem to offer gifts to the infant Jesus. They are so called because their bones are said to repose in the cathedral at Cologne, — having been brought thither from Milan, and presented to the archbishop by Frederick Barbarossa in 1162. See *Balthazar ; City of the Three Kings ; Shrine of the Three Kings.*

Colophon. A city of Ionia in Asia Minor, famed for its cavalry, which, according to Strabo, was so redoubtable that its charge always decided the fate of a battle. On this account the Greek proverb, " to put the colophon to it," meant to terminate an affair; and, accordingly, in old books, any inscription or other device placed at the close, showing the title, writer's or printer's name, and date and place of writing, was called a *colophon.*

Colossus of Independence. An appellation bestowed upon John Adams (1735-1826), on account of his earnest and persistent efforts for colonial independence in the Continental Congress. He is sometimes styled the "Colossus of the Revolution."

Colossus of the Nineteenth Century. A sobriquet bestowed upon Napoleon Bonaparte (1769–1821), because of the colossal power wielded by him during the early part of the present century.

Colossus of Rhodes. A gigantic brass statue of Apollo, which formerly stood near the entrance to the harbor of Rhodes and was considered one of the "Seven Wonders of the World." It was the work of Chares of Lindus, a pupil of Lysippus, and was completed in 280 B.C., after 12 years' labor. Its height was variously estimated at from 90 to 120 feet. In 224 B.C.—56 years after its erection,—it was overthrown by an earthquake, and lay prostrate for centuries—the wonder of the place. When the Saracens captured Rhodes, the Colossus was sold, in 653 A.D., to a Jewish merchant from Edessa, for £36,000. It is said that the brass weighed 720,900 lbs., and, when cut up, required the services of 900 camels to carry it to Alexandria. According to tradition, the statue stood astride the entrance to the harbor of Rhodes, and ships in full sail were able to pass between its legs. This statement, however, is not verified by any of the ancient authors. See *Seven Wonders of the World.*

Columbaria. A name given, by the ancient Romans, to niches used as receptacles for urns holding the ashes of the dead. Each niche contained a pair of cinerary urns (*Lat. ollæ*), and above it were inscribed the names of the persons whose ashes were contained within. The term *columbaria* is derived from *columba* (*Latin for pigeon*), and was thus used on account of the resemblance which these receptacles bore to pigeon-holes. Several columbaria, in a good state of preservation, may be seen at Rome.

It is said that the ashes of favorite dogs were allowed a place in the *columbaria*, while the bodies of slaves were thrown into pits.

Columba's Isle. A name given to the island of Iona—the most famous of the Hebrides — because St. Columba (521–597) founded a monastery there about 563, and introduced Christianity into Scotland. Iona was formerly the burial-place of the Scottish kings. See *St. Columba.*

Columbia. A poetic designation of America, given to it in honor of Christopher Columbus (1440-1506), the discoverer of the New World. The name is, however, generally applied to the United States alone.

Columbiad. See *American Epic Poem.*

Columbian Exposition. Held at Chicago, in 1893, to celebrate the 400th anniversary of the discovery of America. The site of the Exposition covered 633 acres of ground on the shore of Lake Michigan. The 28 principal buildings occupied 142½ acres, while the structure devoted to manufactures and the liberal arts was the largest building in the world, and covered 30¼ acres ; 52 foreign nations participated officially in the Exposition, and appropriated over $6,000,000. The total number of paying visitors amounted to 27,529,400. On October 9th—Chicago Day — 761,942 persons attended the *World's Columbian Exposition.* The Exposition opened on May 1st and closed on October 30th The total receipts were $14,117,382. At the Paris Exposition of 1889, the total number of admissions was 32,354,111, and the total receipts $8,830,000. See *Paris Exposition of 1900.*

Column of July (*Fr. Colonne de Juillet*). A bronze column erected in the Place de la Bastille in Paris, in honor of those that fell in the Revolution of July, 1830. It stands on a massive substructure of white marble, and is 154 feet in height. The capital is crowned with a gilded figure of the Genius of Liberty, poised on one foot. The monument was dedicated, with appropriate ceremonies, by Louis Philippe (1830–1848) on July 28th, 1840. In the vaults beneath are buried the remains of the victims of the Revolutions of 1830 and 1848. It is said that during the Communist " reign of terror " in May, 1871, these vaults were filled with combustibles by the insurgents, for the purpose of destroying the column. Fortunately the attempt was unsuccessful. See *Place de la Bastille.*

Column of the Grand Army. A white marble column at Boulogne, France, erected by the soldiers of the Grand Army, in honor of Napoleon I, to commemorate his projected invasion of England. It is 166 feet in height, and is surmounted by a bronze statue of the Emperor in his coronation robes. The corner-stone was laid by Marshal Soult in 1804, and the work commenced by the Grand Army. See *Boulogne Flotilla.*

Column of Trajan. See *Trajan's Column.*

Column of Vendôme (*Fr. Colonne Vendôme*). A celebrated memorial column in the Place Vendôme in Paris, erected by order of Napoleon I in 1806–1810, to commemorate his victories in the Austro-Russian campaign of 1805. The column is modelled after that of Trajan at Rome, and is 143 feet in height — including the base — and 13 feet in diameter. It is constructed of masonry, and is covered with plates of bronze obtained by melting down 1200 Austrian and Russian cannon. These plates form a spiral band about 300 yards in length, and depict events in the campaign from the breaking up of camp at Boulogne to the battle of Austerlitz. The summit is crowned with a bronze statue of Napoleon in his imperial robes. The

monument was overthrown by the Communists in May, 1871, but the shattered fragments were preserved and the column re-erected in 1875.

Columns of Hercules. See *Pillars of Hercules.*

Columns of St. Mark. The name given to two granite columns standing on the quay of the Piazzetta, near the Doge's Palace, in Venice. They were brought from the Holy Land in 1120 by the Doge Domenico Michiele, and were originally three in number. One, however, was lost in the mud of the lagoon, and the two remaining ones lay prostrate for several years. They were finally reared by one Nicolo Barratiero, a noted gamester, who, in return for his services, was granted the singular privilege of carrying on games of chance in the space between the columns, although such games were prohibited by the laws of Venice. This privilege was, however, neutralized by ordering that all public executions should take place on this same spot. As a result, the superstitious Venetians avoided the place, and considered that even to cross it was ominous of misfortune. When Marino Faliero became doge, the gondoliers landed him between these two columns, and to this fact were attributed all his subsequent misfortunes.

One of the columns is crowned with the Lion of St. Mark — holding in his paw the *Gospel of St. Mark ;* the other is surmounted by a statue of St. Theodore,— the patron-saint of Venice before St. Mark,—erected in 1329. See *Lion of St. Mark ; St. Mark's Column ; St. Theodore's Column.*

Comédie Française. A society of French players, occupying the *Théâtre Français* in Paris. It was founded by Louis XIV (1643–1715) in 1680, and is the only institution of royal France that has survived the Revolution. The association ceased to exist in 1799, but was revived in 1803. It was reorganized by Napoleon I in 1812, and was further remodelled in 1850 and 1859. The *Comédie Française* has been devoted for years to the performance of the masterpieces of Voltaire, Corneille, Racine, and Molière ; and, in more recent times, to the productions of de Musset, Scribe, Legouvé, Dumas père, Dumas fils, and Victor Hugo. Among the famous actors and actresses that have been connected with the society may be named Talma, Mars, Rachel, Got, Delaunay, Coquelin, Mounet-Sully, Worms, Favart, Croizette, and Bernhardt. The *Comédie Française* celebrated its bicentenary in 1880. Its annual subvention is 240,-000 francs. See *Théâtre Français*.

Comedie Humaine. A series of novels projected by Honoré de Balzac (1799-1850), and designed to portray every phase of French society.

"After writing several other novels, he formed the design of presenting in the *Comédie Humaine* a complete picture of modern civilisation. All ranks, professions, arts, trades, all phases of manners in town and country, were to be represented in his imaginary system of things. In attempting to carry out this impossible design, he produced what is almost in itself a literature. The stories composing the *Comédie Humaine* are classified as 'Scènes de la Vie Privée, de la Vie Parisienne, de la Vie Politique, de la Vie Militaire,' &c. . . . Among the masterpieces which form part of Balzac's vast scheme may be mentioned *La Recherche de l'Absolu, Le Père Goriot, Les Illusions Perdues, Les Paysans, Les Marana, La Femme de trente Ans, Les Parents Pauvres,* and *Eugénie Grandet.*" — *Chambers's Encyclopædia.*

"Coming to the Scratch." This expression was originally used by boxers, and referred to the line or *scratch* made in the turf of the prizering, to divide it into two equal parts. "To come to the scratch," accordingly, meant to meet one's antagonist half-way.

Commentaries, Cæsar's. Narratives of the Gallic and Civil Wars, written by Julius Cæsar (100-44 B.C.). The Commentaries on the Gallic War consist of eight books—the first seven of which, entitled *De Bello Gallico*, were written by Cæsar himself ; while the eighth was probably prepared, under his direction, by his friend and fellow-soldier, Hirtius. In addition to the three Commentaries on the Civil War — entitled *De Bello Civile* — of which Cæsar was the author, there are three others, ascribed to Hirtius, treating of the Alexandrian, African, and Spanish Wars, respectively.

Committee of Public Safety. A committee appointed by the *National Convention*, during the French Revolution, on May 27th, 1793. It consisted of nine members, of whom Robespierre, Danton, and Barère were the most influential. Its deliberations were secret. It controlled the proceedings of the ministry ; acted with absolute power in all matters of urgency; and made weekly reports to the Convention. The severe rule of the Committee of Public Safety was termed the "Reign of Terror." It terminated with the overthrow of Robespierre and his associates, on July 28th, 1794. The Parisian communists established a similar committee in March–May, 1871.

Common, Boston. A famous public park in the city of Boston, containing about 48 acres. It is surrounded by an iron fence, and is laid out in sloping lawns and winding paths shaded by magnificent trees. The Common dates from the year 1634, and, according to the city charter, remains a perpetual possession of Boston. It contains a lake, on the site of the ancient and historic Frog Pond, the Soldiers' and Sailors' Monument,— erected to the memory of the men of Boston that fell in the Civil War,—and the beautiful Brewer Fountain, cast in Paris and adorned with statues of Neptune, Amphitrite, Acis, and Galatea.

Common Law of England. The name given to the unwritten law—*lex non scripta*—of England, in contradistinction to the written or statute law.

It consists of a collection of maxims of British, Danish, and Saxon extraction, to which custom has given the force of law ; and derives its origin from King Alfred's code of laws, promulgated in 890 A.D., and afterwards lost. Common law sustained a severe shock after the Norman Conquest. Statute law and equity prevail over common law. The common law of the United States is based on that of England. See *English Law*.

Common Prayer, Book of. The name of the book used in the services of the Church of England and of the Protestant Episcopal Church. It is so called because it contains the prayers used " in common " by the members of those churches, as distinguished from the supplications made use of in their private devotions. It is based on the *King's Primer*, which was published in 1545 and contained the *Creed*, the *Litany*, the *Ten Commandments*, the *Venite*, and the *Te Deum*,— together with a few collects. In 1547, Archbishop Cranmer appointed 12 commissioners to aid him in compiling a liturgy free from popish errors. The book was confirmed by Parliament in 1548, and is known as the *First Prayer-Book of Edward VI*. About the latter part of 1550, exception was taken to parts of this book, and Archbishop Cranmer proposed a new revision. Thus revised and altered, the new liturgy was confirmed by Parliament in 1551, and is known as the *Second Prayer-Book of Edward VI*. Slight revisions of the *Book of Common Prayer* were made in 1559, during the reign of Elizabeth ; and also in 1604, during the reign of James I. Several important changes were made during 1661–1662, after the Restoration. These alterations were ratified by act of Parliament, and received the royal assent, May 19th, 1662. This was the last revision of the *Book of Common Prayer*, made by public authority, and is substantially the form in use at the present time in the Church of Eng-

land. After the American Revolution, the Protestant Episcopal Church was established in the United States in 1784, as an organization separate from the Church of England. The *Book of Common Prayer*, having been modified to suit the institutions peculiar to the United States, was ratified and set forth by a vote of the Convention on October 16th, 1789, and its use prescribed on and after October 1st, 1790. A revision was authorized in 1886, and issued in 1893. See *Missal*.

Common Sense. The name of a celebrated political pamphlet written by Thomas Paine (1737–1809). It appeared in January, 1776, and contributed largely to the diffusion of republican ideas among the American colonies, during the War of the Revolution. In this pamphlet, Paine attacked the British Constitution, opposed the policy of reconciliation, and strongly advocated that of separation from, and complete independence of, the mother-country.

Commons, House of. Had its origin during the reign of Henry III (1216–1272), in 1258, when Simon de Montfort, Earl of Leicester, ordered two knights from each shire, and deputies from certain boroughs, to meet such of the barons and clergy as were favorable to his cause, with the view of strengthening his own power against that of the King. At present, no Parliament is permitted to endure for more than seven years from the time when it is first summoned to meet. Triennial Parliaments were instituted by the law of 1641. On the accession of George I in 1714, the Septennial Act fixed the duration of Parliament at seven years. In accordance with the Reform Act of 1885, the total number of members of the House of Commons at present is as follows :

England	465
Wales	30
Scotland	72
Ireland	103
	670

Commonwealth Avenue. A stately boulevard in the city of Boston, situated in the aristocratic quarter of the town. It is 240 feet wide, and is adorned with handsome churches, club-houses, hotels, and private residences. Through the centre of the avenue extends a parkway shaded by trees. There may be found Warner's statue of William Lloyd Garrison, the great anti-slavery agitator. Upon the pedestal are inscribed the following daring words of the reformer : " I AM IN EARNEST ; I WILL NOT EQUIVO-CATE ; I WILL NOT EXCUSE ; I WILL NOT RETREAT A SINGLE INCH ; AND I WILL BE HEARD.''

Commonwealth of England. The name given to the interregnum between the death of Charles I, on January 30th, 1649, and the restoration of Charles II, on May 8th, 1660. During this period of eleven years, the government of England was nominally a republic,—although in reality a military despotism,—ruled by Oliver Cromwell, assisted by a Council. On December 16th, 1653, Cromwell was made Lord Protector, and held this office for about five years, until his death on September 3rd, 1658, when he was succeeded by his son, Richard Cromwell, who proved to be a weak and inefficient ruler, and soon retired into private life. Monarchy was restored in England on May 8th, 1660, and Charles II returned to London on May 29th of the same year.

Compass, Mariners'. Said to have been known to the Chinese as early as 1115 B.C., and to have been introduced into Europe by Marco Polo, a Venetian traveler, in 1260 A.D. The mariners' compass was familiar, it is claimed, to the Swedes as early as 1250 A.D. To Flavio Gioja, a native of Amalfi, near Naples, is generally given the credit of introducing the suspension of the needle, in 1302. At all events, it is certain that he was the first to use it on a ship. As the king of Naples of that day belonged to the royal family of France, Gioja marked the north point of the compass with a fleur-de-lis, in his honor ; and this symbol is still borne by the mariners' compass among all nations. This story, however, has been contradicted. The territory of Principiato—the birthplace of Gioja—has a compass for its arms, in memory of the discovery. Columbus is said to have been the first to observe the deviation of the needle, in 1492; and Sebastian Cabot is reported to have noticed this same fact in 1540. William Barlowe, an English divine and physicist, invented the compass-box and hanging-compass used by navigators, in 1608.

Complete Angler. A celebrated pastoral by Izaak Walton (1593–1683). It appeared in 1653, and was received with great favor. Hazlitt says that the *Complete Angler* is perhaps the best pastoral in the English language. Owing to its simplicity and sweetness, it has won its way to the hearts of all readers.

Composite Order. An order of architecture introduced by the Romans. It consists of a union of the Corinthian and Ionic Orders, and is also known as the Roman or Italic Order. The capital of the composite column has four volutes—presenting the same face on four sides. The date of the introduction of this order is uncertain. See *Architecture, Orders of.*

Compound Radical. A term applied in organic chemistry to any group, containing two or more elementary atoms, which is capable of entering into a series of different compounds without itself undergoing change or decomposition. Compound radicals cannot exist in a free state, but must be in combination with elements or with other compound radicals. Ammonium, amyl, ethyl, methyl, cyanogen, are all compound radicals. The first compound radical isolated was cyanogen. This was done by Gay-Lussac, in 1815.

Conception, Immaculate.

(1) The doctrine—early taught in the Latin and Greek Churches—that the Virgin Mary was conceived without original sin. The Feast of the Immaculate Conception of the Virgin Mary is celebrated in the Latin Church on the 8th of December, and in the Greek Church on the following day. In the latter Church it is observed under the name of the *Conception of St. Anne*, the mother of the Virgin Mary. On December 8th, 1854, Pope Pius IX (1846–1878) declared this doctrine to be an article of faith, and as such it was universally accepted throughout the Latin Church.

(2) A celebrated painting by Murillo (1617–1682), now in the *Salon Carré* of the Louvre. It was painted in 1678, and is generally considered to be the artist's masterpiece. The picture represents the Virgin Mary, standing in the clouds, supported apparently by a throng of cupids that surround her, and form a garland of infant loveliness. It was purchased at the sale of Marshal Soult's works of art in 1852, for 600,-000 francs ($120,000). Murillo is often called the " Painter of the Conception,"—having portrayed this subject twenty-five times.

Concert Pitch. The name given to the pitch of a certain note adopted by the general body of musicians in various countries. Although it is obviously of great importance to have an accepted standard of pitch by which instruments and voices may be regulated, it is to be regretted that no such uniformity exists. For about two centuries—down to 1827,—the pitch in use remained almost uniform (C = 498 to 515 vibrations per second). The tendency, since then, has been to raise the pitch, until, in 1859, in the Covent Garden orchestra, it was a semitone higher (C = 538). In Steinway's pianos, the pitch of Middle C slightly exceeds this. In 1859, the French government fixed the pitch of C at 522. This is known as French pitch,

and continues in use in France at the present time. An international conference, held at Vienna in 1885, at which representatives from all the leading European countries, except France and England, were present, resulted in the adoption of the French pitch as the standard. Most British orchestras use the higher pitch (known as the Philharmonic); while in music not orchestral and by singers generally, a pitch nearer the French is used.

Conciergerie. An ancient prison connected with the Palais de Justice in Paris, where the victims of the French Revolution were confined before their execution. In the September Massacres of 1792, 288 of the prisoners were killed by the mob. Malesherbes, Bailly, Madame Elizabeth, Madame Roland, Camille Desmoulins, Danton, and Robespierre with seventeen others, were all imprisoned there before they were led to the guillotine. Marie Antoinette also was a prisoner there from August 2nd to October 15th, 1793. The room she occupied for 75 days is still shown, but it has since been turned into an expiatory chapel. Adjoining this chamber and connected with it by an archway is the cell in which Robespierre was afterwards confined, and beyond this is the Hall of the Girondists, — now a prison-chapel. It is claimed that more than 3000 persons passed from the Conciergerie to the guillotine. Louis Napoleon (afterwards Emperor of the French) was confined there for a time, after his fiasco at Boulogne in 1840. See *Palais de Justice.*

Conclave. The name given, both to a set of small chambers (technically called "cells") in the hall of the Vatican at Rome where the cardinals assemble to elect a pope, and to the assembly itself. This practice was instituted by Pope Alexander III (1159–1181) in 1179. The word "conclave" is derived from two Latin words *con* (*with*) and *clavis* (*key*), and means a room that can be locked.

Concordat of 1801. The name given to the famous agreement between Napoleon Bonaparte (as First Consul) and Pope Pius VII (1800–1823) touching the affairs of the Roman Catholic Church in France. In accordance with its provisions, the appointment of bishops was put into the hands of the temporal power, while their " institution " was left with the Pope. A new arrangement of the dioceses of France was also made. The pope, furthermore, renounced all claim to the church lands confiscated during the Revolution, and the government agreed to provide for the maintenance of the clergy. The *Concordat* restored the Roman Catholic religion (though deprived of many of its former privileges) to France, and put an end to the anarchy that existed in the Church. It was signed at Paris on July 15th, 1801. Another concordat between the same parties was signed at Fontainebleau, on January 25th, 1813. After the fall of Napoleon in 1814, these concordats were annulled by a third, signed on November 22nd, 1817.

Concorde, Place de la. A celebrated public square in Paris,—considered by many travelers to be the most beautiful in the world. It is situated between the Jardin des Tuileries and the Champs Elysées, and covers an area 390 yards in length by 235 yards in width. From the centre rises the graceful shaft of the obelisk of Luxor, which once stood before the temple at Thebes, at least 1300 years before Christ. On opposite sides of the obelisk are two beautiful fountains, —the one on the south side being dedicated to the *Seas*, and the one on the north side to the *Rivers*. Around the Place de la Concorde stand eight stone figures representing seven cities of France, and one (Strasburg) which is no longer on French territory. These seven cities are Lille, Bordeaux, Nantes, Rouen, Brest, Marseilles, and Lyons. During the Reign of Terror, the guillotine stood on the site of the obelisk, and it is estimated that between January 21st, 1793, and May 3rd, 1795, more than 2800 persons perished there under the fatal knife. Louis XVI and Marie Antoinette were beheaded there in 1793. There also was proclaimed the Republic in 1848. In 1763, this open space received the name of Place Louis XV, and was adorned by the municipality of Paris with an equestrian statue of the King. Since then, the name of the square has been several times changed. In 1792, it was called the Place de la Révolution ; and in 1799, this name was changed to the Place de la Concorde. On the return of the Bourbons in 1814, the name Place Louis XV was restored ; but the year 1830 witnessed a revival of the name, Place de la Concorde, and this appellation is still retained at the present day.

Confederate Money. The money issued by the Confederate States of America, during the Civil War (1861–1865), at first commanded a slight premium; as the war progressed, however, the value of the dollar steadily declined until, during the last days of the Confederacy, it required from $800 to $1000 in Confederate money to buy a one-dollar greenback. The table given below shows the declining value of the Confederate dollar during the progress of the war :

June 1st, 1861	90 cents.
December 1st, 1861	80 "
December 15th, 1861	75 "
February 1st, 1862	60 "
February 1st, 1863	20 "
June 1st, 1863	8 "
January 1st, 1864	2 "
November 1st, 1864	4½ "
January 1st, 1865	2½ "
April 1st, 1865	1½ "

Confederate States of America. The name given to the Confederacy of eleven States that seceded from the American Union in 1861, and attempted to establish an independent government. This confederation lasted 4 years, 1 month, and 14 days, after which time the seceding States were gradually restored to their places in the Union. In May, 1872, the reconstructed States were once more represented in Congress. The names of these States, together with the dates of the adoption of their new form of government, are as follows:

(1) South Carolina...December 20th, 1860.
(2) Mississippi......January 9th, 1861.
(3) Florida..........January 10th, 1861.
(4) Alabama.........January 11th, 1861.
(5) Georgia.........January 19th, 1861.
(6) Louisiana.......January 26th, 1861.
(7) Texas...........February 1st, 1861.
(8) Virginia.........April 17th, 1861.
(9) Arkansas ....May 6th, 1861.
(10) North Carolina...May 21st, 1861.
(11) Tennessee........June 8th, 1861.

Confederation of the Rhine. A confederation of the Germanic States, formed by Napoleon I, after his successful campaign against Austria in 1805. On the 12th of July, 1806, sixteen princes renounced their allegiance to the old German Empire, and allied themselves to France under the protectorate of Napoleon. The most prominent of these were the Electors of Bavaria and Würtemberg (subsequently raised to the rank of kings), the Elector of Baden, and the new Duke of Cleves and Berg. These were afterwards joined by the Kings of Saxony and Westphalia, and the Elector of Würzburg. In 1811, the Confederation of the Rhine comprised 4 kingdoms, 5 grand-duchies, 11 duchies, and 16 principalities. It had a population of about 15,000,000, and furnished an army of 120,000 men. After Napoleon's disastrous campaign against Russia in 1812, the Confederation of the Rhine crumbled to pieces ; and on the fall of Napoleon (1814) it was succeeded by the Germanic Confederation. See *Germanic Confederation.*

Confessio Amantis (*Lat. Confession of a Lover*). A poem by John Gower (1320–1402), consisting of a dialogue

between a lover and his confessor. It was first printed by Caxton in 1483. Dr. Pauli, the editor of the poem (1857), describes it as " a mixture of classical notions, principally borrowed from Ovid, and of the purely medieval idea, that, as a good Catholic, the unfortunate lover must state his distress to a father confessor." Taine says that the *Confessio Amantis* is " a cartload of scholastic rubbish." Its enormous length (over 30,000 lines) renders it tedious.

Confession of Faith. See *Westminster Confession of Faith.*

Confessions, Les (*Fr. The Confessions*). The name of the famous autobiography of Jean Jacques Rousseau (1712–1778), which contains an account of his early career and presents a series of odd adventures and surprising vicissitudes, narrated in an extremely candid and unreserved manner.

Confessions of an English Opium-Eater. A famous book — purporting to be an autobiography — by Thomas De Quincey (1785–1859). It appeared in 1821, and describes the personal experience of a scholar and man of genius who, like Coleridge, was a slave to the use of opium. In the meridian stage of his career, the amount daily used by De Quincey was 8000 drops of laudanum. In his experience, solid opium required not less than four hours to produce the desired effect, whereas the tincture laudanum acted instantaneously. De Quincey was remarkable for his subtle analytic faculty, as well as for his marvellous power of imagination.

Congé d'élire (*Fr. Permission to elect*). The name originally given in England to the license granted by the sovereign, as head of the Church, to chapters and other bodies, for the purpose of electing bishops and other ecclesiastical dignitaries. Since the act of Henry VIII (1509–1547) in 1534, a *congé d'élire* has always been

13

accompanied by a letter from the sovereign, indicating the person to be chosen; hence it has become in reality a nomination by the Crown, and not a permission to act independently. In case the dean and chapter delay the election of a bishop for a longer period than twelve days, the nomination is made by letters-patent from the Crown. The *congé d'élire* does not exist in the Irish Church.

Congo Free State. An extensive territory in south central Africa, having an area of 1,056,200 square miles and a population of from 8,000,000 to 10,000,000 souls. As a result of Stanley's successful expedition across the continent of Africa from Zanzibar to the mouth of the Congo River, in 1875–1877, there was thrown open to the world the vast territory of the Congo basin, having 12,000 miles of navigable rivers, an area of 1,500,000 square miles, and a population of 30,-000,000 people, speaking 200 different languages and dialects. These discoveries resulted, in 1885, in the formation of the Congo Free State, under the sovereignty of Leopold II, King of the Belgians. The King, however, in 1889, bequeathed to Belgium his sovereign rights in this state. On July 3rd, 1890, a convention between Belgium and the Congo Free State reserved to the former the right of annexation after a period of ten years. It is said that for many years the King of the Belgians has borne the expenses of this great undertaking out of his private purse, and that the public revenue still receives from him an annual subsidy of 1,000,000 francs. On July 31st, 1890, the territories of the Congo Free State were declared inalienable. The central government is located at Brussels ; but there is, in addition, an administrator who presides over local affairs, at Boma, on the Congo River, 66 miles from the sea.

Congressional Cemetery. A finely situated burial-ground in Washington,

D. C., overlooking the Anacostia River, a branch of the Potomac. The first interment was in 1807. It receives its name from having been the place of burial of senators and representatives during the early years of the century. Memorial cenotaphs were also erected to all members of Congress that died while in office. Two vice-presidents—Gerry and Clinton—are buried there, as well as several generals and admirals of national fame.

Congressional Library. The name of a celebrated library in Washington, D. C., intended originally for the exclusive use of members of Congress, but afterwards thrown open to the public, while still serving its original purpose. It was founded in 1800; and contained in 1802 about 1000 volumes. It was burned by the British in 1814. As a nucleus for a new collection, the private library of Thomas Jefferson—containing 6700 volumes — was purchased by Congress for $23,700. In 1850, the Library of Congress contained about 55,000 books,—one-third of which was destroyed by fire in 1851. For many years the library was situated in the west front of the Capitol, and contained space for about 350,000 volumes. These quarters, however, soon became inadequate ; and, in consequence, in 1872, the necessity for a new building was laid before Congress. It was not until 1886, however, that any decided action was taken ; but in that year, the construction of the present superb structure was commenced. It is built of white New Hampshire granite, in the Italian Renaissance style, and occupies an area of 3¾ acres—opposite the east front of the Capitol. The building was completed in 1897, at a cost of $6,360,000, and has accommodations for 4,500,000 books. According to an act of Congress, two copies of every copyrighted work are deposited in the Library. As a result of this requirement, the Congressional Library has grown to be the largest collection of books in America. In 1912, it contained 1,762,393 books, 250,000 pamphlets, 500,000 pieces of music, 25,000 maps, and 256,000 engravings, photographs, etc.,—making a grand total of 2,793,393 publications. The Law Library, established in 1832, contains 85,000 volumes. For the greater convenience of the Supreme Court, which holds its sessions in the old Senate Chamber of the Capitol, this collection has not been removed from its original quarters, although it has always been reckoned a part of the Congressional Library.

Conscript Fathers. A designation given to the senators of Rome during the time of the Republic and the Cæsars, because their names were inscribed on the registers of the Senate. According to Brewer's *Historic Note-Book*, after the Tarquins were expelled from Rome in 509 B.C., a new element was introduced into the Senate. The new senators were called *conscripti*, while the original 300 patricians were still known as *patres*. The new Senate, as thus constituted, was composed of *patres et conscripti*, and was addressed by speakers as *patres, conscripti (fathers, conscripts)*,—a form of address which later was changed to the phrase *patres conscripti (conscript fathers)*.

Conscription. The name given to a method of recruiting armies, derived from the Romans, and adopted during the nineteenth century by the leading nations of Europe. On September 5th, 1798, a conscription of all men from 20 to 25 years of age was ordained in France, and from this number selections were made. In 1813, after Napoleon's disastrous Russian campaign, a conscription of 350,000 men took place ; and in December of the same year, another of 300,000 men. From 1793 to 1813 (a period of twenty years) the estimated conscriptions in France amounted to 4,103,000 men. The law of 1818 (modified in 1824, 1832, and 1868) assigned an annual contingent to each department. In 1872, substitutes were abolished, and military service made obligatory on every Frenchman, not physically incapacitated. All such must enter the army at twenty, and serve for 25 years, as follows: 3 years in the regular army, 6½ years in the army reserve, 6 years in the territorial army (militia), and 9½ years in the territorial reserve. At 45 years of age, liability to service ceases. The number of youths in France that annually reach the age of twenty is about 280,000. Prussia has had a similar law of universal service since 1813 ; in 1887, it was made even more severe throughout the entire German Empire. All the other leading European nations have adopted the same method. Conscription in Great Britain was considered in 1875. During the Civil War in the United States (1861–1865), conscription was ordained by both the Federal and Confederate governments, but in the North especially, large bounties generally furnished a sufficient number of volunteers.

Conservation of Energy. The name given to the doctrine that the total amount of energy in the universe neither increases nor diminishes, although it may assume different forms successively. Tait, in his *Recent Advances in Physical Science*, says: "The grand principle of *Conservation of Energy* . . . is simply a statement of the invariability of the quantity of energy in the universe,—a companion statement to that of the invariability of the quantity of matter." See *Correlation of the Physical Forces.*

Consolations of Philosophy (*Lat. De Consolatione Philosophiæ*). The name of a book written by Boëthius (475–525 A.D.), a celebrated Roman philosopher and statesman, while imprisoned at Pavia just before his execution. It is composed of alternate passages of prose and verse, and is in the form of a dialogue between the author and philosophy personified. The book enjoyed great popularity during the Middle Ages, and was translated into several languages. Alfred the Great, Elizabeth, and Chaucer translated it into English.

Hallam says : "Few books are more striking from the circumstances of their production. Last of the classic writers, . . . he speaks from his prison in the swan-like tones of dying eloquence."

Consolidated Fund of the United Kingdom. The name given to the fund into which nearly the entire revenue of the United Kingdom of Great Britain and Ireland is paid. It was formed in 1786 by the union of the "aggregate," "general," and "South Sea" funds, and was further increased in 1816 by the addition of the Irish revenue. It pays the interest on the National Debt, the Civil List, pensions, salaries, etc.

Consols. This word is an abbreviation of the term *consolidated annuities*, —a kind of stock of which a large portion of the British National Debt is composed. The rate of interest is three per cent., and the market price of consols indicates in a general way the value of all other securities.

Constantine sees Cross. When Constantine was proclaimed Emperor of Rome in 306 A.D., six competitors for the throne arose in different parts of the Empire, and for eighteen years contended with him for the supremacy. Constantine, however, finally triumphed over them all. During his final struggle with Maxentius, he is said to have been converted to the Christian religion by seeing in the sky, at noonday, a flaming cross, inscribed with the words $ Ἐν τούτῳ νίκα$ (*Gr. In this, conquer*). On the night before the battle, a vision appeared to him, and bade him inscribe upon the shields of his soldiers the sacred monogram of the name of Christ. Thenceforth his troops always marched to victory under the standard called the *labarum*,

the top of which was adorned with a mystic X, representing at once the cross and the initial letter of the Greek word $Χρίστος$ (*Christ*). Eusebius says that he heard this story from the lips of the Emperor himself. See *Alonzo Sees Cross; In Hoc Signo Vinces.*

Constellations. The name given to certain fanciful groupings of fixed stars, supposed to resemble living beings or other objects. These groupings have existed from time immemorial, and have received names borrowed mainly from Greek mythology. Some of them are mentioned by Homer and Hesiod, while in the book of *Job* (1520 B.C.) we read of the Pleiades, Orion, and Mazzaroth (meaning, probably, the twelve signs of the zodiac). Hipparchus made a list of 48 constellations, about 147 B.C.; others were added by Tycho Brahe, Hevelius, and Halley. There now exist 29 northern, 12 zodiacal, and 45 southern constellations, which are generally recognized. The following are the names of the constellations of the zodiac : *Aries, Taurus, Gemini, Cancer, Leo, Virgo, Libra, Scorpio, Sagittarius, Capricornus, Aquarius,* and *Pisces.*

Constitution. A celebrated frigate in the American navy, commissioned in 1798. She became famous not only on account of the brilliant work done by her in the attack upon Tripoli in 1804 ; but especially for her capture and destruction of the British frigate *Guerrière*, during the second war between Great Britain and the United States. On the 19th of August, 1812, the *Constitution*, commanded by Captain Hull, met the British vessel under Captain Dacres, and reduced her to a wreck after a desperate fight of 30 minutes. For this signal victory, Hull received ovations in New York, Philadelphia, and Boston, and was rewarded by Congress with a gold medal, and $50,000 for his crew. In December of the same year, the British frigate *Java* surrendered to the *Constitution*. Some years afterwards it was proposed to destroy the *Constitution*, as being no longer fit for service. To remonstrate against such a sacrilege, Oliver Wendell Holmes (1809–1894) wrote the famous poem, entitled *Old Ironsides*, the first line of which is as follows:

"Ay, tear her tattered ensign down!"

The *Constitution* was afterwards removed to the Navy Yard at Philadelphia, and was used for several years as a school ship. See *Old Ironsides*.

Consubstantiation. A doctrine which asserts that, after consecration of the elements, the body and blood of Christ are substantially present in the bread and wine. It differs from transubstantiation in not implying a change in the substance of the elements. This doctrine was maintained by Martin Luther; but theologians of the Lutheran communion uniformly deny that any change takes place in the elements. See *Transubstantiation*.

Continental System. The name given to a method devised by Napoleon I for the purpose of excluding Great Britain from intercourse with the continent of Europe. It commenced with the promulgation of the Berlin Decree on November 21st, 1806. By this system the British Isles were declared to be in a state of blockade, and no European nation was allowed, under pain of war, to receive British goods within its dominions. All merchandise belonging to an Englishman became a lawful prize, and no ship coming fom Great Britain or from any British colony was allowed to enter any continental port. The Continental System collapsed with the fall of Napoleon in 1814. Failure on the part of Russia to comply with the requirements of the Continental System led to the Russian War of 1812, and eventually to Napoleon's downfall. See *Berlin Decree; Milan Decree; Orders in Council*.

Contraband of War. A term applied to all warlike materials, such as arms, ammunition, military or naval supplies, furnished by neutrals to a belligerent, contrary to the law of nations, and liable to seizure and confiscation. The expression is said to have been first used in the Treaty of Southampton between England and France in 1625. The meaning of the words "contraband of war" is not clearly defined, and unless special treaties to this effect exist between nations, the interpretation of the term leads to great embarrassment. During the Civil War in the United States, some negro slaves having penetrated the Union lines at Fort Monroe, Virginia, General Benjamin F. Butler refused to restore them to their owners on the ground that they were "contraband of war." This gave an extension of meaning to the term; and, in consequence, all colored people in and about the Northern army became known as United States contrabands.

Contrat Social (*Fr. Social Contract*). A noted sociological treatise by Jean Jacques Rousseau (1712–1778).

"The 'Social Contract' proceeds on the premise that the basis of society is an original compact by which each member surrenders his will to the will of all, on the condition that he gets protection or defence; and arguing that the community is the true sovereign, that each member of it has equal power and right to make its laws, Rousseau arrives at the conclusion that kings are usurpers, that no laws are binding to which the whole people's assent has not been gained."

Convention held in a Barn. A number of English people that had recently arrived in Boston, Massachusetts, having purchased Quinipiack (now New Haven) fiom the Indians in the autumn of 1637, met there in a barn, held a convention, and adopted the Bible as a constitution. This was the foundation of the city of New Haven. According to tradition, the barn belonged to one Robert Newman, and is supposed to have stood at the corner of Grove and Temple Streets, on land afterwards occupied by the house of Noah Webster, the lexicographer.

Convention, National. See *National Convention of France*.

Convents. Said to have been first founded in 270 A.D. According to Camden, the first convent in England was founded at Folkestone by Eadbald in 630. The first one in Scotland was at Coldingham, where Ethelreda took the veil in 670. Before this date convents had been established in Ireland. They were suppressed, and severely dealt with by Henry VIII (1509-1547), and relatively few now exist in Great Britain. It is said that more than 3000 convents have been suppressed in Europe within recent years. In 1832, the Emperor of Russia abolished 187 convents of monks ; and the King of Prussia, following his example, secularized all those in the Duchy of Posen. Dom Pedro abolished 300 in Portugal in 1834, and Spain put down 1800. In Italy and Sicily, many convents were abolished in 1860, 1861, and 1866 ; and in France, in 1880, convents were abolished by decree.

Conway, Hugh. The pseudonym of Frederick J. Fargus (1847-1885), the popular English author, whose novel entitled *Called Back* enjoyed a remarkable popularity.

Cook's Excursions. These originated with Mr. Thomas Cook, the founder of the system, in 1841, in which year he arranged with the Midland Railway Company of England to convey a party of 570 persons from Leicester to Loughborough, at one shilling each. This system of personally conducted tours was gradually extended by him through Great Britain and Ireland, and eventually to the Continent. In 1856, he conducted a party from Harwich to the Rhine, returning by way of Paris. In later years, he applied his system to America, India, Egypt, and the Holy Land. Mr. Cook died in 1892,

aged 83 years. The system, founded by him, has grown to vast proportions.

Coon's Age. An expression used in the southern part of the United States, meaning *a long time*.

"This child hain't had much money in a
    coon's age."
                         Southern Sketches.

Copernican System. The name given to that theory of the solar system that places the sun in the centre, while the planets and their satellites revolve around it from west to east. This hypothesis, to the development of which Nicolas Copernicus (1473-1543) had given his life, was set forth by him in his famous work, *De Revolutionibus Orbium*, published in 1543—a few days before his death. Although Pythagoras had suggested a similar explanation in 550 B.C., yet the teachings of Ptolemy (150 A.D.) had firmly established the notion that the earth is the centre of the universe, and that the sun, moon, and stars revolve around it. Copernicus's book was condemned by Pope Paul V (1605-1621) in 1616, but this order was revoked by Pope Pius VII (1800-1823) in 1818. Through the labors of Kepler, Galileo, and Newton, the Copernican System was demonstrated to be true, and thus became the cornerstone of modern astronomy.

Cophetua. The name of an imaginary king of Africa, of great wealth, who, though he had previously despised all women, fell in love with a beggar-girl and married her. Her name was Penelophon, although Shakespeare in *Love's Labor 's Lost*, iv, 1, calls her Zenelophon. The legend is extant in Percy's *Reliques ;* and Tennyson has cast the story in modern form in his *Beggar Maid*.

"Young Adam Cupid, he that shot so trim,
  When King *Cophetua* lov'd the beggar-
    maid."
                    Romeo and Juliet, ii, 1.

Copley Medal. A gold medal in the gift of the Royal Society of London, annually awarded for scientific discoveries. It was instituted by Sir Godfrey Copley in 1709. The first Copley medal was awarded to Stephen Gray in 1731. Franklin received the Copley medal in 1753, in recognition of his discoveries in electricity, and the same honor was conferred upon Sir David Brewster in 1815, for his essay on the *Polarization of Light by Reflection*.

Copperheads. A term of reproach conferred, during the Civil War in the United States, upon a faction in the North that was in sympathy with the Rebellion, and secretly abetted the Southern cause. The name is derived from a venomous serpent called the copperhead (*trigonocephalus contortrix*), whose bite is as deadly as that of the rattlesnake, but which, unlike the latter reptile, gives no warning of its approach. Its habitat extends from Florida to 45° north latitude. The name "copperhead" was applied in earlier days, first to the Indians, and, afterwards, as a term of contempt, to the Dutch settlers.

Copyright. Copyright was first established in England by a decree of the Star Chamber, in 1556. In 1585, every book and publication was ordered to be licensed. In the United States, the first copyright law was passed by Congress in 1790. In 1831, this law was amended, and remains in substantially the same form at the present day. By its provisions, copyrights are granted for 28 years, with a renewal of 14 years additional—making in all, 42 years. To secure a copyright, it is necessary to send to the Librarian of Congress a printed copy of the title, before publication,—the fee being one dollar ; while two copies of the book, map, photograph, or other article copyrighted must be deposited in the Congressional Library at Washington. The first movement towards international copyright in the United States was made by Henry Clay, who, in 1837, presented a petition to Congress

to that effect. It was referred to the Senate committee, which reported for full protection. It was not, however, until March 3rd, 1891, after long years of effort and debate, that Congress passed a bill securing international copyright. This law took effect on July 1st, 1891. See *Star Chamber*.

Corcoran Art Gallery. A famous gallery of art in Washington, D. C., founded by the late W. W. Corcoran, a banker of that city, who deeded the building to the city, and presented it with his superb private art-collection, and an endowment fund of $900,000. The Corcoran Art Gallery contains a choice collection of paintings,—some of them masterpieces,—as well as the finest set of casts in America. Among its gems of sculpture may be mentioned Vela's *Dying Napoleon*, and Powers's *Greek Slave*. The collections of bronzes, porcelains, majolicas, and bric-à-brac are especially noteworthy. The building was opened in 1897, and occupies a fine site opposite the State, War, and Navy Department.

Cordeliers (*Fr. Cord-Wearers*). The name of a famous political club in Paris, founded in 1790, during the French Revolution. It derived its name from the fact that it held its meetings in the chapel of the monastery of the Cordelier monks. The club included among its members Danton, Marat, Camille Desmoulins, and Hébert, and was, for a time, a rival of the dreaded Jacobin Club. It was overthrown in 1794, and its leading members guillotined ; and on August 23rd, 1795 it was formally closed by the National Convention. The Cordelier monks were a branch of the Franciscans, —the other branch being the Capuchins,—and were so called because they wore a knotted cord around the waist, in place of a girdle. This name was first given to them by Louis IX (1226–1270) of France, about 1227. See *Capuchins*.

Cordon Bleu. Originally, a knight of the ancient Order of the Saint

Esprit (*Fr. Holy Ghost*), founded by Henry III (1574–1589), on the occasion of his accession to the throne of France. It consisted of 100 knights—exclusive of officers,—and was at one time the highest Order in the kingdom. So called, on account of the color of the ribbon from which the cross of the Order was suspended. In course of time, this appellation was bestowed upon anyone that had achieved eminence in his profession ; and, finally, the term was applied only to first-rate cooks, who, after examination, received a medal suspended from a blue ribbon. Littré says that the blue apron formerly worn by cooks may have helped to earn for them this flattering designation.

Cordon Rouge. A knight of the Order of Saint Louis, founded by Louis XIV (1643–1715) in 1693. So called because the decoration of the Order was suspended from a *red* ribbon.

Corinne. The name of a famous novel by Madame de Staël (1766–1817). It appeared in 1807, and had an immense popularity. *Corinne, ou l'Italie* gives a poetic description of Italy and its people, and displays profound insight and equal sensibility.

Cornice Road. A famous road extending along the Riviera di Ponente, from Nice to Genoa. It derives its name from its situation on the edge or *cornice* of the shore ; and commands, in places, superb views of the Mediterranean. At some points, it attains an elevation of 1600 feet. It was widened by Napoleon I. Since the opening of the railway between Nice and Genoa, the Cornice Road has fallen into disuse. See *Riviera*.

Corn-Laws. The name popularly applied to certain enactments having for their object a restriction on the importation and exportation of grain. They have existed in England since 1360 — during the reign of Edward III (1327–1377),—when the exportation of corn was prohibited, except to Calais and Gascony. In 1393, the right to export was granted ; but, in 1436, this was permitted only when wheat did not exceed 6*s*. 8*d*. a quarter. Various other enactments followed until 1828, when the so-called "sliding scale" was adopted, but without success. In 1839, the famous *Anti-Corn-Law League* — consisting of Richard Cobden, John Bright, Charles Villiers, and others— was formed, and did much to arouse public interest in the question. Sir Robert Peel, the Conservative Premier, became a convert to free-trade principles; and, in 1846, he carried through Parliament a measure to repeal the Corn-Laws. By this act the duty was greatly lowered, and ceased to be imposed in 1849, with the exception of a registration-duty of 1*s*. per quarter, which was finally removed in 1869. See *Free-Trade*.

Coronation Chair. A famous oaken chair in Westminster Abbey, London, in which all the reigning sovereigns of England, since the reign of Edward I (1272–1307), have been crowned. It contains, beneath the seat, the Prophetic or Fatal Stone of Scone, on which the Scottish kings were crowned, and which was brought from Scotland by Edward I in 1297, in token of his complete subjugation of the country. According to tradition, the Scottish Coronation Stone—the "Lia Fail" or "Stone of Destiny"—is the one used by the patriarch Jacob as a pillow. It was originally brought to Tara in Ireland (580 B.C.), and was afterwards taken to Scotland, where it found a resting-place until removed by Edward I. There is a second coronation chair in Westminster Abbey, modelled after the original one, and made for the coronation of Mary, the consort of William III (1689–1702). On coronation days, these chairs are covered with gold brocade, and placed in the choir of the Abbey, before the altar. See *Fenian Oath ; Tara Hill ; Westminster Abbey*.

Coronation of the Virgin. The name given to a number of celebrated paintings by various great masters of the Middle Ages, of which the following may be mentioned as the more famous ones.

(1) *Coronation of the Virgin*, by Fra Angelico (1387–1455). Now in the Louvre, in Paris.

(2) *Coronation of the Virgin*, by Fra Angelico (1387–1455). Now in the Museum of St. Mark in Florence.

(3) *Coronation of the Virgin*, by Fra Angelico (1387–1455). Now in the Uffizi Palace, in Florence.

(4) *Coronation of the Virgin*, by Fra Filippo Lippi (1412–1469). Now in the Academy, in Florence.

(5) *Coronation of the Virgin*, by Raphael Sanzio (1483–1520). At present in the Vatican at Rome. This painting was probably commenced by Raphael, and completed by his pupils, Giulio Romano and Gian Francesco Penni.

(6) *Coronation of the Virgin*, by Raphael Sanzio (1483–1520). This was a cartoon designed for one of the tapestries of the Sistine Chapel. Cartoon and tapestry have both disappeared.

(7) *Coronation of the Virgin*, by Annibale Caracci (1560–1609). Once the property of the poet Rogers, but now in the National Gallery, London.

(8) *Coronation of the Virgin*, by Peter Paul Rubens (1577–1640). Now in Brussels.

Corporal John. A sobriquet conferred by his soldiers upon John Churchill (1650–1722), Duke of Marlborough, who had risen from the rank of corporal.

Corporal Violet. An appellation given to Napoleon Bonaparte (1769–1821), during his stay in Elba in 1814–1815, by his adherents in France. The violet was the floral device of the Empire and was worn by its partisans, who confidently predicted that a certain " Corporal Violet " would return

in the spring. Napoleon was toasted as " Corporal Violet " and " Father Violet," while ladies that longed for the Emperor's return wore violets in their bonnets, and smiled significantly when asked the reason. Little pictures of the flower were sold, which, on raising the petals, disclosed the features of the banished hero. See *Father Violet.*

Corpse Candle. A name given by the Welsh to the *ignis fatuus*, or *Will-o'-the-wisp* (especially when seen in churchyards), because it was supposed to portend death and to show the road that the corpse would take. The expression " corpse candle " was also used to denote a large candle used at wakes.

Corpus Christi (*Lat. Body of Christ*). The name of the most magnificent festival in the Roman Catholic Church. It was instituted in 1264, in honor of the consecrated host and of transubstantiation, by Pope Urban IV (1261–1265), who promised absolution for a period of from 40 to 100 days to the penitent that took part in it; and appointed the Thursday following Trinity Sunday for its celebration. The festival of *Corpus Christi* was afterwards neglected ; but under Pope Clement V (1305–1314) it was re-established, and since then it has been religiously observed. Splendid processions form its distinguishing characteristic. The festival is known in France as *Fête-Dieu*, and in Germany as *Fronleich namsfest.*

Corpuscular Theory of Light. A theory advanced by Sir Isaac Newton (1642–1727) about 1672, to explain the origin of light. It assumes that luminous bodies emit, in all directions, an imponderable substance consisting of molecules of an extreme degree of tenuity. These are propagated in straight lines with enormous velocity, and by direct impingement upon the retina produce the sensation of vision. This theory, owing to the great name of Newton, maintained its vitality until the present century, when it was overthrown by Dr. Thomas Young (1773–1829), and the undulatory theory established in its stead. See *Undulatory Theory of Light*.

Correlation of the Physical Forces. A phrase of recent origin, used to denote the theory that any one of the various forms of physical force (such as gravitation, hesion, light, heat, electricity, magnetism) may be converted into one or more of the other forms. This notion was first suggested by Julius Robert Mayer, a physician of Heilbronn, in 1842, and was more fully developed by Mr. (afterwards Sir) W. R. Grove in his book, *Correlation of the Physical Forces*. The theory was afterwards fully established by experimental researches. The probability is that all forces that exist — whether physical, chemical, vital, or mental— are simply manifestations of one original force appearing under different forms. See *Conservation of Energy*.

Corsica. This is a Phœnician word, meaning the *wooded island*.

Corsican Ogre. An epithet bestowed upon Napoleon Bonaparte (1769–1821), who was a Corsican by birth and family. During the ten years (1804–1814) that he was Emperor, he made Europe tremble by the terror of his name.

Corsican Sesostris. A sobriquet bestowed upon Napoleon Bonaparte (1769–1821), on account of the rapidity and extent of his conquests.

Corso. The name of the principal thoroughfare of Rome, about a mile in length, extending from the Porta del Popolo to the foot of the Capitoline Hill. It is lined with shops, palaces, and private houses, and is the scene of the festivities of the Carnival, which is annually celebrated at Rome, just before the beginning of Lent. Races of riderless horses along the crowded Corso form one of the principal events of the celebration ; while the throwing of flowers and plaster confections (*Il. coriandoli*) from the windows and balconies upon the occupants of carriages in the street below adds much to the merriment of the occasion. See *Carnival*.

Cosmic Dust. A name given to fine particles of matter of a meteoric origin, dissipated throughout the upper regions of the atmosphere, which in their descent and fall upon the earth are easily detected by proper means. Cosmic dust is said to be the source of the dust found on snow, as in the arctic regions.

Cosmos. The name of a famous scientific work, in four volumes, by Alexander von Humboldt (1769–1859), the distinguished scientist and traveler. The first volume appeared in 1845, and the fourth in 1858. The *Cosmos* is universally regarded as one of the greatest scientific works ever published, and presents many of the leading facts of physical science in an orderly sequence. The style, however, is somewhat heavy, and the matter defective from our present standpoint.

"The first volume contains a general view of nature, from the remotest nebulæ and revolving double stars to the terrestrial phenomena of the geographical distribution of plants, of animals, and of races of men,— preceded by some preliminary considerations on the different degrees of enjoyment offered by the study of nature and the knowledge of her laws, and on the limits and method of a scientific exposition of the physical description of the universe."—*Alexander von Humboldt.*

Cossacks. A warlike people of very mixed origin, inhabiting the confines of Poland, Russia, Tartary, and Turkey, first heard of in the tenth century A.D. They distinguished themselves in the wars against the Turks and Tartars, and were known as a powerful military organization, as early as the fifteenth century. They were formed into a regular army by Stephen Batori, in 1576, to defend the frontiers of Russia from the attacks of the Tartars. During the War of 1812–1814 between France and Russia, the Cossacks fought with great fury. They have consisted, in the past, of two main branches—the Little Russian or Ukraine, and the Don Cossacks. It is said that, in intelligence, refinement, and cleanliness, they are superior to the average Russians. At present, they furnish a large contingent of light cavalry to the Russian army, and are thoroughly inured to hunger, thirst, cold, and fatigue. The Cossacks are by many considered to be the finest horsemen in the world. See *Spies of the Czar.*

Cotter's Saturday Night. A celebrated poem by Robert Burns (1759–1796), forming a beautiful picture of a charming phase of Scottish peasant-life.

"The hint of the plan and title of the poem were taken from Ferguson's *Farmer's Ingle.*"

Cotton. This word is said to be derived from the Arabic *qutun, alqutun* (*cotton-wool*).

Cotton Famine. The name given to a period of great distress in the cotton district of England during the American Civil War (1861–1865), occasioned by the secession of the Southern States from the Union. It is said that the annual loss to employers and employees amounted to $200,000,000. Owing to the effectual blockade of the Southern ports maintained by the Federal authorities, the supply of cotton furnished to England nearly ceased. The *Cotton Relief Fund* and the *Cotton Relief Act* aided materially in mitigating the distress.

Cotton-Gin. A machine invented by Eli Whitney in 1793, by which the cotton-wool is separated from the seed, and cleaned with great rapidity and ease. This invention led to such an increase in the cultivation of this staple that the United States soon exported 1,500,000 pounds of cotton annually. Previous to the invention of the cotton-gin, the work was done by hand, and proved to be a tedious process, since one person could clean only a pound or so a day. The invention of the cotton-gin gave slavery the most powerful and insidious impulse that it ever received.

"Cotton is King." An expression much used by the slave-owners of the Southern States before the Civil War (1861–1865), in answer to the arguments of the abolitionists. It was first employed by David Christy in 1855, as the title of his book, *Cotton is King; or, Slavery in the Light of Political Economy.* In March, 1858, James Henry Hammond quoted the phrase in a speech before the United States Senate, whereupon it immediately became a popular byword.

Cottonian Library. A famous collection of ancient MSS., books, and coins, now in the British Museum. It was formed with great care by Sir Robert Bruce Cotton in 1600, and was afterwards added to by his son and grandson. His great-grandson, Sir John Cotton (1679–1731), gave the library to the nation. It was removed to Essex House in 1712, and to Ashburnham House, Westminster, in 1730. In the following year, 114 out of the 958 volumes and MSS. in the library were destroyed, and 98 were damaged. In 1753, the Cottonian Library was transferred to the British Museum. See *Beowulf ; British Museum.*

Counterblast to Tobacco. The name of a treatise against the use of tobacco, written by James I (1603–1625) of England.

The closing paragraph is as follows:

"It is a custom loathsome to the eye, hateful to the nose, harmful to the brain, dangerous to the lungs, and in the black . . . fume thereof, nearest resembling the horrible Stygeian smoke of the pit that is bottomless."

Counter-Jumper. A term humorously applied to a salesman in a drygoods store, in allusion to his supposed habit of jumping over the counter when on his way from one part of the establishment to another.

Country-Dance. This expression has no reference to the country or to country people. It is simply a corruption of the French *contre-danse*, and signifies a dance (as, for instance, the *Sir Roger de Coverley*) in which the partners stand *contre*, or opposite to, each other.

Coup d'État. A phrase signifying a sudden stroke of policy, whereby the existing government of a state is overturned. The expression is generally applied to the successful effort made by Louis Napoleon, on December 2nd, 1851, to subvert the republic of France (which he had solemnly sworn to protect), and to establish a dictatorship in its stead. This conspiracy was planned by Louis Napoleon, Persigny, and De Morny, and carried out by C. de Maupas, minister of police, St. Arnaud, and others. The Legislative Assembly was dissolved, universal suffrage was established, and Paris was declared in a state of siege. The election of a president for a term of ten years was proposed ; 83 members of the Assembly were banished ; and 575 persons were arrested for resistance to the *coup d'état*, and conveyed to Havre for transportation to Cayenne. The *coup d'état* resulted in the restoration of the Empire on December 2nd, 1852.

Court of Lions. A famous apartment in the Alhambra at Granada, Spain, celebrated for the beauty and grace of its architecture. There may be seen the perfection of Moorish art, as little impaired as when it came from the hand of the sculptor, 500 years ago. The court is oblong in shape, and is surrounded by a low gallery resting on 124 columns, remarkable not only for their lightness and elegance, but also for their richness of ornamentation. The square is paved with tiles and the colonnade with white marble, while the walls and capitals of the columns are adorned with arabesques and exquisite filigree work. A pavilion projects into the court at each extremity. The " Court of Lions " takes its name from the fountain that adorns the centre. This consists of an alabaster basin resting upon the figures of twelve lions in white marble. In Moorish days a jet of water rose from the fountain, and, after falling into the basin, passed through the bodies of the lions and issued from their mouths. See *Alhambra*.

Court of St. Germain. When James II (1685–1688) of England fled to France during the Revolution of 1688, he was hospitably received by Louis XIV (1643–1715), and was given the Palace of St. Germain, near Paris, as a royal residence. There he dwelt until his death in 1701. The court of the exiled Stuarts was thereupon known as the Court of St. Germain ; and, during the lifetime of James and that of his son, the Old Pretender, it became the centre of many unsuccessful plots to regain the English throne. See *Pretenders*.

Court of the Great Mogul. An elaborate work of art in the Green Vaults of Dresden, by Dinglinger, jeweler to the court of Saxony. It consists of 138 figures of pure gold, enameled and carved in the most delicate manner, representing the Great Mogul upon his throne, surrounded by his court. Six years were spent by the artist upon this gem. Its cost was about $45,000. See *Green Vaults of Dresden*.

Covenanters. The name given to those Scottish reformers that signed the *National Covenant* and the *Solemn League and Covenant* to resist the aggressions of the Roman Catholic Church and the Church of England, and to secure civil and religious liberty.

(1) *The National Covenant* was drawn up in 1580, at the command of James VI of Scotland, to counteract attempts that were being made by the Roman Catholics to regain possession of that country. It was sworn and subscribed to by all ranks and classes in 1581, and renewed in 1590, 1596, and 1638. The renewal of 1638 was in opposition to the attempt of Charles I to force episcopacy and the prayer-book on Scotland. This covenant was ratified by the Parliament of Charles I, held at Edinburgh in 1640; and was subscribed to by Charles II on his landing in Scotland in 1650, and again at his coronation at Scone in 1651.

(2) *The Solemn League and Covenant.* An international treaty between Scotland and England for the purpose of securing civil and religious liberty for the two kingdoms. It was a modification of the preceding one, and was solemnly adopted by Parliament in 1643. Charles II (1660–1685) accepted it on August 16th, 1650, but repudiated it on his restoration in 1660, when it was declared illegal by Parliament, and copies of it were ordered to be burned.

Covent Garden Theatre. A famous theatre in Bow Street, London, built by Sir W. Davenant, under patent, in 1662. The present structure — the third upon this site — was erected in 1858. It is nearly as large as *La Scala* at Milan, and accommodates an audience of 3500 persons. Covent Garden Theatre is used, at present, almost exclusively for grand opera. See *Drury Lane Theatre; La Scala.*

Coverley, Sir Roger de. The name of a member of an imaginary club, under whose auspices the *Spectator* was supposed to be edited. Sir Roger is the type of an English gentleman of the time of Queen Anne (1702–1714), and figures in thirty papers of the *Spectator*. He is noted for his modesty, generosity, and hospitality. The name *Sir Roger de Coverley* is also given to a dance, similar to the *Virginia Reel*, and supposed to have been the original of it. The title is derived from the English squire described in the *Spectator*.

Cowboys. A name originally given, during the American Revolution, to bands of British marauders and Tories that plundered the people on the east bank of the Hudson River, for a distance of about forty miles north of New York City. This territory was considered neutral ground, and was the scene of many depredations inflicted both by the British and the Americans. The name *cowboys* is now applied to herdsmen on the cattle ranches of the far West. See *Skinners.*

Cracknut Night. A name formerly given to the festival of All Halloween, in allusion to the custom of cracking nuts in the fire on that occasion. See *Halloween.*

Cracow. The name of a city in Austrian Poland, celebrated for the salt-mines of Wieliezka, a village ten miles distant. These mines employ more than 1000 of the 6289 inhabitants of the town, and have an annual output exceeding 50,000 tons. They have been worked for over 600 years, and are the most famous in the world. They extend over an area of about six miles east and west and two miles north and south, and have underground streets and squares, with thirty miles of tramway. They also contain chapels, halls for amusement, caverns, grottoes, and bridges,—all cut out of solid salt. Their greatest depth is 12,000 feet. These mines were almost destroyed by an inundation in 1868.

Cradle of American Liberty. An appellation bestowed upon Faneuil Hall, a large public building in Boston, Massachusetts, in allusion to the many meetings held within its walls by citizens during Revolutionary times, for the purpose of asserting their rights and protesting against British oppression. See *Faneuil Hall.*

Craigenputtoch. The name of a farm near Dumfries, Scotland, famous as the home of Thomas Carlyle (1795–1881), for about nine years (1825–1834). While there he wrote *Sartor Resartus*, as well as the brilliant series of essays contributed to the *Westminster Review*, the *Edinburgh Review*, the *Foreign Quarterly Review*, and *Fraser's Magazine*. In 1867, he bequeathed Craigenputtoch to Edinburgh University.

Crane, Ichabod. The name of a Yankee schoolmaster, whose love-affair with Katrina Van Tassel and subsequent humiliation at the hands of his rival, Brom Bones, are charmingly related by Washington Irving (1783–1859) in the *Legend of Sleepy Hollow*, one of the tales in the *Sketch-Book*.

Cranmer's Bible. The name given to an English version of the Scriptures, which appeared in 1539. It was Tyndale's version, amended by Coverdale, and critically examined by Thomas Cranmer (1489–1556), who also wrote a preface for it. It was printed in 1540, and by royal proclamation, every parish was obliged to have a copy of it in the parish church, under penalty of 40s. per month. See *Tyndale's Bible*.

Crantara. The name of the fiery cross that was passed from place to place in the Scottish Highlands, to rally the clans.

Crapaud, Jean or Johnny (*Fr. Johnny Toad*). A sportive designation of a Frenchman, or of the French nation collectively. It is said to owe its origin to the armorial device of the ancient kings of France—"three toads, erect, saltant." These were afterwards replaced by the fleurs-de-lis. The word *crapaud* was used to designate a Frenchman by Nostradamus (1503–1556) in the line :

"Les anciens *crapauds* prendront Sara."
(The ancient toads shall Sara take.)

Sara is *Aras* reversed ; and when the French, under Louis XIV (1643–1715),

captured that town, they recalled the prophecy.

Crayon, Geoffrey. The *nom-de-plume* under which Washington Irving (1783–1859) published the *Sketch-Book* in 1818.

Crawford Notch. A deep and narrow defile in the White Mountains, New Hampshire. It is about three miles in length, and lies between Mounts Willard and Willey on the west and Mounts Webster and Jackson on the east. The highest point in the Notch is 1915 feet above sea-level, while the massive rocks are visible for 2000 feet above, the peaks being still higher. The scenery throughout this region is grandly impressive. Also called the *White Mountain Notch*. See *Franconia Notch ; Willey House*.

"When we entered the Notch we were struck with the wild and solemn appearance of everything before us. The scale, on which all the objects in view were formed, was the scale of grandeur only. The rocks, rude and ragged in a manner rarely paralleled, were fashioned and piled on each other by a hand operating only in the boldest and most irregular manner. As we advanced, these appearances increased rapidly. Huge masses of granite, of every abrupt form, and hoary with a moss which seemed the product of ages, recalling to the mind the *Saxum vetustum* of Virgil, speedily rose to a mountainous height. Before us, the view widened fast to the S. E. Behind us, it closed almost instantaneously ; and presented nothing to the eye but an impossible barrier of mountains."—Dwight's *Travels in New England*.

Crazy Jane. An epithet conferred upon Joanna la Loca (1479–1555), daughter of Ferdinand and Isabella (of Castile and Aragon). On the death of Isabella in 1504, Joanna inherited the crown of Castile ; but in consequence of her mental imbecility her husband, Philip, exercised the royal power. After the death of her husband in 1506, Joanna spent much of her time in watching his coffin, feeling assured that he would come to life again.

Crécy (or Cressy), Battle of. Fought at Crécy (or Cressy), a village in northern France, on August 26th, 1346, between the English under their king, Edward III (1327–1377), and his son, the Prince of Wales (surnamed the " Black Prince "), and the French under the command of the Count d'Alençon. The English forces numbered about 37,000 men, and the French army 130,000 The battle resulted in a glorious victory for the English ; 30,000 Frenchmen were slain, together with the King of Bohemia (nearly blind) and a number of sovereign princes and French nobles. The English loss was exceedingly small. The Prince of Wales gained his spurs in this battle ; and, according to the commonly received story, adopted, as his crest, that of the slain King of Bohemia—consisting of three ostrich feathers, with the motto *Ich Dien* (*Ger. I Serve*). This has ever since remained the motto and crest of the Princes of Wales. See *Ich Dien*.

Crédit Foncier. The name given to a system of loaning money on the security of real estate, established in France by an edict of February 28th, 1852. The loan is repayable by a terminable annuity,— being so calculated that at the time of the final payment both loan and interest will be extinguished. The borrower is, however, granted the privilege of anticipating repayment. Owing to the terms of the edict, an advance of more than one-half of the value of the property pledged is prohibited. Similar *crédit foncier* companies have been established in Hamburg (1782), western Prussia (1787), Belgium (1841), and England (1863). A system of advancing money on the security of landed property was introduced by Frederick the Great (1740–1786) of Prussia in 1763, to alleviate the distresses in some of the provinces of his kingdom. Three companies were established by the French government in Paris, Marseilles, and Nevers, in 1852, and in December of the same year these were united under the name of the *Crédit Foncier de France.* See *Crédit Mobilier ; Crédit Mobilier of America.*

Crédit Mobilier. The name originally given to a joint-stock company, established at Paris by Isaac and Émile Pereire and others, on November 18th, 1852, for the purpose of advancing money on the security of *movable* property. It was sanctioned by the French government, and received the name of *La Société Générale de Crédit Mobilier,* to distinguish it from the *Sociétés de Crédit Foncier,* which loan money on real or *immovable* property. The avowed object of the society was the promotion of industrial enterprises of all kinds, such as the sinking of mines, the construction of railways, etc. Its operations were conducted on a very large scale, and its early years were ones of great prosperity. In 1854, the society paid a dividend of twelve per cent. In 1855, it made two large loans to the government—one of 250,000,000 and the other of 375,000,-000 francs, and declared a dividend of forty per cent. In 1856, owing to certain necessary restrictions imposed upon the company, the dividends declined to twenty-two per cent., and in 1857 to five per cent. In September of the same year several districts failed, and in 1858 no dividend was declared. Several vain attempts were made to resurrect its credit. In 1871, the company was reorganized, with assets of 48,000,000 francs. In 1878, the capital was reduced from 80,000,-000 francs to 32,000,000 francs, and in 1879 it was raised to 40,000,000 francs. In 1884, the capital was reduced to 30,000,000 francs. Similar companies have been organized in England, Holland, and America. See *Crédit Foncier ; Crédit Mobilier of America.*

Crédit Mobilier of America. The name of a joint-stock company, chartered in Pennsylvania in 1859, to carry on a general loan and contract business, and organized in May, 1863, with a capital of $2,500,000. Four years later (1867), its charter was purchased by the company formed for the construction of the Union Pacific Railroad, and its capital increased to $3,750,000. In 1872, accusations were made in the public press against several members of Congress,— including Vice-President Schuyler Colfax,— who, it was declared, had been bribed, on behalf of the Union Pacific Railroad, by stock of the *Crédit Mobilier of America*. An investigation was immediately ordered by Congress, and consumed a large part of the session of 1872–1873. As a result of their deliberations, the Senate committee (February 27th, 1873) recommended the expulsion of one senator, but no action was taken, as his term of office expired five days later. The House committee, on the same date, passed a resolution, censuring Oakes Ames of Massachusetts and James Brooks of New York for connection with the *Crédit Mobilier*. See *Crédit Mobilier*.

Creedmoor. The name of a village on Long Island, 12 miles east of New York City. Once celebrated for its extensive rifle-range, the largest and most complete in the United States, established in 1871. See *Wimbledon*.

Cremation. Burning the dead was the practice in vogue among the Aryans and their descendants, the Greeks and Romans, Celts, Germans, and Slavs ; and hence may be regarded as the universal custom of the early Indo-European races. Christianity, with its belief in the literal resurrection of the body, is largely responsible for the practice of burying the dead. A return to cremation has, however, been insisted upon by many, mainly for sanitary reasons, during the past 25 years ; and the custom is growing, although slowly, in Europe and America. The crematories of the world have increased from 1 in 1874 to 4 in 1880, and to over 50 in 1890. Of these 17 were in the United States ; and up to May, 1891, over 2200 bodies had

been incinerated. It is estimated that 47 per cent. of the dead in Japan are cremated. The city of Tokio contained, in 1890, 6 crematories which reduced annually 10,000 bodies to ashes. Cremation has been legal in Italy since 1877. Two crematory furnaces were built in the cemetery of Père-Lachaise, at the suggestion of the municipality of Paris, in 1887, at a cost of $50,000. The first incineration at Fresh Pond, Long Island, occurred on December 4th, 1885. There are 23 cremation societies or incineration companies in the United States. In 1895, the number of bodies cremated in the United States was 964. The time required for the reduction of an adult varies from $1\frac{1}{4}$ to $1\frac{3}{4}$ hours, and the ashes weigh from 5 to 7 pounds. Societies for securing the legalization of cremation exist in nearly every country in Europe. It is said that since 1874 more than 3000 books and pamphlets on cremation have been published.

Cremona. A city of northern Italy on the river Po, 60 miles from Milan. It was founded by the Romans in 221 B.C., and in 1859 became part of the kingdom of Italy. Cremona was famous from 1550 to 1750 for the manufacture of violins. Among the most eminent makers were the Amatis (father and son), Stradivarius, and Guarnerius. Cremona lost its reputation for this branch of industry years ago, although violins of the above-named makers still fetch a high price.

Creole. The subjoined extracts are given to show the confusion that exists concerning the meaning of this word.

"In general an individual born in the country, but not of indigenous blood, a term applied, especially in the former Spanish, French, and Portuguese colonies of America, Africa, and the East Indies, to natives of pure European blood (*sangre azul*), in opposition to immigrants themselves born in Europe, or to the offspring of mixed blood, as mulattoes, quadroons, Eurasians, and the like."—*Chambers's Encyclopædia*.

"In the United States (Louisiana), any native of French or Spanish descent by either parent, especially French."—Harper's *Book of Facts*.

"A Creole is a person born in the West Indies or South America *of European parents*. The name is often erroneously applied to persons of mixed white and black parentage."—Edwards's *Words, Facts, and Phrases*.

"In the West Indies, in Spanish America, and in the Southern States, one born of European parents; but as now used in the South it is applied to everything that is native, peculiar to, or raised there. In the New Orleans market, one may hear of *creole* corn, *creole* chickens, *creole* cattle, and *creole* horses. In that city, too, a *creole* is a native of French extraction, as pure in pedigree as a Howard; and great offence has been given by strangers applying the term to a good-looking mulatto or quadroon."—Bartlett's *Dictionary of Americanisms*.

"One born of European parents in the American colonies of France or Spain or in the States which were once such colonies, esp. a person of French or Spanish descent, who is a native inhabitant of Louisiana, or one of the States adjoining, bordering on the Gulf of Mexico."—Webster's *International Dictionary*.

"(1) A native of Spanish America or the West Indies, of European (originally Spanish parentage): distinguished from a negro, aboriginal, or person of mixed blood.

"(2) In Louisiana: 1) a native descended from French or Spanish ancestors by either parent, or a white native who speaks French. 2) A native-born negro, as distinguished from one brought from Africa."—*Standard Dictionary*.

Creole State. An appellation bestowed upon the State of Louisiana, on account of the great number of French and Spanish that originally settled there, and whose descendants still form a large part of the population. See *Creole*.

Crescent and Cross. An expression used to denote Mohammedanism and Christianity,—the crescent being the symbol of the Saracens and the cross that of the Christians.

Crescent City. A name given to New Orleans, Louisiana, on account of the position occupied by the older portion of the city on one of the curves of the Mississippi. In later years, however, the city has been so much extended that the line of its river-front more nearly resembles the capital letter S.

Crescent of Islâm. During the siege of Byzantium — now Constantinople—by Philip of Macedon (359–336 B.C.) in 340 B.C., tradition says that a bright light in the shape of a crescent suddenly appeared and revealed to the Athenian garrison the plans of the besiegers, which in consequence miscarried. To commemorate this event, the Athenians erected a statue to Diana, goddess of the moon, and made the crescent the emblem of the state. When the Turks captured the city of Constantinople in 1453 A.D., they adopted this crescent as their symbol. The crescent is often used to indicate progress and enterprise. In Moscow and other Russian cities, it is seen on churches, surmounted by a cross. According to some, this indicates the Byzantine origin of the Greek Church; according to others, it symbolizes the triumph of Russia over Turkey.

According to another legend, the Sultan Othmân (1280–1326), the founder of the Ottoman dynasty, saw in a vision a crescent moon, which continued to increase until its horns reached from farthest east to farthest west; whereupon he adopted the crescent of his dream as a standard, and took for his motto the Latin words: *Donec repleat orbem* (*Until it shall complete the circle*).

Crichton, Admirable. See *Admirable Crichton*.

Cricket. The English national game, the earliest reference to which is found in the year 1300, during the reign of Edward I (1272–1307). The word *cricket* first occurs about 1550. The game was played at Winchester as early as 1650. Rules were adopted in 1774 by a committee of noblemen and gentlemen, including the Duke of Dorset and Sir Horace Mann. The first English team visited the United States in 1859, and were generally successful. The first English team visited Australia in 1861, and the first Australian team returned the compliment in 1878. A team of Philadelphians made a tour of England in 1897, and played all the leading counties, the Universities, and the "M. C. C." They played, in all, 15 matches,—of which 2 were won, 9 lost, and 4 drawn.

Crimea. This peninsula, extending into the Black Sea, derives its name from a small town established there by the Kimri, or Cymri, and known to the Greeks as *Kimmerikon*.

Crimean War. The name given to a war declared against Russia, on March 28th, 1854, by England and France (afterwards joined by Sardinia), to frustrate the ambitious designs of the Czar Nicholas in the East,—particularly in respect of the Danubian principalities and the protectorate of the Greek Church in the Turkish Empire. Although some naval actions took place in the Baltic and Black Seas, the fighting was mainly confined to the Crimean peninsula, where the allied forces — consisting of about 58,-000 men, under Lord Raglan and Marshal St. Arnaud—landed on September 14th–16th, 1854. Among the battles fought were those of the Alma, Balaklava, Inkermann, and Sebastopol, in which the allies were generally victorious. Peace was declared in March, 1856 ; and by the terms of the Treaty of Paris the Russians lost all that they had gained or attempted to gain in the struggle. The allied forces quitted the Crimea on the 12th of July, 1856.

Crishna. See *Krishna*.

Crisis. The name given to a series of fourteen papers published in Philadelphia by Thomas Paine (1737–1809), during the years 1775–1783. They were extremely patriotic, and did much to revive the drooping spirits of the

colonists during the trying years of the Revolutionary War. The second paper, written just after the hasty departure of the Continental Congress from Philadelphia, begins with the famous words,—" These are the times that try men's souls."

Critique of Pure Reason. A famous philosophic treatise by Immanuel Kant (1724–1804). It appeared in 1781, and laid the foundation of modern German metaphysics. This was followed by the *Critique of Practical Reason*, and the *Critique of the Power of Judgment*. These three *critiques* are, in reality, parts of one great work, and cannot be correctly understood except when studied together.

Crocodile's Tears. A term applied to sham tears or hypocritical sorrow, in allusion to the tale of ancient travelers that crocodiles moan and sigh to allure persons to their vicinity, and even shed tears while devouring them. Although, in point of fact, the crocodile has large lachrymal glands, it has nevertheless acquired a reputation for deceitfulness wholly undeserved.

Spenser, in his *Faerie Queene*, I, v, 18, speaks of the
"Cruell craftie crocodile,
Which, in false griefe hyding his harmefull guile,
Doth weepe full sore, and sheddeth tender teares."

Shakespeare, in *Henry VI, Second Part*, iii, 1, says :
"As the mournful crocodile
With sorrow snares relenting passengers,"

Croesus's Wealth. Crœsus (560–546 B.C.), King of Lydia in Asia Minor, was famous, in antiquity, for his great wealth. Tradition says that this was principally obtained from the golden sands of the river Pactolus, which flowed through his dominions ; but the true source of his riches is probably to be found in the industry of the Lydian people. The value of his landed property has been estimated at $8,333,330. The expression—" As rich as Crœsus"— has passed into a proverb. See *Pactolus*.

Crooked Whiskey. An expression used to denote whiskey on which the excise duty has been evaded, either by frauds or by the connivance of government inspectors. In 1872–1875, large quantities of crooked whiskey were distilled at Chicago, St. Louis, and other western cities, by which the United States government was defrauded out of millions of dollars. In the investigations that followed, several distillers and government officials, having been convicted of fraud, were heavily fined and imprisoned.

Cross, True. The cross on which Jesus Christ suffered death is said to have been dug up on the spot now occupied by the Church of the Holy Sepulchre in Jerusalem, in the presence of the Empress Helena, mother of Constantine, on May 3rd, 326 (termed the *Invention of the Cross*). With the cross were found two others (presumably those of the two thieves), together with the crown of thorns, the nails, and the inscription. The cross was carried off by Chosroes (531–579 A.D.), King of Persia, when Jerusalem was sacked by him ; but was recovered and restored by the Emperor Heraclius I (610–641 A.D.), on September 14th, 615,—a day that has since been celebrated as the *Festival of the Exaltation of the Cross* (instituted in 642). An altar and a crucifix in the Church of the Holy Sepulchre now mark the place of the discovery, and form objects of special interest to all pious pilgrims to Jerusalem. Tradition declares that the Empress Helena cut the cross into three unequal parts,— one of which she gave to Macarius, Patriarch of Jerusalem ; one to Constantinople ; and one to Rome. It is said that this last piece is now inclosed in one of the four pillars that support the dome of St. Peter's Church. The part sent to Constantinople was afterwards given to Louis IX. (1226–1270) of France, and

is now in the Cathedral of Notre Dame de Paris. The piece given to Jerusalem was subdivided into 19 pieces,—4 of which were retained in the city, while the remaining 15 were distributed among other places in the Orient.

According to Brewer's *Historic Note-Book*, at least 79 places claim at present to possess pieces of the true cross. Calvin said that " fifty men could not carry the wood of what is called the true cross," and Luther asserted that there was wood enough " to build an immense house." See *Invention of the Cross ; Santa Croce in Gerusalemme ; Wood of the Cross.*

Crossroads, Burying at. See *Burying at Crossroads.*

Crow, Jim. The name of a popular negro-song first brought out in Louisville, Kentucky, by Thomas D. Rice, the famous delineator of negro character. It proved to be a great success, and was afterwards produced by Rice at the Adelphi Theatre, London, in 1836. There it had an equally great popularity, and Rice soon found himself a celebrity in the London theatrical world. The burden of the song is as follows :

"Wheel about, and turn about, and do just so ;
And every time you wheel about, jump *Jim Crow.*"

Crown of England. The Imperial State Crown of England was made by Messrs Rundell and Bridges in 1838, with jewels taken from old crowns, and others furnished by command of the late Queen Victoria. Its gross weight is 39 oz. 5 dwt. Troy. It contains one large ruby, one large sapphire, 16 ordinary sapphires, 11 emeralds, 4 rubies, 1363 brilliants, 1273 rose diamonds, 147 table diamonds, 4 drop-shaped pearls, and 273 pearls. The large ruby in front, said to have been given to the Black Prince in 1367 by Don Pedro of Castile, was worn by Henry V on his helmet, at the battle of Agincourt, in

1415. The crown of England, together with other crown jewels, is now in the Record or Wakefield Tower, in the Tower of London. The total value of the regalia is estimated at $15,000,000. See *Regalia of England*.

Crown of Scotland. The ancient crown of Scotland, together with the sceptre and the sword of state, is at present in charge of the officers of state for Scotland, and is exhibited in the Crown-room of Edinburgh Castle. These ensigns of royalty were discovered, in 1818, in a chest in the castle, where they had lain hidden since the union of England and Scotland in 1706. The crown is probably of the time of Robert Bruce (1306–1329), but the four gold arches supporting the cross were afterwards added during the reign of James IV (1488–1513). The sceptre is of the time of James V (1513–1542), and the sword of state was a present from Pope Julius II (1503–1513) to James IV in 1507. See *Edinburgh Castle*.

Crowned after Death. See *Castro, Inez de*.

Crucifixion, Relics of the. The following is a list of the relics connected with the crucifixion of Jesus Christ. According to tradition, most of these still exist, and are preserved in various parts of Europe ; but not the slightest reliance can be placed on their claims to genuineness.

The Bandage.	The Robe.
" Blood.	" Spear.
" Cross.	" Sponge.
" Crown of Thorns.	" Staircase.
" Cup.	" Table.
" Grave Clothes.	" Title.
" Handkerchief.	" Tunic or Shirt.
" Nails.	" Whipping-Post.
" Reed.	

See *Relics*.

Cruel. A surname bestowed upon Pedro I (1350–1369), King of Castile and Leon, in allusion to his inhuman treatment of his wife and brothers.

Crusades. The name given to the wars waged by the Christian nations of Europe, to drive the Saracens from Jerusalem and recover possession of the Holy Land. The soldiers that embarked on these enterprises wore a cross on the breast or right shoulder, as a badge of their religious faith ; hence the name *Crusades* (*Fr. croisade*, from *Lat. crux, cross*). These expeditions, according to Haydn's *Dictionary of Dates*, were eight in number, as follows :

(1) *First Crusade* (1095) ended by Jerusalem being taken by assault, July 15th, 1099 ; Godfrey de Bouillon made king.

(2) *Second Crusade* preached by St. Bernard in 1146 ; headed by Emperor Conrad II of Germany and Louis VII of France. Crusaders defeated ; Jerusalem lost in 1187.

(3) *Third Crusade.* Led by Emperor Frederick Barbarossa of Germany, in 1188; joined by Philip II of France and Richard I of England, in 1190. Glorious, but fruitless.

(4) *Fourth Crusade.* Led in 1195, by Emperor Henry VI ; successful till his death in 1197.

(5) *Fifth Crusade.* Proclaimed by Innocent III in 1198. Baldwin, Count of Flanders, attacked the Greeks, and took Constantinople in 1203. His companions returned.

(6) *Sixth Crusade* in 1216. In 1229, Emperor Frederick II obtained possession of Jerusalem on a truce for ten years. In 1240, Richard, Earl of Cornwall, arrived in Palestine, but soon departed.

(7) *Seventh Crusade.* Led by Louis IX (St. Louis) in 1248, who was defeated and taken prisoner at Mansourah, 5th April, 1250 ; released by ransom ; truce of ten years.

(8) *Eighth and Last Crusade*, in 1270, by the same prince, who died of a contagious disease, at Carthage, in Africa, 2nd August. Prince Edward, afterwards Edward I of England, was at Acre, 1271. In 1291, the Sultan took Acre, and the Christians were driven out of Syria.

It is estimated that the Crusades cost the lives of 2,000,000 men.

Crusoe, Robinson. The name of the hero of Defoe's immortal story, who, being shipwrecked on an island in the tropics, leads a solitary life for many years and relieves its monotony by an inexhaustible fertility of resources. The story was founded on the adventures of Alexander Selkirk (1676–1723), a Scottish sailor, who, having quarrelled with his captain during one of his voyages, was left on the island of Juan Fernandez in 1704, with only his gun and ammunition, and a few other necessaries of life. There he remained for over four years, living on game, and clothing himself with the skins of goats. In 1709, he was rescued by Captain Woodes Rogers, and became his mate. He afterwards attained the rank of lieutenant in the navy. Defoe has often been charged with having surreptitiously taken the story of *Robinson Crusoe* from the papers of Alexander Selkirk, but the experiences of the real hero and those of the fictitious one have so little in common that Defoe seems indebted for little more than the suggestion. See *Crusoe's Island ; Juan Fernandez.*

Sir Walter Scott says : " Perhaps there exists no work in the English language which has been more generally read and more universally admired than the *Adventures of Robinson Crusoe.*

Crusoe's Island. The name popularly given to the island of Juan Fernandez, off the coast of Chili, from an erroneous notion that it was the scene of the adventures of Robinson Crusoe. There are shown *Crusoe's Cave*, the beach where he landed his famous raft, and *Crusoe's Lookout*, 3000 feet above the ocean. The island where Defoe placed his hero was in the tropics, off the eastern coast of South America. See *Crusoe, Robinson ; Juan Fernandez.*

Crust of The Earth. Our knowledge of the earth's crust extends to a rela-

tively slight depth below the surface, —the aggregate thickness of the strata or rock-layers already measured, being about 130,000 feet, or nearly 24½ miles. Rocks are divided into two classes, (1) *the unstratified* (which are the older and are nearer the centre of the earth) and (2) the *stratified* (which are the more recent and are nearer the surface). The unstratified rocks (also called *igneous* or *plutonic*) include all rocks that have been fused by heat, or erupted from the earth's interior by volcanic action. The stratified rocks (also called *aqueous* or *neptunic*) include all rocks that have been deposited as sediment by the action of water or of the atmosphere, or that are due to the growth and decay of animals and plants. With the stratified rocks may be grouped the *metamorphic* rocks, consisting, for the most part, of stratified rocks that have been metamorphosed into a crystalline state by the action of heat and pressure,—a change that has resulted in the obliteration of their original character and in the effacement of all traces of organic remains. The depth to which the unstratified rocks extend is unknown, but it is generally considered that at a comparatively short distance from the surface the heat is sufficient to cause all rocks to assume a molten form.

Crutched Friars. A name given to the Trinitarians or Friars of the Holy Trinity, on account of the cross (*Lat. cruciati, crossed*) embroidered on their dress. Other authorities say that they received the name of *Croisiers* (*Fr. croix, cross*), corrupted into *Crouched* or *Crutched* Friars, because of the staff carried by them, the top of which was surmounted by a cross. The Order was founded at Bologna about 1169, and first made its appearance in England in the 13th century. The Crutched Friars had monasteries in London, Oxford, and Reigate.

Crystalline Spheres. The name given, in the Ptolemaic System of astronomy, to a concentric series of immense transparent spheres surrounding the earth,—to each of which was attached a heavenly body. By the revolution of these spheres the sun, moon, planets, and fixed stars were made to move around the earth. The first or innermost sphere was that of the Moon, and after it in order came those of Mercury, Venus, the Sun, Mars, Jupiter, Saturn, and the fixed stars,—eight in all. Later astronomers added a ninth sphere to account for the precession of the equinoxes, and a tenth to produce the alternations of day and night. The tenth sphere—or *primum mobile*, as it was called — was supposed to revolve from east to west in 24 hours, and to carry the remaining crystalline spheres along with it. This fanciful explanation of the movements of the heavenly bodies was accepted as the true one, until the adoption of the Copernican System of astronomy in the seventeenth century. See *Copernican System ; Primum Mobile ; Ptolemaic System.*

Crystal Palace at Sydenham. A gigantic structure, constructed entirely of iron and glass, and situated at Sydenham, Kent, a few miles from London. It stood originally in Hyde Park, and was erected for the Industrial Exhibition of 1851. In December of that year, the building was sold to a company for $350,000, and removed to Sydenham, where it was rebuilt on an enlarged scale. It occupies an area of 17 acres, and consists of a spacious central nave 1608 feet long, with lateral sections, two aisles, and two transepts. The entire cost, including the grounds, has amounted to $7,500,-000. The gardens cover an area of 200 acres, and are beautifully laid out in terraces and adorned with flower-beds, cascades, fountains, and statuary. The fountains are considered the finest in the world, two of the principal ones throwing jets to a height of 280 feet. On special occasions, known as "Grand Displays of the Fountains,"

120,000 gallons are thrown up per minute. The Crystal Palace is used for monster concerts, dramatic entertainments, flower-shows, live-stock shows, etc. It contains an aquarium, well stocked with fish, and an excellent picture gallery.

Crystal Palace, New York. A vast structure — covering five acres — formerly occupying the plot of ground at Sixth Avenue, 40th and 42nd Streets, New York City, now known as Bryant Park. It was opened for a universal industrial exhibition by President Pierce on July 14th, 1853, in the presence of 20,000 persons. The building was afterwards used for the annual fairs of the American Institute, as well as for monster concerts and meetings, and was totally destroyed by fire on October 5th, 1858.

Cucumber Time. The name given to the dull season in the tailoring trade. The Germans call this period *die saure gurken zeit (pickled-gherkin time).* The expression, "Tailors are vegetarians" is said to have arisen because they live on *cucumber* when out of work, and on *cabbage* when fully employed.

Culloden, Battle of. Fought at Culloden, a desolate tract of moorland six miles northeast of Inverness, on April 16th, 1746, between 12,000 English regulars under the Duke of Cumberland, and 5000 Highlanders headed by Prince Charles Edward, called the "Young Pretender," grandson of James II. The battle resulted in a crushing defeat for the Scotch, with a loss of 2500 men killed on the field or in the retreat, while the English loss was only 200. Although the English artillery wrought havoc among the Scotch, it is said that the Highlanders would have won the day, if one of the clans, offended at being placed on the left, had not refused to charge at the crisis of the battle. Prince Charles, after wandering for six months among the wilds of Scotland, while £30,000 were offered for his apprehension, escaped to France, and finally died at Rome on March 3rd, 1778. Since 1881, a cairn 20 feet in height, with an inscription, marks the spot where the battle raged most fiercely, and where many of the slain lie buried. See *Bloody Butcher ; Last Battle.*

Cumberland. This word originally meant the land of *Cymri.*

Cunaxa, Battle of. A battle fought in 401 B.C., at Cunaxa, sixty miles northwest of Babylon, between Artaxerxes Mnemon (405–362 B.C.) and his brother, Cyrus the Younger. The latter was defeated and slain.

Cunctator (*Lat. Delayer*). A surname bestowed upon Quintus Fabius Maximus Verrucosus, the Roman consul, on account of his policy, during the Second Punic War (218–201 B.C.) of avoiding a direct conflict with Hannibal and wearing him out with marches and countermarches. So successful was Fabius in carrying on this strictly defensive system of warfare, that the Carthaginian general was unable to obtain any advantage over him. See *American Fabius ; Fabian Policy.*

Cuneiform Letters (*Lat. cuneus, wedge*). The name given to certain peculiar wedge-shaped or arrow-head characters, inscribed on bricks or clay tablets and found in great numbers among the ruins of Nineveh, Babylon, and Persepolis. They are said to have been invented and introduced into the valley of the Euphrates by the primitive Accadians, and to have been afterwards improved and simplified by the Assyrians and Persians. Sayce says that this form of writing arose when the Accadians, having entered the low country, substituted tablets of clay for papyrus or other similar material, formerly used by them. The earliest date assigned to the use of cuneiform characters is about 3800 B.C., and this use continued until after the Christian

era. Cuneiform letters were also inscribed on bronze, glass, iron, stone, and other substances. These peculiar inscriptions were first successfully deciphered by Grotefend of Hanover, about 1802. Among other scholars that have labored in this direction may be mentioned Burnouf, Lassen, Westergaard, Beer, and Jacquet. Rawlinson not only copied, but also read, the *Behistun Inscription,* consisting of more than 1000 lines. See *Accadians ; Behistun Inscription.*

Cunnersdorf, Battle of. A desperate battle fought on August 12th, 1759, between 50,000 Prussians, commanded by their king, Frederick the Great (1740–1786), and the allied Russians and Austrians, 90,000 in number. The Prussians were the attacking party, and their efforts were at first crowned with success ; but they were finally defeated with a loss of 30,000 killed and wounded, and 200 pieces of artillery.

Cupboard Love. Another name for selfish love, or love from interested motives. It doubtless had its origin in the well-known affection of children for those that feed them on dainties from the cupboard.

Cup of Tantalus. The name of a pretty toy, which illustrates the principle of the siphon in pneumatics. It consists simply of a cup, containing a standing human figure which conceals a siphon. The short branch of the siphon rises in one leg of the figure and reaches the level of the chin, while the long branch descends by the other leg and makes its exit through the bottom of the vessel. When water is poured into the cup, it rises until it reaches the bend of the siphon, whereupon the cup is quickly emptied. Since the lips of the figure are on a level with this bend, it is apparently prevented from drinking in a " tantalizing " way. The toy is said to be a Chinese invention, and derives its name from Tantalus, a noted character in Greek mythology, who, having incurred the wrath of the gods, was condemned to suffer perpetual hunger and thirst. See *Tantalus.*

Curbstone Brokers. Brokers that are not members of any exchange, but transact their business on the street or in offices. They are also known as "street-brokers" or "gutter-snipes." Transactions effected outside the exchanges, or after business hours, are sometimes spoken of as "on the curb." See *Gutter-Snipes.*

Curfew-Bell (*Fr. couvre-feu, cover fire*). A bell formerly rung in England, at sunset in summer and at eight o'clock in winter,—the object of which was to warn the people to *cover up* their fires, extinguish their lamps and candles, and retire to rest. The custom is a Norman one, and is said to have been introduced into England by William the Conqueror (1066–1087) in 1068, as a precaution against fires in the days of chimneyless wooden houses. This enactment was repealed in the reign of Henry I (1100–1135), in 1100. There is good reason, however, for believing that a similar custom existed in England in the days of Alfred the Great (871–901), and that William the Conqueror merely ordained that it should be universally observed, and that penalties should be imposed upon those that neglected to attend to the signal. The custom of ringing the curfew-bell is still observed in various parts of England, although the original purpose no longer exists. The Puritans introduced the custom into New England, and Longfellow speaks, in *The Bells of Lynn*, of the "curfew of the setting sun" as heard at Nahant.

Curiosities. The following interesting facts, concerning the prices paid in recent years for curiosities, are taken from Mulhall's *Dictionary of Statistics :*

(1) *Books.* Mr. Quaritch paid £4900 for a Latin Psalter, and £3900 for a Mazarine Bible at Syston Hall sale.

(2) *Coins.* In 1889, a silver penny of William the Conqueror fetched £32, a half-crown of Elizabeth £44, and one of Charles I £35 sterling.

(3) *Letters and Autographs.* In 1889, at public sale in London, the following prices were paid :

	£		£
Addison	5	Johnson, S.	6
Bolingbroke	9	Kean, E.	9
Bruce (traveller)	6	Keats	14
Burke	8	Lamb, C.	6
Burns	18	Nelson	11
Byron	7	Newton	64
Carlyle	4	Poe, E.	6
Coleridge	3	Pope	16
Dickens	9	Quincey	7
Disraeli	5	Richelieu	5
Elizabeth		Schiller	6
(Queen)	11	Scott	17
Eliot, George	11	Shelley	19
Franklin	6	Smollett	8
Gibbon	6	Sterne	8
Hood	6	Tennyson	7
Hume	5	Thackeray	6
Irving, W.	2	Washington	10

(4) *Manuscripts.* That of Burns's poem, *Scots Wha Hae*, was sold in London in May, 1890, for £70 : that of Wilkie Collins's novel, *The Woman in White*, on the same occasion, for £320.

(5) *Postage Stamps.* A collection was sold in Paris in 1880 for £8000 sterling ; the purchaser was said to be the Duchess Galiera, otherwise known for her princely donations to the poor of Genoa.

(6) *Violins.* At a sale in Paris in 1887 the following prices were paid:

	Date.		£
Stradivarius	1689	....	760
"	1691	....	480
Ruggeri	1650	....	1280

A violin bow by Tourte fetched £44 sterling.

(7) *Walking-Stick.* That of George IV was sold at auction in July, 1890, for £18 sterling.

Curse of Cromwell. The name given to Oliver Cromwell's campaign in Ireland in 1649–1650, on account of the revolting cruelties with which it was stained. Although the awful massacres of Drogheda, Clonmel, and Wexford (in which no quarter was given) were deplored by Cromwell, they were nevertheless justified by him as necessary to the subjugation of the island.

Curse of Scotland. A phrase popularly applied in Great Britain to the nine of diamonds in a pack of playing-cards.

"Perhaps the least worthless of the many explanations offered is that it involves a reference to the detestation entertained in Scotland towards John Dalrymple, first Earl of Stair, on account of his activity in promoting the Union, and especially for his share in the Massacre of Glencoe. His heraldic bearings, 'or, on a saltire azure, nine lozenges of the field,' bore a fanciful resemblance to the nine of diamonds."—*Chambers's Encyclopædia.*

Curtain-Lecture. A private fault-finding administered by a wife to her husband, and supposed to have been originally given behind the curtains of a bed. The *Caudle Lectures* in *Punch* are excellent caricatures of this form of domestic discipline. See *Caudle Lectures.*

Curtain, Painted. Zeuxis and Parrhasius, rival painters of Greece, were each commissioned to paint a picture, as a trial of their skill. On the day appointed, Zeuxis produced a painting of a bunch of grapes,—so cleverly represented that the birds came and pecked at them. Parrhasius was thereupon requested by his rival to remove the curtain that concealed his picture. "The curtain *is* the picture," replied Parrhasius; and Zeuxis was forced to confess himself vanquished, since he had deceived only the birds, while Parrhasius had deceived Zeuxis himself.

Curule Chair. A chair of state in use among the ancient Romans. It was originally in the form of a camp-stool, ornamented with ivory; but afterwards was highly decorated and inlaid with gold. The curule chair was at first used by the ancient kings;

and, in later times, by state-officers, such as dictators, consuls, prætors, senators, and others, who occupied it while presiding over public assemblies. It could be easily moved from place to place, and occupied a position in the chariot of the magistrate, when he rode in state.

Cut One's Eye-Teeth, To. An expression meaning to learn the ways of the world. The eye-teeth are the canine teeth, and Brewer, in his *Dictionary of Phrase and Fable*, says that the phrase means either that the person has cut his *canine* teeth, and consequently can bite as well as bark; or that he has cut his *eye*-teeth, and is necessarily wide-awake and has his wits about him.

Cut One's Wisdom-Teeth, To. A phrase meaning to reach years of discretion. The wisdom-teeth (four in number) are the last ones to make their appearance, and consequently are supposed to do so at a time when the person has attained unto years of wisdom.

Cyclades (*Gr. κύκλος, circle*). A group of islands, about 20 in number, in the Ægean Sea,—so called because, according to the classic legend, they *circled* around Delos (the most important of them) when that island was made stationary by the birth of Diana and Apollo. Strabo (60 B.C.–24 A.D.) says that the Cyclades are 12 in number; but this number is increased by other writers. See *Sporades.*

Cyclopean Masonry. A name given to walls constructed of large, irregular, but closely-fitting stones—unhewn and uncemented,—specimens of which may still be seen at Mycenæ and Tiryns and other parts of Greece, and also in Italy. These walls were probably built by the Pelasgians, a race anterior to the Greeks and Romans, about 1000 B.C.; but later generations, struck by their vast proportions, ascribed their construction to the fabulous race of the Cyclopes, whence their name. Examples of Cyclopean masonry exist also in Sicily, Ireland, and Peru. See *Cyclopes* (3).

Cyclopes (*Gr. Κύκλωπες, Round-Eyed*). The Cyclopes of ancient mythology fall into three groups:

(1) *The Cyclopes of Homer.* These were lawless and impious giants, who inhabited the island of Sicily, and devoured human beings. Their chief, Polyphemus, had one eye only, placed in the centre of his forehead,—which peculiarity was also common to the rest of the race, according to the later poets, although Homer nowhere mentions the fact.

(2) *The Cyclopes of Hesiod.* According to Hesiod, the Cyclopes were three in number: Brontes, Steropes, and Arges, each of whom had one eye, in the centre of his forehead. They were sons of Uranus and Gæa, belonged to the race of Titans, and were hurled into Tartarus, — first by Uranus, and again by Saturn. Eventually they were released by Jupiter, whose servants they afterwards became. They provided Jupiter with thunderbolts, Pluto with a helmet, and Neptune with a trident. They were finally slain by Apollo for having furnished Jupiter with thunderbolts wherewith to kill Æsculapius. According to a later tradition, the Cyclopes were the slaves of Hephæstus, and had their workshops either in Mount Etna or in the volcanoes of Lemnos and Lipari, where they made metal armor for the gods and heroes.

(3) *The Cyclopes of Strabo.* A fabulous race of giants to whom is attributed the construction of the so-called Cyclopean masonry. They are said to have come from Thrace or Lycia into Argolis, and were famous for their skill as builders. See *Cyclopean Masonry.*

Cynics. A sect of Grecian philosophers, founded by Antisthenes (440–376 B.C.) about 396 B.C. The Cynics were noted for their morose and gloomy views of life; for their disregard of all sciences, save that of morality; and for their contempt for the ordinary conventionalities of life. The word *Cynic* is derived either from *Cynosarges* (*Gr. White Dog*), the place where Antisthenes taught; or from κυνικός (*Gr. doglike*), in allusion to the snarling or surly manner affected by the philosophers of this school. To Diogenes of Sinope, the most distinguished disciple of Antisthenes, the Athenians erected a column of Parian marble surmounted by a dog.

Cyprians. A name given to the natives and inhabitants of the island of Cyprus, especially in ancient times. The ancient Cyprians were celebrated for their worship of Venus, and for their devotion to love and pleasure. The word *Cyprians* is at present applied to women of easy virtue.

Cyrenaics. A philosophic sect founded at Cyrene in Africa, by Aristippus (fl. 400 B.C.), a disciple of Socrates. His system of philosophy favored free indulgence in sensual pleasures, and he himself is said to have regarded pleasure as the chief object of life, although he observed moderation in the enjoyment of it.

Cyropædia (*Gr. Κυροπαιδεία, Education of Cyrus*). A political romance by Xenophon (445–355 B.C.), founded on the exploits of Cyrus the Great, founder of the Persian Empire. The *Cyropædia*, from internal evidence and because it contradicts other histories, is not considered authentic, but is rather regarded as a historical romance, wherein the author sets forth his own political opinions, and shows what should be the conduct of a wise and virtuous monarch.

Czar (*Russian tsare, chief*). The principal title borne by the Emperors of Russia, and first assumed by them in 1547, when Ivan IV (1533–1584)—surnamed "The Terrible" — caused himself to be crowned Czar. Previous to that date, this name had been taken by the princes of Moscow as rulers of the Mongols. The word *czar* — more properly spelled *tsar*, *tzar*, or *zar* — is said to be derived from the Latin *Cæsar*. See *Cæsar; Kaiser*.

D

Dagon. The national god of the Philistines,—half man, half fish. According to the *Old Testament*, Dagon had temples at Ashdod, Ascalon, Ekron, Gath, and Gaza (the five principal cities of the Philistines). This deity seems to have been introduced into Canaan from Babylonia, and is probably identical with the Assyrian god, *Dakan* or *Dagan*,—found in the cuneiform inscriptions, and pictured on monuments as having the face and hands of a man and the tail of a fish. In Milton's *Paradise Lost*, Dagon is mentioned as sixth in order in the hierarchy of Hell, — the first five being Satan, Beelzebub, Moloch, Chemos, and Thammuz.

Dagos. The name given originally to people of Spanish parentage, born in Louisiana; but now applied there to all Italians, Sicilians, Spanish, and Portuguese. The word *dago* is said by some to be a corruption of *hidalgo*, a title given to a Spanish nobleman of the lower class.

The following quotation, however, suggests another origin of the word :

"In Spanish America, 'Santiago,' 'San Diego,' 'Iago,' and 'Diego' are such frequently recurring vocables that the Yankee sailor calls natives of these countries *Dago* men, or Diegos."—*Griffis Perry*.

Daguerreotype. The name given to the first successful attempt at photography, in honor of the inventor, Louis Daguerre (1789-1851). This process was perfected in 1839, and consists of a copper plate silvered, and covered, by the action of the vapor of iodine, with a thin film of iodide of silver. By means of the action of light on this iodide of silver, at the focal point of the camera obscura, a picture of the object is formed on the plate. This result is afterwards " developed " by means of vapor of mercury, and " fixed " by treatment in a solution of sodium hyposulphite. In recognition of the importance of his discovery, the French government awarded to Daguerre a life pension of 6000 francs. See *Camera Obscura*.

Dahlia. This flower is named after Andrew Dahl, the Swedish botanist, who discovered it in Mexico in 1784.

Daibutsu. The name of a celebrated idol of Buddha, in Japan, famous both for its size and for its exquisite proportions. It is 50 feet in height and 100 feet in circumference; is made of silver and bronze, and has eyes of gold. Daibutsu is about 600 years old, and is considered the finest idol in existence.

Daltonism. A term sometimes employed to designate color-blindness, and derived from John Dalton (1776–1844), the chemist, who suffered from this defect of vision and who first described it in detail in 1794. Red, blue, and green appeared to him alike ; and it is said that having on a certain occasion dropped a stick of red sealing-wax in the grass, he was unable to distinguish it by its color.

Dam, Don't care a. This expression, contrary to the general belief, is not a profane one. The word *dam*, as here used, means a small coin current in India, and the phrase is merely equivalent to the saying, " don't care a twopence." See *Tinker's Dam*.

Damask Rose. So called because brought from *Damascus* to England by Dr. Linacre in 1540.

Damiens's Bed. An iron or steel bed, in the Conciergerie in Paris, upon which Robert François Damiens (1714-1757), the would-be assassin of Louis XV, was fastened with chains.

He was thereupon horribly tortured, and was finally torn asunder by wild horses. The fragments of his body were then burned, the house in which he was born was demolished, and his family were banished from France. See *Conciergerie ; Procrustes, Bed of.*

Damocles, Sword of. According to Cicero, Damocles, a sycophant at the court of Dionysius the Elder, tyrant of Syracuse, having praised in an extravagant manner the blessings and joys of royalty, was reproved by his master in a singularly effective manner. He was seated at a sumptuous banquet and surrounded by all the trappings of royalty; but on looking upwards, in the midst of his pleasures, he beheld a sharp and naked sword suspended above his head, and held by a single horse-hair. This sight instantly sobered Damocles, and taught him the salutary lesson that the lives of kings are in peril every hour. This story is alluded to by Horace.

Damon and Pythias. Two noble Pythagoreans of Syracuse, famous for their disinterested and unselfish friendship for each other. Pythias (or more properly Phintias), having been condemned to death by Dionysius the Elder, tyrant of Syracuse, about 387 B.C., was permitted to return home to arrange his affairs,—Damon pledging his own life for his friend's reappearance at the time agreed upon. At the appointed hour, Pythias failed to appear, and Damon was, in consequence, led forth to die in his stead. At the last moment, however, Pythias reached the place of execution, and saved Damon from death. The tyrant was so much impressed by this exhibition of disinterested friendship that he not only pardoned Pythias, but begged to be admitted, as a third member, into their sacred communion.

Damson. The word *damson*—meaning a small variety of the common plum—is a corruption of *Damascene*, from Damascus, whence the damson-tree was first brought into Europe.

Danaë. An Argive princess, daughter of Acrisius, and mother of Perseus by Zeus, who visited her in the form of a shower of gold, while she was confined by her father in an inaccessible tower. See *Golden Shower.*

Dance of Death. The name given to an allegorical representation of the triumph of Death over all sorts and conditions of men. It originated in the 14th century, and was a favorite subject with the artists of the Middle Ages. The *Chorea Machabæorum* or *Danse Macabre*, the first printed representation, was published in Paris in 1485, and consisted of a series of woodcuts, representing Death dancing attendance upon all kinds of persons, from Adam and Eve downwards. He is with the judge on the bench, the priest in the pulpit, the nun in the cell, the doctor in the study, the bride, the beggar, the king, and the infant, but is eventually swallowed up. Hans Holbein the Younger (1497–1543) produced a similar series of pictures. They were first published at Lyons, in 41 plates, and subsequently appeared in a new edition, enlarged by 12 additional plates, in 1507. There has been much controversy, however, concerning the authorship of this series of pictures ascribed to Holbein. The celebrated " Dance of Death " on the cloister walls of the Klingenthal, a convent in Basel, was painted probably not earlier than 1312. The " Dance of Death " occurs in rude carvings and pictures in various countries of Europe.

Dancing Chancellor. An appellation conferred upon Sir Christopher Hatton (1540–1591), Chancellor of England, who first won the favor of Queen Elizabeth of England by his graceful dancing at one of the court masques.

Dancing Mania. A form of religious frenzy, manifested by mental aberration and bodily distortion. It was prevalent throughout central Europe during the 13th and 14th centuries, and spread rapidly from city to city. Hundreds, and even thousands, were seized with the epidemic, and continued dancing in wild delirium until they fell exhausted, or dashed out their brains against the surrounding walls. In Italy, the "Dancing Mania" reached its height in the 16th century. It was known there as *Tarantism*, because erroneously supposed to have been caused by the bite of the tarantula spider. It was similar to the " leaping ague " of Scotland; but must not be confounded with the disease of the nerves known as *chorea*, or St. Vitus's dance. It was found that music tended to allay the frenzy, and Paracelsus applied cold water in its treatment with success. At the beginning of the 17th century, the mania commenced to decline, and is at present heard of only in individual cases, —as a form of nervous derangement.

Dandelion. A corruption of the French *dent de lion* (*lion's tooth*), owing to a fancied resemblance of the leaves of this flower to the teeth of a lion. It is called *leontodon* (*lion's tooth*) in Greek, for the same reason.

"There is a difference of opinion as to which part of the plant is supposed to resemble a lion's tooth. Some fancy the jagged leaves gave rise to the name, while others claim that it refers to the yellow flowers, which they liken to the golden teeth of the heraldic lion. In nearly every European country the plant bears a name of similar signification."—Dana's *How to Know the Wild Flowers.*

Dandy King. A nickname given to Joachim Murat (1771–1815), King of Naples, on account of his weakness for dress and personal adornment. Napoleon used to call him " un roi de théâtre," because he was wont to parade the streets of Paris dressed in silks and satins, like a veritable stage king.

Dandy-Traps. A name given to loose stones in the pavements of streets, because, when stepped upon, the muddy water underneath gushes up and soils the shoes and clothing.

Dante and Beatrice. See *Beatrice Portinari.*

Dante's Portrait. A celebrated fresco painting of Dante, by Giotto di Bondone (1276-1336), formerly in the chapel of the Bargello or palace of the Podestà in Florence, and now in the Museo Nazionale. After remaining hidden for many years under a covering of whitewash, it was brought to light in 1840, through the efforts of three gentlemen, and restored — although considerably injured. The picture is a profile likeness, and the eye is wanting,—its place being occupied by a hole, doubtless caused by a nail driven into the wall. The picture is familiar through numberless reproductions, and is especially valuable, being the only likeness of Dante known to have been made during his lifetime.

Carlyle says : "I think it is the mournfulest face that ever was painted from reality ; an altogether tragic, heart-affecting face."

Dante's Stone. A stone in the Piazza del Duomo in Florence, famous as the spot where Dante used to stand or sit, while meditating and gazing upon the cathedral.

Dan to Beersheba, From. A familiar expression, originally used to denote the entire extent of the Holy Land, and afterwards applied to any region, when referring to its whole length. Dan was the most northern city in the " Land of Promise," and Beersheba the most southern one, hence the saying, " From Dan to Beersheba " came to mean the entire extent of the country.

Daphne. A beautiful nymph, pursued by Apollo. When on the point of being overtaken by the amorous god, she prayed for assistance and was met-amorphosed into a laurel-tree, which henceforth became the favorite tree of Apollo.

Daphnis. A Sicilian hero of great beauty, to whom is ascribed the invention of bucolic poetry. He was the son of Mercury, and was brought up by nymphs and taught by Pan to play upon the flute. Afterwards he became a shepherd and tended his flocks, winter and summer, on Mount Ætna. A naiad, having fallen in love with him, made him swear that he would never love another, and threatened him with blindness in case he broke his oath. Daphnis, however, after a time, fell under the spell of a princess, and forgot his promise; whereupon the naiad punished him with blindness, or, as others say, turned him into a stone. He was afterwards raised up to heaven by Mercury, his father, who caused a spring to gush forth at the spot where the ascension occurred.

Darby and Joan. An old-fashioned, conservative married couple, famous for their long life and domestic felicity. They are said to have lived, more than a century ago, in Healaugh, a village in the West Riding of Yorkshire. Darby and Joan are the hero and heroine of a ballad called *The Happy Old Couple*, of uncertain authorship, although sometimes ascribed to Prior. According to Timberley, however, the author was Henry Woodfall, and the originals, John Darby (printer of Bartholomew Close, who died in 1730) and his wife Joan. Woodfall was an apprentice in the service of Darby.

Dardanelles. A narrow passage, which connects the Sea of Marmora with the Ægean Sea, and separates Europe from Asia. It is about 47 miles long, and from 3 to 4 miles broad. The name *Dardanelles* is derived from the ancient city of Dardanus, which formerly occupied the site of the present fortifications at Abydos, on the Asiatic shore, and was founded by Dardanus, the ancestor of Priam and the mythical founder of ancient Troy. The name *Dardanelles* is also applied to the fortifications (Sestos on the European and Abydos on the Asiatic shore) that protect the strait at its narrowest point, and command the entrance to the Sea of Marmora. See *Hellespont.*

Darien Canal. A name formerly applied to the proposed canal across the isthmus of Darien. This narrow strip of land is now known as the isthmus of Panama, and the projected canal as the Panama Canal. See *Panama Canal.*

Dark Ages. A period of about 600 years in European history, commencing with the fall of the Western Roman Empire (476 A.D.) and continuing until the close of the 11th century (1100 A.D.). The Dark Ages comprised the first two-thirds of the Middle Ages, and were characterized by extreme intellectual apathy and gross religious superstition. The sway of the Church was universal, and learning was at its lowest ebb. See *Middle Ages.*

Dark and Bloody Ground. An expression formerly much used in reference to the State of Kentucky, on account of the sanguinary encounters that occurred there between the northern and southern tribes of Indians. Later, the bloody conflicts between the early white settlers and the aboriginal tribes rendered the phrase peculiarly appropriate to that locality. The word *Kentucky*, according to some authorities, means "dark and bloody ground," while others say that the word signifies "at the head of a river."

Dark Continent. A name given to the continent of Africa, on account of the dense ignorance concerning its interior which, until recent years, existed among the peoples of Europe and America. Africa is, at present, more appropriately termed the "Coming Continent."

Dark Day. May 19th, 1780, was so termed on account of the intense darkness that overspread New England on that date. The darkness commenced at 10 o'clock in the morning and continued until the middle of the following night, but varied in duration and intensity in different places. The cause of the phenomenon is unknown. The wind had been variable for several days previous, although blowing principally from the northeast and southwest.

Dark Horse. A term used, in political parlance, in the United States, to denote an unforeseen or compromise candidate,—one that is kept carefully in the background and sprung upon the convention at an opportune moment. The expression is borrowed from the turf, and owes its origin to a custom, among sporting men, of training a horse in secret, or "keeping him dark," so that his merits may be unknown until the day of the race. The phrase "dark horse" is used, in a political sense, by Thackeray in his *Adventures of Philip.*

"A *Dark Horse* is a person not very widely known in the country at large, but known rather for good than for evil. . . . Speaking generally, the note of the *Dark Horse* is respectability verging on colorlessness, a good sort of person to fall back upon when able but dangerous favorites have proved impossible."—Bryce's *American Commonwealth.*

Darwinism. A theory promulgated by Charles Darwin (1809–1882) in 1859, to account for the origin of species in the vegetal and animal kingdoms. It asserts that natural selection has been the principal factor in the evolution of higher from lower organisms, or that species arise from the selective action of external conditions upon individual variations from their specific types. By this means, individual variations or peculiarities that are of advantage in a certain environment tend to become perpetuated in the race. See *Evolution.*

Dauphin. A title borne by the heirs-apparent to the crown of France, under the Valois and Bourbon dynasties. In 1349, Humbert II, the last of the princes of Dauphiné, having no issue, left his domains to Philip of Valois (1328–1350), King of France, on condition that the king's eldest son should be called the "dauphin." The first dauphin was Jean, afterwards John the Good (1350–1364), and the last the Duc d'Angoulême, son of Charles X (1824–1830), who renounced the title in 1830. It is said that Guy VIII (one of the Counts of Vienne and ancestor of Humbert II) was surnamed *Le Dauphin* (*Fr. The Dolphin*), because he wore a dolphin as an emblem on his helmet or shield. This surname remained to his descendants, who were styled Dauphins, and the country they governed was called Dauphiné. The wife of the dauphin was called the dauphine. See *Delphin Classics.*

Davenport Brothers. Two famous spiritualistic mediums, who first became known about 1846. They were natives of America, and practised a remarkable series of impostures, which puzzled observers in every part of the world. They declared that spirits would untie them when bound with cords, and that spirits would play upon all sorts of instruments in a dark cabinet. They were proved to be impostors in 1865.

David. A colossal marble statue by Michael Angelo (1475–1564), in the Academy of Fine Arts in Florence. It stood originally in front of the Palazzo Vecchio. It weighs 1800 pounds, and was completed in 1504. See *Moses.*

Grimm says:

"The erection of this *David* was like an occurrence in nature from which people are accustomed to reckon. We find events dated so many years after the erection of the Giant. It was mentioned in records in which there was not a line besides respecting art."

Davy Jones's Locker. An expression frequently used by sailors to denote the bottom of the ocean, especially as the grave of those drowned at sea. "Davy Jones" is the sailors' synonym for death, and hence it is a common thing among them to say of a person that is dead, that he has gone to "Davy Jones's locker."

"This same *Davy Jones*, according to the mythology of sailors, is the fiend that presides over all the evil spirits of the deep, and is seen in various shapes, warning the devoted wretch of death and woe."—*Peregrine Pickle* (Smollett).

Davy Lamp. A famous safety-lamp invented by Sir Humphry Davy (1778–1829) in 1815, to prevent accidents from the explosion of fire-damp, or hydric carbide, in coal and other mines. It consists of an ordinary oil-lamp, surrounded by a fine wire gauze, and is constructed in accordance with the principle that flame, in passing through fine wire meshes, loses so much of its heat as to be incapable of igniting inflammable gases.

Day of the Barricades. A name given to several occasions in French history when the people of Paris tore up the pavements and piled up barrels filled with stones, behind which they fired at the soldiery. *Barrique* is the French for *barrel*, and hence to barricade a street meant originally to obstruct it with barrels.

(1) May 12th, 1588, when the populace rose against Henry III (1574–1589), and forced him to flee from Paris.

(2) August 27th, 1648, the beginning of the Fronde War.

(3) June 27th, 1830, the first day of the revolution that drove Charles X (1824–1830) from the throne.

(4) February 24th, 1848, when Louis Philippe (1830–1848) was forced to abdicate.

(5) June 23rd, 1848, when Abbé Affre, Archbishop of Paris, was shot while attempting to quell the tumult.

(6) December 2nd, 1851, when Louis Napoleon appealed to the people for re-election to the presidency for ten years.

Day of the Bastille. A name given, in French history, to the 14th of July, 1789, because, on that day, the mob, assisted by the Gardes Françaises, rose in insurrection and destroyed the prison-fortress of the Bastille. During the years 1790–1792, the anniversary of this event was called "La Fête de la Fédération." The "Day of the Bastille" is also known as the "Day of July." See *Bastille*.

Day of the Camel. A name given to the battle of Bassorah, fought on November 4th, 657 A.D., during the first civil war of the Moslems. It was so termed because, on that occasion, Ayesha (the widow of Mohammed) went into battle on a camel, with 70 attendants to hold the bridle. During the contest, the litter or cage in which she rode was pierced by so many darts that, according to Gibbon, it resembled a porcupine with its quills. Other dates given for this battle are 656, 658, and 659.

Day of the Dupes. A term often applied to the 11th of November, 1630, in allusion to the signal triumph achieved by Cardinal Richelieu over his enemies on that day. Maria de' Medici, the mother of Louis XIII, and Anne of Austria, his wife, hating Richelieu, prevailed upon the King to dismiss his "insolent minister" from his council. When next day the cardinal called upon the King to place in his hands the seals of office, Louis relented, refused to accept his resignation, and made him more powerful than ever. The courtiers that had flocked to the residence of the queen-mother at the Luxembourg for mutual congratulations were utterly confounded; while the headsman's axe was long kept busy before the cardinal's vengeance was sated.

Day of the Sections. A name given, in French history, to the 5th of October, 1795, on account of the struggle that occurred in Paris on that day, between the troops under the control of the Convention, commanded by Napoleon Bonaparte and those of the National Guard—acting in the interest of the wards or " sections " of the city. The forces of the Convention were entirely victorious, and the new Constitution and the Directory were firmly established. The Day of the Sections marked the end of the French Revolution and the beginning of the wonderful career of Napoleon Bonaparte. Also known as the *Thirteenth Vendémiare*, from the date (according to the French revolutionary calendar) on which the event occurred.

Dead as a Herring. " It is a rare thing, even for fishermen, to see a really live herring. The fish dies the instant it is taken out of the water."— Edwards's *Words, Facts, and Phrases.*

Dead Heat. A race in which two or more competitors come out even,— there being no winner.

Dead Languages. Languages that are no longer spoken, but exist only in written or printed records. Such are the Latin, Greek, and Hebrew languages.

Dead Men. A term applied to empty bottles, *i. e.*, to those that have been drained of their " convivial " contents. The expression " to lie down among the dead men " means to get so drunk as to slip from one's chair under the table and lie among the empty bottles.

Brewer, in his *Dictionary of Phrase and Fable*, says " the expression is a witticism on the word *spirit*. Spirit means life, and also alcohol (the spirit of full bottles) ; when the spirit is out the man is dead, and when the bottle is empty its spirit is departed."

Dead Men's Shoes. An expression used to denote property that can be obtained only after the present owner's death. " Waiting for dead men's shoes " means looking forward for an

inheritance, or for a position in the line of one's promotion in office.

Dead Sea. A remarkable lake—46 miles long and from 5 to 9 miles wide —situated in the southeast of Palestine, and known from the time of Jerome (340–420 A.D.) as the " Dead " Sea, because no fish of any kind have ever been found in its waters. Its surface, which is lower than that of any other body of water known, is 1292 feet below the level of the Mediterranean. At its northern end it has a depth of about 1300 feet, while the water at the southern extremity is only from 3 to 12 feet deep. The Dead Sea is fed by the Jordan from the north, but has no outlet,— the water being apparently carried off by evaporation. The water of the Dead Sea contains a large amount of the salts of magnesia and soda ; as a consequence, its specific gravity is high, and bathers float in it with ease. The popular notions that the Dead Sea exhales noxious vapors, and that birds cannot fly over its surface and remain unharmed, are not founded on fact. According to tradition, Sodom and Gomorrah — " Cities of the Plain " — stood on the site now occupied by the Dead Sea. This view, however, is no longer entertained, and it is now considered certain that the Dead Sea existed in its present state during the days of Abraham, and even much earlier. See *Cities of the Plain.*

Dead-Sea Fruit. The name given to an imaginary kind of fruit, said by the ancients to grow on the shores of the Dead Sea. It was extremely beautiful to behold, but was bitter to the taste and turned to ashes on the lips. The expression " Dead-Sea Fruit " is used metaphorically to denote hollow and unsatisfactory pleasures. See *Apples of Sodom ; Sodom, Vine of.*

Deaf and Dumb. The first systematic attempt to teach the deaf and dumb was made by Pedro de Ponce, a Spanish Benedictine monk, about

1570. His method of teaching was based on the system of Jerome Cardan, who discovered the theoretical principle on which the instruction of the deaf and dumb is founded. In 1620, Bonet, a monk, published a system of instruction for deaf-mutes, at Madrid. The first school for deaf-mutes in Great Britain was started in Edinburgh, in 1773. In 1817, Thomas H. Gallaudet opened the first institution for the instruction of deaf-mutes in the United States, at Hartford, Connecticut. In 1866, Alexander Melville Bell expounded his system of *Visible Speech* to the Society of Arts at London. The German "oral system" was introduced into England in 1872. According to the *World Almanac*, there are 51 State schools for the deaf in the United States. These schools employ the services of 772 instructors and contain 9037 pupils. The total number of volumes in the libraries of these institutions is 91,271, the value of the scientific apparatus is $12,064, and the value of the grounds and buildings, $16,125,292.

Deaths. The average duration of human life is about 33 years. One-quarter of the people on the earth dies before attaining 6 years of age, one-half before attaining 16 years of age, and only about one person of each 100 reaches the age of 65. Deaths are estimated to occur at the rate of 67 per minute, 97,790 per day, and 35,639,835 per year; births at 70 per minute, 100,800 per day, and 36,792,000 per year.

Dearest Books. The following list of "The Twenty-Seven Dearest Books in the World, Sold by Auction" is taken from *Everybody's Pocket Cyclopædia*. The list was compiled by Bernard Quaritch.

Date of Sale.	Name of Book.	Name of Owner.	Bought by	Price.
1812	The Valdarfer Boccaccio, Venice, 1471	Duke of Roxburghe........	Lord Blandford...	$11,300
1873	The Mazarine Bible, Mentz, 1450–55; printed on paper..................................	Henry Perkins	Bernard Quaritch..	13,450
	The same book printed on vellum...........	" "	Lord Ashburnham	17,000
	Lydgate's Book of the Siege of Troy, MS.....	" "	Bernard Quaritch..	6,600
1881	Augustinus de Civitate Dei, Jenson, 1475; printed on vellum...........................	The Duke of Marlborough.. (*Sunderland Library*) ...	Bernard Quaritch..	5,000
	Aulus Gellius, Rome, 1469; printed on vellum.	" " ...	M. Téchener	3,950
	Biblia Latina, Fust and Schoeffer, 1462.......	" " ...	Bernard Quaritch..	8,000
	Boccaccio, Valdarfer, 1471..................	" " ...	" "	2,925
	Boccace, Ruine des Hommes, Colard Mansion, 1476; printed on vellum..............	" " ...	" "	4,600
	De Bry, Voyages...........................	" " ...	" "	3,600
	Petrarca, Venet., 1488; with engravings after Botticelli.................................	" " ...	" "	9,750
	Durandus, Rationale, Fust and Schoeffer, 1459; printed on vellum....................	" " ...	" "	3,950
	Roman du Roi Artis, MS., about A.D. 1300....	" " ...	" "	2,675
	Virgilius, Venet., 1470; printed on vellum....	" " ...	" "	4,050
	—— Aldus, 1504; printed on vellum.......	" " ...	" "	2,625
1882	Longi Pastoralia, Paris, 1802; printed on vellum, with the drawings..................	The Duke of Hamilton (*Beckford Library*)........	" "	4,500
	Van Dyck's Portraits, plates and etchings....	" "	Thibaudeau........	14,250
1883	Decor Puellarum, Jenson, 1461 (1471)........	" "	Bernard Quaritch..	2,650
	Boece, Croniklis, Edinburgh, 1536; printed on vellum for James V....................	" "	" "	4,000
1884	The Mazarine Bible........................	Sir John Thorold (*Synton Park Library*) ...	" "	19,500
	Biblia Latina, Fust and Schoeffer, 1462......	" " "	Ellis and White ...	5,000
	Psalterium, Fust and Schoeffer, 1459	" " "	Bernard Quaritch..	24,750
1885	The First English Bible, 1535................	Lord Jersey (*The Osterley Park Library*)	" "	3,400
	Recuyell of Troye, printed by Caxton (before 1474)	" " " "	" "	9,750
	Morte Arthur, printed by Caxton, 1485.......	" " " "	" "	9,100
1887	Mazarine Bible............................	Lord Crawford.............	" "	13,000
1889	Mazarine Bible............................	Lord Hopetoun.............	" "	10,000

Death-Warrant of Charles I. The original warrant for the execution of Charles I of England is preserved in the library of the House of Lords, at London. According to Mr. J. H. Pulman, librarian to the House of Lords, " it [the warrant] was produced by Colonel Harker after the Restoration, and was the evidence upon which those who had signed it were excepted from the Indemnity Act."

Death-Warrant of Jesus Christ. During the French rule in Italy, some workmen, while excavating in the ancient city of Amiternum (now Aquila), in the kingdom of Naples, found in 1810 an antique marble vase in which lay concealed a copper plate, bearing on the obverse side a long inscription in the Hebrew tongue. This, when translated, proved to be the death-warrant of Jesus Christ. On the reverse side of the plate were found the words : " A similar plate is sent to each tribe." At the expedition of Naples, it was enclosed in an ebony box, and preserved in the sacristy of the Carthusians. This relic which, if genuine, is to Christians the most impressive and interesting legal document in existence, has been faithfully transcribed, and reads as follows :

"Sentence rendered by Pontius Pilate, acting Governor of Lower Galilee, stating that Jesus of Nazareth shall suffer death on the cross.

In the year seventeen of the Emperor Tiberius Cæsar, and the 27th day of March, the city of the holy Jerusalem,—Annas and Caiaphas being priests, sacrificators of the people of God,—Pontius Pilate, Governor of Lower Galilee, sitting in the presidential chair of the prætory, condemns Jesus of Nazareth to die on the cross between two thieves, the great and notorious evidence of the people saying :

1. Jesus is a seducer.
2. He is seditious.
3. He is the enemy of the law.
4. He calls himself falsely the Son of God.
5. He calls himself falsely the King of Israel.
6. He entered into the temple, followed by a multitude bearing palm-branches in their hands.

Orders the first centurion, Quilius Cornelius, to lead him to the place of execution. Forbids any person whomsoever, either poor or rich, to oppose the death of Jesus Christ.

The witnesses who signed the condemnation of Jesus are :

1. Daniel Robani, a Pharisee.
2. Joannus Robani.
3. Raphael Robani.
4. Capet, a citizen.

Jesus shall go out of the city of Jerusalem by the gate of Struenus."

(I am indebted to Bombaugh's *Gleanings for the Curious* for the above translation.)

De Augmentis Scientiarum. See *Advancement of Learning*.

Debatable Land. A tract of land on the western border of England and Scotland. It was at one time claimed by both countries, and was finally divided between them. The " Debatable Land," owing to its neutral position, was long the residence of thieves and outlaws. Also called the *Batable Land*.

Debonair (*Fr. Le Débonnaire, The Good-Natured*). A title bestowed upon Louis I (814–840) of France on account of his amiability and good-nature. He was, however, weak-minded and irresolute, and ill-adapted to the troublous times in which he reigned.

Decalogue (*Gr. δέκα, ten, λόγος, word*). The name usually given by the Greek Fathers to the Law of the Two Tables, said to have been given by God to Moses on Mount Sinai. They are called in Scripture the " Ten Commandments " (*Exodus* xxxiv, 28; *Deuteronomy* iv, 13), and embrace what is usually called the *Moral Law*.

Decameron (*Gr. δέκα, ten, ἡμέραι, days*). A famous Italian prose work, written by Boccaccio (1313–1375). It consists of 100 tales, 10 of which are supposed to have been told each afternoon for 10 days, by a party of young people of both sexes (seven women and three men) assembled at a country-house, where they had taken refuge during the plague at Florence in 1348. The *Decameron* is the great prose classic of Italy, and has been for many generations the model for Italian writers. Its influence upon European literature has been profound, and Shakespeare and other authors have taken the plots of several of their dramas and stories from it. See *Heptameron*.

De Cive (*Lat. Concerning the Citizen*). The name of a philosophic treatise on government by Thomas Hobbes (1588–1679), written in Latin, and published for private circulation in 1642. The full title is *Elementa Philosophica de Cive*. In 1650, an English treatise — bearing the Latin title *De Corpore Politico* — appeared. Hobbes's ideal form of government is an absolute monarchy.

Declaration of Independence. A famous document, declaring the thirteen American colonies to be "free, sovereign, and independent," and absolved from all allegiance to the British Crown. In June, 1776, the Continental Congress appointed a committee—composed of John Adams, Thomas Jefferson, Benjamin Franklin, Roger Sherman, and Robert R. Livingston—to prepare a formal declaration of independence. The draft of this document was prepared by Thomas Jefferson, and was reported by the committee to Congress on June 28th, 1776. On July 4th of the same year the question of independence came up for final consideration, and the *Declaration* was passed, and ordered to be engrossed for the signatures of the delegates from the different States. On August 2nd, 1776, the *Declaration of Independence* was *signed* by all the members of the Continental Congress present (54), and later in the year by the remaining members—Thomas McKean of Delaware and Matthew Thornton of New Hampshire. Independence Day, therefore, is not the anniversary of the *signing* of the Declaration, but

of its *adoption* by the Continental Congress. See *Independence Day*.

Declaration of Independence, where Written. The original draft of the *Declaration of Independence* was prepared in Philadelphia, by Thomas Jefferson (1743–1826), in 1776. The house in which it was written was a plain three-story brick building on the southwest corner of Market and Seventh Streets. It was erected in 1775, and demolished in 1883. The site is now occupied by the Penn National Bank, on the front of which may be seen a bronze tablet commemorating this important event.

Decline and Fall of the Roman Empire. The title of a celebrated history by Edward Gibbon (1737–1794), universally acknowledged to be one of the greatest masterpieces of historical composition. The first volume was published in 1776, and had an immediate success. The second and third volumes appeared in 1781, after an interval of five years; and the final publication of the entire work in six volumes took place in 1788. The author's uncompromising hostility to Christianity, however, gave great offence to many readers, and was the occasion of several attacks by English divines. Alison, the historian, declared the *Decline and Fall* to be the greatest historical work in existence. Gibbon's profit from the sale of his work was £6000; that of his publisher, £60,000.

The author says : " It was at Rome, on the 15th of October, 1764, as I sat musing amidst the ruins of the Capitol, while the barefooted friars were singing vespers in the temple of Jupiter, that the idea of writing the decline and fall of the city first started to my mind."

De Consolatione Philosophiæ. See *Consolations of Philosophy*.

Decoration Day. A day set apart, in many of the States of the American Union, for the purpose of decorating the graves of the Union soldiers that fell in the Civil War. This beautiful custom originated with the women of the South during the Rebellion, and has been observed ever since. On May 5th, 1868, General John A. Logan, Commander-in-chief of the G. A. R., appointed May 30th for this purpose. Although *Decoration Day* is not a *national* legal holiday, it has been made a holiday in many of the Northern States by legal enactment. Congress always adjourns on this date " as a mark of respect to the memory of the illustrious dead." A similar celebration — known as *Memorial Day* — is held throughout the South on April 26th, on which occasion the graves of the Confederate dead are strewn with flowers. Alabama was the first State to celebrate *Memorial Day*, on April 26th, 1866 ; and New York the first State to declare *Decoration Day* a legal holiday. See *Memorial Day*.

Decuman Gate. One of the four gates in a Roman camp. It was opposite to the prætorian or front gate, and was the farthest from the enemy. It was called *decuman* (from *Lat. decumus*, another spelling of *decimus, tenth*), because the tenth legion was posted near it. Every Roman camp had four gates, as follows : the one that faced the enemy, called the *prætorian gate ;* the one opposite to it, called the *decuman gate ;* and the gates on the right and left sides of the camp, called respectively the *porta principalis dextra* and the *porta principalis sinistra*. See *Prætorian Gate*.

Deepest Mine. The deepest mine in the world is said to be in the Lake Superior copper-mining district, where, in 1890, the Calumet shaft attained a depth of 3900 feet.

Deerslayer. The hero of James Fenimore Cooper's novel of the same name. He appears under five different names, in five of Cooper's novels, as follows :

(1) As Natty Bumppo in *The Pioneers* (1823).

(2) As Hawkeye in *The Last of the Mohicans* (1826).

(3) As the Trapper in *The Prairie* (1827).

(4) As the Pathfinder in *The Pathfinder* (1840).

(5) As the Deerslayer in *The Deerslayer* (1841).

The *Deerslayer* is one of nature's noblemen—brave in action, honorable in conduct, and pure in motive. See *Leatherstocking ; Natty Bumppo*.

Defender of the Faith. A title conferred upon Henry VIII (1509–1547) of England by Pope Leo X (1513–1522) in 1521, in consequence of a Latin treatise, entitled *A Defence of the Seven Sacraments*, written by the King, in confutation of Martin Luther. Although this title was revoked by Pope Paul III (1534–1550), it was legally confirmed by Parliament in 1543, and is still borne by the English sovereigns. Other kings of England —Richard II (1377–1399) and Henry VII (1485–1509)—had borne the same title; but it had not been made hereditary in their cases, and had, in consequence, died with them. The original copy of Henry VIII's treatise is in the Vatican, and contains the following inscription in the King's handwriting : *Anglorum rex Henricus, Leoni X, mittit hoc opus et fidei testem et amicitiæ* (Henry, King of England, sends this work to Leo X as a witness of faith and friendship).

Degrees of Drunkenness. In Brewer's *Dictionary of Phrase and Fable*, we find given the following seven degrees of drunkenness :

(1) Ape drunk.
(2) Lion drunk.
(3) Swine drunk.
(4) Sleep drunk.
(5) Martin drunk.
(6) Goat drunk.
(7) Fox drunk.

De Imitatione Christi (*Lat. Concerning the Imitation of Christ*). A famous devotional work, generally attributed to Thomas à Kempis (1380 (?)–1471). The question of its authorship has, however, been much disputed, and many volumes have appeared on the subject. Among others named as possible authors may be mentioned one Abbot Gersen (whose very existence is in doubt), and Jean Charlier de Gerson, Chancellor of Paris, who died in 1429.

Hallam says: "The book itself is said to have gone through 1800 editions, and has probably been more read than any one work after the Scriptures."

Delaware. This State received its name from Thomas West, Lord de La Warre, Governor of Virginia, who visited the bay in 1610.

Delectable Mountains. A range of mountains mentioned in Bunyan's *Pilgrim's Progress*, from the summit of which a view of the Celestial City could be obtained.

"These Mountains are Immanuel's land, and they are within sight of His City; and the sheep also are His, and He laid down His life for them."—*Pilgrim's Progress.*

"Delenda Est Carthago" (*Lat.* "*Carthage must be destroyed*"). A famous saying of Porcius Cato, the Censor (234–149 B.C.), the inveterate enemy of Carthage, and one of the chief promoters of the Third Punic War. He is said for years to have ended every speech before the Roman Senate (no matter upon what subject) with the words "*Delenda est Carthago*" (*Lat.* "*Carthage must be destroyed*").

Delight of Mankind.

(1) An appellation bestowed upon Titus (79–81 A.D.) the Roman Emperor, because of the wisdom and gentleness of his rule. It is said that at the close of any day on which he had performed no act of kindness he was accustomed to exclaim : " My friends, I have lost a day ! "

" I 've lost a day ! "—the prince who nobly cried,
Had been an emperor without his crown."
Edward Young.

(2) The same title was conferred upon Maximilian II (1564–1576) of Austria, on account of his wisdom, justice, and magnanimity.

Della Cruscans. A school of sentimental poetasters of both sexes, which arose in Florence about 1785, and was afterwards transferred to England, where its lucubrations appeared in two daily newspapers, the *World* and the *Oracle.* Although these productions were marked by insipidity and affectation, yet such was the poetic poverty of the time that they soon became the fashion, and were followed by a host of imitations. The Della Cruscans derived their name from the signature *Della Crusca,* adopted by Robert Merry, one of the founders of the school, and a member of the famous Della Crusca Academy at Florence. The fame of the school was, however, of short duration. In 1794, William Gifford produced his *Baviad* and in 1796 his *Mæviad,*—two political satires which so severely criticised the Della Cruscans that their very name became a byword for literary puerility.

Delphi. An ancient Greek town in Phocis, chiefly famous for its oracle of Apollo. It was situated on the southern slope of Mount Parnassus, and was shut in on the north by a rocky mountain barrier, through a cleft in which issued the waters of the Castalian Spring. Delphi was considered by the Greeks to be the central spot of the earth, and hence was called the "navel of the earth." The Pythian Games were celebrated there, and it was also one of the two meeting-places of the Amphictyonic Council. The famous temple of Apollo was situated at Delphi, and was the seat of the celebrated Delphic Oracle. The building contained vast treasures,—having been enriched with gifts from kings and private individuals. It was plundered on several occasions,—once by the Phocians, and later by Brennus and Sulla. Nero carried off from the temple 500 bronze statues, and Constantine despoiled it of many of its works of art. In the time of Pliny, the town of Delphi contained as many as 3000 statues, while within the temple there stood for a long time a golden statue of Apollo. See *Delphic Oracle.*

Delphic Oracle. A celebrated oracle of Apollo, at Delphi in Phocis. It was situated in the centre of the temple of Apollo, and consisted of a small opening in the ground, from which arose from time to time intoxicating vapors, believed to come from the well of Cassotis. A three-legged stool, or tripod, was placed over the opening, and upon this the pythia or priestess took her seat when the oracle was to be consulted. The words uttered by her, after inhaling the vapor, were supposed to be the revelations of Apollo, and were carefully recorded by the priests. They were afterwards communicated in hexameter verse to those that had come to consult the oracle. If the priestess spoke in prose, her words were immediately turned into poetry by a poet employed for the purpose. It is said that the oracle was discovered through the actions of some goats that were thrown into convulsions on breathing this vapor. No traces of the chasm nor of the exhalations are to be found anywhere at present. See *Delphi.*

Delphin Classics. A famous edition of 39 Latin authors, in 64 volumes, prepared by order of Louis XIV (1643–1715) of France, for the education of his son, the dauphin (*Lat. delphinus*), and published in 1674–1730. It was edited by 39 of the best scholars of France under the direction, originally, of Bossuet and Huet, and bore on the title-pages the words *In Usum Delphini* (*Lat. For the Use of the Dauphin*). Each " author " is accompanied by notes and an index of words. The *Delphin Classics* are esteemed of little value by classical scholars. An edition, with notes, etc.,

was published by Valpy of London in 1818 *et seq.* See *Dauphin.*

Demijohn. This word is from the French *dame-jeanne* (*Lady Jane*), a corruption of the Arabic *damajana, damjana,*—probably from *Damaghan,* a town in Khorassan, a province of Persia, once famous for its glass-works.

Democracy in America. The title of a famous philosophic work on democratic institutions in America, by Alexis de Tocqueville (1805–1859), an eminent French statesman and economist, who visited the United States in 1831. It appeared in four volumes during the years 1835–1840, and had a prodigious success. Royer - Collard declared that, since Montesquieu, nothing comparable to it had appeared.

The *Edinburgh Review,* speaking of the book in 1861, said : " Far from having suffered from the lapse of a quarter of a century, it has gained in authority and interest, from the inexhaustible depth, the unflinching truth, and the extraordinary foresight which are its characteristics."

Democritus of the Sixteenth Century. A title bestowed upon John Calvin (1509–1564), the reformer, because, like the Greek philosopher, he took serious and austere views of life, and had a fondness for solitude and philosophic contemplation.

Denain, Battle of. A battle fought at Denain, France, on July 27th, 1712, between the French commanded by Marshal Villars, and the allies under Prince Eugene. The latter were defeated.

De Natura Deorum (*Lat. Concerning the Nature of the Gods*). A theological work, in three volumes, by Marcus Tullius Cicero (106–43 B.C.), the Roman orator and statesman. It contains an account of the speculations of the Epicureans, the Stoics, and the Academicians concerning the existence and attributes of the Divine Being. In theology, Cicero strove to eliminate whatever seemed mythical, but endeavored to retain the great doctrines which most men accept,—especially the belief in an all-seeing providence, and in immortality. But even these views he holds with some hesitation.

Denderah, Temple of. A famous temple at Denderah, a village of Upper Egypt, near the left bank of the Nile. It was built in the time of Cleopatra and the early Roman Emperors, and exists, at the present day, in a remarkable state of preservation. The structure is 220 feet long and 50 feet broad, and is adorned with hieroglyphics and figures, among which may still be seen profile portraits of Cleopatra and her son Cæsarion.

"The building of the *Temple of Denderah* was begun in the reign of the eleventh Ptolemy, and completed in that of the Emperor Tiberius; but the sculptures and decorations were not finished till the time of Nero."— Murray's *Handbook*.

Dentistry. The art of treating the teeth when diseased and of replacing them when lost is a very ancient one. Herodotus speaks of the ancient Egyptians as practising this art, and the *Laws of the Twelve Tables* (5th century, B.C.) provided that where "teeth bound with gold" were found, it was lawful to burn or bury the gold with the body of the dead person. An Etruscan skull, with a set of animal's teeth artificially inserted in it, was exhumed in 1885. The first physician to speak of treating the teeth is Galen (131–200 (?) A.D.). The science of dentistry, however, may be said to date from 1839, when Professor Richard Newton pointed out "the organic connection between the vascular and the vital soft parts of the frame and the hard substance of the teeth." His work appeared in 1840–1845. The first dental school in the United States was established in Baltimore, in 1839. The National Dental Association was founded in 1897, by the union of the American Dental Association and the Southern Dental Association. See *Twelve Tables, Laws of the.*

De Profundis (*Lat. Out of the Depths*). The 130th Psalm is so called from the first two words in the *Vulgate Version*. It is one of the seven "Penitential Psalms," and forms a portion of the Roman Catholic liturgy. It is sung when the bodies of the dead are committed to the grave. The authorship of the 130th Psalm is ascribed to King David. See *Penitential Psalms.*

Depth of the Ocean. The average depths of the main divisions of the ocean are as follows :

(1) Pacific Ocean......	2500	fathoms.	
(2) Atlantic "	 2200	"	
(3) Indian "	 2300	"	
(4) Southern "	 2200	"	
(5) Antarctic "	 630	"	
(6) Arctic "	 630	"	

The greatest known depth of the ocean is midway between the islands of Tristan d'Acunha and the mouth of the Rio de la Plata, South America. The bottom there was reached at a depth of 46,236 feet, or 8¾ miles,—exceeding by more than 17,000 feet the height of Mount Everest, the loftiest mountain on the globe. Nearly 78 per cent. of the bottom of the ocean lies between the depths of 1000 and 3000 fathoms ; about 17½ per cent. is found in depths less than 1000 fathoms ; and about 4½ per cent. in depths greater than 3000 fathoms. The volume of water in the entire ocean is estimated at 323,800,000 cubic miles.

Derby Day. The day on which the race for the famous Derby stakes (instituted by Lord Derby in 1780) takes place on Epsom Downs, in Surrey, England. It is generally run on the Wednesday in the week preceding Whitsunday, — the second day of the summer meeting. The course, which is about a mile and a half in length, was gone over by W. H. McCalmont's *Isinglass* in 1893 in 2 minutes and 33 seconds, — the fastest running ever known on that course. Under the new regulations (which went into effect in 1890), the "Derby" is at present a stake of £6000—£5000 to the winner, £500 to the nominator of the same, £300 to the second, and £200 to the third horse. *Derby Day* is a great English holiday. Almost all London empties itself to be present, and proceeds to the Downs by every kind of vehicle imaginable. See *Epsom Races.*

De Rerum Natura (*Lat. Concerning the Nature of Things*). A celebrated philosophic and didactic poem by Lucretius (95–51 B.C.), one of the greatest of the Latin poets. The work is in six books (containing upwards of 7000 lines), and unfolds the physical and ethical doctrines of Epicurus, of whom Lucretius was a follower. He denies all design in nature, and accounts for the universal prevalence of law and arrangement in the universe by the theory of natural selection : '' Atoms wrought on by impulse and gravity, and excited in every mode to cohere, and having been tried in all possible aggregations, motives, and relations, *fell at last into those that could endure.*''

It is interesting to observe how many of the modern truths of evolution are anticipated by Lucretius in this poem. He remains the favorite poet of rationalism to this day, and the *De Rerum Natura* is undoubtedly the greatest didactic poem ever written.

Descent from the Cross.

(1) The name of a famous picture in the cathedral at Antwerp. It is the work of Rubens (1577–1640), the most celebrated of the Flemish painters, and is generally considered his masterpiece. Besides the dead Christ, five persons are represented, viz.: the three Marys, Nicodemus, and Joseph of Arimathea. The distinguishing feature of the painting is the pallor of the dead body resting against a white sheet. Rubens received the order for this picture from the Company of Archers in 1611, and completed it three years later.

(2) The name of a painting by Daniele da Volterra, in the Church of Trinità de' Monti, at Rome. It was regarded by Poussin as the third picture in the world. See *Elevation of the Cross.*

Hawthorne says, however : ''I never should have had the slightest suspicion that it was a great picture at all, so worn and faded it looks, and so hard, so difficult to be seen, and so undelightful when one does see it.''

De Senectute (*Lat. Concerning Old Age*). A charming essay, written by Marcus Tullius Cicero (106–43 B.C.), and addressed to his friend Titus Pomponius Atticus. Its object is to show how the burden of old age may be most easily borne. It was written in 44 B.C.

Deseret. A name given by the Mormons to the Territory (now the State) of Utah. The Mormons claim that this word means '' honey-bee,'' in their sacred language. When Edward Everett was Secretary of State of the United States, he forbade the use of this word as the official designation of the Territory.

Desmas. The names Desmas, Dysmas, and Demas are given to the penitent thief, in the ancient *Mysteries.* He is called Dysmas in the apocryphal *Gospel of Nicodemus*, and Demas in the *Story of Joseph of Arimathea.* The impenitent thief is called Gesmas or Gestas. In Longfellow's *Golden Legend*, Titus is the penitent thief, and Dumachus the impenitent one. They were two of a band of robbers that attacked the Holy Family during their flight into Egypt. Titus relented, but Dumachus insisted that Joseph should pay for their release. Whereupon Titus gave his fellow-robber 40 groats, and the infant Jesus said :

'' When thirty years shall have gone by,
   I at Jerusalem shall die,
  By Jewish hands exalted high
    On the accursèd tree,
Then on my right and my left side,
  These thieves shall both be crucified,
And Titus thenceforth shall abide
    In paradise with me.''

See *Thieves, Two.*

Despair, Giant. In Bunyan's *Pilgrim's Progress*, a giant that dwelt with his wife Diffidence, in Doubting Castle. Christian and Hopeful were taken captive by him while sleeping on his grounds, and were confined in a dark dungeon from Wednesday to Saturday, without food or drink. Christian, finally remembering that he had in his bosom a key called *Promise*, with which he could open any lock in Doubting Castle, opened the dungeon-door and, with Hopeful, quickly made his escape.

Deucalion's Flood. According to Greek mythology, Deucalion, King of Phthia in Thessaly, and his wife Pyrrha were preserved by Jupiter from a deluge sent to cover the whole earth, in consequence of man's wickedness. Deucalion and Pyrrha thereupon became the progenitors of a new race by throwing stones behind them, as commanded by the oracle. Men sprang into existence from the stones thrown by Deucalion, and women from those cast by Pyrrha, and thus the world was repeopled.

"There is scarcely any considerable race of men among whom there does not exist, in some form, the tradition of a great deluge, which destroyed all the human race except their own progenitors."—*Chambers's Encyclopædia*.

Deus ex Machina. An expression used to denote unexpected aid in an emergency. It is borrowed from a custom in the ancient Greek theatre, where, during the crisis of a play, a god would sometimes be let down from the air by machinery. Hence, the phrase has come to mean the intervention of a god, or some other unlikely event, by means of which an author is enabled to extricate himself from the difficulties in which he has become involved. The expression means literally " a god [let down upon the stage or flying in the air] by machinery."

Deus Philosophorum (*Lat. God of Philosophers*). A title bestowed upon Plato (429–347 B.C.) by Marcus Tullius Cicero, on account of his great admiration for the learning of the Greek philosopher.

Deus Vult (*Lat. God Wills It*). At the Council of Clermont in 1095, held to consider the project of a crusade against the Saracens, after Pope Urban II (1088–1099) had finished his address advocating the scheme, he was greeted with cheers and cries of *Deus Vult* from the entire assembly. The crowd outside took up the cry, and this eventually became the war-cry of the First Crusade.

Devil upon Two Sticks.

(1) *Asmodeus; or, The Devil upon Two Sticks*, is the English name usually given to Le Sage's famous novel, *Le Diable Boiteux*.

(2) A nickname given to O. P. Morton (1823–1877), United States Senator from Indiana, not only on account of his lameness, which necessitated the use of two canes in walking, but also in allusion to the pugnacious attitude assumed by him in the Senate, after the Civil War, while reconstruction measures were under consideration. See *Asmodeus; Diable Boiteux, Le*.

Devil's Bible. A celebrated MS. of the Bible inscribed on 300 asses' skins, and taken to Stockholm after the *Thirty Years' War* (1618–1648). According to tradition, a poor monk, having been condemned to death, was informed that his sentence would be commuted on condition that he would copy the entire Bible on asses' skins in a single night. During the night he made a compact with the devil, and agreed to exchange his soul for the required manuscript.

Devil's Bridge. A name popularly given, in mountainous countries, to bridges built over wild chasms. The most celebrated of these is the one over the Falls of the Reuss in the Canton of Uri, Switzerland, on the St. Gotthard Road, 4593 feet above sea-level. According to the legend, the devil permitted its construction on condition that the soul of the first person that crossed it should be his. It was built in the 12th century, and consists of a single arch of masonry, which overhangs the river at a height of 70 feet. In 1830, the old bridge was superseded by a new one—20 feet farther up the stream—having a single arch of 26 feet. This fell in 1888, and traffic was renewed for a time on the old moss-covered structure. Severe fighting between the French and the allied Austrians and Russians occurred in that vicinity in 1799.

Diable Boiteux, Le (*Fr. The Lame Devil*). A famous romance by Le Sage (1668–1747). Guevara's *El Diablo Cojuelo* is said to be the original of this story. See *Asmodeus ; Devil upon Two Sticks* (1).

Diamond Necklace. A celebrated piece of jewelry—consisting of 500 diamonds—ordered by Louis XV (1715–1774) as a present for his favorite, Madame Dubarry, who was, however, excluded from court on the death of the King, before the work was finished. The necklace, when completed, was valued at £80,000, but was so costly that no purchaser for it could be found. Boehmer, the court-jeweler, offered it to Marie Antoinette for £56,000, in 1785 ; but the Queen, although she desired it, feared to incur the expense. The Countess de la Motte, an adventuress about the court, knowing the passion entertained for Marie Antoinette by the wealthy and profligate Prince Cardinal de Rohan, induced him to purchase the necklace and present it to the Queen. De la Motte, in this manner, obtained the necklace and made way with it. With her husband, she escaped from Paris, and was soon engaged in selling the separate diamonds. When the time arrived for the payment of the first instalment, Boehmer presented his bill to the Queen. Marie Antoinette denied all knowledge of the affair, and in the trial that ensued it

was proved that the countess had sold the necklace to an English jeweler, and had kept the money. As a punishment, she was branded on each shoulder with the letter V (*Fr. voleuse, thief*), and sentenced to imprisonment for life. She escaped, however, within a year, and fled to England, where she was accidentally killed while trying to escape from a second-story window, when pursued for debt. The cardinal was acquitted of intentional complicity. The Queen was falsely accused, by the populace of Paris, of having had a part in the plot, and was taunted with this accusation even on her way to the guillotine. When Talleyrand heard of the " Affair of the Diamond Necklace," he declared that he should not be surprised if it overturned the throne of France. See *Cagliostro, Count; Œil de Bœuf.*

Diamonds, Famous. The following is a list of the most famous diamonds of the world :

(1) The Braganza.
(2) The Dudley.
(3) The Florentine.
(4) The Great Mogul.
(5) The Hope.
(6) The Koh-i-nur.
(7) The Nassac.
(8) The Orloff.
(9) The Pigott.
(10) The Pitt or Regent.
(11) The Sancy.
(12) The Shah.
(13) The Star of the South.

For particulars, see under the respective names.

Diana. See *Artemis.*

Dickens. A word meaning the Devil. Its origin is variously accounted for.

"Probably a fanciful variation of *deuce.*" —*Standard Dictionary.*

"Perhaps, a contraction of the diminutive *devilkins.*"—Webster's *International Dictionary.*

"A perverted oath, corrupted from 'Nick.' "—Brewer's *Dictionary of Phrase and Fable.*

"I cannot tell what the *dickens* his name is."
　　　　　Merry Wives of Windsor, iii, 2.

Dick's Hatband. An expression applied to the crown of England, which was for a time the hatband of Richard Cromwell (1626–1712), and proved so tight for him that he was forced to resign it. The saying, "As queer as Dick's hatband," refers to the ridiculous figure cut by Richard Cromwell, in his assumption and almost immediate abdication of the sovereignty of England.

Dictator of Letters. A title bestowed upon François Marie Arouet de Voltaire (1694–1778), in allusion to the great influence exerted by him on the literature of France and of Europe.

Dictators. The name given to the supreme magistrates of ancient Rome, appointed by the Senate to act for a period of six months, during critical times, when it became necessary for one man to exercise all the powers of the State. The first dictator was Titus Larcius, or Marcus Valerius, appointed in 501 B.C., eight years after the expulsion of the Tarquins. The early dictators were patricians,—the first plebeian to occupy the office being Caius Marcius Rutilus, appointed in 356 B.C. The office of dictator was abolished in 44 B.C., having become odious through the usurpations of Sulla and Julius Cæsar. Although the dictator enjoyed more extensive power than the consuls, he was nevertheless limited in the following particulars:

(1) He could not touch the public funds.

(2) He could not leave Italy.

(3) He could not ride through Rome on horseback without first obtaining the consent of the people.

The dictator was always preceded by 24 lictors, bearing the *secures* and *fasces*, while the consuls had only 12 lictors.

Dido. Porson, the famous Greek scholar, having declared that he could make a rhyme on any subject, was requested to do so with the three Latin gerund endings, *di, do, dum.* Whereupon, he delivered himself of the following couplet :

"When Dido found Æneas would not come,
She mourned in silence, and was *Di-do dum*(*b*)."

Dido and the Bull's Hide. Dido was the daughter of Belus, King of Tyre, and wife of Sichæus, who, for his wealth, was murdered by Dido's brother, Pygmalion. Dido thereupon fled to Africa, and purchased of the natives as much land as could be encompassed with the hide of a bull. The bargain having been concluded, she carefully cut the hide into narrow strips, and thus enclosed a piece of territory sufficiently large for a citadel. This she called *Byrsa* (*hide*). Thus, according to tradition, was founded the city of Carthage.

"Die is Cast, The." An expression attributed to Julius Cæsar by Suetonius, Lucan, and Plutarch, on the occasion of his passage of the Rubicon, a small river separating Italy from Cisalpine Gaul. The Rubicon formed the limit of Cæsar's command, and to cross it was virtually to declare war against the Republic, since the Senate had expressly decreed that Cæsar should lay down his arms and disband his forces within a limited time, under penalty of being declared an enemy of the commonwealth. It is said that Cæsar lingered for hours on the banks of the Rubicon before making up his mind,—remarking meanwhile to Pollio, one of his generals : "If I pass this river, what miseries I shall bring on my country ! and if I do not pass it, I am undone." Soon after, he exclaimed, "Jacta est alea" (*Lat. The die is cast*), and spurring on his horse he crossed the stream, followed by his soldiers. See *Rubicon.*

Dies Iræ (*Lat. Day of Wrath*). A famous mediæval hymn, descriptive of the Last Judgment. It consists of 18 stanzas, the first of which is as follows :

> " Dies iræ, dies illa !
> Solvet sæclum in favillâ,
> Teste David cum Sibyllâ."

The *Dies Iræ* is generally thought to have been written by Thomas of Celano, a native of Abruzzi, in Naples, who died in 1255. It is also ascribed to Pope Gregory the Great (590–604), and to St. Bernard (1091–1153). It was introducèd into the liturgy of the Roman Catholic Church before 1385. The *Dies Iræ* has been made the subject of musical compositions by Palestrina, Haydn, Cherubini, and Mozart, and has been a favorite poem with translators, none of whom, however, has been able to reproduce the fervor and force of the original. Among the famous translations of this greatest of church lyrics may be mentioned those of Crashaw, Lord Macaulay, Lord Roscommon, Isaac Williams, and Dr. W. J. Irons, among Englishmen, and those of General John A. Dix and Dr. Abraham Coles, among Americans. The version of Dr. W. J. Irons may be regarded as the accepted version at the present day in Great Britain. The hymn is based on the prophetic passage in *Zephaniah* i, 15, 16. See *Stabat Mater Dolorosa.*

Diet of Augsburg. An imperial diet of German princes held at Augsburg in Bavaria, in 1530, by order of the Emperor Charles V, to settle the religious disputes of Germany. On this occasion, the famous *Augsburg Confession*, compiled by Luther, Melancthon, and others, and signed by the Protestant princes, was presented to the Emperor and read before the Diet. Charles, however, again denounced the heresy, and put all that embraced it under the ban of the Empire.

Diet of Spires. An assembly of German princes convoked by the Emperor Charles V of Germany, at Spires in Bavaria, in 1529, principally for the purpose of checking the growth of the Reformation. An edict having been passed prohibiting the further dissemination of the new doctrines, six Lutheran princes, together with the deputies of thirteen imperial towns, formally and solemnly *protested* against the decree. The followers of Luther were accordingly called *Protestants*, which term afterwards came to include all those that seceded from the Church of Rome. See *Protestants.*

Diet of Worms. An imperial diet of German princes, held at Worms in Hesse-Darmstadt in 1521, by order of the Emperor Charles V, to arrest the growth of the doctrines of the Reformation in Germany. Luther was summoned before the Diet, and in the presence of this imperial assembly fearlessly maintained his ground. On refusing to retract his opinions, he was condemned as a heretic, and put under the ban of the Empire. Although the reformer was dismissed under " safe-conduct " from the Emperor, yet to save his life he remained for a year in seclusion, under the protection of the Elector of Saxony. When Luther was informed of the danger that threatened him before the Diet, and was warned not to appear, he declared : " If there were as many devils in Worms as there are tiles upon the roofs of its houses, I would go on."

Dieu-Donné (*Fr. God-Given*). An appellation bestowed upon Louis XIV (1643–1715) in infancy,— his mother, Anne of Austria, having been barren for 23 years previous to her son's birth in 1638. The Comte de Chambord (1820–1883), son of the Duchesse de Berri, was so called also. The title *Adeonatus* (*God's Gift*) was bestowed upon one of the popes, in 672.

Dieu et Mon Droit (*Fr. God and My Right*). The royal motto of England. It was originally the password given by Richard I (1189–1199) of England to his soldiers at the battle of Gisors in France, fought in 1198, on which occasion the French were signally defeated. Henry VI (1422–1461) seems to have been the first English sovereign to use these words as a royal motto.

Dimensions of Heaven. The following fanciful estimate of the dimensions of the Celestial City is taken from Bombaugh's *Gleanings for the Curious*. It is based, of course, upon the statement in *Revelation*, given below.

"And he measured the city with the reed, twelve thousand furlongs. The length, and the breadth, and the height of it are equal." —*Revelation* xxi, 16.

"Twelve thousand furlongs, 7,920,000 feet, which being cubed, 496,793,088,000,000,000,000 cubic feet. Half of this we will reserve for the Throne of God and the Court of Heaven, and half the balance for streets, leaving a remainder of 124,198,272,000,000,000,000 cubic feet. Divide this by 4096, the cubical feet in a room sixteen feet square, and there will be 30,321,843,750,000,000 rooms.

"We will now suppose the world always did and always will contain 990,000,000 inhabitants, and that a generation lasts for 33⅓ years, making in all 2,970,000,000 every century, and that the world will stand 100,000 years, or 1000 centuries, making in all 2,970,000,000,000 inhabitants. Then suppose there were one hundred worlds equal to this in number of inhabitants and duration of years, making a total of 297,000,000,000,000,000 persons, and there would be more than a hundred rooms sixteen feet square for each person."

Diogenes's Tub. The tub in which, according to the common story, Diogenes, the Cynic (412–323 B.C.), made his home, was a huge earthen jar discarded from the Temple of Cybele. It had been used as a receptacle for wine or oil for the sacrifices of the temple, and was sufficiently large to allow the philosopher to recline in it at full length. The truth of this tale has been doubted, although it is said that, during the Peloponnesian War (431–404 B.C.), the Athenians lived in similar vessels; and even after the time of Diogenes such receptacles were used as dwelling-places by the poor.

Diomed's Horses. Diomed, King of the Bistones in Thrace, and son of Mars and Cyrene, owned two horses, Dinos (Dreadful) and Lampon (Bright-Eyed), which he fed on human flesh. For this act he was slain by Hercules, and was himself eaten by his own horse, having been thrown to it by the angry demi-god.

Dircæan Swan. A sobriquet conferred upon Pindar (522 (?) – 442 (?) B.C.), the Greek lyric poet, in allusion to his residence at Thebes, near the river Dirce.

Directory, French. The name given to a body of five individuals (Lépeaux, Letourneur, Rewbell, Barras, and Carnot), to whom was entrusted the administration of public affairs in France. The Directory was established by the Constitution of the 5th Fructidor (August 22nd, 1795), and ruled in conjunction with the Council of Ancients and the Council of Five Hundred. It lasted about four years, when, owing to its corruption and inefficiency, it was overturned by the *coup d' état* of the 18th Brumaire (November 9th, 1799), planned by Napoleon Bonaparte, who, with Cambacérès and Lebrun, established the Consulate,—consisting of three consuls, Bonaparte becoming the first. See *National Convention of France*.

Dis. A contraction of Dives, a name sometimes given to Pluto. He was the son of Saturn and Ops, and ruler of the infernal regions.

"—— Proserpine gathering flowers,
Herself a fairer flower, by gloomy *Dis*
Was gathered,"
          Paradise Lost, iv, 269–271.

Disaster (*Lat. astrum, a star*). A word of astrological origin — meaning originally a baleful or unpropitious aspect of a heavenly body. The word was formed at a time when the stars were supposed to have an influence on human affairs, but is now used simply to denote a calamity or serious mishap.

Discharge Bible. The name given to a version of the Scriptures printed in 1806. It was so called owing to a peculiar error of the printer, whereby the phrase, " I charge thee before God " (1 *Timothy* v, 21), was made to read, " I *discharge* thee before God."

Discipline, Books of. The name given to two books that contain the constitution and order of procedure of the Church of Scotland, from the period of the Reformation (1517).

(1) The *First Book of Discipline*, or the *Policie and Discipline of the Church*, was prepared in 1560–1561 by John Knox and four other ministers, for the practical government of the Church. It was approved by the General Assembly, but was not ratified by the Privy Council. All ministers were required to subscribe to the requirements of the *First Book of Discipline* before admission to office.

(2) The *Second Book of Discipline*, or *Heidis and Conclusiones of the Policie of the Kirk*, was drawn up in 1578 by Andrew Melville and a committee of the leading members of the General Assembly. It is, in a sense, a revision of the *First Book ;* it was not, however, designed to supersede it, but simply to amplify its rules and regulations. This *Second Book* lays down the principles of the Presbyterian form of government as it exists at the present day. Both *Books of Discipline* are still standards in the Church of Scotland, and also in some of the other Presbyterian bodies that have seceded from it.

Discobolus (*Gr. Quoit-Thrower*). A famous bronze statue by Myron, the Greek sculptor. The original was in bronze, and is no longer in existence. Several copies in marble exist, however,— the best of which was discovered on the Esquiline Hill in Rome in 1782, and is now in the Villa Messimi in that city. Other copies may be found in the museums of the Vatican and of the Capitol in Rome, and in the British Museum in London.

" We find in it the most acute observation of life, the most just conception of bold, rapid movement, and the greatest freedom in the expression of the actor."—*Lübke.*

"Ignorance of the laws of momentum leads to analogous errors : as witness the admired *Discobolus*, which, as it is posed, must inevitably fall forward the moment the quoit is delivered."—*Herbert Spencer.*

Discours de la Méthode (*Fr. Discourse upon Method*). The title of a famous philosophic treatise by René Descartes (1596–1650), the celebrated French philosopher. By means of this work, Descartes revolutionized the study of metaphysics, and gained for himself the title of " Father of Philosophy."

Distaff's Day. The name formerly given to the 7th of January (the morrow of the Epiphany), because on that day the Christmas festivities ceased and work was resumed at the distaff.

Distressed Statesman. A nickname given to William Pitt (1708–1778), Earl of Chatham, in 1761, when he found himself compelled to resign his office of Secretary of State.

Dismal Swamp. An extensive morass lying chiefly in southern Virginia, but extending also into North Carolina. It originally measured 40 miles from north to south and 25 miles from east to west, but has been considerably reduced in area by drainage. Its surface was once densely timbered with cypress, cedar, juniper, and pine, but this growth has been greatly thinned during late years. The region is now traversed by a canal connecting Chesapeake Bay and Albemarle Sound, and by two narrow-gauge railroads. The Dismal Swamp rises towards its centre. There may be found Lake Drummond, covering about six square miles.

Divine Comedy (*It. Divina Commedia*). A famous epic poem by Dante Alighieri (1265–1321). It is divided into three parts : the *Inferno* (*Hell*), the *Purgatorio* (*Purgatory*), and the *Paradiso* (*Paradise*). The word *Divina* was not used in the title by the author, but was added after his death, and first appeared in the edition of 1516. The *Divina Commedia* almost created the Italian language, which until that period was so crude that Dante himself hesitated to employ it, and is said to have commenced his poem in Latin.

"In this vision of Hell, Purgatory, and Heaven, we have, as it were, an encyclopedic view of the highest culture and knowledge of the age on philosophy, history, classical literature, physical science, morals, theology. All this, moreover, is expressed in the sublimest and most exquisite poetry, and with consummate power and beauty of language."—*Chambers's Encyclopædia.*

"Dante entitled the saddest poem in the world a Comedy, because it was written in a middle style ; though some, by a strange confusion of ideas, think the reason must have been because it 'ended happily'! that is, because beginning with hell (to some), it terminated with 'heaven' (to others)."—*Leigh Hunt.*

See *Inferno, L' ; Paradiso, Il ; Purgatorio, Il.*

Divine Madman. A sobriquet conferred upon Michael Angelo (1475–1564), who, when meditating upon some great project, secluded himself from the world and its distractions.

Divine Right of Kings. The name given to a doctrine that was promulgated in England in the seventeenth century, and asserted that kings hold their authority by divine appointment and are earthly representatives of the Deity. This principle relieved the sovereign of all responsibility towards his subjects, and gave him absolute claim to their obedience. The chief defenders of this dogma were Salmasius (1640), Hobbes (1642), and Sir Robert Filmer (1653) ; while Milton (1651), Algernon Sydney, and Harrington were its uncompromising opponents. The controversy died a natural death on the accession of the

House of Hanover. In the *Bill of Rights* (1689), the right of the people to depose the sovereign, to alter the order of succession, and to confer the sovereignty on whomsoever they may think proper, is distinctly set forth. See *Bill of Rights ; Passive Obedience.*

Divining-Rod (*Lat. Virgula Divina; Baculus Divinatorius*). A rod with forked branches, usually made of witchhazel, but sometimes of iron or even of brass and copper, and used by those that pretend to locate the existence of water, minerals, and metals, under ground. According to the superstition, the rod is said to dip when held over the desired spot. This nonsense is still believed in, not only by ignorant Cornish miners, but even by intelligent people during these early years of the twentieth century.

Dixie's Land. A famous negro melody, generally considered to be of Southern origin. It is said, however, that it originated in New York City in the early part of the nineteenth century, and, in later years, became identified with the South and Southern institutions. According to the story, Dixie was a slaveholder on Manhattan Island, who was compelled, on account of the growth of the abolition sentiment in that locality, to transfer his slaves to the South. In their new home they were obliged to work harder, and, in consequence, often sighed for their old abode at the North, where the conditions of life were more agreeable. Thus, softened by distance and the lapse of time, the expression " Dixie's Land " became, to the negro race, a synonym for ease and comfort.

The term " Dixie " or " Dixie's Land " is still used to denote the States and Territories south of Mason and Dixon's line. See *Mason and Dixon's Line.*

Dix's Order. A celebrated order issued by John A. Dix (1798–1879), while Secretary of the Treasury in

1861, previous to the outbreak of the Civil War. The U. S. revenue cutter *Robert McClelland*, having been ordered north from New Orleans, was detained by her captain, in anticipation of delivering her to the Louisiana government ; whereupon Dix issued an order commanding Lieutenant Caldwell to arrest Captain Breshwood, to assume command of the cutter, and to bring her north. This order contained the famous words : " If any one attempts to haul down the American flag, shoot him on the spot."

Dizzy. A nickname given by London *Punch* to Benjamin Disraeli (1805–1881), afterwards Earl of Beaconsfield.

Doctor Mirabilis (*Lat. Wonderful Doctor*). A title given to Roger Bacon (1214–1294), the celebrated English philosopher and mathematician, who, by means of his encyclopædic learning and marvellous discoveries in science, contributed materially to the extension of the domain of positive knowledge.

Doctors of the Church. The name given to certain of the Greek and Latin Church Fathers. Among the Greek Church Fathers, Athanasius, Basil, Gregory Nazianzen, and Chrysostom were so called ; and, among the Latin Church Fathers, Jerome, Augustine, Ambrose, and Gregory the Great. Nine additional Doctors of the Church were added by the Roman Catholic Church. See *Church Fathers*.

Doctor Subtilis (*Lat. Subtle Doctor*). A title conferred upon Duns Scotus (1265–1308), the famous theologian and metaphysician, whose writings abound in refined distinctions and manifest consummate dialectic skill.

"The greatest of the Schoolmen were Thomas Aquinas and Duns Scotus. They were founders of rival sects, which wrangled with each other for two or three centuries." —*Hallam*.

Doctor Syntax. The hero of a humorous work by William Combe (1741–1823), entitled *The Tour of*

Doctor Syntax. Doctor Syntax is a simple-minded, henpecked clergyman, unsophisticated, but intelligent and well educated. His adventures in *The Tour in Search of the Picturesque*, in *The Tour in Search of Consolation*, and in *The Tour in Search of a Wife*, are written in eight-syllable verse, and were once extremely popular. Doctor Syntax's horse, *Grizzle*, was a creature of skin and bone.

Doctrinaires. The name given, in French history, to a political party that originated after the restoration of the Bourbons in 1814 and furthered the cause of liberalism and progress. They believed in constitutional liberty, as opposed to the arbitrary will of the sovereign. After the Revolution of July, 1830, the Doctrinaires came into power as the advisers and ministers of Louis Philippe (1830–1848). De Broglie, Royer-Collard, and Guizot were among their number. The term " doctrinaires," as at present used, refers to those persons that would apply abstract theories to the management of the practical affairs of government.

Dodo. A large bird that formerly inhabited the island of Mauritius, and became extinct after 1681. It was somewhat larger than a turkey, but was incapable of flight. Our knowledge of it is derived from the accounts of travelers, from pictures, and, above all, from the skeletons disinterred in 1865–1866, when extensive marshes in the island were drained. Professor Owen has partially reconstructed and described the skeleton. The British Museum contains a foot of the dodo, and in the Ashmolean Museum at Oxford may be seen a head and foot of this extinct bird.

Doe, John, and Richard Roe. In law, two fictitious names given respectively to the plaintiff and defendant in writs of ejectment at common law. This practice continued in England until 1852, when the custom was abolished.

16

"Those mythical parties to so many legal proceedings, *John Doe* and *Richard Roe*, are evidently of forest extraction, and point to the days when forest laws prevailed, and venison was a sacred thing."—*Lower*.

Dog. The question is frequently asked why a dog turns round several times before lying down. In reply, naturalists tell us that the dog, in his wild state, inhabited jungles, as the wolf and the fox do at the present time. Before lying down, nature prompted him to turn around several times in order to bend the leaves away from his body, and thus secure a flat resting-place. This instinct still survives with the dog in his domesticated state, although no reason for the practice exists at the present time.

Dog-Cart. This light one-horse vehicle is so called because, as originally constructed, it contained a box at the back for carrying hunting-dogs to the scene of the sport.

Dog-Days (*Lat. Dies Caniculares*). A name given by the ancient astronomers to the twenty days before and the twenty days after the rising of the dog-star or Sirius with the sun. This period is at present reckoned from the 3rd of July to the 11th of August. It was for years the common opinion that this conjunction of the rising of the dog-star with the rising of the sun was one of the causes of the extreme heat of summer. This conjunction, however, does not occur at the same time in all latitudes, nor is it constant in the same region for a long period ; hence there is much variation as to the limits of the dog-days. It is a mere accident that the rising of Sirius with the sun occurs at the hottest season of the year. In time it will take place in the depth of winter. The Egyptians began their year with the heliacal rising of the dog-star, which event coincided with the flood of the Nile.

Doge. The name of the chief magistrate, possessing princely rank, in the republics of Venice and Genoa.

The office was elective. The first doge of Venice was named Anafesto Paululio or Paoluccio, and was elected in 697 A.D. The Genoese chose their first doge, Simone Boccanegra, in 1339 A.D. Venice has had 122 doges : Anafesto (697) to Luigi Manin (1797). The word *doge* is derived from the Latin *dux* (*leader*). See *Doge's Palace*.

Doge's Palace. A famous palace, formerly occupied by the doges of Venice, and regarded by many as the finest building — architecturally considered—in Europe. It was originally founded in 800 A.D., and was destroyed and rebuilt five times. The present structure dates from 1350. Within may be seen the *Giants' Staircase* —so named from the colossal statues of Mars and Neptune, standing at the top ; the *Hall of the Great Council* —one of the finest rooms in Europe,— containing paintings by Paul Veronese, Tintoretto, and others ; and the *Archæological Museum*, containing bronze and marble statues, sarcophagi, reliefs, urns, etc. At the entrance to the antechamber of the Council of Ten was situated the celebrated *Lion's Mouth*, into which were thrown the secret communications for the Inquisitors. The famous *Bridge of Sighs* connects the Doge's Palace with the ancient state-prisons. See *Bridge of Sighs ; Giants' Staircase*.

Dog-Star. A name frequently given to Sirius, the brightest star in the heavens. It is in the constellation *Canis Major*, or *Greater Dog*, and is also known as *Canicula*, and in astronomical charts as *Alpha Canis Major*.

Dog-Watch (*a corruption of dodge-watch*). The name given to two short watches of two hours each, on shipboard—one from 4 to 6 P.M., and the other from 6 to 8 P.M. The dog-watches were introduced to prevent the same men from always keeping watch at the same hours of the day ; hence on these occasions the sailors are said to *dodge* the routine, or to be doing *dodge*-watch. See *Bell-Time on Shipboard*.

Doldrums. A name given by sailors to a part of the ocean near the equator, abounding in calms, squalls, and light, baffling winds. "To be in the doldrums" means to be in a state of listlessness and ennui.

Dollar-Mark, Origin of. The origin of the sign $ to represent the dollar has given rise to much discussion, and has been variously accounted for. The derivations suggested are given below, as follows :

(1) A combination of the letters U. S. (United States). After the adoption of the Federal Constitution, these initials were prefixed to the Federal currency, and afterwards, in the haste of writing, were run into each other, the U being made first and the S over it.

(2) A modification of the figures ⅞, once used to denote a piece of 8 reals, or, as a dollar was then called, a *piece of eight*.

(3) A form of HS., which marked the Roman unit.

(4) A contraction of P and S, used in Spanish accounts to indicate *peso* (*dollar*).

(5) A device formerly seen on the reverse of the Mexican *Pillar Dollar* (a Spanish coin), representing the Pillars of Hercules connected by a scroll displaying the words *Plus Ultra*.

(6) A contraction for the Spanish *fuertes* (*hard*),—to distinguish silver or hard dollars from paper-money.

Dom-Boc or Doom-Book (*Book of Dooms or Sentences*). A compilation of English laws and customs, made under the authority of Alfred the Great (871–901), from the West Saxon collection of Ina, the Kentish collection of Ethelbert, and the Mercian laws of Offa. The code commences thus : "The Lord spake all these words, saying, I am the Lord thy God." Then follow the *Ten Commandments*, the part of the Mosaic law relating to

criminal offenses, and parts of the *New Testament*, — including the Golden Rule. After these come the ecclesiastical and civil laws.

Domesday Book, or Doomsday Book. The ancient record of the survey of the lands of England, made by order of William the Conqueror (1066–1087), under special commissioners, about 1086. It consists of two volumes — a large folio and a quarto,—and gives the name of every proprietor of land and the extent of his possessions. All of England, except Northumberland, Durham, part of Cumberland, and part of Westmoreland, was included in the survey. The *Domesday Book* was formerly kept in the chapter-house of Westminster, but is now in the public-record office. The taxes were levied by it until 1522, when a more accurate survey was taken, called the *New Domesday Book*. The *Domesday Book* was published at national cost in 1783, in two folio volumes. In 1816, two supplementary volumes were published.

Domine, Quo Vadis Church (*Lat. Lord, Whither Goest Thou ?*). The name of a church on the Appian Way near Rome, erected on the spot where, according to tradition, St. Peter, while fleeing from Rome during the first persecution of the Christians, was met by a vision of the Savior on his way to the city. St. Peter, in amazement, cried aloud, "Domine, quo vadis ?" (Lord, whither goest thou ?)—to which Christ answered : "Venio Romam iterum crucifigi" (I go to Rome to be crucified a second time). The apostle thereupon retraced his steps, re-entered the city, and soon after suffered martyrdom. Within the church may be seen a marble slab on which is engraved a facsimile of the Savior's footprint; while the original stone on which Christ stood is said to be preserved in the basilica of San Sebastiano.

Dominical Letter. "The letter

which, in almanacs, denotes Sunday, or the Lord's day (*Lat. dies Domini*). The first seven letters of the alphabet are used for this purpose, the same letter standing for Sunday during a whole year (except in leap year, when the letter is changed at the end of February). After twenty-eight years the same letters return in the same order. The dominical letters go backwards one day every common year, and two every leap year ; *e. g.*, if the dominical letter of a common year be G, F will be the dominical letter for the next year. Called also *Sunday letter*."— Webster's *International Dictionary*.

The Dominical letters are of use in determining on what day of the week any day of the month falls in a given year.

Dominicans. A religious order founded by Dominic de Guzman (1170–1221 A.D.) at Toulouse in 1215. They were originally a mendicant order, under the rules of St. Augustine, and were established to preach against the Albigenses and other heretics. The Dominicans were called Jacobins in Paris, because their first monastery was in the Rue St. Jacques. In England they were known as Black Friars, on account of the large black mantles worn by them. In 1425, they ceased to be a mendicant order, and attained distinction in theology and politics, until superseded by the Jesuits in the sixteenth century. The Dominicans have been the favorite inquisitors, and one of their number always presided over the cruelties of the Spanish Inquisition. Among famous Dominicans may be named Albertus Magnus, Thomas Aquinas, and Savonarola. See *Franciscans*.

Donatists. A religious sect founded about 313–318 A.D., by Donatus, an African bishop, because of his jealousy of Cæcilianus, Bishop of Carthage. The fundamental doctrines of the Donatists were as follows :

(1) In the Trinity, the Father is superior to the Son, and the Son to the Holy Ghost.

(2) Personal holiness is of greater consequence than apostolic succession.

(3) Excommunicated persons must be rebaptized before they can be again admitted to church membership.

The discipline of the Donatists was extremely severe. The sect was annihilated by the Saracens in the seventh century.

Don Juan. A famous mythical personage whose deeds of refined libertinism have furnished a theme for innumerable playrights and romancers. According to the legend, Don Juan was a member of the celebrated Tenorio family, and a resident of Seville. Having attempted to seduce the daughter of the governor of the city, or of a nobleman of the family of the Ulloas, he is detected in his design by the girl's father, who is killed in the duel that ensues. A statue of the murdered man having been erected in the family tomb, Don Juan forces his way into the vault, and invites the figure to a feast prepared in its honor. At the appointed time, the statue makes its appearance, and, to the great amazement of Don Juan, compels him to follow, and delivers him over to the ruler of the infernal regions.

Goldoni made this story the basis of an Italian play, and Gluck first treated the theme musically in his ballet of *Don Juan*, in 1765. In 1787, appeared Mozart's immortal opera of *Don Giovanni* (*Don Juan*). The name has been made familiar to English readers by Byron's poem entitled *Don Juan*. In this poem the old legends are not followed, and Byron can hardly be said to have done more than borrow the name of the hero.

Donnybrook Fair. A famous fair held annually for centuries in the village of Donnybrook, near Dublin, Ireland. It was established by King John (1199–1216), and was abolished in 1855. Donnybrook Fair was celebrated for the riots and bloodshed that accompanied its observance.

Don Quixote. A famous Spanish romance by Cervantes (1547-1616), written in ridicule of the romantic aspect of chivalry. The hero, Don Quixote, is a country gentleman of La Mancha — full of genuine honor, enthusiastic and impetuous—who has become crazed by the perusal of famous works on chivalry, and believes himself called upon to go forth and do battle for the suffering and the oppressed. His ridiculous attempts in this direction, in company with his esquire, Sancho Panza,— an ignorant and good-natured, but credulous and selfish peasant,—form a series of most amusing adventures. The knight and his esquire are finally brought home to their native village as madmen, and there the author leaves them, while intimating that the narrative of their adventures is not ended. In the second part of the book, we are furnished with another set of experiences, as amusing as the first. As the result of a severe illness, Don Quixote is finally induced to renounce the follies of knight-errantry, and in the end dies peacefully in his bed, as becomes a good Christian.

"Cervantes smiled Spain's chivalry away."
Byron.

Dorr's Rebellion. The name given to an insurrection that took place in Rhode Island in 1841, as the result of an attempt to extend the right of suffrage. From the year 1663, the inhabitants of Rhode Island had lived under a charter granted by Charles II (1660-1685), which bestowed the right of suffrage only on those that owned a certain amount of property. An effort to change this provision led to the formation of two parties, known as the "Suffrage" and the "Law and Order" parties. Each party strove to obtain control of affairs and elected its own State officers. Thomas W. Dorr, having been chosen governor by the "Suffrage" party, seized the State arsenal, but was overpowered by the militia, and obliged to flee. In a second attempt, Dorr's party was defeated by the United States troops, and he himself was arrested, tried, convicted of treason, and sentenced to imprisonment for life. He was afterwards pardoned. A constitution to supersede the Charter of 1663 was framed by a convention that met at Newport in 1842, and was ratified by a vote of the people during the same year. See *Barnburners.*

Dort Bible. A Dutch translation of the Bible, authorized by the Synod of Dort in 1618-1619. The Synod of Dort was a conclave of Protestant divines—86 in number—that sat from November 13th, 1618, to May 19th, 1619. It condemned the doctrines of Arminius, and affirmed those of Calvin.

Dotheboys' Hall. In Dickens's *Nicholas Nickleby,* a school kept by a brute named Squeers, whose system of instruction consisted in alternately beating and starving his pupils. It was, in truth, an institution where the boys were taken in and "done for."

Douay Bible. The name given to the English translation of the Roman Catholic version of the Bible, authorized by the Pope. The *Old Testament* was published in France, in 1609, and the *New Testament* at Rheims in 1582. The text of the *Douay Bible* is copiously explained by notes of Roman Catholic divines, and is a translation of the Latin *Vulgate.* See *Rosin Bible; Vulgate.*

Doubting Castle. The abode of Giant Despair and his wife Diffidence, in Bunyan's *Pilgrim's Progress.* Christian and Hopeful, while sleeping on the grounds adjoining the castle, were seized by the giant and cast into a dungeon, whence they escaped by means of a key called *Promise,* concealed in Christian's bosom. See *Despair, Giant.*

Dough-Face. A contemptuous epithet applied, in ante-bellum days, to those Northern politicians that sympathized with and abetted negro slavery. The expression is said to have originated with John Randolph of Roanoke, and to have been used by him in allusion to those Northern members of Congress that showed a willingness to accede to the demands of the South in matters relating to negro slavery. Referring to them on a certain occasion, he said : " I knew that these men would give way. They were scared at their own *dough-faces*. We had them ; and, if we had wanted more, we could have had them."

This term was also applied to those Southern politicians that were false to the principles of slavery.

" Dover and Calais Meet, When." The expression " When Dover and Calais meet " is frequently used in England to mean *never*.

Downing Street. A street in London, named in honor of Sir George Downing. In its immediate vicinity is the Treasury building, originally erected during the reign of George I (1714–1727), containing the Office of the Prime Minister, the Education Office, the Privy Council Office, and the Board of Trade. The Office of the Chancellor of the Exchequer occupies a separate building in Downing Street. Between Downing Street and Charles Street rise the new Public Offices, erected in 1868–1873, at a cost of £500,-000. They comprise the Home Office, the Foreign Office, the Colonial Office, and the India Office.

Drachenfels (*Ger. Dragon's Rock*). A ruined castle, situated on a mountain of the same name, 850 feet above the level of the Rhine. It is said to have been built in the early part of the twelfth century. During the Thirty Years' War (1618–1648), it was captured and destroyed by Duke Ferdinand of Bavaria. Drachenfels is eight miles southeast of Bonn. Its summit may be reached by a mountain railway, built in 1883. Stone was taken from a quarry on this mountain to build the Cathedral of Cologne. The name *Drachenfels* is said to be derived from the legendary dragon slain by Siegfried, the hero of the *Niebelungen-Lied*. See *Niebelungen-Lied*.

" The castled crag of *Drachenfels*
    Frowns o'er the wild and winding Rhine,
  Whose breast of waters broadly swells
    Between the banks which bear the vine,"
        Childe Harold, iii, LV.

Draco's Laws. A code of laws promulgated by Draco, the Athenian lawgiver and archon, in 621 B.C. According to this code, every violation of the law was made a capital offense; hence arose the saying of Demades concerning Draco's laws, " that they were written not in ink, but in blood." They were abrogated in 594 B.C., and a milder code substituted by Solon in the same year. Draco declared that the smallest offense deserved death, and that he could not find any punishment more severe for more atrocious crimes. The expression " Draconian Laws " is applied at the present time to laws of excessive severity. See *Solon's Laws*.

Draft Riots. The name given to a bloody but ineffectual attempt to resist the enforcement of the draft for Union soldiers in New York City in July, 1863. The insurrection lasted four days (July 13th–16th), during which time the city was in almost complete possession of the rioters. As the militia had been sent to the front to resist Lee in his invasion of Pennsylvania, the defense of the city was left in charge of the police, and these the rioters soon overpowered. Fires broke out in all parts of the city, and many houses were entered and plundered by the mob in search of its victims. Many banks and newspaper offices were fully garrisoned and armed in anticipation of an attack. The negroes especially were severely handled, many of them being stoned or hanged. On the return of the military, however, order was quickly restored. It is estimated that during this four days' carnival of crime about 1000 persons (many of them negroes) were killed and $2,000,000 worth of property destroyed.

Dragonnades. The name given to the cruel persecutions of the French Protestants, commenced by Louis XIV (1643–1715) in 1681. They were so named on account of the prominent part taken in them by the French dragoons. These dragoons were quartered in Protestant villages and houses, and subjected the inhabitants to such cruelties and indignities that many of them were induced to abjure their faith. The persecutions were directed by Louvois, the King's minister, and were consummated by the revocation of the Edict of Nantes (October 22nd, 1685). By this impolitic act, 50,000 families were driven from France. See *Edict of Nantes.*

Dragon's Teeth. An expression used to denote causes of civil dissension and strife. The allusion is to the dragon that guarded the well of Ares. According to the legend, Cadmus slew the monster and sowed some of the teeth, from which sprang the men called Spartans. These all killed one another, with the exception of five, who became the ancestors of the Thebans. The teeth not sown by Cadmus came into the possession of Æetes, King of Colchis, and among the tasks that he enjoined upon Jason was to sow the remaining ones, and slay the armed men that sprang from them.

Drake's Circumnavigation of Globe. Sir Francis Drake, the most famous navigator in the time of Queen Elizabeth (1558–1603), sailed from Falmouth on December 13th, 1577, circumnavigated the globe, and returned to England, after suffering many hardships, on November 3rd, 1580. The queen visited Drake on his ship at Deptford (April 4th, 1581),

and conferred upon him the honor of knighthood. He died at Panama on January 28th, 1596, while engaged in an expedition against the Spaniards, and was buried at sea. See *Circumnavigation of Globe.*

"The waves became his winding-sheet; the
        waters were his tomb;
But for his fame the ocean sea was not
        sufficient room."

Dred Scott Decision. A decision rendered by Chief Justice Taney in the Supreme Court of the United States, in the case of a negro named Dred Scott, who claimed his freedom on the ground that he had lived for some years on free soil, and was consequently a free man. Having been whipped for some offense, he brought suit for assault and battery against his owner, John F. A. Sanborn of New York City. The Supreme Court held that, as a slave, Dred Scott had no right to sue in any United States court; denied the right of Congress to exclude slavery from the Territories; and declared the Missouri Compromise to be null and void. Six of the associate justices supported Chief Justice Taney, and two — McLean of Ohio and Curtis of Massachusetts—dissented. The decision caused intense excitement throughout the country, and produced great dissatisfaction in the free States. See *Missouri Compromise.*

Druid. The word *Druid* is said to be derived from the Celtic word *dru* (*oak*). This tree was especially sacred among the Druids, who frequently performed their religious rites in open spaces surrounded by tall stones, amid oak groves.

Druid Hill Park. A beautiful pleasure-ground, just north of Baltimore, Maryland, containing about 700 acres. The land was purchased by the city at a cost of nearly $800,000, and contains many fine trees. Part of the grounds was laid out before the Revolution.

Drummers. A name given colloquially in the United States to commercial travelers, or persons that travel in the interests of trade. In 1890, it was estimated that there were 250,000 drummers in the United States. During the traveling year (9 months) they spent $382,000,000, or $1,750,000 per day. Out of the 400,000,000 tons of merchandise carried by the railroads 300,000,000 tons were shipped by them.

Drummond Light. So named from Captain Thomas Drummond (1797–1840), who invented it in 1826, and used it in the British Ordnance Survey. It is said to have been seen at a distance of 112 miles. The *Drummond light*—better known as the lime or calcium light — consists of a stick or ball of lime rendered incandescent in the flame of a union of oxygen and hydrogen gases, or of oxygen and coal gas. This name is also given to a heliostat, or mirror, invented by Drummond for throwing rays of light in a given direction. To Captain Drummond is attributed the saying that "property has its duties as well as its rights."

Drunk as Blazes. This expression is a corruption of the saying, "Drunk as Blaizers," and originated in the following way. Bishop Blaize is the patron-saint of wool-combers, who celebrate his festival at Leicester and elsewhere with processions and convivial gatherings. The custom is referred to by Sir Thomas Vyse in his *Impressions of Greece*, in the following words :

"Those who took part in the procession were called *Blaizers*, and the phrase, 'as drunk as Blaizers,' originated in the con-vivialities common on these occasions."

Drunken Parliament. A Scotch parliament that assembled at Edinburgh on January 1st, 1661, and was so named from the fact that its members were almost always drunk. It annulled in a single act all the enactments of its predecessors during the previous 28 years. This measure resulted in a total disintegration of the church system of Scotland.

Burnet, in *His Own Time*, says : "It was a mad, warring time, full of extravagance ; and no wonder it was so, when the men of affairs were almost perpetually drunk."

Drury Lane. A famous street in London, extending from the Strand to Oxford Street and the British Museum. It contains the Drury Lane Theatre, and takes its name from Drury House (now demolished), the home of the Drury family. See *Drury Lane Theatre.*

Drury Lane Theatre. A celebrated theatre in London, first opened in 1663. The present building, the fourth, was completed in 1812. It is the oldest as well as one of the largest theatres in London, and is the only one remaining about which any histrionic traditions linger. Drury Lane Theatre was the scene of the greatest triumphs of Garrick, the Kembles, the Keans, Macready, Wallack, Mrs. Nisbett, Helen Faucit, Ellen Tree, and many others. The greenroom contains busts of Kemble, Kean, and Mrs. Siddons. In the hall are several other busts and statues. The theatre is at present given over mostly to pantomimes and spectacular plays. See *Covent Garden Theatre ; Drury Lane.*

Dryburgh Abbey. A beautiful ruined abbey on the river Tweed in Scotland, five miles southeast of Melrose. It was founded by David I (1124–1153) in 1150, and destroyed by Edward II (1307–1327) of England in 1322, at the time of his unsuccessful invasion of Scotland The abbey was restored by Robert Bruce, and sacked in 1385 ; again destroyed by the English in 1544. In the one transept aisle still remaining lie buried the remains of Sir Walter Scott, his wife, his son, and his son-in-law and biographer, Lockhart.

Dualism. The name given to a philosophic theory that declares that two principles of opposite nature, irreconcilable, and incapable of being derived from each other, lie at the bottom of everything in the universe,—as, for example, the real and the ideal, the material and the spiritual, etc. In a more restricted and theological sense, the term "Dualism" refers to the conflicting powers of good and evil (Ormuzd and Ahriman), that figure in the religion of Zoroaster.

The term "Dualism" was at one time applied to the principles of the advocates of a separate government for Hungary, under the Emperor of Austria. This reform was effected in 1867. See *Monism*.

Duchess, The. The *nom-de-plume* assumed by Margaret Argles, the author of numerous works of fiction.

Ducks and Drakes. "To make ducks and drakes" with one's money is to squander it recklessly and foolishly. The allusion is to the custom, with boys, of taking flat stones and throwing them horizontally along the surface of the water in such a way as to cause them to skim along the surface, touching it and then rising from it several times in succession. The first time the stone rises it is called a *duck*, the second time, a *drake*, and so on, alternately. The meaning of the expression is, of course, that the spendthrift uses his money in a reckless way, even as the boys use stones to make ducks and drakes.

Dudley Diamond. A famous diamond, triangular in shape, but of great brilliancy. In the rough it weighed 88½ carats, but as at present cut it weighs 44½ carats. It was discovered in South Africa by a black shepherd named Swartzboy, who sold it to his master, Nie Kirk, for £400. Nie Kirk afterwards disposed of it for £12,000. It was subsequently purchased by the Earl of Dudley for £30,000, and set in a beautiful tiara. It was originally known as the *Star of South Africa Diamond*.

Duke Humphrey, To Dine with. An old expression, meaning not to dine at all. The phrase is said to have arisen from the fact that a part of the promenade near old St. Paul's in London was known as "Duke Humphrey's Walk," and that persons without the price of a dinner were accustomed to linger there, in the hope of securing an invitation. According to other authorities, the allusion is to Duke Humphrey, the ill-fated son of Henry IV (1399–1413), who was starved to death.

Duke of Exeter's Daughter. The name given to a famous torture-rack in the Tower of London. It was so named because it was invented in 1447 by the Duke of Exeter, when he was high-constable.

Duke of York's Column. A Tuscan column of Scotch granite—124 feet in height—erected in London in 1833, in memory of the Duke of York (second son of George III), who died in 1827. It was designed by Wyatt, and is surmounted by a bronze statue of the duke, by Westmacott. The summit, from which may be obtained a fine view of the western part of the city of London, is reached by a winding staircase.

Duke's Walk. A spot near Holyrood Palace, Edinburgh, celebrated as the favorite promenade of the Duke of York (afterwards James II of England), during his residence in Scotland. It was the common meeting-place for settling affairs of honor; hence an invitation to meet a person in the "Duke's Walk" was considered equivalent to a challenge to a duel. See *Holyrood Palace*.

Dulcinists. A heretical sect that sprang up in Italy, and flourished during the early part of the fourteenth century. Its founder, Dulcino, taught that God had reigned from the beginning to the time of Christ, and that Christ had reigned from His ascension until the beginning of the fourteenth century, at which time He gave up His dominion to the Holy Ghost, and the authority of the Pope ceased. Dulcino and his wife were burned to death in 1307.

Dumbarton Castle. An ancient and picturesque castle situated on a rocky eminence, 280 feet above the river Clyde, near Glasgow, Scotland. Although of no value as a means of defense, it is one of the four Scottish fortresses that must be maintained by the terms of the Treaty of Union. Sir William Wallace, the Scottish patriot, was confined there in 1305, and in one of the apartments of the castle is shown the huge, two-handed sword wielded by the hero. Mary, Queen of Scots, lived there during her childhood, in 1548. Dumbarton Rock has been famous since its capture by the Picts and Northumbrians in 756 A. D.

Dumb-Bell. "The original dumbbell was an apparatus contrived like that for ringing church-bells ; that is, a heavy fly-wheel with a weight attached, which was set in motion like a church-bell, until it acquired sufficient impetus to carry the gymnast up and down, and so bring the muscles into active play. There is one at New College, Oxford, to the present day. The modern weights, so called, produce similar results, in a less cumbrous and more agreeable manner."—Edwards's *Words, Facts, and Phrases.*

Dumb Captain. A sobriquet bestowed by his fellow conspirators on the Prince of Condé (1530-1569), the leader of the plot—known as the Conspiracy of Amboise—to free Francis II (1559-1560) of France from the control of the Guises, and to secure their overthrow. The plot failed through treachery, and Condé's life was saved only by the death of the King.

Dumb Ox. A sobriquet bestowed upon Thomas Aquinas (1227-1274), by his fellow students at Cologne, on account of his apparent dulness and stupidity. His teachers, however, detected the genius that lay hidden beneath this silent and unpromising exterior, and prophesied that this " dumb ox " would some day astonish the world. Aquinas was afterwards known as the " Angel of the Schools " and the " Angelic Doctor."

Dun. This word—meaning to press a creditor for payment—is said to have originated in the name of John Dun, a bailiff of Lincoln, in the reign of Henry VII (1485-1509). Dun was so active and skilful in collecting debts that whenever any one became slow pay, it was the custom to exclaim : " *Dun* him " ; *i. e.,* send Dun after him.

Dunbar, Battle of. A battle fought at Dunbar, Scotland, on September 3rd, 1650, between the Parliamentary forces commanded by Oliver Cromwell and the Royalist Scots under Leslie. The latter were signally defeated, with a loss of 3000 killed and 10,000 taken prisoners. As a result of this battle, Spain recognized the English Commonwealth, and Holland offered its alliance.

Dunce. A word, the origin of which is in doubt. According to the generally accepted opinion, the word is from Duns Scotus (1265-1308), the mediæval Schoolman, whose followers were called *Dunsmen* or *Duncemen,* after their great teacher. At the time of the revival of learning, they strongly opposed the study of the classics ; hence the term *dunce* was applied to any one that despised learning, or was slow in its acquisition. According to Dr. Mackay, the word *dunce* is derived from " the Gaelic *donas,* bad luck ; or in contempt, a poor, ignorant creature."

Dunciad (*Dunce-epic*). A poetical satire by Alexander Pope (1688-1744), in four books, the first three of which were published in 1728, and the fourth in 1742. The poem was written by Pope to revenge himself on his critics and literary enemies, whose name was legion. The satire was most effective, and conferred immortality on Pope's opponents.

Dunderberg (*Thunder Mountain*). A mountain on the Hudson River at the entrance to the Highlands, opposite to Anthony's Nose. According to a well-known legend, the mountain was in the keeping of "a little bulbous-bottomed Dutch goblin, in trunk hose and sugar-loaf hat." He had charge of the thunderstorms in the vicinity; and, in consequence, the skippers for a long time lowered their peaks while passing Dunderberg, in honor of this diminutive Lord of the Mountain. Washington Irving says : " It was observed that all such as paid this tribute of respect were suffered to pass unmolested."

Dunloe, Gap of. A famous pass, about four miles in length, in the county of Kerry, Ireland — near the lakes of Killarney. It is famed for its wild and rugged grandeur.

Dunsinane Hill. A mountain in Perthshire, Scotland, famous from its association with Shakespeare's tragedy of *Macbeth*. It is 1012 feet in height, and on its summit may be seen the ruins of a castle, said to have been Macbeth's fortress. There, according to the play, was fought the battle that resulted in the overthrow and death of the tyrant.

" Macbeth shall never vanquished be until
   Great Birnam wood to high *Dunsinane hill*
Shall come against him."
                         Macbeth, iv, 1.

Dupes, Day of the. See *Day of the Dupes*.

Durability of Perfumes. "Among the curiosities shown at Alnwick Castle is a vase taken from an Egyptian catacomb. It is full of a mixture of gums, resins, etc., which evolve a pleasant odour to the present day, although probably 3000 years old."—Piesse's *Art of Perfumery*.

Durham Terrace. A terrace at Quebec, Canada, 200 feet above the St. Lawrence River. It was named in honor of the Earl of Durham, at one time governor-general of Canada, and occupies the platform formerly occupied by the Château St. Louis, built by Champlain in 1620. Dufferin Terrace—an extension of Durham Terrace —was added some years later, and named in honor of the Marquis of Dufferin, governor-general in 1872–1878. Together with Durham Terrace, it has a length of 1400 feet.

Düsseldorf Gallery. A gallery of paintings at Düsseldorf, Germany, established early in the 18th century. In 1805, its most valuable paintings were carried off by the King of Bavaria, and placed in the *Pinakothek* at Munich, where they still remain. The Düsseldorf Gallery still contains several fine paintings, as well as sketches and drawings by distinguished artists. See *Pinakothek*.

Dutch Auction. The name given to a public sale in which the auctioneer fixes a price upon the article to be sold, —above its value, and then gradually reduces it until some one closes with an offer.

Dutch Courage. A form of courage induced by the free use of intoxicants ; hence sometimes called " pot valor." The expression is often used to denote absence of courage.

Dwarfs, Famous.

(1) *Philetas of Cos* (330 B.C.), poet and grammarian, and tutor of Ptolemy Philadelphus. He is said to have carried weights in his clothing to prevent him from being blown away.

(2) *Coropas*,— a court favorite of Julia, niece of Augustus,— 2 feet 4 inches in height.

(3) *Andromeda*,— a freedmaid of Julia, niece of Augustus,— 2 feet 4 inches in height.

(4) *Alypius of Alexandria*,—logician and philosopher,—1 foot 5¼ inches in height.

(5) *John d'Estrix*, of Mechlin, brought to the Duke of Parma in 1592. He was familiar with several languages, and was not more than three feet tall.

(6) *Geoffrey Hudson*, an English dwarf. When a youth 18 inches tall, he was served up in a cold pie by the Duchess of Buckingham, before Charles I and Henrietta Maria. In 1653, he fought a duel and killed his antagonist.

(7) *Count Borowlaski*, born in November, 1739. He was an accomplished Pole, who lived for many years in England. At thirty years of age, he measured 39 inches in height.

(8) *Charles S. Stratton* (1838–1883), an American dwarf, born in Connecticut. He was known as "General Tom Thumb," and was exhibited in England by P. T. Barnum in 1846. In February, 1863, in New York City, he married Lavinia Warren — aged 21 years, — 32 inches high. Stratton at this time was 31 inches high. Together with his wife and child, and another dwarf named Commodore Nutt, he visited England a second time in 1864.

(9) *Mr. Collard*, aged 22 years, smaller than "Tom Thumb." He sang in concerts in London in 1873, and was called the "Pocket Sims Reeves."

(10) "*Bébé*," dwarf of King Stanislaus of Poland. He was only 23 inches tall, and died in Paris in 1858, at the age of 90.

(11) *Che-mah*, a Chinese dwarf, 42 years old, 25 inches high. He was exhibited at the Westminster Aquarium, London, in 1880.

(12) *Lucia Zarate*, born in 1863, in Mexico ; height 20 inches, weight 4¾ lbs.

(13) *General Mite* (Francis Joseph Flynn), born in 1864 in the State of New York ; height 21 inches, weight 9 lbs.; exhibited in New York City in 1879 *et seq.;* in London, in 1880 *et seq.*

(14) "*Princesse Topaze*," a dwarf of French parentage, born at Buenos Ayres. Weight 15 lbs., height 20 inches. Exhibited at the Westminster Aquarium in 1893. See *Giants, Famous; Tom Thumb.*

Dying Gaul. The name that should properly be given to the statue of the *Dying Gladiator* in the Capitoline Museum at Rome. See *Dying Gladiator.*

Dying Gladiator. A famous marble statue in the Capitoline Museum at Rome. It is the work of some unknown Greek sculptor (possibly Ctesilaus, a contemporary of Phidias), and was found in the gardens of Sallust. Although universally known as the *Dying Gladiator*, the figure is now believed to be that of a wounded Gaul. The right arm is a restoration, possibly by Michael Angelo.

"I do not believe that so much pathos is wrought into any other block of stone."— *Hawthorne.*

Dying Sayings, Real or Traditional. The following list of dying sayings of distinguished persons is taken from Brewer's *Reader's Handbook.*

Addison. "See how a Christian dies !" or, "See in what peace a Christian can die !"

Anaxagoras. "Give the boys a holiday."

Byron. "I must sleep now."

Cæsar (Julius). "Et tu, Brute !"

Charlemagne. "Lord, into Thy hands I commend my spirit !"

Charles II (of England). "Don't let poor Nelly * starve !"

Chesterfield. "Give Day Rolles a chair."

Cromwell. "My desire is to make what haste I may to be gone."

Franklin. "A dying man can do nothing easy."

Goethe. "More light !"

Hobbes. "Now I am about to take my last voyage—a great leap in the dark."

James V (of Scotland). "It † came with a lass, and will go with a lass."

Jesus Christ. "It is finished !"

Knox. "Now it is come."

* Nell Gwynne.   † The Scottish crown.

Mahomet. " O Allah, be it so ! Henceforth among the glorious host of Paradise."

Mirabeau. " Let me die to the sounds of delicious music."

Napoleon I. " Mon Dieu ! La nation Française ! Fête d'armée.*"

Napoleon III. " Were you at Sedan ? "

Nelson. " I thank God I have done my duty."

Rabelais. " Let down the curtain, the farce is over."

Scott, Sir Walter. " God bless you all ! "

Sidney, Algernon. " I know that my Redeemer liveth. I die for the good old cause."

Socrates. " Crito, we owe a cock to Æsculapius."

Talma. " The worst is, I cannot see."

Tasso. " Lord, into Thy hands I commend my spirit ! "

Vespasian. " A king should die standing."

William III of England. " Can this last long ? "

Wolfe, General. " What ! do they run already ? Then I die happy."

Dynamite (*Gr. δύναμις, force*). A powerful explosive compound, consisting of a mechanical mixture of nitro-glycerine with an absorbent, such as sawdust or silicious earth, in the proportion of three of the former to one of the latter. It was first produced by Alfred Nobel in 1867. See *Gun-Cotton ; Nitro-Glycerine.*

E

Eagle of Divines. An appellation sometimes bestowed on Thomas Aquinas (1227-1274), the famous mediæval divine.

Eagle of Meaux. A name given to Jacques Bénigne Bossuet (1627-1704), Bishop of Meaux. Bossuet was the

* Tête d'armée, according to some authorities.

most eloquent of the pulpit orators of France, and was especially famous for his funeral orations. See *Swan of Cambray.*

" The *Eagle of Meaux* and the Swan of Cambray have often been compared. One overawes, the other softens ; one inspires fear of God, the other trust in God ; one, while rejecting the sectarian spirit of the Jansenists, adheres to the harsh ethics of Port-Royal ; the other, not less above suspicion as to his own morals, teaches less gloomy maxims ; he has not that hatred of the present life ; he does not say, like Pascal, that self is detestable ; he wishes us to endure ourselves as we endure our neighbors, to proportion the practices of piety to the strength of the body ; he blames sorrowful austerity, excessive fear of tasting innocent joy and lawful pleasures ; he wishes us to know how to recognize God in the delights of friendship, in the beauties of Nature and Art."—Martin's *History of France.*

Ear of Dionysius. The name given to a celebrated cavern near Syracuse, in Sicily, said to have been constructed by Dionysius the Elder, tyrant of Syracuse, and used by him as a prison for suspected persons. This cave was 250 feet long and 80 feet high. It was fashioned in the shape of a human ear, and was so constructed that the faintest sounds were conveyed from all parts to a central chamber, corresponding to the tympanum or drum of the ear. There the tyrant secreted himself, sometimes, it is said, for days, and listened to the conversations of the unfortunates imprisoned within. The men that built the dungeon were put to death to prevent them from divulging the use to which it was put. A whisper at one end can be distinctly heard at the other, by putting one's ear close to the rock ; while the tearing of paper sounds like a series of explosions. Workmen, while making excavations during recent years, have discovered pieces of iron and lead that are probably the remains of chains and staples used to secure the prisoners.

Ears-to-Ear Bible. The name given to an edition of the Bible, printed in 1810. It is so called on account of an error of the printer, whereby the passage from *Matthew* xiii, 43, "Who hath ears to hear, let him hear," is rendered, "Who hath *ears to ear*, let him hear."

Earthquakes. The following list of the most destructive earthquakes that have occurred since the beginning of the eighteenth century is taken from Mulhall's *Dictionary of Statistics.*

Year.	Place.	Lives Lost.
1703 ...	Yeddo....................	190,000
1716 ...	Algiers	18,000
1726 ...	Palermo..................	6,000
1731 ...	Pekin....................	95,000
1746 ...	Lima....................	18,000
1754 ...	Cairo.	40,000
1755 ...	Lisbon.	35,000
1773 ...	Guatemala	33,000
1797 ...	Quito	41,000
1822 ...	Aleppo..............	22,000
1861 ...	Mendoza (South America).	12,000
1868 ...	Arica....................	6,000
1880 ...	Manila..................	3,000
1883 ...	Ischia...................	2,000

See *Lisbon Earthquake.*

Easter. A festival of the Christian Church, instituted about 68 A.D., in commemorationof the resurrection of Jesus Christ, and at present observed by the Greek, Roman, Anglican, and Lutheran communions. The day for its observance in England was fixed by St. Austin in 597. Owing to the disputes that arose between the Eastern and Western Churches, it was decided by the Council of Nice, in 325 A.D., that "everywhere the Great Feast of Easter should be observed on one and the same day"; following this decision, "Easter Day is always the first Sunday after the full moon which happens upon, or next after, the 21st day of March; and if the full moon happens upon a Sunday, Easter-Day is the Sunday after." In the ancient Church, the festival of Easter lasted eight days; but after the eleventh century it was limited to three days, and in later times generally to two. The word *Easter* is derived from the Saxon goddess *Eostre*, whose festival was in April. From that pagan festival are derived the customs of Easter eggs, Easter fires, etc.

Easter-Day Sun. It was long a belief in England that the sun actually danced on Easter-Day. This notion is referred to in the lines by Sir John Suckling :

"But oh ! she dances such a way,
No sun upon an Easter day
Is half so fine a sight."

Sir Thomas Browne, in his *Vulgar Errors*, ridicules the idea.

Eastern Church. See *Greek Church.*

Eastern Empire. The Eastern Empire was founded by Theodosius the Great, who, at his death in 395 A.D., divided the Roman Empire between his two sons, Arcadius and Honorius. Arcadius received the eastern part, with Constantinople for its capital, and Honorius the western part, with Rome for its capital. The Eastern Empire comprised Asia Minor, Egypt, Asia as far as the Euphrates, the coasts of the Black Sea, the Danube, and all the countries from the Adriatic to the Hellespont. It began to decline in 1057, and finally succumbed to the Turks under Mohammed II in 1453. See *Lower Empire ; Western Empire.*

Eastern Penitentiary. A noted prison in Philadelphia, rendered famous by a somewhat sensational passage in Charles Dickens's *American Notes*, describing the treatment of the criminals imprisoned there during the novelist's first visit to America, in 1842. The penitentiary covers an area of eleven acres, and contains from 1100 to 1200 inmates. It is built on the "radiating" plan, and is conducted on the "individual" system. The prisoners are allowed considerable liberty, as well as many of the comforts (some would say, the luxuries) of life.

"In the outskirts stands a great prison, called the *Eastern Penitentiary:* conducted on a plan peculiar to the State of Pennsylvania. The system here is rigid, strict, and hopeless solitary confinement. I believe it, in its effects, to be cruel and wrong."—Dickens's *American Notes*.

East India Company. A commercial association chartered by Queen Elizabeth on December 31st, 1600, under the title of *The Governor and Company of the Merchants of London Trading with the East Indies*. At that time, its capital was £72,000, and its merchant marine included four vessels. It soon, however, developed a prosperous trade, and in 1683 a share of £100 was sold for £500. Other companies were chartered in 1657, 1688, and 1698, and in 1702 these were all united. In 1773, a governor-general was appointed at Bengal. The East India Company, from a small beginning in Calcutta, extended its territory by gifts from and wars against native princes, until it finally controlled a vast domain. It maintained an army, composed principally of Sepoys, or natives of India. The charter ceased in 1833, but was renewed. The East India Company continued as a corporate body until the outbreak of the Indian Mutiny of 1857, when, owing to the disappearance of the company's army, the government of India was transferred to the Crown. The company's political power ceased on September 1st, 1858, and the queen was proclaimed as Queen of Great Britain and the Colonies, in the principal cities of India, amid great rejoicing, on November 1st of the same year. See *Indian Mutiny*.

East India House. The house of the East India Company. It stood on Leadenhall Street, London, and was demolished in 1862. The famous India Museum was removed to Fife House, Whitehall, and is now in the Kew Gardens Museum. Hoole, the translator of Tasso; Charles Lamb, the humorist; James Mill, the historian of British India; and John Stuart Mill, his son, the distinguished logician and political economist, were clerks in the East India House.

East River Bridge. A gigantic suspension bridge—the longest in the world—connecting the Boroughs of Manhattan and Brooklyn, New York City, and popularly known as the "Brooklyn Bridge." It was commenced in January, 1870, and completed and thrown open to the public in May, 1884, at a cost of $15,000,000. The total length of the bridge (including the approaches) is 1¼ miles, and the width, 85 feet. The central span is 1595 feet in length, and 135 feet above high-water mark. The bridge is suspended on four cables, each of which is 15¾ inches in diameter, and contains 5434 galvanized steel wires. Each cable is 3578½ feet long, and has a supporting power of 122,000 tons in the middle of the sag. The capacity of the bridge is 45,000 pedestrians and 1440 vehicles per hour.

Eblis. The name given by the Arabs to the prince of fallen angels. Before his fall he was called Azazil. According to the legend, he was exiled to the infernal regions for refusing to worship the newly created Adam at the command of the Almighty. To justify his refusal, Eblis declared that he had been formed of ethereal fire, while Adam was merely a creature of common clay. To avenge himself, Eblis tempted Adam and Eve, and caused them to fall from a state of innocence, and, finally, to be separated. The Mohammedans say that when Mohammed was born, the throne of Eblis was precipitated to the lowest part of hell, and all the idols of the Gentiles were overthrown.

"Ecce Homo!" (*Lat. "Behold the Man!"*). The expression made use of by Pilate, when he brought Christ forth from the judgment hall,—wearing the crown of thorns and the purple robe,—and declared that he found no fault in him (see *John* xix, 5).

The term *Ecce Homo* is applied to a number of famous paintings, representing Christ wearing the crown of thorns.

Among these may be mentioned the following :

(1) *Ecce Homo.* A painting by Fra Bartolommeo (1469–1517) in the Pitti Palace, Florence, Italy.

(2) *Ecce Homo.* A painting by Correggio (1494–1534) in the National Gallery, London.

(3) *Ecce Homo.* A painting by Cigoli (1559–1613) in the Pitti Palace, Florence, Italy.

(4) *Ecce Homo.* A painting by Rembrandt (1607–1669).

(5) *Ecce Homo.* A painting by Titian (1477–1576) in the Belvedere Gallery, Vienna, Austria.

The name *Ecce Homo* is also given to a theological treatise, published anonymously in 1865, and attributed to John Robert Seeley (1834–1895), but not acknowledged by him. It is a study of the human character of Jesus Christ (the divine element not being considered).

Echo River. A partly subterranean river, flowing for three-quarters of a mile through the Mammoth Cave, Kentucky, and finally emptying into the Green River. It is 200 feet wide in some places. See *Mammoth Cave.*

École de Médecine (*Fr. School of Medicine*). A famous medical school in Paris, consisting of several buildings erected during the 18th century, with a modern façade fronting on the Boulevard St. Germain. The course of study lasts five years, and is attended by nearly 4500 students, about 250 of whom are women. The École de Médecine contains a library, an amphitheatre seating 1400 persons, and three museums,—the Musée Broca, the Musée Dupuytren, and the Musée Orfila. The faculty is composed of the leading physicians and surgeons of Paris.

École des Beaux-Arts (*Fr. School of Fine Arts*). A noted school in Paris, founded in 1648, for the teaching of architecture, sculpture, painting, engraving, and gem-cutting. It occupies the Palais des Beaux-Arts in the Rue Bonaparte, and is attended by 1600 pupils (66 of whom are women). Those that obtain the *Prix de Rome* are sent to Rome to study for four years, at the expense of the government, and the works sent home by them — termed *Grands Prix de Rome* — are annually exhibited at the École des Beaux-Arts, in October. The museum of the École des Beaux-Arts contains a valuable collection of copies of the principal works of art in foreign museums, and forms an admirable supplement to the Louvre. See *Palais des Beaux-Arts.*

École Polytechnique (*Fr. Polytechnic School*). A celebrated institution in Paris, founded by Monge in 1794, and reorganized and given its present name in 1795. It is designed for the education of military engineers, staff-officers, telegraphists, and officials of the government tobacco-manufactory. Candidates must be between sixteen and twenty years of age, and are admitted only after examination. The school was reorganized a second time in 1816.

Ecstatic Doctor. An appellation bestowed upon Jean de Ruysbroek (1294–1381), the Mystic.

Ecuador. Ecuador is the Spanish for *equator*, and is so called on account of its geographical position.

Ecumenical Councils. The name given to certain general councils of prelates and theologians of the Christian Church, convoked to regulate matters of doctrine and discipline. The following are the ones recognized by the Roman Catholic Church:

(1) *First of Nicæa* (325). Arianism condemned; Nicene Creed promulgated; consubstantiality of the Son of God decreed.

(2) *First of Constantinople* (381). Nicene Creed amended ; bishop of Constantinople declared next in rank to bishop of Rome.

(3) *Ephesus* (431). Nestorius, Bishop

of Constantinople, deposed and anathematized.

(4) *Chalcedon* (451). The doctrine of the two natures (human and divine) of Christ, as defined by Leo of Rome, accepted ; additions to the Nicene Creed made at the Council of Constantinople decreed.

(5) *Second of Constantinople* (553). Condemnation of heretical writings ; doctrines of the first four Ecumenical Councils declared authoritative.

(6) *Third of Constantinople* (680–681). Heresies of the Monothelites condemned ; authority of the six general councils affirmed.

(7) *Second of Nicæa* (787). Iconoclasts condemned.

(8) *Fourth of Constantinople* (869–870). Heretics and Iconoclasts condemned.

(9) *First Lateran* (1123). Right of investiture settled ; 22 canons published.

(10) *Second Lateran* (1139). Marriages of priests declared null and void ; mass forbidden to be heard when celebrated by a married priest.

(11) *Third Lateran* (1179). Schismatics condemned.

(12) *Fourth Lateran* (1215). Albigenses and other heretics anathematized.

(13) *First of Lyons* (1245). Emperor Frederick II deposed.

(14) *Second of Lyons* (1274). Latin and Greek Churches temporarily united.

(15) *Vienne* (1311–1312). Order of Knights Templars suppressed and property confiscated.

(16) *Pisa* (1409). Popes Gregory XII and Benedict III deposed and their acts declared null.

(17) *Constance* (1414–1418). John Huss and Jerome of Prague condemned and burned.

(18) *Basel* (1431–1443). Reunion of all Christians in the Roman Catholic Church attempted.

(19) *Fifth Lateran* (1512–1517). Acts of Council of Pisa condemned, etc.

(20) *Trent* (1545–1563). Doctrines of Luther, Zwinglius, and Calvin condemned ; canon of Scripture decreed ; seven sacraments made authoritative ; Church declared to be the interpreter of the Holy Scriptures; tradition made equal in authority with Scripture.

(21) *Vatican* (1869–1870). Infallibility of the Pope affirmed and promulgated.

Of the 21 councils above enumerated, the Greek Church recognizes the first seven ; and Protestants generally, the first four.

Eddas. The name given to two collections of old Scandinavian literature, written by skalds or bards about the 10th, 11th, or 12th century A.D. Of these, the *Younger* or prose *Edda* treats of Scandinavian mythology, and is supposed to have been compiled by Snorri Sturluson (1178–1241). It is sometimes called the *Resenian Edda*, because it was translated by Resen, in 1640. The work contains quotations from about seventy early poets, and consists of three parts : (1) *Gylfaginning* (*The Deceiving of Gylfi*), a series of stories purporting to have been told by Odin to Gylfi, a Swedish king, and forming the principal source of our knowledge of the Scandinavian theogony ; (2) *Skáldskaparmál*, or the *Art of Poetry ;* and (3) *Háttatál, a System of Prosody.*

The *Elder* or poetic *Edda* contains legends of Scandinavian gods and heroes, and was compiled by Saemund Sigfusson (who lived in Iceland about 1055–1132). It was discovered about 1643 by Brynjulf Sveinsson. The poems belonging to the *Elder Edda* are 33 in number, and deal partly with Scandinavian mythology, partly with heroic and legendary history. Translations of the *Eddas* have been made into English, French, and German. See *Sagas.*

Eddystone Lighthouse. A celebrated lighthouse on the English Channel, nine miles off the coast of Cornwall, and fourteen miles southwest of the Plymouth Breakwater. It is the fourth lighthouse erected on the spot since 1700. The foundation was laid in 1879, and the structure completed in 1882, by Sir James N. Douglass, F.R.S. Like its predecessor, its stones are ingeniously dovetailed throughout. Its light, at an elevation of 133 feet, is equal to 159,600 candles, and may be seen, in clear weather, at a distance of more than seventeen miles. The first Eddystone lighthouse was erected in 1696–1700. It was built of wood with a stone base, and was 100 feet in height. In the great storm of November 20th, 1703, it was washed away with the architect Winstanley. In 1706–1709, it was replaced by a second structure, also of wood with a stone base, 92 feet high. This was burned in 1755. A third, designed by Smeaton, and constructed wholly of stone, was completed in 1759. It was built of Portland oölite encased in granite. The blocks—weighing one or two tons each—were dovetailed into the solid rock forming the base, and each block was dovetailed into its neighbors. The tower was 85 feet in height. The light had an elevation of 72 feet, and was visible at a distance of 13 miles. The rock on which the lighthouse stood became undermined and weakened by the action of the waves, and, in consequence, the structure was removed and the present one erected close at hand.

Eden, Garden of. The site of the Garden of Eden, mentioned in *Genesis*, has been the subject of much speculation among theologians. By some it is placed near Damascus, by others in Armenia. The Caucasus, Hillah near Babylon, Arabia, and Abyssinia are all mentioned as possible sites. The Hindoos say it was situated in Ceylon.

"Many futile attempts have been made to reconcile with modern knowledge the mythical geography of *Genesis* ii, 10–14. . . . It is clear that the writer himself had no exact knowledge of the position of *Eden*, but combined as he found them the special Hebrew legend with the general Asiatic tradition."—*Chambers's Encyclopædia.*

Edgehill, Battle of. Fought in Warwickshire, England, on October 23rd, 1642, between 12,000 Royalists commanded by Charles I (1625–1649) and Prince Rupert, and 10,000 Parliamentarians under the leadership of the Earl of Essex. Edgehill was the first battle of importance in the Civil War; and, although generally regarded as indecisive, was claimed by the supporters of Parliament. The Royalists had the advantage not only in position, but also in cavalry, while Essex was stronger in artillery; 5000 Royalists were killed in this battle.

Edict of Milan. An edict published by the Emperor Constantine (306–337 A.D.), after the conquest of Italy, in 313, "to secure to the Christians the restitution of their civil and religious rights."

Edict of Nantes. A famous edict published, from Nantes, by Henry IV (1589–1610) of France in 1598, granting religious freedom to his Huguenot, or Protestant, subjects. By this edict, the Huguenots were permitted to worship wherever Protestant communities existed, to build churches (except in Paris), and to establish institutions of learning. The Edict of Nantes was confirmed by Louis XIII (1610–1643) in 1610 and by Louis XIV (1643–1715) in 1652, but was afterwards foolishly revoked by the last-named king in 1685. As a result of this rash and impolitic act and of the bloody persecutions that followed, over 500,000 of the most intelligent artisans of France took refuge in England, Holland, Germany, and other parts of Europe, carrying with them the arts of silk-weaving, dyeing, and glass-making, in which they were specially skilled. Many thousands of them settled at Spitalfields, England, where their descendants still remain at the present day. See *Dragonnades; Huguenots.*

Edinburgh Castle. A famous castle —once used as a fortress — in Edinburgh, Scotland. It stands on an eminence 300 feet in height, and, before the days of modern warfare, was deemed impregnable. The castle is said to have been founded by Camelon, King of the Picts, in 330 B.C., and to have been afterwards rebuilt by Edwin, King of Northumbria, in 626 A.D., to protect his dominion from the incursions of the Picts and Scots. It was used as a royal residence as far back as the twelfth century. There James VI,—afterwards James I (1603–1625) of England,—son of Mary, Queen of Scots, was born. The castle contains the regalia of the former kings of Scotland. The castle was captured by Cromwell in 1650, after the battle of Dunbar. See *Crown of Scotland; Dunbar, Battle of.*

Edinburgh Review. A noted quarterly magazine, established in Edinburgh in 1802, by a group of able young writers of Whig principles, among whom may be named Francis Jeffrey, Sydney Smith, Francis Horner, and Henry Brougham. In 1808, the circulation rose to 8000, and reached its maximum in 1813, when 12,000 or 13,000 copies were printed. After that date the circulation and influence of the magazine began to decline. In its palmy days the *Edinburgh Review* exerted a widespread influence, not only in politics but also in literature, where its brilliant style, trenchant criticism, and keen wit excited both wonder and admiration.

Edition of 1611. A name frequently given to the Authorized English Version of the Bible, prepared by a body of eminent scholars, under the direction of King James I (1603-1625) of England. This version was commenced in 1604 and completed in 1611.

Edmund Ironside. Edmund, King of the English during seven months of the year 1016, was called *Ironside*, on account of the complete suit of armor habitually worn by him to protect himself against assassination. Although his death is generally supposed to have

been the result of foul play, this is not the conclusion arrived at by Freeman, the English historian. Other authorities declare that Edmund was surnamed *Ironside* because of his bravery.

Edom (*Heb. red*). The surname of Esau, Isaac's elder son, derived apparently from the current name of the food for which he sold his birthright. Esau settled in the country extending from the mountains south of the Dead Sea to the Gulf of Akabah. This region was called for him the land of Edom, and was afterward known as Idumea. See *Israel.*

"And Esau said to Jacob, Feed me, I pray thee, with the same red pottage; for I am faint; therefore was his name called *Edom.*"
—*Genesis* xxv, 30.

Education and War. The following table, recently compiled, shows the amount per capita expended by the leading nations of the civilized world for military and educational purposes respectively.

Nations.	Military.	Educational.
France.............	$4.00	$ .70
England............	3.72	.62
Holland............	3.58	.64
Saxony.............	2.38	.38
Wurtemberg........	2.38	.38
Bavaria............	2.38	.40
Prussia............	2.04	.50
Russia	2.04	.03
Denmark...........	1.76	.94
Italy	1.52	.36
Belgium............	1.38	.46
Austria............	1.36	.32
Switzerland........	.82	.84
United States.......	.30	1.35

The above table is a striking commentary on the essential barbarism of the professedly civilized nations of Europe and shows the great disparity between the amount of money spent for the maintenance of brute force, and that expended for mental development.

Edward the Confessor. Edward, the last of the Saxon kings of England before Harold, was called the "Confessor," on account of his piety. He reigned from 1041 to 1066. In 1166, one hundred years after his death, he was canonized by Pope Alexander III (1159–1181).

> "The distinction between a CONFESSOR and a MARTYR in the early days of Christianity was simply this : both made an open confession of their faith, and expressed their readiness to die for it ; the former, however, was never called upon to do so, whereas the latter actually suffered martyrdom."—Wagner's *Names and their Meaning*.

Edward the Confessor's Chapel.
A chapel in Westminster Abbey, London, forming the end of the choir. It contains, besides numerous tombs and monuments of English kings and queens, the old coronation chair of the English kings, and the new coronation chair — made for Queen Mary, wife of William III (1689–1702). The old chair contains, under the seat, the famous " Stone of Scone." See *Coronation Chair*.

Égalité (*Fr. Equality*).
A surname assumed, in place of his hereditary title, by Philippe (1747–1793), Duc d'Orléans, cousin of Louis XVI, to express his sympathy with the principles of the French revolutionists, as well as to win the favor of the people. He voted in the Convention, in 1793, for the death of his cousin, but this infamous conduct did not avail him much, and he was himself sent to the guillotine in November of the same year.

Egeria.
The name of a famous nymph, who, according to tradition, instructed Numa Pompilius in the ritual of public worship established by him at Rome. She dwelt in a grove near Aricia, and there the King was accustomed to visit her. According to other accounts, these interviews occurred in a grove before the Porta Capena at Rome, where the grotto of Egeria is still shown. See *Fountain of Egeria*.

Egg of Columbus.
Christopher Columbus, on his return to Spain after his first voyage to America, was made the subject of various disparaging remarks, while dining at the house of a Spanish nobleman. Some of the guests, thinking to lessen the merit of his discovery, declared that the thing itself was easy of accomplishment,—all that was necessary being to have thought of it in the first place. Without deigning to reply directly to his detractors, the great navigator called for an egg and passed it among the guests, asking them to make it stand on end. None of them being able to do so, Columbus took the egg and, breaking the end gently, caused it to stand upright on his plate. The assembled guests with one voice exclaimed that this was a simple thing to do. " Yes," replied Columbus, with a smile, " the only thing necessary was to have *thought* of it ! " The expression " the Egg of Columbus" has since then passed into a proverb, meaning anything that one cannot do and yet finds extremely simple on being shown.

A similar story is related of Brunelleschi, the architect, who, on being told that his plan of building the dome of the cathedral at Florence was not practicable, caused an egg to stand upright by breaking one of its ends, and thus demonstrated that a vault could be upheld without interior support.

> " Many of the historical proverbs have a doubtful paternity. *Columbus's egg* is claimed for Brunelleschi."—*Emerson*.

Egyptian Exploration Fund.
Originated by Miss Amelia B. Edwards to encourage excavations for the purpose of throwing light on the history and arts of ancient Egypt. Sir Francis Wilson was the first president, and Mr. R. S. Poole, the first secretary. Miss Edwards (herself a learned Egyptologist) died in 1892, and bequeathed her property to endow a professorship of Egyptology in University College, London. Several important excavations have been made under the direction of the *Egyptian Exploration Fund*, and many valuable antiquities have been discovered and exhibited in London.

Ehrenbreitstein (*Ger. Broad Stone of Honor*). A fortress on the Rhine, directly opposite Coblenz. It crowns the summit of a precipitous rock, 387 feet in height, and is inaccessible on three sides. The first regular fortifications were begun there in 1672. Ehrenbreitstein was besieged four times by the French during the War of the Revolution, and was finally captured in 1799 by General Jourdain. On the conclusion of the Peace of Lunéville in 1801, the French blew up the fortress and abandoned it. The Congress of Vienna, in 1815, assigned it to Prussia, and in 1816–1826 it was rebuilt and thoroughly fortified. The view from the ramparts of the fortress is one of the finest on the Rhine.

Eiffel Tower. A colossal iron tower —the loftiest structure in the world— erected on the Champ de Mars, Paris, by Gustave Eiffel, in 1887–1889. It was built in honor of the Great Exposition of 1889, and may be called one of the wonders of the world. It is 985 feet high, contains nearly 7000 tons of iron, and cost $1,000,000. Of this amount, the sum of $300,000 was advanced by the French government, while the remainder was supplied by M. Eiffel, who, during the twenty years for which he has been granted a concession of the tower, hopes to recoup himself for his outlay. The tower contains three stories—devoted to restaurants and cafés, and is ascended by a number of elevators. The view from the summit is sublime.

1814. (1) The title of a painting by Jean Louis Ernest Meissonier (1811–1891), representing Napoleon I riding at the head of his staff, accompanied by a portion of his army, during the campaign of 1814, known as the "Campaign of France." The countenance of the Emperor, though resolute, is yet grim with despair, and suggests the closing scenes of his eventful career. Owing to the wintry landscape depicted in this painting,

it is sometimes mistakenly termed the "Retreat from Russia"; but that catastrophe occurred in 1812, almost two years earlier. It will be remembered that the campaign of 1814 was Napoleon's last struggle before his abdication and retirement to the island of Elba. This painting was sold in 1887 for 850,000 francs ($170,000), the highest price ever paid for a picture during the lifetime of the artist. It is, or at least was, owned by M. Chauchard, proprietor of the famous Magasin du Louvre at Paris.

(2) The title of a painting, also by Meissonier, representing Napoleon I mounted on a white horse, with his familiar gray overcoat thrown back from his uniform. The Emperor has left his escort behind him and has ascended a knoll, whence he is viewing the surrounding country. This painting is now the property of Mr. Henry Walters of Baltimore, the possessor of one of the finest private art collections in America. It was formerly owned by Prince Napoleon, and was exhibited in Paris in 1884, among the works of Meissonier.

"His brow is thoughtful, and his eyes wander beyond the ground where the game of his destiny is to be played, trying as it were to read the future. The sky is banked with heavy clouds, and the pale sun which illumines it is no longer the sun of Austerlitz."—*Catalogue of Walters Collection.*

1807. The name of a painting by Jean Louis Ernest Meissonier (1811–1891), representing the first Napoleon at the zenith of his career, during the battle of Friedland, June 14th, 1807. The Emperor is surrounded by a brilliant staff and is acknowledging the salute of a regiment of hussars that is about to charge. It is said that the artist spent fifteen years upon this picture. It was purchased by the late A. T. Stewart of New York for $60,000, and was afterwards presented by the late Henry Hilton to the Metropolitan Museum of Art, New York City.

Eighteen Martyrs of Saragossa.
The name given to eighteen persons
of noble birth, who suffered martyrdom
at Saragossa in 303 A.D., for their devotion to Christianity. According to
the story, Engracia, the daughter of a
Portuguese princess, was betrothed to
a duke of Gallia Narbonensis. While
on her way to her affianced husband,
accompanied by her friend Julia and
sixteen nobles, she stopped at Saragossa to visit her uncle Lupercus.
There she witnessed one of the Christian massacres of Diocletian and Maximian. Regardless of consequences,
Engracia sought out Dacian, told him
her name and rank, and pleaded with
him for the lives of her co-religionists.
Dacian, however, instead of being
moved to compassion, commanded the
princess and all her suite to be cast
into prison, and, after subjecting Engracia to every form of cruelty imaginable, left her to die. Her companions
were all beheaded.

Eighteenth Brumaire. The name
given to the bloodless revolution
whereby Napoleon Bonaparte, on
November 9th, 1799, overthrew the
Directory and the Councils of the
Ancients and of the Five Hundred, established the Consulate in its place,
and had himself chosen First Consul.
This *coup d'état* was so called because
it took place on the 18th day of Brumaire,—the second month of the year
according to the French revolutionary
calendar. See *French Revolutionary
Calendar*.

Eighteenth Fructidor. The name
given to the famous *coup d'état* of
September 4th, 1797, whereby certain
members of the French Directory saved
the Republic from the plots of the Royalists. Two of the Directors—Carnot
and Barthélemy — were proscribed,
while 11 members of the Council of
the Ancients, 42 members of the
Council of the Five Hundred, 35 jour-
nalists, and a host of priests were deported. The Directors that remained
loyal to the Republic, and planned the

coup d'état, were Barras, Laréveillière,
and Rewbell.

Eighth Wonder of the World. An
appellation frequently bestowed upon
the Escorial, a royal palace, mausoleum, and monastery in Spain, 31
miles northwest of Madrid. See *Escorial.*

Eikon Basilike (*Gr. Royal Image*).
A book attributed to Charles I. (1625–
1649) of England, and said to have been
written by him during his imprisonment on the Isle of Wight, but now generally believed to have been the work
of John Gauden (1605–1662), Bishop
of Exeter. It was published in 1649,
and within a year 50,000 copies were sold
in England alone. The *Eikon Basilike*
contains a full account of the trial and
condemnation of the King, and was the
chief means of obtaining for Charles
the title of the " Royal Martyr." The
question of authorship has long been a
matter of discussion, and, according to
some authorities, is not yet settled.
Hume, in his *History of England*,
advocated the claims of the King, in
preference to those of Dr. Gauden.
See *Eikonoklastes.*

"In the *Eikon Basilike* a strain of majestic melancholy is kept up, but the person-
ated sovereign is rather too theatrical for
real nature, the language is too rhetorical and
amplified, the periods too artificially elaborated."—Hallam's *Literature of Europe.*

Eikonoklastes (*Gr. Image-Breaker*).
A celebrated work by John Milton
(1608–1674), prepared, at the request
of the English government, to counteract the effect produced by the *Eikon
Basilike*, and to show that, whether
written by the King or not, its reason-
ings were fallacious. The *Eikonoklastes* appeared in 1649, and is generally regarded as a blot on Milton's
fair fame. See *Eikon Basilike.*

"A book (*Eikon Basilike*) appeared soon
after, which was ascribed to the king, and
contained the most invidious charges against
the parliament. I was ordered to answer
it ; and opposed the *Eikonoklastes* to the
Eikon."—*Milton.*

Ein Feste Burg Ist Unser Gott (*Ger. A Mighty Fortress Is Our God*). A famous hymn by Martin Luther (1483–1546). It is often called "Luther's Hymn." Heine called it the "Marseillaise of the Reformation." It is generally supposed to have been composed by the reformer while on his way to the Diet of Worms (1521); others, however, say it was written at the close of the Diet of Spires (1529).

Elaine. "The lily maid of Astolat," who loved Sir Lancelot, but was not loved in return. Sir Lancelot was sworn to celibacy, and, in addition, his interest was centred in Guinevere, the Queen. Elaine, realizing the hopelessness of her passion, died of a broken heart. In accordance with her last request, her body, clad in white and resting on the bed on which she died, was placed on a barge and guided by an old dumb servitor to King Arthur's palace. In her right hand was placed a lily, and in her left a letter declaring her love. When the "dead steered by the dumb" reached the palace-wharf, the King requested that the body be brought on shore. The letter was then read, and the remains were buried in a manner befitting a queen. On the tomb was inscribed the sad narrative of Elaine's unrequited passion. The story is derived from Sir Thomas Malory's *History of Prince Arthur*, and has been told in blank verse by Tennyson,—forming one of the *Idylls of the King*.

Elba. An island in the Mediterranean, six miles from the coast of Tuscany. It is famous in history as the place of Napoleon's exile from May, 1814, until February, 1815. On the night of February 25th, 1815, the Emperor secretly embarked with 1200 men in hired feluccas, landed at Provence on March 1st, and soon after regained the French throne. The island has an area of 85 square miles and a population of more than 24,000. It was annexed to Italy in 1860.

El Dorado (*Span. The Golden or Gilded Land*). The name given by the Spaniards, during the sixteenth century, to a country supposed to exist in the interior of South America, between the Orinoco and Amazon Rivers. It abounded in gold mines, and in cities built of gold and silver and adorned with precious stones. According to Orellana, a lieutenant of Pizarro, this region contained a city ruled by a king whose garments were made of woven gold. Sir Walter Raleigh organized expeditions in search of this country in 1596 and 1617. The last was that of Antonio Santos, as late as 1780. The expression "El Dorado" has come to mean any fabulous land of boundless wealth.

Eleanor's Crosses. Twelve memorial crosses erected, in accordance with the will of Eleanor of Castile, wife of Edward I of England, to mark the resting-places of her bier, on its way from Hornby in Lincolnshire, where she died (1290), to Westminster Abbey, London, where she was buried. The twelve places, given in their order, from Hornby to Westminster Abbey, are as follows: Lincoln, Grantham, Stamford, Geddington, Northampton, Stony Stratford, Woburn, Dunstable, St. Albans, Waltham, West Cheap, Charing. Of these crosses, three only remain, viz., Geddington, Northampton, and Waltham. See *Charing Cross*.

Eleatic School. A Greek school of philosophy, founded about 535 B.C. by Xenophanes (556–456 B.C.) of Colophon, at Elea in Italy, whither he had been banished. The Eleatics were divided into the Old and New Schools. The "Old School" dealt almost exclusively in abstract speculations. It denied the reality of external phenomena; distrusted all knowledge acquired through the senses; and taught that it is by thought alone that we arrive at truth. Other eminent teachers of the "Old School" were Parmenides (513–430) and Zeno (490–405). The "New School" were students of nature, and experimentalists. Their principal teachers were Leucippus (510–430), Democritus (509–400), and Protagoras (481–411).

Electoral Commission. A commission appointed by the United States Congress on January 29th, 1877, to ascertain the disputed electoral vote of Florida, Louisiana, South Carolina, and Oregon, in the presidential election of 1876. The commission consisted of five associate justices of the United States Supreme Court, five senators, and five representatives,—fifteen persons in all. By a vote of 8 to 7, the commission decided that Hayes and Wheeler (Republican candidates) had been elected by a majority of one electoral vote, viz., by 185 votes to 184.

Electric Eel. The most powerful of the electric fishes. It is found only in the fresh water of the northern countries of South America, and attains a length of about six feet. Its electric shock is sufficiently great to kill its prey, consisting of fishes and amphibians, or to temporarily paralyze a man or large animal. Humboldt's statement of the capture of electric eels by allowing them first to exhaust themselves in attacking horses has never been confirmed. The electric eel was known to the ancients, and was used by them for curative purposes.

Electricity. This word is derived from the Greek ἤλεκτρον (*amber*), and was coined in the sixteenth century by William Gilbert. It owes its origin to the fact, long known to the ancients, that amber, when vigorously rubbed, develops electric properties and has the power of attracting light bodies. Thales (600 B.C.) and Pliny (70 A.D.) were familiar with these facts.

Elements. The ancient Greeks asserted that there were four elements—fire, air, earth, water. Lavoisier (1743–1794) declared that all substances that could not be proved to be compounds

should be regarded as elementary substances, and this view has been adopted by modern chemists. The number of elements now known is about 70 : these, with the exception of fluorine, unite either directly or indirectly with oxygen and form oxides. The elementary substances are somewhat arbitrarily divided into two classes,—metals and non-metals, of which the latter form the larger class. It seems very probable that these so-called elements are simply compounds of simple, primitive atoms, variously distributed as to number and grouping. The thirteen elements given below make up the chief part of the earth's crust, ocean, and the atmosphere. They are as follows : oxygen, hydrogen, nitrogen, carbon, chlorine, sulphur, aluminium, calcium, magnesium, iron, potassium, sodium, and silicon.

Elephanta, Cave-Temples of. The name given to certain famous Brahmanic rock-caves on the island of Elephanta, six miles from the city of Bombay, India. They probably date from the ninth century A.D. Four of these caves are in a good state of preservation. The most important one—known as the Great Temple—is still used by the Hindus on festivals in honor of Siva. This cave is 130 feet in length and 123 feet in width, and is hewn out of the solid trap-rock. The body of the cave was originally supported by 26 columns and 16 half-columns, but most of these have been destroyed. The temple contains a colossal three-headed bust of Siva,—over 17 feet high—measuring 23 feet around the eyes. The Portuguese, in their iconoclastic zeal, placed their cannon at the entrances of these rock-temples, and destroyed many of the columns and other architectural adornments. See *Ellora, Cave-Temples of.*

Eleusinian Mysteries. Secret religious rites and ceremonies in honor of Demeter or Ceres, annually celebrated at Eleusis, near Athens. These ceremonies symbolized the idea of death and resurrection, and are believed to have consisted of certain spectacles, sometimes brilliant and sometimes frightful. Their institution is attributed to Cadmus (1550 B.C.); to Erectheus (1399 B.C.); or to Eumolpus (1356 B.C.). The "Eleusinian Mysteries" were introduced into Rome, and were finally abolished by Theodosius the Great, in 389 A.D. Initiated persons only were permitted to witness them, and were strictly forbidden to divulge what they saw. Those that broke the vow of secrecy were accounted *execrable*. The laws were :

(1) To honor one's parents.

(2) To honor the gods with the fruits of the earth.

(3) To treat brutes with kindness.

Cicero says that the "Eleusinian Mysteries" promoted civilization. See *Gregorian Chant*.

Elevation of the Cross. A famous painting by Peter Paul Rubens (1577–1640), in the cathedral at Antwerp, Belgium. See *Descent from the Cross*.

"Rubens stands forth in all his Titanic greatness as the painter of violent and agitated scenes. The effect of this picture [*The Elevation of the Cross*] is something overpowering, but in all other respects it bears no comparison with *The Descent from the Cross*."—*Handbook of Painting*.

Elevation of the Host. The name given, in the Roman Catholic Church, to the act by which the priest raises the host or consecrated bread of the eucharist with both hands above his head, while the attendant tinkles his bell to call attention to the ceremony, in order that the congregation may worship the body of Christ. According to the doctrine of the "real presence," or transubstantiation, held by the Roman Catholic Church, the bread and wine of the eucharist are changed by consecration into the very body and blood of Christ. See *Real Presence ; Transubstantiation*.

Eleven Thousand Virgins. According to an ancient legend of the Roman Catholic Church, St. Ursula,

the daughter of Dionatus, a British king, was sought in marriage by Holofernes, a heathen prince. St. Ursula accepted the offer, but stipulated that Holofernes should be baptized, and that a period of three years should elapse before the solemnization of the marriage. During this time, the princess was to be allowed to travel with 11 maidens—each attended by 1000 companions. These terms having been agreed upon, St. Ursula, with her retinue, set sail from Britain and visited the tombs of the apostles at Rome. While on their way home, the entire party fell into the hands of Attila the Hun, at Cologne, and were cruelly massacred. St. Ursula, however, was reserved as the wife of Attila, but was subsequently put to death. The Huns were thereupon miraculously destroyed by a host of angels, and the people of Cologne, in gratitude for their deliverance from the invaders, erected the church of St. Ursula, where the bones of the martyrs are shown to this day. See *St. Ursula, Church of*.

Elf-Arrows. A name popularly given to certain triangular pieces of flint, formerly used as arrow-heads by the early inhabitants of Great Britain and Europe generally. It was once believed that these barbs of flint were shot by elves or invisible beings at cattle and men, to bewitch them,—hence the name. Cattle dying suddenly in the fields were said to have been struck by elf-arrows ; and this superstition still lingers in Ireland at the present day. Elf-arrows, set in silver, were frequently worn as talismans, and were considered most efficacious as preventives against poison and witchcraft. They are also called elf-bolts, elf-darts, elf-shot, and elf-stones.

Elgin Marbles. A famous collection of ancient sculptures—principally from the Parthenon at Athens—secured by the Earl of Elgin while ambassador to the Ottoman Porte in 1802, and sold by him to the British government, in 1816, for £35,000. They are now in the British Museum, London. The most admired of the Elgin marbles are part of the frieze and pediment of the Parthenon; these were executed by Phidias, and by others under his direction, about 440 B.C. Lord Byron protested in vain against the removal of these marbles from Greece. See *Arundelian Marbles*.

Elia, Essays of. A series of essays by Charles Lamb (1775–1834), contributed to the *London Magazine*, under the signature of *Elia*, by which designation he is best known in literature.

"The adoption of this signature was purely accidental. Lamb's first contribution to the *London Magazine* was a description of the old South-Sea House, where he had passed a few months' novitiate as a clerk, . . . and, remembering the name of a gay, lighthearted foreigner, who fluttered there at the time, substituted his name for his own."— *Talfourd*.

Elixir of Life (*Lat. Elixir Vitæ*). The name given by the alchemists to an imaginary drug or decoction which, if discovered, would have conferred immortality or, at least, extreme length of life on those that drank it. See *Philosopher's Stone*.

Ellen's Isle. A beautiful island in Loch Katrine, Scotland, famous as the meeting-place of Ellen and Fitz-James, in Sir Walter Scott's poem of *The Lady of the Lake*. See *Lady of the Lake* (2).

Ellora, Cave-Temples of. A series of remarkable rock-cut temples, situated thirteen miles northwest of Aurungabad, India, and excavated, according to Hindoo legends, 7000 years ago, but more probably about 800 A.D. There are 34 temples of large dimensions, some of which are cave-temples proper, *i. e.*, cut out in the interior of the rock, while others are hewn entirely out of the solid rock and have an exterior as well as an interior architecture. The most famous of the latter is called the Kailás, and is dedicated to Siva. The interior is 103 feet long, 56 feet wide, and 17 feet high, and stands in the centre of a vast quadrangular court, embellished with obelisks, colonnades, and sphinxes. See *Elephanta, Cave-Temples of.*

Elm City. A name popularly given to the city of New Haven, Connecticut, on account of the stately elms with which its streets are shaded. See *City of Elms.*

Elmwood. A stately colonial house, surrounded by trees, situated at Cambridge, Massachusetts. It was formerly the home of James Russell Lowell (1819–1891). The house and grounds were recently purchased by popular subscription, and the latter will soon be converted into a public park.

Elocution Walker. A nickname given to John Walker (1732–1807), the famous lexicographer and teacher of elocution.

Elysée, Palais de l'. A palace near the Champs Elysées, Paris, erected in 1718 for the Comte d'Evreux, and now the official residence of the President of the French Republic. During the reign of Louis XV (1715–1774), it was the home of Madame de Pompadour, and afterwards received the name of *Elysée Bourbon*, because of its long occupancy by the Duchesse de Bourbon. Murat, Napoleon I, Louis Bonaparte, King of Holland, and Hortense his wife, the Emperor Alexander I of Russia, and the Duc de Berri all lived there at different times. Napoleon III, while President of the Republic, made the Palais de l'Elysée his home, and enlarged it considerably.

Elysian Fields. An expression frequently used to denote Elysium, the happy land or paradise of the blessed ones after death, according to Greek and Latin mythology. The region in the neighborhood of Cumæ, Italy, abounding in gardens and vineyards, is often so called on account of its resemblance to the description of Elysium given by Virgil. See *Avernus, Lake ; Champs Elysées ; Elysium.*

Elysium. The name given, in classical mythology, to the region where the souls of the good dwell after death. The location of Elysium varied with the fancy of the writer. Homer placed it on the west of the earth, near the ocean, and described it as a happy land, fanned by the delightful breezes of Zephyrus. According to Hesiod and Pindar, Elysium was in the Islands of the Blessed, in the Western Ocean (whence arose the notion of the fabulous island of Atlantis), while Virgil located it in the underworld, with an entrance near Lake Avernus, in Campania. See *Avernus, Lake ; Elysian Fields ; Islands of the Blest.*

Elzevir Editions. Famous editions of the Greek and Latin classics, published by the Elzevirs, a family of printers in Holland, chiefly between the years 1592 and 1681. See *Aldine Editions.*

"Louis, the founder, was born in 1540; began business at Leyden in 1580; he printed about 150 works, and died 4 February, 1617. His sons (especially Bonaventure) and grandsons were celebrated for their work. No fewer than 15 members of this family carried on the business in succession until 1712. Their Pliny (1635), Vergil (1636), and Cicero (1642), are the masterpieces of their press. Their texts, however, were without authority, not resting like those of Aldus and the Stephenses on ancient MSS."—Harper's *Book of Facts.*

Emancipation Proclamation. A celebrated proclamation issued by President Lincoln (1809–1865) on January 1st, 1863, announcing that all persons held in slavery by men in arms against the United States of America were declared free. The number of slaves thus liberated amounted to 3,063,392. Slavery was not disturbed by this proclamation in Delaware, Kentucky, part of Louisiana, Maryland, Missouri, Tennessee, part of Virginia, and West Virginia. The slaves in those States—amount-ing to 831,780—were set free by the XIIIth Amendment to the Constitution, making the total number emancipated 3,895,172.

Embalming. An art, much practised among the ancient Egyptians, owing to their belief that the souls of men would return, after many thousands of years, to their bodies, if these were preserved entire. Some of these bodies, called *mummies*, were buried 3000 years ago, and still exist in a perfect state. Other nations of antiquity practised embalming, but less successfully. The Persians used wax ; the Assyrians, honey ; the Jews, aloes and spices.

"The most perfect specimens of *modern embalming* are preserved in the museum of the royal college of surgeons [London], one being the body of the wife of Van Butchell, preserved by John Hunter by injecting camphorated spirits of wine, &c., into the arteries and veins ; and the other the body of a young woman, who died about 1780 of consumption, in the Lock hospital. The method of embalming royal personages in modern times is fully described in Hunter's 'Posthumous Works.' He died in 1793. During the American war (1861-65), many soldiers' bodies were embalmed and sent home."—Haydn's *Dictionary of Dates.*

Embargo Act. An act passed by the United States Congress on December 22nd, 1807, during Jefferson's second administration, detaining, with few exceptions, all vessels — United States and foreign — then in United States ports, and ordering all United States vessels home. Although the embargo was decreed on account of insults offered to the United States flag by British cruisers, it was repealed in March, 1809, "as ruinous to the States, unsatisfactory to France, and ineffectual as a retaliation upon England." A second embargo, laid in April, 1812, was repealed after ninety days.

Ember Days. Days set apart, in the Roman Catholic and Anglican Churches, to invoke the blessing of God on the fruits of the earth, by means of prayer and fasting. In 1095 A.D., the Council of Placentia appointed as Ember Days the Wednesday, Friday, and Saturday after the following days : the first Sunday in Lent, Whitsunday, the 14th of September (the festival of the Holy Cross), and the 13th of December (the festival of St. Lucia). The expression " Ember Days " is not derived from the ancient custom of putting ashes on one's head, since no such custom ever prevailed in the Christian Church. Its derivation is more probably from the Old English *ym bryne*, meaning *period*, *revolution of time*. See *Ember Weeks*.

Ember Weeks. The name given to the weeks in which the " Ember Days " occur. See *Ember Days*.

Emerald. This precious stone is supposed to derive its name from the Greek σμάραγδος (sometimes μάραγδος), a gem probably the same as that now known as the emerald.

Emerald Isle. An appellation bestowed upon Ireland, on account of the brilliant hue of its herbage and foliage. The expression " Emerald Isle " was first used by Dr. William Drennan (1754-1820), in his poem entitled *Erin*.

" Arm of Erin, prove strong ; but be gentle
  as brave,
And, uplifted to strike, still be ready to
  save ;
Nor one feeling of vengeance presume to
  defile
The cause or the men of the *Emerald Isle*."

Émigrés (*Fr. Emigrants*). The name given to those persons that left France during the Revolution. The royal princes fled in 1789, in consequence of the capture of the Bastille, and were followed, after the adoption of the Constitution of 1791, by all those that felt aggrieved by the extinction of their privileges. The greater number of these refugees returned in 1802, after the Peace of Amiens, owing to an amnesty proclaimed by Napoleon Bonaparte, while First Consul. Many,

however, remained abroad until after the fall of Napoleon. According to the Charter of 1814, the *émigrés* were unable to recover their estates or their privileges. In 1825, however, a compensation of 30,000,000 francs yearly, on a capital of 1,000,000,000 francs, was granted to those *émigrés* that had lost their landed estates. This grant was annulled after the July Revolution of 1830.

Émile, ou de l'Éducation. A noted book on education by Jean Jacques Rousseau (1712-1778). It appeared in 1762, and soon gave offense both to Church and State, on account of its advanced views on mental training. It was accordingly condemned by the Parliament of Paris, and burnt at Geneva. The book, nevertheless, was the cause of many salutary reforms in education and suggested a more *natural* method of developing the faculties, — physical, mental, and moral. It profoundly affected the educational methods of Europe, and bore fruit in the reforms of Pestalozzi and Froebel.

Eminence. A title bestowed upon cardinals, for the first time, by Pope Urban VIII (1623-1644) in 1631. Until that period, these princes of the Church had been called *Illustrissimi* (*Lat. Most Illustrious Ones*).

Éminence Grise, L'. A nickname given to François Leclerc du Tremblay (1577-1638)—better known as "Father Joseph "—to distinguish him from his master, Richelieu. See *Eminence Rouge, L'*.

Éminence Rouge, L'. A nickname conferred upon Cardinal Richelieu (1585-1642), in allusion to his scarlet robe. See *Éminence Grise, L'*.

Emmett's Insurrection. An unsuccessful attempt to seize Dublin and secure the person of the Viceroy, made by Robert Emmett (1778-1803), the Irish patriot, on July 23rd, 1803. The insurrection was a complete failure, only 18 men of the 2000 that had volunteered to participate having put in an appearance. Lord Kilwarden and his nephew were both murdered, but the insurgents were quickly dispersed by a company of soldiers. Emmett, having been arrested, was put on trial on September 19th, 1803, condemned to death, and hanged on the following day. His defense, delivered before sentence was passed upon him, is a fine specimen of noble and touching eloquence.

Empire City. A name popularly given to New York City, because of its pre-eminence in population, wealth, influence, and enterprise among the cities of the United States.

Empire State. An appellation bestowed upon the State of New York, the most populous, wealthy, and influential in the American Union.

Empires of Antiquity, Four Great. By this expression are generally meant the four ancient Empires of Assyria or Babylonia, Persia, Greece or Macedonia, and Rome.

Empress of India (*Lat. Imperatrix Indiæ*). A title conferred upon Queen Victoria by Parliament on May 1st, 1876, at the earnest solicitation of Benjamin Disraeli (1805–1881), then Premier of England, with the understanding that the Queen should confine her imperial rank to India. The principal object of this innovation was to impress the distant subjects of the Crown, as well as to confer additional lustre upon the office of the sovereign. The new title was proclaimed at Delhi, India, on January 1st, 1877, in the presence of the Viceroy of India. Other celebrations were held on the same day at Calcutta, Bombay, and Madras. Not long after this event, at the request of the Queen, Disraeli was elevated to the peerage, with the title of Earl of Beaconsfield.

Empyrean (*Gr. ἔν, in, πῦρ, fire*). The name given by the ancients to the highest heaven, where the pure element of fire was supposed to exist. According to Ptolemy, there are five heavens, as follows :

(1) The sphere of the planets.

(2) The sphere of the fixed stars.

(3) The crystalline sphere, which has a vibratory motion.

(4) The primum mobile sphere, which imparts motion to all the others.

(5) The empyrean sphere, or sphere of fire and home of the Deity. Mediæval and modern poets use the word " empyrean " to denote heaven,—the land of light and the home of the blessed. See *Primum Mobile*.

Enceladus. A son of Tartarus and Gaea, and one of the hundred-handed giants that made war on the gods and tried to scale Olympus. For his impiety, he was overwhelmed by the thunderbolts of Jupiter and buried under Mount Etna, in Sicily. According to tradition, the flames of the volcano are said to proceed from his fiery breath, and whenever he shifts his position under his oppressive load the whole island feels the movement and is shaken to its inmost depths. See *Etna, Mount*.

Longfellow refers to this legend in his poem, *King Robert of Sicily*, as follows :

" Under the Angel's governance benign
The happy island danced with corn and wine,
And deep within the mountain's burning breast
Enceladus, the giant, was at rest."

" Under Mount Etna he lies,
It is slumber, it is not death ;
For he struggles at times to arise,
And above him the lurid skies
Are hot with his fiery breath."
Enceladus (Longfellow).

Enchiridion (*Gr. ἐγχειρίδιον, manual*). The name given to the book containing the maxims of Epictetus (60–120 (?) A.D.), the Roman Stoic philosopher, collected and compiled by his pupil Arrian (146–170 A.D.), the historian of Alexander the Great.

These maxims have been held in high estimation by Christians and pagans for many centuries, and reveal that love of good and hatred of evil that are generally regarded as distinctively Christian sentiments. Epictetus, in the *Enchiridion*, teaches self-renunciation, patience, and the duty of confining one's ambition within the limits of the attainable.

Encore. A French word (meaning *again*) used by English and American audiences to signify their wish for a repetition of some part of the performance. The French, however, do not use this word on similar occasions, but say, instead, *bis* (*twice*).

Encyclopédie, L' (*Fr. The Encyclopædia*). A famous French encyclopædia, which appeared during the years 1751–1772. It consists of 28 volumes ; and was followed by a supplement, in 5 volumes, in 1776–1777, and an analytic index, in 2 volumes, in 1780. Diderot (1713–1784) and D'Alembert (1717–1783) were the editors-in-chief, and were assisted by Voltaire, Grimm, J. J. Rousseau, Dumarsais, Baron d'Holbach, and Jancourt,—a group of brilliant writers, termed " Encyclopédistes." The work was based on Chambers's *Encyclopædia*, published in Edinburgh, but excluded history and biography from its contents. The *Encyclopédie* was made the vehicle of materialistic and atheistic opinions, and was said, owing to its dissemination of these views among the people, to have hastened the coming of the French Revolution.

Endor, Witch of. See *Witch of Endor*.

Endymion. In Greek mythology, a beautiful shepherd-youth of Caria, whose time was passed in perpetual slumber. While he was sleeping in a cave on Mount Latmos, Selene (the Moon) was so touched by his beauty that she came down nightly to kiss him and lie by his side. Various reasons are assigned for this sleep, but the one most generally accepted is that Endymion was kept in this state by Selene herself in order that she might kiss him without his knowledge.

John Keats (1796–1821) has written a poetic romance on this subject, entitled *Endymion*. The first line is as follows:

" A thing of beauty is a joy forever."

Enfield Rifle. So named from the government small-arms factory at Enfield, near London, where it was made. It was introduced in 1853, and superseded the Minié rifle,— being lighter and less cumbersome. The main point of difference between this firearm and the Minié was the great reduction in the diameter of the bore from .702″ to .577″. By this means the barrel was made lighter and the bullet reduced in size, while the charge of powder remained the same. The distribution of Enfield rifles to the native troops of India is said to have led to the Indian Mutiny of 1857,—it being believed at the time by the natives that the grease in the cartridge was cows' or pigs' fat, put there for the purpose of defiling both the Hindus and the Mohammedans. See *Indian Mutiny ; Minié Rifle*.

Engis Skull. A remarkable skull discovered by Dr. Schmerling in the cave of Engis, in the valley of the Meuse, Belgium. It is the cranium of an old person, and, according to Sir Charles Lyell, belongs to a contemporary of the Mammoth (*Elephas primigenius*) and of the woolly Rhinoceros (*Rhinocerus tichorhinus*), with the bones of which animals it was found associated. See *Neanderthal Skull*.

" At whatever conclusion we may arrive as to the origin of the man from whence this fossil skull proceeded, we may express an opinion without exposing ourselves to a fruitless controversy. Each may adopt the hypothesis which seems to him most probable : for my own part, I hold it to be demonstrated that this cranium has belonged to a person of limited intellectual faculties, and we conclude thence that it belonged to a man of a low degree of civilization : a deduction borne out by contrasting the capacity of the frontal with that of the occipital region."—Huxley's *Man's Place in Nature.*

"Thus, as regards the *Engis skull*, there seems no reason to doubt that it really belonged to a man who was contemporaneous with the mammoth, the cave-bear, and other extinct mammalia ; yet it is a perfectly well-developed skull, so that, as Professor Huxley has well pointed out, ' the first traces of the primordial stock whence man has proceeded need no longer be sought, by those who entertain any form of the doctrine of progressive development, in the newest tertiaries ; but that they may be looked for in an epoch more distant from the age of the *Elephas primigenius* than that is from us.' "—Lubbock's *Pre-Historic Times.*

England. This word was originally *Engaland*, the land of the *Engles* or *Angles*, a people that came over from Sleswick, a province of Jutland.

English Cathedrals. " The longest cathedral in England is that of Winchester, which is 545 feet ; the shortest, Oxford, which is 154 feet ; Lincoln is the widest at the transept, 227 feet ; Lichfield the narrowest, 88 feet. The following table gives the length and breadth in feet of some of the largest :

	Internal Length.	Width of Transept.
Winchester	545	186
Ely	517	178
Canterbury	514	154
York	498	222
Lincoln	498	227
Peterborough	480	202
Salisbury	452	210
Durham	420	176
Gloucester	420	144
Norwich	411	191
Lichfield	411	88
Worcester	410	130."

Edwards's *Words, Facts, and Phrases.*

English Language. " The English language has been variously divided into periods by different writers. In the division most commonly recognized, the first period dates from about 450 to 1150. This is the period of full inflection, and is called *Anglo-Saxon*, or, by many recent writers, *Old Eng-*

lish. The second period dates from about 1150 to 1550 (or, if four periods be recognized, from about 1150 to 1350), and is called *Early English*, *Middle English*, or more commonly (as in the usage of this book), *Old English*. During this period most of the inflections were dropped, and there was a great addition of French words to the language. The third period extends from about 1350 to 1550, and is called *Middle English*. During this period orthography became comparatively fixed. The last period, from about 1550, is called *Modern English*."— Webster's *International Dictionary.*

Out of 100,000 words in the English language, 60,000 are of Teutonic origin, 30,000 from the Greek and Latin, and 10,000 from other sources.

English Law. There are three kinds of English law, viz., statute law, common law, and canon law.

(1) *Statute Law* is composed chiefly of statutes or positive enactments passed from time to time by the legislature.

(2) *Common Law* is often defined as " unwritten law," and consists of certain rules of old standing, made binding from immemorial usage and universal acceptance, as ascertained and expressed in the judgments of the courts. It may be superseded by statute law ; but, unless superseded, it controls.

(3) *Canon Law* is derived from the ancient ecclesiastical law that was in force before the Reformation (1517). See *Canon Laws ; Common Law of England ; Roman Law.*

Englishman's Castle. An expression often applied to an Englishman's house, because, according to English law, no bailiff can enter it, either to make him a prisoner or to take forcible possession of his premises.

English Opium-Eater. A sobriquet and *nom-de-plume* of Thomas De Quincey (1785-1859), the famous English author, whose experiences while under the influence of opium are graphically told in his *Confessions*, published in 1821.

English Pope. A sobriquet bestowed upon Pope Adrian IV, the only Englishman that ever occupied the papal chair. His name was Nicolas Breakspear, and his birthplace was at Langley, near St. Albans, Hertfordshire, about 1100. Against his inclination, he was raised to the papal see in 1154. He soon became involved in a quarrel with Frederick I (1152–1190) of Germany, and refused to crown that monarch until he should hold his stirrup as a mark of respect. This the Emperor consented to do, after two days' parley. Adrian IV was about to excommunicate Frederick, when he died in 1159. It was during Adrian IV's pontificate that the doctrine of transubstantiation, advanced by Petrus Lombardus, was established. See *Transubstantiation.*

English Roscius. A title conferred upon David Garrick (1717–1779), the celebrated English actor, poet, and dramatist. Garrick was a performer of marvellous versatility, being equally at home in tragedy, comedy, and farce. The allusion is to Quintus Roscius, the distinguished Roman comedian.

English Solomon. A title bestowed upon James I (1603–1625) of England by his admirers. The Duke of Sully, however, was of a different opinion, and dubbed him "the most learned fool in Christendom."

Henry VII (1485–1509) also received the appellation of "English Solomon" for his skill in uniting the rival houses of York and Lancaster.

Engraved on her Heart. The town of Calais, France, captured by Edward III (1327–1377) of England on August 4th, 1347, after a year's siege, was retaken by the Duke of Guise on January 7th, 1558, during the reign of Mary (1553–1558) of Eng-

land. This loss, it is said, so preyed upon the Queen's mind that it caused her death in November of the same year. "When I am dead," said Mary, "the word *Calais* will be found engraved on my heart."

Enoch, Book of. An apocryphal book, first referred to in the *Epistle of Jude*, 14, 15, and quoted by Clement of Alexandria, Origen, and Tertullian. It purports to be a series of revelations made by God to Enoch, and gives a history of the kingdom of God and of the secret origin of the laws of nature. It was much quoted in Jewish and Christian writings during the first five centuries after Christ; but disappeared, with the exception of a few fragments, about 800 A.D. In 1773, the traveler Bruce found an Ethiopic manuscript-version of this work in Abyssinia, and brought it to England. Archbishop Lawrence published an English translation in 1821, and the Ethiopic text in 1838. The Book of *Enoch* furnishes valuable information concerning Jewish theology and speculation during the centuries immediately preceding the Christian era.

Envelopes. Envelopes for letters were mentioned by Swift in 1726, but did not come into general use until 1840,—the year of the establishment of the penny postal system. Previous to that time, it was the custom to secure the folded sheet of paper on which the letter was written by means of sealing-wax or a wafer. As early as 1844, machinery for the manufacture of envelopes was patented, and came into use.

Eozoön Canadense (*Canadian Dawn-Animal*). The name given to an assumed organism—possibly a large foraminifer—said by some naturalists to be the earliest known form of animal life. It was discovered in the Laurentian Limestone in Canada by Sir William Dawson in 1858, and was named *eozoön* (*Gr. dawn-animal*) by him in 1864. The general impression of scientists at the present day is that this so-called specimen of early animal life is inorganic in nature.

Ephesus, Temple at. A magnificent temple erected at Ephesus in honor of Diana or Artemis, and accounted one of the "Seven Wonders of the World." The original structure was built in the sixth century before Christ, under the direction of the architect Ctesiphon, and was burned in 356 B.C.,—on the night of the birth of Alexander the Great,—by one Herostratus, an Ephesian, who confessed, on the rack, that his sole motive was the desire to immortalize his name. The temple was afterwards rebuilt in a style of greater magnificence than before, and required 220 years for its completion. According to Pliny, it was 425 feet in length and 220 feet in width, and was supported by 127 columns of Parian marble, 60 feet high and weighing 150 tons each. The interior contained innumerable statues and paintings by the masters of Greece, while the altar of the goddess was adorned with the masterpieces of Praxiteles. This temple, plundered by Nero (54–68 A.D.), and afterwards burned by the Goths in 262 A.D., was probably destroyed by the Iconoclasts under Theodosius I (379–395), who issued an edict against the ceremonies of the pagan religion in 381 A.D. The site of the second temple was discovered by Mr. J. T. Wood in April, 1869, and some of the columns were removed to the British Museum. See *Herostratus; Seven Wonders of the World.*

Ephraem Codex. A Greek uncial manuscript, in the National Library in Paris, containing part of the *Septuagint* version of the *Old Testament* and about two-thirds of the *New.* It belongs to the fifth century, and, according to Tregelles, stands next to the Vatican Codex in critical authority. It was carefully edited by Tischendorf in 1843, and printed page for page and line for line. The Ephraem Codex is a palimpsest, and is so called because, in the 13th century, the vellum of the MS., being regarded as of no value, was used to inscribe some of the Greek words of Ephraem, the Syrian theologian. The original writing was first discovered in the latter part of the seventeenth century, but was not revivified until 1834–1835. See *Alexandrian Codex; Sinaitic Codex; Vatican Codex.*

Epic Poems. The following list of epic poems, with a few additions, is taken from Haydn's *Dictionary of Dates*, and includes the most famous ones that have been produced:

(1) *Mahábhárata* (Sanskrit), very ancient; by several authors; the longest epic known (110,000 couplets).

(2) *Rámáyana* (Sanskrit), very ancient; probably the work of one author; superior as a poetical composition to the *Mahábhárata;* contains some 48,000 lines of 16 syllables.

(3) *Iliad* (Greek), presumably by Homer; about 1000 B.C.

(4) *Odyssey* (Greek), presumably by Homer; about 1000 B.C.

(5) *Æneid* (Latin), by Virgil; about 19 B.C.

(6) *Metamorphoses* (Latin), by Ovid; about 1 A.D.

(7) *Pharsalia* (Latin), by Lucan; about 60 A.D.

(8) *Shah Náma* (Persian), by Abú 'l Kasim Mansúr; 1008 A.D.

(9) *Nibelungen-Lied* (German), author unknown; about 1150 A.D.

(10) *Kalevala* (Finnish), author unknown; date unknown.

(11) *Cid* (Spanish), author unknown; about 1150 A.D.

(12) *Divina Commedia* (Italian), by Dante; published in 1472.

(13) *Orlando Furioso* (Italian), by Ariosto; 1516.

(14) *Lusiads* (Spanish), by Camoens; 1572.

(15) *Jerusalem Delivered* (Italian), by Tasso; 1581.

(16) *Faerie Queene* (English), by Edmund Spenser ; 1590–1596.

(17) *Paradise Lost* (English), by John Milton; 1667.

(18) *Henriade* (French), by Voltaire; 1728.

(19) *Idylls of the King* (English), by Tennyson ; 1859–1865.

Epicureans. A school of ancient Greek philosophers, founded in 306 B.C., by Epicurus (341–270 B.C.). Epicurus taught that pleasure is the greatest good and should therefore be sought by all. It is from a misapprehension of the word " Epicurean " that it has come to mean one that indulges his sensual appetites. Although this and similar calumnies were industriously circulated by the Stoics, they were never generally believed. The Epicureans enjoined simplicity in living, and taught that the two greatest evils that afflict mankind are the fear of death and the fear of the gods ; accordingly, to get rid of these two fears was the object of all their speculations. The philosophy of Epicurus appealed strongly to the ancient Romans. Horace, Atticus, and Pliny the Younger were all of this school; while Seneca, although nominally a Stoic, drew much from the speculations of Epicurus. See *Garden Sect.*

Epimenides. A famous poet and prophet, born in Crete in the seventh century B.C., and sometimes reckoned among the " Seven Wise Men of Greece." According to tradition, he was sent, when a boy, by his father in search of a sheep, and while seeking shelter from the midday sun found his way into a cave and there fell into a sleep that lasted 57 years. He is said to have attained the age of 229 years. Epimenides was endowed with supernatural powers, and by his performance of certain mystic rites at Athens in 596 B.C., stayed the plague in that city. See *Seven Wise Men of Greece.*

St. Paul refers to Epimenides, in *Titus* i, 12, as follows : " One of themselves, even a prophet of their own, said, The Cretians are always liars, evil beasts, slow bellies."

Epiphany (*Gr. ἐπιφάνεια, manifestation*). A festival in the Christian Church, celebrating the " manifestation " of Christ to the Gentiles, as revealed by the star that conducted the Wise Men to his birthplace. It is observed on January 6th, the 12th day after Christmas, and is hence often called " Twelfth Day," and sometimes " Christmas of the Gentiles." The word denoted, among the Greeks, the " manifestation " of a god to a worshipper, and was borrowed from them by the Christians. The Epiphany was instituted as a church festival in 813. Until the close of the fourth century, it was observed in honor of Christ's nativity and baptism.

E Pluribus Unum (*Lat. One from Many*). The Latin motto on the obverse of the Great Seal of the United States, and on certain of the coins of that nation. It was first proposed on August 10th, 1776, by Benjamin Franklin, John Adams, and Thomas Jefferson, who had been appointed a committee of three to prepare a device for the seal. This device, however, was not accepted, and it was not until June 20th, 1782, that the motto was adopted as part of the second and successful design submitted by Charles Thompson, Secretary of Congress. In 1796, Congress decreed that the words *E Pluribus Unum* should appear on certain specified coins.

Epping Forest. A pleasure-ground near London, comprising about 5500 acres. It was recently purchased by the corporation of the city, and was opened by Queen Victoria in May, 1882, as a free public park and place of recreation. Epping Forest originally extended from Epping almost to the gates of London, and as late as 1793 contained 12,000 acres. High Beach, one of the finest spots in the Forest, is an elevated tract covered with splendid beech-trees. Tennyson was living there when he wrote *The Talking Oak* and *Locksley Hall.*

Epsom Races. Held annually on the downs near Epsom, a small market-town, fifteen miles southwest of London. The races were established in 1711, and have been a yearly feature since 1730. There are two meetings at Epsom,—the spring meeting, when the " City and Suburban Handicap " is decided, and the summer meeting, at which the " Derby " and " Oaks " are run. The grand stand was built in 1829–1830 at a cost of £20,000 and accommodates 7500 spectators. See *Derby Day.*

" E pur si muove " (*It.* " *Nevertheless it does move* "). A famous phrase attributed to Galileo (1564–1642), the celebrated Italian physicist, when forced by the Inquisition to abjure by oath, on his knees, the doctrine that the earth revolves around the sun. According to the story, the philosopher, on concluding his recantation, exclaimed, *sotto voce*, " e pur si muove " ("nevertheless, it does move "). This legend has been current since 1789, but its truth is doubted by many.

Epworth League. An organization in the Methodist Episcopal Church, founded at Cleveland, Ohio, in 1889. It aims to promote the spiritual welfare of the young, and derives its name from John Wesley's birthplace in Lincolnshire. In 1913, the " Epworth League " numbered 1500 chapters, with a membership of 80,000.

" Its purpose is to promote intelligent and loyal piety in the young members and friends of the church, to aid them in religious development, and to train them in the works of mercy and help. Its constitution provides for development along social, intellectual, and religious lines. Its essential features are the weekly prayer-meeting, the 'intellectual' and 'mercy and help' departments, and its harmony with the officiary of the church. There are no salaried officers, except the General Secretary."—*World Almanac*

Equine Abstinence. " A horse will live 25 days without solid food, merely drinking water ; 17 days without either eating or drinking ; and only 5 days when eating solid food without drinking."—*Everybody's Pocket Cyclopædia.*

Equity. A name used to denote those principles of justice that are not covered by any statute or rule of common law, and require to be dealt with separately. Equity is a system of jurisprudence, supplementary to law, properly so called ; and grew up from the inadequacy of common-law forms to secure justice in all cases.

"In some of the American States, jurisdiction at law and in equity centres in the same tribunal. The courts of the United States also have jurisdiction both at law and in equity, and in all such cases they exercise their jurisdiction, as courts of law or as courts of equity, as the subject of adjudication may require. In others of the American States, the courts that administer equity are distinct tribunals, having their appropriate judicial officers, and it is to the latter that the appellation *courts of chancery* is usually applied ; but, in American law, the terms *equity* and *court of equity* are more frequently employed than the corresponding *chancery* and *court of chancery*."—*Burrill.*

Era of the Olympiads. The era adopted by the ancient Greeks. It dated from July 1st, 776 B.C., the year in which Corœbus was successful in the Olympic Games, and continued to be a basis of reckoning until 440 A.D. The Olympiads were periods of four years, elapsing between two consecutive celebrations of the Olympic Games, and, in marking a date, the year and the Olympiad were both mentioned. The second Olympiad began in 772 B.C. ; the third, in 768 B.C., etc. This method of reckoning was used only by writers, and is never found on coins and rarely on inscriptions.

Erastianism. The name applied to the religious tenets of Thomas Erastus (1524–1583), properly Liebler or Lieber, a learned Swiss theologian and physician. He taught: (1) that the Church is a civil institution and is consequently subject to the State ; (2) that the Church does not possess the right to refuse the sacraments to, nor to excommunicate any person; (3) that the Christian ministry is not a divine institution ; (4) that the right to preach belongs to any person; (5) that Christ and His apostles prescribed no particular form of church government; and (6) that the punishment of all offenses belongs to the civil authorities.

Erato. In Greek and Roman mythology, the muse of erotic poetry and mimic imitation. She is sometimes represented with a lyre. See *Muses*.

Erebus. The name given, in Greek and Roman mythology, to a god of hell and one of the sons of Chaos. The word signifies *darkness*, and was generally used by the poets to denote the dark and gloomy cavern under the earth, through which the shades passed on their way to Hades.

Erechtheum. A celebrated temple (now in ruins) on the Acropolis at Athens, erected in honor of Erechtheus, the Attic hero. The original structure was burned by the Persians in 480 B.C., but a new and more beautiful one was raised on the same site. The building was of the Ionic Order, and formed one of the chief adornments of the Acropolis. The Erechtheum was converted into a Byzantine church during the Middle Ages. See *Acropolis of Athens*.

Erie Canal. A famous canal in New York State, extending from Buffalo to Albany, and connecting Lake Erie with the Hudson River. It was eight years in building (1817–1825), and, as originally constructed, was 40 feet wide at the top, 28 feet wide at the bottom, and 4 feet deep, and cost $9,027,456. The legislature, in 1835, ordered its enlargement to 70 feet wide at the top, 42 feet wide at the bottom, and 7 feet deep. These alterations cost about $25,000,000. The canal contains 72 locks, and can be traversed by vessels of 240 tons. The completion of the Erie Canal was attended with appropriate ceremonies. A group of canal-boats, containing De Witt Clinton (then Governor of New York) and other prominent men, descended the canal from Buffalo to Albany, and were thence towed down the Hudson River to New York City and out to sea, accompanied by many vessels and barges. At Sandy Hook, Governor De Witt Clinton emptied a keg of Lake Erie water into the Atlantic, and thus was effected the union of the waters of the Great Lakes and the Ocean. See *Clinton's Ditch*.

Erigena. A name given to Johannes Scotus (fl. 850 A.D.), the famous philosopher of the ninth century. According to some authorities, Erigena means the "Irishman." At one time Scot and Irish were synonymous terms, so that John Scotus and John Erigena had the same signification. Johannes Scotus Erigena must be distinguished from Johannes Duns Scotus (1265–1308) the Schoolman.

Erin. An ancient name of Ireland, but now used only as a poetic designation.

" There came to the beach a poor exile of
　　Erin,—
　　The dew on his thin robe was heavy and
　　　chill ;
　For his country he sighed, when, at twilight, repairing
　　To wander alone by the wind-beaten hill."
　　　　　　The Exile of Erin (Campbell).

"Erin Go Bragh !" ("*Erin Forever !*"). The ancient war-cry of the Irish.

Erinyes. See *Furies*.

Erl-King. A personification, in German and Scandinavian mythology, of a spirit of evil that haunts the Black Forest of Thuringia and plots mischief and ruin for men, and especially for children. The notion of the Erl-King was introduced into German poetry from the Norse sagas through Herder's translation of the Danish ballad of *Sir Olaf and the Erl-King's Daughter.* Goethe also has a ballad—universally known—called the *Erl-König.*

Erminia. The heroine of Tasso's epic poem, *Jerusalem Delivered.* After the death of her father, the King of Antioch, who was slain at the siege of that city, Erminia fell into the hands of the Crusaders, but was set at liberty by Tancred. This noble deed so touched her heart that she fell in love with the Christian prince. When the Crusaders besieged Jerusalem, Erminia attempted to go to Tancred; but, being discovered, lived for a time with some shepherds on the banks of the Jordan. Accidentally meeting with Vafrino, a spy in the service of the Christian army, she revealed to him a plot against the life of Godfrey, and returned with him to the Crusaders' camp. There she found Tancred wounded, but nursed him so tenderly that he was enabled to take part in the final attack on the city. The ultimate fate of Erminia is not mentioned in the poem. See *Gerusalemme Liberata.*

Ernani. A noted bandit-chief — Lord of Aragon and Count of Ernani— in love with Elvira, who is affianced to Don Ruy Gomez de Silva, whom she detests. Charles V of Spain is also enamored of the maiden, but, his passion being discovered by Silva, the latter joins Ernani in his league against the King. The conspirators are overheard by Charles while in concealment, and are arrested ; but, at the intercession of Elvira, are pardoned and set at liberty. Ernani and Elvira are about to be married, when suddenly the sound of a horn is heard. It is the horn given by Ernani to Silva when he joined the league, saying : "Sound upon this horn, and Ernani shall cease to live." Silva insists upon the fulfilment of the promise, and Ernani, in despair, stabs himself. Verdi has written an opera, and Victor Hugo a play, taking this story for a plot.

Eros. In classic mythology, the Greek name of the deity termed *Cupido* or *Amor* by the Romans. He was the son of Mars and Venus, and was generally represented with golden wings, and armed with a quiver of arrows, which he shot into the bosoms of those gods and men that he would inflame with the passion of love. He was the constant companion of his mother, and was often represented blindfolded. Previous to the time of Alexander the Great (336-323 B.C.), Eros was conceived as a handsome youth ; but in later times, the poets described him as a wanton boy, from whose cruel sports neither gods nor men were safe.

Errors of History. The following list of "Curious Errors of History" is taken from Conklin's *Vest Pocket Argument Settler.*

"William Tell was a myth.

Coriolanus never allowed his mother to intercede for Rome.

Blondel, the harper, did not discover the prison in which Richard I. was confined.

Nero was not a monster ; he did not kill his mother, nor fiddle over burning Rome.

Alfred never allowed the cakes to burn, nor ventured into the Danish camp disguised as a minstrel.

Fair Rosamond was not poisoned by Queen Eleanor, but died in the odor of sanctity in the convent of Godstow.

The Duke of Wellington, at Waterloo, never uttered the famous words, 'Up, Guards, and at them !'

Charles Kingsley gave up his chair of modern history at Oxford because he said he considered history 'largely a lie.'

Chemists have proved that vinegar will not dissolve pearls nor cleave rocks, in spite of the fabled exploits of Cleopatra and Hannibal.

Charles IX. did not fire upon the Huguenots with an arquebus from the window of the Louvre during the massacre of St. Bartholomew.

The siege of Troy is largely a myth, even according to Homer's own account. Helen must have been 60 years old when Paris fell in love with her.

The crew of *Le Vengeur,* instead of going down with the cry of 'Vive la République !' shrieked for help.

The number of Xerxes's army has been grossly exaggerated, and it was not stopped at Thermopylæ by 300 Spartans, but by 7000, or even, as some authors compute, 12,000.

The Abbé Edgeworth frankly acknowledged to Lord Holland that he had never made the famous invocation to Louis XVI. on the scaffold : 'Son of St. Louis, ascend to heaven.'

Philip VI., flying from the field of Crécy, and challenged late at night before the gates of the castle of Blois, did not cry out, 'It is the fortune of France.' What he really said was : 'Open, open ; it is the unfortunate king of France.'

Voltaire, on being asked where he had heard the story that when the French became masters of Constantinople in 1204 they danced with the women in the sanctuary of the Church of Santa Sophia, replied calmly : 'Nowhere ; it is a frolic of my imagination.'

There is no evidence that Romulus ever lived, that Tarquin outraged Lucretia, that Brutus shammed idiocy and condemned his sons to death, that Mucius Scævola thrust his hand into the fire, that Clœlia swam the Tiber, that Horatius defended a bridge against an army."

Erythræan Sea. The name originally given by the ancients to the entire expanse of sea between Arabia and Africa on the west and India on the east,—including the Red Sea and the Persian Gulf. During the rule of the Ptolemies, the name "Erythræan Sea" was confined by some geographers to the gulf between the Straits of Bab-el-Mandeb and the Indian Ocean ; but it was far more generally used as identical with the Mare Rubrum or Red Sea. Even as late as the Christian era, the expression "Erythræan Sea" was used in its original sense.

Esbekeeyah. The principal square in the city of Cairo, Egypt, on or near which are situated the leading hotels, the opera-house, theatres, and European shops. It covers an area of 450,000 square feet and was, at one time, surrounded by a canal to prevent its inundation by the annual rise of the Nile. Since 1866, this canal has been filled up and the central portion of the square converted into a public garden, with cafés and places of amusement. [Written also *Ezbekeyieh*, *Ezbektya*.]

Escorial. A celebrated royal palace, mausoleum, and monastery of Spain, sometimes called the "Eighth Wonder of the World," situated 31 miles northwest of Madrid, at an elevation of 3700 feet. The building, which is constructed of dark gray granite, was erected by Philip II (1555–1598) of Spain as a mausoleum, in accordance with the will of his father. It was commenced in 1563 and completed in 1584, at a cost of about $50,000,000. It is an irregular parallelogram—700 feet long by 550 feet broad—and, according to the current tradition, was planned to represent a gridiron, the object on which St. Laurence suffered martyrdom. Certain it is that it was erected partly to commemorate the victory of St. Quentin over the French on St. Laurence's day (August 10th,1557). The total length of the rooms in this vast structure is above 120 English miles and the building is said to contain 14,000 doors and 11,000 windows. In the Pantheon, or royal mausoleum beneath the church, are buried the remains of the Spanish kings from Charles V (father of Philip II) to Alfonso XII (with the exception of Philip V and Ferdinand VI). The most interesting apartment in the palace is the cell where Philip II spent his last days. The Escorial still contains some fine paintings, although 100 of the best were removed to Madrid in 1837. The library, formerly the richest in Europe, was greatly injured by fire in 1691, and despoiled by the French in 1808, but it still contains over 32,000 volumes and more than 4600 valuable MSS. The Escorial was struck by lightning and severely damaged by the fire that ensued, on October 1st, 1872. The word "Escorial" (less properly, Escurial) is said to be derived from *escoriæ*, the dross of iron mines that still exist in the vicinity. See *Museo*.

Esmeralda. A beautiful gypsy-girl, in Victor Hugo's *Notre Dame de Paris*, who with tambourine and goat dances before the populace in the cathedral close. She is set upon by the mob as a witch, but is rescued by Quasimodo, and concealed for a time in the cathedral. After various adventures she is gibbeted.

Esoteric. A word derived from the Greek, meaning " those within," and used by certain of the ancient philosophers to designate those abstruse or hidden doctrines taught to the initiated, as distinguished from those teachings of a more popular kind designed for the uninitiated and termed " exoteric." Aristotle called those that attended his evening lectures (which were popular in treatment) his *exoteric* pupils, and those that were present at his more abstruse morning lectures his *esoteric* pupils. See *Exoteric*.

Esquire. A title originally bestowed upon the shield-bearer or armor-bearer of a knight ; but at the present day loosely given, both in Great Britain and its colonies and in the United States, to all persons supposed to be in comfortable circumstances.

Wharton says : " Esquires may be divided into five classes; he who does not belong to one of them may or may not be a gentleman, but is no esquire.

(1) Younger sons of peers, and their eldest sons.

(2) Eldest sons of knights, and their eldest sons.

(3) Chiefs of ancient families (by prescription).

(4) Esquires by creation or office, as heralds or serjeants-at-arms ; judges ; justices of the peace ; the higher naval and military officers ; doctors in the several faculties ; and barristers.

(5) Each Knight of the Bath appoints *two* esquires to attend upon him at his installation and at coronations.

No estate, however large, confers this rank upon its owner."

Essay on Criticism. A noted poem by Alexander Pope (1688-1744). It was published in 1711, and at once placed the author in the front rank of the men of letters of his time.

Essay on the Human Understand-ing. A famous essay, in four books, by John Locke (1632-1704), the distinguished English philosopher. It appeared in 1690, and required seventeen years for its preparation. The chief doctrine inculcated in this work is that all our ideas are derived from experience and reflection, and not from intuition.

"The essence of the *Essay* is in its proof that knowledge cannot in any degree have been concisely innate in each man ; for it must be in all cases a gradual growth, dependent upon experience, in which we are liable to error."—*Chambers's Encyclopædia*.

Essay on the Principle of Population. A remarkable essay by Thomas Robert Malthus (1766-1834), the distinguished political economist. Malthus pointed out, in this essay, that the natural tendency of population is to increase more rapidly than the means of subsistence, and that hence the time will come when population will outgrow the means of food-supply. He counsels that governments should pass laws to restrict marriages, and thus limit the increase of population. These views are not original with Malthus, but were enunciated not only by Plato and Aristotle, but also by Franklin, Hume, and others in modern times. It was the merit of Malthus to have presented the doctrine in systematic form, with elaborate proofs derived from history.

Herbert Spencer has robbed the Malthusian Theory of its terrors by demonstrating that, although excess of fertility has been and still remains the cause of man's development, every fresh step in that development itself necessitates in its turn a decline in fertility.

"That human population will forever continue to press upon the means of human subsistence, as Malthus supposed, is therefore not a fact. Individuation and genesis are in necessary antagonism, and advance in the former must be followed by decrease in the latter. Fecundity is thus not a permanent factor, as is implied in the *Malthusian* view, and pressure of population and its accompanying evils, instead of remaining the one problem to be encountered all along the line of human progress, must gradually work itself out altogether." *Introduction to the Philosophy of Herbert Spencer* (Hudson).

Essays on the Nature and Principles of Taste. A series of essays by Archibald Alison (1757–1839). They appeared in 1790. The second edition, published in 1811, was the occasion of an admiring article by Jeffrey in the *Edinburgh Review.*

Essenes. An ascetic Jewish sect, in the time of Christ. They lived in retirement, and asserted that the spirit of religion consists in silence and contemplation. They accepted the Jewish Scriptures, but interpreted them allegorically. The Essenes were probably Pharisees of more decided convictions, and carried out the Pharisaic views with a consistency that made them appear ridiculous in the eyes of the mother-party. They were few in number—never more than 4000—and dwelt in a colony near the Dead Sea.

Estates of the Realm. A phrase often erroneously applied, in England, to the King, Lords, and Commons; but properly given to the Lords, the Clergy or Spiritualty, and the Commons. These three orders—together with the King or Queen—constitute the Parliament of the United Kingdom of Great Britain and Ireland. In France, the three orders were the nobles, the clergy, and the third estate (*tiers-état*), and these remained distinct until the Revolution of 1789. See *Tiers-État.*

État Major. A term in use in France, since the time of Louis XIV (1643–1715), to denote the staff of an army. It includes " all officers above the rank of colonel, also, all adjutants, inspectors, quartermasters, commissaries, engineers, ordnance officers, paymasters, physicians, signal officers, judge-advocates; also, the non-commissioned assistants of the above officers."

Eternal City. An ancient and popular designation of Rome,—a city said to have been built under the direction of the gods, and to enjoy their special favor. This expression, or one equivalent to it, occurs frequently in the Latin authors.

" To them no bounds of empire I assign,
Nor term of years to their immortal line."
                Æneid (Dryden's Translation).

Etesian Winds. Northwest winds that blow in the Ægean Sea and the Levant each year, for forty days, after the rising of Sirius, the dog-star. They are dry and warm.

Ether.

(1) A hypothetical substance of extreme elasticity and tenuity, filling all space and existing even within the densest bodies. Most modern scientists regard its existence as established, and consider it to be the medium through which the vibrations of light, radiant heat, electricity, and magnetism are propagated. Sir William Thomson and James Clerk-Maxwell have given much attention to this question.

(2) An anæsthetic first used in 1846 by Dr. W. T. G. Morton of Boston, Massachusetts, to relieve pain in the extraction of teeth, and soon after employed in surgical operations. It is considered safer than chloroform,— the proportion of deaths to the number of administrations being 1 to 16,677. Ether is a highly volatile, colorless liquid, produced by the action of sulphuric acid on alcohol. It is also called *ethyl ether* and *sulphuric ether.*

Etna, Mount. An active and destructive volcano, near the coast of Sicily, famous for its terrible eruptions both in ancient and modern times. Diodorus Siculus speaks of them as occurring in 1693 B.C., and Thucydides mentions three as happening in 734, 477, and 425 B.C. In 1169 A.D., an awful eruption overwhelmed Catania, and 15,000 persons perished ; in 1669 A.D., 10,000 persons were destroyed in the streams of lava that flowed over the country for forty days. According to classic mythology, the forges of the Cyclopes were under Mount Etna. See *Cyclopes ; Enceladus.*

Eton College. A famous educational institution at Eton, England, founded by Henry VI (1422–1461) in 1440, under the title of " The College of the Blessed Mary of Eton beside Windsor." The endowment exceeds £20,000. The pupils consist of *King's Scholars*, or *Collegers* (of whom there are 70), who enter college between twelve and fourteen years of age, and of *Oppidans*, who enter between ten and fourteen years of age. Until 1851, the education was purely classical, but in that year mathematics was admitted into the curriculum, and in 1869 physical science was added to the course of study. Eton has been, for generations, the favorite school for the sons of the nobility and gentry of England. The number of scholars in 1891 was 1007. Among the famous men that have studied at Eton may be named Horace Walpole, Bolingbroke, Porson, Hallam, Gray the poet, Shelley, Wellington, Canning, Fox, Gladstone, Lord Salisbury, and Sir John Lubbock. The " Eton Montem," or triennial procession of the students to Salt Hill (*ad montem*), was discontinued after 1846.

Ettrick Shepherd. A sobriquet bestowed upon the Scotch poet, James Hogg (1770–1835), who was born in the forest of Ettrick, Selkirkshire, and in his early days followed the calling of a shepherd.

" The *Ettrick Shepherd* was my guide."
Wordsworth.

Euclid Avenue. A noted street in Cleveland, Ohio. It is lined with stately mansions, which stand on a gentle eminence 200 to 500 feet from the Avenue, and is adorned with beautiful shade-trees, smooth lawns, flowers, and shrubbery. Bayard Taylor and other distinguished travelers have declared Euclid Avenue to be the most beautiful street in the world.

Euclid's Elements. A celebrated mathematical work, in thirteen volumes, by Euclid of Alexandria, who flourished about 300 B.C. It treats of plane and solid geometry, proportion, properties of numbers, and incommensurable magnitudes. The work has been translated into many languages, and is probably the best-known mathematical book in existence. It has been used for 150 years in Great Britain as a text-book of geometry, and still holds its ground in spite of the many efforts made to displace it. In France and the United States, it has given place to better treatises. The work is not entirely original ; and contains many demonstrations by Thales, Pythagoras, Eudoxus, and others. Euclid, however, added many theorems of his own, and reduced them all to logical order. The first printed edition of *Euclid's Elements* was a translation from Arabic into Latin, and appeared in Venice in 1482. The first edition in Greek was published at Basel in 1533.

Eugubine Tables. Seven bronze tables, found in a subterranean chamber at Gubbio (the ancient *Iguvium* or *Eugubium*) in Italy, in 1444 A.D. They contain inscriptions relating to the ritual, sacrifices, etc., of the temple of Jupiter, and were probably prepared in the first and second centuries after Christ. Four of the tables are in Umbrian, two in Latin, and one in both languages. They furnish a very comprehensive and interesting memorial of the Umbrian language. The most accurate copy of the inscriptions is given by Lepsius in his *Inscriptiones Umbricæ et Oscæ*, published at Leipsic in 1841.

Eumenides (*Gr. Benign Ones*). A euphemistic term used by the Greeks to denote the Erinyes or Furies, fearful maidens, who dwelt in the depths of

Tartarus and whose mission it was to punish men—both in this world and in the next—for their crimes. It is said that they were first called Eumenides after the acquittal of Orestes by the Areopagus, when the anger of the Erinyes had been appeased. See *Furies*.

Euphues. A famous romance, by John Lyly (1553 (?)–1606), in two parts, —entitled, respectively, *Euphues, or The Anatomy of Wit* (1579), and *Euphues and his England* (1580). The work was written in an affected and bombastic style — fashionable for a time in literature and at court—and was received with great applause. The word *euphuism*—meaning affected elegance and refinement of language—was formed from the title of this work. This unnatural style was not original with Lyly, but was modelled after that of Guevera, the Spanish writer.

Eurasian Plain. A name given by ethnologists, about 1865, to the great central plain of Europe and Asia. The word *Eurasian* is also used to denote the offspring of a European father and an Asiatic mother.

"Eureka" (*Gr. "I have found"*). A word said to have been uttered by Archimedes (287 (?) – 212 B.C.), the Greek philosopher, when the principle of specific gravity first dawned upon him. It is said that the thought first came to him while at the bath, and that he fled half-naked through the streets of Syracuse to his home, shouting : "I have found it ! I have found it !" The problem that had been given him to solve was to determine whether a golden crown made for Hiero, King of Syracuse, had been alloyed with silver. This the King had suspected, and the philosopher afterwards proved it to be true.

Euroclydon. A northeast wind prevailing in the Levant. It was the cause of St. Paul's shipwreck, and is spoken of in *Acts* xxvii, 14, as follows :

"But not long after there arose against it a tempestuous wind, called *Euroclydon*."

In the revised version of the *New Testament*, this wind is termed *Euraquilo*.

Europe's Liberator. A sobriquet conferred upon Arthur Wellesley (1769–1852), Duke of Wellington, who freed Europe from the despotic rule of Napoleon Bonaparte.

Eurydice. The wife of Orpheus, killed by the bite of a serpent on her wedding-night. According to classical mythology, Orpheus followed Eurydice to Hades, where, by the music of his lyre, he so charmed Pluto, the grim ruler of the infernal regions, that he won back his wife from this most inexorable of the deities. His wife, however, was restored to him only on condition that he should not look back at her until they had arrived in the upper world. When they had almost reached the limit of their journey, Orpheus was so overcome by the anxiety of love that he looked around to see if Eurydice were following him, and beheld her being dragged back into the infernal regions.

Euterpe. In classical mythology, the muse of lyric poetry. She is represented in ancient works of art with the flute in her hand. See *Muses*.

Evacuation Day. November 25th, 1783,—the day on which the British troops evacuated New York City. It was at one time celebrated with much enthusiasm, but of late years has been almost entirely neglected. The rear-guard of the British army embarked at the Battery, and the advance-guard of the American forces marched down the Bowery and through Chatham, Queen, and Wall Streets to the corner of Broadway and Rector Street. They were followed by Washington and his generals, the City Council, and other functionaries. A few weeks later Washington bade farewell to his officers at Fraunce's Tavern (still standing), at the corner of Broad and Pearl Streets.

Evangelical Alliance. Founded at Liverpool, in 1845, by Sir Culling Eardley Smith and others for the purpose of promoting unity among Protestant Christians in their efforts against Romanism and infidelity. More specifically, it seeks " to associate and concentrate the strength of an enlightened Protestantism against the encroachments of Popery and Puseyism, and to promote the interests of a scriptural Christianity." The first general conference was held in London in 1846, and was attended by 921 members from all parts of the world,—representing 50 different religious denominations. Several international conferences have been held since then: in London (1851), Paris (1855), Berlin (1857), Geneva (1861), Amsterdam (1867), New York (1873), Basel (1879), and Copenhagen (1885). The " Alliance " holds yearly meetings at present. It has brought the Protestant denominations throughout the world into closer union, and has done effective work in the crusade against slavery, intemperance, and profanity. A week of universal prayer is observed in the early part of January, each year, throughout the world.

Evangeline. A poem by Longfellow (1807–1882), founded on the historic incident of the expulsion of the inhabitants of Acadia (now Nova Scotia) from their homes in 1755. See *Acadia.*

Everglades. " Tracts of land covered with water and grass; peculiar to the Southern States. In Florida, the term is applied to portions of the land lower than the coast and but little above the level of the sea, covered with fresh water. The islands elevated above this swamp are called ' hummocks.' " — Bartlett's *Dictionary of Americanisms.*

Florida is often called the " Everglade State."

Evil Eye. A mysterious power attributed to certain persons, who are thereby able to injure others, or even to cause their death, by simply looking at them. This ancient and widespread superstition was at one time sanctioned by the classical authors, the Fathers of the Church, and the physicians of the Middle Ages; and is still believed in by many nations within the range of Christendom. The belief is widely spread among the Italians and Spaniards at the present day, as well as among the Turks, Chinese, and Japanese. The ancient Greeks called it *Baskania,* and the Romans, *Fascinum.* Virgil, in the *Third Eclogue,* speaks of an " evil eye " that has bewitched the tender lambs; and St. Paul, in *Galatians* iii, 1, makes use of the idea metaphorically to denote the spiritual perversion of the Galatians, as follows:

" O foolish Galatians, who hath bewitched you, that ye should not obey the truth, before whose eyes Jesus Christ hath been evidently set forth, crucified among you ? "

Evolution. The difficulties in the way of framing a satisfactory definition of Evolution are so great that the compiler of the present work deems it best to quote the one given by Herbert Spencer in *First Principles* (§ 145). It is as follows:

" *Evolution* is an integration of matter and concomitant dissipation of motion ; during which the matter passes from an indefinite, incoherent homogeneity to a definite, coherent heterogeneity ; and during which the retained motion undergoes a parallel transformation."

See *Darwinism.*

Exarch of Ravenna. A title borne by the viceroy deputed from Constantinople to govern Italy, while that country remained a dependency of the Byzantine Empire. It was first bestowed by Justinian on Narses, his general - in - chief, who reconquered Italy from the Goths, in 554 A.D. The extent of the exarchate was gradually diminished until it finally embraced only the territory about Ravenna. In 752 A.D. the Byzantine rule at Ravenna came to an end through the conquests of Astulf, King of the Longobards.

Excalibur. The name of the famous mystic sword of King Arthur, which he found inserted in a sheath of stone and pulled out,—although 201 of his bravest knights had singly been unable to withdraw it. An inscription on the stone declared that whoever should succeed in unsheathing the sword would prove to be the rightful heir to the throne; and Arthur was, accordingly, chosen and proclaimed king by general acclamation. The sword was said to be so bright that " it gave light like 30 torches." Arthur, at the approach of death, commanded an attendant to cast the sword into a lake near by; but the order had to be given three times before it was obeyed. As soon as the sword touched the water, a hand " clothed in white samite " appeared, caught it by the hilt, flourished it three times, and then sank beneath the waters of the lake. Tennyson has related this incident in a charming poem, entitled *Morte d'Arthur*. [Written also *Excalibor*, *Excalibar*, *Escalibar*, *Escalibor*, and *Caliburn*.]

Ex Cathedra (*Lat. From the Chair*). An expression usually applied to opinions or decisions of exalted personages, delivered in a solemn and judicial manner. It is also ironically used to denote self-sufficient, dogmatic opinion.

Excelsior State. A name popularly given to the State of New York, in allusion to the motto " Excelsior " on its coat-of-arms.

Exception Proves the Rule. " This proverbial saying is very generally misunderstood. The word *prove* anciently meant ' test,' and is so used in this saying. An old use of the word *prove* occurs in the advice of St. Paul : ' Prove all things,' etc.; which means that we should *test* all things, so

as to know which good ones to ' hold fast ' to. An exception cannot prove a rule in the modern sense, it tends rather to render it invalid; but an exception may *test* a rule and in some cases prove it to be wrong, whilst in others the test may show that the so-called exception may be explained. Another theory on the subject is that the very word ' exception ' implies that there is a rule; so that the word ' prove ' means ' proves the existence of.' " — Edwards's *Words, Facts, and Phrases*.

Exeter Hall. A famous public hall on the Strand, London, capable of accommodating 5000 persons. It was erected in 1830–1831 for meetings of religious and philanthropic societies, concerts, oratorios, and lectures. Exeter Hall was purchased for the Young Men's Christian Association in July, 1880, for £25,000, and was reopened with a jubilee during March of the following year. The " May Meetings " of the various religious societies are held there.

Exodus. The name of the second book of the *Old Testament*. It derives its name from a Greek word meaning *going out* or *departure*, and is so named because it relates the events connected with the sojourn of the Israelites in Egypt, their departure from that country, and their wanderings in the peninsula of Sinai. Tradition for a long time ascribed the authorship of *Exodus* to Moses, but since the 17th century biblical critics have given sufficient reasons for doubting this statement. It is probable that the Book of *Exodus* is the work of several writers.

Exoteric. A word derived from the Greek, meaning " those without," and used by certain of the ancient philosophers to designate those simple and easily comprehended doctrines taught to the uninitiated, as distinguished from those teachings of a more abstruse kind, designed for the initiated, and termed *esoteric*. Aristotle called those that attended his morning lectures (which were abstruse in treatment) his *esoteric* pupils, and those that were present at his more popular evening lectures, his *exoteric* pupils. See *Esoteric*.

Expounder of the Constitution. A title popularly conferred upon Daniel Webster (1782–1852), on account of his masterly interpretation of the Constitution of the United States. This appellation was also bestowed upon John Marshall (1755–1835), because of the famous decisions in constitutional law rendered by him while Chief-Justice of the Supreme Court of the United States.

Extradition Treaties. Treaties between nations, which have for their object the mutual surrender of alleged criminals, are of comparatively recent origin. The United States concluded an extradition treaty with Great Britain, August 9th, 1842; with France, November 9th, 1843; with Switzerland, November 25th, 1850; with Austria, July 3d, 1856; with Norway and Sweden, March 21st, 1860; with Mexico, December 11th, 1861; with Italy, March 23d, 1868; with Turkey, January 5th, 1877; with Belgium, 1882; with Spain, 1887; with Uruguay, 1887; and with Germany, 1892. Extradition is usually granted for forgery, burglary, embezzlement, counterfeiting, perjury, rape, grand larceny, manslaughter, and murder. Political offences are excepted from extradition in the treaty between Great Britain and the United States.

Extreme Unction. One of the seven sacraments of the Roman Catholic Church, the expediency of which is founded on *James* v, 14 : " Is any sick among you ? let him call for the elders of the church; and let them pray over him, anointing him with oil in the name of the Lord." According to the Council of Trent, this sacrament was instituted by Christ Himself; although other authorities say that the practice was introduced by Pope Felix IV (525–530 A.D.). Extreme unction is believed to impart grace and strength to the Christian in his dying hour, and is administered by the priest who, dipping his thumb into the holy oil, anoints the sick person, in the form of the cross, upon the eyes, ears, nose, mouth, hands, and feet,—making use of a special form of prayer at each anointing. The holy oil used in the sacrament of extreme unction is blessed once each year by the bishop, attended by a number of priests, on Maundy-Thursday. See *Seven Sacraments*.

Eye of Greece. A name given by the ancients to Athens, the most celebrated of the cities of Greece.

" Athens the *eye of Greece*, mother of arts
    And eloquence, native to famous wits
    Or hospitable, in her sweet recess,
    City or suburban, studious walks and
        shades."
                Paradise Regained, iv, 237–240.

Eye of a Needle. " Lord Nugent, when at Hebron, was directed to go out by '*the Needle's eye*,' that is, by the small gate of the city. This explains an obscure passage of Scripture on *riches*, for the gate in question would hardly be high enough to allow a camel to pass, and the animal would have to go down on its knees and crawl to be able to pass." — Edwards's *Words, Facts, and Phrases*.

Eylau, Battle of. A sanguinary contest between the French, commanded by the first Napoleon, and the Russians and Prussians under Benningsen. It was fought at Eylau, a village 25 miles south of Königsberg, on February 7th–8th, 1807, and terminated in favor of Napoleon. The allies lost 20,000 men, and the French nearly 15,000. The victory, however, was barren of results, and the French were so reduced that they retired to the Vistula. The battle of Eylau was the first check sustained by Napoleon in his career of conquest.

F

Fabian Policy. A term originally applied to the method of warfare pursued by Quintus Fabius Maximus Verrucosus, the Roman consul, in his struggles with Hannibal during the Second Punic War (218 – 201 B.C.). Instead of coming to an open engagement, Fabius harassed the Carthaginian commander by marches, counter-marches, and ambuscades, and by these delays enabled the Roman army to assemble in greater strength. The expression " Fabian Policy " is used, at the present time, to denote any policy of delays and cautions. See *American Fabius ; Cunctator.*

Fabliaux. A group of over 100 short metrical tales, peculiar to the early literature of France. They are generally humorous or satiric, and deal with passing events or familiar topics. The oldest one preserved seems to be *Richeut* (about 1156), but the greater number belong to the latter part of the 12th and the beginning of the 13th century. The authors of the *Fabliaux* are, in most cases, unknown. Most of these stories are of Indian origin, and reached Europe either by way of Byzantium or of Arabia. They were widely circulated orally throughout Europe, and found their way also into books and discourses. The *Fabliaux* poets were wandering minstrels much inferior in position to the Trouvères and Troubadours. The best of these tales that have come down to us is the fabliau of *Aucassin and Nicolette*, which is naturally conceived and replete with interesting situations. See *Troubadours ; Trouvères.*

Facial Angle. The name given to the angle included between one line drawn from the centre of the forehead to the most projecting part of the upper jaw above the incisor teeth, and a second line from the opening of the ear to the base of the nasal aperture. It was suggested by Peter Camper (1722–1789), a Dutch anatomist, as a method of estimating mental capacity, and long served as a principle of classification in the science of Ethnology. In negroes, the angle is 70 degrees; in Europeans, from 75 to 85 degrees.

" The higher the average cerebral development in man, the larger is the average facial angle."

Factory King. A nickname conferred upon Richard Oastler (1789–1861) of Bradford, England, in allusion to his successful promotion of the " Ten Hours' Bill."

Faerie Queene. An allegorical romance in six books, by Edmund Spenser (1552–1599). It was the author's original purpose to complete the poem in twelve books, setting forth the twelve moral virtues worthy of practice by a knight or gentleman; and there is a tradition to the effect that these were all produced. The first part was published in 1590, and the second in 1596. The plan of the *Faerie Queene* is borrowed from the *Orlando Furioso* of Ariosto; but Spenser far surpasses his Italian prototype in creative genius. To Spenser has been accorded the high distinction of being called the " Poets' Poet."

Fainéants, Rois (*Fr. Do-Nothing Kings*). A term applied in reproach to the last seven kings of the Merovingian line in France, under whom the Mayors of the Palace were the real rulers of the country. These sovereigns were Thierry III, Clovis III, Childebert III, Dagobert III, Chilpéric II, Thierry IV, and Childéric III. The last of these was dethroned by Pepin le Bref, who caused himself to be proclaimed king and founded the Carlovingian line. Louis V—the last of the Carlovingian dynasty and a descendant of Pepin le Bref—also received the title of " Le Roi Fainéant."

Fair Helen. A sobriquet conferred upon Helen of Troy, the most beautiful woman of ancient times. She was the daughter, according to tradition, of Jupiter and Leda, and the wife of Menelaus, King of Sparta. Her abduction by Paris, son of Priam, King of Troy, was the immediate cause of the Trojan War, which lasted ten years and resulted in the destruction of the city. After the death of Paris—which occurred not long before the fall of Troy—Helen married his brother, Deiphobus, whom she afterwards betrayed to Menelaus, and thus regained her first husband's love. With him she returned to Sparta, and there lived, during the rest of her life, in tranquil happiness.

Fair Maid of Anjou. A sobriquet conferred upon Lady Edith Plantagenet, wife of David, Prince Royal of Scotland.

Fair Maid of Galloway. A sobriquet conferred upon Margaret, only daughter of Archibald, fifth Earl of Douglas.

Fair Maid of Kent. A title bestowed upon Joan, Countess of Salisbury (1326–1385), only daughter of the Earl of Kent, on account of her great beauty. She was the wife of Edward, the Black Prince, and mother of Richard II of England. She had been twice married before she gave her hand to the Prince of Wales.

Fair Maid of Norway. A title conferred upon Margaret, daughter of Eric II of Norway, and granddaughter of Alexander III of Scotland.

Fair Maid of Perth. A sobriquet given to Catherine or Katie Glover, the most beautiful young woman in Perth, Scotland. She is the heroine of Walter Scott's novel of the same name.

Fairmount Park. An extensive pleasure-ground in Philadelphia, containing nearly 3000 acres. It was acquired by purchase and gift during the years 1844–1867, and was the site, in 1876, of the Centennial Exposition. Its entire length of 10 miles is bisected by the Schuylkill River and its tributary, the Wissahickon Creek. Memorial Hall and Horticultural Hall —buildings of the Centennial Exposition—are still standing in the Park.

Fair Perdita. A sobriquet conferred upon Mrs. Mary Robinson, the actress, in allusion to her successful impersonation of this character in Shakespeare's *Winter's Tale*. It was while performing in this play that she attracted the attention of the Prince of Wales (afterwards George IV), and eventually became his mistress.

Fair Rosamond. A name given to the daughter of Lord Clifford, and mistress of Henry II (1154–1189) of England. She died about 1176, and was buried at Godstow Abbey, near Oxford. According to a legend that first appears in the 14th century, Rosamond dwelt in a secret bower, or maze, at Woodstock, whose labyrinthine approaches were so intricate that they could be discovered only by means of a silken thread used by the King for that purpose. Queen Eleanor, having artfully gained access to the bower, poisoned Rosamond in 1173.

Fairs. " In that of Leipzig, the annual average of sales is four millions sterling, comprising 20,000 tons of merchandise, of which 8000 tons are books. The fair of Nijni-Novgorod is the greatest in the world, the returns showing:

Year.	Goods Offered.	Goods Sold.
1841	£ 8,000,000	£ 7,000,000
1857	13,000,000	12,000,000
1876	30,000,000	28,000,000

The fair is attended by 150,000 dealers from all parts of the world, and the goods sold in 1876 were:

Cottons, linens, etc.	£ 8,000,000
Furs, leather, etc.	7,000,000
Ural metals.	7,000,000
Flour, fish, brandy.	3,000,000
Tea and luxuries.	3,000,000
Total	£28,000,000 "

Mulhall's *Dictionary of Statistics*.

Falernian Wine. One of the favorite wines of the ancient Romans, so called because it was made in a district of northern Campania, known as the *Falernus Ager,* or Falernian Field. Its merits were highly extolled by Virgil, Horace, and other poets. Falernian wine began to decline in quality during the time of Pliny the Elder (23–79 A.D.).

Falling Stars. According to the religion of Islâm, falling stars are firebrands flung by good angels, to prevent evil spirits from drawing too near to the gates of Paradise.

False Prophet. A name given to Mohammed Ahmed (1841 (?) – 1885), who appeared at the age of 40, and claimed to be the Mahdi, or Mohammedan restorer of all things. In 1881, he advanced into the Soudan with 1500 followers, and defeated the Egyptian forces; in 1883, he seized El-'Obeyd and made it his capital. In November of the latter year, Hicks Pasha was defeated, and his army annihilated; in 1885 Khartoum was treacherously taken, and General Gordon, sent by Great Britain to pacify the Soudan, was killed. The Mahdi died of smallpox, at Omdurman, on June 25th, 1885.

Famous Old People of 1901. The following list is taken from the *World Almanac* for 1901.

(*Age at the last birthday is given. The list was made up for January 1, 1901.*)

Age.

98. Ex-Senator Bradbury, of Maine.
97. Thomas Sidney Cooper, R.A.; Rev. Dr. Thomas L. Sawyer, oldest minister of Universalist Church.
96. Hon. David Wark, "Father of the Canadian Senate."
95. Benjamin D. Silliman, oldest living graduate of Yale.
93. Ernest W. G. B. Legouvé, oldest French Academician.
91. Cassius M. Clay; Admiral Keppel, R.N.
90. Pope Leo XIII.; Lord Armstrong.
88. Samuel Smiles, biographer; Bishop Clark, of Rhode Island; Charles L. Tiffany, jeweler; ex-Senator John H. Reagan of Texas.

86. Verdi, the composer; Baroness Burdett-Coutts.
85. Elizabeth Cady Stanton; Adolf Menzel, German painter.
84. Ex-Senator Dawes; Rev. Newman Hall; Daniel Huntington, painter; Philip James Bailey, poet; Parke Godwin; Russell Sage.
83. Professor Mommsen, historian; King Christian of Denmark; Sir Joseph Hooker, botanist; Erastus Dow Palmer, sculptor, of Albany, N. Y.; George F. Watts, R.A.
82. Ex-Senator Evarts; ex-Senator Hampton; Professor Bain; ex-Secretary Boutwell; Bishop Watson of East Carolina.
81. Queen Victoria; ex-Prime-Minister Crispi; General Longstreet; Duke of Cambridge; Julia Ward Howe; Bishop Huntington; Dr. Thomas Dunn English.
80. Herbert Spencer; John Tenniel, cartoonist; Florence Nightingale; Mrs. G. H. Gilbert, actress; Princess Mathilde Bonaparte; Susan B. Anthony.
79. Professor Virchow; Duc de Broglie; Sir William H. Russell, journalist; Sir Charles Tupper; Ristori, tragic actress; Prince Hohenlohe-Schillingfuerst.
78. Bishop Whipple; Got, French comedian; Edward Everett Hale; Professor Alfred R. Wallace; Abram S. Hewitt; Rev. Henry M. Field; Donald G. Mitchell; Rev. Dr. Theodore L. Cuyler; Fitz-John Porter.
77. Thomas Wentworth Higginson; Professor Goldwin Smith; ex-Senator Grow; Li Hung Chang; Rev. Dr. Robert Collyer; Miss Yonge, novelist.
76. Professor Huggins, astronomer; Eastman Johnson, painter; ex-Vice-President Levi P. Morton; George Macdonald, novelist; Senator Morgan; General Franz Sigel.
75. Sir William Aitken, pathologist; Richard H. Stoddard, poet; Professor March, philologist.
74. Karl Blind; Marquis of Dufferin; ex-Empress Eugénie; Senator Hoar.
73. Sir William Harcourt, statesman; Père Hyacinthe; General Lew Wallace; Sagasta, Spanish statesman; J. H. Stoddart, comedian; Marquis of Ripon.
72. Sir Henry James, lawyer; De Freycinet, French statesman; ex-Senator Edmunds; General Gourko, Russian commander; Ibsen, dramatist; ex-President Dwight, of Yale; Jules Verne; Count Tolstoi; Justice Gray, of the Supreme Court; King Albert of Saxony; Berthelot, French statesman; Lord Pauncefote; Clara Barton; Edward Atkinson.

71. General Booth, Salvation Army leader; Joseph Jefferson; Carl Schurz; Senator Allison; Senator Cullom; King Oscar of Sweden and Norway; Viscount Peel; Murat Halstead.

70. President Diaz, of Mexico; Emperor Francis Joseph; ex-Queen Isabella; J. Q. A. Ward, sculptor; Rev. Joseph Parker, English pulpit orator; Marquis of Salisbury; Albert Bierstadt; Louise Michel, French agitator; Salvini, tragedian; ex-Secretary Tracy; Mme. Janauschek, actress; General Oliver O. Howard; Bishop Doane; Cardinal Satolli; Senators Vest, Teller, and Jones of Nevada.

69. Archdeacon Farrar; General Galliffet, French soldier; President Gilman, of Johns Hopkins; George J. Goschen; Frederick Harrison, positivist; Henry Labouchère, journalist; Henri Rochefort; Victorien Sardou; General Schofield; Senator Frye; Joachim, violinist; Sir George Nares, Arctic explorer; Ambassador Choate.

68. Field-Marshal Lord Roberts, British Army; Rev. Dr. Talmage; Maggie Mitchell, actress; Sir Edwin Arnold, poet; Professor Vambéry; Andrew D. White; Justice Shiras; Professor William Crookes; General Gordon, of Georgia; ex-Senator Quay; General Ignatieff; George H. Boughton, R.A.; G. W. Custis Lee.

67. Chief-Justice Fuller; Field-Marshal Lord Wolseley; Denman Thompson, actor; Justice Harlan; ex-President Harrison; Duke of Devonshire; Edmund Clarence Stedman, poet; John L. Toole, comedian; Lewis Morris, poet; Frank Stockton, novelist; ex-Secretary Bliss; Senator Platt of New York.

66. Senator Depew; President Eliot of Harvard University; Augustus J. C. Hare, author; Sir John Lubbock; Cardinal Gibbons; Ignatius Donnelly; Whistler, painter.

65. Leopold II, King of the Belgians; Rev. Lyman Abbott; President Charles K. Adams; Bouguereau, French painter; ex-Secretary Carlisle; Andrew Carnegie; Bishop Potter; Theodore Thomas; Paul Du Chaillu; "Mark Twain"; Charles Francis Adams; Alfred Austin, poet; General Shafter; General Fitzhugh Lee; Richard Olney; ex-Vice-President Stevenson; General Stewart L. Woodford.

64. Edward John Poynter, President of the Royal Academy; Professor C. F. Chandler; Thomas Bailey Aldrich; Alma-Tadema, painter; W. S. Gilbert, dramatist; General Joseph Wheeler; General Merritt; Joseph Chamberlain; ex-Secretary Alger; William Winter, dramatic critic.

63. Ex-President Cleveland; Whitelaw Reid; General Horace Porter; W. D. Howells, novelist; William L. Alden, author; Dr. Angell, ex-Minister to Turkey; Edward Eggleston, novelist; Justices Brewer and Peckham; Miss Braddon; Swinburne, poet; Admiral Dewey.

62. Sir Walter Besant, novelist; Professor James Bryce; ex-Queen Liliuokalani; John Hay, Secretary of State; Sir Henry Irving; Lecky, historian; John Morley; John Wanamaker; President Loubet; Bret Harte; Generals Brooke and E. S. Otis.

61. Rear-Admiral Schley; General Sir Redvers Buller; General Miles; ex-Speaker Thomas B. Reed; Archbishop Corrigan; ex-Senator Gorman; Bishop Keane; John D. Rockefeller.

60. Captain A. T. Mahan; Rear-Admiral Sampson; Henry Watterson; Labor Commissioner Wright; Clemenceau; Empress Frederick of Germany; Palmer Cox; Hiram Maxim; King Leopold of Belgium; Émile Zola; "Ouida."

"At what age does one become 'old'? Five centuries ago a man was old at fifty. But the hale and hearty gentleman of to-day who has just turned sixty would probably protest against being classed among old people, even if famous. That his susceptibilities may not be wounded, therefore, a separating dash has been discreetly introduced after age sixty-five."

Faneuil Hall. A celebrated public hall in Boston, Massachusetts, sacred to the cause of liberty. It was erected by Peter Faneuil, a Huguenot merchant, in 1742, and presented by him to the town of Boston. The original building was destroyed by fire in 1761, and rebuilt three years later. During Revolutionary times, it was so frequently used for political meetings that it became known as the "Cradle of American Liberty." James Otis, Daniel Webster, Louis Kossuth, and Wendell Phillips have all spoken there. The hall is capacious, and is adorned with portraits of eminent Americans. See *Cradle of American Liberty*.

19

Fanny Fern. A *nom-de-plume* assumed by Mrs. Sarah Payson Parton (1811–1872), the wife of James Parton and sister of Nathaniel P. Willis.

Farmer George. A nickname bestowed upon George III (1763–1820), King of England, because of his bucolic tastes and proclivities.

Farnese Bull. A colossal group of antique sculpture—the largest known—now in the National Museum at Naples. It is the work of Apollonius and his brother Tauriscus (of the Rhodian school of sculpture, which flourished about 300 B.C.), and represents Dirce bound by Zethus and Amphion to the horns of a bull for ill-using her mother. The group, which is carved from a single block of marble, was discovered, in a mutilated state, in the Baths of Caracalla, during the sixteenth century. It was restored by Bianchi, working under the direction of Michael Angelo, in 1546, and was placed in the Farnese Palace at Rome, whence its name. In 1786, it was removed to Naples. See *Baths of Caracalla.*

Farnese Hercules. A colossal antique statue—now in the National Museum at Naples—representing Hercules resting on his club and holding in his right hand the apples of the Hesperides. It is said to be the work of Glycon of Athens, and a copy of the original by Lysippus. The statue was discovered in the Baths of Caracalla in 1540, during the reign of Pope Paul III (1534–1550), and was placed in the Farnese Palace at Rome, whence its name. The legs were not discovered until twenty years after. The Farnese Hercules was transferred to Naples in 1786. See *Baths of Caracalla ; Garden of the Hesperides ; Wilhelmshöhe.*

Farnese Palace. A magnificent palace of vast extent, at Rome, commenced by Pope Paul III (1534–1550), one of the illustrious Farnese family.

It is constructed of materials taken from the Theatre of Marcellus and the Coliseum, and is, as Hillard says, " a shameless receiver of stolen goods." In the great hall or gallery may be seen the masterpieces in fresco of Annibale Caracci, upon which he spent eight years, and for which he was rewarded with the trifling sum of $600. The gallery of sculpture was at one time famous, but its masterpieces were removed to Naples in the latter part of the eighteenth century.

Fasti Capitolini. The name given to certain marble tablets discovered in the Forum at Rome in 1547, 1817, and 1818. They contain a list of the Roman chief-magistrates and triumphs, from the beginning of the Republic until the close of the reign of Augustus (14 A.D.), and have proved of great value in verifying important historical data. They were deposited in the Capitol (whence their name), and may still be seen there.

Fata Morgana. The Italian name given to a species of mirage seen, under certain atmospheric conditions, in the Straits of Messina between Calabria and Sicily. It consists of images—some erect and some inverted—of hills, groves, buildings, ships, and other objects in the vicinity. These are seen sometimes in the water and sometimes in the air, and form a kind of moving spectacle. This mirage is so called, because it is supposed to be the work of the fairy (*It. fata*), Morgana, the pupil of Merlin and sister of King Arthur.

Fates. In classic mythology, the name given to Clotho, Lachesis, and Atropos, the three daughters of Nox. They were sometimes called the " Destinies," and were believed to determine the course of human life. The Fates were usually represented as young women of serious mien—Clotho holding the spindle, Lachesis drawing out the thread of life, and Atropos cutting it off. Temples consecrated to them existed throughout Greece and elsewhere.

Father Abraham. A sobriquet bestowed upon Abraham Lincoln (1809–1865), the sixteenth President of the United States, during the Civil War.

Father Fritz. A term of endearment conferred upon Frederick the Great (1740–1786) of Prussia by his loyal and devoted subjects.

Father of America. A sobriquet conferred upon Samuel Adams (1722–1803), the American Revolutionary patriot and statesman.

Father of American Shipbuilding. A sobriquet conferred upon John Roach (1813–1887), the famous American shipbuilder.

Father of Church History. A title bestowed upon Eusebius (260(?)–339(?) A.D.), Bishop of Cæsarea.

Father of Comedy. A sobriquet given to Aristophanes (444–380 B.C.), the celebrated Greek comic poet. His comedies are of the highest order of excellence, and furnish an instructive commentary on the evils existing in Athens in his day. They are written in the purest Attic dialect, with great simplicity of style, and abound in wit and humor.

Father of English Poetry. A title conferred by John Dryden upon Geoffrey Chaucer (1328–1400), the first great English poet.

Father of English Printing. A sobriquet conferred upon William Caxton (1422 (?)–1492), the earliest English printer.

Father of Epic Poetry. A title conferred upon Homer (fl. 1000 B.C.), the Greek poet and reputed author of the *Iliad* and *Odyssey*.

Father of German Literature. A title conferred upon Gotthold Ephraim

Lessing (1729–1781), the distinguished German author.

Father of Greek Prose. A title conferred upon Herodotus (484–420 B.C.), the Greek historian.

Father of his Country. A title frequently bestowed upon rulers and military commanders for distinguished services rendered to the state. Cicero was proclaimed *Pater Patriæ* (*Lat. Father of his Country*) by the Roman Senate, on account of his courage and skill in overthrowing the conspiracy of Catiline. The same title was offered to Marius, the Roman general, but was declined by him. It was afterwards borne by several of the Cæsars, and later by Cosmo de' Medici and Andronicus Palæologus. With Americans the title is most intimately associated with the name of George Washington, who, as founder and first President of the American Republic, richly deserves this appellation.

Father of his People. An appellation given to Louis XII (1498–1515) of France, in allusion to the genuine interest manifested by him in the welfare of his subjects. The same title was borne by Christian III (1533–1559) of Denmark.

Father of History. The name given by Cicero to Herodotus (484–420 B.C.). If not the earliest writer on history, he was at least the first to present the subject in a systematic manner.

Father of Landscape-Gardening. A title conferred upon André Lenôtre (1614–1700), the French architect and garden-designer.

Father of Lies. A sobriquet conferred upon Herodotus (484–420 B.C.), the Greek historian, whose statements, according to many, should be taken with a grain of allowance.

Father of Medicine. A title given to Hippocrates (468–367 (?) B.C.), the most famous physician of ancient Greece, through whose efforts the art of medicine was first established upon scientific principles.

Father of Moral Philosophy. An appellation conferred upon Thomas Aquinas (1227–1274 A.D.), the noted Schoolman.

Father of Orthodoxy. An appellation bestowed upon Athanasius (296 (?)–373 A.D.), Primate of Egypt, who defended the so-called "orthodox" doctrines of the Trinity against the assaults of the Arians.

Father of Satire. A title conferred upon Archilochus (714 (?)–676 B.C.), the Greek lyric poet.

Father of Song. An appellation conferred upon Homer (fl. 1000 B.C.), the famous Greek poet.

Father of Symphony. A sobriquet conferred upon Joseph Haydn (1732–1809), who excelled in this form of musical composition.

Father of the Faithful. A title conferred upon Abraham, the founder of the Hebrew race. He is the chief biblical example of faith.

"And he [Abram] believed in the Lord; and he counted it to him for righteousness." —*Genesis* xv, 6.

Father of Tragedy. A sobriquet bestowed by the Athenians on Æschylus (525–456 B.C.), the Greek tragic poet. He was their earliest great writer of tragedies, and excelled in force, majesty, and passion. In the "Great Tragic Trio," Æschylus was the poet of the sublime, Sophocles of the beautiful, and Euripides of the pathetic.

Father of Waters. A name popularly given to the Mississippi River, on account of its great length (2804 miles) and the number of its tributaries. The word "Mississippi" is of Indian origin, and means "Great and Long River." The name of the famous river of Burmah—the Irrawaddy—is also said to mean "Father of Waters." Its length is estimated to be 1200 miles.

Fathers of the Greek Church. The name given to the Christian writers of the Greek Church, who lived during the fourth and fifth centuries. The principal ones are as follows:
  (1) Athanasius.
  (2) Basil the Great.
  (3) Chrysostom.
  (4) Cyril of Alexandria.
  (5) Cyril of Jerusalem.
  (6) Ephrem of Edessa.
  (7) Epiphanius.
  (8) Eusebius of Nicomedia.
  (9) Gregory of Nazianzus (Cappadocia).
  (10) Gregory of Nyssa.

Fathers of the Latin Church. The name given to the Christian writers of the Latin Church, who flourished during the fourth and fifth centuries. They are as follows:
  (1) Ambrose of Milan.
  (2) Augustine of Hippo.
  (3) Hilary.
  (4) Jerome.
  (5) Lactantius.
To these is frequently added St. Bernard (1091–1153), the last of the Latin Fathers.

Father Thames. An epithet popularly applied to the river Thames in England, as being the source of much of the prosperity and wealth of the great city on its banks.

Father Violet. A nickname bestowed upon Napoleon Bonaparte (1769–1821) during his exile at Elba in 1814–1815. It was mysteriously whispered throughout France at that time that a certain Corporal, or Father, Violet would return in the spring with the violets, and that flower became, in consequence, the badge of his adherents and was publicly worn by them. It is still the symbol of the French Imperialists. See *Corporal Violet.*

Faubourg St. Antoine. An industrial section of Paris, situated on the right bank of the Seine. It was famous during the French Revolution as the centre and source of the insurrectionary faction, and in every subsequent revolt it has been the hotbed of the disaffected elements of society. In 1854, its character was materially altered, and at present it contains some of the most extensive manufacturing establishments in the city.

Faubourg St. Germain. An aristocratic quarter of Paris, situated on the left bank of the Seine. It was the residence, before the French Revolution, of the old noblesse of France, many of whose stately mansions are still standing. At present, it is the section of the city where the ministers, ambassadors, and many of the ancient nobility have their homes. It adjoins the *Quartier Latin* on the east.

Faun of Praxiteles. A famous antique marble statue by Praxiteles, the Greek sculptor, now in the Capitoline Museum at Rome. It was discovered in Hadrian's Villa at Tivoli, and represents a youth of seventeen leaning against the trunk of a tree and holding in his right hand a short flute. This statue furnished the title of Hawthorne's romance of *The Marble Faun*.

Faust. The hero of a celebrated tragedy by Goethe (1749–1832), based on the semi-legendary story of Doctor Faustus, a famous necromancer of the sixteenth century. He is often confounded with Johann Faust, or Fust, the associate of Gutenberg in the invention of the art of printing. According to the play, Doctor Faustus is a student who, after vainly toiling for years to learn the secrets of alchemy, grows weary of his search, and makes a compact with the Devil (in the shape of Mephistopheles), whereby, in exchange for his soul, he is granted plenary indulgence in all sensual pleasures. When the hour of his doom arrives, Mephistopheles appears on the scene, claims his victim, and disappears with him to the infernal regions. Faust, on one occasion, was furnished with a mantle by means of which he was wafted through the air in whatever direction he desired.

It is said that Goethe thought out his tragedy as early as 1774, but did not publish the first part until 1808. The second part appeared in 1831. The drama of *Faust* depicts the struggle between the lower and the higher natures, which is ever going on in the human breast, and is justly regarded as one of the masterpieces of German literature. *Faust* is also the title of a charming opera by Gounod, based practically on the same story.

Favored Child of Victory. An epithet conferred upon André Masséna (1758–1817), Duke of Rivoli and Prince of Essling, the greatest of the first Napoleon's marshals, because of his uninterrupted career of victory in Italy, Switzerland, Germany, and Poland.

Feather in One's Cap. An expression which, doubtless, owes its origin to the wellnigh universal custom, among savage tribes, of adding a new feather to the head-dress for every enemy slain. In Scotland, it is still customary for the sportsman that kills the first woodcock to pluck a feather from the bird and stick it in his cap.

In the *Lansdowne MS.* in the British Museum is a description of Hungary in the year 1599, in which occur these words : " It hath been an ancient custom among them that none should wear a feather but he who had killed a Turk." Hence the phrase came to mean an honor or mark of distinction, and is so used at the present day.

Federalist. The name given to a series of political essays—eighty-six in number — that first appeared in the *New York Gazette*, under the signature of " Publius," and strongly advocated the adoption of the Federal Constitution. More than half of these essays were written by Alexander Hamilton (1757–1804), and the remainder by

James Madison (1751–1836) and John Jay (1745–1829).

Federal States. The name given to those States of the American Union that were loyal to the Federal government during the Civil War (1861–1865) and opposed the attempts of the eleven Confederate States to secede and establish a government of their own.

Fenian Oath. The name given to a secret oath taken by the Fenians, the motive of which is said to be the recovery of the " Lia Fail " or " Stone of Destiny," and its return to the Irish people. This historic stone, generally known as the " Scone," is at present under the Coronation Chair in Westminster Abbey. According to tradition, it was brought from Egypt to Ireland by a beautiful princess, and placed in Tara's Hall, in 580 B.C. See *Fenians; Coronation Chair.*

Fenians. A political society, organized in 1857 by Irishmen in Ireland and the United States, for the purpose of overthrowing English rule in Ireland and establishing a republic. The movement first attracted attention in the United States in 1863, and in November of that year a Fenian Congress —consisting of 200 delegates — met at Chicago. In 1866, Fenian meetings were held in all parts of the United States. Two risings were planned in Ireland in 1865 and 1866, but were frustrated by the vigilance of the British government. These were followed in 1867 by a general insurrection throughout Ireland, which also was quickly suppressed. In the United States, raids into Canada were attempted in 1866, 1870, and 1871, but were all utter failures. The Skirmishing Fund—raised to encourage the use of dynamite in the destruction of English public buildings and English commerce — and the Clan-na-Gael, an extreme party, were later developments of the Fenian spirit. The word " Fenian " is derived from Fionna Eirinn, an ancient military organiza-

tion, which took its name from the famous Irish legendary hero, Finn or Fionn Mac - Cumhail. See *Clan-na-Gael ; Fenian Oath.*

Ferney, Patriarch of. An epithet bestowed upon Voltaire (1694–1778), the famous French writer, who during the last twenty years of his life resided at Ferney, a small village near Geneva, Switzerland. During the period of his residence there, Voltaire was considered the autocrat of French literature, and his château became a Mecca for literary and political pilgrims from all parts of Europe.

Feudal System. A military and social organization of the Middle Ages, based on the tenure of land. It had its origin among the German tribes about the 9th century A.D., and later spread over western Europe and the British Isles. According to this system, the sovereigns of the various countries made extensive gifts of land to their nobles, on condition that they and their heirs should render military service to the Crown in times of need. William the Conqueror (1066–1087) introduced feudalism into England in 1068, although the principle of tenure of land by suit or service to the owner had been established by the Saxons as early as 600 A.D. Vassalage, limited by Henry VII (1485–1509) in 1495, was abolished by statute in 1663. The Feudal System was introduced into Scotland by Malcolm II (1003–1033) in 1008, and was abolished in that country in 1746–1747, during the reign of George II (1727–1760). In France it was established by Clovis I (481–511) about 486, and suppressed by Louis XI (1461–1483) in 1470.

Feuillants. A celebrated revolutionary club in Paris, founded in 1790 by Lafayette, Sieyès, Larochefoucauld, and other French republican leaders holding moderate views, to counteract the intrigues of the Jacobins. It derived its name from the convent of the *Feuillants* — a religious order of reformed Cistercians—where its meetings were held. The *Feuillants* were forcibly dispersed by a furious mob on March 28th, 1791, while in session in the cloister, and were disbanded in 1792. Their original name was the " Company of 1789," and their nickname the " Club Monarchique."

F. F. V. These initial letters of the phrase " First Family of Virginia " are used in a humorous sense to denote those that lay claim to ancient lineage in the Old Dominion.

"The famous initials F. F. V. have had their significance changed by some of our boys in the last campaign, in consequence of their constant alacrity in running, to Fast Footed Virginians."—*New York Tribune*, August 2nd, 1861.

Fidus Achates (*Lat. Faithful Achates*). An expression used to denote a faithful and devoted friend. In Virgil's *Æneid*, Achates is the bosom-companion of Æneas and accompanies him in all his wanderings.

Field of Lies. The name sometimes given to the battle fought in 833 A.D. near Colmar, in which Louis le Débonnaire (814–840), while battling against his three sons, was deserted by his own army.

Field of the Cloth of Gold. A plain between Suisnes and Ardres, near Calais, France, famous as the place of meeting between Henry VIII (1509–1547) of England and Francis I (1515–1547) of France, on June 7th–25th, 1520. The splendor and magnificence displayed on that occasion gave the field its name. For 18 days the two monarchs feasted and played like schoolboys,—each sovereign declaring that he would not cut his beard until he should again visit his " good brother." Many of the nobility of both countries embarrassed themselves financially by their senseless extravagance on that occasion, and were forced to live lives of penury during their remaining years.

Fifteen Decisive Battles. The following, according to Sir E. S. Creasy, are the fifteen decisive battles of the world, from Marathon to Waterloo,—a period of 2305 years :

(1) Marathon (490 B.C.).
(2) Syracuse (413 B.C.).
(3) Arbela (331 B.C.).
(4) Metaurus (207 B.C.).
(5) Teutoberg (9 A.D.).
(6) Châlons (451 A.D.).
(7) Tours (732 A.D.).
(8) Hastings (1066 A.D.).
(9) Orleans (1429 A.D.).
(10) Armada (1588 A.D.).
(11) Blenheim (1704 A.D.).
(12) Pultowa (1709 A.D.).
(13) Saratoga (1777 A.D.).
(14) Valmy (1792 A.D.).
(15) Waterloo (1815 A.D.).

See *Sixteen Memorable Battles.*

Fifteen Great American Inventions. The following list of fifteen great American inventions is taken from Killikelly's *Curious Questions*. It is as follows :

(1) The Cotton Gin.
(2) The Planting Machine.
(3) The Grass Mower and Reaper.
(4) The Rotary Printing-Press.
(5) Steam Navigation.
(6) The Hot-Air Engine.
(7) The Sewing-Machine.
(8) The India-Rubber Industry.
(9) The Machine Manufacture of Horseshoes.
(10) The Sand-Blast for Carving.
(11) The Gauge Lathe.
(12) The Grain Elevator.
(13) Artificial Ice-Making on Large Scale.
(14) The Electric Magnet and its Practical Application.
(15) The Telephone.

Fifteen Mysteries. In the Roman Catholic Church, fifteen mysteries are enumerated—five joyous, five dolorous, and five glorious.

The " Five Joyous Mysteries " are as follows :

(1) The Annunciation to the Virgin Mary.

(2) The Visitation of the Virgin Mary to Elizabeth, wife of Zacharias.

(3) The Birth of Jesus Christ at Bethlehem, in Judea.

(4) The Purification and Offering of the Virgin Mary in the Temple.

(5) The Visit of Jesus Christ to the Temple, at the age of twelve.

The "Five Dolorous Mysteries" are as follows :

(1) The Agony in the Garden.

(2) The Scourging.

(3) The Crowning with Thorns.

(4) The Bearing of the Cross to Calvary.

(5) The Crucifixion.

The "Five Glorious Mysteries" are as follows :

(1) The Resurrection.

(2) The Ascension.

(3) The Descent of the Holy Ghost on the Day of Pentecost.

(4) The Assumption of the Virgin Mary.

(5) The Consummation of the glory of the Virgin Mary.

Fifth Avenue. A splendid avenue in New York City, extending from Washington Square to the Harlem River. It was at one time a street of private residences exclusively, but has suffered of late years from the encroachments of trade. From Washington Square to 59th Street — a distance of nearly three miles—the avenue is lined with handsome private houses, churches, clubs, hotels, and shops. South of 59th Street, the thoroughfare is fast becoming a business centre; but north of this point are located many of the finest private residences in the city.

Fifth Doctor of the Church. A sobriquet conferred upon Thomas Aquinas (1227–1274), the famous scholastic teacher.

Fifth Monarchy Men. The name given to a sect of English fanatics who, about 1645, declared that the "mil-lennium " was at hand, and that Jesus Christ would appear a second time on earth and establish the fifth universal monarchy or world-kingdom, as successor to the four great monarchies of ancient times,—the Assyrian, Persian, Græco-Macedonian, and Roman. They acknowledged no earthly king but Christ, whom they actually elected as their ruler at London. They attempted to murder Oliver Cromwell, but were dispersed by him in 1653. In 1661—during the reign of Charles II (1660–1685)—the " Fifth Monarchy " men attempted to seize the kingdom by force, without waiting for the advent of the Messiah, but were quickly suppressed. The ringleaders were captured and executed in 1661, and the sect exterminated.

Fifty Years of Human Life. "According to a French statistician, taking the mean of many accounts, a man of 50 years of age has slept 6000 days, worked 6500 days, walked 800 days, amused himself 4000 days, was eating 1500 days, was sick 500 days, etc. He has eaten 17,000 lbs. of bread, 16,000 lbs. of meat, 4600 lbs. of vegetables, eggs, and fish, and drunk, in all, 7000 gallons of liquid — namely, water, tea, coffee, beer, wine, etc."—*Everybody's Pocket Cyclopædia.*

Figaro. A dramatic character first introduced on the Parisian stage in 1785, by Beaumarchais, in his dramas, *Le Barbier de Séville* and *Le Mariage de Figaro.* *Figaro* is at first a barber and afterwards a valet-de-chambre, and has become a type of extraordinary cunning and intrigue. These plays by Beaumarchais were made the basis of classic operas by Mozart and Rossini. The name *Figaro* is also given to a Paris journal established in 1854.

Fighting Joe. An epithet conferred upon Joseph Hooker (1814–1879), an American general during the Civil War, on account of the dash and bravery shown by him at the battle of Manassas in 1862. He was placed in command of the Army of the Potomac in January, 1863; but was disastrously defeated by General Lee at Chancellorsville on May 2nd–4th of the same year, and was soon after superseded by General Meade.

Fighting Nat. An appellation bestowed upon Nathaniel Fitz-Randolph, a bold and intrepid soldier during the American Revolutionary War.

Fighting Phil. A sobriquet conferred upon General Philip Kearny (1815–1862), on account of his bravery and dash in battle.

Filia Dolorosa (*Lat. Daughter of Sorrow*). An epithet conferred upon Marie Thérèse Charlotte (1778–1851), Duchesse d'Angoulême, daughter of Louis XVI. See *Orphan of the Temple.*

Filibusters. A name originally given to those freebooters that plundered the coast of America during the sixteenth and seventeenth centuries; but, in more recent times, applied to certain lawless adventurers from the United States, who attempted to seize upon various countries of Spanish America. The most famous of these were Narcisso Lopez (1799–1851), and William Walker (1824–1860). Lopez, after several unsuccessful attempts to invade Cuba, organized in 1850 an expedition of 600 men and landed at Cardenas, which he captured but was obliged soon afterwards to relinquish. Shortly after, he returned to New Orleans. A second attempt in 1851 was even less successful. After landing some miles west of Havana, he appealed in vain to the people to rise in revolt, but was forced to surrender, having accomplished nothing. He was garroted on September 1st, 1851.

William Walker led several filibustering expeditions into Lower California, Nicaragua, and Honduras, during the years 1853–1860. He was finally captured on September 30th, 1860, and delivered up to the Honduras government, by whom he was tried and shot on October 12th, 1860, but his followers were set at liberty.

Filioque Controversy. The name given to a controversy that long disturbed the Christian Church. It took its name from the Latin words *Filioque* (*and from the Son*), and turned on the question whether the Holy Ghost proceeded from the Father alone or from the Father and the Son,—the Greek Church maintaining the former dogma and the Latin Church the latter. These words (*Filioque*) were inserted in the Nicene Creed by Recared, at the Council of Toledo in 589 A.D., and were adopted by the Western or Latin Church, but were rejected by the Eastern or Greek Church after 662 A.D. The Athanasian Creed (arranged in its present form between 813 and 850 A.D.) asserts the procession of the Holy Ghost from the Father and the Son. See *Athanasian Creed; Greek Church; Latin Church; Nicene Creed.*

Fingal's Cave. A celebrated cavern on the island of Staffa, off the west coast of Scotland, consisting of huge columnar blocks of black basalt, which support a lofty arch. The entrance of the cave is 42 feet wide and 66 feet high above the water at mean tide, and its length about 227 feet. The entire floor is covered by the sea, and is accessible to boats at certain states of the tide. Fingal's Cave is much visited by tourists on account of its marvellous formation, which resembles that of the Giants' Causeway in Ireland. See *Giants' Causeway.*

Finland. This word is properly Fenland, the land of *fens* or marshes.

Firebrand of the Universe. A title conferred upon Tamerlane (1336–1405 A.D.), the famous Asiatic conqueror.

Fire-Eaters. A name given, before the Civil War in the United States, to those inhabitants of the Southern States that held extreme views on slavery and States' Rights. The term was applied to them by their Northern political opponents. See *State Rights*.

Fire of London. See *Great Fire of London*.

First Book Printed in England. *The Dictes and Wise Sayings of the Philosophers* is said to have been the first book printed in England. It was the work of William Caxton (1422–1491) and appeared in 1477. A facsimile was published by Elliot Stock in 1877. Caxton doubtless learned the art of printing from Colard Mansion, a well-known printer at Bruges, and while living there published, in 1474 the first book printed in the English language,—entitled the *Recuyell of the Historyes of Troye*, a translation of Raoul Lefèvre's work.

First Czar. Ivan IV (1533–1584) of Russia—surnamed " The Terrible "—was the first Russian sovereign that assumed the title of czar. He did much for the development of his country in commerce and the arts, and added considerable territory to his dominions. During his reign, the first annexation of Siberia took place.

First Gentleman of Europe. An epithet conferred upon George IV (1820–1830) of England by his admirers, in allusion to his courtly manners and exquisite taste in dress.

" A nickname given to George IV., who certainly was first in rank, but it would be sad indeed to think he was ever the most gentlemanly man in feeling, manners, and deportment. Louis d'Artois was so called also."—Brewer's *Dictionary of Phrase and Fable*.

First Grenadier of the Republic. A nickname given by Napoleon Bonaparte to Latour d'Auvergne (1743–1800), the famous French grenadier, on account of his surpassing bravery.

" La Tour d'Auvergne, named by the First Consul as the *First Grenadier of the Republic*, was distinguished alike for his modesty and bravery ; he was killed June 27, 1800, and thereafter up to 1814 at every roll-call of his company the color-bearer answered to

his name, ' Dead on the field of honor.' "—Chandler's *Encyclopedia*.

First King of Jerusalem. An honorary title bestowed upon Godfrey of Bouillon (1061–1100 A.D.), the hero of the First Crusade. In 1099—eight days after the capture of Jerusalem—he was proclaimed King by his troops, but declined to be crowned, saying : " I cannot wear a crown of gold where my Savior wore a crown of thorns." He accordingly accepted, instead, the title of " Defender and Guardian of the Holy Sepulchre." His tomb is still pointed out in Jerusalem, near the Holy Sepulchre, which he was the first to rescue from the hands of the Infidel. In 1187, Jerusalem was captured by Saladin, and was never retaken by the Crusaders.

First Picture in the World. An expression frequently applied to Raphael's painting of the " Transfiguration," in the Vatican at Rome. See *Transfiguration*.

" It is generally regarded as being the first painting in the world, although the double scene on one canvas has been severely criticised."—Loomis's *Index Guide*.

First Steamship to Cross the Atlantic. The first steamship that succeeded in crossing the Atlantic Ocean was the *Savannah*,—a vessel of about 350 tons' burden, measuring 100 feet in length. She was built in New York City by Francis Pickett in 1818, and was a full-rigged ship, with side paddle-wheels that could be unshipped and taken on deck in stormy weather. Under the command of Captain Stevens Rogers, this vessel sailed from Savannah on May 20th, 1819, but did not venture on the high seas until the 25th of the month. She reached Liverpool on June 20th, after an ocean voyage of 26 days—during 16 of which she used her paddles. Off Cape Clear she was mistaken for a ship on fire, and was pursued by the British cutter *Kite*. The *Savannah* afterwards visited St. Petersburg, Copenhagen, Stockholm, and other foreign ports. Captain Rogers, having failed to dispose of his vessel to the King of Sweden, started for home and reached Savannah on November 30th, 1819. The engines and boilers were afterwards removed and the ship was used as a sailing-packet between New York and Savannah. She was finally wrecked off the south coast of Long Island.

First Version of the English Bible. The first complete version of the English Bible was that of Myles Coverdale. It appeared in 1535, and was based on the Swiss-German version published at Zurich in 1524–1529. In 1382, there had appeared a version attributed to Wycliffe ; but the gospels alone can be identified as the work of Wycliffe himself. The translation of the *Old Testament* and the *Apocrypha* is the work of Nicolas de Hereford. The translation of the *New Testament* by William Tyndale appeared at Worms in 1525 ; later editions in 1534–1535.

Fishes, Sounds Produced by. It is a well-known fact that fishes emit various sounds. These are due primarily to the action of the pneumatic duct and swimming bladder ; but are produced also by the lips or the pharyngeal or intermaxillary bones, as in the tench, carp, and a large number of other fishes. Dufosse enumerates 50 species of fish that produce sounds of some sort ; and Abbot has increased the number, in this country. Among these may be named the drum-fish, the sea-horse, the mud sun-fish, the gizzard-shad, the mullet, and the cat-fish.

"It should also be noticed that the organs of hearing in many musical fishes are said to be unusually well developed, hence these sounds are probably love-notes ; and Abbot notices the fact that these fishes are dull-colored during the reproductive season, as well as at other times, while voiceless fishes, such as the perch, common sun-fish, chub, roach, etc., are highly colored during the breeding season, and thus the sexes are mutually attracted, in the one case by music, and in the other by bright colors. Finally

the sounds of fishes may be said to be homologous with those of reptiles, birds, and mammals, the air-bladder being homologous with the lungs of the higher vertebrates, while the pneumatic duct is comparable with the trachea of birds and mammals."—Packard's *Zoölogy.*

Five. "Five, or the pentad, the great mystic number, being the sum of $2 + 3$, the first *even* and first *odd* compound. Unity is God alone, *i. e.,* without creation. Two is diversity, and three (being $1 + 2$) is the compound of unity and diversity, or the two principles in operation since creation."—Brewer's *Dictionary of Phrase and Fable.*

Five Christian Verities.
(1) The Child Jesus, conceived in the womb of the Virgin Mary and called Jesus, was verily and indeed the Son of God, and the Second Person of the Trinity.
(2) This Jesus is true God, one with the Father and the Holy Ghost.
(3) The two perfect natures coexist in one only Person. The divine nature was received from God the Father; the human nature from His mother Mary.
(4) All that pertains to the Person of Christ as a substance is *unique ;* but all that pertains to His nature is *double.*
(5) The Virgin Mary is veritably and properly the mother of God.

Five Forks, Battle of. A sanguinary battle fought near Richmond, Va., on April 1st, 1865, between the Federals under General Sheridan and the Confederate forces. After a desperate struggle of several hours, the Confederate line was turned and overwhelmingly defeated. As a result of this battle, Richmond was evacuated on the following day.

Five Good Emperors. A term applied to the five Roman Emperors that succeeded the Flavian line. They ruled from 96 to 180 A.D., and by their wise and just administration of affairs raised the Roman Empire to its highest point of prosperity and renown. Their names are as follows : Nerva, Trajan, Hadrian, Antoninus Pius, and Marcus Aurelius Antoninus. Two centuries later, the Senate, at the accession of each Emperor, expressed the wish that he might be "more fortunate than Augustus, more virtuous than Trajan."

Five Great Powers of Europe. An appellation conferred on certain nations of Europe, in allusion to their pre-eminence in wealth, population, and military resources. They may be named in the order of their importance, as follows : Great Britain, Germany, France, Russia, and Austria.

Five Hundred, Council of. A French legislative assembly of 500 members, whose duty it was to propose laws, which were afterwards accepted or rejected by the Council of the Ancients. It was established August 22nd, 1795, and was dissolved November 9th, 1799, by Napoleon Bonaparte, who, with the assistance of the army, abolished the Directory, established the Consulate, and caused himself to be elected First Consul. See *Ancients, Council of.*

Five Kings of France. A term applied to the body of five men constituting the French Directory. To them was entrusted the executive government of France from October 26th, 1795, to November 9th, 1799,—a period of four years. They were frequently styled "Their Five Majesties of the Luxembourg." The Directory was overthrown by Napoleon Bonaparte on the 18th Brumaire (November 9th, 1799), and the Consulate established in its stead. See *Directory, French.*

Five Points. A section of New York City between Centre Street and the Bowery, at the junction of Baxter, Worth, and Park Streets, notorious for many years as the home of poverty, vice, and crime. As early as 1830, efforts were made to improve this degenerate neighborhood, but it was not until 1850, when the *Five Points House*

of Industry and the *Five Points Mission* were established, that the locality began to show signs of improvement. At the present time, however, the "Five Points" is no longer a dangerous quarter of the city, but is filled with chapels, mission-schools, manufactories, and the homes of law-abiding people. Open squares and streets have been laid out by the municipal authorities, and the region has been in every way greatly improved.

Five Points of Calvinism. The name given, in church history, to the five points of doctrine laid down by John Calvin (1509–1564), and held by his followers in opposition to the doctrines taught by Arminius (1560–1609), the Dutch theologian. They are as follows :
(1) Predestination.
(2) Irresistible Grace.
(3) Original Sin.
(4) Particular Redemption.
(5) Perseverance of the Saints.
The Synod of Dort, a conclave of Protestants that sat during 1618–1619, condemned the doctrines of Arminius as heretical, and affirmed those of Calvin. See *Arminians.*

Five P's. A nickname given to William Oxberry (1784–1824), who was at once poet, printer, publisher, publican, and player.

Five Sacraments. A term applied to certain sacraments recognized by the Roman Catholic and Greek Churches, but rejected by the Church of England and by Protestants generally. These are confirmation, penance, holy orders, matrimony, and extreme unction. The only sacraments recognized by the Protestant communions are baptism and the eucharist.

"There are two Sacraments ordained of Christ our Lord in the Gospel, that is to say, Baptism, and the Supper of the Lord.
"Those five commonly called Sacraments, that is to say, Confirmation, Penance, Orders, Matrimony, and Extreme Unction, are not to be counted for Sacraments of the Gospel, being such as have grown partly out of the cor-

rupt following of the Apostles, partly are states of life allowed in the Scriptures ; but yet have not like nature of Sacraments with Baptism and the Lord's Supper, for that they have not any visible sign of ceremony ordained of God."—*Thirty-nine Articles (Art. xxv).*

Five Wits. An old-time enumeration of certain of the powers of the mind. They are common wit, imagination, fantasy, estimation, and memory.

" These are the five witts removyng inwardly—
First ' Common Witte,' and then ' Ymagination,'
' Fantasy ' and ' Estimation ' truely,
And ' Memory.' "
    The Passe-tyme of Plesure, xxiv.
        (Stephen Hawes).

Flag, United States. The first legislation on the question of a national flag was in the form of a congressional resolution, passed June 14th, 1777, declaring " that the flag of the 13 United States be 13 stripes alternate red and white ; that the union be 13 stars, white in a blue field, representing the new constellation." In 1794, Congress decreed that after May 1st, 1795, " the flag of the United States be 15 stripes, alternate red and white, and that the union be 15 stars, white in a blue field." This change was made to mark the admission of Vermont and Kentucky into the Union. The stars and stripes were then equal, and a star and stripe were to be added with the admission of each State. It was realized, however, that the addition of a stripe for each new State would soon render the flag too large, and a resolution was accordingly passed in Congress on April 4th, 1818, reducing the number of stripes to 13 (representing the original Union), and making the stars 20 in number,—there being at that time 20 States. It was furthermore enacted that a new star should be added for each new State admitted into the Union. The flag now contains 45 stars,—a number equal to that of the States composing the American Union.

Flagellants. The name given to certain groups of religious fanatics that appeared in various countries of Europe from the thirteenth to the sixteenth century, and declared that self-inflicted scourgings or flagellations were the only means of atonement for sin. They publicly enforced their teachings by inflicting upon themselves the discipline of scourging, and marched in large companies from town to town, chanting denunciatory hymns. The " Flagellants " were declared heretics by Pope Clement VI (1342–1352) in 1349, and 90 of them, with their leader, Conrad Schmidt, were burned in 1414. Their doctrines were condemned by the Council of Constance (1414–1418).

Flaminian Way. A celebrated road of ancient Italy, extending from the Flaminian Gate at Rome to Ariminum (*Rimini*) on the Adriatic. It was built in 220 B.C., by Caius Flaminius while censor, to secure free communication with the recently conquered territory of the Gauls, and was afterwards extended to Milan under the name of the *Via Æmilia.* Augustus Cæsar, in 27 B.C., renewed the Flaminian Way throughout its entire length. See *Roman Roads.*

Flavian Emperors. A name given to the Roman Emperors, Vespasian, Titus, and Domitian,—the last three of the "Twelve Cæsars." They ruled during 69–96 A.D., and were so called from Titus *Flavius* Vespasian, the first of the line. See *Cæsars, Twelve.*

Fleet, The. A famous prison in London, built over the Fleta or Fleet, once a small creek, but at present a sewer. It was founded in 1189, and became a debtors' prison in 1640. It was burned during the Great Fire of 1666, and again in the Gordon Riots of 1780; was rebuilt in 1781–1782 ; and finally demolished in 1845. In 1864, the site was sold to the " London, Dover, and Chatham Railway Company " for £60,000, and in 1868 the last vestige was removed. During the eighteenth century the Fleet Prison was the scene of every kind of atrocity and cruelty, and its horrors were brought to public notice in 1726 by the trial of the warden for murder. Many distinguished men were confined there, and Pope called it the " Haunt of the Muses," from the number of poets imprisoned within its walls. Fleet Prison was notorious for the so-called " Fleet Marriages," performed irregularly by clergymen imprisoned there for debt. These marriages were solemnized without license or banns, for fees ranging from a dram of gin to a large sum of money. They were the occasion of innumerable scandals, and were finally declared illegal by an Act of Parliament passed in 1753. It is said that on the day before this Act went into effect 217 such marriages were recorded in one register alone. See *Gretna Green.*

Fleet Captured by Cavalry. During the war between France and Holland in 1793–1795, Pichegru led the French soldiers into Amsterdam in midwinter, and was met by the citizens shouting: " Vive la République Française! " As the Dutch fleet was at that time ice-bound in the Zuyder Zee,—the harbor of Amsterdam,—Pichegru surrounded it with his cavalry and forced it to surrender. Thus was witnessed the unique spectacle in war, of a fleet of war-ships surrendering to a land force. It has been wisely suggested that if the Dutch had been as fertile in resource as Napoleon I at Austerlitz, they might easily have destroyed the ice and thus have made their capture impossible.

Fleet Marriages. See *Fleet, The.*

Fleet Street. A famous thoroughfare in London, extending from Ludgate Hill to the Strand. It derives its name from the Fleet — formerly a stream and now a sewer—which empties into the Thames near Blackfriars Bridge. Fleet Street has been celebrated for centuries for its printers,

booksellers, banking-houses, taverns, and coffee-houses, and is at present the centre of the London newspaper world. It was for years the favorite promenade of Dr. Samuel Johnson, the great lexicographer. See *Fleet, The.*

Fleshly School. A term applied to certain English poets of the nineteenth century, in allusion to the sensuous character of their writings. Among them may be mentioned Morris, Swinburne, and Rossetti.

Fleur-de-lis. The heraldic device of the Bourbons, first adopted as the symbol of the French monarchy by Louis VII (1137–1180), when setting out on the Second Crusade. According to Littré, the fleur-de-lis represents, in a very imperfect manner, three flowers of the white lily (*Lat. lilium*) joined together ; but by other authorities it is said to be a representation of the white iris which, on this supposition, is called the flower-de-luce. Givillim, in his *Display of Heraldrie* (1611), says that the device is " Three toads erect, saltant," and Nostradamus, referring to this legend in the sixteenth century, calls Frenchmen *crapauds* (*Fr. toads*). Some writers, in more recent times, have thought this emblem to be " a bee flying," because certain ornaments resembling bees were found in the tomb of Childéric I (458–481), father of Clovis, when it was opened in 1653; while still others have claimed that the fleur-de-lis is the flower of the reed placed in the hand of Christ by the soldiers when they crowned him King of the Jews. According to a tradition, the fleur-de-lis was brought by an angel from heaven to Clovis (481–511), as the result of a vow made by him that if successful in battle against the Alemanni he would embrace Christianity. It is claimed by some authorities that when Louis VII (1137–1180) chose the iris as his heraldic emblem, it received the name of the *fleur-de-Louis* (*Fr. Louis's flower*); and that this was first corrupted into *fleur-de-luce* and afterwards into *fleur-de-lis* (*Fr.* lily), although having no affinity with that flower. The royal standard was at one time thickly sown with these emblems, but Charles VI, it is further declared, reduced the number to three, to typify the Trinity.

The fleur-de-lis remained the national emblem of France until the Revolution of 1789, when it was superseded by the tricolor. Napoleon Bonaparte, when he became Emperor, introduced the bee as the Imperial emblem. Written also *fleur-de-lys*. See *Napoleonic Bee.*

Flodden Field, Battle of. A famous battle fought in Northumberland on September 9th, 1513, between 30,000 Scots commanded by their King, James IV (1488–1513), and 32,000 English under the Earl of Surrey. The Scots were routed with dreadful slaughter and suffered the most serious defeat in their history. James IV, together with the flower of his nobility and 9000 of his army, was slain, while the English loss amounted to about 4000 men. A stirring and reasonably accurate account of this battle may be found in the sixth canto of Sir Walter Scott's *Marmion.* It is said that, as a result of the battle, there "was not a worshipful Scots family that did not own a grave on Brankstone Moor."

Florentine Diamond. The fourth largest cut diamond in the world. It has a pale yellow tint, weighs 139½ carats, and forms one of the crown-jewels of the Emperor of Austria. It is valued at over $500,000. It originally belonged to Charles the Bold, Duke of Burgundy, and was picked up after the battle of Granson by a Swiss peasant and sold by him to a priest for a gulden (about forty cents). The priest sold it to Bartholomew Day, a merchant of Berne, for $1000. After passing through several hands, it finally came into the possession of Pope Julius II (1503–1513), who presented it to the Emperor of Germany.

Flour City. A name popularly given to the city of Rochester, New York, on account of its extensive mills devoted to the manufacture of flour. This title might be applied with much greater appropriateness, at the present day, to the city of Minneapolis, Minnesota.

Flower City. An appellation sometimes given to the city of Springfield, Illinois, on account of the beauty of its suburbs.

Flowery Kingdom. The words *Hwa Kwoh* — meaning "Flowery Kingdom" — are often applied to China by the inhabitants of that country. The Chinese, in their overweening national vanity, consider themselves the most cultivated and enlightened of nations and, hence, the *efflorescence* of all civilization.

Flume, The. A picturesque ravine in the Franconia Mountains, New Hampshire, 700 feet in length, through which flows a stream in a series of beautiful cascades. The walls of this miniature cañon are 70 feet in height in some places. A large granite boulder, which was long wedged between the rocks at a place where the passage is only ten feet wide, was dislodged and swept away by a spring freshet a few years ago.

Fluxions. A branch of the higher mathematics developed by Sir Isaac Newton (1642–1727) in 1665. It differs from the differential and integral calculus developed by Leibnitz (1646–1716) simply in its method of notation. Leibnitz made known his discovery in 1684, and a controversy at once ensued as to the priority of the discovery. It is now generally admitted that the work was done independently by each philosopher. Owing, however, to the greater simplicity of the notation used by Leibnitz, his system has proved more practical and has been fruitful of greater results. The finest applications of the calculus have been made by

Newton, Euler, Lagrange, and La-place.

Flying Dutchman. A phantom ship seen by sailors in tempestuous weather off the Cape of Good Hope, and considered the forerunner of ill-luck. The generally accepted tradition, as stated by Sir Walter Scott, is "that she was originally a vessel loaded with great wealth, on board of which some horrid act of murder and piracy had been committed ; that the plague broke out among the wicked crew, who had perpetrated the crime, and that they sailed in vain from port to port, offering, as the price of shelter, the whole of their ill-gotten wealth ; that they were excluded from every harbor for fear of the contagion which was devouring them ; and that, as a punishment of their crimes, the apparition of the ship still continues to haunt those seas in which the catastrophe took place."

According to another legend, the *Flying Dutchman* was a vessel whose captain met with baffling winds while trying to round the Cape of Good Hope on his return from the East Indies in 1806 ; and, although advised to put back, swore that he would round the cape in spite of God and the devil, even if he strove until the Day of Judgment. He was accordingly taken at his word, and his doomed ship still struggles in vain against head winds, and brings disaster on all that behold her. Captain Marryatt's novel, *The Phantom Ship*, is founded on this legend.

Fontainebleau, Palace of. A celebrated château at Fontainebleau, 37 miles southeast of Paris, famous for many years as the residence of the sovereigns of France. It was founded in 999 by Robert the Good (996-1031); rebuilt in 1169 by Louis VII (1137-1180) ; and enlarged by Louis XI (1461-1483) and his successors. The present structure is mainly the work of Francis I (1515-1547), although Henry IV (1589-1610) made extensive additions to it. Napoleon I (1804-1814) resided at Fontainebleau for several years, and signed his abdication there on April 4th, 1814. Pope Pius VII (1800-1823) was detained there as a prisoner for nearly two years, and there also was signed, in 1685, the revocation of the Edict of Nantes. In the *Cour du Cheval Blanc*—a courtyard in front of the palace—Napoleon bade farewell to his guard on April 20th, 1814, the eve of his departure for the island of Elba. The palace contains a fine library, choice collections of paintings and sculpture, and abounds in objects of historic interest. The forest of Fontainebleau, surrounding the château, covers an area of 65 square miles. It is beautifully kept, and abounds in superb views.

Fontenoy, Battle of. A sanguinary battle fought near Tournay, Belgium, on May 11th, 1745, between the French, commanded by Marshal Saxe, and the allies (English, Austrians, and Dutch), under the Duke of Cumberland. The allies were forced to retreat with a loss of about 7000 men. The French lost the same number.

Fool's Paradise. An expression used, at the present day, to denote the mental condition of any person that indulges in vain hopes and elusive expectations. Such a one is said to live in a " Fool's Paradise." The origin of the term is as follows: According to the Schoolmen, the Latin word *limbus* (*hem* or *border*) was used to denote a region near the abode of the blessed, but not a part of it,—a sort of borderland, where dwell " the praiseless and the blameless dead." This region, they taught, had four divisions, as follows :

(1) *The Limbus Puerorum*, or paradise for unbaptized children.

(2) *The Limbus Patrum*, or paradise for the patriarchs and good men that lived before the coming of Christ.

(3) *The Limbus Purgatorius*, or

paradise where the mildly wicked are cleansed of their sins.

(4) *The Limbus Fatuorum*, or paradise of fools, idiots, and lunatics, who not being responsible for their sins, cannot be consigned to purgatory or hell, and, not having done anything to deserve salvation, cannot be admitted into heaven.

In the modern acceptation of the term, a " Fool's Paradise " is no longer a place, but simply a mental state. See *Limbo* or *Limbus*.

Forbidden Fruit. According to the Mohammedan doctors, the forbidden fruit (called *Paradisaica*) eaten by Adam and Eve was not the apple, but the banana or Indian fig. The reason assigned for this belief is that when the eyes of the guilty pair were opened as the result of their disobedience, " they sewed fig leaves together, and made themselves aprons." See *Genesis* iii, 7.

Ford's Theatre. A theatre in Washington, D. C., famous as the scene of the assassination of President Lincoln on April 14th, 1865. After that tragic event it was closed by order of the United States government. In the following year, the building was purchased by Congress for $100,000, and converted into the *Army Medical Museum*. This collection of curiosities —said to be one of the finest in the world—was removed in August, 1887, to a structure specially erected for it, and the Ford's Theatre building was given over to the *Pension and Record Bureau of the War Department*, which still occupies it. On June 9th, 1893, the building partially collapsed,— causing considerable loss of life. See *Booth's Conspiracy*.

Forefathers' Day. The name given to the anniversary of the landing of the Pilgrim Fathers on Plymouth Rock, Massachusetts (December 22nd, 1620).

Forest City. A name given to three cities in the United States, viz.,

Cleveland, Ohio ; Portland, Maine ; and Savannah, Georgia ; in allusion to the great number of shade-trees with which their streets are adorned.

Forest Laws. The name given to a series of severe enactments of William the Conqueror (1066–1087) relating to the royal forests and the preservation of the game therein. From these Norman enactments are derived the " game-laws " of modern days. The Forest Laws, however, were not reduced to a regular code until the granting of the Forest Charter of 1217. In that charter the penalties for killing game were greatly modified. No man could be deprived of his life for killing a deer,—the penalty being restricted to a fine or to imprisonment for a year and a day.

Forlorn Hope. This expression— meaning a body of men specially chosen to lead the way in some dangerous warlike enterprise—is, according to Professor Skeat, derived from the Dutch *de verlooren hoop* (*a lost band or troop*). The French equivalent of this phrase is *enfants perdus*. The name is given on account of the extreme peril to which the leaders of such a party are necessarily exposed.

"In huntsman's language, a hound that goes before the rest of the pack, and follows the chase, is called a *forlorn*, or *forloyne* one."—Brewer's *Dictionary of Phrase and Fable*.

Formic Acid. First obtained from the red ant (*Lat. formica rufa*), whence its name. It is found in ants, in the stings of bees, wasps, and nettles, in fir-needles, and in certain animal secretions. Formic acid was first produced in the laboratory by Pelouze in 1831. Its artificial production marked an era in the history of organic chemistry.

Fornarina, La. The name given to several portraits by Raphael (1483– 1520), supposed to represent one Margarita, daughter of a turf-burner named Fornajo (whence the name), and mistress of the artist. The painting in the Barberini Palace at Rome is said to be the earliest portrait, and bears the name of Raphael on the armlet. There is another in the Pitti Palace at Florence, which is said to have served as a model for the Sistine Madonna. "La Fornarina," in the Tribune of the Uffizi Palace at Florence, is declared by Missirini to be a portrait of Vittoria Colonna, the friend of Michael Angelo, and is said to have been painted by Sebastian del Piombo, and not by Raphael, as was once supposed. Among other pictures bearing the name of "La Fornarina" may be named one — called also "Dorothea" —at Blenheim, England. It is dated 1512, and is supposed to be the work of Sebastian del Piombo.

Forrest-Macready Riot. See *Astor Place Riot.*

Fort Donelson. A fort on the Cumberland River, Tennessee, held by the Confederates during the early part of the Civil War. It was defended by about 15,000 men under General Floyd, and, after a desperate resistance, was surrendered to General Grant, with 10,000 prisoners and 40 guns, on February 16th, 1862. Of the garrison, 2000 men were killed, while many others, together with Generals Floyd, Pillow, and Forrest, escaped down the river at night. The Federal loss was about 2000 men. The fall of Fort Donelson led to the immediate evacuation of Nashville and Columbus.

Fort Duquesne. A French fort, erected in 1754 at the junction of the Alleghany and Monongahela Rivers, now Pittsburg, and named in honor of Duquesne, the Governor of Canada. There was fought, July 9th, 1755, a desperate battle between the English, commanded by General Braddock, and the French and Indians,—resulting in the utter defeat and rout of the English, with a loss of 57 officers (including General Braddock) and 710 men. The

French loss amounted to about 70 men. George Washington, then a young man of twenty-two, participated in this engagement and escaped without injury. When Fort Duquesne finally fell into the hands of the English it was rebuilt and named Fort Pitt.

Fort Lafayette. A fort, on an artificial island in the Narrows, at the entrance of New York Bay. It was commenced in 1812, and was originally called Fort Diamond ; but, in 1823, its name was changed to Fort Lafayette. During the Civil War, Fort Lafayette was used as a place of detention for political prisoners, and, on that account, became known as the "American Bastille." It is used at present as an ordnance-depot and as a place for experimental work in torpedoes.

Fort Monroe. A famous fort at Old Point Comfort, Virginia, erected to protect the navy-yard at Norfolk. It occupies an area of about eighty acres, and is surrounded by a moat from 75 to 150 feet wide, with tide-water from 8 to 15 feet deep. The shape of the fort is that of an irregular heptagon. It cost about $3,000,-000, and was commenced in 1817, after designs by General Bernard (1779–1839), a celebrated military engineer under Napoleon I, who afterwards served in the United States army (1816–1831). Fort Monroe remained in possession of the Federal government during the Civil War.

Fort Sumter. A fort in the harbor of Charleston, South Carolina, famous as the scene of the first conflict during the Civil War. After a bombardment of two days, it was surrendered on April 14th, 1861, by Major Robert Anderson, who, with his garrison, sailed northward. The fort accordingly fell into the hands of the Confederates and remained in their possession until the evacuation of Charleston, February 17th, 1865. Several unsuccessful attempts to capture Fort Sumter were made during the war. Admiral

Dupont, with a fleet of monitors, attempted to destroy the fort, April 7th, 1863, but failed, on account of obstructions in the harbor. In the summer of the same year, Admiral Dahlgren reduced Fort Sumter to a heap of ruins, but was unable to capture it. On February 18th, 1865, the United States flag was again raised over the ruins, and on April 14th, 1865 (the fourth anniversary of the surrender), the original flag that had been lowered by Major Anderson was again unfurled by him, amid general rejoicing.

Forty. The number "forty" occurs very frequently in the Bible and in Mohammedan writings, and seems to have been held in superstitious veneration by the Jews, Christians, and Moslems alike. The following interesting examples cited are from W. A. Clouston's *Group of Eastern Romances and Stories* (1889):

(1) The Flood continued 40 days.

(2) Isaac was 40 years of age when he took Rebekah to wife.

(3) Esau was 40 years of age when he wedded the two Hittite damsels.

(4) Joseph and his kinsmen fasted 40 days for their father Jacob.

(5) Moses fasted 40 days on three occasions.

(6) The Hebrew spies searched Canaan for 40 days.

(7) The Israelites wandered 40 years in the wilderness.

(8) Eli was judge of Israel for 40 years.

(9) Goliath defied the army of Saul for 40 days.

(10) David and Solomon each reigned 40 years.

(11) Elijah fasted 40 days.

(12) Nineveh was to be destroyed after 40 days.

(13) Ezekiel bore the iniquities of the house of Judah 40 days,—a day for a year.

(14) Christ was tempted by Satan in the wilderness, after having fasted 40 days.

(15) Christ remained on earth 40 days after his resurrection.

According to Christian tradition, Christ remained 40 hours in the tomb.

Forty Immortals. A name often given to the forty members of the French Academy. These members are elected for life, after personal application and the submission of their nomination to the head of the State. The "French Academy" meets twice weekly in Paris, and is "the highest authority on everything appertaining to the niceties of the French language, to grammar, rhetoric, and poetry, and the publication of the French classics." Membership is the highest literary distinction within the power of the nation to bestow. See *Academy, French.*

The following is a list of the "Forty Immortals" of the French Academy.

Year elected.	Name.
1. 1855..	Ernest Wilfred Gabriel Baptiste Legouvé.
2. 1862..	Jacques Victor Albe, Duc de Broglie.*
3. 1870..	Émile Ollivier.
4. 1874..	Alfred Jean François Mézières.
5. 1876..	Marie Louis Antoine Gaston Boissier.
6. 1877..	Victorien Sardou.
7. 1878..	Edmond Armand, Duc d'Audiffret-Pasquier.
8. 1880..	Aimé Joseph Edmond Rousse.
9. 1881..	René François Armand Sully-Prudhomme.
10. 1882..	Adolphe Louis Albert Perraud.
11. 1884..	François Edouard Joachim Coppée.
12. 1884..	Ludovic Halévy.
13. 1886..	Vallery Clément Octave Gréard.
14. 1886..	Othénin P. de Cléron, Comte d'Haussonville.
15. 1888..	Jules Arnaud Arsène Claretie.
16. 1888..	Eugène Marie Melchior, Vicomte de Vogüé.
17. 1890..	Charles Louis de Saulses de Freycinet.
18. 1891..	Louis Marie Julien Viaud (Pierre Loti).
19. 1892..	Ernest Lavisse.
20. 1893..	Vicomte Henri de Bornier.*

* In May, 1901, Charles Jean Melchior, Comte de Vogüé, and Edmond Rostand were elected members of the Academy in place of the Duc de Broglie and the Vicomte Henri de Bornier.

Year elected.	Name.
21.	1893..Paul Louis Thureau-Dangin.
22.	1893..Marie Ferdinand Brunetière.
23.	1894..Albert Sorel.
24.	1894..José Maria de Heredia.
25.	1894..Paul Bourget.
26.	1894..Henri Houssaye.
27.	1895..Jules Lemaitre.
28.	1896..Jacques Anatole Thibault (Anatole France).
29.	1896..Marquis Marie C. A. Costa de Beauregard.
30.	1896..Gaston Bruno Paulin Paris.
31.	1896..Claude-Adhémar (André Theuriet).
32.	1896..Louis Jules Albert, Comte Vandal.
33.	1897..Albert, Comte de Mun.
34.	1897..Gabriel Hanotaux.
35.	1898..Claude Jean Baptiste Guillaume.
36.	1899..Henri Léon Émile Lavedan.
37.	1899..Paul Deschanel.
38.	1900..Paul Hervieu.
39.	1900..Émile Faquet.
40.	1900..Eugène Marcellin Berthelot.

Forty Thieves. The name of one of the most celebrated of the *Arabian Nights' Entertainments*, also called the *Tale of Ali Baba*. These forty thieves, according to the story, concealed their treasure in a cave in the forest,—the door of which opened and closed only at the sound of the magic word *Sesame*. Their secret having been accidentally discovered by an old woodchopper, they were robbed of a great part of their wealth ; and, in their efforts to wreak vengeance on their despoiler, were all exterminated.

Forty-Two Articles. The name given to the original number of the *Articles of the Church of England*, set forth by the King's authority in 1553. In 1562, 7 of these were dropped—reducing the number to 35—and 4 new ones were added, making the final total 39. The four new articles are those numbered V, XII, XXIX, and XXX. See *Thirty-Nine Articles*.

Forum of Trajan. See *Trajan's Forum*.

Forum Romanum. An oblong space, originally containing 2½ acres,

situated at the base of the Capitoline and Palatine Hills in Rome. In the days of the Republic it was the centre of the public life of the city, and in course of time became occupied and surrounded by superb public edifices, the ruins of many of which still remain. Among these structures may be mentioned the eight granite columns of the Temple of Saturn, erected in 491 B.C. and restored in 44 B.C; the Temples of Concord (388 B.C.), of Castor and Pollux, of Vesta (496 B.C.), of Julius Cæsar Deified, and of Antoninus and Faustina (141 A.D.). There also may be seen the foundations of the Arch of Augustus ; the extensive ruins of the Basilica Julia; the bases of Domitian's statue and of the column of Phocas ; and the milestone, from which point all Roman roads were measured. North of the Forum Romanum stands the Arch of Septimius Severus; and south, the Arch of Titus. The Forum was traversed by the *Via Sacra*, along whose winding way the triumphal processions passed on their way to the Capitol. It was paved with large blocks of lava, most of which remain in their original position. Among the other forums in Rome may be named those of Augustus, Vespasian, and Trajan. In the centre of the last-named stands the beautiful Column of Trajan. See *Trajan's Column ; Trajan's Forum*.

Forwards, Marshal. A nickname bestowed by the Russians, during the campaign of 1813, upon Field-Marshal von Blücher (1742–1819), the famous Prussian general, on account of his energy and promptness in attack and his amazing celerity of movement.

Foscari, Two. A historical tragedy by Lord Byron (1788–1824), produced in 1820. It is based on the tragic story of Francesco Foscari (for 35 years Doge of Venice) and his son Giacopo. Verdi has written an opera with the same title, and Miss Mitford (1786–1855) has produced a tragedy entitled *The Foscari*.

Fotheringay Castle. A castle in Northamptonshire, England, famous as the place of confinement, for nearly nineteen years, of Mary, Queen of Scots, who was beheaded there by order of Queen Elizabeth in 1587. It was erected about 1400, and demolished by order of James I (1603–1625) in 1604. Richard III (1483–1485) was born at Fotheringay Castle in 1452.

Founding of Rome. According to Varro (116–28 B.C.), Rome was founded by Romulus on the 20th of April, in the year 3961 of the Julian period, 3251 years after the creation of the world, 753 years before the birth of Christ, 431 years after the Trojan War, and in the fourth year of the sixth Olympiad. Other dates given are as follows : Cato, 751 ; Polybius, 750 ; Fabius Pictor, 747; and Cincius, 728 B.C.

"Of the early history of Rome there is no reliable account, as the records were burned when the city was destroyed by the Gauls (390 B.C.), and it was five hundred years after the founding of the city (A. U. C., *anno urbis conditæ*) before the first rude attempt was made to write a continuous narrative of its origin. The names of the early monarchs are probably personifications, rather than the appellations of real persons. The word Rome itself means *border*, and probably had no relation to the fabled Romulus. The history which was accepted in later times by the Romans and has come down to us is a series of beautiful legends."—Barnes's *General History.*

Fountain of Arethusa. A famous fountain anciently existing in Ortygia, a small island in the harbor of Syracuse. Cicero speaks of it as " a fountain of fresh water, which bears the name of Arethusa, of incredible magnitude, and full of fish ; this would be wholly overflowed and covered by the waves were it not separated from the sea by a strongly built barrier of stone." According to the legend, Arethusa was a nymph of Arcadia, who, being pursued by Alpheus, an amorous water-god, prayed to Artemis for protection. She was, accordingly, changed by the goddess into a fountain that flowed under the land and sea, and

finally reappeared near Syracuse. The river-god, however, still pursued her, and mingled his stream with the fountain.

Shelley (1792–1822) produced, in 1820, an exquisite poem founded on this legend, entitled *Arethusa.* See *Ortygian Shore.*

Fountain of Castalia. See *Castalian Spring.*

Fountain of Egeria. The name given to a vaulted chamber in the valley of the Almo, about a mile from Rome, said to be the site of the ancient fountain of the nymph Egeria, with whom Numa Pompilius conferred, and from whom he received instruction in the ritual of public worship established by him at Rome. Modern discoveries, however, have located the site of the fountain and grove of Egeria near the ancient Porta Capena, within the present walls of the city. See *Egeria.*

Fountain of Trevi. A celebrated fountain in Rome, near the Quirinal. It was built by Pope Clement XII (1730–1740) in 1735, after designs by Niccolò Salvi, and consists of a mass of rocks grouped together at the base of the façade of a palace. In a niche in the centre of this façade is a statue of Neptune in his car,—drawn by horses and accompanied by Tritons. Water spouts from the conchs of the Tritons and the nostrils of the horses, and, mingling with that flowing from the crevices between the rocks, produces a brilliant effect. It is a tradition at Rome that a draught of water taken at this fountain on departing from the city insures a safe return.

Fountain of Youth. An imaginary fountain said to be endowed with the marvellous power of restoring to youth all those persons that bathed in its waters. Tradition placed it in several regions of the New World, and expeditions headed by Ponce de Leon and other Spanish navigators went in serious quest of its rejuvenating waters. By many it was supposed to be situated on the island of Bimini, one of the Bahamas.

Four Attributes. The four attributes of glorified bodies acknowledged by the Roman Catholic Church are subtility, agility, luminosity, and immortality.

Four Cardinal Virtues. The four cardinal virtues recognized in the Roman Catholic Church are fortitude, justice, prudence, and temperance. A second enumeration, consisting of the following six, has also been suggested: conscientiousness, courage, justice or justness, modesty, reverence, and sympathy.

Four-Eyed George. A nickname conferred upon General George Gordon Meade (1815–1872) during the Civil War, in allusion to the spectacles worn by him.

Four Great Heresies. A name given to four important heresies in the early Christian Church, all of which concerned the doctrine of the Incarnation. They were as follows :

(1) *The Arian Heresy.* According to the doctrines promulgated by Arius, Bishop of Alexandria, Christ was created inferior to the Father, and the Holy Ghost was created by the Son and hence was not God. This heresy was condemned by the Council of Nice, in 325 A.D.

(2) *The Apollinarian Heresy.* According to the teachings of Apollinaris the Younger, Bishop of Laodicea, the divine nature of Christ took the place of the rational human soul, and the body of Christ was a spiritualized and glorified form of humanity. These doctrines were condemned by the Council of Constantinople in 381 A.D.

(3) *The Nestorian Heresy.* Nestorius, Patriarch of Constantinople, taught that Jesus Christ was a union of two persons, one human and one divine. He denied the title of " Mother

of *God* " to the Virgin Mary, and asserted that she was the mother of the *man* Jesus only. The Council of Ephesus condemned this heresy in 431 A.D.

(4) *The Eutychian Heresy.* Eutyches, Abbot of Constantinople, taught that Christ was not man, but God only, —a view condemned by the Council of Chalcedon in 451 A.D.

Four Hundred. An expression first made use of, about the year 1889, by Ward McAllister, a New York society leader, to denote the number of persons who, in his opinion, were actually " in society " in that city. A few years later this number was reduced by him to 150. See *Upper Ten Thousand.*

Fourierism. A communistic system devised by Charles Fourier (1772– 1837), the celebrated French socialist. According to this scheme, society, throughout the world, was to be divided into groups called *phalanges*, consisting of 1800 individuals each,— a number deemed sufficient to include all human capacities, but not too great to interfere with the conveniences of a common life. Each group was to live in a spacious edifice, called a *phalanstère*, containing workshops, studios, etc., located in the centre of a highly cultivated domain, a square league in extent. These several groups or *phalanges* were to be united in a central government, not unlike that of the Swiss cantons or the United States of America. Labor was to be made attractive by a special study of the tastes and capacities of each individual and by a constant change of occupation. One language only was to be spoken. All the gains of each *phalanstère* were to be held in common, and, in distributing the profits of labor, *necessary* labor was to receive the highest reward, *useful* labor the second, and *pleasant* labor the lowest. An attempt was made to establish a society on these principles near Versailles,

France, in 1832, but the effort resulted in a complete failure. This, according to its advocates, was owing to the limited scale on which the system was tried.

Four Kings. A pack of playing-cards is sometimes called the "History of the Four Kings." In a French pack, the four kings are as follows :

(1) David, King of Israel.
(2) Alexander, King of Macedon.
(3) Cæsar, King of Rome.
(4) Charlemagne, King of France.

Four Letters. The name given to "four letters containing the name of God, and called by Rabbins 'tetragrammaton.' Thus, in Hebrew, J H V H (JeHoVaH) ; in Greek $\theta\epsilon\sigma s$; in Latin, *Deus ;* in French *Dieu ;* in Assyrian *Adat ;* Dutch, *Godt ;* German, *Gott ;* Danish, *Godh ;* Swedish, *Goth ;* Persian, *Soru ;* Arabic, *Alla ;* Cabalistic, *Agla ;* Egyptian, $\theta\omega\nu\theta$; Spanish *Dios ;* Italian, *Idio,* etc."— Brewer's *Dictionary of Phrase and Fable.*

Four Symbols. A name given to the four creeds or symbols of worship acknowledged by the Roman Catholic Church. They are as follows :

(1) *The Symbol of the Apostles,* also known as the *Apostles' Creed.*
(2) *The Symbol of Nice,* also called the *Nicene Creed.* It was formulated at the Council of Nice, 325 A.D.
(3) *The Symbol of Constantinople,* so named because it was formulated at the Council of Constantinople, 381 A.D.
(4) *The Symbol of Athanasius,* also called the *Athanasian Creed.* It is supposed to formulate the teachings of Athanasius against the Arian heresy. It did not appear until 670 A.D.

Fourth Estate. An expression which, according to Thomas Carlyle (1795–1881), is said to have been applied to the newspaper press by Edmund Burke, while speaking in the House of Commons.

"Burke said there were three estates in Parliament, but in the Reporters' Gallery yonder there sat a *fourth estate,* more important far than they all."—*Hero Worship,* Lecture V.

Fra Diavolo (*It. Brother Devil*). A sobriquet bestowed upon Michele Pezza (1760–1806), a famous Calabrian insurgent. In his early days, he is said to have been a monk under the name of Fra Angelo, and to have been expelled from the monastery for misconduct. He defended the kingdom of Naples against the French, and was made a colonel by Cardinal Buffo in 1799. While attempting to rouse the Calabrians against the French, he was taken prisoner by treachery at San Severino, and hanged in 1806, despite the efforts of the English to secure his release. Auber has composed an opera, entitled *Fra Diavolo,* based on some of the traditions that have clustered about his name.

Francesca da Rimini. A beautiful daughter of Guido da Polenta, Lord of Ravenna, who was given in marriage to Lanciotto Malatesta, Lord of Rimini, on the conclusion of the peace between the two houses in the latter part of the thirteenth century. Lanciotto, having discovered a criminal intimacy between his wife and his brother Paolo, revenged himself by putting them both to death. This story of " Francesca " is narrated in Dante's *Inferno,* and forms the plot of a tragedy by Silvio Pellico (1789–1854). George H. Boker (1823–1890) also wrote a play, and Leigh Hunt (1784–1859) a poem, on the same subject.

Franciscans. A religious order founded by St. Francis d'Assisi (1182–1226) about 1209. In England they were called *Grey Friars,* in allusion to the grey mantles worn by them. They appeared in Great Britain in 1220; and at the time of their suppression by Henry VIII (1509–1547) in 1536, they had more than 60 abbeys. The Franciscans were vowed to chastity, poverty, and obedience, and lived an austere and ascetic life. Among their number may be named Duns Scotus, Roger Bacon, St. Bonaventure, Cardinal Ximenes, Alexander of Hales, and William of Ockham. St. Francis was canonized by Pope Gregory IX. (1227–1241) in 1228. The Franciscans are still one of the largest orders in the Roman Catholic Church. See *Capuchins; Cordeliers; Dominicans.*

Franconia Notch. A picturesque mountain-pass in the Franconia Mountains, New Hampshire. Near the entrance of the Notch is the famous Profile, or Old Man of the Mountain, and near by are the lovely Profile and Echo Lakes. The entire region is grandly impressive, and is visited annually by thousands of tourists. See *Crawford Notch; Old Man of the Mountain.*

Frangipani. The name of an illustrious Roman family, whose authentic history dates from 1014 A.D., and which figured conspicuously in the quarrels of the Guelphs and Ghibellines during the twelfth and thirteenth centuries. It is said to have derived its name from its beneficent distribution of bread during a famine at Rome. The name " frangipani " is also given (1) to a kind of pudding made of broken bread ; (2) to a perfume, derived from or imitating the odor of the *Plumeria alba*, discovered by Mercutio Frangipani, the Italian botanist, in the West Indies in 1493; and (3) to a kind of pastry containing cream and almonds.

Frankenstein. A psychological romance by Mary Wollstonecraft Shelley (1797–1851). It describes a monster in human form, created by a young student of physiology out of the remains of bodies found in churchyards and dissecting-rooms. This being is endowed with animal passions and muscular strength, and has an intense craving for human companionship ; but it is soulless and, owing to its hideous aspect, is shunned by all. Realizing its deficiencies and weary-ing of its vain search after human sympathy, it inflicts dreadful retribution upon the person that brought it into existence.

Frankfort-on-the-Main. A city of central Germany, situated on the right bank of the river Main. It was founded in the fifth century after Christ, and was long famous as the place of election of the German Emperors, and as the seat of the Diet from 1816 to 1866. It became a part of Prussia in 1866, at the close of the " Seven Weeks' War " with Austria. The Peace of Frankfort, which marked the termination of the Franco-German War of 1870, was signed at Frankfort-on-the-Main by Prince Bismarck and Jules Favre on May 10th, 1871. The city is said to owe its name to Charlemagne, who led his army of *Franks* across a ford of the river at that point in order to attack the Saxons beyond the Main. It is the city generally referred to when the name Frankfort alone is used, and should be carefully distinguished from *Frankfort-on-the-Oder*, which see.

Frankfort-on-the-Oder. A town in the province of Brandenburg, Prussia, on the right bank of the Oder. It was a member of the Hanseatic League during the fourteenth and fifteenth centuries, and suffered greatly during the "Thirty Years' War " (1618–1648). At Cunnersdorf, 4½ miles east of Frankfort, Frederick the Great sustained a serious defeat at the hands of the Russians and Austrians on August 12th, 1759. Frankfort-on-the-Oder should be carefully distinguished from *Frankfort-on-the-Main*, which see.

Franklin, Search for. Sir John Franklin, an English explorer, having been placed in command of an expedition to discover the Northwest Passage —consisting of the vessels *Erebus* and *Terror*, with 134 picked officers and men—sailed from Greenhithe, England, on May 19th, 1845, and was last seen by a whaler in Baffin's Bay on July 26th of the same year. As many as fifteen expeditions were fitted out and despatched by England and America between 1848 and 1854, to rescue, or at least find traces of, the missing explorers. On May 6th, 1859, Lieutenant Hobson found at Point Victory, near Cape Victoria, a tin case containing a paper signed by Captain Fitzjames on April 25th, 1848,—certifying that the *Erebus* and *Terror* were surrounded by ice, that Sir John Franklin had died on June 11th, 1847, and that the ships had been abandoned on April 22nd of that year. Captain McClintock continued the search, and discovered skeletons and other relics. In 1878–1880, Lieutenant Schwatka of the United States Army found other remains of Sir John Franklin's men. To Franklin is entitled the honor of being the first discoverer of the Northwest Passage.

Franks. The name applied, about 240 A.D., to a confederation of German tribes dwelling on the middle and lower Rhine. During the fifth century, they invaded Gaul and founded the kingdom that afterwards became known as *France*. According to some authorities, the word " Frank " means *freeman*, while others contend that it is derived from *franca*, a kind of javelin carried by them.

Frascati's. The name of an aristocratic gaming-establishment in Paris during the early part of the last century. It was situated on the Rue de Rivoli, and was frequented by both sexes. It was suppressed by Louis Philippe (1830–1848), in accordance with a decree ordering all gaming-houses in Paris to be closed after January 1st, 1838.

Frederick the Great, Statue of. A bronze equestrian statue of Frederick II (1740–1786) of Prussia situated on the Unter den Linden, opposite the Imperial Palace, at Berlin. It was modelled by Christian Rauch (1777–1857) and erected in 1851. The statue is seventeen feet in height and stands upon a pedestal twenty-five feet high, the sides of which are adorned with life-size portrait-figures. It is said that Rauch devoted ten years to the modelling of this statue.

Frederick the Noble. An epithet bestowed upon Frederick III (1888), Emperor of Germany, not only on account of his liberal views on government, literature, and theology, but also because of the bravery and patience manifested by him while battling with a mortal disease. He reigned from March 9th, 1888, to June 15th, 1888. See *Unser Fritz*.

Fredericksburg, Battle of. A battle fought at Fredericksburg, Virginia, between the Federals commanded by General Burnside and the Confederates under General Lee. The Union forces were defeated with a loss of 12,353 killed, wounded, and missing. The total Confederate loss was 5207.

Freedmen's Bureau. A bureau organized in 1865, at the close of the Civil War, to protect and care for the newly made freedmen as well as the loyal refugees throughout the South. It was managed by a commissioner appointed by the President of the United States, and an assistant commissioner from each of the States that had been in rebellion against the Federal government, and was divided into four departments, as follows : (1) Lands, (2) Records, (3) Finance, and (4) Medical Affairs. During four years, the Freedmen's Bureau distributed over 20,000,000 rations, established many schools throughout the South, and provided 1,000,000 freedmen with medical treatment. About $400,-000 were collected as rent from the lands confiscated by the United States government and leased to the freedmen or refugees for a period of three years at an annual rental of six per cent. of their appraised value. After January 1st, 1869, the work of the Freedmen's Bureau was entirely educational. It was abolished by Act of

Congress and ceased to exist in July, 1870. The total expenditures from March, 1865, to August, 1870, were $15,359,092.27.

Free Imperial Cities. A name given to certain towns, in the old German Empire, that owed allegiance to no one except the Emperor, and were allowed to exercise sovereign rights within their own territories, as well as to sit and vote in the Imperial Diet. In 1790 they numbered 51, but in February, 1803, all the free imperial towns of Germany, except Hamburg, Lübeck, Bremen, Augsburg, Nuremberg, and Frankfort-on-the-Main, lost these privileges ; and, of those last-named, Augsburg, Nuremberg, and Frankfort ceased to be free imperial towns in 1806.

"In 1815, however, the three Hanse towns, together with Frankfort, were admitted into the German Confederation as free towns. But by the incorporation of Frankfort with Prussia in 1866 there were left but three free cities in Germany—Lübeck, Bremen, and Hamburg. . . . In 1870, each of these was made an integral part of the German empire, and by 1889 all had joined the German imperial customs union."—*Chambers's Encyclopœdia.*

Freemasonry. Freemasonry is of very ancient origin. It is variously traced to the Knights Templars, to the Crusades, to the Rosicrucians, to the patriarchs, to the pagan mysteries, to the Roman college of artificers, to Cromwell, to Prince Charles for political purposes, to Sir Christopher Wren, to masonry as a craft in the Middle Ages, to the Pharaohs, to Solomon's Temple, and even to the Tower of Babel and Noah's Ark. According to some authorities, it was introduced into England in 674 A.D., and into Scotland in 1140 A.D. The first grand lodge at York was established in 926. Freemasonry was forbidden in England in 1424. It was introduced into France in 1725, into America in 1730, into Russia in 1731, and into Germany in 1740. Grand lodges exist in all the principal countries of Europe and America, and lodges in connection with the main bodies may be found in India, China, Japan, Africa, Polynesia, Turkey, the West Indies, Syria, Newfoundland, and New Zealand. Freemasonry is under the ban of the Church in Spain, Italy, and other Catholic countries, and the membership in those lands is small and scattered. The total number of members in the grand lodges of the United States of America and Canada, in 1912, amounted to 1,522,478.

According to Edwards's *Words, Facts, and Phrases,* " freemason " is a corruption of the French *frère-maçon* (*brother-mason*).

Free-Soilers. A political party in the United States, founded in 1848—as a result of the Wilmot Proviso — to oppose the extension of slavery to the Territories. It comprised the Liberty party, the anti-slavery Whigs, and the Barnburners or anti-slavery Democrats in the State of New York. The Free-Soilers nominated Martin Van Buren for President in 1848, and John P. Hale in 1852, but without success. In 1856, they became merged in the newly formed Republican party. See *Wilmot Proviso.*

Freestone State. A name sometimes given to the State of Connecticut, on account of the extensive quarries of freestone found within its borders.

Free-Trade. The principles of free-trade were first advocated by Adam Smith (1723–1790) in his *Wealth of Nations,* published in 1776. Until 1846 the doctrine made slow progress, but after the repeal of the Corn-Laws in that year, through the instrumentality of Richard Cobden, the new views made rapid progress in public favor. A commercial treaty between England and France, based on the principles of free-trade, was signed in Paris on January 23rd, 1860, by Lord Cowley and Richard Cobden, and by the French ministers, Baroche and Rouher. It is said that British exports have tripled since 1830. Cobden predicted that all other nations would follow England's example within twenty years; but this, it is needless to say, has not happened. Free-trade has been a dominant question in American politics during the past fifteen years, and was made the main issue in the presidential elections of 1888 and 1892. At the present time, the policy of lower duties, championed by the Democratic party finds most favor in the United States.

It is said that the expression "free-trade" originated with Henry Grattan (1750–1820) in the Irish Parliament in 1779, and was used in reference to the restrictions placed on Irish trade by the British Parliament. See *Corn-Laws*.

Freischütz, Der (*Ger. The Free-Shooter*). A German marksman who, according to a legend, made a compact with the devil and received from him seven bullets — six of which were to hit without fail whatever was aimed at, while the seventh was to be directed at the will of the "Evil One." Weber, in 1821, produced an opera entitled *Der Freischütz*, which made this legend known in all civilized countries. The libretto is by Kind, and is taken from Apel's *Gespensterbuch* (*Ger. Ghostbook*).

French Academy. See *Academy, French; Forty Immortals.*

"French Language Has Only Five Words." An expression made use of by Cardinal de Retz (1614–1679) in describing the general sentiment of the French court on the accession to power of Maria Theresa, wife of Louis XIV. Referring to her efforts to conciliate all political parties and to the good feeling thereby produced, de Retz wittily said that the French language at that time contained only five words —" *The Queen is so good.*"

French Revolution. The French Revolution commenced on July 14th, 1789, with the destruction of the Bastille, and lasted until July 27th, 1794, when the National Convention deposed Robespierre and put an end to the Reign of Terror. In November of the next year the Directory was established, and remained in power until overthrown by Napoleon Bonaparte on the 18th Brumaire (November 9th, 1799).

French Revolutionary Calendar. The name given to the calendar adopted in France, by a decree of the National Convention in 1793, whereby a new era was established, commencing from the foundation of the Republic, September 22nd, 1792. According to this calendar, the year was divided into twelve months of thirty days each, —leaving the five remaining days in ordinary years, and the six in leap-years, to be devoted to festivals or holidays. These were known as complementary days. Every fourth or "Olympic" year was to have a sixth complementary day called "Revolution Day," and every period of four years was to be called a "Franciade."

The following are the names of these twelve months, and also the dates of the Gregorian Calendar within which they are included.

(1) AUTUMN.

(1) Vendémiaire.(Vintage month)..22 Sept. to 21 Oct.
(2) Brumaire.....(Fog month)......22 Oct. to 20 Nov.
(3) Frimaire.....(Sleet month)......21 Nov. to 20 Dec.

(2) WINTER.

(4) Nivôse........(Snow month).....21 Dec. to 19 Jan.
(5) Pluviôse......(Rain month).....20 Jan. to 18 Feb.
(6) Ventôse.......(Wind month).....19 Feb. to 20 Mar.

(3) SPRING.

(7) Germinal....(Sprouts' month)..21 Mar. to 19 Ap'l.
(8) Floréal.......(Flowers' month). 20 Ap'l to 19 May.
(9) Prairial......(Pasture month)..20 May to 18 June

(4) SUMMER.

(10) Messidor ....(Harvest month)..19 June to 18 July.
(11) Fervidor or
     Thermidor..(Hot month)......19 July to 17 Aug.
(12) Fructidor....(Fruit month).....18 Aug. to 16 Sept.

SANSCULOTIDES, OR FEASTS DEDICATED TO

Les Vertus.............(The Virtues)........17 Sept.
Le Génie.............(Genius)..............18 Sept.
Le Travail............(Labor)..............19 Sept.
L'Opinion ....(Opinion)............20 Sept.
Les Récompenses......(Rewards)............21 Sept.

Each month was divided into three parts of ten days each. These parts were called *decades*, from the Greek word *deka* (*ten*). The names of the days, with the exception of the last, were taken from the Latin numerals and signified *first day*, *second day*, etc. They were as follows: *Primidi, Duodi, Tridi, Quartidi, Quintidi, Sextidi, Septidi, Octidi, Nonidi*, and *Decadi*. The last day, *Decadi*, from the Greek numeral *deka* (*ten*), was the day of rest. The "French Revolutionary Calendar" continued in force until January 1st, 1806, when the use of the Gregorian Calendar was restored by order of Napoleon I.

French Roscius. A sobriquet conferred upon François Joseph Talma (1763–1826), the greatest of French tragedians. The allusion is to Roscius, the famous Roman actor.

Fresco-Painting. A method of painting with water-colors—consisting chiefly of natural earths—on freshly laid plaster. By this means the pigments unite with the moist plaster and produce a vivid effect. The word *fresco* is Italian, and means *fresh, cool.* Fresco-painting was the method employed by the great Italian masters to express their grandest conceptions of religion. It is said that when Michael Angelo was commanded to paint his *Last Judgment* in the Sistine Chapel in oils and not in fresco, as had been originally agreed upon, he declared that oil-painting was for women and indolent artists, but that fresco was for men and painters, and was allowed to have his own way.

Friar Bacon's Brazen Head. According to a legend prevalent during the Middle Ages, Roger Bacon (1214–1292) spent seven years in constructing a brazen head, which he fancied would tell him how to surround the island of Great Britain with a wall of brass. This head was to speak within a month after its completion, but no special hour was set for its so doing. Bacon, accordingly, set his servant to watch, while specially enjoining him to notify his master in case the head should speak. At the end of the first half-hour the servant heard the head exclaim, "Time is"; at the end of the second half-hour, "Time was"; and at the end of the third half-hour, "Time's past"; whereupon it fell with a loud crash and was shattered to pieces. The servant neglected to call Bacon, thinking he would not care to be disturbed for such a trifle, and thus the knowledge necessary to build the brazen wall was never acquired.

This belief in the existence of a talking brazen head was widely spread during the Middle Ages. Gerbert, a famous French Churchman, is said to have made such a head; and Albertus Magnus is alleged to have constructed an entire man of brass.

Friar Tuck. The chaplain and steward of "Robin Hood," and one of his constant companions. He is jolly, self-indulgent, and combative, and dresses in a russet habit of the Franciscan order, with a red cord girdle and red stockings. He is introduced by Sir Walter Scott into *Ivanhoe*, as the Holy Clerk of Copmanhurst; and is also mentioned by Ben Jonson in his *Sad Shepherd*.

Friedland, Battle of. A battle fought at Friedland, a town in northern Prussia, on June 14th, 1807, between the allied Russians and Prussians under Bennigsen, and the French commanded by Napoleon I. The allies were defeated with a loss of 18,000 men and 80 pieces of cannon, while the victors lost about 10,000. This battle was followed by the Peace of Tilsit, whereby Prussia lost nearly half of her dominions, and Napoleon became virtual master of Europe.

Friendly Islands. So named by Captain Cook, (1728–1779), the famous navigator, because of the friendly disposition manifested by the natives.

Friend of the People (*Fr. Ami du Peuple*). See *Ami du Peuple*.

'Frisco. A name familiarly given to the city of San Francisco, California, throughout the State.

Fritz, Alte (*Ger. Old Fritz*). An epithet affectionately bestowed upon Frederick II (1740–1786), King of Prussia, by his admiring subjects.

Frogmore Lodge. A royal residence near Windsor, England, the grounds of which contain the magnificent mausoleum of Queen Victoria (1837–1901) and the Prince Consort (1819-1861). The remains of the Prince Consort were removed to Frogmore on December 18th, 1862, and deposited in a sarcophagus, said to be composed of the largest known block of granite without a flaw.

Frog-Pond. A small body of water in Boston Common, regarded with affectionate reverence by the inhabitants of that city. Oliver Wendell Holmes humorously likens it to the "Palladium" of ancient Troy, and says that even as the Trojan gazed with rapturous pride on the image of the heaven-descended goddess, so may the dweller at the "Hub" look into the placid depths of the Frog-Pond, and there contemplate Himself,—the Native of Boston !

Fronde, Wars of the. The name given, in French history, to the civil wars that occurred in 1648-1654, during the minority of Louis XIV (1643-1715), between the parliamentary party led by Marshal Turenne and Cardinal de Retz, and the court faction headed by Cardinal Mazarin, the Prime-Minister, and supported by the Queen-Regent. These wars had their origin in the despotic policy of Mazarin, to whom the Queen-Mother had entrusted the entire management of affairs. The populace of Paris demanded the abolition of monopolies, the reduction of taxes, and the recognition of the rights of Parliament; but, these requests having been refused, the people revolted against the authorities and erected barricades in the city. Mazarin and the Queen-Regent fled, and civil war was declared. The Frondeurs (as the parliamentary party was called) soon disagreed among themselves, and Mazarin, with a force of 8000 men, returned to Paris in triumph. An agreement was thereupon reached between the court and Parliament, whereby the people were relieved from oppressive taxation, and Mazarin was allowed to retain his office. Thus ended the civil contest known as the *Old Fronde*. A second contest—called the *New Fronde*—broke out soon after, and was at bottom a struggle between Mazarin and Condé. As before, Mazarin was forced to flee from the country, but was once more recalled and reinstated in power. The *New Fronde* resulted in the complete triumph of the court party and the utter humiliation of the Parliament of Paris.

The name *Frondeurs* (*Fr. slingers*) was given to the parliamentary party, on account of an incident in a street quarrel.

Fuchsia. The fuchsia was named in honor of Leonard von Fuchs (1501–1566), the German botanist, who discovered it in Mexico in 1542.

Fugitive Slave Law. An act passed by the Congress of the United States in September, 1850. It imposed a fine of $1000, and an imprisonment of six months, on all persons harboring fugitive slaves or aiding in their escape. The law was declared unconstitutional by the Supreme Court of Wisconsin, February 3rd, 1855 ; and was repealed by Congress on June 23rd, 1864.

Fulton's Folly. An epithet derisively conferred upon the *Clermont*, the first successful vessel propelled by steam. She was built by Robert Fulton (1765–1815), and made her first trip up the Hudson River, from New York to Albany, in September, 1807. See *Clermont*.

Funeral Customs. The following list of curious funeral customs is taken from Conklin's *Vest-Pocket Argument Settler.*

"The music kept up at Irish wakes used to be for the purpose of driving away evil spirits.

The Mohammedans always, whether in their own country or one of adoption, bury without a coffin of any kind.

The primitive Russians placed a certificate of character in the dead person's hand, to be given to St. Peter at the gates of heaven.

The natives of Australia tie the hands of the corpse and pull out the finger nails—this for fear that the dead will scratch their way out of the grave and become vampires.

In India, up till within the past few years, the devoted wife ascended the funeral pyre of her dead husband, and was incinerated by the same flame that reduced her loved one to ashes.

During the time of the old Roman empire the dead bodies of all except suicides were burned. The Greeks sometimes buried their dead in the ground, but more generally cremated them in imitation of the Romans.

When a child dies in Greenland the natives bury a living dog with it—the dog to be used by the child as a guide to the other world. When questioned about their strange custom they say: 'A dog can find his way anywhere.'"

Funk, Peter. An individual employed at petty auctions to bid on articles put up for sale, and thus increase their price. Such a person is called a *Peter Funk*, probably because this name was frequently given as that of an ostensible purchaser, when the article was really bought in by the auctioneer.

Furies. The name given, in classic mythology, to the three avenging goddesses, Alecto, Megæra, and Tisiphone, —daughters of Earth or of Night,— whose function it was to punish murder, perjury, filial ingratitude, and violation of the rite of hospitality. They bore lighted torches, and presented an appalling aspect,— having serpents twined in their hair, and blood dripping from their eyes. The Furies were called by the Greeks *Erinyes* and *Eumenides.* See *Eumenides.*

Furioso (*It. Violent One*). A nick-

name conferred upon Jacopo Robusti (1512 – 1594), the famous Italian painter, in allusion to the rapidity with which he worked. See *Tintoretto.*

Fusillades. The name given to the wholesale massacres committed at Lyons, France, in 1792, after that city had surrendered to the forces of the National Convention. The guillotine proving too slow a method of execution, the unfortunate victims were brought out in crowds, and mowed down with musketry and cannon. The name of the city was changed to "Ville-Affranchie"; its principal buildings were destroyed, and 6000 of its citizens were butchered under the direction of Fouché, Couthon, and Collot d'Herbois. The Convention further decreed that a monument should be erected on the ruins, with the inscription: "Lyons made war upon liberty; Lyons is no more!" See *Noyades.*

G

Gabriel. In Christian and Jewish tradition, one of the seven archangels, —the other six being Michael, Raphael, Uriel, Chamuel, Zophiel, and Zadkiel. Gabriel is mentioned in the *Old* and *New Testaments*, generally as a minister of sympathy and hope to man. He interpreted the vision of Daniel, and as the "Messenger of the Messiah" bore the glad tidings of the "Annunciation" to the Virgin Mary. Gabriel is held in great reverence by the Mohammedans. He is called by them the "Spirit of Truth," and is said to have dictated the *Koran* to Mohammed. He is often mentioned in Milton's *Paradise Lost*, and is placed at the "eastern gate of Paradise" where, as "chief of the angelic guards," he keeps watch.

"Go, Michael, of celestial armies prince:
    And thou in military prowess next,
    Gabriel; lead forth to battle these my sons
    Invincible, . . ."
                    Paradise Lost, vi, 44-47.

Gadsden Purchase. The name given to a section of Mexican territory, south of the Gila River, purchased by treaty through the efforts of James Gadsden, while United States Minister to Mexico, and now included in Arizona and New Mexico. It contains 45,535 square miles, and cost $10,000,000. The treaty and purchase were approved December 30th, 1853.

Gadshill. A town three miles northwest of Rochester, England, commanding a splendid prospect, and noted as the scene of Falstaff's famous encounter. It was famous forty years ago as the place of residence of Charles Dickens (1812–1870). The house (an old-fashioned brick structure) was coveted by Dickens when a boy, and was purchased by him in 1856.

Galen. A name sometimes given, in disparagement, to an apothecary or medical man. The allusion is to Galen (130–200 A.D.), the famous Greek physician and author of medical treatises.

Galerie d'Apollon (*Fr. Gallery of Apollo*). A superb apartment in the Louvre at Paris, 210 feet in length. It was constructed during the reign of Henry IV (1589–1610), was burned in 1661, and rebuilt under Louis XIV (1643–1715); but was not completed until 1848–1851. It is the most beautiful hall in the palace, and one of the finest in the world, and derives its name from the central ceiling-painting by Delacroix, depicting Apollo's victory over the Python. The room contains superb furniture of the time of Louis XIV, gems, jewels, and other objects of art, as well as the most valuable collection of enamels in existence.

Galerie des Glaces (*Fr. Gallery of Mirrors*). A magnificent hall in the palace of Versailles, 240 feet long, 35 feet wide, and 42 feet high. It faces the garden with its ornamental fountains, and is lighted by 17 large windows, opposite which are as many superb mirrors in gilded niches, whence its name. The ceiling is decorated with scenes from the life of Louis XIV (1643–1715), painted by Charles Lebrun in 1679–1683. The Galerie des Glaces was used for balls, fêtes, etc., until the time of the Revolution (1789). On the occasion of the marriage of the Duc de Bourgogne, in the reign of Louis XIV, the hall was lighted with 4000 candles, and the ladies were attired in black velvet adorned with diamonds. In August, 1855, a grand ball in honor of Queen Victoria was given there by Napoleon III ; and on January 18th, 1871, King William I of Prussia was proclaimed Emperor of Germany in this same apartment.

Galileo's Lamp. A famous bronze swinging lamp in the nave of the Cathedral at Pisa, whose oscillations first suggested to Galileo (1564–1642) the theory of the pendulum.

"It was while he was still at the University, and before he was twenty years of age, that Galileo made his first discovery. When watching a lamp one day which was swinging from the roof of the cathedral, he noticed that whether it made a long or a short swing, it always took the same time to go from one side to another. To make quite sure of this he put his finger on his own pulse, and, comparing its throbs with each swing of the lamp, found that there was always the same number of beats to every swing."—Buckley's *Short History of Natural Science.*

Galileo's Tower. A building near Florence, Italy, where, according to tradition, Galileo studied with his telescope the movements of the heavenly bodies.

"At a short distance from the convent is a tower, which was used by Galileo as an observatory, and near the tower is a villa in which the illustrious philosopher resided, and where Milton is said to have visited him."—Hillard's *Six Months in Italy.*

Galleys. A system of punishment in vogue among the ancients, and introduced into France in 1564 by a decree of Charles IX (1560–1574). The "bagnes," or convict prisons, were substituted for the galleys in 1748, and the name *travaux forcés* was given them by the French government in 1798. According to the *Code Napoléon*, adopted in 1810, this term included branding, infamy, and forfeiture. Branding was abolished in 1832, and *travaux forcés* in 1852,— the imperial government substituting for them deportation to Guiana. Toulon, Rochefort, and Brest were the places of the last existing bagnes.

Gallican Church. A name often applied to the Roman Catholic Church in France, which has always manifested a certain degree of independence in respect of the Roman See.

Gallic Cæsar. An appellation bestowed upon Napoleon Bonaparte (1769–1821), in allusion to the many points of resemblance between his career of conquest and that of his great Roman prototype.

Gallows Hill. See *Witch Hill.*

Gantlet, Running the. This expression — meaning to suffer ill-treatment at many hands — is derived from a form of military punishment once in vogue, in which the culprit, stripped to the waist, was obliged to run repeatedly between two lines of soldiers facing inwards, each one of whom struck at him with a short stick or switch. The custom is said to have originated during the "Thirty Years' War," (1618–1648), and to have been adopted by the European armies as a mode of punishment. The word "gantlet," as here used, has not the meaning usually given it — that of an iron glove,—but is simply a corruption of *gantlope* or *gatlope*, and is derived from the Swedish *gatlopp*, meaning *a running down a lane.* Some etymologists, however, derive the word from the German *gassenlaufen* (*running the lane*), and others from the Dutch *gangloopen*, having the same signification.

Gaol. This word is interesting as being the only one in the English language in which the digraph *ao*

occurs. *Jail* is the preferred spelling in Great Britain and Ireland, and the usual one in the United States.

Garden City. An appellation sometimes given to Chicago, Illinois, on account of the number and beauty of its private gardens. Other authorities declare that this appellation was bestowed upon the city because of the fertile territory that surrounds it.

Garden of Europe. A name frequently given to Italy, on account of its fertile soil, delightful climate, beautiful scenery, and luxuriant vegetation.

Garden of Italy. An appellation bestowed upon the island of Sicily, on account of its charming scenery and fertile soil. The name is also given to Campania and Lombardy, for similar reasons.

Garden of the Gods. A tract of land, about 500 acres in extent, near Colorado Springs, Colorado. It abounds in weird and fantastic pinnacles and towers of red and white sandstone, some of them more than 300 feet in height. Among the chief features of interest are the Cathedral Spires, the Balanced Rock, etc. The gateway of the garden consists of two enormous masses of red sandstone, 330 feet high, sufficiently far apart for the roadway to pass between them.

Garden of the Hesperides. In classic mythology, a garden situated in the Atlantic Ocean, beyond Mount Atlas. It was famous as the dwelling-place of the sisters known as the "Hesperides," who were commissioned to guard the golden apples of Juno, given her by Terra on her marriage to Jupiter. These apples were also protected by the dragon Ladon. The "Eleventh Labor of Hercules" consisted in securing these apples of the Hesperides ; but they were afterwards restored by Minerva to their proper guardians. See *Farnese Hercules.*

Garden Sect. An appellation frequently bestowed upon the followers of Epicurus (341–270 B.C.), the Greek philosopher, who in 307 B.C. established his school at Athens in a garden which he had purchased and laid out for that purpose. See *Epicureans.*

Garfield Monument. A memorial to the late President Garfield (1831–1881), at Cleveland, Ohio, erected by voluntary subscriptions. The monument consists of a circular tower, 148 feet high and 50 feet in diameter, in the centre of which stands a heroic marble statue of Garfield. The memorial was dedicated on May 30th, 1890, and cost $134,755.

Gargantua. A famous satirical romance by François Rabelais (1495–1553). It narrates the wonderful adventures of a celebrated giant named Gargantua, who lived for several centuries and begot a son, Pantagruel, as remarkable as himself. The story is a satire on all classes of society, and has had an immense influence. It is said that the character of the hero is drawn from an old Celtic tradition. See *Gargantuan Curriculum.*

Gargantuan Curriculum. A phrase signifying an encyclopædic course of study, *i. e.,* one including all languages, sciences, and arts. The allusion is to Gargantua's advice to his son Pantagruel, as recorded in the following words : " There should not be a river in the world, no matter how small, thou dost not know the name of, with the nature and habits of all fishes, all fowls of the air, all shrubs and trees, all metals, minerals, gems, and precious stones. I would, furthermore, have thee study the Talmudists and Cabalists, and get a perfect knowledge of man, together with every language, ancient and modern, living or dead." See *Gargantua.*

Garisenda, La. One of the two leaning towers at Bologna, Italy, so named from its builders, the Garisendi

brothers. The structure is 137 feet high and leans 8 feet 2 inches from the perpendicular. It was erected about the beginning of the 12th century, and furnished Dante with a characteristic and picturesque simile for his *Divine Comedy :*

" As seems the *Garisenda,* to behold
  Beneath the leaning side, when goes a cloud
  Above it so that opposite it hangs ;
  Such did Antæus seem to me."
Divine Comedy (Longfellow's Translation).

" The leaning towers of brick, one of which furnished Dante a most picturesque and characteristic illustration, impressed me the more, as I had never happened to hear of them, and they quite startled me as I came upon them unawares. . . . These towers in Bologna are very ugly, and one half suspects them to have been over on purpose to attract that attention which, in their normal state, they could not secure."—Hillard's *Six Months in Italy.* See *Torre degli Asinelli.*

Garnet. This precious stone is supposed to derive its name from the Latin *granatus (having many seeds or grains),* and is so called from its resemblance in form and color to the seeds or grains of the pomegranate.

Garrick Club. A famous club in Garrick Street, Covent Garden, London, founded in 1831, and named in honor of David Garrick, the eminent English actor. It contains a valuable collection of portraits of famous English players, and has been since its foundation the resort of many distinguished men. The celebrated " Garrick Club Controversy," in 1858, between Thackeray and Edmund Yates, which, through Dickens's championship of the latter, led to an estrangement between himself and Thackeray, occurred there, and was the literary event of the day.

Garter, Order of the. The highest order of English knighthood, instituted by Edward III (1327–1377) on April 23rd, 1349, in honor of his past and future successes, and as a means of rewarding his successful companions-in-arms. It was called, until the reign of Edward VI (1547–1553), the *Order*

21

of *St. George*, in honor of the patron saint of England. According to the original constitution, the Knights Companions were to be 25 in number, exclusive of the sovereign, and were to assemble yearly at St. George's Chapel, Windsor, where each knight was provided with a stall. The statutes of the Order were revised in 1522 and in 1560 ; in 1805, the Order was reconstituted so as to consist of the sovereign, the Prince of Wales, 25 Knights Companions, and lineal descendants of George III. Subsequent statutes authorized the admission of foreigners of distinction.

The principal badge of the Order is a garter about an inch wide, worn on the left leg, a little below the knee. It is made of dark blue velvet bordered with gold, and has inscribed upon it the Old-French motto : *Honi soit qui mal y pense* (*Evil be to him that evil thinks*). Other insignia are the gold medallion of St. George and the Dragon ; the collar ; the star, consisting of the cross of St. George surrounded by the garter ; the mantle ; the hat ; the sword ; etc. See *Honi Soit Qui Mal Y Pense*.

Gas, Illuminating. First made and used in Cornwall, England, in 1792, and at Birmingham, in 1798. It was introduced into London in 1807, and was in general use in that city in 1820. First introduced into Dublin in 1818 ; Paris, 1819; New York, 1821; Boston, 1822 ; Philadelphia, 1835 ; Sydney, Australia, 1841 ; Moscow, 1866.

Gasconade. This word — meaning vainglorious boasting—is derived from *Gascon*, an inhabitant of Gascony, an ancient province of France, whose people were noted for their vanity and braggadocio. See *Rodomontade*.

Gaspar ("The White One"). The name of one of the three "kings," "magi," or "wise men," led to the manger at Bethlehem by the Star in the East. Tradition says that Gaspar was the one that offered frankincense,

in token of divinity. See *Balthazar ; City of the Three Kings ; Cologne, Three Kings of ; Melchior ; Star in the East.*

Gate City. A name given to Keokuk, Iowa, a city at the natural head of navigation on the Mississippi River, just below the Des Moines Rapids. These rapids are now passed by a canal eleven miles long, constructed at a cost of $5,000,000. The name "Gate City" was also applied by Jefferson Davis to the city of Atlanta, Georgia, a noted railroad centre, considered by him to be the most important city in the Southern States, strategically considered.

Gate of Tears. An epithet bestowed upon the Strait of Bab-el-Mandeb, which connects the Red Sea with the Gulf of Aden, on account of the many shipwrecks that have occurred there. The channel is only twenty miles wide, and, owing to its rocks and fierce currents, is exceedingly dangerous to small vessels in rough weather.

" Like some ill-destined bark that steers
  In silence through the *Gate of Tears*."
  Lalla Rookh (Moore).

Gate of the Lions. The name of a famous gateway in the wall of the citadel of Mycenæ, Greece, forming the principal entrance to the Acropolis of the ancient city. It was a ruin in the time of Pausanias, the traveler and geographer (who flourished in the second century after Christ), and was described by him as being the work of the Cyclopes. The blocks of stone forming this gateway are of enormous size, being fifteen feet in height and nine feet in width. The huge lintel surmounting the opening contains two lions, sculptured in bas-relief, resting on their hind feet and facing each other. Many important excavations were made at Mycenæ in 1876 by Dr. Schliemann.

Gate of the Mediterranean. A name frequently applied to the Strait of Gibraltar, which connects the Mediterranean Sea with the Atlantic Ocean. See *Gibraltar*.

Gatling Gun. A famous revolving battery gun, usually having 10 parallel barrels, and capable of firing as many as 1000 shots per minute when the crank is worked by hand, and 1500 when it is turned by electricity. It was invented by Richard Jordan Gatling, an American, in 1861–1862, and was exhibited at the Paris Exposition of 1867. It was tried in England, and declared inferior to a field-gun firing shrapnel. Of late years, it has been greatly improved. See *Mitrailleuse*.

Gautama. One of the names given to Siddartha [624 (?)–543 (?)] B.C.), a prince of Kapalivastu, central India, of the family of Sakya, and, according to a legend, the founder of Buddhism. Gautama is the name of the great " solar " race to which the family belonged. See *Buddha*.

Gavotte. The name given to a dance that originated among the *Gavots*, the people of the Pays de Gap, France.

Gehenna. The Greek name of the Valley of Hinnom, situated south and west of the city of Jerusalem. Sacrifices to Moloch, instituted by Solomon (1015–975 B.C.), were offered there, and for years after, it was the place chosen by the Jewish Kings for the practice of their idolatrous rites. When Josiah (641–609 B.C.), King of Judah, restored the national worship, he made Gehenna a place of defilement by covering it with human bones; after this, it became the cesspool of the city. Fires were kept constantly burning there to consume the bodies of malefactors, carcasses of animals, and whatever other offal had been cast out from the city. The word " Gehenna " occurs frequently in the Scriptures ; and, in the *New Testament* (Version of 1611), is always translated " hell." See *Hinnom*.

General Grant. Ulysses S. Grant (1822–1885) was the youngest President of the United States, having been 46 years of age when inaugurated on March 4th, 1869.*

Geneva Award. The name given to the amount ($15,500,000) awarded by the tribunal of five arbitrators that met at Geneva, Switzerland, in 1871–1872, to settle the claims made by the United States for injuries to American commerce during the Civil War, inflicted by the *Alabama* and other Confederate privateers built in English shipyards. See *Alabama Claims*.

Geneva Bible. A translation of the Bible, printed in 1560. It was the work of the English exiles (Knox, Coverdale, and others) that had taken refuge in Geneva, Switzerland, during the reign of Queen Mary (1553–1558). The edition was furnished with racy notes, and became, in consequence, a great favorite with the common people. Sometimes called the *Breeches Bible* because of its peculiar rendering of *Genesis* iii, 7. See *Breeches Bible*.

Geneva Catechisms. The name given to two catechisms prepared by John Calvin (1509–1564). The *Smaller Catechism* was published in French in 1536 ; and the *Larger Catechism* in the same language, in 1541 or 1542. The latter was soon after translated into various languages, and became the standard in the Reformed churches of Switzerland, France, the Low Countries, Scotland, and Hungary. A Latin edition of the *Smaller Catechism* was published in 1538, and one of the *Larger Catechism* in 1545.

Génie du Christianisme (*Fr. Genius of Christianity*). A famous work by François René (1768–1848), Vicomte de Châteaubriand, devoted to the vindication of the Roman Catholic Church. It appeared in 1802, and, according to Sainte-Beuve, " its publication was the great literary event of the first half of our century." The

* This was previous to the inauguration of Theodore Roosevelt, who became **President** at **43** years of age.

book is celebrated rather for its brilliant passages of description than for its soundness of reasoning or depth of thought ; but appearing, as it did, at the time of the reaction from the atheistic views of earlier days, it did much to reconcile France to the conciliatory policy adopted by Napoleon I toward Pope Pius VII (1800–1823).

Genista, Planta. A species of broom, belonging to the class of leguminous plants. It is said that the word " Plantagenet " is derived from this botanical name ; but what special plant is referred to is not certainly known. See *Plantagenet*.

Genre-Paintings. A term applied to paintings that depict every-day life and manners, as distinguished from those that represent landscapes, marine views, or historical subjects. Among the famous genre-painters that have flourished may be mentioned Teniers, Ostade, and Jan Steen, among the Dutch ; Watteau, Greuze, and Chardin, among the French; and Hogarth, Wilkie, and Mulready, among the English.

Gentiles. A word used by the ancient Hebrews to denote all tribes of men that had not received the true faith, and had not been circumcised. The early Christians borrowed the term from the Jews, and applied it to all persons that were neither Jews nor Christians. In the writings of St. Paul, the Gentiles are generally called Greeks. The word " Gentiles " is also used by the Mormons to denote all persons that are not of their faith.

Geoffrey Crayon. A *nom-de-plume* assumed by Washington Irving (1783–1859), the celebrated American author.

George Eliot. A *nom-de-plume* assumed by Mary Ann Evans Lewes Cross (1819–1880), the distinguished English novelist.

George Sand. A pseudonym adopted by Armandine Lucile Aurore Dupin (1804–1876), " Baronne " Dudevant, the famous French novelist.

Georges's Conspiracy. The name given to a famous conspiracy to assassinate Napoleon Bonaparte while First Consul, and restore the Bourbons, in the person of Louis XVIII, to the throne of France. It was discovered in February, 1804, and the prime movers, Georges Cadoudal (commonly known as " Georges "), Pichegru, and Moreau, were immediately arrested. The conspirators were tried in June, when seventeen were condemned to death and many others to imprisonment. Pichegru was found strangled in prison ; Cadoudal, with eleven others, was guillotined on June 25th ; and Moreau was exiled and went to America. He returned to Europe in 1813, and fell at the battle of Dresden, while assisting the allies in the war against Napoleon. Sometimes called *Pichegru's Conspiracy*.

Georgia. This State of the American Union—one of the original thirteen—received its name in honor of George II (1727–1760) of England. It was settled by James Oglethorpe in 1733, and was designed as a refuge for insolvent persons and persecuted Protestants of Germany.

German Empire. The present German Empire comprises 25 states and a Reichsland (Alsace-Lorraine). It has an area of 211,108 square miles, and a population of about 57,000,000. It was established on January 1st, 1871, by the union of Bavaria, Würtemberg, Baden, Hesse-Darmstadt, and Saxony with the North German Confederation, —consisting of Prussia and the states north of the Main. According to the Constitution of April 16th, 1871, the Empire is a confederation, under the presidentship of the King of Prussia, who bears the hereditary title of Emperor of Germany. The first Chancellor of the Empire, Prince Otto von Bismarck, was appointed May, 1871, and resigned March 18th, 1890. William I (1861–1888), King of Prussia, was proclaimed Emperor of Germany at Versailles on January 18th, 1871.

Germanic Confederation. The name given to a league of the states of Germany — including Austria and Prussia — established in place of Napoleon's "Confederation of the Rhine." It was formed June 8th, 1815, and held its first Diet at Frankfort, November 16th, 1816. The Confederation was declared dissolved by Prussia, June 14th, 1866 ; but continued its sittings, until renounced by Austria at the Peace of Nikolsburg, July 26th, 1866. The last meeting of the Diet was held August 24th, 1866. On August 18th, 1866, the " North German Confederation"—consisting of the North German states, under the leadership of Prussia — was established, and continued to exist until the re-establishment of the German Empire, January 1st, 1871. See *Confederation of the Rhine.*

German Plato. An epithet conferred upon Friedrich Heinrich Jacobi (1743–1819), on account of the high religious tone of his metaphysical writings.

Germ Theory of Disease. The name applied to the theory that most, if not all, infectious or zymotic diseases are caused by the introduction into the organism of living germs of ferments, or ferments already developed, by means of which are set up processes of fermentation injurious to bodily health. Similar views were held during the Middle Ages, and were promulgated in the 16th century; but the germs themselves were not discovered until the 19th century, when they were first made known by Professors Tyndall, Lister, and others. Professor Huxley, at the meeting of the " British Association " on September 14th, 1870, announced his belief in the germ theory of disease. In 1879 *et seq.*, Dr. Koch identified the germs of cholera, consumption, and cattle-diseases. Louis Pasteur had marked suc-

cess in treating diseases by inoculation. The influenza bacillus was discovered by Richard Pfeiffer in 1892.

Gerrymander. A word, meaning to divide a State into districts for the choice of representatives in such a way as to give the political party in power an advantage over the other, even though the latter may have a majority of votes in the State. The term originated in Massachusetts in 1812, when the Democratic-Republicans so arranged the senatorial districts as to control most of them and thus secure the election of a United States senator. The word is derived from Elbridge Gerry, who was Governor of the State at the time and approved of the apportionment. It is said that one of the senatorial districts was so distorted in shape as to resemble a salamander ; whereupon the Federalists called it a " gerrymander," from the Governor's name.

Gerusalemme Liberata (*It. Jerusalem Delivered*). A celebrated Italian epic poem by Torquato Tasso (1544–1595), in 24 books. It narrates the exploits and experiences of the Crusaders during the First Crusade, and the triumphal entry of the Christian army into Jerusalem. Although the *nominal* hero of the poem is Godfrey of Bouillon, yet it is to the lives and loves of the fictitious characters introduced that the poem owes its charm and vitality.

Gesta Romanorum (*Lat. Deeds of the Romans*). The title of a collection of short stories, derived from Oriental and classical sources, and written in the Latin tongue. Their authorship is unknown, but they are thought to have been produced about the beginning of the 14th century. Pierre Bercheur (better known by his Latin name of *Petrus Berchorius*), a Benedictine prior, and Helinandus, a monk, have been mentioned as possible compilers or authors of these tales ; but their claims may be safely disregarded.

Boccaccio, Shakespeare, and many of the early English poets borrowed extensively from the *Gesta Romanorum*. In its modern form, the work consists of 181 stories,—first printed in 1473.

Gestas. See *Desmas ; Thieves, Two.*

Gethsemane. A garden near Jerusalem, located, according to early tradition, at the foot of the Mount of Olives beyond the brook Kidron, and famous as the scene of Christ's agony on the night before the crucifixion. The exact spot is not known, but a small square enclosure of about 200 feet, containing a few old olive-trees and surrounded by a high wall, is pointed out to travelers as the site of the " garden."

Getting into a Hole. This proverbial expression is said to arise from an accident that sometimes occurs in playing golf, in which game, if the player's ball " gets into a hole," he is almost certain to lose the game.

Gettysburg, Battle of. The most famous battle of the American Civil War, and the turning-point of the Rebellion. It was fought on July 1st, 2nd, and 3rd, 1863, between 80,000 Federal troops, under General Meade, and an equal number of Confederates, commanded by General Lee, and resulted in the complete defeat of the latter, who, however, were suffered to retreat unmolested. The Federal losses were 23,190 men, 7000 of whom were missing ; while the Confederates lost about 36,000 men, nearly 14,000 of whom were taken prisoners. Lee's entire loss during the campaign amounted to 60,000 men. It is claimed that prompt action on the part of the Federals, after the battle, would have resulted in a complete dispersion of the Confederates. On November 19th, 1863, part of the field was converted into a national cemetery for the soldiers that had fallen in the struggle. See *Cemetery Hill ; Little Round Top ; Seminary Ridge.*

Ghauts.

(1) The name given to two converging mountain-ranges of Hindustan, which run parallel with the eastern and western coasts respectively, and meet near Cape Comorin, at the southern extremity of the peninsula. The Eastern Ghauts have an average elevation of 1500 feet, and lie at a distance of from 50 to 150 miles from the coast. The Western Ghauts attain an average height of from 3000 to 7000 feet,—the peak of Dodabetta being 8760 feet above the sea-level. They are famed for the beauty of their scenery, and contain extensive forests, which furnish the finest timber.

(2) The name " Ghauts " is also given to the long flights of steps—used as bathing-stairs or as landing-places —that line the river-banks of many of the cities and towns of central India. These flights of steps are adorned, either at the base or at the top, with temples and shrines, and furnish a place of resort not only for the idle and devout, but also for those engaged in the transaction of business. Benares, Hardwar, and Maheswar are celebrated for these landing-places. Cawnpore and Sadullapur possess " burning ghauts,"—used for cremation. The word " Ghauts " is also written *Ghâts.*

Ghetto. The Jews' quarter, in an Italian town or city, to which they were at one time confined. The " Ghetto " of Rome was established by Pope Paul IV (1555-1559) in 1556, and existed until 1885, when it was removed to make way for the new embankment of the Tiber. The Jews were at one time closely confined to that section of the city, and were not allowed outside its limits, unless distinguished from the Christians by wearing, the men a yellow hat, and the women a veil of the same color. The streets in this section were narrow and filthy ; yet, strange to say, the " Ghetto " was one of the most healthful portions ot the city. It was enclosed by walls, containing gates that were locked every night.

Ghibellines. See *Guelphs and Ghibellines.*

Giants, Famous.

(1) *Og, King of Bashan* (1451 B.C.). Mentioned in *Deuteronomy* iii, 11. His bedstead was nine cubits long and four cubits wide.

(2) *Goliath of Gath.* His height was " 6 cubits and a span."

(3) *Four Sons of Goliath,* killed about 1018 B.C.

(4) *Emperor Maximin* (235 A.D.); 8½ feet high, and of vast bulk. According to some, he was between 7 and 8 feet: according to others, over 8 feet.

(5) *Gabara,* brought from Arabia in the days of Claudius (41–54 A.D.), the Roman Emperor. Said by Pliny to have been 9 feet 9 inches tall.

(6) *John Middleton,* called the " Child of Hale " (Lancashire); 9 feet 3 inches tall. His hand from the carpus to the tip of the middle finger measured 17 inches, and the palm measured 8½ inches in breadth.

(7) *Patrick Cotter,* surnamed the " Irish Giant," was born in 1761, and measured 8 feet 7 inches in height : hand, to the tip of the middle finger, measured 12 inches : shoe, 17 inches long.

(8) *Charles Byrne,* called O'Brien; 8 feet 4 inches tall. Died in 1783 ; skeleton in Museum of Royal College of Surgeons.

(9) *Big Sam,* porter of Prince of Wales (George IV) at Carlton Palace ; nearly 8 feet tall.

(10) *M. Brice,* born among the Vosges ; 7 feet 6 inches tall.

(11) *Robert Hales,* surnamed the " Norfolk Giant." Was 7 feet 6 inches tall, and weighed 452 lbs.

(12) *Chang-Woo-Gow,* a Chinese giant, 8 feet tall. Exhibited at Westminster Aquarium, London, in 1880.

(13) *Martin Van Buren Bates* of Kentucky, 7 feet tall.

(14) *Ann Haven Swann* of Nova Scotia, 7 feet tall. After exhibiting with Bates in London in 1871, married him.

(15) *Marian,* surnamed the " Amazon Queen," born in 1866. She was 8 feet 2 inches tall. Exhibited in London in 1882.

(16) *Joseph Winkelmaier,* a native of Austria, 8 feet 9 inches tall. Exhibited in London in 1887.

(17) *Elizabeth Lyska,* a Russian, aged 12, exhibited in London in 1889, and again in 1893. Height 6 feet 8 inches.

See *Dwarfs, Famous.*

Giants, Battle of the. The name given to a battle fought at Marignano (now Malegnano), near Milan, on September 13th–14th, 1515, between the allied French and Venetian forces under Francis I of France, and the Italians and Swiss, commanded by the Duke of Milan. The battle was hotly contested, and resulted in a victory for Francis. The total number of slain is said to have exceeded 20,000 men. Trivulzio, who had been present at eighteen pitched battles, called them all child's play as compared with this " battle of the giants."

Giants' Causeway. A famous promontory of columnar basalt, projecting from the northern coast of Antrim, Ireland, and extending into the North Channel. The uncovered portion comprises several acres, and recedes from the water to a height of about 50 feet. The surface is uneven, and is formed of the tops of vertical, polygonal columns, about 40,000 in number, most of which are hexagonal in shape, although pentagonal, heptagonal, octagonal, and nonagonal ones occur. These columns vary from 15 to 20 inches in diameter, and are divided into joints or sections,— the concave surface at the end of one section fitting perfectly upon the convex surface of the next section. The entire plateau, covering many square miles and extending from 300 to 500 feet in depth, is composed of basalt which, in cooling at the surface, has crystallized into these polygonal columns. This marvellous natural formation is called the "Giants' Causeway," because of the ancient legend that it was the beginning of a mole or causeway to be constructed by giants across the channel to Scotland. See *Fingal's Cave.*

Giants' Staircase. A noted staircase in the Doge's Palace, Venice, so named from the colossal statues of Mars and Neptune, standing at the top. It was at the summit of this staircase that the Doges of Venice were crowned, and there also that the Doge, Marino Faliero, was beheaded on April 16th, 1355. See *Doge's Palace ; Lion's Mouth.*

Gibraltar. A rocky promontory on the southwest coast of Spain, jutting out into the Mediterranean Sea and rising to an altitude of 1439 feet. It is about three miles long and three-fourths of a mile broad, and is connected with the mainland by a low, sandy isthmus. Gibraltar has been in the possession of the English since 1704, and is considered impregnable, —vast sums of money having been expended in adding to its natural defenses, particularly on the western side. It is regarded as the " key of the Mediterranean," and is, strategically considered, the most celebrated fortress in the world, although, since the days of steamships and long-range guns its military importance has materially declined. In 1720, 1727, and 1779, it successfully resisted severe attacks by the French and Spaniards. The regular garrison, in time of peace, numbers about 7000 men. The cost of maintaining the garrison and fortifications averages £330,000 annually. The name " Gibraltar " is a corruption of *Jebel al Tarik* (*Ar. The Mount of Tarik*). See *Pillars of Hercules.*

Gibraltar of America. A term frequently applied to the city of Quebec,

in allusion to its wellnigh impregnable position and strong means of defense, both natural and artificial.

Giessbach Falls. A series of beautiful cascades—seven in number—near Lake Brienz, Switzerland, about thirty miles southeast of Berne. They are much visited by tourists, and, when illuminated at night with lights of various colors, present an enchanting appearance. Their total height is more than 1100 feet. See *Staubbach Fall.*

Gig. The name of this vehicle is said to be derived from the French *gigue* (*jig*), and is applied to it on account of its rocking motion.

Gil Blas. A celebrated romance, in four volumes, by Alain-René Le Sage (1668–1747). The first two volumes appeared in 1715, the third in 1724, and the fourth in 1735. Although Le Sage has been accused of lack of originality by Voltaire and others, and has even been declared to be nothing more than a translator, yet as a novelist he stands in the front rank in the estimation of the majority of readers of all nations.

"This novel, which has perhaps been a more universal favorite than any other, has enjoyed uninterrupted popularity for more than 150 years."—Wheeler's *Who Wrote It?*

Gilly-flower. A corruption of July-flower.

Gilpin, John. A London linen-draper and " train-band captain," whose amusing adventures are related by Cowper (1731–1800) in his ballad entitled *The Diverting History of John Gilpin, Showing how he Went further than he Intended, and Came safe Home again.* The original of the poem is said to have been a Mr. Bayer or Beyer, a famous linen-draper, whose establishment was on Paternoster Row, where it joins Cheapside. The story was related to Cowper by Lady Austen (who remembered it from her childhood), to divert the poet from his melancholy. The poem first appeared in 1782, and was afterwards included in the second volume of Cowper's works.

Gin. This word is a contraction of *Geneva*, the city in Switzerland where this spirituous liquor was first distilled.

Ginevra.

(1) The title of a metrical tale by Samuel Rogers (1763-1855). It narrates the tragic fate of a young Italian bride, who, while in a frolicsome mood, secretes herself, on her wedding-day, in an old oaken chest, which closes with a spring-lock and buries her alive. This same tradition has been made the subject of a ballad by T. Haynes Bayley, entitled *The Mistletoe Bough;* and forms also one of the narratives given by Collet, in his *Causes Célèbres*.

(2) A lady in Ariosto's *Orlando Furioso*, who is falsely accused by the duke and is condemned to die, unless some valiant knight does battle for her within a month. Rinaldo, being assured of Ginevra's innocence, slays the duke in combat, and restores the lady to Ariodantes, her lover.

Giotto's Campanile. The name given to the famous campanile or bell-tower of the Duomo at Florence, erected about the middle of the fourteenth century by Giotto di Bondone (1276-1336), but not completed until after his death. It is 275 feet high, and consists of four stories,—the first and fourth of which are the tallest. This structure is in the Italo-Gothic style, and is entirely veneered with marble. Giotto's original design called for the erection, upon the summit, of a spire 90 feet high ; and the four piers on which this superstructure was to rest may be seen at the present day.

Giralda, La. The campanile of the cathedral at Seville, Spain. It is called La Giralda (*Span. The Weather-cock*), from the bronze figure of Faith on the summit, which turns with the wind, although weighing a ton and a quarter. The tower is 275 feet high,

and consists of two sections,—the lower of which (185 feet high) was built as a minaret by Abu Yusuf Yakub in 1196, while the upper was added in 1568.

Girandola. The name given to the superb fireworks formerly displayed from the Castle of St. Angelo at Rome, at Easter and on the Festival of St. Peter. The exhibition, which as a pyrotechnic display surpassed all others in the world and was rivalled only by the illumination of St. Peter's, was afterwards made on the Pincian Hill.

Charles Dickens, in his *Pictures from Italy*, speaking of this display, says : "The concluding burst—the *Girandola*—was like the blowing up into the air of the whole massive fortress without smoke or dust."

Girard College. A superb structure in Philadelphia, erected in 1833-1847, and devoted to the purposes of education. It is constructed of white marble, in the Corinthian style of architecture, and represents a Greek temple. Girard College was founded by Stephen Girard (1759-1831), a Philadelphia merchant, who left $2,-000,000 and forty-five acres of land for an asylum " for poor white male children without fathers, and between six and ten years of age." By the terms of Girard's will, no minister of any sect is permitted to serve on the board of trustees or even to enter the college premises. In 1900 there were 67 instructors, 1731 pupils, and a library of 17,000 volumes. The course of study requires eight years for its completion.

Girondists. A party of moderate republicans in the National Assembly and National Convention, during the French Revolution, so called because their earliest leaders—Vergniaud, Guadet, Gensonné, Grangeneuve, and Ducos—came from the department of *La Gironde*. Their opposition to the " September Massacres " and to the execution of the King drew upon them the hatred of the Jacobin or Mountain party ; and on July 2nd, 1793, the

Girondists, after an ineffectual attempt to impeach Marat, were overthrown and 31 of their deputies were arrested. On October 30th, 21 of their number were tried and sentenced to death, and of these, 20 perished by the guillotine on the following day, Valazé, one of their number, having stabbed himself on hearing his sentence pronounced. See *Jacobins* (2).

Girton College. The most famous college for women in England. It was founded at Hitchin in 1869, removed to Cambridge in connection with the " Association for Women's Lectures " in Cambridge, and incorporated in 1873. It numbers about 115 students, and has about 30 lecturers,—the majority being connected with Cambridge University. The course of instruction, to which students are admitted after an examination, includes " divinity, modern languages, classics, mathematics, moral science, natural science, history, vocal music," and extends over three years. The college fees are £105 per annum. Students may attend " University " lectures in Cambridge, in addition to those provided by the college. Newnham College, in connection with Girton, was founded in 1871–1875. See *Newnham College.*

Gis. This, according to Brewer's *Dictionary of Phrase and Fable*, is a corruption of " Jesus " or J. H. S. In *Hamlet*, iv, 5, Ophelia says:
" By *Gis*, and by Saint Charity,
    Alack, and fie for shame."

Gitche Manito. The name given by some tribes of North American Indians to the Spirit of Good, or Ruler of Mankind. He is symbolized as an egg. See *Mitche Manito.*
" *Gitche Manito* the Mighty,
He, the Master of Life, was painted
As an egg, with points projecting
To the four winds of the heavens.
Everywhere is the Great Spirit,
Was the meaning of this symbol."
        Longfellow's *Hiawatha.*

Gladiators' War. A formidable insurrection in Italy, which broke out in 73 B.C., and lasted for two years. It was headed by Spartacus, a renowned Thracian, who had served in the Roman army, but, having deserted and been subsequently captured, was reduced to slavery and made a gladiator. At the head of a small band he escaped from the training-school at Capua, and took refuge in the crater of Vesuvius. There he was joined by malcontents of every class, and was soon in command of a powerful army, with which he twice defeated the Roman forces, and ravaged the provinces of southern Italy. He was finally slain in battle by Crassus (71 B.C.), and his army put to flight. A body of 5000, who were trying to escape into Gaul, were intercepted by Pompey on his return from Spain, and cut to pieces. It is said that Crassus hanged 6000 of the captives on the highway between Rome and Capua. Called also the *Servile War.*

Gladstone's Umbrella. An expression frequently heard during the English political campaign of 1885, and used to personify Gladstone's marvellous power in so harmonizing the conflicting elements composing the Liberal party as to present a united front to the enemy in the impending contest.

" Is *Mr. Gladstone's umbrella* worn out beyond repair? Will it no longer protect the various wings of the Liberal party from the downpour of disintegration which must inevitably fall on a collection of such incongruous elements as whigs, radicals, and semi-socialists?"—*Daily Paper.*

Glen, The. A picturesque locality in the White Mountains, New Hampshire, situated at the foot of Mount Washington, and commanding a superb view of the Presidential range. The carriage-road to the summit of Mount Washington begins at this point which, before the erection of the inclined railway, was the rendezvous of all tourists that made the ascent.

Globe Theatre. A noted playhouse near Bankside, London, erected in

1594. It was built in the shape of a horseshoe, and was partly covered with thatch. Shakespeare's plays were produced there about that time,—the great dramatist himself taking part in some of them. The building was destroyed by fire on June 29th, 1613, during a performance of the play of *Henry VIII*, and although a large audience was present at the time, all escaped without injury. A new structure was erected in the following year, but was removed on April 15th, 1644.

Ben Jonson says of the Globe Theatre that it was the " glory of the Bank, and the fort of the whole parish." In old prints it is represented as a tower-like building, having long, narrow windows, and surmounted by a turret.

Gloria in Excelsis (*Lat. Glory [be to God] in the Highest*). One of the most ancient doxologies in the Christian Church, — often spoken of as the " Angelic Hymn." It is called the *Doxologia Major* (*Greater Doxology*), to distinguish it from the *Gloria Patri*, also known as the *Doxologia Minor* (*Minor Doxology*). The *Greater Doxology* is of Eastern origin, and is probably more than 1500 years old. The Church of England has used it in its liturgy for over 1200 years.

Glorious First of June, Battle of. A naval battle fought off the island of Ushant on June 1st, 1794, between the English fleet of 25 ships-of-the-line, commanded by Lord Howe, and the French fleet of 26. The contest resulted in a complete victory for the English, who captured 7 of the enemy's vessels, and dismasted 10 more.

Glorious Revolution. The name given in England to the bloodless Revolution of 1688–1689, whereby James II was deposed and William and Mary chosen joint-sovereigns in his stead. This date marks the end of despotic government in England. William and Mary, on their accession to the throne, agreed to a " Bill of Rights," which guaranteed to the people all that they had earnestly striven to obtain during the previous 85 years ; and thus the government of Great Britain was firmly established as a constitutional monarchy. See *Bill of Rights*.

Glyptothek. A famous gallery in Munich, Bavaria, containing a superb collection of ancient and modern sculpture. The building was completed in 1830, and forms a hollow square,— lighted entirely from the inner side. There may be seen the celebrated marbles, brought from the temple of Minerva (Pallas Athene) on the island of Ægina, and restored by Thorwaldsen. The word is derived from the Greek γλυπτός (*carved*), θήκη (*collection*). See *Æginetan Marbles ; Pinakothek*.

Gnostics. A group of ancient heretics, famous from the rise of Christianity. They did not constitute a distinct sect, but were more nearly a complication of many sects. The Gnostics claimed to interpret the teachings of Christianity in a philosophic manner ; and in so doing, combined Oriental theology and Greek philosophy with its doctrines. The principal tenets of the Gnostics were as follows :

(1) Belief in one Eternal God.

(2) Countless generations of *æons* emanating from God, and representative of the Divine attributes.

(3) The essential evil of material substance.

(4) The existence of a *demiurge* (*inferior God*) by whom the world was governed. He was the *Old Testament* God, and hostile to the Supreme Being.

These tenets were revived in Spain by the " Priscillianists," in the fourth century. See *Adamites ; Agnosticism*.

Gobelin Tapestry. A kind of tapestry named after Jean Gobelin, a wooldyer, who lived in Paris during the reign of Francis I (1515–1547), and discovered the famous Gobelin dyes. In the following century, the family added a tapestry department to their dyeing establishment, and by skilful work amassed a fortune. The factory was purchased by Louis XIV (1643–1715) in 1662, and converted into an establishment for the manufacture of tapestry for the adornment of palaces, under the title of "The Royal Hotel of the Gobelins." Colbert, the famous minister, was placed in charge, and the artists Lebrun and Vouet were employed as designers. After 1697, the manufacture of tapestries alone was continued. The factory was closed during the Revolution and until the restoration of the Bourbons; but since that time it has been in active operation, although at present much reduced in size. The present building is situated on the Avenue des Gobelins, Paris; it was severely damaged by the Communists in 1871,—70 pieces of valuable tapestry having been destroyed. Highly wrought pieces of Gobelin tapestry cost as much as $30,-000, and require five or ten years for their completion,—a piece six inches square being considered an average day's work.

Goddess of Reason. The name given by the French Revolutionists to a personification of those intellectual attributes that distinguish man from the lower orders of animal life,—raised to the rank of a goddess and worshipped in place of the God of Christianity. On November 10th, 1793, the Cathedral of Notre Dame was converted into a "Temple of Reason," and the statue of the Virgin Mary was replaced by one of Liberty. On a mound, thrown up in the choir, was erected a "Temple of Philosophy," adorned with busts of Voltaire, Rousseau, and others, and within it was enthroned the Goddess of Reason (represented by Maillard, the ballet-dancer), who received the homage of her worshippers. She was clothed in white and adorned with an azure mantle, while her glowing hair was surmounted by the cap of liberty. Damsels clad in white and carrying torches surrounded the temple and ministered to her, or marched in

solemn procession to the music of the patriotic hymns of the National Guard. The cathedral was closed on May 12th 1794, and was reopened in 1802, by Napoleon Bonaparte, as a place of Christian worship. See *Notre Dame.*

God of All Philosophers. A title conferred by Cicero upon Plato (429–347 B.C.), the famous Greek philosopher.

God of the Gypsies. The name given by these wandering tribes to the Supreme Being is Baro Dével, whose son, Alako, will eventually restore them to their native land. Alako is represented as holding a pen in his left hand, and a sword in his right. The word "Dével" means *sky,* and suggests a pantheistic conception of the universe. So far as the gypsies of the present day possess a religion, it is generally that of the land of their adoption. They are Mohammedans in Mohammedan countries, Christians in Christian lands, and Protestants or Catholics, according to the prevailing belief. See *Gypsies.*

God's Acre. An ancient Saxon phrase, meaning a churchyard or cemetery.

" I like that ancient Saxon phrase, which calls
　　The burial-ground *God's Acre!* It is just;
　It consecrates each grave within its walls,
　　And breathes a benison o'er the sleeping dust."
　　　　　　　God's Acre (Longfellow).

Gods, Among the. A phrase used to denote the topmost gallery of a theatre, on account of its proximity to the ceiling, which is frequently painted to represent the sky. This expression is said to have originated at the Drury Lane Theatre, London.

God Save the King. Although the question of the origin of the English National Anthem has been much debated and is still in doubt, the words and music are generally supposed to have been written about 1740 by Henry Carey (1696–1743), in honor of a birth-day of George II (1727–1760). It is also claimed that the *melody* was com-posed by Dr. John Bull in 1606, during the reign of James I (1603–1625), but that it was not used at that time as a national air. Handel (1685–1759) translated and adapted the anthem *God Save the King* for the use of the House of Hanover.

God Tempers the Wind to the Shorn Lamb. This proverbial ex-pression, which is frequently credited to the Bible, was first used in its present form by Laurence Sterne in his *Senti-mental Journey* (1768). The phrase, however, is not original with him, but is a paraphrase of the French proverb, " Dieu mesure le froid à la brebis tondue," or " À brebis près tondue Dieu lui mesure le vent."

Gog and Magog. The name given to two colossal wooden figures, about fourteen feet high, in the Guildhall, London, erected in 1708 to replace two that had been burned in 1666, during the " Great Fire." The original figures were made of pasteboard and wickerwork, and were carried in pro-cession on grand city occasions. Their earlier names were Corinæus and Gogmagog ; but at some time in their history they apparently agreed to drop the high-sounding name of Corinæus, and divide that of Gogmagog between them. According to Mother Shipton's prophecy, when Gog and Magog fall, London will fall also. Gog and Magog are also the names of giants mentioned several times in the Scriptures. See *Guildhall ; Mother Shipton ; Tutelary Deities of London.*

Gold Coast. A portion of Guinea, on the west coast of Africa, where gold is found. It is bounded on the east by the Slave Coast and on the west by the Ivory Coast, and has a coast-line of 350 miles. The popula-tion is about 1,500,000, and the area, including the protected States, 29,400

square miles. See *Ivory Coast ; Slave Coast.*

Golden Age. " One of the four ages into which the life of the human race was divided ; the simple and patriarchal reign of Saturn, a period of perpetual spring, when the land flowed with milk and honey, and all things needed to make life happy were produced spontaneously ; when beasts of prey lived peaceably with other animals, and man had not yet, by indulging his vices and passions, lapsed from a state of innocence. It was succeeded by the ages of silver, brass, and iron; but a belief prevailed, that when the stars and planets had performed a complete revolution around the heavens, the Golden Age would return."—Wheeler's *Dictionary of the Noted Names of Fiction.* See *Ages, Mythologic ; Saturnian Days.*

Golden Book. The name given to the Register of the Venetian nobility during the Republic. All persons whose names were enrolled in it, if twenty-five years of age, were mem-bers of the " Grand Council." When Venice fell before the conquering arms of Napoleon Bonaparte in 1797, the *Golden Book* was burned at the foot of a Tree of Liberty.

Golden Bull.
(1) An edict issued by the Emperor Charles IV (1347–1378) of Germany, at Nuremberg in the year 1356, mainly for the purpose of establishing the laws regulating the imperial elections. It is preserved at Frankfort-on-the-Main.
(2) A constitutional edict promul-gated in 1222 by Andrew II (1205–1235), King of Hungary, whereby the government was transformed from an absolute to an aristocratic monarchy. It was regarded as a national constitu-tion, and remained in force until the dissolution of the German Empire in 1806. Like *Magna Charta*, it was wrung from the unwilling King by his nobles, and fixed their rights and privileges.

A " Golden Bull " is so called from the golden capsule that enclosed the *bulla* or seal attached to the document.

Golden Cave. The fertile land of Scobellum was, according to the legend, peopled by inhabitants that surpassed all the other nations of the world in cruelty, pride, luxury, lying, and drunkenness. As a punishment for their wickedness, the gods transformed all the people into beasts, and promised to restore them to human form when the fire of the Golden Cave should be quenched. This cave contained a cistern, guarded by two giants and two centaurs, and its waters were considered of great service in quenching the fire.

Golden Fleece. In Greek mythology, the fleece of the ram Chrysomallus, which transported Phrixus over the sea to Colchis, whither he had fled to escape his father's wrath. Phrixus, on his arrival, sacrificed the ram to Zeus and gave the fleece to King Aëtes, who hung it in a grove of oak trees sacred to Ares, where it was guarded by a terrible dragon that never slept. It was afterwards stolen by Jason, the leader of the Argonautic Expedition. See *Argonauts.*

Golden Fleece, Order of. An order of knighthood, founded by Philip III, Duke of Burgundy and the Netherlands, in 1429, at the time of his marriage with Isabella, daughter of John I (1385–1433) of Portugal. It was established for the protection of the Church, and consisted of 31 members, with whom rested the sole right of filling vacancies. Subsequently, however, Pope Gregory XIII (1572–1585) granted to Philip II (1555–1598) of Spain the right of nominating the knights himself. It is at the present day the highest order in Spain and Austria.

Golden Gate. The name given to a channel five miles long and two miles wide, forming the entrance from the Pacific Ocean to the Bay of San Francisco, and washing the northern shore of the peninsula on which the city is built.

Golden Horn. The name given to a celebrated curved inlet on the Bosporus, on which the city of Constantinople is situated. It extends in a northwesterly direction, and is so called, not only on account of its surpassing beauty, but also because of the wealthy cities that line its shores.

Gibbon, however, says: "The epithet of *golden* was expressive of the riches which every wind wafted into the capacious port."

Golden House. A famous palace of great extent, erected at Rome by Nero (54–68), but now in ruins. According to Suetonius and others, it was roofed with golden tiles and was surrounded by a triple portico, supported by 1000 columns. The vestibule contained a colossal statue of the Emperor, 120 feet in height. The interior of this superb edifice was profusely gilded and embellished with mother-of-pearl and precious stones, and was adorned with the choicest paintings and statues. It contained a circular banqueting-hall that revolved in imitation of the sun's motion, while from openings in its vaulted ivory ceiling flowers were showered upon the guests, and perfumes sprinkled upon them from golden pipes. The princes and popes of the Farnese family used the materials of this superb edifice to construct their own palaces and villas.

Golden Legend.

(1) A celebrated mediæval collection of "lives of the saints" by Jacobus Voragine (1230–1298), a Dominican, who was archbishop of Genoa during the last six years of his life. It was written in Latin, and had an immense popularity, having passed through more than 100 editions and been translated into most of the European languages. It contains 182 chapters, and was first printed in 1470. A translation, printed by Caxton, appeared in

1483 ; and a second by Wynkyn de Worde, in 1498.

(2) The title of a dramatic poem by Henry Wadsworth Longfellow (1807–1882). It appeared in 1851.

Golden-Mouthed. An appellation conferred upon John Chrysostom (347–407), Archbishop of Constantinople, on account of his wonderful eloquence. The word " Chrysostom " is from the Greek, and signifies *golden-mouthed*.

Golden Number. The name given to the number showing the year of the lunar or metonic cycle. It is reckoned from 1 to 19, and is so called from having been formerly written in the calendar in gold. According to other authorities, however, these numbers were called *golden*, because the Greeks ordered the number of each of the nineteen years composing the " Metonic Cycle " to be inscribed in letters of gold on a pillar of marble. The " Table of Golden Numbers," in the *Book of Common Prayer*, is still used to determine the date of the festival of Easter. See *Metonic Cycle*.

Golden Rose. A rose of pale gold, blessed with great solemnity by the Pope in person on the Fourth Sunday in Lent, and usually presented to some church or distinguished person, in recognition of special services rendered to the Holy See. The rose weighs two ounces, and was at one time colored red, to represent the blood of Christ shed for the sins of the world. This custom is said to have been instituted in the 13th century. Henry VIII and Mary of England, Maria Theresa, Napoleon III, and Isabella II of Spain were all recipients of the " golden rose." Venice, at one time, possessed five " golden roses "; but during the wars waged by the Republic they were either lost, stolen, or destroyed.

Golden Rule.

(1) A name given by the ancient mathematicians to the rule of propor-tion, or " rule of three," in allusion to its great usefulness.

(2) A term frequently applied to Christ's doctrine of doing to others as we should wish them to do unto us. See *Luke* vi, 31.

Golden Shower. Acrisius, King of Argos, having been informed by an oracle that his daughter Danaë would bear a child destined to kill its grandfather, locked her up in a brazen tower or, as some say, in a subterranean cavern. Jupiter, however, being enamored of her, visited her in her prison in the form of a golden shower. From this union sprang Perseus, who, while taking part in the celebrated games in honor of Acrisius, accidentally struck his grandfather with a discus and killed him,—thus fulfilling the prediction of the oracle. See *Danaë*.

Golden State. A term frequently applied to California, one of the States of the American Union, in allusion to its extensive and valuable deposits of gold.

Golden Temple. A famous temple of the Sikh faith, at Umritsur, Hindustan. It is situated in the midst of the Pool of Immortality, a holy reservoir or tank, and is reached from the mainland by a marble causeway. The structure is of granite, the lower portion of which is covered with white marble and the upper portion with copper plates. The four entrances are provided with silver doors. The roof is adorned with cupolas at the corners, and is surmounted by a low dome. The interior of the temple consists of a large, elaborately frescoed apartment devoted to the religious services of the Acalis, or " Immortals," an order established by Goroo Govind.

Goldy. A pet name given to Oliver Goldsmith (1728–1774) by Dr. Samuel Johnson, and the one by which he was familiarly known.

Golgotha. The Hebrew name for *Calvary*, an eminence in or near Jerusalem, famous as the scene of the crucifixion of Jesus Christ. The place where Christ suffered death on the cross is unknown. Many persons, however, identify it with the rock of Calvary in the Church of the Holy Sepulchre. The name "Golgotha" signifies a *skull*, and was probably given to the place on account of its round, bare, skull-like appearance. See *Calvary*.

Good-by. This expression is a contraction of *God be with you*, and is similar to the French *adieu*, which is *à Dieu* ([I commend you] *to God*).

"The common phrase 'good-by' is equivalent to *farewell*, and would be better written *good-bye*, as it is a corruption of *God be with you* (*b' w' ye*)."

Good Gray Poet. A sobriquet conferred upon Walt Whitman (1819–1892), the American poet.

Good Friday. The name given to the Friday before Easter, observed as a solemn fast since the earliest days of Christianity, in memory of the crucifixion of Jesus Christ, which event is said to have occurred on Friday, April 15th, 29 A.D., or on Friday, April 3rd, 33 A.D. The expression "Good [probably God's] Friday" is said to be peculiar to the Church of England; the Anglo-Saxons usually called the day "Long Friday," on account of the length of the services on that occasion. In the United States, Good Friday is a legal holiday in Alabama, Louisiana, Maryland, Pennsylvania, and Tennessee.

Good Queen Anne. A sobriquet bestowed upon Anne of Bohemia, wife of Richard II (1377–1399) of England; and not upon Anne (1702–1714), daughter of James II, and Queen of England, as is commonly supposed.

Good Queen Bess. An appellation conferred upon Queen Elizabeth (1558–1603) of England, in allusion to the affectionate regard in which she was held by her loyal subjects.

Good Wine Needs No Bush. A proverbial expression, which owes its origin to the ancient custom of hanging out an ivy-bush at the doors of taverns—probably in honor of Bacchus, to whom the ivy was sacred—to inform travelers that "good cheer" might be found within. Many references to this custom are found in the old poets and dramatists. In Lily's *Euphues*, A. 3, we read: "Things of greatest profit are set forth with least price. Where wine is neat, there needeth no ivie-bush." In Allot's *English Parnassus*, we find the following lines :

" I hang no ivie out to sell my wine;
The nectar of good wits will sell itselfe."

During the reign of Edward III (1327–1377), all the "taverners" in the city of London were summoned to Guildhall, and solemnly warned that in future no bush or signboard would be allowed to "extend over the king's highway beyond the length of seven feet."

Goody Two-Shoes. The authorship of this famous nursery-tale, which appeared in 1765, is generally ascribed to Oliver Goldsmith (1728–1774). It was published by Newbery, a famous bookseller in St. Paul's Churchyard, London, renowned for his children's picture-books.

Gordian Knot. Gordius, a poor peasant of Phrygia, having been chosen king in accordance with the prediction of the oracle at Delphi, consecrated his chariot to Zeus in the acropolis of Gordium. The pole of the chariot was fastened to the yoke by an intricate knot of bark, which no one could untie, although an oracle had declared that whosoever was able to unloosen this knot should become master of all Asia. Alexander the Great, after obtaining possession of the city, addressed himself in vain to the difficulty; whereupon he severed the knot with his sword and calmly applied the prediction of the oracle to himself.

Gordon Riots. The name often applied to the London "No Popery" Riots of 1780, instigated by Lord George Gordon (1751-1793), in his efforts to force the House of Commons to repeal the bill passed (1778) for the relief of the Roman Catholics. The riots lasted five days, and occasioned the destruction of much valuable property. The churches and chapels of the Roman Catholics were first destroyed ; and, later, Newgate prison, the mansion of the Chief-Justice, Lord Mansfield, together with many private dwellings, shared the same fate. During this insurrection, most people, to save their houses from being destroyed, wrote over the doors the words "No Popery." The riots were finally quelled on the 8th of June, by armed bands of citizens, aided by the King's troops and the militia of several counties. More than 200 rioters were killed, 248 wounded, and 135 arrested—21 of whom were afterwards executed. The injury to property was estimated at £180,000. Lord Gordon was tried for high-treason, but was acquitted through the efforts of Erskine, on February 5th, 1781. Dickens has given a graphic account of the "Gordon Riots" in his novel, *Barnaby Rudge.*

Gorgons. The name given, in classic mythology, to Stheno, Euryale, and Medusa, the daughters of Phorcus and Ceto ; on which account they are sometimes called "Phorcydes." They were frightful monsters, possessing wings, brazen claws, and enormous teeth ; their bodies were covered with impenetrable scales, while their heads were entwined with hissing serpents. According to Hesiod, they dwelt on the edge of the Western Ocean, but later traditions mention Libya as their home. According to some legends, Medusa was a very beautiful maiden and the only one of the sisters that was mortal. Having borne a child to Neptune in one of Minerva's temples, the outraged goddess changed her hair into serpents, and gave her so frightful an aspect that whoever looked upon her was changed to stone. Perseus slew Medusa, and Minerva affixed her head to the centre of her shield. From her blood sprang the winged horse Pegasus. See *Pegasus.*

Gossamer Days. "A maiden was accustomed to spin late on Saturday in the moonlight. At one time the new moon on the eve of Sunday drew her up to itself, and now she sits in the moon and spins and spins. And now, when the 'gossamer days' set in late in the summer, the white threads float around in the air. These threads are the spinning of the lunar spinner."— Reddall's *Fact, Fancy, and Fable.*

Gotham. A colloquial term used to denote the city of New York, and first so employed in *Salmagundi*, a humorous work by Washington Irving, William Irving, and James K. Paulding. It is doubtless an allusion to the parish of Gotham in Nottinghamshire, England, famed for the marvellous stupidity of its people,—a characteristic which gained for them the sarcastic appellation of the "Wise Men of Gotham."

> "Three wise men of *Gotham*
> Went to sea in a bowl ;
> And if the bowl had been stronger,
> My song would have been longer."
> *Mother Goose's Melodies.*

Goths. A warlike race which, at one time, inhabited the country in the vicinity of the Baltic, and afterwards moved toward the Black Sea and the lower Danube, where, about 250 B.C., it divided into two branches. Those that remained in the eastern part of the Roman Empire were called Eastern (Ostro) Goths, while those that migrated westward were termed Western (Visi) Goths. The Ostrogoths, after ravaging eastern Europe, established, under Theodoric, a kingdom in Italy, which lasted from 493 to 554 A.D., when the country was recovered by Narses, and annexed to the Eastern Empire. The Visigoths, after various successes against the Romans, sacked Rome, under Alaric, in 410. They afterwards settled in Spain and founded a kingdom that lasted until that country was conquered by the Saracens.

Grace at Meat. A custom in vogue among the ancient Greeks, who refused to partake of any meat until they had first offered part of it to their gods —as first‑fruits. The custom, in Christian countries, of offering a short prayer before, and sometimes after, meat is in keeping with Christ's example. See *John* vi, 11.

Grace Darling of America. A sobriquet conferred upon Ida Lewis Wilson (b. 1841), the keeper of Lime Rock lighthouse, Newport, Rhode Island. Like her famous English prototype, she has been the means of saving several lives from shipwreck.

Grand Mufti. In Turkey, the supreme head of the Ulemas or interpreters of the *Koran*, and the officer next in importance and dignity to the Grand Vizier. He is the chief spiritual authority, and in that capacity is denominated Sheik-al-Islâm (*Lord of the Faith*). The Grand Mufti is chosen by the Sultan, who presents him with a vest of rich sables and grants him a salary of about $25 per day. He alone has the honor of kissing the Sultan's left shoulder, and enjoys the special prerogative of girding him with the sword on his ascension to the throne. The office of Grand Mufti has, however, declined in dignity and importance in recent times.

Grace Greenwood. A pseudonym adopted by Mrs. Sara Jane (Clarke) Lippincott (b. 1823), a popular American author and lecturer.

Graces. The name given, in classic mythology, to Aglaia, Thalia, and Euphrosyne, the three daughters of Zeus and Euronyme. They attended on Venus and sometimes on Apollo, and were famous for their beauty, refinement, and gentleness. In early times they were represented as clad in elegant drapery, but at a later period were only partially draped or entirely nude.

Grail, Holy. A miraculous chalice —made of a single emerald—said to be the cup from which Christ drank at the Last Supper, and which was afterwards filled with the blood that flowed from his wounds on Calvary. According to other accounts, it was the platter or dish that held the paschal lamb at the last Passover celebrated by Christ and his disciples. As the story goes, the " Holy Grail " was preserved and carried by Joseph of Arimathea to England, where it remained for many years as an object of worship, but finally disappeared—its keepers having failed to fulfil the conditions imposed upon those that had it in charge. Many knights-errant, especially those of the " Round Table," spent their lives in searching for it, and finally Sir Galahad was successful in his quest. The " Holy Grail " possessed miraculous properties, and was said to have the power of preserving chastity and prolonging human life. According to certain legends, it was brought down from heaven by angels, and placed in the keeping of a body of knights, who guarded it in a castle on the summit of an inaccessible mountain, called Montsalvage. Also called *St. Graal* and *Sangreal*. See *Lancelot du Lac; Round Table.*

Granary of Europe. A name given, in ancient times, to the island of Sicily, on account of the fertility of its soil.

"The soil of Sicily was very fertile, and produced in antiquity an immense quantity of wheat, on which the population of Rome relied to a great extent for their subsistence." —Smith's *Classical Dictionary.*

Gran Capitan. A sobriquet conferred upon Gonsalvo di Cordova (1453–1515 A.D.), the famous Spanish warrior.

Grand Alliance. A treaty between Leopold I (1658–1705), Emperor of Germany, and the States-General of Holland, to resist the aggressions of Louis XIV (1643–1715) of France. It was signed at Vienna on May 12th, 1689, — England, Spain, and Savoy afterwards acceding to it. Its objects were:

(1) To prevent the union of the monarchies of France and Spain.

(2) To prevent the French from getting possession of the Spanish possessions in America.

(3) To secure to the English and Dutch their dominions and commerce.

(4) To procure satisfaction to the Emperor Leopold in regard to the Spanish Succession.

Grand Army of the Republic. A society of veteran Union soldiers of the Civil War, organized at Springfield, Illinois, in 1865–1866, under the direction of Dr. B. F. Stephenson, surgeon of the 14th Illinois Infantry. It consisted (1902) of 6416 Grand Army Posts,—the first of which was organized at Decatur, Illinois, on April 6th, 1866. The total number of members (1902) was 263,745. A national encampment is held annually, at which a new commander-in-chief is chosen.

Grand Canal. The name given to the principal canal and main water-thoroughfare of Venice, Italy. It is nearly two miles in length, is in shape like the letter S, and divides the city into two nearly equal parts. The "Canalazzo," as it is called in Italian, is spanned by the Rialto, and is lined with palaces which, although appearing stained and battered in the daytime, loom up grandly in the moonlight. See *Rialto.*

Grand (or Imperial) Canal of China. A famous artificial waterway in China, extending from Peking to Hang-chau, a distance of nearly 700 miles. It dates back to the 13th century A.D., and is probably the work of Kublâ, the first sovereign of the Yüan dynasty (1280–1367). Since the introduction of steam navigation along the seaboard of China, the "Grand Canal" has fallen into disuse, and portions of it are sadly in need of repair.

"In point of magnitude, our most extensive inland navigation in England can no more be compared to the grand trunk that intersects China than a park or garden fishpond to the great lake of Winandermere."— *Barrow* (1806).

Grand Climacteric. The name given to the 63rd year of a man's life, which was formerly considered the most critical period of his existence. Its peculiar influence was attributed to the fact that it consists of the multiple of 7 and 9,—two sacred numbers. See *Climacteric Years.*

Grand Corrupter. A nickname given to Sir Robert Walpole (1676–1745), Whig politician and Prime-Minister of England.

Grande Lunette (*Fr. Great Telescope*). The name given to the colossal telescope constructed for the Paris Exposition of 1900, but still in an unfinished condition. Its tube is 197 feet in length, weighs 20 tons, and has a lens diameter of 49¼ inches. This tube is mounted on a fixed horizontal base,—the objects examined being reflected into it by means of a movable mirror entirely disconnected from the telescope proper.

Grande Mademoiselle. An appellation conferred upon Anne Marie Louise d'Orléans (1627–1693), Duchesse de Montpensier and cousin of Louis XIV (1643–1715) of France.

Grandes Reliques (*Fr. Grand Relics*). The name given to certain sacred relics preserved in the sacristy of the cathedral at Aix-la-Chapelle, a city of Rhenish Prussia. They are exhibited to the public from the 10th to the 24th of July, once in every seven years, and attract great numbers of spectators,—as many as 180,000 having visited the spot on one occasion.

These relics were presented to Charlemagne (768–814) by the Patriarch of Jerusalem and by Haroun-al-Raschid, and consist of the following objects :

(1) The cotton robe—five feet long —worn by the Virgin Mary at the time of the Nativity.

(2) The swaddling-clothes of the infant Jesus.

(3) The scarf worn by Christ at the crucifixion.

(4) The cloth on which was placed the head of John the Baptist.

In addition to these may be mentioned the following, often known as the " Lesser Relics ":

(1) The skull of Charlemagne.

(2) The hunting-horn of Charlemagne.

(3) A locket containing hair of the Virgin Mary.

(4) A piece of the true cross.

(5) A nail of the true cross.

(6) The cord with which Christ was bound.

(7) The sponge that was dipped in vinegar.

(8) The leathern girdle of Christ.

(9) A piece of Aaron's rod.

(10) Manna from the wilderness.

Aix-la-Chapelle remained until 1558 the place of coronation of the Emperors of Germany, and it was upon these " Relics " that they swore allegiance to the Empire.

Grand Lama. The supreme highpriest — regarded as divine — in the Lamaistic hierarchy. Lamaism is the name of the religion prevailing in Mongolia and Thibet ; it is a form of Buddhism, corrupted by Sivaism, and by Shamanism or spirit-worship. The Grand Lama is also called the *Dalailama*, *i. e.*, the ocean-priest, or priest as wide as the ocean.

Grand Monarque. An appellation often bestowed upon Louis XIV (1643–1715) of France, who, during his long reign of 72 years, was the most powerful European sovereign, and raised France to the summit of military

renown. He left the country burdened with debt, and died amid the execrations of all classes of the community.

Grand Old Man. A sobriquet conferred upon William Ewart Gladstone (1809–1898) by his admirers, during his administration of 1881–1885. The expression is said to have originated with John Bright in a speech at Northampton, but is also credited to Mr. Labouchère and Lord Rosebery.

Grand Opera-House. An imposing place of amusement in the Borough of Manhattan, New York City, corner of Eighth Avenue and 23rd Street, erected by Samuel N. Pike of Cincinnati, Ohio, and opened on January 9th, 1868, under the name of " Pike's Opera-House." It has seats for 2000 people, and standing - room for 1500 more. The auditorium is finely proportioned, and the stage—one of the largest in the city—is 80 feet wide and 70 feet deep.

Grand Prix. A famous horse-race for a purse of 100,000 francs, annually run at Longchamp, near Paris, early in June of each year. It is also styled the " French Derby," and marks the close of the gay season, since immediately after its occurrence the fashionable world of Paris prepares for its departure to the country or the seashore.

The " Grand Prix de Paris " was established in 1863 by the Duc de Morny, half-brother to Napoleon III. In 1881, Foxhall, James R. Keene's horse, won the " Grand Prix " for America, after a desperate struggle.

Grands Mulets (*Fr. Big Mules*). The name given to a number of dark-colored rocks on the slope of Mont Blanc, because of their fancied resemblance to a train of mules, when seen from a distance. Alpine climbers, when making the ascent of Mont Blanc, are accustomed to spend the night at that place.

Grand Tour. The name given, in former days, to the conventional European pleasure-trip made by wealthy English tourists. The itinerary included France, Switzerland, Italy, and Germany.

Grand Trianon. A handsome one-story villa near the palace of Versailles, erected by Louis XIV (1643-1715) for Madame de Maintenon in 1688. Louis XIV, Louis XV, Louis XVI, and Napoleon I all resided there. The building is in the form of a horse-shoe, and contains several sumptuously furnished apartments and a few choice works of art. The celebrated trial of Marshal Bazaine took place there in 1873. See *Petit Trianon.*

Grangers. A national association of American farmers, founded in 1867 under the title of "Patrons of Industry," by a government clerk named Kelly, to improve the social and industrial condition of the farmer. Each "grange" corresponds to a lodge in free-masonry, and when properly organized comprises 13 officers. Meetings, devoted to music and literature, are held periodically, while questions of politics are strictly prohibited. In 1880, there were 25,000 granges with 2,000,000 members in the United States. At the 25th annual meeting of the National Grange, held in 1891, it was reported that during its existence it had established 27,379 subordinate granges in 44 States and Territories. The number of granges is at present (1901) about 27,700.

Granicus, Battle of the. A famous battle fought near the river of the same name in Asia Minor on May 22nd, 334 B.C., between 35,000 Macedonian troops led by Alexander the Great (336-323), and over 600,000 Persians commanded by the satraps of the neighboring provinces. The Macedonians defeated the Persians with great slaughter and lost only 55 foot-soldiers and 60 horse. As a result of this battle, Sardis, Miletus, and Hali-

carnassus, together with other great towns, fell into the hands of the conqueror.

Granite Redoubt. The name given to the invincible front presented by the grenadiers of the Consular Guard at the battle of Marengo (June 14th, 1800).

Granite State. A name popularly given to the State of New Hampshire, in allusion to the extensive granite formations in its northern part.

Grant Mausoleum. A massive granite tomb, containing the remains of General Ulysses S. Grant (1822–1885), situated on Riverside Drive, New York City. The corner-stone was laid on April 27th, 1892, by President Harrison, and the monument was dedicated on April 27th, 1897,— precisely five years later. The total cost was about $600,000, contributed by about 90,000 persons; and, with the exception of about $40,000, this entire amount was subscribed by the people of the city of New York. The monument consists of a lower story, in the Doric style of architecture, 90 feet square and 72 feet high,—surmounted by a cupola, supported on Ionic columns. The total height of the structure is 150 feet above the grade, or 280 feet above mean high-water of the Hudson River. The interior is much more impressive than the exterior, and resembles Napoleon's Tomb in the Hôtel des Invalides, Paris. In the open crypt beneath the centre of the dome is placed a red porphyry sarcophagus containing the ashes of the hero; and by its side is a similar one destined to receive the remains of Mrs. Grant, in accordance with the General's wishes. Mrs. Grant buried, Dec. 21, 1902.

Grapes, Painted. See *Curtain Painted.*

Grass-Widow. This phrase — denoting a woman temporarily separated from her husband—is a corruption of "grace widow," *i. e.*, a widow by grace or courtesy.

Gravelotte, Battle of. A sanguinary and fiercely contested battle, fought on August 18th, 1870, at Gravelotte, a village of Lorraine, 7 miles west of Metz, between the Germans commanded by the King in person and the French under Marshal Bazaine. The right wing of the French having been outflanked after 12 hours' desperate fighting, they fell back under cover of Metz with a loss of 19,000 men. The German loss was 25,000. This battle is sometimes called the *Battle of Rézonville*.

Great American Traveler. A self-bestowed title, by which Daniel Pratt (1809–1887) was popularly known. Pratt was originally a carpenter, and was noted for his harmless eccentricities. He spent much of his time lecturing through the United States, and lived upon charity.

Great Bed of Ware. A famous piece of furniture, formerly preserved at the inn called the "Saracen's Head" at Ware, but removed to Rye House in 1869. It is considered one of the curiosities of England, and measures 12 feet square. It is made of oak, — elaborately carved,— and is surmounted by a heavy canopy, supported by a lofty headboard and by two massive bedposts at the foot. Twelve persons can occupy it comfortably at one time. The bed bears the date of 1460, but is not considered by antiquaries to be older than the time of Elizabeth (1558–1603). When some years ago it was offered at auction, Charles Dickens bid £100 for it ; but being valued at a higher sum, it was bought in by the owner.

Shakespeare refers to this celebrated bed in *Twelfth Night*, iii, 2, in the following words : "as many lies as will lie in thy sheet of paper, although the sheet were big enough for the *bed of Ware* in England, set 'em down."

Great Bell of Moscow. See *Bell of Moscow*.

Great Bell of St. Paul's. A famous bell in St. Paul's Cathedral, London, hung in 1882 and familiarly known as "Great Paul." It is 8 feet 10 inches in height, weighs about 17½ tons, and cost £3000. It is used only at the time of the death or funeral of one of the members of the royal family, the bishop of London, the dean of the cathedral, and the lord-mayor of London (while in office). The original bell was cast in 1716, and weighed over 5 tons. It measured 6 feet 10½ inches in diameter at the mouth.

Great Britain, Last Battle in. The last battle in Great Britain was that of Culloden Moor, fought on April 16th, 1746, between the English commanded by the Duke of Cumberland and the Scotch under Prince Charles Edward, surnamed the "Young Pretender." See *Culloden, Battle of*.

Great Bullet-Head. A nickname conferred upon Georges Cadoudal (1771–1804), the leader of the Chouans. See *Chouans ; Georges's Conspiracy*.

Great Commoner. A sobriquet conferred upon William Pitt (1708–1778), first Earl of Chatham, a famous parliamentary orator and, for more than twenty-five years, the leader of the House of Commons. This title has also been bestowed upon the American statesmen, Henry Clay (1777–1852) and Thaddeus Stevens (1798–1868).

Great Crystal. A famous crystal, four feet long, two feet wide, and one foot thick, formerly in the *diwan-i-khas*, or private audience hall of the Citadel at Delhi, India. It then stood upon a large marble table, and was used by the Great Moguls as a throne. The table is still in the *diwan-i-khas*, but the crystal was removed to London many years ago.

Great Dauphin. A name given by the French historians to Louis the Dauphin (1661–1711), son of Louis XIV. Neither he nor his son, the Duc de Bourgogne (surnamed the " Little Dauphin "), ever lived to reach the throne. At the death of Louis XIV (1715), the crown of France descended to his great-grandson, Louis XV.

Great Divide. A name often given to the Rocky Mountains, which extend from north to south throughout the western part of North America, and form the principal watershed of the continent.

Great Duke. A title often applied to the Duke of Wellington (1769–1852).

" Bury the *Great Duke*
   With an empire's lamentation,
Let us bury the *Great Duke*
   To the noise of the mourning of a mighty
      nation,
Mourning when their leaders fall,
Warriors carry the warrior's pall,
And sorrow darkens hamlet and hall."
    Ode on the Death of the Duke of
        Wellington (Tennyson).

Great Earl of Cork. A title conferred upon Richard Boyle (1566–1643), first Earl of Cork, who by his own exertions acquired great wealth and expended it freely in promoting public improvements.

Great Eastern. This vessel—the largest ever constructed — was designed by Brunel and built by Messrs. Scott Russell & Company, for the Australian trade by way of the Cape of Good Hope. After several unsuccessful attempts, she was launched in 1858 and completed during the following year. The *Great Eastern* was 692 feet long, 83 feet broad, and was divided into 11 water-tight compartments. The height of her hull was 60 feet. She had 6 masts, 5 funnels with 100 furnaces, and was provided with 10 boilers. Her propelling power comprised both paddle-wheels and screw, while her engines were estimated to

work up to 11,000 horse-power. She had capacity for 1000 passengers, 5000 tons of merchandise, and 15,000 tons of coal. Altogether, the vessel was estimated to have cost £732,000. Her trial trip across the Atlantic Ocean occurred in June, 1860, and required 11 days. In 1861, she conveyed 2000 troops from England to Canada, but her voyages were all losing ventures, since the receipts failed to meet the current expenses and the outlay for necessary repairs. In 1864, the vessel was first employed to lay the Atlantic cable, and served repeatedly in that capacity in later years. After serving as a coal-hulk at Gibraltar in 1884, the *Great Eastern* was sold at auction in London for £26,200, and was used for a time as a " show " ship. In 1888, she was a second time disposed of at auction for £58,000, and was broken up.

Great Elector. A sobriquet conferred upon Frederick William (1640–1688), second Elector of Brandenburg, who, by his talent and energy, raised the Electorate to a position of supremacy among the German states, and laid the foundations of Prussian greatness. His son Frederick (1688–1713), third Elector of Brandenburg, was proclaimed King Frederick I of Prussia, in 1701.

Great Fire of Hamburg. A serious conflagration, which occurred at Hamburg in May, 1842, and in three days destroyed one-third of the city,—including numerous churches, public buildings, and 2000 houses. Although the estimated loss exceeded £2,000,-000, the part of the city destroyed was immediately rebuilt. A singular phenomenon during the fire was the simultaneous ringing of all the great bells of the city — occasioned, it is said, by the currents of air produced by the conflagration.

Great Fire of London. A disastrous conflagration, which broke out in London on September 2nd, 1666, the year after the "Great Plague," and raged for five days. During this time, there were destroyed 88 churches (including St. Paul's), 4 city gates, the Guildhall, the Royal Exchange, Sion College, and 4 stone bridges, together with 13,200 houses. The ruins covered 396 acres and embraced 400 streets, while the losses sustained were estimated at £4,000,000. Only 8 persons perished, but over 200,000 were rendered homeless and encamped in the fields of Islington and Highgate. See *Monument, The*.

Great Gun of Moscow. A famous cannon in the Kremlin at Moscow, Russia, sometimes called the "pocket-piece" of the Empress Anne. The diameter of the bore is said to be three feet. The gun has never been used.

Great Harry. The name given to the first ship of the English navy. She was built by Henry VII (1485–1509) in 1509, and named in his honor. The *Great Harry* was 1000 tons' burden, and cost £15,000. She was the first double-decker and the first war-vessel built in England, had 4 masts, carried 80 guns, and measured 138 feet in length and 38 feet in breadth. Accidentally burned at Woolwich in 1553.

Great-Heart, Mr. In Bunyan's *Pilgrim's Progress*, the name of the guide and protector of Christiana (the wife of Christian) and her family, on their journey to the Celestial City.

Great Magician of the North. A sobriquet conferred upon Sir Walter Scott (1771–1832), the celebrated poet and novelist, and first bestowed upon him by Professor John Wilson ("Christopher North") in a poem entitled *The Magic Mirror*, published in 1812. See *Magician of the North*.

Great Minstrel. An epithet bestowed upon Sir Walter Scott (1771–1832) by the *Edinburgh Review*, in 1815.

"Here is another genuine lay of the *Great Minstrel*, with all his characteristic faults,

beauties, and irregularities."— *Edinburgh Review*.

Great Mogul. The title of the chief of the Mogul Empire, founded in Hindustan in 1525 A.D., by Baber, a descendant of Tamerlane, the famous Mongol conqueror. For more than two centuries, the Mogul Emperors ruled India and lived in great magnificence at Delhi, which continued to be their capital until the reign of Akbar (1555–1605), when it was transferred to Agra. They were finally conquered by the English, and in 1806, Shah Allum, the last person to whom the title of "Great Mogul" rightly belonged, having died, the Mogul Empire ceased to exist. The religion of the Moguls was Mohammedan, but, although introduced by them into India, it was never accepted by the native Hindus.

Great Mogul Diamond. A celebrated Indian diamond, whose history is said to date from 56 B.C. In the 14th century, it fell into the hands of the Rajah of Malwa, and later became the property of the Mogul Emperors, at Delhi. The French jeweler, Tavernier, says that he saw this diamond at the court of Aurungzebe in 1665, and declares that it weighed, in the rough state, $793\frac{5}{8}$ carats. It is generally described, however, as a round white rose-cut stone, of 280 carats. It was probably stolen and broken up at the sack of Delhi by Nadir Shah, in 1739. By some authorities it is identified with the Koh-i-nur, and by others with the Orloff.

Great Moralist. A title often bestowed upon Dr. Samuel Johnson (1709–1784), the famous author, in allusion to the ethical character of some of his writings—especially his *Essays*, from which, according to Goldsmith, a complete system of morality may be deduced.

Great Mother. The Earth. It is related of Lucius Junius Brutus and the sons of Tarquin that, having consulted the oracle at Delphi to ascertain who should succeed Superbus on the throne of Rome, they received the following answer : " He that shall first kiss his mother ! " The two princes hastened to fulfil what seemed to them to be the meaning of the oracle ; but Brutus, prostrating himself upon the ground, exclaimed : " Thus do I kiss thee, O Earth, the great Mother of us all ! "

Great Pacificator. A nickname given to Henry Clay (1777–1852), the American statesman, in allusion to his great skill in reconciling sectional differences by his passage of the Missouri Compromise. See *Missouri Compromise.*

Great Paul. See *Great Bell of St. Paul's.*

Great Plague of London. The name given to a fearful pestilence that ravaged London in 1665, and carried off nearly 100,000 persons. The population of the city at that time numbered 500,000 ; hence it will be seen that about one-fifth of the inhabitants perished. Fires were kept burning day and night for three days, to purify the air. The infection was not, however, entirely stamped out until the " Great Fire " of the following year. The plague is supposed to have been introduced into England by certain Dutch merchants, and to have been brought into the city in bales of cotton. Daniel Defoe has written a *Journal of the Plague in London*, which is graphic in style, but highly imaginative.

Great Pyramid. A gigantic mausoleum standing, in company with eight others, on the west bank of the Nile, near Memphis, Egypt. Its age is not definitely known, but it is tolerably certain that it was built by Chufu or Cheops, the second king of the Fourth Dynasty in 3733 B.C. (according to Brugsch). Other authorities assign 1082 B.C. as the date of its erection. Herodotus says that 30 years were required for its completion, during which

time 100,000 men worked steadily upon it. The height was originally 481 feet, and the base 774 feet square,—the entire structure covering an area of about 12 acres, or more than twice that of St. Peter's at Rome. The pyramid has been greatly despoiled and stripped of its exterior blocks to furnish stone for the walls and mosques of Cairo. The interior contains several apartments, the principal of which is the King's Chamber, containing the broken red sarcophagus of the monarch, 7 feet 6¼ inches long, 3 feet 3 inches broad, and 3 feet 5 inches high. The Great Pyramid was entered by the Caliph El Manûn, in the 9th century A.D. See *Pyramids of Gizeh.*

Great Seal of England. The symbol of office of the Lord Chancellor,—used for giving assent to all charters, grants, letters-patent, etc. The earliest regular " Great Seal " was that of Edward the Confessor (1042–1066) ; it was called the " Broad Seal," and was affixed to the grants of the Crown. The most ancient seal with *arms* on it was that of Richard I (1189–1199). When Littleton, the Lord Keeper, joined Charles I in 1642, he took the " Great Seal " with him ; whereupon Parliament ordered a new one to be made. Charles II, on his accession in 1660, commanded another to be made. James II, in his flight, threw the " Great Seal " into the Thames, but it was soon after recovered. In 1784, the " Great Seal " was stolen from the house of Thurlow, the Lord Chancellor. It was never recovered, but was replaced next day. On the Union of Great Britain and Ireland, in 1801, a new seal came into use. Since 1757 the " Great Seal " has been in charge of the Lord Chancellor. On the accession of a new sovereign, the old seal is solemnly destroyed, and is replaced by a new one. See *Privy-Seal.*

Great Seal of the United States. Adopted June 20th, 1782, by a committee appointed to secure a suitable device for a Great Seal of the United

States. It consists, on the obverse side, of a spread-eagle, having on its breast a shield with 13 stripes and a chief azure, and in its beak a scroll bearing the motto *E Pluribus Unum*. In one talon is a bundle of arrows, and in the other an olive branch. Above the head is a " glory " emerging from the clouds and surrounding 13 stars. On the reverse side is an unfinished pyramid—symbolic of the strength and growth of the Union ; above it is an eye, surrounded by a triangle. Around the rim are the mottoes *Annuit Cœptis* (*Lat. He [God] Has Favored the Undertaking*) and *Novus Ordo Seclorum* (*Lat. A New Order of Things*). The " Great Seal " has never been altered, and is in the custody of the Secretary of State. See *E Pluribus Unum*.

Great Seer. A sobriquet conferred upon Dr. Samuel Johnson (1709–1784), the famous lexicographer and man of letters.

Great Sow. An epithet bestowed upon Isabella of Bavaria, wife of Charles VI (1380–1422) of France, on account of the dissoluteness of her life.

Great Tom. A famous bell at Christ-Church College, Oxford, England. It was cast in 1680, weighs 7⅜ tons, and measures 7 feet in diameter at the mouth. It is said to be faulty in tone.

Great Triumvirate. Dante, Petrarch, and Boccaccio are sometimes called the " Great Triumvirate of Italian Literature."

Great Unknown. A name given by James Ballantyne to Sir Walter Scott (1771–1832), the author of the Waverley novels, which, although published anonymously, attained great popularity. Speculation was long rife as to the authorship of these charming romances ; but it was not until the failure of Scott's publishers in 1825 that the secret was finally divulged.

Great Unwashed. A phrase first used by Edmund Burke (1729–1797),

to denote the artisan class. The expression was afterwards popularized by Sir Walter Scott (1771–1832).

Great Verulam. A title conferred upon Francis Bacon (1561–1626), the English philosopher, who, in 1618, was raised to the peerage as Baron Verulam.

Great Wall of China. See *China, Great Wall of*.

Great Western. A famous steamship, built by J. K. Brunel for the Great Western Steamship Company, and launched at Bristol, England, in July, 1837. She was 212 feet long, 35 feet 4 inches broad, and had a depth of hold of 23 feet 2 inches. Her registry was 1340 tons and her engines were of 1440 horse-power. On April 8th, 1838, the *Great Western* started from Bristol on a voyage across the Atlantic, and reached New York in fourteen days. This virtually reduced the time between England and America about one-half, and demonstrated the feasibility of transatlantic steam-navigation.

Greek Author, Emaciated. Philetas of Cos, the famous dwarf, was also a Greek poet and grammarian, and flourished about 330 B.C. He was the preceptor of Ptolemy Philadelphus (263–246 B.C.), and, according to tradition, was so emaciated that his sandal-soles were made of lead to prevent him from being blown away. According to other accounts, he carried weights in his pockets for the same purpose. Ælian shrewdly wonders how the poet could muster sufficient strength to carry ballast, if he was too weak to withstand the wind.

Greek Church. The Greek Church —also called the Eastern or Byzantine Church — is the name given to that part of Christendom that separated from the Roman or Western Church in 1054, in which year Pope Leo IX (1048–1054) issued a formal excommunication against the patriarch, Michael Cerularius. As early as the 5th century, however, jealousies and differences in doctrine had led to an estrangement between the two wings of the Christian Church, but these did not result in a complete rupture until the 11th century. The principal difference in doctrine between the two Churches turns upon the question whether the procession of the Holy Ghost is from the Father only, or from both the Father and the Son, — the Greek Church teaching the former doctrine and the Roman Church the latter. The Greek Church accepts the doctrines set forth by the first seven Ecumenical Councils ; administers the eucharist in both kinds to the laity ; accepts the Bible and tradition as the rule of faith ; worships the Virgin Mary and the saints; permits the use of pictures, but not of images ; denies the existence of Purgatory, but offers prayers for the repose of the soul after death ; and believes in penance, confession, and absolution. The Church further accepts transubstantiation and worships the Host, but rejects the celibacy of the clergy and the infallibility of the Pope. Confirmation follows immediately after baptism, even in the case of infants. Priests are obliged to marry, but before ordination. They cannot marry after ordination, and hence cannot contract a second marriage. The Greek Church flourishes in Russia (of which it is the state-church), Austria, Hungary, Greece, Roumania, Bulgaria, Eastern Roumelia, Servia, Montenegro, and Turkey in Europe, and numbers about 98,000,000 adherents. See *Filioque Controversy ; Latin Church.*

Greek Fire. A highly inflammable substance, probably composed of bitumen, sulphur, naphtha, and nitre, — the invention of which is generally ascribed to Callinicus of Heliopolis, in 668 A.D. It was first used by the Greeks of the Byzantine Empire to repel the attacks of the Saracens on Constantinople in 673 A.D., and caused the destruction of the invaders' ships and 30,000 of their troops. The process of manufacture of Greek Fire was carefully guarded for several centuries; but the secret became gradually known, and, in consequence, its use spread slowly throughout western Europe, where it continued to be of service until the 14th century, when it was superseded by the more efficient agent, gunpowder. At the siege of Charleston, South Carolina, during the American Civil War, the Federals used a substance called " Greek Fire," composed of sulphur, nitre, and lampblack.

Greek Calends. An expression, among the Romans, meaning *never.* The Calends were the first day of each Roman month, and were the customary days for the payment of rents, interest, etc. As there were no Calends in the Greek system of reckoning the months, a postponement of any payment until the Greek Calends (*Lat. Ad Calendas Græcas*) meant simply a refusal to pay altogether. It is said that this expression was much used by the Emperor Augustus (27 B.C.–14 A.D.), and afterwards passed into a proverb.

Greek Meets Greek, When. This expression, slightly altered, is derived from the line, " When Greeks *joined* Greeks, then was the tug of war." The quotation is from the drama of *Alexander the Great* by Nathaniel Lee (1655–1692), and refers to the stubborn resistance offered by the cities of Greece to Philip and Alexander of Macedon.

Greek Slave. A famous marble statue by Hiram Powers (1805–1873), the American sculptor, completed in 1843. Five replicas are said to have been made by the artist,—the first of which was sold to Captain Grant and taken to England, and is now in the gallery of the Duke of Cleveland. The second copy is now in the Corcoran Art Gallery at Washington ; the third is in the possession of the Earl of Dudley; the fourth was purchased by A. T. Stewart of New York for $11,000 ; and the fifth became the property of the Hon. E. W. Stoughton.

Greenbacks. A name said to have been given by the Hon. S. P. Chase, Secretary of the Treasury, to the legal-tender notes first issued by the United States government in 1862, during the Civil War, in allusion to the color of the ink used in printing their reverse sides. This green tint was first produced by a Canadian, and is said to be difficult either to photograph or to counterfeit. See *Bluebacks.*

Green Grotto. A famous cavern situated on the island of Capri, at the entrance of the Bay of Naples, and reached through an archway twenty feet in height. It derives its name from the dazzling green color produced by the refraction and reflection of the sun's rays. See *Blue Grotto ; Capri.*

Greenhorn. This word, which is at present figuratively used to denote a raw and inexperienced lad (*i. e.,* one unused to the ways of the world), was originally applied to an ox with undeveloped horns, and hence unfit to be put to the plow.

Green-Mountain Boys. A band of Vermont settlers, organized in 1773, under the leadership of Ethan Allen, Seth Baker, and others, for the purpose of protecting themselves against the attempts of the Governor of New York to drive them from their lands and take possession of their territory, on the ground that it belonged to New York, under the charter granted by Charles II (1660-1685). During the Revolutionary War, the " Green-Mountain Boys," 300 in number, led by Ethan Allen, rendered great service in securing the passes into Canada, and thus preventing the British troops from overrunning Vermont. See *Green-Mountain State.*

Green-Mountain State. A name popularly given to the State of Vermont, on account of the range of hills —known as the Green Mountains— that extend through it from north to south. The word " Vermont " is derived from the French *vert mont (green mountain).* See *Green-Mountain Boys.*

Green Sea. A name given by Oriental geographers to the Persian Gulf, in allusion to a remarkable strip of bright green water that lies along the Arabian coast.

Green Thursday. Maundy-Thursday. It is the great day of absolution in the Lutheran Church. See *Maundy-Thursday.*

Green Vaults of Dresden. A series of apartments in the royal palace at Dresden, so called from the paper or hangings with which they were originally adorned. They contain a superb collection of jewels, gold and silver work, ivory carvings, and curios. There may be seen the largest known onyx,—valued at $30,000,—as well as the regalia used at the coronation of Augustus. See *Court of the Great Mogul.*

Greenwich Hospital. An asylum for aged and disabled sailors, situated on the Thames, six miles below London. It occupies the site of an ancient palace, and was opened as a retreat for seamen in 1705. Until the end of 1865, the number of inmates in the hospital averaged about 2700, but after that year it decreased to 350 in consequence of a decision of the Admiralty, giving to pensioners the option of remaining in the hospital or of receiving an outdoor pension. The hospital contains the relics of Lord Nelson,—notably the coat and waistcoat worn by him at the battle of Trafalgar.

Greenwich Observatory. The Royal Observatory at Greenwich, England, was founded by Charles II (1660–1685) in 1675, at the earnest request of Sir Jonas Moore and Sir Christopher Wren. It crowns a hill, 180 feet high, in Greenwich Park—named Flamsteed Hill, in honor of the first astronomer-royal, who took up his residence there in 1676. The observatory contains a fine refracting telescope — having an aperture of 28 inches and a length of 28 feet—erected in 1893–1894. The correct time for the whole of England is settled at Greenwich every day at 1 P.M. The meridian of Greenwich is used by all English astronomers in making their calculations, while English geographers and seamen have adopted it in reckoning longitude on the earth's surface. Greenwich was recommended as the universal meridian not only by the *Geodetic Congress* at Rome in 1883, but also by the *International Conference* held at Washington in 1884. See *Astronomer-Royal.*

Greenwood Cemetery. A beautiful cemetery in the Borough of Brooklyn, New York City, comprising 475 acres. It was opened in 1840, and since that time about 300,000 interments have been made in it. Its control is vested in a board of public trustees, who have for its maintenance a fund of nearly $1,000,000. Among the noted monuments in Greenwood Cemetery may be mentioned those erected in memory of Horace Greeley, James Gordon Bennett, John Matthews, the Brown Brothers, S. F. B. Morse, Mary M. Danser, Charlotte Canda, Captain Correja, and A. S. Scribner. The Soldiers' Monument, the Firemen's Monument, the Brooklyn Theatre Monument, the Pilot's Monument, and the bronze statue of De Witt Clinton are also worthy of notice.

Gregorian Calendar. The name given to the reformed calendar introduced by Pope Gregory XIII (1572–1585) in 1582 to correct an error in the civil year, which, according to the Julian Calendar, had been made 11 minutes and a few seconds too long. This disparity—although a small one—increased as the years rolled by, so that in the 16th century the civil year was ten days in arrear of the solar year. To remedy this difficulty, ten days were omitted from the Julian Calendar, thus causing the vernal equinox to fall on March 21st (the day on which it fell at the time of the Council of Nice in 325 A.D.), instead of on March 11th. Between the years 1582–1753, the Gregorian Calendar was introduced into all the principal countries of Europe, except Russia, Greece, Turkey, and some of the smaller states belonging to the Greek Church, which still retain the Julian Calendar. See *Julian Calendar; New Style; Old Style.*

Gregorian Chant. The name given to certain choral melodies introduced into the ritual of the early Christian Church by Pope Gregory I (590–604), surnamed " The Great." It is said to be an improvement on the Ambrosian Chant, which was taken from the Greek Chant used in the Eleusinian Mysteries. The Ambrosian Chant had only four tones, and was extended to eight by Gregory I. See *Ambrosian Chant; Eleusinian Mysteries.*

Gretna Green. A village of Dumfriesshire, Scotland, near the border, famous for years as the scene of runaway marriages. Until the year 1856, the Scotch law ruled that a marriage was valid, if the contracting parties declared their willingness before witnesses ; but after that date Parliament declared such marriages illegal, unless one of the parties had lived in Scotland for 21 days previous to the ceremony. It is said that sometimes as many as 200 couples were united in matrimony there during one year. After the abolition of the Fleet marriages in 1753, Gretna Green became a favorite spot for clandestine unions. See *Fleet, The.*

Grimm's Law. The law discovered by Jacob L. Grimm (1785–1863), the famous German philologist, illustrating the manner in which the mute consonants interchange in corresponding words in the various branches of the Aryan or Indo-European family of languages. The following table, taken from Haydn's *Dictionary of Dates*, illustrates the working of this law:

	(1) LABIALS.	(2) DENTALS.	(3) GUTTURALS.
Greek, Latin,			
Sanskrit.....	p b f	t d th	k g ch
Gothic.........	f p b	th t d	k
Old High			
German	b (v) f p	d z t	g ch k

Examples: Sanskrit, *pitri;* Greek and Latin, *pater;* Italian, *padre;* Spanish, *padre;* French, *père;* Gothic, *fadrein (pl.)*: Old High German, *vatar;* English, *father.*

Grog. " Admiral Vernon, whose ardent devotion to his profession had endeared him to the British naval service, was in the habit of walking the deck, in bad weather, in a rough *grogram* cloak, and thence had obtained the nickname of *Old Grog.* Whilst in command of the West India station, and at the height of his popularity on account of his reduction of Porto Bello with six men-of-war only, he introduced the use of rum and water among the ship's company. When served out, the new beverage proved most palatable, and speedily grew into such favor that it became as popular as the brave admiral himself, and in honor of him was surnamed by acclamation ' Grog.' "—*Gleanings for the Curious* (Bombaugh).

Grotto de la Vièrge (*Fr. Grotto of the Virgin*). A cave at Lourdes, France, where the Virgin Mary is said to have appeared to Bernadette Soubirous, a poor girl, fourteen years of age, at noon on February 11th, 1858. During the succeeding six months, the Virgin is reported to have appeared seventeen additional times. In the following year over 200,000 persons visited the spot, which, since then, has been a noted place of pilgrimage. The cave contains a spring, whose waters are believed to possess miraculous powers of healing. See *Lourdes, Our Lady of.*

Grotto del Cane (*It. Grotto of the Dog*). A small cave in the vicinity of Lake Agnano, near Naples, Italy, from whose walls and floor are constantly issuing clouds of vapor mingled with carbonic-acid gas. The latter, having a greater specific gravity than the atmosphere, sinks to the bottom and leaves the upper part of the cave perfectly free. The cavern derives its name from the cruel practice of subjecting dogs to the effect of this gas for the amusement of tourists and others, and afterwards reviving them by exposure to the air. This grotto was known to the ancients, and was called by Pliny " the breathing-place of Pluto."

Grotto of Ephesus. A grotto near Ephesus, used by the ancients as a test of female chastity. It contained a statue of Diana, to which was fastened a reed, said to have been presented by Pan. If, after a young woman had entered this grotto, the reed emitted musical tones, she was adjudged innocent ; but if, on the contrary, hideous sounds came from the instrument, the poor wretch was condemned, and passed forever from the sight of men.

Grotto of Posilippo. The name given to a tunnel through which passes the road from Naples to Pozzuoli. It is 2265 feet long, from 20 to 30 feet wide, and varies in height from 20 to 80 feet or more. It extends under the hill of the same name, and is traditionally believed to have been constructed in the time of Augustus (27 B.C.–14 A.D.). The probability, however, is that it belongs to an earlier period. About midway of the tunnel is a niche, forming a temple of the Virgin Mary. Above the eastern entrance is situated the so-called Tomb of Virgil. See *Tomb of Virgil.*

Grub Street. A street near Moorfields, London, at one time famous for literary " hacks " and inferior literary productions. Dr. Samuel Johnson, in his *Dictionary,* thus describes it : " Originally the name of a street near Moorfields in London, much inhabited by writers of small histories, dictionaries, and temporary poems, whence any mean production is called *Grub-Street.*" The expression was freely used, in this sense, by Marvell, Pope, Swift, and others. In 1830, the name was changed to Milton Street, but authorities are not agreed as to whether this new appellation was bestowed in honor of the poet or of one Milton, a builder. John Foxe, the author of the *Book of Martyrs*, and Speed, the historian, lived in Grub Street.

Grundy, Mrs. A person mentioned in, but not introduced as a character into, Morton's play of *Speed the Plough.* She is a near neighbor of one Dame Ashfield, who, in all the concerns and doings of her daily life, manifests great solicitude as to what " Mrs. Grundy " would say. " What will Mrs. Grundy say ? " has accordingly passed into a proverb, meaning, " What opinion will the eminently virtuous and respectable portion of society pass upon our actions ? "

Grütli. A meadow on the western shore of Lake Lucerne, Switzerland, where, according to tradition, Werner Stauffacher of Schwyz, Walter Fürst of Uri (father-in-law of William Tell), and Arnold Welchthal of Unterwalden met on November 7th, 1307, and solemnly swore to free their country from the Austrian yoke. The spot now belongs to the Swiss nation,—having been purchased in 1859 with the penny-subscriptions of the Swiss school-children. The field contains a fine monument of Schiller, the author of *Wilhelm Tell*, erected in 1860, and one in commemoration of the oath, —placed there in 1884.

"Guard Dies but Never Surrenders." A saying attributed to General Cambronne, at the battle of Waterloo, when summoned to surrender the remnant of the Imperial Guard. It is said that these words were never uttered, but were simply a fabrication of one Rougemont, a maker of *mots*, who published them in *L'Indépendant* two days after the battle. This utterance was persistently denied by General Cambronne himself, on several occasions.

Guardian. A daily journal, founded by Richard Steele in 1713. It extended to 175 numbers,—82 of which were written by Steele and 53 by Addison, while the remaining ones were contributed by Pope, Berkeley, Budgell, and others.

Guelphs and Ghibellines. The names given to two great political parties, whose conflicts form a large part of the history of Italy and Germany, during the 12th, 13th, and 14th centuries. In the struggles that ensued in Italy,—the chief scene of the conflicts between these two factions,— the Ghibellines championed the cause of the German Emperors, while the Guelphs maintained the supremacy of the Pope. The word " Guelph " is the Italian form of *Welfe*, and the word " Ghibelline " the Italian form of *Waiblingen.* It is said that these words were first adopted as party-names at the battle of Weinsberg, in Swabia, in 1140, on which occasion the Emperor Conrad of Hohenstaufen, and Welf, uncle of Henry the Lion, Duke of Saxony, rallied their respective followers with the war-cries, " Hie Waiblingen ! " " Hie Welfe ! " Guelph is the name of the present royal family of England. Its origin is uncertain.

Guides. A name given in the French army, as early as 1744, to a small company of men detailed as messengers on active service. In 1796, a corps of " guides " was formed by Bessières, under the direction of Napoleon Bonaparte, as a personal body-guard of the Commander-in-chief, who had been nearly carried off by the enemy on the 30th of May of that year. The " guides " were gradually increased in number by Napoleon, and were finally converted by him into a guard 10,000 strong. Napoleon III made the *Corps des Guides* a part of the Imperial Guard.

Guildhall. The Council-Hall of the city of London. It was originally erected in 1411–1431, but was totally destroyed by the Great Fire of 1666 ; was rebuilt in 1789, and restored in 1865–1868. The Great Hall, 153 feet long, 48 feet wide, and 55 feet high, is a finely proportioned room, capable of accommodating 7000 persons. It contains a handsome open-timber roof, superb stained-glass windows, and monuments to Chatham, Wellington, Nelson, Pitt, and others. In corners, on lofty pedestals, stand the colossal wooden figures of the giants Gog and Magog. On the 9th of November of each year, a dinner, attended by nearly 1000 guests, is given there by the Lord Mayor, on the occasion of his accession to office. The banquet necessitates the services of 20 cooks, the slaughter of 40 turtles, and the consumption of 14 tons of coal. The Guildhall contains, in addition, a library, reading-room, art-gallery, and museum. There also may be found the Common Council Chamber, the Court of Aldermen, the Chamberlain's Office, and the Chamberlain's Parlor. See *Gog and Magog ; Lord Mayor's Day.*

Guilds. The name given to certain corporations or fraternities of traders that grew up in the free-cities and towns of Europe, during the Middle Ages. Free-cities of this kind in England were called " Boroughs." These corporations were most powerful in the towns of Flanders and South Germany. Each guild exercised a monopoly in its own particular craft, in return for which privilege the members rendered military service in defending the towns from attack. The right to exercise one's trade independently depended upon membership in a guild, which membership carried with it the rights of citizenship. The guild was expected to supervise the work of its members,

and to see that it was of reasonable quality. Henry VIII (1509–1547) of England gave a death-blow to the guilds by confiscating their property, on the ground that it was used for superstitious purposes. The word " guild " is derived from the Anglo-Saxon *gild* (*payment*), which is also the correct spelling of the English form,—the letter *u* being superfluous.

Guillotine. An instrument devised for painless decapitation, and introduced during the French Revolution by the National Convention. It received its name from its supposed inventor, Joseph Ignace Guillotin (1738–1814), a physician who, as a member of the Convention, simply *recommended* its adoption from motives of humanity. The statement that Guillotin was a victim of the instrument whose use he had suggested is untrue. He lived to become one of the founders of the Academy of Medicine in Paris, and died peacefully at the age of seventy-six. The guillotine was first used in Paris to execute a criminal named Pelletier on the Place de Grève, on April 25th, 1792. The first political victim to suffer death by this means was Dangremont, who was guillotined on August 21st of the same year. See *Place de Grève.*

Guinea. An English gold coin in use from 1664 to 1817, when it was superseded by the sovereign. It derived its name from the fact that, when first coined, the gold used in its manufacture was brought from the coast of Guinea, in West Africa. Its value varied considerably at different periods, but in later years was fixed by law at 21 shillings.

" It is still customary in Great Britain to estimate professional fees, honoraria of all kinds, complimentary subscriptions, prices of pictures, race-horses, etc., in guineas."— *Chambers's Encyclopædia.*

Guinever, Queen. The wife of King Arthur, and the most beautiful woman of her time. She was generally called the "Grey-Eyed," and was famous for her amours with Sir Lancelot du Lac and others. After the departure of her husband to the war, she " married " Modred, the King's nephew, who had been left in charge of the kingdom. When this fact became known to Arthur, he hastened home and fought a great battle with Modred at Cambula, in Cornwall, wherein the latter was slain. Meanwhile Guinever had fled and taken the veil in the nunnery of Julius the Martyr. She was buried at Meigle, in Strathmore. This account of Guinever, as found in Geoffrey's *British History*, differs from that given by Tennyson in the *Idylls of the King*. See *Lancelot du Lac.*

Gulf, Largest. The Gulf of Mexico is said to be the largest gulf in the world,—covering an area of 800,000 square miles.

Gulf of Curtius. A yawning chasm that opened in the Forum at Rome—probably as the result of an earthquake—in 362 B.C. According to the legend, the soothsayers declared that the gulf would not close until there had been cast into it the most precious things in Rome, whereupon Mettus Curtius, a noble Roman youth, appeared on horseback in full armor, and, exclaiming, " Rome has no greater riches than courage and arms," dashed over the precipice into the abyss, which at once closed over him.

Gulf States. A name often given, in the United States of America, to those States that border on the Gulf of Mexico, viz., Florida, Alabama, Mississippi, Louisiana, and Texas.

Gulf Stream. A remarkable oceanic current, which derives its name from the Gulf of Mexico, out of which it flows. The Gulf Stream passes into the Atlantic Ocean between the coasts of Florida and Cuba, and, after flowing along the coast of North America until it reaches Newfoundland, turns abruptly eastward. One portion then passes southwards towards the Azores, but the larger stream washes the coasts of the British Isles, and even reaches to the shores of Spitzbergen and Nova Zembla. The Gulf Stream varies in velocity at different points of its course. It has an average speed of four or five miles an hour as it issues from the Gulf of Mexico ; off Cape Hatteras the velocity is about three miles an hour, while off Newfoundland it is reduced to one and one-half miles per hour. In its passage across the Atlantic, the rate is only four or five miles per day. The Gulf Stream is said to be 50 miles wide, as it flows through the narrowest part of the strait between Florida and Cuba ; 150 miles wide off Charleston, S. C. ; and 300 miles wide off Newfoundland; while in crossing the Atlantic it spreads fan-like over the surface. The total length of the Gulf Stream is estimated at 3000 miles.

Gulliver's Travels. The name of a famous satirical romance by Jonathan Swift (1667–1745). It appeared in 1726, and was immediately recognized as a work of superior merit. The book is divided into four parts, which are as follows :

(1) A Voyage to Lilliput.

(2) A Voyage to Brobdingnag.

(3) A Voyage to Laputa, Baluibarbi, Luggnagg, Glubbdubdrib, and Japan.

(4) A Voyage to the Country of the Houyhnhnms.

Gun-Cotton. A highly explosive substance, invented by Schönbein, a German chemist, and made known by him in 1846. It consists of purified cotton, steeped in a mixture composed of equal parts of nitric and sulphuric acids, and afterwards dried. Its explosive power is said to be more than fifty times that of gunpowder of equal weight. See *Dynamite.*

Gunpowder, When Discovered. The discovery of gunpowder is generally ascribed to Berthold Schwarz, a monk of Goslar in Germany, about

1320 A.D. It is claimed, however, that it was known to the Hindus and Chinese centuries before that date. Roger Bacon (1214–1292) gives the composition of gunpowder in his treatise, *De Nullitate Magiæ*. The probability is that Schwarz introduced some method of manufacture whereby the ingredients (saltpetre, charcoal, and sulphur) were thoroughly mixed and the substance rendered fit for practical use. Gunpowder was first used in England by Edward III (1327–1377), in his war against the Scotch, in 1327.

Gunpowder Plot. A conspiracy formed by a small number of English Roman Catholics, during the reign of James I (1603–1625), to blow up by gunpowder the King, Lords, and Commons, at the opening of Parliament on November 5th, 1605. The plot was fortunately discovered on the evening before it was to have been carried into effect, and Guy Fawkes, who was employed to fire the train, was apprehended in the vaults under the Houses of Parliament, where the gunpowder was stored. Robert Catesby, the principal conspirator, escaped, but was shot at Worcester on November 8th, while attempting to raise an insurrection. Guy Fawkes and several others were executed on January 31st, 1606. See *Guy Fawkes's Day*.

Gun, Son of a. "A jovial fellow. A gun is a large flagon of ale."— Brewer's *Dictionary of Phrase and Fable*.

Gutter-Snipes. A Wall Street expression, used to denote those brokers that transact their business on the sidewalk, and are not members of the New York Stock Exchange. They are sometimes called "curbstone brokers." See *Curbstone Brokers*.

Guy Fawkes's Day. The name given in England to the 5th of November, famous as the anniversary of the attempted destruction of the Houses of Parliament, in 1605. The day was originally celebrated with religious services, in memory of the providential deliverance of the King and Parliament ; but at the present time its observance is limited to the peculiar custom of parading straw - stuffed effigies of Guy Fawkes through the streets of London and other English cities. These grotesque figures, seated in chairs supported on poles, are carried about the streets by men and boys, who go from house to house soliciting alms or firewood. In the evening the effigy is burned in a big bonfire, amid scenes of general rejoicing. See *Gunpowder Plot*.

Guy's Hospital. A celebrated hospital in Southwark, London, founded in 1725 by Thomas Guy, a city bookseller, who amassed a vast fortune by speculation in South Sea stock. The hospital contains at present over 700 beds, and annually relieves 5000 in-patients and over 80,000 out-patients. The yearly income is about £40,000. Sir Astley Cooper, the famous surgeon, is buried in the chapel, where may also be seen a fine marble statue of the founder. See *South Sea Bubble*.

Gwynne, Nell. One of the favorites of Charles II (1660–1685) of England, whose real name was said to be Margaret Symcott (1660–1687). She was at first an orange-girl, and afterwards an actress ; and it was while serving in the latter capacity that she first attracted the attention of the King. By Charles, she was the mother of Charles Beauclerk, afterwards the Duke of St. Albans. During her days of prosperity she was noted for her benevolence and kindness of heart. Almost the last words of the King, as he lay dying, were: "Don't let poor Nelly starve!"

Gyges's Ring. Gyges was a young Lydian shepherd who, according to a fable related by Plato, obtained possession of a golden ring that rendered its wearer invisible. Herodotus says that Candaules, King of Lydia, having married Nyssia, showed Gyges the Queen while in her bath. Indignant at this act of impropriety, Nyssia prevailed upon Gyges to murder her husband, which he easily accomplished by entering the King's chamber unseen. Gyges afterwards usurped the throne and married Nyssia. He reigned for many years (716 – 678 B.C.), and amassed great wealth. See *Helmet of Invisibility*.

Gypsies. A nomadic race, whose various tribes came from India into Europe during the 14th or 15th century, and are now widely scattered throughout Turkey, Russia, Hungary, Spain, England, and other countries. By many authorities they are thought to be the descendants of low-caste Hindus, expelled by Timur about 1399 A.D. The name " gypsies " was given them in England, because they were originally supposed to have come from Egypt. See *God of the Gypsies.*

According to Mulhall's *Dictionary of Statistics*, the number of gypsies in Europe is as follows :

(1) Great Britain................... 18,000
(2) Russia........................ 15,000
(3) Scandinavia................... 7,000
(4) Spain........................ 40,000
(5) Austria 197,000
(6) Roumania 193,000
(7) Turkey....................... 200,000
(8) Germany, etc................. 42,000

H

Habeas Corpus. This Writ of Right — protecting British subjects against arbitrary and false imprisonment — was passed May 27th, 1679, during the reign of Charles II (1660–1685). By virtue of this act, " if any person be imprisoned by the order of any court, or of the queen, he may have a writ of *habeas corpus*, to bring him before the queen's bench, or common pleas, which shall determine whether his committal be just. This act (founded on the old common-law) is next in importance to *Magna*

Charta. Parliament may suspend the *Habeas Corpus* act for a specified time in a great emergency. Then the nation parts with a portion of liberty to secure its permanent welfare, and suspected persons may then be arrested without cause assigned." — Harper's *Book of Facts.*

"The constitution of the United States provides that 'the privilege of *habeas corpus* shall not be suspended, unless when, in cases of rebellion or invasion, the public safety may require it' ; but does not specify the department of the government having the power of suspension. A series of contests on this subject between the legal and military authorities began in Maryland, May, 1861."— Haydn's *Dictionary of Dates.*

Habitans (*Fr. Inhabitants*). A word used to denote Canadian farmers of French descent or origin, especially in the Province of Quebec. Their language is a *patois* which more nearly approximates the French of the 17th century than that of the present day. The word is generally used in the plural, and is also written *habitants.*

Haddon Hall. A famous mansion in Derbyshire, England, 23 miles northwest of Derby. It has been occupied successively by the Avenells, Vernons, and Rutlands ; and is at present the seat of the Duke of Rutland. The building is in an excellent state of preservation, and represents three different styles of architecture,— the Pointed Gothic, the Tudor, and the Elizabethan. No additions to the structure have been made since the 16th century. Reference to Haddon Hall is made in Sir Walter Scott's *Peveril of the Peak.*

Hades. In Greek and Latin mythology, Hades or Pluto was the god of the lower world, or infernal regions. He was the son of Saturn and Rhea, and the brother of Jupiter and Neptune. The word " Hades " is also used to denote the lower regions, or place of departed spirits. In the *Septuagint* translation, "Hades" is the Greek word by which the Hebrew *sheol* (*the abode* *of the dead*) is translated ; and, in this sense, it is frequently used in the *New Testament*. In the *Apostles' Creed*, the words, " he descended into Hell," mean he descended into Hades, or the place of departed spirits.

Hadrian's Mausoleum. A stately tomb at Rome, erected by the Emperor Hadrian (117–138 A.D.) in 130. It contained the remains of Hadrian, Lucius Verus, the Antonines, Commodus, and Septimius Severus. The building consisted originally of a quadrangular base, surmounted by a circular tower two stories in height and covered with Parian marble. About 423 A.D., during the reign of the Emperor Honorius (395–423), the tomb was converted into a fortress ; and later it became the citadel of papal Rome, under the name of the Castle of St. Angelo. The basement of the present structure is all that remains of the ancient mausoleum. See *Castle of St. Angelo.*

Hadrian's Villa. The name given to a great number of superb structures —now in ruins—erected at Tivoli (the ancient *Tibur*), 18 miles east of Rome, by the Emperor Hadrian (117–138 A.D.), who wished to reproduce the most striking objects that he had met with in his extensive travels. According to antiquaries, the space enclosed in this way was about eight or ten miles in circumference. When, about seventy years after the time of Hadrian, the Emperor Caracalla (212–217 A.D.) built at Rome the celebrated baths that bear his name, the famous buildings of Hadrian's Villa were rifled of their superb marbles for purposes of decoration. See *Baths of Caracalla.*

Hadrian's Wall. An ancient Roman wall in England, which extended from Solway Frith to the mouth of the Tyne,—a distance of nearly seventy miles. It was erected by the Emperor Hadrian (117–138 A.D.) in 121, to prevent the incursions of the Picts and Scots ; and was probably added to by the Emperor Septimius Severus (193–211 A.D.) in 208. Extensive remains exist at the present day. The wall was 80 miles long, 12 feet high, and 8 feet thick ; and contained fortresses or " mile-castles," at intervals of a Roman mile, with smaller sentry - boxes between. A ditch, 36 feet wide and 15 feet deep, extended along the northern side of the wall; while a Roman military road, connecting the garrisons of the different stations, ran along the southern side. The wall required ten or fifteen years for its construction, and was garrisoned by 10,000 soldiers. See *Roman Walls.*

Hagiographa (*Gr.Sacred Writings*). One of the three Jewish divisions of the *Old Testament,*—the other two being the *Law* and the *Prophets*. It consists of *Psalms, Proverbs, Job, Song of Songs, Ruth, Lamentations, Ecclesiastes, Esther, Daniel, Ezra, Nehemiah,* and *Chronicles.*

Haidee. A beautiful Greek maiden in Byron's poem of *Don Juan,* " whose hair was auburn, and whose eyes were black as death." During the absence of her father, she and Don Juan fell in love with each other; but on his return the lovers were separated. Don Juan was imprisoned and afterwards sent from the island, while Haidee lost her reason and died after a lingering illness.

Hail, Columbia ! A patriotic ballad written by Joseph Hopkinson (1770–1842) on April 29th, 1798, when war between France and the United States seemed imminent. The words were written for the benefit of a young actor and singer named Fox, then playing at the Philadelphia Theatre, and were set to the music of the *President's March,* composed by one Fayles, the leader of the John Street Theatre orchestra in New York. The song soon became extremely popular.

Halcyon Days. An expression meaning a period of peace, happiness, and tranquillity. It is derived from a notion, prevalent among the ancient Sicilians, that during the seven days before and the seven days after the winter solstice (December 21st), the kingfisher, or halcyon-bird, laid its eggs and hatched them in a floating nest on the surface of the sea, which during that period remained perfectly calm.

" Amidst our arms as quiet you shall be
    As halcyons brooding on a winter's sea."
                                        Dryden.

" Birds of a color sat brooding on the
    charmed wave."   *Milton.*

Half-Breeds. A term of reproach applied by the " Stalwarts " in New York State to those Republicans that supported Garfield's administration and opposed the re-election of Conkling and Platt to the United States Senate. They were also called " Feather-Heads." See *Stalwarts.*

Halidon Hill, Battle of. A battle fought near Berwick, Scotland, on July 19th, 1333, between the English, commanded by Edward III (1327–1377), and the Scots under the Regent Douglas. The latter were defeated with a loss of 10,000 (according to some authorities, 14,000) killed. The English loss was insignificant.

Halloween. The name given to the evening before All Hallows or All Saints' Day,—the night of October 31st. In England and Scotland it was long devoted to certain harmless fireside revelries, and to pastimes engaged in by young people to ascertain their future husbands or wives. Burns, in his poem of *Halloween*, admirably summarizes the customs in vogue on this occasion, during the latter half of the 18th century. See *All Saints' Day ; Cracknut Night.*

Ham, Citadel of. An ancient fortress near St. Quentin, France, rebuilt by the Comte de St. Pol in 1470, and used at the present time as a state prison. The central tower is 100 feet high, and the walls are 36 feet in thick-ness. It was the place of confinement of Joan of Arc, Moncey, and others ; of M. de Polignac and the Count de Peyronnet, ministers of Charles X (1824–1830) ; and of Louis Napoleon [afterwards Napoleon III (1852–1870)] from 1840 until his escape in 1846. From his long incarceration there, the French Emperor was often spoken of as the " Prisoner of Ham." See *Prisoner of Ham.*

Hamites. One of the three great families of the White or Caucasian race,—the two others being the Aryans and the Semites. They are supposed to have been closely allied to the Semitic family, and to have broken away from it at a very remote epoch ; but when and where this separation took place are matters of pure conjecture. According to one theory, they formerly occupied the regions of the Euphrates and the Tigris and made their way thence through Syria and Arabia into Africa. Their leading historic representatives are the Egyptians, and probably the Chaldeans. See *Aryans ; Semites.*

Hamitic Languages. The name given to a family of related languages closely allied to the Semitic stock. It comprises three groups: (1) the *Egyptian*, including the Old Egyptian and Coptic ; (2) the *Libyan*, including the Libyan, Berber, Kabyle, Tuareg, and Guancho ; (3) the *Ethiopian*, including the Somali, Galla, Beja, Dankali, and Agau. According to some authorities, the Old Egyptian and Coptic are grouped with the Semitic languages. See *Aryan Languages ; Semitic Languages.*

"The family . . . is styled the Hamitic (by a name correlative to Semitic and Japhetic) : its constitution and relations, however, are still matters of no little difference of opinion among linguistic scholars, and can be fully established only by continued research." — Whitney's *Language and the Study of Language.*

Hamlet's Grave. On the terrace in the grounds of the royal castle of

Marienlyst (now a seaside resort), a few miles north of Elsinore, may be seen a portion of a column surrounded by trees. This is reverently shown to travelers as the grave of Hamlet. No credence, however, is placed in this statement, which is simply a story invented for the gratification of tourists.

"In fact, Hamlet's identification with this enchanting spot is at best but a Shakespearian fiction. Hamlet's country was not Zealand but Jutland."—Murray's *Hand-Book*.

"Everywhere the vandals are; but on the whole," says Jacob A. Riis, "I rather think that Elsinore has turned the tables on them. Hamlet being dead, there had to be a *Hamlet's grave*, of course. The English tourists demanded it, and in due course of time there appeared a mound on the bluff, marked with a plain granite shaft that bore the name of the melancholy Dane. The relic-hunters chipped it to pieces in one brief season. The hotel keepers provided another, and it went the same way. When last I stood at Hamlet's grave I beheld it a mighty heap of stones and slag, several cartloads. My friend, one of the solid citizens of the town, nodded knowingly at my look of amazement.

"'We caught up with them at last,' he said. 'We just have enough carted out from the glass-works every year to fill up the holes they made the season before; then let them go ahead. Want to go and look at Ophelia's spring?'"—*Century Magazine.*

Hammer-Cloth. The name given to the cloth that covers the box of a coach. The origin of this expression is variously accounted for. According to some authorities, the cloth was so called because it covered the box in which a *hammer* and other tools were formerly carried for use in case of accident, when breakdowns were frequent, owing to the bad condition of the roads. Other writers, however, say that hammer-cloth is a corruption of "hamper-cloth"; and that, in olden days, it was the custom of travelers to place on the front of the carriage a *hamper* filled with provisions, over which a cloth was thrown,—known as a hamper-cloth. Others, again, derive the word "hammer" from the Icelandic *hamr* (*skin*),—skin being

used for this purpose,—and say that our "yellow-hammer" means yellow-skin.

A fanciful suggestion, found in Brewer's *Dictionary of Phrase and Fable*, is "that the word *hammer* is a corruption of 'hammock,' the seat which the cloth covers being formed of straps or webbing stretched between two crutches like a sailor's hammock."

Webster's *International Dictionary* says that the word is probably from the Danish *hemel* (*heaven, canopy, tester*), akin to German *himmel*, and perhaps also to English *heaven*.

Hampton Court Palace. A palace on the Thames, fifteen miles southwest of London, erected by Cardinal Wolsey (1471–1530) and presented by him to Henry VIII (1509–1547), in 1526. Mary, Elizabeth, Cromwell, the Stuarts, and other English sovereigns at times resided there. Since the reign of George II (1727–1760), however, Hampton Court has ceased to be a royal residence, and is now occupied by pensioners of the Crown. Part of the original structure was torn down and the grand Inner Court built by William III (1689–1702) in 1694. This sovereign also laid out the park and gardens—comprising 40 acres —in the formal Dutch style. The palace contains a gallery of paintings, rich in Italian works of art,—especially of the Venetian School.

Hampton Roads. The name given to the broad channel between Chesapeake Bay and the mouth of the James River in Virginia, famous during the Civil War as the scene of conflict between the *Monitor* and the *Merrimac*, on March 9th, 1862. Hampton Roads is defended by Fort Monroe. See *Merrimac (1); Monitor.*

Hampton Roads Conference. A conference held on board a United States vessel, in Hampton Roads, on February 3rd, 1865,—during the Civil War,—between President Lincoln and Secretary Seward, representing the

North, and Messrs. Alexander H. Stephens, R. M. T. Hunter, and John A. Campbell, the South. The interview was brought about by Francis P. Blair, who had twice visited Jefferson Davis at Richmond, in January, 1865, with the hope that a suspension of hostilities and an ultimate restoration of the Union might be effected by a common attempt on the part of the North and the South to enforce the Monroe Doctrine and expel the French from Mexico. The conference, however, was purely informal, and resulted in nothing.

Handsome Englishman. A nickname bestowed by the French forces, under Marshal Turenne, upon John Churchill (1650 – 1722), afterwards Duke of Marlborough, in allusion to his distinction of person and grace of manner.

Handsome Swordsman. See *Beau Sabreur.*

Hanging Gardens of Babylon. Anciently considered one of the " Seven Wonders of the World," and attributed both to Semiramis and to Nebuchadnezzar, the latter of whom is said to have built them for Nitocris, his Median Queen, to remind her, in the midst of the Chaldean plain, of the hills of her native land. The " Hanging Gardens " were built in the form of a square, and rose, in a series of terraces supported on brick arches, to a height of 75 feet. There were five gardens,—each having an area of four acres, arranged in the form of an amphitheatre. The surface of each garden consisted of large, flat stones, covered with sheets of lead and overspread with earth, on which flourished trees, shrubs, and flowers of every description. The different terraces were adorned with fountains and banqueting-halls, while groves and parterres of flowers added to the beauty of the scene. Water, for purposes of irrigation, was raised from the Euphrates to a reservoir at the top, by means of a screw. Pliny

the Elder (23–79 A.D.), who visited the spot during the first century of the Christian era, says that the region was then a wilderness. The ruins of the " Hanging Gardens " may be recognized in the mound called El-Kasr.

Hanseatic League. A politico-commercial association, established in 1241 A.D. by certain cities of northern Germany, for mutual benefit and protection. It was organized by Hamburg, Bremen, and Lübeck, and ultimately included 85 towns. Its affairs were controlled by a diet called the Hansa, which met every three years — generally at Lübeck — and dictated the policy of the Association. In 1348, the League proclaimed war against Waldemar, King of Denmark; and in 1428 against Eric, with 40 ships and 12,000 troops, exclusive of seamen. It virtually dissolved in 1630, having been greatly injured by the Thirty Years' War (1618-1648). The rise of commerce in the Low Countries, during the 15th century, also contributed materially to its decline. In 1870, Hamburg, Bremen, and Lübeck — the last remaining cities of the League — were incorporated into the German Empire.

Hanse Towns. A name formerly given to the three maritime cities of Germany — Hamburg, Bremen, and Lübeck,—which were the chief towns of the Hanseatic League. See *Hanseatic League.*

Hansom Cabs. So named from their inventor, Hansom, who was also the architect of the town-hall at Birmingham, England. The first patent was taken out in 1834, and the second in 1836.

Happy Valley. A delightful region, mentioned in Dr. Samuel Johnson's *Rasselas* as the residence of the princes of Abyssinia. It was reached through a rocky cave, and was accessible from no other point.

Hapsburg, House of. A noted family, of which the Imperial House of Austria is the present representative. This name—also written *Habsburg*—is a contraction of *Habichts-burg* (*Hawk's Tower*), an ancient castle on the Aar in Switzerland, erected in the 11th century A.D. It was built by Werner, Bishop of Strasbourg, whose nephew (Werner II) first assumed the title of Count of Hapsburg. The real founder of the family, however, was Albert, first mentioned in the *Annals* as Count of Hapsburg, in 1153. Rudolph, Count of Hapsburg, became Archduke of Austria and Emperor of Germany in 1273.

Hara-kiri. A term applied to the peculiar Japanese custom of official suicide,—obsolete since 1868. According to this institution, every person holding military or civil office was bound, when disgraced by the government, to commit suicide by disembowelling himself. In point of fact, however, these self-inflicted wounds—consisting of one or two crosswise gashes given with a sharp sword or dagger—were supplemented by the well-directed blow of a superior executioner, who, with a longsword, beheaded the hapless victim. The Japanese estimated the number of these official suicides at 500 annually. The word *hara-kiri* is also written *hari-kiri*, and means *belly-cut*. It is also called " happy despatch."

Hardshell Baptists. A name given, in the southern States of the American Union, to a sect of Baptists noted for their rigid and narrow religious views. In England, the term is applied to the *Anti-Mission Baptists*, who object to organized mission-work of all kinds, as not being sanctioned by Scripture. See *Softshell Baptists*.

Hardshell Democrats. The name given to one of the two rival factions into which the Democratic party in New York State was divided from 1848 to 1854,—the other faction being known as the " Softshells." The " Hardshells " were strong pro-slavery men, and favored the enforcement of the Fugitive Slave Law. They included the Cass Hunkers of 1848, of the national school of politics. See *Softshell Democrats*.

Harleian Collection. A famous collection of rare manuscripts and printed books, collected by Robert Harley (1661–1724), afterwards Earl of Oxford and Mortimer. It was purchased by the English government for £10,000, during the reign of George IV (1820–1830), and is now in the British Museum. The collection contains 14,236 original rolls, charters, and other deeds, exclusive of 7639 volumes. Although miscellaneous in its character, the leading feature is historical literature in all its departments. There may be seen one of the earliest MSS. of Homer's *Odyssey ;* two very early copies of the Latin gospels, written in gold letters ; besides 200 MS. Bibles or biblical works, and 300 volumes of writings of the Church Fathers.

Harlot, Northern. An epithet conferred upon Elizabeth Petrovna (1709–1762), Empress of Russia, daughter of Peter the Great and Catherine I, in allusion to her gross immorality. She is also called " The Infamous."

Haroun-al-Raschid (*Ar. Aaron the Just*). A famous caliph of Bagdad (786–809 A.D.), belonging to the Abbasside dynasty. His imaginary adventures are related in the *Arabian Nights' Entertainments*. See *Abbassides*.

Harpies. In Greek and Roman mythology, Aello, Celæno, and Ocypete, daughters of Neptune and Terra. They were disgusting winged monsters, having the bodies of vultures and the heads of maidens. They had pale faces, were armed with long claws, and polluted everything with which they came in contact. The Harpies were regarded as the avenging ministers of the gods.

Harrow. A famous grammar-school at Harrow, Middlesex County, England, founded and endowed by John Lyon in 1571. The school was originally intended to afford free education to 30 poor parish-boys ; but has, at present, upwards of 500 pupils. The study of mathematics was introduced in 1837, and that of modern languages in 1851–1855. Lord Palmerston, Sir Robert Peel, Lord Byron, Sheridan, Sir William Jones, and Cardinal Manning were educated at Harrow.

Harry of the West. A sobriquet conferred upon Henry Clay (1777–1852), the American statesman, who for many years represented Kentucky in the United States Senate.

Hartford. The name of the flagship of Admiral Farragut (1801–1870) at the naval battle of New Orleans (April, 1862), and afterwards at that of Mobile Bay (August, 1864).

Harvard University. Founded October 28th, 1636, by an act of the General Court of Massachusetts, whereby the sum of £400 was granted towards the establishment of a school or college. The institution was named in honor of the Rev. John Harvard, a native of England, who died at Charlestown, Massachusetts, in 1638, and bequeathed his library of over 300 volumes and £779 (one-half of his estate) to the college. The purpose of Harvard College, during the colonial period, was "the education of the English and Indian youth in knowledge and godliness," particularly as a preparation for entering the Puritan ministry. In point of fact, however, only one Indian was ever graduated (in 1665). In 1913, Harvard University had 707 instructors, 5045 students, and 980,275 volumes in its library. The 250th anniversary of its foundation was celebrated on November 6th–8th, 1886.

Harvest Moon. "The moon near the full at the time of harvest in England, or about the autumnal equinox, when, by reason of the small angle that is made by the moon's orbit with the horizon, it rises nearly at the same hour for several days."—Webster's *International Dictionary*.

The name "harvest moon" is given in England to this phenomenon, because it occurs at the time of the annual harvest and enables the farmer to continue his labors after sunset. See *Hunter's Moon*.

Hastings, Battle of. Fought, October 14th, 1066, between the Saxons under their King, Harold II, and the Normans under William, Duke of Normandy. The battle resulted in the defeat of the Saxons and the death of Harold, whose right eye was pierced by an arrow. More than 30,000 men perished in the struggle. As a result of this contest, William — surnamed the Conqueror—became King of England under the title of William I (1066–1087), and established the Norman line of English sovereigns.

Hastings, Impeachment of. The most famous trial in the annals of English jurisprudence is that of Warren Hastings (1732–1818), who, while Governor - General of India (1773–1785), was charged with high crimes and misdemeanors, the chief of which was the acceptance of £100,000 from the Nabob of Oude. The trial commenced in Westminster Hall on February 13th, 1788, and lasted 7 years and 3 months,—requiring nearly 150 sittings. Hastings was acquitted on April 23rd, 1795. Burke, Sheridan, and Sir James Erskine distinguished themselves in the prosecution. Sheridan's speech on the impeachment lasted five hours, and produced so great a sensation that the House of Commons arose after it, and adjourned until the following day. The expenses of Warren Hastings's trial were defrayed by the East India Company, and a pension was afterwards granted to him.

Hat of Gessler. According to the Swiss legend, Hermann Gessler, a tyrannical steward in the service of Albert II, Duke of Austria and Emperor of Germany, who was striving to annex the Forest Cantons of Switzerland to his possessions, placed the ducal hat of Austria on a pole in the market-place of Altorf, and commanded all that passed it to uncover and do reverence to it. William Tell, a famous archer, refused to submit to this indignity, and was thereupon condemned to death unless he should pierce with an arrow an apple placed on his son's head. Tell successfully accomplished this feat, and, when asked by Gessler what he had purposed to do with the second arrow, found on his person, replied : " To have shot you if I had killed my child !" A few days later, while Gessler and his men were conveying Tell to the castle of Küssnacht, the patriot escaped, and, carefully watching his opportunity, shot the tyrant through the heart. According to the legend, the episode of the " Hat of Altorf " caused the wars with Austria that resulted in the liberation of Switzerland. See *Tell's Chapel; William Tell.*

Hatred of the Jews for the Samaritans. The Samaritans were thoroughly despised by the Jews, and their very name became a term of reproach among the people of Judea. They were the descendants of those Israelites that remained after the dispersion of the Ten Tribes, and intermarried with the colonists sent from Mesopotamia by the King of Assyria to occupy the land. They accepted the *Pentateuch* as inspired, and made it the foundation of their faith and practice. They also erected a temple at Mount Gerizim, where they practised idolatry. The Jews, on their return from the Babylonian Captivity in 536 B.C., refused to have any intercourse with these idolaters, and ever after remained their bitter enemies. This state of affairs existed at the time of Christ ;

and He Himself was reproached by the Jews with being one of that hated race, in the words : " Say we not well that thou art a Samaritan, and hast a devil ? "—*John* viii, 48.

Hatto, Bishop. According to tradition, Hatto was a cruel archbishop of Mayence, who in 970 A.D., at the time of a severe famine in Germany, collected many of the starving people in a barn and burned them to death, in order to free himself from their importunities,— saying that they were like mice, fit only to consume corn. Fleeing afterwards to his tower at Bingen-on-the-Rhine to escape from the plague, he was pursued by hundreds and thousands of mice, and devoured by them. Southey has made this story familiar by his well-known ballad of *Bishop Hatto*, in which, however, the invaders are rats, and not mice. The Mouse-Tower, or Maüsethurm, near Bingen, is still pointed out as the scene of this occurrence. It is situated on a small island, in the midst of the Rhine. See *Mouse-Tower.*

Hatter, Mad as a. " In the Anglo-Saxon the word ' mad ' was used as a synonym for violent, furious, angry, or venomous. In some parts of England, and in the United States particularly, it is still used in this sense. *Atter* was the Anglo-Saxon name for an adder, or viper. The proverbial saying has therefore probably no reference to hat-makers, but merely means ' as venomous as an adder.' The Germans call the viper *Natter*."—Edwards's *Words, Facts, and Phrases.*

Hauser, Casper, Case of. " There appeared in the streets of Nuremberg, 20 May, 1828, a boy in the garb of a peasant, helpless and bewildered. He carried 2 letters. One purporting to be by a laborer said that the boy was given into his custody on 7 Oct., 1812, and by agreement he had instructed him in reading, writing, and the Christian religion, and kept him in close confinement from that time.

The other letter purported to be from his mother, saying he was born on 30 Apr., 1812, that his name was Casper, and that his father, an officer in the 6th Nuremberg regiment, was now dead. The appearance of the youth corresponded with these credentials. He was detained in prison as a vagrant until July, 1828, when he was given into the care of prof. Daumer, who, as guardian, took charge of his education. On 17 Oct., 1829, he was found wounded on his forehead, as he said, by a man with a blackened face. He was placed under surveillance. The earl of Stanhope became interested, and sent him to Anspach to school. After this he became clerk to the president of the court of appeals. The case again attracted notice by his receiving a death wound at the hands of some person unknown to him while walking in the outskirts of the town on the afternoon of 14 Dec., 1833. Prof. Daumer, and Feuerbach, president of the court of appeals, believed that he was son of the grand-duke Charles Frederick ; but this was contradicted in 1875, and an official record of the baptism, post-mortem examination, and burial of the heir were published. It is still uncertain who the boy was, but the prevailing belief connects him closely with the grand-duke of Baden. Much interest has been excited among students of psychology by prof. Daumer's record of Casper's intellectual growth after his release from solitude. A monument was erected to him at Anspach.''
—Harper's *Book of Facts*.

Hawkeye State. A name popularly given to the State of Iowa, in memory of a famous Indian chief whose name was at one time a terror to the early settlers within its borders.

Hawthorn. Henry VII (1485–1509) of England is said to have chosen hawthorn for his device, because the crown of Richard III was found in a hawthorn bush on the field of Bosworth, after the battle. According to

an old English tradition, Christ's crown of thorns was made of hawthorn, which, for this reason is called by the French *l'épine noble*. In south Germany, blackthorn was believed to have been the wood used, while other traditions pointed to some kind of buckthorn.

Hawthornden. An antique house, with quaint, lofty gables and gray walls, situated on the edge of a precipice overlooking the river Esk, near Dalkeith, Scotland, and famous as the residence of the poet, William Drummond (1585–1649).

Haydn. Haydn (1732–1809), the famous composer, was the happy possessor of a diamond ring presented to him by Frederick II (1740–1786) of Prussia. This article of adornment became so necessary to him in his work that, it is said, he could not compose a single bar of music unless he could see this ring glistening on his finger.

Hayseeds. A term often used in American politics, to denote farmers or their representatives and delegates. The " hayseed delegation " in a State legislature means the representatives of the rural districts.

Head of Oliver Cromwell. Shortly after the restoration of Charles II (1660–1685), the body of Oliver Cromwell, which had been interred with great ceremony in Westminster Abbey, was taken from its grave and exposed on the gibbet at Tyburn,—being afterwards buried beneath it. The head was severed from the body and exposed, with those of Ireton and Bradshaw, on the top of Westminster Hall. There it remained for 30 years, and was finally carried to the ground by a high wind. As the story goes, it was picked up by a sentry, and some years after was sold by his family to one of the Russells, a distant descendant of Cromwell. According to a letter that appeared in the London *Times* of December 31st, 1874, signed " Senex," this ghastly trophy came into the possession of a Mr. Wilkinson, a medical man, "in whose family it still remains." In another letter, which appeared in the *Globe* of September, 1874, it is stated that the head "is now in the possession of Mr. Horace Wilkinson of Sevenoaks, Kent."

Heart of Heart. This phrase, meaning the inmost part of one's heart, is almost always erroneously written "heart of hearts."

> "Give me that man
> That is not passion's slave, and I will wear
>   him
> In my heart's core, ay, in my *heart of heart*,
> As I do thee."
>
> *Hamlet*, iii, 1.

Heart of the Andes. A famous painting by Frederick Edwin Church (1826-1900), the American artist.

Heathens. A word originally meaning those that dwell on the *heaths*, or in the country. It acquired its peculiar signification because of the fact that, at the time of the introduction of Christianity into Germany, the dwellers on the *heaths* were those that most strenuously opposed the new teachings. As at present used, the word "heathens" refers to all people except the Christians, Jews, and Mohammedans; but, in the Scriptures, the Jews are the only people not included in the meaning of the term. See *Pagans*.

He-Bible. The name given to the first edition of the "Authorized Version of the Bible," so called because the word "he," instead of "she," occurs in *Ruth* iii, 15,—the passage reading, "And *he* went into the city." See *She-Bible*.

Hecla, Mount. An active volcano in Iceland, 5102 feet in height. The first recorded eruption occurred in 1004 A.D. Eighteen outbreaks are said to have taken place,—that of 1784-1785 having been perhaps the most terrible one ever experienced. Twelve rivers

were dried up, 21 villages were totally destroyed, and 34 seriously damaged. The last violent eruption took place in 1845, and lasted for more than a year. On that occasion fine dust from the volcano was scattered over the Orkney Islands,—situated at a distance of 500 miles from Mount Hecla.

Heel-tap. A small segment of leather in the heel of a shoe, which is taken out when the shoe is finished. The word is figuratively used to denote a small portion of wine or liquor left in a glass after drinking, and which must be drained before the drinker can set it down as "finished."

Hegira (*Ar. hijrah, flight*). The hegira or flight of Mohammed from Mecca to Medina occurred on September 13th, 622 A.D. (subsequently established as the first year of the Moslem Era). See *City of the Prophet*.

> "The starting point of the Era was made to begin, not from the date of the flight, but from the first day of the Arabic year, which corresponds to July 16, A.D. 622."—Webster's *International Dictionary*.

Heidelberg Castle. A famous castle now in ruins, occupying a height near the city of Heidelberg, Germany, 330 feet above the town. It was commenced at the close of the 13th century, and was added to in 1410, 1559, and 1607. Partly destroyed by the French in 1689 and 1693, and seriously damaged by lightning in 1764. Since then it has never been rebuilt. Heidelberg Castle was for many years the palace of the Electors Palatine, and was deemed one of the most impregnable fortresses in Europe. Parts of the structure are said to have been designed by Michael Angelo. See *Heidelberg Tun*.

Heidelberg Catechism. A famous summary of religious doctrines, sometimes called the *Palatinate Catechism*. It was compiled by the Heidelberg theologians, Caspar Olenianus and Zacharias Ursinus, at the request of the Elector Frederick III of the Palatinate, and was published in 1563. It was approved by several synods, and revised by the Synod of Dort in 1619. The *Heidelberg Catechism* has been translated into all the leading European languages, and is used in America as the standard of faith in the Dutch and German Reformed churches. A tercentenary edition of this catechism was published in Latin, English, and German, in New York City in 1863.

Heidelberg Tun. A monstrous cask in the cellar of Heidelberg Castle, capable of holding 49,000 gallons, or 283,000 bottles, of wine. It is made of copper, fastened with iron hoops, and is 36 feet in length and 24 feet in height. For nearly twenty years after its completion in 1751, it was kept filled with Rhine wine of the best quality, and was annually replenished at the time of the vintage. This occasion was celebrated with dances and other festivities, which took place on a platform surmounting the top. The tun has been empty since 1769. It is said that the beer-vats at Barclay & Perkins's Brewery in London are much larger than the Heidelberg Tun,—one of these having a capacity of 108,000 gallons. See *Barclay and Perkins's Brewery ; Heidelberg Castle.*

Heir-Apparent. The name given to a person whose right to inherit an estate is beyond question, if he survives the ancestor. See *Heir-Presumptive.*

Heir of the Republic. A title conferred upon Napoleon Bonaparte (1769–1821), who, after ruling the French Republic for nearly five years as First Consul, assumed the title of Emperor and, by his despotic measures, destroyed the last vestiges of liberty.

Heir - Presumptive. The name given to a person whose right to inherit an estate is indefeasible, in case he survives and no nearer relative is born. Thus, the Princess - Royal (eldest daughter of Queen Victoria) was heir-

presumptive to the crown of England until the birth of the Prince of Wales.

Webster's *International Dictionary* defines an heir-presumptive as "one who, if the ancestor should die immediately, would be his heir, but whose right to the inheritance may be defeated by the birth of a nearer relative, or by some other contingency." See *Heir-Apparent.*

Heldenbuch (*Ger. Book of Heroes*). A collection of old German poems by various writers, many of whom are unknown.

"This is the title of a collection of old German poems, embodying a great variety of national traditions, from the time of Attila and the irruption of the German nations into the Roman Empire. They were written at different times, by various poets, the oldest of them belonging to the Swabian period. Among their authors, the names of Heinrich von Ofterdingen and Wolfram von Eschenbach are enumerated. Some of the old poems were remodelled in 1472, by Kaspar von der Roen, a Frank, and the oldest printed copies give the revised text. . . . But what is usually understood by the 'Heldenbuch' is the collection of poems, as it was reproduced under this title by Kaspar von der Roen, consisting of four parts."—*Poets and Poetry of Europe* (Longfellow).

Helicon. A mountain range—5736 feet in height — in the southwest of Bœotia, in ancient Greece, sacred to Apollo and the Muses. The village of Ascra, at the foot of the range, was the residence of Hesiod, and the early home of Greek poetry. The two fountains, Aganippe and Hippocrene,—whose waters gave poetic inspiration,—were situated on the slopes of this mountain range. See *Ascræan Poet ; Hippocrene.*

"From *Helicon's* harmonious springs
A thousand rills their mazy progress take."
Gray.

Heligoland. A miniature island in the North Sea, situated about thirty miles northwest of the mouth of the Elbe. It is about one mile long and one-third of a mile wide, and has a superficial area of three-fourths of a square mile. Heligoland came into the possession of the English in 1807, and was ceded to Germany in 1890. The resident population is considerably over 2000 ; but during the bathing-season the island is visited by more than 12,000 tourists.

Heliopolis (*Gr. City of the Sun*).
(1) The name given by the Greeks, during the rule of the Seleucidæ, to the city of Baalbek in Syria.
(2) The Greek name of the city, called On or An by the ancient Egyptians. It was situated near the apex of the Delta, and was one of the oldest and most important of the cities of Egypt. See *Baalbek.*

Heliotrope. According to Greek mythology, Apollo, who was in love with Clytia, forsook her for her sister Leucothoë. Clytia thereupon pined away, and after her death Apollo changed her into a flower that always turned its face towards the sun-god, and was accordingly called *heliotrope* (*Gr. ἤλιος, sun, τρόπος, turning*).

Helium. A hypothetical gaseous element supposed to exist in the sun, owing to the presence of certain lines in the solar spectrum. It was discovered by Professor Ramsay, in the mineral *cleveite,* in 1895, and was liquefied by him in 1898, by means of liquid hydrogen. See *Chromosphere.*

Hellespont (*Gr. Ἕλλη, Helle, πόντος, sea*). The ancient name of the Dardanelles, a narrow strait between Europe and Asia, connecting the Sea of Marmora with the Ægean Sea. It derives its name from Helle, daughter of Athamas, King of Thebes, who was drowned there. See *Dardanelles.*

Hell Gate. A narrow channel in the East River, between Long Island and Great Barn Island, famous during two centuries for its dangerous reefs and rapid currents. As early as 1851, blasting operations were commenced there, and between 1870 and 1885

many of the ledges were undermined and blown up with nitro-glycerine by General Newton and a corps of engineers, at a cost of millions of dollars. Since that time the passage of the channel has been robbed of most of its terrors.

Helmet of Invisibility.
(1) The helmet of Pluto or Hades, worn by Perseus when he slew Medusa. Through the assistance of Mercury and Minerva, Perseus obtained this helmet from the Grææ, the sisters of the Gorgons, and restored it to them after he had accomplished his purpose.
(2) The helmet of Mambrino, a Moorish King, mentioned in the poems of Bojardo and Ariosto. It was made of pure gold, and, like the helmet of Pluto, rendered its wearer invisible. It was eagerly sought by the paladins of Charlemagne, and was finally borne away by Rinaldo. Reference is made to this helmet in *Don Quixote,* the hero of which, as Cervantes tells us, imagined that he had discovered it in the shape of a highly polished brass basin worn by a barber in a shower of rain, to protect his new hat, while on his way to bleed a patient. See *Gyges's Ring.*

Helmuth the Taciturn. A sobriquet conferred upon Helmuth, Count von Moltke (1800–1891), who, although master of several languages, never betrayed himself in any one of them.

Helots. The name given to the ancient Spartan serfs, the lowest of the four classes into which the population of Laconia was divided. They are supposed to have constituted the aboriginal population of the country, and to have been subdued at the time of the Dorian Invasion. The Helots belonged to the state, and tilled the soil,— with which they were bought and sold. After the conquest of Messenia in 668 B.C., their number was greatly increased, and at one time they are said to have composed four-fifths of the inhabitants of Laconia. In 464

B.C., they revolted and nearly gained possession of the city of Sparta. They distinguished themselves during the Peloponnesian War (431–404 B.C.), and were granted their liberty in return for their valuable aid; but, shortly after, 2000 of them were treacherously slain. The Helots were annually whipped to remind them of their state of servility, and were frequently massacred to reduce their numbers.

Helvetia. The old Latin name for Switzerland, now used principally in a poetic sense. It is derived from the *Helvetii*, a warlike people of Celtic origin, who, according to Julius Cæsar, inhabited the region corresponding to the western part of modern Switzerland.

" See from the ashes of *Helvetia's* pile
The whitened skull of old Servetus smile."
O. W. Holmes.

Helvetian Republic. The name given to Switzerland, after it was conquered by the French in 1797. The new government was established in 1798, and lasted until 1814, the year of the first Napoleon's downfall. During this period, Switzerland, although nominally a republic, was really a vassal of France; but by the Treaty of Vienna (1815) its old constitution was restored and its independence and neutrality guaranteed.

Hempen Widow. The widow of a man that has suffered death by hanging. The allusion is, of course, to the material of which the rope is made.

Hen and Chickens. An expression sometimes applied to the cluster of seven stars, known as the Pleiades, in the constellation Taurus.

Hengist and Horsa. The names of the two brothers—Saxon chiefs— that led the first band of Teutonic invaders into Britain in 449 A.D., at the request of King Voltigern, to assist him in repelling the invasions of the Picts. They rendered effective aid and

freed Britain from the invaders, for which service they were rewarded with the isle of Thanet; but soon after they turned against Voltigern and made themselves masters of a large part of the island. In the battle of Aylesford, Horsa was slain ; Hengist, however, survived, and founded the kingdom of Kent, with Canterbury for his capital. Although mentioned by Nennius and the *Anglo-Saxon Chronicle*, many historians regard Hengist and Horsa as mythical characters.

" German *hengst* (a stallion), and Horsa is connected with an Anglo-Saxon word *hors* (horse). If the names of two brothers, probably they were given them from the devices borne on their arms."—Brewer's *Dictionary of Phrase and Fable.*

Henriade. An epic poem by Voltaire (1694 – 1778), celebrating the achievements of Henry IV (1589–1610) of France. Owing to the liberal religious views expressed in the poem, its publication was forbidden by the French authorities, and it was accordingly surreptitiously printed at Rouen in 1723 and secretly conveyed to Paris, where, under the title of *La Ligue ou Henri le Grand, Poème épique*, it was widely read. During his stay in England in 1726–1728, Voltaire dedicated the poem, in a revised form, to Queen Caroline, consort of George II (1727–1760), under the title of *La Henriade.*

Henrietta. A famous yacht, formerly owned by James Gordon Bennett. In December, 1866, the *Henrietta* was victor in a transatlantic race with the yachts *Fleetwing* and *Vesta*, and sailed a distance of 3106 miles in 13 days 21 hours and 55 minutes. This is said to be the quickest ocean voyage ever made by a sailing vessel.

Henry VII's Chapel. A superb chapel in the Gothic style of architecture, in Westminster Abbey, London, erected by Henry VII (1485–1509), as a burial-place for himself and his successors. It contains about 100 statues and figures, as well as tombs of royal and distinguished persons. There lie buried the remains of Henry VII, Edward V, Edward VI, Elizabeth, Mary Queen of Scots, James I, Charles II, William III and Queen Mary his wife, and George II. The Knights of the Bath are installed there, and above their dark oaken stalls hang the tattered banners of many distinguished members of the Order.

Heptameron (*Gr. ἑπτά, seven, ἡμέραι, days*). A collection of tales, modelled after the *Decameron* of Boccaccio, and generally considered by critics to be the joint production of Marguerite de Valois (1492–1549), Queen of Navarre, Des Périers, and others. They are supposed to have been related by a party of ladies and gentlemen, to beguile the time while detained by bad weather on their return from Cauterets. The stories are 72 in number, and are separated by "interludes"—serving to introduce the narrators. The subjects are similar to those of the *Decameron*, but are worked out in an original manner.

"These stories are the best known and most popular in the French language, a celebrity for which they were probably as much indebted to the rank and character of the author, as to their intrinsic merit."—*Dunlop*.

Heptarchy. The name given to the seven principal kingdoms established by the Saxons in England, at various times from the 5th to the 9th century. They were as follows : Essex, Sussex, Wessex, Kent, East Anglia, Mercia, and Northumbria. In 828 A.D., these various petty kingdoms were united under one government by Egbert, King of Wessex, who was from that time styled King of England. The word "heptarchy" means seven governments.

Heptateuch. A term (meaning seven volumes) applied, in a collective sense, to the first seven books of the *Old Testament*, which are as follows: *Genesis, Exodus, Leviticus, Numbers, Deuteronomy, Joshua,* and *Judges*. The

word is derived from the Greek *ἑπτά, seven, τεῦχος, book*. See *Pentateuch*.

Herculaneum. An ancient city of Campania, situated at the foot of Mount Vesuvius, five miles east of Naples. It was overwhelmed, together with Pompeii and Stabiæ, by an awful eruption of the volcano in 79 A.D., during the reign of Titus (79–81 A.D.). The city of Herculaneum now lies at a depth of from 50 to 100 feet below the surface, and is covered with volcanic tufa,—consisting of sand and ashes consolidated by water. The buried city was first discovered in 1706, when, on deepening a well, excavations were made to the depth of 90 feet, revealing an ancient amphitheatre. In 1738, explorations were systematically begun under royal authority, and many valuable art-relics — including the statues of Æschines, Agrippina, the Sleeping Faun, the group of the Satyr and the Goat, and busts of Plato, Demosthenes, Augustus, Seneca, and Scipio Africanus — were discovered. These are at present in the National Museum at Naples. There also may be seen 150 rolls of MS. papyri, found in 1754. The modern villages of Resina and Portici are situated on the present surface, directly over the entombed city ; and this circumstance, together with the hardness of the tufa, has caused the excavations to be carried on to a limited extent only. Enough, however, has been accomplished to reveal an amphitheatre capable of accommodating 8000 persons, a forum, a colonnade, two small temples, and a few dwelling-houses. See *Museo Nazionale ; Pompeii*.

Hercules, Twelve Labors of. Hercules, having been informed by the oracle at Delphi that immortality awaited him if he would serve Eurystheus for twelve years and do his bidding, bound himself to the Argive King, who imposed upon him the following difficult tasks, which he successfully accomplished. They are known in classic fable as the "Twelve

Labors of Hercules," and are as follows :

(1) *The Fight with the Nemean Lion.*

(2) *The Fight against the Lernæan Hydra.*

(3) *The Capture of the Arcadian Stag.*

(4) *The Destruction of the Erymanthian Boar.*

(5) *The Cleansing of the Stables of Augeas.*

(6) *The Destruction of the Stymphalian Birds.*

(7) *The Capture of the Cretan Bull.*

(8) *The Capture of the Mares of the Thracian Diomedes.*

(9) *The Seizure of the Girdle of the Queen of the Amazons.*

(10) *The Capture of the Oxen of Geryones in Erythia.*

(11) *The Fetching of the Golden Apples of the Hesperides.*

(12) *The Bringing of Cerberus from the Lower World.*

Hermes Trismegistus (*Gr. Hermes Thrice-greatest*). The Greek name of the Egyptian god Thoth, the reputed author of numerous works, some of which are still extant. They were probably compiled by the Egyptian Neo-Platonists. Thoth was regarded as the fountain head of Egyptian culture, the god of writing, of religion, and of the arts and sciences. See *Hermetic Books.*

Hermetic Books. The name given to the sacred canon of the ancient Egyptians, consisting of 42 books, divided into 6 sections. They derive their name from their reputed author, Hermes Trismegistus ; and are an encyclopædia of theology, religion, arts, and sciences. Their authorship and time of production are alike unknown, but they are supposed to have been written by Egyptian Neo-Platonists during the fourth century after Christ. Jamblichus gives their number as 20,000, and Manetho as 36,525. According to some of the ancients,

Pythagoras and Plato derived all their knowledge from these "Hermetic Books." See *Hermes Trismegistus.*

Hermitage.

(1) An imperial palace of vast extent, at St. Petersburg, Russia, connected with the Winter Palace by several covered galleries. It was erected by the Empress Catherine II (1762–1796) as a place of retirement from the worries and fatigues of government and court-life, and was enlarged by her in 1775. In its present form, however, the palace dates only from 1840–1850. It forms a parallelogram of vast and noble dimensions—being 515 feet long by 375 feet wide,— and contains a superb gallery of paintings, a collection of statuary, a theatre seating 500 persons, and a library of rare books and MSS.

(2) A mansion, about twelve miles from Nashville, Tennessee, on the Cumberland River, formerly the residence of Andrew Jackson (1767–1845), the seventh President of the United States. A vault, not far from the house, contains the remains of Jackson and his wife, and is marked by a simple monument. Some years ago, the women of Tennessee purchased the part of the "Hermitage" estate containing the homestead and the tomb, and presented it to the State authorities.

Herodians. A political sect among the Jews, friendly to Herod the Great (40 B.C.–1 A.D.) and his dynasty. According to Dr. Prideaux, they believed (1) that the Roman dominion over Judea was lawful and just and that it was their duty to submit to it ; and (2) that, under the existing state of affairs, they might practise heathen observances.

"The sect so called in the New Testament was composed of Jews, who believed that Herod was the Messiah, because 'when the sceptre departed from Judah,' he was declared king by a decree of the Roman Senate." — Edwards's *Words, Facts, and Phrases.*

24

Herod's Temple. A superb structure of white marble, erected by Herod the Great (40 B.C.–1 A.D.), at Jerusalem, on the site of the Temple of Zerubbabel. Work was commenced in 19 B.C.; and in nine years and a half the temple was ready for use. The building was much larger than the preceding one, and measured 100 cubits in length, 70 cubits in breadth, and 100 cubits in height. The stones composing this edifice were of large dimensions, some of them being 25 cubits long, 8 cubits high, and 12 cubits thick. This magnificent structure, "which rose like a mount of gold and of snow," was totally destroyed by the Romans under Titus, in 70 A.D. The site is now occupied by the Mosque of Omar. See *Mosque of Omar; Mount Moriah; Solomon's Temple; Zerubbabel's Temple.*

Heroic Age. An imaginary period, in the history of nations, occurring between the mythical and the historic ages, when heroes, or those called the "children of the gods," are supposed to have lived. According to Hesiod, the Heroic Age was the age of the heroes that fought at Troy. See *Ages, Mythologic.*

Hero of Modern Italy. A title conferred upon Giuseppe Garibaldi (1807–1882), in allusion to his noble and disinterested services in the cause of Italian independence.

Hero of the Nile. A sobriquet bestowed upon Horatio Nelson (1758–1805), on account of his brilliant naval victory over the French in Aboukir Bay, on August 1st, 1798. With a greatly inferior force, Nelson attacked and wellnigh destroyed the entire French fleet under Admiral Brueys. See *Nile, Battle of the.*

Herostratus. An Ephesian who, in order to immortalize his name, set fire to the Temple of Diana at Ephesus (one of the "Seven Wonders of the World"), in 356 B.C., on the night, it is said, of the birth of Alexander the Great. For this infamous deed, he was put to death by torture, and a decree was passed by the Ephesians, making it a penal offense even to mention his name. The contrary effect, however, was produced; and at the present day, the name of the builder of the temple is forgotten, while that of its destroyer is vividly remembered. See *Ephesus, Temple at.*

" The aspiring youth that fired the Ephesian
    dome
 Outlives in fame the pious fool that raised
   it."
                          Colley Cibber.

Hesperia (*Gr. Western Land*). A name given by the Alexandrian grammarians to Italy, because it lay to the west of Egypt, and sometimes applied by them to the whole of western Europe. The Romans, in after years, gave this name to Spain for a similar reason (*i. e.*, because it was to the west of Italy).

Hesperides, Garden of the. See *Garden of the Hesperides.*

Hesperus. The name given by the Greeks to the planet Venus, when it was the evening star. See *Phosphorus.*

Hetman. The title of the commander-in-chief of the Cossacks, annually chosen from among their number. The Cossacks in assembly threw their fur caps at the candidates for whom they voted, and the one receiving the greatest number was declared elected. The office of Hetman or Attaman was abolished by the Emperor Nicholas I (1825–1855), except as a hereditary title in the imperial family.

H. H. The initials by which Helen M. Jackson (1831–1885), the popular author, was widely known.

Hiawatha, Song of. The title of a poem by Longfellow (1807–1882), based on the deeds of Hiawatha, the legendary hero of the Iroquois Indians. It appeared in 1855, and soon obtained a wide popularity. It is sometimes called the Indian Epic of America. See *American Epic Poem.*

"I have at length hit upon a plan for a poem on the American Indians, which seems to me the right one, and the only. It is to weave together their beautiful traditions into a whole. I have hit upon a measure, too, which I think the right and only one for such a theme."—Longfellow's *Diary.*

Hibernia. The ancient Roman name for Ireland, now used only in a poetic sense. The island was known to the Greek geographers as Ierne.

Hicksites. A numerous body of rationalistic Quakers in America, founded by Elias Hicks (1748–1830), who, in 1827, seceded from the *Society of Friends* and created a schism in that body by his promulgation of Unitarian doctrines. About one-half of the "Friends" in America adopted his views. The Hicksites deny the miraculous conception, the divinity and the atonement of Christ, as well as the inspiration and authenticity of the Scriptures.

Higher Law. An expression first made use of by the Hon. William H. Seward (1801–1872), in a speech delivered by him in the United States Senate, March 11th, 1850, on the question of the admission of California into the Union. As employed by him on that occasion, the phrase denoted a law higher than the Constitution, viz., a law of God ; and in that sense it was caught up and used with telling effect by the Abolitionists, whose purposes were set at naught by the laws in force at that time.

Highest Monument. The highest monument in the world is the Eiffel Tower, erected in Paris in honor of the French Exposition of 1889. It is 985 feet in height,—nearly twice the altitude of the Washington Monument, which, until the completion of the Eiffel Tower, was the loftiest structure on the globe. See *Eiffel Tower ; Washington Monument (1).*

Highest Mountain in Europe. The highest mountain in Europe is Mount Blanc, 15,782 feet above sea-level. Although popularly associated with Switzerland, this mountain is situated in Savoy, a province of France. The Caucasus range, which is really Asiatic in character, is sometimes treated as part of the boundary line between Europe and Asia, and contains six peaks considerably over 16,000 feet,— Mount Elburz (the highest) attaining an elevation of 18,000 feet above the level of the sea.

Highland Laddie. An epithet conferred by his Scottish admirers upon Prince Charles Edward Stuart (1720– 1788), the "Young Pretender," during his residence in Holyrood Palace, Edinburgh, after his capture of that city in 1745. The cause of the Stuarts was then at its height, and the name of the "Young Pretender" was on every lip. The ladies of the Jacobite party adorned themselves with ribbons on which the Prince was represented as "The Highland Laddie," while the more fortunate ones procured locks of his hair or miniatures of his person.

Highland Mary. A poem by Robert Burns (1759–1796), beginning with the words :

"Ye banks, and braes, and streams around
    The castle o' Montgomery."

"Highland Mary" is generally thought to be Mary Campbell, the poet's first love. She lived as a dairy-maid in the "castle o' Montgomery," near Tarbolton, the residence of Colonel Hugh Montgomery, and was affianced to Robert Burns. During her absence from the castle, while on a visit to her relatives, she was seized with a malignant fever, and died before Burns could reach her side. According to other authorities, "Highland Mary" is said to be Mary Morison, one of the poet's early loves.

High Seas. A term usually applied to that part of the ocean distant three miles or more from the coast-line of any country. According to international law, every country bordering on the ocean has exclusive control of the sea for a distance of three miles from its shores. This is known as the "territorial sea" of the country, or *mare clausum*. Beyond that point, the ocean is the common property of all nations. This distinction between "high seas" and "territorial seas" is not maintained in respect of navigation, but as regards fishing it is otherwise. In Great Britain and Ireland, foreign fishermen are not allowed to fish within three miles of the coast, unless special arrangements have been made either by treaty or by license from the Crown.

Highwaymen, Noted English. The following list is compiled principally from Brewer's *Reader's Handbook :*

(1) *Claude Duval* (1643–1670).
(2) *James Whitney* (1660–1694).
(3) *Jonathan Wild* (1682–1725).
(4) *Jack Sheppard* (1701–1724).
(5) *Dick Turpin* (1705–1739).
(6) *Jerry Abershaw* (1773–1795).
(7) *Swift Nick Nevison* (hanged at York in 1684).
(8) *Galloping Dick* (executed at Aylesbury in 1800).
(9) *Captain Grant* (executed at Maryborough in 1816).
(10) *Samuel Greenwood* (executed at Old Bailey in 1822).
(11) *William Rea* (executed at Old Bailey in 1828).

Hind and Panther. An allegory in verse by John Dryden (1631–1700). It appeared about 1686, soon after the poet's conversion to the Roman Catholic Church, and was written in defense of his new opinions. In this poem the "Hind" is the Church of Rome, the "Spotted Panther" is the Church of England, while the Independents, Quakers, Anabaptists, and Calvinists are represented as bears, hares, boars, and wolves, respectively.

Hinnom. A narrow valley situated south and west of Jerusalem, forming part of the boundary line between Judah and Benjamin. It is known at the present day as *Wady Jehennam.* See *Gehenna ; Tophet.*

Hippocrates's Sleeve. A kind of strainer, used by the early chemists for straining syrups, making decoctions, etc. It was conical or sleeve-shaped in form, and was made by stitching together the adjacent sides of a square piece of linen or flannel.

Hippocratic Face. A condition of the human face produced by death, long illness, excessive hunger, and the like. The nose is pinched, the temples hollow, the eyes sunken, the ears cold and retracted, the skin of the forehead dry, the complexion livid, and the lips relaxed and cold. This appearance is so named from having been accurately described by Hippocrates [468–367 (?) B.C.], the "Father of Medicine."

Hippocratic Oath. A solemn oath said to have been administered by Hippocrates himself [468–367 (?) B.C.] to his disciples, when they were about to enter upon the practice of medicine. According to the terms of this oath, the asseverator pledged himself to absolute purity of morals, and solemnly promised to practise his profession in accordance with the principles of humanity and honor. The novice further pledged himself to the most disinterested brotherhood with all persons legitimately connected with the healing art, and to deeds of kindness towards their offspring.

According to Webster's *International Dictionary*, "such an oath is still administered to candidates for graduation in medicine."

Hippocrene (*Gr. Ἱπποκρήνη, Fountain of the Horse*). A fountain near Mount Helicon, in Bœotia, sacred to the Muses, said to have been miraculously produced by a stroke of the hoof of Pegasus. See *Helicon ; Pegasus.*

Hobbes's Voyage. An expression meaning a leap in the dark. It is derived from the last words of Thomas

Hobbes (1568–1679), the English philosopher, who, on his death-bed, exclaimed : " Now I am about to take my last voyage—a great leap in the dark." See *Dying Sayings, Real or Traditional*.

Hobson's Choice. An expression meaning a choice without an alternative. It is said to have had its origin in the name of one Tobias Hobson, who kept a livery-stable at Cambridge, England, in the time of Charles I (1625–1649), and required each customer to take, in his turn, the horse that stood nearest the stable-door. In this way no favoritism was shown, —all customers being served alike. Milton wrote two humorous epitaphs on the death of this eccentric carrier.

" Mr. Hobson kept a stable of forty good cattle, always ready and fit for travelling ; but when a man came for a horse, he was led into the stable, where there was great choice, but he obliged him to take the horse which stood next to the stable-door ; so that every customer was alike well served according to his chance, and every horse ridden with the same justice : from whence it became a proverb, when what ought to be your election was forced upon you, to say, ' Hobson's choice.' "—*Spectator*, No. 509.

Hog, To Go the Whole. An expression, meaning to go to the utmost limit, the origin of which is variously accounted for.

" This phrase probably arose from the Arabian story versified in Cowper's *Love of the World Reproved*. Mohammed allowed his followers to eat pork, except one portion of the animal, which he did not specify, and consequently strict Mohammedans were debarred from eating any. Others, however, through one piece being forbidden,

—thought it hard
From *the whole hog* to be debarred,

and so, one taking a leg, another a shoulder, and so on,

With sophistry their sauce they sweeten,
Till quite from tail to snout 't is eaten."
—Walsh's *Handy-Book of Literary Curiosities*.

" Carlyle . . . suggested that *going the whole hog* was probably a phrase of Irish origin. Hog he found was a synonym in Ireland for a tenpenny piece when that coin

was in common use in the country."—*Standard Dictionary*.

It is said that in Virginia, the wholesale dealer in meat asks the retail butcher if he intends " to go the whole hog " or to take certain joints only, and regulates his price accordingly.

Hohenlinden, Battle of. A bloody battle fought on December 3rd, 1800, between 70,000 French and Bavarians commanded by Moreau, and 60,000 Austrians under the Archduke John. The contest resulted in a signal victory for the French, who lost 5000 men killed and wounded. The Austrian loss was 17,000 men and 74 guns. This victory led to the Treaty of Lunéville, which was signed in February of the following year. Campbell has commemorated this battle in his famous lyric, *The Battle of Hohenlinden*, published soon after the sanguinary event.

" On *Linden* when the sun was low,
All bloodless lay the untrodden snow,
And dark as winter was the flow
Of Iser rolling rapidly."

Hohenstaufen, House of. The name of the German princely house that occupied the imperial throne from 1138 to 1254 A.D. It was preceded by the Saxon and Franconian dynasties. The House of Hohenstaufen was founded by Frederick von Büren, who lived about the middle of the 11th century, and the name was first assumed by his son Frederick, from a castle built by him on the hill of Staufen, near Stuttgart. Conrad III, the first Emperor of this house, was elected in 1138, and was succeeded by Frederick I (1152–1190), Henry VI (1190–1197), Philip I (1198–1208), Frederick II (1212–1250), and Conrad IV (1250–1254).

Hohenzollern, House of. The name of the present reigning family of Prussia. It claims a greater antiquity than any other dynasty in Europe, and traces its descent from Count Thassilo, who, in the early part of the 9th century, built a castle on the Zollern hill, whence the family derives its name. In 1415, Frederick VI, the representative of the younger branch of the Hohenzollerns, was invested with the electorate of Brandenburg by the Emperor Sigismund, and thus was founded the present dynasty of Prussia. In 1870, Prince Leopold of Hohenzollern was a candidate for the throne of Spain, but as his nomination gave umbrage to France, he voluntarily withdrew in July of the same year.

Holborn Viaduct. A causeway in the city of London, 465 yards long and 27 yards wide, extending from Newgate to Hatton Garden. It was completed in 1869, and was built to overcome the inconvenience to traffic between Oxford Street and the City, occasioned by the steep descent of Holborn Hill. As a result of the building of this viaduct, Oxford Street and Holborn form one continuous thoroughfare. The structure is considered the finest piece of street-architecture in London. It is constructed almost entirely of iron, but is not visible,—its sides being lined with rows of buildings. Holborn was formerly known as *Oldbourne*, and was so called from being built on the edge of a brook or "bourne" that emptied into Fleet Ditch.

Holiday. A corruption of "Holy Day, ' and still sometimes spelled *holyday*. Holidays were originally days set apart by the Roman Catholic Church, either as religious festivals or in commemoration of some event of importance.

Holland House. A famous mansion, built in the Tudor style, standing at the west end of Kensington Gardens, London. It was erected in 1607, and, soon after its completion, passed into the hands of Henry Rich, first Earl of Holland, from whom it derived its name. After his execution for treason, the house came into the possession of Fairfax and Lambert, two Parliamentary generals ; but was restored to

Lady Holland in 1665. Addison resided there from 1716 to 1719 ; and, later, the mansion became the property of Henry Fox, afterwards Baron Holland, the father of the famous Charles James Fox. William III and Mary lived there for a brief period. During the first half of the 19th century, Holland House was the rallying-place of the literary and political celebrities of the Whig party, who were lavishly entertained by the distinguished third Baron Holland. No other private dwelling in England, says Macaulay, can boast of so great a number of inmates famous, in their day, for political influence or literary attainments.

Hollands. A name popularly given to Dutch gin, and also to a kind of linen first manufactured in Holland.

Holy Alliance. An alliance formed in 1815, after the fall of Napoleon I, by the Emperors of Russia and Austria and the King of Prussia, ostensibly for the purpose of governing their respective nations in a paternal manner, in accordance with the principles of Christianity. In reality, however, the league was simply another name for a compact entered into with the object of suppressing the growth of free institutions and of preventing the development of liberal ideas throughout the Continent. The Kings of England and France afterwards joined the Alliance, and in 1818 a Congress was held at Aix-la-Chapelle, on which occasion a declaration was issued, asserting that the purpose of the Alliance was to insure peace and legitimate stability. A special article excluded forever the members of the Bonaparte family from any throne in Europe. England and France afterwards withdrew from the Holy Alliance, which, after the lapse of a few years, came to an end. It was, in general, censured in England as inimical to the principles of freedom.

Holy and Apostolical Crown. The ancient crown of the Kings of Hungary,—regarded as the palladium of the Hungarian nation. It is surmounted by two ribs of gold, which are said to have been part of a crown presented to St. Stephen, King of Hungary, by Pope Sylvester II (999–1003) in 1000 A.D., and are believed by the faithful to be the work of angels. This diadem is kept in the chapel of the royal castle at Buda-Pesth, in Hungary. During the struggle for Hungarian independence in 1848–1849, the crown was removed for safe-keeping by Kossuth, but subsequently fell into the hands of the Austrians, who in 1867 restored it to the Hungarians.

Holy City. An appellation bestowed by any sect or nation upon the city that is identified with its religious beliefs and observances, and that has, in consequence, become a place of veneration and worship. Among such cities may be mentioned :

(1) *Allahabad*, the " Holy City " of the Indian Mohammedans.

(2) *Benares*, of the Hindoos.

(3) *Cuzco*, of the ancient Incas.

(4) *Jerusalem*, of the Jews and Christians.

(5) *Mecca*, *Medina*, and *Damascus*, of the Mohammedans generally.

(6) *Moscow* and *Kief*, of the Russians.

(7) *Rome*, of the Roman Catholics.

Holy Coat of Trèves. A seamless garment preserved in the cathedral at Trèves in Rhenish Prussia, and said to be the one worn by Jesus Christ on the day of his crucifixion. According to tradition, it was discovered by the Empress Helena while on a visit to the Holy Land in the 4th century, and was afterwards deposited by her for safe-keeping in the cathedral at Trèves. In the 9th century, the Holy Coat was concealed from the Normans in the crypt of the church, but was brought to light and solemnly exhibited in 1196. It was not shown again until 1512 when, owing to the vast crowds

that flocked to see it, Pope Leo X (1513–1522) decreed that it should be exhibited only once every seven years thereafter. It is said that in 1844 the Holy Coat was viewed by 1,000,000 devout pilgrims in the course of a single week. In 1891—the first time of its exhibition since 1844—it was seen by nearly 2,000,000 pilgrims. A Holy Coat is also shown at Argenteuil and at 19 other places.

" Christ is always represented in the Gospels as a very poor man, but the shirt of Trèves is that of a prince, and must have been of fabulous price. The same inconsistency is remarkable in numerous other sacred ' relics.' "—Brewer's *Historic Note-Book.*

Holy Cross Day. A name sometimes applied to the festival of the Exaltation of the Cross (September 14th), which commemorates the restoration of the cross to Jerusalem in 628.

Holy Family. The name given to any scriptural painting representing the infant Jesus, surrounded by his attendants. These are, generally, Joseph and Mary, John the Baptist, Elizabeth, and Anna. All of these persons, however, do not figure in every picture of the Holy Family.

Holy Grail. See *Grail, Holy.*

Holy Grotto. A grotto in Nazareth, where, according to Roman Catholic tradition, the Virgin Mary stood when she received from the Angel Gabriel the message of the Annunciation. A monastery now covers the spot, and there, it is claimed, originally stood the house in which Mary was born, and which was afterwards miraculously transported to Loretto, in Italy. The grotto is reached by a flight of 15 steps, and is 20 feet long, 20 feet wide, and 10 feet deep. Its sides are encased with marble, and on the altar (also of the same material) are seven vases of flowers, while above it nine silver lamps are kept constantly burning.

The Greek Christians at Nazareth have identified another spot with the scene of the Annunciation, and over the Fountain of the Virgin have erected a church, in commemoration of the event. See *Loretto.*

Holy Handkerchief. The handkerchief or napkin lent by St. Veronica to Jesus Christ while on his way to Calvary, to wipe the bloody sweat from his brow. According to the legend, a perfect image of Christ's features was imprinted upon it. This precious relic is preserved in St. Peter's Church at Rome, in a chapel under the dome, dedicated to St. Veronica. A second handkerchief — said also to be the original one — is in the cathedral at Milan. See *Sudarium ; Veronica.*

Mark Twain, in his *Innocents Abroad,* says : " . . . we saw this handkerchief in a cathedral in Paris, in another in Spain, and in two others in Italy. In the Milan cathedral it costs five francs to see it, and at St. Peter's at Rome it is almost impossible to see it at any price. No tradition is so amply verified as this of St. Veronica and her handkerchief."

Holy Land. A term used especially by Christians to designate Palestine, as being the scene of the birth, ministry, and death of Jesus Christ; but also employed by other religious sects to describe the places sacred to them from association. Thus, the Mohammedans speak of Mecca as the Holy Land, it being the birthplace of Mohammed. The Chinese Buddhists call India the Holy Land, because the founder of their religion was born there ; while the Greeks bestowed this same title on Elis, where was situated the temple of Olympian Zeus.

Holy League.
(1) A league, formed in 1510, by Pope Julius II (1503–1513), Ferdinand V (1461–1519) of Spain, and the Republics of Venice and Switzerland, against Louis XII (1498–1515) of France, — its object being to dispossess Louis of Venice and expel him from Italy. The French army, under the command of Gaston de Foix, the King's nephew, gained the three great victories of Bologna, Brescia, and Ravenna over the League, in the course of as many months ; but, in the last-named battle, Gaston de Foix was killed, and the French successes came to an end. The League was dissolved on the death of Pope Julius II in 1513.
(2) A coalition, formed at Peronne in France, in 1576, to prevent the accession of Henry of Navarre (a Protestant prince) to the throne of France. It lasted until 1593, when Henry embraced the Roman Catholic faith. The objects of the League were : (1) to exterminate the Huguenots ; (2) to confine Henry III in a monastery ; and (3) to make the Duke of Guise King of France. See *Cambrai, League of.*

Holy Maid of Kent. An appellation conferred upon Elizabeth Barton (1506–1534), who, during the reign of Henry VIII (1509–1547), incited the Roman Catholics of England to oppose the Reformation. She was beheaded at Tyburn on April 20th, 1534. Elizabeth Barton was believed at one time to be possessed of the gift of prophecy, and her prediction, that if Henry VIII should divorce Catharine of Aragon and marry Anne Boleyn England would suffer direful calamities caused widespread apprehension. So successful was she for a while in her impostures that she even deceived Cardinal Wolsey and Sir Thomas More, but as the awful consequences of Henry's marriage — predicted by her—never came to pass, her reputation as a prophetess was hopelessly destroyed. She confessed on the scaffold that she was " ' a poor wench without learning,' who had been puffed up by praises to her own undoing and that of her companions." See *Nun of Kent.*

Holy of Holies. The name given to the innermost apartment in the

Temple at Jerusalem. It was the most sacred spot in the entire edifice, and was entered only by the high-priest once every year. The Holy of Holies was separated from the Sanctuary, or Holy Place, by an impervious veil, and was probably entirely dark. According to St. Mark, this veil " was rent in twain from the top to the bottom " at the instant of the death of Jesus Christ on the cross.

" In the Temple, the only light that could penetrate to the *Holy of Holies* was from the front ; and though the Holy Place was partially lighted from the sides, its principal source of light must have been through the eastern façade."—*Fergusson.*

Holy Oil. A name given, in the 4th century A.D., to oil brought from Jerusalem to Europe ; and, afterwards, to oil blessed at the tombs of the saints. At the present day, the term more particularly refers to the baptismal oil with which children are anointed throughout the Russian Empire. It is said that two gallons are annually required for this purpose, in Russia alone. The oil is kept at the Kremlin at Moscow, and is stored in 33 massive jars of solid silver.

Holy Places in Palestine. The name given to those places in the Holy Land, chiefly in or near Jerusalem, that are identified with the principal events in the life of Jesus Christ, and are on that account greatly venerated by Christians. Among them may be mentioned the Church of the Nativity, the Church of the Holy Sepulchre, the Church of the Ascension, the Tomb of the Virgin, the Fountain of the Virgin, the Via Dolorosa, the Garden of Gethsemane, and the Mount of Olives.

Holy Roman Empire. The official title of the German Empire from 962 to 1806 A.D.—a period of more than eight centuries,—when Francis II of Hapsburg renounced the imperial dignity and retained the title of Emperor of Austria, which he had assumed in 1804. Although the Western Empire of the Romans ceased to exist in 476 A.D., Charlemagne, more than 300 years later, sought to revive it and was crowned Emperor of the Romans by Pope Leo III (795–816) at Rome, in 800 A.D. The Empire, however, fell to pieces soon after his death in 814 ; but was again revived by Otho the Great, who in 962 was crowned at Rome by Pope John XII (956–963). For more than 800 years thereafter the Empire flourished, and was governed by an unbroken succession of German princes, who claimed and, to some extent, exercised, the prerogatives of the ancient Roman Emperors. The word " Holy " was added to the title to suggest that the Empire had been christianized, and the words " of the German Nation " were sometimes appended to indicate that the nation had attained control of the ancient imperial realm. When the German Empire was revived in 1871, the titles " Holy " and " Roman " were both quietly dropped.

Holyrood Palace. A celebrated palace at Edinburgh, Scotland, once an abbey and, for several centuries, the residence of the Scottish sovereigns. The abbey—vestiges of which still remain—was founded by David I (1124–1153) in 1128. The palace, which is built in the form of a quadrangle with a central court, was commenced in the reign of James IV (1488–1513), and is especially famous as the residence of Mary Queen of Scots, whose favorite, Rizzio, was murdered almost before her very eyes by Lord Darnley and other conspirators on March 9th, 1566. Holyrood was nearly destroyed by Cromwell's soldiers in 1650, but was rebuilt by Charles II (1660–1685), after the Restoration. The apartments once occupied by Queen Mary are still preserved in their original condition. Holyrood ceased to be a royal residence on the accession of James VI (1567–1625) to the throne of England in 1603. George IV (1820–1830), however, dwelt there for a while in 1822, and Queen Victoria (1837–1901) occasionally spent the night within its walls.

Holy Saturday. The name frequently given to the Saturday immediately preceding Easter Sunday.

Holy Stone. A celebrated stone, sacred to St. Patrick, preserved at Ardmore, Waterford County, Ireland. According to tradition, it was miraculously floated across the ocean from Rome, together with the saint's vestments, a bell for his tower, and a lighted taper for his celebration of the mass.

"The people crowd to the *Holy Stone*, and, having gone on their bare knees several times round it, creep under it, lying flat. The painful contortions of some of these poor people it is distressing to witness, as they force themselves through the narrow passage. It is only at low water that this part of the ceremony can be performed. The stone, which weighs perhaps four or five tons, rests upon two small rocks, leaving a passage under it."—*Mr. and Mrs. Hall.*

Holy Thursday. A name frequently given to Ascension Day, which occurs forty days after Easter and ten days before Whit-Sunday. The name "Holy Thursday" is often erroneously applied to Maundy-Thursday, the Thursday in Holy Week. See *Maundy-Thursday.*

Holy Wars. A term frequently used to denote the Crusades or military expeditions, organized to rescue the Holy Sepulchre at Jerusalem from the hands of the Mohammedans. See *Crusades.*

Holy Water. The name given in the Roman Catholic and Greek Churches to water blessed by a priest or bishop for certain religious purposes. This custom was prescribed by Jewish law, and was also a part of the ritual of many pagan nations. Holy Water is said to have been used in Christian churches as early as 120.

Holy Week. The name given to the week immediately preceding Easter, which commemorates the principal events in the passion and death of Jesus Christ. This institution is of very early origin in the Christian Church, and is also known as the "Week of Indulgences," the "Still Week," the "Great Week," the "Week of the Holy Passion," the "Vacant Week," and the "Penitential Week." In the English Church, Holy Week is also called Passion Week; but this last term is used by the Roman Catholics to denote the week before Palm Sunday. The days specially observed in Holy Week are Palm Sunday, Spy-Wednesday, Maundy-Thursday, Good Friday, and Holy Saturday or the Great Sabbath. See *Passion Week.*

Homer, British. An epithet conferred upon John Milton (1608–1674), reference to which is made, in the epitaph on Thomas Gray's monument in Westminster Abbey, in the following lines:

"No more the Grecian muse unrivall'd reigns,
  To Britain let the nations homage pay:
  She felt a Homer's fire in Milton's strains,
  A Pindar's rapture in the lyre of Gray."

Homeric Hymns. Poems supposed by the ancients to have been written by Homer, but considered by modern critics to have been the work of other hands. Of those now extant, the five best known are the *Hymns to the Delian Apollo, to the Pythian Apollo, to Aphrodite, to Hermes,* and *to Demeter.* The *Homeric Hymns* are vastly inferior to the *Iliad* and *Odyssey,* and probably contain fragments by writers of every century, from the time of Homer (*fl.* 1000 B.C.) to that of the Persian War (490 B.C.).

Homeric Times. An expression sometimes used to denote a period prior to that of recorded history. The minute description of social and economic life given in the poems of Homer, reinforced by the facts brought to light by the researches of Schliemann, have placed before us a mass of information concerning the civilization of the prehistoric Greeks. This people possessed vessels of copper and ornaments of gold, pottery and vases, knives and keys of iron, wrought leather-goods, and head-dresses of gold. Spinning, weaving, and fine embroidery were arts practised by the women ; while relief-sculpture, and wood and ivory carving manifested the skill attained by the Greeks in the fine arts.

Homeric Verse. A name sometimes given to hexameter verse—the epic or heroic verse of the Greeks and Romans—because it was adopted by Homer in his two great poems,—the *Iliad* and *Odyssey*. Hexameter verse —as its name implies—consists of six feet, the first four of which may be either dactyls or spondees, while the fifth must regularly be a dactyl and the sixth a spondee. When, however, the fifth foot is a spondee, the verse is said to be spondaic. A spondee consists of two long syllables, and a dactyl of one long syllable and two short ones. Virgil's *Æneid* also is written in hexameter verse.

Homer of Portugal. A sobriquet conferred upon Luis de Camoëns (1524–1580), the author of *The Lusiad*, and the greatest poet of Portugal. See *Apollo of Portugal.*

Homer's Iliad. See *Iliad.*

Homer's Odyssey. See *Odyssey.*

Home, Sweet Home. A popular ballad by John Howard Payne (1792–1852), an American actor and dramatist. It was composed as a song for one of his dramas, entitled *Clari ; or, The Maid of Milan,* which was presented for the first time in 1813. The music of the ballad is said to have been adapted from a Sicilian air, by Sir Henry Bishop.

It is a singular fact that the man that wrote this touching ballad was without a home during the last 40 years of his life, and died in a foreign land. He himself says : " How often have I been in the heart of Paris, Berlin, London, or some other city, and have heard persons singing or heard organs playing *Home, Sweet Home,* without having a shilling to buy myself the next meal or a place to lay my head ! The world has literally sung my song till every heart is familiar with its melody, yet I have been a wanderer from my boyhood, and, in my old age, have to submit to humiliation for my bread."

Homœopathy. A theory of medicine, promulgated by Dr. Samuel Hahnemann (1755–1843), of Leipsic, in 1810. It asserts that any disease should be treated by medicines, in minute doses, that would produce in a healthy patient symptoms similar to those manifested by the disease requiring treatment. This is the principle of " like diseases are cured by like remedies " (*Lat. Similia similibus curantur*), and is based on the theory that two similar diseased conditions cannot subsist in the same organ at the same time. Homœopathy was introduced into England in 1827, and into the United States about the same time. The Hahnemann Hospital was opened in Bloomsbury Square, London, on September 16th, 1850. The American Institute of Homœopathy, organized in 1844, is the oldest medical organization in the United States, and has (1913) 3000 members.

Honeycomb, Will. One of the members of the imaginary club by whom the *Spectator* was said to be edited. He was an authority on all affairs connected with the gay world, and was noted for his courtly manner and graceful bearing. See *Spectator.*

Honeymoon. The name given to the first moon or month after marriage. The word is derived, according to good authority, from the custom with newly married couples among the ancient Teutones, of drinking metheglin or mead (a kind of wine made with honey) for thirty days after marriage. Attila the Hun is said to have drunk so much mead at his wedding-feast that he died from its effects.

Honi Soit Qui Mal Y Pense (*Old-French, Evil to him that evil thinks*). The motto of the Order of the Garter and of the Crown of England. See *Garter, Order of the.*

"The order was established by Edward III on April 23, 1349. But why the garter was selected as its name and symbol, and what is the special significance of the motto, have long been moot questions with historians. Camden and others suggest that as Richard Cœur de Lion had once distinguished some chosen knights by causing them to tie a thong or garter round the leg, Edward had reminiscently given his own garter as the signal for a battle, probably Crécy, in which he was successful. Polydore Virgil, whose history appeared in 1536, nearly two hundred years after the event, is the first authority for the familiar story that the Countess of Salisbury, the king's mistress, dropped her garter at a ball, and that Edward picked it up and handed it back to the lady, with the remark, "Honi soit qui mal y pense," and forthwith founded the order. Polydore's authority, therefore, is no authority at all. It is extremely unlikely that such an incident would have been suppressed by Froissart, who makes no mention of it, though he relates the story of the countess's amour with the king. The motto, it may be added, is an old French one, proverbial in France before Edward's day."—Walsh's *Handy-Book of Literary Curiosities.*

Hoosac Tunnel. The longest and most notable railroad tunnel in America. It is near North Adams, Massachusetts, on the line of the Fitchburg Railroad, and pierces the Hoosac Mountains, a spur of the Berkshire Hills. The tunnel is 4¾ miles long, averages 25 x 25 feet, and cost the State about $16,000,000. It was commenced in 1855, and completed, after several interruptions, in 1874. The tunnel is the property of the State, and was built to shorten the distance between Boston and the West.

Hoosier State. A name popularly applied to the State of Indiana, the inhabitants of which are frequently called *Hoosiers.* The word *hoosier* is said to be a corruption of *husher*, a common term for a *bully* throughout the West.

Hope Diamond. The name given to a superb blue diamond, valued at from $100,000 to $150,000. It weighs 44⅜ carats, and is owned by the family of Mr. H. T. Hope. It is said to have been cut from a larger stone, weighing, in its rough state, 112¼ carats. This original stone was sold to Louis XIV (1643–1715) by Tavernier, but disappeared during the time of the French Revolution.

Horatius Cocles of the Tyrol. A sobriquet conferred by Napoleon Bonaparte upon Alexandre Davy Dumas, the father of the novelist, and an officer in the army of Dumouriez, who, alone, in 1798, defended the passage of the bridge at Brixen, and thus contributed materially to the success of the day.

Horicon. The Indian name of Lake George,—meaning "Silvery Waters." Wheeler, however, in his *Dictionary of the Noted Names of Fiction*, denies the truth of this statement, and says that *Horicon* is "a fanciful name sometimes given to Lake George, and commonly supposed to be the original Indian name, but really an invention of the American novelist, James Fenimore Cooper. The ancient Iroquois name of this lake was *Andialarocte*, which is said to mean 'there the lake shuts itself.' The French missionary, Father Jogues, called it *Saint Sacrement*, because he discovered it on the eve of that festival." When the lake came into the possession of the English, they gave it its present name, in honor of George II (1727–1760), who was then on the throne.

Horizon. "Objects at sea are visible at the following distances:

Elevation.		Elevation.	
Feet.	Miles.	Feet.	Miles.
5	3	200	18
10	4	300	23
20	6	500	30
50	9	800	37
100	13	1000	42."

Mulhall's *Dictionary of Statistics.*

Hornbook. The alphabet-book or primer for learning to read, in universal use in England before the days of printing, and common even down to the time of George II (1727-1760). It consisted of a single leaf set in an oaken frame (9 x 5 inches), covered with a thin sheet of transparent horn to protect it from being defaced,— whence its name. The leaf contained on one side the alphabet, in large and small letters, also the Lord's Prayer and the nine digits, together with a large number of monosyllables. The frame had a handle, and this was generally provided with a hole for a string, by means of which the hornbook could be suspended from the scholar's girdle. The back of the frame was ornamented with a rude sketch of St. George and the Dragon. Hornbooks are now very rare. Frequent allusions to them are found in the older writers, and Shenstone, in his *Schoolmistress*, speaks of them as follows :

> " Their books of stature small they take in hand,
> Which with pellucid horn secured are,
> To save from fingers wet the letters fair."

Horn Gate. In Virgil's *Æneid*, a gate of horn in the lower regions, through which are sent up to earth visions and dreams that come true. See *Ivory Gate.*

> " Sunt geminæ Somni portæ, *quarum altera fertur*
> *Cornea*, qua veris facilis datur exitus Umbris ;
> Altera candeati perfecta nitens elephanto,
> Sed falsa ad cœlum mittunt insomnia Manes."
>
> *Æneid*, vi, 893-896.

Horse, Enchanted. An artificial horse, richly caparisoned, whose marvellous exploits form one of the tales of the *Arabian Nights' Entertainments.* This horse, which was presented by a Hindu to the Shah of Persia as a New Year's gift, was worked by two pegs. One of these—in the hollow of the horse's neck, near the pommel of the saddle,—when turned, caused the animal to rise into the air and to take whatever course the rider desired ; while the other, behind the right ear, when operated brought the animal to the ground, but not as swiftly as he had mounted.

Horse, Fifteen Points of a Good. " A good horse sholde have three propyrtees of a man, three of a woman, three of a foxe, three of a haare, and three of an asse. Of a *man*, bolde, prowde, and hardye. Of a *woman* fayre-breasted, faire of heere, and easy to move. Of a *foxe*, a fair taylle, short eers, with a good trotte. Of a *haare*, a grate eye, a dry head, and well rennynge. Of an *asse* a bygge chynn, a flat legge, and a good hoof."— *Wynkyn de Worde* (1496).

Horse Latitudes. A belt of calms in the North Atlantic Ocean, lying between 30° and 35° north latitude. The name is said to be derived from the fact that, during Colonial times, ships bound from New England to the West Indies, with a deck-load of horses, were often delayed in these regions of calms, and were obliged, from want of water, to throw overboard a portion of the animals.

Horseshoe. The belief in the horseshoe, as an " earnest " of good fortune and as a protection against evil spirits, is widely spread among the inhabitants of Great Britain and the United States, and exists in Germany and Scandinavia as well as in far distant Hindustan. The origin of this superstition is variously accounted for. According to Walsh's *Handy - Book of Literary Curiosities*, " the horseshoe unites within itself three lucky elements : it is crescent-shaped, is a portion of a horse, and is made of iron."

From the earliest times, ornaments fashioned in the shape of a crescent have been regarded as potent charms to ward off evil spirits. This belief is referred to in Butler's *Hudibras*, in the following couplet :

> " Chase evil spirits away by dint
> Of sickle, *horseshoe*, and hollow flint."

Iron has long been considered to be a metal possessed of protecting powers, and hence has given to the horseshoe an additional charm ; while the horse, in the old English mythology, was regarded as a harbinger of good luck. It is also stated that the horseshoe derives its mystic property from its resemblance to the halo that surrounded the head of the patron saint once placed in every church and home. This halo frequently remained after the image of the saint had disappeared, and finally became itself the symbol of that protection which the saint was supposed to give. Horseshoes are still nailed up over doors as a protection against witches. Lord Nelson nailed one to the mast of the *Victory*.

Horseshoe Curve. A famous curve on the Pennsylvania Railroad, near Kittanning Point.

" At one point there is a curve as short as the letter U, and that, too, where the grade is so steep that in looking across from side to side it seems that, were the tracks laid contiguous to each other, they would form a letter X. The road hugs the sides of the mountains, and from the windows next to the valley, the traveler can look down on houses and trees dwarfed to toys, while men and animals appear like ants from the great elevation."—Appletons' *Guide to the United States and Canada.*

Horseshoe Fall. The name given, in consequence of its shape, to the larger of the two cataracts composing the Falls of Niagara. It is 2200 feet across, and has a perpendicular plunge of 158 feet. It is estimated that 13,-500,000 cubic feet of water pass over the precipice every minute. The boundary line between the United States and Canada passes through the middle of the Horseshoe Fall, which is, on this account, frequently called the Canadian Fall. See *Niagara Falls.*

Horse, Wooden. A gigantic horse which, according to the legend, figured in the siege of Troy, and caused the fall and destruction of the city. It was devised by Ulysses and Diomed, was built of wood, and was filled with armed men. Sinon, a cunning Greek, " informed the Trojans that the wooden horse had been constructed as an atonement for the Palladium which had been carried off by the Greeks, and that if they would drag it into their own city, Asia would gain the supremacy over Greece." The Trojans believed the story, and introduced the monster within the walls ; whereupon Sinon, at night, released the soldiers, who immediately opened the gates to the Greeks. The sentinels were slain, the city sacked and burned, and the inhabitants put to the sword. The story of the Wooden Horse is not found in the *Iliad*, but is related by Æneas in the Second Book of the *Æneid.* See *Sinon.*

Hospice of St. Bernard. A famous monastery and inn for the accommodation of travelers, situated near the summit of the pass of the Great St. Bernard, in Switzerland. It was founded in 962, by Bernard de Menthon, a pious nobleman, as a place of shelter and entertainment for pilgrims journeying to and from Rome. The present building—erected in 1125—is in charge of fifteen or twenty young and vigorous Augustinian monks, who devote themselves, with the aid of their dogs, to the task of rescuing unfortunate travelers who are in danger of perishing in the snows of that region. According to some authorities, the dogs at present used are not St. Bernards, but Newfoundlands. It is said that during recent years from 15,000 to 20,000 people have been entertained annually at the Hospice of St. Bernard. The building has sleeping accommodations for 80 travelers, and can shelter about 300. The monks accept no compensation for their services, although it is the custom for departing visitors to drop some gift into the alms-box. The Hospice is the highest habitation in Europe, being about 8000 feet above sea-level.

Hospital Sunday. The name given to a certain Sunday in the year, set apart by churches of almost every denomination in London and the provinces, for special collections in support of the hospitals of the country. The movement was formally started in 1873, although something in this direction had been done in Glasgow as early as 1844. This custom was introduced into the United States in 1874. The Sunday chosen in England for this purpose is the one nearest the 15th of June ; but, in the United States, it is the last Sunday of the year.

Host, Elevation of the. See *Elevation of the Host.*

Hôtel de Cluny. A handsome building in Paris, now used as a museum of mediæval works of art and products of industry. It occupies part of the site of a Roman palace, said to have been erected by the Emperor Constantius Chlorus (305–306 A.D.), who resided in Gaul from 292 to 306. Julian the Apostate (361–363 A.D.) was there proclaimed Emperor by his soldiers in 360. The present structure derives its name from the wealthy abbey of Cluny, into whose possession the ruins came, in 1340. This building was erected on the site of the ancient palace, about 1500, and still exists in a remarkable state of preservation. It was used successively as a royal residence, a theatre, and a convent, and, during the Revolution, Marat held his meetings there. In 1833, the Hôtel de Cluny passed into the hands of M. du Sommerard, a learned antiquary, and on his death, in 1842, it was purchased by the French government, and converted into a public museum. Since that time the collection has been greatly extended. Its treasures consist of sculptures, tapestries, wood and ivory carvings, enamels, glass, ironwork, and pottery. See *Thermes, Les.*

Hôtel de Rambouillet. The residence of the Marquis de Rambouillet, at Paris, famous, during the 17th century and later, as a political and literary centre. This salon was originally formed in opposition to the court party during the reign of Henry IV (1589–1610), and strove, by means of elegance of manners and purity of speech, to offset the vulgarity and barbarity of the court. Subsequently it became the rendezvous of the most famous wits and celebrities of the day, and, owing to the indifference of Louis XIII (1610–1643) to letters, soon rose to be the arbiter of taste in literature. Ladies of the highest rank sought admission to these *réunions,* and were termed " Les Précieuses." In later years, this salon fell from its high estate and became the scene of frivolous and affected discussions. Molière, in his plays *Les Précieuses Ridicules* and *Les Femmes Savantes,* ridiculed the literary pretensions of the Hôtel de Rambouillet, and caused the name to be used only as a derisive epithet.

Hôtel des Invalides. An asylum for wounded and maimed soldiers, in Paris, founded by Louis XIV (1643–1715) in 1670, and completed in 1675. In the time of the Revolution, it was called the *Temple of Humanity,* and, during the first Napoleon's reign (1804–1814), the *Temple of Mars.* It has accommodation for 5000 inmates, but there are not more than 400 at present, as most of the " Invalides " prefer to live independently on their pensions. Admission to the Hôtel des Invalides is not granted unless the applicant has lost one or more of his limbs in battle, has served in the army for thirty years, or is 60 years of age. The building contains, besides the quarters of the men, a church, a library, a museum, and a council-chamber. Under the dome — beyond the church — may be seen the superb mausoleum of the first Napoleon. See *Tomb of Napoleon.*

Hôtel des Monnaies. The name given to the Mint of Paris—sometimes called *La Monnaie.* It stands near the Pont Neuf, and was erected in 1771–1775. The building contains a museum in which may be seen: (1)

a collection of *French Coins*, arranged chronologically from the earliest times to the present day ; (2) a collection of *Foreign Coins* of every country ; and (3) a collection of *Medals* of various kinds. In the ateliers are shown the engines, furnaces, and machinery used in the processes of coining. The machines invented by M. Thonnelier are extremely ingenious, and are capable of producing 2,000,000 francs per day.

Hôtel de Ville. A magnificent structure in Paris, devoted to the affairs of the municipality, and erected by the architects Ballu and Deperthes, to replace the one destroyed by the Communists in 1871. The building is in the French Renaissance style, and is rectangular in shape. It has dome-covered pavilions at the angles, mansard-windows, tall decorated chimneys, and a graceful tower. The façade is richly adorned with sculptures, and in the niches of the principal stories are statues of famous Parisians. The first floor contains *La Salle du Conseil Municipal*, or *Council Chamber*, and the apartments of the Prefect of the Seine. On the floor above is the vast *Salle des Fêtes*. The old Hôtel de Ville, occupying this site, was completed during the reign of Henry IV (1589-1610). It was the scene of many stirring events during the French Revolution. Louis XVI (1774-1789), on his return from Versailles, came to the Hôtel de Ville and declared his allegiance before the National Assembly ; and Robespierre, to escape the guillotine, shot himself, in this same building, but only succeeded in shattering his jaw. See *Pétroleuses.*

Hôtel Dieu. A magnificent hospital in Paris, near the river Seine, recently erected at a cost of 45,000,000 francs, almost one-half of which amount was paid for the site. It contains 839 beds, is richly endowed, and is admirably appointed throughout. The original hospital was founded by Clovis II (638-655 A.D.), and is the oldest institution of the kind in Paris, and probably in Europe.

Hot Gospeller. A nickname conferred upon Edward Underhill, an ardent Protestant, who was imprisoned in 1553 in consequence of a ballet made by him against the Roman Catholics, immediately after Mary (1553-1558) was proclaimed Queen in London. The term "Hot Gospellers" was applied to the Puritans after the Restoration (1660).

Hotspur. A sobriquet conferred upon Henry Percy (1364-1403), in allusion to his fiery and ungovernable temper. He rebelled against Henry IV (1399-1415) of England, and was killed at the battle of Shrewsbury. Hotspur is introduced as a character in Shakespeare's *Henry IV*, Part I. See *Hotspur of Debate.*

Hotspur of Debate. A nickname conferred upon Lord Stanley (1799-1869), afterwards the fourteenth Earl of Derby, owing to his unsparing use of invective. Bulwer-Lytton, in his *New Timon*, speaks of him as " frank, haughty, bold, the Rupert of Debate." See *Hotspur ; Rupert of Debate.*

Hougoumont. A château, with orchards and gardens, situated on the right of the English line at Waterloo. It was a point of great strategic importance and formed Napoleon's first object of attack. Although the French succeeded in gaining possession of the orchards and holding them for a time, the château itself remained in possession of the English during the entire battle. The word *Hougoumont* is said to be a corrupted form of *Château Goumont ;* but Victor Hugo, in *Les Misérables*, says it was originally written *Hugo-mons*, and that the house was built by one Hugo, Sire de Sommeril. See *Waterloo, Battle of.*

Hounslow Heath. A desolate region, at one time open and infested with highwaymen. It is situated west from Hounslow, a village in Middlesex County, ten miles southwest of London, and in 1546 contained 4293 acres. It is now, for the most part, enclosed.

Houris. The name given to the black-eyed damsels of Paradise, whose charms are set forth in the *Koran.* They are possessed of perpetual youth and beauty, and are capable of renewing their virginity at pleasure. Intercourse with these lovely women is promised to all true believers, and seems to constitute the chief delight of the Moslem heaven. Every believer will have 72 of these houris, and his union with them will be fruitful or otherwise according as he may elect. In case offspring is desired, they will attain their full stature and development in an hour. The word " houri" is said to be derived from the Arabic *hûr al oyûn (the black-eyed).*

House of Commons. See *Commons, House of.*

House of Keys. In the Isle of Man, an assembly having both legislative and judicial powers, composed of 24 principal commoners of the island. This body was originally self-elective; but, in 1866, election by the people, every seventh year, was established by act of Parliament The House of Keys is one of the two co-ordinate branches of the General Assembly called the Court of Tynwald, — the other branch consisting of the Lieutenant-governor and Council. A bill is separately considered by each branch; and, after being passed by both, is transmitted for the royal assent. It does not, however, become a law until it has been promulgated in both the English and Manx languages on the Tynwald Hill. See *Manx Laws.*

House of Lords. See *Lords, House of.*

House of Peter. A small house at St. Petersburg, Russia, on the north bank of the Neva, occupied by Peter

the Great (1682–1725) during the building of the city. It was the first structure erected at the time of the founding of the Russian capital in 1702. The house is entirely covered with a protective casing, and consists of three small apartments, — a reception-room, bedroom, and chapel. These contain numerous relics of the great Czar.

House of Pilate. See *Casa de Pilatos.*

Houses of Parliament. An imposing pile of buildings in London, in the Tudor-Gothic style of architecture, sometimes called " The New Palace of Westminster." It covers an area of eight acres, and has been erected since 1840, at a cost of $15,000,000, to replace the original structure burned down in 1834. The building contains 11 courts, 100 staircases, 1100 apartments, and has an imposing river-front of 940 feet, adorned with statues of the English monarchs from William the Conqueror to Victoria. It is surmounted by three lofty towers: the Clock Tower, sometimes called St. Stephen's Tower, 318 feet high; the Middle Tower, 300 feet in height; and the Victoria Tower, 340 feet in altitude. Within are the House of Lords or Peers, the House of Commons, the royal apartments, the Speaker's residence, libraries, conference and committee rooms, and various other apartments devoted to the requirements of the legislature of the United Kingdom. See *Commons, House of; Lords, House of; Westminster Palace.*

House that Jack Built. The name of a famous nursery-tale of a cumulative character, in which each preceding statement is repeated after the introduction of a new one, as follows.

(1) This is the house that Jack built.

(2) This is the malt that lay in the house that Jack built.

(3) This is the rat that ate the malt that lay in the house that Jack built.

(4) This is the cat that killed the

25

rat that ate the malt that lay in the house that Jack built.

(5) This is the dog that worried the cat that killed the rat that ate the malt that lay in the house that Jack built.

(6) This is the cow with the crumpled horn that tossed the dog that worried the cat that killed the rat that ate the malt that lay in the house that Jack built.

(7) This is the maiden all forlorn that milked the cow with the crumpled horn that tossed the dog that worried the cat that killed the rat that ate the malt that lay in the house that Jack built.

(8) This is the man all tattered and torn that kissed the maiden all forlorn that milked the cow with the crumpled horn that tossed the dog that worried the cat that killed the rat that ate the malt that lay in the house that Jack built.

(9) This is the priest all shaven and shorn that married the man all tattered and torn that kissed the maiden all forlorn that milked the cow with the crumpled horn that tossed the dog that worried the cat that killed the rat that ate the malt that lay in the house that Jack built.

Houyhnhnms. The name given by Jonathan Swift (1667–1745), in the fourth part of *Gulliver's Travels*, to a race of horses, endowed with reason, which ruled over a degraded race of mankind, called Yahoos. The word *houyhnhnms* is a dissyllable, and suggests the whinnying of a horse.

Howadji. A *nom-de-plume* adopted by George William Curtis (1824–1892) in his books of Eastern travel, entitled *Nile Notes of a Howadji* and *A Howadji in Syria*. The word *howadji* is Arabic, and means a merchant or traveler.

Howe's Cave. A famous cave in Schoharie County, New York, 39 miles from Albany,—considered the most remarkable cavern in existence, after the Mammoth Cave in Kentucky. It was discovered in 1842 by Lester Howe, who is said to have penetrated into its interior for a distance of twelve miles. The farthest point reached by the visitor is about four miles from the entrance. The cave contains some remarkable stalactites and stalagmites, and abounds in curious and fantastic formations. Howe's Cave is sometimes called Otsgaragee Cavern. See *Mammoth Cave.*

How to Find Easter-Day. "Easter-day . . . is always the First *Sunday* after the Full Moon which happens upon or next after the Twenty-first Day of *March;* and if the Full Moon happen upon a *Sunday, Easter-Day* is the *Sunday* after."— *Book of Common Prayer.*

Easter-Day, therefore, can never fall earlier than March 22nd nor later than April 25th.

Hub of the Universe. A sportive appellation bestowed by Oliver Wendell Holmes (1809–1895) upon the State-House in Boston, Massachusetts, and afterwards extended in its application to the city itself. The allusion is, of course, to the hub of a wheel, to which the other parts are subservient. During the visit of the Prince of Wales to India in 1876, the special correspondent of the London *Daily News* applied this same term to the city of Calcutta.

"Boston State-house is the hub of the solar system. You could n't pry that out of a Boston man if you had the tire of all creation straightened out for a crowbar."— *The Autocrat of the Breakfast-Table.*

"Calcutta, with no trivial infusion of downright vulgarity, swaggers as if it were the *hub of the universe*, the veritable salt of the earth."

Hudibras. The title of a satiric poem by Samuel Butler (1612–1680). It relates the adventures of one Hudibras, a Presbyterian justice, who, during the days of the Commonwealth, sallied forth in company with his squire, Ralph, a clerk of the Independent sect, with the quixotic notion of correcting evils and enforcing a strict observance of the laws laid down by Parliament for the suppression of harmless sports and amusements.

"*Hudibras* was incomparably more popular than *Paradise Lost;* no poem in our language rose at once to greater reputation." —*Hallam.*

"Butler is said to have taken the name of his hero from the old romances of chivalry, Sir Hugh de Bras being the appellation of one of the knights of Arthur's fabulous Round Table."—Wheeler's *Dictionary of the Noted Names of Fiction.*

Huguenots. The name given in derision to the French Protestants, or followers of Calvin. Being cruelly treated during the reign of Francis II (1559–1560), they finally took up arms against their persecutors. Although by the Edict of January, 1562, the Huguenots were granted toleration, yet in March of the same year great numbers of them were massacred at Vassy by the party of Guise. This infamous act led to the civil wars, which continued, with some interruptions, until the promulgation, by Henry IV (1589–1610) in 1598, of the Edict of Nantes, whereby civil and religious liberty was confirmed to the Huguenots. It was during a truce in these civil wars that the fearful massacre of St. Bartholomew took place, on August 24th, 1572. The power of the Huguenots, as a political party in the state, was destroyed by Louis XIII (1610–1643) and his minister, Richelieu. Louis XIV (1643–1715), in 1685, revoked the Edict of Nantes, and, as a result of this impolitic act, half a million Huguenots—the best blood of France — fled to England, Germany, the Netherlands, Switzerland, and America.

The origin of the word *Huguenot* is variously accounted for. According to some, it is derived from the German *Eidgenossen* (*Oath-Companions*), while others trace it to *Hugues,* a Calvinist of Geneva. A third derivation of the word is from *Hugon,* a gate in Tours, near which, it is said, the Huguenots were wont to assemble. See *Edict of Nantes; St. Bartholomew, Massacre of.*

Human Body, Wonders of. "The skin contains more than 2,000,000 openings, which are the outlets of an equal number of sweat glands. The human skeleton consists of more than 200 distinct bones. An amount of blood equal to the whole quantity in the body passes through the heart once every minute. The full capacity of the lungs is about 320 cubic inches. About two-thirds of a pint of air is inhaled and exhaled at each breath in ordinary respiration. The stomach daily produces 9 pounds of gastric juice for digestion of food ; its capacity is about 5 pints. There are more than 500 separate muscles in the body, with an equal number of nerves and blood-vessels. The weight of the heart is from 8 to 12 ounces. It beats 100,000 times in 24 hours. Each perspiratory duct is one-fourth of an inch in length; of the whole, about 9 miles. The average man takes $5\frac{1}{2}$ pounds of food and drink each day, which amounts to one ton of solid and liquid nourishment annually. A man breathes 18 times in a minute, and 3000 cubic feet, or about 375 hogsheads of air every hour of his existence." — Conklin's *Vest - Pocket Argument Settler.*

Humanities. The name given to those studies comprising polite or elegant learning, as language, rhetoric, poetry, grammar, and the ancient classics. More commonly known at the present day as *belles-lettres.*

"The cultivation of the languages, literature, history, and archæology of Greece and Rome were very commonly called *literæ humaniores,* or, in English, the *humanities,* . . . by way of opposition to the *literæ divinæ,* or divinity."—*George P. Marsh.*

Human Race. The following estimate of the population of the earth according to race, made by John Bartholomew of Edinburgh, is taken from the *World Almanac* for 1901:

(1)	*Indo-Germanic or Aryan (White)*	545,500,000
(2)	*Mongolian or Turanian (Yellow and Brown)*	630,000,000
(3)	*Semitic or Hamitic (White)*	65,000,000
(4)	*Negro and Bantu (Black)*	150,000,000
(5)	*Hottentot and Bushman (Black)*	150,000
(6)	*Malay and Polynesian (Brown)*	35,000,000
(7)	*American Indian (Red)*	15,000,000
	Total	1,440,650,000

Humble Pie, To Eat. A phrase meaning to humiliate oneself ; to submit or apologize in an abject manner. The " humbles " or " umbles " are the heart, liver, and entrails of the deer, and were served in the form of a pie to the servants and retainers at a hunting-feast, while the lord and his household dined on the venison-pasty. Hence, " to eat *humble* or *umble* pie " came to mean to occupy a subordinate and menial position, and, later, was applied to degradations of other kinds.

Hundred Days. An expression frequently applied to the period of time that elapsed between the arrival of Napoleon I in Paris (March 20th, 1815), after his escape from Elba and his departure (June 29th, 1815), after his second abdication. See *Champ de Mai.*

Hundred Years' War. The name given to the long contest between England and France (1337-1453), beginning in the reign of Edward III (1327-1377) and ending in the reign of Henry VI (1422-1461). This war resulted from the claim of Edward III to the throne of France, and lasted, with intervals of peace, for more than 100 years. During this prolonged struggle the English gained the great victories of Crécy (1346), Poictiers (1356), and Agincourt (1415).

Hunkers. A term applied to the conservative or pro-slavery wing of the Democratic party in the State of New York (1844-1848), as distinguished from the younger radical element, known as the " Barnburners." The

term is said to be derived from the Dutch word *honk* (*home*). Other authorities, however, say that this wing of the Democratic party was called " Hunkers " or " Old Hunkers," because it was in possession of a large " hunk " of the spoils. See *Barnburners.*

Hunter's Moon. The name given to the lunation immediately following the harvest moon. Owing to the small angle that is made by this moon's orbit with the horizon, it rises, like the harvest moon, at the same hour for several days. It is so called, however, not because it enables the hunter to pursue his game at night (as is generally supposed), but because, the crops having been harvested in September, there is nothing to interfere with the sportsman's pleasure. See *Harvest Moon.*

Hurricane. A sobriquet conferred upon the Comte de Mirabeau (1749–1791), the French statesman and orator, in allusion to the overpowering energy and tumultuous flow of his eloquence. See *Modern Gracchus.*

Hyades. A group of nymphs (3, 5, or 7 in number) who, according to Greek mythology, were the guardians of Dionysus. Their names were Ambrosia, Eudora, Pedile, Coronis, Polyxo, Phyto, and Thyene or Dione. Zeus placed them in the heavens, where they form the head of the constellation Taurus. Their rising with the sun was thought by the ancient Greeks to portend rain, and hence they were known as the " rainy Hyades." The brightest of them—a red star of the first magnitude—was called by the Arabs Aldebaran. It forms the eye of Taurus.

Hybla Honey. A kind of honey, famous among the ancients, and frequently mentioned by the Latin poets and those of later times. It derives its name from Hybla, a name given to three cities of ancient Sicily; but from which one of these three the famous honey came is a matter of doubt. The expression "Hyblean bliss," meaning "honeyed bliss" is frequently used by the poets.

"From friendship the wise extract
Earth's most *Hyblean bliss*."
Night Thoughts (Young).

"But for your words, they rob the *Hybla* bees,
And leave them honeyless."
Julius Cæsar, v, 1.

Hyde Park. A famous pleasure-ground in London, a mile and a half long and three-fourths of a mile wide, extending westward from Piccadilly to Kensington Gardens and covering an area of 390 acres. It was formerly the ancient manor of Hyde, belonging to the abbey of Westminster, and was laid out as a park and enclosed in 1535, during the reign of Henry VIII (1509–1547). In Elizabeth's time (1558–1603), stags were still hunted there, and under Charles II (1660–1685) it was used for horse-races. The "Serpentine," an artificial sheet of water, was introduced by Queen Caroline, wife of George II (1727–1760). Hyde Park is the fashionable drive of London, and on fine afternoons during the "season" it is densely thronged with equipages, moving at little more than a walking pace.

Hydrogen. A highly inflammable gas, forming one of the 70 elements. It is colorless and odorless, but can be liquefied when subjected to great pressure at an extremely low temperature. This was first successfully accomplished by Raoul Pictet and Cailletet, in 1877. Hydrogen is rarely found in nature in the free state, but enters into combination with other elements,—forming an important constituent in vegetal and animal tissues. In combination with oxygen, it constitutes one-ninth, by weight, of water. As it is the lightest of all the gases, its density is generally taken as the standard by which to measure the density of all the others. The density of atmos-pheric air is $14\frac{1}{2}$ times as great as that of hydrogen. Hydrogen was first described by Paracelsus, about 1500 A.D., under the name of "combustible air," and was also familiar to Boyle and others; but to Cavendish is accorded the honor of being the discoverer of this elementary substance. In the *Transactions of the Royal Society for 1766*, he gave the first accurate description of its properties, and suggested the best methods of obtaining it. The word *hydrogen* means "water-producer," and is derived from the two Greek words ὕδωρ(*water*)and γεννάω (*I produce*).

Hydropathy. The name given to the treatment of diseases by the use of water, externally and internally. This method of curing bodily ailments was practised by Hippocrates as early as the 4th century before Christ; by Galen in later times; and in the 10th century by the Arabs, who introduced the treatment into Europe, where it had many followers during the Middle Ages. It was revived by Dr. Currie of Liverpool in 1797, and was first applied by him to the treatment of fevers and febrile disorders. In 1825, one Vincenz Priessnitz, a farmer of Grafenberg, in Austrian Silesia, achieved a remarkable success by means of water as a remedial agent,—although insisting also on plain food, prolonged exercise, and pure air as adjuvants. According to *Chambers's Encyclopædia*, there are 50 hydropathic establishments in England, 15 in Scotland, and 1 in Ireland. The first hydropathic establishment in London was founded in 1842; the first in New York, in 1844.

Hydrophobia. A word popularly applied to the disease known as *rabies*, but in reality the name simply of one of the symptoms of that malady. In the case of a human being suffering from the disease, the symptom known as hydrophobia is characterized by contraction of the throat and spasms of the pharynx if anything is offered to drink. Its manifestation is evidence that the death of the patient is at hand, and will occur in a few days. The word "hydrophobia" means "dread or fear of water," and is derived from the two Greek words ὕδωρ (*water*) and φόβος (*fear*).

Hygrometer. An instrument used for measuring the amount of moisture in the atmosphere. The first hygrometer, made by de Saussure (1740–1799), is known as a hair-hygrometer. It consists of a human hair, boiled in lye, which expands or contracts in length, according as the air is more or less moist. It is connected with an index that registers the variations. Later, Deluc made a similar instrument in which a piece of whalebone was substituted for the hair. Such hygrometers, however, being affected by other influences besides that of moisture, are not accurate indicators. Daniell's hygrometer (1820) is, theoretically, the most perfect instrument made. It was used at the Royal Observatory at Greenwich until 1847, when it was superseded by a more practical instrument, known as the Wet and Dry Bulb Thermometer.

Hyksos. The name given to a race —possibly of Tartars, although its origin is unknown — who invaded Lower Egypt, overthrew the reigning dynasty, captured Memphis, and held possession of the country, according to Manetho, for five centuries (2080–1525 B.C.). They established themselves in the city of Avaris (afterwards called Tanis), where some of their monuments may still be seen. In the opinion of other authorities, however, they held the country only from 1842 to 1591 B.C. Eusebius, who is supported by many of the best Egyptologists, says that Joseph was Vizier of Egypt, during the rule of the Hyksos, or "Shepherd Kings." The Hyksos were conquered and almost entirely driven out of Egypt by Ahmes, the founder of the XVIIIth dynasty, under whose rule Egypt be-

came a great centralized power, having Thebes for its capital.

Hymen. The god of marriage, among the Greeks and Romans. His origin is variously accounted for, but he is generally considered to have been the son of Apollo and Calliope. Other legends, however, make him the son of Dionysus and Aphrodite. Hymen is properly the bridal-song personified. He is first mentioned by Sappho, and is represented as a larger and more serious - looking Cupid, clad in a golden - hued mantle, and carrying a torch and a veil in his hands.

Hymettus, Mount. A mountain in Attica, three miles south of Athens, famous for its bluish marble, but more especially for its honey, which is still in repute.

" And the brown bees of *Hymettus*
  Make their honey not so sweet."
  Wine of Cypress (Mrs. Browning).

Hyperboreans. The name given by the ancients to an imaginary people— favorites of Apollo—who lived beyond Boreas, or the North Wind. Virgil placed them under the North Pole. This favored race dwelt in a terrestrial paradise under a cloudless sky, and enjoyed a fruitful land, unending peace, and perpetual youth and health. The Hyperboreans were said to live in an atmosphere composed entirely of feathers. Herodotus and Pliny both refer to this fiction, but say that it was suggested by the amount of snow that fell in those northern regions. The word " Hyperboreans " has been used, in the modern science of anthropology, to designate certain peoples that dwell in the northeast of Asia and the northwest of America, and that cannot be classified either as Mongolians or as North American Indians.

Hyperion. One of the Titans, son of Uranus and Gaea, and father of Helios, Selene, and Eos. Homer and the later poets, however, use the word as a patronymic of Helios or Apollo:

hence the name has become the synonym for manly beauty and grace.

" So excellent a king; that was, to this,
Hyperion to a satyr."

Hamlet, i, 2.

I

Iberia. A name given by the ancient Greeks to the territory including Spain, Portugal, and southwestern France, but now used as a poetic term for Spain only. The word " Iberia " was also employed by the Greeks and Romans to designate the southern part of Georgia,—a country in Asia, south of the Caucasus Mountains, between the Black and the Caspian Seas.

Ice Palace. A stately structure, built on a frozen lake in Russia, and composed entirely of blocks of ice. It was erected by command of the Empress Anne (1730-1740) of Russia, during the winter of 1739-1740. In this cheerless abode the Empress compelled one of her disgraced nobles, Prince Galitzin (whom she had forced to marry a second time), to remain with his newly made bride during his wedding-night. The building lasted for many months, owing to the severity of the climate.

Ichabod. The title of a poem by John G. Whittier (1807-1892), supposed to have been written as a rebuke to Daniel Webster on account of his betrayal of the anti-slavery cause during the last years of his life. Ichabod (meaning, *Where is the glory?*) was the son of Phinehas, and the grandson of Eli; and was so named by his mother when the tidings reached her of the capture of the Ark of the Covenant and the death of her husband and father-in-law.

" And she said, the glory is departed from Israel : for the Ark of God is taken."—1 *Samuel* iv, 22.

Ich Dien (*Ger. I Serve*). The motto of the Prince of Wales, — said to have been adopted by Edward, the Black Prince, from John, the blind King of Bohemia, who was slain by him at the battle of Crécy, August 26th, 1346. This story, however, does not rest on good authority.

According to Welsh tradition, Edward I (1272-1307), having conquered Wales, promised to provide its people with a prince that "could speak no word of English." Accordingly when his son Edward was born, he presented him to the assembly, saying in Welsh, *Eich dyn* (*Behold the man*). See *Crécy* (or *Cressy*), *Battle of.*

Ichthys (*Gr. Ἰχθύς, fish*). A Greek word meaning a fish, frequently used as a symbol of Christ by the early Christians, because its letters form the initials of our Savior's names and titles, as follows:

Ἰησοῦς (*Jesus*).
Χριστός (*Christ*).
Θεοῦ (*of God*).
Ὑιός (*Son*).
Σωτήρ (*Savior*).

It is found on ancient seals, rings, lamps, and tombs, and came into general use in the 4th century. It is said that Aptatus, Bishop of Milesia (who lived about that time), was the first to construct this acrostic. Baptismal fonts were often ornamented with the figure of a fish,—several of which may be found in French cathedrals at the present day. Augustine says that ἰχθύς is the mystical name of Christ, " because he descended alive into the depths of this mortal life—into the abyss of waters." Julius Africanus speaks of Christ as " the great fish taken by the fish-hook of God, and whose flesh nourishes the whole world."

Icon Basilike. See *Eikon Basilike.*

Iconoclasts (*Gr. Image-Breakers*). A party of religious enthusiasts who, in 726 A.D., at the instigation of the Byzantine Emperor, Leo Isaurus (716-741), destroyed the images, pictures, statues, and other emblems, in the churches of Constantinople. This movement spread to Italy, but was stoutly resisted by the Latin Church and the people generally. Leo, although condemned by a Council at Rome under Pope Gregory III (731–741), persevered in his opposition to the use of images, and this policy was continued by his successor Constantine (741–775), surnamed Copronymus. The Council of Constantinople, held in 754, forbade the use of all images, except that of Christ in the eucharist ; but this decision was revoked at the Council of Nicæa, in 787, during the reign of Irene, widow of Leo. Subsequent Emperors, however, returned to the policy of iconoclasm, which finally led to the separation of the Eastern and Western Churches. The Eastern Church, at the present day, permits the use of pictures, but rejects all sculptured or graven images of sacred objects.

Ides. One of the divisions of the Roman month,—the other two being the *Calends* and the *Nones.* The *Ides* generally fell on the thirteenth of the month; but in March, May, July, and October they occurred on the fifteenth.

" Beware the *ides* of March."
Julius Cæsar, i, 2.

Idler. A periodical established by Dr. Samuel Johnson in 1758. It extended to 103 numbers, 12 of which were contributed by Thomas Warton, Langton, and Sir Joshua Reynolds.

"The *Idler* was the last experiment on the public taste in England of periodical essays published separately."— *Chambers's Cyclopædia of English Literature.*

Idylls of the King. A series of poems by Alfred, Lord Tennyson (1809–1892), illustrative of the *Arthurian Legend.* A first series—comprising *Enid, Vivien, Elaine,* and *Guinevere*—appeared in 1859, and was continued by instalments during 1870, 1872, and 1885. In their present form, the *Idylls of the King* consist of twelve poems, arranged in the following order :

(1) The Coming of Arthur.
(2) Gareth and Lynette.
(3) The Marriage of Geraint.
(4) Geraint and Enid.
(5) Balin and Balan.
(6) Merlin and Vivien.
(7) Lancelot and Elaine.
(8) The Holy Grail.
(9) Pelleas and Ettarre.
(10) The Last Tournament.
(11) Guinevere.
(12) The Passing of Arthur.

If, Château d'. A celebrated castle, used in former years as a place of incarceration, chiefly for prisoners of state, and situated on the island of If in the Mediterranean, near Marseilles. It figures conspicuously in the novel of *Monte Cristo,* by Alexandre Dumas père. There the hero, Edmond Dantès, was unjustly imprisoned for 14 years.

" It was fourteen years day for day since Dantès's arrest. He was nineteen when he entered the Château d'If; he was thirty-three when he escaped."—*Monte Cristo,* Chapter XXI.

Ignis Fatuus (*Lat. Foolish Fire*). A phosphorescent light, occasionally seen in the vicinity of marshy places and churchyards. It is usually observed in the autumn evenings soon after sunset; and is common in northern Germany, Italy, western Scotland, and southern and northwestern England. The " ignis fatuus" is popularly known as *Jack o' Lantern, Spunkie, Will o' the Wisp, Walking Fire,* and *The Fair Maid of Ireland.* Milton refers to it as *Friar's Lanthern,* and Scott, as *Friar Rush with a Lantern.* The expression is figuratively used to denote any quixotic or utopian scheme. The Germans, in one of their legends, identify the " ignis fatuus " with the soul of an unbaptized infant; and the Irish, with a soul that has escaped from Purgatory. This phenomenon is much less common than it was a century ago, and its disappearance is probably due to the general improvement in the drainage of bogs and fens.

I. H. S. Originally I (iota), H (eta), Σ (sigma), the first three letters (or, as some authorities say, the first two and the last letters) of the Greek word 'ΙΗΣΟΥΣ (Jesus). In later years, the origin of these letters having been lost, they were mistaken for the *Latin* capitals I. H. S., and a Latin word was found for each letter, as follows: Iesus Hominum Salvator (*Lat. Jesus, Savior of Men*). This anagram is said to have originated with St. Bernardine of Siena in 1347. According to other authorities, the letters I. H. S. are the initials of the words *In Hoc Signo* (*Lat. In This Sign*), miraculously displayed in the sky before Constantine and his army. See *In Hoc Signo Vinces*.

"Formerly it was customary to put the horizontal abbreviation mark over the letters, thus : I. H. S. This mark was afterwards altered into a cross, and it became I. Ħ. S., as it now frequently appears in Roman Catholic publications. In this form, it forms the initials of 'In hâc salis,' meaning 'In this [cross] salvation.' "—Edwards's *Words, Facts, and Phrases*.

Ile de la Cité (*Fr. Island of the City*). An island in Paris in the river Seine, forming the most ancient part of the city. When Julius Cæsar conquered Gaul (58–51 B.C.), the *Parisii* were a tribe living on the banks of the Sequana or Seine, and their chief town was Lutetia, occupying the present island of *La Cité*. This island formed the principal part of Paris during the Middle Ages ; and although now no longer the centre of the city's life, it still possesses numerous famous buildings. Among these may be mentioned the churches of Notre Dame and La Sainte-Chapelle, the Palais de Justice (occupying the site of the old royal palace), the Tribunal de Commerce, the Préfecture de Police, the Hôtel Dieu, and the Morgue.

Iliad. The oldest, and probably the most famous, epic poem in existence. It is attributed to Homer, the Greek poet, who flourished about 1000 B.C., and describes, in 24 books, certain important events that occurred during the tenth and last year of the siege of Troy. Agamemnon, the Commander-in-chief of the allied Greeks, having quarrelled with Achilles, the latter retires in anger from the contest, and sulks in his tent. As a result of his defection, the Trojans are victorious ; and Achilles, accordingly, sends his friend Patroclus to turn the tide of battle. Patroclus, however, is slain by Hector ; whereupon Achilles, rushing forth in rage to avenge the death of his friend, kills Hector, and drags his body—fastened to his chariot—towards the Grecian ships. The poem of the *Iliad* closes with the restoration of the body of Hector to Priam, and the funeral ceremonies in honor of the Trojan hero. See *Odyssey*.

"F. A. Wolf, in his 'Prolegomena,' in 1795, regarded the poems as a composite of epic songs, formed by Pisistratus about 550 B.C. This was the beginning of the 'Homeric controversy,' in which the leading scholars of Europe have been engaged ever since. The Germans have generally accepted the theory of Wolf, with some modifications, while the British have until very recently defended the unity of each epic, and the individuality of Homer, under the lead of Col. Mure, the historian of Grecian literature, Mr. Gladstone ('Homer and the Homeric Age'), and others. Grote, the historian of Greece, believed that the *Iliad* was originally a poem of moderate length on 'the wrath of Achilles,' and had been pieced out, after the art of writing became general, with several shorter poems. More recently Paley and others in England have adopted extreme views as to the late date of the poems in their present form, and the multiplicity of authors of their constituent parts."—Harper's *Book of Facts*.

Iliad of France. An appellation sometimes conferred upon the *Romance of the Rose*, a poetic allegory by Guillaume de Lorris and Jean de Meung. See *Romance of the Rose*.

Illustrious Infidel. A title conferred upon Robert G. Ingersoll (1833–1899), the famous American agnostic.

Imitation of Christ. See *De Imitatione Christi*.

Immortal Dreamer. An appellation bestowed upon John Bunyan (1628–1688), the famous author of the *Pilgrim's Progress*.

Immortal Four of Italy. An appellation frequently bestowed upon the four greatest poets of Italy : Dante (1265–1321), Petrarch (1304–1374), Ariosto (1474–1533), and Tasso (1544–1595).

" The poets read he o'er and o'er,
And most of all the *Immortal Four
Of Italy*."
Tales of a Wayside Inn (Longfellow).

Immortals. The body-guard of the Persian Kings (500 B.C.), recruited wholly from the nobility. It constituted a *corps d'élite*, and numbered 10,000 men. The name " Immortals " was also given to the body-guard of the Byzantine Emperors, during the 4th and 5th centuries. See *Forty Immortals*.

Immortals, Forty. See *Forty Immortals*.

Immortal Tinker. A sobriquet conferred upon John Bunyan (1628–1688), the illustrious author of the *Pilgrim's Progress*, and a tinker by trade.

Impeachment. According to the Constitution of the United States, the House of Representatives has the sole power of impeaching the President, Vice-President, and other Federal civil officials ; but by a numerical majority only. To the Senate is granted the sole power of *trying* all impeachments. In such cases, the Senate sits as a court, with a new organization ; and each member is required to take a special oath or affirmation applicable only to the impeachment proceedings. A vote of two-thirds of the Senate is necessary for a conviction, and from its decision there is no appeal. The Constitution limits the punishment to removal from office and disqualification from holding office under the United States government. When the President is tried, the Chief-Justice presides. Andrew Johnson, having been impeached by the House of Representatives in 1868, was duly tried by the Senate; but was acquitted by a vote of 35 for conviction and 19 for acquittal (one vote of the required two-thirds having been lacking).

Impending Crisis. The title of a famous book by Hinton Rowan Helper, a native of North Carolina, published in 1857. It had a sale of over 140,000 copies, and exerted a widespread influence. Its purpose was to show the evil effects of slavery upon the whites. Helper, however, was no friend of the negro, and declared in a later work, *Nojoque*, published in 1867, that his primary object in preparing it [*The Impending Crisis*] was to write the negro out of America, and his secondary one to write him out of existence. In December, 1859, Mr. Clark of Missouri introduced a resolution in the House of Representatives to the effect that no one that had approved of Helper's *Impending Crisis* was fit to be Speaker.

Imperial Guard. Organized in 1799 by Napoleon Bonaparte (1769–1821) while First Consul, and called at first the Consular Guard. After his accession to the throne as Emperor, it was termed the Imperial Guard. It consisted originally of 9775 men ; but in 1814 the number was increased to 102,706 men. In 1809, the Guard was subdivided into the *Old* and the *Young Guard*, and admission to it was granted only as a reward for meritorious service in three campaigns. The Imperial Guard was abolished by Louis XVIII (1814–1824), in 1815, but was revived by Napoleon III in 1854. It served in the Crimean War in 1855, and continued to exist during the days of the Second Empire. As a result of its surrender with Metz to the Germans in 1870, it was soon after abolished by the " Government of Defense."

Imperial Library of St. Petersburg. A famous library at St. Petersburg, founded during the latter part of the eighteenth century. It contains, at present, about 1,200,000 volumes, and is especially rich in ancient MSS.

Improvisatori. An Italian word applied to persons that extemporize on a given theme, and sometimes accompany their voice with a musical instrument. The ancient Greeks were skilled in the practice of this art, as are also the Arabs and many tribes of negroes at the present day ; but in modern Europe improvisation has been confined almost entirely to Italy, where Petrarch introduced the practice of composing verses without previous preparation, — accompanying himself with the lute. Although such productions are not limited to short poems of simple structure, but often have the form and dignity of epic poems, it is remarkable that none of them rise above the level of mediocrity. The most famous " improvisatori " of Italy have come either from Tuscany or from Venetia.

In Cœna Domini (*Lat. At the Lord's Supper*). The name of a famous papal bull, so called from the ancient day of its annual publication—Holy Thursday, at the Lord's Supper. It is not considered to be the work of any one pope, but dates back to the Middle Ages, and is variously attributed to Popes Martin V (1417–1424), Clement V (1305–1314), and Boniface VIII (1294–1303). It probably received its present form from the Popes Julius II (1503–1513), Paul III (1534–1550), and Urban VIII (1623–1644). From the year 1627, it continued to be annually issued on Holy Thursday for a century and a half, and may be briefly described as a summary of ecclesiastical censures, especially against all heretical sects. Being regarded by the European potentates as an interference with their rights, it was vigorously opposed by them during the seventeenth century. In 1770, Pope Clement XIV (1769–1775) discontinued its publication, since which date it has been generally considered a dead letter. According to some eminent travelers that have visited Rome this bull of censure is still read, though in a simpler form.

Incorruptible. An epithet conferred by his admirers upon Robespierre (1758–1794), the celebrated French demagogue, because he was proof against pecuniary temptations.

" Probably called the *Incorruptible* from his denunciations against corruption at the outbreak of the Revolution." — Brewer's *Historic Note-Book.*

Incunabula (*Cradle Books*). A word specifically applied to all specimens of printing and block-engraving that appeared up to the end of the year 1500. According to Didot, 13,000 independent works appeared during the 15th century, with an average issue of 300 copies, making the total number of " incunabula " about 4,000,000. More recent investigators (Hain, Van der Linde, and others) have increased this estimate to 30,000 separate publications, with an average issue of 500 each, making a total of 15,000,000.

Independence Day. The name of the national holiday in the United States of America, set apart to commemorate the adoption of the Declaration of Independence by the Continental Congress on July 4th, 1776. Independence Day is popularly known as the " Fourth of July," and is a legal holiday in all the States and in the District of Columbia. See *Declaration of Independence.*

Independence, Declaration of. See *Declaration of Independence.*

Independence Hall. A historic building on Chestnut Street, Philadelphia, rich in Revolutionary memories, and revered as the cradle of American independence. The Continental Congress met there, and appointed George Washington commander-in-chief of the American army in June, 1775. There also the Declaration of Independence was adopted by Congress on July 4th, 1776, and was afterwards proclaimed to a vast multitude assembled in the adjoining square, amid great enthusiasm. The building is now used as a museum, and contains many interesting souvenirs of Revolutionary days. Among these, may be mentioned articles of furniture used by Washington, Lafayette, Franklin, and John Hancock ; letters, swords, wearing-apparel, and authentic portraits of the heroes of '76. In the corridor is placed the famous " Liberty Bell," which announced the adoption, by Congress, of the Declaration of Independence, and proclaimed " liberty throughout the land to all the inhabitants thereof." In an apartment in the second story, called " Congress Hall," Washington delivered his farewell address. See *Liberty Bell*.

Independents. A large and influential religious body, in England, that came into existence during the reign of Elizabeth (1558–1603), and played a conspicuous part during the Civil War. They were also called Congregationalists, and derived their name from the distinctive principle of church polity advocated by them, that every Christian church or congregation " is entitled to elect its officers, to manage its own affairs, and to stand independent of, and irresponsible to, all authority, saving that only of the Supreme and Divine Head of the Church, the Lord Jesus Christ." The Independents were originally called " Brownists " and " Barrowists " from their founders Brown and Barrow. They were cruelly treated during their early history, but in the time of the Commonwealth they received religious toleration and protection against the Presbyterians from Oliver Cromwell, who was of their number. As a result of the

passage of the *Act of Uniformity* in 1662, the Independents were persecuted under Charles II (1660–1685) and James II (1685–1688) ; but were granted religious liberty by the *Act of Toleration*, passed in 1689. The first Independent or Congregational Church in America was founded at Plymouth, Massachusetts, in 1620, by the followers of John Robinson.

" Congregationalism is the ruling sect of the six northeastern states [of the American Union], and has exerted, and still exerts, a beneficial influence upon the religious, social, and political life of the whole nation."— *Philip Schaff.*

Index Expurgatorius. The name given to a catalogue prepared by the Roman Catholic Church, containing a list of books forbidden by papal authority to be read by any of its members, unless in editions that have been freed from objectionable passages. This *Index* was introduced by Pope Sixtus V (1585–1590), and was first published by the Duke Alba, at Antwerp, in 1751. It was republished in 1828, and is constantly receiving additions. Similar lists—modelled after that of Rome—were published in other countries, especially in Italy and Spain. See *Index Librorum Prohibitorum.*

Index Librorum Prohibitorum. The name given to a catalogue prepared by the Roman Catholic Church, containing a list of books forbidden by command of the Pope to be read, owing to their heretical contents. Although the reading of heathen books had been prohibited by the Council of Carthage in 400, it was not until the time of Pope Paul IV (1555–1559) that the first Roman *Index* appeared. This was officially prepared by the Inquisition, by order of the Pope, and was published in the years 1557 and 1559. It was approved by the Council of Trent, and was referred to Pope Pius IV (1559–1566), with the request that it be completed and published on his own authority. This was accordingly done in 1564. Many subsequent editions—containing numerous additions —have since appeared, the best-known of which is that of Rome (1819). The reading of the books named in the *Index Librorum Prohibitorum* is punishable with excommunication and degrading penances. See *Index Expurgatorius.*

Indian Bible. A translation of the Bible into the Algonquin language of the North American Indians by John Eliot (1604–1690), surnamed the "Apostle to the Indians." The translation of the *New Testament* appeared in 1661, and that of the *Old Testament* in 1663. This was the first Bible printed in the New World, and remained for nearly 100 years the only version issued in the colonies. Eliot took a special interest in the North American Indians,—believing them to be the descendants of the long-lost Ten Tribes of Israel,—and labored zealously among them for years.

Indian File. Another name for single file. So called, on account of a custom among the North American Indians, who, when traveling through the woods, especially on the war-path, moved in single file,—the one behind treading exactly in the footsteps of the one ahead, and the last man carefully effacing the footprints of those that had preceded him. Thus the Indians were able to conceal not only their numbers, but also even their whereabouts.

Indian Mutiny. A fierce insurrection which broke out in British India in 1857, and was quelled during the following year, at a cost of £40,000,-000. Various causes were assigned for this terrible outbreak, but the principal one may doubtless be found in the fact that the Sepoys in the Indian army outnumbered the Europeans six to one. The immediate provocation, however, was the widely spread report that the cartridges served out to the Bengal troops were greased with bullock fat, and that every Sepoy would

lose caste on biting off the end. Among the thrilling incidents of the "Mutiny" may be mentioned the siege of Delhi, the massacre of Cawnpore, and the relief and capture of Lucknow. After the suppression of the Indian Mutiny, the East India Company ceased to exist and the government of India was assumed by the British Crown. The army was totally reorganized and, as a result, the European soldiers outnumbered the native ones two to one. All the strategic points were placed in the hands of European soldiers, and almost the entire artillery was manned by European artillerymen. See *Cawnpore, Massacre of; East India Company; Enfield Rifle.*

Indians. The name properly applied to the natives of India, but also erroneously given to the aborigines of America by Columbus, who imagined, on reaching the island of San Salvador, that he had discovered the eastern shore of India. The confusion resulting from the improper use of this word has been partially remedied by prefixing the word *American,* or using the compound *Amerind.*

Indian Summer. In North America, a period of mild, balmy weather, —usually occurring in November,— characterized by a clear sky and a hazy or smoky atmosphere, especially near the horizon. The name is said to be derived from the custom, among the Indians, of using this delightful time of year to harvest their corn. According to one of their traditions, "they always had a second summer of nine days just before the winter set in." Indian summer corresponds to a similar season prevailing during the late autumn in England and the Mediterranean countries, called "St. Martin's Summer," from St. Martin's Festival, which falls on November 11th. Shakespeare refers to this in *Henry VI,* Part First, as follows :

" This night the siege assuredly I 'll raise ;
    Expect *St. Martin's summer,* halcyon
        days."

Inductive Philosophy. A system of philosophy based on observation and experiment. It was first expounded by Francis Bacon (1561–1626), in his work, the *Novum Organum*, published in 1620, and is, on that account, frequently called the " Baconian " Philosophy. See *Baconian Philosophy*.

Indulgences. The name given, in the Roman Catholic Church, to remissions—partial or plenary—of temporal penalties of sin, which remain due after the eternal punishment has been remitted. Grants of absolution were first issued by Pope Leo III (795–816) about 800; and were continued by Pope Gregory VII (1073–1080) and by Pope Urban II (1088–1099) in the 11th century, and by pontiffs in the 12th century as rewards for those persons that joined the Crusades. Indulgences were publicly *sold* for the first time by Pope Clement V (1305–1314) in 1313. This practice was revived and greatly abused by Pope Julius II (1503–1513) and Pope Leo X (1513–1522), with a view to raising the necessary funds for the erection of St. Peter's Church at Rome. In fact, it was the sale of indulgences throughout Germany by the Dominican monk, Tetzel, in 1517, that roused the ire of Martin Luther and became the inciting cause of the Reformation. The Council of Trent in 1563 condemned the abuse of the practice, and restricted it by fixed laws.

Inez de Castro. See *Castro, Inez de.*

Infallibility, Papal. The doctrine of papal infallibility in matters of faith and morals was taught as early as 750, and led to the famous disputes between the Gallican and Ultramontane divines—the former denying and the latter asserting the infallibility of the papal judgment. It was not, however, until July 18th, 1870, that this dogma was decreed to be an article of faith, and was promulgated by the Vatican Council. The doctrine was stoutly opposed in Germany, and led to the formation of the " Old Catholic Church." Dr. von Döllinger, one of the leaders of the new movement, was excommunicated on April 18th, 1871, and was chosen rector of the University of Munich on July 29th of the same year. The Bavarian government protested against the new doctrine on September 27th, 1871. See *Old Catholics.*

Infanticide. A practice common among the nations of antiquity, but limited in modern times to barbarous and semi-civilized peoples. It existed in Greece and Rome, and found supporters in Plato and Aristotle. Until recent times, infanticide was general throughout the South Sea Islands. It prevailed in India to a fearful extent, but was repressed during the rule (1798–1805) of the Marquis of Wellesley and is now gradually dying out. Infanticide was prohibited in China in June, 1873.

Infant Roscius. A sobriquet conferred upon William Henry Betty (1791–1874), the famous histrionic prodigy, who made his *début* at the age of twelve, and amazed the theatre-loving public by the brilliancy and power of his acting.

Inferno, L'. The title of the first part of Dante's *Divine Comedy*. It is in 34 cantos, and gives a vision of Hell, which, according to the poet, consists of an enormous funnel-shaped pit, divided into circular stages, and entered by seven gates. Under the guidance of Virgil, Dante visits these different circles in succession, and beholds the famous perpetrators of earthly crimes and the various methods devised for their punishment. See *Divine Comedy ; Paradiso, Il ; Purgatorio, Il.*

Inflected Languages. Languages in which relations are expressed, not only by prefixes and suffixes, but also by modification of the form of the roots. The inflected languages include the languages of the more highly developed nations of history, and are divided into two great classes : (1) the *Aryan* (including the *Sanskrit, Persian, Greek, Latin, Slav, Keltic, Teutonic,* etc.), and (2) the *Semitic* (including the *Hebrew, Arabic, Syriac,* etc.). See *Agglutinative Languages ; Monosyllabic Languages.*

In Hoc Signo Vinces (*Lat. In This Sign Thou Shalt Conquer*). The motto adopted by the Emperor Constantine (306–337) after his final struggle with Maxentius, the last of the six competitors that contended with him for the possession of the imperial throne. According to the legend, Constantine was one day riding at the head of his army, when suddenly he beheld in the sky, at noonday, a flaming cross, inscribed with the above words. This vision so impressed the conqueror that he immediately became a convert to Christianity, and was thereafter known as the first Christian Emperor of Rome. See *Constantine Sees Cross ; I. H. S.*

Innocents, Massacre of the. The name given to the slaughter of all the children of two years and under in Bethlehem, Judea, soon after the birth of Christ. This crime was committed by Herod for the purpose of destroying the infant Jesus, who, he feared, would reign as King of the Jews in his stead. According to the account given by St. Matthew, Joseph, having been warned in a dream of the King's intention, fled to Egypt with the child Jesus and his mother, and remained there until after Herod's death. " Innocents' Day "—in memory of this event—occurs on December 28th, the third day after Christmas, and is observed in the Roman Catholic and Protestant Episcopal Churches. See *Childermas Day.*

Inoculation. Inoculation for smallpox was introduced into England from Turkey by Lady Mary Wortley Montagu, in 1721. In 1718 her son was successfully inoculated at Adrianople, and three years later her daughter was publicly inoculated in England. In the same year seven condemned malefactors were inoculated, and, as a result of these successes, two children of Caroline, Princess of Wales, were inoculated soon after. This gave sanction to the practice, although it was publicly condemned by the clergy until 1760. Catherine II (1762–1796) of Russia was inoculated in 1768. Of 5964 persons inoculated in 1797–1799, only three died. The merits of vaccine inoculation were discovered by Dr. Jenner in 1796, and successfully introduced three years later. Direct inoculation was forbidden by law in 1840. See *Vaccination.*

Inquisition. A tribunal—officially styled " The Holy Office "—instituted by the Roman Catholic Church for the discovery and punishment of heresy and unbelief. It was first established in the south of France in 1210–1215, by Pope Innocent III (1198–1216), who appointed a commission to aid in checking the growth of the Albigensian heresy. Pope Gregory IX (1227–1241), at a council held at Toulouse in 1229, reorganized this commission and committed it to the care of the bishops ; but, afterwards, thinking them too lenient in their treatment of heretics, he placed the matter in charge of the Dominicans. The Inquisition was established in Aragon in 1233, in Venice in 1249, in France in 1255, in Castile in 1290, and in Portugal in 1526. It was in Spain and Portugal and their dependencies that the greatest cruelties were inflicted. Torquemada was appointed inquisitor-general of Spain in 1483, and during his term of office—lasting 16 years—9000 persons were committed to the flames. His successor, Diego Dega, in 8 years, put 1600 persons to a similar death. According to the historian Llorente, 32,000 persons were put to death in 236 years by the Spanish Inquisition, and 291,000 were punished in other ways. The Inquisition in

Spain was suppressed in 1820, was partially restored in 1825, and was finally abolished in 1834-1835,—its property having been applied to the payment of the national debt. The Holy Inquisition still exists at Rome, but its activity is limited to an examination of heretical books and to trials for ecclesiastical offenses. Since 1870, its jurisdiction has been limited to the Vatican. The Inquisition was never established in England. See *Auto da Fé*.

I. N. R. I. The initial letters of the words composing the Latin inscription, IESUS NAZARENUS REX IUDÆORUM (*Lat. Jesus of Nazareth, King of the Jews*), placed by Pilate on the cross.

"And Pilate wrote a title, and put it on the cross. And the writing was JESUS OF NAZARETH, THE KING OF THE JEWS. This title then read many of the Jews; for the place where Jesus was crucified was nigh to the city: and it was written in Hebrew, and Greek, and Latin."—*John* xix, 19, 20.

Insane Root. An expression used to denote hemlock, which, when eaten, was said to play strange pranks with the imagination. According to the legend, those that partook of it were enabled to see objects otherwise invisible. Shakespeare refers to this superstition in the following words :

"Were such things here, as we do speak about,
Or have we eaten on the *insane root*,
That takes the reason prisoner?"
Macbeth, i, 3.

Insects. Insects form the largest class of animals, numerically, being estimated by some naturalists to compose four-fifths of the animal kingdom.

"It is impossible at present to give any secure estimate of the number of insects, though it is probably safe to say that they exceed all other animals taken together. Over 80,000 species of beetles or Coleoptera and about 15,000 moths and butterflies have been recorded ; and Speyer estimates the total census at 200,000, while M'Lachlan concludes that future entomological industry will raise the sum total of insect species to a million."—*Chambers's Encyclopædia*.

Instauratio Magna (*Lat. Great Instauration or Restoration*). A celebrated treatise by Lord Francis Bacon (1561-1626), planned by him to consist of six parts, and designed to form a complete exposition of his system of philosophy. Owing to its vastness, the work was never completed. The following are the names of the parts that have actually appeared :

Part I. *De Augmentis Scientiarum* (*On the Advancement of Learning*).
Part II. *Novum Organum* (*The New Instrument or Method*).
Part III. *Sylva Sylvarum* (*The History of Nature*).
Part IV. *Scala Intellectus* (*Steps of the Understanding*).

Institute of France. A French national association for the promotion of the arts and sciences. It was founded by the Directory in 1795, under the name of the *Institut National*, and was successively reorganized in 1803, 1816, and 1832. The French Institute embraces five different academies : *L'Académie Française, L'Académie des Inscriptions et Belles-Lettres, L'Académie des Sciences, L'Académie des Beaux-Arts*, and *L'Académie des Sciences Morales et Politiques*. Members are elected by ballot, and each election must be confirmed by the government. Each member receives an annual salary of 1500 francs, and the secretary of each academy, 6000 francs. The Institute is composed of 229 members, 36 académiciens libres, 32 associés étrangers, and 238 correspondants. To become a member of the French Institute is the highest ambition of every literary and scientific Frenchman. See *Academy, French ; Palais de l'Institut*.

Institutes of the Christian Religion. A theological work by John Calvin (1509-1564). It was published in 1536, and had for its object to expound and vindicate the doctrines of the Reformed Church. Calvin's *Institutes* was the first systematic and thorough defense of Protestantism.

Invention of the Cross. A festival in the Greek and Roman Catholic Churches, annually celebrated on May 3rd, in commemoration of the miraculous " invention," or discovery, of the true cross at Jerusalem in 326, by Helena, the mother of Constantine the Great. See *Cross, True.*

Invincible Doctor. A sobriquet conferred upon William of Occam or Ockham (1270–1347), the distinguished English philosopher and theologian. He was excommunicated by Pope John XXII (1316–1334) for his bold defense of the Emperor Louis of Bavaria against the encroachments of the papal power. Also termed *Doctor Singularis et Invincibilis.*

Iodine. A substance discovered by Courtois in 1811, and proved to be an elementary body by Gay-Lussac a few years later. It derives its name from its beautiful violet-colored vapor. Iodine is much used in medicine to scatter cutaneous eruptions and to reduce glandular swellings, and was first successfully applied in the treatment of goitre by Dr. Coindet of Geneva in 1820. A prize of 3000 francs for this discovery was awarded him by the Academy of Sciences at Paris.

Ionian School. The earliest of the Greek schools of philosophy. It existed for about 200 years (600–400 B.C.), and was materialistic and empiric. The Ionian philosophers speculated on the outer world, and sought the first principle that lies beneath its changing phenomena. This Thales claimed to find in water ; Anaximander, in heat ; Anaximenes and Diogenes of Apollonia, in air ; Heraclitus, in fire ; and Anaxagoras, in atoms influenced by mind.

Iran. The official designation of the Kingdom of Persia at the present day. The name *Iran* was originally given to the great plateau in western Asia, comprising modern Persia, most of Afghanistan, and Beluchistan.

It extends from the Elburz and Hindu Kush Mountains on the north to the Persian Gulf and Arabian Sea on the south, and from Kurdistan and the Tigris on the west to the Indus on the east.

Ireland Forgeries. The name given to certain Shakespearian autographs, private letters, and plays, which a youth named Ireland claimed to have discovered ; but which he had in reality forged. One of the plays, called *Vortigern,* was produced at the Drury Lane Theatre on April 2nd, 1796 ; but proved to be a vapid and senseless production. Ireland soon after acknowledged the forgery, and published his *Confessions* in 1805. He died in obscurity and poverty in 1835.

Ireland's Three Saints. An appellation conferred upon Ireland's three great saints,—St. Patrick, St. Columba, and St. Bridget.

Iridium. A hard, brittle, silver-white metallic element, belonging to the platinum group, discovered by Tennant in 1803. Sometimes found native and nearly pure, but generally combined with osmium. It is, with the exception of osmium, the heaviest metal known, and is used for pen-points, contact-points in telegraphy, and points of scientific instruments liable to wear. Its specific gravity is 22.4. See *Osmium.*

Irish Agitator. A sobriquet conferred upon Daniel O'Connell (1775–1847), the apostle of Irish liberty.

Irish Language. The native language of Ireland is the Irish-Gaelic, —one of the three divisions forming the Goidelic branch of the Celtic family. During the past 300 years, the native Irish language has been steadily declining and giving way to the English. According to *Chambers's Encyclopædia*, it is estimated that in 1881 only 64,167 spoke Irish-Gaelic alone (and this in a corrupt form), as against

26

103,562 in 1871 ; while the number that spoke both English and Irish-Gaelic (called " bilinguals ") was 885,765 in 1881, as against 714,313 in 1871. So that, during the decade from 1871 to 1881, although the number of " bilinguals " increased considerably, there was a falling off of about one-third of those that spoke Irish-Gaelic alone. The oldest forms of the language are preserved in the *Ogham Inscriptions* (500 A.D.). The *New Testament* was translated into Irish-Gaelic in 1603, and the *Old Testament* in 1685. A society for the preservation of the Irish-Gaelic tongue exists in England at the present day.

Iron Age. See *Ages, Mythologic.*

Iron Cage. When Bayazeed, Sultan of the Ottomans, was defeated and taken prisoner by the famous Tamerlane at the battle of Angora in 1401 A.D., he was at first treated by the conqueror with great clemency, and was even offered the restoration of his throne on condition that he would lay aside his hostility. Bayazeed, however, abused Tamerlane's generosity, and, having been detected in a plot to assassinate the Tartar chief, was loaded with chains and placed in an iron cage. In that condition he was forced to accompany the conqueror's victorious army.

Iron Chancellor. An appellation conferred upon Prince Otto von Bismarck (1813–1898), Chancellor of the German Empire, in allusion to his inflexible purpose and indomitable will.

Iron Chest. A secret compartment in the wainscot of the bedchamber of Louis XVI (1774–1789), in the palace of the Tuileries. It was constructed by Gamain, the King's locksmith, and was so skilfully concealed that its presence defied detection. Gamain, however, revealed its existence to the National Convention, and an examination of its contents was immediately made. Among the papers found were some so compromising to Mirabeau's loyalty to the Republic, that his bust was ordered to be removed from the hall of the Convention and ground into powder.

Iron City. A term popularly applied to the city of Pittsburg, Pennsylvania, on account of its extensive iron industries. It is estimated that one-fifth of all the iron and steel made in the United States is produced in and near Pittsburg. See *Smoky City.*

Ironclad Oath. An oath of office prescribed by Congress in 1867—after the Civil War—as a protection against future disloyalty to the United States government on the part of the citizens of the reconstructed States. It excluded from the right of franchise those persons that had borne arms against the Federal government, as well as those that had rendered direct or indirect aid to persons engaged in the act of rebellion.

Iron Cross. A Prussian order of merit instituted by Frederick William III (1797–1840) of Prussia on March 10th, 1813, as a reward for bravery during the " War of Liberation " against France. The decoration is a Maltese cross of iron, edged with silver, and worn either around the neck or in the button-hole. This Order was revived by William I, King of Prussia (1861–1888), on July 19th, 1870, on the eve of the Franco-German War, and was bestowed by him on his son, the Crown Prince, for his victory of Wissembourg, August 4th, 1870. During 1870–1871, 40,000 persons were decorated with the Iron Cross.

Iron Crown of Lombardy. A famous crown, composed principally of gold and precious stones, so called on account of a thin circular band of iron that forms part of it. This iron band is said to have been forged from a nail of the true cross given by the Empress Helena to her son, Constantine the

Great. It was first used at the coronation of Agilulf, King of the Longobards, in 591. Charlemagne was crowned with it in 774, and so were all the later Emperors of Germany that were Kings of Lombardy. When Napoleon I was crowned King of Italy, at Milan, in 1805, he himself placed this iron crown upon his head, saying : "God has given it to me ; woe to him that touches it." This precious relic remained in the cathedral at Monza until 1859, when it was removed to Mantua. After the Peace of Vienna in 1866, the "Iron Crown" was presented by the Emperor of Austria to Victor Emmanuel, King of Italy, and was restored to the church at Monza for safe-keeping.

Iron Duke. A sobriquet conferred upon Arthur, Duke of Wellington (1769–1852), during his later years. It is said that this nickname was originally given to the *Duke of Wellington*, an iron steam-vessel that plied between Liverpool and Dublin. The expression, however, was so well suited to the old soldier, on account of his sternness of character and want of sympathy with the masses, that it was applied to him also.

Iron Mask, Man with the. A mysterious French prisoner of state, whose identity has never been satisfactorily established. He was closely confined (under the charge of M. de St. Mars) at Pignerol (1679); at Exilles (1681); at Sainte - Marguerite (1687) ; and finally was transferred to the Bastille (1698), where he died on November 19th, 1703, and was buried the following day in the cemetery of St. Paul, under the name of Marchiali. He wore a mask of black velvet while journeying from prison to prison ; and, although treated with the utmost deference, was forbidden to uncover himself, under penalty of instant death. According to some authorities, he was forced to wear his mask at all times. See *Bastille.*

"Notwithstanding the appellation given

him, the mask he wore was not of iron, but of black velvet, strengthened with whalebone, and secured behind the head with steel springs, or, as some assert, by means of a padlock. Many conjectures have been hazarded as to who this mysterious personage could have been. One opinion is, that he was a son of Anne of Austria, queen of Louis XIII, his father being Cardinal Mazarin (to whom that dowager queen was privately married), or the Duke of Buckingham. Others suppose him to have been a twin-brother of Louis XIV, whose birth was concealed to prevent the civil dissensions in France which it might one day have caused. The latter view was adopted by Voltaire, in common with many others. Some Dutch writers assert that the prisoner was a young foreign nobleman, the chamberlain of Queen Anne, and the real father of Louis XIV. It has more recently been surmised that Fouquet was the mask ; but M. Delort and the Right Honorable Agar Ellis (afterward Lord Dover) identify him with a Count Matthioli, a minister of Charles III, Duke of Mantua. This minister had been largely bribed by Louis XIV, and had pledged himself to urge the duke to give up to the French the fortress of Casale, which gave access to the whole of Lombardy. But Louis, finding that Matthioli was playing him false, lured him to the French frontier, and had him secretly arrested and imprisoned. Being a minister plenipotentiary at the time, his seizure was a flagrant violation of international law, which it was safer to be able to deny than to attempt to justify ; and the denial once made, the honor of France was involved in upholding it. This opinion is the one generally received at the present day by those who have investigated the subject."—Wheeler's *Dictionary of the Noted Names of Fiction.*

Ironside. See *Edmund Ironside.*

Ironsides. The name given to a famous regiment of one thousand horse that served under Oliver Cromwell, in allusion to the iron courage displayed by it at the battle of Marston Moor (1644). The "Ironsides" were chiefly recruited in the eastern counties of England. They were religious fanatics, almost to a man, and enjoyed the proud distinction of never having been defeated in battle. Cromwell said of them in a speech, the year before his death, "truly they were never beaten, but whenever they were engaged against the enemy they beat continually." See *Marston Moor, Battle of.*

Iron Virgin. An instrument of torture in use during the Middle Ages. It was a hollow wooden figure, fashioned to represent a maiden of the 15th century, and opened like a cupboard, revealing an interior studded with sharp iron spikes. After the victim had been forced within, the lid gradually closed upon him and brought his body in contact with these spikes, which pierced him through and through. There he lingered in dreadful agony, until death relieved him from his sufferings. Underneath the figure was a trap-door, through which the dead body fell.

Irrepressible Conflict. An expression said to have originated with the Hon. William H. Seward (1801–1872), in a speech delivered by him at Rochester on October 25th, 1858. The allusion was to the growing struggle between freedom and slavery, which a few years later developed into the Civil War.

Isaiah's Tree. An aged mulberry-tree, which stands near the Pool of Siloam in Jerusalem, and is traditionally associated with the death of Isaiah. There, according to the legend, the prophet was sawn asunder by order of King Manasseh. The trunk is gnarled, bent, and yellow, and is supported by a pile of loose stones. See *Pool of Siloam.*

Isiac Table. A flat, rectangular copper plate, about four feet eight inches long, containing several rows of Egyptian emblems and divinities. According to the story, it was found by a soldier at the siege of Rome in 1525 A.D., and, two years later, was sold by him to Cardinal Bembo. Although generally regarded as spurious, it is carefully preserved in the Royal Gallery of Turin.

Isis. An Egyptian goddess, the sister-wife of Osiris and the mother of Horus. She was worshipped not only in Egypt, but also in Greece and Rome and other parts of Europe, and was identified with Io by the Greeks. She was generally regarded as the Queen of Heaven, and was often represented as wearing a veil, — the emblem of secrecy. See *Osiris.*

"Plutarch considers *Isis* to be the earth, the feminine part of nature, while Diodorus says that the Egyptians, considering the earth to be the parent of all things born, called her Mother, just as the Greeks called the earth Demeter." — Murray's *Manual of Mythology.*

Isis, Temple of. A noted temple at Philæ, Egypt, founded by Ptolemy Philadelphus (284–246 B.C.). Many of its sculptures, however, are of the time of the Roman Emperors.

"Through the propylon you enter a court and proceed through a pylon into a portico with ten columns. This is the gem of the temple and is really of great beauty. The colors are marvellously fresh, the capitals being of vivid blue and green, with delicate mixtures of red, crimson, and orange. The ceiling is light blue with bright stars set upon it. Round and about are many small chambers, all covered with excellent sculptures— some representing the king slaying hostile nations, others describing the death and resurrection of Osiris, and still others covered with mythological hieroglyphics. In the courtyard is a great block of red granite giving the famous Rosetta Stone inscription, though unfortunately without the Greek text. Very many of the sculptures have been defaced with hammers by the early Christians. In 579 A.D., the interior of this temple became, under Bishop Theodorus, the church of St. Stephen, and at a later period a Coptic church was built from the ruins."—*Actual Africa* (Vincent).

Islâm (*also written Eslâm*). An Arabic word, meaning "complete and entire submission of body and soul to God, His will and His service, as well as to all those articles of faith, commands, and ordinances revealed to and ordained by Mohammed his prophet." It is the proper name of the religion generally known as Mohammedanism, and consists in an observance of the following five duties:

(1) Declaring that there is but one God.

(2) Reciting prayers daily.

(3) Giving legal alms.

(4) Observing the month of Ramadan as a fast.

(5) Making one pilgrimage to Mecca during a lifetime. See *Ramadan.*

Island City. An appellation sometimes bestowed upon Montreal, the commercial metropolis of British North America, because situated on the island of the same name.

Island of the Seven Cities. An imaginary island, abounding in gold, and adorned with superb houses and temples, whose lofty towers were visible at a great distance. According to a legend that prevailed at the time of Columbus, this island was settled by seven bishops who, having fled with a great number of people from Spain and Portugal, when those countries were conquered by the Moors, took to the ocean, and finally landed on an unknown island. After their arrival, the bishops burned the ships, to prevent the return of their followers, and founded seven cities. It is said that those navigators that visited the island in after years were never permitted to return.

Islands of the Blest. An imaginary group of islands in the Atlantic Ocean, beyond the Pillars of Hercules, whither the favorites of the gods were conveyed without dying, and where they dwelt in unending bliss. The region was one of surpassing loveliness, and abounded in nature's richest and rarest products. They were called by the Greeks the "Happy Islands," and by the Romans the "Fortunate Islands." See *Elysium.*

" Their place of birth alone is mute
 To sounds that echo further west
 Than your sires' *Islands of the Blest.*"
 Byron.

Isola Bella (*It. Beautiful Island*). The most celebrated of the Borromean Islands, situated on Lake Maggiore in northern Italy. It commands a charming prospect of the lake, and contains a superb palace—filled with objects of art—situated in the midst of beautiful gardens, which rise in terraces from the water's edge, and are adorned with tropical plants. See *Borromean Islands.*

" *Isola Bella* looks like a gentleman's villa afloat. A boy would throw a stone entirely over it in any direction. It strikes you as a kind of toy, as you look at it from a distance : and, getting nearer, the illusion scarcely dissipates ; for, from the water's edge, the orange-laden terraces are piled, one above another, like a pyramidal fruit-basket ; the villa itself peers above like a sugar castle, and it scarce seems real enough to land upon."—*N. P. Willis.*

Israel (*Heb. Prince with God*). The surname of Jacob, Isaac's younger son, bestowed upon him after his successful wrestle with an angel at Peniel. It became the distinctive name of his descendants, and afterwards of the Kingdom of the Ten Tribes. See *Edom; Israel, Kingdom of; Israel, Twelve Tribes of.*

" And he said, Thy name shall be called no more Jacob, but *Israel*: for as a prince hast thou power with God and with men, and hast prevailed."—*Genesis* xxxii, 28.

Israel, Kingdom of. In 975 B.C., during the reign of Rehoboam (975–958 B.C.), son of Solomon, the Hebrew monarchy was split into two sections —known, respectively, as the Kingdom of Judah and the Kingdom of Israel. The former of these kingdoms remained under the rule of Rehoboam, and comprised the two tribes of Judah and Benjamin, with Jerusalem for its capital; while the latter—consisting of the remaining ten tribes—chose Jeroboam (975–954 B.C.) for its King, and made Shechem its capital. The Kingdom of Israel was ruled by 19 kings of different dynasties, and lasted until 721 B.C., when it was conquered by Shalmaneser, King of Assyria. Hoshea, the ruling King, was cast into prison, and the mass of the people was carried captive into the mountainous regions of Media. Their place was taken by Assyrian colonists; and these, mingling and intermarrying with the few remaining Israelites, formed the mixed race known as Samaritans. See *Judah, Kingdom of.*

Israel, Twelve Tribes of. The name given to the descendants of the twelve sons of Jacob, surnamed *Israel,* who were as follows : Reuben, Simeon, Levi, Judah, Dan, Naphthali, Gad, Asher, Issachar, Zebulun, Joseph, and Benjamin. When Canaan was conquered by the Israelites, the land was divided among the tribes by lot. Two of these, however, received no inheritance, viz., Levi, whose descendants became priests and were supported by the nation in common, and Joseph, whose two sons, Ephraim and Manasseh, were adopted by Jacob, and gave names to separate tribes. So far as the occupancy of the land was concerned, the following are the names of the Twelve Tribes of Israel : Reuben, Simeon, Judah, Dan, Naphthali, Gad, Asher, Issachar, Zebulun, Benjamin, Ephraim, and Manasseh. See *Israel; Sons of Israel.*

Issus, Battle of. A famous battle, fought in Asia Minor in 333 B.C., between Alexander the Great and Darius, King of Persia, in which the former was completely victorious. According to Justin, the Persian army consisted of 400,000 foot and 100,000 horse; 61,000 of the former and 10,000 of the latter were slain, and 40,000 taken prisoners. Diodorus Siculus says the Macedonian loss was only 450. After the battle, the family of the Persian King fell into the hands of Alexander, and were treated by him with the utmost consideration and respect.

Isthmian Games. A series of athletic contests in ancient Greece, so called because celebrated on the Isthmus of Corinth. They were instituted about 1406 B.C., by Sisyphus, in honor of Melicertes, a sea-god, and were re-established in 1239, by Theseus, in honor of Poseidon. These games were observed on the first and third years of each Olympiad, and were held so sacred

that not even a public calamity was permitted to prevent their celebration. The contests comprised foot and chariot races, boxing, wrestling, leaping, and the *pancration* (a combination of wrestling and boxing). The victors were at first crowned with garlands of pine-leaves, but in later years with wreaths of ivy. The Isthmian Games were continued by the Greeks until a late period, and were revived by Julius Cæsar in 60 B.C. and by the Emperor Julian in 362 A.D. See *Nemean Games; Olympic Games; Pythian Games.*

Ithuriel (*Heb. God's Discovery*). One of two angels, mentioned in Milton's *Paradise Lost,* sent by Gabriel to find Satan, who had eluded the vigilance of the heavenly guards and had effected an entrance into the Garden of Eden. Satan was discovered, " squat like a toad, close at the ear of Eve "; but, when touched by Ithuriel's spear, he immediately resumed his natural form. The angel commissioned by Gabriel to accompany Ithuriel in his search was called Zephon.

" Him thus intent *Ithuriel* with his spear
  Touch'd lightly ; for no falsehood can endure
  Touch of celestial temper, but returns
  Of force to its own likeness. Up he starts,
  Discover'd and surprised."
            Paradise Lost, iv, 810–814.

Ivan Ivanovitch. A popular nickname of the Russian people,— corresponding to the *John Bull* of the English, the *Johnny Crapaud* of the French, and the *Brother Jonathan* of the Americans. He is generally described as an indolent, good-natured person.

Ivan Veliki. A celebrated bell-tower, over 200 feet in height, in the Kremlin at Moscow. It is surmounted by a gilded dome, and contains 34 bells, varying in weight from 36 tons to half a ton. In front of the Ivan Veliki stands (unmounted) the Tzar Kolokol, or Great Bell of Moscow. See *Bell of Moscow; Kremlin.*

"When they all sound at once, as on an Easter morn, the very tower must rock on its foundation."—*Bayard Taylor.*

Ivory Coast. A part of Guinea, on the west coast of Africa, famous for its trade in ivory. It is bounded on the west by Liberia, and on the east by the Gold Coast. The western portion belongs to Liberia, while the eastern is shared between Great Britain and France. The term "Ivory Coast" has no political significance. See *Gold Coast; Slave Coast.*

Ivory Gate. In Virgil's *Æneid,* a gate of gleaming white ivory, in the lower world, through which false and delusive dreams are sent up to earth by the deities of the infernal regions. See *Horn Gate.*

" From *gate of horn or ivory,* dreams are sent :
These to deceive, and those for warning meant."

Æneid.

Ivry, Battle of. A famous battle fought near Ivry, France, on March 14th, 1590, between the Huguenots under Henry of Navarre [afterwards Henry IV (1589–1610) of France], and the army of the League, commanded by the Duke of Mayenne. Henry's forces consisted of 8000 foot and 2000 horse, while the Leaguers numbered 12,000 foot and 4000 horse. The Huguenot army, encouraged by the valor of their dashing leader, won a brilliant victory, while Mayenne, thoroughly beaten, fled across the river Eure, leaving on the field 12,000 men, dead, wounded, or prisoners of war.

" I Want to Meet my God Awake." An expression attributed to Maria Theresa (1740–1780), Empress of Germany, who, on her deathbed, refused to take a dose of opium to mitigate her sufferings, owing to her desire to meet the end in the full possession of her faculties.

J

Jack Horner. A famous personage in nursery literature, whose merry deeds are described by Halliwell in his *Nursery Rhymes of England.*

The lines—
" Little *Jack Horner* sat in a corner,
Eating his Christmas pie ;
He put in his thumb, and pulled out a plum,
Saying, ' What a good boy am I ! ' "—

are said to veil a satire ; and in Brewer's *Reader's Handbook* we read the following : " In *Notes and Queries,* xvi, 156, several explanations are offered, ascribing a political meaning to the words quoted—Jack Horner being elevated to a king's messenger or king's steward, and the 'plum' pulled out so cleverly being a valuable deed which the messenger abstracted."

Jack of Clubs. A sobriquet conferred upon General Philip H. Sheridan (1831–1888) by his soldiers during the Civil War (1861–1865).

Jack of Spades. A title conferred upon General John A. Logan (1826–1886) by his troops during the Civil War (1861–1865).

Jack Robinson. The origin of the saying, " Before you can say Jack Robinson,"—meaning "immediately," —is variously explained.

" Grose says that the saying had its birth from a very volatile gentleman of that name, who used to pay flying visits to his neighbourhood, and was no sooner announced than he was off again ; but the following couplet does not confirm this derivation.

' A warke it ys as easie to be done
As tys to saye *Jacke! robys on.'*
An old Play, cited by Halliwell,
' Arch. Dict.' "
Dictionary of Phrase and Fable (Brewer).

" This current phrase is said to be derived from a humorous song by Hudson, a tobacconist in Shoe Lane, London. He was a professional song-writer and vocalist, who used to be engaged to sing at supper-rooms and theatrical houses.

A warke it ys as easie to be done
As tys to saye Jacke ! robys on.
HALLIWELL, *Arch. Dictionary.*"
Fact, Fancy, and Fable (Reddall).

"Lord Eldon relates that during the parliamentary debates on the India Bill, when Mr. John Robinson was Secretary to the Treasury, Sheridan, one evening when Fox's majorities were decreasing, said: ' Mr. Speaker, this is not at all to be wondered at, when a member is employed to corrupt everybody in order to obtain votes.' Upon this there was a great outcry by almost everybody in the house. 'Who is it?' 'Name him! Name him!' 'Sir,' said Sheridan to the Speaker, 'I shall not name the person. It is an unpleasant and invidious thing to do; and, therefore, I shall not name him. But don't suppose, Sir, that I abstain because there is any difficulty in naming him ; I could do that, Sir, as soon as you could say Jack Robinson.' "—*Gleanings for the Curious* (Bombaugh).

Jack Tar. A popular designation of a sailor, given him on account of the tarpaulin overalls donned by him in stormy weather.

Jacobins.

(1) The name of the French Dominicans, so called because their first convent was situated in the *Rue St. Jacques*, Paris, where they established themselves in 1219.

(2) A political club formed at Versailles in 1789, at the beginning of the French Revolution, and at first called the *Club Breton*, because organized by deputies from Brittany. It was afterwards removed to Paris, and held its meetings in a former convent of the *Jacobins* in the Rue St. Honoré, from which circumstance it received from its enemies the name of the *Jacobin Club*, although its proper designation was the *Society of Friends of the Constitution*. The club held extreme political views, and took a leading part in the French Revolution. It favored the death of the King and the destruction of the Girondists, and encouraged the atrocities of the Reign of Terror. Among its members were Marat and Robespierre. After the execution of the latter, in August, 1794, the influence of the Jacobin Club steadily declined ; and on November 9th of the same year its meetings were suppressed. See *Girondists*.

Jacobites. The name given in England, after the Revolution of 1688, to the adherents of James II (1685–1688) and his son and grandson—the "Old" and "Young Pretenders." The word is derived from *Jacobus*, the Latin form of *James*.

The name "Jacobites" was also applied to a sect, among the Eastern Christians, that spread widely during the 6th and 7th centuries. It derived its name from *Jacob* Baradæus, a Syrian heresiarch.

Jacob's Ladder. The name given to a vision beheld by Jacob when a fugitive from his brother Esau, described in *Genesis* xxviii, 12–15. While the patriarch slept, he beheld a ladder reaching from earth to heaven, on which ascended and descended the angels of God. This dream assured Jacob of God's omnipresent providence and of His communication of all needed good.

The name "Jacob's Ladder" is also applied to a herbaceous, perennial plant of the Order *Polemoniaceæ*. It is found in the centre and south of Europe, and in the temperate regions of Asia and North America. See *Jacob's Stone*.

Jacob's Sons. The twelve sons of Jacob, in the order of their seniority, were as follows : Reuben, Simeon, Levi, Judah, Dan, Naphthali, Gad, Asher, Issachar, Zebulun, Joseph, and Benjamin. See *Israel*, *Twelve Tribes of*.

Jacob's Stone. The name sometimes given to the famous Stone of Scone in the Coronation Chair, at Westminster Abbey. It is so called because tradition declares it to be the identical stone on which Jacob rested his head when he beheld the vision of the ladder reaching from earth to heaven. See *Coronation Chair ; Jacob's Ladder*.

Jacob's Well. A famous well — about 9 feet in diameter and 75 feet deep — near Nablûs, Syria, in the vicinity of Mount Gerizim. It is hewn out of the living rock, and, according to tradition, was dug by the patriarch Jacob while living in that vicinity. There Jesus rested during the heat of the day, and held his famous conversation with the woman of Samaria. A large church was erected over the well in the 4th century, but was probably destroyed before the time of the Crusades. Nothing but a heap of ruins now remains. The well is dry at certain times, but at others contains several feet of water.

Jacquard Loom. Invented by Joseph Marie Jacquard (1752–1834), a native of Lyons, France, and patented by him on December 23rd, 1801. By means of this loom, the most complex pattern can be woven as easily and as rapidly as a piece of plain cloth. So great was the opposition to the introduction of the Jacquard loom in Lyons, that the inventor almost lost his life in the attempt, while his machine was publicly destroyed by a body of men called the Conseil des Prud'hommes. A monument now stands on the spot where this outrage was committed, and manifests the appreciation of a more enlightened generation.

Jacquerie. The name given to an insurrection that broke out among the peasants of France in 1358, while the French King (John the Good) was detained as a prisoner of war in England. This revolt, which was caused by the oppressions of the privileged classes, took its rise in the vicinity of Paris, and soon assumed such threatening proportions that the nobles were compelled to make common cause against it. The insurgents, 20,000 strong, were headed by one Caillot (surnamed Jacques Bonhomme), and for six weeks committed frightful depredations, — having in that time destroyed 30 castles. They were finally defeated with great slaughter near Meaux, where 7000 of them, including their

leader, were slain. The word "Jacquerie" is derived from "Jacques" Bonhomme, the surname of Caillot.

Jaffa Massacre. The name given to a massacre of Turkish troops by order of Napoleon Bonaparte (1769–1821) in 1799, during the Egyptian campaign. After the fall of Jaffa, a large number of soldiers — variously estimated at from 1200 to 3800 — who had voluntarily surrendered themselves as prisoners of war, were marched some distance from the town and shot down in cold blood. Their bodies were then heaped in pyramids, and for half a century their bones were visible in the glistening sand. This deed, which remains one of the darkest stains on Napoleon's name, was defended by him on the plea of necessity. He declared at St. Helena that he would do the same thing to-morrow, and that any other general would act similarly under similar circumstances.

Jamaica. This name is a corruption of *xaymaco*, a West Indian expression meaning "the country abounding in springs."

Janiculum Hill. A famous hill in the city of Rome, situated on the right bank of the Tiber, and south of St. Peter's Church. It affords a fine prospect of the city and its environs, and derives its name, according to tradition, from *Janus*, the Sun-god of the Latins. Numa Pompilius, the second King of Rome, was buried there; and Ancus Martius, the fourth King, fortified the hill, and connected it with the city by means of the Pons Sublicius, the first Roman bridge. This is the bridge that was so valiantly defended by Horatius Cocles against the Etruscans commanded by Porsenna. The Janiculum is not one of the "Seven Hills of Rome." See *Seven Hills of Rome*.

Janizaries (*Turk. Iéni Tchéri, New Soldiers*). The first regular militia or standing army of the Ottoman Empire,

—organized by the Sultan Orkhan (1326-1360) in 1330, and remodelled by his son Amurath I (1360-1389) in 1360. It consisted originally of Christian prisoners, forced to embrace Mohammedanism, and of the children of Christians, compelled to become Moslems. The Janizaries were of two classes. One of these, thoroughly organized, was stationed in barracks in Constantinople and other cities, and numbered 100,000; while the other class, scattered throughout the Empire, numbered from 300,000 to 400,000. They formed the infantry of the army in time of war, and acted as a police-force in time of peace. The Sultan's body-guard was composed of them. Owing to their many privileges, they finally became more dangerous to the state than any foreign enemies; and repeated attempts were made, but in vain, to dissolve the organization. Finally, in 1826, the Sultan Mahmoud II (1808-1839), having organized a new army on a European basis, defeated the Janizaries in a sanguinary conflict, and drove them to their barracks, which were then set on fire; 8000 perished in the flames, 15,000 were afterwards executed, and more than 20,000 were banished. On June 17th, 1826, the Janizaries were abolished by proclamation, and in their place was established the *Nigam*, a body of soldiers organized on the European plan.

Jansenists. The name given to the followers of Cornelius Jansen (1585-1638), Bishop of Ypres, France, whose book—entitled *Augustinus*—was published in 1640, and taught the doctrine of free grace. This view was contrary to that held by the Jesuits, and resulted in a long and bitter religious controversy. The book was prohibited by a decree of the Inquisition in 1643, and was condemned by Pope Urban VIII (1623-1644) in 1644, and again by Pope Innocent X (1644-1655) in 1653. Pascal, in 1656, published his famous *Lettres Provinciales* in defense of the Jansenists, and accused the Jesuits of immorality, simony, and other crimes. Such, however, was the influence of the Jesuits that the Jansenist doctrines were again condemned by Pope Clement XI (1700-1721) in his famous bull *Unigenitus*, issued in 1713. The Jansenists were persecuted by Louis XIV (1643-1715), and in 1720 they were banished from France by the Regent, the Duke of Orleans. As a result of these harsh measures, many of them fled to the Netherlands and established at Utrecht, in 1713, an archbishopric, which they retain at the present day. Jansenism still exists in Haarlem and Utrecht, but is rapidly declining in influence. See *Jesuits; Unigenitus.*

Janus, Temple of. Erected at Rome by Caius Duilius during the First Punic War; restored by Augustus; and dedicated by Tiberius. Its doors were kept open in time of war and closed in time of peace. They were closed at the end of the First Punic War (235 B.C.), and again in 29, 25, and 5 B.C. Janus was an ancient Latin divinity, worshipped both by the Etruscans and the Romans. He presided over the beginnings of things, and was always invoked at the commencement of any undertaking,—even before Jupiter.

Jardin d'Acclimatation. An enclosed portion of the Bois de Boulogne, Paris, devoted to the reproduction and acclimatization of useful and rare vegetal and animal species. It covers an area of fifty acres, and constitutes one of the most attractive spots in the neighborhood of the city. The Jardin d'Acclimatation contains extensive conservatories, aquariums, aviaries, cattle-sheds, and kennels. It suffered severely during the siege of Paris in 1870-1871.

Jardin des Plantes. A celebrated scientific institution in Paris, founded in 1626 by Guy de Labrosse, an eminent botanist. It covers an area of 75 acres, and contains extensive botanical and zoölogical gardens, as well as galleries of mineralogy, geology, human and comparative anatomy, and anthropology. Free lectures on natural history are given in an amphitheatre holding 1200 persons. Buffon, Lamarck, Cuvier, and Geoffroy de St. Hilaire all taught there. The Jardin des Plantes was seriously injured during the siege of Paris in 1870–1871.

Jardin Mabille. A celebrated open-air garden, formerly existing in Paris in the neighborhood of the Champs-Elysées. It was much resorted to by women of the *demi-monde*, and by strangers in their desire to see Parisian " life." The garden was brilliantly illuminated with colored lights, and was adorned with fountains and parterres of flowers. There was also a large covered apartment used for dancing in inclement weather.

Jarley, Mrs. One of the characters in Dickens's novel, *The Old Curiosity Shop*. She was a kind-hearted woman of the " stout and comfortable kind," and befriended " Little Nell " in her wanderings. Mrs. Jarley was sole proprietress of a traveling wax-show consisting of " one hundred figures the full size of life." This, she asserted, was " the only stupendous collection of real waxwork in the world " and " the genuine and only Jarley."

One of the hand-bills read as follows:

" If I know'd a donkey wot would n't go
  To see *Mrs Jarley's wax-work show*,
  Do you think I 'd acknowledge him ? oh,
    no, no !
          Then run to Jarley's——' "

Jasher, Book of. A lost Hebrew book, twice quoted in the *Old Testament* (*Joshua* x, 13; 2 *Samuel* i, 17, 18). Its author and contents are both unknown, and have given rise to much speculation. According to many scholars, the book perished during the captivity of the Jews in Babylon (606–536 B.C.). As the word *Jasher* means *just* or *upright*, the book is generally

thought to have been a history of *just men*.

"Two rabbinical works under the name *Book of Jasher* are extant, one written in 1394 A.D. by R. Shabbatai Carmuz Levita, the other by R. Tham, printed in 1544. An anonymous work was also printed in 1625 at Venice and Prague.

"In 1751 an English forgery was issued by Jacob Ilive, an English printer, under the title of the *Book of Jasher*, professedly translated from the Hebrew by Alcuin, with a fictitious attestation by Wickliffe."—*Who Wrote It?* (Wheeler).

Java. A Malay word, meaning the " Land of the Nutmegs."

Jean Crapaud. See *Crapaud, Jean or Johnny.*

Jeanie Deans. The heroine of Sir Walter Scott's novel, *The Heart of Mid-Lothian*. The character is founded on fact, and portrays a young woman of sterling sense, sound judgment, and warm affections, who rises superior to danger and misfortune.

Jean Jacques. The Christian name of J. J. Rousseau (1712–1778), the famous French philosopher, and the one by which he is frequently designated by English writers.

"That is almost the only maxim of *Jean Jacques* to which I can cheerfully subscribe."—*Bulwer-Lytton.*

Jean Paul. The name adopted as a pseudonym by Jean Paul Richter (1763–1825), the eminent German author, and the one by which he is generally known.

Jemappes, Battle of. A battle fought at Jemappes, a village in Belgium, on November 6th, 1792, between 40,000 French under Dumouriez, and 19,000 Austrians, intrenched in woods and hills and defended by redoubts. The latter were defeated, and, as a result, Belgium was placed under the control of France. The loss on each side was reckoned at about 5000.

Jena, Battle of. A sanguinary battle fought on October 14th, 1806, between 90,000 French under the first Napoleon and 70,000 Prussians commanded by the Prince of Hohenlohe. On the same day, a second battle was fought at Auerstädt, 14 miles north of Jena, between 30,000 French under Davoust and 48,000 Prussians led by the aged Duke of Brunswick. The Prussians were signally defeated in both contests, and lost 20,000 in killed and wounded, nearly as many prisoners, and 200 cannon. The French loss was about 14,000. As a result of these victories, Napoleon effected the complete subjugation of Prussia.

Jersey Lily. An appellation bestowed upon Mrs. Langtry (b. 1852), the noted English beauty. According to Wagner's *Names and their Meaning*, she is so called because she is a native of the island of Jersey and bears the Christian name of " Lillie.''

Jerusalem Chamber. An apartment in Westminster Abbey, probably so called from the tapestries or pictures of the history of Jerusalem with which it was at one time adorned. The Upper House of Convocation of the Province of Canterbury meets there. The chamber dates from 1376-1386, and is famous as the scene of the death of Henry IV (1400-1413), March 20th, 1413.

"*King Henry.*   Doth any name particular belong
            Unto the lodging where I first did swoon ?

Warwick.   'T is call'd Jerusalem, my noble lord.

King Henry.   Laud be to God ! — even there my life must end.
            It hath been prophesied to me many years,
            I should not die but in Jerusalem,
            Which vainly I suppos'd the Holy Land.—
            But, bear me to that chamber ; there I 'll lie :
            In that Jerusalem shall Harry die.''

Henry IV, Part II, iv, 4.

Jerusalem Delivered. See *Gerusalemme Liberata*.

Jesuits. A religious order in the Roman Catholic Church, properly called the *Society of Jesus*. It was founded by Ignatius Loyola in 1534, and confirmed by a papal bull in 1540. The vows of the order comprise (1) chastity, (2) poverty, (3) obedience, and (4) implicit submission to the Holy See. The members are divided into four classes : novices, scholastics, coadjutors, and professed members, and are governed by a general or " Præpositus Generalis,'' who holds office for life. The objects of the society are fourfold : (1) education of youth ; (2) education of adults by preaching ; (3) defense of the true faith against all heretics and unbelievers ; and (4) missionary work among the heathens. The Jesuits acquired great influence in the Roman Catholic Church, and finally came to wield extensive political power. As a result, they were suppressed, or banished, from Portugal, Spain, France, Italy, and other European countries, as detrimental to the public interests. Pope Clement XIV (1769-1775) issued a bull abolishing the order in 1773, but it was revived by Pope Pius VII (1800-1823) in 1814. In 1872 the Jesuits were banished from Germany, and in 1880 from France. They are an active force in the Ultramontane movement at the present time. See *Jansenists*.

Jesus and the Clay Bird. According to a legend mentioned in Horne's *Apocryphal New Testament* (1820), the infant Jesus, while amusing himself with other children by making clay birds, breathed upon the one that he had fashioned, whereupon it instantly became endowed with life, and flew away.

Reference to this tradition is made in the *Koran*, chapter v, as follows :

" When God shall say, O Jesus, son of Mary, remember my favour towards thee, and towards thy mother ; . . . when thou didst create of clay as it were the figure of a bird, by my permission, and didst breathe thereon, and it became a bird by my permission."

Jesus, Child Blessed by. According to tradition, the child that Jesus called unto him and set in the midst of his disciples was Ignatius, afterwards Bishop of Antioch. He was surnamed "Theophoros," which was interpreted by Jerome and other writers to mean the "God-borne." This story, however, was unknown in the early days of the Christian Church. Eusebius makes no mention of it, and Chrysostom positively declares that Ignatius had never seen Christ. He suffered martyrdom at Rome in 107 A.D., during the reign of the Emperor Trajan (98–117), for refusing to renounce the Christian religion.

Jeunesse Dorée. An association of young men, chiefly of the upper classes, formed in Paris in 1794, after the fall of Robespierre, to take summary vengeance upon the Jacobins. On the 9th of October, they attacked the hall of the Jacobin Club, forced the doors, and, after a brief contest, drove the members into the street. The hall was then closed by order of the Convention, and the Jacobin Club was soon after abolished, to the joy of the whole nation. The phrase "jeunesse dorée" is at present applied to young men of wealth and fashion, with whom amusement is the principal object in life.

Jewel in Toad's Head. "*The toad, ugly and venomous, wears yet a precious jewel in its head.* Fenton says: 'There is to be found in the heads of old and great toads a stone they call borax or stelon, which being used as rings give forewarning against venom' (1569). These stones always bear a figure resembling a toad on their surface. Lupton says : 'A toad-stone, called *crepaudia*, touching any part envenomed by the bite of a rat, wasp, spider, or other venomous beast, ceases the pain and swelling thereof.' In the

Londesborough Collection is a silver ring of the fifteenth century, in which one of these toad-stones is set. The stone was supposed to sweat and change colour when poison was in its proximity."—*Dictionary of Phrase and Fable* (Brewer).

Jewels of Cornelia. An appellation bestowed upon Tiberius and Caius Gracchus, tribunes of Rome, and sons of Cornelia, a distinguished Roman matron. Being left a widow with twelve children, she devoted her entire time to their education, and declined, it is said, an offer of marriage from Ptolemy, King of Egypt. It is related that, on a certain occasion, a wealthy lady, after displaying her jewels and other ornaments to Cornelia, asked the Roman matron to show hers ; whereupon Cornelia called her sons Tiberius and Caius to her side, and, pointing to them, exclaimed, "These are my jewels !" She survived her two sons, and was held in such honor by the Romans that, after her death, they erected a monument to her memory, with the inscription, CORNELIA, MOTHER OF THE GRACCHI.

Jew, Wandering. See *Wandering Jew.*

Jezebel. An infamous woman, the wife of Ahab (931–909 B.C.), King of Israel. She introduced idolatry into the kingdom, and tried to put an end to the worship of Jehovah. She was thrown from the window of the palace, and was trampled under foot by the horses of Jehu. The expression "a painted Jezebel" has been used, since the days of the Puritans, to denote a woman of brazen appearance and loose morals.

Jim Crow. See *Crow, Jim.*

Jingoes. A term first used, during the Russo-Turkish War of 1877–1878, to denote that branch of the Conservative party in England that endeavored to force the country into a war with

Russia. The word was adopted from McDermott's music-hall song — then popular in London — beginning with the words :

" We don't want to fight, but by *jingo* if we do,
We 've got the ships, we 've got the men, we 've got the money too."

Jingoism corresponds to the French *Chauvinism*, and has lately been applied in the United States to the sentiment that favors an aggressive foreign policy. The word *Jingo* is derived, according to some authorities, from a corruption of *St. Gingulph*. Other authorities, however, say that it is a corruption of *Jainko*, the Basque term for the Deity ; hence the expression "By Jingo " may be considered a direct appeal to the Supreme Being. See *Chauvinism*.

Joan, Pope. See *Pope Joan*.

Job, Book of. One of the poetical books of the *Old Testament*, whose date and authorship are unknown. Although considered by many to be the oldest book in existence, it is now generally referred to the 16th century before Christ. The work was written in Hebrew, with a mixture of Arabic. Whether Job was an allegorical figure or a real personage has never been determined.

Job's Comforter. An expression, ironically used, to denote any person who, under pretense of sympathizing with another's afflictions, attributes them to his misdeeds, and thus aggravates his sorrow. The allusion is to Eliphaz, Bildad, and Zophar, friends of Job, who visited him in his distress, and declared that his misfortunes resulted from his sins and iniquities.

"Then Job answered and said, I have heard many such things : miserable comforters are ye all."—*Job* xvi, 1, 2.

Job's Turkey, As Poor as. This simile—suggestive of extreme poverty —has reference to the deplorable state to which Job was reduced, when de-livered by God into the hands of Satan. According to the popular notion, " Job's turkey " had but one feather in its tail, and was obliged to lean against the fence to gobble. The fact that Job possessed no turkey (since the bird is a native of America) does not seem to have been realized by the originator of the saying. Judge Haliburton of Nova Scotia — popularly known as " Sam Slick " — refers to " Job's turkey " in some of his writings.

John Brown's Farm. A tract of land near North Elba, Essex Co., New York, formerly the home of John Brown (1800–1859), the noted Abolitionist. The property was purchased some years ago by an association headed by Kate Field, and was converted into a public park. John Brown's grave — near the house—is annually visited by hundreds of tourists.

John Brown, Song of. A song, the authorship of which is unknown, popular in the Northern States of the American Union previous to and during the Civil War. The chorus is as follows :

" Glory, halle—hallelujah ! Glory, halle—hallelujah !
Glory, halle—hallelujah !
His soul is marching on ! "

" The origin of this senseless farrago—as senseless as the equally popular ' Lillibulero ' of the times of the great civil commotion in England — is, I believe, quite unknown. But sung to a degraded and jiggish form of a grand and simple old air, it was a great favorite in the early part of the war. It was heard everywhere in the streets ; regiments marched to it ; and the air had its place in the programme of every barrel-organ grinder. In fact no song was sung so much during the rebellion."—*Richard Grant White*.

John Bull. The popular personification of the English people. He is represented as a bluff, corpulent, irascible old fellow, clad in leather breeches and top boots, and carrying a stout oaken cudgel. This nickname is derived from Dr. Arbuthnot's satire, entitled *The History of John Bull*, written to ridicule the Duke of Marlborough, and published in 1712. It is generally attributed to Dean Swift, and is frequently published in his works.

John Chinaman. See *Chinaman, John.*

Johnny Crapaud. See *Crapaud, Jean or Johnny.*

Johnny Rebs. A nickname conferred upon the Confederate soldiers by the Federal troops, during the American Civil War. Its origin is said to be as follows : A Southern picket, having been taunted with the remark that the South was depending on the assistance of the English to secure its independence, and that he himself was no better than a " John Bull," indignantly denied the statement, and declared that he should as soon be called a " nigger " as a " Johnny Bull."

Johnstown Flood. An appalling catastrophe that occurred at Johnstown, Pennsylvania, on May 31st, 1889, and caused the death of 2142 persons. It was occasioned by the bursting of a dam at Conemaugh Lake, 275 feet above the city and 18 miles distant. The advancing column of water traversed this distance in seven minutes, and reached the Pennsylvania Railroad bridge below the city. This obstruction acted as a dam and greatly increased the loss of life. Fire soon broke out and added to the havoc wrought. The loss of property occasioned by the flood was estimated at $9,674,105 : and the amount collected to relieve the sufferers, $2,912,346.30. All the States of the Union, as well as many European nations, sent contributions.

Jones, Davy. See *Davy Jones's Locker.*

Joule's Law. A physical law discovered by Dr. Joule (1818–1889), the distinguished English physicist, and sometimes called the " law of the mechanical equivalent of heat." It asserts that when heat is transformed into energy, or energy into heat, the quantity of heat is equivalent to the quantity of energy. The discovery of this law led to the grand generalization of the conservation of energy. See *Conservation of Energy.*

Jovial. This word had its origin in the ancient belief in astrology. According to that pseudo-science, every person was born under the influence of some planet, which governed his character and conduct through life. Hence, happy and good-natured persons were called " jovial," because those born when Jupiter [or Jove] was in the ascendant were believed to be so disposed. See *Martial ; Mercurial ; Saturnine.*

Juan Fernandez. An island in the Pacific Ocean, about 400 miles west of the coast of Chili, famous as the residence, for over four years (1704–1709), of Alexander Selkirk, a buccaneer of Scotch extraction, whose solitary life there is said to have suggested to Daniel Defoe the story of *Robinson Crusoe.* Although sailors generally believe this island to have been the scene of Crusoe's imaginary adventures, Defoe expressly mentions an island on the east coast of South America, near the mouth of the Orinoco. See *Crusoe, Robinson ; Crusoe's Island.*

Judah, Kingdom of. The name given to that part of the Hebrew monarchy that remained after the revolt of the ten tribes, in 975 B.C. It comprised the tribes of Judah and Benjamin, together with some Danite and Simeonite cities, and had Jerusalem for its capital. The kingdom of Judah was ruled over by 20 kings, and lasted until 588 B.C. (a period of 387 years), when Nebuchadnezzar captured Jerusalem, destroyed and plundered the temple, and carried the inhabitants into captivity. When Babylon fell under the conquering arms of Cyrus, that monarch permitted the Jews to return to their homes, and rebuild their temple (536 B.C.). From that time the Jews remained a subject nation, and were ruled successively by the Persians, Macedonians, Egyptians, and Romans. See *Israel, Kingdom of.*

Judas Tree. A small tree of the Order *Leguminosæ*, found in the temperate regions of Asia and Europe, and in the middle and western parts of the United States. Its name is popularly believed to be derived from the legend that Judas Iscariot hanged himself on a tree of this kind.

"A corruption of *kuamos* tree—*i. e.*, the leguminous or bean tree. The corrupt name has given rise to the tradition that it was upon one of these trees 'that Judas Iscariot hanged himself."—Brewer's *Dictionary of Phrase and Fable.*

Judges. The name given to the rulers that exercised supreme control over the Israelites at intervals from the death of Joshua (1425 B.C.) to the accession of Saul (1095 B.C.), a period of 330 years. These "Judges" were fifteen in number, as follows: (1) Othniel ; (2) Ehud : (3) Shamgar ; (4) Deborah and Barak ; (5) Gideon ; (6) Abimelech ; (7) Tola ; (8) Jair ; (9) Jephthah ; (10) Ibzan; (11) Elon ; (12) Abdon ; (13) Samson ; (14) Eli; (15) Samuel. They were chosen for life, and ruled with an authority little inferior to that of kings.

Judgment of God. An appellation conferred upon the battle of Fontenaille or Fontenay. See *Battle of the Brothers.*

Juggernaut. An idol in the temple at Puri, in Orissa, India,—one of the incarnations of Vishnu as Krishna. It consists of an irregular block of stone, pyramidal in shape, having two large diamonds for eyes, and is lodged in a magnificent temple built in 1198 A.D., at a cost of $2,500,000. On festal days, this idol is conveyed to its country home on a magnificent car (45 feet high and 35 feet square), having 16 wheels, each 7 feet in diameter. The statement that the fanatical devotees of Vishnu throw themselves under the wheels of the advancing car — hoping thereby to attain eternal bliss — is branded as a calumny of English writers. Such loss of life as may occur on these occasions is the result of accident, and not of design. The number of pilgrims that formerly visited the temple was reckoned at 1,200,000 annually. At the present day, as many as 100,000 assemble there on great festivals, while the annual offering may amount to as much as £37,-000. In addition to this sum, the temple of Juggernaut derives an annual income of £31,000 from its lands and various religious establishments. The word *Juggernaut* or *Jaggernaut* is a corruption of the Sanskrit *Jagannâtha,* and means the *Lord of the World.*

Julian Calendar. The name given to a reformation of the Roman calendar, effected in 46 B.C. by Julius Cæsar (100-44 B.C.), with the assistance of Sosigenes, the Alexandrian astronomer. It was an adoption of the Greek mode of reckoning, and made the year consist of 365 days and 6 hours, with an extra day added every fourth year, —known as bissextile or leap-year. The Julian Calendar remained in use among the nations of Europe until the close of the 16th century, after which it was gradually supplanted by the Gregorian Calendar. Russia, Greece, and Turkey still adhere to the Julian Calendar, or Old Style of reckoning. See *Gregorian Calendar ; New Style ; Old Style.*

Julienne Soup. A clear meat soup, containing chopped vegetables, chiefly carrots. It was named after its inventor, Julien, a famous French caterer who settled in Boston about the time of the French Revolution (1789) and established a restaurant there.

Juliet's Tomb. A rude marble sarcophagus in the chapel of an old Franciscan monastery (now suppressed) at Verona, Italy, which is pointed out as the tomb of Juliet, the daughter of Capulet and wife of Romeo. Its genuineness is generally doubted by travelers.

"That which is shown as *Juliet's Tomb* has about as much claim to the honor as the barber's basin in Don Quixote had to be Mambrino's helmet. But as a man thinks, so it is. A porcelain nest-egg is to the eye as good as any other, and an old washtrough serves well enough to call forth that unimaginative enthusiasm which is only aroused by some object addressed to the senses. The tomb which Shakespeare has built will outlast the amphitheatre, and endure as long as love and grief twine the rose and the cypress in the garland of life."— *Six Months in Italy* (Hillard).

July. "This month is generally believed to have been so named in honour of Julius Cæsar. There is good reason, however, for believing that it bore a similar name (Jule) before Julius Cæsar was born, and that the name was derived from *huil*, a wheel, . . . the symbol of the summer solstice. There is no doubt that the name *Jule*, being already in use in some parts of the Empire, induced the courtiers at Rome to suggest that the name *Julius*, which so closely resembled it, should supersede *Quintilis* in all; and that the same reason induced the Roman Senate to adopt the idea."—Edwards's *Words, Facts, and Phrases.* See *August.*

July Column. See *Column of July.*

Junius, Letters of. A series of political letters, which appeared from 1769 to 1772 in the *Public Advertiser*, a popular English newspaper, over the signature of "Junius." They attacked public men and measures with unsparing severity, and acquired great popularity on account of their brilliant style, clear and cogent reasoning, just censure, and intimate knowledge of public affairs. The writer has always remained unknown, although strong circumstantial evidence points to Sir Philip Francis as their author. Among other persons to whom the authorship of these letters has been ascribed may

be mentioned Edmund Burke, Lord Shelburne, Barré, Lord George Sackville, Wilkes, Horne Tooke, Lord Lyttleton, William Gerard Hamilton (commonly called " Single - Speech Hamilton"), Mr. Dunning (afterwards Lord Ashburton), Sergeant Adair, the Rev. J. Rosenhagen, John Roberts, Charles Lloyd, Samuel Dyer, General Lee, the Duke of Portland, and Hugh Boyd.

In a letter to his publisher the author says : " It is not in the nature of things that you, or anybody else, should know me unless I make myself known : all arts, or inquiries, or rewards, would be ineffectual." Again he says : " I am the sole depositary of my secret, and it shall die with me." Pitt declared to Lord Aberdeen that he knew who wrote the *Letters of Junius*, but that it was not Francis ; and Lady Grenville made the same statement in a letter to the editor of *Diaries of a Lady of Quality*. Macaulay, however, considers the evidence presented to prove Sir Philip Francis to be the author of these philippics, sufficiently strong " to support a verdict in a civil, nay, in a criminal proceeding."

Jupiter Scapin. A nickname conferred upon Napoleon Bonaparte (1769–1821) by the Abbé de Pradt, in allusion to the strange mixture of greatness and pettiness manifested in his character. "Scapin" is a knavish and thievish valet in Molière's comedy, *Les Fourberies de Scapin.*

"In short, when you have penetrated through all the circles of power and splendor, you were not dealing with a gentleman, at last ; but with an impostor and a rogue : and he fully deserves the epithet of *Jupiter Scapin*, or a sort of Scamp Jupiter."—Emerson's *Representative Men* (article *Napoleon*).

Jury, Trial by. Trial by jury was introduced into England during the Saxon Heptarchy (455–828 A.D.), but is said by most authorities to have been instituted by Alfred the Great (871–901 A.D.) about 886. Dr. Stubbs, however, in his *Constitutional History*,

27

traces the modern jury system to a Frankish origin. It was established in France in 1791, in Russia in 1886, and in Spain in 1889. Civil cases in Scotland were first tried by a jury in 1815. Trial by jury was abolished by imperial decree in Austria in 1852. In Scotland, France, and the islands of Guernsey and Jersey, a majority of the jury is necessary for a decision ; in France, since 1831, a majority of two-thirds is required. The original Constitution of the United States instituted trials by jury for criminal cases, but made no such provision for civil cases. This omission was rectified by the adoption of the seventh amendment, whereby trial by jury can be secured in all suits-at-law in which the value in controversy exceeds $20.

Justinian's Code. See *Code of Justinian.*

K

Kaaba. See *Caaba.*

Kaiser (*Ger. Cæsar*). A title borne by the Emperors of the Holy Roman Empire, on the dissolution of which, in 1806, this appellation was retained by the Emperors of Austria. It was assumed by William I, King of Prussia, when crowned sovereign of the new German Empire in 1871. See *Cæsar ; Czar ; Holy Roman Empire.*

Kaiser Wilhelm Canal. A waterway of great strategic and commercial importance, connecting the North Sea with the Baltic. It was commenced in 1887 and completed in 1895, at a cost of 7,800,000 pounds sterling. It is 61 miles in length and 29 feet 6 inches in depth, and has a surface breadth of 213 feet. The canal enables the Imperial fleets to concentrate themselves, either on the North Sea or the Baltic, in a few hours. It is also known as the " Baltic," the " North Sea and Baltic," and the " Kiel " Canal.

Kansas, Bleeding. A phrase applied to the Territory of Kansas, previous to the Civil War, in allusion to the sanguinary contests that occurred there on the question of admitting slavery within its borders. Kansas was finally admitted as a free State in 1861. See *Kansas-Nebraska Bill.*

Kansas - Nebraska Bill. A bill passed by the United States Congress, on May 30th, 1854, organizing the Territories of Kansas and Nebraska, and providing " that the people of the Territories, in forming their constitutions, should decide for themselves whether the new States should be free or slaveholding." This measure aimed at extending the domain of slavery, and was in direct opposition to the " Missouri Compromise," passed in 1821, by which slavery (except in Missouri) was forever excluded from that part of the United States north of latitude 36° 30'. Kansas was at once settled by colonists from the Northern and Southern States, and became the battle-ground between the partisans of slavery and those of freedom. Desperate contests to obtain political control of the Territory ensued; and, after years of lawlessness and bloodshed, Kansas was admitted into the Union as a free State in 1861. Nebraska followed suit in 1867. See *Kansas, Bleeding ; Missouri Compromise.*

Karnak, Temple of. A stupendous ruin, situated in the ancient city of Thebes, Egypt, on the eastern bank of the Nile. It covers an area of nine acres, and consists of temples, courts, obelisks, and avenues of sphinxes. Karnak was built in part by Osirtasen I of the XIIth dynasty, and was greatly added to by the monarchs of the XVIIIth dynasty. The grand hypostyle hall of the temple contains twelve massive columns, 62 feet high and 12 feet in diameter, together with 122 smaller columns and 2 obelisks. The walls are adorned with sculptures depicting the victories of Seti I and Rameses II. These walls are said to have been originally 80 feet high, and 25 feet thick at the base. See *Luxor, Temple of.*

"The palace temple at Karnak—perhaps the noblest effort of architectural magnificence ever produced by the hand of man. Its principal dimensions are 1200 feet in length by about 360 in width ; and it covers, therefore, about 430,000 square feet, or nearly twice the area of St. Peter's at Rome, and more than four times that of any mediæval cathedral existing. This, however, is not a fair way of estimating its dimensions ; for our churches are buildings entirely under one roof, but at Karnak a considerable portion of the area was uncovered by any buildings, so that no such comparison is just. The great hypostyle hall, however, is internally 340 feet by 170, and with its two pilons it covers more than 88,000 square feet, a greater area than the cathedral of Cologne, the largest of all our Northern cathedrals ; and when we consider that this is only a part of the great whole, we may fairly assert that the entire structure is among the largest, as it undoubtedly is one of the most beautiful, buildings in the world."—*Fergusson.*

Kathleen Mavourneen. A charming ballad, written by Caroline Elizabeth Sarah Norton (1808–1877), the granddaughter of Richard Brinsley Sheridan.

Kazan Cathedral. A famous church at St. Petersburg—dedicated to Our Lady of Kazan —standing on the Nevskoi Prospekt, the principal thoroughfare of the city. The building is 238 feet long and 182 feet wide, and measures about 230 feet to the top of the cross. It is built of gray Finland granite, in imitation of St. Peter's at Rome, and cost about $3,000,000. In the ikonostas may be seen the image of "Our Lady of Kazan," blazing with gems. It was brought from Kazan in 1579, and placed there in 1821. The church contains numerous paintings by Russian academicians, as well as military trophies captured from various European nations.

Kearsarge. A United States warvessel famous for her destruction of the Confederate privateer *Alabama,* near Cherbourg, France, on June 19th, 1864. The *Kearsarge* was commanded on that occasion by Captain Winslow, and carried 7 guns and a crew of 163 men. She was totally wrecked on a reef in the Caribbean Sea, on February 2nd, 1894, but without loss of life. See *Alabama.*

Keely Motor. A machine which the inventor, John W. Keely, of Philadelphia, claimed was capable of generating its own power without cost. The high-sounding name, Pneumatic-Pulsating-Vacuo-Engine was given to it, and large sums of money were sunk by capitalists in the vain attempt to apply this so-called invention to practical use. In 1872, Keely commenced experiments with the view of attaining some practical result ; but all these efforts proved fruitless up to the time of his death, in 1899. Scientific men always regarded Keely's claims with extreme suspicion ; and a careful examination of his premises, made shortly after his death, proved the entire enterprise to be a colossal humbug.

Kenilworth Castle. A beautiful and picturesque ruin in Warwickshire, England, familiar to every reader of Sir Walter Scott's novel of the same name. The castle was founded in 1120 by Geoffroy de Clinton, Treasurer of Henry I (1100–1135), and was afterwards enlarged and fortified by Simon de Montfort, to whom it was given by Henry III (1216–1272) as a weddingportion, with his [the King's] sister Eleanor. Queen Elizabeth (1558–1603) presented it to her favorite, Robert Dudley, Earl of Leicester, and there, in 1575, the sovereign was entertained by her subject for 18 days at a daily cost of £1000. After Leicester's death, Kenilworth was seized by the Crown, and was demolished by the Roundheads, during Cromwell's time, for the sake of the materials. Since then it has belonged to the Earls of Clarendon. The only part of the original fortress remaining is Cæsar's Tower, the walls of which are 16 feet thick in places.

"Of this lordly palace, where princes feasted and heroes fought, now in the bloody earnest of storm and siege, now in the games of chivalry, where beauty dealt the prize which valor won, all is now desolate. The massy ruins of the castle only serve to show what their splendor once was, and to impress on the musing visitor the transitory value of human possessions."—*Sir Walter Scott.*

Kensington Palace. A royal palace —formerly the residence of the English sovereigns—situated in the western part of London. It was originally the seat of Heneage Finch, Earl of Nottingham and Lord Chancellor of England, and was sold by his successor to William III (1689-1702) in 1689. Kensington Palace was the residence of William and Mary (1689-1702), of Queen Anne (1702-1714) and her consort, Prince George of Denmark, and of George II (1727-1760)—all of whom died within its walls. There Queen Victoria (1837-1901) was born and reared, and there also she received the tidings of the death of William IV (1830-1837) and of her own accession to the throne. Kensington Gardens, surrounding the palace, originally comprised 26 acres, but have been repeatedly enlarged and are now 2½ miles in circuit. They adjoin Hyde Park, with which they are connected by a stone bridge over the Serpentine.

Kent's Hole. A cavern in the vicinity of Torquay, England, famous not only for its relics of primitive man, but also for its remains of extinct animals. Although the existence of this cave had been known from time immemorial, it did not attract the attention of scientists until 1825. Excavations were carried on by Pengelly from 1865 to 1880, at a cost of nearly £2000, and yielded results of the highest importance to the science of anthropology. There were found flint tools of the Palæolithic Age, and implements of bone—such as needles, awls, and harpoons. The animal remains discovered comprised those of the lion, hyena, bear, wolf, fox, rhinoceros, mammoth, Irish elk, reindeer, etc., showing that these animals once lived in Britain, and were contemporaneous with men of the Stone Age.

Kepler's Laws. Three laws of planetary motion discovered by Johann Kepler (1571-1630), the distinguished German astronomer. They place the science of the heavenly bodies on a solid basis, and form " the three arches of the bridge over which Astronomy crossed the gulf between the Ptolemaic and Copernican Systems." These laws are as follows :

(1) Each planet revolves in an ellipse, with the sun at one of the foci.

(2) Each planet moves in such a way that the radius vector (*i. e.*, the line drawn from the centre of the sun to the centre of the planet) passes over equal areas in equal periods of time.

(3) The square of the time of a planet's revolution around the sun is proportional to the cube of its mean distance from the sun.

Kew Gardens. The Royal Botanic Gardens and Arboretum at Kew, 5 miles west of London, were founded by the mother of George III in 1760, and made a national institution in 1840. Including the Arboretum, they cover an area of 248 acres, and are maintained at an annual cost of about £20,000. The Gardens contain a superb collection of plants, and are particularly rich in ferns, orchids, and cacti. Among the buildings may be mentioned the Palm House, the Water - Lily House, the Temperate House or Winter Garden, the Tropical House, and the Pagoda. There are also four Botanical Museums in different parts of the Gardens. Dr. Joseph D. Hooker, the famous botanist, was director of Kew for 20 years (1865–1885), and was succeeded by Mr. W. T. Thistleton Dyer.

Key of Bastille. This interesting relic was presented to Washington by Lafayette during his first stay in

America. It is antique in shape, and hangs in the principal hall of Washington's mansion at Mount Vernon.

Key of Death. A large key preserved in the Arsenal at Venice. It was invented by one Tibaldo, a Venetian merchant, who, being disappointed in love, used it to destroy not only his rival, but also the parents of the woman he had unsuccessfully sought in marriage. He even attempted the life of the woman herself, but, fortunately, was brought to justice, and ended his career on the scaffold. The key contains a secret spring which, when pressed, forces a poisoned needle into the flesh. Owing to its extreme fineness this needle leaves no trace of its entrance, but soon causes death. See *Arsenal of Venice*.

Key of the Mediterranean. A term applied to the rock and fortress of Gibraltar, which, owing to its position, controls the passage between the Atlantic Ocean and the Mediterranean Sea. See *Gibraltar.*

Keys of Knowledge. A term applied to five things enumerated in the *Koran* as known to God alone. They are as follows :
(1) The time of the day of judgment.
(2) The time of rain.
(3) The sex of an animal previous to birth.
(4) What will happen on the morrow.
(5) The place where any person shall die. See *Koran.*

Keystone State. An appellation conferred upon the State of Pennsylvania, because it occupies a central position among the thirteen States that adopted the Constitution. If the names of the following States—New Hampshire, Massachusetts, Connecticut, Rhode Island, New York, New Jersey, Pennsylvania, Delaware, Maryland, Virginia, North Carolina, South Carolina, and Georgia—be arranged in the form of an arch, Pennsylvania will occupy the central part, or " keystone.'' According to other authorities, the State is so called on account of its influence and importance. Another reason assigned is that when the question of adopting the Declaration of Independence came before the Continental Congress on July 4th, 1776, six States voted for it and six against, whereupon Pennsylvania cast her vote in the affirmative and thus secured the adoption of the measure.

Khasne. A famous rock-temple at Petra, a ruined city of Arabia Petræa. Its façade comprises two stories, and is highly ornamented in the Roman style of architecture. The purpose of the temple and the time of its construction are alike matters of conjecture. The name *Khasne* — meaning *Treasure* — was given to it by the Arabs in allusion to a tradition that the urn on the top of the façade contains precious jewels and vast sums of money, which are jealously guarded by genii.

Khuttub Minar. A famous column of sandstone and white marble, situated about 10 miles south of Delhi, India. It is 238 feet high, and tapers gracefully from a diameter of 47 feet at the base to one of 9 feet at the summit. The column contains a winding staircase, and is adorned with inscriptions from the *Koran*. It was erected during the 13th century. Bayard Taylor declares the Khuttub Minar to be, " beyond question, the finest shaft in the world.''

Kiblah. The point towards which Mohammedans turn their faces in prayer. It is in the direction of the Caaba at Mecca, and is indicated in mosques by a niche in the wall. The point was originally Jerusalem, but this was afterwards changed by Mohammed. Written also *Keblah.* See *Caaba.*

Kick the Bucket, To. " A slang phrase common on both sides of the

Atlantic, meaning to die. The allusion is probably to the way in which a slaughtered pig is hung up, viz., by passing the ends of a bent piece of wood behind the tendons of the hind legs and so suspending it to a hook in the beam above. This piece of wood is locally termed a bucket, and so, by a coarse metaphor, the phrase came to have its present meaning."—Walsh's *Handy-Book of Literary Curiosities.*

" The tradition among the slang fraternity as to the origin of this phrase is that ' One Bolsover, having hung himself to a beam while standing on the bottom of a pail, or bucket, kicked the vessel away in order to pry into futurity, and it was all UP with him from that moment—*Finis!* ' "—Bombaugh's *Gleanings for the Curious.*

Kilkenny Cats. The Irish fable of the two cats of Kilkenny that fought so fiercely that only their tails remained, is said to be a satire on the contentions of the municipalities of Kilkenny and Irishtown, which, in the 17th century, struggled so fiercely over their boundary lines and other rights that they finally became impoverished. Other authorities, however, say that this story is based on fact, and had its origin during the Irish Rebellion of 1803. According to their account, it was a custom with the Hessian soldiers garrisoned at Kilkenny to tie two cats together by their tails and throw them across a clothesline to fight. Being, on a certain occasion, surprised in this cruel sport, one of their number cut the animals' tails in two as they hung across the line, and coolly explained the presence of the caudal appendages by saying that the two cats had been fighting and had devoured each other, with the exception of the tails.

Killed by Kindness. Brewer, in his *Dictionary of Phrase and Fable*, explains the origin of this phrase in two ways. They are as follows :

(1) " It is said that Draco, the Athenian legislator, met his death from his popularity, being smothered in the theatre of Ægina by the number of caps and cloaks showered on him by the spectators (B.C. 590).

(2) The allusion is to the ape, which not unfrequently strangles its young ones by hugging them too hard."

Kinchinjinga. A lofty peak of the Himalayas, at one time supposed to be the tallest mountain on the globe. Its height is estimated at 28,176 feet,—826 feet lower than Mount Everest.

" *Kanchinginga*, properly speaking, consists of three peaks, which are sharp, serrated, precipitous, and apparently composed of solid rock from the snow-limit to the summit. Its immense height is not thoroughly appreciated by the traveler for two causes—its great distance (fifty miles ' as the crow flies '), and the fact that the point of observation itself is one-fourth the height of the mountain. Had I risen earlier and ridden to Mount Senchal, fifteen hundred feet above Darjeeling, I might have obtained a view of Mount Everest, which is nearly thirty thousand feet (above five and a half miles) in perpendicular height above the level of the sea, and is the loftiest point upon our globe. Until quite recently *Kanchinginga* was supposed to be the higher of the two, but it is now found to be eight hundred feet less. Mount Everest is a single peak— a cone—and the summit appears like a small white tent among the clouds. In grandeur and sublimity, however, it is excelled by *Kanchinginga.*"—*Through and Through the Tropics* (Vincent).

Kindergarten. A natural system of education for young children, devised by Friedrich Wilhelm August Froebel (1782–1852), and first unfolded by him in 1826, in his work entitled *Die Menschenerziehung.* It was first practically applied in Germany by Mr. and Mrs. Ronge in 1849, and was introduced into England in 1851. The Kindergarten System is a reaction against the traditional methods of infant education, and aims to develop all of the powers of the child in complete equilibrium. Singing, dancing, and the use of toys are much resorted to. The system has made great headway in the United States during the past few years.

King Arthur. See *Arthur, King.*

King Cole. " Cole, Coël, or Coïlus, was a legendary British prince who flourished, according to the old chroniclers, about the middle of the third century after Christ. Assuming independence, he attacked and took possession of the Roman colony at Camelodunum, which he named after himself Colechester, that is, *Cole castrum*, or Cole's camp. The Roman general Constantinus Chlorus endeavored to regain the place, and immediately laid siege to it. This lasted for three years, when, having seen Helena, Cole's daughter, who is described as being very beautiful, he made peace with Cole, on condition of receiving Helena in marriage. This was agreed to, and it is asserted that Constantine the Great was the fruit of the union. At Colchester there is a large earthwork,— probably the remains of a Roman amphitheatre,— which is popularly called 'King Cole's Kitchen.' " — *Mother Goose's Melodies* (edited by G. A. R.).

> " Old *King Cole*
> Was a merry old soul,
> And a merry old soul was he ;
> He called for his pipe,
> And he called for his bowl,
> And he called for his fiddlers three."
> *Mother Goose's Melodies.*

King Cotton. See "*Cotton is King.*"

King Lear. A legendary king of Britain, who, according to tradition, died about 800 B.C. The story of his last days, taken from Holinshed's *Chronicle*, forms the basis of Shakespeare's sublime tragedy of *King Lear*, written probably in 1605 or 1606.

"Leir, the son of Baldud, was admitted ruler over the Britons in the year of the world 3105. At what time Joas reigned as yet in Juda. This Leir was a prince of noble demeanour, governing his land and subjects in great wealth. He made the town of Carleir, now called Leicester, which standeth upon the river Dore. It is writ that he had, by his wife, three daughters, without other issue, whose names were Gonorilla, Regan, and Cordilla, which daughters he greatly loved, but especially the youngest, Cordilla, far above the two elder." — Holinshed's *Chronicle*.

King Log. A term sometimes applied to a lazy or do-nothing king, in allusion to Æsop's fable, in which the frogs are represented as petitioning Jupiter to send them a ruler. According to the apologue, the king of gods and men gave them a log of wood for a monarch, but this proved so displeasing to them because of its passivity that they soon entreated Jupiter to send them another king. See *King Stork.*

King-Maker. An epithet conferred upon Richard Nevil (1420–1471), Earl of Warwick, who deposed Henry VI in 1460, and raised Edward, Duke of York, to the throne as Edward IV, in the following year. In 1470, he drove Edward from the throne and restored Henry. He was slain on April 14th, 1471, at the battle of Barnet by Edward IV, who thereupon became king a second time.

King of Bath. A sobriquet conferred upon Richard Nash (1674–1761), commonly known as " Beau Nash." He was appointed master of ceremonies and director of amusements at Bath, England, and for 15 years presided over the social affairs of that fashionable resort. See *Beau Nash.*

King of Beggars. A title bestowed upon Bampfylde Moore Carew [1692(?)–1758 (?)], a notorious English vagabond and adventurer. He ran away from home when a boy, and joined a band of gypsies, who elected him king.

King of England. In 828 A.D., Egbert, King of Wessex, united the States of the Saxon Heptarchy into one kingdom under the name of England. The first monarch, however, to assume the title of " Rex Anglorum," or " King of the English," was Edmund the Elder, son of Alfred the Great, who ascended the throne in 901.

King of Painters. A title assumed by Parrhasius, the famous Greek painter, who flourished during the fifth century before Christ. His vanity was equal to his artistic skill.

King of Rome. A title bestowed, at the time of his birth, upon Napoléon François Charles Joseph, son of Napoleon I and Marie Louise. After the fall of Napoleon in 1814, the King of Rome was taken in charge by his grandfather, the Emperor of Austria, and carefully educated as an Austrian prince. His title was changed to that of the Duke of Reichstadt in 1818. He died of pulmonary disease at Schönbrunn, near Vienna, on July 22nd, 1832, in his twenty-second year.

"It is thought that this title was given in imitation of Charlemagne. If so, it was a blunder; Charlemagne was never 'king of Rome,' but he was 'patrician of Rome.' In the German empire, the heir-apparent was 'king of the Romans,' not 'king of Rome.' This latter title was expressly conferred on the German kings, and sometimes on their heirs, by a coronation at Milan. The German title equivalent to 'dauphin,' or 'prince of Wales,' was 'King of the Romans.'"—*Reader's Handbook* (Brewer).

King of Shreds and Patches. In the old *Moralities,* or moral dramas, the buffoon, who impersonated Vice or Iniquity, was dressed as a mimic king in a parti-colored suit, and hence was often called a *king of shreds and patches.* Hamlet uses this expression in speaking of his uncle, the infamous Claudius.

King of Terrors. A term frequently applied to Death, as being of all misfortunes the one most dreaded by mankind.

King of the Barricades. A nickname conferred upon Louis Philippe (1830–1848), King of the French, whose accession to the throne in 1830 was preceded in Paris by a three-days' revolution, during which the people erected 10,000 barricades.

King of the Courts. A sobriquet conferred by Cicero upon Quintus Hortensius (114–50 B.C.), the famous Roman advocate.

King of the Feds. A title conferred upon Alexander Hamilton (1757–1804), the American statesman, and leader of the Federalist party.

King of the French. The title assumed by Louis Philippe (1830–1848), when called to the throne, to show that he reigned not by divine right, but by the will of the people. See *Citizen King.*

"Thus did France repudiate forever the venerable but antiquated principle of the 'Divine right of Kings.' The throne of Louis Philippe was founded avowedly upon the contrary theory—that sovereignty resides primarily in the *people,* and may consequently be granted or withdrawn at pleasure; that the sovereign is in fact only the delegate and nominee of the nation."—*Student's History of France.*

King of the King. A sobriquet conferred upon Cardinal Richelieu (1585–1642), who, as Prime Minister of France during the reign of Louis XIII (1610–1643), made that sovereign the first man in Europe, but the second man in France.

King of the World (*Shah Jehan*). A title assumed by Khorrum Shah (1627–1666), the fifth Emperor of the Mogul dynasty at Delhi, India.

King of Waters. A name given to the Amazon, as being the largest, but not the longest, river in the world. See *Amazon ; Father of Waters.*

King of Yvetot (*Fr. Roi d' Yvetot*). A title conferred by Clotaire I in 534 A.D. upon the lord of the petty French principality of Yvetot, near Rouen. According to a tradition, Clotaire, having murdered Gaulthier, Lord of Yvetot, before the high altar of Soissons, bestowed this title upon his heirs by way of atonement for his crime. This singular dignity was formally annulled in 1681, although the people of Yvetot continued to enjoy certain special privileges until the time of the Revolution. Béranger's celebrated poem, *Le Roi d' Yvetot*—written in 1812—is a satire on the first Napoleon. It describes a good little king, unknown to fame and satisfied with his condition, and hence happier than the average monarch. The term "King of Yvetot" is often used to denote a king of vast pretensions, but of limited authority.

King Oliver. A nickname bestowed upon Oliver Cromwell (1599–1658), the Lord Protector of the English Commonwealth.

King Pétaud. The ruler of an assembly of beggars, chosen from among their number as being either the poorest or the most adroit of them all. The name is derived from the Latin *petere* (*to beg*), and is found only in the phrase *La Cour du Roi Pétaud* (*Fr. The Court of the King Pétaud*), meaning an assembly where no order is observed and all are masters.

King Philip's War. The name given to a desperate attempt made by Philip, son of Massasoit, sachem of the Wampanoags, to exterminate the white settlers of New England, on account of real and imaginary wrongs committed by them. The war broke out on July 4th, 1675, with an attack on Swansea, Rhode Island, and continued with varying fortune until August of the following year. The Indians were finally defeated; and Philip, becoming a fugitive, was shot in a swamp by a renegade Indian, and his son sold into slavery in Bermuda. It is said that 13 towns and 600 dwellings were destroyed, and 600 colonists killed, by the Indians. The expenses of the war were estimated at $500,000. As a result of King Philip's War, the power of the Indians in New England was completely broken. See *Mount Hope.*

King's Daughters. An unsectarian Christian sisterhood, organized in New York City on January 18th, 1886. Its object is to make women more helpful to society in every possible way, and it welcomes to its membership all that are willing to assist in this Christian work. The organization has spread widely throughout the United States, and has been established in Canada, England, France, Italy, India, etc. The badge of the sisterhood is a silver Maltese cross worn on a purple ribbon, and the watchword is—"In His Name."

King's Evil. A name given to scrofula, owing to the belief, prevailing in England from the time of Edward the Confessor (1041–1066) to that of Queen Anne (1702–1714), that this disease could be healed by royal touch. The Jacobites, however, asserted that this power did not descend to William III and Anne, because they were not sovereigns by divine right. The practice reached its height during the reign of Charles II (1660–1685), when 92,107 persons were touched; and most of whom, according to the King's physician, were cured. Queen Anne continued the practice, and on March 30th, 1714, touched 200 persons, among them Samuel Johnson (then three years old), whom, however, she did not heal. The practice of "touching" ceased entirely with the accession of the House of Hanover, although Charles Edward, the "Young Pretender," touched a female infant in 1745. Henry VII (1485–1509) introduced the custom of presenting each person "touched" with a gold coin, called a touch-piece.

The French Kings claimed this same miraculous power from the time of Clovis I (481–511). On Easter-Sunday, 1686, Louis XIV (1643–1715) touched 1600 persons, using the words, "Le roy te touche, Dieu te guérisse."

King's King. A nickname given to Anne de Joyeuse, in allusion to his great ascendancy over Henry III (1574–1589), King of France.

Kings of Cologne, Three. See *Cologne, Three Kings of.*

King Stork. A term sometimes applied to a rapacious king that devours the substance and destroys the lives of his subjects, without the least regard for their welfare. The allusion is to the stork mentioned in Æsop's fable. It was sent by Jupiter to rule over the frogs when they became dissatisfied with King Log, and devoured them voraciously. See *King Log*.

Kitchen Cabinet. See *Cabinet, Kitchen*.

Kitchen - Middens (*Danish, kjökken, kitchen, mödding, heap of refuse*). A name given to great mounds—some of them 1000 feet in length and 250 feet in width—first observed in Denmark and afterwards found in England, Scotland, France, and other parts of Europe, as well as in North and South America, and in Australia. They are supposed to be the refuse-heaps of prehistoric races, and are composed chiefly of oyster-, mussel-, cockle-, and periwinkle-shells. In them are found implements of wood, bone, and stone, together with bones of animals, cinders, and fragments of pottery. These "kitchen-middens" were doubtless formed by man during the Polished Stone Epoch. In the Museum at Copenhagen may be seen many interesting specimens found in these refuse-heaps.

Kit-Kat Club. A club formed in London in 1703 by Jacob Tonson, an eminent publisher—ostensibly for the purpose of encouraging literature and the fine arts, but really to promote the interests of the House of Hanover. Among its members were the Duke of Marlborough, Sir Robert Walpole, Congreve, Steele, Addison, and Dr. Garth. The club was so named because it met for a time at the house of one Christopher Katt, a pastry-cook in King Street, Westminster ; although, according to other authorities, the name was derived from the sign of the Cat and the Fiddle. See *Kit-Kat Pictures*.

Kit-Kat Pictures. A name given to portraits measuring 36 inches in length by 28 or 29 inches in width. The origin of this expression is as follows : On the dissolution of the Kit-Kat Club, about 1720, each member presented Jacob Tonson, the founder, with a portrait of himself, painted by Sir Godfrey Kneller. These portraits were all uniform in size and were painted in three-quarter lengths, in order that one room might contain them all. On this account, any portrait thus reduced in size is called a kit-kat portrait. See *Kit-Kat Club*.

Klaus, Peter. The hero of an old German tradition, whose experiences—almost identical with those of Rip Van Winkle—are related in Otmar's *Volcks-Sagen*. He is represented as being a goatherd from Sittendorf, who, while leading his flock to pasture, is lured by a young man to a deep dell, surrounded by crags, where he finds twelve mysterious personages playing at bowls, but without uttering a word. Having drunk some wine from a can near at hand, he is overpowered with sleep, and finally awakens only to find everything about him changed. After making his way to the village near at hand, he learns to his consternation that he has been asleep for twenty years. See *Rip Van Winkle ; Sleeping Beauty in the Wood*.

Knickerbocker. A word frequently used to denote any old resident of New York City, but properly restricted to a person descended from one of the Dutch families that settled Manhattan Island. " Diedrich Knickerbocker " is the imaginary author of Washington Irving's *History of New York*.

" Originally the name of an old Dutch burgher family of New York, the name has come to be bestowed as an honorary epithet on all worthy descendants of Dutch stock." —*Fact, Fancy, and Fable* (Reddall).

Knight of the Rueful Countenance. A nickname bestowed upon Don Quixote, by Sancho Panza, his esquire. See *Don Quixote ; Knight of the Sorrowful Countenance*.

Knight of the Sorrowful Countenance. A nickname conferred upon Don Quixote. He is also called the " Knight of the Woeful Countenance." See *Don Quixote ; Knight of the Rueful Countenance.*

Knights of Labor. One of the largest labor organizations in the United States. It was established in Philadelphia in 1869, by Uriah S. Stevens, as a secret order for the protection of working people and the development of skilled labor throughout the United States, and some time after was called the " Knights of Labor." In 1878, the General Assembly was organized at Reading, Pennsylvania, with a supreme office of General Master Workman. The society claims a membership of 200,000.

Knights of Malta. A religious and military order — properly called the " Knights of St. John of Jerusalem "— founded in 1048 at Jerusalem for the protection of pilgrims to the Holy Sepulchre. Pope Pascal II (1099–1118) instituted the order in 1113. The members were of three classes,—knights, priests, and servitors,— and were vowed to chastity, obedience, and poverty. After the capture of Jerusalem by Saladin, the knights established themselves at Acre in 1191 ; but were driven thence in 1291, and found an asylum in Cyprus for some years. In 1309, they captured the island of Rhodes, and were thenceforth known as the " Knights of Rhodes." In 1523, they were compelled to surrender Rhodes to the Sultan Solyman, and retired to the island of Candia (Crete). In 1530, Charles V (1516–1558) gave them the island of Malta. At that time they became known as the " Knights of Malta." After the capture of Malta by Napoleon Bonaparte in 1798, and its subsequent surrender to the English in 1800, the Knights of Malta made their headquarters at Ferrara (1826) and at Rome (1834). The order commenced to decline morally and politically about the time of the Reformation (1517), and continued during the 19th century to drag on a lingering existence in France, Spain, Italy, Germany, and England.

Knights of the Round Table. An order of knighthood said to have been founded by King Arthur in 540 A.D. It was so called because, on occasions of state, the King and his knights sat at a large circular table, in order that no dispute over the question of precedency might arise. The number of these knights is variously estimated. According to a popular notion, there were 12 of them ; other authorities say 40; while the *History of Prince Arthur* places the number at 150. The chief adventures of the Knights of the Round Table occurred while in search of the Holy Grail, said to have been brought into Britain by Joseph of Arimathea. See *Grail, Holy ; Round Table ; Twelve Knights of the Round Table.*

Knights Templars. An order of religious knighthood, founded in the Holy Land in 1118, during the time of the Crusades, and confirmed by Pope Honorius II (1124–1130) in 1128. It was formed to protect pilgrims to the Holy Sepulchre from the attacks of the Saracens, and derived its name from the fact that Baldwin II (1118-1131), King of Jerusalem, established the headquarters of the order in his palace, which stood on the site of Solomon's Temple. The Templars became numerous in several European countries, and settled in England in 1125. Their vast wealth and power, acquired during the 13th century, raised up for them hosts of enemies, and they were, in consequence, cruelly persecuted, especially in France, where large numbers were burned alive or hanged. The order was abolished by Pope Clement V (1305 – 1314) in 1312. Molay, the grand master of the order, was burned alive at Paris in March, 1314. In England the property of the

Knights Templars was given to the Hospitallers, and the head of the order perished in the Tower.

Knitters. See *Tricoteuses.*

Know-Nothings. An epithet popularly conferred upon the " American " or " Native - American " party, a secret political organization in the United States, because its members, when questioned as to its principles and purposes, professed " to know nothing." The party was organized about 1854, showed considerable strength in the following year, and in 1856 nominated Millard Fillmore for re-election to the presidency. The " Know-Nothings " split on the slavery question, and became divided into the " North " and " South Americans." They were merged into the Constitutional Union party in 1860.

The following propositions, embodying the principles of the " American " party, is taken from Harper's *Book of Facts :*

(1) Americans shall rule America.

(2) The Union of these States.

(3) No North, no South, no East, no West.

(4) The United States of America—as they are—one and inseparable.

(5) No sectarian interferences in our legislation or in the administration of American law.

(6) Hostility to the assumption of the Pope, through bishops, etc., in a republic sanctified by Protestant blood.

(7) Thorough reform in the naturalization laws.

(8) Free and liberal educational institutions for all sects and classes, with the Bible, God's Holy Word, as a universal text-bok.

Koh-i-nur (*Mountain of Light*) **Diamond.** A famous Indian diamond, found in the mines of Golconda in 1550, and said to have belonged at one time to the Mogul Emperors, Shah Jehan and Aurungzebe the Great. Nadir Shah obtained it in 1739, and called it the Koh-i-nur. It next passed into the hands of the Afghan rulers, and finally became the property of Dhuleep Singh, the last ruler of the Punjab. Upon the annexation of his dominions to the British Empire in 1849, the Koh-i-nur was surrendered to Queen Victoria, and was formally presented to her in 1850. It originally weighed about 800 carats ; but, as a result of the unskilful cutting of Hortensio Borghese, a Venetian, it was reduced to 279 carats. The diamond was again cut in England in 1852, and now weighs 102¼ carats. It is " rose cut," but is too thin to display much fire. It is valued at £2,000,000.

Kolin (or Kollin), Battle of. A battle fought at Kolin (or Kollin), in Bohemia, on June 18th, 1757, between 31,000 Prussians commanded by Frederick the Great (1740–1786), and 54,000 Austrians under General Daun. The latter won a signal victory.

Königgrätz, Battle of. See *Sadowa (or Königgrätz), Battle of.*

Koran (*Ar. kara, the reading, i. e., the book*). The sacred book of the Mohammedans, portions of which are said to have been revealed to Mohammed (570–632 A.D.) by the angel Gabriel, during a period of 23 years. It was written about 610 A.D., and was collected and published by Abu-Bekr about 635, — three years after the death of the Prophet. The *Koran* is fluently and concisely written in Koreish Arabic, and teaches that there is but one God, and that Mohammed is his prophet. Among the Mohammedans it is regarded with great veneration, and is the authority on all questions of faith, morals, and jurisprudence. It is divided into 114 chapters (*surâs*), and these are again subdivided into 600 verses (*ayats*). The *Koran* was translated into Latin in 1143, into French in 1647, and into English in 1734. Translations into other European languages appeared in 1763 *et seq.*

"The word of God and of the apostle was diligently recorded by his [Mahomet's] disciples on palm-leaves and the shoulder-blades of mutton ; and the pages, without order or connection, were cast into a domestic chest in the custody of one of his wives. Two years after the death of Mahomet, the second volume was collected and published by his friend and successor Abubeker."—*Gibbon.*

Kouyunjik Gallery. An apartment in the British Museum, containing the Assyrian collections of Messrs. Layard, Rassam, and Loftus, brought from Nimroud, Khorsabad, and Kouyunjik. There may be seen a collection of bas-reliefs dating from 721–625 B.C., and belonging to the royal palace of Sennacherib at Nineveh, afterwards occupied by Assurbanipal or Sardanapalus, the grandson of Sennacherib.

Krag-Jörgensen Rifle. A breech-loading magazine rifle recently adopted by the United States army and navy. It is used also in Denmark, Norway, and Venezuela.

Kremlin (*Russian, krema, fortress*). A celebrated palace and citadel at Moscow, occupying a triangular area about two miles in circumference. This enclosure contains palaces, churches, monasteries, and towers, and is enclosed within lofty walls—pierced by five gates and crowned with eighteen towers. The Kremlin was built in 1300, and was surrounded by walls in 1376. It was burned by Rostopchin, the Russian governor, in 1812,—at the time of Napoleon's occupation of the city,—and was rebuilt in 1816. It is the most sacred spot in the entire Russian Empire. There the Russian Emperors have been crowned for 300 years ; and there also are buried the Czars down to Ivan Alexievitch, brother of Peter the Great.

Krishna. The eighth avatar or incarnation of Vishnu—the second god of the Hindu Triad,—usually considered the most glorious of all the manifestations of that deity. His mortal parents were Văsudêvă and Dêvăkî ;

and his place of birth, the kingdom of Mathura.

"Kansa, demon-king of Mathura, having committed great ravages, Brahman complained to Vishnu, and prayed him to relieve the world of its distress ; whereupon Vishnu plucked off two hairs, one white and the other black, and promised they should revenge the wrongs of the demon-king. The black hair became Krishna."—Brewer's *Dictionary of Phrase and Fable.*

Kriss-Kringle (*Ger. Kristkindlein, Christ-child*). "The infant Christ. The German for child is *kind*, of which the diminutive is *kindlein* or *kindchen.* This, in some parts of Germany and in Pennsylvania, has been formed into *kindel*, and the children are promised gifts at Christmas from ' *Christ kindel.*' The corruption of this last into *Kriss-Kringle*, as a name for the babe of Bethlehem, is neither English nor bad German, but a mere jargon or gibberish of the vilest kind."—Bartlett's *Dictionary of Americanisms.*

Ku-Klux-Klan. A secret society formed, in the Southern States of the American Union after the Civil War, to prevent the negroes from exercising the right of franchise, and to intimidate, by threats of assassination, such persons as were obnoxious to the organization. It began its outrages in 1868, but was suppressed in 1871.

Kulturkampf. A term applied to the contest between the Roman Catholic Church and the German Empire, owing to the attempt of the latter to vindicate its right to interfere with the affairs of all religious societies in the country. The struggle commenced with the expulsion of the Jesuits in 1872, and ended in certain concessions granted by Prince Bismarck in revisions of the politico-ecclesiastical legislation of 1886–1887.

Kunnersdorf, Battle of. See *Cunnersdorf, Battle of.*

Kyrie Eleison (*Gr. Lord, Have Mercy upon Us !*). "The well-known form of earnest and pathetic penitential appeal of the Scriptures, of frequent occurrence in the services of the early Church, and in the liturgical formulæ of the Eastern and Western Churches, and, since the Reformation, retained even in many Protestant churches."— McClintock and Strong's *Cyclopædia*.

L

Labor, American Federation of.
One of the largest labor unions in the world. It was organized in 1886 at Columbus, Ohio, and claims a membership of 2,000,000

"The objects and aims of the *American Federation of Labor* are officially stated to be to render employment and the means of subsistence less precarious by securing to the workers an equitable share of the fruits of their labor."— *World Almanac* (1903).

Labors of Hercules, Twelve. See *Hercules, Twelve Labors of.*

Labyrinth.
(1) A remarkable structure in Egypt, near Lake Mœris, the ruins of which were explored in 1845 by Lepsius, the German Egyptologist, but without satisfactory results. According to Herodotus, it surpassed the Pyramids, and contained 3000 chambers, half of which were below ground. Manetho (*fl.* 275 B.C.), the Egyptian historian, says that the Labyrinth was built by King Mœris (1400 B.C.), as a sepulchre for himself; but historians are by no means agreed on this point. The earliest name found among the ruins is that of Amenemhat III of the XIIth dynasty (2080–1900 B.C.). He is generally regarded as the builder of the Labyrinth and of Lake Mœris as well. According to Fergusson, this mysterious building measured about 1150 feet east and west, by 850 feet north and south.

(2) A structure in the neighborhood of Cnossus in Crete, said to have been built by Dædalus in 1210 B.C., for the confinement of the fabled Minotaur. Although the Cretan Labyrinth is frequently mentioned by ancient writers, none of them speaks of it as an eye-witness, and Diodorus and Pliny expressly say that no trace of it remained in their time. The general opinion of modern writers is that no such structure ever existed. See *Lake Mœris; Minotaur.*

Lachesis. See *Fates.*

Lachine Rapids (*Fr. La Chine, China*).
These rapids, near Montreal, Canada, were so named by the early explorers, who hoped to find a passage to *China* by sailing up the St. Lawrence River.

Lackland.
A surname given, at his birth, to King John (1199–1216) of England by his father, Henry II (1154–1189), because he received no fiefs, like his elder brothers. It is said that Henry intended to confer upon him the Lordship of Ireland.

Lacrosse.
A Canadian field-game played by 24 persons,— 12 on each side. It originated among the North American Indians, and was named *Lacrosse* by the Jesuit missionaries to Canada, on account of the resemblance of the curved stick used in the game to a bishop's crozier. This sport is still popular among the Indians of Canada, and is widely cultivated by the Canadians themselves, who consider it their national game. The "National Lacrosse Association of Canada" was founded in 1867, and the first association in the United States in 1879. Lacrosse clubs have also been established in England and Scotland.

Lacryma Christi (*Lat. Tear of Christ*).
A Neapolitan red or white wine made from grapes that grow on the slopes of Mount Vesuvius, Italy. It is sweet but piquant, and is famed for the delicacy of its flavor. The name "lacryma Christi" is also given to the vine from which this wine is produced.

"The famous vine, the wine of which is called *Lacryma Christi*, is found in this spot beside land devastated by lava."— *Corinne* (Madame De Staël).

Ladies' Peace. A name given to the Treaty of Cambrai (1529) between Francis I (1515-1547) of France and Charles V (1519-1556) of Germany, because negotiated, without the intervention of any other agents, by the Duchess of Angoulême, mother of the French King, and Margaret of Austria, aunt of the Emperor of Germany. By this treaty Italy was surrendered to Charles, while Francis recovered his sons, and paid 2,000,000 crowns for Burgundy.

Ladies, Withdrawal of. The custom, with ladies, of retiring to the drawing-room at the close of dinner and leaving the men to themselves, is said to have been introduced into England by the Norsemen, who always dismissed all women from their convivial assemblies.

Lady Day. A title given, in England, to the Feast of the Annunciation —a festival celebrated in the Greek, Roman Catholic, and Anglican Churches in memory of the tidings of the incarnation of the Messiah, brought by the angel Gabriel to the Virgin Mary. It is observed on March 25th, but the date of its establishment by the Christian Church is in doubt. By some it is assigned to 350, and by others to the seventh century. Chrysostom and Bernard speak of it as "the root of all festivals." The Jews apply the expression "Lady Day" to a part of the ceremony of the Passover.

Lady of Shalott. A young and beautiful maiden, who spent her life in seclusion on the island of Shalott. She fell in love with Lancelot du Lac, but, realizing that her passion was hopeless, died of a broken heart. Tennyson's poem of this name is one of the tenderest of his minor songs.

Lady of the Lake.
(1) A name given to Vivien, the mistress of the enchanter Merlin. She dwelt in a palace in the midst of an imaginary lake, and was surrounded by a court of brave knights and fair ladies. In Tennyson's *Merlin and Vivien* (*Idylls of the King*), the enchantress, having induced Merlin to reveal his secrets to her, enclosed him in a hollow oak, where "he lay as dead, and lost to life and use and name and fame."

(2) A title bestowed upon Ellen Douglas, the daughter of a disgraced favorite of King James V (1513-1542) of Scotland, who dwelt with her father in seclusion, in the vicinity of Loch Katrine. She is the heroine of Sir Walter Scott's poem, *The Lady of the Lake.* See *Ellen's Isle; Vivien.*

Lafitte, Château. A château, or farmhouse, on the left bank of the Gironde, in the district of Medoc, France. It is in the centre of the famous vine district, and gives its name to one of the finest red wines produced. See *Margaux, Château.*

Lagado. An imaginary city,—the capital of Baluibarbi, a continent subject to the kingdom of Laputa. It is mentioned in *Gulliver's Travels* as being famous for an academy where learned men spend their time in extracting sunbeams from cucumbers, transmuting ice into gunpowder, and making pincushions from softened rocks. See *Laputa.*

Lager Beer. A light German beer, so called because kept in a *lager* (*Ger. storehouse*) for some months before use.

Laissez Faire. A phrase used to denote the attitude taken by those economists that believe that the state should abstain from all interference with trade and industry. The words are generally traced to one Gournay, an economist of the Physiocratic School; but are said to have been first used by the vine-growers of France in remonstrance against the system of Colbert, which established a minute regulation of industry by the state. This saying has been adopted in England as a watchword of free-trade, as opposed to the theory of protection.

"Lord John Russell said : ' Colbert, with the intention of fostering the manufactures of France, established regulations which limited the webs woven in looms to a particular size. He also prohibited the introduction of foreign manufactures. The French vine-growers, finding they could no longer get rid of their wine, began to grumble. Then Colbert asked a merchant what relief he could give, and received for answer ' *Laissez faire, laissez passer*'—Don't interfere with our mode of manufactures and don't stop the introduction of foreign imports.' "—Brewer's *Dictionary of Phrase and Fable.*

Lake Country or District. The name given to a region in the northwestern part of England,—comprising the counties of Westmoreland and Cumberland, together with a small part of Lancashire. It contains as many as sixteen lakes or meres; among which may be mentioned Windermere, Esthwaite Water, Coniston, Grasmere, Ullswater, Ennerdale Water, Derwentwater, and Rydal Water. The Lake District extends about 30 miles north and south and 25 miles east and west, and abounds in picturesque and sublime scenery. It is annually visited by thousands of tourists. See *Lake Poets.*

Lake-Dwellings. The name given to the remains of habitations of prehistoric man erected on the shallow margins of lakes, and supported by piles or other substructures. They were first observed at Meilen on Lake Zurich, Switzerland, during the winter of 1853–1854, and were afterwards found in large numbers on the borders of Lakes Geneva, Neuchâtel, and Constance. These relics of early days belong to the Stone, Bronze, and Iron Ages of Civilization. They were first described by Dr. Keller of Zurich in 1854–1856, and, according to him, were probably erected from 1000 to 2000 years before Christ. Herodotus (*fl.* 450 B.C.) speaks of the Pæonians as living in similar structures on Lake Prasias. Lake-dwellings have also been found in Italy, France, Austria, Germany, Ireland, and Scotland. See *Ages, Archæologic.*

Lake Mœris. A vast reservoir, near ancient Memphis, Egypt, built by Amenemhat III of the XIIth dynasty (2080–1900 B.C.). It was used to store up the waters of the Nile during the rainy season, and afterwards to distribute them over the land, by means of canals, during the period of drought. According to Herodotus, its circumference was 3600 furlongs, and its greatest depth 50 fathoms. From its centre rose two pyramids, each surmounted by a colossal statue. The revenue derived from the fisheries of Lake Mœris furnished the Queens of Egypt with an annual revenue of $200,000. See *Labyrinth* (1).

Lake Poets. A term derisively applied by the *Edinburgh Review,* early in the nineteenth century, to a group of poets whose chief representatives—Wordsworth, Southey, and Coleridge—dwelt in the Lake District of England. The Lake Poets protested against the stiff and formal poetry in vogue, and were distinguished for their simplicity of style and close adherence to nature. Lamb, Lloyd, and Wilson were also included under the designation of Lake Poets. See *Lake Country or District.*

Lake State. A name popularly given to the State of Michigan because it borders on Lakes Superior, Michigan, Huron, and Erie.

Lake Superior. Lake Superior—lying between the United States and Canada—is the largest body of fresh water on the surface of the globe. It covers an area of 31,200 square miles,—almost that of Ireland. Its greatest length is 412 miles, and its greatest width 167 miles.

Lama, Grand. See *Grand Lama.*

Lambeth Palace. A stately structure in London, on the banks of the Thames, used as the official residence of the archbishops of Canterbury since 1197. It was commenced in that year, and completed in the 15th century. The building contains a fine set of portraits of the archbishops, and a valuable library of 30,000 volumes and 2000 MSS. The Lollards' Tower (properly called the Water Tower), so named because the Lollards, or followers of Wycliffe, are said to have been imprisoned and tortured there, is a massive, square keep, erected in 1434. See *Lollards' Tower*.

Lammas-day (*Anglo-Saxon, hlaf, loaf, moesse, mass*). A name given to the first of August, owing to the early English custom of offering, on that day, bread made of new wheat as a thanksgiving for the first-fruits of the harvest. Lammas-day is one of the four cross-quarter days of the year, —the three others being Whitsuntide, Martinmas, and Candlemas.

Lammas-day is also the name of a festival celebrated in the Roman Catholic Church on the first of August, in memory of the imprisonment of St. Peter, and is otherwise known as the Feast of St. Peter ad Vincula.

Lamourette's Kiss. A name given in derision to a sudden but short-lived reconciliation of the opposing factions of the French National Assembly, on July 7th, 1792. It was brought about by an eloquent appeal made by the Abbé Lamourette (whose name signifies " sweetheart "), Constitutional Bishop of Rhone-et-Loire. This event is also called the " Norman Reconciliation," from Normandy, the native country of Lamourette.

" The deputies of every faction, Royalist, Constitutionalist, Girondist, Jacobin, and Orleanist, rushed into each other's arms, and mixed tears with the solemn oaths by which they renounced the innovations supposed to be imputed to them. The king was sent for to enjoy this spectacle of concord, so strangely and so unexpectedly renewed. But the feeling, though strong,—and it might be with many overpowering for the moment,—was like oil spilt on the raging sea, or rather like a shot fired across the waves of a torrent, which, though it counteracts them by its momentary impulse, cannot for a second alter their course. The factions, like Le Sage's demons, detested each other the more for having been compelled to embrace."—*Sir Walter Scott.*

Lamp, Safety. See *Davy Lamp.*

Lancelot du Lac. The surname " du Lac " is said to have been given to Lancelot, son of King Ban of Benwicke, because he was stolen in infancy by Vivien, called " La Dame du Lac," and educated at her court. On reaching man's estate, he was presented by Vivien to King Arthur, and became one of his trustiest knights. He was celebrated for his exploits while in search of the Holy Grail, and also for his amour with Guinever, wife of King Arthur. See *Grail, Holy; Guinever, Queen.*

Lancers. A set of quadrilles, said to have been improvised by a company of *Lancers* for their own amusement.

Landau. A four-wheeled covered vehicle, the top of which is divided into two sections, which can be let down in such a way as to make an open carriage. The word is derived from *Landau*, a town in Bavaria, where such vehicles were first made.

Land o' Cakes. A name frequently given to Scotland, where oatmeal cakes form an important article of diet, especially among the lower classes. The phrase was made famous by Robert Burns in 1789, in his poem *On Captain Grose's Peregrinations through Scotland*, which commences with the following lines :

" Hear, *Land-o'-Cakes* an' brither Scots, Frae Maidenkirk to Johnny Groats."

Land of Beulah. See *Beulah, Land of.*

Land of Bondage. A name sometimes given to Egypt, in allusion to the cruelties inflicted upon the Israelites during the latter years of their sojourn in that country.

"And they made their lives bitter with hard bondage, in mortar, and in brick, and in all manner of service in the field : all their service, wherein they made them serve, was with rigour."—*Exodus* i, 14.

Land of Great Peace. A title conferred upon the Empire of Japan, on account of the long immunity from war enjoyed by that country. From 660 B.C., the date of the establishment of the present dynasty, until 1192, the rise of Tycoonism—a period of almost 1900 years—there was no war in Japan. The next four centuries were years of bloodshed ; but in 1603, Iyeyasu organized a government that gave peace and stability to the Empire for 200 years. In 1806, a public festival was decreed in commemoration of this long period of tranquillity,—a period probably without precedent in history during the Christian era.

Land of Inverted Order. A term popularly applied to Australia, on account of the strange inversions of nature seen in the flora and fauna of that island-continent.

Sydney Smith, in his *Essays*, thus humorously refers to these peculiarities :

"In this remote part of the earth Nature (having made horses, oxen, ducks, geese, oaks, elms, and all regular and useful productions for the rest of the world) seems determined to have a bit of play, and to amuse herself as she pleases. Accordingly, she makes cherries with the stones on the outside ; and a monstrous animal, as tall as a grenadier, with the head of a rabbit, a tail as big as a bedpost, hopping along at the rate of five hops to a mile, with three or four young kangaroos looking out of its false uterus to see what is passing. Then comes a quadruped as big as a large cat, with the eyes, color, and skin of a mole, and the bill and web-feet of a duck,—puzzling Dr. Shaw, and rendering the latter half of his life miserable, from his utter inability to determine whether it was a bird or a beast. Add to this a parrot with the legs of a sea-gull ; a skate with the head of a shark ; and a bird of such monstrous dimensions that a side bone of it will dine three real carnivorous Englishmen ; together with many other productions that agitate Sir Joseph and fill him with mingled emotions of distress and delight."

The sobriquet "Land of Inverted Order" might, with more propriety, be applied to Japan and Holland.

Land of Nod. This figurative expression, meaning *sleep*, is doubtless borrowed from the English word *nod*, meaning an inclination of the head in drowsiness. The attempt to connect it with the "Land of Nod," mentioned in *Genesis* iv, 16, as the country to which Cain fled after the murder of his brother Abel, seems rather strained,— to say the least.

Land of Promise. A name frequently given to Canaan, or that part of the Holy Land lying west of the Jordan, in allusion to the biblical promise made by Jehovah to the patriarchs Abraham, Isaac, and Jacob, that their posterity should possess it.

Land of Steady Habits. A name formerly given to the State of Connecticut, in allusion to the settled customs and grave deportment of its inhabitants. See *Blue Laws of Connecticut*.

Land of the Rose. A name sometimes given to England, in allusion to the rose, which is the national emblem of that country.

Land of the Shamrock. A name sometimes given to Ireland, in allusion to the shamrock, which is the national emblem of that country.

Land of the Thistle. A name sometimes given to Scotland, in allusion to the thistle, which is the national emblem of that country.

Landsturm (*Ger. Land - Attack*). The name given to a final reserve-force in Germany, Austria, and other European countries, subject to call only in cases of great emergency, such as invasion. It is composed of all able-bodied males between 17 and 45 or thereabouts, not otherwise enrolled. See *Landwehr*.

Landwehr (*Ger. Land - Defense*). The name given to a military force in the German and Austrian Empires and other European countries, constituting an army-reserve, and composed of men that have at some time served in the standing-army. In Germany and Austria the term of service is five years. During this period the members are engaged in civil pursuits, and are called upon for service only in time of war. The Austrian Landwehr was organized in 1805, and the Prussian in 1813. The latter did effective work in the Austro-Prussian War of 1866, and also in the Franco-Prussian War of 1870. The German Landwehr consists of 500,000 men. See *Landsturm*.

Language of Precious Stones. " The ancients attributed marvellous properties to many of the precious stones. We give in tabular form the different months, and the stones sacred to them, with their respective meanings. It has been customary among lovers and friends to observe the significance attached to the various stones in making birthday, engagement, and wedding presents.

" *January* — Garnet. — Constancy and fidelity in every engagement.

" *February* — Amethyst. — Preventive against violent passions.

" *March* — Bloodstone. — Courage, wisdom, and firmness in affection.

" *April*—Sapphire.—Free from enchantment; denotes repentance.

" *May*—Emerald.—Discovers false friends, and insures true love.

" *June*—Agate.—Insures long life, health, and prosperity.

" *July*—Ruby.—Discovers poison ; corrects evils resulting from mistaken friendship.

" *August*—Sardonyx.—Insures conjugal felicity.

" *September* — Chrysolite. — Free

from evil passions and sadness of the mind.

" *October* — Opal. — Denotes hope ; sharpens the sight and faith of the possessor.

" *November* — Topaz.—Fidelity and friendship ; prevents bad dreams.

" *December* — Turquoise. — Prosperity in love." — *Everybody's Pocket Cyclopædia* (Harper).

Language, Primeval. The verse found in *Genesis* xi, 1, — "And the whole earth was of one language, and of one speech,"—has given rise to much speculation as to the language spoken on the earth previous to the " Confusion of Tongues." According to many authorities, Hebrew was the language spoken by Adam ; while others state that Hebrew, Arabic, and Chaldee are simply dialects of the original tongue. The Persians assert that there were three primitive languages—the Arabic, the Persian, and the Turkish. The Arabic—being the most persuasive—was used by the serpent in addressing Eve ; the Persian—being the most poetic—was spoken by Adam and Eve ; and the Turkish—being the most menacing—was employed by Gabriel when driving the guilty pair from the Garden of Eden. Herodotus says that Psammetichus, King of Egypt, wishing to learn the language that would be naturally spoken by a person, caused two infants to be carefully guarded and kept from all verbal intercourse whatsoever. When brought before him, the first word uttered by the children was *bekos* (Phrygian for *bread*) ; whereupon it was at once asserted that Phrygian was the primeval or oldest tongue. There is a tradition current near Manchester, England, to the effect that King John, wishing to discover the language natural to man, confined several children in a lonely fortress, under the care of a single attendant, who was forbidden to speak with them under pain of death. Desiring some years after to ascertain the outcome of his experiment, the King approached the tower unobserved, when to his amazement he heard the children singing :

> " King John
> Has many a whim ;
> And this is one."

Languages, Number of.

It is estimated that there are more than 3000 languages in the world,—the greater number of which are those of savage and semi-civilized tribes and nations. English is said to be spoken by over 100,000,000 people ; French by over 41,000,000 ; German by 69,000,000 ; Italian by 30,000,000 ; Spanish by 41,000,000; Portuguese by 13,000,000; and Russian by 67,000,000.

"There are 3424 known languages, or rather dialects, in the world. Of these, 937 are Asiatic ; 587 European ; 276 African ; and 1624 American languages and dialects. *Adelung.*"—Harper's *Book of Facts.*

Language, Universal.

See *Volapük.*

Langue d'Oc.

The name given to the Provençal dialect, formerly spoken in the south of France and the north of Spain. It was so called from the use of the word *oc* (*Lat. hoc*), instead of *oui* (*yes*). The troubadours used this dialect in the composition of their lyrics and romances. See *Langue d'Oïl; Provençal Language ; Troubadours.*

Langue d'Oïl.

The name given to a dialect formerly spoken north of the Loire. It was so called from the use of the word *oyl* or *oïl* (*Lat. illud*), instead of *oui* (*yes*). The Langue d'Oïl is the basis of the modern French, and the dialect in which the trouvères composed their romances. See *Langue d'Oc ; Trouvères.*

Lantern of Diogenes.

A name popularly given to the choragic monument at Athens, erected by Lysicrates in honor of a victory won by himself in 334 B.C. It is a small circular building of exquisite proportions, about 8 feet in diameter and 34 feet in height. See *Choragic Monuments.*

"Notwithstanding the smallness of its dimensions, one of the most beautiful works of art of the merely ornamental class to be found in any part of the world."—*Fergusson.*

Laocoön.

A famous group of ancient sculpture, now in the Vatican at Rome, representing Laocoön and his two sons struggling in the coils of two enormous serpents. It was discovered in the ruins of the Baths of Titus on the Esquiline Hill in 1506, and was purchased by Pope Julius II (1503–1513) for the Vatican. Napoleon Bonaparte removed it to Paris in 1797, but after his fall in 1814 it was returned. Pliny says the Laocoön was carved out of a single block of marble, in accordance with the command of the Roman Senate, and was the work of the three Rhodian sculptors, Agesander, Athenodorus, and Polydorus. Various dates—between 200 B.C. and 200 A.D.—have been assigned to it ; but the one accepted by the best authorities is about 100 B.C. Michael Angelo was the first to observe that the group is in three pieces. The upraised arms of the figures and portions of the serpents are restorations.

Laocoön was a son of Priam and Hecuba, and a priest of Apollo and afterwards of Neptune. He married, contrary to the will of Apollo, and warned the Trojans against admitting the Wooden Horse within the walls of the city. As a punishment for one or both of these crimes he, together with his two sons, was destroyed by two gigantic serpents that came up out of the sea. The legend of Laocoön is post-Homeric, and is frequently met with in Greek poetry. Virgil introduces it in the Second Book of the *Æneid.* See *Baths of Titus.*

"The group of *Laocoön* and his sons—so justly denominated, by Michael Angelo at the time of its discovery, the miracle of art, ' il portento dell' arte '—is one of those productions which would have been pronounced impossible had they never been executed. It stands upon the very line by which the art of sculpture is divided from poetry and painting. There is no other work of Greek art, of high rank at least, which resembles it."—*Six Months in Italy* (Hillard).

Laputa. An imaginary aërial island, mentioned in *Gulliver's Travels*. It contained 10,000 acres and was inhabited by a set of dreamy philosophers, who occupied themselves with music and mathematics. Owing to their habitual absent - mindedness, these sages employed attendants, known as "flappers," to rouse them from their reveries by flapping them on the mouth and ears with blown bladders, whenever their attention was to be withdrawn from "high things" and bestowed upon mundane affairs. See *Lagado*.

Lares. Tutelary deities, derived from the Etruscan religion and worshipped by the ancient Romans as the guardians of particular localities. They were of two classes : (1) the domestic *Lares* or household divinities, whose images stood either on the hearth or in a small chapel, and who were regarded as the disembodied souls of pious ancestors ; (2) the public *Lares*, who were protectors of streets and highways, cross-roads, and the country. See *Manes ; Penates*.

La Scala. A famous opera-house at Milan, Italy. It contains six rows of boxes, and has accommodations for 3600 persons. The depth of the auditorium from the curtain to the front of the centre box is 95 feet, and the width 73 feet. The stage is 150 feet deep.

"We wished to go to *La Scala*, the largest theatre in the world, I think they call it. We did so. It was a large place. Seven separate and distinct masses of humanity—six great circles and a monster parquette."—*Innocents Abroad* (Mark Twain).

Last Astrologer. A sobriquet given to William Lilly (1602–1681), a famous English astrologer. He was employed as a servant in London, during his youth, and in 1632 began the study of astrology. He soon acquired fame as a fortune-teller, and was frequently consulted on political affairs, not only by Charles I (1625–1649), but also by those of the opposite party. He claimed to foresee the fate of Charles I, the Great Plague, and the Great Fire of London. He was pensioned for a time by Parliament for his services. He published annually from 1644 to 1681 an almanac, entitled *Merlinus Anglicus Junior*.

Last Battle. A term sometimes applied to the battle of Culloden Moor, fought near Inverness, Scotland, on April 16th, 1746. It received this appellation on account of its being the last battle fought on the soil of Great Britain. See *Culloden, Battle of*.

Last Judgment. A superb fresco-painting by Michael Angelo (1475–1564), on the wall opposite to the entrance of the Sistine Chapel, in the Vatican at Rome. It is 60 feet high and 30 feet wide, and was completed in 1541—after a labor of eight years. The painting contains nearly 300 figures, and presents "a confused mass of naked bodies in the most violent attitudes and most admired disorder, and excels chiefly in energy of expression." The "Last Judgment" has been much injured by the dampness, but more especially by the smoke from the incense and altar candles. Fra Angelico, Andrea Orcagna, Fra Bartolommeo, and Peter Paul Rubens, among others, have left masterpieces on this same subject.

Last Man. A sobriquet conferred by the Parliamentary party on Charles I (1625–1649) of England, meaning that he was the last man that should ever sit on the English throne. His son—Charles II—was called the "Son of the Last Man." See *Son of the Last Man*.

Last of the Fathers. A title conferred upon St. Bernard (1091–1153), Abbot of Clairvaux.

Last of the Goths. A title bestowed upon Roderick, King of the Visigoths in Spain, who was defeated and slain by the Moors in 711 A.D.

He was the 34th and last of the Visigothic line of kings, who reigned in Spain from 414 to 711 A.D. Southey has written a historical poem on this subject, entitled *Roderick, the Last of the Goths*.

Last of the Greeks. A sobriquet conferred upon Philopœmen [252 (?) – 183 B.C.], a native of Arcadia, who, as commander-in-chief of the Achæan League, strove to allay the domestic troubles in Greece, and thus protect his country against the aggressions of Rome. His efforts, however, were thwarted by the vigor of the Roman policy and the vacillation of his countrymen. Within fifty years after his death, Greece became a Roman province under the name of Achaia. According to Pausanias, " Miltiades was the first, and Philopœmen the last, benefactor to the whole of Greece." See *Achæan League*.

Last of the Incas. An appellation conferred upon Atahualpa, Inca of Peru, who was treacherously murdered by Pizarro, on August 29th, 1533.
Prescott, in his *Conquest of Peru*, says :

" The blood-stained annals of the conquest afford no such example of cold-hearted and systematic persecution, not of an enemy, but of one whose whole deportment had been that of a friend and benefactor."

Last of the Knights. An epithet conferred upon Maximilian I (1493–1519), Emperor of Germany, in allusion to his valiant deeds in tournament and battle.

Last of the Mohicans. A sobriquet given to Uncas, the Indian chief and hero of James Fenimore Cooper's novel of the same name. Sometimes written *Last of the Mohegans*.

Last of the Puritans. A sobriquet conferred upon Samuel Adams (1722–1803), the American Revolutionary patriot and statesman.

Last of the Romans. A title conferred upon several distinguished persons in ancient and modern times. They are as follows :
(1) Marcus Junius Brutus (85–42 B.C.), the leader of the conspiracy against Julius Cæsar.
(2) Caius Longinus Cassius (*d.* 42 B.C.), a fellow conspirator. He is said to have been so called by Brutus.

" The *last of all the Romans*, fare thee well !
It is impossible that ever Rome
Should breed thy fellow."
Julius Cæsar, v, 4.

(3) Ætius [396 (?) –454 A.D.], a Roman general, in the service of the Emperor Valentinian, who defeated Attila the Hun on the plains of Châlons, and saved Gaul from the encroachments of the barbarians. He was so called by Procopius.
(4) Colas di Rienzi (1313–1354 A.D.), the Roman tribune, who championed the cause of the people in their struggles against the oppressions of the nobles.

" Redeemer of dark centuries of shame,—
The friend of Petrarch,—hope of Italy,—
Rienzi! *last of Romans !* "
Childe Harold, iv, 114.

Desbillons, Congreve, Horace Walpole, and Charles James Fox were all so called by their admirers. See *Last of the Tribunes*.

Last of the Saxons. A title bestowed upon Harold II (1066), the last Saxon king. He was defeated and slain at the battle of Hastings on October 14th, 1066.

Last of the Schoolmen. A sobriquet conferred upon Francisco Suarez (1548–1617), a Spanish Jesuit and teacher of philosophy.

Last of the Stuarts. An epithet applied to Henry Benedict Stuart (1725–1807), Cardinal York. He was a grandson of James II (1685–1688) of England and brother of Charles Edward, the " Young Pretender." He died at Rome, and with him the line of the Stuarts became extinct. See *Pretenders*.

Last of the Tribunes. A name given to Colas di Rienzi (1313-1354 A.D.), who was chosen tribune by the citizens of Rome in 1347, and was confirmed in his authority by Pope Clement VI (1342-1352). After a brief rule of seven months—characterized by oppression and extravagance—he was deposed and driven from the city by the infuriated populace. See *Last of the Romans* (4).

Last of the Troubadours. A sobriquet conferred upon Jacques Jasmin (1798-1864), the noted Gascon poet.

Last Rose of Summer. The title of a popular song by Thomas Moore (1779-1852), forming one of his *Irish Melodies*.

Last Supper. A noted painting by Leonardo da Vinci (1452-1520), on the wall of the refectory of the Dominican convent of the Madonna delle Grazie at Milan, Italy. It is, without doubt, the most famous picture in the world, and was executed in 1496-1498 by order of the Duke of Milan. Owing to abuse and neglect, it is almost entirely obliterated,—so much so that, at the present time, little more than the outlines of the figures remain. In 1652, the monks cut a doorway through the wall, thus destroying portions of the central part of the painting ; and in 1796 the refectory was used as a stable for the cavalry of Napoleon Bonaparte, although contrary to his orders. The best copy of Leonardo's " Last Supper " is by his pupil Marco d'Oggiono (about 1510), and hangs in the Royal Academy of Arts in London. This is the picture from which Morghen's famous steel engraving was taken.

"It is probably the most celebrated picture in the world ; that is, the most talked of and written about, . . . a work full of melancholy interest,—a picture in ruins ; and the imagination peoples the denuded walls with forms not inferior to those which time has effaced."—*Six Months in Italy* (Hillard).

Lateran Councils. A term used to denote all the councils of the Roman Catholic Church convened in the basilica of St. John Lateran at Rome, but sometimes applied only to the " ecumenical " or general councils held there. The dates of these latter are as follows :

(1) First Lateran Council, 1123.
(2) Second Lateran Council, 1139.
(3) Third Lateran Council, 1179.
(4) Fourth Lateran Council, 1215.
(5) Fifth Lateran Council, 1512-1517.

See *Ecumenical Councils*.

Lateran, Palace of the. The ancient palace of the Popes of Rome, occupying the site of the residence of Platius Lateranus, a noble implicated in the conspiracy of the Pisos. It was presented to Pope St. Sylvester (314-336) by the Emperor Constantine, and was used as a papal residence until the removal of the Popes to the Vatican in 1377,—a period of nearly 1000 years. Pope Sixtus V (1585-1590) demolished the original building in 1586, and erected the present one from plans by Fontana. In 1693 it was used as a hospital; and in 1843 it was converted into a museum for classical sculpture and early Christian antiquities. The chapel of the Popes and a part of the dining-hall are all that remain of the original structure. See *St. John Lateran, Church of*.

Latin Church. A name given to the Roman Catholic Church to distinguish it from the Greek or Eastern Church, from which it separated in 1054 A.D. The term is chiefly used by Oriental Christians. See *Filioque Controversy ; Greek Church*.

Latin Union. An alliance formed in 1865 by France, Belgium, Switzerland, and Italy—afterwards joined by Greece—for the purpose of establishing and maintaining a uniform system of gold and silver coinage. Spain, Russia, Servia, Bulgaria, and Roumania have adopted the same system in part, but are not members of the "Union."

Latter-Day Pamphlets. A series of political tracts by Thomas Carlyle (1795–1881), attacking the general policy of the government of Great Britain. They appeared in 1850, and were occasioned by the revolutionary events of 1848.

"In these the censor appeared in his most irate and uncompromising mood, and with his peculiarities of style and expression in greater growth and deformity. He seemed to be the worshipper of mere brute-force, the advocate of all harsh, coercive measures. Model-prisons and schools for the reform of criminals, poor-laws, churches, as at present constituted, the aristocracy, parliament, and other institutions, were assailed and ridiculed in unmeasured terms, and, generally, the English public was set down as composed of sham-heroes and a valet or *flunkey* world. On some political questions and administrative abuses, bold truths and merited satire appear in the Pamphlets; but on the whole, they must be considered, whether viewed as literary or philosophical productions, as unworthy their author."— *Chambers's Cyclopædia of English Literature.*

Latter-Day Saints. "The Church of Jesus Christ of Latter-Day Saints," or, briefly, "Latter-Day Saints," is the proper designation of the religious community popularly known as the Mormons. This latter title, derived from their sacred book—*The Book of Mormon,*—is strenuously objected to by them. See *Book of Mormon; Mormons.*

Laughing Philosopher. An epithet conferred upon Democritus of Abdera, [470(?)–362(?) B.C.], the Greek philosopher, because he ridiculed the feeble efforts of men and believed that all their acts were governed by fate. See *Weeping Philosopher.*

"His claim to the title of Laugher (ὁ γελασῖνος) has been disputed, and by moderns generally rejected. Perhaps the native stupidity of his countrymen, who were renowned for abusing the privilege of being stupid, afforded him incessant matter for laughter. Perhaps he was by nature satirical, and thought ridicule the test of truth."— Lewes's *Biographical History of Philosophy.*

Laura de Noves. A French lady of rank and beauty, immortalized by Petrarch in his sonnets and canzoni. She was a native of Avignon, and was first seen by the poet in that city on April 6th, 1327, in the Church of St. Clara. This date, together with that of Laura's death on April 6th, 1348—21 years later to a day,—is inscribed in Petrarch's handwriting on the fly-leaf of his *Virgil,* now preserved as a priceless treasure in the Ambrosian Library at Milan.

"Think you, if *Laura* had been Petrarch's wife,
He would have written sonnets all his life?" *Don Juan,* iii, 8.

Laureate, Poet. See *Poet-Laureate.*

Laurel Hill. A beautiful cemetery in Philadelphia, adjoining Fairmount Park. It contains 200 acres, and is adorned with fine monuments. It is especially famous, however, for its beautiful landscape-gardening and its profusion of shrubs and flowers. Among its trees are some fine cedars of Lebanon,—the first to bear fruit in the United States. See *Fairmount Park.*

Lauterbrunnen. A deep and narrow valley in the Canton of Berne, Switzerland, enclosed by perpendicular walls of sandstone from 1000 to 1600 feet in altitude. From these heights descend cascades on every side, chief among which may be mentioned the famous *Staubbach* ("dust-stream"). The sun is hardly seen at all there in winter, and even in July not before seven A.M. Through the valley flows the Weisse Lütschine, one of the tributaries of the Aar. See *Staubbach Fall.*

La Vendée. See *Vendée, Rising of La.*

Lavender. The name of this plant is derived from the Latin *lavere* (*to wash*). It is so called in allusion to the extensive use of this perfume in washing and bathing.

Law of Gravitation. " Shakespeare evidently understood the law of gravitation, although he lived before Newton. In *Troilus and Cressida*, Act. iv, Sc. 2, it is thus alluded to :

" The strong base and building of my love
  Is as the very centre of the earth,
  Drawing all things to it."
  Edwards's *Words, Facts, and Phrases.*

Law's Bubble. A term sometimes applied to the " Mississippi Scheme," a wild speculative enterprise planned by John Law (1671–1729), the famous financier, for the purpose of liquidating the French debt. This scheme, although successful at the start, collapsed totally in 1720, and spread financial disaster throughout the land. Law was compelled to leave France, and died in poverty at Venice some years later. See *Mississippi Scheme.*

Layamon's Brut. See *Brut.*

Lazzaroni. The name given to a class of vagabonds in Naples, Italy, which, during the 17th and 18th centuries, formed a distinct caste. They annually elected a chief, called Capo Lazzaro, who was recognized by the authorities and frequently took an active part in political affairs. In 1647, headed by Masaniello, they overthrew the government, and, for a few days, held possession of the city. In 1798, instigated by Cardinal Ruffo, and led by Michele Sforza, they successfully resisted the attacks of the French. The lazzaroni had no homes nor regular occupations. They wore ragged clothes, were filthy in their habits, and slept in the open air. They were so called—either from *Lazarus*, the beggar, or more probably from the hospital of *St. Lazarus*, which served as a place of refuge for the destitute of the city. Other authorities say the word is derived from the Italian *lazzaro* (*leper* or *pauper*).

Lead Pencils. This is a misleading expression. Lead pencils contain no lead, properly so called, but are composed of graphite or plumbago, an allotropic form of carbon.

"They received their name from the leaden plummets which were used for ruling faint lines on paper, before the discovery of the mines of graphite in Cumberland."—Edwards's *Words, Facts, and Phrases.*

League, The. A term applied, by way of pre-eminence, to the Holy League formed by the Roman Catholic party in France, in 1576, to prevent the accession of Henry of Navarre and to place the Duke of Guise on the throne. See *Holy League* (2).

Leaning Tower of Pisa. A name often given to the campanile or bell-tower of the Cathedral of Pisa, Italy, owing to its marked deviation from the perpendicular. This inclination is said by competent judges to result from a defective foundation, and to be in no sense intentional. The tower was commenced in 1174, but was not completed until the middle of the 14th century. It is built of white marble, and is 188 feet in height and 50 feet in circumference. It is cylindrical in shape, and consists of eight stories, each of which is adorned with columns. Galileo, about 1635, made experiments in gravitation from this tower.

" *The Tower of Pisa* may claim to be the noblest tower of Southern Romanesque. The round form doubtless comes from Ravenna ; but the Pisan tower is a Ravenna tower glorified."—*Freeman.*

Learned Blacksmith. An epithet bestowed upon Elihu Burritt (1810–1879), the American reformer, author, and linguist. He began life as a blacksmith about 1827, and worked at that trade for many years, during which time he made himself proficient in numerous ancient and modern languages.

"Elihu Burritt acquired a mastery of eighteen languages and twenty-two dialects, not by rare genius, which he disclaimed, but by improving the bits and fragments of time which he could steal from his occupation as a blacksmith."—Mathews's *Getting on in the World.*

Leatherstocking. A sobriquet bestowed upon Natty Bumppo, a famous character in Cooper's novels entitled *The Pioneers, The Last of the Mohicans, The Prairie, The Pathfinder,* and *The Deerslayer,*—which are on this account called the *Leatherstocking Tales.* See *Deerslayer ; Natty Bumppo.*

"*Leatherstocking* stands half-way between savage and civilized life ; he has the freshness of nature, and the first-fruits of Christianity ; the seed dropped into vigorous soil. These are the elements of one of the most original characters in fiction, in whom Cooper has transplanted all the chivalry, ever feigned or practiced in the Middle Ages, to the rivers, woods, and forests of the unbroken New World."—*Duyckinck.*

Lebel Rifle. A breech-loading magazine rifle in use in the French army at the present day. It was adopted in 1887, and superseded the Gras rifle.

Lee-Metford Rifle. A breech-loading magazine rifle introduced into the British army in 1888, and still in use in the service.

Legal Holidays. "There is no regular national holiday in the United States. Congress has at various times appointed special holidays. Thanksgiving day, designated by the president by proclamation, is a holiday in those states that so provide by law. The following are the principal days observed in most of the states as a holiday :

"New-Year's day, Jan. 1. Washington's Birthday, 22 Feb. Decoration Day, 30 May in most states. Independence day, 4 July. General election day, 1st Tuesday after 1st Monday in Nov. Thanksgiving day, last Thursday in Nov. Christmas day, 25 Dec. Labor day, 1st Monday in Sept., made national legal holiday 1894.

"Arbor day is a legal holiday in some states, although the month and date of its observance vary. Every Saturday after 12 o'clock noon is a legal holiday in New York, New Jersey, Pennsylvania, and Maryland. Good Friday is observed in Alabama, Florida, Louisiana, Maryland, Pennsylvania, Minnesota, and Tennessee."— Harper's *Book of Facts.*

Legion. A division of the ancient Roman army, corresponding to what is known, at the present day, as a *corps d'armée.* During the reign of Romulus, by whom the legion is said to have been founded in 720 B.C., it consisted of 3000 foot and 300 horse ; but was increased, in the time of Marius (88 B.C.), to 6200 foot and 700 horse. At that date, the manipular formation was abolished and the legion was divided into ten cohorts, each cohort into three maniples (companies), and each maniple into two centuries. The standard of the Roman legion was generally an eagle. The standing army of Augustus Cæsar (27 B.C.–14 A.D.), about 5 B.C., was composed of 45 legions, 25,000 cavalry, and 37,000 light-armed troops. See *Phalanx.*

Legion of Honor. An order of merit instituted as a reward for civil and military services, by Napoleon Bonaparte when First Consul, in 1802, and confirmed by Louis XVIII (1814–1824) on his accession to power. It originally embraced four classes, but a fifth was added in 1852. As at present constituted, it comprises the following five classes :

(1) Grand Crosses (70 members).
(2) Grand Officers (200 members).
(3) Commanders (1000 members).
(4) Officers (4000 members).
(5) Chevaliers or Knights (25,000 members).

In each class, 60 per cent. of the members must be soldiers or sailors. The decoration of the Order consists of a five-rayed white enamelled cross, on the obverse of which is a female head representing the Republic, surrounded by the words *République Française ;* on the reverse side are two flags crossed, and the legend *Honneur et Patrie.* This is suspended from a wreath of oak and laurel leaves by a ribbon of scarlet watered-silk.

During the "Hundred Days," the Order embraced 48,000 members. In the reign of Napoleon III (1852–1870) the number of members rose to 64,800, and in the year 1872 to 69,179. In 1890, the membership was reduced to 53,848. The annual expenditure of the Order (in pensions, medals, etc.) amounts to 7,000,000 francs.

Legitimists. The name given, during the years 1814–1883, to the supporters of the claims of the elder branch of the Bourbon family to the throne of France, as opposed to the Orleanists. In 1862, they held a congress at Lucerne, and decided to pursue a pacific policy. During the years 1871–1875, they displayed great political activity, but failed in their efforts to re-establish themselves in power. Their last representative, Henri, Duc de Bordeaux—styled Comte de Chambord,—died childless in 1883 ; whereupon the Legitimists accepted the Orleanist Comte de Paris in his stead, as head of the House of Bourbon. The Comte de Paris died in 1894, and was succeeded by his son Robert, Duc d'Orléans, who is at present the head of the royal family of France. See *Bourbon, House of ; Orleanists.*

Leipsic, Battle of.
(1) One of the most sanguinary battles of modern times,—called the "Battle of the Nations,"—fought on October 16th, 17th, 18th, and 19th, 1813, between the French and their allies (180,000 strong) commanded by Napoleon I, and the combined forces of Austria, Russia, and Prussia (almost 300,000 in number), under Prince Schwarzenberg, Marshal Blücher, and Bernadotte, Crown-Prince of Sweden. The French—owing to the conduct of the Saxons, who went over to the enemy in the heat of the engagement—were totally defeated with a loss of 30,000 killed and wounded and 38,000 taken prisoners. The loss of the allies was estimated at 52,000. As a result of this battle, Leipsic was taken by the allies, and Napoleon, with the remnants

of his shattered army, retreated across the Rhine. Soon after, the Confederation of the Rhine was dissolved, and Germany was freed from the tyranny of the Napoleonic rule. The fiftieth anniversary of the battle was celebrated on October 18th, 1863.
(2) During the "Thirty Years' War" (1618–1648), the Imperialists were defeated near Leipsic by Gustavus Adolphus, on September 7th, 1631, and again by the Swedes under Torstensen, on October 23rd, 1642. See *Battle of the Nations.*

Lemuria. A hypothetical prehistoric continent, now submerged in the Indian Ocean. It was so named by Sclater, in allusion to its being the original home of the *lemurs*, a family of nocturnal mammals allied to the monkeys. Madagascar is said to be a remnant of it.

"The Indian Ocean formed a continent which extended from the Sunda Islands along the southern coast of Asia to the east coast of Africa. This large continent of former times Sclater, an Englishman, has called *Lemuria*, from the monkey-like animals which inhabited it, and it is at the same time of great importance from being the probable cradle of the human race, which in all likelihood here first developed out of anthropoid apes."—Haeckel's *History of Creation*, vol. i, p. 361.

Lenormand, Mdlle. "A famous *tireuse de cartes*. She was a squat, fussy little old woman, with a gnarled and knotted visage, and an imperturbable eye. She wore her hair cut short and parted on one side, like that of a man ; dressed in an odd-looking *casaquin*, embroidered and frogged like the jacket of an hussar ; and snuffed continually. This was the little old woman whom Napoleon I regularly consulted before setting out on a campaign. Mdlle. Lenormand foretold to Josephine her divorce ; and when Murat, king of Naples, visited her in disguise, she gave him the cards to cut, and he cut four times in succession *le grand pendu* (king of diamonds); whereupon Mdlle. rose and said, ' La séance est terminée ; c'est dix louis pour les rois ' ; pocketed the fee, and left the room taking snuff.

("In cartomancy, *le grand pendu* signifies that the person to whom it is dealt, or who cuts it, will die by the hands of the executioner.")—Brewer's *Reader's Handbook*.

Lenox Library. A superb collection of books, paintings, statuary, rare manuscripts, and specimens of early printing and binding, formerly the private property of James Lenox, a New York merchant, and presented by him to the city of New York. The building occupied a block on Fifth Avenue, facing Central Park, and was opened to the public in 1875. The number of volumes is about 110,000. This collection at present forms part of the New York Public Library, now at Fifth Avenue and 42nd Street. See *Astor Library; New York Public Library.*

Lent. A penitential season lasting 40 days — observed in the Roman Catholic, Anglican, and other Christian Churches, from Ash-Wednesday to Easter-Day, exclusive of Sundays. It is said to have been instituted by Pope Telesphorus (127–139) in 130. In early days, Lent commenced on Sunday—now known as the first Sunday in Lent; but in 487 the four days preceding were added by Pope Felix III (483–492), thus increasing the number of fast-days to 40. Lent was first observed in England in 640. Previous to 1543, the use of meat was prohibited during this season, but in that year Henry VIII (1509–1547) of England issued a proclamation, permitting the use of *white* meat. The use of meat was wholly forbidden by James I (1603–1625) in 1619 and 1625, and again by Charles I (1625–1649) in 1627 and 1631. The word "Lent" is derived from the Anglo-Saxon *Lencten (Spring).*

Leonora d'Este. A noble lady, sister of Alfonso II d'Este, reigning Duke of Ferrara, for whom the poet Tasso (1544–1595) cherished a romantic passion, and to whom he addressed a number of sonnets expressive of his admiration. Leonora never married, but lived with her sister Lucrezia, who had separated from her husband. She died in 1581, and during her fatal illness Tasso wrote as follows to her chaplain, from the prison in which he was confined : "If my Lady Leonora is better, as it comforts me to believe, and I greatly desire, humbly kiss her hands in my name, most reverend father, letting her know that I have grieved much for her illness, the which I have not bewailed in verse, because of I know not what repugnance of my mind."

"It is not known whether she had any feeling for him beyond that of simple friendship ; but the difference in their rank was such that he could not hope to marry a princess of the proud and sovereign house of Este. Some writers ascribe his misfortunes and imprisonment to this love for Leonora ; and others suppose that he offended Alfonso by his irritable temper, or that he was actually insane."—Lippincott's *Biographical Dictionary.*

Lesbian Kiss. An expression sometimes used to denote an immodest kiss. The allusion is to the ancient Lesbians, who were noted for their licentiousness.

"The general character of the people was so debauched and dissipate, that the epithet of *Lesbian* was often used to signify debauchery." — Lemprière's *Classical Dictionary.*

"**L'État, c'est moi !**" (*Fr.* "*The State, that is myself !*"). An expression used by Louis XIV (1643–1715), when requested to convene the States-General. These words sum up the policy of "Le Grand Monarque," which was to make the rule of the sovereign absolute. He aimed to concentrate in himself all the powers and functions of government ; and deemed himself not only the guardian and dispenser, but also the source and origin of all law and justice.

Lethe. In classic mythology, one of the five rivers of the lower regions, —the other four being Acheron, Cocytus, Phlegethon, and Styx. Its waters, when drunk by the souls of the departed before their passage into the Elysian Fields, caused them to forget entirely the affairs of the upper world. Dante makes Lethe the boundary line between Purgatory and Paradise. The word is from the Greek, and means *forgetfulness.*

" Far off from these a slow and silent stream,
Lethe, the river of oblivion, rolls
Her wat'ry labyrinth ; whereof who drinks,
Forthwith his former state and being forgets,
Forgets both joy and grief, pleasure and pain."

Paradise Lost, ii, 583–587.

Lettres de Cachet. See *Cachet, Lettres de.*

Leuctra, Battle of. Fought near the village of Leuctra in Bœotia, on July 8th, 371 B.C., between the Thebans under Epaminondas, and the Spartans commanded by their King, Cleombrotus. The Spartans were totally defeated with a loss of 4000 killed— including their King,—while the Thebans lost only 300. This battle forever destroyed the Spartan supremacy, and made Thebes the leading power in Greece.

Leuthen, Battle of. A battle fought in Silesia, on December 5th, 1757, between 34,000 Prussians commanded by Frederick the Great (1740–1786), and 90,000 Austrians under Prince Charles of Lorraine. The latter were totally defeated, with a loss of 10,000 killed and wounded, and 12,000 taken prisoners. The Prussian loss was 6500 killed and wounded.

Levant. The name given to the eastern part of the Mediterranean Sea and to those countries (Asia Minor, Syria, and Egypt) that border upon it. In a wider sense, the term is applied to all the region between Italy and the Euphrates. The word *Levant* is derived from the Italian *Levante (Rising)*, *i. e.*, the East.

"The lands of the *Levant* are properly those that lie upon and stretch away from the eastern shores of the Mediterranean, the lands of the sunrise ; but these comprise territories so important and historic that the word *Levant* has come to be applied to the whole East."—*Zigzag Journeys in the Levant* (Butterworth).

Lever of Archimedes. Archimedes (287–212 B.C.), the famous mathematician of ancient Syracuse, was so impressed with the tremendous power of the lever — the principle of which was discovered by him—that he exclaimed on one occasion, "Give me where I may stand and I will move the world." Had this opportunity been afforded him, " the fulcrum being nine thousand leagues from the centre of the earth, with a power of 200 lbs., the geometer would have required a lever 12 quadrillions of miles long, and the power would have needed to move at the rate of a cannon-ball to lift the earth one inch in 27 trillions of years."

Leviathan. A profound philosophic treatise by Thomas Hobbes (1588– 1679), published in 1651. It gave great offense to theologians and even to Royalists, and was publicly censured by Parliament in 1666.

"This treatise, which reduces all theory of government to blind submission to the ruling power, has been the subject of more attention and more denunciation than any other political work in the language. At the time of its appearance it was denounced by writers of all classes. His system of ethics was declared to be pure selfishness, reducing the conscience and emotions to a mere judgment of what succeeds or fails. Of late years, however, there is a tendency to reopen the judgment passed on Hobbes and to consider his position more carefully. Certain it is that Hobbes is one of the most vigorous, independent thinkers in the annals of England, anticipating more than one of the discoveries of recent political science, while in point of style he may serve as a model for any age."—*Hart's Manual of English Literature.*

Lexington, Battle of. Fought at Lexington and Concord, Massachusetts, on April 19th, 1775, between the American patriots and the British regulars, and famous as being the first battle in the War of the Revolution. The victory is generally considered to have remained with the patriots. The British loss was 273, and the American, 103.

Libby Prison. An old tobacco warehouse in Richmond, Virginia, used by the Confederates during the American Civil War, as a place of confinement for military prisoners. During the years 1861–1865, more than 12,000 Union soldiers were imprisoned there. The building was purchased by Chicago capitalists in 1889 and removed to Chicago, where it was converted into a National War Museum—filled with interesting relics of the Civil War.

Liberal Republicans. A political party in the United States, organized in 1872. It was principally composed of Republicans that were dissatisfied with the administration of President Grant and favored greater toleration in dealing with the South. Horace Greeley (1811–1872) was nominated for President by the Liberal Republicans in May, 1872, and was endorsed by the Democrats in the following July. He suffered an overwhelming defeat in the election that followed, and General Grant was triumphantly chosen for a second term. The Liberal Republicans ceased to have any influence as a political party after that event.

Liberator.
(1) A sobriquet conferred upon Simon Bolivar (1783–1830) by the Peruvians in 1823, because of his success in freeing Peru from the dominion of Spain.
(2) A title given to Daniel O'Connell (1775–1847), the famous orator and political agitator, in allusion to his successful attempts to relieve the Roman Catholics of Ireland from political disabilities.

(3) The name given to an anti-slavery journal in the United States, founded by William Lloyd Garrison (1804–1879) in 1831, and edited by him until 1866. Its motto was: "My country is the world; my countrymen are all mankind."

Liberator of Italy. A title popularly bestowed upon Giuseppe Garibaldi (1807–1882), the distinguished patriot, on account of his life-long devotion to the cause of Italian unity and independence.

Libertines (*Lat. Freedmen*). A fanatical sect that arose in the Netherlands in 1525 A.D., and spread thence into France and Switzerland. They called themselves *Spiritualists*, and had as leaders, Coppin, Quintin of Hennegau, Bertrand, and Pocquet. They advocated a community of goods and wives ; and held that, when the soul is united to God through the acceptance of religion, man is at liberty to gratify any sensual appetite,—such desires being no longer evil. Through the efforts of Calvin, this baneful sect left France, and took refuge in the Netherlands, where it disappeared entirely.

Liberty Bell. A famous bell, which now hangs in the corridor of Independence Hall, Philadelphia. It was cast in England in 1752, and bore the inscription : "Proclaim liberty throughout the land and unto all the inhabitants thereof" (*Leviticus* xxv, 10). Owing to a flaw it was recast in America, with the same inscription, and was hung in the belfry of the State-House about 1755. More than twenty years later — in 1776 — it announced to the multitudes assembled the glad tidings of liberty, on the occasion of the adoption of the Declaration of Independence by the Continental Congress. The bell was cracked in 1835, and was exhibited at the Columbian Exposition at Chicago, in 1893. See *Independence Hall*.

Liberty Enlightening the World.
See *Bartholdi's Statue.*

Lick Observatory. A noted astronomical observatory situated on the summit of Mount Hamilton (4210 feet), California, 26 miles east of San José, with which place it is connected by a fine mountain-road. It was founded by James Lick (1796–1876), a California millionaire, whose remains are interred (but not at his request) in a vault within the foundation-pier of the great equatorial telescope. This instrument—ordered in his trust-deed to be " superior to and more powerful than any telescope ever yet made "— is one of the largest and most powerful refractors in existence. It has an object-glass 36 inches in diameter (made by Alvan Clark & Company of Cambridgeport, Mass.), and a tube 56 feet long. The Observatory is endowed with a fund of $700,000, and forms the astronomical department of the University of California. The time-service of all the Pacific railroads, from Ogden to El Paso, is given out from the Lick Observatory. See *Yerkes Observatory.*

Life, Expectation of. The following table, taken from Mulhall's *Dictionary of Statistics*, shows the expectation of life in various countries at different ages :

YEARS TO LIVE.

Age.	England.	United States.	Belgium.	Holland.	Saxony.	Sweden.
10	49.2	48.7	44.3	46.5	47.0	48.0
20	41.0	42.2	37.1	38.9	39.3	40.1
30	33.6	35 3	31.2	32.1	32.1	33.2
40	26.7	28.2	25.5	26.2	25.0	25 9
50	20.2	20.9	19.6	20.0	18.0	19.1
60	13.9	14.1	13.2	13 3	11.7	12 9
70	8.9	8.5	8.2	8.0	6.9	8.0
80	5.5	4.4	5.3	4.6	3.9	4.1

Lifting the Hat, Origin of. " The custom of lifting the hat had its origin during the age of chivalry, when it was customary for knights never to appear in public except in full armor.

" It became a custom, however, for a knight, upon entering an assembly of friends, to remove his helmet, signifying, ' I am safe in the presence of friends.'

" The age of chivalry passed away with the fifteenth century ; but among the many acts of courtesy which can be traced back to its influence, none is more direct in its origin than that of lifting the hat to acknowledge the presence of a friend. "— Killikelly's *Curious Questions.*

Light of the World. A title conferred upon Sigismund (1411–1437), Emperor of Germany, on account of his enlightenment and intelligence.

Ligurian Republic. The name given to a republic composed of Genoa, Venetia, and part of Sardinia, established by Napoleon Bonaparte in 1797. It was united to France in 1805, and later became a part of the newly founded Kingdom of Italy. Liguria is the ancient name for this region.

Lilis or Lilith. According to Jewish tradition, the wife of Adam before the creation of Eve. Refusing to submit to Adam, she was turned out of Paradise into a region of the air, where she still dwells. She haunts the abodes of men, and is especially inimical to new-born children. Superstitious Jews were accustomed to place in their wives' chambers four coins, to which were attached labels bearing the names of Adam and Eve and the words *Avaunt thee, Lilith !* The word " lullaby " is said by some authorities to be a corruption of *Lilla, abi* (*Lat. Lilith, avaunt*). Lilis is introduced as a famous witch in the Walpurgis-Night scene in Goethe's *Faust.*

Lily Maid of Astolat. A sobriquet conferred upon Elaine, the heroine of *Lancelot and Elaine.* See *Elaine.*

" Elaine the fair, Elaine the loveable,
Elaine, the *lily maid of Astolat,*

High in her chamber up a tower to the east
Guarded the sacred shield of Lancelot."
Tennyson's *Lancelot and Elaine.*

Limbo or Limbus (*Lat. limbus, border*). A region said by the School-men to be situated on the confines of Hell, and occupied, according to the Roman Catholic Church, by some of the souls of the departed. It is a neutral land, where dwell those whose wickedness is not sufficiently great to consign them to Hell, and who yet are not fitted to enter into the joys of Heaven. There abide the souls of the patriarchs and other pious persons that lived before the birth of Christ, as well as those of unbaptized infants, mildly wicked persons, and fools, idiots, and lunatics. There are four regions in "Limbo," whose names are as follows:
(1) Limbus Puerorum.
(2) Limbus Patrum.
(3) Limbus Purgatorius.
(4) Limbus Fatuorum.
See *Fool's Paradise.*

Lime-Light. See *Drummond Light.*

Lincoln Monument. An imposing granite monument erected at Oak Ridge Cemetery, Springfield, Illinois, in memory of Abraham Lincoln (1809–1865), the Martyr-President, who is buried there. It measures 119 feet in length by 72 feet in breadth, and has a total height of 120 feet. It is adorned with groups of statuary, above which stands a bronze statue of Lincoln. The monument cost $264,000 (some authorities say $206,550), and was unveiled in October, 1874.

Lincoln Tower. A beautiful tower and spire on Westminster Bridge Road, London, erected by the combined sub-scriptions of English and American admirers, as a memorial of Abraham Lincoln and the abolition of slavery. It is 220 feet high and cost about £7000. The corner-stone was laid by General Schenck, the American Minis-ter to Great Britain, in 1874, and the headstone was placed by the Rev.

Newman Hall in the following year. Lincoln Tower adjoins the Noncon-formist chapel—called Christchurch—erected, with the assistance of Ameri-can contributions, for the congregation of the late Rowland Hill.

Liner. "The ships belonging to the regular lines of London, Liverpool, or Havre packets are called *liners*, to distinguish them from transient ships sailing to the same ports."—Bartlett's *Dictionary of Americanisms.*

Lingua Franca. A term applied to a corrupt Italian dialect, intermingled with words from the Arabic, Turkish, and modern Greek, and used through-out the Mediterranean Sea since the palmy days of Venice and Genoa, as the language of commercial intercourse between the Levantines and the nations of modern Europe. The expression *Lingua Franca* is used also to denote any language that serves a similar pur-pose, as, for instance, the Swahili in Africa and the Chinook in the north-western part of the United States.

Linnæan System. A system of plant-classification devised in 1725–1730 by Carl von Linné or Linnæus (1707–1778), the celebrated Swedish botanist. It classifies plants mainly according to their sexual organs, and separates them into 24 classes. It is often called the *Artificial System*, be-cause it disregards the natural relations of plants and simply groups them ac-cording to certain obvious external characteristics. The *Linnæan System* remained in use for about 100 years; but is now almost entirely superseded by the *Natural System*, introduced by Antoine de Jussieu (1748–1836) in 1788.
"The Artificial System was invented by Carl von Linné, of Sweden (1707–1778), better known by his Latinized signature *Linnæus;* this is thence called also the Linnæan System. Linnæus revised the crude materials which in his day formed the extent of research in both Botany and Zoölogy. He gave to each genus and species a name; he established rules for the forma-tion of these names; and so happy was he

in this nomenclature—which has been universally adopted—that he should be called the poet-laureate, as well as the high-priest, of science. His artificial classification of plants was made because it was the best that could then be adapted to the masses, who had neither time nor opportunity for deeper investigation. But it was much more respected by his successors than by himself; for he says in his 'Botanical Philosophy,' 'The first and last desideratum is studious inquiry into the methods of nature.' Still, his system was in almost universal use for nearly a hundred years; the most valuable botanical books written during that period are based upon it. And though it has long been superseded by the *Natural Method*, the Linnæan nomenclature has become so identified with botanical science that no student can pursue the study successfully—certainly none can examine these valuable old works intelligently—without some knowledge of the classes and orders of the Artificial System."—Ketchum's *Botany*.

Lion and Unicorn. The English lion and the Scottish unicorn became the "supporters" of the Royal Arms of the United Kingdom, on the accession of James I of England in 1603.

Lion, Nemean. See *Nemean Lion*.

Lion of Lucerne. A famous piece of sculpture at Lucerne, Switzerland, hewn out of the sandstone rock in the side of a cliff. It represents a colossal lion, transfixed with a spear and dying, but still endeavoring to protect with its paw the Bourbon fleur-de-lis. This monument was designed by Thorwaldsen (1770-1844), and was dedicated in 1821 to the officers and soldiers of the ill-fated Swiss Guard,—nearly 800 in number,—who were slain on the 10th of August, 1792, while defending the Palace of the Tuileries from the attack of the mob. See *Swiss Guards*.

Lion of St. Mark. A winged lion of bronze, surmounting one of the famous granite columns in the Piazzetta at Venice, and holding between its fore-paws the Gospel of St. Mark. When the city fell into the hands of the French in 1797, Napoleon Bonaparte removed this lion to Paris, where it remained until his fall. In 1815 it

29

was restored to Venice, and, although injured on the journey, was carefully repaired. This bronze lion must not be confounded with the two marble lions standing before the gates of the Arsenal in that city. The winged lion was the heraldic device of the ancient Republic of Venice. See *Arsenal of Venice; Columns of St. Mark; St. Mark's Column.*

" Sullen old *lion of grand St. Mark*
  Lordeth and lifteth his front from the
  dark." *Joaquin Miller.*

Lion of Sweden. A nickname bestowed upon Johan Gustafsson Banér or Banier (1595-1641), the Swedish field-marshal, on account of his bravery and impetuosity.

Lion of the North. A sobriquet conferred upon Gustavus Adolphus (1611-1632) of Sweden, the Protestant champion during the "Thirty Years' War," in allusion to his courage, prudence, and generosity. See *Star of the North.*

" In the intoxication of his fortune he was still a man and a Christian, and in his devotion still a hero and a king."—*Schiller.*

Lion of the Tribe of Judah. A title conferred upon Jesus Christ, who sprang from the tribe of Judah and the house of David, and overcame death, the world, and the devil. The lion is supposed to have been the emblem of the tribe of Judah.

" For it is evident that our Lord sprang out of Juda; of which tribe Moses spake nothing concerning priesthood."—*Hebrews* vii, 14.
" And one of the elders saith unto me, Weep not: behold, the *Lion of the tribe of Judah*, the Root of David, hath prevailed to open the book, and to loose the seven seals thereof."—*Revelation* v, 5.

Lion's Mouth. An opening in the wall, at the head of the Giants' Staircase in the Doge's Palace at Venice, into which were dropped secret accusations against persons that had incurred suspicion. See *Doge's Palace; Giants' Staircase.*

" If a man had an enemy in those old days, the cleverest thing he could do was to slip a note for the Council of Three into the *Lion's mouth*, saying ' This man is plotting against the Government.' If the awful Three found no proof, ten to one they would drown him anyhow, because he was a deep rascal, since his plots were unsolvable. Masked judges and masked executioners, with unlimited power, and no appeal from their judgments, in that hard, cruel age, were not likely to be lenient with men they suspected yet could not convict."—*Innocents Abroad* (Mark Twain).

Lion's Share. An expression meaning the whole or, at least, the greater part of anything. The saying is derived from one of Æsop's fables, wherein the lion is represented as claiming all the spoil, although he has been assisted in the hunt by a number of beasts. He demanded one-quarter as his own special prerogative ; one-quarter for his superior strength ; and one-quarter for his courage. As for the remaining quarter, he defied any one to dispute its possession with him.

Lisbon Earthquake. One of the most appalling catastrophes of modern times. It occurred on All Saints' Day, — November 1st, 1755,—and within eight minutes caused the deaths of 50,-000 persons (Mulhall says 35,000), and the destruction of most of the houses of the city of Lisbon. Nearly 3000 persons that had taken refuge from the falling buildings on a quay, on the banks of the Tagus, were engulfed by a wave, forty feet in height, that came rushing in from the sea. The damage was estimated at 20,000,000 sterling. The shock was felt as far as Scotland on the north, Asia Minor on the east, Morocco on the south, and the West Indies on the west. Humboldt says that the entire surface disturbed by this earthquake amounted to four times the area of Europe. See *Earthquakes.*

Lis, Fleur-de-. See *Fleur-de-lis.*

Lit de Justice (*Fr. Bed of Justice*). See *Bed of Justice.*

Literary Colossus. A sobriquet conferred upon Dr. Samuel Johnson (1709–1784), in allusion to the pre-eminent position occupied by him among the literary men of his day.

Little Blue Cloak. A nickname given to Edme Champion (1764–1852), the French philanthropist, in allusion to the short blue cloak worn by him as a protection from the cold.

Little Britain. A part of the city of London, so called from having been at one time the residence of the Dukes of Brittany. In the days of the Stuarts, this region was given over to book-sellers. The expression " Little Britain " is sometimes used as a designation of the French province of Bretagne or Brittany.

Little Church around the Corner. A name popularly given to the Protestant Episcopal Church of the Transfiguration in New York City, from the fact that the Rev. William T. Sabine, rector of the Church of the Atonement, on Madison Avenue, refused to read the funeral services over the body of George Holland, the actor (*d.* Dec. 22nd, 1870), and referred the friends of the deceased to " a little church around the corner where they did that sort of thing." Dr. Houghton, the rector of the Church of the Transfiguration, readily consented to officiate, and thereby endeared himself to the members of the dramatic profession, many of whom have manifested their interest in the church in a substantial manner. Since that time, most of the famous actors that have died in or near New York City, have been buried from the " Little Church around the Corner."

Referring to this incident, Dr. Houghton said : " It drew toward the church, to which my life had been given, a world of kindly tender feelings, and it opened wide for personal ministration and usefulness such a door as few of you can imagine. . . . From the prison and the gambling-house and the house of ill-repute the message or the messenger has hither come that might not have elsewhere gone. God's blessing has rested upon this our parish and church by reason of the effort made to make the most of the greater opportunity thus offered for ministering to those who had need."

Little Corporal. A title familiarly bestowed upon Napoleon Bonaparte (1769–1821) by his admiring soldiers after the battle of Lodi (1796), in allusion to his small stature, youthful appearance, and surpassing bravery.

This sobriquet clung to him throughout his career as Consul and Emperor and, as Las Casas, his biographer, says: "Perhaps this very nickname contributed to his miraculous success on his return in 1815. While he was haranguing the first battalion, which he found it necessary to address, a voice from the ranks exclaimed, 'Vive notre petit Caporal! we will never fight against him!'"

Little Dorritt. A name given to Amy Dorritt, in Charles Dickens's novel of *Little Dorritt*.

Little Em'ly. A beautiful girl in Dickens's novel of *David Copperfield*. She was a niece of Mr. Peggotty, and was induced to elope with Steerforth, but was afterwards deserted by him.

Little Giant. A sobriquet conferred upon Stephen A. Douglas (1813–1861), the American politician and statesman, on account of his small stature and commanding intellect.

Little Mac. A nickname given to General George B. McClellan (1826–1885) by his soldiers during the Civil War. It was also popular as a political sobriquet during the presidential campaign of 1864, in which McClellan figured as the Democratic candidate. The refrain of one of the political songs of that year was as follows:

"O, clear the track for *Little Mac*,
For he'll give Old Abe the sack,
On next November, Tuesday!"

Little Magician. A nickname conferred upon Martin Van Buren (1782–1862), the eighth President of the United States, in allusion to his mastery of the politician's art.

Little Napoleon.
(1) A sobriquet conferred upon General George B. McClellan (1826–1885) by his troops during the Civil War.
(2) A title bestowed upon General P. G. T. Beauregard (1819–1893) by his soldiers during the Civil War.

Little Nell. A child in Charles Dickens's novel of *The Old Curiosity Shop*. She was her grandfather's companion in all his wanderings, and, although living amid scenes of crime and vice, never lost the purity of character and sweetness of nature that distinguished her.

Little Queen. A sobriquet conferred upon Isabella of Valois, who, at the age of eight, was married to Richard II (1377–1399) of England.

Little Red Fox. A nickname given to Alexander II (1214–1249), King of Scotland.

Little Red Riding-Hood. A widely diffused nursery-tale, common to Sweden, Germany, and France. The version familiar to us comes from the French, and is entitled *Le Petit Chaperon Rouge*. It is found in *Les Contes des Fées*, by Charles Perrault (1628–1703). The Grimm Brothers give this story in the *German Popular Tales*, under the title of *The Little Red Cap*, and derive the legend from the region lying along the river Main in Germany. Ludwig Tieck reproduces the same tale in his *Volksmärchen* (*Popular Stories*), published in 1795. According to the Swedish version, Red Riding-Hood is a young woman that takes refuge in a tree to escape from a wolf; the wolf, however, gnaws the tree, and the lover reaches the spot only to see his sweetheart eaten by the monster.

Little Rhody. An appellation bestowed upon the State of Rhode Island, the smallest in the American Union. Its area, including water as well as land surface, is only 1250 square miles. Texas, the largest State in the Union, contains 265,780 square miles.

Little Round Top. An eminence of great strategic importance, the possession of which was hotly contested during the battle of Gettysburg (July 1st, 2d, and 3rd, 1863). It occupied a position on the left of the Union line, and was gallantly defended by Sickles's corps against the flower of the Southern army under Longstreet, during the second day of the battle. With this hill in their possession, the Confederates would have turned the left flank of the Union army, and rolled it back in defeat. See *Gettysburg, Battle of.*

Little Villain. A phrase used on several occasions by Horace Greeley (1811–1872), in the columns of the *New York Tribune,* when alluding to Henry J. Raymond (1820–1869), the editor of the *New York Times.*

Liverpool Landseer. A sobriquet conferred upon William Huggins (1821–1884), the famous painter of animals.

Lives Sacrificed. The following extract from Alison's *History of Europe* gives the number of victims said to have perished during the Reign of Terror in France :

"The extent to which blood was shed in France during this melancholy period will hardly be credited by future ages. The republican, Prudhomme, whose prepossessions led him to anything rather than an exaggeration of the horrors of the popular party, has given the following appalling account of the victims of the Revolution:

Nobles..................	1,278
Noble women..........	750
Wives of laborers and artisans	1,467
Religieuses.............	350
Priests.................	1,135
Common persons, not noble.................	13,623

Guillotined by sentence of the revolutionary tribunals.............. 18,603	18,603
Women who died from illness produced by excitement and grief....	3,748
Women killed in La Vendée..............	15,000

Children killed in La Vendée..............	22,000
Men slain in La Vendée.	900,000
Victims under Carrier at Nantes	32,000

Of whom were :	Children shot.....	500
	Children drowned.	1,500
	Women shot......	264
	Women drowned..	500
	Priests shot......	300
	Priests drowned...	460
	Nobles drowned..	1,400
	Artisans drowned.	5,300

Victims at Lyons	31,000
Total.....................	1,022,351

" In this enumeration are not comprehended the massacre at Versailles, at the Abbey, the Cannes, or other prisons, on the 2d of September, the victims of the Glacière of Avignon, those shot at Toulon and Marseilles, or the persons slain in the little town of Bedouin, of which the whole population perished. It is in an especial manner remarkable, in this dismal catalogue, how large a proportion of the victims of the Revolution were persons in the middling and lower ranks of life. The priests and nobles guillotined are only 2,413, while the persons of plebeian origin exceed 13,000 ! The nobles and priests put to death at Nantes were only 2,160 ; while the infants drowned and shot are 2,000, the women 764, and the artisans 5,300 ! So rapidly, in revolutionary convulsions, does the career of cruelty reach the lower orders ! and so wide-spread is the carnage dealt out to them, compared to that which they have sought to inflict on their superiors."

Living, Cost of. The following table, taken from Mulhall's *Dictionary of Statistics,* gives the cost of a workman's food in various countries, in 1880 :

	SHILLINGS PER WEEK.		PERCENTAGE OF FOOD COST.
	Food.	Wages.	
Great Britain....	14	31	45
France	12	21	57
Germany........	10	16	62
Belgium.........	12	20	60
Italy	9	15	60
Spain	10	16	62
United States....	16	48	33
Australia........	11	40	28

Lloyd's. A famous establishment in London, devoted to navigation, maritime trade, marine insurance, and shipping intelligence. It derives its name from a coffee-house in Tower Street, kept by one Edward Lloyd, in the 17th century. In 1692, this coffee-house was removed to Lombard Street, and became the meeting-place of shipping-merchants and underwriters. In 1774, *Lloyd's* established itself in the Royal Exchange, occupying the rooms previously used by the *East India Company*. There the institution remained until the destruction of the building by fire in 1838, when it sought temporary quarters, until the completion of the present Royal Exchange in 1844.

The objects of the institution are (1) to transact the business of marine insurance ; (2) to protect the interests of its members in all matters relating to shipping, cargoes, and freight ; and (3) to collect, publish, and diffuse information in regard to maritime affairs. To accomplish this last named object, *Lloyd's* keeps a staff of about 1500 agents in all parts of the world, constantly employed in the collection and transmission of news. See *Royal Exchange*.

Lochleven Castle. An ancient castle situated on an island in Loch Leven, Scotland, famous not only as the place of imprisonment of Mary Queen of Scots, in 1567–1568, but also as the scene of her escape on Sunday, May 2nd, 1568. While there, Mary was compelled to sign her abdication in favor of her infant son, James, and to accept the Earl of Murray as Regent of the kingdom. An interesting account of these events is given in Sir Walter Scott's novel, *The Abbot*. The castle was built in 1257, and served as a royal residence in the time of Alexander III (1249–1286). It was besieged by the English in 1301, and again in 1335. Patrick Graham, first archbishop of St. Andrew's, and the Earl of Northumberland, were imprisoned there. The former died within its walls in 1447.

Locksmith King. A nickname given to Louis XVI (1774–1789), King of France, in allusion to his devotion to the art of lock-making.

Locofocos. A nickname given to the Democratic party by the Whig newspapers of New York City in 1835, as the result of an incident that occurred at a stormy political meeting in Tammany Hall in that year. Owing to a difference of opinion that arose between the factions present, the chairman left his seat, and the lights were extinguished in the hope of dispersing the assembly; whereupon the opposing faction produced candles and *loco-foco* matches, relighted the hall, and continued the meeting. This term was in vogue throughout the country until the outbreak of the Civil War.

Lodi, Battle of. See *Bridge of Lodi*.

Lodore. A celebrated waterfall, near Keswick, in the Lake District of England. It descends through a thickly wooded gorge and has a fall of 120 feet. Southey has made it famous by his graphic and humorous poem entitled *The Cataract of Lodore*, —the closing lines of which are as follows:

" And gleaming and streaming and steaming and beaming,
And rushing and flushing and brushing and gushing,
And flapping and rapping and clapping and slapping,
And curling and whirling and purling and twirling ;
Retreating and beating and meeting and sheeting,
Delaying and straying and playing and spraying,
Advancing and prancing and glancing and dancing,
Recoiling, turmoiling, and toiling and boiling,
And thumping and flumping and bumping and jumping,
And dashing and flashing and splashing and clashing ;
And so never ending, but always descending,
Sounds and motions for ever and ever are blending,

All at once and all o'er, with a mighty
uproar—
And this way the water comes down at
Lodore."

Log-Cabin Harrison. A nickname
familiarly given to William Henry
Harrison (1773-1841), during the
political campaign of 1840, which resulted in his election as President of
the United States.

The origin of this expression, according
to Frey's *Sobriquets and Nicknames,* is as
follows : " During the excitement which
preceded his election as the ninth President
of the United States, a Washington correspondent of the *Baltimore Republican,* in
one of his letters, sneeringly remarked that
give the candidate a pension of a thousand
dollars and a barrel of hard cider and he
would sit contented in his log cabin for the
rest of his days. To ridicule the log cabin
in which every Western man was born, ill
became the party whose best representative
was Jackson. Some happy observer seized
the unfortunate sneer and used it as a rally-
ing cry for the Harrison party. Log cabins
large enough to hold great crowds of people
were built in many places. Small ones
mounted on wheels and decorated with rac-
coon skins were used in processions, and a
barrel marked ' Hard Cider' was conspicuous at the public meetings, Politicians wore
log-cabin buttons and handkerchiefs, log-
cabin cigars were smoked, and even laun-
dresses advertised to do up shirts in log-cabin
style. Log-cabin songs, introducing the
hard cider, were sung, and a collection of
these songs was published in a book."

Loggie of Raphael. A name given
to a series of arcades—13 in number—
facing the court of San Damaso in the
palace of the Vatican at Rome. They
are so called because they are decorated
with frescoes and arabesques by Raphael and his pupils. There are 52
of these frescoes in 13 sections, 12 of
which represent scenes from the *Old
Testament* and one from the *New Testament.* The entire collection is frequently termed " Raphael's Bible."

Log-Rolling. An expression, used
in American politics, to denote mutual
coöperation in the passage of bills
in Congress, and State legislatures,
whereby one faction supports a measure (not its own) in return for aid

given it by another faction. The term
is derived from the custom in vogue
among the early settlers, of helping
one another to clear the land by combining to roll the logs away.

" Two members, each of whom has a bill
to get through, or one of whom desires to
prevent his railroad from being interfered
with while the other wishes the tariff on an
article which he manufactures kept up, make
a compact by which each aids the other.
This is *Log-rolling;* You help me to roll my
log, which is too heavy for my unaided
strength, and I help you to roll yours."—
American Commonwealth (Bryce).

Loi des Suspects (*Fr. Law of the
Suspected.*) A measure enacted by the
National Convention of France (September 17th, 1793), during the Reign
of Terror, whereby suspected persons
were rendered liable to immediate
arrest. As a result of this law, the
liberty and property of the entire
population of France were placed at
the disposal of the government, and
the prisons were filled with more than
200,000 wretched captives. A similar
enactment, called the *Public Safety
Bill,* was passed on February 18th,
1858, after Orsini's attempt to murder
Napoleon III.

Lokman, Fables of. A collection
of Arabic fables, supposed to have
been written by Lokman, who is
variously said to have been a Nubian
slave, contemporary with David and
Solomon, and a nephew or grandson
of Job. Others identify him with
Balaam, and still others with Æsop.
The fables attributed to Lokman are
now generally believed to be of Greek
origin. They were edited and translated into Latin by Erpenius in 1615.
See *Æsop, Fables of ; Pilpay, Fables of.*

Lollards. A society formed in Antwerp, about 1300 A.D., for the purpose
of ministering to the sick and dying.
Their name was probably taken from
Walter Lollard, the reformer, who was
publicly burned for heresy, at Cologne,
in 1332. They afterwards spread into
England, and espoused the cause of

Wickliffe, with whose doctrines they appear to have had much in common. For this reason, all of Wickliffe's followers were derisively called *Lollards*. Owing to their growth in numbers and influence, the Lollards became formidable rivals of the Roman Catholic Church, and were persecuted during the reign of Henry V (1413–1422). After that time, they merged into the reformed religion and lost their identity. See *Wickliffites*.

Lollards' Tower. A massive square keep, forming part of Lambeth Palace, London, so called because certain of the Lollards, or followers of Wyckliffe, are said to have been imprisoned there. In the upper part of the tower is shown a room, 13½ feet long, 12 feet wide, and 8 feet high, called the "prison." It still contains inscriptions by the prisoners, and is furnished with eight large rings, to which the heretics were chained. It is claimed, however, that the real Lollards' Tower was the southwest tower of old St. Paul's Cathedral, destroyed by fire in 1666. See *Lambeth Palace*.

Lombard Street. A street in London, famous for many centuries as the financial centre of Great Britain. It derives its name from the Lombard money-lenders of Genoa and Florence, who, in the 14th and 15th centuries, took the place of the persecuted and discredited Jews of "Old Jewry."

"*Lombard Street* constituted the colony of the Jews of Lombardy sent over to England by Pope Gregory IX for the purpose of advancing money to those who were unable to pay the taxes so vigorously demanded throughout the country in 1229."—Wagner's *Names and their Meaning*.

London Bridge. The most famous and important bridge in the city of London and, with the exception of Tower Bridge, the one nearest the sea. The present structure is built of granite, and was opened to the public by William IV (1830–1837) in 1831. It is 928 feet long and 54 feet wide, and cost about £2,500,000. Until about a century

ago, it was the only bridge across the Thames in the city of London. Various wooden bridges existed at this spot during Saxon, and perhaps Roman, times; but the first stone structure was commenced in 1176, in the reign of Henry II (1154–1189), and completed in 1209. For many years, London Bridge was lined with houses on both sides, and resembled a continuous street. It is estimated that 20,000 vehicles and 120,000 pedestrians cross London Bridge in the course of 24 hours.

London Docks. A vast establishment, in London, on the left bank of the Thames, completed in 1805, at a cost of £4,000,000. It covers an area of 120 acres, and contains water-space for 300 large vessels, exclusive of lighters; warehouses with a storage capacity of 220,000 tons; and cellars capable of holding over 8,000,000 gallons of wine. The number of men employed at the "Docks" in one day varies from 1000 to 3000. The capital of the "London and St. Katherine's Docks Company" amounts to £13,-000,000. See *St. Katherine's Docks*.

"Nothing will convey to the stranger a better idea of the vast activity and stupendous wealth of London than a visit to these warehouses, filled to overflowing with interminable stores of tea, coffee, sugar, silk, tobacco and other foreign and colonial products; to these enormous vaults, with their apparently inexhaustible quantities of wine; and to these extensive quays and landing-stages, cumbered with huge stacks of hides, heaps of bales, and long rows of casks of every conceivable description." — *London and its Environs* (Baedeker).

London Fire. See *Great Fire of London*.

London Plague. See *Great Plague of London*.

London Stone. A stone said to have been placed by the Romans in Cannon Street, London, in 15 B.C.; and removed to the opposite side of the way in 1742. In 1798, it was built into the south wall of St. Swithin's Church, where it still remains.

It is said to be a fragment of the central *milliarium*, or mile-stone, of London, from which were measured distances on the high-roads that radiated from it. According to tradition, it was brought from Troy by Brutus, and laid by him as the foundation-stone of the city. In 1450, Jack Cade struck London Stone with his staff, exclaiming as he did so, " Now is Mortimer lord of this city ! "

London University. An examining-board instituted by the English Government in 1836, for the purpose of conferring degrees in the different arts and sciences upon candidates of either sex, wherever educated. The teaching establishment connected with the London University is known as University College. It has an attendance of about 2000 students, and offers a curriculum including the arts and sciences, law, and medicine.

London Wall. The ancient wall, built by the Romans to defend the city of London, was erected between 350 and 369 A.D., and enclosed an area of about 380 acres.

"It extended from the site of the present Tower of London on the E. to Ludgate Hill on the W., and inland from the Thames as far as the marshy ground known in later times as Moorfields and Finsbury or Fensbury. . . . This wall was maintained in parts until modern times, but has almost entirely disappeared before the alterations and improvements which taste and the necessities of trade have introduced. The most prominent remaining piece of the Roman wall is in London Wall, between Wood Street and Aldermanbury, where an inscribed tablet calls attention to it. Another fragment may be seen in the churchyard of St. Giles, Cripplegate, about 100 yards farther to the west."—*London and its Environs* (Baedeker).

Lone-Star State. A name popularly given to the State of Texas, in allusion to the single star on its coat-of-arms. This star was originally the device on the flag and seal of the Republic of Texas, and was adopted to denote the political isolation of that commonwealth. It was retained by the State on its admission into the American Union.

Long Acre. A well-known street in London, extending from Drury Lane to St. Martin's Lane.

"Mr. Rimbault says that ' Long Acre, in Henry VIII's time, was an open field called "The Elms," from a line of those trees growing upon it, as shown in Aggas's plan. It was next called "Leven Acres," and since 1612, from the length of a certain slip of ground then first used as a pathway, "*Long Acre*." '"—Edwards's *Words, Facts, and Phrases.*

Long Bridge. A famous old bridge, about a mile long, crossing the Potomac River into Virginia, at Washington, D. C. It is a shabby structure, but is historically important as having been the main avenue of communication with the Army of the Potomac during the Civil War. At that time it was strongly fortified, and afforded the principal highway for the transportation of troops and provisions.

Longchamp, Hippodrome de. A famous racecourse in Paris, France, adjoining the Bois de Boulogne. It is 1500 metres in length by 300 in breadth, and was established in 1857, having been granted to the Jockey Club by the city. The *Grand Prix* of 100,000 francs, styled the " French Derby," is annually competed for there, early in June, and marks the close of the fashionable season in Paris. One-half of this sum is furnished by the city, and the remaining half by the five great railway companies and the individual entries. The races at Longchamp attract great crowds, and on *Grand Prix Day* one would imagine that all Paris and half of London were in attendance.

Longevity, Human. The following list of instances of remarkable longevity, given on the authority of Prichard, Whitehurst, Bailey, and others, is taken from Bombaugh's *Gleanings for the Curious :*

	Died.	*Age.*
(1) Apollonius of Tyana....	99 A.D.	130
(2) St. Patrick..............	491 "	122
(3) Attila	500 "	124

		Died.	Age.
(4)	Llywarch Hên	500 A.D.	150
(5)	St. Cœmenge	618 "	120
(6)	St. Mongah or Kentigern	781 "	185
(7)	Piastus, King of Poland.	861 "	120
(8)	Countess of Desmond	1612 "	145
(9)	Thomas Parr	1635 "	152
(10)	Thomas Damme	1648 "	154
(11)	Dr. Mead, Hertfordshire	1652 "	148
(12)	James Bowles, Kenilworth	1656 "	152
(13)	Henry Jenkins	1670 "	169
(14)	William Edwards	1688 "	168
(15)	Petrarch Czartan	1724 "	185
(16)	Margaret Patten	1739 "	137
(17)	John Roven	1741 "	172
(18)	Mrs. John Roven	1741 "	164
(19)	John Effingham, Cornwall	— "	144
(20)	Thomas Winslow, a captain under Cromwell	1766 "	146
(21)	Draakenburg, a Dane	1772 "	146
(22)	Jonas Warren, Ballydole	1787 "	167
(23)	Jonas Surington, Bergen, Norway	1797 "	159
(24)	Demetrius Grabowsky, Poland	1830 "	169
(25)	Bridget Devine	1845 "	147

Longfellow's House. A colonial mansion at Cambridge, Massachusetts, doubly renowned as the headquarters of Washington during the Revolutionary War, and later as the home of the poet Longfellow. It was built in 1759, by Colonel John Vassall, a British officer, and was abandoned by him in 1775, on his return to England at the outbreak of the Revolution. The house was occupied by Washington and his wife for eight months, during the siege of Boston. In 1837, it was purchased by Longfellow, who resided there until his death in 1882.

"Not far from Elmwood, Lowell's lifelong home, is the house which is doubly renowned as the headquarters of Washington and the home of Longfellow."—*Address on James Russell Lowell* (G. W. Curtis).

Long Friday. A name given by the Anglo-Saxons to Good Friday, perhaps in allusion to the length of the fast enjoined on that day.

Long Parliament. The name given by historians to the English Parliament assembled by Charles I (1625-1649) on November 3rd, 1640, and forcibly dissolved by Oliver Cromwell on April 20th, 1653, after an existence of nearly 13 years. It was not legally dissolved, however, until the "Restoration" in 1660. The Long Parliament sat throughout the Civil War and part of the Protectorate. It impeached Strafford and Laud ; brought Charles I to trial on the charge of treason ; abolished the monarchy and the House of Lords ; and established a republic under the name of "The Commonwealth," the executive power of which was lodged in a Council of State composed of 41 persons. See *Pride's Purge ; Rump Parliament.*

Longshanks. A nickname conferred upon Edward I (1272-1307) of England, on account of his spindle legs.

Longshoreman. This word—meaning a person engaged in loading and unloading the cargoes of vessels—is an abbreviated form of *alongshoreman.*

Long Tom. A nickname conferred upon Thomas Jefferson (1743-1826), in allusion to his tall stature and slender figure.

Long Vacation. An expression used in the English courts-of-law and the universities to denote the summer vacation. In courts of common law it extends from August 10th to October 24th; in chancery courts, from August 10th to October 28th ; and at the universities, from the end of Easter term to October, a period of more than three months.

"The *Long Vacation* is a relic of Norman usages in the English Courts. The time of the long vacation in Normandy was adapted to the season of the vintage, and the same period was fixed in England by the Normans, and has remained unaltered to the present day."—Edwards's *Words, Facts, and Phrases.*

Long Walk. A celebrated avenue in Windsor Park, England, extending in a straight line, for a distance of nearly three miles, from the principal entrance of Windsor Castle to Snow Hill, an eminence crowned by a colossal statue of George III. It is finely shaded with elms, and is considered the finest avenue of its kind in the world.

Long Walls. The name given to the walls that, in ancient times, connected Athens with the seaport towns of the Piræus and Phalerum. These walls were three in number, but the term " Long Walls " seems to have been confined to the two parallel ones that connected Athens with the Piræus, —the one leading to Phalerum being called the Phalerian Wall. These parallel walls were about five miles long, 12 feet thick, and 550 feet apart. The enclosure between them formed a continuous street—at one time lined with houses—between the city and the port. The " Long Walls " were constructed in the fifth century B.C., during the administration of Pericles. They were in ruins when visited by Pausanias, the Greek traveler, during the second century after Christ. Traces of the northern wall still remain.

Longwood. The name of the residence occupied by Napoleon Bonaparte at St. Helena, from December 10th, 1815, until his death on May 5th, 1821. The ex-Emperor reached the island on October 16th, 1815, and took up his residence at " The Briers "—the home of Mr. Balcombe, where he remained until Longwood was made ready for his occupancy.

Lookout Mountain, Battle of. A battle fought on November 24th, 1863, —during the Civil War,—resulting in a victory for the Union forces. General Hooker, with about 10,000 men, advanced against Lookout Mountain, a lofty eminence on the Tennessee River, 2400 feet above the sea-level, and by a bold movement secured possession of its frowning heights. The Confederates were driven out of Wauhatchie Valley, and the Federals effected a junction with General Thomas at Chattanooga. This contest, owing to the elevation at which it occurred, is often called the " Battle in the Clouds." See *Chattanooga, Battle of.*

Lord Mayor's Day. November 9th, on which occasion the ancient and picturesque custom is maintained of conducting the newly elected mayor of London through the streets from the City to the new Courts of Justice, where he is solemnly sworn into office. This is one of the characteristic sights of London, and is followed by a dinner at Guildhall, given by the lord mayor to the members of the Cabinet and the chief civic dignitaries. See *Guildhall.*

Lords, House of. The peers of England were summoned to consult with the sovereign in matters of state in early times, but the earliest writ in existence dates from 1265, during the reign of Henry III (1216–1272). The House of Lords consists of the temporal and spiritual peers of the realm, and is presided over by the Lord Chancellor of England. He is the Keeper of the Great Seal, and acts as Speaker of the House for formal purposes. As at present constituted, the House of Lords comprises 6 princes of the blood, 2 archbishops, 24 bishops, 21 dukes, 22 marquises, 116 earls, 25 viscounts, 299 barons, 16 Scottish representative peers chosen for each Parliament, and 28 Irish representatives elected for life, —in all 559 members. The House of Lords is the court of final appeal for all parts of the kingdom, and exercises original jurisdiction in trials of its members for treason or felony, and in cases of impeachment brought by the House of Commons.

" Peers of England are free from all arrests of debts, as being the king's hereditary counsellors ; therefore a peer cannot be outlawed in any civil action, and no attachment lies against his person ; but execution may be taken upon his lands and goods. For the same reason, they are free from all attendance at courts leet or sheriff's turns ; or, in case of a riot, from attending the *posse comitatus.* He can act as a justice of the peace in any part of the kingdom."—Haydn's *Dictionary of Dates.*

Lords, Number of. See *Lords, House of.*

Lorelei. A rock, near St. Goar on the Rhine, which rises perpendicularly to a height of 427 feet above the river. In early days, it was dangerous to boatmen, and this fact gave rise to the legend of a siren that dwelt upon its summit and, by her ravishing voice, enticed sailors and fishermen to a whirlpool at its base, where they perished. Goethe has written a charming ballad, and Heinrich Heine, a lyric,—entitled the *Lorelei,*—concerning this legend.

" Yonder we see it from the steamer's deck,
 The haunted mountain of the *Lorelei*.
 The o'erhanging crags sharp-cut against a
  sky
 Clear as a sapphire without flaw or rack."
     Thomas Bailey Aldrich.

Loretto. A city in Italy, near Ancona, famous as the site of the *Santa Casa,* or *Holy House,* said to be the house in which the Virgin Mary dwelt during her residence in Nazareth. According to the legend, the *Santa Casa* was miraculously transported,— first to Fiume in Dalmatia in 1291, thence to a wood near Recanati in 1294, and finally to its present site in 1295. This shrine was at one time annually visited by 200,000 pilgrims, but at the present day the number averages 50,000. The image of the Virgin, called "The Lady of Loretto," within the *Santa Casa,* is said to have been carved by St. Luke. When the city fell into the hands of the French in 1797, this image was taken to France, but was restored with much ceremony in 1803. See *Holy Grotto.*

Lost Arts. A term applied to certain processes of manufacture, known to ancient and mediæval peoples, but not understood by those of modern times. Among such processes may be mentioned the manufacture of Tyrian purple, Damascus steel, and malleable glass. Wendell Phillips (1811–1884), in a brilliant lecture, entitled *The Lost Arts,* showed that many of the methods of production in present use, claimed as discoveries of modern times, were known and practised by the ancients.

Lost Atlantis. See *Atlantis.*

Lost Cause. The name often given to the cause for which the people of the South fought during the Civil War. It may be briefly denominated as the belief in negro - slavery and State-sovereignty. The expression is said to have originated with E. A. Pollard, who employed it as the title of a history of the War of the Rebellion, written by himself.

Lost Pleiad. See *Pleiades.*

Lost River. The name given to a river in Hampshire Co., West Virginia, famous as a natural curiosity. On reaching the base of a mountain, the stream suddenly disappears and continues on its course through subterranean channels.

Lost Tribes. The Kingdom of Israel—comprising the Ten Tribes— was overthrown by Shalmaneser, King of Assyria, in 721 B.C., and the inhabitants were carried captive into the mountainous regions of Media. Various speculations have been indulged in concerning the fate of that people, and most fanciful theories as to their whereabouts have been held. According to some authorities, they may be found in China at the present day, while others place them in the region of the Caspian Sea. The ancient Nestorians, the Afghans, the Mexicans and Peruvians, the North American Indians, and even the inhabitants of Great Britain and Ireland, have all been identified (?) in turn as the descendants of that unfortunate people. In all probability, the great mass of the transported nation adopted the customs and usages of the people among whom they were planted, and were eventually absorbed by them. See *Red Men.*

"The 'lost tribes of Israel' have been sought for in almost every quarter of the globe, and as one nation answered the conditions of the theory about as well as another, 'the remnants of the ten tribes were found marauding in the Afghan passes, wandering with the reindeer in Lapland, chasing buffaloes on the American prairies, or slaughtering human victims on the teocallis of Mexico.' But the enthusiasm of Rudbeck, Garcia, and Adair had at least one good result: it caused evidence about the facts of manners and customs—afterwards to be, in the hands of scientific students, of great value for the history of civilization—to be preserved before it was lost before advancing European influences. The ten tribes delusion has now, however, sunk to a lower level than when Lord Kingsborough spent his fortune in publishing the Mexican pictures and chronicles. In spite of all the new real knowledge as to races, it has even now more votaries than ever. 'There is indeed no doubt,' says Dr. Tylor, 'that this abject nonsense has a far larger circulation than all the rational ethnology published in England.' "—*Chambers's Encyclopædia.*

Lotophagi (*Gr. Λωτοφάγοι, Lotus-Eaters*). A race of people, mentioned in Homer's *Odyssey* as dwelling on the northeast coast of Africa, and visited by Ulysses in his wanderings after the fall of Troy. They lived upon the fruit of a plant called the *lotus*, the taste of which was so delightful as to cause utter forgetfulness of home on the part of those that partook of it. In historic times, the Greeks gave this name to a people that dwelt on the northern coast of Africa, between the Syrtes, and used as an article of food a plant supposed to be identical with the lotus of Homer.

Lot's Wife. The name given to a round pillar of solid stone, capped with limestone, standing on the southwest shore of the Dead Sea. It is about 40 feet high, and stands upon a lofty pedestal. The column bears a striking resemblance to an Arab woman with a child on her shoulder, and has received its name in allusion to the events narrated in *Genesis* xix, 26. It was discovered by an American party under Lieutenant Lynch, and is simply the result of the action of the winter rains on the hills of rock-salt in the vicinity of the Dead Sea. In the present instance, the salt has been protected by the cap of limestone, which has allowed the surrounding parts to wash away until a pillar has been formed.

Lotus-Eaters. See *Lotophagi.*

Louisa. A nickname given to General Lew Wallace (*b.* 1827) by his soldiers during the American Civil War.

Louisiana. The name formerly given to a vast region in North America, comprising nearly all the territory in the United States at present occupied by Louisiana, Arkansas, Missouri, Iowa, Minnesota, North Dakota, South Dakota, Nebraska, Kansas, Indian Territory, Oklahoma, Colorado, Wyoming, Montana, Idaho, Oregon, and Washington. It was first explored by De Soto in 1541, and was visited by La Salle, the French explorer, who, in 1682, sailed down the Mississippi and took possession of the country, naming it Louisiana in honor of Louis XIV. In 1717, it fell into the hands of John Law, the speculator, and originator of the "Mississippi Scheme"; but after the collapse of that bubble, the territory reverted to the Crown. It was ceded to Spain in 1762, but was retroceded to France in 1800. In 1803, it was sold to the United States by Napoleon Bonaparte (then First Consul) for $15,000,000. This extensive region was disposed of by the French to prevent its falling into the hands of the English, who had concentrated a formidable squadron in the Gulf of Mexico, evidently for the purpose of taking possession of the Mississippi River. With the exception of Texas and the Mexican territory (acquired either by conquest or purchase), the ancient province of Louisiana includes all the region of the United States west of the Mississippi River.

Lourdes, Our Lady of. The title under which the Virgin Mary is worshipped at Lourdes, France. It was authorized in 1862 by Monseigneur Laurence, Bishop of Tarbes, who published at the same time the recital of "seven undoubted miracles" performed in the year 1858, which, according to his statement had been strictly investigated by a committee of ecclesiastics and scientists. See *Grotto de la Vièrge.*

Louvre. A famous palace in Paris, originally the residence of the French Kings ; but, since the French Revolution, used as a museum of art and antiquities. It contains one of the finest collections in existence. The Louvre derives its name from an ancient hunting-château that stood on the site of the present palace, in the midst of a forest infested with wolves and known as the *Lupara* (*Lat. lupus, wolf*), or *Louverie* (*Fr. loup, wolf*). It is said to have been a royal residence in the time of Dagobert (628). In 1204, Philip Augustus (1180–1223) erected a prison-tower there, which was afterwards fitted up as a palace by Charles V (1364–1380) about 1364. The foundation of the present building was laid by Francis I (1515–1547) in 1541, and the structure was enlarged and adorned by successive kings, particularly by Henry IV (1589–1610), Louis XIII (1610–1643), and Louis XIV (1643–1715). After the death of Louis XIV, the Louvre was no longer used as a royal residence, Louis XV (1715–1774) and Louis XVI (1774–1789) preferring St. Germain, Versailles, and the Tuileries. Napoleon I (1804–1814) converted the palace into a museum and filled it with the finest paintings and statuary in the world, brought thither from all parts of Europe. After his fall in 1814, the most valuable of these art-treasures were restored to their rightful owners. The work of uniting the Louvre with the Tuileries, commenced by the Bourbon Kings and continued by Napoleon I, was completed by Napoleon III (1852–1870) in 1857, at an estimated cost of $15,000,000. The palaces of the Louvre and the Tuileries cover an area of 48 acres.

Loveliest Face. The statue of Psyche, in the National Museum at Naples, is considered by many connoisseurs to have the loveliest face in antique sculpture. It was discovered in the amphitheatre at Capua.

Lovers, Romantic. The following list of distinguished men and their favorites is taken from Brewer's *Reader's Handbook :*

(1) Aristotle and Hepyllis.

(2) Boccaccio and Fiammetta [*Maria,* daughter of Robert of Naples].

(3) Burns and Highland Mary [either *Mary Campbell* or *Mary Morison*].

(4) Byron and Teresa [Guiccioli].

(5) Catullus and the Lady Clodia, called "Lesbia."

(6) Charles II of England and Barbara Villiers [Duchess of Cleveland]; Louise Renée de Kerouaille [Duchess of Portsmouth] ; and Nell Gwynne.

(7) Charles VII of France and Agnes Sorel.

(8) Cid (*The*) and the fair Ximena, afterwards his wife.

(9) Dante and Beatrice [Portinari].

(10) Epicurus and Leontium.

(11) François I and la Duchesse d'Étampes [*Mdlle. d'Heilly*].

(12) George I and the Duchess of Kendal [*Erangard Melrose de Schulemberg*].

(13) George II and Mary Howard, Duchess of Suffolk.

(14) George III and the Fair Quakeress [*Hannah Lightfoot*].

(15) George IV and Mrs. Mary Darby Robinson, called "Perdita" (1758–1800) ; Mrs. Fitzherbert, to whom he was privately married in 1785 ; and the Countess of Jersey.

(16) Goethe and the frau von Stein.

(17) Habington, the poet, and Castara [*Lucy Herbert*, daughter of Lord Powis], afterwards his wife.

(18) Hazlitt and Sarah Walker.

(19) Henry II [of France] and Diane de Poitiers.

(20) Henry IV [of France] and La Belle Gabrielle (d'Estrées).

(21) Henry II [of England] and the fair Rosamond [Jane Clifford].

(22) Horace and Lesbia.

(23) Johnson (*Dr.*) and Mrs. Thrale.

(24) Lamartine and Elvire, the Creole girl.

(25) Louis XIV and Mdlle. de la Vallière; Mde. de Montespan; Mdlle. de Fontage.

(26) Lovelace and the divine Althea, [*Lucy Sacheverell*], also called Lucasta.

(27) Mirabeau and Mde. Nehra.

(28) Nelson and Lady Hamilton.

(29) Pericles and Aspasia.

(30) Petrarch and Laura [*wife of Hugues de Sade*].

(31) Plato and Archianassa.

(32) Prior and Chloe, or Cloe, the cobbler's wife, of Linden Grove.

(33) Raphael and La Fornarina, the baker's daughter.

(34) Rousseau and Julie [*la Comtesse d' Houdetot*].

(35) Scarron and Mde. Maintenon, afterwards his wife.

(36) Sidney and Stella [*Penelope Devereux*].

(37) Spenser and Rosalind [*Rose Lynde*, of Kent].

(38) Sterne (in his old age) and Eliza [*Mrs. Draper*].

(39) Stesechoros and Himera.

(40) Surrey [*Henry Howard, Earl of*] and Geraldine, who married the Earl of Lincoln.

(41) Swift and (1) Stella [*Hester Johnson*]; (2) Vanessa [*Esther Vanhomrigh*].

(42) Tasso and Leonora or Eleanora [d'Este].

(43) Theocritos and Myrto.

(44) Waller and Sacharissa [*Lady Dorothea Sidney*].

(45) William IV as Duke of Clarence and Mrs. Jordan [*Dora Bland*].

(46) Wolsey and Mistress Winter.

(47) Wyat and Anna [*Anne Boleyn*], purely Platonic.

Lower Empire.   A name sometimes given to the Byzantine, or Eastern Roman Empire, from the time of its establishment in 395 A.D. to the fall of Constantinople, its capital, in 1453. See *Eastern Empire.*

"Some historians make it begin with the reign of Valerian, 253; others with that of Constantine, 323."—Haydn's *Dictionary of Dates.*

Low Sunday.   The name given, in the Roman Catholic Church, to the first Sunday after Easter.   It was so called because some of the solemnities observed on Easter were repeated on that day, which was, accordingly, regarded as a feast, but of *a lower degree*, than Easter itself.   See *Quasimodo Sunday.*

Lucrezia di Borgia.   Although Lucrezia di Borgia—daughter of Pope Alexander VI (1492-1503) and sister of Cæsar Borgia — has been generally represented as a monster of wantonness and crime, it is nevertheless, at the present time, the opinion of accurate and unprejudiced historians that her crimes have been unduly magnified, and that she was a too willing tool in the hands of her unprincipled father and brother.   As Duchess of Ferrara, in after years, she won the love and esteem of her subjects, and became renowned as the patron of literature and the arts.   The closing years of her life were in marked contrast with her early days at the Vatican.

Lucus a Non Lucendo (*Lat. A grove from not shining*).   An expression used to denote anything absurdly derived or reasoned out.   The allusion is to Servius, the ancient grammarian, who, either sportively or in earnest, derived the word *lucus* (*grove*) from *lucere* (*to shine*), on the ground that a grove is dark and gloomy and does n't shine.   This derivation was received with favor by some and derided by others, and the phrase came, in consequence, to be applied to any far-fetched etymology or ridiculous *non sequitur.*

Luddites.   The name given, in

England, to bands of riotous workmen who, in 1811–1816, went about the manufacturing districts of Yorkshire, Lancashire, and Nottinghamshire, destroying the power-looms, from the mistaken notion that the introduction of machinery tended to lessen the demand for manual labor. They derived their name from one Ned Lud of Lancashire, an imbecile boy, who had, in a fit of anger, destroyed some stocking-frames thirty years before. The real leaders of these bands assumed female attire and were called " Lud's Wives."

Lumber State. A name popularly given to the State of Maine, in allusion to the extensive lumbering trade in which its inhabitants are engaged. About one-half of the surface of the State is covered with forests of pine, spruce, hemlock, and birch.

Lunacy. A term originally used to denote intermittent insanity, from the mistaken notion that this form of mental aberration was dependent upon the changes of the moon (*Lat. luna*). The ancient Romans thought that insane persons became more violent as the moon increased to the full. The word " lunacy," as at present used, denotes any form of mental unsoundness except idiocy.

Lundy's Lane, Battle of. Fought at Lundy's Lane, Canada, near Niagara Falls, on July 25th, 1814, between 3000 Americans commanded by General Brown, and 4500 British under General Rial. The British were finally driven from the field, but managed to regain their position during the night. The American loss in killed and wounded was 743, and the British, 878. In this contest, which is sometimes called the battle of Bridgewater, the victory is generally considered to have remained with the Americans. Colonel (afterwards General) Winfield Scott greatly distinguished himself in this engagement.

Lunéville, Peace of. A treaty of peace, concluded between Austria and the French Republic, February 9th, 1801. By this treaty the Emperor of Austria ceded to France the Belgic Provinces and the west bank of the Rhine as far as Holland, and acknowledged the independence of the Batavian, Cisalpine, Helvetic, and Ligurian Republics.

Lupercalia. A festival annually celebrated among the ancient Romans on February 15th, in honor of Lupercus, the god of fertility. According to Plutarch, however, it was instituted in honor of Romulus and Remus ; while Livy says that it was brought into Italy by Evander, the Arcadian. During this festival, the rites of which were of the most primitive sort, large numbers of goats and dogs were sacrificed and their skins cut up and twisted into thongs. The priests (called *Luperci*) ran through the city with these thongs, striking all persons (especially women) that placed themselves in their way in the hope of thereby rendering the god of fertility propitious to them. The celebration of the Lupercalia was abolished by Pope Gelasius (492–496) in 496.

" Forget not, in your speed, Antonius,
To touch Calphurnia ; for our elders say,
The barren, touched in this holy chase,
Shake off their sterile curse."
Julius Cæsar, i, 2.

Lusiads, The (*Portuguese, Os Lusiados, The Lusitanians*). The national epic poem of Portugal, written by Luis de Camoens (1524–1580), in honor of the Portuguese discoveries in India. Its hero is Vasco da Gama, the noted navigator, whose adventures, in rounding the Cape of Good Hope, constitute the main feature of the poem. *The Lusiads* appeared in 1572, and was dedicated to King Sebastian (1557–1578). It is in ten books, and is sometimes called the Epic of Commerce. See *Lusitania*.

" In this poem Camoens did for the Portuguese language what Chaucer did for English and Dante for Italian, and made himself, moreover, the interpreter of the deepest feelings and aspirations of the Portuguese nation."—*Chambers's Encyclopædia.*

Lusitania. The ancient name of Portugal, said by Pliny the Elder to be derived from *Lusus*, a companion of Bacchus in his travels, who established a colony in Portugal and named it *Lusitania* and the colonists *Lusians.* The word is used in modern poetry. See *Lusiads, The.*

Lutetia. The ancient name of Paris, —meaning a collection of mud-huts. At the time of the conquest of Gaul by Julius Cæsar (100–44 B.C.), Lutetia was the chief town of the tribe of the Parisii, settled on the banks of the Sequana (Seine). The Romans called it *Lutetia Parisiorum* (*i. e., the mud-town of the Parisii*), whence is derived the modern name Paris.

Luther's Hymn. See *Ein Feste Burg Ist Unser Gott.*

Lützen, Battle of.

(1) A memorable battle, during the "Thirty Years' War," fought on November 6th, 1632, between the Swedes, commanded by Gustavus Adolphus (1611–1632), and the Imperialists, led by Wallenstein. The victory remained with the Swedes, who, however, lost their King during the engagement.

(2) A sanguinary battle, fought on May 2nd, 1813, between 102,000 French, commanded by the first Napoleon, and 69,000 Russians and Prussians, led by Wittgenstein. The French were victorious ; but, owing to a lack of cavalry, were unable to follow up their success. The allies retired in good order, without the loss of a wagon or a gun. The French loss was about 12,000 and that of the allied forces, 20,000.

Luxembourg Palace. A famous palace in Paris, erected in 1615–1620 by Marie de Médicis, widow of Henry IV (1589–1610). It remained a royal residence until the time of the Revolution, when it was converted into a state-prison by the National Conven-

tion. There were confined Maréchal de Noailles and his wife, Vicomte de Beauharnais and his wife Josephine (afterwards Empress of the French), Hébert, Camille Desmoulins, Danton, Robespierre, the artist David, and others. In 1795, the building was called the *Palais du Directoire ;* and in 1799 this title was changed to that of the *Palais du Consulat.* In the time of the Empire (1804–1814), it was named the *Palais du Sénat-Conservateur*, and during the reigns of Louis XVIII (1814–1824), Charles X (1824–1830), and Louis Philippe (1830–1848), it was styled the *Chamber of Peers.* In the days of Napoleon III (1852–1870), it again became known as the *Palais du Sénat.* After the destruction of the *Hôtel de Ville* in 1871, the Luxembourg Palace was occupied by the Prefect of the Seine ; but in 1879 the Chambers removed their sittings from Versailles to Paris, and the Senate once more took possession of its old quarters. The famous Gardens of the Luxembourg, adjoining the palace, are adorned with fountains, statues, terraces, and balustrades, and resemble the Boboli Gardens at Florence. Part of the palace is occupied by the Luxembourg Gallery, a superb collection of paintings and statuary. See *Musée du Luxembourg.*

Luxor, Temple of. A stupendous temple in Egypt, situated at Luxor, two miles south of Karnak. It was founded by Amenophis III of the XVIIIth dynasty, and was enlarged by succeeding monarchs. These ruins have remained covered with rubbish for centuries, and it is only within recent years that excavations have been made by the Egyptian Government. The temple, although inferior in size and majesty to that at Karnak, is by some authorities reckoned superior in point of architectural merit. Two granite monoliths—one of which still remains —formerly stood in front of the palace; its companion now adorns the Place de la Concorde in Paris. Karnak and

Luxor were at one time united by an avenue of sphinxes—80 feet wide. See *Karnak, Temple of ; Obelisk of Luxor.*

Lyceum. A place at Athens, near the banks of the Ilissus, consecrated to *Apollo Lyceius (the Wolf-slayer).* It was famous for its shady woods and beautiful gardens, but especially for its gymnasium, where Aristotle taught. The word " lyceum " was applied in mediæval times to certain higher Latin schools where the Aristotelian philosophy was taught. In the United States it denotes any literary association organized for popular instruction, and is also applied to any hall or building used for that purpose. Aristotle's philosophy is often called the " philosophy of the Lyceum."

Lycurgus's Laws. A code of laws drawn up by Lycurgus *(fl.* 850 B.C.,) the Spartan lawgiver, and adopted by the Lacedæmonians. Lycurgus rescued his country from anarchy, remodelled the constitution, and exacted from the citizens of Sparta a promise not to make any changes in his laws until his return. He then went into voluntary exile, and was never seen afterwards.

Lynch Law. A term said to be derived from the name of Charles Lynch (1726–1796), a patriotic Virginian, who, in company with Robert Adams and Thomas Calloway, undertook to inflict summary punishment on outlaws and Tories during the War of the Revolution. These punishments were limited to flogging and banishment. The origin of this term, however, is in doubt.

" The phrase has been variously traced to a Virginia soldier and to a Virginia farmer of that name, to one Lynch, who was sent out from England about 1687 to suppress piracy, and to a mayor of Galway in Ireland ; while yet another tradition refers it to Lynch Creek, in North Carolina, where the forms of a court-martial and execution were gone through over the lifeless body of a Tory, who had already been precipitately hanged to prevent a rescue."—*Chambers's Encyclopædia.*

30

M

Macadamizing. A system of road-building devised by John Loudon Macadam (1756–1836), a Scotch engineer, who, to acquire the requisite knowledge, traveled 30,000 miles and spent £5000. This method — introduced in 1810—consists in laying small pieces of flint or granite, from one to two ounces in weight, at a depth of from six to eight inches. This " road-metal," as it is termed, is then thoroughly pressed and rolled, and produces a covering as solid as a wall. Macadam also introduced the practice of making the centre of the road higher than the sides, by which means the drainage of highways was greatly improved. He was appointed Surveyor-general of Metropolitan Roads in 1827, and received a government grant of £10,000. He published, in 1819, an essay on *The Scientific Repair and Preservation of Public Roads.*

Macaronic Verse. A kind of humorous poetry, consisting of a mixture of Latin or Greek with words from living languages, to which are given the inflections of the dead tongues. Sometimes, however, the vernacular of the author is introduced in an unadulterated form. Although Odassi, or Odaxius, of Padua, born about 1450, was the originator of this kind of poetry, his disciple Teofilo Folengo (1491–1544), a Benedictine, who wrote under the name of Merlinus Coccaius, is generally considered to be the inventor of macaronic verse. He, at least, was the first to use the word in this sense His *Maccaronea,* which appeared in 1517, is a mingling of Latin and Italian. It has considerable literary merit, and gave the author a respectable standing among the writers of his time. Macaronic poetry was cultivated in Italy, France, and Germany, and was introduced into England during the reign of Henry VII (1485–1509). Excellent specimens may be found in *Le Malade Imagi-*

naire, and in the *Epistolæ Obscurorum Virorum*. The best-known English example is the *Polemo-Middinia* (1683), ascribed to Drummond of Hawthornden.

Macaulay's New Zealander. An imaginary figure referred to by Lord Macaulay (1800–1859), in his review of Ranke's *History of the Popes*.

The words of the passage are as follows :

"She [the Roman Catholic Church] was great and respected before the Saxon had set foot on Britain, before the Frank had passed the Rhine, when Grecian eloquence still flourished in Antioch, when idols were still worshipped in the temple of Mecca. And she may still exist in undiminished vigor when some traveller from New Zealand shall, in the midst of a vast solitude, take his stand on a broken arch of London Bridge to sketch the ruins of St. Paul's."

This last sentence is said to be a repetition of similar ones by Horace Walpole and Mrs. Barbauld. Allusions to the "Decay of Empire" in Great Britain may also be found in the writings of Volney, Shelley, Kirke White, and Goldsmith; but to Macaulay is due the credit of making this thought famous in English literature.

Maccabees. The name of a family in Syria, which, during the second century before Christ, resisted the persecutions inflicted upon the Jewish nation by the Seleucidæ. After the death of Mattathias, the leader of the revolt, in 166 B.C., his son, Judas Maccabæus, defeated the Syrians in three battles, reconquered Jerusalem, purified the Temple, and restored the worship of Jehovah. He was slain in ambush in 161 B.C., and was succeeded by his brother Jonathan, who was raised to the dignity of high-priest, but was afterwards treacherously slain at Ptolemais in 144 B.C., by Tryphon, the guardian of the young prince Antiochus Theos. His brother Simon then succeeded to the leadership of the Commonwealth, and completely established the independence of the Jews.

After seven years of beneficent rule, he was foully murdered, together with his two sons, by his son-in-law Ptolemy, who vainly hoped to be chosen his successor. John Hyrcanus, son of Simon, was the next ruler. He renewed the alliance with Rome, conquered Idumæa, and took the title of king, 107 B.C. Syria became a Roman province in 63 B.C.

Macedonian Phalanx. A tactical organization invented by Philip (359–336 B.C.) of Macedon, about 360 B.C. The rank was 16 men deep. The men were armed with short swords and with spears 24 feet long, and were so arranged that the spears of those in the fifth rank projected three feet beyond the front rank. The front rank was accordingly protected by five formidable rows of spears. The Macedonian phalanx was especially suited for service against cavalry in the open plains of Asia, and proved of great service to Alexander the Great in his campaigns against Darius, King of Persia. See *Phalanx*.

Macedonia's Madman. A sobriquet conferred upon Alexander the Great (336–323 B.C.), King of Macedon, not only because of his lust of conquest, but also on account of his ungovernable passions and uncontrollable temper.

"Heroes are much the same, the point 's agreed,
From *Macedonia's Madman* to the Swede."
Pope.

McFingal. The title of a humorous epic sketch of the American Revolution by John Trumbull (1750–1831). It was modelled after Butler's *Hudibras*, and held the Tories of the time up to ridicule. John Adams predicted that it would "live as long as *Hudibras*." It was published in 1775, and acquired great popularity which, however, proved to be only temporary.

McFlimsey, Flora. The heroine of the poem, *Nothing to Wear*, a sharp but good-natured satire on the follies and extravagances of women's dress. It is by William Allen Butler (d. 1902), a lawyer of New York City.

Machiavellian Principles. The name given to certain principles of government promulgated by Niccolo Machiavelli (1469-1527) of Florence, and laid down in his famous work entitled *Del Principe (The Prince)*. The book appeared at Rome in 1532 ; and was translated into English in 1761.

"The broad scheme of the book is everywhere the same—viz., that for the establishment and maintenance of authority all means may be resorted to, and that the worst and most treacherous acts of the ruler, however unlawful in themselves, are justified by the wickedness and treachery of the governed. Such being the moral of the book, a question has arisen as to the intention of the writer, and a favourite theory for a time prevailed, that *The Prince* was but a satire upon absolutism, and was designed to serve the cause of liberty, of which Machiavelli was an ardent friend, by making arbitrary power odious and contemptible. This theory, however, besides being utterly irreconcilable with the tone of the work, is completely disproved by a letter of Machiavelli to his friend Vettori (1513), which was discovered only in 1810, and which shows that *The Prince* was written by Machiavelli in all seriousness, in order to recommend himself to the Medici (for whose private perusal it was designed, and not for publication) as a master in the art of government."—*Chambers's Encyclopædia*.

Madame Tussaud's. A famous wax-work exhibition in London, founded by Madame Tussaud (1760-1850), early in the last century, and still in existence. It contains, in addition to a large collection of wax-figures of ancient and modern notabilities, numerous relics of the first Napoleon, — comprising the military carriage (captured by the Prussians after Waterloo) in which he made the memorable Russian campaign ; the camp-bedstead used by him for almost six years at St. Helena ; his favorite garden-chair ; the cloak worn by him at Marengo ; and the cradle of the King of Rome. In the " Chamber of Horrors " may be seen the famous guillotine used in Paris during the French Revolution, and bought by Madame Tussaud from Samson, the grandson of the famous executioner, surnamed " Monsieur de Paris." It is estimated that upwards of 22,000 persons—including Louis XVI, Marie Antoinette, Madame Elizabeth, the Duke of Orleans, and Robespierre—were decapitated by this instrument.

Madame Véto. A nickname given to Marie Antoinette (1755-1793), during the French Revolution, in allusion to the great influence exercised by her over her husband, Louis XVI (1774-1789), whereby she frequently induced him to place his constitutional veto upon the acts of the Legislative Assembly. See *Monsieur Véto*.

Mad Anthony. A sobriquet conferred upon Major-General Anthony Wayne (1745-1796), on account of his intrepid courage and reckless valor during the American Revolutionary War. Although daring and impetuous in battle, he was nevertheless not lacking in prudence and judgment.

·Mad as a Hatter. See *Hatter, Mad as a*.

Mad Cavalier. A title bestowed upon Prince Rupert of Bavaria (1619-1682), nephew of Charles I (1625-1649) of England, and commander of the King's forces during a part of the Civil War. He displayed great energy and courage in battle ; but, unfortunately, his disregard of authority and impatience of advice resulted in his defeat in several engagements, and his consequent removal from the command of the Royalist army.

Madeleine, La (*Fr. The Magdalen*). A beautiful church in Paris, constructed after the model of a Greek temple. It forms a parallelogram, 350 feet long and 147 feet wide, and has a height of 54 feet. It stands upon a basement 23 feet high, and is surrounded by 52 massive Corinthian columns with richly carved capitals.

The building was commenced in 1764
—during the reign of Louis XV (1715-
1774)—and was designed for a parish
church. Owing to the Revolution,
work was suspended and was not resumed until the time of the Empire,
when Napoleon I (1804-1814) decided
to complete the edifice and convert it
into a Temple of Glory in honor of
the Grand Army. After the fall of
Napoleon, Louis XVIII (1814-1824)
proposed to convert the building into
an expiatory chapel to Louis XVI,
Louis XVII, and Marie Antoinette ;
but finally returned to the original intention of making it a church. The
work was continued in 1816, and the
building was finally completed in 1842,
at a cost of nearly $3,000,000. La
Madeleine contains some fine frescoes,
and several sculptures and paintings
illustrating events in the life of Mary
Magdalen. It is famed for its sacred
music on great church festivals and
during Passion Week.

Madman. A sobriquet bestowed
upon Sebastian (1557-1584), King of
Portugal, from his wild desire to emulate the warlike deeds of Alexander
the Great. He was slain in battle
against the Moors in Africa ; but his
countrymen refused to believe the report of his death, and declared that he
would eventually return and restore
his country to its former power and
glory.

Madman of the North. An epithet
conferred upon Charles XII (1682-
1718) of Sweden, not only on account
of the rashness and impetuosity of his
character, but also because of his
strange eccentricities of conduct. He
was the most peculiar personage of the
18th century, and should be regarded,
as his biographer Voltaire has truly
said, as an old Norse Sea-King, born
ten centuries after his time. See *Brilliant Madman.*

Madonna della Candelabra (*It.
Madonna of the Candlestick*). A famous picture by Raphael Sanzio
(1483-1520), representing the Virgin
and Child, with an angel on each side
holding a lighted torch. It is supposed to have been painted in 1515,
and was at one time in the Borghese
Palace at Rome. It was afterwards
owned by Lucien Bonaparte, the Duke
of Lucca, and Mr. Monroe of England,
and finally came into the possession of
the Hon. H. Butler Johnstone of London. The *Madonna della Candelabra*
was exhibited at the Metropolitan
Museum of Art, New York City, in
1883.

Madonna della Sedia (*It. Madonna
of the Chair*). A famous Madonna by
Raphael Sanzio (1483-1520), in the
Pitti Palace at Florence. It is considered the loveliest of this artist's
Madonnas, and is perhaps the most
celebrated, owing to the many engravings and copies that have been made
of it. The Virgin is represented as
seated in a low chair, with the infant
Jesus in her arms, and the youthful
John the Baptist at her side. This
picture is sometimes known as the
Madonna della Seggiola (*It. Madonna
of the Low Chair*). See *Christian
Venus.*

"She is a beautiful Grecian or Circassian
Sultana ; her head is covered with a sort of
turban, while striped oriental stuffs of bright
colors and embroidered with gold wind
around her form ; she bends over her child
with the beautiful action of a wild animal,
and her clear eyes, without thought, look
you full in the face."—*Taine.*

Madonna di Foligno. A celebrated
altar-piece by Raphael Sanzio (1483-
1520), now in the Vatican at Rome.
It was painted for the Church of Ara
Cœli, and was placed over the high
altar there in 1511. In 1565, it was
removed to the convent of Foligno,
and, in 1797, was transferred to Paris.
It was restored to Italy in 1815, and
was placed in the Vatican, where it has
since remained. The painting is a
votive offering of Sigismund Conti,—
private secretary of Pope Julius I
(1503-1513),—and commemorates his
miraculous preservation when his lif

was endangered by a thunderbolt. In the background of the picture—below the figure of the Madonna—is represented the city of Foligno, the native place of Sigismund, whence its name.

Madonna di San Sisto.

A marvellous work of art painted in 1518 by Raphael Sanzio (1483–1520), as an altar-piece for the monastery of San Sisto at Piacenza, Italy, whence its name. It was purchased by Augustus III (1733–1763), Elector of Saxony and King of Poland, for $40,000 in 1753, and was placed in the Dresden Gallery where it still remains. The Virgin is represented as standing on the clouds and holding the infant Jesus in her arms. On the left of the picture is St. Sixtus, and on the right, St. Barbara. The two cherubs in the lower part of the painting are often called Raphael's "Afterthoughts." These figures are all of heroic size.

"This masterpiece of Raphael has, by many critics, been regarded as the first painting in the world. In force and sentiment, as an altar-piece, and in the ease and harmony of its composition, this work has hardly an equal; whilst in the dignity and grandeur of the Divine Mother, no work can be compared with it. The peculiarly 'divine' expression of the Madonna's face is due in part to an exaggerated breadth between the eyes, a characteristic which the Greek sculptors were wont to make use of to give divinity of expression to the statues of their gods, and partly to the non-focusing of the eyes, by which they are made to look at no particular point, but into infinite distance."—Loomis's *Index Guide*.

Maelström.

A famous whirlpool, or more properly a current, off the northwest coast of Norway, between Moskenäs and Mosken, two of the Lofoden Isles. This current flows alternately six hours from north to south and six hours from south to north, and produces angry whirls, the sound of which may at times be heard at a distance of several miles. The strait is navigated by vessels either at low tide or at high tide, and is generally traversed with little apprehension. When, however, the wind and tide are contrary, the passage becomes extremely dangerous, especially during a northwest wind or at the time of spring-tides. The stories of ships being engulfed in the vortex may be dismissed as fables, although a vessel once within the influence of the Maelström would probably either founder or be dashed upon the rocks. The depth of water, supposed at one time to be too great to admit of soundings, does not exceed 20 fathoms.

Mæonian Swan.

An appellation conferred upon Homer (*fl.* 1000 B.C.), the Greek poet, who was supposed by some to have been born in *Mæonia*, a district of Lydia, in Asia Minor. He is also called *Mæonides* and *Mæonius Senex*.

Mafia.

A secret society in Sicily, organized for private revenge, robbery, and opposition to all forms of government. It became prominent in 1860. It exacts from its members implicit obedience to the will of its leaders; absolute silence as to its membership, objects, and ends; and the rendering of succor—pecuniary or moral—to such of their colleagues as may be in distress. The Mafia controls elections, shields members from the consequences of their crimes, and even organizes strikes, and attempts to regulate the wages of workingmen. The efforts of the Italian government to extirpate this society have thus far failed; but many of its members have emigrated to America and settled in New York and New Orleans. In 1891, a dispute arose between Italy and the United States, in consequence of the action of some of the citizens of New Orleans in lynching certain members of the Mala Vita section of the Mafia, who had been tried for murder and acquitted. The difficulty was amicably settled, and the sum of $25,000 was paid by the government of the United States to that of Italy for the benefit of the heirs of the lynched Italians. See *Camorra.*

Magazine, First English. The first monthly magazine of the modern type published in England was brought out by Edward Cave in 1731, and was entitled *The Gentleman's Magazine.* Dr. Samuel Johnson was one of its contributors. This magazine still continues to flourish.

Magdeburg Hemispheres. The name given to two hollow hemispheres of brass, so made as to fit each other with an air-tight joint ; but separable at pleasure. If, however, the air within be exhausted by means of an air-pump, the external atmospheric pressure will no longer be counteracted by an expansive pressure from within, and considerable force will be required to effect their separation. They are so named from Magdeburg, a city in Germany, where Otto von Guericke, their inventor, lived. He constructed two hemispheres of copper, about two feet in diameter, and, having exhausted the air, found that it required the strength of several horses to pull them apart. See *Royal Library of Berlin.*

"In the Museum at Berlin the hemispheres used by Guericke in his experiments are preserved. They are of copper, and, by the author's measurements 22 inches interior diameter with a flange an inch wide, making the entire diameter 2 feet. Accompanying is a Latin book by the burgomaster describing numerous pneumatic experiments which he had performed, and containing a wood-cut representing three spans of horses on each side trying to separate the hemispheres." — Steele's *Physics.*

Magellanic Clouds. Two cloudy masses of light, oval in shape and unequal in size, seen at night in the heavens, in the vicinity of the South Pole. They are supposed to be nebulæ, or dense aggregations of stars, so far distant as to give to the unassisted eye the impression of cloud-like masses. They cover areas of about 42 and 10 square degrees respectively, and are so named in honor of Ferdinand Magellan (1470 – 1521), the great Portuguese

navigator, who first observed them in 1520, during his voyage around the globe.

Magenta, Battle of. A sanguinary battle of the Franco-Austrian War, fought on June 4th, 1859, near Magenta, a town in Lombardy, 18 miles west of Milan. There the French and Sardinians, 55,000 strong, commanded by Napoleon III, defeated the Austrians, 75,000 in number. The Austrians lost in this engagement 10,000 in killed and wounded, and 7000 prisoners, while the allied losses were only 4000. For his distinguished valor on the field of battle, General MacMahon was created a marshal of France and Duke of Magenta.

Magi. The name given to the hereditary priests of the ancient Persian religion. They were not only " the keepers of the sacred things, the learned of the people, the philosophers and servants of God," but also astrologers and diviners. They exercised a commanding influence in public affairs, superintended the education of the young, and were the constant companions of the sovereign. This order of priesthood, having lapsed into luxury and indolence, was reorganized by Zoroaster about 550 B.C., and reestablished on its ancient basis of simplicity and severity. During the rule of the Sassanian Kings, the Magi declined in importance, and became reduced to the ranks of wandering fortune-tellers and quacks. The word finally came to be used as a generic term for astrologers in the East, and was given to the " Wise Men " that went to Bethlehem to seek the infant Jesus. See *Wise Men of the East.*

Magician of the North. A title assumed by Johann Georg Hamann (1730–1788), a German thinker and writer of original power and genius. See *Great Magician of the North.*

"The great *Hamann* is a deep sky full of telescopic stars, with many a nebula which no eye can resolve."—*Jean Paul Richter.*

Magna Charta (*Lat. Great Charter*). A famous charter, or document, extorted from King John (1199–1216) by the barons of England, and designed to protect the liberties of the English people against the encroachments of the Crown. It was sealed by the King at Runnymede, near Windsor, on June 15th, 1215; and is justly regarded as the foundation-stone of British liberty. The fundamental parts of the Charter were derived from certain Saxon charters continued in force by Henry I (1100–1135) and his successors. The original MS. of *Magna Charta* is lost, but the copy preserved in Lincoln Cathedral is considered to be the most accurate one in existence. A fac-simile of it, reproduced by photographs in the *National MSS.*, was published in 1865. See *Runnymede*.

"The most important provisions [of *Magna Charta*] are: (1) no scutage or aid shall be raised, except in the case of the king's captivity, the knighting of his eldest son, or the marriage of his eldest daughter, except by the general council of the kingdom; (2) no freeman shall be imprisoned or disseised, outlawed or proceeded against other than by the legal judgment of his peers, or by the law of the land; (3) that right or justice shall not be sold, delayed or denied to any; (4) that the civil court shall be stationary, and not follow the king's person. Other provisions were directed against the abuse of the power of the king as lord paramount, the tyranny of the forest laws, and grievances connected with feudal tenure."—*Pearl Cyclopædia.*

Magna Græcia (*Lat. Great Greece*). The name given, in ancient times, to the Greek colonies of southern Italy, most of which were founded during the 8th century B.C. According to some authorities, the Greek colonies in Sicily were also included under this designation. The following is a list of the principal Greek colonies in southern Italy, with the dates of their foundation.

(1) Cumæ	1034	B.C.
(2) Sybaris	720	"
(3) Crotona	710	"
(4) Locri	710	"
(5) Tarentum	707	"
(6) Rhegium	—	"
(7) Metapontum	700–650	B.C.
(8) Siris	—	"
(9) Velia	540	"

Magnet. This word is generally said to be derived from *Magnesia*, a city of Lydia, in Asia Minor, where the peculiar properties of the magnetic ore of iron—known as lodestone—were first discovered. According to another authority, however, the origin of the word is traced to *Magnes*, a shepherd, who was detained on Mount Ida by the iron in his shoes, and found himself unable to move.

Magnetic Mountain. A lodestone mountain, described in the *Arabian Nights' Entertainments* as attracting all vessels to it, by virtue of the iron in them. When ships came within a certain distance of this mountain, the magnetic attraction proved so great that it drew all the nails and bolts from their sides and bottoms, and caused the vessels to fall apart and sink. This fable of the "Magnetic Mountain" is found in the writings of several Arabic authors, and appealed strongly to the imagination of the romancers of the Middle Ages.

"The mountain is very rugged; on the top of it there is a dome of fine brass, supported by pillars of the same metal; and on the top of the dome stands a horse, likewise of brass, with a rider on his back, who has a plate of lead fixed to his breast, upon which some talismanic characters are engraved. There is a tradition that this statue is the chief cause why so many ships and men have been lost and sunk in this place; and people say that it will continue to be fatal to all those who have the misfortune to come near it until the statue is thrown down."—*Arabian Nights' Entertainments* (*The Story of the Third Calender*).

Magnificat. A canticle in praise of the Virgin Mary, used in the evening service of the Roman Catholic, Lutheran, and Anglican Churches. It is so named from its first word in the *Vulgate* (*Luke* i, 46): *Magnificat anima mea Dominum* (*Lat. My soul doth magnify the Lord*). It was first used in the public worship of the Church about 506 A.D.

Mahábhárata. A famous Hindu epic poem — probably the longest in existence — containing, in its present form, 110,000 couplets of 32 syllables each. Although traditionally ascribed to Vyása, it is evident that this vast work is the production of successive ages, and not the composition of a single author. Moreover, the word " Vyása " means simply the distributor or arranger. The poem relates the struggles of the celebrated families of the Kauravas and Pándavas for the supremacy, — ending in the success of the latter, and the establishment of their rule over the northern part of India. The date of this poem is involved in obscurity, although some critics have assigned to it the year 500 B.C. The *Mahábhárata* contains, in addition to the narrative portions, much incidental matter relating to the philosophy, religion, law, and morals of the ancient Hindus, and constitutes a complete cyclopædia of India in early times. See *Ashtavakra ; Bhagavad-Gîta ; Rámáyana.*

Mahdi, El (*Ar. The Well-Directed One*). The Messiah of Islâm, not mentioned in the *Koran*, but said to have been promised by Mohammed. According to the prediction of the Prophet, the Mahdi will rule the world temporally and spiritually, and convert it to the true faith. The Shiites believe that he has already appeared, but the Sunnites claim that he is yet to come. Among the many that have arisen, claiming to be the Mahdi, may be mentioned Mohammed Ahmed (1841(?)–1885), who raised an insurrection in eastern Soudan in 1881. His victorious career caused the annihilation of Hicks Pasha's army in 1883, the capture of Khartoum in 1885, and the death of General Gordon in the same year.

Mahomet's Coffin. According to tradition, Mahomet's coffin, in the Mausoleum, or Hujrah, of Medina, rests suspended in mid-air. The faithful say that it is supported by relays of angels, relieved every hour; while others assert that the coffin is made of iron and is held in place by two magnets. The story is an idle Christian fable. See *Tomb of Mohammed.*

" Burckhardt visited the sacred enclosure, and found the ingenuity of science useless in this case, as the coffin is not suspended at all."—Brewer's *Dictionary of Phrase and Fable.*

Mahrattas. A Hindu people inhabiting western and central India, where they founded an empire in 1674. In 1761, they were defeated, with a loss of 50,000 men, on the field of Panipat by Ahmed Shah Duráni, ruler of Afghanistan. In 1804, they became involved in a long and bloody war with the British, and in 1818 were reduced to a state of servitude. One chief, however, named Sindhia, held out for a number of years, but was finally subdued in 1843.

" Where in wild *Mahratta*-battle fell my
    father evil-starr'd ; —
I was left a trampled orphan, and a selfish
    uncle's ward."
           Locksley Hall (Tennyson).

Maiden Queen. An appellation popularly conferred upon Queen Elizabeth (1558–1603) of England, who died unmarried after a reign of nearly 45 years. See *Virgin Queen.*

Maid Marian. The name assumed by Matilda, daughter of Robert, Lord Fitzwalter. She was the paramour of Robin Hood, the famous English outlaw, and is said to have been poisoned by King John (1199–1216) because she rejected his suit. Douce believes Maid Marian to be a creation of the imagination, and says that " none of the materials that constitute the more authentic history of Robin Hood prove the existence of such a character in the shape of his mistress."

" Robin's mistress dear, his loved *Marian*,
    Was sovereign of the woods, chief lady of
    the game ;
    Her clothes tucked to the knee, and
    dainty-braided hair,
With bow and quiver armed."
           Drayton.

The term " Maid Marian " was frequently used to denote a personage dressed in girl's clothes, and introduced into the morris-dances as the Queen of the May. She wore a golden crown and carried a flower in her left hand. Hence the use of the expression to describe a woman of bold and masculine character.

Maid of Athens. The title by which Lord Byron (1788–1824) addressed Theresa Macri, a beautiful Athenian maiden, in his song of the same name. Twenty-four years after the poem was written, an Englishman sought out the " Maid of Athens," and found her living in abject poverty, surrounded by a numerous family, and bereft of every trace of her former beauty.

> " *Maid of Athens*, ere we part,
> Give, oh give me back my heart!
> Or, since that has left my breast
> Keep it now, and take the rest!
> Hear my vow before I go,
> Ζώη μου', σᾶς ἀγαπῶ."

Maid of Bath. A sobriquet conferred upon Miss Linley, an accomplished and charming singer, who, in 1772, became the wife of Richard Brinsley Sheridan, the famous orator and dramatist.

Maid of Orleans. A surname given to Joan of Arc (1411–1431), because of her success in raising the siege of Orleans, which feat she accomplished in one week.

Maid of Perth. See *Fair Maid of Perth*.

Maid of Saragossa. An epithet conferred upon Agustina Zaragoza, a maiden famous for her heroism at the siege of Saragossa, Spain, in 1808–1809. After the fall of her lover, she calmly mounted the battery and worked the gun in his stead.

Lord Byron has commemorated this incident in the following lines :

> " Her lover sinks—she sheds no ill-timed tear ;
> Her chief is slain—she fills his fatal post ;
> Her fellows flee—she checks their base career ;
> The foe retires—she heads the sallying host ;
> Who can avenge like her a lover's ghost ?
> Who can avenge so well a leader's fall ?
> What maid retrieve when man's flush'd hope is lost ?
> Who hang so fiercely on the flying Gaul,
> Foil'd by a woman's hand, before a batter'd wall ? "
>
> *Childe Harold*, i, lvi.

Maid of the Mist. The name of a little steamer that formerly navigated the Niagara River below the Falls, and served to convey adventurous tourists as near to the cataract as safety permitted. In 1867, her owner, fearing that the little craft might be seized for debt, in company with two other men, ran the *Maid of the Mist* through the whirlpool-rapids into the placid waters of Lake Ontario,—out of the sheriff's jurisdiction. During this perilous passage, she lost her smokestack, and, for a part of the time, was submerged from stem to stern ; but finally emerged from her trying ordeal without serious injury. The name *Maid of the Mist* is applied, at the present time, to a small steamer that conveys tourists nearly to the foot of the Horseshoe Fall.

Maine Law. The name given, in the State of Maine, to an act " to prohibit drinking-houses and tippling-shops." It was passed in May, 1851; received the signature of the governor on June 2nd; and was first enforced at Bangor on July 4th of the same year. This law was re-enacted, in all its parts, in 1858, and was made more stringent in 1867, and again in 1870. It was so amended in 1872 as to bring cider, and wine made from grapes grown in the State, within the prohibition. In 1884, an amendment was added to the constitution prohibiting forever the sale of intoxicating liquors within the limits of the State. Since 1851, the expression "Maine Law" has been used colloquially to denote any State enactment prohibiting the sale of intoxicating drinks.

Maison Carrée (*Fr. Square House*). A beautiful Corinthian temple at Nîmes, in southern France, erected during the time of the Roman occupation of the country. It has been carefully restored ; and is used, at the present time, as a museum. The structure is rectangular in shape, measuring 85 by 45 feet, and is exquisite in its proportions and elegant in every detail. It contains some beautiful statues and several fine paintings. The *Maison Carrée* was at one time attributed to Augustus (27 B.C.–14 A.D.); but a closer study of its architecture has led to the opinion that it was erected during the period of the Antonines (138–180 A.D.). It is said to have suggested to Thomas Jefferson the plan of the State Capitol at Richmond, Virginia.

Maison Dorée (*Fr. Golden House*). A famous café standing on the Boulevard des Italiens, Paris. It derives its name from the liberal amount of gold-leaf used in the decoration of its façade. A restaurant of the same name occupied a fine mansion on Union Square, New York City, during the "sixties."

Majolica. Majolica is the Italian name for *Majorca* (one of the Balearic Isles), and was given to a kind of coarse enamelled pottery of the Moors, —introduced into Italy after the conquest of that island by the Pisans in 1115 A.D. Lucca della Robbia of Florence is said to have been the first to use stanniferous glaze on majolica ware, about 1425. Also written *Maiolica*.

Major Prophets. The name given to the *Old Testament* prophets Isaiah, Jeremiah, Ezekiel, and Daniel, on account of the length of their writings as compared with those of the "Minor Prophets." The term is also applied to the books containing their prophecies. According to the Jewish classification of the books of the *Old Testament*, the "Major Prophets" include *Isaiah, Jeremiah*, and *Ezekiel*,—*Daniel* being numbered among the *Hagiographa*. See *Minor Prophets*.

Malachite. A native green carbonate of copper, well adapted for purposes of ornament, and capable of receiving a high degree of polish. It is generally sawed into thin slabs, and is used as a veneer for table-tops, mantels, and other kinds of household decoration. A mass of solid malachite weighing about 25 tons was found in the Ural Mountains about 1835. The ancients used malachite as a talisman to protect infants against the baleful influences of witchcraft and sorcery.

"*Malachite* . . . varies in colour from emerald to grass-green, and exhibits all degrees of transparency down to perfect opacity. It takes a high polish, and when in large masses is cut into tables, snuff-boxes, vases, etc."—Watts's *Dictionary of Chemistry*.

Malakhoff. A famous hill and redoubt, forming one of the principal defenses of the city of Sebastopol during the Crimean War (1854–1856). It was unsuccessfully attacked by the allied French and English on June 17th–18th, 1855, but was finally carried by assault by the French and Sardinians, after five hours' desperate fighting, on September 8th of the same year. The French and Sardinian loss was 1646 killed, 4500 wounded, and 1400 missing. See *Redan*.

Malbrouk. The hero of an ancient French song of the same name, identified in the popular mind with John Churchill (1650–1722), Duke of Marlborough, famous for his victories over the French. According to Châteaubriand, however, the music is of Arabic origin, while the story is as old as the Crusades, and narrates the exploits of one Mambron, a crusader, who was killed in battle, and whose return was vainly awaited by his wife. The song became popular in France shortly before the Revolution (1789), and was sung to the son of Louis XVI by his foster-mother, Mme. Poitrine. It was a favorite also with Napoleon I, who, according to Las Casas, was heard to hum the air a few years before his death. Arago says that when Monge, the French savant who accompanied Napoleon to Egypt, sang it to a company of Arabs at Cairo, they immediately recognized it.

" *Malbrouk* s'en va-t-en guerre,
Mironton, mironton, mirontaine ;
Malbrouk s'en va-t-en guerre,
Ne sait quand reviendra,
Il reviendra z'à paques—
Mironton, mironton, mirontaine,
Ou à la Trinité."

Malingerer. "This word, brought much into use by the exigencies of our civil war, is from the French 'malin gré,' and signifies a soldier who from 'evil will' shirks his duty by feigning sickness, or otherwise rendering himself incapable: in plain words, a poltroon."—*Gleanings for the Curious* (Bombaugh).

Mall.

(1) A broad avenue, planted with rows of elms, limes, and planes, on the north side of St. James's Park, London. It was at one time the fashionable resort of the city, and derives its name from the French game of *paillemaille*, formerly played there. This sport was introduced into England during the reign of Charles I (1625–1649), and may be regarded as the forerunner of modern croquet.

(2) A stately promenade, shaded with graceful elms, and adorned with statues and groups of sculpture, in Central Park, New York City. It is about a quarter of a mile in length and 200 feet in width, and extends to the Terrace—the chief architectural feature of the Park. See *Pall Mall*.

Malmaison. A château on the left bank of the Seine, ten miles west of Paris, famous as the favorite residence of Josephine, wife of Napoleon I. Napoleon himself sought rest and relaxation at Malmaison during the period of the Consulate, and spent several days there after the disaster of Waterloo. The palace was assigned to Josephine after her divorce in 1809, and there she died on the 29th of May, 1814. Malmaison was owned for a time by Queen Christina of Spain, and was purchased and restored by Napoleon III in 1861. The Germans, while besieging Paris, repulsed a sortie made there under General Ducrot, on October 21st, 1870. Malmaison fell into decay after the Franco-German War, and was offered at auction a few years ago. Fortunately, it was purchased by M. Osiris, a wealthy Parisian, who resolved to restore the château to its former condition and to present it to the French Government as a museum of Napoleonic relics. This worthy object has now been accomplished.

Malplaquet, Battle of. A bloody battle fought at Malplaquet in northern France, on September 11th, 1709, between the allies commanded by the Duke of Marlborough and Prince Eugene, and the French under Marshal Villars. The French were utterly routed with a loss of 12,000 men, while the allied loss exceeded 20,000.

Malthusian Theory. See *Essay on the Principle of Population*.

Malvern Hill, Battle of. The name given to the last of the "Seven Days' Battles" of the Peninsular campaign, during the American Civil War. It was fought on July 1st–2nd, 1862, between 90,000 Federals commanded by General McClellan and 60,000 Confederates under General Lee. The battle resulted in a repulse of the Confederate forces with a loss of 900 killed and 3500 wounded. The Federal loss was 375 killed and 1800 wounded. McClellan failed to take advantage of this success, and continued his retreat to Harrison's Landing.

Mambrino. A Moorish king, whose imaginary exploits are related in the poems of Bojardo and Ariosto. He was famed for his possession of an enchanted helmet of gold, which rendered its wearer invisible. See *Helmet of Invisibility* (2).

Mamelon (*Lat. mamma, breast*). A fortified mound, forming one of the defenses of Sebastopol during the Crimean War (1854-1856). It was captured by the French on June 7th, 1855. Artificial mounds, used as fortifications and called *mamelons*, from their resemblance to a woman's breast, were common at the siege of Sebastopol.

Mamelukes (*prop. Mamlûks*). Originally, Turkish and Circassian slaves imported into Egypt by the Sultan Es-Sâlih-Ayyûb in 1240 A.D., and formed by him into a body-guard. In 1250, they murdered Touran-Shah, the reigning sultan, and placed one of their own number upon the throne. From that year until the Ottoman conquest of Egypt in 1517—a period of 267 years—the country was ruled exclusively by Mameluke sultans, whose reigns were generally stained with violence and bloodshed. After the establishment of Turkish supremacy, the Mamelukes gradually declined in power and importance. They were disastrously defeated by Napoleon Bonaparte in 1798, at the battle of the Pyramids, and, after the French occupation of Egypt, they retreated into Nubia. On the retirement of the French and English from the country, the Mamelukes returned and, aided by the Arnauts, reconquered Egypt from the Turks. In 1805 and 1811, they were virtually exterminated by the Turkish Pasha, Mehemet Ali, at Cairo, and their power was finally broken. The remnant escaped to Nubia, but were massacred in 1820.

Mamertine Prison. A famous state-prison of ancient Rome,—for a long time the only one existing in the city. It is situated on the slope of the Capitoline Hill, and consists of two cells—one above the other—excavated in the living rock. The upper cell is said to have been constructed by Ancus Martius about 600 B.C., and the lower cell by Servius Tullius in 578 B.C. Jugurtha is said to have been starved to death by Marius in the Mamertine Prison ; and there also Vercingetorix, the commander of the Gauls, Sejanus, the minister and favorite of Tiberius, the accomplices of Catiline, and Simeon Barjoras, the defender of Jerusalem, were put to death.

According to Christian tradition, Peter and Paul were imprisoned there. The visitor is shown the pillar to which the apostles were chained for months ; the dent in the stone-wall made by Peter's head when thrust against it by his jailer; and the spring of water that gushed forth miraculously, and furnished the apostle with the water needed to baptize his jailers. Unfortunately for the story, Plutarch says that this spring was in existence 150 years before the event. The Mamertine Prison is reached through the Church of San Pietro in Carcere, which has been built over it.

Mammon. The Syrian god of riches. The word is used in the *New Testament* to denote either wealth or the personification of wealth. Milton makes *Mammon* one of the principal fallen angels, and thus describes him :

" *Mammon*, the least erected Spirit that fell
From Heav'n : for e'en in Heav'n his looks and thoughts
Were always downward bent, admiring more
The riches of Heav'n's pavement, trodden gold,
Than aught divine or holy else enjoy'd
In region beatific."
Paradise Lost, i, 679-684.

Mammoth Cave. A vast cavern in Kentucky, situated about 85 miles southwest of Louisville. It is the largest cave known,—extending below the surface of the earth for a distance of ten miles, although the various avenues and passages already explored have a total length of about 175 miles. The main portion of the cave is 4 miles long, and varies in width from 40 to 300 feet. It contains a vast series of halls, domes, cloisters, grottos, and caverns, to which appropriate names have been given. There are also several streams and lakes, among which may be mentioned the River Styx, Echo River, Lake Lethe, and the Dead Sea. The air within is pure and healthful, while the temperature remains at 52–56° Fahrenheit, throughout the year. The curiosities of the cave include eyeless fish and crawfish, and blind insects. Professor Shaler asserts that the carboniferous limestone forming the Mammoth Cave covers an area of 8000 square miles, and contains 100,000 miles of open caverns beneath it. Mammoth Cave was accidentally discovered by a hunter in 1809, and is annually visited by 5000 tourists. See *Echo River; Howe's Cave*.

Manchester School. The term applied to a party of English Radicals, organized at Manchester about 1848. It was an outgrowth of the "Anti-Corn-Law League," and advocated resistance to government interference, electoral reform, free-trade, non-intervention in foreign affairs, and general economy. Richard Cobden (1804–1865) and John Bright (1811–1889) were its foremost representatives.

Manchester Ship-Canal. A famous ship-canal connecting the city of Manchester, England, with the sea. It was commenced in November, 1887, and opened for navigation in May, 1894,—at a cost of about £15,000,000. The canal is 35½ miles in length, has an average depth of 26 feet, an average width of 172 feet, and contains three locks, or rather three sets of locks. The time required to make the entire

passage, allowing 25 to 35 minutes for passing through the locks, is about seven hours. See *Bridgewater Canal*.

Mandats. See *Assignats*.

Man-Eating Tree. The man-eating tree of Madagascar is simply a product of the imagination. Mr. Frank Vincent, the distinguished American traveler, who, within recent years, has spent considerable time in Madagascar, pronounces the tree a fake, and says that all accounts of it are the purest Munchausenism. He investigated the matter carefully for his own personal satisfaction, during his stay on the island, and found that all tales told of the existence of the "man-eating tree" were entirely without foundation.

Manes. The name given by the ancient Romans to the souls of the departed. They were regarded as gods, and were worshipped with divine honors. At certain seasons sacrifices were offered to these spirits, and on February 19th of each year a general festival, called *Feralia* or *Parentalia*, was celebrated in honor of all the Manes. On that occasion, it was the duty of all children and heirs to offer sacrifices to the spirits of their parents and benefactors. The term *Manes* was also applied to the benevolent gods of the Lower World, in contrast to the malevolent spirits known as *Larvæ* or *Lemures*. See *Lares; Penates*.

Man in the Moon. The name given to a fanciful figure observed on the surface of the moon, when looked at with the naked eye. When examined with a telescope, however, these outlines resolve themselves into shadows cast by the lunar mountains. This figure is supposed to represent a man leaning on a fork, on which is supported a bundle of sticks, for gathering which on Sunday he was imprisoned in the moon. Chaucer, Shakespeare, and other poets refer to this superstition; and in *Numbers* xv, 32–36, we read of a man that was stoned to death for gathering sticks on the Sabbath. According to many authorities, this passage has given rise to the fable of the " Man in the Moon."

Man-Milliner. A nickname given to Henry III (1574-1589), King of France, who neglected affairs of state and employed his time in devising new fashions in dress. See *Mignon*.

Mannlicher Rifle. A breech-loading magazine rifle in use at the present time in the armies of Austria-Hungary, Brazil, Bulgaria, Ecuador, Greece, Holland, Peru, Roumania, Russia, and Siam.

Man of Blood. A name applied to Charles I (1625-1649), King of England, by the Puritans, because he waged war against Parliament. The expression " Bloody Man " (*Heb. Man of Blood*) is found in *2 Samuel* xvi, 7, and is there applied to King David.

Man of Blood and Iron. An appellation bestowed upon Otto von Bismarck (1815-1898), Prime-Minister of Prussia, in allusion to his remark that the vexed question between Austria and Prussia—resulting in the War of 1866—could be settled only by " blood and iron."

Man of Chios. A title bestowed upon the poet Homer (*fl.* 1000 B.C.), who lived in the city of Chios, on the island of the same name, in the Ægean Sea, and was possibly born there. It is now called *Chio* by the natives, and has been italianized into *Scio*.

Byron speaks of Homer, in the *Bride of Abydos*, Canto II, as

" The blind old man of *Scio's* rocky isle."

Man of December. An appellation conferred upon Napoleon III (1852-1870), in allusion to the *coup d' état* of December 2nd, 1851, which led to his elevation to the imperial throne in the following year.

Man of Destiny. An epithet conferred upon Napoleon Bonaparte (1769-1821), who declared that all his actions were guided by fate and that he was the chosen instrument of destiny.

At a public banquet given at Buffalo, New York, in the spring of 1883, Grover Cleveland, then Governor of the State, was introduced by the toast-master, Congressman Farquhar, as the "Man of Destiny." The appellation clung to him, and was fully justified by his subsequent political successes.

Man of Ross. A sobriquet bestowed by Alexander Pope upon John Kyrle (1664-1754) of Ross, Herefordshire, England, on account of the many philanthropic acts performed by him in the neighborhood of his estate.

Man of Sedan. Napoleon III (1852-1870) is so called in allusion to the battle of Sedan—fought August 29th-September 1st, 1870—where he was signally defeated and suffered the loss of his empire. His dying words to his life-long friend, Dr. Conneau, were : " *Étiez-vous à Sedan?* " (" *Were you at Sedan?* ")

Man of Sin. An expression found in *2 Thessalonians* ii, 3, and variously interpreted by Christian writers.

" Whitby says the ' Man of Sin ' means the Jews as a people.
"Grotius says it means Caius Cæsar or else Caligula.
" Wetstein says it is Titus.
" Olshausen thinks it is typical of some one yet to come.
" Roman Catholics say it means Antichrist.
" Protestants think it refers to the pope.
"The Fifth-Monarchy men applied it to Cromwell."—Brewer's *Reader's Handbook*.

Man of the People. A sobriquet conferred upon Charles James Fox (1749-1806), the English statesman and orator.

Man on Horseback. A nickname popularly conferred upon Georges Ernest Jean Marie Boulanger (1837-1891), the famous French agitator and demagogue, from the fact that he was rarely seen in public except when mounted on his favorite black charger. For some years he enjoyed great popularity, and was by many regarded as the coming man of France, but having been charged by the Senate with appropriating, while Minister of War, the sum of 250,000 francs for purposes of his own propaganda, he fled to England and afterwards retired to Belgium, where he committed suicide.

The phrase " Man on Horseback " is also used to denote any person that curbs the violence of mob-rule, and re-establishes law and order. See *Robespierre on Horseback.*

" The *Man on Horseback* is not a demagogue ; he is an organizer. He restores order out of chaos, he reinstitutes legal forms and the courts ; by his will and power he checks the violence of mobs ; if the currency has been debased, and it usually has, he restores it. He does all this without argument, without debate, but nobody notices that he is using a despotic power, for all are on their knees thanking God for blessed peace and security once more. So they throw garlands before the advancing footsteps of their emperor. Thus the demagogue, ever professing his devotion to liberty, becomes in effect its executioner."— *New York Tribune.*

Mansion House. The official residence of the Lord Mayor of London, during his year of office. It was erected on the site of the Old Stocks Market in 1739–1752, at a cost of £42,638. The building has the general appearance of a Roman palazzo and contains, in addition to a long suite of state- and reception-rooms, the famous Egyptian Hall, an apartment used for public and private banquets, and capable of seating 400 guests. It was designed by the Earl of Burlington from a description of an Egyptian chamber furnished by Vitruvius, and is adorned with several statues by British sculptors. The Mansion House contains an excellent collection of portraits and other paintings, and several fine pieces of statuary. Among its curiosities may be enumerated a huge state-bed that cost 3000 guineas, and a kitchen famous for its vast size.

Mantinea, Battle of. A famous battle, fought near Mantinea, a city of Arcadia, in 362 B.C., in which the Thebans, commanded by Epaminondas, defeated the combined forces of Lacedæmon, Athens, Achaia, Elis, and Arcadia. Epaminondas was killed in the moment of victory, and, with his death, the period of Theban supremacy in Greece came to an end.

Mantuan Bard. A sobriquet conferred upon Virgil (70–19 B.C.), the Roman poet, who was born at Mantua, Italy. See *Mantuan Swan.*

Mantuan Swan. An epithet conferred upon Virgil (70–19 B.C.), the Roman poet, who was a native of Mantua, Italy. See *Mantuan Bard.*

" Ages elapsed ere Homer's lamp appeared,
And ages ere the *Mantuan Swan* was heard ;
To carry Nature lengths unknown before,
To give a Milton birth, asked ages more."
          Cowper.

Man without a Skin. A nickname given by David Garrick to Richard Cumberland (1732–1811), the famous English dramatist, whose extreme sensitiveness of nature rendered him incapable of enduring even the slightest amount of unfavorable criticism.

Man with the Iron Mask. See *Iron Mask, Man with the.*

Manx Laws. The name given to the laws at present in force in the Isle of Man, many of which were enacted during the 6th century A.D. The Isle of Man has its own constitution and government, which is, to a certain extent, independent of the British Parliament. It has its own legislative body, styled the Court of Tynwald, consisting of two branches : (1) the Lieutenant-governor and Council, and (2) the House of Keys (or Keepers). The House of Keys was formerly self-elective ; but in 1866 an act of parliament was passed substituting election by the people every seventh year. All bills must be separately considered by each branch, and, after being passed by both, must receive the royal assent. According, however, to an ancient custom, they do not become laws until they have been promulgated in the English and Manx languages on Tynwald Hill. See *House of Keys.*

Marathon, Battle of. One of the most famous and extraordinary battles of ancient or modern times. It was fought (490 B.C.) on the plain of Marathon, 22 miles northeast of Athens, between 11,000 Greeks commanded by Miltiades and about 110,000 Persians under Mardonius, a lieutenant of Darius, King of Persia. The Persians were signally defeated, with a loss of 6400 men, and fled in terror to their ships. The Greek loss was only 192 men, and these were buried on the field under a large tumulus, or mound, which remains to the present day. Marathon is justly considered one of the decisive battles of the world.

"It broke forever the spell of Persian invincibility, which had previously paralyzed men's minds. It secured for mankind the intellectual treasures of Athens, the growth of free institutions, the liberal enlightenment of the Western world, and the gradual ascendency for many ages of the great principles of European civilization."

Marble Faun. See *Faun of Praxiteles.*

Marblehead Turkeys. Codfish are sometimes so called in Massachusetts. See *Cape Cod Turkeys.*

Marble Statue with Eyelashes. See *Ariadne, Sleeping.*

Marcus Aurelius, Statue of. A famous bronze equestrian statue, standing in the centre of the Piazza del Campidoglio, at Rome. It represents the Emperor as if about to address his soldiers, and is considered the finest specimen of ancient art in existence. Michael Angelo professed great admiration for this statue, and caused it to be removed from the front of the Lateran and placed in its present position, in 1538. During the Middle Ages, it was supposed to be a statue of Constantine; and this error, fortunate for the interests of art, doubtless preserved it from destruction. It is said that Michael Angelo, on a certain occasion, was so much impressed with the lifelike action of the horse, that he addressed to it the word *cammina* (*It.* go along).

Mardi-Gras (*Fr. Fat-Tuesday*). A name frequently applied to Shrove-Tuesday, the day before Ash-Wednesday, the first day of Lent. It is the last day of the carnival, and is noted for its merrymakings throughout Italy and the south of France. The celebrated Carnival of Mardi-Gras at New Orleans is celebrated with great splendor, and is, without doubt, the most picturesque festival in the United States. See *Carnival; Shrove-Tuesday.*

Marengo, Battle of. A desperate battle fought on June 14th, 1800, near Marengo, a town of northern Italy, between 30,000 French commanded by Napoleon Bonaparte and 30,500 Austrians under Melas. The French, through the opportune arrival of Desaix, achieved a glorious victory, but lost 7000 men — killed and wounded. The Austrian loss was 6000 killed, 12,000 taken prisoners, and 45 cannon. As a result of this battle, Bonaparte secured possession of twelve strong fortresses and became master of Italy.

Margaux, Château. A handsome Italian villa on the left bank of the Gironde, in the district of Medoc, France. It is in the centre of the famous vine district, and gives its name to one of the finest red wines produced. This is obtained from a small grape, similar to a black currant in flavor. See *Lafitte, Château.*

Marian Persecution. The name given to the persecution inflicted on the Protestants of England during the reign of Queen Mary (1553–1558). It is estimated that, within the period of three years, 277 persons were burned at the stake,— among whom were 5 bishops, 21 clergymen, 8 laymen, 84 tradesmen, 100 husbandmen, laborers, and servants, 55 women, and 4 children. The chief agents of the Queen were Bishops Gardiner and Bonner.

Marigold. This yellow flower was named in honor of Queen Mary (1553-1558) of England.

Mariners' Compass. See *Compass, Mariners'*.

Mariotte's Law. The name commonly given, on the continent of Europe, to the famous law of the compressibility of gases, discovered by Mariotte in 1679. It may be stated as follows : *The temperature remaining the same, the volume of a given quantity of gas is inversely as the pressure which it bears.* This law has been proved, within recent years, to be only approximately true. It was first discovered in 1662 by Robert Boyle, the celebrated physicist ; and is, on that account, known in England as "Boyle's Law." See *Boyle's Law*.

Mark Twain. The pseudonym adopted by Samuel Langhorne Clemens (*b.* 1835), the American humorist.

"The *nom-de-plume* of Mark Twain, derived from an expression used in sounding the lead on the Mississippi, is said by Mr. Clemens to have been at first used by a certain Captain Sellars, as a signature to paragraphs contributed by him to the 'New Orleans Picayune.' After his death it was adopted by Mr. Clemens, 'without asking permission of the proprietor's remains.' "— Wheeler's *Dictionary of the Noted Names of Fiction*.

Marlborough House. A palace in Pall Mall, London, erected by Sir Christopher Wren, in 1709-1710, for John Churchhill, first Duke of Marlborough. It was purchased by the Government in 1817, and, after being put to various uses, became the property and residence of the Prince of Wales (now Edward VII) in 1863.

Maroons. The name given to the fugitive negro slaves of Jamaica, who, after the conquest of the island by the English in 1655, fled to the mountains, and maintained a continuous warfare with the colonists for 140 years. In 1795 they were finally subdued, and a part of them were transported to Nova Scotia and afterwards to Sierra Leone. The remainder became free in 1834, and eventually fraternized with their manumitted brethren. The Bush negroes of Guiana — about 4000 in number — are also called Maroons. The word is said to be derived from the Spanish *cimmarron* (from *cima, mountain top*).

Marriage à la Mode. The name given to a series of six paintings by William Hogarth (1697-1764), depicting, with rare satire, a variety of occurrences in the high life of the time. They were sold at auction by the artist in 1750, for the modest sum of £126 (the frames alone having cost him over £24). In 1797, they realized the sum of £1381, and in 1824 were acquired by the National Gallery at London. They are generally considered to be the artist's masterpiece.

Marriage at Cana.

(1) A colossal painting (30 x 20 feet) by Paolo Cagliari (1528-1588), called *Paolo Veronese*, in the *Salon Carré* of the Louvre in Paris. It was painted in 1563, and is especially famous for the portraits of the noted persons introduced. Among these may be mentioned Francis I of France and his Queen, Eleanor; Mary, Queen of England ; Charles V of Germany ; Sultan Soliman ; and the artists Titian, Bassano, Paolo Veronese, and Tintoretto.

"Paolo Veronese was the real master of Rubens. His works, however, have their defects: he was, as Algarotti observes, careless in design, and in costume extremely licentious; but these faults are completely concealed by the absorbing magnificence of his coloring, which, added to his noble fancy and inexhaustible invention, renders his defects as a grain of sand in the balance."— *Wornum*.

(2) A famous painting by Jacopo Robusti (1512–1594), surnamed *Il Tintoretto*, in the sacristy of the Church of Santa Maria della Salute in Venice.

Tintoretto's motto was : "The coloring of Titian, the drawing of Michael Angelo."

Marriage-Knot, Origin of. The word "knot," as used in this sense, is said to be derived from *nid* or *nod*, a Norse rune-stave corresponding to our letter N, and meaning necessity or compulsion. At Scandinavian weddings, the bridegroom drew this rune-stave on the finger-nail of the bride, to denote her union with him in marriage.

Marriage of the Adriatic. See *Adriatic Sea Wedded to the Doge.*

Marriage of St. Catherine. A celebrated painting by Antonio Allegri da Correggio (1494–1534), in the *Salon Carré* of the Louvre in Paris. It represents the betrothal of the saint to the infant Jesus in the presence of the Virgin Mary and St. Sebastian, and is said to be connected with a domestic incident in the artist's life, viz., the marriage of his sister, Caterina Allegri, in 1519. The painting belonged at one time to Cardinal Mazarin, but was purchased from him by Louis XIV (1643–1715) and placed in the gallery of the Louvre.

Marriages. "According to Mulhall, in each year in England, 15 people out of every thousand marry. Of each 1000 men who marry, 861 are bachelors and 139 widowers, while of each 1000 women only 98 have been married before and 902 are spinsters ; 12 marriages out of 100 are second marriages. The average age at which men marry is 27.7 years, while the average age at which women marry is 25½ years. Out of every 1000 persons in England, 602 are unmarried, 345 are married, and 53 widowed. In England, over one-half of all the women between 15 and 45 are unmarried. In all countries about 5 per cent. of marriages prove barren. Among the English nobility 19 per cent. are childless. Married women live 2 years longer than single ones, although 1 in 70 dies in childbirth. If the mother dies first, the father survives 9½ years ; but if the father dies first, the survival of the mother is 11½ years as an average; 2441 births occur in England daily, about 33 for each 1000 inhabitants. February is the month in which the greatest number of births occur, June the month in which occur the fewest. The average number of births for each marriage is 4.33. Out of every 1000 births, 11 are twins and 45 are illegitimate."—*Everybody's Pocket Cyclopædia.*

Mars, Canals in. The name given to certain long, thin, straight lines seen on the surface of the planet Mars. They were first observed by M. Schiaparelli of Milan in 1879, and since that time have been carefully studied by many other astronomers. Some of them measure 3000 or 4000 miles in length, and more than 60 miles in width. From their tint they are generally assumed to be water-courses, although no reason exists for supposing them to be artificial.

Marseillaise Hymn. A French political hymn, the words and music of which were composed on April 24th, 1792, by Rouget de Lisle (1760–1836), a young French officer of engineers then stationed at Strasburg. It was called by him *Le Chant de l'Armée du Rhin*, but received its present name because sung with great fervor by a body of volunteers from Marseilles, who entered the French capital on July 20th of the same year and thus made the song known to the Parisians. This statement, however, is doubted by some. The *Marseillaise* was forbidden to be sung under the Restoration and the Second Empire, but speedily became the national song on the outbreak of the Franco-German War. Louis Philippe (1830–1848) pensioned the author in 1830. See "*Ça Ira*"; *Carmagnole.*

"There is no national air that will compare with the *Marseillaise* in sublimity and power : it embraces the soft cadences full of the peasant's home, and the stormy clangor of silver and steel when an empire is overthrown ; it endears the memory of the vine-dresser's cottage, and makes the Frenchman, in his exile, cry, 'La Belle France!' forgetful of the sword, and torch, and guillotine, which have made his country a spectre of blood in the eyes of nations. Nor can the foreigner listen to it, sung by a company of exiles, or executed by a band of musicians, without feeling that it is the pibroch of battle and war."—Bombaugh's *Gleanings for the Curious.*

Marshalsea. An old prison in London, no longer standing. It was originally attached to the Marshalsea Court, established for the trial of servants of the King's household ; but later became a place of incarceration for debtors, defaulters, and persons convicted of piracy and other crimes committed on the high seas. It was abolished by act of parliament in 1849. The Marshalsea figures prominently as the home of *Little Dorritt*, in Dickens's novel of that name.

Marshals of Napoleon I. The following is a list of the Marshals of France appointed by Napoleon I (1804–1814) during his reign :

(1) Augereau (1757–1816), Duke of Castiglione.

(2) Bernadotte (1764–1844), Prince of Ponte-Corvo, King of Sweden.

(3) Berthier (1753–1815), Prince of Neufchâtel and Wagram.

(4) Bessières (1768–1813), Duke of Istria.

(5) Brune (1763–1815).

(6) Davoust (1770–1823), Duke of Auerstadt, Prince of Eckmühl.

(7) Gouvion Saint-Cyr (1764–1830).

(8) Grouchy (1766–1847).

(9) Jourdan (1762–1833).

(10) Kellerman (1735–1820), Duke of Valmy.

(11) Lannes (1769–1809), Duke of Montebello.

(12) Lefebvre (1755–1820), Duke of Dantzic.

(13) Macdonald (1765–1840), Duke of Tarentum.

(14) Marmont (1774–1852), Duke of Ragusa.

(15) Masséna (1758–1817), Duke of Rivoli, Prince of Essling.

(16) Molitor (1770–1849).

(17) Moncey (1754–1842), Duke of Conegliano.

(18) Mortier (1768–1835), Duke of Treviso.

(19) Murat (1771-1815), Grand Duke of Berg and Cleves, King of Naples.

(20) Ney (1769–1815), Duke of Elchingen, Prince of the Moskwa.

(21) Oudinot (1767–1847), Duke of Reggio.

(22) Pérignon (1754–1818).

(23) Poniatowski (1762–1813), Prince Josef Anton.

(24) Serrurier (1742–1819), Count.

(25) Soult (1769–1851), Duke of Dalmatia.

(26) Suchet (1770–1826), Duke of Albufera.

(27) Victor (1764–1823), Duke of Belluno.

"It is asserted that Arrighi, duc de Padoue (died 21 March, 1853), H. J. W. Clarke, duc de Feltre (died Oct. 1818), and Andoche Junot, duc d'Abrantes (suicide 29 July, 1813), were only titular marshals, and that G. Christophe Michel Duroc (killed at the battle of Mackersdorff, 23 April, 1813) was only marshal of the palace."—Haydn's *Dictionary of Dates.*

Mars's Satellites. Previous to 1877, Mars was supposed to be without satellites, but in August of that year Prof. Asaph Hall of the Washington Observatory discovered two small bodies revolving around the planet, and named them *Deimos* (*Gr. Terror*) and *Phobos* (*Gr. Flight*). They are the smallest celestial bodies known, and revolve around Mars in orbits nearly circular and almost in the plane of its equator. *Phobos* — the nearer satellite—has a diameter of 7.2 miles, and a mean distance of 5850 miles; while *Deimos* has a diameter of 5.2 miles, and a mean distance of 14,650 miles.

"*The larger of these worlds is scarcely larger than Paris.* Should we honour them with the title of worlds? They are not even terrestrial continents, nor empires, nor kingdoms, nor provinces, nor departments. Alexander, Cæsar, Charlemagne, or Napoleon might care but little to receive the sceptre of such worlds. Gulliver might juggle with them. Who knows, however! The vanity of men being generally in the direct ratio of their mediocrity, the microscopical reasoning mites which doubtless swarm on their surface have also, perhaps, permanent armies which mutilate each other for the possession of a grain of sand." —Flammarion's *Popular Astronomy*.

Marston Moor, Battle of. A desperate battle fought near York, England, on July 2nd, 1644, between the Royalists—22,000 strong—commanded by Prince Rupert and the Marquis of Newcastle, and the Scotch and Parliamentary armies — numbering 24,000 men—under Fairfax and the Earls of Leven and Manchester. The Royalists were signally defeated, and fled in confusion to York, leaving 4000 men dead on the field. It was at Marston Moor that Oliver Cromwell, with his famous " Ironsides," decided the issue of the contest, and first gave proof of his remarkable military talent. See *Ironsides*.

Martel (*The Hammer*). A surname conferred upon Charles, the son of Pepin d'Héristal, for the valor with which he pounded the Saracens at the battle of Tours, in 732 A.D. It is said that he " knocked down the foe, and crushed them beneath his axe, as a martel or hammer crushes what it strikes." See *Tours, Battle of*.

M. Collin-de-Plancy, however, in his *Bibliothèque des Légendes*, makes the following statement concerning the origin of this word : " It is surprising that almost all our modern historians, whose profound researches have been so highly vaunted, have repeated the little tale of the *Chronicle of St. Denis*, which affirms that the surname of Martel was conferred on Charles for having hammered (*martelé*) the Saracens. Certain writers of the present day style him, in this sense, Karle-le-Marteau. The word

martel, in the ancient Frank language, never bore such a signification, but was, on the contrary, merely an abbreviation of Martellus, Martin."

Martial. According to astrology, a person of " martial" tendencies is supposed to derive his warlike disposition from the influence of the planet Mars, which was in the ascendant at the time of his birth. See *Jovial; Mercurial; Saturnine*.

Martini-Henry Rifle. A breech-loading rifle introduced into the British army in 1874. It was superseded by the Lee-Metford rifle in 1888.

Martinmas. A church festival celebrated on the eleventh of November, in honor of St. Martin of Tours [316 (?)–396 (?)], a prelate of the Roman Catholic Church. Martinmas is one of the cross-quarter days of the year, —the others being Whitsuntide, Lammas, and Candlemas. Luther derived his first name from the circumstance of having been born on the eve of this festival, which, in Germany, is also called *Martinalia*.

Marvellous Boy. A sobriquet conferred upon Thomas Chatterton (1752–1770), the juvenile poet, whose precocious talent, strange career, and early death have rendered him one of the marvels of English literature.

"I thought of Chatterton, the *marvellous boy*,
The sleepless soul that perished in his pride."
Wordsworth.

Maryland. This State of the American Union was named by George Calvert (1580–1632), Lord Baltimore, in honor of Henrietta Maria, Queen of Charles I (1625–1649) of England.

Masaniello. A corruption of Tommaso Aniello (1622–1647), a fisherman of Amalfi, Italy, who incited a successful revolt against the Duke of Arcos, Spanish Viceroy of Naples, and compelled him to abolish a tax imposed on fruit and vegetables. Masaniello remained master of Naples for seven days, but during this brief period so alienated his friends by his excesses and despotic acts, that he was betrayed by them to the agents of the Viceroy, and assassinated. His body was flung into a ditch, but on the following day it was interred with great pomp and ceremony. Auber has composed an opera on this subject, entitled *La Muette de Portici.* See *Seven Days' King.*

Mason and Dixon's Line. The name given to the boundary-line between Pennsylvania and Maryland, surveyed in 1763–1767, by Charles Mason and Jeremiah Dixon, two English engineers, for the purpose of settling the long-standing border disputes between the two colonies. It ran due west in north latitude 39°43′ 26.3″ for 245 miles, and for the first 132 miles was marked with stone-posts at intervals of one mile. Each fifth stone was larger than the rest, and bore on one side the arms of the Penn family and on the other those of the Baltimore family. The line was resurveyed in 1849, but so accurately had the work been done in the first instance, that no error of importance was discovered. John Randolph of Roanoke (1773–1833) made frequent use of this phrase during the exciting debates in Congress in 1820, on the question of excluding slavery from the State of Missouri, and referred to it as the boundary-line between slavery and freedom. The expression was taken up by every newspaper, and soon became immensely popular. See *Dixie's Land ; Old Line State.*

" Freedom's Keystone is slavery, thet ther 's
 no doubt on,
 It 's suthin' thet 's—wha' d' ye call it?—
 divine,—
An' the slaves thet we ollers make the
 most on
 Air them north o' *Mason an' Dixon's
 Line.*"
 Lowell's *Biglow Papers.*

Mason and Slidell Affair. See *Trent Affair.*

Masorah (*Heb. tradition*). A collection of notes — critical, exegetical, and grammatical — bearing upon the Hebrew text of the *Old Testament.* According to Jewish tradition, the *Masorah* was commenced by Moses and continued by the learned men of the nation; but in all probability it is the work of Jewish doctors that dwelt in Palestine, between the 6th and 10th centuries after Christ. These notes were written in Chaldee, around the margins of the MSS. of the *Old Testament.* The first Rabbinical Hebrew Bible, containing the *Masorah* carefully prepared and arranged, was printed at Venice in 1526.

Massacre of St. Bartholomew. See *St. Bartholomew, Massacre of.*

Massacre of the Innocents. See *Innocents, Massacre of the.*

Matterhorn. An Alpine peak in south Switzerland, 14,705 feet in height. After several unsuccessful attempts by Prof. Tyndall and others in 1860, it was finally scaled by Mr. Edward Whymper and party on July 14th, 1865. While making the descent, four of the number — Lord Francis Douglas, Rev. C. Hudson, Mr. Hadow, and Michael Croz, a guide — met their death by falling from a precipice 4000 feet high. The first woman to ascend the Matterhorn was Miss Walker, who, with her father, reached the summit on July 22nd, 1871. Dr. W. O. Mosely, an American, was killed on August 14th, 1879, while ascending the mountain. On September 12th, 1890, three persons lost their lives in attempting to make the ascent.

Matthew Buckinger.

" Of all the imperfect beings brought into the world, few can challenge, for mental and acquired endowments, anything like a comparison to vie with this truly extraordinary little man. Matthew Buckinger was a native of Nuremberg, in Germany, where he was born, June 2, 1674, without hands, feet, legs, or thighs ; in short, he was little more than the trunk of a man, saving two excrescences growing from the shoulder-blades, more resembling fins of a fish than arms of a man. He was the last of nine children, by one father and mother, viz., eight sons and one daughter ; after arriving at the age of maturity, from the singularity of his case and the extraordinary abilities he possessed, he attracted the notice and attention of all persons, of whatever rank in life, to whom he was occasionally introduced. . . . Mr. Buckinger was but twenty-nine inches in height and died in 1722."—*Ten Thousand Wonderful Things.*

Maundy - Thursday. The name given to the Thursday before Good Friday. According to Spelman, the word "Maundy" is derived from *mande* (*a hand-basket*), from which the King distributed alms to the poor on that day. Others, however, say its origin may be traced to the Latin phrase *dies mandati*, the day on which Christ gave to His disciples His great *mandate* that they should love one another as He had loved them (*John* xiii, 34). Maundy-Thursday is often erroneously called Holy Thursday. See *Holy Thursday ; Green Thursday.*

"This is a Roman Catholic festival, and in that church the name originated. The epistle in the Mass of *Maundy-Thursday* is taken from 1 Cor. xi. In the 24th verse are these words : 'Take, eat' ; in Latin, '*Accipite et manducate.*' This is believed to be the original of *Maundy*, and the word was certainly used to signify the Last Supper of the Lord."—Edwards's *Words, Facts, and Phrases.*

Mauritius. This island was colonized by the Dutch, and was named in honor of *Maurice*, Prince of Orange.

Mauser Rifle. A breech-loading magazine rifle adopted by Germany in 1871 and still used by that nation. It superseded the needle - gun. The Mauser rifle is in use also in Belgium, Colombia, Chile, Costa Rica, Hayti, Morocco, Persia, Paraguay, Spain, Sweden, San Salvador, Turkey, and Uruguay.

Mausoleum. A celebrated marble tomb erected at Halicarnassus to the memory of Mausolus, King of Caria, by his widow, Artemisia, in 353 B.C., and accounted one of the "Seven Wonders of the World." It remained in an excellent state of preservation until the 12th century A.D., but during the succeeding 200 years fell into decay. In the 16th century, the ruins were used for building materials by the Knights of St. John. The original site was identified by C. T. Newton, Esq., in 1857, and, through his efforts, some of the remains of the structure, —including a portion of the statue of Mausolus—were removed to the British Museum. The word "mausoleum" became, in course of time, the generic term applied to any splendid sepulchral monument.

Mausoleum of Augustus. A stately tomb, now in ruins, erected on the Campus Martius, Rome, by the Emperor Augustus (27 B.C.–14 A.D.), and designed by him as the burial-place of the Imperial family. There were interred Augustus, Tiberius, Claudius, Nerva, Germanicus, and many others.

Mausoleum of Hadrian. See *Hadrian's Mausoleum.*

Mausoleum at Charlottenburg. See *Charlottenburg.*

Mayfair. A fashionable district in London, east of Hyde Park. It derives its name from an annual six days' fair formerly held there in May, for the benefit of the leper hospital of St. James the Less, Bishop of Jerusalem, now St. James's Palace.

Mayflower. A vessel of 180 tons that conveyed the "Pilgrim Fathers," or early settlers of Massachusetts, to the New World. The *Mayflower* set sail from Southampton, England, with 101 passengers, on September 17th, 1620, and after a tempestuous voyage of 63 days anchored in the harbor of Cape Cod. On December 21st of the same year, the company landed on

Plymouth Rock and established a settlement there. See *Pilgrims.*

Mayors of the Palace. The name given to certain high dignitaries, who became the virtual rulers of France during the reigns of the later Merovingian kings. In 752, Pepin le Bref, son of Charles Martel, and Mayor of the Palace, confined Childéric III in a convent, and caused himself, with the consent of the Pope, to be proclaimed King of the Franks. Thus commenced the Carlovingian line of French monarchs, which lasted 235 years. The office of Mayor of the Palace was curtailed by the Carlovingian kings, and abolished by Hugh Capet (987–996). See *Carlovingian Dynasty ; Merovingian Dynasty.*

Max O'Rell. The pseudonym of Paul Blouët (*b.* 1848), the popular French writer and lecturer. He is the author of several semi-humorous works on the institutions and customs of Great Britain and the United States of America.

Mazarine Bible. The name given to an edition of the Bible in Latin, printed by John Gutenberg, and so called because a copy of it was found in the library of Cardinal Mazarin. It is probably the first book printed from movable types, and although undated is assigned to some year between 1450 and 1455. About twenty copies are known to exist. The Mazarine Bible is in two volumes of 324 and 317 pages respectively, and is printed in large Gothic characters, resembling a manuscript. In June, 1873, a copy on vellum was sold for £3400, and one on paper for £2690. In December, 1884, a copy belonging to Sir John Thorold brought £3900. See *Dearest Books.*

Mazeppa. A hetman (1644–1709) of the Cossacks, who, while a page at the court of Jan Casimir, King of Poland, was detected in an intrigue with the wife of a Podolian noble. As a punishment for his crime, he was lashed to a wild horse and borne to the country of the Cossacks, where the animal dropped dead from exhaustion. Mazeppa was rescued and kindly treated by this people, and finally rose to be a prince and commander-in-chief of their armies. He fought against the Russians in the battle of Pultowa in 1709, and later took refuge in Turkey, where he soon afterwards died. In Byron's poem of *Mazeppa,* the hero relates the story of his life to Charles XII after the battle.

Meal-Tub Plot. A pretended conspiracy against the Duke of York (afterwards James II), concocted by one Dangerfield in 1679, and attributed by him to the Presbyterians, whom he charged with attempting to destroy the government and establish a republic. When captured and thrown into prison he asserted that the plot was really formed by the Roman Catholics against the life of the King (Charles II), and declared that the treasonable papers would be found in the bottom of a meal-tub in the house of one Mrs. Collier, his mistress. Dangerfield finally confessed the entire affair, and was sentenced to be whipped and pilloried. He died in 1685, as the result of an injury inflicted upon him by a barrister named Robert Francis, who struck out one of his eyes, and was afterwards hanged for the crime.

Mécanique Analytique (*Fr. Analytical Mechanics*). A famous work on general astronomy and celestial physics by Jean Louis Lagrange (1736–1813), published in 1788. It is considered one of the masterpieces of the human intellect, worthy to rank with Newton's *Principia* and Laplace's *Mécanique Céleste.*

Mécanique Céleste (*Fr. Celestial Mechanics*). A treatise on the physics of the universe by Pierre Simon Laplace (1749–1827), in five volumes. It appeared in 1799–1825, and was justly regarded as the capital monument of the astronomer's genius.

Mecca. A city of Arabia, situated 245 miles south of Medina. It is famous as being the birthplace of Mohammed (571 A.D.), and the holy city of Islâm. Mecca contains the Great Mosque, or Caaba, a magnificent temple, which is annually visited by hundreds of thousands of pilgrims. Near the city is a cave where, it is said, the prophet was accustomed to retire to perform his devotions, and where, in 604, the *Koran* was revealed to him by the angel Gabriel. In 622, Mohammed, to escape from his enemies, fled from Mecca, and after a journey of 16 days entered Medina amid the acclamations of the populace. This event is called the Hegira, and marks the commencement of the Mohammedan era. See *Caaba; Hegira; Medina.*

Medal of Christ. See *Christ, Likeness of.*

Medea. A famous sorceress, the daughter of Aëtes, King of Colchis, and wife of Jason, the leader of the Argonautic expedition, whom she assisted in finding the Golden Fleece. She accompanied Jason to Greece, but was deserted by him in order that he might marry Creusa. Medea, thereupon, took fearful vengeance on her faithless spouse by murdering the two sons she had borne him. She is said to have become immortal, to have been honored with divine worship, and to have married Achilles in Elysium. Sophocles and Euripides among the ancients, and Corneille among the moderns, have made the story of Medea the subject of tragedies, but the one written by Sophocles is lost.

Medici. A distinguished Florentine family, which rose to supreme power in the 15th century, and became famous as the restorers of literature and the fine arts throughout Italy. Its most illustrious members were Cosimo de' Medici (1389–1464), surnamed *Il Vecchio* (*The Ancient*) and *Pater Patriæ*, and Lorenzo (1448–1492)

his grandson, surnamed *The Magnificent* and *The Father of Letters.* This latter ruled Florence from 1469 to 1492, and proved himself a most munificent patron of art and literature. The family of the Medici became extinct on the death of its last male representative, Gian Gastone, seventh Grand-Duke of Tuscany, in 1737.

" Lorenzo was a worthy descendant of his famous grandfather, just in his government, magnanimous to his enemies, and not only a munificent patron of art and literature, but himself a man of wide culture and a distinguished lyric poet. To enlarge on the institutions, universities, and schools founded by him, and on the famous names of painters, sculptors, architects, philosophers, and poets who surrounded him would be to write the history of the Renaissance." —*Chambers's Encyclopædia.*

Medina. A city of Arabia, situated 245 miles north of Mecca, famous as the place to which Mohammed fled for refuge in 622 A.D. Medina is, after Mecca, the most holy city in the Mohammedan world, and contains the mosque El-Haram (*Ar. The Sacred*), said to have been erected on the spot where the Prophet died, and to enclose his tomb. Medina is known as the City of the Prophet. See *Mecca; Tomb of Mohammed.*

Mediterranean Sea (*Lat. medius, middle, terra, land*). So called because nearly enclosed by the continents of Europe, Asia, and Africa.

Meister, Wilhelm. The hero of Goethe's philosophic romance entitled *Wilhelm Meister's Lehrjahre* (*Ger. Apprenticeship*), published in 1795.

" *Wilhelm Meister's Apprenticeship,* . . . whatever may be thought of it in other respects, has a deeper object than many a poem which has called itself epic : nor was it hastily or carelessly huddled together without study; for this novel, it would appear, lay ten years in the author's mind and hand, one year longer than even the Horatian period."—*Carlyle.*

Meistersingers (*Ger. meister, master, singer, singer*). The name given to certain artisan-poets in Germany, who formed themselves into guilds—similar to the trade-guilds of the time—and composed verses, chiefly on moral and religious subjects, in accordance with fixed and rigid rules. The meistersingers were the successors of the minnesingers, and endeavored to revive the national minstrelsy, which had fallen into decay with the decline of those love-singers. They claimed to have been founded by Frauenlob during the 13th century, and were in the zenith of their popularity at the time of the Reformation (1517). The most famous representative of the meistersingers was Hans Sachs (1494–1576). He was a cobbler at Nuremberg, and has been immortalized by Wagner in his comic opera entitled *Die Meistersinger von Nürnburg*. See *Minnesingers*.

Melchior (" King of Light "). The name of one of the three " kings," " magi," or " wise men " led to the manger at Bethlehem by the Star in the East. According to the tradition, Melchior offered gold to the infant Jesus, in token of royalty. See *Balthazar; City of the Three Kings; Cologne, Three Kings of; Gaspar; Star in the East.*

Melchizedek. A king of Salem and priest of the most high God, mentioned in *Genesis* xiv, 18–20. He met Abraham on his return from his victory over Chedorlaomer, and gave him his blessing, receiving tithes in return.

" It has been matter of great inquiry among commentators, who *Melchizedek* really was. He has been variously supposed to be the Holy Spirit, the Son of God, an angel, Enoch, and Shem. But the safest and most probable opinion is that which considers *Melchizedek* as a righteous and peaceful king, a worshipper and priest of the most high God, in the land of Canaan ; a friend of Abraham, and of a rank elevated above him."—*Dictionary of the Holy Bible.*

Mellifluous Doctor. An epithet conferred upon St. Bernard (1091–1153), the noted ecclesiastic, whose writings have been called " a river of Paradise."

Melpomene. In classical mythology, the muse that presided over tragedy. She is generally represented standing, with her left foot raised on a rock, and holding in her right hand a mask, such as was worn by tragedians. See *Muses.*

Melrose Abbey. A beautiful abbey—now in ruins—on the bank of the river Tweed, Scotland, 40 miles southwest of Edinburgh. It was founded by David I (1124–1153) for the Cistercian monks in 1136, and became the mother-church of the Order in that country. After being twice injured by the English, it was rebuilt in a style of increased magnificence, between the years 1322 and 1505, but was again devastated by the English, under the Earl of Hertford, in 1545, and was totally ruined during the Scotch Reformation. Since that time no attempt at restoration has been made, and the ruins have served as a quarry for the neighboring town of Melrose. The ruined church is all that remains at the present day, and is greatly admired for the beauty of its architecture, which belongs to the Second Pointed Style. Melrose Abbey is the burial-place of Michael Scott, the wizard of the *Lay;* Alexander II and Johanna, his queen; William Douglas, the " Dark Knight "; and the second abbot, St. Waltheof. The heart of Robert Bruce is said to be buried before the high-altar.

" If thou would'st view fair *Melrose* aright,
  Go visit it by the pale moonlight ;
For the gay beams of lightsome day,
  Gild, but to flout, the ruins grey.
When the broken arches are black in night,
  And each shafted oriel glimmers white ;
When the cold light's uncertain shower
  Streams on the ruined central tower ;
When buttress and buttress, alternately,
  Seem framed of ebon and ivory ;
When silver edges the imagery,
  And the scrolls that teach thee to live and die ;
When distant Tweed is heard to rave,
  And the owlet to hoot o'er the dead man's grave,

Then go—but go alone the while—
Then view St. David's ruined pile ;
And, home returning, soothly swear,
Was never scene so sad and fair ! "
    Scott's *Lay of the Last Minstrel*.

Memento Mori (*Lat. Remember, you must die*). " The ancient Egyptians, at their grand festivals and parties of pleasure, always had a coffin placed on the table at meals, containing a mummy, or a skeleton of painted wood, which, Herodotus tells us, was presented to each of the guests with this admonition : ' Look upon this, and enjoy yourself; for such will you become when divested of your mortal garb.' This custom is frequently alluded to by Horace and Catullus; and Petronius tells us that at the celebrated banquet of Trimalcion a silver skeleton was placed on the table to awaken in the minds of the guests the remembrance of death and of deceased friends."—*Gleanings for the Curious* (Bombaugh).

"A reminder of our latter end. The Egyptians passed round a skull at their feasts for this purpose: and behind the Roman general in his triumphal chariot stood a slave whispering in his ear, *Respice post te, hominem memento te*, Look behind you, remember that you are but a man. The Russian Tsars used to be presented with specimens of marble at their coronation, from which to select one for their tombs."—King's *Classical and Foreign Quotations*.

Memnon. A celebrated colossal statue, about 60 feet in height, situated near Thebes in Egypt, and commonly known as the " Vocal Memnon." It stands on the left bank of the Nile, and with its companion, was erected in honor of Amenoph III, of the XVIIIth dynasty, in front of his now vanished temple. It was originally a monolith, but, having been overthrown either by Cambyses (*fl.* 525 B.C.) or by the earthquake of 27 B.C., the upper part was restored by means of sandstone blocks. According to ancient tradition, this statue, when first touched by the rays of the rising sun, emitted a musical tone, like the snapping of a harp-string, which the imaginative Greeks concluded was the voice of Memnon greeting his mother Eos (the Dawn). Strabo, who visited this statue about 18 B.C., was the first to mention this remarkable fact. See *Memnon's Harp*.

"These sounds . . . were said to be produced either by a priest hidden in the Colossus or by the expansion of fissured portions under the influence of the sun's rays. Though many celebrated persons of antiquity—such as Strabo, Ælius, Gallus, and Hadrian—testified as to hearing this peculiar music, its particular character and cause have never been satisfactorily explained." —Vincent's *Actual Africa*.

Memnon's Harp. A term sometimes applied to the statue of Memnon at Thebes, Egypt, which was said by the ancients to emit musical tones— like those of a harp—at the rising of the sun. See *Memnon*.

Memorabilia of Socrates. The Latin title of the memoirs of Socrates by Xenophon, wherein he defends the great moralist against the charges of impiety and of corrupting the Athenian youth. The *Memorabilia* (*Lat. Things worthy of remembrance*) is highly esteemed as a *résumé* of the practical features of the Socratic philosophy.

Memorial Day. A day set apart by the States that seceded from the American Union during the Civil War, for the purpose of decorating with flowers the graves of those that fell in behalf of the " Lost Cause." The custom originated among the women of the Southern States during the Rebellion, and is annually observed on April 26th. Decoration Day (May 30th) is also known as Memorial Day. See *Decoration Day*.

Memorial Hall. A handsome edifice —forming part of Harvard University —erected by the alumni and friends of the institution, at a cost of $575,000, in memory of the students and graduates that lost their lives in the Civil War. It contains, in addition to the Memorial Hall proper, a semi-circular theatre, used for class-day and commencement exercises, and a spacious Gothic dining-hall, capable of seating 1000 students, adorned with portraits and busts of distinguished men and friends of the University. The building was dedicated in 1874.

Menai Suspension Bridge. A celebrated suspension bridge — spanning the Menai Strait — built by Thomas Telford, and completed in 1825, at a cost of £120,000. The total length of the structure is 1710 feet, and the span between the points of suspension 579 feet, while the total weight of iron used in its construction amounts to 2187 tons. It was designed for the use of vehicles and foot-passengers only, but the necessity for railway communication finally led to the building of the Britannia Bridge, which was completed in 1850. Until that date, however, the Menai Suspension Bridge was the only means of communication — save by boats—between Carnarvon and the island of Anglesea. It is chiefly famous at the present day as being the first important suspension bridge erected. See *Britannia Bridge*.

Mendicant Orders. The name given in the Roman Catholic Church to certain religious orders that renounce the ownership of all property—real or personal—and subsist wholly upon the alms of the faithful. Such associations originated during the 13th century, and spread extensively throughout Europe; but, at the general council held by Pope Gregory X (1271–1276) at Lyons in 1272, these orders were reduced to four, viz., Dominicans, Franciscans, Carmelites, and Augustinians.

Men of Grütli. See *Grütli*.

Mentone Man. A fossil human skeleton, found in a cave at Mentone, near Nice, in France, on March 26th, 1872. It lay buried 21½ feet below the surface, and when discovered was in an almost perfect state of preservation. The height of the original figure is estimated to have been six feet. The skull was dolichocephalic or "long-headed," with a facial angle of nearly 85 degrees ; but, owing to a fracture before and behind, a perfect measurement was impossible. Alongside the skull were found 22 perforated teeth, which are supposed to have formed a network or chaplet about the head. The cave contained, in addition, flint implements, and bones of the cave-bear, cave-lion, and other extinct animals. The Mentone Man — supposed to belong to the Palæolithic Age —was placed in the Museum of Natural History in Paris. See *Ages, Archæologic.*

Mentor. A wise and faithful friend and counselor of Ulysses, King of Ithaca, who, on his departure for the Trojan War, entrusted to him the supervision of his household and the education of Telemachus, his son. Minerva, under the guise of Mentor, plays a prominent part in Fénelon's romance of *Télémaque*. The word "mentor" has consequently come to mean a wise and prudent adviser of the young.

Mephistopheles. A mocking, jeering fiend, who figures prominently in Goethe's poem of *Faust*, and in Gounod's opera of the same name. He is also familiar to modern readers as the attendant evil-spirit in Marlowe's tragedy of *Faustus*. In the old demon lore, Mephistopheles is one of the seven fallen archangels, and is next in power to Satan. It is to Goethe's *Faust*, however, that he owes all his modern vitality. See *Faust*.

Mercantile System. An economic theory of long standing, based upon the belief that a nation grows rich in proportion as it accumulates gold and silver. In consequence, it is considered advantageous for every nation to import as little as possible of the produce of other nations, and to export as much as possible of its own, since thereby more money will be received than parted with. This excess of the money value of exports over imports is called the " balance of trade." See *Balance of Trade*.

Mercator's Projection. A map or chart of the world, for nautical purposes, devised by Gerard Kauffmann (1512–1594), whose surname, Latinized, was Mercator (*The Merchant*). It is a cylindrical projection in which all the meridians are straight lines *perpendicular* to the equator, and all the parallels are straight lines *parallel* to the equator. As a result, the shapes of countries are greatly distorted, and the polar regions, especially, immensely exaggerated. Mercator's Projections were published in 1556, and applied to navigation about 1599.

" This device of representing a globe in perspective on a flat surface is due to Edward Wright, an Englishman ; but the chart so arranged by Wright was printed and published by Gerard Mercator, a printer of maps in Flanders, who died at the age of 82, in 1594."—Brewer's *Historic Note-Book*.

Mercurial. A person of " mercurial " temperament was supposed, according to astrology, to derive his active and sprightly disposition from the influence of the planet Mercury, which was in the ascendant at the time of his birth. See *Jovial ; Martial ; Saturnine*.

Mercury, Flying. A celebrated bronze statue of Mercury by Giovanni da Bologna (1524–1608), surnamed *Il Fiammingo*, in the National Museum at Florence. It was executed in 1598 for a fountain at the Villa Medici at Rome, and represents the god lightly poised on one foot, as if in the act of springing into the air. He wears a winged cap, and carries a caduceus, or wand, in his left hand.

" It seems a wonder that he did not absolutely fling himself into the air when the artist gave him the last touch. No bolder work was ever achieved ; nothing so full of life has been done since."—*Hawthorne*.

Mercy's Dream. A painting by Daniel Huntington (*b.* 1816), now in the Metropolitan Museum of Art in New York City. It was for several years in the private art-collection of Marshall O. Roberts, a retired New York merchant ; and, after his death, was purchased by the artist and presented by him to the Museum.

Mer de Glace (*Fr. Sea of Ice*). A famous glacier, which fills the upper gorges of the chain of Mont Blanc in Savoy, and extends into the valley of Chamouni, a distance of over twelve miles. It is annually visited by thousands of tourists during the summer season.

Meredith, Owen. The pseudonym adopted by Edward Robert, Earl of Lytton (1831–1891), the poet and novelist.

Merlin. A famous British prophet and enchanter, who is supposed to have flourished during the time of King Arthur, about 450 A.D. According to Geoffrey of Monmouth, he sprang from the intercourse of a Welsh princess with a demon ; but was baptized by Blaize, and thus rescued from the powers of darkness. He early displayed the gifts of prophecy and divination. According to Ariosto, Merlin made " the fountain of love " mentioned in the *Orlando Innamorato*, as well as " one of the four fountains " spoken of in the *Orlando Furioso*. He is also said to have made King Arthur's Round Table with seats for 150 knights, and to have brought from Ireland the stones found at Stonehenge on Salisbury Plain. Spenser refers to Merlin in the *Faerie Queene*, and Tennyson relates some of his adventures in the *Idylls of the King*. Allusion is also made to him in Ellis's *Specimens of Early English Metrical Romances*, in Drayton's *Polyolbion*, and in Sir Walter Scott's *Kenilworth*. The manner of his death is variously related, and his grave is shown at Drummelzier on the Tweed, where, in attempting to escape from his adversaries, he was impaled on a hidden stake. See *Vivien*.

Merovingian Dynasty. The first dynasty of French kings, founded in 481 A.D. by Clovis (481–511), a Frankish chieftain of great energy. It was so called from Merovich or Merowing, the grandfather of Clovis, who was the leader of the Franks at the battle of Châlons (451). The Merovingian dynasty lasted from 481 to 752 (a period of 271 years), when it was succeeded by the Carlovingian line of kings. See *Carlovingian Dynasty; Mayors of the Palace*.

Merrilies, Meg. A half-crazy gypsy, who figures prominently in Sir Walter Scott's novel of *Guy Mannering*. She was the nurse of Harry Bertram, and the ruler of the gypsy race.

Merrimac.

(1) A Confederate iron-clad vessel, which destroyed the Federal frigates *Congress* and *Cumberland* in Hampton Roads, Virginia, on March 8th, 1862, but was driven off by the *Monitor* on the following day. When the Federals abandoned the Norfolk Navy-Yard in 1861, they scuttled and sank the frigate *Merrimac*. She was, however, soon after raised by the Confederates, protected with four inches of iron to the water's edge, armed with a prow of iron, and mounted with ten heavy guns. To this iron-clad the Confederates gave the name of *Virginia*. After her contest with the *Monitor*, the *Merrimac* did no further damage, and was blown up on the evacuation of the Norfolk Navy-Yard by the Confederates, May 11th, 1862. As a result of this naval contest, there was a general substitution of iron-clads for wooden vessels, in the navies of the world.

(2) A steam collier purposely sunk at the entrance of the harbor of Santiago, Cuba, under the direction of Richmond P. Hobson (*b.* 1870), on June 3rd, 1898, to prevent the escape of Cervera's fleet. Although the vessel failed to obstruct the channel, the daring deed was hailed with applause throughout the United States. Hobson, together with his crew of seven men, escaped from the sinking ship in a small craft, but was soon after captured by the Spaniards, and confined in the fortress of Santiago until July 6th of the same year. See *Monitor*.

Merry Andrew. A sobriquet originally conferred upon Andrew Borde (1500–1549), a learned and eccentric physician of the time of Henry VIII (1509–1547), who, according to Hearne, frequented " markets and fairs, where a conflux of people used to get together, to whom he prescribed; and, to induce them to flock thither the more readily, he would make humorous speeches, couched in such language as caused mirth and wonderfully propagated his fame."

The expression " Merry Andrew " was afterwards applied to any clown or buffoon, or more specifically, to any jester in attendance on a traveling mountebank.

Merry England. A popular designation of England. The word " merry," as used in this phrase, does not mean *gay* or *lively*, as is generally supposed, but *agreeable* or *pleasant*, in accordance with its earlier signification. Thus Spenser speaks of " *merry* London," and Chaucer of a

> " citee
> That stood full *merry* upon a haven side."

" The word ' merrie ' in this phrase [*Merrie England*] did not originally mean cheerful or gay, as is commonly supposed. It was anciently *mere*, probably from an Anglo-Saxon adjective meaning excellent, illustrious, famous, or renowned. Hence, ' merry men,' in the address of a chief to his followers, meaning not men of mirth, but of renown. Spenser uses the word ' merry ' in the sense of excellent or agreeable in the couplet,

> Then eke my feeble bark awhile may stay,
> Till *merry* wind and weather call her thence away."

Edwards's *Words, Facts, and Phrases*.

Merry Monarch. A nickname conferred upon Charles II (1660–1685) of England.

"Honor and shame, to him, were scarcely more than light and darkness to the blind."
—*Macaulay.*

Messalina. The infamous wife of the Roman Emperor Claudius (41–54 A.D.), whose name has become a synonym for profligacy and incontinency. See *Modern Messalina.*

Messiah.

(1) An epic poem, in 15 books, describing the principal events in the passion of Jesus Christ. It was written by Friedrich Gottlieb Klopstock (1724–1803), the eminent German poet, and appeared during the years 1748–1773.

"When the reader commences this poem, he receives an impression like that of a person entering a grand cathedral filled with the music of an organ."—*Madame de Staël.*

(2) A famous oratorio by Handel (1684–1759), considered his masterpiece. It appeared in 1742.

Metaphysics (*Gr. μετά τά φυσικά, after the things that relate to nature*). A term first used by the disciples of Aristotle to designate that part of his writings that came *after*, or followed, the part that treated of *physics* (or nature). The word, however, has been generally interpreted to mean " matters above or beyond physics," in importance.

"Commonly, in the schools, called *metaphysics*, as being part of the philosophy of Aristotle, which hath that for title ; but it is in another sense ; for there it signifieth as much as 'books written or placed after his natural philosophy'. But the schools take them for 'books of supernatural philosophy'; for the word *metaphysic* will bear both these senses."—*Hobbes.*

Metaurus, Battle of. A battle fought in central Italy in 207 B.C., between the Carthaginians commanded by Hasdrubal, the brother of Hannibal, and the Romans under the consuls Livius and Claudius Nero. The Romans were signally victorious ; and, after the battle, tossed the head of Hasdrubal into the Carthaginian camp. This victory is believed to have saved Rome, and is accounted one of the fifteen decisive battles of the world by Professor Creasy. See *Fifteen Decisive Battles.*

Methodists. A nickname given to Charles Wesley (1708–1788) and his associates by their fellow-students at Oxford, in 1729, on account of their *methodical* strictness in all religious matters. The word is said, however, to have been used in Cromwell's time by one John Spencer, librarian of Zion College, London, who published a book wherein he asks the question : " Where are now our Anabaptists, and plain pack-stuff *Methodists*, who esteem all flowers of rhetoric in sermons no better than stinking weeds ? "

Metonic Cycle. A period of almost exactly 19 years—6939 days, 14 hours, 27 minutes—at the end of which the sun, moon, and earth will bear the same relation to one another as at the beginning ; and, in consequence, the new moons will recur at seasons of the year exactly corresponding to those of the preceding cycle. This fact was discovered by Meton, the Athenian astronomer, in 433 B.C., and was used by the Greeks in the regulation of their calendar. It is still employed by the Western Church in determining the festival of Easter. See *Golden Number.*

Me Too. An epithet contemptuously applied to Thomas C. Platt (*b.* 1833) in the days when he and Roscoe Conkling were United States Senators from New York,— the implication being that he was the mere tool and puppet of the abler man.

Metric System. A decimal system of weights and measures, which originated in France with a committee appointed by the Academy of Sciences, at the request of the Constituent Assembly, on May 8th, 1790. The system was completed in 1799, and declared to be the only legal one on November 2nd, 1801. It is so named because it is based upon the *meter*, a measure equal to 39.37 inches. This fundamental unit of length and basis of the system is very nearly $\frac{1}{10000000}$th part of the distance on the earth's surface from the equator to the pole, measured on the meridian passing through France from Dunkirk to Barcelona. A standard meter, made of platinum, was placed in the Palace of the Archives at Paris in 1799. The unit of surface is the *are*, which equals 100 square meters. The unit of volume is the *stere*, or cubic meter ; the unit of capacity is the *liter*, or cubic decimeter ; the unit of weight is the *gramme*—the weight of a cubic centimeter of distilled water at 4° Centigrade (the temperature of maximum density) ; while the unit of money is the *franc*—a silver coin weighing 5 grammes. The multiples of these units are expressed by the Greek numerals *deca* (10), *hekato* (100), *kilo* (1000), *myria* (10,000) ; while the divisors are denoted by the Latin numerals *deci* (10), *centi* (100), *milli* (1000).

The metric system has been legalized in Great Britain and the United States, and is now in use in every civilized country except Montenegro.

Metropolis of Great Britain. The name given to the cities of London and Westminster, and the parliamentary boroughs of Battersea, Bethnal Green, Camberwell, Chelsea, Clapham, Deptford, Finsbury, Fulham, Greenwich, Hackney, Hammersmith, Hampstead, Islington, Kensington, Lambeth, Lewisham, Marylebone, Newington, Paddington, St. Pancras, Shoreditch, Southwark, Tower Hamlets, Wandsworth, West Ham, and Woolwich. This gigantic city covers an area of 122 square miles, and contains a population (1911) of 7,252,963 persons.

Metropolitan Museum of Art. Situated in Central Park, near Fifth Avenue and 82nd Street, New York City. It was founded in 1870, and for some years occupied the Douglas Mansion in West 14th Street; but, in 1880, the collections were removed to the present building, which was formally opened by President Hayes in March of the same year. The Museum contains fine collections of Egyptian antiquities, casts of ancient sculpture, statuary, paintings, gems and miniatures, oriental porcelains, glass and ancient pottery, and specimens of carved wood. The total value of its possessions is estimated at over $4,-000,000. The building has been several times enlarged. See *Cesnola Collection*.

Metropolitan Opera House. A superb temple of amusement in New York City, occupying the block bounded by Broadway, Seventh Avenue, 39th, and 40th Streets. It was erected by a number of capitalists at a cost of about $1,500,000, and was opened in the autumn of 1883. The interior of the building was destroyed by fire in August, 1892, but was restored at a cost of $500,000. It has a seating capacity of 3500. The stage is one of the largest in the country, and the auditorium is surrounded by two tiers of boxes and three balconies,— making in all five galleries. The Metropolitan Opera House is the home of the German and Italian opera, and is also used for concerts, balls, banquets, lectures, and meetings of various kinds.

Metternich's Maxim. To Prince von Metternich (1773–1859) is attributed the saying: "All *for*, but not *through*, the people." As the foe of popular government and the friend of absolutism, Metternich believed that the king and his council should make the laws. These should, of course, be in the interests of the people, who, however, were to have no voice either in their enactment or in their repeal.

"In schools and private families, *Metternich's maxim* is acted on ; but nations are clubs, not schools or families ; and in clubs the members, not the elected chairman, make the laws."—Brewer's *Historic Note-Book*.

Michael. An archangel mentioned several times in the Bible, where he is described as the special protector of the Jewish nation (*Daniel* x, 13–21), and the leader of the angelic host in their contest with the powers of darkness (*Revelation* xii, 7–9). Michael is the minister of peace and plenty, and the chief of the seven archangels that stand before the throne of God. He figures prominently in Milton's *Paradise Lost*, where, in company with Gabriel, he does battle against Satan and his angels ; and afterwards prophesies to Adam all that shall happen until the second coming of Christ. He is also commissioned to lead Adam and Eve out of Paradise. Michael is canonized in the calendar of the Roman Catholic Church, and his festival, termed Michaelmas, is celebrated on September 29th. According to tradition, he appeared to the Virgin Mary to announce to her the time of her death, and afterwards bore her soul to Jesus. See *Michaelmas*.

Michaelmas. A festival in the Roman Catholic Church, celebrated on the 29th of September, in honor of St. Michael and All Angels. It was instituted, according to Butler, in 487 A.D. In England and Ireland it is one of the four quarterly days on which rents are paid,—the three others being Lady Day (March 25th), Midsummer Day (June 24th), and Christmas Day (December 25th). The Lord Mayor of London is elected on Michaelmas Day. See *Michael*.

" The custom in England of eating goose at *Michaelmas* has been explained by saying that Queen Elizabeth heard of the destruction of the Spanish Armada while eating the bird at dinner on 29 Sept., 1588, at the house of Sir Neville Umfreyville. The custom is much older, and extends to the other countries of Europe."—*Clavis Calendaria*.

Microphone. An instrument used in connection with the telephone for making faint sounds audible. It was invented by Professor D. E. Hughes in December, 1877, and exhibited before the Royal Society on May 9th, 1878. By means of this instrument, the tread of a fly or the fall of a piece of tissue-paper may be rendered audible for miles.

" An electric current is established between two moderately conducting bodies (such as pieces of charcoal, metallised by being plunged when heated into mercury) resting slightly upon each other, mounted on a piece of thin wood. If the contact is so made that one of the bodies may be easily displaced, minute sounds produced on the wood disturb the electric conductivity at the place of contact, and may be heard by the help of the telephone. The sonorous and electric waves are thus rendered synchronous, and become convertible. The tread of a fly sounds like that of a large quadruped."—Haydn's *Dictionary of Dates*.

Microscope. Although the early history of this instrument is obscure, the first microscope is generally believed to have been made by Zacharias Jansen, a Dutchman, in 1590. The invention is also attributed to Galileo about 1610, and to Fontana and van Drebbel in 1621. Microscopes with double glasses appeared soon after the discovery of the law of the refraction of light, about 1624 ; but it was not until the invention of the achromatic lens and its application to the microscope by Lister and others, that this instrument became of positive value in the cause of science. The binocular microscope was invented by Professor Riddell in 1851. A millionth of a grain of blood was detected by means of the spectrum microscope exhibited by Mr. H. Sorby in 1865.

Midas. A king of Phrygia, to whom Dionysus granted the request that everything he touched should be turned to gold. Since, however, his food was transmuted into the precious metal the moment he touched it, the unhappy monarch was forced to beg the god to take back his fatal gift.

Midas was afterwards told to bathe in the river Pactolus, — the sands of which, according to the fable, yielded grains of gold ever after. Having been called upon to decide between the musical merits of Apollo and Pan, Midas gave a verdict in favor of the latter, whereupon Apollo changed his ears into those of an ass. This deformity he concealed, by means of a Phrygian cap, from all persons but his barber, who, however, became so oppressed with his knowledge of the fact that he is said to have dug a hole in the ground and to have whispered into it : " King Midas has an ass's ears ! " Greatly relieved in mind, he filled up the hole; but on the spot there sprang up a reed that whispered the secret to the breeze. See *Pactolus.*

Middle Ages. A period of about 1000 years in the history of Europe, beginning with the fall of the Western Roman Empire in 476 A.D., and ending with the fall of the Eastern Roman Empire in 1453 A.D. The Middle Ages include the years between the close of classic times and the dawn of the modern era, and constitute the epoch of Feudalism, Chivalry, and the Crusades. According to Hallam, the Middle Ages comprise about 1000 years, from the invasion of France by Clovis in 486 to that of Naples by Charles VIII in 1494. See *Dark Ages.*

Middle Kingdom (*Chinese, Tchang-Kooe*). A name given to China by the inhabitants themselves, who believe that their Empire is situated in the exact centre of the earth.

"China is so called sometimes with the sense of the Land of the Happy Mean, from the habits of mediocrity its inhabitants are supposed to have imbibed from the Confucian philosophy teaching the choice of the middle course in all things."—Walsh's *Handy-Book of Literary Curiosities.*

Middle States. At the time of the adoption of the Federal Constitution (1787–1790), the States of New York, New Jersey, Pennsylvania, Delaware, and Maryland occupied a central position between the New England Commonwealths and those of the South, and hence were popularly called the Middle States. Owing to the growth of the country, this term has lost its geographical significance, but is still retained for reasons of convenience.

Midsummer Day. A Church festival in honor of the nativity of John the Baptist, occurring on June 24th. In England and Ireland, it is the second of the four quarterly days on which rent is paid,—the three others being Lady Day (March 25th), Michaelmas (September 29th), and Christmas Day (December 25th). The eve of St. John, or Midsummer Eve (June 23rd), was celebrated with great rejoicing throughout Europe during the Middle Ages.

From early days John the Baptist was regarded as the patron saint of the masses in England, and even at the present time imposing masonic festivals continue to be held on Midsummer Day.

Mignon. A nickname given to Henry III (1574 – 1589), King of France, who, accompanied by a band of effeminate young men, called " Les Mignons," marched through the streets of Paris, in the garb of a penitent,— following the shrines of the saints. See *Man-Milliner.*

Mignonette. This word is a diminutive of the French *mignon* (*charming*), and is given to the flower that bears its name, on account of its delicate perfume.

Milan Cathedral. A magnificent Italo - Gothic structure at Milan, Italy, built entirely of white marble from the quarries of the Gandoglia, beyond Lake Maggiore. It was founded in 1366, under the direction of the architect, Heinrich von Gmünd, and was virtually completed by order of Napoleon I (1804–1814) in 1805–1813. The cathedral is in the form of a Latin cross, and measures 490 feet in

32

length and 180 feet in breadth. Fifty two columns, varying from 8¼ to 10 feet in diameter, support the roof. The height of the nave is 152 feet, and that of the tower 354 feet above the pavement. The exterior is adorned with upwards of 3000 statues (Baedeker), and the interior with 700, while the roof is a forest of exquisitely carved Gothic turrets—98 in number. Milan Cathedral is the largest church in the world, with the exception of St. Peter's at Rome.

"Howsoever you look at the great Cathedral, it is noble, it is beautiful! Wherever you stand in Milan, or within seven miles of Milan, it is visible—and when it is visible, no other object can claim your whole attention. Leave your eyes unfettered by your will but a single instant and they will surely turn to seek it. It is the first thing you look for when you rise in the morning, and the last your lingering gaze rests upon at night. Surely, it must be the princeliest creation that ever brain of man conceived." —Mark Twain's *Innocents Abroad.*

"There are accommodations for several thousand statues, but the precise number we are unable to give, not having had time to count them ; however, for the benefit of those who would like to judge for themselves, we will give the statement of different authors : McCulloch says 4500; Dr. S. I. Prime, author of *Travels in Europe and the East,* affirms that there are already 7000, and places for 3000 more ; Murray says 4400, which is the more correct." — *Harper's Hand-Book to Europe and the East.*

Milan Decree. A decree issued by Napoleon I (1804–1814) from Milan, on December 17th, 1807. It declared that any vessel that submitted to British search, or consented to any pecuniary exactions whatever, was liable to confiscation. See *Berlin Decree ; Continental System ; Orders in Council.*

Milesians.

(1) The inhabitants of the ancient Greek city of Miletus in Asia Minor.

(2) The ancient inhabitants of Ireland, from the tradition that the country was conquered and colonized by two sons of Milesius, or Miled, an imaginary king of Spain, about 2000 years before the Christian era. According to another account, the Milesians were the Scots, who, in prehistoric times, invaded Ireland ; and were so called from a fabled ancestor Milesius, whose name is a modified form of Miles (a Latin translation of the Keltic *Gulam*).

Military Academy, United States. See *United States Military Academy.*

Milk Grotto. A grotto or cave at Bethlehem, where, according to tradition, the Virgin Mary and the infant Jesus hid themselves from the wrath of Herod, previous to their flight into Egypt. The grotto is hewn out of the limestone rock, — the whiteness of which is said to have been caused by a few drops of Mary's milk. It is stated that a visit to this cave or the possession of a small piece of the stone has the miraculous power of increasing the flow of a woman's milk. As a result of this belief, small fragments are eagerly sought by the many pilgrims that visit the cave, and are also sent to all parts of Europe and the East.

Milky Way. An irregular luminous belt that encircles the Celestial Sphere, and has the general shape of a great circle, inclined at an angle of 63° to the Equinoctial. Its luminosity is due to the myriads of stars or suns composing it, many of which have been revealed to us by means of the telescope. It varies in width from 4 to 20 degrees, and at one point of its course splits up into two nearly parallel branches of unequal brightness, which do not reunite for a distance of 150 degrees. Democritus first taught that the Milky Way is composed of stars, and Galileo proved it with the telescope. Modern astronomers assert that the stars composing the universe are grouped in great clusters, called nebulæ ; according to this theory, the Milky Way is simply the nebula in which our sun is placed.

"In the midst of this gigantic collection of stars lost in this vortex of worlds, our little solar system lies. The dimensions of the centre of this system—the sun which appears to us so great, but which in reality is that of a star of the second or third magnitude—are found to represent but an atom of the luminous sand of the Milky Way."— *Proctor.*

Mill Boy of the Slashes. A nickname given to Henry Clay (1777–1852), the eminent statesman and orator, who, when a boy, made frequent visits to a grist-mill in the "Slashes," a low swampy region in Hanover County, Virginia,—the place of his birth.

Millenarians. A name given to believers in the Millennium, or second coming of Christ. They are also called Chiliasts from the Greek χίλιοι (*one thousand*). See *Millennium.*

Millennium (*Lat. mille, one thousand; annus, year*). A period of one thousand years, during which, according to the belief of many Christians, Satan will be bound, and the Messiah, in company with the resurrected saints and martyrs, will reign upon the earth in a state of blessedness and peace. This will be followed by the resurrection of the wicked and the final judgment. At the close of the Millennium, Satan will be released and will make a final attempt to regain his power ; but, with the wicked, will be cast into the lake of fire. See *Adventists; Millenarians.*

Referring to the passage in *Revelation* xx, 1–5, the *Standard Dictionary* says :

"Theologians are divided as to whether 1000, 360,000, or an indefinite number of years is meant, and also as to whether the period will precede or follow Christ's second coming, or is identical with the present dispensation, or is already past."

Millerites. See *Adventists.*

Millionaires. The following table, taken from Mulhall's *Dictionary of Statistics* (1891), is interesting as an attempt, on the part of the author, to furnish a list of the world's wealthy men, and an estimate of their fortunes.

NAME.	PROFESSION.	ESTIMATED WEALTH, £.	RESIDENCE.	DIED.
Seneca	Philosopher	3,400,000	Rome	65
Fugger	Banker	6,500,000	Augsburg	1506
Goldsmid	Banker	10,000,000	London	—
Astor	Furrier	6,000,000	New York	1848
Stewart	Haberdasher	16,000,000	New York	1873
Vanderbilt	Railroad Director	36,000,000	New York	1877
Overstone	Banker	4,000,000	London	1883
Rothschild	Banker	3,500,000	London	1879
Brassey	Contractor	5,000,000	London	1870
Krupp	Founder	3,000,000	Essen	—

Million of Facts, A. The following interesting statement concerning Sir Richard Phillips's *A Million of Facts* (published in 1835), is taken from Edwards's *Words, Facts, and Phrases.*

"In the introduction to this celebrated work of Sir Richard Phillips, it is stated that the volume contains far more than a million of *facts*. A correspondent of 'Notes and Queries' (January 23, 1875) points out that the volume contains only 403,650 *words*."

Milton of Germany. A title conferred upon Friedrich Gottlieb Klopstock (1724–1803), the famous German poet.

Mine Explosion. While the Federal forces were besieging Petersburg, Virginia, in the summer of 1864, an attempt was made to penetrate the Confederate lines by blowing up a part of the fortifications. For this purpose, a subterranean gallery, 511 feet in length, with lateral passages extending under the Confederate works, was constructed and stored with 8000 pounds of gunpowder. Early in the morning of July 30th, the mine was successfully exploded ; but, in the charge that followed, the Union forces were repulsed with a loss of about 4400 men in killed, wounded, and missing. Although General Burnside, in front of whose corps the mine was constructed, approved of the scheme, it was condemned as impracticable by the leading officers and engineers of the Army of the Potomac.

Mines, Deepest.

(1) Ashton Moss Colliery, near Manchester, England, 2850 feet.

(2) Adalbert Silver-Lead Mine, at Przibram, Bohemia, 3432 feet.

(3) Calumet Copper Mine, near Lake Superior, United States, 3900 feet.

"The deepest mine in the world is the rock-salt bore hole at Spesenberg, near Berlin, which is 4175 feet in depth. It is not, however, quite perpendicular. The deepest perpendicular shaft is that of Adalbert, at Prisbram, in Bohemia, which is 3280 feet. The deepest British mine is Dunhill Colliery, near Wigan, which is 2824 feet. The deepest boring in the world is the artesian well at Potsdam, Missouri, in the United States, which is 5500 feet, or 220 feet beyond a mile.—*Times*, Jan. 17, 1881."—Edwards's *Words, Facts, and Phrases*.

Miniatures. Miniatures were originally the small pictures with which manuscripts were illuminated during the Middle Ages. They received this name, not on account of their *minute* size, but because they were colored with *minium* (*Lat. red lead*), whence was derived the Italian word *miniatura*.

After the invention of printing and engraving, this art entered on a new phase, and the word "miniature" came to mean, in popular parlance, simply "a very small portrait."

Minié Rifle. An improved form of rifle invented by Claude Étienne Minié (1814–1879), a French soldier, and brought out by him in 1849. It was adopted by the French army about 1850 ; and, with certain modifications, by the British army in 1851. It was superseded in the British army by the Enfield rifle in 1853. The Minié rifle weighed 9 lbs. 13 ounces, and was 4 feet 7 inches in length,—the diameter of the bore being .702″. See *Enfield Rifle*.

Minnesingers (*Ger. minne, love ; singer, singer*). The name given to certain lyric poets of Germany that flourished during the 12th and 13th centuries. They were generally men of noble birth, and sang of love, friend-ship, religion, war, and adventure, at the courts of kings and feudal barons. Although akin to the troubadours of Provence, the minnesingers treated love in a more refined spirit, and manifested a greater reverence for woman. They wrote principally in the Swabian dialect of Middle High German. The most famous of their number were Walther von der Vogelweide and Wolfram von Eschenbach. The Hohenstaufens, the dukes of Austria, and Hermann of Thuringia were the chief patrons of the minnesingers. See *Meistersingers*.

Minor Prophets. The name given to the group of *Old Testament* prophets from Hosea to Malachi inclusive, in allusion to the brevity of their writings. The term is also applied to the books containing their prophecies. These are *Hosea, Joel, Amos, Obadiah, Jonah, Micah, Nahum, Habakkuk, Zephaniah, Haggai, Zechariah, and Malachi*. See *Major Prophets*.

Minotaur. A hideous monster, having the body and limbs of a man and the head of a bull, confined in the labyrinth near Cnossus in Crete, where it was fed with human victims sent periodically by tributary states. The Minotaur was the fruit of a most unnatural passion entertained by Pasiphaë, wife of Minos, for a bull; the animal was finally slain by Theseus, with the help of Ariadne. See *Labyrinth* (2).

Minstrel of the Border. A sobriquet conferred upon Sir Walter Scott (1771–1832), the distinguished poet and novelist. See *Border Minstrel*.

" Once more by Newark's castle gate,
    Long left without a warder,
I stood, looked, listened, and with thee,
    Great *Minstrel of the Border*."
               Wordsworth.

Minstrels. The name given during the Middle Ages, in England, Scotland, France, and Normandy, to strolling singers that accompanied themselves upon the harp, and added dancing, mimicry, and other devices for the entertainment of their patrons. In England, they fell into disrepute during the reign of Henry VIII (1509–1547), and were adjudged rogues and vagabonds in the time of Queen Elizabeth (1558–1603). The minstrels were the successors of the skalds, bards, and minnesingers. According to Haydn's *Dictionary of Dates*, they were originally pipers appointed by lords of manors to entertain their copyholders while at work, and owed their origin to the glee men or harpers of the Saxons. See *Minnesingers*.

Mint Sauce. " Eating mint sauce with lamb is probably a remnant of the custom of eating bitter herbs with the paschal lamb. It is a custom unknown on the Continent, and peculiarly English."—Edwards's *Words, Facts, and Phrases.*

Minuet. This graceful dance derives its name from the Latin *minutus* (*small*), and is so called on account of the short steps that characterize it.

Minute-Men. The name given, during the American Revolutionary War, to the militia of 12,000 men enrolled by enactment of the Provincial Congress of Massachusetts, on November 23rd, 1774, and so called because pledged to be ready for service at " a minute's notice." They were afterwards increased to 20,000.

"This was the *minute-man* of the Revolution, the rural citizen trained in the common school, the church, and the town-meeting; who carried a bayonet that thought, and whose gun, loaded with a principle, brought down, not a man, but a system."—*George William Curtis.*

Mirabeau of the Mob. A title conferred upon Georges Jacques Danton (1759–1794), the French revolutionist, whose character bore a striking resemblance to that of Mirabeau.

Miracle of Nature. A sobriquet conferred upon Christina (1632–1654),

Queen of Sweden, noted for her ability and eccentricity.

Miracle of Our Age. A title conferred upon Sir Philip Sidney (1554–1586), the English statesman and poet.

Miracle - Plays. Rude dramas founded on the historical events in the *Old* and *New Testaments* and the lives of the saints, and performed at first in the churches, and afterwards on fixed or movable platforms in the streets. They were extremely popular during the Middle Ages, and were frequently written and acted by the clergy. The earliest known specimen is the *Christos Paschon*, assigned, but somewhat questionably, to Gregory Nazianzen (328–389). The Miracle-Plays were designed as a means of religious instruction for the people ; but were finally so mixed up with irreverence and buffoonery as to become the means of inducing contempt rather than reverence for the Church. They were suppressed in Austria and Bavaria during the latter part of the 18th century ; but an exception was made in favor of the Passion-Play at Ober-Ammergau, which is still regularly performed every ten years,—the last representation having been given in 1900. See *Moralities ; Mysteries ; Ober-Ammergau.*

Misérables, Les. A famous novel by Victor Hugo (1802–1885). It appeared in 1862, and is by many considered to be his masterpiece.

Miserere. A paraphrase of the 50th Psalm in the *Vulgate* (51st in the *Authorized Version*), beginning with the words *Miserere mei, Deus*, and forming a liturgic prayer set to music. It is used in the Roman Catholic Church on penitential occasions and especially in Passion Week. The most famous arrangement is that by Gregorio Allegri (1580–1652), in which two choirs, one of four and one of five parts, sing alternately until the finale, when both join in *pianissimo*, the measure gradually becoming slower.

This piece, from the time of its composition, has always been sung on Wednesday and Friday of Passion Week, in the Sistine Chapel at Rome. It was formerly the exclusive property of the Chapel, but was written down by Mozart after two hearings. Since then it has been repeatedly published. See *Penitential Psalms.*

Misnomers. The following misnomers are taken from a list in Brewer's *Dictionary of Phrase and Fable.*

(1) *Absalom* means a *Father's Peace,* a fatal name for David's rebellious son.

(2) *Arabic Figures* were not invented by the Arabs, but by the Indians.

(3) *Baffin's Bay* is no bay at all.

(4) *Brazilian Grass* does not come from Brazil, nor even grow in Brazil, nor is it a grass at all. It consists of strips of a palm leaf (*Chamærops argentea*), and is chiefly imported from Cuba.

(5) *Catgut* is not the gut of cats, but of sheep.

(6) *China,* as a name for porcelain, gives rise to the contradictory expressions British China, Sèvres China, Dresden China, Dutch China, Chelsea China, etc., like wooden mile-stones, iron mile-stones, brass shoe-horns, iron pens, etc.

(7) *Cleopatra's Needles* were not erected by Cleopatra nor in honor of that queen, but by Thothmes III.

(8) *Dormouse* is *dormeuse,* the sleepy animal.

(9) *Galvanized Iron* is not galvanized. It is simply iron coated with zinc, and this is done by dipping it in a zinc bath containing muriatic acid.

(10) *German Silver* is not silver at all, nor was the mixture invented by a German, but has been in use in China time out of mind.

(11) *Indians (American).* A blunder of geography on the part of the early discoverers of the New World, who set their faces westward from Europe to find India, and believed they had done so when they discovered America.

(12) *Irish Stew,* a dish unknown in Ireland.

(13) *Iron-Mask* was made of velvet.

(14) *Lunar Caustic* is not a substance from the moon, but is simply nitrate of silver, and silver is the astrological symbol of the moon.

(15) *Lunatics* are not affected by the changes of the moon more than other invalids. No doubt their disorder has its periodicities, but it is not affected by the moon.

(16) *Meerschaum* is not petrified " sea-foam," as the word implies, but a composition of silica, magnesia, and water.

(17) *Mother of Pearl* is the inner layer of several sorts of shell. It is not the mother of pearls, as the name indicates, but in some cases the matrix of the pearl.

(18) *Pen* means a feather (*Lat. penna, wing*). A steel pen is not a very choice expression.

(19) *Pompey's Pillar,* in Alexandria, was erected neither by nor to Pompey. It was set up by the Emperor Diocletian, according to its inscription.

(20) *Prussian Blue* does not come from Prussia, but is the precipitate of the salt of protoxide of iron with red prussiate of potass.

(21) *Rice Paper* is not made from rice, but from the pith of Tung-tsau, or hollow-plant, so called because it is hollow when the pith has been pushed out.

(22) *Salt of Lemon* is in reality a binoxalate of potash, with a little of the quadroxalate.

(23) *Sand blind* is a mere corruption of *sam* (*half*) blind.

(24) *Sealing Wax* is not wax at all, nor does it contain a single particle of wax. It is made of shellac, Venice turpentine, and cinnabar.

(25) *Slave* means noble, illustrious (*slavi*), but is now applied to the most ignoble and debased.

(26) *Turkeys* do not come from Turkey, but North America, through Spain, or India. The French call them "dindon," *i. e., d' Inde* or *coq d' Inde,* a term equally incorrect.

(27) *Turkey Rhubarb* neither grows in Turkey, nor is it exported from Turkey. It grows in the great mountain chain between Tartary and Siberia, and is a Russian monopoly.

(28) *Turkish Baths* are not of Turkish origin, nor are they baths, but hot-air rooms or thermæ.

(29) *Vallambrosa.* Milton says—

" Thick as autumnal leaves that strew the brooks
In Vallambrosa."

Paradise Lost, i, 302.

But the trees of Vallambrosa, being pines, do not shed thickly in autumn, and the brooks are not strewed with their leaves.

(30) *Ventriloquism* is not voice from the stomach at all, but from the mouth.

(31) *Whale-bone* is no bone at all, nor does it possess any properties of bone. It is a substance attached to the upper jaw of the whale, and serves to strain the water which the creature takes up in large mouthfuls.

Misquotations. The following list, chiefly of misquotations from Scripture, is taken from Bombaugh's *Gleanings for the Curious :*

" God tempers the wind to the shorn lamb." From Sterne's *Sentimental Journey to Italy.* Compare *Isaiah* xxvii, 8.

" In the midst of life we are in death." From the Burial Service ; and this, originally, from a hymn of Luther.

" Bread and wine which the Lord hath commanded to be received." From the English Catechism.

" Not to be wise above what is written." Not in Scripture.

" That the Spirit would go from heart to heart as oil from vessel to vessel." Not in Scripture.

" The merciful man is merciful to his beast." The scriptural form is, " A righteous man regardeth the life of his beast."—*Prov.* xii, 10.

" A nation shall be born in a day." In *Isaiah* it reads, " Shall a nation be born at once ? "—lxvi, 8.

" As iron sharpeneth iron, so doth a man the countenance of his friend." " Iron sharpeneth iron ; so a man sharpeneth the countenance of his friend."—*Prov.* xxvii, 17.

"That he who runs may read." " That he may run that readeth."—*Hab.* ii, 2.

" Owe no man anything but love." " Owe no man anything, but to love one another."—*Rom.* xiii, 8.

" Prone to sin as the sparks fly upward." " Born unto trouble, as the sparks fly upward."—*Job* v, 7.

" Exalted to heaven in point of privilege." Not in the Bible.

Eve was not Adam's *helpmate*, but merely a help meet for him ; nor was Absalom's long hair, of which he was so proud, the instrument of his destruction ; his head, and not the hair upon it, having been caught in the boughs of the tree. (2 *Samuel* xviii, 9.)

" Money is the root of evil." Paul said, 1 *Timothy* vi, 10, " The love of money is the root of all evil."

" In the sweat of thy face shalt thou eat bread."—*Gen.* iii, 19. Commonly quoted " brow."

" Cleanliness akin to godliness." Not in the Bible.

Missal. The mass-book of the Roman Catholic Church. It was probably compiled at the close of the fifth century, and was amplified by Pope Gelasius I (492–496), and by Pope Gregory I (590–604). Various missals, differing in minor details, were in use in the Church until 1570 ; but, in that year, Pope Pius V (1566–1572), in virtue of a decree of the Council of Trent (1545–1563), ordered that all churches that did not possess a mass-book, whose use they had enjoyed uninterruptedly for 200 years, should adopt the Roman Missal. Several churches in Germany, France, and Italy availed themselves of this privilege ; but at the present day the great majority have conformed to the Roman Catholic requirement. The

Roman Missal was revised by Pope Clement VIII (1592–1605) in 1604, and again by Pope Urban VIII (1623–1644) in 1634. In England, the Missal was superseded by the Book of Common Prayer in 1549. See *Common Prayer, Book of ; Trent, Council of.*

Missing Link. An expression used in zoölogy to denote a hypothetical form of life assumed to have existed between two related types : more specifically, a term applied to some individual intermediate in development between the ape and man, and forming a bond of union between them. Evolution, however, does not teach that man is descended from the ape ; but simply that both these types have evolved from some more primitive form, which is regarded as their common ancestor.

Mississippi River. The Mississippi is the longest river in North America, and has a total length of 2804 miles. The Missouri affluent, with the lower Mississippi, gives a total of 4382 miles, and forms the longest river on the globe. See *Father of Waters.*

Mississippi Scheme. A scheme devised by John Law (1671–1729), a famous Scotch financier, under the patronage of the Duke of Orleans, Regent of France, for the purpose of liquidating the national debt of that country by means of the resources of the province of Louisiana, bordering on the Mississippi River. The project was launched in 1716, by the establishment of a bank ; and in 1717, the West India Company was incorporated with a capital of 200,000 shares of 500 livres each. In 1719, this company obtained exclusive control of the trade to the East Indies, China, and the South Seas, and all the possessions of the French East India Company. An additional issue of 5000 shares was created, but so wild was the speculative craze that more than 300,000 persons applied for them. As a result, the shares rose to 20 times their original value, and in 1719 were nominally worth more than 80 times the amount of all the specie current in France. The " bubble " burst in 1720, and the notes of the bank fell to one-tenth of their nominal value. Law was obliged to flee the country, and died in poverty at Venice. The Mississippi Scheme was the most disastrous speculation of modern times, and nearly precipitated a revolution. It must not be confounded with the South Sea Bubble, which see. See *Law's Bubble.*

Missouri Compromise. The name popularly given to an act of the United States Congress, passed February 27th, 1821, admitting Missouri into the Union as a slaveholding State, but expressly declaring that slavery should thenceforth be prohibited in any State lying north of latitude 36° 30′,—the southern boundary of Missouri. Although Henry Clay was one of the most prominent supporters of this measure, it originated, not with him, but with John W. Taylor of New York. See *Buncombe or Bunkum ; Kansas-Nebraska Bill.*

" Like compromises of principles generally, it only postponed the evil day. At the time of that agreement, slavery was comparatively weak, and might have been abolished, or at least restricted by the nation. By letting it grow, it was allowed to reach such power, that it required for its abolition a great civil war and the lives of many thousand men."—Higginson's *Young Folks' History of the United States.*

Mistletoe. According to an old Celtic tradition, the mistletoe was originally a forest tree ; but having furnished the wood for the Savior's cross, it was thenceforth condemned to exist as a parasite. It was closely connected with many of the druidical superstitions, and was held in high esteem for its magical properties. It was styled " all heal " by the Druids, and was considered an antidote for all diseases. Traces of this ancient respect linger in certain old English Christmas customs, such as kissing under the mistletoe.

Mistral. A cold northwest wind that prevails at certain seasons of the year in southern France and northern Italy, and does great damage to crops and fruit. It is especially violent from the close of autumn to the beginning of spring. It dries up the soil, clears the atmosphere, and raises dangerous storms on the Mediterranean.

Mistress of the Adriatic. An appellation conferred upon the city of Venice, which, in the days of its supremacy, ruled the Adriatic with its fleets, and controlled the commerce of that sea.

"The nations of the Baltic and of farthest Ind now exchanged their products on a more extensive scale and with a wider sweep across the earth than when the *Mistress of the Adriatic* alone held the keys of Asiatic commerce."—*Motley.*

Mistress of the Seas. A name frequently given to Great Britain, in allusion to her supremacy on the ocean. This sentiment finds expression in the familiar line :

"Britannia rules the waves."

Mistress of the World. A title frequently bestowed upon the city of ancient Rome, which rose gradually from humble beginnings to almost universal empire, and finally surpassed in the extent of its dominions all the great sovereignties that had preceded it. The Roman Empire, during the reign of Augustus, is supposed to have contained 100,000,000 inhabitants — one-half of whom were slaves. It included the modern countries of Portugal, Spain, France, Belgium, western Holland, Rhenish Prussia, parts of Baden and Wurtemberg, most of Bavaria, Switzerland, Italy, the Tyrol, Austria proper, western Hungary, Croatia, Slavonia, Turkey in Europe, Greece, Asia Minor, Syria, Palestine, Idumæa, Egypt, Cyrenaica, Tripoli, Tunis, Algeria, and most of Morocco.

Mitche Manito. The name given by certain tribes of North American Indians to the supreme Spirit of Evil.

He is symbolized as a serpent. See *Gitche Manito.*

"*Mitche Manito* the Mighty,
He the dreadful Spirit of Evil,
As a serpent was depicted,
As Kenabeek, the great serpent,
Very crafty, very cunning,
Is the creeping Spirit of Evil,
Was the meaning of this symbol."
Longfellow's *Hiawatha.*

Mitrailleuse. A breech - loading machine-gun invented in Belgium. It was introduced into the French army by Napoleon III (1852–1870) after the Austro-Prussian War of 1866, and was much used during the Franco-Prussian War of 1870. It consists of 37 rifle-barrels (inclosed in a steel cylinder), which can be discharged either separately or simultaneously by the turn of a crank-handle. Reloading requires five seconds ; and ten discharges can be fired in one minute, with an effective range of about 1000 yards. The mitrailleuse did not render efficient service during the War of 1870,—being either destroyed by the long-range shell fire of the German batteries, or captured by the cavalry without serious loss. See *Gatling Gun.*

Mitre. A tavern in Fleet Street, London, famous as the meeting-place of Dr. Samuel Johnson, Goldsmith, Boswell, and others. It is no longer in existence.

"The *Mitre* was Dr. Johnson's favourite supper-house, the parties including Goldsmith, Percy, Hawkesworth, and Boswell; there was planned the tour to the Hebrides. Johnson had a strange nervous feeling, which made him uneasy if he had not touched every post between the *Mitre* and his own lodgings. Johnson took Goldsmith to the *Mitre*, where Boswell and the Doctor had supped together in the previous month, when Boswell spoke of Goldsmith's 'very loose, odd, scrambling kind of life,' and Johnson defended him as one of our first men as an author, and a very worthy man ;— adding, 'he has been loose in his principles but is coming right.' "—Timbs's *Clubs and Club Life in London.*

Mnemosyne. In classical mythology, the goddess of memory, and by Zeus the mother of the Muses.

"The mother of the Muses was called . . . *Mnemosyne*, that is, 'Memory,' and especially the memory or recollection of great events, such as the war with the Titans, that was said to have occurred at the commencement of the world's history, and must continue to occur until the universe is brought into perfect harmony. In later times she came to be viewed merely as goddess of memory, and worshipped along with the Muses."—Murray's *Manual of Mythology*.

Moab. A region east and southeast of the Dead Sea, formerly inhabited by the descendants of Moab, the son of Lot. The country is frequently mentioned in the Bible. The Moabites were gross idolaters — worshipping Chemosh and Baalpeor with obscene rites and ceremonies. They treated the Israelites with great inhumanity during their approach to the "Land of Promise," and were constantly at war with them. They were subdued by Ehud about 1336, by David about 1040, and by Jehoshaphat in 895 B.C.

Moabite Stone. A black basalt tablet—3 feet 10 inches long, 2 feet broad, and 14½ inches thick — discovered among the ruins of Dhibân in ancient Moab, by the Rev. F. Klein, in 1868. It belongs to the 9th century B.C., and bears an inscription of 34 lines in Hebrew-Phœnician characters, recording the successful revolt of Mesha, King of Moab, against Jehoram, King of Israel,—referred to in 2 *Kings* iii, 4, 5. The stone was purposely broken by the Arabs, whose cupidity had been aroused by M. Clermont-Ganneau in his indiscreet eagerness to obtain possession of it. It has, however, been carefully mended, and is now in the museum of the Louvre, at Paris.

Modern Athens.

(1) An appellation conferred upon the city of Edinburgh, Scotland, not only on account of its resemblance to the capital of ancient Attica, but also because of its many famous institutions of learning, its cultivated society, and its distinguished representatives in the fields of letters and science.

(2) A name given to Boston, Massachusetts, a city famous not only for its many educational, literary, and scientific institutions, but also for the intelligence and refinement of its citizens.

Modern Babylon. A name given to London, the metropolis of the British Empire, which in size, population, wealth, and influence surpasses all other cities of the modern world as Babylon did those of ancient times.

Modern Gracchus. A sobriquet conferred upon the Count de Mirabeau (1749–1791), who espoused the cause of the people against the aggressions of the privileged rulers. See *Hurricane*.

Modern Messalina. An epithet bestowed upon Catherine II (1762–1796), of Russia, in allusion to her cruelty and licentiousness. See *Messalina*.

"Though extremely profligate and cruel, she had too strong a mind to be enslaved by her passions or to allow them to interfere with her ambitious policy."—Lippincott's *Biographical Dictionary*.

Mogul, Great. See *Great Mogul*.

Mohair. This word is said to be a corruption of *moorhair*, or hair of the Angora goat of Asia Minor, introduced into Spain by the Moors. Other authorities derive the word from the Arabic *mukhayyer*, a kind of haircloth, or from the Latin *marmoreus* (*resembling marble*).

Mohammed's Coffin. See *Mahomet's Coffin*.

Moll Cutpurse. A nickname bestowed upon Mary Frith, a notorious thief in the time of Charles I (1625–1649). She possessed great physical strength, and frequently assumed man's attire. Having on one occasion "held up" Lord Fairfax on Hounslow Heath, she was captured and sent to Newgate, but escaped by means of bribery. She died of dropsy at the age of 74 years.

Moll Flanders. "A woman of extraordinary beauty, born in the Old

Bailey. She was twelve years a courtezan, five times a wife, twelve years a thief, eight years a transport in Virginia ; but ultimately grew rich, lived honestly, and died a penitent (Charles II's reign)."—Brewer's *Dictionary of Phrase and Fable*.

Daniel Defoe has written a tale entitled *Moll Flanders*.

Molly Maguires.

(1) Members of a secret society in Ireland, organized in 1843 to resist the efforts of officials employed by the landlords to distrain for rent. They were called "Maguires" from Cornelius Maguire, Baron of Inniskillen, who, in 1641, took part with Sir Phelim O'Neil in the Irish Rebellion,—and received the additional name of "Molly," because they frequently committed their depredations while attired in women's clothes.

"*Molly Maguires* were generally stout active young men, dressed up in women's clothes, with faces blackened or otherwise disguised. . . . In this state they used suddenly to surprise the unfortunate grippers, keepers, and process-servers, and either duck them in bog-holes, or beat them in the most merciless manner, so that *Molly Maguires* became the terror of our officials."—Trench's *Realities of Irish Life*.

(2) A secret society — composed almost entirely of Irishmen — which, during the ten years preceding 1877, terrorized the inhabitants of the coal-mining regions of Pennsylvania.

"Murders were committed, and great quantities of coal and other property destroyed by incendiarism. In 1875, they terrorized over the whole country, threatened whole towns, and compelled the ordering out of the militia. On the withdrawal of the troops, a series of the most cruel murders was committed, until, at length, by strategy, ten of the members of the society were arrested for the crime. Notwithstanding the efforts made by the members, who appeared to swear an alibi, but who were advised by counsel to go home and not be prosecuted for perjury, all were convicted of murder, and on the 20th of June, 1877, executed."—*Providence Journal*.

Moloch (*more properly*, *Molech*). The chief deity of the Ammonites,

mentioned in 1 *Kings* xi, 7, as the "abomination of the children of Ammon." The worship of Moloch, which consisted chiefly in the sacrifice of human victims, was established in Jerusalem by Solomon (1015–975 B.C.), and abolished by Josiah (641–610 B.C.). It was not abandoned, however, by the Jews, until the time of the Babylonish Captivity (606–536 B.C.). The word "Moloch" is figuratively used to denote any pernicious influence that entails loss of life or sacrifice of principle, as the Moloch of war, the Moloch of ambition, etc.

" First *Moloch*, horrid king, besmear'd with blood
Of human sacrifice and parents' tears,
Though for the noise of drums and timbrels loud
Their children's cries unheard, that passed thro' fire
To his grim idol. Him the Ammonite
Worshipp'd in Rabba and her wat'ry plain,
In Argob and in Basan, to the stream
Of utmost Arnon. Nor content with such
Audacious neighborhood, the wisest heart
Of Solomon he led by fraud to build
His temple right against the temple of God,
On that opprobrious hill ; and made his grove
The pleasant vale of Hinnom, Tophet thence
And black Gehenna call'd, the type of Hell."

Paradise Lost, i, 392–405.

Momus. In classical mythology, the son of Nox, and god of mockery and ridicule. He delighted to rail at the actions of men and gods, sparing no one except Aphrodite, in whom he could find nothing to criticise, and in consequence vexed himself to death. It is said that he found fault with the man made by Hephæstus, because there was no window in his breast through which his secret thoughts might be seen.

Monaco. The smallest sovereign principality in Europe, situated on the Mediterranean, nine miles east of Nice. It has an area of eight square miles, and a population of about 13,000.

This principality has been in possession of the Genoese family of Grimaldi since 968 A.D. In 1793 it became subject to France, but in 1815 regained its independence. Monaco has its own system of coinage, and issues its own postage-stamps. It is especially famous for the casino or gaming-establishment at Monte Carlo. See *Monte Carlo*.

Mona Lisa. See *Belle Joconde*.

Monarchy Abolished. The English monarchy was abolished by the House of Commons early in February, 1649 (a few days after the execution of Charles I), and was restored in the person of Charles II, his son, on May 29th, 1660. The French monarchy was abolished by the National Convention on September 21st, 1792, and was restored in the person of Louis XVIII, on May 3rd, 1814. On the return of Napoleon from Elba in March, 1815, the French King proceeded to Lille and afterwards to Ghent, where he remained during the brief period of the Emperor's second reign. See *Hundred Days*.

Money. The word "money" is derived from *moneta*, a name given by the Romans to their silver pieces, because coined in a building on the Capitoline Hill attached to the temple of Jupiter Moneta. The officers in charge of the mint were called triumviri monetales, and Niebuhr thinks that they were introduced at the time when the Romans first began to coin silver, *i. e.*, 269 B.C.

Monism. The name given to the philosophic theory that refers all phenomena to a single ultimate principle. See *Dualism*.

"The doctrine has been held in three generic forms : matter and its phenomena have been explained as a modification of mind, involving an idealistic *monism*; or mind has been explained and resolved into matter, giving a materialistic *monism*; or, thirdly, matter, mind, and their phenomena have been held to be the manifestations or modifications of some one substance, like the substance of Spinoza, or a supposed unknown something of some evolutionists, which is capable of an objective and subjective aspect." — Webster's *International Dictionary*.

Monitor. An armored vessel of novel construction, famous for her contest with the Confederate iron-clad *Merrimac* in Hamptom Roads, on March 9th, 1862. The *Monitor* was built for the United States Government by John Ericsson (1803-1889), a Swedish engineer, and was launched at Greenpoint, Long Island, on January 30th, 1862. This peculiar structure — consisting of a sea-going iron raft surmounted by a revolving turret—was 141 feet 6 inches in length, 41 feet 6 inches in breadth, with a depth of hold of 11 feet 6 inches. The deck was raised a few inches only above the water, and the turret contained two eleven-inch shell guns, each weighing 15,668 pounds. The vessel was propelled by a powerful steam-engine. She was lost in a gale off Cape Hatteras, on December 31st, 1862. See *Merrimac (1)*.

Monosyllabic Languages. Languages in which the words are composed of simple monosyllabic roots, isolated, and, as a rule, independent of one another. In this elementary form of language, the root-words correspond in their essence with general conceptions only, and are unrestricted by any notions of person, gender, number, time, mood, or relationship. The principal monosyllabic languages are the Chinese, Annamese, Siamese, Burman, and Tibetan. To these may be added the Pegu in British Burma, and the Kassia, confined to a small district in the south of Assam. See *Agglutinative Languages; Inflected Languages*.

Monroe Doctrine. The name given to a scheme of national policy outlined by James Monroe (1758–1831), while President of the United States, and promulgated by him in his message to

Congress, dated December 2nd, 1823. It embodies the principle of non-intervention of European powers in the affairs of the Western Hemisphere, and has been practically, though not formally, adopted by the United States. The Monroe Doctrine was asserted against Napoleon III's attempt to found an empire in Mexico in 1863–1867, and was frequently referred to at the time of the boundary disputes between Venezuela and British Guiana in 1895–1896. The following passage is from President Monroe's famous message :

"We owe it therefore to candor, and to the amicable relations existing between the United States and those Powers, to declare that we should consider any attempt on their part to extend their system to any portion of this hemisphere, as dangerous to our peace and safety. With the existing Colonies or Dependencies of any European Power we have not interfered, and shall not interfere. But with the Governments who have declared their Independence, and maintained it, and whose Independence we have, on great consideration, and on just principles, acknowledged, we could not view any interposition for the purpose of oppressing them, or controuling in any other manner their destiny by any European Power, in any other light than as the manifest ation of an unfriendly disposition towards the United States."

Monsieur Véto. A nickname conferred upon Louis XVI (1774–1789), during the French Revolution, in allusion to the privilege granted him by the Constitution of 1791 of vetoing all measures passed by the Legislative Assembly. See *Madame Véto*.

Mons Meg. A famous old cannon, on the esplanade of Edinburgh Castle, supposed to have been forged at Mons, in Flanders, in 1486, during the reign of James II (1437–1460) of Scotland. It was used at the siege of Norham Castle in 1514; but afterwards fell into the hands of the English, and for a century and a half was one of the most admired relics in the Tower of London. The cannon was restored to Edinburgh Castle by George IV (1820–1830) in 1829. Mons Meg is 13 feet 3¼ inches

long, with a bore of 20 inches. According to some authorities, it was named " Mons " from the blacksmith that forged it, and " Meg " from his wife.

Mons Sacer (*Lat. Sacred Mount*). An eminence, three miles distant from Rome, to which the plebeians, smarting under the indignities offered them by the privileged classes, retired in 494 B.C., with the intention of founding a new city. The patricians, thoroughly alarmed at this step, settled the difficulty by cancelling the debts of the commons, and setting at liberty those held in slavery. In addition, two magistrates — called tribunes, and chosen from the people — were appointed to watch over the plebeians, and protect them from the injustice of the patrician magistrates. It was on that occasion that Menenius Agrippa related to the plebeians, with telling effect, the fable of the belly and the members.

The plebeians withdrew a second time to *Mons Sacer* in 449 B.C., after the death of Virginia, and demanded the resignation of the decemvirs and the restoration of the consulate and tribunate. As a result, eight of the decemvirs were driven into exile, while Appius Claudius and one other were imprisoned and eventually committed suicide.

Mon Soldat (*Fr. My Soldier*). A term of endearment applied to Henry IV (1589–1610), King of France, by his favorite, Gabrielle d'Estrées.

Montagnards (*Fr. mountaineers*). The name given, during the first French Revolution, to the extreme radicals of the National Convention, because they occupied the most elevated seats in the hall of the assembly. The body included both the Jacobins and Cordeliers, and was led by Robespierre, Danton, Marat, St. Just, and Collot d'Herbois. The Montagnards triumphed over the Girondists on July 2nd, 1793 ; but were themselves overthrown on the Ninth Thermidor (July

27th, 1794). During the Revolution of 1848, the name " Montagnards " was assumed by the radical party in the National Assembly. See *Mountain*.

Montanists. Followers of Montanus, a heretic, who appeared at Ardaban in Phrygia in 156 A.D., and endeavored to reform and purify the Christian Church. He favored a rigorous discipline, advocated celibacy, discountenanced second marriages, encouraged martyrdom, and enjoined rigid fasts. Montanus, moreover, called himself the " Paraclete " ; claimed to possess the gift of prophecy (which he shared with two women, Prisca and Maximilla) ; and lived in daily expectation of the Second Advent. Tertullian, the eminent Church Father, joined the sect of the Montanists, which survived in the East until the 4th century.

Mont Blanc. The name of the highest mountain in Europe (if we regard the Caucasus range as Asiatic). It is 15,782 feet above the level of the sea, and is situated in France (40 miles south of the Lake of Geneva), and not in Switzerland, as is popularly supposed. Mont Blanc was successfully ascended for the first time by Balmat and Paccard, two guides, in June, 1786. Saussure reached the summit in the following year, and since that time the mountain has been frequently ascended. It is said that, down to 1886, 24 persons had perished in the attempt. More than 50 parties climb Mont Blanc, annually, at the present day. The construction of a railway up the mountain is now under consideration.

Mont Cenis Road. A famous military road over the Mont Cenis Pass between Savoy and Piedmont. It was constructed in 1802–1810 by Fabbroni, at the command of Napoleon I (1804–1814), and cost $1,500,000. See *Simplon Road*.

Mont Cenis Tunnel. A railway tunnel, 7½ miles long, piercing the Alps under the Col de Fréjus. It was begun on the Italian side in 1857, and on the French side in 1863; was completed in 1870 at a cost of $15,000,000, and opened on September 17th, 1871. The tunnel starts on the French side from a point 3904 feet above the level of the sea, rises gradually to an elevation of 4377 feet, and then slopes downward to the opening on the Italian side, 4334 feet above the level of the sea. About 2000 workmen were constantly employed in the work of excavation, which is estimated to have cost $1100 per lineal yard. See *Simplon Tunnel; St. Gotthard Tunnel*.

Mont-de-Piété. A national pawn-broking institution in Paris, founded in 1777, by a royal ordinance of Louis XVI (1774–1789). It enjoys a monopoly of lending money on pledges for the benefit of the " Assistance Publique," and charges seven per cent. on all loans, to pay the current expenses of the establishment.

" The loans are not made for less than a fortnight, but articles may be redeemed within that time on payment of the fees. The sums advanced vary from two-thirds to four-fifths of the value of the articles, the maximum lent being 10,000 francs at this establishment, and 500 francs at the branch-offices. The interest and fees, which before 1885 were as high as 9½ per cent., are now reduced to 7 per cent., with a minimum of 1 franc. The pledges are sold after fourteen months from the time when the borrower has failed to redeem them or to renew his ticket or ' reconnaissance ' ; but within three years more the excess of the price realised over the sum lent may still be claimed. The *Mont-de-Piété* lends upwards of 50,000,-000 francs annually."—Baedeker's *Paris and its Environs*.

Monte Carlo. A small town in the principality of Monaco, famous for its casino or gaming establishment, built on ground leased by the Prince of Monaco to a French stock company. This palatial structure is open during the entire year, and contains play-rooms, dancing-rooms, and reading-rooms. It is annually visited by over 400,000 persons, and employs the services of 1000 attendants. See *Monaco*.

Montenotte, Battle of. Fought on April 12th, 1796, between the Austrians commanded by General Argentan and the French led by Napoleon Bonaparte, who, in this battle, won his first victory over the Austrians.

"My patent of nobility," said Napoleon, on one occasion, to the Emperor of Austria, "dates from the *battle of Montenotte*."

Montereau, Battle of. Fought on February 18th, 1814, near Paris, between the Austrians under Schwartzenberg and the French commanded by Napoleon I (1804–1814), who, in this battle, won his last victory over the allies. It was on this occasion that the Emperor, when entreated by his artillerymen to retire to a place of safety, exclaimed : " Courage, my friends ; the ball that is to kill me is not yet cast ! "

Monticello. A fine colonial mansion, about three miles from Charlottesville, Virginia, formerly the residence of Thomas Jefferson (1743–1826), the third President of the United States. It stands upon a hill 600 feet above the town, and commands a superb view of the Blue Ridge Mountains for 150 miles. Not far from the house is a small private graveyard, where the author of the Declaration of Independence lies buried.

Montmartre. A hill in the northern part of Paris, rising 330 feet above the Seine, and commanding an extensive view of the city. The word is said to be derived from *Mons Martyrum (Lat. Mountain of the Martyrs)*, a name given to this elevation because St. Denis and his companions were, according to tradition, martyred there in 270 A.D. Other authorities, however, say that the word is derived from *Mons Martis (Lat. Mountain of Mars)*, from a temple of Mars that once stood there. Gypsum has long been quarried at Montmartre, and has, on that account, received the name of plaster of Paris.

"The heights of *Montmartre* witnessed the final struggle between the French troops and the Prussian and Russian allies on 30th March, 1814, and also played an important part in the sieges of 1870–71. On 18th March, 1871, the insurgent soldiers, having assassinated the generals Clément-Thomas and Lecomte, took possession of the cannon on the Montmartre, which had been entrusted to a body of the National Guard. Thus began the Communist rebellion of 18th March to 28th May, 1871, a period of horror almost without parallel in the chequered annals of Paris. The insurgents were dislodged by the victorious troops on 24th May, and the batteries of *Montmartre* were then directed against the Communists who occupied Les Buttes - Chaumont and Père - Lachaise."—Baedeker's *Paris and its Environs*.

Montmorenci Falls. A picturesque waterfall, eight miles northeast of Quebec, Canada. It is 250 feet high, and 50 feet wide. An ice cone, formed every winter below the falls, sometimes attains a height of 200 feet. A mile above the precipice may be seen the " Natural Steps," a succession of ledges worn by the action of the water, and as regularly formed as if they were the work of human hands.

Mont St. Michel. A picturesque rocky islet in the bay of St. Michel, off the coast of Normandy. It consists of a mass of granite—3000 feet in circumference and 242 feet in height—surmounted by an ancient castle and monastery, founded by the Benedictines during the 8th century. This structure, after successfully withstanding desperate sieges by Henry II (1154–1189) and Henry V (1413–1422) of England, was converted into a prison during the French Revolution, and continued to be so used until 1863. In 1874, it was declared a " monument historique," and large sums were expended upon its restoration. Mont St. Michel bears a striking resemblance to St. Michael's Mount, off Cornwall, on the opposite side of the English Channel. See *St. Michael's Mount*.

Monument, The. A fluted stone

column, 202 feet high, designed by Sir Christopher Wren, and erected in Fish Street, London, in 1671–1677, in commemoration of the Great Fire of 1666. A winding staircase leads to a platform,—enclosed in an iron cage to prevent suicides,—above which rises a huge gilded urn. Inscriptions and allegorical reliefs adorn the pedestal. It is said that the height of the column equals the distance from the foot of the base to the house in Pudding Lane where the conflagration commenced. The cost of this structure was about £14,500. See *Great Fire of London.*

Monumental Church. A memorial church in Richmond, Virginia, erected on the site of the Richmond Theatre, at the burning of which, in 1811, 60 persons—including Governor Smith and some of the most eminent men and women of the State — lost their lives. The remains of these victims are interred beneath a mural tablet in the vestibule of the church.

Monumental City. A name frequently applied to the city of Baltimore, Maryland, from the number of its monuments,—the principal of which are the Washington Monument, the Battle Monument, the Wildey Monument, the Wells and McComas Monument, and the Poe Monument. See *Battle Monument; Washington Monument (2).*

Moody and Sankey. Two famous evangelists, whose labors were chiefly confined to Great Britain and the United States. In 1873, and again in 1883, they visited England and conducted enthusiastic revivals in that country. In the winter of 1876, they appeared at the Madison Square Garden, New York City, and in 1877 in Boston,—attracting vast crowds on both occasions. In later years, Mr. Moody (1837–1899), although engaged in evangelistic work, was chiefly occupied with his training-schools at Northfield, Massachusetts.

Moon Calf. An inanimate human monster, or shapeless mass, superstitiously believed to have been produced by the influence of the moon, but, according to Pliny, engendered by woman only. The word is also used to denote a dolt or stupid fellow.

Moon Hoax. The name given to a series of articles published in the New York *Sun* of August 26th–31st, 1835, under the title of *Great Astronomical Discoveries Lately Made by Sir John Herschel, LL.D., F.R.S., etc., at the Cape of Good Hope.* These articles professed to be extracts from reports in the *Supplement of the Edinburgh Scientific Journal,* of remarkable observations and discoveries concerning the moon, made by Sir John Herschel at the Cape of Good Hope, with his famous reflecting telescope. They were prepared by Locke, the editor of the *Sun,* and Lewis Gaylord Clark, then editor of the *Knickerbocker Magazine,* in the form of a literary romance, and were written with great care. The public was completely deceived by the narrative, and even scientific men credited the marvellous story. M. Arago, the eminent French savant, went so far, it is said, as to request the French Academy, of which he was a member, to send a deputation from that body to confer with the English astronomer at the Cape.

Moors. In European history, a term generically applied to the inhabitants of the Barbary States under Turkish rule, and to the actual inhabitants of Morocco, but specifically used to denote the Arab and Berber conquerors and occupants of Spain from 711 to 1492 A.D. During the first four centuries of their control of the Spanish peninsula, the Moors surpassed all the nations of northern Europe in literature, science, and the arts.

Moralities. Religious dramas (succeeding the *Miracle-Plays*) in which the *dramatis personæ* were personifications of the Virtues and Vices. These allegorical personages at first appeared in the *Miracle - Plays*, along with scriptural or legendary characters, but afterwards entirely supplanted them. The *Moralities* were first introduced into England during the time of Henry VI (1422–1461), and remained in favor until the reign of Elizabeth (1558–1603). They were inferior in interest to the *Miracle-Plays*, and led the way to the introduction and establishment of the regular English drama. See *Clerks of the Revels ; Miracle-Plays ; Mysteries.*

Mora Stones. A pile of stones near Upsala, the centre of ancient Sweden, where the old kings used to take the oath of office and receive the homage of their loyal subjects. These stones —eleven in number—are inscribed with the names and the dates of accession of these kings. Gustavus III (1771–1792) erected a building over this interesting historic relic, in 1780.

Moravians. A body of evangelical Protestants(otherwise known as *Herrn-huters, The Church of the Brethren,* or *The Unity of the Brethren*) that withdrew into Moravia in the 15th century. They were originally Hussites; but in 1467, under the leadership of Peter Chelczicky, they established a separate religious community based on the apostolic model. They spread rapidly during the 15th century, and flourished in Bohemia, Moravia, and Poland; but were finally either crushed, or absorbed into the Reformed Church. The Moravians founded an abode—called *Herrnhut* (*the Watch of the Lord*)—on Count Zinzendorf's estate in Saxony, in 1722, and were introduced by him into England about 1738. In this same year a number of Moravians came to the United States, and established a settlement in Georgia; but the majority removed to Pennsylvania soon after, and founded the town of Bethlehem in 1741. The Moravians have always been zealous in missionary work, and have labored extensively among the Indians of the New World.

33

Morey Letter. A letter that appeared, on the eve of the presidential election of 1880, in one of the morning journals in the interior of New York State. It purported to have been written by James A. Garfield (1831–1881), the Republican candidate, to H. L. Morey, Employers' Union, Lynn, Massachusetts, and declared that the interests of large employers of labor would be advanced by the free admission of Chinese immigrants. The letter was widely copied by the Democratic newspapers throughout the country—especially on the Pacific Slope,— and, although promptly denounced as a forgery by Garfield and subsequently proved to be such, nevertheless, in the opinion of many, its existence gave the six electoral votes of California to the Democratic candidate. The name and address of Morey proved to be fictitious.

Morganatic Marriage. A matrimonial union between a man of rank and a woman of inferior social position, in which it is stipulated that the woman and her children shall not enjoy the rank nor inherit the possessions of the man. The offspring, however, are considered legitimate. Morganatic marriages are solemnized by giving the left hand instead of the right. In Germany, this form of union is permitted to royalty and the higher nobility only ; in Prussia, to the lower nobility also. It is asserted that George I (1714–1727) of England was married in this way to the Duchess of Kendal; the Duke of Sussex to Lady Cecilia Underwood; and Frederick VI (1808–1839) of Denmark to the Countess of Danner.

Morgan Excitement. " In 1826, William Morgan and a David C. Miller of Batavia, N. Y., announced an *exposé* of Freemasonry. Before the book was produced Morgan was arrested for a trifling debt and confined in Canandaigua jail, from whence he was secretly taken on the night of 12 Sept. 1826, to fort Niagara, at the mouth of the Niagara river, and was never heard of afterwards. Probably violence to a person so obscure never produced so much excitement ; but the outrage was cruel and wanton. An earnest attempt was made to discover the perpetrators, but without success. Such was the feeling against the order of Freemasons, that it created a political party antagonistic to it (Anti-masonic) which nominated state and national tickets, 1829–31.''—Harper's *Book of Facts*.

" Suddenly, Morgan disappeared one evening, and it was soon proved that he had been forcibly abducted. Excitement naturally arose, committees of vigilance and safety were organized, and he was traced westward to Fort Niagara, near Lewiston, N. Y., where he was temporarily imprisoned, and whence, it was ultimately testified, he was taken out into deep water in Lake Ontario and there sunk, though this was strenuously denied, and various stories from time to time affirmed that he was subsequently seen alive at Smyrna in Asia, and other places."—*Horace Greeley*.

Morgarten, Battle of. A famous battle, fought on the mountain-slope of the same name in the Canton of Zug, Switzerland, on November 15th, 1315, in which 1300 Swiss from Schwyz, Uri, and Unterwalden engaged 20,000 Austrians, commanded by Duke Leopold, and completely defeated them.

Morgue. A small building on the Ile de la Cité, Paris, where the bodies of unknown persons are exposed to public view for the purpose of identification. It was erected in 1864, and is admirably adapted to its purpose. The bodies are placed on marble slabs—after having been frozen at 5–7° Fahrenheit—and may be thus preserved for at least three months. The annual number received is about 750,—one-seventh being those of women. Similar places for the reception of the unclaimed dead exist in all large cities.

Mormons. A religious community founded by Joseph Smith (1805–1844) in Fayette, Seneca Co., New York, in 1830. In 1831, the Mormons settled in Kirtland, Ohio, and soon after founded Zion, Missouri. In 1838, they removed to Nauvoo, Illinois, where Smith was shot while in jail. After enduring much persecution, they migrated in 1847 to Utah, under the guidance of Brigham Young (who was soon after chosen seer), and founded Salt Lake City. Several ineffectual attempts having been made by the Mormons for the admission of Utah into the Union, President Woodruff, in 1890, issued a proclamation declaring that the Church no longer enjoins polygamy, and this declaration was afterwards confirmed in conference. In consequence of this proclamation, Utah was admitted as a State in 1896. The Mormons throughout the world number about 250,000, — 100,000 of whom are in Utah. See *Book of Mormon ; Latter-Day Saints*.

Mormon Tabernacle. See *Mormon Temple*.

Mormon Temple. A superb granite structure in Salt Lake City, Utah, erected in 1853–1893, at a cost of over $4,000,000. The building is 186 feet long and 99 feet wide, and is adorned at each end with three pointed towers, —the loftiest of which, in the centre of the eastern façade, is 210 feet high and is surmounted by a colossal gilded figure of the Mormon angel Moroni. The interior (not accessible to strangers) is artistically decorated.

A little to the west of the Temple is the famous Mormon Tabernacle, built in 1864–1867. It is in the shape of an ellipse—250 feet long, 150 feet wide, and 70 feet high—and can accommodate about 12,000 persons. The building is surmounted by a wooden roof with iron shingles, resembling the shell of a turtle or the inverted hull of a ship.

Morning Star of the Reformation. An appellation frequently bestowed upon John Wickliffe (1324–1384), the first of the reformers that inveighed against the doctrines and practices of the Roman Catholic Church.

"Wyckliffe will ever be remembered as a good and great man, an advocate of ecclesiastical independence, an unfailing foe to popish tyranny, a translator of Scripture into our mother tongue, and an industrious instructor of the people in their own rude but ripening dialect. May he not be justly styled the *Morning Star of the Reformation ?*"—*Eadie.*

Morpheus. In classical mythology, the son of Somnus, or Sleep, and god of dreams. The word "Morpheus" means fashioner or moulder, and was applied to this divinity because he gave to these bodiless creations an apparent form and substance.

Mortal Sins. A term applied in the Roman Catholic Church, to wilful and deliberate trangressions,—"sins gross, knowingly, wilfully, deliberately committed." They bring spiritual death to the soul, and eternal punishment upon the sinner. See *Seven Deadly Sins ; Venial Sins.*

Morus Multicaulis Mania. The name given to a fever of speculation that raged in the United States during 1835, and caused many persons to engage extensively in the planting of mulberry trees, even at ruinous prices, for the purpose of rearing silkworms. The excitement soon subsided, but not until large sums of money had been sacrificed in the attempt. *Morus multicaulis* is the Latin name of the variety of mulberry tree planted on that occasion.

Mosaic Work. The word "mosaic"—when used to denote ornamental work consisting of small pieces of stone, glass, or other substances harmoniously inlaid—is not derived from the proper name *Moses ;* but comes, through the Italian *mosaico,* from the Greek Μοῦσειος (*belonging to the Muses*). Pliny says that decorative work of this kind was so called, because first used for tessellated floors in the grottoes dedicated to the Muses.

Moses. A celebrated colossal statue by Michael Angelo (1475–1564), in the Church of San Pietro in Vincoli in Rome. It was originally designed as one of 30 statues to adorn the tomb of Pope Julius II (1503–1513) in St. Peter's ; of these, three only—Moses, Leah, and Rachel — were executed by Michael Angelo, and the monument was never completed. The "Moses" is generally considered to be one of the masterpieces of the great sculptor. See *David.*

"He seems to be beholding the worship paid to the golden calf; his head turns to the left, with flashing eyes ; his beard, agitated by the inward commotion, falls heavily down upon his breast ; the right hand rests upon the tables of the law, and with the left he presses the beard to himself, as though he would check the violent outburst of passion. But the advanced position of the right foot, and the backward movement of the left, give us to understand that in a moment this powerful form will spring to its feet and vent upon the apostates his fierce and withering indignation."—*Lübke.*

Mosque of Mohammed Ali. A superb Moslem temple at Cairo, Egypt, commenced by Mohammed Ali (1769–1849), Viceroy of Egypt, and completed after his death. The interior walls are faced with alabaster, while the magnificent dome is supported by four massive square columns of rose-tinted marble. In one corner is the gorgeous tomb of Mohammed Ali. According to some authorities this mosque surpasses St. Peter's at Rome, or its more famous rival, St. Sophia at Constantinople, in the splendor of its architecture and the beauty of its decorations.

Mosque of Omar. A famous mosque on Mount Moriah, Jerusalem, occupying the site of the ancient Jewish temple. It was built by the Caliph Omar, or, as some authorities assert, by the Caliph Abd-el-Malek, in the 7th century. It is octagonal in shape, and has a diameter of 170 feet. The lower part is constructed of various-colored marbles, while the upper part is covered with porcelain tiles and pierced with 56 windows. The structure is surmounted by a beautifully proportioned dome, — so light and graceful in design that it seems to rest like a balloon of silk upon the mosque. The interior is adorned with arabesques. In the centre — beneath the dome — is a large, irregular stone, nearly 50 feet in diameter, surrounded by an iron railing. This is called the "Sacred Rock"; and, before the advent of the Mohammedans, was regarded by the Jews and Christians alike as the very spot where Abraham bound Isaac, and where the sacrificial altar of the Temple stood. The Moslems, however, assert that Mohammed knelt there in prayer, and ascended thence to heaven. On this rock are shown not only the footprint of the Prophet as he mounted heavenward, but also the mark left by the archangel Gabriel's hand, as he seized the rock to prevent it from following Mohammed. See *Calvary ; Mount Moriah.*

Mosquito Coast. A strip of territory lying on the east coast of Nicaragua. It was discovered by Columbus in 1502, and was claimed by Spain, although never conquered by that country. During the 17th century, the Mosquito Coast was the headquarters of the buccaneers, and in 1650 became subject to Great Britain. In 1850, as a result of the Bulwer-Clayton Treaty between the United States and Great Britain, these two nations agreed not "to occupy or fortify or colonize, or assume or exercise any dominion over, any part of Central America." In 1855, the United States charged Great Britain with non-fulfilment of the treaty, and in 1859 the English agreed, with certain reservations, to cede the territory to Honduras. Nicaragua now claims the sovereignty of this territory. The Mosquitoes, who now number only 10,000, were at one time able to muster an army of 40,000 men. See *Bulwer-Clayton Treaty.*

Mossbacks. "A *sobriquet* for the old-liners and fossils in the Democratic party, most common in Ohio, but also used in other parts of the country. They are supposed to be the remnants of the ante-bellum Democracy. The derivation is from an old snapping-turtle, in the popular vernacular called a ' mossback,' because of the covering of its shell by a growth of moss-like aquatic vegetation, induced by its sluggish habits and long living in stagnant water." — Walsh's *Handy-Book of Literary Curiosities.*

Most Costly Painting in the World. The Madonna degli Ansidei, painted by Raphael about 1505, for the chapel of the Ansidei family in the Servite Church at Perugia, and now in the National Gallery in London, is probably the most costly painting in the world. It was purchased from the Duke of Marlborough in 1884, for £70,000, the largest sum ever paid— so far as is known — for any single picture. The painting is eight feet high, and represents the Virgin and Child seated upon a throne, flanked by life-size figures of John the Baptist and St. Nicholas of Bari—the latter in his episcopal robes. This is one of the best preserved specimens of Raphael's work, and is often called the Blenheim Madonna. See *Blenheim.*

Most Faithful Majesty. A title conferred upon John V (1707–1750), King of Portugal, by Pope Benedict XIV (1740–1758).

Most Learned of the Romans. An honorary title conferred upon Marcus Terentius Varro (116–27 B.C.), the celebrated Latin author, on account of his almost universal erudition. His learning was highly esteemed by Cicero, Quintilian, and St. Augustine. According to his own statement, he wrote 490 books — nearly all of which are lost.

Most Methodical Doctor. A sobriquet conferred upon John Bassol (*d.*

1347), the noted Scotch theologian, in allusion to the method and order displayed in his writings.

Most Profound Doctor. A title conferred upon Ægidius de Columna (1247–1316), a famous Sicilian schoolman.

Most Resolute Doctor. A title conferred upon Durand de St. Pourçain (*d.* 1332), a noted schoolman and philosopher.

Most Useful Tree. The palm tree, in its different varieties, probably furnishes man with the greatest number of useful products.

"Linnæus, whose knowledge of palms was limited to the more arborescent species, very appropriately named them the 'Princes of the Vegetable Kingdom.' Their stately habit, the elegant proportion of the stems, and the grace and beauty of the leaves of the majority of the larger species, coupled with the great variety and utility of the products of all, mark them as a most distinguished and valuable group of plants, gratifying the eye by their adornment of the landscape, and ministering abundantly to the necessities and the pleasures of both savage and civilised man. The stems when young and tender are delicious and nutritious food; when old and mature those of certain species yield valuable farinaceous substances; some are valuable as timber trees, and the terminal bud of several consists of a mass of tender mucilaginous leaves, which are esteemed a delicate and delicious vegetable. Many yield by incision or otherwise an abundance of sweet sap, from which sugar, refreshing drinks, wines, spirits and vinegar are obtained. Their leaves are used for thatch and for the making of mats, baskets, hats, umbrellas, thread, cord, and clothing. They yield excellent and inexhaustible materials, and they are in some cases a natural substitute for writing-paper, the records and writings of many eastern peoples being inscribed on them."—*Chambers's Encyclopædia.*

Mother Ann. A title bestowed by her followers upon Ann Lee (1735–1784), the founder and "spiritual mother" of the society of Shakers. She is regarded by them as the female incarnation of Christ,—Jesus being the male manifestation. See *Shakers.*

"Ann was . . . accepted as the only true leader of the Church of Christ—not in the common acceptation of that term, but as the incarnation of infinite wisdom and the 'second appearing of Christ,' as really and fully as Jesus of Nazareth was the incarnation of infinite power, or Christ's first appearing, and she now hesitated not to style herself '*Ann, the Word,*' signifying that in her dwelt the *Word.*"—McClintock and Strong's *Cyclopædia.*

Mother Carey's Chicken. A name familiarly given by sailors to the stormy petrel, a small oceanic bird, vulgarly supposed to be the unfailing harbinger of bad weather. The expression "Mother Carey" is said to be a corruption of *mater cara* (*Lat. dear mother*), a phrase used by Italian sailors when speaking of the Virgin Mary, the patroness of sea-faring men, to denote their gratitude for her kindness in sending these forerunners of tempestuous weather. According to Yarrell, the famous ornithologist, the phrase "Mother Carey's chicken" was first used by the sailors of Captain Carteret, and probably had reference to some hag of that name.

Mother Goose. Mother Goose—the author of the *Melodies for Children*—was a veritable personage, and not an imaginary character, as is generally supposed. Her maiden name was Elizabeth Foster, and she was born in Boston in 1665. She married Isaac Vergoose, otherwise Goose, in 1692, and lived to the advanced age of 92 years. The nursery rhymes bearing her name were composed by her for the entertainment of her grandchildren, and were collected and published in Boston in 1719, by her son-in-law, Thomas Fleet.

Chandler's *Encyclopædia*, however, takes a different view of the matter, and says: "There is no satisfactory evidence that the songs were written by a person named Goose. It is probably a collection of nursery rhymes of the times."

Mother Hubbard. *Mother Hubbard's Tale* is a satiric poem, in the style of Chaucer, written by Edmund

Spenser (1552–1599). It assumes to have been recited to the poet, during a time of sickness, by an old woman called Mother Hubbard, and recounts the adventures of an ape and a fox that formed a union to better their fortunes. After meeting with a variety of experiences, they finally came to grief at the court of King Lion. The nursery tale of *Mother Hubbard*, who

" Went to the cupboard
To get her poor dog a bone,"

is the one usually associated with the above title.

Mother of Believers. A sobriquet conferred upon Ayeshah (611–678 A.D.), the favorite wife of Mohammed.

Mother of Books. A sobriquet conferred upon the city of Alexandria, Egypt, in allusion to its vast library, which constituted one of the wonders of ancient times. See *Alexandrian Library*.

Mother of Presidents. A name popularly given to the State of Virginia, in allusion to the number of chief magistrates furnished by that Commonwealth to the American Union. They are as follows : George Washington, Thomas Jefferson, James Madison, James Monroe, William Henry Harrison, and John Tyler.

Mother of States. Virginia is sometimes so called, not only because it is the oldest of the original thirteen colonies that adopted the Declaration of Independence, but also because, from the large amount of territory included in its original grant, were afterwards formed the States of Kentucky, Ohio, Indiana, Illinois, and West Virginia.

Mother of the Beautiful Child. An epithet conferred by the Florentines upon Elizabeth Barrett Browning (1809–1861), whose son was a model of beauty and grace. It is said that the poetess was more proud of this appellation than of her literary reputation, and declared in a letter to a friend that it was worth twenty *Aurora Leighs*.

Mother Shipton. A title bestowed upon Ursula Southiel Shipton (1488–1560), an English prophetess, whose prognostications exerted a powerful influence over the common people, and were heeded by the higher classes also. Henry VIII (1509–1547) and Elizabeth (1558–1603) consulted her. According to tradition, she predicted the death of Lord Percy and of Cardinal Wolsey, the suppression of the monasteries, the marriage of Henry VIII to Anne Boleyn, the execution of Mary Queen of Scots, and the accession of James VI of Scotland to the throne of England. In 1684, Richard Head published a book containing many apocryphal tales in which Mother Shipton figures as the heroine; and in 1797 S. Baker issued in book-form her prophecies, together with those of Nixon, the Cheshire prophet. See *Gog and Magog*.

Mottoes, Royal. The following are some of the mottoes adopted by royal personages in modern times :

(1) *Dieu et Mon Droit.* Used as a pass-word by Richard I (1189–1199) at the battle of Gisors in 1198, but first adopted as a royal motto by Henry VI (1422–1461).

(2) *Ich Dien.* Adopted by Edward, the Black Prince, at the battle of Crécy (1346).

(3) *Honi Soit Qui Mal Y Pense.* The motto of the Order of the Garter and of the Crown of England, adopted by Edward III (1327–1377) in 1349.

(4) *Je Maintiendrai.* Originally the motto of the House of Nassau, and adopted by William III (1689–1702) of England when he came to the throne. To it he added the words " *the liberties of England and the Protestant religion.*"

(5) *Semper Eadem.* A motto assumed by Queen Elizabeth (1558–1603), and adopted by Queen Anne (1702–1714) in 1702.

Mound-Builders. An extinct race of North America, whose remarkable earth-mounds still exist in the United States from the Great Lakes to the Gulf of Mexico and from the Appalachian to the Rocky Mountains, but are especially numerous in Ohio, Illinois, Indiana, and Missouri. In the State of Ohio alone there are said to be 10,000 mounds of this kind. Their average height is from 6 to 30 feet, with a diameter of 50 to 100 feet. Excavations have revealed the presence of pottery, copper tools and ornaments, stone implements, and knives of obsidian. Much speculation has been indulged in concerning the origin, time of existence, and social condition of this mysterious people, but satisfactory evidence does not exist. Owing to the presence of similar mounds in North Asia, James Fergusson has suggested that the " Mound-Builders" came from that continent. See *Mound City ; Serpent Mound.*

Mound City. A name sometimes given to the city of St. Louis, Missouri, on account of the artificial mounds in its vicinity, said to have been the work of the ancient Mound-Builders. See *Mound-Builders.*

Mountain. A name often given, during the first French Revolution, to the party of extreme radicals in the National Convention, because they occupied the highest seats in the assembly - hall. The " Mountain " perished with Robespierre on the Ninth Thermidor (July 27th, 1794). See *Montagnards ; Plain.*

Mountain Dew. A phrase frequently applied to whiskey, and especially to Scotch whiskey, which, in former times, was illicitly distilled among the mountains.

Mountain of Fire. A name given to Mount Etna in Sicily, by the Saracens.

Mount Ararat. A mountain in Armenia, having an altitude of about 17,000 feet above the sea-level. According to the commonly accepted tradition, it was the resting-place of Noah's ark after the Deluge. The *Chaldæan* legend of the Flood says that the ark rested in Gordyene, northeast of Nineveh.

Mount Auburn. A beautiful cemetery at Cambridge, Massachusetts,— perhaps the most widely-known burial-place in the United States. It was consecrated in 1831. Mount Auburn occupies an area of 125 acres, and has more than 30 miles of avenues and paths. The grounds are beautifully laid out, and contain many fine monuments. Within the chapel — a handsome Gothic structure — may be seen marble statues of John Winthrop, James Otis, John Adams, and Joseph Story. Among the illustrious dead buried at Mount Auburn may be named Longfellow, Lowell, Motley, Edward Everett, Rufus Choate, Charles Sumner, Margaret Fuller, Phillips Brooks, William Ellery Channing, Edwin Booth, Charlotte Cushman, and Nathaniel Bowditch.

Mount Everest. The name of the loftiest peak of the Himalayas, and the highest ascertained point on the surface of the globe. According to the measurement of Waugh in 1856, the altitude of Mount Everest is 29,002 feet above the level of the sea. It was named in honor of Sir George Everest (1790–1866), Surveyor-general of India, by his successor Sir Andrew Scott Waugh. See *Kinchinjinga.*

Mount Hope. An eminence in Rhode Island, nearly opposite the city of Fall River, Massachusetts. It is famous as the residence of Philip (*d.* 1676), Sachem of the Wampanoags, who carried on a long and desperate struggle with the early settlers of New England,— known as King Philip's War. See *King Philip's War.*

Mount Moriah. An eminence in the eastern part of the city of Jerusalem, famous as the site of the three

Jewish temples successively erected by Solomon, Zerubbabel, and Herod. It is at present occupied by the Mosque of Omar. See *Herod's Temple; Mosque of Omar; Solomon's Temple; Zerubbabel's Temple.*

Mount of Olives. A ridge—also called Olivet—on the east side of Jerusalem, distant from the city about half a mile, and separated from it by the Valley of Jehoshaphat. It is intimately associated with some of the most important events narrated in the *Old* and *New Testaments*, such as the flight of David during Absalom's rebellion, the idolatry of Solomon, the triumphal entry of Christ into Jerusalem, His agony and betrayal, and His ascension. The hill was at one time covered with olive-trees, a few only of which remain at the present day. Gethsemane lay at its foot on the western side, and Bethany on its eastern slope. The central summit is crowned with a church which, according to tradition, marks the spot of the Ascension. Other authorities, however, say that this event occurred near Bethany. See *Church of the Ascension.*

Mount Pilatus. A mountain, 7290 feet high, near Lake Luzerne, Switzerland. According to tradition, it derives its name from Pontius Pilate, the Roman Governor of Judea at the time of Christ's crucifixion. Having been banished from Rome by the Emperor Tiberius (14-37 A.D.), he wandered into Switzerland, where he was seized with remorse for his crime, and threw himself from the summit of the mountain into the lake. According to other authorities, the word *Pilatus*, as here used, is simply a corruption of the Latin *pileatus* (*wearing a cap*). If this be the origin of the word, Mount Pilatus means simply "the mountain wearing a cap of snow."

Mount St. Elias. A mountain in southeast Alaska, having an elevation of 19,500 feet. It is the highest mountain in North America.

Mount Sinai. A sacred mountain in Arabia Petræa, between the Gulfs of Suez and Akabah, on the summit of which, according to the *Old Testament* (*Exodus* xix), Moses received from Jehovah the tables of stone, inscribed with the *Ten Commandments.*

"In this mountain-mass there are three separate mountains clearly distinguishable—Mount Serbal (6750 feet); Mount Catherine (8540 feet), lying south-east of Serbal; and Uram Shomer (some 8000 feet). Authorities, ancient theologians and historians and modern travellers and commentators, are greatly divided on the identification of the Sinai of Moses, some (Eusebius, Jerome, Lepsius, Ebers, &c.) upholding the claims of Serbal, others (Farrar, Tischendorf, Strauss, Stanley, Palmer, Sir Charles Warren, Hull, &c.) contending for Mount Catherine. Tradition has pointed to the latter ever since the time of Justinian, but the vexed question is yet far from being settled. The mountain known as Jebel Katherin has two well-marked peaks, a northern one called Horeb, and a southern called Jebel Musa (Mountain of Moses). It is this last summit which tradition has selected as the sacred mountain of the Hebrew law-giving."—*Chambers's Encyclopædia.*

Mount Tabor, Battle of. A battle fought near Mount Tabor, Syria, on April 16th, 1799, between the Turks and the French, commanded by Napoleon Bonaparte, assisted by Murat and Klêber. The Turks were defeated with great slaughter. Tradition makes Mount Tabor the scene of the "Transfiguration" of Jesus Christ.

Mount Vernon. The home and burial-place of George Washington, situated in Fairfax County, Virginia, 15 miles below Washington City. It was originally called the "Hunting Creek Estate," but received its present name from Lawrence Washington, in honor of Admiral Vernon, under whom he had served in the Spanish Wars. The estate came into the possession of George Washington (1732-1799) in 1752. The central part of the building was built by Lawrence, and the wings by George. The house commands a fine view of the Potomac, and contains many interesting historic relics, — among which may be mentioned the key of the Bastille presented to Washington by Lafayette. In a retired spot near the mansion stands the Tomb of Washington. It is a plain brick structure with an iron gate, between the bars of which may be seen the marble sarcophagi containing the remains of Washington and his wife.

In 1856, Mount Vernon (including the mansion and six acres) was purchased from the descendants of Washington for $200,000. This amount was raised by subscription, under the auspices of the "Ladies' Mount Vernon Association," assisted by the eloquence of Edward Everett, the famous orator. Thanks to these efforts, Mount Vernon is now the property of the nation.

Mount Zion. A hill in the southwest part of Jerusalem, separated from Mount Moriah by the valley Tyropœon. It formed the oldest part of the city, and was a fortified town of the Jebusites, until captured by David, 1049 B.C. From that time it was often called the "City of David." That monarch erected a palace on Mount Zion, which continued to be the royal residence for more than 1000 years. There also David was buried, with 14 of his successors, in the royal tomb. During the siege of Jerusalem by Titus (70 A.D.) Zion was the last spot to surrender.

"Beautiful for situation, the joy of the whole earth, is *Mount Zion*, on the sides of the north, the city of the great King."—*Psalms* xlviii, 2.

Mouse=Tower (*Ger., Mäusethurm*). A tower, on a small island in the Rhine, whither, according to the legend, Hatto, the wicked archbishop of Mayence, fled for refuge from the mice, and where he was devoured by them. See *Hatto, Bishop*.

"It appears to have been built in the thirteenth century by a Bishop Siegfried (full 200 years after the death of Bishop Hatto), along with the opposite castle of Ehrenfels, as a watch-tower and toll-house for collecting the duties upon all goods which passed the spot. The word *maus* is probably only an older form of *mauth*, duty or toll; and this name,

together with the very unpopular object for which the tower was erected, perhaps gave rise to the dolorous story of Bishop Hatto and the rats."—Murray's *Handbook*.

Moyamensing Prison. A massive granite structure in the city of Philadelphia. It is in the Indo-Gothic style of architecture, and is used as a place of confinement for persons that are either awaiting trial or serving short sentences.

Mrs. Grundy. See *Grundy, Mrs.*

Mrs. Partington. See *Partington, Mrs.*

Muckross Abbey. A beautiful ruined abbey, situated in Kerry County, Ireland, near the Lakes of Killarney. It was founded in 1440. The church contains the tombs of many of Ireland's most renowned chieftains, as well as those of several of the kings of Munster. The cloisters are in an excellent state of preservation and enclose a courtyard, the whole area of which is shaded by an immense yew-tree of great age, measuring twelve feet in circumference.

Mudie's. A famous circulating library in London — containing hundreds of thousands of volumes — founded by Charles Edward Mudie (1818–1890), an English bookseller, in 1842.

Mudsill. The name given to the timber laid directly on the ground to form the foundation of a railroad. The word was first used figuratively, to denote a person of low social position, in a speech delivered by Senator Hammond of South Carolina on March 4th, 1858. During the Civil War, the aristocratic Southerners frequently alluded to the inhabitants of the manufacturing states of the North as "Northern Mudsills."

"In all social systems there must be a class to perform the drudgery of life; that is, a class requiring but a low order of intellect and but little skill. Such a class you must have, or you would not have that other class which leads progress, civilization, and refinement. It constitutes the very *mud-sill* of society and of political government; and you might as well attempt to build a house in the air as to build either the one or the other except on this *mud-sill.*"—*Speech of Senator Hammond, March 4, 1858.*

Mugwumps. A term of reproach applied, during the presidential campaign of 1884, to those Republicans that bolted the nomination of James G. Blaine and gave their support to Grover Cleveland, the candidate of the Democratic party, in the interests of Civil-Service Reform. The word "Mugwump" is said to be a corruption of the Algonquin *Mugquomp*, employed in John Eliot's Indian translation of the Bible (1661) to denote a duke or great leader (*Genesis* xxxvi). It was probably first used, in a political sense, by the *New York Sun* (June 15th, 1884).

Mulatto. A Spanish word, derived from the Latin *mulus* (*mule*), meaning the offspring either of a white woman and a negro, or of a negress and a white man.

Mulligan Letters. Two series of letters written by James G. Blaine to Warren Fisher of Boston, in relation to the affairs of the " Little Rock and Fort Smith Railroad.'' These letters passed into the hands of one Mulligan, the bookkeeper of Mr. Fisher, and when, in 1876, the congressional committee, charged with an inquiry into the alleged corrupt practices of Mr. Blaine in his endeavor to secure favorable legislation for this railroad, met in Washington, Mulligan was requested to produce these letters before the committee. Blaine, however, secured possession of them beforehand, and went himself before the committee of investigation with an explanatory statement. Soon after, he suffered a severe sunstroke, the investigation was, in consequence, dropped. During the campaign of 1884, when Blaine was the presidential

candidate, the affair was revived and a new series of " Mulligan Letters " was published. They played an important part in the campaign, and were cited by the Democrats and Mugwumps as proofs of the candidate's corrupt practices, while his supporters stoutly declared that nothing compromising could be found in them.

Mumbo Jumbo. A hideous demon greatly feared by the negro women of western Africa, and frequently invoked as a means of keeping them in subjection. The expression is used at the present day in civilized communities, to denote any senseless jargon or absurd object of popular idolatry.

"This is a strange bugbear, common to the Mandingo towns, and much employed by the pagan natives in keeping their women in subjection; for, as the Kaffirs are not restricted in the number of their wives, every one marries as many as he can conveniently maintain; and, as it frequently happens that the ladies do not agree among themselves, family quarrels sometimes rise to such a height that the authority of the husband can no longer preserve peace in his household. In such cases, the interposition of *Mumbo Jumbo* is called in, and is always decisive."—*Mungo Park.*

Münchausen, Baron. The imaginary author and hero of a series of wonderful tales, entitled *The Adventures of Baron Münchausen.* They were first published in England in 1785 by Rudolf Erich Raspe, an expatriated German, and were followed by translations and imitations in German and other languages. The name of the hero is said to be derived from Jerome Charles Frederick von Münchhausen (1720-1797), a German officer in the service of Russia, who became notorious for his ridiculous tales of adventure. It is said that by dint of repetition he came finally to believe implicitly in the truth of his most extravagant stories.

The authorship of these extravaganzas is in dispute, although Brewer, in his *Dictionary of Phrase and Fable*, says: "The author is Rudolf Erich Raspe, and the sources from which the adventures were compiled are Bebel's *Facetiæ*, Castiglione's *Cortegiano*, Bildermann's *Utopia*, and some of the baron's own stories."

Münchausen of the West. A nickname given to David Crockett (1786–1836), the American pioneer, in allusion to the many improbable tales related by him.

Munda, Battle of.

(1) A battle fought at Munda (now *Monda*) in southern Spain, in 216 B.C., between the Carthaginians and the Romans, commanded by Cneius Scipio. The latter were victorious.

(2) A desperate battle fought at Munda (now *Monda*) in southern Spain, in 45 B.C., between the army of Julius Cæsar and the forces of the Senatorial party commanded by Cneius and Sextus, sons of Pompey the Great. The latter were utterly routed with great loss of life.

Murderers' Bible. A term popularly applied to a version of the Scriptures, published in 1801. It derived its name from an error in *Jude*, 16, where the word "murmurers" is rendered "murderers."

"These are *murderers*, complainers, walking after their own lusts; and their mouth speaking great swelling words, having men's persons in admiration because of advantage."—*Jude*, 16.

Muscular Christianity. A phrase first used by Charles Kingsley (1819–1875), the English author, to denote the kind of Christianity that teaches "that a man's body is given him to be trained and brought into subjection, and then used for the protection of the weak, the advancement of all righteous causes, and the subduing of the earth which God has given to the children of men."

Musée du Luxembourg (*Fr.*, *Museum of the Luxembourg*). A gallery of fine arts in the palace of the Luxembourg, Paris, devoted to the works of living artists. See *Luxembourg Palace*.

"The works of the most distinguished masters are generally transferred to the Louvre, or sent to provincial galleries, about ten years after their death ; so that a comprehensive survey of modern French art cannot be obtained in one place."—Baedeker's *Paris*.

Musen-Almanach (*Ger.*, *Almanac of the Muses*). "Several publications bearing this title appeared in Germany between the middle of the 18th century and the middle of the 19th century. Gotter (1746–1797) and Boje (1745–1806), two of the poets of the Göttingen Union, were the principal projectors of the celebrated *Musen-Almanach*, issued at Gotha in 1770. In the years 1801, 1802, Tieck, in conjunction with A. W. Schlegel and others, composed a *Musen-Almanach*, published at Tübingen. In 1804–06, Chamisso, with Varnhagen von Ense, edited an Almanac of the Muses. Schiller and Goethe may also be mentioned as Musen - Almanach contributors." — Wheeler's *Who Wrote It?*

Museo (*Span.*, *The Museum*). A gallery of fine arts in Madrid, Spain, containing probably the most superb collection of paintings in the world. Among these treasures may be mentioned more than 60 of the masterpieces of Velasquez, 46 of the works of Murillo, together with fine specimens of the work of Raphael, Rubens, Titian, Correggio, Paul Veronese, Vandyke, and many others. The gallery was founded by Ferdinand VII (1808–1833), to whom is due the credit of endeavoring to unite in one vast collection all the paintings scattered throughout the palaces of Madrid. His daughter Isabella (1833–1868) continued this work, and, in addition, transferred to the Museum the most celebrated paintings of the Escorial. See *Escorial*.

Museo Capitolino (*It. Capitoline Museum*). A famous gallery of sculpture in the Capitol at Rome, founded by Pope Clement XII (1730–1740). Among its gems may be named the *Dying Gladiator*—found in the Gardens of Sallust ; the *Faun of Praxiteles*—discovered in the Villa d'Este at Tivoli ; the *Antinous*—found at Hadrian's villa; the *Cupid and Psyche;* the *Infant Hercules ;* the *Venus of the Capitol ;* the group of *Leda and the Swan;* and the *Doves of Pliny*—one of the finest pieces of antique mosaic in existence.

Museo Chiaramonti. A gallery of ancient sculpture in the Vatican at Rome, arranged by Canova. It was founded by Pope Pius VII (1800–1823), and named in honor of that pontiff's family. The gem of the collection is the bust of the young Augustus, discovered at Ostia early in the 19th century, by Mr. Fagan, the British Consul. It represents the Emperor at the age of 16 or 18, and compels the admiration of all beholders.

"The face is of delicate and dreamy beauty. The brow is intellectual and thoughtful, but the chief charm of the work is in the exquisite refinement of the mouth. The maiden in the fairy tale, who spoke pearls and diamonds, must have had such lips. It is the face of a poet, and not of a statesman. The expression is that of one dwelling in a soft, ideal world. It looks as Virgil might have looked when the genius of Latin poetry met him on the banks of the Mincius, and threw her inspiring mantle over him."—Hillard's *Six Months in Italy*.

Museo Nazionale (*It.,National Museum*). A vast treasure-house of art in Naples, Italy, founded by Ferdinand I (1759–1825) in 1816, and originally called the *Museo Borbonico* (*It. Bourbon Museum*). It contains a gallery of paintings, an extensive collection of marble and bronze statuary, and a large library; but it is especially noted for its wonderful display of antiquities found in the ruined cities of Pompeii and Herculaneum.

"These possessions are absolutely unique. They defy rivalry, and can never be damaged by comparison. A large part of all that we know of the private life of the Romans has been revealed to us from these open graves of the past."—Hillard's *Six Months in Italy*.

Museo Pio-Clementino. A museum in the Vatican at Rome, containing the finest collection of ancient sculpture in existence, among which may be mentioned the *Torso Belvedere*, the *Perseus*, the *Meleager*, the *Antinous Belvedere*, the *Laocoön*, the *Apollo Belvedere*, the *Ariadne* (formerly called *Cleopatra*), and the sarcophagus of L. Scipio Barbatus. The Museum was named in honor of the Popes Pius VI (1775–1799) and Clement XIV (1769–1775), who contributed liberally to its foundation and support.

Muses. In Greek and Roman mythology, the name given to the female divinities that presided over poetry, art, and science. They were originally three in number, although Homer at one time speaks of one only, and on another occasion alludes to nine. The "Nine Muses," as we know them, were first mentioned by name by Hesiod in his *Theogony*. They are as follows :

(1) *Clio*, the muse of history.

(2) *Melpomene*, the muse of tragedy.

(3) *Thalia*, the muse of comedy and burlesque.

(4) *Calliope*, the muse of epic poetry.

(5) *Urania*, the muse of astronomy.

(6) *Euterpe*, the muse of lyric poetry.

(7) *Polymnia*, or *Polyhymnia*, the muse of song and oratory.

(8) *Erato*, the muse of erotic poetry.

(9) *Terpsichore*, the muse of dancing and the choral song.

The fountains of Aganippe and Hippocrene on Mount Helicon, and the Castalian spring, at the foot of Mount Parnassus, were spots sacred to the *Muses*.

Museum. A celebrated institution of learning at Alexandria, Egypt, founded by Ptolemy Soter (323–283 B.C.) for the perpetuation, increase, and diffusion of human knowledge. It contained a library of 700,000 volumes, a botanical and zoölogical garden, an anatomical dissecting-room, and an astronomical observatory, and was at one time attended by nearly 14,000 students. The corps of instructors was divided into the four faculties of literature, mathematics, astronomy, and medicine; and instruction was given by lectures, conversations, and other appropriate methods. The *Septuagint Version* of the Hebrew Scriptures is said to have been prepared at the Museum of Alexandria, at the request of Ptolemy Philadelphus (283–247 B.C.). See *Alexandrian Library ; Septuagint.*

Mysteries. Properly speaking, the rude dramas founded on historical events in the *Old* and *New Testaments*, as distinguished from the *Miracle-Plays*, based chiefly on legends in the lives of the saints. This distinction, however, has never been strictly observed. See *Clerks of the Revels ; Miracle-Plays ; Moralities.*

N

Naboth's Vineyard. A vineyard in Jezreel, greatly coveted by Ahab (917–898 B.C.), King of Israel. Naboth — the owner — declined, however, either to sell the vineyard to the King or to exchange it for another, and was, in consequence, cruelly murdered on a false charge of blasphemy—trumped up by the infamous Queen, Jezebel. Ahab thereupon took immediate possession of the vineyard, but was met by the prophet Elijah, who denounced the wickedness of the King and Queen, and foretold the awful doom that awaited Jezebel and her children.

The phrase "Naboth's Vineyard" is used at the present day to denote any possession greatly coveted by others.

Nameless City. Ancient Rome is sometimes so called, because it had a mysterious appellation of great antiquity, which it was death to utter. This name is said to have been *Valentia*, afterwards translated into the Greek word Ῥώμη (*Rome*), and first used, among the Greek authors, either by Aristotle or Theophrastus.

Names of Puritans. The following are some of the grotesque names formerly in use among the Puritans of England :

Swear-not-at-all Ireton.

Glory-be-to-God Pennyman.

Hew - Agag - in - pieces - before - the-Lord Robinson.

Obadiah- bind- their- kings-in - chains-and-their-nobles-in-irons Needham.

Praise-God Barebone.

Fear-God Barebone.

Jesus- Christ-came-into-the-world-to-save Barebone.

If- Christ- had- not- died-for-thee-thou-hadst-been-damned Barebone.

Nantes, Edict of. See *Edict of Nantes.*

Naples. The Greek colony of Parthenope—founded about 1000 B.C. — comprised two settlements, Palæopolis (*Old City*) and Neapolis (*New City*), which existed side by side for many years. From the latter of these, the name Naples (*It. Napoli*) is derived.

Naples Museum. See *Museo Nazionale.*

Napoleon. If the name " Napoleon " be written in Greek characters, the six following words may be formed from it by dropping the initial letter of each word in succession, thus : Ναπόλεων, Ἀπολέων, Πόλεων, Ὄλεων, Λέων, Ἐών, Ὤν,—which, being translated, signifies : *Napoleon, the destroyer of entire cities, was the lion of his people.*

Napoléon, Code. See *Code Napoléon.*

Napoleonic Bee. This emblem of sovereignty, adopted by Napoleon I (1804–1814), is said to be derived from the *fleurons*, discovered in the tomb of Childéric I (458–481 A.D.)—father of Clovis—in 1653. These small ornaments, used to adorn the harness of the royal war-horse, were mistaken for *bees* by the antiquaries of that day, and were sent to Louis XIV (1643–1715).

Napoleon I, while laboring under the same delusion, adopted them as emblems of activity and enterprise, and congratulated himself that he had secured a device of greater antiquity than the fleur-de-lis. See *Fleur-de-lis*.

Napoleon Memorial. A statue in St. George's Chapel, Windsor, erected in May, 1881, in memory of Prince Louis Napoleon (1856–1879)— son of Napoleon III—who was slain by the Zulus.

Napoleon of Peace. A sobriquet bestowed upon Louis Philippe (1830–1848), King of the French, whose peaceful and prosperous reign of eighteen years was in marked contrast to the warlike days of the Empire.

Napoleon's Return from Elba. The following quotation from Edwards's *Words, Facts, and Phrases* is interesting as showing the marked change that took place in the tone of the French newspapers, when Napoleon's return from Elba was crowned with success.

" Napoleon escaped from Elba on March 1, 1815, reaching Paris on the 20th. His progress was marked by some strange alterations in the tone of the French newspapers. On March 9 the ' Journal des Débats ' spoke of him as the ' poltroon of 1814 '; on the 15th occurs the sentence, ' Scourge of generations, thou shalt reign no more.' On the 16th he is described as 'a Robespierre on horseback '; on the 19th as 'the adventurer from the island of Corsica '; but on the 21st the tone is changed, and we are told that ' THE EMPEROR has pursued his triumphant course,' and ' THE EMPEROR has found no other enemies than the miserable libels which were vainly scattered in his path to impede his progress.' "

Napoleon's Tomb. See *Tomb of Napoleon*.

Narva, Battle of. A battle fought at Narva, Russia, on November 30th, 1700, between 50,000 Russians under Peter the Great (1682–1725), and 8000 Swedes commanded by Charles XII (1697–1718). The Russians were routed with a loss of 18,000 slain and 30,000 taken prisoners.

Naseby, Battle of. A hotly contested battle, fought at Naseby, England, on June 14th, 1645, between 7500 Royalists commanded by Charles I (1625–1649) and Prince Rupert, and 14,000 Parliamentarians under Cromwell and Fairfax. The King was signally defeated and fled, leaving his baggage, cannon, and 5000 prisoners in the hands of the victors. He finally escaped into Scotland, but was soon after handed over to the English Parliament.

Nassac Diamond. A famous diamond, at one time in the possession of the East India Company. Before coming into the hands of its present owner, the Duke of Westminster, it weighed 89¾ carats ; but since then it has been recut, and now weighs only 78⅝ carats. Its present value is about £30,000.

Natal. This territory,—now a British colony, — on the southeast coast of Africa, received its name from Vasco da Gama [1450 (?) –1524], the famous Portuguese navigator, who first saw it on Christmas Day, 1497; and, in consequence, named it *Natal* in honor of *Christi dies natalis* (*Lat. the birthday of Christ*).

Natick Cobbler. A nickname popularly conferred upon Henry Wilson (1812–1875), the American statesman, who, during his early manhood, followed the shoemaking trade at Natick, Massachusetts.

National Assembly of France. On June 17th, 1789, the *Tiers-État*, or Commons, of the States-General of France established themselves as the National Assembly, with legislative powers. On the 20th, their hall was closed by order of the King, whereupon the members withdrew to a tennis-court near by, and swore not to disband until they had given a new constitution to France. The King refused to ratify the decrees of the Assembly, and threatened to dissolve it; but soon after yielded to its authority. The following day, the clergy and nobles joined the *Tiers-État*. The National Assembly proclaimed liberty of conscience and freedom of the press, abolished the State religion, annulled monastic vows, abrogated laws of primogeniture, divided France into departments, established a national bank, and issued assignats. It dissolved itself on September 21st, 1792, and was succeeded on the same day by the National Convention. See *National Convention of France; States-General ; Tennis-Court Oath.*

National Convention of France. Incorporated in the hall of the Tuileries, Paris, on the dissolution of the National Assembly of France, on September 21st, 1792, when M. Grégoire announced that the Assembly had ceased to exist. The National Convention abolished royalty and established a republic, guillotined Louis XVI and Marie Antoinette, crushed the Girondists and the Cordeliers, and finally overthrew Robespierre and the infamous Reign of Terror. It was dissolved on October 26th, 1794, and gave place to the Directory. See *Directory, French ; National Assembly of France.*

National Debts.
(1) Austria-Hungary, $2,821,706,-000.
(2) France, $5,829,742,000.
(3) Germany, $2,573,585,000.
(4) Great Britain, $3,090,427,000.
(5) Italy, $2,388,662,000.
(6) Russia, $3,837,156,000.
(7) Spain, $1,742,857,000.
(8) United States, $2,104,875,000.

National Gallery. A famous picture-gallery in Trafalgar Square, London, erected in 1832–1838, at a cost of £100,000, and considerably enlarged in 1861, 1869, 1876, and 1887. The collection dates from 1824, when the Angerstein pictures—38 in number—were purchased by the Government for £57,000. Since then, it has been greatly extended by means of purchases, donations, and legacies ; and contains at the present time about 1300 works of art. Among the most important additions may be mentioned the collections of Robert Vernon (1847), J. M. W. Turner (1856), and Wynn Ellis (1876). The National Gallery contains excellent examples of the leading representatives of Italian, Spanish, Flemish, and Dutch art.

National Hymns.
(1) Austria.—*The Austrian National Anthem.*
(2) Belgium.—*La Brabançonne.*
(3) Denmark.—*Kong Christian.*
(4) England.—*God Save the King.*
(5) France.—*La Marseillaise.*
(6) Holland.—*Wien Neerlandsch Bloed.*
(7) Hungary.— { *Szózat (The Appeal). Magyar Hymnusz.*
(8) Norway.— { *Sönner of Norge. Ja, vi elsker dette Laudet! (Yes, we love this land!).*
(9) Portugal.—*Hymno Constitucional.*
(10) Russia.—*Russian National Anthem.*
(11) Sweden.—*King Karl, the Young Hero.*
(12) United States.—*The Star-Spangled Banner.*

National Monument. A superb granite monument in the National Cemetery, Gettysburg, Pennsylvania, erected in memory of the Union soldiers that fell in the battle of July 1st–3rd, 1863. The shaft is surmounted by a colossal marble figure of Liberty, and the base is surrounded by marble statues of History, War, Peace, and Plenty. It was dedicated on July 1st, 1869. The National Cemetery covers an area of 17 acres on Cemetery Hill, and contains the graves of 3572 soldiers, belonging to 18 States of the Union. It was consecrated with impressive ceremonies on November 19th, 1863, on which occasion Edward Everett delivered the oration and President Lincoln made his famous Gettysburg address,— the words of which were afterwards inscribed on the base of the National Monument. See *Gettysburg, Battle of.*

Nation of Gentlemen. A complimentary appellation bestowed upon the Scotch people by George IV (1820–1830), in allusion to the kind and respectful attention that he received from them on the occasion of his visit to that country in 1822.

Nation of Shopkeepers. A term of contempt frequently used by Napoleon Bonaparte (1769–1821), in speaking of the English people. Louis XIV (1643–1715) is said to have made use of the same expression when referring to the inhabitants of Holland. The phrase occurs also in the writings of Adam Smith (1723–1790).

Nations That Eat Most. "Among modern nations, the greatest eaters are the English, Germans, French, and the Americans—the ruling peoples of our civilization. The diet of the Spaniards and the Italians is notably less substantial than that of the English and Germans, just as their brains are less active and original.

"The Americans are, on the average, the greatest eaters in the world. Said Carlyle to Emerson : ' The best thing I know of that country is, that in it a man can have meat for his labor.' " — *Everybody's Pocket Cyclopædia.*

Natty Bumppo. The hero of James Fenimore Cooper's novel, *The Pioneers* (1823). He figures, under other names, in the other novels of the Leatherstocking Series. Carlyle calls him " one melodious synopsis of man and nature in the West." See *Deerslayer ; Leatherstocking.*

Natural Bridge of Virginia. A remarkable natural curiosity in Rockbridge County, Virginia, about 125 miles west of Richmond. It is a huge limestone arch, 100 feet wide and 90 feet in span, crossing Cedar Brook at a height of 215 feet above the surface of the stream. The sides of the arch are almost perpendicular, and present an imposing aspect when seen from below. George Washington, when a youth, carved his name on the west side of the arch, about 25 feet above the creek, and this remained for nearly three-quarters of a century the highest point reached by any adventurous spirit; but in 1818, James Piper, a student in Washington College, actually climbed from the base to the top of the arch.

Natural System. See *Linnæan System.*

Navarino, Battle of. A desperate naval battle fought in the bay of Navarino, Greece, on October 20th, 1827, in which the Turkish and Egyptian navies were completely annihilated by the combined fleets of Great Britain, France, and Russia, commanded by Sir Edward Codrington. The Turks blew up more than 30 of their ships to prevent them from falling into the hands of the enemy. The Duke of Wellington characterized this victory as an " untoward event," since it weakened the power of Turkey and encouraged Russia in her hope of eventually obtaining possession of Constantinople.

Nazarenes. A set of Jewish Christians, during the first century after Christ, whose members observed the precepts and obligations of the Mosaic law, after these had been abandoned by the mother-church at Jerusalem. There is no conclusive evidence that they denied the divinity of Christ.

"For we have found this man a pestilent fellow, and a mover of sedition among all the Jews throughout the world, and a ringleader of the sect of the *Nazarenes.*"—*Acts* xxiv, 5.

Nazarites. The name given, among the Israelites, to such persons — male or female—as consecrated themselves to the service of Jehovah, in accordance with a peculiar vow prescribed in *Numbers* vi. They abstained from the use of wine, refrained from shaving their heads, and avoided the defilement resulting from contact with the dead. The usual period of the Nazaritish vow was 30 days, although Samson, Samuel, and John the Baptist are mentioned in the Bible as " Nazarites for life."

Neanderthal Skull. A remarkable skull discovered in a limestone cavern, in the Neanderthal Valley in Rhenish Prussia, in 1857. Its peculiar formation has given rise to wide difference of opinion among ethnologists,—some of whom assert that this cranium belongs to the race of cave-dwellers of prehistoric times, while others declare that its abnormal features were caused by disease during the individual's lifetime. See *Engis Skull.*

"It has been suggested that this *Neanderthal skull* may have been that of an idiot. There is not, however, any sufficient reason for this hypothesis; and though the shape of the skull is so remarkable, the brain appears to have been of considerable size, and, indeed, is estimated by Professor Huxley at about seventy-five cubic inches, which is the average capacity of the Polynesian and Hottentot skulls. It must, however, be admitted that though the antiquity of this skull is no doubt great, there is no satisfactory proof that it belonged to the period of the extinct Mammalia."—Lubbock's *Pre-Historic Times.*

Nearest Fixed Star. The fixed star nearest the earth is Alpha Centauri, whose estimated distance from us is 25,000,000,000,000 miles. Notwithstanding its tremendous velocity of 186,400 miles per second, light requires 4 years and 128 days to cross this vast abyss, while sound would take more than 3,000,000 years to travel the same distance. It is said that an express-train, starting from Alpha Centauri, and moving uninterruptedly at a uniform velocity of 37 miles per hour, would not reach this earth in less than 75,000,000 years.

Nebular Hypothesis. A theory of the origin of the universe, first propounded by Kant (1724–1804), and later by Laplace (1749–1827) and Sir William Herschel (1738–1822). It asserts that all the heavenly bodies (stars, planets, satellites, etc.) have been formed by the cooling, condensing, and revolving of nebulous matter, through long ages. This theory is generally accepted by astronomers, and has been virtually established by the investigations of recent spectroscopists.

"An hypothesis to explain the process of formation of the stars and planets, presented in various forms by Kant, Herschel, Laplace, and others. As framed by Laplace, it supposed the matter of the solar system to have existed originally in the form of a vast, diffused, revolving nebula, which, gradually cooling and contracting, threw off, in obedience to mechanical and physical laws, successive rings of matter, from which subsequently, by the same laws, were produced the several planets, satellites, and other bodies of the system. The phrase may indicate any hypothesis according to which the stars or the bodies of the solar system have been evolved from a widely diffused nebulous form of matter."—Webster's *International Dictionary.*

Necessitarians. A philosophic term used to denote those persons that deny the freedom of the will, and assert that in human conduct all volitions are determined by motives that obey the law of causation as invariably as do the forces of nature. The word "Determinists" was suggested as a substitute, by John Stuart Mill (1806–1873), and has been very generally adopted.

Neck-Verse. A name given to the first verse of Psalm li, because formerly used as a reading test with those persons that claimed exemption from capital punishment on the ground of "Benefit of Clergy." If the condemned criminal could read the passage, he *saved his neck,* and was simply branded on the left hand and set at liberty. See *Benefit of Clergy.*

Nectar. In classical mythology, the drink of the Olympian gods. The Greek poets generally thus described it, but Sappho and Alcman declared that ambrosia was the beverage of these divinities, and nectar their food. It resembled red wine, according to Homer, and diffused a delicious odor. Its continued use conferred immortality. See *Ambrosia.*

Needle-Gun. A breech-loading rifle, invented by Johann Nikolaus von Dreyse (1787–1867), in 1836. It is so called because the charge is ignited by means of a fine steel bolt or needle, which is pressed through the cartridge and strikes against a percussion cap in the base. The needle-gun was introduced into the Prussian army in 1841, in place of the old muzzle-loading smooth-bore musket. It rendered effective service during the Danish War of 1864 and the Austrian War of 1866, but was superseded by the Mauser rifle in 1871. See *Chassepot-Rifle.*

Nelson's Last Signal. Nelson's famous signal before the battle of Trafalgar (October 21st, 1805), as indicated by "Sir Home Popham's Telegraphic Code," ran as follows:

Nos.	253	269	863	261	471
	England	Expects	That	Every	Man
	958	220	374	4 21 19 24
	Will	Do	His	D U T Y.

Nem. Con. A contraction of the Latin phrase *nemine contradicente* (*no one contradicting*), i. e., *unanimously.*

Nem. Diss. An abbreviation of the Latin phrase *nemine dissentiente* (*no one dissenting*), i. e., *unanimously.*

Nemean Games. A series of athletic contests in ancient Greece, celebrated in honor of Zeus, at Nemea in Argolis, on the first and third year of each Olympiad (some authorities say on the third year only). According to tradition, they were instituted by the Argives in honor of Archemorus, and were revived by Hercules ; history, however, gives 570 B.C. as the date of their establishment. The Emperor Julian (361–363 A.D.) revived them in 362 A.D., but they ceased to be celebrated in 396. The games comprised horse- and chariot-races, archery, spear-throwing, boxing, wrestling, and contests in music and poetry. The victors were at first crowned with olive-leaves; but, in after years, with garlands of parsley. Eleven of Pindar's Odes are in honor of the victors in these games. See *Isthmian Games ; Olympic Games ; Pythian Games.*

Nemean Lion. A famous lion of Nemea in Argolis, the slaying of which constituted the first of the "Twelve Labors of Hercules." It was the offspring of Typhon and Echidna, and had been sent by Hera to devastate the region about Nemea. Hercules, knowing that the hide of the monster was proof against his arrows, approached it from behind, caught it in his arms, and squeezed it to death. He thereupon stripped the skin from the body, and wore it ever afterwards as a means of defense.

> "My fate cries out,
> And makes each petty artery in this body
> As hardy as the *Nemean lion's* nerve."
> *Hamlet,* i, 4.

Nemesis. According to Hesiod, a daughter of Nox, or Night. She was originally a personification of the moral faculty, or conscience, but was afterwards regarded as the goddess of retributive justice.

> "She was the goddess of punishment, and as such a figure of her was placed beside the bench of the judges. A mysterious power watching over the propriety of life, she was conceived as shaping the demeanour of men in their times of prosperity, punishing crime, taking luck away from the unworthy, tracking every wrong to its doer, and keeping society in equipoise."—Murray's *Mythology.*

Neo-Platonism. A school of Greek philosophy founded at Alexandria, the third century after Christ, by Ammonius Saccas (204–269 A.D.). It was the last attempt of the ancient world to solve the great problems of speculative inquiry, and flourished until the 6th century, when all the schools of heathen philosophy were closed by the Emperor Justinian (527–565). Neo-Platonism is a blending of Plato's doctrine of "Ideas" with the Oriental doctrine of "Emanation." Its principal teachers were Ammonius Saccas, Plotinus, Porphyry, Jamblichus, and Proclus.

Neptune, Temple of. A ruined Doric temple at Pæstum, in southern Italy, first made known in 1755. It probably dates from the 6th century B.C., and is the finest specimen of Doric architecture outside of Greece.

Neptune's Staircase. A fanciful name given to a series of eight locks at the western extremity of the Caledonian Canal, Scotland, forming a cyclopean stairway of eight steps, each step or lock being 8 feet high, 170 feet long, and 40 feet broad. See *Caledonian Canal*.

Neri e Bianchi (*It., Black and White*). The names given to two political factions in Florence, Italy, in 1300 A.D., headed respectively by Corso di Donati and Vieri di Cerchi. In the struggle between these factions the *Neri* prevailed, and condemned Dante (who had favored the *Bianchi*) to perpetual banishment on a charge of peculation.

Nestor. The son of Neleus and Chloris, and King of Pylos. When an old man, he joined the Grecian chiefs at the siege of Troy, where, according to Homer, he was renowned not only for his wisdom, justice, and eloquence in council, but also for his valor on the field. Having ruled over three generations of men, his influence and advice were considered well-nigh equal to those of the immortal gods. He survived the fall of Troy, and returned to his native land, where Zeus granted him the enjoyment of a serene old age. The word "Nestor," as used at the present day, denotes any aged and wise counsellor.

" *Nestor*, the leader of the Pylian host,
The smooth-tongued chief, from whose persuasive lips
Sweeter than honey flowed the stream of speech.
Two generations of the sons of men
For him were past and gone, who with himself
Were born and bred on Pylos' lovely shore,
And o'er the third he now held royal sway."
Iliad, i, 294–300 (Derby's Translation).

Nevskoi Prospekt (*Russian, Neva Perspective*). The most fashionable, as well as the most animated, thoroughfare in St. Petersburg, Russia. It extends, almost in a straight line, from the Admiralty to the Neva, near the Smolnyi convent, and is lined with public buildings, churches, private dwellings, and handsome shops. It has a width of 130 feet,—with a double roadway,— and presents, during the winter season, a scene of gayety and animation unsurpassed in Europe.

New Atlantis. See *Atlantis, New*.

New Connecticut. A name formerly given to the "Western Reserve," a tract of land—comprising about 3,700,-000 acres—bordering on Lake Erie, in the State of Ohio, which at one time belonged to the State of Connecticut. See *Western Reserve*.

New England Primer. An almanac for the year 1691—now in the library of the Massachusetts Historical Society, Boston—contains the following advertisement :

"There is now in the Preff, and will fuddenly be extant, a Second Impression of *the New England Primer enlarged*, to which is added, more *Directions for Spelling*, the *Prayer of K. Edward the 6th*, and *Verses made by Mr. Rogers the Martyr, left as a Legacy to his Children*. Sold by *Benjamin Harris*, at the *London Coffee-House* in *Boston*."

The origin of the book is involved in

obscurity. The oldest copy known bears the date of 1775.

Newgate. A famous old jail in the city of London, originally used as a place of imprisonment for malefactors and debtors, and afterwards as a house of detention for persons awaiting trial at the Old Bailey Court. It is said to be the oldest prison in England,— having been commenced during the reign of Henry I (1100–1135). In 1241, the building had fallen into decay, and was restored by extorting the sum of 20,000 marks from the wealthy Jews of the city. Newgate was destroyed during the Great Fire of 1666. The present building was commenced in 1770; the interior was ruined by fire during the Lord Gordon riots of 1780, but was restored in 1782. Among the noted prisoners confined within its walls in times past, may be mentioned George Wither, Daniel Defoe, Jack Sheppard, and Titus Oates. Newgate demolished, 1902. See *Old Bailey (2)*.

New Jersey. This State of the American Union was so named in honor of the valorous defense of the island of Jersey against the Parliamentary forces, made by Sir George Carteret in 1664.

New Learning. A name given to the study, in their original tongues, of the Bible and the masterpieces of Greek and Latin literature, during the revival of letters in Europe, in the 15th and 16th centuries.

Newnham College. A college for the higher education of women at Cambridge, England, established in 1871–1875, and incorporated in 1880. It has at the present time about 160 students, who are under the charge of a principal, two vice-principals, and five instructors, and receive instruction partly by lectures delivered at the college and partly by such lectures at the University of Cambridge as are open to them. In 1881, the University threw open to the students of Newn-

ham College its tripos and previous examinations, at which many have taken high rank. In the Mathematical Tripos of 1890, Miss Fawcett's position was "above the senior wrangler." The majority of the students remain for three or four years. See *Girton College*.

News. It is said that the initial letters of the cardinal points of the compass, arranged thus : $W + E$, used

$$\begin{array}{c} N \\ W + E \\ S \end{array}$$

to be placed on the first page of the newspapers of olden times (*i. e.*, between the years 1595–1730) to indicate that they contained information from the four quarters of the globe. These letters were afterwards placed on a straight line, thus: NEWS; and from this practice the sheets were called "news - papers." Brewer, however, in the *Dictionary of Phrase and Fable*, says that the old spelling of the word, *newes*, is fatal to this conceit.

Newspapers, Number of. The total number of newspapers published in the world at the present time is about 50,000, — more than half of which are printed in the English language. They are distributed as follows :

  (1) United States and Canada......21,360
  (2) Great Britain 8,000
  (3) Germany...................... 6,000
  (4) France...................... 4,300
  (5) Japan 2,000
  (6) Italy 1,500
  (7) Austria-Hungary................ 1,200
  (8) Asia, exclusive of Japan......... 1,000
  (9) Spain 850
 (10) Russia 800
 (11) Australia...................... 800
 (12) Greece 600
 (13) Switzerland.................... 450
 (14) Belgium....................... 300
 (15) Holland....................... 300
 (16) All other countries............. 1,000

Newstead Abbey. An ancient structure, formerly a monastery, 10 miles northwest of Nottingham, England, on the edge of Sherwood Forest. It was founded for the Augustinian by Henry II (1154–1189) in 1170, in atonement for the murder of Thomas à Becket, and came into the possession of the Byron family in 1540. Lord Byron (1788–1824), the famous poet, made it his home in 1808, but sold it in 1818. Since that time, about $500,-000 have been expended upon its restoration.

New Style. A phrase used to denote the Gregorian Calendar, introduced by Pope Gregory XIII (1572–1585) in 1582. It was adopted by France, Italy, Spain, Denmark, Holland, Flanders, and Portugal, in 1582 ; by Germany in 1584 ; by Switzerland in 1583–1584 ; by Hungary in 1587 ; by Scotland in 1600; and by England in 1752. See *Gregorian Calendar ; Julian Calendar ; Old Style.*

New York. The City and State of New York received their present names in 1664, in honor of the Duke of York (afterwards James II of England), to whom this territory was given by his brother, Charles II (1660–1685).

New York Public Library (Astor, Lenox, and Tilden Foundations). A public library in New York City, formed by a consolidation of the Astor and Lenox Libraries, the Tilden Trust Fund, and the New York Free Circulating Library. This union was chiefly effected during the year 1895 ; and soon after that date the old distributing reservoir, extending from 40th to 42nd Street on Fifth Avenue, was chosen as the site for a suitable building. This structure, now entirely completed, is 366 feet long, and 246 feet deep, and has shelf-room for 1,250,000 volumes. It contains, in addition, reading-rooms, music- and map-rooms, special study-rooms, and picture-galleries. The New York Public Library now contains 536,381 volumes and 177,646 pamphlets in the reference department, and 155, 777 volumes in the circulating department,—making a total of 869,804 publications. See *Astor Library; Lenox Library.*

Niagara Falls. This stupendous cataract, situated on the Niagara River, about 22 miles from Lake Erie and 14 miles from Lake Ontario, was first described by Father Hennepin, a French Jesuit missionary, who visited it in 1678. Niagara Falls is divided by Goat Island into two cataracts of unequal size: (1) the Horseshoe, or Canadian, Fall—with a descent of 158 feet, and (2) the American Fall—1100 feet in width, with a descent of 164 feet. It is estimated that 15,000,000 cubic feet of water pass over these ledges each minute,—nine-tenths of which sweep over the Horseshoe. The average depth of water at the brink is 4 feet ; although in the centre of the Horseshoe it is not less than 20 feet. The falls are said by geologists to have worn their way back from Lake Ontario, and thus to have formed the chasm of the Niagara River. The American Fall recedes at the present time at the rate of 6 inches annually, and the Horseshoe Fall at the rate of from 3 to 5 feet annually. See *Horseshoe Fall.*

" The waters which fall from this horrible precipice do foam and boil after the most hideous manner imaginable, making an outrageous noise more terrible than thunder." —*Father Hennepin.*

Nibelungen-Lied. A famous German epic poem, of unknown authorship, consisting of ancient ballads, termed sagas. In its present form it dates from the middle of the 12th century A.D. It is divided into two parts—the first ending with the death of Siegfried and the second with the death of Kriemhild, his widow. Interest in the *Nibelungen-Lied* declined after the Reformation (1517), but revived at the close of the 18th century; it was not, however, until the early part of the 19th century that scholars realized the great literary treasures contained in this poem. Richard Wagner founded his musical dramas, entitled the *Ring of the Nibelungen*, on this epic.

"The 'Nibelungenlied' is the greatest and most complete of all the German popular epics. The historical basis of the poem is found in the fifth and sixth centuries of the Christian era; and the name, Nibelungen, is said to be derived from an ancient and powerful Burgundian race, whose terrible downfall is the subject of the work. . . . It belongs partly to the same cycle of adventures, characters, and traditions as the 'Heldenbuch,' and springs from the same great heroic age of Germany. The present form of the poem is undoubtedly the work of a single author, who, with a soundness of judgment and felicity of genius rarely equalled, combined the separate songs, sagas, and traditions relating to Attila and the Huns, and their connexions with the Burgundian tribe, into one beautiful and harmonious whole; and this poet, according to the conjecture of William Schlegel, von der Hagen, and others, was the Minnesinger, Heinrich von Ofterdingen. . . . The scene of the poem is on the Rhine and in Austria and Hungary."—Longfellow's *Poets and Poetry of Europe*.

Nicaragua Canal. A ship-canal, projected to connect the Atlantic and Pacific Oceans, by using the waters of Lake Nicaragua and the San Juan River. Excavations were commenced in the autumn of 1889, and by October, 1890, $2,000,000 had been expended. Work was suspended in 1893. When completed, the canal will have a length of 170 miles, of which distance 28 miles only will require excavation. The elevation of the summit-level above tide-water will be 110 feet, and this will be surmounted by eight locks. The average depth of the canal will be 30 feet, and its minimum width 100 feet. The estimated cost of construction is $125,-000,000, and the time required for its completion, five years. The time-limit from ocean to ocean will be about 44 hours. It is said that a saving of 10,753 miles in the journey by water from New York to San Francisco will be effected by means of this canal. See *Bulwer-Clayton Treaty*.

Nicene Creed. A creed of the Christian Church, adopted by the Council of Nicæa in 325, and completed by the Council of Constantinople in 381. It was drawn up as a protest against the heresies of Arius and Macedonius, and asserted belief in the divinity of Christ and of the Holy Ghost. The words *filioque* (*Lat. and from the Son*)—teaching that the Holy Ghost proceeds from the Son as well as from the Father—were added by the Latin Church in the sixth century. See *Apostles' Creed; Athanasian Creed; Filioque Controversy*.

Nicomachean Ethics. An ethical treatise by Aristotle (384–322 B.C.), forming part of his system of philosophy. Cicero's supposition that this work was written by Nicomachus, the son of Aristotle, was probably occasioned by the peculiar title,—the origin of which may be otherwise explained.

Nigger in the Woodpile. A colloquialism used to denote the hidden cause of any transaction, which is not regarded as open and above-board. The expression originated in the South, and refers to the thievish tendencies of the negro race.

Nightmare of Europe. An appellation conferred upon Napoleon Bonaparte (1769–1821), who, in the exercise of his despotic power, oppressed the nations of Europe for many years.

"So it came about that we, who watched him dart from place to place, like the shuttle of destiny, and who heard his name always in connection with some new achievement and some new success, had come at last to look upon him as something more than human, something monstrous, overshadowing France and menacing Europe. . . . Even now, after the long gap of years and the knowledge of his downfall, that great man casts his spell upon you, but all that you read and all that you hear cannot give you an idea of what his name meant in the days when he was at the summit of his career."—Conan Doyle's *Uncle Bernac*.

Nihilists. A secret body of revolutionists in Russia, who aim at the overthrow of imperialism and the establishment of government on a communistic basis. The name wa first applied by the novelist Turgue-nieff (1818–1883) in 1862, to those socialists that denounce the institution of marriage ; but since 1892 it has been given to all persons desirous of overthrowing civil and religious authority throughout the Russian Empire. Nihilism is said to have come into being in 1860, under the influence of one Herzen, a follower of Hegel; but other authorities say it originated in 1848. The assassination of the Emperor Alexander II (1855–1881) in 1881 was universally attributed to the Nihilists. Of late years their dogmas have been gradually spreading, especially among the lower classes.

"In 1868 the following manifesto was circulated :

(1) Tear out of your hearts the belief in the existence of God, or you can never know what freedom is.

(2) The second lie to get rid of is *Right*, which is only the bastard of Might. Might makes Right. Without Might there is no such thing. Away with it !

(3) Having got rid of these two lies, civilization, property, marriage, morality, and justice will snap like pack-thread.

(4) Let your own happiness be your only law ; but, in order to enjoy this law, you must destroy everything that exists in the shape of government and social organization. Annihilate everything as it now exists—the good with the bad,—make a clean sweep of all ; for if but one atom of the old leaven is suffered to remain, it will corrupt the new order, and all the work will have to be done again."—Brewer's *Historic Note-Book.*

Nike-Apteros, Temple of. A small temple of great beauty, in Athens, Greece, standing on the right of the entrance into the Acropolis. It is 27 feet long, 18 feet broad, and 23 feet high from the lowest step to the top of the pediment. This structure was probably erected by Cimon (*fl.* 460 B.C., anterior to the time of Pericles), and was demolished by the Turks in 1687 for the purpose of constructing a battery, when besieged by the Venetians. The temple had totally disappeared about one hundred years ago ; but, in 1835, the fragments were discovered and were carefully restored to their proper places,—partly by the government and partly by private contributions received from England. Also known as the " Temple of Wingless Victory."

Nile. A colossal group in marble, representing Father Nile in a recumbent attitude,—surrounded by 16 children, or cupids. It was discovered near the Church of Santa Maria sopra Minerva in Rome, during the pontificate of Leo X (1513–1522), and is now in the Vatican.

"The principal figure is in a reclining posture, and represents a man in the ripe autumn of life, with a flowing beard and a grave expression, while around him sixteen children are sporting in every possible variety of attitude ; some climbing on his knees ; some clasping his neck ; some nestling in his lap ; some bestriding his arms ; and some playing with his feet. Most of these little creatures are restorations, but they are very cleverly executed. They seem to be really enjoying the fun ; and the 'fine, old gentleman' with whom they are frolicking appears like an indulgent grandpapa, surrendering himself to a game of romps with his grandchildren. The number sixteen is said to be in allusion to the sixteen cubits at which the rise of the river begins to irrigate the land."—Hillard's *Six Months in Italy.*

Nile, Battle of the. A desperate naval battle fought on August 1st, 1798, in the Bay of Aboukir (near the Rosetta mouth of the Nile), Egypt, between the British fleet commanded by Admiral Nelson, and the French fleet under Admiral Brueys. The French were overwhelmingly defeated with a loss of 5225 men drowned, burned, and missing. Nine of their ships were captured, two were destroyed, and two escaped. The English loss was 218 killed and 677 wounded. Nelson was created a baron, with a pension of £2000 a year, for his services in this engagement. The battle of the Nile proved fatal to the success of Bonaparte's Egyptian Expedition. See *Aboukir, Battle of (3)* ; *Orient, L'.*

Nile, Inundation of the. This phenomenon occurs regularly every year, and lasts from the 15th of June to the 17th of September. After this period, the river gradually subsides, leaving a rich alluvial deposit for six miles on each side of the stream. A rise of 16 cubits is necessary to furnish the proper irrigation. An excessive rise of the river means great loss of crops and property, and sometimes of human life ; while the failure of a few feet may occasion almost a famine during the ensuing year. In 1829, the Nile rose 26 cubits, and caused the deaths of 30,000 persons by drowning, as well as the destruction of a great amount of property. The average rise at Thebes is 40 feet ; at Cairo, 27 feet. An attempt is now being made, by the construction of extensive storage-basins, to supply the Nile valley during the time of low water.

" On the island of Rhoda, opposite to Cairo, is a square well, connected with the river by a canal, and containing a graduated marble pillar, divided into 24 cubits, each measuring 21.386 inches. A rise of 18 cubits is traditionally regarded as the height of the lowest inundation ; 19 cubits is considered tolerable, 20 excellent, 21 adequate, and 22 complete, but 24 is ruinous."— *Chambers's Encyclopædia*.

Nîmes, Arena of. A famous Roman ruin in the town of Nîmes, in southern France. It is 437 feet in length, 332 feet in breadth, and 72 feet in height. It accommodated 20,000 people. In 1810, an act was passed, ordering the débris to be removed ; and, at the present day, there is no obstruction remaining. The structure is supposed to be of the same age as the Coliseum at Rome. It was occupied as a fortress by the Visigoths and Saracens, and is now occasionally used for a bull-fight. See *Coliseum*.

Niña. One of the three ships with which Christopher Columbus sailed for America from Palos, Spain, on August 3rd, 1492. She was commanded by Vincente Yanez Pinzon. See *Pinta ; Santa Maria*.

Nincompoop. This word, meaning a *fool*, a *blockhead*, a *simpleton*, is a corruption of the Latin phrase (*non compos* [*mentis*], *not sound of mind*). See *Non Compos Mentis*.

Nine Days' Wonder. This expression—meaning a short-lived sensation—is said to have originated in some reference to the nine days (July 10th–18th, 1553) during which Lady Jane Grey was styled Queen of England. Another authority, however, says the phrase refers to the nine days after birth, during which a puppy is unable to see.

" A wonder lasts nine days, and then the puppy's eyes are open."
      Bohn's *Handbook of Proverbs*.

Nine Orders of Angels. The pseudo-Dionysius (4th or 5th century after Christ), in his *Celestial Hierarchy*, divides the angels into three classes, and each class into three orders, as follows :

First Class.	*Second Class.*
(1) Thrones.	(4) Dominions.
(2) Cherubim.	(5) Authorities.
(3) Seraphim.	(6) Powers.

Third Class.
(7) Principalities.
(8) Archangels.
(9) Angels.

See *Ephesians* i, 21; *Colossians* i, 16.
" In heaven above
The effulgent bands in triple circles move."
      Tasso's *Jerusalem Delivered*.

Nine Planets. Including the planetoids (which by many are regarded as fragments of a larger planet destroyed by contact with some other celestial body), the planets composing the solar system are nine in number, as follows : Mercury, Venus, the Earth, Mars, the Planetoids, Jupiter, Saturn, Uranus, and Neptune.

Nine Points of the Law. The following are the nine requisites for success in a suit-at-law, enumerated in Brewer's *Dictionary of Phrase and Fable*.

(1) A good deal of money.

(2) A good deal of patience.
(3) A good cause.
(4) A good lawyer.
(5) A good counsel.
(6) Good witnesses.
(7) A good jury.
(8) A good judge.
(9) Good luck.

Nine Tailors Make a Man.

" In North's ' Church Bells of Leicestershire,' the author, in speaking of tolling for the dead, says: ' These tolls are called "tellers," and it has been suggested that the old saying " Nine tailors make a man " is a corruption of "Nine tellers mark a man," meaning that three times three tolls or tellers are struck on the passing bell for a man.' At Wimbledon it is still the custom to strike three times three for an adult male and three times two for a female on the tenor bell ; but for children under twelve the treble bell is used, and the strokes are twice three for a male, and twice two for a female." — Edwards's *Words, Facts, and Phrases.*

" The present scope of this expression is that a tailor is so much more feeble than another man, that it would take nine of them to make a man of average stature and strength. There is a tradition that an orphan lad, in 1742, applied to a fashionable London tailor for alms. There were nine journeymen in the establishment, each of whom contributed something to set the little orphan up with a fruit barrow. The little merchant in time became rich, and adopted for his motto ' Nine tailors made me a man,' or ' Nine tailors make a man.' This certainly is not the origin of the expression, inasmuch as we find a similar one used by Taylor a century before that date, and referred to as of old standing even then :

' Some foolish knave, I thinke, at first began
The slander that three taylers are one man.'
Taylor, " Workes," iii, 73 (1630)."

Brewer's *Reader's Handbook.*

Nine Worthies.

The name given to nine famous persons, distinguished as embodiments of sterling worth. They are as follows :

(1) Three Gentiles.
{ (1) Hector.
{ (2) Alexander the Great.
{ (3) Julius Cæsar.

(2) Three Jews.
{ (4) Joshua.
{ (5) David.
{ (6) Judas Maccabæus.

(3) Three Christians.
{ (7) Arthur.
{ (8) Charlemagne.
{ (9) Godfrey of Bouillon.

The expression " Nine Worthies " is also applied to the privy councillors of William III of England (1689–1702), four of whom — Devonshire, Dorset, Monmouth, and Edward Russell — were Whigs. The remaining five — Caermarthen, Pembroke, Nottingham, Marlborough, and Lowther — were Tories.

Nine Worthies of London.

(1) Sir William Walworth (slew Wat Tyler. Twice Lord Mayor).
(2) Sir Henry Pritchard (entertained Edward III, with 5000 followers ; and other sovereigns).
(3) Sir William Sevenoke (fought the Dauphin of France ; built almshouses and school).
(4) Sir Thomas White (kept the Londoners loyal to Queen Mary during Wyatt's Rebellion).
(5) Sir John Bonham (commander of army raised to oppose progress of Solyman).
(6) Christopher Croker (famous at siege of Bordeaux).
(7) Sir John Hawkwood (one of the knights of the Black Prince).
(8) Sir Hugh Caverley (freed Poland from the presence of a huge bear).
(9) Sir Henry Maleverer (a Crusader, and guardian of Jacob's Well).

Ninth Thermidor.

The Ninth Thermidor of the year II, in the French Revolutionary Calendar, corresponds to the 27th of July, 1794. It is historically memorable as the day on which the National Convention deposed Robespierre (1758–1794), and thus put an end to the Reign of Terror. On the following day, the tyrant and 22 of his partisans were guillotined.

It is said that the following epitaph for Robespierre was written by one that understood his character : "Passer-by, lament not for Robespierre ; for, were he living, thou wouldst be dead." See *Reign of Terror*.

Niobe. A noble group of ancient sculpture in the gallery of the Uffizi Palace, Florence, Italy, representing Niobe lamenting the death of her children, slain by the arrows of Apollo and Diana. It was discovered in Rome in 1583, and is supposed to be the work either of Praxiteles or of Scopas.

"No wonder the strength of that woe depicted on her countenance should change her into stone. One of her sons—a beautiful, boyish form—is lying on his back, just expiring, with the chill languor of death creeping over his limbs, We seem to hear the quick whistling of the arrows, and look involuntarily into the air to see the hovering figure of the avenging god."—*Bayard Taylor*.

Nirvâna (*Sanskrit, Blowing Out*). In Brahmanism, a synonym of *Moksha*, meaning spiritual freedom and ecstasy. In the Buddhist religion, it means the final release of the soul from the necessity of transmigration, and its consequent enfranchisement from the ills of existence by absorption into the divine essence.

"Every Sanskrit scholar knows that *Nirvâna* means originally the blowing out. . . . The human soul, when it arrives at its perfection, is blown out, if we use the phraseology of the Buddhists, like a lamp."—*Max-Müller's Chips from a German Work-Shop*.

"Complete *Nirvâna* or extinction cannot, of course, take place till death ; but this state of preparation for it, called simply *Nirvâna*, seems attainable during life, and was, in fact, attained by Gautama himself. The process by which the state is attained is called *Dhyana*, and is neither more nor less than ecstasy or trance, which plays so important a part among mystics of all religions. The individual is described as losing one feeling after another, until perfect apathy is attained, and he reaches a region 'where there are neither ideas, nor the idea of the absence of ideas !' "—*Chambers's Encyclopædia*.

Nitrate King. A nickname conferred upon Colonel J. T. North of Eltham, England, because of his successful speculations in that commodity.

Nitrogen. A colorless, tasteless, inodorous gas, forming one of the elements. It was formerly regarded as permanent or non-condensable ; but it can now be liquefied when subjected to great pressure, at an extremely low temperature. This was first successfully accomplished in 1877, by Cailletet and Pictet. In the free state, it shows little disposition to enter into direct combination with the other elements. It forms an important constituent of many compounds, as well as of all vegetal and animal organisms, and comprises four-fifths of the total volume of the atmosphere. It cannot, however, support animal life, and its function seems to be simply to dilute the oxygen with which it is associated. Nitrogen is 14 times as heavy as hydrogen. It was discovered by Dr. Rutherford of Edinburgh, in 1772, and was afterwards carefully studied by Lavoisier, Priestley, and Scheele. The word means " nitre-producer," and is derived from the Greek words νίτρον (*nitre*) and γεννάω (*I produce*). This element was so called because it was found to be a necessary constituent of nitre, or potassium nitrate. See *Azote*.

Nitro-Glycerine. A highly explosive substance discovered by Sobrero, a young Italian chemist, in Paris in 1846, but not rendered serviceable as a blasting-agent for industrial purposes until about 15 years later. It is formed by dissolving glycerine in equal amounts of strong nitric and sulphuric acids and pouring this solution into water, whereupon the nitro-glycerine forms a precipitate. The many accidents resulting from its transportation caused the British Parliament to forbid its use in 1869.

This prohibition led to the introduction of dynamite, *i. e.*, nitro-glycerine, absorbed by some inert, porous solid—like infusorial earth, sawdust, etc., and thus rendered less liable to explosion from moderate shocks. See *Dynamite.*

Noctes Ambrosianæ.

A series of papers — in the form of dialogues — contributed by John Wilson (" Christopher North ") and others to *Blackwood's Magazine*, between the years 1822–1835. Of the 71 articles constituting the original series, 39 are said to be the genuine contributions of the poet Wilson.

"There is not so original and curious a work in the English and Scotch languages. It is a most singular and delightful outpouring of criticism, politics, and descriptions of feeling, character and scenery, of verse and prose, and maudlin eloquence, and especially of wild fun. It breathes the very essence of the bacchanalian revel of clever men ; and its Scotch is the best Scotch that has been written in modern times."— *Lord Cockburn.*

No Man's Land.

(1) Formerly, a strip of public land in the United States, lying north of Texas, east of New Mexico, south of Colorado and Kansas, and west of Indian Territory. It is 167½ miles long and 34½ miles wide, and forms, at the present day, a part of the Territory of Oklahoma,—organized in 1890. Previous to that time, it was beyond the jurisdiction of the United States courts, and became a place of refuge for outlaws and desperadoes. It was ceded to the United States by Texas in 1850, because it lay north of Mason and Dixon's Line (36° 30′), and hence could not be admitted into the Union as part of a slave State.

(2) A strip of territory on the boundary line between Pennsylvania and Delaware. Although officially declared to be a part of Pennsylvania, the inhabitants of this section, nevertheless, vote in Delaware and record their title-deeds and legal papers in that State. It is said that some of the people dwelling on this strip of land insist that they are not the legal inhabitants of any State, and, consequently, neither pay taxes nor vote.

(3) A small uninhabited island, near Martha's Vineyard, off the coast of Massachusetts.

(4) A region in British South Africa, now called East Griqualand.

(5) A territory of 80,000 square miles in South Australia. See *Oklahoma.*

Nom-de-Plume.

This expression —meaning a fictitious name assumed by an author—is frequently used in England and America, but not in France. The French use the term *nom-de-guerre* instead. The following extract from *L'Intermédiaire*, a French periodical, furnishes conclusive evidence on this point.

"We do not know in our language the expression *nom de plume*, and there is no need of borrowing it from the English. We have the phrase *nom de guerre*, which is thoroughly French, and which clearly enough indicates literary pseudonymity. The very origin of this phrase is thoroughly French. Formerly a soldier in enlisting took a surname, which he retained so long as he served under the flag. It was a true *nom de guerre*. The extension is natural. Under certain *régimes* of self-will (*bon plaisir*) or terror, is not the literary arena a field of battle where one fights for his liberty or his life?"—Walsh's *Handy-Book of Literary Curiosities.*

Non Compos Mentis (*Lat. Not sound of mind*).

A corruption of the first two words of this expression has given rise to the word *nincompoop*. See *Nincompoop.*

Nonconformists.

A term applied to those clergymen — 2000 in number — that left the Church of England in 1662, two years after the Restoration, rather than submit to the conditions of the *Act of Uniformity*. This Act required : (1) that every clergyman should be reordained, if he had not already received episcopal ordination ; (2) that he should declare his assent to everything contained in the *Book of Common Prayer ;* (3) that he should take the oath of canonical obedience ; (4) that he should abjure the *Solemn League and Covenant;* and finally, (5) that he should renounce the principle of taking arms, on any pretense whatsoever, against the King.

The word "Nonconformists" is used at the present time to denote all dissenters from the Anglican Church.

Nonjurors. A name given to those bishops and clergymen of the Anglican Church that refused to take the oath of allegiance to William and Mary in 1689, after the deposition of James II. Their refusal was based on the belief that James was the "Lord's anointed," and could not be justly and lawfully set aside. The Nonjurors comprised Sancroft, Archbishop of Canterbury, eight bishops, and 400 of the inferior clergy,—all of whom were ejected from their livings in 1691.

Norfolk Boy. A nickname given to Richard Porson (1759–1808), the famous Greek scholar, while a student at Eton, in allusion to the place of his birth.

Norman's Woe. A sombre mass of rocks, situated near the entrance to the harbor of Gloucester, Massachusetts. It has been immortalized by Longfellow in his ballad, *The Wreck of the Hesperus.*

" Such was the wreck of the Hesperus,
In the midnight and the snow !
Christ save us all from a death like this,
On the reef of *Norman's Woe !* "

North American Review. Founded in Boston, Massachusetts, in 1815, and published bi-monthly until 1818, when it became a quarterly magazine. In 1879, it was removed to New York and issued as a monthly.

" From 1815, for sixty years, though receiving some contributions from other parts of the country, the *North American* practically represented the culture which centred in Boston and Cambridge. Successive editors were William Tudor, Willard Phillips, Edward Tyrrell Channing, Richard Henry Dana, Senior, Edward Everett, Jared Sparks, Alexander H. Everett, Francis Bowen, Andrew P. Peabody, James Russell Lowell, Charles Eliot Norton, and Henry Adams. These Boston and Cambridge men wrote much for the *Review,* a single individual sometimes contributing several papers to a number. Culture and critical spirit certainly existed in a land and in a time when a single periodical could print articles by such representative men as Everett, Sparks, and Lowell among its editors, and Irving, Prescott, Bancroft, Motley, Parkman, Emerson, Longfellow, Holmes, and Curtis among its contributors. Their work may fairly enough be said, in the words of a later editor of the *Review,* to 'represent the growth of native thought and scholarship in the United States from the close of the second war with Great Britain down to the close of the great civil war.' "—Richardson's *American Literature.*

Northeast Passage. See *Northwest Passage.*

Northern Homer. A sobriquet conferred upon Sir Walter Scott (1771–1832), the famous poet and novelist.

North German Confederation. See *Germanic Confederation.*

North River. A name given to the Hudson River by the early Dutch settlers to distinguish it from the Delaware, which was called by them the South River. This name is sometimes applied to the Hudson at the present day, especially in the neighborhood of New York City.

Northumberland. This word originally denoted the land north of the river Humber in England.

Northumberland House. The noble mansion of the Duke of Northumberland, which, until 1874, stood on the southeast side of Trafalgar Square, London. It was erected by Henry Howard, Earl of Northampton, who, in 1614, bequeathed it to his nephew, Thomas Howard, Earl of Suffolk. It then received the name of *Suffolk House,* and afterwards passed into the hands of Algernon Percy, Earl of Northumberland, by whom it was called *Northumberland House.* The building was purchased, in 1873, by the "Metropolitan Board of Works" for £497,000, and was demolished to make way for Northumberland Avenue, a new street extending from Charing Cross to the Victoria Embankment. The Grand Hotel occupies a part of the site of Northumberland House.

Northwest Passage. The name given to an ocean-passage for ships from the Atlantic to the Pacific, by way of North America. The attempt to discover such a route was first made, about 1500, by Corte Real, a Portuguese navigator, and was renewed later, though without success, by Hudson, Baffin, Foxe, Ross, Back, Parry, Sir John Franklin, and others. In 1850–1852, Captain McClure, while in search of Franklin, succeeded in passing from Behring's Strait into Baffin's Bay, and thus demonstrated the existence of a Northwest Passage. Several other routes have been discovered since that time, but from a commercial point of view they are all valueless. The Northeast Passage from the Atlantic to the Pacific, by way of Europe and Asia, was first accomplished by an expedition under Prof. Nordenskjöld, in 1878–1879.

Northwest Territory. A name given, during the early history of the United States of America, to a territory of 420,000 square miles, lying northeast of the Ohio River, and comprising at the present day the States of Ohio, Indiana, Wisconsin, and Michigan. After the Revolutionary War, the States that laid claim to this region ceded it to the General Government, and in 1787, Congress adopted an ordinance providing for its organization. This organization, however, was not fully completed until 1799. In accordance with one of the articles of the ordinance, slavery was forever excluded from the Northwest Territory. See *Western Reserve*.

Notre Dame. The cathedral church of Paris. It was founded in 1163,

during the pontificate of Alexander III (1159–1181), but was not completed until 1420. The church is a Gothic structure—in the form of a Latin cross —and has a length of about 420 feet, a width of 155 feet, and a height of nave of 110 feet. The façade—which is the finest part of the structure—is flanked by two towers, 223 feet high. The south one contains the great *Bourdon de Notre Dame*, one of the largest bells in the world, weighing 16 tons ; the clapper alone weighs nearly 1000 lbs. The interior of the church is somewhat disappointing; it is adorned with paintings, sculptures, bas-reliefs, and stained-glass windows depicting scenes from sacred history. Notre Dame was converted into a "Temple of Reason" during the French Revolution. It was closed in 1794, and reopened by Napoleon Bonaparte as a place of Christian worship in 1802. The building was beautifully restored in 1866 and the following years, under the superintendence of Viollet-le-Duc, at a cost of £250,000 ; but was cruelly desecrated by the Communists of 1871, and narrowly escaped destruction by fire. Napoleon I was crowned Emperor at Notre Dame on December 2nd, 1804. See *Goddess of Reason*.

Notus. See *Auster*.

Novum Organum (*Lat., New Instrument, or Method*). A philosophic treatise, in two volumes, by Lord Francis Bacon (1561–1626), forming the second and most important part of the *Instauratio Magna*. It was written in Latin, and appeared in 1620. The object of the *Novum Organum* is to furnish mankind with a better method of investigating truth, *i. e.*, a better Logic than the so-called Aristotelian, or syllogistic, method. It is designed to be "the science of a better and more perfect use of reason in the investigation of things, and of the true aids of the understanding." See *Baconian Philosophy ; Instauratio Magna*.

"Previous to the publication of the

'Novum Organum' of Bacon, natural philosophy, in any legitimate and extensive sense of the word, could hardly be said to exist."—*Sir John Herschel.*

Noyades. The name given to the method of wholesale drowning adopted by Jean Baptiste Carrier at Nantes, France, in 1793. To accomplish his purpose a vessel, fitted with a movable bottom, was filled with victims and towed out into the Loire at night, where it was scuttled with all on board. This inhuman act was repeated 25 times. By means of these summary executions — called also " vertical deportations " — more than 10,000 persons perished. In addition, men and women were frequently bound together and flung into the Loire,— a device called " Republican Marriage." It is said that the river became so polluted by the presence of corpses that the use of the water for drinking and cooking was prohibited. Carrier, although his crimes were condoned by Robespierre, was guillotined on December 16th, 1794, some months after the fall of the tyrant. See *Fusillades; Republican Marriages.*

Nullification Doctrine. A doctrine prevalent among the Southern States of the American Union, previous to the Civil War. It maintained the right of any State to *nullify* any act of the Federal Government, which it deemed prejudicial to the interests of the commonwealth. The doctrine of Nullification rests upon the principle of State rights, which asserts that the States are sovereign commonwealths, and owe merely a nominal allegiance to the General Government. In 1832, South Carolina, holding the recently enacted tariff to be oppressive to the State as well as unconstitutional, attempted to nullify the act by legislation and declared that any attempt at force would be followed by secession from the Union. Andrew Jackson, then President of the United States, pronounced this conduct treasonable, and sent General Scott to Charleston, S. C., to maintain the authority of the Federal Government and to protect the Custom House officials in the performance of their duties. In 1833 Congress passed a bill for a gradual reduction of the duties of which South Carolina complained, and the dangers of civil war were for the time averted. See *State Rights.*

Nun of Kent. A sobriquet conferred upon Elizabeth Barton (1506–1534). She was also known as the *Holy Maid of Kent.* See *Holy Maid of Kent.*

Nutmeg State. A sobriquet conferred upon the State of Connecticut, the shrewd inhabitants of which have been jocosely charged with manufacturing cedar nutmegs, in imitation of the genuine article, and palming them off on unsuspecting customers.

O

Oak, To Sport One's. A phrase signifying that one is " not at home to visitors." The saying originated at the English universities, where the students' " chambers " have two doors,—an inner and an outer one. The *outer* door is made of oak ; and, when this is closed or " sported," it denotes either that the occupant of the apartment is out or that he does not wish to be disturbed.

". . . Young Wardlaw went down to Oxford and shut himself up in his own room, a prey to fear and remorse. *He sported his oak,* and never went out. All his exercise was that of a wild beast in its den, walking restlessly up and down."— *Foul Play* (Charles Reade and Dion Boucicault).

Oates's Plot. An imaginary plot, concocted in England by Titus Oates (1620–1705) during the reign of Charles II (1660–1685), having for its object the massacre of the King and the members of Parliament, the burning of London, the re-establishment of the Roman Catholic Church, and the invasion of Ireland by a French army.

This pretended conspiracy was revealed by Oates on August 12th, 1678; and upon his false testimony and that of his confederates eighteen Roman Catholics were accused, convicted, and executed, —among them, the aged Viscount Stafford. Oates became the hero of the day ; he was hailed "Savior of his Country," received a pension of £600, and was granted a suite of apartments at Whitehall. A reaction soon after set in, and Oates was tried for perjury. Being found guilty (May, 1685), he was publicly whipped, pilloried, and imprisoned for life; but, on the accession of William and Mary (1689), he was pardoned and a pension of £300 was granted him. The excitement occasioned by this supposed plot led to the passage by Parliament of the *Test Act*, which excluded Roman Catholics from the House of Lords. This disability was not removed until the reign of George IV (1820–1830). See *Popish Plot.*

Oath of Strasburg. The name given to an oath taken, soon after the battle of Fontenay (841 A.D.), by Charles and Louis, sons of Louis le Débonnaire, wherein they formally renewed their allegiance to their brother Lothaire, the Emperor. See *Battle of the Brothers.*

"Louis first explained the oath to his men in the German speech ; Charles did the same to his warriors in Franco-Roman, the parent of the present French language. Then Charles, standing before the Germans, took oath in their language, while Louis, confronting the Frenchmen, took the same oath in the Romance tongue. This incident shows how, already, the two nations were becoming distinct in speech, The oaths still remain, and that taken by Louis before his brother's troops is the oldest monument of the French language."—Steele's *Brief History of France.*

Obelisk in London. An Egyptian monolith, standing on the Victoria Embankment, between Charing Cross and Waterloo Bridges, London, where it was placed on September 12th, 1878. It weighs somewhat more than 186 tons, and is 68 feet 5½ inches high, from base to apex. This obelisk is one of two monoliths erected at On (Heliopolis) by Thothmes III (*fl.* 1600 B.C.), and removed to Alexandria by Augustus about 23 B.C. According to some authorities, however, these obelisks were removed to Alexandria by Rameses II, and while there they were long popularly, but erroneously, known as "Cleopatra's Needles." One of these, after lying prostrate in the sand for ages, was acquired for the British Government by Sir Ralph Abercromby in 1801, but was not removed. It was offered by Mehemet Ali (1769–1849), and again by the Khedive in 1877, and was finally conveyed to England, where it arrived on January 20th, 1878. See *Obelisk in New York ; Victoria Embankment.*

Obelisk in New York. A granite monolith in Central Park, New York, presented to the city, through the Department of State, by the late Ismail Pasha, Khedive of Egypt, in 1877. It was brought to this country by Lieutenant - Commander Gorringe, U.S.N., and placed in position on January 22nd, 1881,—the entire expense of removal and erection ($103,-732) having been borne by the late William H. Vanderbilt. Its height from base to apex is 69 feet 2 inches, and its weight about 220 tons, or 440,-000 lbs. It is the sixth in size of the famous monoliths of Egypt, and is one of two obelisks erected at On (Heliopolis) by Thothmes III (*fl.* 1600 B.C.), and removed to Alexandria by Augustus about 23 B.C., or, as some authorities say, by Rameses II. See *Obelisk in London.*

Obelisk of Luxor. A celebrated obelisk in the Place de la Concorde, Paris, presented to the French Government by Mehemet Ali (1769–1849), Khedive of Egypt, and placed in position in October, 1836,—in the presence of Louis Philippe (1830–1848) and thousands of spectators. It is a monolith of syenite, or reddish granite, the sides of which are inscribed with hieroglyphics, and rests on a pedestal of Breton granite, 13 feet high. The obelisk proper is 76 feet high, and weighs 240 tons, or 480,000 lbs. Its removal to France required the services of 800 men, and entailed an expense of 2,000,000 francs. It is one of two obelisks erected by Rameses II about 1350 B.C., at the entrance of the famous Temple of Luxor. See *Luxor, Temple of.*

Obelisk of Orsotasen. A celebrated Egyptian obelisk of red granite, 70 feet in height, still standing near the village of Matareieh, eight miles north of Cairo. It bears the name of Orsotasen (Usurtesen) I, the second king of the XIIth dynasty.

Obelisk of St. Peter's. A famous obelisk of red granite — 132 feet in height — standing in the centre of the Piazza of St. Peter's at Rome. It is sometimes called the Obelisk of the Vatican. It was brought from On (Heliopolis) to Rome by the Emperor Caligula (37–41 A.D.), and placed in the Vatican Circus. In 1586, during the pontificate of Sixtus V (1585–1590), this huge monolith — estimated to weigh about 500 tons — was moved on rollers from its original position and placed on its present site. This great triumph of mechanical skill was accomplished under the superintendence of Domenico Fontana (1543–1607). The Obelisk of St. Peter's enjoys the unique distinction of being the only monument of the kind at Rome that has never been overthrown.

Obelisk of the Lateran. A superb monolith of red granite—the largest in existence — standing in the Piazza of St. John Lateran at Rome. It is 104 feet in height, or, with the pedestal, 153 feet, and about 600 tons (1,200,000 lbs.) in weight. It was originally erected by Thothmes III (*fl.* 1600 B.C.) of Egypt, in front of the Temple of the Sun at Thebes, and was brought by Constantine to the Circus Maximus

in 357 A.D. In 1587, during the pontificate of Sixtus V (1585–1590), it was discovered there in three pieces, and in 1588 was removed to its present site.

Obelisk of the Monte Cavallo. An Egyptian obelisk of red granite—without hieroglyphics — situated in the Piazza di Monte Cavallo, in Rome. It is said to have been brought from Egypt to Rome by the Emperor Claudius (41–54 A.D.).

Obelisk of the Piazza del Popolo. A noble Egyptian obelisk of red granite, 116 feet in height, in the Piazza del Popolo at Rome. It was brought from the Temple of the Sun at On (Heliopolis) by the Emperor Augustus (27 B.C.–14 A.D.), and erected in the Circus Maximus. In 1589 it was removed, and placed in its present position. It is said to be the oldest obelisk in Rome.

Ober = Ammergau. See *Passion-Play.*

Occult Sciences. A name given, during the Middle Ages, to those sciences that were supposed to be subject to the action or influence of hidden qualities or supernatural powers, — such as magic, divination or fortune-telling, necromancy, alchemy, and astrology. In modern times, the expression " occult sciences " has been applied to all forms of mysticism and esoteric philosophy.

Ocean, Depth of. According to Dr. John Murray, the greatest depths of the ocean, as ascertained during the "Challenger Expedition" (1872–1876), are as follows :

(1) Atlantic Ocean, 27,366 feet.
(2) Pacific Ocean, 30,000 feet.
(3) Indian Ocean, 18,582 feet.
(4) Southern Ocean, 25,200 feet.
(5) Arctic Ocean, 9,000 feet.

Ocean, Ownership of. Although the ocean is the common property of mankind and, as such, is free to all, yet, according to a generally recognized law, every country exercises the right of ownership and jurisdiction over the sea within three miles of the shore.

Ocean Records. The following is the list of record-breaking ocean passages between New York and Queenstown, east or west, during the years 1856–1894 inclusive.

Date.	Steamer.	D.	H.	M.
1856	Persia	9	1	45
1866	Scotia	8	2	48
1869	City of Brussels	7	22	3
1873	Baltic	7	20	9
1875	City of Berlin	7	15	48
1876	Germanic	7	11	37
1877	Britannic	7	10	53
1880	Arizona	7	7	23
1882	Alaska	6	18	37
1884	Oregon	6	11	9
1884	America	6	10	0
1885	Etruria	6	5	31
1887	Umbria	6	4	42
1888	Etruria	6	1	55
1889	City of Paris	5	19	18
1891	Majestic	5	18	8
1891	Teutonic	5	16	31
1892	City of Paris	5	15	58
1892	City of Paris	5	14	24
1893	Campania	5	12	7
1894	Lucania	5	7	23

Odd Fellows. The name adopted by the members of a social and benevolent order, founded in London in 1745. The " Independent Order of Odd Fellows " was formed in Manchester in 1813, and was introduced into the United States in 1819. The " Grand Lodge of Maryland and the United States " was established in 1821. In 1842 the American branch severed its connection with the Manchester Unity. The membership of the " Independent Order of Odd Fellows " in the United States was estimated in 1910 at 1,562,-829. The English order, entitled the " Manchester Unity of Odd Fellows," numbers 1,048,683. For the year ending December 31st, 1899, the I. O. O. F. disbursed, for benevolent purposes, the sum of $3,695,488.32. Grand Lodges

35

also exist in Australasia, Germany, Denmark, Sweden, and Switzerland. The " Grand United Order of Odd Fellows of America " (colored) has a membership of 492,906 and property valued at $2,150,500.

Odéon. A famous theatre in Paris, built during the reign of Louis XVI (1774–1789), and chiefly devoted to the classic drama. It receives from the Government an annual subvention of 100,000 francs. The theatre has been several times destroyed by fire. In 1818 it was rebuilt by order of Louis XVIII (1814–1824), who granted the management permission to perform all the classic plays,—hitherto the exclusive privilege of the " Comédie Française." On this account, it was called the " Second Théâtre Français,"—a title which it retains at the present day. Certain of the plays of Casimir Delavigne, Ponsard, George Sand, and Victorien Sardou were performed there for the first time. " L'Odéon," in its early days, was occupied for a while by the " Comédie Française."

Odeum. A theatre designed for musical purposes, erected at the southeastern foot of the Acropolis at Athens, during the rule of Pericles, and completed about 437 B.C. The structure was surmounted by a circular roof, said to have been made of the masts and spars of the Persian ships captured at the battle of Salamis (480 B.C.). According to other accounts, however, the building was, in its original state, actually covered with the tent of Xerxes. No remains of the Odeum exist at the present day.

Odyssey. A famous epic poem of great antiquity, attributed to Homer, the Greek poet, who flourished about 1000 B.C. It narrates, in 24 books, the wanderings and adventures of Odysseus (Ulysses) during his journey to Ithaca after the fall of Troy. See *Iliad*.

"The authorship of these great epics [the *Iliad* and *Odyssey*] and the existence of

Homer have been made the subject of prolonged controversy. In ancient times no doubt was felt in regard to either of these points, but shortly before the close of the last century, Wolf, in his *Prolegomena*, advocated the theory that these poems were not written by Homer, or any single poet, but were the productions of various authors and were subsequently united into one continuous whole. The question may be regarded as still unsettled."—Wheeler's *Who Wrote It ?*

Œcumenical Councils. See *Ecumenical Councils*.

Œil de Bœuf. A spacious antechamber in the palace at Versailles, where the courtiers used to await the "*Lever*" of the King. It received its name from the two bull's-eye windows level with the ceiling. The Salle de l'Œil de Bœuf was the scene of numerous court intrigues and quarrels. From this apartment, the Cardinal de Rohan was summoned to attend the King (Louis XVI) in his private cabinet, and explain the part played by him in the mysterious affair of the Diamond Necklace. See *Diamond Necklace*.

O. K. "These letters in America signify 'all right.' Their use, it is said, originated with old John [Jacob] Astor, the millionaire of New York. He was looked upon in commercial circles as a man of great information and sound judgment, and was a sort of general referee as to the solvency or standing of other traders. If a note of enquiry as to any particular trader's position came, the answer to which he intended to be satisfactory, he was accustomed to write across the note the letters ' O. K.,' and return it to the writer. The letters O. K. he supposed to be the initials of ' all correct,' and in this sense they are now universally current in the States."—Edwards's *Words, Facts, and Phrases*.

Oklahoma. A Territory of the United States of America, originally formed from the western part of Indian Territory and the Public Land Strip, or No Man's Land. It was opened for

settlement by proclamation of President Harrison, on April 22nd,1889, and organized as a Territory on May 2nd, 1890; enlarged in 1891, and again in 1893, when the Cherokee Outlet or Strip (containing 9409 square miles) was added. The area of Oklahoma is 38,958 square miles, and the population (1900) 404,172. See *No Man's Land* (*1*).

Old Abe. A nickname familiarly bestowed upon Abraham Lincoln (1809–1865), while President of the United States.

Old Bailey.
(1) A street in London, extending from Ludgate Street to Newgate Street. It derives its name from the *ballium*, or open space, in front of the old City Wall, along which it extended from Lud Gate to New Gate.
(2) A famous old criminal court on Old Bailey Street, London, erected in 1773, and enlarged in 1808. It is officially known as the *Central Criminal Court*, and consists of two divisions,— the *Old Court*, for the trial of serious offenses, and the *New Court*, for the trial of petty offenses. The Old Bailey adjoins Newgate Prison. See *Newgate*.

Old Beeswax. A nickname jocosely conferred upon Raphael Semmes(1809–1877), commander of the privateer *Alabama*, whose formidable mustache, thoroughly waxed, was an object of great merriment among the officers and crew. See *Alabama*.

Old Bory. A nickname bestowed upon General P. G. T. Beauregard (1819–1893) during the Civil War.

Old Buck. A sobriquet conferred upon James Buchanan (1791–1868), the fifteenth President of the United States.

Old Buena Vista. A nickname given to Zachary Taylor (1784–1850), twelfth President of the United States, in allusion to his victory at Buena

Vista, Mexico (February 23rd, 1847), where, with only 5000 men, he held Santa Anna, the Mexican commander, with 20,000 men, in check for two days, and finally defeated him.

Old Bullion. A sobriquet conferred upon Thomas H. Benton (1782–1858), United States Senator from Missouri, because of his steadfast advocacy of a gold and silver currency as the only remedy for the financial ills that, in his opinion, had come upon the country as a result of President Jackson's unwillingness to renew the charter of the United States Bank. See *Bank of the United States ; Bullion State.*

Old Catholics. The title assumed by a number of Roman Catholics in Germany, who protested against the dogma of the personal infallibility of the Pope, as proclaimed by the Vatican Council of 1870. Under the leadership of Dr. Döllinger and Professor Friedrich, they established a separate communion in 1871 ; Dr. Reinkens, the first bishop of the Old Catholics, was chosen in 1873, and was recognized by the Emperor of Germany. A conference of Old Catholics, held at Cologne in 1873, was attended by the Bishops of Ely and Lincoln and Dean Stanley of the Anglican Church. At the Synod held at Bonn in 1874, auricular confession and compulsory fasting were abolished, and commissions were appointed to draw up a new ritual in the vulgar tongue and to frame a Catechism and Bible History. The Old Catholic movement was at its height in 1875 ; but since that time it has steadily declined. A somewhat similar movement was advocated in France by Père Hyacinthe. See *Infallibility, Papal.*

Old Chapultepec. A nickname conferred upon General Winfield Scott (1786–1866), whose victory at Chapultepec (September 13th, 1847) opened the way to the City of Mexico, and brought the Mexican War to a successful termination.

Old Chickamauga. A sobriquet conferred upon General James B. Steedman (1820–1864) during the American Civil War.

Old Chief. A sobriquet bestowed upon Henry Clay (1777–1852), the famous American statesman and orator.

Old Cities. It is stated in Taylor's *Words and Phrases* that " the names of five of the oldest cities of the world, Damascus, Hebron, Gaza, Sidon, and Hamath, are still pronounced by the inhabitants exactly in the same manner as was the case thirty or perhaps forty centuries ago."

Old Colony. An expression originally applied to that part of Massachusetts included within the limits of the Plymouth Colony, but afterwards used to designate the entire State. In 1692, the Plymouth and Massachusetts Bay Colonies, which, for many years, had been independent of each other, were united in one province, bearing the name of Massachusetts.

Old Country. An expression used in the United States and Australia to denote the British Isles ; but sometimes restricted in its application to Ireland proper.

Old Dominion. A nickname familiarly bestowed upon the State of Virginia, one of the United States. The following explanation of the origin of this term is generally regarded as the most plausible.

" In Captain John Smith's 'History of Virginia,' edition of 1629, there is a map of the settlements of Virginia, which, at that time, included New England, as well as every other part of the British settlements in America. He there calls our present Virginia ' *Ould* Virginia,'—the word *old* being so spelt at that time,—in contradistinction to the New England colony, which is called 'New Virginia.' Here, then, we have the word ' ould,' the distinctive word of the title. Now, we know that, from the settlement of the colony to the Revolution, every act of parliament, every letter of the king to the governor, always designated Virginia as the

'Colony and *Dominion*' of Virginia. Here is found the other word; and the change in common talk from 'Ould Virginia' to 'Old Dominion' was easy, imperceptible, and almost inevitable."—*Historical Magazine.*

Acording to another explanation, the title "Old Dominion" was bestowed upon Virginia by Charles II (1660–1685), because the colony had refused to recognize the government of Cromwell, and, after the execution of Charles I, had transferred its allegiance to his son. In gratitude for this loyalty, Charles II caused the arms of Virginia to be quartered with those of England, Scotland, and Ireland, as a distinct portion of the Old Dominion and an independent member of the United Kingdom.

Old Douro. A sobriquet conferred upon the Duke of Wellington (1769–1852), on account of his brilliant passage of the river Douro (May 11th, 1809) in the presence of an army of 10,000 Frenchmen. As a result of this achievement, Marshal Soult was taken by surprise and put to flight.

Old Elm. A famous tree of unknown age, formerly standing on Boston Common. It was more than 72 feet in height, and measured over seven feet in diameter at a distance of one foot above the ground. This tree, which is supposed to have been standing at the time of the settlement of Boston in 1630, was blown down during the winter of 1876. An iron railing encloses the spot where it once stood. In its day it was frequently spoken of as the "oldest inhabitant" of the city.

Old English Holidays. The following holidays originated in mediæval England before the time of the Reformation (1517), and are still observed in various parts of Great Britain and Ireland.

(1) Twelfth-Day or Twelfth-Tide (sometimes called Old Christmas-Day): January 6th.
(2) Candlemas : February 2nd.

(3) Old Candlemas : February 14th.
(4) Lady-Day : March 25th.
(5) Midsummer-Day : June 24th.
(6) St. Swithin's-Day : July 15th.
(7) Lammas-Day : August 1st.
(8) Michaelmas : September 29th.
(9) Allhallowmas : November 1st.
(10) All Souls' - Day : November 2nd.
(11) Martinmas: November 11th.
(12) Childermas : December 28th.

In addition to these may be mentioned :

(1) Old Lady-Day: April 6th.
(2) Old Midsummer-Day: July 7th.
(3) Old Lammas-Day: August 13th.
(4) Old Michaelmas : October 11th.
(5) Old Martinmas: November 23rd.

Oldest Christian Hymn. The oldest Christian hymn, in the opinion of many, is the one mentioned in *Luke* ii, 14, as sung by a multitude of the heavenly host at the time of the birth of Christ at Bethlehem.

Of this hymn Jeremy Taylor says: "As soon as the blessed Choristers had sung their Christmas carol and taught the Church a hymn to be put into her offices forever on the anniversary of this festivity, the Angels returned into heaven."

Oldest Dynasty in Europe. See *Hohenzollern, House of.*

Oldest Ruin in Rome. The name given to the fragment of wall discovered on the Palatine Hill at Rome, and supposed by some archæologists to be part of the original structure erected by Romulus to enclose the city at the time of its foundation (753 B.C.). The early history of Rome, however, is so largely an affair of tradition that little faith can be placed in the above statement. Certain it is, nevertheless, that the so-called "Wall of Romulus" shares, with the Mamertine Prison and the Cloaca Maxima, the honor of being one of the few relics of the early history of the city.

Oldest Statue. A wooden statue of a man, supposed to be at least 6000 years old, may be seen in the Museum of Antiquities at Boulak, Egypt. It was discovered by Mariette - Pasha (1821–1881) at Memphis, and placed by him in the museum. It is a little over three feet in height and stands erect, holding a staff in its left hand. The eyes consist of pieces of opaque white quartz, with pupils formed of rock-crystal, imparting a lifelike appearance to the figure. The statue is said to have been originally covered with a thin coating of plaster of Paris and then painted. Nothing is known of its history, although by some authorities it is considered to be the oldest figure in existence.

Old Father Nile. See *Nile*.

Old Fox. A sobriquet conferred upon Marshal Soult (1769–1851) by his soldiers, in allusion to the crafty methods employed by him in his campaigns.

Old Fritz (*Ger., Alte Fritz.*) A popular name for Frederick the Great (1740–1786) among the German people, even at the present day.

Old George. An appellation conferred upon General George Monk (1608–1670), Duke of Albemarle, who restored Charles II to the English throne.

Old Glorious. A title conferred upon William III (1689–1702), King of England.

Old Glory. A patriotic expression frequently made use of by the American people, when referring to the Stars and Stripes.

Old Grimes. The title of a ballad by Albert G. Greene (1802–1867), the American poet.

"*Old Grimes* is dead ; that good old man ;—
　We ne'er shall see him more :
　He used to wear a long black coat,
　　All buttoned down before."

B. P. Shillaber (Mrs. Partington) has written a parody upon this poem, entitled *Young Grimes*. See *Partington, Mrs.*

Old Grog. See *Grog*.

Old Harry. A slang name for the Devil,—the origin of which is variously accounted for.

"It has been suggested ('Notes and Queries,' xii, 229) that this appellation comes from the Scandinavian *Hari* or *Herra* (equivalent to the German *Herr*), names of Odin, who came in time (like the other deities of the Northern mythology) to be degraded from his rank of a god to that of a fiend or evil spirit. According to Henley, the hirsute honors of the Satan of the ancient religious stage procured him the name 'Old Hairy,' corrupted into 'Old Harry.'"— Wheeler's *Dictionary of the Noted Names of Fiction*.

"To harry (*Saxon*) is to tear in pieces, whence our *harrow*. There is an ancient pamphlet entitled 'The Harrowing of Hell.' I do not think it is a corruption of 'Old Hairy,' although the Hebrew *Seirim* (hairy ones) is translated devils in Lev. xvii, 7, and no doubt alludes to the he-goat, an object of worship with the Egyptians. Moses says the children of Israel are no longer to sacrifice to devils (*seirim*), as they did in Egypt."—Brewer's *Dictionary of Phrase and Fable*.

"It is a corruption of the words 'Old Hairy.'"—Edwards's *Words, Facts, and Phrases*.

Old Hickory. A sobriquet popularly bestowed upon Andrew Jackson (1767–1845), the seventh President of the United States, because of his tough and unyielding disposition. According to another version, he was so called because, while engaged in war with the Creek Indians in 1813, he fell short of rations and fed his men on hickory nuts.

James Parton, in his *Life of Andrew Jackson*, writes as follows, in regard to the origin of this nickname : "The name of *Old Hickory* was not an instantaneous inspiration, but a growth. First of all, the remark was made by some soldier, who was struck with his commander's pedestrian powers, that the General was tough. Next, it was observed that he was as tough as hickory. Then he was called *Hickory*. Lastly, the affectionate adjective 'old' was prefixed, and the General thenceforth rejoiced in the completed nickname, usually the first-won honour of a great commander."

Old Ironsides. A name given to the United States frigate *Constitution*, launched at Boston, September 20th, 1797, and commissioned during the following year. See *Constitution.*

Old Jack. A sobriquet conferred upon General Thomas J. Jackson ("Stonewall" Jackson) by the Confederate forces during the American Civil War. See *Stonewall Jackson.*

Old Lady of Threadneedle Street. A popular designation of the Bank of England, which is situated on Threadneedle Street, London. See *Bank of England.*

Old Line State. A name popularly given to the State of Maryland, in allusion to the boundary line, known as "Mason and Dixon's Line," between it and Pennsylvania. See *Mason and Dixon's Line.*

Old Man Eloquent.

(1) An expression first made use of by Milton in one of his *Sonnets,* in allusion to Isocrates (436–338 B.C.), the Athenian orator, who died of grief on hearing of the defeat of the Athenians at Chæronea.

" When that dishonest victory
  At Chæronea, fatal to liberty,
Killed with report that *old man eloquent.*"
                 Sonnet X (Milton).

(2) A sobriquet conferred upon John Quincy Adams (1767–1848), sixth President of the United States, during the latter part of his career.

Old Man of Hoy. An insulated pillar of rock, of natural formation, 450 feet high, bearing a marked resemblance to the human form. It is situated on the island of Hoy, one of the Orkneys.

Old Man of Storr. A natural curiosity on the island of Skye, Scotland, consisting of a columnar basalt formation, 160 feet high.

Old Man of the Mountain. A wonderful semblance of the human face, seen in profile, in the Franconia range of the White Mountains of New

Hampshire. It is situated in the famous Franconia Notch, 1500 feet above Profile Lake, and consists of three disconnected ledges of granite, which have an aggregate height of about 40 feet. One ledge forms the forehead, another the nose and upper lip, and a third the chin. According to tradition, this remarkable phenomenon was worshipped by the Indians. See *Franconia Notch.*

Hawthorne, in his tale, *The Great Stone Face,* refers to it in the following words: "The Great Stone Face then was a work of Nature in her mood of majestic playfulness, formed on the perpendicular side of a mountain by some immense rocks, which had been thrown together in such a position as, when viewed at a proper distance, precisely to resemble the features of the human countenance. It seemed as if an enormous giant or a Titan had sculptured his own likeness on the precipice."

Old Man of the Sea. In the *Arabian Nights' Entertainments,* an old man—apparently very weak and infirm—encountered by Sindbad the Sailor during his fifth voyage. Under pretense of a desire to be carried across a brook, he fastened himself so firmly upon the back of his unfortunate victim that the sailor was unable to shake him off. After several ineffectual attempts to free himself from his burden, Sindbad managed to intoxicate the monster; and, after loosening his hold upon him, threw him upon the ground and crushed his head with a stone. Sir Walter Scott speaks of the "Old Man of the Sea" as the greatest bore on record. The expression is frequently used to denote any burden that cannot be shaken off. See *Sindbad the Sailor.*

Old Manse. An old house at Concord, Massachusetts, erected in 1765, and famous as the birthplace of Ralph Waldo Emerson and the home of Nathaniel Hawthorne. In the study, on the floor above the dining-room, Emerson wrote his famous essay on *Nature,* and Hawthorne his *Mosses from an Old Manse.* Adjoining the house is the bridge over the Concord River, "where the embattled farmers stood and fired the shot heard round the world."

"He [Hawthorne] lived in close retirement in this old spot, concentrating his mind upon his habitual fancies for three years, during which time, if we are to take literally, and it is probably not far from the truth, the pleasant sketch of his residences by his friend, Mr. G. W. Curtis, he was not seen by more than a dozen of the villagers."—Duyckinck's *Cyclopædia of American Literature.*

Old Noll. A term of contempt applied to Oliver Cromwell (1599-1658) by his contemporaries.

"Nay, *Old Noll*, whose bones were dug up and hung in chains here at home, has not he, too, got to be a very respectable grim bronze figure, of whom England seems proud rather than otherwise?"—*Thomas Carlyle.*

Old North. A name familiarly applied to Christ Church, Boston, Massachusetts,— the oldest ecclesiastical edifice now standing in the city. It was dedicated in 1723, and received its Bible, prayer-books, and communion-service (still in use), from George II in 1733. It was from the original steeple of this church (blown down in 1804, but immediately replaced) that the lanterns of Paul Revere were hung out to warn the people of Middlesex of the march of the British on Lexington and Concord (April 18th, 1775). A tablet on the front of the church commemorates this event in the following words:

"THE SIGNAL LANTERNS OF PAUL REVERE, DISPLAYED IN THE STEEPLE OF THIS CHURCH, APRIL 18, 1775, WARNED THE COUNTRY OF THE MARCH OF THE BRITISH TROOPS TO LEXINGTON AND CONCORD."

According to some authorities, the North Church referred to by Paul Revere, in an account prepared by him twenty years after the event, was the North Church then standing on North Square. Christ Church, however, was also known as the "North Church," in Revolutionary times; and, to support its claim, it brought forward evidence showing that Captain John Puling, one of the wardens, received the signal to display the lanterns, and that Robert Newman, the sexton, hung them out. See *Old South.*

"The modest spire yet stands, reverend relic of the old town of Boston—of those brave men and of their deeds. Startling the land that night with the warning of danger, let it remind the land forever of the patriotism with which that danger was averted, and for our children, as for our fathers, still stand secure, the Pharos of American liberty."—*Oration at Concord, April 19th, 1875* (George William Curtis).

Old Oaken Bucket. The title of a popular lyric by Samuel Woodworth (1785 – 1842), beginning with the words :

"How dear to this heart are the scenes of
    my childhood,
When fond recollection presents them to
    view."

"It will hold its place among the choice songs of the country."—Duyckinck's *Cyclopædia of American Literature.*

Old Put. A sobriquet conferred upon General Israel Putnam (1718-1790) by his soldiers, during the War of the American Revolution.

Old Reliable. A nickname conferred upon General George H. Thomas (1816-1870) during the Civil War.

Old Rosey. A sobriquet bestowed upon General William S. Rosecrans (1819-1898) during the Civil War.

Old Rough-and-Ready. A nickname given to General Zachary Taylor (1784-1850), afterwards President of the United States, by his soldiers during the Mexican War.

Old Rowley. A nickname conferred upon Charles II (1660-1685) of England, who was famous for his intrigues with the fair sex. The allusion is to Rowley, a famous stallion in the royal stud. Other authorities say that the word "Rowley," as here used, is derived from "Roland," and refers to the proverb "A Roland for an Oliver," —wherein Roland is made to apply to the King and Oliver to Cromwell, the Lord Protector. See *Roland for an Oliver, A*.

Old Scratch. This expression, frequently used to denote the Devil, is said to be a corrupted form of *Skratti, Schrat,* or *Schratz,* a demon of the Old Norse mythology.

Old South. A familiar appellation of the Old South Meeting-House in Boston, Massachusetts. This historic church, erected in 1729, has played an important part in the history of the city, and is often called the " Temple of Freedom." It was frequently used as a meeting-place of the disaffected, previous to the outbreak of the Revolution ; and from its doors went forth, in 1773, the band of disguised Bostonians that threw the tea into the harbor. During the British occupation of Boston in 1775, the " Old South " was converted into a riding-school for the cavalry; but, on the evacuation of the city, it was restored to its original use. The church barely escaped destruction in the Boston Fire of 1872 ; and, at a later period, was used temporarily as a post-office. The Old South Society worshipped there from 1729 to 1875, when it removed to a new structure at the corner of Boylston and Dartmouth Streets,—costing about $500,000. In 1876, the "Old South Meeting-House" was sold,—the intention being to tear it down and replace it with a business building. It was, however, purchased by the Preservation Committee for $430,000, and converted into a loan museum of historic relics,—including portraits, old furniture, flags, and weapons. A tablet on the tower, placed there in 1867, bears the following inscription :

OLD SOUTH

CHURCH GATHERED 1669
FIRST HOUSE BUILT 1670
THIS HOUSE ERECTED 1729
DESECRATED BY BRITISH TROOPS
1775-6.

See *Old North*.

Old Stars. An appellation conferred upon General O. M. Mitchel (1810–1862), during the Civil War, in allusion to his fame as an astronomer.

Old State House. A famous old building in Boston, Massachusetts, erected in 1748. In early days, the first floor was used as the Merchants' Exchange, and the second story as the meeting-place of the governors of the Province and the Royal Council. A few feet from the eastern porch occurred the Boston massacre (March 5th, 1770). In 1789, Washington reviewed from this building a procession in his honor, and in 1835 William Lloyd Garrison took refuge there to escape from the mob that had broken up the anti-slavery meeting and threatened his life. In later years, the State House was turned into business offices, and was so much altered, inside and outside, as almost to destroy the original architectural effect. In 1880–1881, however, it was purchased by a number of public-spirited citizens, and restored as nearly as possible to its original condition. The rooms, including the old Council-Chamber and the Hall of Representatives, contain a collection of relics and paintings of Revolutionary times.

Old Stone Mill. A circular stone tower in Touro Park, Newport, supposed by some antiquaries to have been erected by the Norsemen during the 11th century, but more generally thought to have been built for a windmill by Governor Benedict Arnold during the 17th century. Certain it is that, in his will, he described the structure as " my stone-built windmill."

Longfellow refers to it in his poem of *The Skeleton in Armor :*

> " There for my lady's bower
> Built I the lofty tower,
> Which, to this very hour,
> Stands looking seaward."

Old Style. A phrase used to denote the Julian Calendar, introduced by Julius Cæsar (100–44 B.C.) in 46

B.C. Although this method of reckoning time has been superseded by the Gregorian Calendar in most of the countries of Europe, it is still in use in Russia, Greece, Turkey, and some of the smaller states belonging to the Greek Church. See *Gregorian Calendar ; Julian Calendar ; New Style.*

Old Tecumseh. A nickname given to General William Tecumseh Sherman (1820-1891) by his troops, during the Civil War.

Old Three Stars. A sobriquet conferred upon General Ulysses S. Grant (1822-1885) during the Civil War, in allusion to the three stars that indicated his rank as lieutenant-general.

Old Tip. A nickname given to General William Henry Harrison (1773-1841), ninth President of the United States, in allusion to the victory gained by him over the Indians at the battle of Tippecanoe, November 6th, 1811.

Old Tom. This expression, now used to denote gin of a superior quality, is said to have originated in the following way:

"One of the partners in 'Hodge's' distillery at Millbank was Thomas Chamberlain, familiarly known in the distillery as Old Tom. His department was the superintendence of the distillery operations. One of the employés of the firm, a man named Norris, left their service and opened a 'gin-palace' in Great Russell Street, Covent Garden, and he,—out of respect to his old master,—christened a cordial of Hodge's make 'Old Tom,' a name which is now general for a fine quality of gin."—Edwards's *Words, Facts, and Phrases.*

Old Zach. A nickname bestowed upon Zachary Taylor (1784-1850), a distinguished American general and twelfth President of the United States.

Olla Podrida (*Span., Rotten Pot*). The name given in Spain to a peculiar dish, consisting of stewed meat and vegetables, highly prized by the inhabitants of that country. It resembles the French *pot-au-feu* and the Scotch *hotch-potch.* The expression *olla podrida* is frequently used, at the present day, to designate any collection of stories, anecdotes, and odds and ends,— grouped without reference to any special object or plan. See *Pot-Pourri.*

Olmütz, Conference of. Held at Olmütz, the ancient capital of Moravia, on November 29th, 1850, under the Czar Nicholas (1825-1855), for the purpose of settling the difficulties between Austria and Prussia, relative to the affairs of Hesse-Cassel. Lafayette was confined at Olmütz by the Austrians from 1792 until 1797.

Olympiads. See *Era of the Olympiads.*

Olympian Jove, Statue of. A colossal ivory and gold statue of Jupiter, carved by Phidias [500 (?) –432 (?) B.C.], the Greek sculptor, and placed in the temple of the god at Olympia in Elis. It was generally regarded as the masterpiece of Phidias, and was accounted one of the "Seven Wonders of the World." The statue was 60 feet in height, and represented Jupiter seated on a throne of cedar—adorned with gold and precious stones,—holding in his right hand a chryselephantine statue of Victory and in his left a sceptre surmounted by an eagle. The statue was removed to Constantinople by the Emperor Theodosius I, and was destroyed by fire about 475 A.D.

"The idea which Phidias essayed to embody in this, his greatest work, was that of the supreme deity of the Hellenic nation, no longer engaged in conflicts with the Titans and the Giants, but having laid aside his thunderbolt, and enthroned as a conqueror, in perfect majesty and repose, ruling with a nod the subject world."—Smith's *Classical Dictionary.*

Olympic Games. A series of athletic contests in ancient Greece, celebrated every fifth year in honor of Zeus, at Olympia in Elis. They were instituted, according to tradition, by Hercules ; and, although established in very early times, did not become a truly national festival until 776 B.C. The games at first comprised chariot-races, foot-races, boxing, wrestling, leaping, running, etc.; but after 456 B.C. dramas were prepared and works of art exhibited, in addition. The victors were crowned with garlands of olive-twigs, cut from a sacred tree, and were welcomed home with triumphal processions. The festival of the Olympic Games was abolished by the Emperor Theodosius I in 394 A.D. In 1876 A.D.,—the 75th anniversary of Greek independence,—the Olympic Games were successfully revived, and several of the events were won by Americans. See *Isthmian Games ; Nemean Games ; Era of the Olympiads ; Pythian Games.*

Olympus, Mount. A famous mountain range, lying between Thessaly and Macedonia,—the highest peak of which is 9750 feet above the sea. The Greeks regarded Mount Olympus as the chief abode of the gods : there Jupiter had his palace and held his court. In later times, however, the philosophers transferred the abode of the gods to the planetary spheres.

"Homer describes the gods as having their several palaces on the summit of Olympus ; as spending the day in the palace of Zeus (Jupiter), round whom they sit in solemn conclave, while the younger gods dance before them, and the Muses entertain them with the lyre and song. They are shut in from the view of men upon the earth by a wall of clouds, the gates of which are kept by the Hours. The same conceptions are found in Hesiod, and to a great extent in the later poets ; with whom, however, even as early as the lyric poets and the tragedians, the idea becomes less material, and the real abode of the gods is gradually transferred from the summit of Olympus to the vault of heaven (*i. e.*, the sky) itself."—Smith's *Classical Dictionary.*

Ommeyyades. See *Ommiades.*

Ommiades. A dynasty of Arabian caliphs founded by Moawiyah (610–680 A.D.) in 661 A.D. They were 14 in number, and ruled at Bagdad from 661 until 750, when they were overthrown by the Abbassides. The Ommiades of Spain were founded by Abdurrahman in 753. They were 18 in number and reigned until 1031. See *Abbassides.*

Omnibus. The word " omnibus "— meaning " for all " — is the dative plural of the Latin adjective *omnis* (*all*).

Omnium Gatherum. " Dog Latin for a *gathering* or collection *of all* sorts of persons and things; a miscellaneous gathering together without regard to suitability or order."— Brewer's *Dictionary of Phrase and Fable.*

One-Armed Devil. A nickname given to General Philip Kearny (1815–1862), the Union commander, by the Confederate troops during the Civil War. See *One-Armed Phil.*

One-Armed Phil. A sobriquet conferred upon General Philip Kearny (1815–1862), who lost his arm in the Mexican War. See *One-Armed Devil.*

Oneida Community. A society, practising a community of wives as well as of goods, founded at Oneida Creek, New York, by John H. Noyes (1811–1886) in 1848. The organization soon numbered about 300 members, — living on thoroughly communistic principles. The community was also known as *Free-Lovers, Perfectionists,* and *Bible-Communists.* Owing to the pressure of outside opinion, the peculiar practices of the organization were greatly modified : marriage was introduced ; community of goods was abandoned ; property was divided ; and reorganization effected as a joint-stock company under the laws of the State. Since 1881, the " Oneida Community " has been simply a business corporation.

Only, The. A sobriquet lovingly conferred upon Jean Paul Friedrich Richter (1763 – 1825), the poet and humorist, by the German people, on account of the tender and refined sentiments manifested in his writings.

Opal. This word is derived from the Latin *opalus* (*precious stone*).

Opera in the United States. The first performance of Italian opera in the United States was given in New York City in 1825. The opera was Rossini's *Barber of Seville*.

Ophir. A region, famous for its gold, frequently visited by the ships of Solomon and of the Phœnicians. It is several times mentioned in the *Old Testament*, but its location has never been satisfactorily determined. Among the many places which, in the writings of travelers, have been identified with Ophir, may be mentioned Armenia, the Moluccas, Peru, Iberia, Phrygia, Africa, India, Arabia, Malacca, San Domingo, Mexico, New Guinea, and Ormuz. In all probability, however, Ophir was situated either on the east coast of Africa, in Arabia, or in India. Ritter, who accepts Lassen's view and devotes 80 octavo pages to a consideration of the question, places Ophir in India, at the mouth of the Indus River.

Opus Majus (*Lat. Greater Work*). A celebrated philosophic treatise, in Latin, by Roger Bacon (1214–1292), written about 1265, and first printed in 1733. The work was condemned as heretical by a council of Franciscans in 1278, and Bacon was cast into prison, where he languished for ten years. He also wrote the *Opus Minus* and the *Opus Tertium*. See *Admirable Doctor*.

Orange-Blossoms. The origin of the custom of wearing orange-blossoms as bridal ornaments has been variously accounted for :

(1) This custom is said to have originated among the Saracen brides, and to have been introduced into Europe by the Crusaders. The Saracens regarded the orange-tree as the emblem of fecundity, since it bore blossoms and fruit at the same time.

(2) According to another theory, orange-blossoms were worn by brides, not only on account of their agreeable odor, but also on account of their rarity and consequent high price.

(3) This custom is said to have taken its rise in Spain, where oranges have been successfully cultivated for centuries, and to have spread thence all over Europe.

Orangemen. An association of Irish Protestants, founded in 1795 in the north of Ireland, for the purpose of sustaining the Protestant religion and upholding the authority of the sovereign and the laws of the United Kingdom. It derives its name from William III (1689–1702) of England, the Prince of Orange. It was dissolved as a secret society in 1830, but was revived in 1845. Branches exist in the British colonies and the United States. The red-letter days of the Orangemen are July 1st and 12th— the anniversaries of the battles of the Boyne and of Aughrim—and November 5th, the anniversary of the arrival of William, Prince of Orange, at Torbay. Frequent encounters between the Roman Catholics and the Orangemen have occurred on these occasions. A serious riot took place in New York City on July 12th, 1871, in which 60 lives were lost. See *Orange-Peel*.

Orange=Peel. A nickname given to Sir Robert Peel (1788–1850), when Chief Secretary for Ireland (1812– 1818), on account of the strong anti-Catholic spirit displayed by him in his administration of affairs. See *Orangemen*.

Oratorio, First. The first oratorio is ascribed to St. Philip Neri (1515– 1595), an Italian ecclesiastic. It appeared about 1550, and was so called from having been first performed in a chapel, or " oratorio." The first true oratorio, however, is Emilio del Cavaliere's *La Rappresentazione della' Anima e del Corpo*, performed at Rome about 1600. See *Oratory, Priests of the*.

Orator of the Human Race. A sobriquet conferred upon Baron Jean Baptiste Clootz (1755–1794), the Prussian-French Revolutionist. See *Anacharsis Clootz.*

Oratory, Priests of the. An order founded by St. Philip Neri (1515–1595), at Rome, about 1550. The members were not required to take any vow, but were simply to live a devotional life and to apply themselves to theological study. In 1558, the meetings were transferred from Neri's private apartments to an " oratory," or chapel, built over the nave of the Church of San Girolamo, whence is derived the name of the Order. The Congregation of the Oratory was introduced into Paris in 1611, and into England by Cardinal Newman in 1847. It was suppressed in France in 1790, but was restored in 1853 under the title of the *Oratory of the Immaculate Conception.* See *Oratorio, First.*

Orchestra. " The foundation of the modern orchestra is the *string quartet*, composed of the first and second violins, viola, and violoncello, with the double bass (contra basso, doubling the bass at an octave beneath). Next follow the *wood wind quartet*, composed of oboe, flute, clarionet, and bassoon. The *brass wind* comes next, including the horns, trombones, and trumpets. Finally, the drums (kettledrums) are a department by themselves."—*Pearl Cyclopædia.*

Orders, Holy. The Roman Catholic Church recognizes seven holy orders in the ministry, — three of which (bishops, priests, and deacons) are termed major, or holy, orders, while the remaining four (readers, exorcists, acolytes, and doorkeepers) are denominated minor, or secular, orders. In the Anglican Church, the major orders only are recognized. The Greek Church also has the distinction of major and minor orders, but unites all the functions of the four minor orders of the Roman Catholic Church in one single order, that of " reader."

Orders in Council. A term applied to orders issued by the sovereign of the British Empire, with the advice of the Privy Council. The most celebrated of these Orders in Council are the ones issued in 1807, as reprisals for the Berlin Decree of Napoleon I. According to the one issued January 7th, 1807, all neutral vessels were prohibited from entering any port of France or of her allies, under pain of confiscation. On November 11th, 1807, a second Order in Council declared that all the ports of France and of her European allies, as well as those of all countries with which England was at war, were in a state of blockade. See *Berlin Decree ; Continental System ; Milan Decree.*

Orders of Architecture. See *Architecture, Orders of.*

Orient, L'. The name of the French flag-ship at the battle of the Nile, fought on August 1st, 1798. She blew up during the engagement and caused the death of Admiral Brueys and more than 900 men. Mrs. Hemans has commemorated an event connected with the destruction of the vessel, in her poem *Casabianca*, which begins with the well-known line :

"The boy stood on the burning deck."

See *Nile, Battle of the.*

Original Sin. " Various views on Original Sin were held by the fathers in the early Christian Church, it being generally understood to imply the corruption of man's nature by the fall. The Pelagian controversy (5th cent.) caused the doctrine to be more sharply defined. Augustine, the great opponent of Pelagius, declaring that ' as all men have sinned in Adam, they are justly exposed to the vengeance of God, because of this hereditary sin and guilt of sin.' Pelagius held that the posterity of Adam were not involved in his transgression, and that consequently infants came into the world as innocent as Adam prior to his fall. Also that man's unaided efforts were sufficient to enable him to keep God's commandments. The doctrine of Pelagius was finally condemned at the council of Ephesus (431). While the later Eastern Church inclined to Pelagius' views of the freedom of the human will, the Western generally followed the doctrine of Augustine, the Churches of the reformation maintaining a similar belief (see Art. IX, Book of Common Prayer). The Arminian doctrine, held by the Wesleyan Methodists and some other religious bodies, in a more or less modified form, teaches that man by the fall has not lost his ability for good, and that natural corruption derived from Adam is not of the nature of sin. The Roman Catholic doctrine of Original Sin declares that ' the fall caused only the loss of the divine gifts, the natural consequence of which is man's imperfection and infirmity.' The Roman Catholic Church also holds that the effects of Original Sin are entirely destroyed by baptism."—*Pearl Cyclopædia.*

Orlando Furioso. The title of a celebrated romantic epic poem by Ludovico Ariosto (1474–1533). The poet commenced the work at the age of 30, and spent eleven years in its composition. It was first published in 1516. The *Orlando Furioso* is, in a sense, a continuation of Boiardo's *Orlando Innamorato*, and deals with the fabulous wars between Charlemagne and the Saracens ; the love of Orlando for Angelica ; and his madness on learning of her infidelity. Interwoven with these stories are many incidents and episodes which, although marked by great vivacity and beauty of invention, yet detract from the unity of the work. See *Orlando Innamorato.*

"The 'Orlando Furioso,' as a great single poem, has been very rarely surpassed in the living records of poetry. He must yield to three, and only three, of his predecessors. He has not the force, simplicity, and truth to nature of Homer, the exquisite style and sustained majesty of Virgil, nor the originality and boldness of Dante."—Hallam's *Introduction to the Literature of Europe.*

Orlando Innamorato. The title of a romantic epic poem by Matteo Maria Boiardo (1434–1494), dealing with the adventures of the paladins of Charlemagne and the love of Orlando for the Eastern princess, Angelica. It was left unfinished by the author and was published about 1495, but was afterwards so greatly improved by Berni (1490–1536) that the original was nearly forgotten. Ariosto continued the story in his *Orlando Furioso,* and thereby did much to obscure the fame of the earlier poem. See *Orlando Furioso.*

"The 'Orlando Innamorato' of Boiardo has hitherto not received that share of renown which seems to be its due. In point of novel invention and just keeping of character, especially the latter, he has not been surpassed by his follower Ariosto ; and whatever of this we find in the 'Orlando Innamorato' is due to Boiardo alone."—Hallam's *Introduction to the Literature of Europe.*

Orleanists. The name formerly given to the supporters of the Orleans branch of the royal family of France, descended from Philippe, Duc d'Orléans, younger brother of Louis XIV. The Orleanists believed in a constitutional monarchy, repudiated the doctrine of the " divine right of kings," and declared that sovereignty resides in the people. Louis Philippe (1830–1848), the first and only king of the House of Orleans, was chosen by the Chambers, and ascended the throne with the title of " King of the French." After the death, in 1883, of the Comte de Chambord, the heir of the House of Bourbon, the two Houses became united in the person of the Comte de Paris (1838–1894), grandson of King Louis Philippe. The present heir of the Bourbon-Orleans family is Robert, Duc d'Orléans, born in 1869. See *Bourbon, House of ; Legitimists.*

Orleans, Battle of. A battle, or series of battles, fought at Orleans,

France, in 1429, between the French led by Joan of Arc (1411–1431) and the English commanded by the Duke of Bedford. On the 29th of April, the "Maid of Orleans" raised the siege of Orleans and entered the town with provisions, and on the 8th of May following the English were forced to abandon the enterprise.

Orloff Diamond. A celebrated diamond, weighing 193 carats, now in the imperial sceptre of the Czar of Russia. It formed at one time the eye of an idol in a temple in the island of Seringham in Mysore, and was stolen by a French soldier, who sold it to an English sea-captain for £2000. After passing through several other hands, it was purchased at Amsterdam, in 1772, by Count Orloff for £90,000, and presented by him to Catherine II of Russia on her birthday.

Ormulum. A metrical work written about 1220 A.D., and so called from the name of its author, Brother *Orm* or *Ormin*, a canon of the Order of St. Austin. It consists of a series of homilies, having for subject-matter those portions of the *New Testament* appointed to be read in the daily service of the Church. According to Professor Marsh, ninety-seven per cent. of the words used are of Saxon origin.

"The history of this work is rather curious. Only a single manuscript copy exists, and that apparently the original copy or autograph of the author. It was found at the Hague, in Holland, in 1659, among the books of the deceased book-collector, Van Vliet, and was purchased by the eminent scholar, Francis Junius, and by him was bequeathed, among other treasures, to the Bodleian Library, at Oxford. It was supposed by Van Vliet to be an old Gothic or Swedish manuscript. As it is not broken up into verses, it was supposed to be in prose until 1775, when Tyrwhitt discovered that it was in verse. Since the announcement of this discovery, the *Ormulum* has attracted increasing attention, as an important document in early English literature; and finally, in 1852, it was printed in handsome style by the Oxford University press, under the editorial care of Dr. White, formerly Professor of Anglo-

Saxon in that University."—Hart's *Manual of English Literature*.

Ormuzd, or Oromasdes. The name given, in the Zoroastrian religion, to the supreme deity and creator of all things. He is also the personification of the principle of good, and is in perpetual conflict with Ahriman, the spirit of evil, whom he will finally overcome. See *Ahriman or Ahrimanes*.

"According to the Persian myths, the world—which is to last 12,000 years, during which the war between the good and the evil principle is to go on increasing—is at length to be consumed, the evil principle exterminated, and a new world created in its room, over which Ormuzd is to reign as the supreme and sole monarch."—Wheeler's *Dictionary of the Noted Names of Fiction*.

Orphan of the Temple. A sobriquet conferred upon Marie Thérèse Charlotte (1778–1851), Duchesse d'Angoulême, the unfortunate daughter of Louis XVI, in allusion to her three years' imprisonment in the Temple. Louis XVIII called her the "Modern Antigone," and Napoleon I declared that she was the only "man" of her race. See *Filia Dolorosa*.

Orpheus. See *Eurydice*.

Orphic Mysteries. Mystic ceremonies in honor of Bacchus (Dionysus) Zagreus, observed by the followers of Orpheus at a very early period in the history of Greece. These Orphic worshippers of Bacchus, however, did not practise the licentious rites usually characteristic of the "Dionysia" or "Bacchanalia"; but aimed rather at an ascetic purity of life. They dressed in white linen garments, and ate no animal food save what was yielded by the ox sacrificed to Dionysus.

Orphic Poems. The name given to certain mystic poems, still extant, at one time regarded as the genuine productions of Orpheus (the mythical hero), but now known to be the work, mainly, of Christian writers of the Alexandrian School during the 3rd and 4th centuries A.D.,—based upon a few primitive snatches.

Orsini's Conspiracy. An infamous attempt to assassinate Napoleon III (1852–1870), made on January 14th, 1858. It was planned by Orsini and his associates, Pieri, Rudio, and Gomez, who believed that Napoleon's death would further the cause of Italian liberty. Three bombs were thrown under the imperial carriage, at the moment of its arrival at the opera, and in the explosions that followed 10 persons were killed and 156 wounded, although the Emperor and Empress escaped unhurt. Orsini, Pieri, and Rudio were sentenced to capital punishment, and Gomez to penal servitude for life. At the intercession of the Empress, Rudio's life was spared, but Orsini and Pieri were guillotined, March 13th, 1858.

Ortygian Shore. A phrase used by Shelley (1792–1822) in his poem *Arethusa*, to denote the eastern shore of Sicily, near Syracuse. The expression is derived from Ortygia, an island near Syracuse. This was the original site of the city, and contained the celebrated fountain of Arethusa. See *Fountain of Arethusa.*

Osborne House. A favorite residence of the late Queen Victoria, situated near East Cowes, on the Isle of Wight. It was purchased from Lady Blachford in 1840, by the Queen and the Prince Consort, and was enlarged and beautified by them at a cost of £200,000. The estate comprises an area of 5000 acres. Queen Victoria died at Osborne House on January 22nd, 1901. Presented to the nation in 1902.

Osiris. The chief of the Egyptian deities. He was the son of Seb (Earth) and Nut (Heaven), and married his sister Isis. Together they reigned over Egypt and were greatly beloved; but Osiris, having incurred the envy of his brother Set, was murdered by him. Set thereupon usurped the throne, but was slain by Horus, son of Osiris, and his body cast into Lake Sirbon. Osiris, after death, became the judge of the dead in the lower world. He has been identified with the god Ra, with the Moon, and with the Nile, and is generally regarded as the fountainhead of life and fecundity. See *Isis.*

Osmium. This metal—interesting as being the heaviest known—has a specific gravity of 22.447. It was discovered in 1803 by Tennant, as an alloy of iridium in platinum ores. The metal is rare, and is not used in the arts. The alloy of osmium and iridium (known as osmiridium) resists the action of acids, and is used for the tips of gold pens. See *Iridium.*

Os Sacrum (*Lat. Sacred Bone*). A triangular bone at the lower extremity of the vertebral column, wedged in between the two innominate bones in such a way as to form the keystone of the pelvic arch. Various reasons have been given to account for the origin of this name. Littré favors the view that this bone was so called because it had a special significance in the sacrifices of the ancients; but, according to other authorities, it received its name because of its identification with *Luz*, the resurrection-bone of the ancient Jewish rabbis. See *Resurrection-Bone.*

Ossa, Mount. A mountain in Thessaly, near Mount Pelion. In classic myth, the Giants, in their war with the gods, piled Pelion on Ossa, in their attempts to scale Olympus. See *Pelion, Mount.*

" Now pile your dust upon the quick and
    dead ;
Till of this flat a mountain you have made
To o'ertop old Pelion, or the skyish head
Of blue Olympus.

Hamlet, v, 1.

Ossian's Poems. Poems said to have been written by Ossian, the son of Fingal, a Scottish warrior-bard of the third century A.D., and first given to the world by James Macpherson

(1738–1796) in 1760–1763. They profess to be translations from manuscripts of Gaelic poetry collected in the Highlands of Scotland, but are regarded at the present day as essentially the work of Macpherson himself. They excited great interest among the literary men of their day,— Dr. Johnson, Hume, Gibbon, and others denouncing them as forgeries, while Dr. Blair, Lord Kames, and others declared them to be genuine productions. Ossian's poems consist of *Fingal*, an epic poem in six books ; *Temora*, an epic poem in eight books ; and a number of shorter epic and dramatic productions. These had been translated into almost every European language by the close of the 18th century, and speedily became favorites on account of their wild and rugged beauty.

Ostend Manifesto. A paper drawn up at Ostend in October, 1854, by the United States Ministers to Great Britain, France, and Spain, and forwarded to their Government at Washington. It declared that the possession of Cuba was necessary to the safety and welfare of the United States, and that if Spain would not sell the island it should be taken by force. The manifesto was ineffective.

Ostrogoths. A term applied to the Eastern Goths as opposed to the Visigoths, or *Western* Goths. This distinction arose about 330 A.D. See *Goths ; Visigoths.*

Oudenarde, Battle of. A battle fought at Oudenarde, Belgium, on July 11th, 1708, between the allies commanded by the Duke of Marlborough and Prince Eugene, and the French under the Duke of Burgundy and Marshal Villars. The battle resulted in a disastrous defeat for the French.

Oui (*Fr. yes*). This word is a contraction of the Latin *hoc illud.* The successive changes undergone by these words are said to be as follows : *hoc-ill'*, *ho'-il, o'-il, oïl, oï, oui.*

Ouida. The pseudonym adopted by Louise de la Ramée (*b.* 1840), the French novelist.

"Her actual name is Louise de la Ramée (born in 1840) ; but remarking the infantile conversion of Louise into ' Ouida,' she was struck by the novelty of such a *nom de plume,* and immediately adopted it."— Wagner's *Names and Their Meaning.*

Overland Route.

(1) A term applied to the route between England and India by way of Dover, Paris, the Mont Cenis Tunnel, Brindisi, and the Suez Canal,— as opposed to the voyage around the Cape of Good Hope.

(2) A name given to the route from the Eastern States to California by way of the plains,—as opposed to the voyage around Cape Horn.

Over the Left. This expression, which is generally considered to be of modern origin, dates back at least to 1682, as is evidenced by the following words, written in that year : " What the Protestant religion gets by lives and fortunes spent in the service of a Popish successor will be *over the left* shoulder."

The records of the County Court at Hartford, Connecticut, state that, on September 4th, 1705, an action was brought by one James Steel against Bevell Waters, and that a verdict was found for the plaintiff. On leaving the court-room, Waters addressed the Court, saying : " God bless you *over the left* shoulder,"—for which offense he was fined £5 for contempt at the next session. Waters appealed, and, pending trial, the Court asked the opinion of the Rev. Messrs. Woodbridge and Buckingham, ministers of Hartford, as to the meaning of this obnoxious phrase. These reverend gentlemen replied that (1) the words were profane, and (2) that they carried " great contempt in them, arising to the degree of an imprecation or curse, the words of a curse being the most contemptible that can ordinarily be used."

Ovid of France. A sobriquet conferred upon Du Bellay (1524–1560), the French poet. He was one of the seven contemporary French poets—known as the "Pleiades of France"—who flourished in the reign of Henry III (1574–1589).

Owens College. A college at Manchester, England, founded by John Owens, a liberal Churchman, who died in 1846,—leaving about £100,000 as an endowment. The institution was opened in 1851, on an absolutely unsectarian basis, and furnished instruction in science, law, and medicine. In 1880, it was made a constituent part of the Victoria University.

Oxford's Assault. The name given to the attempted assassination of Queen Victoria and the Prince Consort in London, June 10th, 1840, by one Edward Oxford, a youth of low degree. Although Oxford discharged two pistols at short range, the Queen and her husband were unharmed. The miscreant was captured and tried at the Old Bailey, on July 10th of the same year. Being adjudged insane, he was sentenced to confinement in Bethlehem Hospital, but was afterwards removed to Broadmoor. He was liberated in 1868, on condition of leaving the country.

Oxford-Cambridge Boat Race. This contest between the students of the Universities of Oxford and Cambridge occurs annually on the second Saturday before Easter. The course is on the Thames, from Putney to Mortlake,—a distance of about 4¼ miles, and the time occupied in covering it varies from a trifle under 19 minutes to something more than 25 minutes,—this difference depending on the state of the wind and tide. The first race between the universities was rowed at Henley in 1829, and the second in 1836. Since 1849 the races have been rowed from Putney to Mortlake (in 1856 and 1863 from Mortlake to Putney); and since 1856 they have been annual events. In the 47 races rowed during the years 1856–1902 inclusive, Oxford has won 28 times and Cambridge 18 times,—the race of 1877 having resulted in a dead heat. The following is the complete record up to date:

Year.	*Winner.*	*Course.*	*Time.*	*Won by*
1829..	Ox.	Henley.	14 m. 30 s.	Easily
1836..	Cam.	W.* to P.	36 m.	1 m.
1839..	Cam.	W. to P.	31 m.	1 m. 45 s.
1840..	Cam.	W. to P.	29 m. 30 s.	¾ length
1841..	Cam.	W. to P.	32 m. 30 s.	1 m. 4 s.
1842..	Ox.	W. to P.	30 m. 45 s.	13 s.
1845..	Cam.	P. to M.	23 m. 30 s.	30 s.
1846..	Cam.	M. to P.	21 m. 5 s.	2 lengths
1848..	Cam.	P. to M.	22 m.	Easily
1849..	Ox.	P. to M.	....	Foul
1852..	Ox.	P. to M.	21 m. 36 s.	27 s.
1854..	Ox.	P. to M.	25 m. 29 s.	11 strokes
1856..	Cam.	M. to P.	25 m. 50 s.	½ length
1857..	Ox.	P. to M.	22 m. 35 s.	35 s.
1858..	Cam.	P. to M.	21 m. 23 s.	22 s.
1859..	Ox.	P. to M.	24 m. 40 s.	C. sank
1860..	Cam.	P. to M.	26 m. 5 s.	1 length
1861..	Ox.	P. to M.	23 m. 30 s.	48 s.
1862..	Ox.	P. to M.	24 m. 41 s.	30 s.
1863..	Ox.	M. to P.	23 m. 6 s.	43 s.
1864..	Ox.	P. to M.	21 m. 40 s.	26s.
1865..	Ox.	P. to M.	21 m. 24 s.	4 lengths
1866..	Ox.	P. to M.	25 m. 35 s.	15 s.
1867..	Ox.	P. to M.	22 m. 40 s.	½ length
1868..	Ox.	P. to M.	20 m. 56 s.	6 lengths
1869..	Ox.	P. to M.	20 m. 5 s.	3 "
1870..	Cam.	P. to M.	22 m. 4 s.	1¼ "
1871..	Cam.	P. to M.	23 m. 5 s.	1 length
1872..	Cam.	P. to M.	21 m. 15 s.	2 lengths
1873..	Cam.	P. to M.	19 m. 35 s.	3¼ "
1874..	Cam.	P. to M.	22 m. 35 s.	3 "
1875..	Ox.	P. to M.	22 m. 2 s.	10 "
1876..	Cam.	P. to M.	20 m. 20 s.	Easily
1877..	{Ox. Cam.}	P. to M.	24 m. 8 s.	Dead heat
1878..	Ox.	P. to M.	22 m. 13 s.	10 lengths
1879..	Cam.	P. to M.	21 m. 18 s.	3½ "
1880..	Ox.	P. to M.	21 m. 23 s.	3¾ "
1881..	Ox.	P. to M.	21 m. 51 s.	3 "
1882..	Ox.	P. to M.	20 m. 12 s.	7 "
1883..	Ox.	P. to M.	21 m. 18 s.	3½ "
1884..	Cam.	P. to M.	21 m. 39 s.	2½ "
1885..	Ox.	P. to M.	21 m. 36 s.	2½ "
1886..	Cam.	P. to M.	22 m. 29 s.	⅔ length
1887..	Cam.	P. to M.	20 m. 52 s.	2½ lengths
1888..	Cam.	P. to M.	20 m. 48 s.	7 "
1889..	Cam.	P. to M.	20 m. 14 s.	2¾ "
1890..	Ox.	P. to M.	22 m. 3 s.	Bare lgth.
1891..	Ox.	P. to M.	21 m. 48 s.	½ length
1892..	Ox.	P. to M.	19 m. 21 s.	2¼ lengths
1893..	Ox.	P. to M.	18 m. 47 s.	1 lgth. 4 ft.
1894..	Ox.	P. to M.	21 m. 39 s.	3½ lengths
1895..	Ox.	P. to M.	20 m. 50 s.	2¼ "
1896..	Ox.	P. to M.	20 m. [illegible] s.	⅖ length
1897..	Ox.	P. to M.	19 m. 12 s.	2⅓ lengths
1898..	Ox.	P. to M.	22 m. 15 s.	Easily
1899..	Cam.	P. to M.	21 m. 4 s.	4 lengths
1900..	Cam.	P. to M.	18 m. 47 s.	20 "
1901..	Ox.	P. to M.	22 m. 31 s.	⅖ length
1902..	Cam.	P. to M.	19 m. 9 s.	Easily

* Westminster.

Oxford Street. A leading thoroughfare in London, extending from the Marble Arch (Hyde Park) to Holborn, a distance of 1½ miles, and forming the principal artery of traffic between the City and the northwest quarter of the metropolis.

Oxford University. One of the two famous universities in England. It is situated at Oxford, 52 miles northwest of London. Tradition assigns its foundation to Alfred the Great (871–901), but this statement is now generally discredited. The university received its first charter from Henry III (1216–1272) in 1248 ; was incorporated by Elizabeth (1558–1603) in 1570 ; and sent two members to Parliament for the first time, in 1604, —a privilege which it still enjoys. It has 23 colleges (14 of which were founded before the Reformation) and 6 halls ; and includes, in addition, museums, laboratories, libraries, and chapels. The number of students in attendance is about 3500. See *Cambridge University.*

Oxygen. A colorless, tasteless, inodorous gas, constituting one of the elements. It was long regarded as permanent, or non-condensable; but it can now be liquefied, when subjected to great pressure at a very low temperature. This was first successfully accomplished in 1877 by Raoul Pictet. Oxygen, in its free state (*mixed*, but not chemically *combined*, with nitrogen), constitutes about one-fifth of the volume, and more than one-fifth of the weight, of the atmosphere. It is the most abundant and widely distributed of all the elements, and enters into combination with every other elementary substance except fluorine. Oxygen is necessary for the support of animal life, and for this reason was called " vital air " by the older chemists. It was discovered independently by Priestley and Scheele in 1774. Lavoisier in 1789 proved, by a series of carefully conducted experiments, that the so-called combustion, or "burning," of bodies is simply the result of their rapid chemical union with oxygen. This important discovery over-

threw the " phlogiston theory," and laid the foundation of modern chemistry. The word *oxygen* means *acid-producer ;* it was given to this gas by Lavoisier, from his erroneous notion that it was the essential principle of all acids. It is derived from the Greek ὀξύς (*sharp*) and γεννάω (*I produce*). See *Phlogiston.*

Ozone. An allotropic and active form of oxygen, discovered by Schonbein of Basle in 1840. It is artificially produced by the slow oxidation of moist phosphorus, or by electrolysis of water by means of a current of high tension. Ozone is a more powerful oxidizing agent than oxygen, and, when breathed, is highly irritating to the throat and lungs. It occurs in minute quantities in the atmosphere, especially during electric disturbances. Ozone was liquefied by Hautefeuille and Chappuis in 1880.

" Ozone is still more corrosive than oxygen. It tarnishes mercury, which oxygen does not attack at ordinary temperatures ; it bleaches powerfully, and it is a rapid disinfectant. A piece of tainted meat plunged into a jar of it is instantly deodorized, and it is probable that, even in minute quantities, this gas exercises a powerful influence in purifying the atmosphere. Ozone is condensed oxygen."—Steele's *Popular Chemistry.*

P

Pacific Ocean. So named by Ferdinand Magellan [1470 (?) –1521], the famous navigator who, in 1520, entered it through the straits that bear his name. So deeply impressed was he with its calmness and placidity, as contrasted with the stormy and tempestuous weather encountered by him in the adjoining straits, that he conferred upon it the name of " Pacific," —a title which it has borne ever since

" Admiring its illimitable but placid sur face, and exulting in the meditation of i secret perils soon to be tried, he courteous imposed upon it the name it is forever bear, 'the Pacific Ocean.' "—Draper's *Intelectual Development of Europe.*

Pactolus. The ancient name of a small river in Lydia, Asia Minor, whose waters were said to flow over golden sands. In classic myth, Midas, King of Phrygia, foolishly besought Dionysus that all things he touched should be changed to gold. His prayer was granted, but as even the food he touched was transmuted into the precious metal, Midas implored the god to revoke the gift. He was thereupon ordered to bathe in the river Pactolus, which ever after flowed over golden sands.

The gold found in the bed of this river was, in reality, from Mount Tmolus, and, according to tradition, was the principal source of wealth of the Lydian kings. See *Crœsus's Wealth ; Midas.*

Pædobaptists (*Gr.*, παῖς, *child*, βαπτίζω, *I baptize*). A term applied to those persons that advocate *infant* baptism, in contradistinction to those that permit *adult* baptism alone. The vast majority of Christians are Pædobaptists. See *Anabaptists.*

Pagans (*Lat. paganus, peasant*). A word originally meaning " dwellers in the country," but afterwards used by the early Christians to denote those persons that practised idolatrous rites. It acquired its peculiar meaning from the fact that the dwellers in the rural districts, being remote from the centres of instruction, remained for a long time unconverted to Christianity. See *Heathens.*

Palace of Diocletian. A palace of vast dimensions, at Salona, on the Adriatic, erected by the Emperor Diocletian (284–305 A.D.), after his abdication. The modern Austrian town of Spalato was founded upon the ruins of this ancient palace.

Palace of the Cæsars. A mass of shapeless ruins on the Palatine Hill at Rome, constituting the remains of the palace of the Roman Emperors. The original structure was erected by the Emperor Augustus (27 B.C.–14 A.D.), and was greatly enlarged and adorned by Tiberius, Caligula, and Nero. It was probably the most magnificent palace that ever existed, and, in its palmy days, was one of the wonders of the world.

"Imagine a hill, upwards of a mile in circuit, and less than 200 feet high, strewn with shapeless ruins and yawning with excavations, to such an extent that the original soil is almost displaced by fragments of brick and mortar ; intersperse it with kitchen gardens, for the growing of such matter-of-fact vegetables as cauliflower, artichokes, and lettuce ; throw in occasionally the vine, the laurel, the cypress, and the ivy ; overshadow it with here and there a stately oak ; crown the whole with a smart, modern villa ;—and you will have some notion of the *Palace of the Cæsars.* . . . It is a labyrinth of vaults, arches, broken walls, and fragments of columns ; a mighty maze of desolation without a plan. Portions of stucco, mosaic and fresco, are still found in many places to attest the imperial splendor of a former age."—Hillard's *Six Months in Italy.*

Palais de Justice. A historic pile of buildings, comprising the Law-Courts, the Conciergerie, the Sainte-Chapelle, and the Préfecture de Police, situated on the Ile de la Cité, Paris. The site was originally occupied by an ancient palace of the French kings, presented by Charles VII (1422–1461) to the Parliament of Paris; that building, however, was so much injured by fire in 1618, 1630, and 1776, that little of it remains at the present day besides the square tower known as La Tour de l'Horloge. This tower contains the oldest clock in France, constructed in 1370 by Henri de Vic, a German clock-maker. It was restored during the 18th century, and again in 1852. The famous bell, which repeated the signal given by the Church of St. Germain l'Auxerrois for the Massacre of St. Bartholomew (August 24th, 1572), also hung in this tower.

The Court of Cassation holds its sittings in the Palais de Justice, and has several halls appropriated to its use. See *Cassation, Court of ; Conciergerie ; Sainte-Chapelle.*

Palais de l'Elysée. See *Elysée, Palais de l'*.

Palais de l'Industrie. A large building of stone, iron, and glass, formerly standing in the Champs Elysées, Paris. It was erected for the first International Exposition, held in 1855, and was afterwards used for exhibitions of various kinds, and for public functions. The annual exhibit of paintings and sculptures—known as *Le Salon*—was annually held in this building from the 1st of May to the 20th of June. The Palais de l'Industrie was removed for the Exposition of 1900, and the Great Hall of Fine Arts was erected in its place. See *Salon, Old*.

Palais de l'Institut. A building in Paris, devoted to the uses of the Institute of France. It was erected during the latter part of the seventeenth century, by the will of Cardinal Mazarin, as a place of instruction for youths from the newly acquired provinces of Roussillon, Pignerol, Flanders, and Alsace ; and hence was popularly known as the *Collège des Quatre Nations*, but more correctly as the *Collège Mazarin*. During the Revolution it was used as a prison, but in 1795 it was ceded by the National Convention to the Institute of France. This body, however, held its meetings in the Louvre until 1806. The Palais de l'Institut contains the famous Mazarin Library, comprising more than 200,000 volumes. See *Institute of France*.

Palais des Beaux-Arts. A building in the Rue Bonaparte, Paris, occupied by the École des Beaux-Arts. It was commenced in 1829, during the reign of Louis XVIII (1824–1830), but was not completed until 1839. It occupies the site of the old Couvent des Petits Augustins. See *École des Beaux-Arts*.

Palais des Thermes. See *Thermes, Les*.

Palais des Tuileries. See *Tuileries, Palace of the*.

Palais du Louvre. See *Louvre*.

Palais du Luxembourg. See *Luxembourg Palace*.

Palais du Quai d'Orsay. A palace on the Quai d'Orsay, Paris, commenced by Napoleon I (1804–1814) in 1810, and completed by Louis Philippe (1830–1848) in 1835. It was designed as a palace for the exhibition of the products of French industry, but was used in later years by the *Conseil d'État* and the *Cour des Comptes*. The building was burned in 1871, and is still in ruins.

Palais Royal. An extensive palace in Paris, erected by Cardinal Richelieu in 1620–1636, and originally called the Palais Cardinal. After Richelieu's death (1642), it was occupied by Anne of Austria (widow of Louis XIII), with her two sons, Louis XIV and Philip of Orleans, and since that time has been known as the Palais Royal. Louis XIV (1643–1715) afterward presented the Palace to his brother Philip; and until the time of the Revolution it continued to be the residence of the Orleans family. After the execution of Philippe Égalité (1793), the Palais Royal was confiscated, and was put to various uses during the Republic and the Empire. On the return of the Bourbons in 1814, the building was restored to its original owners, and there Louis Philippe resided until his accession to the throne in 1830. The royal apartments were wrecked by the mob during the Revolution of 1848 and the name of the building was changed to that of the Palais National. During the Second Empire, the original name was restored, and part of the Palace was assigned as residence to Jerome Bonaparte, ex-King of Westphalia. The Palais Royal was seriously damaged by fire during the Commune in 1871, but has since been completely restored. The gardens, shops, and restaurants adjoining the Palace were long a favorite resort for idlers about town and visitors to Paris ; but of late years the tide of fashion has set in the direction of the Boulevards, and, as a consequence, the attractions of the Palais Royal have greatly diminished.

Palatinate. A political division of the old German Empire,— ruled by counts - palatine. In 1623 it was divided into two parts, the Upper or Bavarian Palatinate, and the Palatinate-on-the-Rhine, lying on both sides of the river. This latter division became known as the Palatinate proper ; but in later years the name was applied only to that portion lying on the west bank of the Rhine.

Pale. A district in Ireland within which English sovereignty and law were acknowledged after the invasion of the island by Henry II (1154–1189) in 1172. This territory varied in extent at different times ; but may be said, in a general way, to have comprised the counties of Dublin, Meath, Carlow, Kilkenny, and Louth. The word "pale" is derived from the Latin *palus* (*stake*), and is often used figuratively, as in the expressions, "To walk the studious cloister's *pale*." "Without the *pale* of civilization."

Palefaces. A nickname bestowed upon the Europeans by the North American Indians.

Palimpsest. The name given to any parchment from which the original writing has been removed so that it may be used a second time. This device was frequently resorted to by the monks and others during the Middle Ages, owing to the scarcity of parchment. Where the original has been only partially erased, it has been found possible in some MSS. to recover it by carefully removing the second writing. Many valuable productions have been thus recovered, — among which may be mentioned Cicero's *De republica*. This had been partially

erased and covered by a treatise of Lactantius. The restoration was published by Mai in 1821.

Palindrome. The name given to any word, sentence, or verse, that reads the same whether the letters composing it are taken in direct or reverse order. The following are considered fair specimens of this kind of composition :

Madam, Hannah, noon, civic, tenet.

Madam I 'm Adam.

Live was I ere I saw evil.

Lewd did I live & evil I did dwel.

Able was I ere I saw Elba.

Odo tenet mulum, madidam mulum tenet Odo.

Anna tenet mappam, madidam mappam tenet Anna.

Sator arepo tenet opera rotas.

Signa te, signa ; temere me tangis et angis ; Roma tibi subito motibus ibit amor.

Palisades. A ridge of columnar trap-rock, varying in height from 300 to 500 feet, and extending along the west bank of the Hudson River from Fort Lee (opposite New York City), for a distance of over twenty miles. The beauty of these cliffs has been considerably marred by blasting and quarrying operations ; but the surrounding territory has been recently purchased, and will eventually be converted into a public park, under the control of the States of New York and New Jersey.

Palladium. A famous wooden image of Pallas (Minerva), said to have been hurled from heaven by Zeus, and to have fallen near the tent of Ilus, while he was engaged in building Ilium (Troy). The oracle of Apollo having declared that the city should never be taken so long as the Palladium was retained within its walls, the statue was placed in a sanctuary and carefully guarded. It was, however, finally stolen by Ulysses and Diomedes about 1184 B.C., and thus victory was secured to the Greeks. According to some accounts, Troy contained two Palladia,

—one of which was stolen and conveyed to one of the Greek cities, while the other was taken to Italy by Æneas, and secretly guarded by the Romans in the Temple of Vesta. The word "palladium" is frequently used at the present day to signify a pledge of security and protection.

Pall Mall. A famous street in London, the centre of club-life, and often called the "street of modern palaces." It derives its name from *paille-maille*, a game introduced from France during the reign of Charles I (1625–1649), and first played in England about 1630. Pall Mall was a fashionable suburban promenade at that period, and it was not until the close of the 17th century that it became a street. See *Mall.*

Palmers. A name given to those persons, during the Middle Ages, that had made pilgrimages to the Holy Sepulchre at Jerusalem, and had brought home palm-branches in token of having accomplished the journey. On his return home from the Holy Land, the pilgrim repaired to the church to render thanks for his successful journey, and gave the palm-branch to the priest, who placed it upon the altar.

Palmetto City. A sobriquet conferred upon the city of Charleston, South Carolina, in allusion to the great number of palmetto trees that adorn its streets.

Palmetto State. A sobriquet conferred upon the State of South Carolina, in allusion to the great number of palmetto trees within its borders. The palmetto figures conspicuously on the seal of that commonwealth.

Palm Sunday. The Sunday before Easter, so called in commemoration of the entry of Christ into Jerusalem, when the people strewed palm branches in his way. In the Greek and Roman Catholic Churches, the day is celebrated by processions of the clergy, bearing blessed branches of the palm tree, or of other trees in countries where the palm cannot be procured. In the Roman Catholic Church, palms are also distributed to the people, and are carefully preserved by them during the year. They are afterwards burned, and the ashes used on Ash-Wednesday. At Rome, the Pope personally distributes the palms to all the churches in the city. The name "Palm Sunday," is found as early as the fifth century, but processions in honor of the day cannot be traced back farther than the eighth century.

Palmyra, Ruins of. Situated in an oasis in northern Syria, about 150 miles northeast of Damascus. These stupendous ruins comprise the Temple of the Sun (or Baal); the famous colonnade, nearly a mile in length, and consisting at one time of more than 1500 Corinthian columns; and the sepulchral towers overlooking the ancient city. These ruins were visited in 1751 by Messrs. Wood and Dawkins, who published an account of them in 1753. Tradition assigns the founding of Palmyra to Solomon (1015–975 B.C.); but the probability is that it is an Arab settlement, conveniently planted on the great caravan route between the Persian Gulf and the Mediterranean Sea. It attained its greatest prosperity under the famous Queen Zenobia (266–272 A.D.). The city was destroyed by the Emperor Aurelian (270–275 A.D.) in 273, and the inhabitants put to the sword. Tadmor was the original name of the city, and was preserved until the time of Alexander the Great (336–323 B.C.), who conquered it; whereupon its name was changed to Palmyra. Both names mean the "City of Palms."

Pan, Legend Concerning. It was currently believed among the early Christians that, at the time of the crucifixion of Christ, a loud voice was heard throughout the isles of Greece proclaiming that the great Pan was dead and that the rule of the Olympian gods was at an end.

"Plutarch . . . is the first to tell the story that in the reign of Tiberius one Thamus, a pilot, when steering near the islands of Paxæ, was commanded by a loud voice to proclaim that 'the great Pan is dead.' As soon as he had reached Palodes he cried the news aloud from the poop of his ship, whereupon was heard a great noise of lamentation, as of nature itself expressing its grief. The coincidence of this story with the birth or the crucifixion of Christ gave occasion to an explanation that it marked the end of the old world and the beginning of the new when the old oracles became dumb. Rabelais has the story, there is a well-known allusion to it in Milton's *Ode on the Nativity*, and it has been finely treated by Schiller and Mrs. Browning."—*Chambers's Encyclopædia.*

Panama Canal. A ship-canal, 46½ miles long, projected across the Isthmus of Panama and partially completed. The sum of $275,000,000 has already been expended upon the enterprise, and it is estimated that $325,000,000 additional will be necessary to complete it. The portion finished is about 14 miles long. The width of the canal will be 160 feet at the top and 72 feet at the bottom, except where it passes through the Culebra ridge ; there the widths at top and bottom will be 78 feet and 29 feet respectively. The estimated time required to complete the work was ten years. A company was formed and a concession obtained from the United States of Colombia in 1877, and in 1881 the work of excavation was commenced. The company was forced into liquidation in 1889. At that time work on the canal was abandoned, but has since been resumed. See *Darien Canal.*

Pan-American Congress. A congress of American nations, proposed by James G. Blaine, Secretary of State during the administration of President Harrison (1889–1893), and held at Washington, D. C., November 18th, 1889–April 19th, 1890. The Congress dealt with questions of international interest, — recommending reciprocity treaties and uniform systems of weights, measures, and coinage. It led, however, to no practical results. The following countries sent representatives to the Conference : Hayti, Nicaragua, Peru, Guatemala, Colombia, Argentine Republic, Costa Rica, Paraguay, Brazil, Honduras, Mexico, Bolivia, Venezuela, Chili, San Salvador, Ecuador, and the United States of America.

Pandects of Justinian. A digest of the writings of Roman jurists, compiled by Tribonian at the request of the Emperor Justinian (527–565 A.D.), and promulgated in 534 A.D. They comprise 50 volumes, and contain more than 9000 extracts from 39 authors, classified under 429 titles. From the date of their publication, the Emperor decreed that all citations of passages not found in the *Pandects* would be declared null and void. A copy of the *Pandects* was found in the ruins of Amalfi in 1137 ; it was taken to Pisa, and afterwards removed to the library of the Medici at Florence. See *Code of Justinian.*

Panem et Circenses (*Lat., Bread and the Circus-Games*). A favorite cry among the ancient Romans,—meaning that all they desired was to be fed and entertained at the public expense. The phrase occurs in Juvenal's *Satires*, xi, 81.

Pan-Handle. A fanciful name given to the narrow wedge-shaped strip of land, lying between Pennsylvania and Ohio, and forming part of the State of West Virginia. This phrase is sometimes applied to the northwest projection of Texas.

Pansy. An Anglicized form of the French word *pensée* (*thought*).

Pantheism. A system of speculation which, in its material aspect, identifies God with the Universe, and, in its spiritual aspect, identifies the Universe with God. This form of belief is of great antiquity, and is found in the Hindu, Egyptian, Persian, and Greek systems of religion and philosophy. Xenophanes of Elea, who flourished about 538 B.C., was the first classical thinker who taught the higher, or idealistic, form of pantheism. The theory was subsequently revived by Giordano Bruno (1548–1600), and, in more recent times, by Spinoza, Kant, and Fichte. Pantheism implies the non-existence of conscious mind outside of nature, and hence is incompatible with personal immortality.

Pantheon. A superb temple in Rome, erected in 27 B.C. by Marcus Agrippa, son-in-law of the Emperor Augustus, and famous as the only structure of the ancient city that has escaped destruction. It is supposed to have been designed as part of the Baths of Agrippa ; but to have been transformed, after completion, into a temple for the gods of conquered nations, whence its name. In 399 A.D. it was closed as a temple by decree of the Emperor Honorius (395–423), and in 608 was consecrated as a Christian church by Pope Boniface IV (608–615), under the name of *Santa Maria della Rotunda*, or *ad Martyres*. The Pantheon is a circular building—having an interior diameter of 142 feet—and is surmounted by a dome. This is pierced by a circular opening—28 feet in diameter—for the admission of light. Raphael, Annibale Caracci, Victor Emmanuel, and other distinguished Italians are buried in the Pantheon. See *Panthéon*.

Panthéon. A magnificent building in Paris, founded as a church by Louis XV (1715–1774) in 1764, in pursuance of a vow, and dedicated to Sainte Geneviève, the patron-saint of the city, in 1790. In 1791, it was converted by the National Convention into a mausoleum for the eminent men of France, and was named Le Panthéon. In 1806 it was reconsecrated as a church, and in 1821 was renamed Sainte Geneviève. In 1831, it was

renamed Le Panthéon ; in 1852 it was again made a church ; and in 1885 it was once more secularized for the obsequies of Victor Hugo. The building is in the form of a Greek cross—276 by 370 feet—and is surmounted by a dome, 272 feet high. The interior is decorated with frescoes, paintings, statues, mosaics, and other works of art. In the vaults are buried the remains of Voltaire, Rousseau, Victor Hugo, Lagrange, Bougainville, Marshal Lannes, and several senators of the First Empire. Marat and Mirabeau were also interred there, but their bodies were afterwards removed by order of the Convention. See *Pantheon*.

Pantisocracy. The name given by Coleridge in 1794 to a Utopian republic — based on communistic principles — which he and his friends, Southey, Robert Lovell, and George Burnet, dreamed of founding on the banks of the Susquehanna River in Pennsylvania. This romantic scheme was never realized, mainly for want of capital; and, not long after, Coleridge and Southey married, and accepted life as they found it.

"It was imagined that they and others of congenial tastes and principles should join together and leave the Old World for the woods and wilds of the young republic of the West. Possessions were to be held in common : each would work for all. The daily toil was to be lightened by the companionship of the best books and the discussion of the highest things. Each young man would take to himself a fitting helpmeet, whose part it should be to prepare their food and rear a new race in pristine hardihood and innocence."—Walsh's *Handy-Book of Literary Curiosities*.

Papal Infallibility. See *Infallibility, Papal*.

Papal States. See *Church, States of the*.

Paper House. A phrase used in theatrical parlance to denote an audience consisting principally of "dead heads," or persons admitted free of charge.

Paper King. A nickname conferred upon John Law (1671–1729), the originator of the famous Mississippi Scheme, in allusion to his pretended belief in the efficacy of a paper currency issued greatly in excess of the specie held for its redemption. See *Mississippi Scheme.*

Paper-Saving Pope. A nickname given by Dean Swift to Alexander Pope (1688–1744), the English poet, whose MS. of the translation of the *Iliad* and the *Odyssey* was written on scraps of old paper.

Papua. A Portuguese term, meaning *frizzled*, applied to this island, in allusion to the frizzled heads of hair borne by the natives.

Paraclete. The name of an abbey in Champagne, France, founded by Abélard (1079–1142) in 1122, and afterwards converted into a sisterhood, of which Héloïse became the first prioress. It was the burial-place of these ill-starred lovers until 1800, when their remains were taken to Paris and deposited in the Museum of French Monuments. In 1817 they were buried in one tomb in the cemetery of Père-Lachaise, where they still lie. See *Abélard and Héloïse.*

The word *Paraclete* is also used to denote the Holy Spirit, as comforter of mankind. In the early Church, it was currently believed that the *Paraclete* would appear bodily on the earth.

Paradise. In Christian theology, paradise means either (1) the Limbo of the Schoolmen, (2) Heaven itself, or (3) the intermediate estate, or place, where the souls of the saved await the resurrection and the final judgment. The word " paradise " is derived from the Greek παράδεισος (*park* or *pleasure-ground*), and is used in the *Septuagint* to denote the terrestrial Garden of Eden ; in the *New Testament*, the word means the place where the souls of the blessed enjoy happiness. See *Limbo or Limbus ; Purgatory.*

Paradise Lost. An epic poem in twelve books, or cantos, by John Milton (1608–1674). It appeared in ten books in 1667, but in 1674 it was so divided as to make twelve books. The composition of the poem occupied over seven years, *i. e.*, from 1658 to 1665.

" The MS. of *Paradise Lost* was sold by Milton to Samuel Simmons, April 27, 1667, for an immediate payment of five pounds, with a stipulation to receive five pounds more when thirteen hundred of the first edition should be sold, and the same sum after the sale of the same number of the second and third editions. Two years elapsed before the sale of thirteen hundred copies." —Wheeler's *Who Wrote It ?*

" With a singsong chuckle the auctioneer at the Arnold book sale, at No. 91 Fifth Avenue, yesterday disposed of a yellow, dog-eared book, which an untutored eye might expect to find mouldering in any old bookstore. But the sale of this dog-eared volume, according to Bangs & Co., the auctioneers, broke all records, and brought the highest price ever paid for a copy of Milton's masterpiece. The record price up to yesterday, it was said, was $525, which was given at the recent Foote book sale.

The following figures show how the blind poet's works have increased in value with the years :

In 1667 Milton sold his manuscript of *Paradise Lost* at £5 for the first 1300 copies.

In 1681 Milton's widow sold out all rights in the book for £8, or something less than $40.

In 1901 $830 is paid for a single volume.

The volume sold yesterday has the original blank leaf before the title, which is lacking in almost all other copies. The title page reads as follows :

'PARADISE LOST
A
POEM
Written in
TEN BOOKS
By John Milton.
Licensed and Entred according to Order.
LONDON
Printed, and are to be sold by Peter Parker under Creed Church near Aldgate ; And by Robert Boulter at the Turks Head in Bishopsgate-Street ; And Matthias Walker, under St. Dunstans Church in Fleet-Street, 1667.'"

—New York *Tribune* (May 9th, 1901).

Paradise Regained. An epic poem in four books, or cantos, by John Milton (1608–1674). It was probably written in 1665–1666, and appeared in 1671. Milton esteemed this poem his most perfect production, but this preference of the poet has not been shared by either the critics or the public.

". . . I will content myself with noting that the universal consent of readers places the *Paradise Regained*, in point of interest and variety, very far below the *Paradise Lost*."—Shaw's *Complete Manual of English Literature.*

Paradiso, Il. The title of the third part of Dante's *Divine Comedy.* It is in 33 cantos, and gives a picture of Heaven, which, acccording to the poet, is a region divided into ten spheres,— each one of which is appropriated to a special order of beings, as follows :

(1) The Sphere of the Moon (for Angels).

(2) The Sphere of Mercury (for Archangels).

(3) The Sphere of Venus (for Virtues).

(4) The Sphere of the Sun (for Powers).

(5) The Sphere of Mars (for Principalities).

(6) The Sphere of Jupiter (for Dominions).

(7) The Sphere of Saturn (for Thrones).

(8) The Sphere of the Fixed Stars (for Cherubim).

(9) The Sphere of the Primum Mobile (for Seraphim).

(10) The Sphere of the Empyrean (for the Virgin Mary and the Triune God).

See *Divine Comedy ; Inferno, L' ; Purgatorio, Il.*

Parallel Lives. The title of a celebrated work by Plutarch [50 (?)–120 (?) A.D.], the Greek philosopher and moralist, consisting of 46 biographical accounts of eminent Greeks and Romans, arranged in pairs. The biography of each Greek is accompanied by that of some distinguished Roman, and this is followed by a critical estimate wherein the two characters are carefully compared, trait for trait.

Parcæ. A term used by the ancient Romans to designate the Fates. The word is derived from *pars* (*Lat., lot*), and was applied to these imaginary beings, because they were supposed to determine the lot of all mankind. See *Fates.*

Parc=aux=Cerfs. A name originally given to a deer-park near Versailles, France, laid out by Louis XII (1498–1515), and afterwards appropriated by Louis XIV (1643–1715) for building purposes. The term is, however, generally applied to an infamous establishment founded there by Louis XV (1715–1774), and maintained by him for immoral purposes.

Pariahs. The name given to the lowest grade of society among the Hindus of Southern India. They are below the four great castes of Brahmanism, and are, on that account, frequently called "out-castes." The Pariahs are presumed to represent the aboriginal race of India, conquered by the Sûdras. These last constitute the fourth and lowest caste, and were themselves conquered by the Vedic peoples. See *Caste.*

Parian Inscription. See *Arundelian Marbles.*

Parian Marble. A superior quality of white marble, much used by the architects and sculptors of ancient Greece, and formerly obtained from the quarries of Mount Marpessa on the island of Paros, in the Ægean Sea. These quarries, although not exhausted, are no longer worked. The Parian marble of the present day is not marble, but simply a kind of clay, baked in an oven, like porcelain. The famous statue of the Venus de' Medici at Florence is made of Parian marble. See *Pentelic Marble.*

Paris Exposition of 1900. The beginning of the Paris Exposition of 1900 dated officially from July 13th, 1892, on which occasion a decree was issued by President Carnot, announcing a "universal exposition of works of art and of industrial and agricultural products," to be held in Paris from May 5th to October 31st, 1900: this was subsequently changed to April 15th –November 5th, 1900. The number of persons that visited the Exposition is estimated at about 50,000,000, and the greatest number of attendances on a single day at more than 600,000. The Exposition was closed on November 12th,—one week later than the date originally set. See *Columbian Exposition*.

Paris Opera House. A superb temple of amusement in Paris, bearing the inscription " Académie Nationale de Musique." It was designed by Garnier, was commenced in 1861, and completed in 1874. The building covers an area of nearly three acres, and has a seating capacity of 2200— being surpassed in this respect by the opera house at Vienna and the theatres of La Scala at Milan and San Carlos at Naples. The edifice, including the site, cost 37,000,000 francs. The façade is adorned with superb groups of statuary and medallion busts of many of the principal composers, while the grand staircase, foyer, and auditorium are unequalled by those of any other structure. The stage is 196 feet high, 178 feet wide, and 74 feet deep. Back of this is the ballroom (*foyer de la danse*), containing portraits of twenty famous danseuses.

Parliament of Religions. A conference of representatives of various religious bodies, held at the World's Fair in Chicago, September 11th–27th, 1893. The sittings were largely attended, and intense interest was manifested in the proceedings.

The objects aimed at by the conference were:

(1) To define the cardinal truths held and taught in common by the religions of mankind.

(2) To promote fraternal relations among all religious bodies.

(3) To strengthen the grounds for belief in God and immortality.

(4) To consider the present condition and outlook of the religious world.

Parnassus, Mount. A mountain in ancient Phocis, 65 miles northwest of Athens,—celebrated as one of the principal seats of Apollo and the Muses, and as an inspiring source of poetry and song. The Delphic oracle and the Castalian spring were on its southern slope. The expression, " to climb Parnassus,"—meaning to write poetry —is sometimes used at the present day.

Parsees. Adherents of the ancient Zoroastrian religion, descended from Persian refugees settled in India. After the overthrow of the Sassanian dynasty of Persian kings by the Caliph Omar in 651 A.D., great numbers of the people fled to Western India—principally to Bombay,—where their descendants still reside and form an active and enterprising community. The Parsees decline to eat food not cooked by one of their own religion, abstain from the use of beef and pork, and contract marriages with persons of their own creed only. They do not bury their dead, but expose them on towers—called " Towers of Silence "— to the birds of the air. After the bones have been denuded of flesh, they are collected and buried in a subterranean cave. The number of Parsees at Bombay is estimated at about 85,000. See *Towers of Silence*.

Partant pour La Syrie (*Fr.*, *Departing for Syria*). The title of a popular French song, written by the Count Alexandre de Laborde and set to music by Hortense de Beauharnais, Queen of Holland, in 1809. It attained great popularity during the reign of Napoleon III (1852–1870).

Parthenon (*Gr.*, παρθένος, *virgin*). A magnificent temple on the Acropolis at Athens, erected in 444–438 B.C., in honor of Minerva, the tutelary goddess of the city. It was built by the architects Ictinus and Callicrates, under the supervision of Phidias, and cost 6000 talents (about $7,200,000). The structure was of Pentelic marble, in the Doric style of architecture, and was adorned, both within and without, with exquisite works of sculpture. In the *cella* of the temple stood the renowned chryselephantine statue of Minerva, placed there by Phidias in 438 B.C. The building was 228 feet in length by 101 feet in width, and measured 64 feet to the top of the pediment. The sculptures of the pediment, metopes, and frieze were the work of Phidias ; many of these were removed by Lord Elgin in 1812, and placed in the British Museum. During the Middle Ages, the Parthenon became successively a Christian church and a Turkish mosque. In 1687 it was used by the Turkish Government as a powder magazine, and was almost totally destroyed in that year by a shell thrown by the Venetians while besieging the city. Even in its present ruined state, the Parthenon is considered the most perfect specimen of Doric architecture in existence. See *Elgin Marbles.*

Parthenopean Republic. A short-lived republic, established at Naples by the French, January 23rd, 1799, and overthrown in June of the same year. It derived its name from *Parthenope*, the ancient name of Naples before its conquest by the Romans in 328 B.C.

Parthian Warfare. A mode of warfare among the ancient Parthians, which consisted in the discharge of arrows backwards during pretended flight, as well as forwards in direct attack. The phrase " Parthian arrow " is frequently used to denote a parting shot.

Partington, Mrs. A *nom-de-plume* adopted by B. P. Shillaber (1814–1890), the noted American humorist. The name is said to have been suggested by a remark of Sydney Smith in a speech delivered in 1831, wherein he compared the attempt of the House of Lords to prevent the passage of the Reform Bill with the effort of a certain Mrs. Partington to drive back the Atlantic Ocean with her mop and pattens. This incident is said to have actually occurred at Sidmouth, England, in the winter of 1824, when the tide rose to an unusual height and threatened several of the houses with ruin.

Pasquinades. A term frequently applied to anonymous publications of a satiric or libellous nature,—sometimes written and sometimes printed. They derive their name from one *Pasquino*, a witty tailor, who dwelt at Rome at the close of the 15th century, and delighted his patrons with his sarcastic humor. Not long after his death, a mutilated statue — supposed to represent Menelaus supporting the dead Patroclus—was dug up near his former home, and was named Pasquino in his honor. It was placed near the Piazza Navoni, and its pedestal soon after became a place for affixing satires and lampoons reflecting upon the doings of the Pope and cardinals.

Passion-Play. A dramatic representation of the chief events in the Passion of Christ, performed every tenth year by the inhabitants of the village of Ober-Ammergau, Bavaria, in accordance with a vow made by them in 1633, to express their gratitude at the cessation of the plague. This vow has been religiously kept, with few interruptions, ever since. The play depicts the events recorded in the Gospels, and is interspersed with tableaux from the *Old Testament* and choral odes. It occupies about seven hours and a half in its representation ; enlists the services of 500 persons ; and is performed in an open-air theatre, accommodating 6000. The Passion-Play is probably the only " miracle-play," or "mystery," in existence ; and attracts great numbers of tourists, as well as peasants from all parts of the Tyrol and Bavaria. The last performance took place in 1910.

Passionspiel. The German for *passion-play.* See *Passion-Play.*

Passion Week. The name properly given to the week preceding Holy Week, but commonly used in the Anglican Church, since the Reformation (1517), to denote the week immediately preceding Easter, *i. e.*, Holy Week. See *Holy Week.*

Passive Obedience. A political doctrine inculcating entire submission of the subject to those in authority. It is a corollary of the doctrine of the " divine right of kings," and first came into prominence in English history during the time of the Stuarts. It was defended by Hobbes, the famous philosopher, and opposed by Algernon Sidney, Milton, Locke, and Harrington. On the accession of the House of Hanover in 1714, the doctrine of " Passive Obedience " died a natural death. See *Divine Right of Kings.*

Passover. The chief festival of the Jews, instituted in 1491 B.C. to commemorate the departure of the Israelites and their deliverance from the bondage of Egypt, and so called because on the night before the exodus the angel of the Lord smote the firstborn of all the Egyptians, but *passed over* the houses of those Israelites that had done as Moses had commanded them. The Passover is celebrated on the first full moon of the vernal equinox, occurring between the 14th and the 21st of the month *Nisan,*—the first of the sacred year (*Exodus* xii, 1–51). See *Pentecost ; Tabernacles, Feast of.*

Pasteur Institute. An international hospital in Paris, for the inoculation of persons suffering from hydrophobia, founded by Louis Pasteur (1822–1895) in May, 1886, and formally opened in November, 1888. The remains of the founder were transferred from the Cathedral of Notre Dame to a crypt in the Pasteur Institute, on December 26th, 1896.

" Reported number of patients by M. Pasteur since 1885, 6,950, to 28 June, 1889; 1,830 patients, 7 deaths, in 1889 ; 1,520 patients, 5 deaths, in 1895 ; 1,308 patients, 4 deaths, in 1896; 1,521 patients, 6 deaths, in 1897."—Haydn's *Dictionary of Dates.*

Pater - Noster (*Lat., Our Father*). The name given to the *Lord's Prayer* in the Roman Catholic Church, from the first two words in the Latin version. See *Ave Maria.*

" In the Rosary of the Virgin Mary it is combined with the Hail Mary, the prayer addressed to the Virgin (whence the larger beads of the 'Rosary' are sometimes called *Pater-Nosters*), and perhaps the most usual of all the formal shorter devotions among Roman Catholics is the recitation of *a stated number of times* of the ' Pater,' with one or more ' Ave Marias,' generally concluding with the Doxology."—McClintock and Strong's *Cyclopædia.*

Paternoster Row. A street in London, near St. Paul's Cathedral, at present the centre of the retail book-trade. Early in the last century, it was the seat of the great publishing houses ; but, in later years, these moved away to the neighborhood of the Strand and Piccadilly, and left the " Row " to the booksellers of the metropolis. The origin of the name is variously accounted for. According to some, the street was so called from the rosary- or paternoster-makers that dwelt there; others, however, say that it was so named because all funeral processions, *en route* for St. Paul's, commenced their pater-nosters on entering this street, and continued to say them until they reached the gate of the cathedral. See *Pater-Noster.*

Pathfinder.
(1) The hero of James Fenimore Cooper's novel of the same name.
(2) A sobriquet conferred upon Major-General John C. Fremont (1813–1890), who, between 1840 and 1850, conducted four exploring expeditions across the Rocky Mountains for the purpose of opening an overland route between the Atlantic and the Pacific Oceans. See *Deerslayer.*

Patricians. The nobles, or hereditary aristocracy, of Rome. During the early days of the Republic, they held possession of all political rights, which, however, after a struggle of nearly 200 years (494–300 B.C.), they were finally forced to share with the plebeians. See *Plebeians*.

Patron Saints. The name given, during the Middle Ages, to those saints that were supposed to watch over and protect the interests of particular persons, places, and trades. The following is a list of some of the more prominent of these patrons of countries, cities, and towns :

(1) Aberdeen, St. Nicholas.
(2) Antwerp, St. Norbert.
(3) Austria, SS. Colman and Leopold.
(4) Brussels, St. Gudule.
(5) Cologne, St. Ursula.
(6) Edinburgh, St. Giles.
(7) England, SS. George and Mary.
(8) Flanders, St. Peter.
(9) France, SS. Mary, Michael, and Denis.
(10) Genoa, St. George.
(11) Germany, SS. Martin, Boniface, and George.
(12) Holland, St. Mary.
(13) Ireland, St. Patrick.
(14) Italy, St. Anthony.
(15) Lisbon, St. Vincent.
(16) Milan, St. Ambrose.
(17) Naples, St. Januarius.
(18) Paris, St. Geneviève.
(19) Portugal, SS. Sebastian, James, and George.
(20) Prussia, SS. Mary, Adalbert, and Andrew.
(21) Rome, SS. Peter and Paul.
(22) Russia, SS. Nicholas, Andrew, Wladimir, and Mary.
(23) Scotland, St. Andrew.
(24) Spain, SS. James the Great, Michael, Thomas à Becket, and Edward.
(25) Venice, SS. Mark, Justina, and Theodore.
(26) Vienna, St. Stephen.
(27) Wales, St. David.

Patronymics. Surnames derived from the names of parents or other ancestors. They are formed by adding prefixes or suffixes to proper names, as follows :

(1) *Atrides*, son of Atreus.
(2) *FitzOsborne*, son of Osborne.
(3) *Heraclidæ*, descendants of Heracles.
(4) *Johnson*, son of John.
(5) *MacPherson*, son of Pherson.
(6) *O'Grady*, son of Grady.
(7) *Petrovitch*, son of Peter.

Paul et Virginie. The title of a celebrated romantic tale by Bernardin de St. Pierre (1737–1814), published in 1788. It passed through 50 editions in a single year, and was quickly translated into the principal languages of Europe. Napoleon Bonaparte is said to have taken the book with him on his Italian campaign (1796–1797), and to have re-read it during his captivity at St. Helena (1815–1821).

Paul Pry. The name of the principal character in Poole's comedy of the same name. He is an officious, meddling busybody, who has no occupation of his own and is constantly interfering with the affairs of others. According to Brewer's *Dictionary of Phrase and Fable*, the original of the character was one Thomas Hill.

Paul Veronese. The real name of this artist was Paolo Cagliari, or Caliari,—the surname *Veronese* having been conferred upon him in honor of *Verona*, his birthplace.

Pavonia. The name formerly given to a tract of land in New Jersey, extending from Jersey City to Perth Amboy. It was ceded by the Indians in 1630 to Michael Pauw, Burgomaster of Amsterdam and Lord of Achtienhoven, and was called by him *Pavonia*, a Latinized form of his name. The old Dutch settlement of Communipaw, south of Jersey City, is also indebted for its name to this same Michael Pauw.

Pawnbrokers' Balls. The three golden balls, forming the pawnbrokers' sign, are derived from the armorial bearings of the Medici family, the earliest and most famous of the money-lenders of Lombardy. This device was first used by the agents of the Medici in London, and was afterwards adopted by others.

"They [the three balls] represent three gilded pills; and were used by the Medici in allusion to the profession of medicine, in which that family was eminent, and from which they derived their name."—Edwards's *Words, Facts, and Phrases*.

"Everyone knows that these balls are the arms of the Medici family, but it is not so well known that they refer to an exploit of Averardo de Medici, a commander under Charlemagne. This bold warrior slew the giant Mugello, whose club he bore as a trophy. This mace or club had three iron balls, which the family adopted as their device."—Brewer's *Reader's Handbook*.

Peabody Fund.

(1) A fund of $3,500,000, established by George Peabody (1795–1869), the American philanthropist, in 1867–1869, to aid the cause of education in the Southern States of the Union. Of this amount, $1,380,000 was unfortunately invested in Mississippi and Florida bonds, which these States afterwards repudiated. During the thirty-two years that have elapsed since the establishment of the Trust, more than $2,669,755 have been distributed for educational purposes. In its early history the income of the Peabody Fund was expended in establishing public schools throughout the South; but, this having been accomplished, the money is now spent in the training of teachers by means of Normal Schools and Teachers' Institutes.

(2) A fund of £500,000 ($2,500,000), contributed at various times during the years 1862–1869, by George Peabody, for the purpose of benefiting the poor of London. Large dwelling-houses for the working classes of the city—called Peabody Buildings—have been erected at Spitalfields, Islington, Shadwell, Westminster, Chelsea, Bermondsey, etc., and furnish accommodation for 20,000 persons,—each family

paying an average weekly rent of four shillings.

It is estimated that the grand total of Mr. Peabody's philanthropic gifts amounts to nearly $10,000,000.

Peaceful Prelate. A sobriquet bestowed upon Jean Baptiste Massillon (1663–1742), Bishop of Clermont, in allusion to his pacific method of settling ecclesiastical quarrels.

Peacock Throne. A famous throne, formerly standing in the diwan-i-khas, or audience-hall, of the Citadel at Delhi, India, in the days of Shâh-Jehân (1627–1658 A.D.) and Aurungzebe (1658–1707 A.D.), Mogul emperors. It measured six feet in length by four feet in width, and was supported by six feet of solid gold, encrusted with gems. The throne itself—also of gold —was inlaid with diamonds, emeralds, and rubies, and surmounted by a canopy of the same metal. It received its name from the figures of two peacocks — with outspread wings blazing with precious stones — placed behind it. Between these was a figure of a parrot (life-size), said to have been cut from a single emerald. The cost of the "Peacock Throne" is variously estimated at from ten to fifty million dollars.

Pearl. This precious stone is said to derive its name from the Latin *pirula* (*little pear*).

Pearl Mosque. A small, but exquisitely proportioned Mohammedan temple at Agra, India, so called on account of its surpassing beauty. Its architecture is the purest Saracenic. The edifice is built of polished white marble, and is crowned with three domes of the same material, surmounted by slender golden spires. See *Akbar's Palace*.

"The Motee Musjid, erected by Shah Jehan, was seven years in building, and furnished employment for three thousand workmen, among whom were many Persians, also a few Italians, Portuguese, and French. The marble was presented to the emperor by the Rajah of Jeypoor, and the simple cost of erection is said to have been as much as thirty lakhs of rupees, or one million five hundred thousand dollars. This, however, seems an exaggerated tradition, when we remember the cheapness of labor and the necessities of life at that period."— Vincent's *Through and Through the Tropics*.

Peculiar Institution. A phrase used, before the American Civil War, to designate negro slavery in America as being an institution peculiar to the Southern States.

"Urgent appeals were sent to the sympathizers of Senator Douglas in Missouri to attend and do honor to the champion of the *peculiar institution* at the meeting in Quincy, Illinois." — New York *Tribune* (Oct. 19th, 1854).

Peculiar People. A small sect of Faith-Healers, founded in London in 1838. They reject medical assistance in cases of illness (but not in those requiring surgical aid), and rely upon prayer, anointing by their elders, and careful nursing. The sect is recruited from the humble classes of the community, and bears an excellent reputation for morality and honesty. In 1868, two of its members were tried for manslaughter, but were acquitted; in 1872, a father, whose child died of smallpox, was convicted for neglecting to summon medical aid. Establishments for the healing of disease by prayer exist also in Germany. The Faith-Healers and Christian Scientists in the United States are similar communities. See *Christian Science*.

Peeler. A slang term for a policeman. It is derived from Sir Robert Peel (1788–1850), the English statesman, who, as Home Secretary, established the Irish constabulary in 1814, and reorganized the London police-force in 1829.

The word "peeler" was used to denote a thief or robber during the 16th century.

Peeping Tom of Coventry. A phrase used to denote a person of ungovernable inquisitiveness. When, according to the legend of Coventry,

the Lady Godiva rode naked through the town, to relieve the inhabitants of certain grievous oppressions, she commanded all persons to remain indoors and away from the windows, under pain of death. One person, however, being unable to resist the temptation to take a peep, lost his sight in consequence, and has ever since been known as "Peeping Tom of Coventry." Tennyson has told the story in his poem *Godiva*.

Peep o' Day Boys. A nickname given to the Irish insurgents of 1784, from their habit of breaking into the dwellings of the "Defenders" at the dawn of day, in search of arms or plunder.

Pegasus. In classic myth, the famous winged horse that sprang from the blood of Medusa, the mortal Gorgon, when she was slain by Perseus. Pegasus dwelt at Olympus, and carried thunder and lightning for Zeus. By his aid, Bellerophon conquered the Chimæra. Pegasus was regarded by later writers as the horse of Eos, and was said to have revealed the famous fountain of Hippocrene on Mount Helicon by a kick of his hoof. According to a modern poetic fancy, Pegasus became the horse of the Muses, and thence arose the saying, "to mount one's Pegasus," — meaning to write poetry. See *Gorgons; Hippocrene*.

Pelagians. A heretical sect among the early Christians, founded by Pelagius, a native of Britain, who visited Rome in 400. The Pelagians maintained:

(1) That Adam was created mortal, and would have died whether he had sinned or not.

(2) That Adam's sin injured himself alone, and not the human race.

(3) That new-born infants are in the same condition as Adam was before his fall.

(4) That the whole human race will not rise again from the dead on account of Christ's resurrection.

(5) That the Law, as well as the Gospel, qualifies men for the kingdom of heaven.

(6) That there were men that lived without sin before the advent of Christ.

(7) That the grace of God is not necessary to salvation.

(8) That grace is given to men in proportion to their merit.

These doctrines were condemned by the Synods of Jerusalem (415) and Carthage (416), and by the Council of Ephesus (431).

Pelasgians. A prehistoric people, probably belonging to the Aryan race. They dwelt in Asia Minor, Greece, and Italy, and made their first appearance in Europe about 2000 B.C. The ancient Greeks were doubtless a mixture of the Hellenes and the Pelasgians.

"The nation was widely spread over Greece and the islands of the Grecian archipelago, and the name of *Pelasgia* was given at one time to Greece. One of the most ancient traditions represented Pelasgus as a descendant of Phoroneus, king of Argos; and it seems to have been generally believed by the Greeks that the Pelasgi spread from Argos to the other countries of Greece. . . . The most ancient architectural remains of Greece, such as the treasury or tomb of Atreus at Mycenæ, are ascribed to the Pelasgians, and are cited as specimens of Pelasgian architecture, though there is no positive authority for these statements."— Smith's *Classical Dictionary*.

Pelican. The fable of the pelican feeding its young with blood from its own breast has been variously accounted for. It probably arose from the fact that this bird presses the red tip of its bill against its breast in order the more easily to empty its pouch in feeding its young. Another explanation is that the flamingo disgorges a bloody-looking secretion, which it discharges into the mouths of its young, and that this characteristic, having been transferred to the pelican, gave rise to the story.

Pelican State. A popular name of the State of Louisiana, derived from the Arms of the State, which show a pelican protecting her young and feeding them with blood from her own breast. See *Pelican*.

Pelion, Mount. A mountain in Thessaly, near Mount Ossa. It is famous, in classic myth, as the mountain that the Giants piled on Ossa in their frantic attempts to scale Olympus. See *Ossa, Mount*.

Peloponnesian War. A famous struggle between Athens and Sparta, with their respective allies, for the control of Greece. The war lasted for 27 years (431–404 B.C.), and resulted in the complete overthrow of the Athenian ascendancy. After several crushing defeats on land and sea, the Athenians surrendered their city in 404 B.C., and the war came to an end. The three principal causes assigned for the defeat of Athens were:

(1) The early death of Pericles, her most famous statesman.

(2) The foolish attempt of Athens to conquer Sicily.

(3) The acceptance of Persian gold by Sparta.

The history of the Peloponnesian War has been brilliantly told by Thucydides.

Peloponnesus (*Gr., Island of Pelops*). This word is said to be derived from the mythical Pelops, King of Pisa in Elis. The Peloponnesus formed the southern part of ancient Greece, and was united with Hellas proper by the Isthmus of Corinth. It was called Morea in the 13th century A.D., on account of its fancied resemblance to a mulberry-leaf (*Lat. morus, mulberry*), and still retains that name.

Penates. The old tutelary deities of the ancient Romans, supposed to have been brought by Æneas from Troy into Italy, and preserved, first at Lavinium, afterwards at Alba Longa, and finally at Rome. They were of two kinds: (1) the domestic *Penates*, or guardians of the household, and (2)

37

the public *Penates*, or protectors of the state—regarded as the great family of citizens. See *Lares; Manes*.

"These divinities (*i. e.*, Lares, Manes, Penates) were by no means exactly differentiated from each other, and obviously all owed their existence to the fundamental ideas underlying the worship of ancestors, with its altar, the domestic hearth—the most persistent and perhaps the oldest of all the religions of man." — *Chambers's Encyclopædia*.

Penelope's Shroud. During the long absence of Ulysses, King of Ithaca, at the siege of Troy, his wife, Penelope, was beset by numerous suitors for her hand. To put them off, she declared that she could not choose from among them, until she had finished weaving a shroud, or robe, for Laërtes, her aged father-in-law. Penelope was careful to undo by night what she had woven by day, and thus managed to keep her suitors at a distance. This stratagem was finally discovered by her admirers, who thereupon renewed their attentions; but the timely return of Ulysses, after an absence of twenty years, put an end to their importunities.

Peninsular War. The name given to the war waged in Spain and Portugal in 1807–1814, between the armies of Napoleon I (1804–1814) and the English and Spanish forces under the command of Sir Arthur Wellesley (afterwards Duke of Wellington). The war grew out of an attempt on the part of Napoleon to partition Portugal, and place his brother Joseph on the throne of Spain. The Spaniards rose in opposition to this tyrannical measure, and solicited aid from England, which was freely granted. After losing the great battles of Douro, Talavera, Salamanca, and Vittoria, the French were driven out of the peninsula, and the rightful king, Ferdinand VII, was established on the Spanish throne.

Peninsula State. A name popularly given to the State of Florida, in allusion to its shape. It is also called the " Everglade State," from one of its natural features.

Penitential Psalms. A term applied to seven of the Psalms of David, so called from being peculiarly adapted to the expression of sorrow for sin. They are Psalms vi, xxxii, xxxviii, li, cii, cxxx, cxliii of the *Authorized Version*, and correspond with vi, xxxi, xxxvii, l, ci, cxxix, and cxliii of the *Vulgate*. These psalms were set apart for this purpose as early as 200 A.D., and are referred to by Origen (185–254 A.D.). Pope Innocent III (1198–1216) decreed that they should be recited during Lent. The most deeply penitential, and the one most frequently used, is the fifty-first Psalm, known as the *Miserere* (Psalm l in the *Vulgate*). See *De Profundis; Miserere*.

Penitent Thief. See *Desmas*.

Pen-Names. The following list of pen-names of popular authors is taken from *Everybody's Pocket Cyclopædia :*

A. L. O. E. (a lady of Eng.)..Mrs. C. Tucker
Artemus Ward...........Charles F. Browne
Arthur Sketchley.............George Rose
Asa Trenchard...........Henry Watterson
Barry Cornwall.......Bryan Waller Procter
Betsy B................Mrs. Mary Austin
Bibliophile..................S. A. Allibone
Bill Nye.....................Wm. E. Nye
Boz........................Charles Dickens
Brick Pomeroy.........Mark M. Pomeroy
Burleigh.............Matthew Hale Smith
Carleton.......................C. C. Coffin
Clara Belle.........Mrs. Wm. Thomson
Colley Cibber.................James Rees
Currer Bell..............Charlotte Brontë
Dick Tinto.................F. B. Goodrich
Doesticks....................M. Thompson
Elia.........................Charles Lamb
Eli Perkins..................M. D. Landon
Fanny Fern............Mrs. James Parton
Fat Contributor...........A. M. Griswold
Father Prout........Rev. Francis Mahoney
Frank Forrester.........Henry W. Herbert
Gail Hamilton............Mary A. Dodge
Gath................Geo. Alfred Townsend
George Eliot.....Mrs. Lewes or Mrs. Cross
George Sand..............Mme. Dudevant

Grace Greenwood . .	Mrs. S. J. C. Lippincott
Hans Breitmann	Charles G. Leland
Harper's Easy Chair	Geo. Wm. Curtis
H. H.	Helen Hunt
Ik Marvel	Donald G. Mitchell
Irenæus	Rev. Dr. S. I. Prime
Jacob Omnium	M. J. Higgins
Jenny June	Mrs. J. C. Croly
John Phenix	G. H. Derby
Josh Billings	H. W. Shaw
Joshua Coffin	H. W. Longfellow
J. S. of Dale	F. J. Stimson
Junius	J. H. Brown
Knickerbocker	Washington Irving
Laicus	Rev. Lyman Abbott
Marion Harland	Mrs. M. V. Terhune
Mark Twain	Samuel L. Clemens
Max Adler	C. H. Clark
Max O'Rell	Paul Blouët
Miles O'Reilly	C. G. Halpine
Miss Mulock	Mrs. Dinah M. Craik
M. Quad	Charles B. Lewis
Mrs. Partington	B. P. Shillaber
Nym Crinkle	A. C. Wheeler
Oliver Optic	William T. Adams
Orpheus C. Kerr	R. H. Newell
Ouida	Louise de la Ramée
Our Member for Paris	H. Labouchère
Owen Meredith	Lord E. R. Lytton
Perley	Ben. Perley Poore
Peter Parley	Samuel G. Goodrich
Peter Pindar	John Wolcott
Petroleum V. Nasby	D. R. Locke
Philip Quilibet	George E. Pond
Pisistratus Brown	William Black
Porte Crayon	D. H. Strother
Sam Slick	Judge T. C. Haliburton
Saxeholm	Miss Rush Ellis
Shirley Dare	P. C. Dunning
Sophie Sparkle	Jennie E. Hicks
Susan Coolidge	Miss Woolsey
Sylvanus Urban	Ed. *Gent. Magazine*
Sylvanus Cobb, Jr	S. Cobb
Thomas Ingoldsby	R. H. Barham
Timothy Titcomb	Dr. J. G. Holland
Trusta	Elizabeth S. Phelps
Veteran Observer	E. D. Mansfield
Warrington	W. P. Robinson
Warwick	F. B. Ottarson

Pennsylvania. The name given by William Penn (1644–1718) to the territory granted to him by Charles II (1660–1685) of England in 1681. Penn wished to call the province Sylvania (*Lat., wooded country*) on account of its extensive forests ; but was over-ruled by the King, who insisted on the addition of the prefix Penn, in honor of Admiral Penn, the founder's father.

Pennsylvania Avenue. The principal street in Washington, D. C., extending from the eastern branch of the Potomac to Georgetown,—a distance of nearly five miles. The part of the avenue between the Capitol and the Treasury Department is 1⅓ miles long, and forms the busiest and most fashionable thoroughfare in the city. It is 160 feet broad, is paved with asphalt, and is lined with shops, hotels, and restaurants.

Pensées, Les (*Fr., The Thoughts*). A celebrated theological work by Blaise Pascal (1623–1662), the French philosopher, consisting of fragments of an extensive and systematic treatise on the fundamental truths of Christianity, which, however, the author did not live to complete. It was published in 1669 (seven years after his death) by a committee of influential Jansenists, but was so much garbled in the interests of orthodoxy that the author's original meaning is greatly obscured. A more accurate edition, published by M. Prosper Faugère, appeared in 1844.

"*The Thoughts* of Pascal are to be ranked, as a monument of his genius, above the 'Provincial Letters,' though some have asserted the contrary. They burn with an intense light ; condensed in expression, sublime, energetic, rapid, they hurry away the reader, till he is scarcely able or willing to distinguish the sophisms from the truth they contain. For that many of them are incapable of bearing a calm scrutiny is very manifest to those who apply such a test. The notes of Voltaire, though always intended to detract, are sometimes unanswerable ; but the splendour of Pascal's eloquence absolutely annihilates, in effect on the general reader, even this antagonist."—Hallam's *Introduction to the Literature of Europe.*

Pensions, United States. On June 30th, 1912, there were 860,294 pensioners on the pension-rolls of the United States ; and, during the twelve months previous to that date, the sum of $152,-986,433.72 had been disbursed. The total number of claims allowed during the years 1867–1912 inclusive was 2,078,340, and the total sum disbursed during the same period was $4,286,- 922,719.65. During the fiscal year ending June 30th, 1912, the number of pensioners was decreased by 31,804.

"Mrs. U. S. Grant and Mrs. J. A. Garfield receive pensions of $5000 a year; Mrs. Phil. Sheridan has $2500; eight, including Mrs. John C. Fremont, Mrs. Logan, and Mrs. George B. McClellan, receive $2000 a year, and forty-five receive $1200 a year. Among these are the widows of Generals Banks, Gresham, Custer, Doubleday, Hartranft, Robert Anderson, Casey, Gibbon, Kilpatrick, Mower, Paul, Ricketts, Warren, and Rousseau, and Admiral Wilkes. Among the notable pensioners who receive pensions of $100 a month are ex-Senator John M. Thayer, of Lincoln, Neb.; Franz Sigel, of New York; and John C. Black, of Chicago."—*World Almanac* for 1901.

Pentateuch (*Gr., πέντε, five, τεῦχος, book*). A term collectively applied to the first five books of the *Old Testament*,— ascribed by Jewish tradition to Moses. They are *Genesis, Exodus, Leviticus, Numbers,* and *Deuteronomy*. See *Heptateuch.*

Pentecost (*Gr., πεντηκοστή, fiftieth*). The name given to the Jewish feast held on the *fiftieth day* after the Passover, to render thanks for the ingathered harvest. The Jews called it also the " Feast of Weeks," because it was observed seven complete weeks (or fifty days) after the Passover. This festival was introduced into the Christian Church to commemorate the descent of the Holy Spirit upon the apostles, which event took place on that day; and from early times the feast of Pentecost was chosen as one of the occasions for the administration of the rite of baptism. The name " Whitsunday " given to this festival in England is derived from the *white* robes worn by the candidates for baptism on that day. Pentecost is observed by the Jews at the present day on the 6th and 7th of the month *Sivan, i. e.,* between the second half of May and the first half of June. See *Passover ; Tabernacles, Feast of ; Whitsunday.*

Pentelic Marble. A celebrated variety of white marble, quarried from Mount Pentelicus, near Athens, and much esteemed by the ancient Greeks. The Parthenon, the Propylæa, the Temple of Wingless Victory, and other buildings on the Acropolis, were built of this material. Several ancient statues, executed in Pentelic marble, still exist. See *Parian Marble.*

People's Friend. A sobriquet conferred upon William Gordon (1801–1849), a noted philanthropist of Hull, England.

Pepys's Diary. A unique work by Samuel Pepys (1632–1703), giving a curious and faithful account of the times in England from 1659 to 1669. It includes almost every phase of public and social life, from the gayeties of the court to the pettiest detail of every-day existence. The book was written in shorthand, and was not discovered until a century after the author's death. It was deciphered and published (although in a mutilated form) by Lord Braybrooke in 1825.

"The best book of its kind in the language. . . . Pepys is marvellously entertaining ; the times and the man peep out in a thousand odd circumstances and amusing expressions. . . . The ablest picture of the age in which the author lived, and a work of standard importance in English literature."—London *Athenæum.*

Perdita. The pseudonym of Mrs. Mary Robinson, *née* Darby (1758–1800), the English poetess and actress. She became the mistress of the Prince of Wales (afterwards George IV).

Père Duchesne. A nickname given to Jacques René Hébert (1755-1794), a notorious Jacobin demagogue. He acquired this sobriquet from his scurrilous journal entitled *Père Duchesne,* in which were published the vilest insinuations against the character of Marie Antoinette.

Père - Lachaise. The name of a famous cemetery in Paris, so called from Lachaise, the Jesuit confessor of Louis XIV (1643 – 1715), whose country-seat occupied the site of the present chapel. The cemetery was laid out in 1804, and covers an area of about 110 acres. It is handsomely adorned with well-shaded walks and avenues, and affords a fine view of the city. Père - Lachaise contains about 20,000 monuments ; it is visited on All Souls' Day (November 2nd) by fully 100,000 people. Among the illustrious dead buried there may be named Abélard and Héloïse, Casimir-Périer, Talma, Mars, Rachel, Alfred de Musset, Racine, Molière, Lafontaine, Michelet, Garnier-Pagès, Béranger, Déjazet, Balzac, Arago, Laplace, Casimir-Delavigne, Charles Nodier, Monge, Champollion, Kellermann, Ney, Masséna, Dupuytren, Larrey, Nélaton, Ricord, and St. Hilaire. The two other leading cemeteries of Paris are those of Montmartre and Montparnasse.

Perfidious Albion. An expression said to have been used by Napoleon Bonaparte (1769–1821), as he watched the receding shores of England from the ship *Northumberland*, which was conveying him to St. Helena.

Brewer, in his *Historic Note-Book*, says that this expression is not original with Napoleon I, but that it probably refers to the homage exacted from Edward III (1327–1377) of England by Philip VI (1328–1350) of France in 1329. Edward was sorely wounded by this indignity, and subsequently avenged it to the bitter end. The saying also occurs in one of the sermons of Bossuet (1627–1704). See *Albion.*

Peripatetic Philosophy. A term often applied to the philosophy of Aristotle and his followers. It is of doubtful origin, but is supposed to be derived either from the philosopher's custom of walking about (*Gr.* περιπατέω, *to walk about*) while instructing his disciples, or from the place in which he lectured, which was a shaded

walk (*Gr.* περίπατος). See *Aristotelian Philosophy.*

" It is curiously illustrative of his restless, vivacious temperament that he could not stand still and lecture, but delivered his opinions whilst walking up and down the shady paths of the Lyceum, attended by his eager followers. Hence his disciples were called the Walking Philosophers—*Peripatetics.*"—Lewes's *Biographical History of Philosophy.*

Periplus. The name given to the Greek version of a narrative of voyage and discovery, said to have been written by Hanno, the Carthaginian navigator, about 500 B.C. He is represented as sent with a fleet of 60 vessels and 30,000 colonists to explore the western coast of Africa, and as having continued the voyage until his store of provisions began to fail. The age and authenticity of the *Periplus* have been much discussed by geographers and critics. It is considered by many to be merely an abstract of a larger work.

Perpetual Motion. A continuous motion conceived as attainable by a machine that supplies its own motive power wholly from within. The impossibility of attaining perpetual motion has been repeatedly demonstrated by physicists, but the solution of the problem still remains a subject of experiment with many fanatics.

" Every machine is constructed to transmit motion or force. The machine, further, modifies the transmitted force, so as to overcome certain resistances, some 'useful' and some 'prejudicial.' In every instance the motion of the machine is derived from without, and the energy so conveyed is to be at once referred to muscular action, or the weight of falling water, or a current of air, or the expansive force of steam, or some other natural power. Some such force is at once implied by the action of any machine, whether the motion is only commencing or has continued for an indefinite time. In an ordinary clock, for example, action is due to the muscular force expended in coiling a spring or raising a weight. The sight of motion in wheels or levers compels us to believe that force has been exerted upon them, and they are merely vehicles for transmitting it. The machine has gained so much motion and energy, but only at the expense of some exterior agent. The quantity of force in existence being fixed, no new stock can be created, and therefore a self-moving machine is absurd even in name. . . . In the words of the French Academy (Histoire, 1775): 'Neglecting friction and resistance (of the air), a body to which motion has been given will retain it for ever, but only on condition that it does not act on other bodies; and the only perpetual motion possible, even on this hypothesis, would be useless for the purpose of the devisers. . . . Numerous mechanics who might have been of great service have wasted (on this kind of research) their means, time, and talents.'"—*Chambers's Encyclopædia.*

Persecutions of Christians. See *Ten Persecutions.*

Perseverance of the Saints. In the Calvinistic system of theology, a doctrine that teaches that the elect of God shall never totally and finally fall from grace, but shall *persevere* to the end and thus attain unto salvation. This doctrine has been the occasion of much controversy between the Calvinists and Arminians,—the former maintaining a belief in the doctrine of the "Final Perseverance of the Saints," and the latter denying it.

"This *perseverance of the saints* depends not upon their own free-will, but upon the immutability of the decree of election, flowing from the free and unchangeable love of God the Father; upon the efficacy of the merit and intercession of Jesus Christ; the abiding of the Spirit, and of the seed of God within them; and the nature of the covenant of grace—from all which ariseth also the certainty and infallibility thereof."—*Westminster Assembly's Confession of Faith.*

Peshito Version. An ancient Syriac translation of the *Old Testament* and the greater part of the *New Testament,*—supposed to date from the end of the second or the beginning of the third century A.D. The books lacking are the *Second Epistle of Peter,* the *Second* and *Third Epistles of John,* and *Revelation,*—these probably not constituting, at that time, part of the Canon of Scripture. The *Peshito Version* holds the same place among Syriac Christians as the *Vulgate* among the Roman

Catholics and the *Authorized Version* among English-speaking Protestants. The *Old Testament* version was made direct from the Hebrew, and is regarded by theologians as an extremely faithful rendering of the original.

Pestalozzian System. A system of education devised by Johann Heinrich Pestalozzi (1746–1827), the famous Swiss teacher and educational reformer. Pestalozzi believed that the true object of education consists in the gradual unfolding of the mental faculties in their proper order, and that, among these, the perceptive powers are the first to be developed. In his teaching of the young, he adopted concrete methods of instruction,—using objects themselves, and not lessons about objects. Despite his many quixotic notions and his marked incapacity in practical affairs, Pestalozzi gave a mighty impulse to primary education.

Peterhof Palace. A palace near St. Petersburg, Russia, erected by Peter the Great (1682–1725) as a suburban residence in 1720. It is filled with innumerable objects of art, and contains a remarkable collection of portraits of Russian ladies, 368 in number, painted by Count Rotari and presented by him to Catherine II (1762–1796). The gardens and fountains are scarcely inferior to those of Versailles. Near by are the Hermitage, the Cottage of Catherine II, and the English Garden.

Peterloo. A name formed in imitation of *Waterloo,* and sarcastically given to the dispersal, by the military, of a reform meeting of 60,000 persons —principally operatives— held in St. Peter's Field, Manchester, England, on August 16th, 1819. Soon after the meeting had been called to order, it was charged by the cavalry,— all outlets having been guarded by troops. Eleven persons were killed, and many were wounded.

Peter Parley. The *nom-de-plume* assumed by Samuel Griswold Goodrich (1793–1863), the American author, whose juvenile works on geography, history, travel, etc., enjoyed a great popularity during the middle period of the nineteenth century.

Peter's Fish. A name popularly given to the haddock, on account of the belief once entertained that the spots on its sides were the marks of Peter's fingers when he caught the fish from whose mouth he took the tribute-money.

"An ancient legend ascribes these spots to the finger and thumb of St. Peter, and states the haddock to be the fish from the mouth of which he took the tribute-money, 'the inventors of the legend never adverting to the improbability of a marine fish living in the fresh-water lake of Gennesaret.' The haddock, indeed, is not found even in the Mediterranean."—*Chambers's Encyclopœdia.*

Peter's Pence. The name given to the annual tribute to the Pope of Rome, so called because collected during the five weeks intervening between SS. Peter and Paul's Day and August 1st. By some authorities its origin is ascribed to Ina, King of Wessex, in 721; by others, to Offa, King of Mercia, in 777; while Lingard traces it to Alfred the Great (871–901). At all events, the custom originated in Anglo-Saxon England, and was introduced into Ireland by Henry II (1154–1189). The tax consisted of a silver penny, and was paid by all families possessed of land or cattle having an annual value of 30 pence. "Peter's Pence" was annually claimed by the Popes, and was regularly paid until 1534, when it was abolished by Henry VIII (1509–1547). It practically ceased at the time of the Reformation (1517). Traces of a similar tribute are found in Denmark, Sweden, Norway, and Poland. Of late years the payment of "Peter's Pence," as a voluntary offering, has been revived in several of the Roman Catholic countries of Europe, and with signal success. In 1877, on the occasion of the Pope's Jubilee, the sum of £660,000 was contributed for that purpose.

Peter the Great, Statue of. A colossal bronze equestrian statue of Peter the Great (1682–1725) of Russia, situated at the western extremity of the Admiralty Square, at St. Petersburg. It was modelled by Falconet, and erected by Catherine II (1762–1796) in honor of the founder of the city. The statue represents the Czar seated upon a prancing steed, and rests upon a huge block of Finland granite weighing 1500 tons. This was brought from a marsh four miles distant from the city, and was removed at great labor and expense. The Czar is clad in a simple tunic and mantle, and is seated on a bearskin, emblematic of the country he regenerated. His head is bare and crowned with laurel, while his right hand is outstretched, as if in benediction of his people.

Peter, the Wild Boy. A half-savage human being, discovered in the forest near Hameln in Hanover, in July, 1724 (while George I of England and his friends were hunting there), and supposed at that time to be about 13 years of age. When found, "he was walking on his hands and feet, climbing up trees like a squirrel, and feeding upon grass and moss of trees." He was taken to England in 1726 by the King, and placed under the care of the famous Dr. Arbuthnot, who expended much labor in unavailing attempts to teach him the ways and customs of civilized persons. He preferred wild herbs and grasses to the fare of the King's table, and could never be taught to articulate a single word distinctly. He manifested, however, a taste for music. In 1737, he was placed with one Tom Fen, a Hertfordshire farmer, with whom he lived until the latter's death in 1786. This shock, however, proved so great for "Peter" that he soon after took to his bed, refused food, and died. He was visited in 1782 by Lord Monboddo, and is described by him in his *Ancient Metaphysics* as about 70 years of age, 5 feet 3 inches tall, docile, and healthy. To prevent his being lost while rambling about the country he wore a brass collar, with the inscription " Peter the Wild Boy, Broadway Farm, Berkhampstead.''

Petition of Right. A declaration of certain inalienable rights and privileges of British subjects, drawn up by the House of Commons and granted by Charles I (1625–1649) on June 26th, 1628. Its leading clauses were :

(1) That no taxes should be levied by royal authority, without the consent of Parliament.

(2) That no person should be detained in prison, except by the law of the land or by due process of law.

(3) That soldiers and mariners should not be billeted in private houses against the laws and customs of the realm.

(4) That commissions for proceeding by martial law should be abolished.

The *Petition of Right* was regarded as the second *Magna Charta*, and constituted the first check on the prerogatives of the Crown since the accession of the House of Tudor. See *Bill of Rights*.

Petit Trianon. An attractive little structure, near the palace of Versailles, built by Louis XV (1715–1774) for Madame du Barry in 1766, and afterwards presented by Louis XVI (1774–1789) to Marie Antoinette. It is tastefully fitted up, and contains several fine paintings and other works of art. In the garden of the Petit Trianon, near by, may be seen the famous Swiss village where Marie Antoinette and her court played at peasant life. See *Grand Trianon*.

Petrarch and Laura. See *Laura de Noves.*

Petrarch's House. A country-house still standing in the village of Arqua, Italy, famous as the home of Petrarch during his last years. There

he was found dead in his library on July 19th, 1374. The tomb of the poet — a simple monument of red marble — may be seen in the churchyard of the village.

The following is an almost literal translation of his epitaph:

" THIS STONE COVERS THE COLD BONES OF FRANCIS PETRARCH. VIRGIN MOTHER, RECEIVE HIS SOUL ; O THOU SON OF THE VIRGIN, HAVE MERCY; AND MAY [HIS SOUL], WEARY WITH EARTH, NOW FIND REPOSE IN THE CITADEL OF HEAVEN.''

Petrified City. Ishmonie, a ruined city in Upper Egypt, is popularly so called because it contains a vast number of statues of human beings and animals which, according to tradition, were originally alive and were subsequently changed into stone. They maintain, so the superstitious declare, the same attitudes and postures that were assumed by them at the time of their miraculous change. Reference is first made to this city in Kircher's *Mundus Subterraneus* (1664).

Pétroleuses. The name given, during the Paris Commune of 1871, to those women charged with the crime of helping to set fire to the public buildings of the city by pouring petroleum on them. Many of these female incendiaries were shot. The Palais des Tuileries, the Hôtel de Ville, and other historic edifices were destroyed in this manner.

Petronius. See *Arbiter Elegantiæ.*

Petrossky Palace. A small palace near the city of Moscow, Russia, founded by the Empress Elizabeth (1741–1762). It is surrounded by beautiful gardens, which, on summer evenings, are the favorite resort of the middle classes of the city. Napoleon I retired to the Petrossky Palace during the burning of Moscow; and there, in sight of the blazing city, he dictated the news of the conflagration to France.

Phædo. The title of a celebrated dialogue of Plato (429–347 B.C.), setting forth the views of Socrates on the immortality of the soul. It takes the form of a conversation between Socrates and his friends on the last day of the philosopher's life, and presents his arguments for a belief in immortality. The *Phædo* closes with a touching description of the last hours of Socrates. Also written *Phædon*. See *Phædon*.

" I did not feel the pity which it was natural I should feel at the death of a friend : on the contrary, he seemed to me perfectly happy as I gazed on him and listened to him : so calm and dignified was his bearing. And I thought that he only left this world under the protection of the gods, who destined him to a more than mortal felicity in the next."—*Phædo.*

Phædon. A dialogue on the immortality of the soul by Moses Mendelssohn (1729–1786). It appeared in 1767, was received with great favor, and was translated into the principal European languages. It bears a striking resemblance to the *Phædo* of Plato, from which it is in part taken. See *Phædo.*

" The *Phædon* of the latter [Mendelssohn], in its chaste precision and simplicity of style, may almost remind us of Xenophon : Socrates, to our minds, has spoken in no modern language, so like Socrates, as here, by the lips of this wise and cultivated Jew."—*Carlyle.*

Phaëthon. The son of Helios (the Sun) who, being entrusted with his father's chariot for a single day, lost control of the fiery steeds and almost set the earth on fire. For this presumptuous conduct Zeus smote Phaëthon with a thunderbolt, and flung his body down into the river Eridanus, or Po. His sisters, the Heliades, or Phaëthontiades, who had yoked the horses to the car, were changed into poplars and their tears into amber. Also written *Phaëton.*

Phalanx. An ancient Greek formation for heavy infantry, consisting of 8000 men—in parallel columns, standing close one behind the other, with spears one crossing another, and shields united. In the Lacedæmonian, or Spartan, phalanx, the men stood four, six, and more often eight deep, while in the Macedonian phalanx (introduced by Philip of Macedon about 360 B.C.) the men stood sixteen deep. See *Legion ; Macedonian Phalanx.*

Pharaoh. A word used to denote any one of the ancient kings of Egypt. It occurs in the *Old Testament* as a proper name, without the article, and refers to the monarch ruling at the time. The name is popularly used to mean either the king that befriended Joseph, or the dynasty under which occurred the oppression of the Israelites and their subsequent departure from Egypt.

Pharisees. An ancient Jewish sect, which dates as a distinct body from about 160 B.C. The Pharisees believed that God had revealed to Moses an oral Law (*Masorah*), which supplemented the written Law, and taught the existence of life after death and the resurrection from the dead. The Pharisees derived their name from the Hebrew *perûshim* (*separated*), because they set themselves apart and pretended to a greater degree of holiness than the rest of the Jews. They paid great attention to forms and ceremonies, inculcated the strictest observance of all religious duties, and placed great reliance in fasting, ablutions, and long prayers. According to the *Talmud* there were seven classes of Pharisees. See *Sadducees.*

Pharos of Alexandria. A famous lighthouse on the island of Pharos at the mouth of the harbor of Alexandria, commenced by Sostratus of Cnidus in 298 B.C., and completed under Ptolemy Philadelphus (283–247) about 283 B.C. It consisted of a white marble column, 550 feet in height, on the top of which fires were kept constantly burning. The cost of this structure was 800 talents, which is equivalent to $850,-000, if Attic, or $1,700,000, if Alexandrian. The Pharos of Alexandria has always been included among the " Seven Wonders of the World."

Pharsalia, Battle of. A famous battle fought at Pharsalia in Thessaly, on August 9th, 48 B.C., between the forces of Julius Cæsar and those of Cneius Pompey. It resulted in a memorable victory for the former, and secured for him the mastery of the Roman world. The battle of Pharsalia is one of the most important in Roman history, since from it dates the virtual establishment of the Empire.

Phi Beta Kappa (*Φ B K*). A famous college fraternity in the United States, and the oldest of the Greek-letter societies,—founded at William and Mary College, Virginia, in 1776, and at present composed of fifty different chapters. It was originally a secret organization ; but of late years its innocent mysteries have become open secrets. Meetings are held at the various colleges at Commencement times, when those students composing the first third of the graduating classes are elected members. The total membership, at the present time, is estimated at over 6000. The name of the society is derived from the initial letters of its motto, which is said to be *Φιλοσοφία Βίου Κυβερνήτης* (PHILOSOPHY IS THE GUIDE OF LIFE).

Phigalian Marbles. A collection of twenty-three marble bas-reliefs, originally forming part of the frieze of the temple of Apollo Epicurius at Phigalia, in Arcadia. They are said to be works of the earlier school of Phidias, and represent contests of the Centaurs and Lapithæ and of the Amazons and Greeks. The Phigalian marbles were purchased for the British Museum by the Prince Regent (afterwards George IV), in 1815.

Philadelphia Lawyer. " ' That beats a Philadelphia lawyer.' ' He knows as much as a Philadelphia lawyer.' These are common sayings, whence it is to be inferred that the bar of the Quaker City are distinguished for their learning and shrewdness."—Bartlett's *Dictionary of Americanisms*.

Philippe Égalité. See *Égalité*.

Philippi, Battle of. A desperate conflict waged at Philippi, in Thrace, in 42 B.C., between the army of Mark Antony and Octavius Cæsar and the republican forces commanded by Brutus and Cassius. The levies of the conspirators were signally defeated in two successive engagements, whereupon Brutus and Cassius — believing the cause of the Republic forever lost — committed suicide. Octavius and Antony divided the Roman world between them,—the former taking the West, and the latter the East. To Lepidus, the third triumvir, was given Africa ; but he was soon after deprived of his possessions.

Philippics. A term originally applied to the three famous orations delivered by Demosthenes against Philip of Macedon, and, later, to the fourteen orations of Cicero against Mark Antony. The word is now used to denote any severe or violent invective, whether spoken or written.

Philippine Islands. So named by Ferdinand Magellan, the famous navigator, in 1521, in honor of Philip II (1555–1598) of Spain.

Philistines. An ancient warlike people, who inhabited the seacoast of Canaan from Joppa to Gaza. They were constantly at war with the Israelites ; but maintained their independence until finally subdued by David (1045–1015), King of Israel, in 1040 B.C. About 63 B.C. they were conquered by Pompey, the Roman general, and made part of the province of Syria. The word " Palestine " denotes, in the *Old Testament*, " the land of the Philistines."

Heine and others of the liberal party in Germany in 1830 applied the term "Philistines" to the opponents of progress; and later (in 1867 *et seq.*) Matthew Arnold used the same expression to designate the opponents of culture and refinement among the upper-middle classes.

Phillips Academy.

(1) A famous college preparatory-school at Exeter, New Hampshire, founded by John Phillips in 1781. It has ten instructors and more than 300 students, and has enrolled among its former pupils the names of Daniel Webster, George Bancroft, and Edward Everett. Its list of graduates — more than 6000 in number — includes the names of many men distinguished in professional and mercantile life.

(2) A well-known college preparatory-school at Andover, Massachusetts, founded and endowed by the Phillips family in 1778.

Philosopher, The.

(1) An appellation conferred by Justin Martyr on Marcus Aurelius Antoninus (161-180 A.D.), the Roman Emperor, in allusion to his wisdom, learning, and virtue.

(2) A surname given to Porphyry (233-304 A.D.), the Neo-Platonist and opponent of Christianity.

(3) A title bestowed upon Leo VI (886-911 A.D.), Emperor of the East and author of several moral treatises.

Philosopher of Chelsea. See *Chelsea Philosopher.*

Philosopher of Ferney. See *Ferney, Patriarch of.*

Philosopher of Malmesbury. An

epithet conferred by Lord Byron upon Thomas Hobbes (1588-1679), the celebrated English philosopher, in allusion to the place of his birth.

"In short, upon that subject I've some qualms very
Like those of the *philosopher of Malmesbury.*"

Don Juan, xv, 96.

Philosopher of Sans-Souci. An

appellation bestowed upon Frederick the Great (1740-1786), King of Prussia, in allusion to his devotion to literature. He left many and various works, which were published in 23 volumes, in 1790. Voltaire called him the "Philosopher-Prince," the "Solomon and Alexander of the North," the "Marcus Aurelius of Potsdam," the "Trajan and Pliny Combined," etc. See *Potsdam ; Sans-Souci.*

Philosopher's Stone. A universal

solvent, vainly sought by the alchemists of old for the purpose of changing the baser metals into gold and silver. See *Elixir of Life.*

"Their [the alchemists'] conception was that gold was the perfect metal, and that all other metals were so many removes or deflections from gold, in consequence of arrestment, corruption, or other accidents. Now, though gold, being simply perfect, could not, if mixed with the imperfect, perfect the latter, but would rather share its imperfections ; yet, were a substance found many times more perfect than gold, it might well perfect the imperfect. Such a substance would be composed of purest mercury and sulphur, commingled into a solid mass, and matured by wisdom and artificial fire into possibly a thousand thousand times the perfection of the simple body. This was the *philosopher's stone* which so many devotees of alchemy in the middle ages toiled in vain to fabricate." —*Chambers's Encyclopædia.*

Phlegethon. In classic mythology,

one of the five rivers of the lower world,—the other four being Acheron, Cocytus, Lethe, and Styx. It rolled with waves of flame, and nothing grew upon its scorched and dreary shores.

" . . . fierce *Phlegethon,*
Whose waves of torrent fire inflame with rage."

Paradise Lost, ii, 580-581.

Phlogiston (*Gr.* φλογιστόν, *set on*

fire). An imaginary substance which, by union with a body, rendered it combustible, and by disengagement from a body caused its combustion. To explain the fact that bodies became heavier when burned, it was assumed that phlogiston conferred upon them the so-called principle of "Levity." This theory was first proposed by Stahl (1660–1734) in 1697, and was firmly held by all chemists until the time of Lavoisier (1743–1794) who, in 1789, by means of a series of experiments, proved that the combustion of bodies results, not from the disengagement of phlogiston, but from the chemical union of oxygen with them. This discovery overthrew the phlogistic theory, and established that of oxygenation in its stead. See *Oxygen*.

Phœbe. In classic myth, a surname of Artemis (Diana), in her capacity as goddess of the moon. See *Phœbus*.

Phœbus. In classic myth, a surname of Apollo, in his capacity as sun-god. The word is derived from the Greek φοῖβος (*the bright or pure*). See *Phœbe*.

Phœnician Stone. A famous imposture, in the shape of a stone, bearing a bilingual inscription in Greek and in pretended Phœnician, and purporting to be a genuine tablet of the 5th century B.C. In 1824, the stone was sent from Malta to Raoul Rochette, curator of the Cabinet of Antiquities at Paris, and was declared to be genuine by him. A copy of the inscription was sent to several of the learned men of Europe for decipherment and translation. Among the savants imposed upon, in addition to Rochette, may be mentioned Gesenius of Halle and Hamaker of Leyden. The "Phœnician Stone" was afterwards proved to be simply a base hoax.

Phœnix. A mythical bird of ancient Egypt, which, according to Herodotus, visited Heliopolis once in every 500 years after its father's death, and buried the body in the temple of Helios. This it accomplished by placing the remains in an egg, or case, of myrrh, and then closing up the egg. It is further related that the Phœnix, when about to die, withdrew into Arabia, and there built for itself a nest, to which it imparted the power of generation, and from which a new and young Phœnix afterwards arose. As soon as the latter was grown, like its predecessor it proceeded into Egypt, and burned and buried its father. According, however, to the popularly known account, the Phœnix burned *itself*, and a new Phœnix arose from the ashes. Another received version is that a worm crawled out of the body of the dead Phœnix, and became the new one. The bird was represented as resembling an eagle, with feathers partly red and partly golden.

" I have re-created France ; and from the ashes
Of the old feudal and decrepit carcase,
Civilization on her luminous wings
Soars, *phœnix*-like, to Jove ! "
        Richelieu, i, 2.

Phœnix and Turtle. The title of a poem attributed to William Shakespeare (1565–1616). It first appeared in Chester's *Love Martyr* in 1601, and is supposed to have been written shortly before that date.

"There is no other external evidence that these verses are Shakespeare's than their appearance with his signature in a collection of his poems published in London while he was living there in the height of his reputation."—*Richard Grant White*.

Phœnix Park. A fine public pleasure-ground in Dublin, Ireland, covering an area of nearly 2000 acres. It contains many superb trees and fine drives and walks, and is well stocked with fallow deer. The principal object of interest in the park is the Wellington Testimonial,— a massive obelisk placed on a granite pedestal, on which are inscribed the names of the victories won by England's famous warrior. The monument is about 200 feet high, and cost $100,000. The word " Phœnix "— as here used — is a corruption of the Gaelic *Fion-uisc* (*fair water*), a name applied to a chalybeate spring at one time visited as a spa. See *Phœnix Park Murder*.

Phœnix Park Murder. An infamous crime committed in Phœnix

Park, Dublin, on May 6th, 1882, whereby Lord Frederick Cavendish, newly appointed Secretary for Ireland, and Thomas A. Burke, permanent Under-Secretary, were fatally stabbed by four men known as " Invincibles." The murderers belonged to a gang of miscreants, secretly banded together for the commission of such crimes. One of their number, named Carey, gave queen's evidence, and revealed the fact that 21 persons were implicated in the plot. Several of these individuals were found guilty and executed. It was afterwards proved that the leaders of the Home Rule movement had nothing to do with the murder. See *Phœnix Park*.

Phonetic Spelling. Any system of spelling in which the articulate sounds of a language are represented by an unvarying set of symbols,—the fundamental principles being (1) that each sound shall have a separate symbol and (2) that no symbol shall be used for any sound except its own. The illogical nature of English spelling has long been realized by the ablest linguistic scholars in England and America, and the warmest sympathy with its reform has been manifested by them.

On this subject the late Professor Max-Müller of Oxford said:

" The question, then, that will have to be answered sooner or later is this ; ' Can this unsystematic system of spelling English be allowed to go on forever?' Is every English child, as compared with other children, to be mulcted in two or three years of his life in order to learn it? Are the lower classes to go through school without learning to read and write their own language intelligently? And is the country to pay millions every year for this utter failure of national education? I do not believe or think that such a state of things will be allowed to go on forever, particularly as a remedy is at hand. I consider that the sooner it is taken in hand the better. There is a motive power behind these phonetic reformers which Archbishop Trench has hardly taken into account. I mean the misery endured by millions of children at schools, who might learn in one year, and with real advantage to themselves, what they now require four or five years to learn, and seldom succeed in learning after all."

Phonograph. An instrument for reproducing vocal and other sounds, invented by Thomas A. Edison in 1877, and greatly improved by him in 1888 by the substitution of wax for tinfoil in the sheet for receiving impressions.

"Linear indentations are made by a pin pressed by the voice in speaking or singing in a sheet of tin foil, fixed on a revolving cylinder, and from these casts may be taken. When these are placed upon another cylinder revolving before a telephone, the sounds may be reproduced."—Harper's *Book of Facts*.

Phonography. Although systems of shorthand had been in use since the days of Greece and Rome, it was not until 1837 that a method, based entirely upon phonetic principles, made its appearance. This was known as the " Phonography " of Isaac Pitman, and soon became deservedly popular. Up to 1890, this indefatigable reformer had issued 150 different shorthand books ; and his *Phonographic Teacher* was selling at that time at the rate of 150,000 copies annually. From the date of issue the total sale of the volume amounted to 1,370,000. It is estimated that as many as 80 different systems had appeared by 1850.

"About 95 per cent. of reporters in England, the colonies, and America use Pitman's system, which has been adapted to the Welsh, French, German, Italian, Spanish, Dutch, Japanese, and Malagasy languages. It is estimated that its practitioners all over the world number above half a million."—*Chambers's Encyclopædia*.

Graham's System (1858) and Munson's System (1866) are founded on Pitman's.

Phosphorus. The name given by the Greeks to the planet Venus, when it was the morning star. The word means " light-bearer." See *Hesperus*.

Photosphere. The name given to the luminous envelope surrounding the solid or liquid nucleus of the sun.

It consists of incandescent gases, and is the seat of solar light and heat. According to Wilson's theory, the so-called sun-spots are simply rents in the photosphere (made by powerful upward currents), revealing the dark body of the sun as a nucleus at the centre. The more modern theory, however, is that the spots are cavities in the photosphere, produced by the pressure of vast descending masses of vapor. Although these spots sometimes last for months, they often form and vanish in a few days or even hours.

As viewed with a telescope of low power, the photosphere has an apparently smooth surface ; but when examined with an instrument of higher power it presents a granulated structure,—resembling a gravel heap, seen from a little distance. See *Chromosphere.*

Phrenology. A system of psychology founded by Dr. Gall (1758–1828), a German physician, and afterwards expounded and developed by his pupil, Dr. Spurzheim. It is based on four fundamental principles :

(1) The brain is the organ of the mind.

(2) The mental faculties can be analyzed and reduced to a definite number.

(3) Different parts of the brain are appropriated to these different mental faculties.

(4) Capacity and character are indicated by the external form of the skull.

According to phrenologists, the mind is commonly divided into 35 faculties, associated with a corresponding number of areas on the cranium. These faculties are as follows :

(1) Amativeness.
(2) Philoprogenitiveness.
(3) Inhibitiveness or Concentrativeness.
(4) Adhesiveness.
(5) Combativeness.
(6) Destructiveness and Alimentiveness.
(7) Secretiveness.
(8) Acquisitiveness.
(9) Constructiveness.
(10) Self-esteem.
(11) Love of approbation.
(12) Cautiousness.
(13) Benevolence.
(14) Veneration.
(15) Firmness.
(16) Conscientiousness.
(17) Hope.
(18) Wonder.
(19) Ideality.
(20) Wit.
(21) Imitation.
(22) Individuality.
(23) Form.
(24) Size.
(25) Weight.
(26) Coloring.
(27) Locality.
(28) Number.
(29) Order.
(30) Eventuality.
(31) Time.
(32) Tune.
(33) Language.
(34) Comparison.
(35) Causality.

See *Physiognomy.*

" But anatomy and physiology have proved that the exterior surface of the brain is by no means an index to mental processes or characters ; still less is such a guide furnished by the minute variations in the shape of the skull, which in a general way correspond to the exterior surface of the brain. Size of brain does not correspond directly to mental power or activity ; nor is the superficial conformation the most important feature of the brain. Parts of the external surface are known to have functions other than those attributed by phrenologists ; the frontal sinus of the skull is sometimes large enough to occupy the region allotted to four or five phrenological organs ; and there are many osteological differences in the various bones of the skull which obviously have nothing to do with brain-functions or mental processes."—*Chambers's Encyclopædia.*

Phryne. A famous Bœotian courtesan of the 4th century B.C., celebrated for her beauty and wealth. She offered to rebuild the walls of Thebes, if she might be allowed to place upon them the following inscription : ALEXANDER DESTROYED THEM, BUT PHRYNE, THE HETÆRA, REBUILT THEM. Phryne numbered among her admirers many of the most famous men of the day ; while her beauty of face and form gave rise to some of the noblest works of art. She posed for the celebrated picture of Apelles, known as the *Venus Anadyomene*, and for the equally renowned statue of Praxiteles, entitled the *Venus of Cnidus*. See *Venus Anadyomene ; Venus of Cnidus*.

Physiognomy. A pseudo-science, which professes to judge character from the external appearance, especially from the countenance. It is of considerable antiquity, having originated with Aristotle (384–322 B.C.). In modern times, Lavater (1741–1801) attempted to raise physiognomy to the dignity of a science, but without success. His famous work, entitled *Physiognomic Fragments for the Promotion of the Knowledge and Love of Mankind* was published in 1775–1778. In Darwin's *Expression of the Emotions in Men and Animals* (1872) may be found the first successful attempt to place physiognomy on a firm scientific basis. See *Phrenology*.

Pianofortes. The invention of the pianoforte is properly accredited to Bartolomeo Cristofali (or Cristofori) of Padua, Italy, whose first instrument appeared in 1714. Other claimants for this honor are J. C. Schröter, a German, and Marius, a Frenchman. The pianoforte was first introduced into England about 1766. The name is derived from two Italian words meaning *soft* and *loud*, respectively, and is given to this instrument because the notes (which are produced by the action of hammers on wires) may be increased or diminished in loudness at will.

Pibroch. A kind of bagpipe-music heard among the Highlands of Scotland. It is chiefly of a martial charac-

ter, and includes marches, dirges, etc. The earliest mention of the bagpipe in war is in 1594, at the battle of Glenlivet.

Picayune Butler. So General Benjamin F. Butler (1818–1893) was called by the inhabitants of New Orleans, during his military occupation of that city at the time of the American Civil War.

Piccadilly. A noted street in London, about a mile in length, extending from Haymarket to Hyde Park Corner. It derives its name from Piccadilla Hall, where a certain kind of lace—called *piccadilly*—much in vogue during the reign of Queen Elizabeth (1558–1603), was sold.

Pichegru's Conspiracy. See *Georges's Conspiracy*.

Pickwickian Sense. A humorous phrase sometimes used to designate some peculiar or technical mode of expression. It is found in Dickens's *Pickwick Papers*, where it is used both by Mr. Blotton and Mr. Pickwick to explain away the unparliamentary and personal language used by them. See *Pickwick Papers*, Chapter I.

Picnic. "This is a corruption of the French *pique-nique*. In its native country it signifies an entertainment in which each person contributes to the general supply of the table. It is not in France, as with us, confined to out-of-door entertainments. The 'Literary World,' August 1, 1879, gives the following as an extract from a French newspaper : ' Pique-nique of Saint Henri. The list of subscribers at fifteen francs a head will be closed at four o'clock. Evening dress and white ties are *de rigueur*. They will sit down to table at eight o'clock.' "—Edwards's *Words, Facts, and Phrases*.

Picts and Scots. Two warlike tribes of Celtic origin, formerly inhabiting Scotland, whose destructive inroads into Southern Britain were a continual source of alarm to the inhabitants during the 4th and 5th centuries A. D. They were several times driven back, but after the withdrawal of the Roman forces from the island, these northern barbarians renewed their incursions with increased vigor. Finally, the Britons called to their assistance the Saxons, Angles, and Jutes; and these Teutonic peoples —after repelling the Picts and Scots— finally succeeded in establishing themselves in the country which they were summoned to defend. See *Hengist and Horsa*.

Pictured Rocks. A natural curiosity, consisting of a series of sandstone cliffs, extending for about seven miles along the southern shore of Lake Superior. They rise vertically from the water's edge to a height varying from 50 to 300 feet, and present a remarkable exhibition of the eroding power of water, combined with brilliant hues imparted by certain minerals.

"The *Pictured Rocks* are a series of seven miles of sandstone cliffs, rising 300 feet sheer from the waters of Lake Superior, worn by the waves into many strange and fantastic shapes, as of castles, towers, chapels, gates, sails, and profiles, in vivid tints of gray and green, amber and vermilion, blue and yellow, and extending eastward from the beautiful Munising harbor to the desolate yellow sand-hills of the Sables, 30 miles west of Sault Ste. Marie. At one point the Silver Cascade plunges 175 feet sheer over the cliffs, and scores of other waterfalls gem the lonely walls of rock. This is in the heart of Hiawatha's country, and the wigwam of Nokomis stood on the site of the half-ruined and deserted port of Munising, facing the Big Sea Water."—King's *Handbook of the United States*.

"Westward by the Big-Sea-Water,
Came unto the rocky headlands,
To the *Pictured Rocks* of sandstone
Looking over lake and landscape."
Longfellow's *Hiawatha*, xvii.

Pidgin-English (*probably a corruption of Business-English*). A grotesque jargon of English intermingled with Chinese, Malay, and Portuguese words, —employed in the commercial cities of China and the Far East to facilitate the business intercourse of natives and foreigners. This extraordinary dialect is passing away, owing to the increasing number of Chinese that know English and of Englishmen that are familiar with Chinese.

"*Pidgin-English* has nothing to do with pigeons. The word 'pidgin' is simply the Chinese pronunciation of the word 'business.'"—*New York Tribune.*

Pied Piper of Hamelin. The hero of a celebrated old German legend, whose deeds are narrated by Robert Browning, in his poem of the same name. According to the story, he was a fantastically attired musician, who appeared at Hamel, in the country of Brunswick, and offered, in return for a certain sum of money, to rid the town of rats with which it was infested. After performing his part of the bargain, the money was denied him ; whereupon he blew upon his pipe, and was at once followed by the children of the town, 130 in number, to a cave near at hand, the entrance to which immediately closed upon them and imprisoned them forever.

"To blow the pipe his lips he wrinkled,
And green and blue his sharp eyes twinkled . . .
And ere there are three notes his pipe had uttered . . .
Out of the houses rats came tumbling—
Great rats, small rats, lean rats, brawny rats,
Brown rats, black rats, gray rats, tawny rats—
And step by step they followed him dancing,
Till they came to the river Weser. . . ."
Robert Browning.

Pietà, La. A famous marble group by Michael Angelo (1475-1564), representing the Virgin Mary, with the body of the dead Christ resting upon her knees. The work was commissioned by the Cardinal of San Dionigi, and was completed by the sculptor at the age of 24, who by this production quickly passed from the rank of an esteemed artist to the position of foremost sculptor of the day. The group of *La Pietà* is at present in one of the chapels of St. Peter's at Rome, but is so unfortunately placed that a satisfactory view of it cannot be obtained.

Pigott Diamond. A celebrated diamond, weighing 49 carats, brought to England from India by Lord Pigott. Before cutting, it weighed 82¼ carats. In 1801 this diamond was disposed of in a lottery, for £30,000 ; and in 1818 it passed into the hands of Messrs. Rundell and Bridge. Its present estimated value is £40,000.

Pig Tails. A nickname bestowed upon the Chinese, in allusion to their braided queues.

Pike's Peak. A lofty peak (14,147 feet) of the Rocky Mountains, six miles west of Colorado Springs, Colorado. The summit is reached by a bridle-path, a carriage-road, and an inclined railway having a length of 8¾ miles and a total ascent of 7,500 feet.

Pilgrims. A body of English Nonconformists, who emigrated from Holland (whither they had fled to escape persecution), and settled Plymouth Colony in 1620. They are to be distinguished from the " Puritans," a body of non-separatist religious reformers from England, who, in 1629–1630, founded and settled the Massachusetts Bay Colony. These two colonies remained independent of each other for many years, but were finally united in 1692, under the name of Massachusetts. See *Mayflower; Puritans.*

Pilgrim's Progress. A famous allegory, in two parts, by John Bunyan (1628–1688). The first part describes the journey of Christian from this world to that which is to come, while the second deals with the setting out of his wife and children and their safe arrival at the Celestial Country. The work passed through ten editions between 1678 and 1685. It has been translated into almost every language

38

of Europe, and still enjoys a marvellous popularity. A rare first edition of *Pilgrim's Progress* was sold in London on May 9th, 1901, at the record price of 1475 guineas. The book measures 6 x 3¾ inches, and was printed in Cornhill in 1678. Only five copies are known to be in existence.

"In one particular and most difficult department of writing, Allegory, he [Bunyan] stands unrivalled, not only in English, but in all literature. Shakespeare is not. so clearly the first of Dramatists, as is John Bunyan the Prince of Dreamers. His Dream of the *Pilgrim's Progress* is confessedly the greatest of all Allegories, ancient or modern ; it has been translated into almost every language that has a religious literature of its own, and it probably has been more read, and been instrumental of more spiritual good, than any other book, the Bible only excepted. Bunyan was a Baptist; but he is a favorite among all Protestant denominations."—Hart's *Manual of English Literature.*

"After the Bible, the book most widely read in England is the *Pilgrim's Progress,* by John Bunyan. The reason is, that the basis of Protestantism is salvation by grace, and that no writer has equalled Bunyan in making this doctrine understood."—Taine's *English Literature.*

Pillar-Saints. A class of religious ascetics — principally Syrian — in the early Christian Church, who mortified the flesh by dwelling upon pillars in the open air. Their founder, Simeon Stylites (390–460), is said to have lived in this manner for thirty years. Pillar-saints were found in the East as late as the 12th century, but after that time they ceased to exist. They were called " Stylites " by the Greeks.

Pillars of Heaven. A term used by the ancient inhabitants of Africa to denote the Atlas Mountains, because they were supposed to support the sky. The myth of Atlas, bearing the heavens upon his head and shoulders, is said to have sprung from the notion that lofty mountains support the celestial vault. See *Atlas.*

Pillars of Hercules. The name given by the ancient Greeks and

Romans to Calpe and Abyla, two mountains, standing—the one in Europe and the other in Africa—on opposite sides of the strait connecting the Mediterranean Sea and the Atlantic Ocean. They are known respectively, at the present day, as the Rock of Gibraltar and Jebel Zatout.

According to tradition, these mountains were raised by Hercules, while on his journey in search of the oxen of Geryones. They were long regarded by the ancients as marking the extreme western limit of the habitable world. See *Atlantis; Atlas; Gibraltar.*

Pilpay, Fables of. A collection of fables attributed to Pilpay (Pilpai or Bidpai), a Brahman gymnosophist, of whom little is known. They were originally written in Sanskrit (several centuries before the Christian era), and were afterwards translated into Arabic, and, subsequently, into most of the languages of Europe. The *Hitopadêsa (i. e., Friendly Counsel)*, a Sanskrit collection, was translated into English by Wilkins in 1787. The *Fables of Pilpay* were freely drawn upon by La Fontaine and other European fabulists. See *Æsop, Fables of; Lokman, Fables of.*

Pinakothek. The name given to two celebrated galleries of paintings in Munich, Bavaria,—known respectively as the *Old Pinakothek* and the *New Pinakothek.* The *Old Pinakothek* (completed by Klenze in 1836) is a magnificent sandstone structure, 520 feet long, and contains a superb collection of 1500 paintings,—the works of old masters. The *New Pinakothek* is a repository of modern paintings and antiquities. The word is derived from the Greek πίναξ (*picture*), θήκη (*repository*). See *Glyptothek.*

Pinchbeck. An alloy, consisting of 75 per cent. of copper and 25 per cent. of zinc, much used in the early part of the 19th century as a cheap substitute for gold. It derives its name from its inventor, Christopher Pinchbeck, a London clockmaker, who died in 1732. The word is figuratively used to denote anything pretentious or spurious.

Pincian Hill. A famous elevation in the city of Rome, forming a pleasure-ground much resorted to by the fashionable people of the city. It consists of a park covering a few acres, laid out in gardens, walks, and drives, and commands a superb prospect on every side. In the centre of the grounds stands the Obelisk of the Pincian. It is not one of the celebrated "Seven Hills of Rome." See *Seven Hills of Rome.*

Pine-Tree Flag. A flag carried by the first war-vessels commissioned by Washington at the commencement of the Revolution. It originated with the Massachusetts Colony, and consisted of a white field with a pine-tree in the centre, and the motto, APPEAL TO HEAVEN.

Pine-Tree Money. Silver money coined in Boston, Massachusetts, during the 17th century. The coins were in denominations of three, six, and twelve pence, and received their names from the rude figure of a pine-tree on the obverse side.

Pine-Tree State. A name popularly given to the State of Maine, in allusion to the extensive forests of pine-trees that cover the central and northern portions of the State.

Pin-Money. Originally, an allowance made by a husband to his wife for the purchase of pins, which, in early days, were so expensive that only the wealthy could afford to use them. The makers of pins were allowed to sell them only on January 1st and 2nd; and, in consequence, on those days the ladies provided with "pin-money" flocked to the shops to purchase them. The expression is used, at the present day, to denote an allowance to wife, daughter, or sister, for personal expenses. See *Pins.*

Pins. Brass pins were brought from France into England in 1540, and were first used by Catherine Howard, wife of Henry VIII (1509–1547). They were first made in England in 1543. In 1824, Wright's machine for making solid-headed pins (an American invention) was introduced into England. About 1500 tons of iron and brass wire are annually made into pins in that country. The value of the yearly production in the United States is estimated at over $1,000,000.

"It is quite an error to suppose that pins were invented in the reign of François I., and introduced into England by Catharine Howard, the fifth wife of Henry VIII. In 1347, just two hundred years before the death of François, 12,000 pins were delivered from the royal wardrobe for the use of the princess Joan, and in 1400 (more than a century before François ascended the throne) the duchess of Orléans purchased of Jehan le Breconnier, *espinglier,* of Paris, several thousand long and short pins, besides five hundred *de la façon d'Angleterre.* So that pins were not only manufactured in England, but were of high repute even in the reign of Henry IV."—Brewer's *Dictionary of Phrase and Fable.*

Pinta. One of the three vessels with which Christopher Columbus set sail for America from Palos, Spain, on August 3rd, 1492. Her commander was Alonzo Pinzon, a distinguished Spanish navigator. See *Niña ; Santa Maria.*

Pipe-Laying. An expression used, in political parlance, to denote any underhand method of procedure whereby party schemes are helped forward. The phrase is said to be derived from certain letters brought forward in New York by the Democrats many years ago, to prove an attempt on the part of the Whigs to colonize voters in that city. In those letters, the number of men engaged to visit New York and to vote were spoken of as so many yards of "pipe,"—the work of pipe-laying for the introduction of Croton water being at that time under way.

Pipe-of-Peace. See *Calumet.*

Piræus. The harbor of ancient and modern Athens, five miles distant from the city,—with which it was connected, in olden days, by the famous Long Walls. The Piræus was planned by Themistocles, laid out by Hippodamus of Miletus, and built by Pericles. It was at one time a commercial port, as well as a town of considerable importance ; but, as a result of the destruction of its arsenal and fortifications by Sulla in 86 B.C., it gradually fell into decay. The Piræus of the present day is connected with the city of Athens by a railway, 5½ miles long, built in 1869. The town is known as the Manchester of Greece, on account of its growth as a commercial centre. See *Long Walls.*

Pisa, Leaning Tower of. See *Leaning Tower of Pisa.*

Pitcairn's Island. A solitary island in the South Pacific Ocean—measuring 2½ miles by 1 mile—colonized by mutineers from the ship *Bounty* in 1789. The colony was unknown to the world until 1814, when it was accidentally discovered by the captain of an English vessel. The island was annexed to Great Britain in 1839; but eventually proved too small for the support of the colony, which had rapidly increased in numbers. Accordingly, in 1856, about 200 of the islanders were transferred to Norfolk Island, which had been previously prepared for their reception. The inhabitants of Pitcairn's Island—numbering 126 in 1890—bear an excellent reputation for uprightness and morality. See *Bounty.*

Pitt Diamond. A celebrated diamond—one of the most perfect known—found in 1701 by a slave in the Parteal mines in India. After passing through several hands, it was purchased for £20,400 by Thomas Pitt (grandfather of the famous Earl of Chatham), from which circumstance it derives its name. The original weight of this diamond was 410 carats; but by judicious cutting this was reduced to 136¾. In 1717, the stone was sold by Pitt for £135,000 to the Duke of Orleans — then Regent of France; on which account, it is often called the "Regent" diamond. It adorned the hilt of the first Napoleon's sword of state, and afterwards passed into the possession of the King of Prussia. It is now in Paris, among the national jewels of France, and is valued at £480,000 ($2,400,000).

Pitti Palace. A superb structure in Florence, Italy, containing one of the finest collections of paintings in the world. It was commenced in 1435 by Lucca Pitti (an opponent of the Medici family), and was not completed until the following century. In 1530, the building passed into the hands of the Medici family, and it is to their munificence that we owe the collection of pictures that grace its walls. See *Ponte Vecchio; Uffizi Palace.*

"The *Pitti Palace*, a splendid structure, was commenced for himself, by Lucca Pitti, a vain, weak man, elevated to great power by a sudden turn of political fortune. It finally passed by purchase, and while yet unfinished, into the possession of the rival family of the Medici, and furnishes an instructive commentary upon the saying, that fools build houses and wise men buy them. Johnson might have found, in the varying fortunes of the founder of this palace, a vivid illustration of the vanity of human wishes. . . . Here are nearly five hundred pictures, many of them of the highest merit, and very few that are not good. No other collection of paintings which I have seen approaches it in excellence, with the single exception of the Dresden Gallery; and between these two it would not be easy to award the palm of superiority."—Hillard's *Six Months in Italy.*

Pittsburg Landing, Battle of. See *Shiloh, Battle of.*

Place de Grève. The name formerly given to the Place de l'Hôtel de Ville, Paris, which, prior to the French Revolution (1789), was the place of public execution. The Huguenot chiefs, Briquemont and Cavagnes were hanged there in 1572, by order of Catherine de' Medici; and there Comte Montgomery was executed for having accidentally caused the death of Henry II (1547–1559). Ravaillac, the assassin of Henry IV; Cartouche, the highwayman; and Damiens, who attempted to kill Louis XV, paid the penalty of their crimes on the Place de Grève.

Place de la Bastille. A public square in Paris, occupying the site of the Bastille, which was demolished in 1789—at the beginning of the French Revolution. In its centre stands the famous Column of July, dedicated in 1840 to the memory of those that fell in the Revolution of July, 1830. The Place de la Bastille marks the termination of the old boulevards, and the beginning of the Faubourg St. Antoine. It was the scene of fierce fighting during the Revolution of 1848. See *Bastille; Column of July.*

Place de la Concorde. See *Concorde, Place de la.*

Place du Carrousel. A large open space between the palaces of the Louvre and the Tuileries in Paris,— so named from a tournament, or equestrian ball, held there by Louis XIV (1643–1715) in 1662. It is open to traffic, and generally has a lively and animated appearance. Until the beginning of the last century, this space was covered with houses, churches, etc., and was a labyrinth of narrow streets. The work of removing these unsightly structures was commenced by Napoleon I (1804–1814), and continued by Louis Philippe (1830–1848). Napoleon III (1852–1870) completed the work in 1858 at an expense of $8,000,000, and divided the square thus cleared into three parts — the Square du Carrousel, near the Louvre; the Place du Carrousel proper, in the centre ; and the Cour des Tuileries at the western end. At the entrance of the Cour des Tuileries stands the Arc du Carrousel, erected by Napoleon I in 1806. See *Arc du Carrousel.*

Place-Makers' Bible. The name given to a version of the Scriptures, printed in 1561-1562, wherein the words *peace-makers* are rendered *place-makers*. " Blessed are the *place-makers*: for they shall be called the children of God."—*Matthew* v, 9.

Walsh, in his *Handy-Book of Literary Curiosities*, says that this is "a version that should be in great request with practical politicians of all parties."

Place of Wailing. A small, quadrangular area near the Mosque of Omar, in Jerusalem, enclosed by ordinary dwellings on the west and by the ancient wall of Haram on the east. This wall — consisting of several courses of huge stones—is believed by the Jews to be a portion of the court of Solomon's Temple, and the only part of that structure now remaining. For centuries, the descendants of Abraham have repaired to this spot on Fridays and also on other days, to mourn over the calamities that have befallen Israel, and to pray for the coming of the Messiah. In former years they were forced to pay a large sum for this melancholy privilege.

Place Vendôme. An octagonal place in Paris, formerly occupied by the palace of the Duc de Vendôme, son of Henry IV (1589-1610) and Gabrielle d'Estrées. This building was removed by Louis XIV (1643-1715) in 1688, and an open square laid out on its site. The Place Vendôme has been successively known as the Place des Conquêtes, the Place Louis le Grand, and the Place des Piques ; and received its present appellation from Napoleon I (1804-1814). In its centre stands the Column of Vendôme, erected by Napoleon I in 1806-1810, in commemoration of his victories over the Austrians and Russians in 1805. The buildings surrounding the Place Vendôme are in the Corinthian style of architecture, and, although somewhat severe in appearance from their uniformity, still present a general aspect not unpleasing. See *Column of Vendôme.*

Plague of London. See *Great Plague of London.*

Plain. A name given during the French Revolution to the Girondists in the National Convention, because they occupied the lowest benches on the floor of the assembly-hall. See *Montagnards ; Mountain.*

Plantagenet. The name of the royal house that occupied the throne of England from Henry II (1154-1189) to Richard III (1483-1485) inclusive, —a period of 331 years. This word is said to be derived from the *planta genista (the Spanish broom-plant)*,—a sprig of which was adopted as a device by the Earl of Anjou, great-grandfather of Henry II, during a pilgrimage to the Holy Land, and was commonly worn by him in his helmet. According to the story, the Earl chose this emblem for penitential reasons,— having offered himself to be scourged with the stems of the broom-plant in atonement for a murder that he had committed. See *Genista, Planta.*

Platæa, Battle of. A battle fought at Platæa in Bœotia, in 479 B.C., between 300,000 Persians under Mardonius and 110,000 Athenians and Lacedæmonians commanded by Aristides and Pausanias. The Persians were utterly routed and, in the massacre that ensued, scarcely 3000 escaped with their lives. The Greek loss was small. This victory, together with that of Mycale—fought on the same day—put an end to the Persian invasions of Greece.

Plato. The real name of this philosopher was *Aristocles*, after his grandfather ; but he was surnamed *Plato (Gr. πλατύς, broad)*, from the great breadth of his forehead, **or, as some** say, of his shoulders.

"Some writers incline to the opinion that 'Plato' was the epithet of broad-browed; others of broad-shouldered; others, again, that it was expressive of the breadth of his style. This last is absurd. The author of the article *Plato* in the *Penny Cyclopædia* pronounces all the above explanations to be 'idle, as the name of Plato was of common occurrence among the Athenians of that time.' But surely Aristocles was not endowed with this surname of Plato without cause. Unless he derived the name from a relation, he must have derived it from one of the above causes."—Lewes's *Biographical History of Philosophy*.

Plato and the Bees. According to a legend, the infant Plato, while sleeping in his cradle, was visited by a swarm of bees, which settled on his lips, and thus predicted that " honeyed words " would flow from his mouth in after years.

" Even the notions respecting his [Plato's] style are erroneous. It is not the ' poetical ' metaphorical style usually asserted. It has unmistakable beauties, but not the beauties popularly attributed to it. Its immense power is dramatic power. The best dialogues are inimitable scenes of comedy. Character, banter, irony, and animation are there, but scarcely any imagery, and that seldom beautiful."—Lewes's *Biographical History of Philosophy*.

Platonic Love. An expression commonly used to denote a pure, spiritual love—devoid of carnal desire—subsisting between persons of opposite sexes. This kind of affection is believed by many to have been warmly advocated by Plato, hence the name it has received. Lewes, however, in his *Biographical History of Philosophy*, says that this notion is utterly false, and writes as follows:

"The bond which unites the human to the divine is Love. And Love is the longing of the Soul for Beauty ; the inextinguishable desire which like feels for like, which the divinity within us feels for the divinity revealed to us in Beauty. This is the celebrated Platonic Love, which, from having originally meant a communion of two souls, and that in a rigidly dialectical sense, has been degraded to the expression of maudlin sentiment between the sexes. Platonic love meant ideal sympathy ; it now means the love of a sentimental young gentleman for a woman he cannot or will not marry."

Platonic Year. A term used in astronomy to denote the period of time required for the equinoxes to complete their revolution. The duration of this period is estimated at about 26,000 years,—at the expiration of which time the various stars and constellations occupy the same positions, relative to the equinoxes, that they did at the beginning. Tycho Brahe computed the length of the Platonic Year at 25,-816 years ; Ricciolus at 25,920 years ; and Cassini at 24,800 years. Also called the *Great Year*.

Plebeians. The Commons of Rome, who were originally forbidden all political rights. They were, for the most part, poor, and were not allowed to intermarry with the Patricians. They served in the army without pay, were sold into slavery for debt, and could even be cut in pieces for distribution among their creditors. Finding their condition intolerable, the Plebeians, in 494 B.C., seceded to Mons Sacer, near Rome, where they resolved to build a new city ; but this step so alarmed the privileged classes that they granted to the Commons the right of annually choosing, from their own number, two magistrates—called tribunes—with power to protect them against the aggressions of the Patricians. After the lapse of about 200 years, the disabilities of the Plebeians were almost entirely removed; and between the years 356–300 B.C. they secured the dictatorship, the censorship, and the prætorship, as well as the right to be pontiff and augur. Thus, the Roman Republic, after two centuries of existence, finally secured a democratic form of government. See *Patricians*.

Plebiscitum. A term used in ancient Roman history, to denote a law passed by the *comitia tributa* (*assembly of the plebs or commons*), established in 491 B.C. Within recent years the name " plébiscite " has been given to any national decree obtained by an appeal to universal suffrage. Louis Napoleon was chosen President in 1848 and Emperor in 1852, by a *plébiscite;* and later, in 1870, he appealed to the French people to confirm, in the same manner, the Imperial power and to sanction the adoption of the new Constitution. Although over 7,000,000 persons voted to support the Empire and less than 2,000,000 against it, yet the fact that 50,000 of the army voted with the minority caused great alarm at the Tuileries, and did much to convince Napoleon III that the salvation of his dynasty lay in the desperate expedient of war.

Pleiades. In classic myth, the seven daughters of Atlas and Pleione, whose names are as follows : Electra, Maia, Taygete, Alcyone, Celæno, Sterope, and Merope. Their history is variously told, but all authorities agree that after their death, or translation, they were placed in the heavens, where they now shine as a group of stars in the constellation " Taurus." Six only of the Pleiades are visible to the naked eye. The ancients believed that the missing one was Sterope, who hid herself from shame at having married a mortal, while her sisters had become the wives of gods. Others, however, say that Electra is the " Lost Pleiad," —she having left her place to avoid seeing the ruin of Troy, which had been founded by her son, Dardanus. It is thought by many astronomers that our entire solar system has an orbital movement,—the centre of which is the group of the Pleiades.

Pliny's Doves. A superb and perfectly preserved specimen of ancient mosaic in the Capitoline Museum at Rome. It is described in Pliny's writings, and is, on that account, called " Pliny's Doves." This mosaic—representing four doves in the act of drinking—was discovered in the Villa Adriana in 1737 by Cardinal Furietti, and was purchased from him by Pope Clement XIII (1758–1769) for the museum of the Capitol. The stones composing it are so minute that, on an average, 160 pieces are required to cover one square inch.

Plon - Plon. An appellation bestowed upon Prince Napoleon (1822–1891), son of Jerome Bonaparte, King of Westphalia, by his second wife, Frederica Catherine of Würtemberg. It is said to be a euphonic corruption of *Craint-plomb* (*Fr., Fear-bullet*), a nickname given to him on account of cowardice during the Crimean War.

Plumed Knight. A sobriquet of James G. Blaine (1830–1893), conferred upon him by Colonel Robert G. Ingersoll, in a speech nominating Mr. Blaine for the presidency at the Republican Convention of 1876.

"Like an armed warrior, like a *plumed knight*, James G. Blaine marched down the halls of the American Congress and threw his shining lance full and fair against the brazen foreheads of the defamers of his country and the maligners of his honor."— *Robert G. Ingersoll.*

Plymouth Brethren. The name applied to a body of Christians, calling themselves simply " Brethren," who first appeared at Plymouth, England, about 1830, and afterwards extended themselves among the Protestants of France, Switzerland, Italy, and the United States. Their founder, John Nelson Darby (1800–1882), afterwards withdrew from the communion. The Plymouth Brethren believe in original sin and predestination, the atonement, and the sanctifying power of the Holy Ghost ; but reject utterly all forms of church organization, and have no official ministry. They entertain premillenarian views, and practise adult baptism.

Plymouth Church. A large brick building of extreme architectural simplicity, in the Borough of Brooklyn, New York City, famous for 40 years (1847–1887) as the scene of the pastoral labors of the late Henry Ward Beecher (1813–1887). It seats 2800 persons, and contains one of the largest church-organs in America.

Plymouth Rock. A ledge of rock near the waterside at Plymouth, Massachusetts, on which the Pilgrims are said to have stepped when they first landed (December 21st, 1620). It is surmounted by a handsome granite canopy, in the attic of which have been placed the bones of several of the colonists that died during the first year of settlement. In 1774, Plymouth Rock was raised from its bed, but unfortunately was broken in the operation. In the following year, the upper part was removed to the public square, where it remained until 1834, when it was again removed and placed in front of Pilgrim Hall. There it rested until 1880, when it was taken and reunited with the original portion. This fragment bears the names of the forty-one signers of the famous *Mayflower Compact*.

"This work has become an object of veneration in the United States."—*De Tocqueville.*

Pnyx. A meeting-place for the public assemblies of ancient Athens, occupying the slope of a low, rocky hill, at a distance of a quarter of a mile from the Areopagus. It was semicircular in form, and covered an area of about 12,000 square yards. A solid rectangular block of stone, from which the Athenian orators used to address the multitude assembled in the arena before them, still stands there.

Poet-Laureate. An office in the gift of the sovereign of England, said to have been created during the reign of Edward IV (1461–1483). The appellation is derived from a custom of the English universities, which continued until 1512, of presenting a laurel leaf to graduates in rhetoric and versification,—the "King's Laureate" being a graduated rhetorician in the service of the king. It was formerly the duty of the poet-laureate to write an ode on the birthday of the king, but this custom has been discontinued since the reign of George III (1760–1820). The first poet-laureate, in the modern sense, was Edmund Spenser [1552(?)–1599], who was granted a pension of £50 by Queen Elizabeth (1558–1603) in 1591. Ben Jonson (1574–1637) was the first to receive the office by formal letters-patent.

The following is a list of the poets-laureate of England—beginning with Spenser—together with their years of incumbency :

(1) Edmund Spenser (1591–1599).
(2) Samuel Daniel (1599–1619).
(3) Ben Jonson (1619–1637).
(4) William Davenant (1660–1668).
(5) John Dryden (1670–1689).
(6) Thomas Shadwell (1689–1692).
(7) Nahum Tate (1692–1715).
(8) Nicholas Rowe (1715–1718).
(9) Lawrence Eusden (1718–1730).
(10) Colley Cibber (1730–1757).
(11) William Whitehead (1757–1785).
(12) Thomas Warton (1785–1790).
(13) Henry James Pye (1790–1813).
(14) Robert Southey (1813–1843).
(15) William Wordsworth (1843–1850).
(16) Alfred Tennyson (1850–1892).
(17) Alfred Austin (1896–).

Poets' Corner. A name popularly given to a portion of the south transept of Westminster Abbey, from the fact that it contains the tombs of several of the principal English poets, as well as monuments and memorial tablets to many that are buried elsewhere.

"In the reign of Richard II, the practice of burying court favourites and others in the abbey commenced, and the first poet to be laid in the south transept, often called the *Poets' Corner,* was Geoffrey Chaucer, who probably owed this distinction as much to the fact that he was clerk of the works in the abbey, and occupied a house on the site of the chapel of Henry VII., as to his poetry. In the same transept are buried Spenser, Dryden, Garrick, Johnson, Dickens, Browning, Tennyson, and others of less note ; and many monuments commemorate poets and literary men buried elsewhere."—*Chambers's Encyclopædia.*

Poictiers, Battle of. A famous battle fought near Poictiers, in the west of France, on September 19th, 1356, between 14,000 English and Gascons under Edward, the Black Prince, and 60,000 French commanded by King John. The English were completely victorious,—killing 11,000 and taking more than 2000 prisoners, among whom were the King himself and one of his sons. Also written *Poitiers*.

Poison of Mithridates. It is related of Mithridates VI, King of Pontus, that in his last extremity he took poison to avoid falling into the hands of his enemies; but that owing to his long-continued use of antidotes, the draught failed in its effect, and the King was in consequence forced to throw himself upon the sword of a slave (63 B.C.). Racine's tragedy, entitled *Mithridate* (1673), deals with this theme.

Poisson d'avril (*Fr., April Fish*). The French expression for April Fool.

"The *poisson d'avril* is the mackerel, and we have the expression 'You silly mackerel,' and silly indeed are those who allow themselves to be caught by the palpable jokes engendered on the first of April."—Brewer's *Dictionary of Phrase and Fable*.

Poland, Partitions of. Three separate partitions of Poland have taken place, as follows :

FIRST PARTITION (1772).

	English Square Miles.	*Population.*
(1) Russia	42,000	1,800,000
(2) Prussia	13,000	416,000
(3) Austria	27,000	2,700,000

SECOND PARTITION (1793).

	English Square Miles.	*Population.*
(1) Russia	96,000	3,000,000
(2) Prussia	22,000	1,100,000

THIRD PARTITION (1795).

	English Square Miles.	*Population.*
(1) Russia	43,000	1,200,000
(2) Prussia	21,000	1,000,000
(3) Austria	18,000	1,000,000

In 1795, Stanislaus II (Augustus Poniatowski), the last sovereign of Poland,—a king without a country,—resigned his sovereignty, and on February 12th, 1798, died, a prisoner of state, at St. Petersburg.

Polaris. A steamer, fitted up for polar exploration by the United States Government, which sailed for the Arctic Ocean in 1871, under command of Captain Charles Francis Hall. Captain Hall died in Greenland in 1871, and after fearful suffering and privation the *Polaris* was abandoned by those on board. Part of the crew sought refuge on floating ice and were finally picked up by the steamer *Tigris* on April 30th, 1873, after drifting about for 195 days. The remainder constructed boats and put to sea, where they were rescued on June 23rd, 1873, and taken to Dundee, Scotland. It is said that Captain Hall reached north latitude 82° 16′ by means of sledges.

Pole-Star. A star of the second magnitude, at the extremity of the handle of the " Little Dipper." It is in the constellation *Ursa Minor* (*Little Bear*), and is distant 1° 17′ from the north pole of the heavens. Owing to the movement of the pole of the celestial equator around that of the ecliptic, it follows that this star will eventually (2100 A.D.) approach within 28′ of the north pole ; after which it will gradually recede from it. Twelve thousand years hence, *Vega*, in the constellation of the *Lyre*, will be within five degrees of the north pole, and will be the polar star.

"The polar-star enjoys a certain fame, like all persons who are distinguished from the common, because, among all the bodies which scintillate in the starry night, it alone remains motionless in the heavens. At any moment of the year, by day or by night, when you observe the sky, you will always find it.' All the other stars, on the contrary, turn in twenty-four hours round it, taken as the centre of this immense vortex. The pole star remains motionless at the pole of the world, from whence it serves as a fixed point to navigators on the trackless ocean, as well as to travellers in the unexplored desert."—Flammarion's *Popular Astronomy*.

"The distance of Polaris is so great, that though the star is moving through space at the rate of ninety miles per minute, this tremendous speed is imperceptible to us. It requires nearly fifty years for its light to reach the earth ; so that when we look at Polaris, we know that the ray which strikes our eye set out on its journey through space half a century ago. We cannot state positively that the star is now in existence, since if it were destroyed to-day it would be fifty years before we should miss it."—Steele's *Astronomy.*

" But I am constant as the *northern star*,
Of whose true-fix'd and resting quality
There is no fellow in the firmament.
The skies are painted with unnumber'd
    sparks,
They are all fire, and every one doth
    shine ;
But there 's but one in all doth hold his
    place : "
                    Julius Cæsar, iii, 1.

Polish Byron. A sobriquet conferred upon Adam Bernard Mickiewicz (1798–1855), the Polish poet.

Polish Franklin. A title bestowed upon Thaddeus Czacki (1765–1813), the Polish historian and philosopher.

Polish Voltaire. An appellation conferred upon Ignatius Krasicki (1734–1801), the Polish satirical poet.

Political Assessments in the United States. In 1876, the Congress of the United States enacted a law, forbidding the soliciting or receiving of political assessments by government officials. In 1877, President Hayes, soon after his inauguration, issued an order, forbidding all persons in the service of the government from taking any part in political campaigns, except voting at primaries and elections.

" The Civil Service act contains provisions forbidding any person in the service of the United States from levying upon or collecting from persons in the Executive Civil Service contributions to be devoted to political objects, the collection of such contributions by any person in any public building of the United States, or discrimination against persons who do not make such contributions or render political service. A violation of any of the provisions concerning political assessments, or their collection in a public building in the United States, is declared to be a misdemeanor, punishable by a fine not exceeding five thousand dollars, or by imprisonment for a term not exceeding three years, or by such fine and imprisonment both in the discretion of the court. The act also declares that when rules to carry its provisions into effect shall have been promulgated, ' it shall be the duty of all officers of the United States in the departments and offices to which any such rules may relate, to aid, in all proper ways, in carrying such rules, and any modifications thereof, into effect.'

An executive order of July 14, 1886, which is still in force, warns office-holders that, while individual interest and activity in political affairs are by no means condemned, they must bear in mind that their time and labor are due to the Government, and that they should scrupulously avoid, in their political action as well as in the discharge of their official duty, offending, by obtrusive partisanship, their neighbors who have relations with them as public officials."
—*World Almanac* (1901).

Polka. A popular dance in ¾ time, which is said to have originated in Bohemia about 1834. It was introduced into England in 1843, and into the United States soon after.

Polo. An Oriental game of high antiquity, which, it is claimed, can be traced back to 600 B.C. It was first played by Europeans at Calcutta in 1863, and was introduced into England in 1871, and into the United States in 1876. The game has long been popular among wealthy men of sporting proclivities, but is too expensive a pastime to become common. Polo may be briefly described as hockey on horseback.

Polymnia, or Polyhymnia. In classic mythology, one of the nine Muses. She presided over song and oratory. See *Muses.*

Pompeii. A ruined city of Campania, situated at the foot of Mount Vesuvius, 15 miles east of Naples. After experiencing a severe earthquake-shock in 63 A.D., Pompeii was suddenly overwhelmed by a terrible eruption of the volcano in 79 A.D. The entire city was buried under a layer of ashes and cinders from 20 to 70 feet deep, and lay undisturbed for more than 1600 years. In 1689, the accidental discovery of a bronze figure led to further research ; but it was not until 1755 that excavations were really commenced. These proceeded fitfully until 1860, when the Italian Government took the matter in hand, and accomplished wonders in the unearthing of the ancient city. About one-third of the space within the walls has been excavated,—revealing the presence of an amphitheatre, a theatre, a forum, three triumphal arches, besides innumerable private houses, schools, shops, and factories. Many of the portable curiosities — including frescoes, mosaics, reliefs, statues, bronzes, etc.—have been placed in the National Museum at Naples, founded by Ferdinand I in 1816. See *Herculaneum ; Museo Nazionale.*

Pompey's Pillar. An imposing column of red granite, standing on an eminence near the city of Alexandria, Egypt. It is of the Corinthian order of architecture, and has a total height of 98 feet 9 inches,—the shaft proper having an altitude of 73 feet and a circumference of 29 feet 8 inches. The name " Pompey's Pillar," given to this monument, was conferred upon it by ancient travelers, who erroneously supposed it to have been reared in honor of Pompey, the Roman triumvir. According to an inscription on the base, it was erected by Publius, Prefect of Egypt, in honor of Diocletian (284–305 A.D.), the Roman Emperor. It is supposed to commemorate the conquest of Egypt by Diocletian in 296 A.D.

" It is generally believed that the column has no reference to Pompey, to whom a mark of honor was, nevertheless, set up somewhere in this vicinity. One supposes that the pillar was dedicated to Vespasian, another to Severus ; and Mr. Clarke, from a half-effaced inscription on the base, considers that Hadrian is the person honored; while many assert, from the same inscription, that it is dedicated 'to Diocletian Augustus, most adorable emperor, tutelar deity of Alexandria.' "—Harper's *Book of Facts.*

" It has about as much right to be called *Pompey's* pillar as the obelisk of Heliopolis, re-erected by Rameses II at Alexandria, has

to be called *Cleopatra's Needle,* or Gibraltar Rock a pillar of Hercules."—Brewer's *Dictionary of Phrase and Fable.*

Pompey's Statue. A colossal marble statue, discovered in 1553, and now in the Palazzo Spada at Rome. It is generally supposed to be a statue of Pompey, and is perhaps the identical one at the base of which " great Cæsar fell."

" On this last point, the evidence is quite sufficient to allow a willing faith to rest upon it ; and in such cases faith is always willing. . . . This statue was found entire, with the exception of the right arm ; yet the head had evidently been separated from the trunk, and seems not to be that which originally belonged to it. During the French occupation of Rome, Voltaire's tragedy of Brutus was acted in the Colosseum ; and this statue was transported there, that the mock Cæsar might fall at the foot of the real statue,— though in doing this, it was necessary to saw off the restored right arm,—a piece of dramatic enthusiasm, like that of the London manager who, to give due effect to a melodrama founded upon the murder of Weare, introduced into one of the scenes the very horse and gig which belonged to him."— Hillard's *Six Months in Italy.*

Pons Asinorum. See *Asses' Bridge.*

Pont du Gard. A famous Roman aqueduct, 14 miles northeast of Nîmes, supposed to have been built about 27 A.D. It crosses the river Gard, or Gardon, at a height of 180 feet, on a structure composed of three tiers of arches,—the topmost one of which is 885 feet in length. This aqueduct conveyed the waters of the Eure and Airan to Nîmes,—a distance of about 25 miles.

" The stones of which it is constructed are of immense size, and devoid of all ornament. The wildness and picturesqueness of the valley over which this stupendous structure stands make it one of the most desirable curiosities to visit in the south of France. This is confessedly one of the proudest monuments of Roman greatness. It is of the Tuscan order, little ornamented, but of a very picturesque appearance. Having very fortunately escaped destruction during the Middle Ages, it sustained only one serious injury, in 1600, when a portion of the second tier of arches was broken away by the Duke of Rohan in making a passage for his artillery. This has since been repaired at the expense of the states of Languedoc, and it is now difficult to see in what part the injury took place."—Harper's *Hand-Book to Europe and the East.*

Ponte Vecchio (*It., Old Bridge*). A famous old structure, crossing the river Arno at Florence, Italy. It is lined on both sides with jewelers' and goldsmiths' shops, and forms an almost continuous street of ancient houses. Supported upon arches above the bridge proper runs the "Gallery of the Grand Duke," a covered passageway built to connect the Uffizi and Pitti Palaces, on opposite sides of the river. This passage is now freely used by tourists. See *Pitti Palace; Uffizi Palace.*

" I can remember when the Medici
  Were driven from Florence ; longer still ago
The final wars of Ghibelline and Guelf.
Florence adorns me with her jewelry;
And when I think that Michael Angelo
Hath leaned on me, I glory in myself.
  Longfellow's *Old Bridge at Florence.*

Pontifex Maximus. The chief of the college of pontiffs, among the ancient Romans. The institution of the pontiffs is traditionally ascribed to Numa ; but as they were found in all the Italian communities, they probably originated in the early religious development of the Latin race. The "college" at first consisted of four patricians, with a chief (*pontifex maximus*); but in 300 B.C. the Ogulnian Law increased the number to nine, four of whom were to be plebeians. In 81 B.C., this number was further increased by Sulla to fifteen ; and again to sixteen by Julius Cæsar. The first plebeian to attain the dignity of *pontifex maximus* was Tiberius Coruncanius (254 B.C.). During the Empire, the functions of this office were generally discharged by the emperors themselves ; but, after the establishment of Christianity, the title was dropped by them, and was afterwards assumed by the bishops of Rome. It forms, at the present day, one of the

designations of the Pope. The word "pontifex" is by many supposed to be derived from the Latin *pons* (*bridge*) and the root of *facio* (*I make*) ; but in what way the pontifices were connected with bridge-building is, to say the least, obscure.

"The word has nothing to do, as was supposed, with the *making of bridges* (pontes facere), but it is only another form of pompifex, the *orderer of processions* and other religious rites."—Smith's *Glossary of Terms and Phrases.*

Pontine Marshes. A low-lying, malarial region—27 miles long by 17 broad — occupying the southern part of the Roman Campagna and extending in a southeastern direction from Velletri to the sea at Terracina. It is traversed by the Appian Way. Many attempts have been made to drain these marshes, but without success,— the surface being too level. Appius Claudius attempted it as early as 312 B.C., and since that time renewed efforts have been made by the Emperors Augustus and Trajan as well as by several of the Popes of Rome. This region was at one time highly cultivated, and contained towns of considerable size. Before the opening of the railway between Rome and Naples, the road traversing the Pontine Marshes formed the great highway between central and southern Italy.

Pont Neuf (*Fr., New Bridge*). A handsome stone bridge in Paris, crossing both arms of the Seine and connecting the Ile de la Cité with the mainland. It was commenced by Henry III (1574–1589) in 1578, and completed by his successor Henry IV (1589–1610) in 1604. The bridge was remodelled in 1852, and the end adjoining the left bank was restored in 1886. In an open space on the Ile de la Cité stands an equestrian statue of Henry IV, erected by Louis XVIII in 1817. The original statue of Henry IV—placed there by Louis XIII in 1635—was melted down and converted into cannon in 1792. In retaliation for this insult, Louis XVIII caused the statue of Napoleon on the Column of Vendôme and that of Desaix in the Place des Victoires to be used in making the present statue of the king.

Pool of Bethesda. A pool or fountain in Jerusalem, near the temple, alluded to in *John* v, 2-7. Tradition locates the Pool of Bethesda in what is now a large dry reservoir, bordering on the outside of the north wall of the temple enclosure ; but Dr. Robinson and others identify it with the Fountain of the Virgin,—an intermittent spring in the lower part of the Valley of Jehoshaphat. We are told that, at a certain season of the year an angel went down and troubled the water of the pool, and that whoever first stepped in, after the troubling, was made whole.

Pool of Siloam. A rock-cut pool, near the Valley of Jehoshaphat, Jerusalem. It is, at present, an artificial stone reservoir, and is fed by a fountain high up in the cliff. The waters of the Fountain of the Virgin flow into the Pool of Siloam through a subterranean passage, 1750 feet in length, and are thought to be derived from the reservoirs under the area of the ancient temple, and in part from Mount Zion. The water of Siloam was formerly sacred to the temple, but is now used for purposes of irrigation. See *Isaiah's Tree.*

"The Pool is a deep, walled ditch, through which a clear stream of water runs, that comes from under Jerusalem somewhere, and passing through the Fountain of the Virgin, or being supplied from it, reaches the place by way of a tunnel of heavy masonry. The famous pool looked exactly as it looked in Solomon's time, no doubt, and the same dusky, Oriental women came down in the old Oriental way, and carried off jars of water on their heads, just as they did three thousand years ago, and just as they will do fifty thousand years hence if any of them are still left on earth."—*Innocents Abroad* (Mark Twain).

Poor Richard's Almanac. A popular almanac first published in 1732 by Benjamin Franklin, under the assumed name of "Richard Saunders," and continued by him for 26 years. It contained, in addition to the matter usually found in such publications, a vast amount of common sense and worldly wisdom, expressed in a pithy and sententious manner. See *Saunders, Richard.*

"Benjamin Franklin, printer, as 'Richard Saunders, Philomath,' for a quarter of a century provided the people with saws, proverbs, and bits of homely advice which were conned and repeated by thousands, and so effectively taught principles of common-sense, economy, and prudence that they actually increased Philadelphia's stock of ready money, and helped to make its vicinity the home of frugality and 'forehandedness.' Ten thousand copies made a great circulation for those days ; and the pamphlets were worn to pieces by their eager owners."—Richardson's *American Literature.*

Pope Joan. An imaginary female, who is said to have concealed her sex, and to have succeeded to the papacy as John VIII, in 855. According to the latest version of the story, she was the daughter of an English missionary, and was born at Mainz, or Ingelheim. Having formed an illicit union with a young monk at Fulda she assumed male attire and fled with him to Athens, where her lover soon died. Later, she made her appearance at Rome where, owing to her extensive learning, she was chosen pope to succeed Leo IV (847-855). Her sex was discovered by the premature birth of a child during a solemn procession to the Lateran Basilica. This monstrous tale was universally believed in Italy during the 15th and 16th centuries. See *Boy Popes.*

Pope of Philosophy. An appellation conferred upon Aristotle (384-322 B.C.), the Greek philosopher, in allusion to the despotic influence which his system of philosophy exerted for centuries on the thought of Europe.

"The great master mind of antiquity. Less lofty and imaginative than Plato, less ideal, less grand ; but with a keener insight, a more sharp and subtle penetration, a more thoroughly scientific spirit ; of wider erudition and vaster learning, content to deal with facts and phenomena, but content with nothing short of a thorough comprehension and complete mastery and scientific arrangement of these ; a mind that has left its impress more thoroughly on all succeeding time and all succeeding progress of the race than any one mind, beside, that was ever created."—Haven's *History of Philosophy.*

Pope of the Huguenots. A sobriquet conferred upon Cardinal Richelieu (1585–1642), who destroyed the Huguenots as a political party, but granted them the free exercise of their worship, to the disgust of the extreme Roman Catholics.

Popes of Rome. According to Gams's *Series Episcoporum,* there have been 260 occupants of the pontifical chair. These include only the popes canonically chosen. Tradition represents St. Peter as the first Pope, or Bishop, of Rome (41–67 A.D.). See *Antipopes.*

Popish Plot. A pretended conspiracy on the part of the Roman Catholics in England, during the reign of Charles II (1660–1685), the object of which was declared to be the massacre of the King and Parliament, the burning of London, and the restoration of the Roman Catholic religion. It was concocted by one Titus Oates, and is frequently called Oates's Plot. See *Oates's Plot.*

Popular Sovereignty. A phrase meaning the supreme governmental authority in a state, considered as vested in the will of the people. The expression " popular sovereignty " was much used in the United States, before the Civil War, to denote the political doctrine that each Territory had the right to decide for itself—either as a Territory or on its admission as a State into the Union—whether negro slavery should be permitted or prohibited within its limits. See *Squatter Sovereignty.*

Population of the United States. The population of the United States at each census from 1790 to 1900, inclusive, as given below, is taken from the *World Almanac* (1901).

(1) 1790.. 3,929,214	(7) 1850..23,191,876
(2) 1800.. 5,308,483	(8) 1860..31,443,321
(3) 1810.. 7,239,881	(9) 1870..38,558,371
(4) 1820.. 9,633,822	(10) 1880..50,155,783
(5) 1830..12,866,020	(11) 1890..63,069,756
(6) 1840..17,069,453	(12) 1900..76,304,799
	(13) 1910..95,410,503

Population of the Roman Empire. The population of the Roman Empire at the death of Augustus (14 A.D.) is estimated by Bodio thus :

Italy	6,000,000
Spain	6,000,000
Greece	3,000,000
Gaul	3,400,000
Other Countries	4,600,000
Europe	23,000,000
Asia	19,500,000
Africa	11,500,000
Total	54,000,000

Population of the World. The following table of the estimated population of the world, in millions, is taken from Harper's *Book of Facts :*

Year.	Author.	World.	Europe.	America.	Asia.	Africa.	Australia.
1810	Gotha	682	180	21	380	99	2
1828	Balbi	847	214	40	481	109	3
1845	Michelot	1009	245	50	620	90	4
1874	Behm-Wagner	1391	301	85	798	203	4
1886	Levasseur	1483	347	112	822	197	5

Estimates vary widely ; that of Wagner and Lupan in the *Bevölkerung der Erde* for 1891, is 1,479,000,000,—less than that of Levasseur in 1886.

Porcelain Tower. A famous tower at Nanking, China, built in 1411–1430 A.D., by Hoang-li-Tai, as a present for the Empress ; and destroyed in 1856, during the Tae-Ping Rebellion. It was an octagonal structure of nine stories, and rose to a height of 260 feet. The outer surface was covered with porcelain slabs of various colors, while from the cornices of the different stories hung bells, which gave forth sweet tones when agitated by the breeze. More than 125 lamps were suspended on the outside, and illuminated the tower at night. The cost of the structure is said to have been $4,000,000.

Porta del Popolo (*It., Gate of the People*). A gate on the north side of the city of Rome, erected in 1561 from designs by Michael Angelo.

"The gate itself, though designed in part by Michael Angelo, is not a structure of any conspicuous excellence; but the Piazza del Popolo, upon which it opens, is an imposing square, though not corresponding to the ideal image of Rome which the scholar forms."—Hillard's *Six Months in Italy*.

Portage Bridge. A famous wooden bridge, formerly existing on the line of the Erie Railway (New York, Lake Erie, and Western Railway) and crossing the gorge of the Genesee River, about a mile north of the town of Portage, New York. It was 800 feet in length and 234 feet in height, and was said to be the largest wooden railway-bridge in the world. It was afterwards replaced by an iron structure.

Porta Santa. (*It., Holy Door*). A walled-up doorway in the façade of St. Peter's at Rome, adjoining the principal entrance to the cathedral. It has been broken down by the Pope, in person, on the Christmas eve of each of the jubilees that have taken place at intervals of 25 years (with the exception of 1850), since the time of Sixtus IV (1471–1484). The Pope, after appropriate preliminary services, strikes the wall with a silver hammer; whereupon, the masonry, having been previously loosened, immediately falls inward. The Pope, bareheaded and holding a torch, then passes in—followed by his cardinals and other attendants—and proceeds at once to the high altar where vespers are chanted. Meanwhile, the other doors of the cathedral are thrown open to the congregation.

This jubilee was instituted by Pope Boniface VIII (1294–1303), and was ordered by him to be held at the close of each century, on which occasions plenary indulgence and remission of sins would be granted to all those that should visit the shrines of the saints and martyrs at Rome. Owing to the immense amount of treasure offered by wealthy penitents on these days of jubilee, they were increased in number from one to four in each century.

Porte St. Denis. A triumphal arch in Paris, on the line of the Boulevards, erected in 1672, to commemorate the victories of Louis XIV (1643–1715) in Holland and the district of the Lower Rhine. It is 81 feet high, 82 feet wide, and 16 feet thick, and is pierced by a single archway, 50 feet high and 26 feet wide. The piers are adorned with obelisks in relief, covered with military trophies. See *Porte St. Martin*.

Porte St. Martin. A triumphal arch in Paris, on the line of the Boulevards, erected in 1674, in honor of the victories of Louis XIV (1643–1715) in Franche-Comté. It is 57 feet high, 57 feet wide, and 14 feet thick, and is adorned with inscriptions and reliefs commemorating the triumphs of the King. After the abdication of Napoleon I (1804–1814), the Russian and Prussian armies entered Paris by way of the Porte St. Martin, and proceeded thence to the Place de la Concorde. The Porte St. Martin and the Porte St. Denis were the scenes of desperate and sanguinary contests during the Revolutions of 1830, 1848, and 1871. See *Porte St. Denis*.

Portland Cement. A hydraulic cement, generally made by calcining limestone with clay or shale. It receives its name from its resemblance to Portland stone.

Portland Vase. A famous ancient Roman vase, or cinerary urn, found, during the pontificate of Urban VIII (1623–1644), in a marble sarcophagus —presumably that of the Emperor Alexander Severus (222–235 A.D.) and his mother Mammæa—in the Monte del Grano, near Rome. It was deposited in the Barberini Palace at Rome, where it remained until 1770, when it was purchased by Sir William Hamilton, from whose possession it passed into that of the Duchess of Portland in 1787. At the sale of her effects, the vase was bought by the Duke of Portland and deposited in 1810 in the British Museum, where it still remains. On February 27th, 1845, it was smashed to pieces with a stone by a lunatic named William Lloyd ; but the fragments were so carefully united as to leave little trace of the injury. The ground of the Portland vase is of dark blue glass, and the figures that adorn it are cut in cameo on an outer layer of opaque white glass. It is 10 inches high, with a diameter of 7 inches at the widest part, and has two handles. The designs that ornament the vase are said to represent, on the obverse side: Thetis consenting to be the bride of Peleus in the presence of Poseidon and Eros ; and, on the reverse side: Peleus and Thetis on Mount Pelion. The bottom is adorned with a bust of Paris. Josiah Wedgwood (1730–1795), the celebrated potter, made copies in earthenware of the Portland vase, which originally brought 25 guineas each, but are now valued at £200. See *Barberini Vase.*

Porto Rico. This name of the recently acquired possession of the United States in the West Indies is the Spanish for " rich port."

Port Royal des Champs. A noted convent of Cistercian nuns, about eight miles from Versailles, France, founded in 1204 by Matthieu de Montmorency. Soon after its establishment, it obtained, by papal dispensation, the privilege of receiving lay persons who, without assuming monastic vows, desired to live in religious seclusion. In 1626, the religious part of the community was removed to Paris, and in 1633 was placed in a new convent,

while the old establishment became exclusively devoted to the uses of the lay members, some of whom were the famous *Port Royalists.* The institution, being a stronghold of Jansenism, incurred the bitter enmity of the Jesuits, and was finally destroyed through their influence, in 1709. Pope Clement XI (1700–1721) issued a formal bull for its suppression, and the buildings were razed to the ground by order of Louis XIV. See *Port Royalists.*

Port Royalists. The name given to a community of learned men of Jansenist tendencies, who established themselves at the convent of *Port Royal des Champs,* during the 17th century, for purposes of study and religious meditation. Among them may be mentioned Antoine Arnauld, Arnauld d'Antilly, Pascal, Tillemont, Nicole, De Sacy, and Lancelot. These ascetics also founded a school, and produced the famous " Port Royal " works on grammar, logic, and mathematics,—long and justly famed for their excellence. See *Port Royal des Champs.*

Positivism. " A system of philosophy elaborated in Paris by Auguste Comte (1798–1857), having as its foundation the doctrine that man can have no knowledge of anything but phenomena, and that our knowledge of phenomena is relative, not absolute. It thereby excludes all metaphysics and philosophy, all knowledge of the supernatural, of cause and First Cause, of mind human and divine, and all except empirical knowledge of nature. In Comte's view all knowledge proceeds by three stages: first, *the theological,* in which phenomena are regarded as due to a supernatural agency : second, the *metaphysical,* in which they are referred to metaphysical causes; and third, the *positive,* in which an explanation of phenomena by experience is sought in mere law or the relations of facts. Positivism aims at a *classification* of sciences by purely experimental and historical methods, and at a *sociology* having as its ethical basis a utilitarian altruism. Comte attempted later to construct a cult, somewhat analogous to the worship of the Roman Catholic Church, but without recognition of Christian dogma. Thus, in effect, he returned to his first or theological stage, somewhat after the manner of Vico's (1725) law of cycles." — *Standard Dictionary*.

See *Religion of Humanity*.

Postage Stamps. Adhesive postage stamps were invented by James Chalmers of Dundee (1782–1853) in 1834. After the passage of the Uniform Penny Postage bill by Parliament in 1840, envelopes bearing an *impressed* stamp, or mark, for postage were introduced at the suggestion of Rowland Hill, but failed to find favor with the public. The adhesive postage stamp of Chalmers was thereupon substituted, and did much to insure the success of the Penny Postage scheme. Postage stamps were introduced into America in 1847.

Postal Union. At the International Postal Convention, held at Berne, Switzerland, on September 15th, 1874, a treaty was concluded on October 9th of the same year, whereby the principal nations of Europe and America agreed to adopt a uniform rate of postage. The rates determined upon were as follows : letters, 5 cents for each half-ounce or fraction thereof ; postal cards, 2 cents each ; newspapers and periodicals, 1 cent for each 2 ounces. This arrangement went into effect on July 1st, 1875, and was adopted by France on July 1st, 1876, and by Australia on October 1st, 1891. Matter mailed in the United States for Canada and Mexico is subject to United States postage. The International Postal Union was formed in 1885.

Posthumous Trial. After the death of Pope Formosus (891–896),

39

his successor, Stephen VII (896–897) had the body of Formosus exhumed, and put on trial for some alleged political offense. Stephen appeared in person as accuser and secured a verdict against the dead pontiff ; whereupon the body of Formosus was stripped, mutilated, and finally cast into the Tiber, while all his official acts—even those of consecration—were annulled. These atrocities so enraged the people of Rome that they rose against Stephen and cast him into prison, where he was soon after strangled by the friends of Formosus.

This trial of the dead Pope formed the subject of a famous painting by J. P. Laurens, the French artist, exhibited at the Paris Exposition of 1878, where it attracted great attention and was awarded the medal of honor at the École des Beaux-Arts. At the close of the Exposition, the picture was shipped to Nantes, where it belonged ; but all trace of it was lost from that day. Several fine engravings of the painting have been obtained, however, and preserve its most striking details.

Potato. The potato is a native of South America, and is generally supposed to have been introduced into England by Sir John Hawkins in 1565, although others ascribe its introduction to Sir Francis Drake in 1586. Sir Walter Raleigh (1552–1618) cultivated the potato in Cork County, Ireland, where he had large estates. Its culture did not become general in England until the latter part of the 18th century.

Pot-Pourri. Originally, a name given to a dish composed of various kinds of meat and vegetables, cooked together. In this sense, it corresponds to the Spanish *olla podrida* and the Scotch *hotch-potch*. The phrase is also used to denote any mixture of dried flowers, spices, etc., preserved in a vase with a perforated top, and used to perfume the air of a room. In music, the term "pot-pourri" means a medley of popular airs strung together, without much attempt at arrangement. See *Olla Podrida.*

Potsdam. A city of Prussia, 18 miles southwest of Berlin, chiefly famous as the home of Frederick the Great (1740–1786). There may be seen the palace of Sans-Souci—surrounded by a splendid park and gardens—erected by the king in 1745–1747 ; the historic windmill ; the old palace, or *Residenz ;* and the garrison-church, or *Garnisonkirche*, where lie the remains of Frederick. About 2½ miles from Potsdam is the new palace, with nearly 200 rooms, built by Frederick the Great in 1763–1770, after the "Seven Years' War." See *Sans-Souci.*

Pot-wallopers. An expression used in England before the Reform Act of 1832, to denote those persons that proved themselves housekeepers, and hence electors, by boiling their pots over their own fireplaces. At Taunton, during the 18th century, according to Defoe's *Tour through Great Britain*, " several inmates or lodgers would, some little time before the election, bring out their pots, and make fires in the street, and boil their victuals in the sight of their neighbours, that their votes be not called in question." The expression is derived from *pot*, and *wallop (to sway or move to and fro like boiling water).*

Pound. The word " pound "—as used in England to denote a certain sum of money — is derived from the pound-weight of silver, used as a money-standard by the ancient Romans, and introduced by them into their conquered provinces. Originally, this pound of silver was coined into 20 shillings, but from the time of Edward II (1307–1327), these coins were gradually reduced in size, until finally as many as 288 shillings were coined from the same weight of bullion. In the time of Elizabeth (1558–1603) 60, and in the time of George I (1714–1727), 66 shillings were coined

to the pound. This ratio still continues; but the term " pound " has lost its original meaning, and simply signifies 20 shillings of the present coinage.

Prado.
(1) A broad, well-shaded boulevard in Madrid, Spain, originally a meadow (as its name indicates), but converted to its present use by Charles III (1759–1788). It is nearly two miles long, and is finely adorned with elm-trees and beautiful fountains. The broadest part—called El Salon—is about 1400 feet long, and 200 feet wide. The Prado is the principal resort of beauty and fashion during the afternoon, especially on Sunday, when it is crowded with the best citizens of Madrid, either on foot, on horseback, or in carriages.
(2) A name applied to the Museo, or Royal Museum, at Madrid. See *Museo.*

Prætorian Gate. The name of the front gate in a Roman camp. It was always the gate that faced the enemy. See *Decuman Gate.*

Prætorian Guard. The body-guard of the Roman Emperors, instituted in 13 B.C., by Augustus (27 B.C.–14 A.D.), and composed of nine or ten cohorts of 1000 men each,—three of which were stationed at Rome, and the remaining ones in adjoining cities. Tiberius (14–37 A.D.) assembled them all at Rome, and placed them in a permanent camp, and Vitellius (69 A.D.) increased their number to 16 cohorts. They served at first for 12 and afterwards for 16 years, and received double pay. The privates ranked with the centurions of the regular army, and, on their retirement, received 20,000 sesterces. The Prætorians were at first the servants of the Emperors, but eventually became their masters,— elevating and deposing the " Cæsars " at their will, and finally selling the imperial purple for a sum of money to Didius Julianus in 193 A.D. Their power was curtailed by Septimius

Severus (193–211), and their privileges greatly decreased by Diocletian (284–305). In 312, they were disbanded by Constantine the Great (306–337).

Pragmatic Sanction. A solemn edict issued by the head of a state, and operating as a fundamental law. The expression seems to have been originally applied to certain decrees of the Byzantine Emperors; but, as at present used, it refers to several important European treaties, the principal of which are as follows :

(1) The ordinance of Louis IX (1226–1270) of France, establishing the liberties of the Gallican Church, in 1269.

(2) The ordinance of Charles VII (1422–1461) of France, confirming the decrees of the Council of Basle, whereby the papal power in France was limited and defined, in 1438.

(3) The decree that secured the succession of the German Empire to the House of Austria, in 1439.

(4) The ordinance by which Charles VI (1711–1740), Emperor of Germany, —having no male issue, — settled his dominions on his daughter, the Archduchess Maria Theresa, in 1713.

(5) The decree by which Charles III (1759–1788) of Spain ceded his right of succession to the Kingdom of Naples to his third son and his descendants, in 1759.

Prairie State. A name popularly given to the State of Illinois, on account of its uniformly level surface, which practically forms one vast prairie.

Praise-God Barebone. A Puritan fanatic, who was the leader of the Parliament convened by Cromwell on July 4th, 1653, and dissolved on December 13th of the same year. The Christian name borne by this enthusiast bears witness to the peculiar custom of naming in vogue among the English Puritans. It is said that his son, Dr. Barebone, was generally known as "Damned Dr. Barebone,"

from the fact that he was named "If-Christ-had-not-died-for-thee-thou-hadst-been-damned." See *Barebone's Parliament ; Names of Puritans.*

Prater. A park and forest in the city of Vienna, Austria, 4270 acres in extent. It became the property of the imperial family in 1570, and was used as a *chasse* until 1766, when it was opened by the Emperor Joseph II (1742–1790) as a public pleasure-ground. The principal avenue — known as the *Haupt Allee* — has a quadruple row of superb chestnut trees. It is about 2½ miles in length, and is the favorite promenade of the Viennese, especially during the month of May, when it is thronged with the fashion and beauty of the city.

Prayer-Test. The name given to a proposal to test the efficacy of prayer, anonymously made in the name of science, in the *Contemporary Review* for July, 1872. This proposal received the strong endorsement of Professor Tyndall, and was couched in the following terms :

"I ask that one single ward or hospital, under the care of first-rate physicians and surgeons, containing certain numbers of patients afflicted with those diseases which have been best studied, and of which the mortality rates are best known, whether the diseases are those which are treated by medical or by surgical remedies, should be, during a period of not less, say, than three or five years, made the objects of special prayer by the whole body of the faithful ; and that at the end of that time the mortality rates should be compared with the past rates, and also with the rates of other leading hospitals similarly well managed during the same period."

This suggestion gave rise to a protracted and energetic debate, but the experiment was not made.

Praying Wheel. A mechanical contrivance in use among the Lamaist Buddhists, who believe that the efficacy of a prayer depends upon the frequency of its repetition. These instruments vary greatly in size, from small cylinders turned by hand to large ones driven by wind or water. Long strips of paper or cloth — inscribed with petitions repeated hundreds and even thousands of times—are wound round these cylinders ; and as they revolve, the rolls uncoil and thus the prayer is said.

"This notion arises from a misconception. Sakyamuni, the Buddha, is said to have 'turned the wheel of the law'—*i. e.*, to have preached Buddhism incessantly—we should say as a horse in a mill."—Brewer's *Dictionary of Phrase and Fable.*

Pre-Adamites. The name given to a race of men, which, according to Eastern legend, is said to have lived upon the earth previous to the time of Adam. As a result of the twofold account of creation given in *Genesis*, it has been declared by certain writers of modern times that there were two separate creations of men,—the first, a defective race, from which sprang the entire Gentile world, and the second, the Adamic race, from which the Jewish people are descended. This view was elaborately set forth by Isaac de la Peyrère, in his work entitled *Præadamitæ* (*Pre-Adamites*), published in 1655. Whatever view may be held concerning the biblical Adam, it is certain that man has existed on the earth for hundreds of thousands of years. See *Adamites.*

Precious Stones, Language of. See *Language of Precious Stones.*

Predestination. A theological doctrine, which asserts that all events— including the salvation or perdition of human beings—are preordained by God from all eternity. This view— which originated in the attempt to reconcile the freedom of man's will with the belief in divine omnipotence—was maintained by St. Augustine and opposed by Pelagius, in the early part of the fifth century A.D. In later years, the doctrine was defended by the Augustinians, Jansenists, and Calvinists, and opposed by the Dominicans, Jesuits, Arminians, and

Wesleyan Methodists. **The Roman Catholic Church regards the question as one rather of metaphysics than of faith.**

"Predestination to Life is the everlasting purpose of God, whereby (before the foundations of the world were laid) he hath constantly decreed by his counsel secret to us, to deliver from curse and damnation those whom he hath chosen in Christ out of mankind, and to bring them by Christ to everlasting salvation, as vessels made to honor. Wherefore, they which be endued with so excellent a benefit of God, be called according to God's purpose by his Spirit working in due season : they through Grace obey the calling : they be justified freely : they be made sons of God by adoption : they be made like the image of his only-begotten Son Jesus Christ : they walk religiously in good works, and at length, by God's mercy, they attain to everlasting felicity."—*Book of Common Prayer, Article of Religion xvii.*

Prehistoric Time. An expression used to denote the period of time prior to that covered by *recorded* history. It has no definite chronological significance, since historic records extend back in different places to different times.

Sir John Lubbock says that "Prehistoric Time" may be divided into four periods, or epochs, as follows:

(1) The Palæolithic or Early Stone Period.

(2) The Neolithic or Polished Stone Period.

(3) The Bronze Period.

(4) The Iron Period.

See *Ages, Archæologic.*

Pre-Raphaelites. The name given in England about 1850, to a group of painters, including Millais, Holman Hunt, Alma Tadema, and Dante Gabriel Rossetti, who rebelled against the conventionality of routine-teaching in art, and sought to return to the natural method, as practised previous to the time of Raphael (1483–1520). The Pre-Raphaelites were ably championed by the famous art-critic, John Ruskin (1819–1900). As a school they were severely criticised, but their work was productive of much good.

Presburg, Treaty of. A treaty of peace concluded between France and Austria, December 26th, 1805. By the terms of this treaty, Austria surrendered Venetia to the newly created Kingdom of Italy ; ceded the Tyrol and the Vorarlberg to Bavaria ; and transferred her provinces in Suabia to the Electors of Würtemberg and Bavaria, who were afterwards raised to the rank of kings.

President. The name of an American steamship that sailed from New York for Liverpool in the spring of 1841, but was never heard of afterwards.

Presidents of the United States. The following is a list of the Presidents of the United States, with their terms of office :

(1) George Washington. Two terms: 1789–1797.

(2) John Adams. One term : 1797–1801.

(3) Thomas Jefferson. Two terms : 1801–1809.

(4) James Madison. Two terms : 1809–1817.

(5) James Monroe. Two terms : 1817–1825.

(6) John Quincy Adams. One term : 1825–1829.

(7) Andrew Jackson. Two terms : 1829–1837.

(8) Martin Van Buren. One term : 1837–1841.

(9) William Henry Harrison. One month : 1841.

(10) John Tyler. Three years and eleven months : 1841–1845.

(11) James K. Polk. One term : 1845–1849.

(12) Zachary Taylor. One year and four months: 1849–1850.

(13) Millard Fillmore. Two years and eight months : 1850–1853.

(14) Franklin Pierce. One term : 1853–1857.

(15) James Buchanan. One term : 1857–1861.

(16) Abraham Lincoln. One term and one month : 1861–1865.

(17) Andrew Johnson. Three years and eleven months : 1865–1869.

(18) Ulysses S. Grant. Two terms : 1869–1877.

(19) Rutherford B. Hayes. One term : 1877–1881.

(20) James A. Garfield. Six months and fifteen days : 1881.

(21) Chester A. Arthur. Three years, five months, and thirteen days : 1881–1885.

(22) Grover Cleveland. Two terms : 1885–1889 ; 1893–1897.

(23) Benjamin Harrison. One term : 1889–1893.

(24) William McKinley. One term, six months, and nine days: 1897–1901.

(25) Theodore Roosevelt. One term, three years, five months, and 21 days (1901–1909).*

Prester John. The title of an imaginary Christian sovereign, who, according to mediæval tradition, ruled over an extensive empire in the interior of Asia during the 12th century. This myth is supposed to have originated in the stories of the Nestorian missionaries, who, in the 11th and 12th centuries, penetrated into Eastern Asia and converted to Christianity one Oong, a Khan of Tartary. In 1177, Pope Alexander III (1159–1181) dispatched an envoy to Prester John, but the ambassador never returned ; and in 1254 Louis IX (1226–1270) of France sent Rubruquis, a French friar, to search for him, but the journey proved fruitless. In later years, tradition transferred Prester John to Abyssinia, where he continued his mythical existence as king of that country.

According to certain authorities, he was called Prester [*i. e.*, Priest or Presbyter] John, because he favored the Nestorian Christians.

Pretenders. The name given to those princes of the Stuart family that laid claim to the English crown after the Revolution of 1688. They were James Francis Edward Stuart (1688–1765), son of James II, and Charles Edward Stuart (1720–1788), grandson of James II, known respectively as the

* (26) William H. Taft. One term: 1909–1913.
(27) Woodrow Wilson. 1913–19—.

"Old Pretender" and the "Young Pretender." The House of Stuart became extinct by the death of Cardinal York, brother of the "Young Pretender," at Rome in 1807. See *Court of St. Germain ; Last of the Stuarts ; Tombs of the Stuarts ; Young Chevalier.*

Pride's Purge. The name given to an act of Colonel Thomas Pride, who, with a body of soldiers, "purged" the Long Parliament of its Presbyterian royalist members on December 6th, 1648, on which occasion 41 members were arrested and 160 were excluded on the following day. The House of Commons, now reduced to about 80 Independents, appointed a commission to try the King (Charles I) on a charge of treason. See *Long Parliament ; Rump Parliament.*

Primate of All England. An ancient ecclesiastical title still borne by the Archbishop of Canterbury. The Latin form is *Metropolitanus et Primus Totius Angliæ.*

Primate of England. An ancient ecclesiastical title still borne by the Archbishop of York. The Latin form is *Primus et Metropolitanus Angliæ.*

Primrose. This name, meaning the *first rose*, is given to one of the earliest flowering plants.

Primrose Day. April 19th,—the anniversary of the death of Lord Beaconsfield (1805-1881)—so called in allusion to the statesman's fondness for that flower. Its observance was proposed by Sir George Birdwood. An abundant display of primroses is made on that day,—particularly by members of the Primrose League, organized November 17th, 1883.

Primum Mobile. A term used in the Ptolemaic system of astronomy to denote the tenth or outermost sphere, which was supposed to revolve from east to west every 24 hours, and to carry the other spheres along with it. See *Crystalline Spheres.*

Prince, The (*It. Del Principe*, or *Lat. De Principatibus*). A celebrated political treatise by Niccolo Macchiavelli (1469-1527). It is said to have been written for the private use of Lorenzo de' Medici, and not for publication.

"The 'Prince' is the best known of his [Macchiavelli's] political works, and from the infamous principles which he has here developed, though probably with good intentions, his name is allied with everything false and perfidious in politics. The object of the treatise is to show how a new prince may establish and consolidate his power, and how the Medici might not only confirm their authority in Florence, but extend it over the whole of the Peninsula. . . . His 'Prince' reduced to a science the art, long before known and practised by kings and tyrants, of attaining absolute power by deception and cruelty, and of maintaining it afterwards by the dissimulation of leniency and virtue."— Botta's *Hand-Book of Universal Literature.*

Prince John. A sobriquet conferred upon John Van Buren (1810–1866), the son of Martin Van Buren, eighth President of the United States.

Prince of Destruction. An appellation conferred upon Timour, or Tamerlane (1336–1405), the famous Mongol warrior, whose career of conquest was accompanied by indiscriminate pillage, widespread devastation, and frightful loss of life. It is said that on one occasion, after quelling a revolt at Bagdad, he erected a pyramid composed of 90,000 human heads, as a warning against rebellion.

Prince of Musicians. A title conferred upon Giovanni Pierluigi da Palestrina (1524–1594), one of the greatest of Italian musical composers.

Prince of Orators. A title conferred upon Demosthenes (384–322 B.C.), the greatest orator of antiquity.

Prince of Painters. A title said to have been assumed by Parrhasius (*fl.* 400 B.C.) ; also conferred upon Apelles (*fl.* 330 B.C.).

Prince of Peace. A name often conferred upon the Messiah, who came to proclaim on earth peace and good will toward men.

"For unto us a child is born, unto us a son is given : and the government shall be upon his shoulder : and his name shall be called Wonderful, Counsellor, The mighty God, The everlasting Father, The *Prince of Peace*."—*Isaiah* ix, 6.

Prince of Philosophers. A sobriquet conferred upon Plato (429–347 B.C.), the famous Greek philosopher.

Prince of Princes. A sobriquet conferred upon George IV (1820–1830), King of England, by Byron in *Don Juan*.

Prince of Showmen. A sobriquet often conferred upon Phineas Taylor Barnum (1810–1891), the American showman, in allusion to the great success attained by him in his efforts to amuse and entertain the public.

Prince of Story-Tellers. A sobriquet conferred upon Boccaccio (1313–1375), the author of the *Decameron*.

Prince of the Peace. A title conferred by Charles IV of Spain upon his prime-minister, Manuel de Godoy (1767–1851), who successfully negotiated a treaty of peace with France in 1795.

"In one year this obscure garde-de-corps received the titles of lieutenant-general, admiral of the Spanish fleet, duke of Alcudia, knight of the Golden Fleece ; and on the marriage with the king's niece he was created 'Prince of the Peace.' "—Brewer's *Historic Note-Book*.

Prince of Wales. The title borne by the eldest son of the sovereign of England.

"After the fall of the last native princes of Wales, Llewelyn in 1282 and David in 1283, Wales came fully under the dominion of Edward I, who in 1284 is fabled to have presented the Welsh with a prince in his infant son, Edward, really born at Carnarvon Castle. Edward, by the death of his elder brother four months later, became heir-apparent ; but it was not till 1301 that he was created *Prince of Wales*. Edward III in 1343 invested his son Edward the Black Prince with the principality, and from that time the title of *Prince of Wales* has been borne by the eldest son of the reigning king. Till the time of Charles II the Welsh connection was oddly maintained by the arrangement that the *Prince of Wales* always had a Welsh wet-nurse. The title is not inherited, and has usually been bestowed by patent and investiture, though in a few instances the heir to the throne has become *Prince of Wales* simply by being so declared."—*Chambers's Encyclopædia*.

Prince Rupert's Drops. The name given to tadpole-shaped pieces of glass, which have been formed by melting the glass and allowing it to drop into cold water. If the point of the tail of one of these be broken off, the whole will at once shiver to pieces with a loud report. Owing to the sudden cooling, the particles have not had sufficient time to arrange themselves in a stable manner, and hence they fly asunder as soon as the skin is broken. These curious drops are commonly supposed to have been discovered by Prince Rupert (1619–1682), the grandson of James I of England ; but Faraday says that they were simply brought by him into England in 1660.

Princes Street. A famous street in the city of Edinburgh, Scotland, and one of the finest in Great Britain. It is lined with public buildings, monuments, and hotels, and commands a superb view of the old castle.

Principia. A world-renowned mathematical treatise by Sir Isaac Newton (1642–1727), published either by the Royal Society or by Halley, in 1687. Its full title is *Philosophiæ Naturalis Principia Mathematica* (*Lat., The Mathematical Principles of Natural Philosophy*). The work consists of three parts,—the first and second of which deal with the motions of bodies, and the third with the solar system. Laplace regarded the *Principia* as " pre-eminent above all other productions of the human intellect."

"The great discovery which characterizes the 'Principia' is that of the principle of universal gravitation, that every particle of matter in the universe is attracted by, or gravitates to, every other particle of matter, with a force inversely proportional to the squares of their distances."—*Sir David Brewster.*

Printing-House Square. A small triangular space in New York City, at the intersection of Park Row and Nassau Street — adjoining City Hall Park. It is the newspaper-centre of the metropolis, and in its immediate neighborhood are located the offices of the *Tribune, Times,** *World, Sun, Journal, Press, News,* and *Staats-Zeitung.*** In the centre of the square stands a bronze statue of Benjamin Franklin, unveiled in 1872.

Prisoner of Chillon. A name given to François de Bonnivard (1496–1570), a Frenchman, who, having espoused the cause of the Genevese in their struggles against Charles III, Duke of Savoy, was confined by that prince for six years (1530–1536) in a dungeon of the Castle of Chillon. At the expiration of that period he was liberated by the Bernese, who were at war with Savoy, and had captured the castle. Byron's poem, the *Prisoner of Chillon,* is doubtless founded on this incident; but his addition of the two brothers who were imprisoned with François, and who died in consequence of hunger and confinement, is purely an invention of the poet, and without historic foundation. It was probably suggested to Byron by Dante's story of Count Ugolino and his two sons. See *Chillon, Castle of.*

> " Chillon ! thy prison is a holy place,
> And thy sad floor an altar—for 't was trod,
> Until his very steps have left a trace
> Worn, as if thy cold pavement were a sod,
> By Bonnivard ! May none those marks efface
> For they appeal from tyranny to God."
>   *Prisoner of Chillon* (Byron).

Prisoner of Ham. An appellation conferred upon Napoleon III (1852–1870), who, on account of his attempt at Boulogne in 1840 to restore the Empire, was condemned to perpetual imprisonment in the citadel of Ham, and,

* *Times* now located at Times Square.
** *Staats-Zeitung* now located at William and Beekman Streets.

after six years' confinement, escaped and fled to England. See *Ham, Citadel of.*

Prisoner of the Vatican. A title conferred by his adherents upon Pope Pius IX (1846–1878), who in 1870 was deprived of his temporal possessions, and was assigned the Vatican as a place of residence, where he remained professedly a prisoner.

Prison of Socrates. The name given to several rock-hewn dungeons at the foot of the Musæum Hill at Athens, Greece. In one of these, Socrates is said to have been imprisoned, and to have drunk the fatal hemlock ; but of this there is no proof. According to some authorities, these excavations are the remains of ancient baths.

Privateer. A privately owned vessel, licensed by a government by letters of marque to make war upon the shipping of a hostile power. To make war upon an enemy without letters of marque, or upon the shipping of a nation not mentioned in them, is piracy. Privateering was authorized by Edward I (1272–1307) of England against the Portuguese, and became very general during the 17th and 18th centuries. In 1856 it was abolished by the leading nations of Europe, and in 1871 by the United States of America.

Privy Council. A body of advisers on matters of state, appointed by the English sovereign. It is said to have been instituted by Alfred the Great (871–901) in 895, and to have been originally composed of twelve persons. It consists, at the present time, of about 200 members, and includes the royal family, lords temporal and spiritual, great officers of state, judges, ambassadors, colonial governors, and others. Privy Councillors are appointed without grant or patent, and must be natural-born British subjects. Immediately after the death of the sovereign, the Privy Council proclaims his successor.

Privy Seal. In Great Britain, the term applied to the seal subsidiary to the Great Seal. It is affixed to all charters, grants, and pardons that are afterwards to pass the Great Seal, or to documents that do not require the latter. The Privy Seal is in the custody of an officer, at one time called the Keeper and afterwards the Lord Privy Seal. He is now the fifth officer of state, and is generally a member of the Cabinet. See *Great Seal of England.*

Probability, Theory of. The theory of probability has for its object, according to Jevons, " the determination of the number of ways in which an event may happen or fail, in order that we may judge whether the chances of its happening or failing are greater." It originated with Pascal, and since that time has been discussed by some of the most eminent mathematicians,— among whom may be named D'Alembert, Euler, Lagrange, Laplace, and Quetelet.

"The mathematical expression of a *chance* is the ratio of frequency with which an event happens in the long run. If an event may happen in a ways, and may fail in b ways, and each of these $a + b$ ways is equally likely, the *chance*, or probability, that the event will happen is measured by the fraction $\frac{a}{a + b}$, and the *chance*, or probability that it will fail is measured by $\frac{b}{a + b}$."—*Chambers's Encyclopædia.*

Procopius Sees Cross. According to the legend, Procopius, a captain in the service of Diocletian (284–305 A.D.), was proceeding towards Antioch with a band of soldiers to extirpate the Christians of that city, at the Emperor's command, when he suddenly felt the earth tremble beneath his feet, and, amid thunder and lightning, heard a voice exclaim : " Neanius, whither goest thou, and against whom art thou marching with such fury ? " Immediately after, a blazing cross appeared in the sky, and the same voice exclaimed: " I am Jesus Christ, the Son of the living God, who was crucified "; whereupon Procopius was at once converted, and became known as St. Procopius of Jerusalem. See *Alonzo Sees Cross.*

"This exaggerated parody of Saul's conversion is given by Mgr. Guérin as a fact, and appears in the *Acta Sanctorum* of the Bollandists. It is quite impossible to read it and not pity the bad taste of the writer who concocted the story, for notwithstanding the high and mighty names that vouch for it, no one can possibly believe it to be a fact. Alban Butler, with his usual want of fidelity, suppresses it, forgetting that his duty was to give the lives of the saints as he found them in books sanctioned by the pope and cardinals, and not to trim these biographies according to his own judgment, and pander to Protestant ' prejudices.' "—*Brewer's Dictionary of Miracles.*

Procrustes, Bed of. An iron bed, owned by Damastes, or Polypemon, surnamed Procrustes (*Gr., The Stretcher*), a famous legendary robber of Attica, on which he tied all his victims, and adjusted them to its length either by cutting off their legs if they were too long or by stretching them if they were too short. He was killed by Theseus, after being made to suffer the tortures that he had inflicted upon others. See *Damiens's Bed.*

Profile. See *Old Man of the Mountain.*

Prometheus. In classic mythology, the son of the Titan Iapetus and of Clymene, and brother of Atlas, Menœtius, and Epimetheus. According to one tradition, he stole fire from heaven, for which offense Zeus chained him to a rock on Mount Caucasus, where an eagle preyed daily upon his liver, which was restored on each succeeding night. Hercules finally slew the eagle, and, by permission of Zeus, released the long - suffering Prometheus. Other legends make Prometheus the creator of man out of earth and water, either at the beginning of the human race or subsequent to the deluge of Deucalion.

Propaganda. A religious establishment for the propagation of the Roman Catholic faith—not only among the heathen, but also among heretics — founded at Rome by Pope Gregory XV (1621–1623) in 1622. His successor, Urban VIII (1623–1644) enlarged and endowed the institution, and, in 1627, added a college for the education of missionaries to foreign countries. This college of the *Propaganda* is attended by about 200 pupils from all parts of the globe, who are carefully educated at the expense of the Church, and fully equipped for the missionary work to which they are assigned. It possesses a library of 30,000 volumes, a valuable museum, and a polyglot printing-press. On the festival of the Epiphany, recitations are delivered by the pupils in every language represented in the college — numbering sometimes 50 or 60.

Prophet. A title conferred upon Mohammed (570–632 A.D.), and also upon Joachim, Abbot of Fiore (1130–1202 A.D.).

Propylæa. A magnificent structure, now in ruins, forming the entrance or vestibule of the Acropolis at Athens. It was constructed of Pentelic marble, and was commenced in 437 B.C., under the auspices of Pericles, and completed by the architect Mnesicles in 432,— about the beginning of the Peloponnesian War.

"The *Propylæa* were themselves one of the masterpieces of Athenian art. They were entirely of Pentelic marble, and covered the whole of the western end of the Acropolis, having a breadth of 168 feet. The central portion of them consisted of two porticoes, of which the western one faced the city, and the eastern one the interior of the Acropolis, each consisting of a front of six fluted Doric columns. This central part of the building was 58 feet in breadth, but the remaining breadth of the rock at this point was covered by two wings, which projected 26 feet in front of the western portico. Each of these wings was in the form of a Doric temple. The northern one, or that on the left of a person ascending the Acropolis, was called the *Pinacotheca*, from its walls being

covered with paintings. The southern wing consisted only of a porch or open gallery. Immediately before its western front stood the little temple of Niké Apteros."—Smith's *Smaller History of Greece.*

Prospect Park. A fine pleasure-ground in the Borough of Brooklyn, New York City, covering an area of 550 acres. It was commenced in 1866, and completed at a cost of $12,000,000. The park contains 8 miles of drives, 3½ miles of bridle-paths, and 11 miles of pathways for pedestrians. A lake having an area of 61 acres, a carriage concourse 186 feet above the sea-level, fine old shade-trees, wooded hills, and extensive meadows are among the attractions offered to the visitor. In point of natural beauty, Prospect Park is considered to surpass its more showy rival in the Borough of Manhattan. The Ocean Parkway —a superb boulevard, 210 feet wide— leads from Prospect Park to the ocean, a distance of six miles.

Protector. A title conferred upon Oliver Cromwell (1599–1658), who in 1654 was formally proclaimed Lord Protector of the Commonwealth. The appellation "Protector" was also bestowed upon John, Duke of Bedford, and his brother Humphrey, Duke of Gloucester, in 1422 ; upon Richard, Duke of Gloucester, in 1483; and upon Edward Seymour, Duke of Somerset, in 1547.

Protestant Duke. An appellation conferred by his admirers upon James Scott, Duke of Monmouth (1649–1685), the natural son of Charles II, who, although reared a Catholic, embraced the Protestant faith. He raised the standard of rebellion against James II, whom he denounced as a tyrant and a popish usurper; was defeated at Sedgemoor; and beheaded on Tower Hill.

Protestant Pope. A title bestowed upon Pope Clement XIV (1769–1774), in allusion to a bull issued by him in 1773, ordering the suppression of the Order of the Jesuits, or the Society of

Jesus. This act gave great offense to the more devout Roman Catholics, who regarded it as a concession to Protestantism.

Protestants. A name originally given to the six Lutheran princes and the deputies of the thirteen imperial towns, who, at the Diet of Spires in 1529, formally and solemnly *protested* against the decree forbidding any further innovations in religion until the meeting of a general council. Since then, the term has come to be applied to all religious sects that *protest* against the doctrines and practices of the Church of Rome. See *Diet of Spires*.

Proteus. In classic mythology, a sea-god, — the son of Oceanus and Tethys. According to Homer, he dwelt on the island of Pharos, near the mouth of the Nile; but Virgil placed his favorite residence on the island of Carpathos, between Crete and Rhodes. Proteus tended the sea-flocks of Poseidon (Neptune), and possessed the gift of vaticination as well as the power of endless transformation. He showed great unwillingness to prophesy, and, when caught, assumed every possible shape to avoid the necessity of doing so ; but on realizing that escape was impossible, he resumed his natural shape, and foretold the future with accuracy.

Protoplasm (*Gr.*, πρῶτος, *first*, πλάσμα, *formed substance*). A viscid, jelly-like substance, forming the principal part of vegetal and animal cells. It was so named by Von Mohl in 1846 ; and, in 1863, was identified with the *sarcode* of animal tissues, discovered by Dujardin in 1835. Huxley, in 1868, called it " the physical basis of life." Protoplasm may be conveniently studied in the amœbæ and foraminifera (low forms of animal life); in the colorless blood-cells ; in tender vegetal shoots ; and in the ova of animals. The essential properties of life, viz., irritability, contractility,

assimilation, variability, heredity, and reproduction, — all inhere in protoplasm, but require for their manifestation moisture, a temperature ranging between 32° and 110° Fahrenheit, and the presence of certain complex food-compounds.

"The name was first applied in 1846 to the matter in vegetable cells, which was identified later with the animal substance previously known as *sarcode*. The protoplasm of most cells appears under high powers of the microscope as a network (spongioplasm or reticulum) containing a more fluid substance (hyaloplasm or enchylema) in its meshes. Chemically it is a mixture of 80 to 85 per cent. water and 15 to 20 per cent. solids, chiefly proteids, as albumoses, globulins, and peptones, with small quantities of fat, carbohydrates like glycogen and inosite, and mineral salts, especially those of potassium, which cause it to yield an alkaline reaction. Protoplasm has been called by Huxley the 'physical basis of life,' and some have held that its phenomena show that the difference between organized and unorganized matter is simply a difference of complexity of chemical constitution."—*Standard Dictionary*.

Provençal Language. A Romance dialect — sometimes called the *langue d'Oc*—spoken in France, south of the Loire, and also in eastern Spain, Savoy, Piedmont, and part of Switzerland. The Provençal was the language of the troubadours, and developed a considerable literature during the 12th and 13th centuries. A revival of Provençal literature, during the nineteenth century, was marked by much poetic activity. The modern Provençal is more simply inflected than the ancient, and has a large admixture of French. See *Langue d'Oc ; Troubadours*.

Provence. A former maritime province of France, bounded on the south by the Mediterranean Sea. It included a portion of the Roman province of Gaul, often called *Provincia* (*Lat.*, *the Province*), whence it derived its name. It was overrun in the fifth century by the Visigoths and Burgundians, and later by the Saracens. In 1486, it was united to France under Charles VIII (1483–1498). Ancient Provence comprised the French departments of

Bouches du Rhône, Var, Basses-Alpes, and portions of Alpes Maritimes and Vaucluse.

Proximate Principles. The name given in chemistry to certain organic compounds which, " from their being supposed to stand, in order of simplicity, nearest to the elements," are termed *proximate principles*. They form a series of compounds having a definite chemical composition, which may be isolated from vegetal and animal bodies after death, or may, in some cases, be artificially built up out of inorganic materials in the laboratory of the chemist. The principal proximate principles found in plants are starch, cellulose, sugar, gluten, and legumin ; while the chief ones found in animals are albumen, casein, fibrin, and certain fats.

Psalms, Book of. A collection of lyrics, 150 in number, forming one of the books of the *Old Testament*. The dates of the *Psalms* vary greatly,— ranging from the time of Moses to that of the Captivity, or, in the opinion of some critics, even to the days of the Maccabees. It was believed by the early Jews and Christians that all the *Psalms* were composed by David ; but an examination of their contents shows that they were written at various periods, and that David was simply the chief contributor. To him are ascribed 73 psalms in the Hebrew text, and 84 in the *Septuagint*. Among the other authors may be named Asaph, the sons of Korah, Jeduthun, Heman, Ethan, Moses, and Solomon.

P's and Q's," " Mind Your. This cautionary saying is generally believed to have originated in the public-houses of olden days, where it was the custom to keep a tally in chalk, on the wall, of the potations indulged in,—the letter "P" being used to denote the pints consumed, and the letter "Q" the quarts. As these scores were supposed to be settled weekly, the appli-

cation of the phrase, " Mind your P's and Q's," is extremely obvious.

Ptolemaic System. The name given to the theory of the solar system that places the earth at rest in the centre, while the heavens revolve around it from east to west once in 24 hours,—carrying with them the sun, moon, planets, and fixed stars, in their respective spheres. This theory received its name from Ptolemy Claudius (*fl.* 140 A.D.), the celebrated Greek astronomer, and held its place until superseded by the Copernican System. See *Copernican System ; Crystalline Spheres.*

"As soon as astronomers came to understand and test the Copernican Theory, this venerable and disorderly pile of hypotheses, which had received the papal seal of infallibility, and had in various forms held supreme sway over the minds of men for twenty centuries, at once crumbled to atoms and sank into oblivion."—*Chambers's Encyclopædia.*

Ptolemies. The name given to a dynasty of Greek rulers that governed Egypt from 323 to 30 B.C.,—a period of 293 years. It was founded by Ptolemy Lagus, surnamed also Soter, who, at the time of the death of Alexander the Great (323 B.C.), was Governor of Egypt, and after the division of the Empire into four monarchies, became king of that country. The dynasty of the Ptolemies comprised 14 sovereigns. On the death of Cleopatra —the last of the line—in 30 B.C., Egypt became a province of Rome.

Ptolemy's Mirror. A large mirror, said to have been placed in the tower of the Pharos of Alexandria by Ptolemy Euergetes (247–222 B.C.). Aboolfeda (1273–1331 A.D.), the famous Arabian writer, says that this mirror was made of Chinese iron, and that shortly after the Saracen conquest of Egypt it was destroyed by the Christians to prevent it from falling into the hands of their oppressors. In Buffon's opinion, Ptolemy's Mirror was made of polished steel. It reflected the greater part of Lower Egypt and a portion of the

Mediterranean Sea, and enabled the observer to detect either the approach of a hostile fleet or the existence of a disturbance on land. This account of Ptolemy's Mirror is generally regarded as fabulous.

Pucelle, La (*Fr.*, *The Maid*). A sobriquet conferred upon Joan of Arc (1411–1431), the Maid of Orleans.

Pulpit of Pisa. A famous hexagonal pulpit of white marble in the Baptistery of Pisa, executed by Nicolo Pisano in 1260. It is adorned with bas-reliefs, representing scenes from the *New Testament*. See *Baptistery of Pisa ; Pulpit of Siena.*

Pulpit of Siena. A superb octagonal pulpit of white marble in the Cathedral of Siena, Italy, carved by Nicolo Pisano, and completed in 1268. The sides are adorned with elaborately carved panels, depicting scenes from the Nativity, the Passion, and the Final Judgment. See *Pulpit of Pisa ; Siena Cathedral.*

Pulse. The following table, compiled from the observations of Dr. Guy, shows the differences in the rapidity of the pulse at different ages :

AGES.	MALES.	FEMALES.
	Average Pulsations.	*Average Pulsations.*
From 2 to 7 years.....	97	98
" 8 " 14 "	84	94
" 14 " 21 "	76	82
" 21 " 28 "	73	80
" 28 " 35 "	70	78
" 35 " 42 "	68	78
" 42 " 49 "	70	77
" 49 " 56 "	67	76
" 56 " 63 "	68	77
" 63 " 70 "	70	78
" 70 " 77 "	67	81
" 77 " 84 "	71	82

"Dr. Guy found the pulsations of the heart in the fœtus to be pretty uniformly 140 per minute. At birth, the pulse is 136. It gradually diminishes during the first year to about 128. The second year, the diminution is quite rapid, the tables of Dr. Guy giving 107 as the mean frequency at two years of age. After the second year, the frequency progressively diminishes until adult life, when it is at its minimum, which is about 70 per minute. It is a common but erroneous impression that the pulse diminishes in frequency in old age. On the contrary, numerous observations show that at the later periods of life the movements of the heart become slightly accelerated, ranging from 75 to 80.

During early life there is no marked and constant difference in the rapidity of the pulse in the sexes ; but, toward the age of puberty, the development of the sexual peculiarities is accompanied with an acceleration of the heart's action in the female, which continues even into old age."—Flint's *Text-Book of Human Physiology.*

Pultowa, Battle of. A desperate battle fought at Pultowa, Russia, on June 27th, 1709, between the Russians commanded by Peter the Great (1682–1725) and the Swedes under Charles XII (1697–1718). The latter were utterly defeated.

Punch. The name of this beverage is derived from the Hindu *panch* (*five.*) It is so called because it originally consisted of five ingredients, viz., sugar, arrack, spice, lemon-juice, and water.

Punch and Judy. The origin of this comic puppet-show has been the subject of much discussion. Punch has been identified with Pontius Pilate, Judy with Judas the betrayer, or with the Jews, and the play with one of the old "Mysteries." This notion is entirely without foundation. The name *Punch* is simply a contraction of *Punchinello* (for *Pulcinello*, the buffoon of Neapolitan comedy), while *Judy* is probably derived from *Judith*,—at one time a common female name. It is said that a character similar to Punch is found in the puppet-plays of Italy, Egypt, Persia, India, China, and Japan. Punch-and-Judy shows were introduced into London in 1666 by an Italian, who erected a booth near Charing Cross for their performance.

Punic Faith (*Lat. Fides Punica*). An ironical phrase used by the ancient Romans to denote treachery and faithlessness. The allusion is to their Punic or Carthaginian neighbors, whom they represented as wanting in integrity and honor. The word *Punica* is derived from *Pœni* (the Latin form of the name *Phœnicians*), from whom the Carthaginians were descended.

Punic Wars. The name given to the three great contests waged between Rome and Carthage for the supremacy of the Mediterranean Sea. They covered a period of more than 100 years (264–146 B.C.), and resulted in the defeat and destruction of Carthage.

(1) *First Punic War* (264–241 B.C.). Carthage gave up all claim to the island of Sicily, and paid an indemnity of 3200 talents.

(2) *Second Punic War* (218–201 B.C.). Carthage surrendered all her warships, except ten ; was forbidden to wage war on any state without the consent of Rome ; and was compelled to pay an indemnity of 10,000 talents, and a yearly tribute of 200 talents.

(3) *Third Punic War* (149–146 B.C.). Carthage fell after a siege of two years. The city was razed to the ground, and the country was made a Roman province.

Puránas. Sacred poetical books of the Hindus, popularly believed to have been arranged by Vyása, the reputed compiler of the *Vedas* and the author of the *Mahábhárata*. They contain mythological traditions, cosmogonic theories, epic narratives, and legendary lore ; and are supposed to have been prepared for the instruction of the lower castes. In their present form they probably belong to the earlier centuries of the Christian era, although containing materials much more ancient. The *Puránas* are 18 in number, and are subdivided into 3 groups of 6 each. They are written in epic couplets, and are estimated to contain 800,000 lines. See *Vedas*.

Purgatorio, Il. The title of the second part of Dante's *Divine Comedy*. It is in 33 cantos, and gives a picture of Purgatory, which, according to the poet, is situated in a mountain in mid-ocean, near the antipodes of Judea. This mountain is divided into terraces and terminates in Paradise, from which it is separated by the rivers Lethe and Eunoe. See *Divine Comedy ; Inferno, L' ; Paradiso, Il.*

Purgatory. In the theology of the Roman Catholic and Greek Churches, a place of purgation where souls, after death, are cleansed from venial sins or undergo the temporal punishment due to remitted mortal sins, before admittance into heaven. The Roman Catholics believe that the sufferings of the souls in Purgatory may be alleviated by the prayers and alms of the faithful and by the sacrifice of the mass. They further believe that this suffering is " by fire " ; in which notion they differ from the Greek Christians, who do not determine the manner of punishment, but regard it as simply " through tribulation." Protestants generally deny the existence of Purgatory, and hold that the scriptural passages and the writings of the Fathers, quoted in support of the doctrine, are insufficient to establish its validity. See *Paradise.*

Puritan City. An appellation bestowed upon the city of Boston, Massachusetts, in allusion to the strict notions of life and conduct entertained by its founders and early inhabitants.

Puritans. A name originally given in 1564 to those clergymen of the Church of England that refused to conform to the liturgy and discipline, as arranged by Archbishop Parker and his coadjutors, and insisted on a return to a *purer* form of faith and worship. In later years, the name " Puritans " was applied to those persons that actually separated from the Church of England, and eventually became Presbyterians, Independents, Baptists, etc. See *Pilgrims.*

" The *Puritans* as a body were strong upholders of freedom of conscience and of popular rights, disliked vestments, pomp, and ritualism, advocated simplicity in worship, and opposed anything that seemed to them to approach looseness of morals."—*Standard Dictionary*.

Purple Island. An allegorical poem by Phineas Fletcher (1584–1650), published in 1633. It is in 12 cantos, and constitutes an elaborate anatomical description of the body and mind of man, considered in the light of an island-kingdom.

"The title of the *Purple Island* is most attractive and most fallacious. If a reader should take it up (as would probably be the case with those ignorant of its nature) with the expectation of finding some delightful story or romantic fiction, what must be his disappointment to plunge at once into an anatomical lecture in verse on the human frame—to find that the poet has turned topographer of an island founded upon human bones, with veins for its thousand small brooks, and arteries for its larger streams; and that the mountains and valleys with which it is diversified are neither more nor less than the inequalities and undulations of the microcosm."—*Retrospective Review*.

Puseyism. A name given to the Tractarian movement in England in 1831–1845, principally by its opponents. The word is derived from Dr. Edward Bouverie Pusey, Regius Professor of Hebrew in the University of Oxford, one of the leaders of the movement and one of the chief contributors to the *Tracts for the Times*. See *Tractarianism*.

Puss in Boots. The hero of an old nursery tale of the same name, written by Charles Perrault (1628–1703). This story, which appeared in the author's *Contes des Fées* (1697), under the title of *Le Chat Botté*, narrates the adventures of a remarkably intelligent cat, which, by its ready wit, secures a fortune and a royal bride for its master, an impecunious young miller, who passes under the name of the Marquis de Carabas. Perrault borrowed the story from an Italian work entitled *The Nights*, by Straparola,—translated into French in 1585. A similar nursery tale is found in the German and Scandinavian. See *Carabas, Marquis of*.

Pygmalion.

(1) In classic mythology, a king of Cyprus, who fell in love with an ivory image of a young maiden that he had made, and besought Venus to endow it with life. The request was granted; whereupon Pygmalion married the maiden and became by her the father of Paphus.

(2) A king of Tyre, and brother of Dido. He murdered Sichæus, the husband of Dido, for his wealth; but Dido sailed secretly from Tyre with the treasure and crossed to Africa, where she founded the city of Carthage.

Pyramids of Gîzeh. The name given to a group of pyramids—nine in number—standing on the west bank of the Nile, near Memphis, Egypt. Like the other pyramids, they were simply tombs of the Egyptian monarchs that flourished from the First to the Twelfth Dynasty. The largest and most famous one of the group is the First or Great Pyramid, built by Chufu, or Cheops, the second king of the Fourth Dynasty, in 3733 B.C. (according to Brugsch). Its original height was 481 feet, and its base 774 feet square. The Second Pyramid was built by Chafra, or Chephren, the third king of the Fourth Dynasty, in 3666 B.C. (according to Brugsch). It is 450 feet high by 700 feet at the base. It contains two sepulchral chambers, opened by Belzoni in 1816. Its masonry is inferior to that of the First Pyramid. The Third Pyramid was erected by Menkaura, or Mycerinus (3633 B.C.), king of the Fourth Dynasty. It is much smaller than the other two, being only 215 feet high, on a base of 350 feet. The other six pyramids are greatly inferior in size and interest. It is estimated that there are about 75 pyramids in Egypt, situated between 29° and 30° north latitude. See *Great Pyramid*.

Pyramids, Battle of the. A sanguinary battle fought near Cairo, Egypt, between the French commanded by Napoleon Bonaparte (1769-1821), and the Mamelukes and their Arab auxiliaries under Mourad Bey. These superb horsemen of the desert were unable, after repeated charges, to break the French squares, and were mowed down on every side by the rolling fire of musketry and artillery. As a result of this victory, Bonaparte entered Cairo in triumph ; and, soon after, the whole of Lower Egypt submitted to his rule. It was at this battle that Bonaparte uttered the famous words : " Soldiers, from yonder pyramids forty centuries look down upon you ! "

Pyramus and Thisbe. In classic mythology, two ill-starred lovers of ancient Babylon, whose misfortunes are related in Ovid's *Metamorphoses.* They lived in adjoining houses, but, being prevented by their parents from meeting, they held frequent conversations through a hole in the wall. On a certain occasion they agreed upon a meeting at the tomb of Ninus. Thisbe was the first to arrive at the spot, and, while waiting for her lover, beheld a lioness that had recently devoured an ox. In her flight, she dropped a garment, which the lioness soiled with blood. Pyramus, on finding this, imagined that Thisbe had been murdered, and stabbed himself under a mulberry-tree,—the fruit of which, according to tradition, has ever since been blood-red. Soon after, Thisbe returned and, finding the dead body of her lover, killed herself with the same weapon. Shakespeare has introduced a burlesque of *Pyramus and Thisbe* in the *Interlude* in his *Midsummer Night's Dream.*

Pyrrhic Victory. A victory obtained at such a cost as to amount practically to a defeat. The allusion is to the battle of Asculum (279 B.C.), where the Romans, although defeated by Pyrrhus, made him pay so dearly for his triumph as to extort from him the words : " Another such victory and I am lost ! "

Pythagorean Theorem. The name given, in geometry, to the theorem that the square described on the hypothenuse of a plane right-angled triangle is equivalent to the sum of the squares described on the other two sides. Pythagoras [580 (?) –500 (?) B.C.], the famous Greek philosopher, is universally credited with the invention of this theorem. See *Asses' Bridge.*

Pythian Games. One of the four great festivals of ancient Greece, celebrated every fifth year, in honor of Apollo, in the Crissæan plain near Delphi. They were instituted, according to tradition, by Apollo, in commemoration of his victory over the serpent Python,—whence the name. These festivals were at first limited to singing, with cithern accompaniment ; but afterwards they came to include athletics, horse-racing, and contests in poetry and art. The victors were crowned with a laurel-wreath, or presented with a palm-branch. The Pythian Games were continued until 394 A.D. See *Isthmian Games ; Nemean Games ; Olympic Games ; Python.*

Pythias. See *Damon and Pythias.*

Pythium. A chasm, or opening, in the earth in the temple of Apollo, at Delphi, from which arose intoxicating vapors,— supposed to come from the well of Cassotis. See *Delphic Oracle.*

Python. In classic mythology, a huge serpent, formed from the mud left on the earth after the deluge of Deucalion. This monster dwelt in the caves of Mount Parnassus, but was slain by Apollo, who established the Pythian Games in commemoration of his victory, and received, in consequence, the surname "Pythius." See *Pythian Games.*

Pyx, Trial of the. A term applied in Great Britain to the official inquiry annually made to determine the weight and fineness of the standard coins issued from the Mint during the preceding year. It is so called from the *pyx*, *i. e.*, the box or chest in which are preserved the specimen gold and silver coins of the realm. The first trial is said to have been ordered during the reign of Henry II (1154-1189). The earlier tests occurred at irregular intervals ; but since the passage of the Coinage Act of 1870, the examination has been annually made at Goldsmiths' Hall, by a jury of goldsmiths presided over by the King's or Queen's Remembrancer. A similar examination takes place annually at the Philadelphia Mint, on the second Wednesday in February.

Q

Quadragesima Sunday. The first Sunday in Lent,—so called because it is about the fortieth (*Lat.*, *quadragesima, fortieth*) day before Easter.

Quadrilateral. The name given in modern history to four fortresses of northern Italy, in the valley of the Po, viz., Peschiera and Mantua on the Mincio, and Verona and Legnago on the Adige. They were surrendered to Italy by Austria on October 16th, 1866. The Prussian Quadrilateral is formed by the fortresses of Luxemburg, Coblentz, Sarre-Louis, and Mayence. See *Seven Days' War.*

Quadruple Alliance. An alliance between Great Britain, France, Austria, and Holland, formed in 1719. By it were guaranteed the succession of the House of Hanover to the English throne; the renunciation of the Spanish claim to the French crown ; and the succession of the princes of the Orleans family to the French throne, in case Louis XV (1715-1774) should die without issue. These conditions were accepted by Spain in 1720.

Quaker City. A name popularly conferred upon the city of Philadelphia,

40

which was settled by William Penn and a company of Friends, or Quakers, in 1682.

Quaker Poet.
(1) A name often given to Bernard Barton (1784-1840), the English poet, who was a member of the Society of Friends.
(2) A popular appellation of John Greenleaf Whittier (1807-1892), the American poet, who was a member of the Society of Friends.

Quakers. A word originally used, in a derisive sense, to designate the members of the " Society of Friends "; but no longer regarded by them as a term of opprobrium. It was first employed by Judge Bennet of Derby, who, in 1650, called George Fox and his associates " Quakers," because they bade the magistrates " *tremble* at the word of the Lord."

" Fox's teaching was primarily a preaching of repentance. . . . The trembling among the listening crowd caused or confirmed the name of *Quakers* given to the body; men and women sometimes fell down and lay struggling as if for life."—*Encyclopædia Britannica.*

Quarantine. This word is derived from the Italian *quarantina (forty)*, and originally denoted the period of 40 days, during which all merchants and others from the Levant—arriving at Venice—were obliged to remain in the house of St. Lazarus, before being admitted into the city.

Quartier Latin (*Fr.*, *Latin Quarter*). A district in the city of Paris, lying on the south side of the Seine. It is the centre of numerous learned institutions, and is inhabited by thousands of students, whose bohemian ways of life in olden days are described in the pages of Murger, Balzac, and De Musset.

" Due allowances made, there is still reason to believe that students and other men in the *Quartier Latin* of Paris present nowadays a quieter and, it must be acknowledged, often a more dignified appearance than that which they bore two generations since."—Dickens's *Dictionary of Paris.*

Quashee. A name sometimes given to a West Indian negro. It is said to be derived from Quassi, or Coissi, a black man of Surinam, who prescribed the bark of the quassia plant as a remedy for fever, and attained a great reputation for skill among the natives.

Quasimodo Sunday. The name usually given in France and Germany to Low Sunday, because the *Introit* in the mass used on that day begins with the words : *Quasimodo geniti infantes* (*Lat., As new-born babes*), 1 *Peter* ii, 2. See *Low Sunday.*

Quatre-Bras, Battle of. Fought at the village of Quatre-Bras, Belgium, 10 miles southeast of Brussels, on June 16th, 1815,—two days before the battle of Waterloo,—between the allies under the Duke of Brunswick, the Prince of Orange, and Sir Thomas Picton, and the French commanded by Marshal Ney. The French Marshal, after an ineffectual attempt to secure possession of Quatre-Bras, withdrew with a loss of over 4100 men. The loss of the allies was 5200, and included the Duke of Brunswick, to whose memory a bronze lion was erected in 1890.

Quebec, Battle of. A desperate battle fought on the Plains of Abraham on September 13th, 1759, between the French, commanded by the Marquis of Montcalm and the English under General Wolfe. The French were signally defeated and forced to evacuate the city of Quebec. Both commanders fell in the action. The battle of Quebec marked the close of French rule in North America. See *Abraham, Heights (or Plains) of.*

"With the triumph of Wolfe on the Heights of Abraham began the history of the United States. By removing an enemy whose dread had knit the colonists to the Mother-Country, and by breaking through the line with which France had barred them from the basin of the Mississippi, Pitt laid the foundation of the great Republic of the West. Nor were these triumphs less momentous to Britain. The Seven Years' War is, in fact, a turning-point in our National

History, as it is a turning-point in the history of the world."—Green's *History of the English People.*

Quebec Citadel. An impregnable fortress, crowning Cape Diamond,— 333 feet above the St. Lawrence River, —and constituting the chief defense of the city of Quebec, Canada. It covers an area of 40 acres, and commands a superb prospect of the river and the surrounding country. The original citadel was designed by Vauban ; the present one — built in 1823—is said to have been planned by the Duke of Wellington.

Queen Anne's Farthings. The name given to certain pattern farthings struck during the years 1713–1714, in accordance with suggestions for the improvement of the coinage made to the British Government by Dean Swift. It is currently believed in parts of England that only three of Queen Anne's farthings are in existence, and that of these, two are in the possession of the Government. The missing one is consequently assumed to be of enormous value, but the truth is that it is no rarer than any other coin of equal antiquity.

Queen Bess. See *Good Queen Bess.*

Queen City. A popular name of Cincinnati, Ohio,—conferred upon it when it was the commercial metropolis of the West. Although the city has lost its supremacy since the rise of Chicago and St. Louis, it retains this sobriquet at the present day. Also called the " Queen of the West."

> " And this song of the Vine,
>   This greeting of mine,
> The winds and the birds shall deliver
>   To the *Queen of the West,*
>   In her garlands dressed,
> On the banks of the beautiful river."
>   *Longfellow.*

Queen City of the Lakes. An appellation bestowed upon the city of Buffalo, New York, on account of its commercial importance and its commanding position on the Great Lakes

The title might, with more appropriateness, be conferred upon Chicago, Illinois.

Queen Dick. A nickname given to Richard Cromwell (1626–1712), whose brief rule as Lord Protector was characterized by timidity and incapacity.

"Queen of Spain Has No Legs." When Margaret of Austria, queen-consort and wife of Philip III (1598–1621) of Spain, made her entry into that country in 1599, she passed through a town famous for the manufacture of silk stockings. The authorities, as a mark of loyalty and respect, presented the Queen with a superb pair, but these were indignantly declined by the chamberlain, who declared that the Queen of Spain had no legs! Margaret of Austria, hearing of this, became very indignant, and threatened to return home,—declaring that she would not have left her native country if she had expected to lose her legs. The story is, in all probability, a joke on Spanish etiquette.

Queen of the Adriatic. A title conferred upon the city of Venice, Italy, which for centuries ruled the Adriatic Sea, and, until the discovery of the ocean route to India in 1498, controlled the commerce between Europe and the East.

Queen of the Antilles. A name given to the island of Cuba, which, in point of size, population, beautiful scenery, natural fertility, and capacious harbors, surpasses all the other islands of the West Indies.

Queen's Shilling. A coin, ordinarily an English shilling, handed to a recruit on his verbal declaration of intention to enter the British military service. Its acceptance is considered equivalent to signature of the contract. Sometimes, and since the death of Victoria, called the King's shilling.

Quid Rides ? "Quid Rides, the motto of Jacob Brandon, tobacco-broker, who lived at the close of the eighteenth century. It was suggested by Harry Calendon of Lloyd's coffee-house. *Quid Rides* (Latin) means 'Why do you laugh ?' *Quid Rides, i. e.,* 'the tobacconist rides.' "—Brewer's *Reader's Handbook.*

Quilp. A cruel, cunning, and ferocious dwarf in Dickens's *The Old Curiosity Shop.*

"The child was closely followed by an elderly man of remarkably hard features and forbidding aspect, and so low in stature as to be quite a dwarf, though his head and face were large enough for the body of a giant. His black eyes were restless, sly, and cunning ; his mouth and chin, bristly with the stubble of a coarse hard beard ; and his complexion was one of that kind which never looks clean or wholesome. . . . His dress consisted of a large high-crowned hat, a worn dark suit, a pair of capacious shoes, and a dirty white neckerchief sufficiently limp and crumpled to disclose the greater portion of his wiry throat. Such hair as he had was of a grizzly black, cut short and straight upon his temples, and hanging in a frowsy fringe about his ears. His hands, which were of a rough coarse grain, were very dirty ; his finger-nails were crooked, long, and yellow."
—Dickens's *The Old Curiosity Shop.*

Quinquagesima Sunday. The first Sunday before Lent,— so called because it is about the fiftieth (*Lat., quinquagesima, fiftieth*) day before Easter.

Quintessence. The ancient Greek philosophers recognized four elements in nature, viz., fire, air, earth, and water. To these the Pythagoreans added a fifth and called it ether, the fifth substance. This they asserted was more subtile than fire; it had an upward motion at creation, and formed the substance out of which the stars were made. The alchemists of the Middle Ages gave the name *quintessence* to alcohol and to the ferment oils.

" Swift to their sev'ral quarters hasted then
 The cumbrous elements, Earth, Flood,
  Air, Fire ;
 And this ethereal *quintessence* of Heav'n
 Flew upward, spirited with various forms,
 That roll'd orbicular, and turned to stars
 Numberless, as thou seest, and how they
  move : "

Paradise Lost, iii, 714-719.

Quirinal Palace. An immense structure on the summit of the Quirinal Hill at Rome. It was begun by Pope Gregory XIII (1572–1585) in 1574, and continued by a long series of succeeding pontiffs. The Quirinal Palace is at present the residence of the King of Italy and his family ; but prior to 1870 it was the summer residence of the Popes. The meetings of the conclaves of cardinals for the election of a new pope were, at one time, held there; and from the balcony of the palace—facing the Piazza del Quirinale—the name of the newly elected pope was announced to the people. Pope Pius VII (1800–1823) died there.

Quo Vadis Church. See *Domine, Quo Vadis Church.*

R

Rabbinical Literature. A term erroneously applied to the literature of the Jews after their return from the Captivity (536 B.C.). It consists of innumerable works—principally in Hebrew and Arabic—by learned rabbis ; and treats mainly of questions dealing with the Law of Moses, although occasionally branching out into poetry, philosophy, ethics, history, and grammar. Among the more famous rabbinical works may be mentioned the *Septuagint Translation*, the *Jerusalem Talmud*, the *Babylonian Talmud*, the *Midrash*, and the *Targums.*

Races of Men. The foremost naturalists of modern times — including Linnæus, Blumenbach, Huxley, Virchow, Flower, Broca, and Topinard—practically agree in classifying the entire human family in three, four, or, at most, five primary groups. These are (1) the *Caucasic* (white) ; (2) the *Mongolic* (yellow) ; (3) the *Ethiopic* (black) ; (4) the *American* (red) ; and (5) the *Malayo-Polynesian* (brown). Many modern authorities, however, regard the *American* and *Malayo-Poly-*nesian as remote branches of the *Mongolic* ; and Professor Flower, who, in 1885, adopted the threefold division of *Caucasic, Mongolic,* and *Ethiopic,* says that primitive man, in the course of time, became differentiated into " the three extreme types represented by the Caucasian of Europe, the Mongolian of Asia, and the Ethiopian of Africa, and that all existing members of the species can be ranged around these types, or somewhere or other between them."

Radcliffe College. A collegiate institution for the higher education of women, at Cambridge, Massachusetts, —founded in 1893. It is an outgrowth of the "Harvard Annex," or "Society for the Collegiate Instruction of Women," organized in 1879,—the instructors being members of the Harvard faculty. Radcliffe College has, at present, 114 instructors, 407 students, and a library of 13,000 volumes. Its diplomas are signed by the President of Harvard University. The college is named in honor of the Englishwoman, Anne Radcliffe (Lady Moulson), the first woman to give a scholarship (1640) to Harvard University.

Rail-Splitter. A nickname conferred upon Abraham Lincoln (1809–1865), who, during the year 1830, is said to have supported himself by splitting rails for his father.

" One of the first duties was to fence in a field on the rich bottom-lands, which had been selected for cultivation. For this purpose, with the help of one laborer, Abraham Lincoln, it is said, split three thousand rails —the crowning work of a long, laborious period of his life. The hand who aided him in this exploit, named John Hanks, a distant relative of his mother, bears earnest testimony to the strength and skill with which the maul and the wedge were employed on this occasion."—Barrett's *Life of Abraham Lincoln.*

Railway King. A title bestowed upon George Hudson (1801–1871) of York, England, whose railway speculations were among the boldest and most daring of modern times. After amassing great wealth, he became involved in the railway-panic of 1847–1848, and lost the principal part of his vast fortune. In 1859, he retired to the Continent, where he lived for several years in straitened circumstances.

Raised to the Purple. An expression used to denote elevation to the rank of emperor among the ancient Romans. The allusion is, of course, to the purple robe, or mantle, worn by the Roman emperors as a badge of imperial dignity.

Rake's Progress. The name given to a series of eight paintings by William Hogarth (1697–1764), depicting, with rare skill, the career of a dissipated man of fashion of the time.

Ramadan. The ninth month of the Moslem year, observed as a fast in commemoration of the first revelation received by Mohammed. It commences with the new moon of the ninth month of the year, and ends on the day preceding the great festival of Bairam. From dawn to sunset of each day during this period, the strictest abstinence is enjoined, — all eating, drinking, bathing, smoking, and other bodily pleasures—even swallowing one's saliva, being forbidden. At night, however, the satisfaction of the most necessary desires is permitted. As the Mohammedan year is lunar—consisting of 354 days, 21 hours—it follows that, in the course of 33 years, the *Ramadan* passes through all the seasons. It is said that the fast of the *Ramadan* is much less strictly observed than in former times. See *Islâm*.

Rámáyana. A celebrated Hindu poem, narrating the adventures of Ráma, one of the incarnations of the god Vishnu. It contains 48,000 lines of 16 syllables each, and is traditionally ascribed to Valmíki, who is said to have recited the poem to the sons of Ráma. The *Rámáyana* is the work of a single mind; and ranks, as a poetic composition, far above the *Mahábhá-*

rata. Its date is unknown, but it is generally believed to have been written prior to 500 B.C. Unlike the *Mahábhárata*, the *Rámáyana* contains little incidental matter ; but deals almost exclusively with the history of the Ráma incarnation of Vishnu. See *Mahábhárata*.

"The great Hindoo epic entitled *Rámáyănă* is chiefly occupied with the adventures and exploits of Rama and his famous minister Hânumân, the monkey king. The consort of Rama was Sîtâ, eminent for her purity and other virtues. Her deliverance from the power of the great giant Râvana, and the triumphant issue of the ordeal by fire, by which her perfect virtue was completely established, form perhaps the most interesting portion of the great poem or romance above named."—Lippincott's *Biographical Dictionary*.

Rambouillet, Hôtel de. See *Hôtel de Rambouillet.*

Ramillies, Battle of. A battle fought at Ramillies, a village in Belgium, on May 23rd, 1706, between the allied forces commanded by the Duke of Marlborough and the French under Marshal de Villeroy and the Elector of Bavaria. The French were defeated with a loss of 13,000 killed and wounded, while about 4000 of the allies were slain in the action. As a result of this battle, the French were obliged to evacuate the whole of the Spanish Netherlands.

Ranks in the Peerage. The higher nobility, or peerage, of England consists of five ranks, viz., duke, marquis, earl, viscount, and baron. All persons holding these titles are members of the Upper House of Parliament, where they sit as Lords Temporal. The archbishops and bishops of the Established Church are termed Lords Spiritual. They are not peers of the realm, but have seats in the Upper House.

Ranz des Vaches. The French name given to the simple native airs played on the Alphorn or Kuh-horn, and sung by the herdsmen of the Swiss Alps, while driving their herds to and from pasture. The pastoral associations called forth by these melodies, when heard by the Swiss in foreign lands, are said to produce in them an irresistible longing for home.

Rape of the Sabines. A famous group in marble, by John of Bologna (1524-1608), in the Loggia di Lanzi at Florence, Italy. It represents a young man holding a young woman in his arms, with an old man lying at his feet. It is generally regarded as the sculptor's masterpiece.

Raphael. According to Christian and Jewish tradition, one of the seven archangels that stand around the throne of God,—the other six being Gabriel, Michael, Uriel, Chamuel, Zophiel, and Zadkiel. He is mentioned in the apocryphal book of *Tobit* as the friend of Tobias ; through his aid Sara was delivered from her plague, and Tobit from his blindness. Raphael is introduced by Milton into *Paradise Lost*, where he figures as the guardian-angel of humanity, sent by God to warn Adam of the danger of sin and its unhappy consequences.

"*Raphael*, the sociable Spirit, that deign'd
To travel with Tobias, and secured
 His marriage with the sev'ntimes-wedded
 maid."
                    Paradise Lost, v, 221-223.

Raphael of Cats. A nickname given to Godefroi Mind (1768-1814), the Swiss painter, noted for his pictures of cats.

Raphael of England. A sobriquet conferred upon Sir Joshua Reynolds (1723-1792), the famous English painter.

Raphael of France. An appellation bestowed upon Eustache Lesueur (1617-1655), a French painter of mediocre ability, who was raised to fame by the low state of art during his time.

Raphael of Music. An appellation conferred upon Wolfgang Amadeus Mozart (1756-1791), the eminent musical composer.

Raphael's "Hours." A series of twelve pictures, in the Pompeiian style, generally ascribed to Raphael (1483-1520), although, in the opinion of many critics, no valid reason exists for connecting his name with them. The originals are thought to be lost, and are known to us only from engravings. The "Hours" are represented by twelve female figures floating in space: they are gracefully draped, and symbolize the varying moods manifested by man during the passage of time. According to some authorities, the "Hours" were sketched by Raphael and completed by his pupils ; while others assert that they are simply copies of Pompeiian pictures, to which the name of Raphael was added to render their sale more easy and profitable.

"It is asserted that they were painted in an inner room in the Vatican, now altered ; but Passavant rejects the idea of their genuineness, and insists that they were engraved from mural remains of Pompeii."—*Radcliffe*.

Rare Ben. An epithet conferred by William Shakespeare upon Ben Jonson (1574-1637), the celebrated English poet and dramatist. It is stated by John Aubrey, in his *Letters*, that the inscription, "O Rare Ben Jonson," over the poet's grave in Westminster Abbey, was placed there at the suggestion of one Jack Young, an eccentric gentleman, who, at the time of the burial, gave a workman eighteen pence to engrave it. Jonson is buried, in an upright position, beneath the pavement of the north aisle of the abbey ; but a medallion in his honor may be seen in the south transept, or Poets' Corner. See *Poets' Corner*.

Ratio of Diameter to Circumference. See *Squaring the Circle*.

Reading Magdalen. A famous painting by Correggio (1494-1534), in the Gallery at Dresden, Saxony. It is a small picture—14 by 18 inches—and represents the Magdalen lying upon the ground, with one hand supporting the head, while the other holds a book on which the eyes are attentively fixed. It was purchased by Augustus III, Elector of Saxony, from the Duke of Modena in 1745, for 6000 louis-d'or ($30,000). The picture, which is painted on copper, is hung on hinges so that it may be seen in different lights. According to *Chambers's Encyclopædia* it is now regarded as merely a 17th-century copy of the original, painted in 1528.

Real Presence. The doctrine that teaches the actual presence of the body and blood of Jesus Christ in the Eucharist, after the consecration of the elements. This view is held by the Roman Catholic, the Greek, and other Eastern Churches, and also by certain members of the Anglican Communion. See *Consubstantiation; Elevation of the Host; Transubstantiation.*

Reason, Goddess of. See *Goddess of Reason.*

Rebecca of Ivanhoe. The heroine of Scott's *Ivanhoe* is said to have been named in honor of Rebecca Gratz (1781–1869), a Jewess of Philadelphia, famous for her beauty, her philanthropy, and her steadfast devotion to the faith of her fathers. Washington Irving, who was an intimate friend of the Gratz family, spoke of her during his visit to Abbotsford in the autumn of 1817, and his description of the fair Jewess's charms so captivated Walter Scott that he resolved to introduce a character similar to hers into one of his forthcoming novels. In 1819, appeared his *Ivanhoe*, in which the heroine received the name of Rebecca, in honor of Irving's friend.

Rebekah's-Camels Bible. The name given to an edition of the Bible, published in 1823, from an error in *Genesis* xxiv, 61, where the word *damsels* is rendered *camels*.

"And Rebekah arose, and her *camels*, and they rode upon the camels, and followed the man: and the servant took Rebekah, and went his way."

Rebel Brigadiers. A nickname conferred by Northern politicians upon those Southern Congressmen that had served in the Confederate army during the Civil War.

Rechabites. The descendants of Jonadab, son of Rechab, who were forbidden by him to drink wine, to build houses, to sow seed, or to plant or own vineyards. They were further commanded to dwell in tents all their days, as remembering that they were strangers in the land. The Rechabites were of Midianite origin, and dwelt at Jerusalem about 600 B.C. They were probably carried into captivity by Nebuchadnezzar (606 B.C.), and after their return to Judea settled in the city of Jabez, beyond Jordan. The name "Rechabites" has been adopted by several bodies of total abstainers from alcoholic drinks, in England and America. See *Jeremiah* xxxv.

Recusants. A term first applied in England, during the reign of Elizabeth (1558–1603), to those persons that refused or neglected to attend the services of the Established Church. Harsh measures were enacted against them, —especially in the case of the Roman Catholic Recusants, who were fined 100 marks (£66 13s. 4d.) for wilfully *hearing* mass and double that amount for *saying* mass, with a year's imprisonment in addition, in both cases. They were, furthermore, disabled from inheriting, purchasing, or in any way acquiring lands ; were forbidden to teach school ; to hold public office ; to keep arms in their houses ; or to come within ten miles of London, under penalty of £100. They were not permitted to travel more than five miles from home without a special license, and could bring no action at law or in equity. Protestant Recusants were relieved from their disabilities by the *Toleration Act of 1689;* and Catholic Recusants were relieved partially in 1791, and completely by the *Emancipation Act of 1829.*

Redan. A fortification, forming one of the chief defenses of the city of

Sebastopol during the Crimean War (1854–1856). It was unsuccessfully assaulted by the English on September 8th, 1855 ; but, owing to the capture of the Malakhoff by the French on the same day, and the consequent abandonment of Sebastopol by the Russians, the Redan fell into the hands of the allies soon after. See *Malakhoff.*

Red-Book. A name popularly given in Great Britain to a volume containing the names of all persons holding office under the Government in the civil, military, and naval service,— with their birthplaces, salaries, and other particulars. The term " Red-Book " is also applied to a volume that contains similar information respecting the 14,000 officials of the Chinese Empire. See *Blue-Books ; Yellow-Book.*

Red Cap. See *Bonnet Rouge.*

Redcoats. A nickname given by the American colonists to the British soldiers during the Revolutionary War, in allusion to the color of their uniforms.

Red Cross Society, American National. A society organized in the United States of America for the relief of suffering occasioned by war, pestilence, famine, flood, fire, or other far-reaching calamity. It was incorporated under the laws of the District of Columbia on October 1st, 1881, and re-incorporated on April 17th, 1863. The society acts under the Geneva Treaty,—signed in 1864, — whereby every society of whatever nation, organized for the aid of the sick and wounded in time of war and recognized by the military authorities of its own nation, is granted the rights of neutrality. The badge adopted by these various relief organizations is a red cross on a white ground. This symbol is respected on the battle-field by all civilized nations.

Red Hat. This symbol of office— not *worn* by cardinals, but suspended

in the church of their title and finally buried with them—was first presented to these princes of the Roman Catholic Church by Pope Innocent IV (1243–1254) in 1243 or 1245. The color was chosen for the purpose of reminding them that they should be willing to shed their blood in the defense of the Church, if necessary. See *Cardinals.*

Red-Letter Days. This expression —meaning happy, fortunate, or auspicious days—finds its origin in the old Anglican Calendar, where the greater Festivals and Saints' Days were printed in red letters, and the lesser ones in black. See *Black-Letter Days.*

Red Man.
(1) According to a superstition current in France, and especially in Brittany, a demon that controls the elements and casts into the sea those that disturb his solitude. It was popularly believed in France that a little Red Man mysteriously appeared to the first Napoleon and foretold his downfall.
(2) A name often given to the American Indian, on account of the color of his skin.

Red Men. William Hepworth Dixon (1821–1879) says that the Mormons, or Latter-Day Saints, regard the Red Men, or North American Indians, as descendants of the ancient Hebrews, who, as a punishment for their disobedience, were deprived of their priestly functions and changed in physiognomy and color. It is further believed that, after a time, they will assume their original hue, and will be reinstated in the priestly office.

Red Prince. A nickname given to Prince Frederick Charles of Prussia (1828–1885), nephew of the Emperor William I, in allusion to the color of his favorite hussar uniform. He was an able soldier, and rendered efficient and valuable service during the wars with Austria (1866) and France (1870).

Red Republicans. A name given in France to the advocates of extreme republican doctrines. They are so called, in allusion to the red cap of liberty worn by them during the French Revolution. See *Bonnet Rouge*.

"The *Red Republicans* were so called for a two-fold reason. In the first place, they did not hesitate to steep their hands in human blood to accomplish their political aims; and, secondly, they wore the red cap, symbolical of Liberty from the days of the Romans downwards."—Wagner's *Names and their Meaning*.

Red Riding-Hood. See *Little Red Riding-Hood.*

Red Sea. The origin of this term is much disputed. In the opinion of some, this body of water is so called from the large amount of red coral and pink-colored fuci found in it, while others declare that the name comes from the red soil that forms the bottom of the sea. The term is, however, with greater probability, derived from the ancient *Idumæa (Sea of Edom)*,—Edom signifying *red*. Haydn's *Dictionary of Dates* is authority for the statement that Ehrenberg, in 1826, discovered that the color was due to the presence of the marine plant, *Trichodesmium erythræum*.

Redskins. A nickname conferred upon the American Indians by the Europeans.

Red Snow. A name popularly given to the *Protococcus nivalis*, a microscopic red plant of the subkingdom *Protophyta*, found in the arctic and alpine regions, the snow of which it tinges with large patches of scarlet,—whence its name.

Redwood Library. A beautiful old Doric structure at Newport, Rhode Island, built in 1750 by Peter Harrison, assistant architect of Blenheim Palace. The library was incorporated in 1747. It contains about 35,000 books,—some of which were presented by the King of England and Bishop Berkeley—and several choice works of art.

Referendum. A political institution peculiar to Switzerland, by means of which all legislation enacted in the Federal and Cantonal Assemblies may be *referred* to the people for their ratification or rejection. In some Swiss Cantons a similar method of *Referendum* has been practised since the 16th century; but the present form was not adopted until 1830, when it was introduced into the Canton of St. Gallen. In 1848, the *Referendum* was incorporated into the Swiss Federal Constitution ; and in 1874, its application was extended. At the present day, the *Referendum* exists in all the Cantons except Freiburg. In the majority of the Cantons, 5000 signatures are necessary to obtain a *Referendum* for Cantonal laws. Swiss voters enjoy, in addition, the right of *Initiative*, whereby they may commence proceedings for the enactment of new laws, or the repeal or amendment of old ones. At least 50,000 signatures are required to exercise this privilege in federal affairs ; and, in most of the Cantons, 5000 signatures are necessary for Cantonal legislation. *Referendum* and *Initiative* mark the highest developments of democracy thus far attained.

Reformation. The name given to the great religious revolution of the 16th century, which resulted in the establishment of Protestantism throughout a great part of western Christendom. Although the Reformation originated during the Renaissance, it did not assume definite shape until 1517, when Martin Luther (1483–1546) vigorously protested against the sale of indulgences under papal sanction, and roused the people of Germany to a realization of the corrupt practices of the Church. The Reformation achieved its greatest success in Germany, Switzerland, Holland, Denmark, Sweden, Scotland, and England. In Spain and Italy, it was crushed by the Inquisition; in France, it gave rise to the Huguenot Wars ; while in

Bohemia and parts of Germany, its development was greatly retarded by the " Thirty Years' War." Speaking broadly, the Teutonic peoples accepted the reformed faith, while those of Latin origin adhered to the Roman Catholic religion.

Reformed Episcopal Church. An ecclesiastical organization founded in the United States in 1873, by the Right Reverend George David Cummins, D.D. (1822–1876), Assistant Bishop of the Protestant Episcopal Church in the diocese of Kentucky, and established in England four years later. It is composed principally of seceders from the Protestant Episcopal Church, and numbers, in this country, 8 bishops, 103 ministers, 104 churches, and about 10,000 communicants. It adopts the *Prayer-Book of 1785 ;* and condemns the following doctrines held, in substance, by the parent organization :

(1) That the Church of Christ exists only in one order or form of ecclesiastical polity.

(2) That Christian ministers are " priests " in another sense than that in which all believers are a " royal priesthood."

(3) That the Lord's table is an altar on which an oblation of the body and blood of Christ is offered anew to the Father.

(4) That the presence of Christ in the Lord's Supper is a presence in the elements of bread and wine.

(5) That regeneration is inseparably connected with baptism.

Re Galantuomo (*It., Honest King*). A title conferred upon Victor Emmanuel II (1849–1878), King of Sardinia and afterwards of United Italy, in allusion to the generous manner in which he redeemed his promise to maintain a constitutional government, a free press, and a fair degree of religious liberty.

Regalia of England. The name given to a superb collection of crowns and other emblems of royalty, carefully preserved in the Jewel-Room of the Tower of London. The Regalia at present consists of the following articles:

(1) St. Edward's Crown, made for the coronation of Charles II,—the original crown of King Edward having been sold after the execution of Charles I.

(2) Queen Victoria's Crown.
(3) The Prince of Wales's Crown.
(4) The Queen Consort's Crown.
(5) The Queen's Crown.
(6) St. Edward's Staff.
(7) The Royal Sceptre.
(8) The Sceptre of the Dove, or Rod of Equity.
(9) Queen Victoria's Sceptre.
(10) The Ivory Sceptre.
(11) The Sceptre of Queen Mary.
(12) The Orbs of the King and Queen.
(13) The Model of the Koh-i-nur Diamond (original at Windsor Castle).
(14) The Curtana, or Pointless Sword of Mercy.
(15) The Swords of Justice.
(16) The Coronation Bracelets.
(17) The Royal Spurs.
(18) The Coronation Oil Vessel, or Ampulla.
(19) The Anointing Spoon (probably the only existing relic of the ancient Regalia).
(20) The Salt-cellar of State.
(21) The Baptismal Font.
(22) The Wine Fountain.
(23) The Basin.

The total value of the Regalia is estimated at $15,000,000. See *Crown of England ; Tower of London.*

Regalia of Scotland. See *Crown of Scotland.*

Regent Diamond. See *Pitt Diamond.*

Regent's Park. An extensive pleasure-ground in the northwest part of London,—laid out during the last years of George III (1760–1820), and opened to the public in 1838. It covers an area of 472 acres, and derives its name from the Prince-Regent, afterwards George IV (1820–1830). A large part of the park is occupied by the Zoölogical Gardens, the Botanical Gardens, the Baptist College, and various private villas.

Regent Street. A famous street in London, devoted to the fashionable retail trade. It is about one mile long, and extends from Waterloo Place to Portland Place. Regent Street was laid out by John Nash in 1813, and named by him in honor of his patron, the Prince-Regent, afterwards George IV (1820–1830).

Regicides. The name given in English history to the 150 commissioners chosen by Parliament to try Charles I (1625–1649) of England. Of this number, 70 actually sat in trial upon the King, and 59 signed the death-warrant (January, 1649). Of these last, 29 were afterwards tried and condemned to death, but only 10 were executed,— the remaining 19, together with 6 others (who were not granted a trial), being imprisoned, some of them for life. Three of the Regicides, Whalley, Goffe, and Dixwell, escaped to New England, where they dwelt for some time in concealment. See *Regicides' Cave*.

Regicides' Cave. A cavern on the summit of West Rock, near New Haven, Connecticut, where Goffe and Whalley — two of the Regicides that had escaped from England after the restoration of the Stuarts — lay concealed for some time in 1661. See *Regicides*.

Regius Professor (*Lat.*, *regius*, *royal*). In the Universities of Oxford and Cambridge, a professor that occupies a chair founded by Henry VIII (1509–1547). In the Scotch universities, regius professors are appointed by the Crown.

Règne Animal (*Fr.*, *Animal Kingdom*). A famous scientific treatise on zoölogy by Georges Cuvier (1769–1832), published in 1817.

" The work immediately took the highest rank among books of the kind, and became generally the basis or guide of zoölogical studies throughout Europe."—Lippincott's *Biographical Dictionary*.

Regular Clergy. A term applied, in the Greek and Latin Churches, to the body of ecclesiastics that have assumed monastic vows, and live apart from the world, in accordance with some *regula*, or rule. As distinguished from these are the secular clergy, who do not follow any religious rule, but have the care of parishes.

Reichsrath. The name given to the representative council of the Austrian Empire. It consists of an Upper and a Lower House,—the former of which contains 225 members, and is composed of princes of the Imperial family that have attained the age of 21 years, hereditary nobles, archbishops and bishops, and certain life-members nominated by the Emperor for distinguished services in Church or State, science or art. The Lower House contains 353 members, chosen as popular representatives of the 16 provinces that constitute the Austrian Empire. All bills, to become laws, must pass both Houses of the Reichsrath and, in addition, must obtain the sanction of the Emperor.

Reichstag. The name given to one of the two legislative bodies in the German Empire,— the other being known as the Bundesrath, or Federal Council. The Reichstag is composed of 397 members, elected by universal suffrage and ballot, for a term of five years. It must be convened annually, but cannot meet unless the Bundesrath is also in session. All bills, to become Imperial laws, must pass both Houses by a clear majority ; and must, in addition, be signed by the Emperor and countersigned by the Chancellor of the Empire, who is, *ex officio*, the President of the Bundesrath. See *Bundesrath*.

Reign of Terror. A term applied to the period during the French Revolution, included between the fall of the Girondists (May 31st, 1793), and the overthrow of Robespierre and his associates (July 27th, 1794). It lasted 420 days, and was characterized by anarchy, violence, and bloodshed. It is estimated that in Paris alone, 1285 persons were guillotined between June 10th and July 17th, 1794,—the closing days of the "Terror." See *Ninth Thermidor*.

Reinecke Fuchs. See *Reynard the Fox*.

Relics. The following list of famous relics is taken from Brewer's *Reader's Handbook*. It is given on the authority of John Brady (1839), and may be found in his *Clavis Calendria*.

"COAL. One of the coals that roasted St. Lawrence.

FACE. The face of a seraph, with only part of the nose. (See below, 'Snout.')

FINGER. A finger of St. Andrew; one of John the Baptist; one of the Holy Ghost; and the thumb of St. Thomas.

HANDKERCHIEFS (*Two*), with impressions of the face of Christ: one sent by our Lord Himself, as a present to Agbarus, prince of Edessa; and the other given to St. Veronica, as the 'Man of sorrows' was on His way to execution. The woman had lent it to Jesus to wipe His brow with, and when He returned it an impression of His face was photographed on it.

HEAD. Two heads of John the Baptist.

HEM. The hem of our Lord's garment which the woman with the issue of blood touched; and the hem of Joseph's garment.

LOCK OF HAIR. A lock of the hair with which Mary Magdalene wiped the Saviour's feet.

NAIL. One of the nails used in the Crucifixion, set in the 'iron crown of Lombardy.'

PHIAL OF SWEAT. A phial of the sweat of St. Michael, when he contended with Satan.

RAYS OF A STAR. Some of the rays of the guiding star which appeared to the Wise Men of the East.

RIB. A rib of the 'Verbum caro factum,' or the Word made flesh.

ROD. Moses' rod.

SEAMLESS COAT. The seamless coat of our Lord, for which lots were cast at the Crucifixion.

SLIPPERS. A pair of slippers worn by Enoch before the Flood.

SNOUT. The 'snout' of a seraph, supposed to have belonged to the face (see above).

SPOON. The pap-dish and spoon used by the Virgin Mary for the child Jesus.

SWORD AND SHIELD. The short sword of St. Michael, and his square buckler lined with red velvet.

TEAR. The tear shed by Jesus over the grave of Lazarus. It was given by an angel to Mary Magdalene.

TOOTH. A tooth of our Lord Himself.

WATER-POT. One of the water-pots used at the marriage at Cana, in Galilee."

See *Crucifixion, Relics of the.*

Relics of the Crucifixion. See *Crucifixion, Relics of the.*

Religio Medici (*Lat. Religion of a Physician*). A famous and somewhat singular book written by Sir Thomas Browne (1605-1682), an eminent English physician, and anonymously published in 1642. It contains a minute statement of the author's opinions,—not only on religion, but also on a variety of philosophic and fanciful questions. The book gave rise to numerous imitations, and was speedily translated into Latin, French, Italian, German, and Dutch. Owing to certain heterodox statements, the *Religio Medici* was placed in the *Index Expurgatorius*.

"The *Religio Medici* was no sooner published, than it excited the attention of the public by the novelty of paradoxes, the dignity of sentiment, the quick succession of images, the multitude of abstruse allusions, the subtilty of disquisition, and the strength of language."—*Samuel Johnson*.

Religion of Humanity. A form of religion advocated by Auguste Comte (1798-1857), in his system of Positive Philosophy. It proposed the worship of Humanity as an object of love and reverence, in place of a Deity whose existence (according to Comte) it is impossible either to affirm or deny. Comte's conception of Humanity is that of a collective entity,—comprising all the men and women, past, present, and to come, whose lives have been, are, or shall be devoted to the well-being of mankind. Love is the leading principle of the Religion of Humanity, order its foundation, and progress its object. See *Positivism*.

"Comte looked on the *religion of Humanity* as fulfilling all the highest aims sought by the religions of the past, and especially as succeeding naturally to Christianity, the historical value of which he thoroughly appreciated as a transitional phase of religious development."—*Chambers's Encyclopædia*.

Religions of the World. The following statistics concerning the chief religions of the world are taken from the *World Almanac* for 1901. They were prepared by M. Fournier de Flaix, and are the latest estimates made by a competent and reliable authority.

(1) Christianity................ 477,080,158
(2) Ancestor-Worship and Confucianism.............. 256,000,000
(3) Hinduism.................. 190,000,000
(4) Mohammedanism.......... 176,834,372
(5) Buddhism.................. 147,900,000
(6) Taoism.................... 43,000,000
(7) Shintoism................. 14,000,000
(8) Judaism................... 7,186,000
(9) Polytheism 117,631,669

It is estimated that there are more than 1000 religions in the world at the present day.

"Remember the Vase of Soissons!" At a division of spoil after the battle of Soissons (486 A.D.), Clovis (481–511), King of the Franks, asked for himself a costly vase, which had been stolen by the soldiers from one of the churches of Rheims, and which he desired to restore. All present consented except one, who, raising his battle-axe, shattered the vase at one blow, exclaiming : "Never shalt thou have more than thy allotted share !" The King concealed his anger, but in the following year, at a general review of his troops, he approached this soldier that had insulted him, and, taking from him his axe, threw it upon the ground, in reproof for not keeping it in proper condition. As the unfortunate offender stooped to pick up his weapon, Clovis, with one blow of his

battle-axe, cleft his skull, exclaiming as he did so: " Remember the vase of Soissons ! "

" Remember Thou Art a Man ! " It was customary in ancient Rome, whenever a successful general was awarded the honor of a public triumph, to place in the chariot with him a public slave who, according to Tertullian, ever and anon whispered into the ear of the conqueror the words, "*Hominem memento te*" ("*Remember thou art a man*").

Vespasian, the Roman Emperor, had a slave, who said to him daily, as he left his apartment, " *Remember thou art only a man*," and thus reminded him of the transitory nature of earthly glory.

It is said that as the Roman Emperors passed in state through the streets of the Imperial city, they were preceded by an officer, who carried burning flax, and uttered from time to time the words, " *Sic transit gloria mundi*" ("*Thus passes away the glory of the world*"). See *Skulls at Banquets*.

Renaissance. The name given to the great intellectual movement that took place in Europe during the 15th and 16th centuries, and marked the transition from the Middle Ages to the modern era. It was, substantially, a revolt against the ecclesiastical tradition and intellectual tyranny of mediævalism, and was characterized by a revival of philosophy, letters, art, science, and political and religious thought.

" From the nature of the case, it is impossible to fix a definite date for the beginning of the *Renaissance ;* long before the close of the dark ages there were isolated scholars and thinkers who anticipated the new light. In its main elements, however, the movement originated in Italy towards the end of the 14th century, and, attaining its full development there in the early half of the 16th, the *Renaissance* communicated itself throughout the whole of the rest of Europe; France, Germany, England, and other countries participating later in the movement, which in each of them took a somewhat different shape. But Italy was specially the nursing - mother of the *Renaissance*."— *Chambers's Encyclopædia*.

Republic. A celebrated dialogue by Plato (429–347 B.C.), presenting that philosopher's conception of an ideal commonwealth.

"The *Republic* is unquestionably one of the most interesting of his works; and so slow has been the progress of social science, compared with every other science, that many of the views Plato has there put forth are still entertained by very serious thinkers; whereas his views on morals seldom, his views on physics never, find a defender."— Lewes's *Biographical History of Philosophy*.

Republican Marriages. A name frequently given to a method of drowning devised by the infamous Carrier, at Nantes in 1793. It consisted in tying men and women together by their hands and feet, and casting them into the Loire. See *Noyades*.

Republican Calendar of Brazil. A calendar adopted by the Republic of Brazil in 1890. It is taken from Comte's *Système de Politique Positive*, and is frequently called the *Positivists' Calendar*. In it the days of the week and the months of the year are renamed, as follows :

Sunday	Humanidi.
Monday	Maridi.
Tuesday	Patridi.
Wednesday	Filidi.
Thursday	Fratridi.
Friday	Domidi.
Saturday	Matridi.

January	Moses.
February	Homer.
March	Aristotle.
April	Archimedes.
May	Cæsar.
June	Paul.
July	Charlemagne.
August	Dante.
September	Gutenberg.
October	Shakespeare.
November	Descartes.
December	Frederick the Great.

Restoration. The name given to the re-establishment of the monarchical form of government in England, in the person of Charles II, who, in 1660, was recalled by Parliament to the throne of his ancestors. On May 29th of the same year, the King entered London amid the rejoicings of the populace.

Resurrection Bone. The name given to a bone in the human body, known as *Luz* by the ancient Jewish rabbis, and believed by them to be the nucleus of the resurrection body, on account of its fancied indestructibility. According to the common belief, this bone could be neither dissolved, broken, ground to pieces, nor burned. Its location is a matter of much dispute, although some authorities identify it with the *os sacrum*. See *Os Sacrum*.

"The learnèd Rabbins of the Jews
    Write, There 's a bone, which they call
        Luz,
No force in nature can do hurt thereto ;
And therefore at the last great day,
All th' other members shall, they say,
Spring out of this, as from a seed.
                Butler's *Hudibras*.

Retreat of the Ten Thousand. The name given to the famous retrograde march of the Greek mercenaries, under Xenophon [445 (?)–355 (?) B.C.] and others, from Cunaxa—where Cyrus fell in his attempt to dethrone his elder brother, Artaxerxes, King of Persia, in 401 B.C.— to Kotyora, on the southern shore of the Black Sea. The time consumed in this memorable march was 215 days, and the distance covered was 3465 miles. Xenophon has left a graphic account of this expedition and retreat in his *Anabasis, or History of the Expedition of Cyrus the Younger*. See *Anabasis*.

Revised Version of the Bible. The name given to a version of the English Bible, recommended by the convocation of bishops at Canterbury in 1870. Work was commenced at Westminster in June of the same year by a committee of about 50 scholars of various denominations, divided into two companies,—one for the revision of the *Old Testament* and one for the revision of the *New*. The co-operation of the American clergy, and of scholars generally, was invited, and in 1871 a committee of 32 revisers was organized in the United States, under the presidency of Dr. Philip Schaff (1819–1893), and rendered valuable assistance. The revision of the *New Testament* was completed on November 11th, 1880, and published on May 17th, 1881 ; that of the *Old Testament* was finished in July, 1884, and published on May 19th, 1885. See *Authorized Version of 1611.*

"There seems no likelihood that the *Revised Bible* will ever supersede the Authorised Version. Whatever its critical value, it is sadly defective in style, and is not to be compared to the older book in rhythm and simplicity. It is equally defective in arrangement, and we greatly miss the tables of contents at the heads of the chapters."— Brewer's *Historic Note-Book.*

Revolutionary Calendar. See *French Revolutionary Calendar.*

Revolutionary Songs. The following is a list of the most popular songs composed during the French Revolution.

(1) *La Marseillaise* (1792).
(2) *Veillons au Salut de l'Empire* (1791).
(3) *Ça Ira* (1789).
(4) *Le Chant du Départ* (1794).
(5) *La Carmagnole* (1792).
(6) *Le Vengeur* (1794).

Revolutionary Tribunal. A court of judgment established in Paris, France, in 1793, by the National Convention, to try the enemies of the French Republic. Up to July 27th, 1794, when Robespierre and his associates were deposed, the Revolutionary Tribunal had caused the deaths of 2774,—ranging in age from 14 to 97 years. During the last three months of the Reign of Terror, the Revolutionary Tribunal was a mere tool in the hands of Robespierre.

Reynard the Fox (*Ger., Reinecke Fuchs*). A celebrated German beast-epic of unknown authorship and uncertain origin. It is a satire on German society during the Middle

Ages, and is supposed to have originated among the Franks at some unknown period. It was first made known in the 15th century, through the medium of a Low-German version attributed to Hinrek van Alkmar. Caxton translated the *Reinecke Fuchs* into English in 1481.

"This remarkable poem contains a humorous account of the adventures of *Renard the Fox* at the court of King Nodel (the lion); and it exhibits the cunning of the former, the means which he adopted to rebut the charges made against him, and the hypocrisy and lies by which he contrived to gain the favor of his sovereign, who loaded him with honors. The plot turns chiefly on the long struggle between Renard and his uncle Isengrin, the wolf, who typifies the feudal baron, as Renard does the Church. Renard is swayed by a constant impulse to deceive and victimize everybody, whether friend or foe, but especially Isengrin ; and, though the latter frequently reduces him to the greatest straits, he generally gets the better of it in the end."—Wheeler's *Dictionary of the Noted Names of Fiction.*

Rhapsodists. A class of men in ancient Greece, who wandered from place to place, and recited the productions of Homer, Hesiod, and other poets. They were held in high esteem, and it is to them, doubtless, that is due the credit of the wide diffusion of the Homeric poems throughout the Greek world. After these ballads were collected and reduced to connected epics by Pisistratus [612 (?)–527 B.C.], the occupation of the Rhapsodists gradually declined in importance.

Rheims, Cathedral of. A superb Gothic cathedral at Rheims, France, erected between 1212 and 1430, and famous as the place of coronation of all the kings of France (except Henry IV), from 1179 to 1774. In 496, Clovis (481–511), the first of the Merovingian line, was baptized, with 3000 of his men, at Rheims ; and owing to this fact the city became, in subsequent years, the place for the coronation of all the kings of France.

Rheinfels (*Ger., Rock of the Rhine*). An imposing ruined castle on the

Rhine, near St. Goar. It was built in 1245 by Count Diether III of Katzenellenbogen, and belonged alternately to the Hessians and French until 1794, when it fell into the hands of the French Revolutionary army. In 1797, it was blown up, and sold for $300. It is now the property of the King of Prussia.

Rhemish Testament. A Roman Catholic version of the *New Testament*, so called because published at *Rheims*, France, in 1582. It is translated from the Latin *Vulgate*, and forms part of the *Douay Bible*. See *Douay Bible*.

Rhine, Confederation of the. See *Confederation of the Rhine*.

Rhododendron. This word means literally a rose-tree, and is derived from the Greek ῥόδον (*rose*), δένδρον (*tree*).

Rialto. A famous marble bridge across the Grand Canal at Venice, built by Antonio da Ponte in 1590. It consists of a single arch, 90 feet wide and 24 feet high, and rests upon 12,000 piles. The name *Rialto* is derived from *Rivo-Alto*, — one of the islands on which Venice is built. This island was long the financial and commercial centre of the city, and gave its name to the bridge that connects it with the mainland. There was situated the Exchange; and it is probably to that building (and not to the bridge) that Shakespeare refers in his comedy of *The Merchant of Venice*, i, 3, as follows :

" Signor Antonio, many a time and oft,
   In the *Rialto*, you have rated me
   About my money and my usances :
   Still have I borne it with a patient shrug ;
   For sufferance is the badge of all our
      tribe."

See *Grand Canal*.

Richard Cœur-de-Lion. A name popularly conferred upon Richard I (1189-1199), King of England, on account of the mighty deeds of valor performed by him during the Third Crusade.

"Richard I (1189 to 1199), styled Cœur de Lion, otherwise 'The Lion Hearted,' is traditionally said to have torn the living heart out of the mouth of a lion to whose fury he was exposed by the Duke of Austria for having killed his son in battle. This extraordinary exploit surpasses the bounds of reason ; still there is no doubt that he performed prodigies of valor during the Wars of the Crusades." — Wagner's *Names and their Meaning.*

Rideau Hall. The official residence of the Governor-General of the Dominion of Canada. It is an old-fashioned, unattractive building, situated about a mile from the city of Ottawa.

Rider. In legislative parlance, an additional section, or clause, annexed to a bill while in course of passage, and frequently foreign to its original purport.

"Late in the Session the Senate passed the General Appropriation Bill for government expenses, with a 'rider,' organizing the Territories of New Mexico and California, permitting Slavery." — Johnston's *American Politics.*

Rienzi's House. A brick building in Rome, Italy, said to be the house in which Rienzi (1313-1354), the orator and tribune, may have lived. It is also, but without apparent reason, called the House of Pilate. See *Casa de Pilatos*.

"On the other side of the cross-street is the picturesque *House of Crescentius,* or *Casa di Rienzi,* or *di Pilato,* as it is commonly called, constructed of brick with a singular admixture of antique fragments. On the side, . . . a long inscription records that this lofty house was erected by Nicholas, son of Crescens, not from motives of ambition, but as a reminiscence of the ancient glory of Rome! The Crescentii were the most powerful noble family in Rome at the close of the 10th century, but the house, the oldest existing specimen of mediæval domestic architecture, is not earlier than the 11th or 12th century. The building was originally much larger, and was intended to command the bridge over the Tiber."—Baedeker's *Central Italy.*

Right Foot Foremost. The origin of this saying is traced to the ancient Romans, with whom it was considered to be a bad omen to cross the threshold with the left foot, on entering a house. Accordingly it was customary with them to station boys at the entrances of mansions, to caution visitors and guests against this mistake.

Rights of Man. A famous statement, in 17 clauses, adopted by the French National Assembly in August, 1789. It was modelled after the American *Declaration of Independence*, and marked out the leading principles of a limited monarchy based upon a constitution. It was severely criticised by Edmund Burke (1729–1797) in his *Reflections on the French Revolution*, and warmly defended by Thomas Paine (1737–1809), in his *Rights of Man.*

Rigi-Kulm. The highest point of the Rigi, a mountain near Lake Lucerne, Switzerland, 5909 feet high. It is reached by two railways, and is annually visited by more than 50,000 tourists. The Rigi-Kulm is famous not only for its superb sunrise and sunset effects, but also for a peculiar atmospheric phenomenon, known as the Spectre of the Rigi.

"The Rigi, although only 5909 feet above the level of the sea, has this advantage over many of its higher neighbors—the view is unobstructed in every direction: it is a perfect Mount Tabor on a large scale."—Harper's *Hand-Book for Travellers in Europe and the East.*

Rijks Museum. A famous gallery of art at Amsterdam, Holland, containing nearly 600 paintings — mostly belonging to the Dutch School—together with a fine collection of engravings and etchings by Rembrandt and other masters. The gems of the collection are the *Night Watch*, by Rembrandt, the *Banquet of the Guard*, by Van der Helst, and the *Evening School*, by Gerard Dow. This last cost $800 in 1766, and was purchased for the Museum in 1808 for $3,700.

4I

Rinaldo. A famous warrior, who figures prominently in Tasso's *Jerusalem Delivered*, Pulci's *Morgante Maggiore*, Bojardo's *Orlando Innamorato*, Ariosto's *Orlando Furioso*, and other Italian and French romances. See *Armida.*

Ring in Marriage. "Clemens tells us its use in the marriage service began in Egypt, and then, as now, signified a transfer of property. 'With all my worldly goods I thee endow.' The marriage-ring gave to an Egyptian woman the power to issue commands in the name of her husband, and made her in every way his representative.

Among the Anglo-Saxons, the bridegroom gave a pledge, or 'wed' (a term from which we derive the word wedding), at the betrothal ceremony. This wed consisted, among other things, of a ring, which was placed on the maiden's right hand, and remained there until transferred at the marriage ceremony to the left hand. At this ceremony the bridegroom put the ring first on the end of the thumb, then on the first, and then on the second finger, naming the Trinity; and lastly placed it on the third or marriage finger, to signify that, next to God, her duty was to her husband. Our marriage ceremony is very nearly the same as that used by our forefathers, a few obsolete words being changed."—Killikelly's *Curious Questions.*

Ring of Gyges. See *Gyges's Ring.*

Ring-Strasse. In Vienna, a series of handsome boulevards, nearly three miles long, occupying the site of an ancient line of fortifications which, until 1858, separated the old or inner portion of the city (called the *Stadt*) from the new or outer portion. They are 165 feet in width, and form the boundary-line of five sides of an irregular hexagon,— the sixth side being bounded by the Franz-Josef Quay on the Danube Canal.

Rip Van Winkle. A simple, good-natured man, of shiftless habits, whose strange adventures are related in the *Sketch-Book* of Washington Irving (1783–1859). He was a descendant of the early Dutch colonists of New York, and dwelt in a village at the foot of the Kaatskill Mountains, with a termagant wife and a troop of ragged children. While wandering through the mountains, on a certain occasion, he fell in with a strange-looking, dwarfish fellow, who was carrying a keg filled with liquor. Rip readily offered his assistance, and accompanied the stranger to a natural amphitheatre, where a party of odd-looking persons were gravely playing at ninepins, in perfect silence. After recovering somewhat from his fear, Rip Van Winkle ventured to taste of the beverage that he had helped to carry, and repeated the experiment so often that he finally fell into a deep sleep that lasted twenty years, although it seemed but a night. On his return to the village, he found everything greatly changed: his wife had died, his daughter was married, and his old friends had passed away. Most wonderful of all, the War of the Revolution had been fought, and Rip found himself no longer a subject of King George III, but a free citizen of the United States of America. See *Klaus, Peter; Sleeping Beauty in the Wood.*

River of Natural Ink. A natural curiosity said to exist in Algeria. It is caused by the junction of two streams,—one of which drains a region strongly impregnated with iron, while the other flows from a peat-bog and holds a large quantity of gallic acid in solution. The union of these two streams causes the iron and the gallic acid to combine, and thus produces a genuine ink.

Riviera (*It., Seashore*). The name given to a narrow strip of coast-land in France and Italy, bordering upon the Gulf of Genoa. Strictly speaking, it extends only from Nice to Spezzia; but, as generally understood, it includes the entire coast from Cannes to Leghorn. It is divided at Genoa into the western coast, or *Riviera di Ponente*, and the eastern coast, or *Riviera di Levante*. The former is the milder, and is consequently more frequented by tourists and valetudinarians. It abounds in beautiful scenery, and contains numerous resorts of health and fashion,—among which may be mentioned Nice, Monaco, Mentone, and San Remo. See *Cornice Road; Monaco.*

Rivoli, Battle of. A desperate battle fought at Rivoli, a town of northern Italy, 12 miles northwest of Verona, on January 14th–15th, 1797, between 60,000 Austrians commanded by Alvinzi and 30,000 French under Napoleon Bonaparte, who there won one of his most brilliant victories. As a result of this battle, Mantua surrendered to the French on February 2nd, 1797, and 20,000 Austrians were made prisoners of war.

Rivoli, Rue de. A noted street in Paris, named in honor of Napoleon Bonaparte's victory over the Austrians at Rivoli, in 1797. It extends parallel with the Seine for a distance of about two miles, from the Place de la Concorde to the Rue St. Antoine, which connects it with the Place de la Bastille. The Rue de Rivoli was opened in 1802, but was not completed until 1865,—during the Second Empire. It is estimated that the making of this street cost the sum of $8,000,000, and caused the removal of more than 414 houses.

Roaring Forties. A term used, in nautical parlance, to denote a stormy region of the Atlantic, Pacific, and Indian Oceans, lying between 40° and 50° *south* latitude. It is characterized by strong north-northwest and northwest winds. The same name is also given, by analogy, to a rough part of the Atlantic Ocean, lying between 40° and 50° *north* latitude.

Robbing Peter to Pay Paul. In 1540, the abbey-church of St. Peter at Westminster (now Westminster Abbey), was raised by letters-patent to the dignity of a cathedral; but in the year 1550 it was reunited with the diocese of London, and several of its estates were appropriated to the repairs of St. Paul's Cathedral. This act met with considerable opposition, and gave rise to the proverbial saying : "Why rob St. Peter to pay St. Paul?"

Robe, Crucifixion. See *Holy Coat of Trèves.*

Robert le Diable (*Fr., Robert the Devil*). The hero of a French metrical romance of the 13th century,—identical with Robert, first Duke of Normandy and father of William the Conqueror, whose ferocious cruelty in war gave rise to numerous legends. According to the story, he was pledged to the Devil before his birth ; and, after running a career of unprecedented wickedness, became miraculously converted, did penance of the most humiliating kind, and finally married the daughter of the Emperor. This romance was converted into prose during the 14th century. There was also a miracle-play on the same subject. Meyerbeer's opera, *Robert le Diable*, was composed in 1826.

Robert Macaire. A sportive designation of a Frenchman, or of the French nation collectively. It is derived from the name of a character in a great number of French plays,—among which may be mentioned *Le Chien de Montargis* and *Le Chien d'Aubry.* The character has always been a favorite one with Parisian audiences.

Robespierre on Horseback. A phrase used to denote any ruthless leader that would willingly trample the people under foot, if his own selfish ends. The expression is said to have been first used by Barras in speaking of Napoleon Bonaparte. See *Man on Horseback.*

Robespierre's Weavers. The name given to the fishwomen and other female rabble of Paris during the French Revolution. They were partisans of Robespierre, and joined the *sans-culottes* in demanding from the National Assembly the arrest of the Girondist deputies (June 2nd, 1793.) See *Sans-Culottes; Tricoteuses.*

Robin Goodfellow. A merry, domestic sprite, famous for his mischievous pranks and practical jokes. He is the same as *Puck*, the jester of Fairy Court.

"The constant attendant upon the English fairy court was the celebrated Puck, or *Robin Goodfellow*, who, to the elves, acted in some measure as the jester or clown of the company,—a character then to be found in the establishment of every person of quality,—or, to use a more modern comparison, resembled the Pierrot of the pantomime. His jests were of the most simple, and, at the same time, the broadest comic character; to mislead a clown on his path homeward, to disguise himself like a stool, in order to induce an old gossip to commit the egregious mistake of sitting down on the floor when she expected to repose on a chair, were his special employments."—Wheeler's *Dictionary of the Noted Names of Fiction.*

Robin Gray, Auld. The title of a tender and touching ballad of humble life, written by Lady Anne Lindsay (1750-1825) — afterwards Lady Barnard—about 1771, and set by her to the old Scotch air, *The bridegroom grat when the sun gaed doun.*

"It instantly became popular, but the lady kept the secret of its authorship for the long period of fifty years, when, in 1823, she acknowledged it in a letter to Sir Walter Scott, accompanying the disclosure with a full account of the circumstances under which it was written."—Chambers's *Cyclopædia of English Literature.*

Robin Hood. A noted English freebooter and outlaw who, according to tradition, dwelt with his followers in Sherwood Forest, Nottinghamshire, during the reign of Richard I (1189-1199), and later. Many of the old ballads and stories commemorate his deeds of valor, his generosity, his gallantry, and his skill in archery. His principal companions were Little John, Friar Tuck, Will Scarlet, and Maid Marian; while his chief enemies were the Abbot of St. Mary's and the Sheriff of Nottingham. According to some historians, Robin Hood was a name assumed by the Earl of Huntingdon, who was disgraced and banished from court by Richard I, at the time of his accession. See *Sherwood Forest; Maid Marian.*

Robin Redbreast. According to tradition, a robin pecked a thorn out of the crown worn by Christ on his way to Calvary, and the blood that flowed from the wound fell upon the bird's breast and dyed it red. Another legend states that the robin carries dew in its beak to the sufferers in the burning lake, and that its breast is red from the scorching produced by the fire of Gehenna.

Robinson, Jack. See *Jack Robinson.*

Robinson Crusoe. See *Crusoe, Robinson.*

Rob Roy (*Gaelic, Robert the Red*). A nickname given to Robert Macgregor [1660 (?)–1734], a Scotch adventurer, who assumed the name Campbell in consequence of the proscription of his clan by the Scottish Parliament in 1662. He is the Robin Hood of Scotland, and the hero of one of Sir Walter Scott's most popular novels. He was a partisan of the "Old Pretender" during the Jacobite Rebellion of 1715.

Robsart, Amy. The daughter of Sir John Robsart, and wife of Robert Dudley, Earl of Leicester. On September 8th, 1560, she was found dead, with her neck broken, at the foot of a staircase. It is generally believed that she was the victim of foul play, and that Dudley, and even Queen Elizabeth herself, were accessories to the crime. Certain it is that the Queen continued to favor Leicester after this affair, in spite of his unpopularity throughout England. Amy Robsart is a prominent character in Scott's novel of *Kenilworth.*

Rocking Stone of Tandil. A natural curiosity in the Argentine Republic, consisting of a gigantic quartz bowlder, so delicately poised as to move backward and forward at the slightest touch. The following account of this interesting phenomenon is taken from Vincent's *Around and About South America* (1890).

"Among many wonders of nature in the Argentine Republic, I saw an especially interesting geological phenomenon. It was a great *rocking-stone*—perhaps the largest in the world—three miles from Tandil, a small village, which may be reached by railway, two hundred and fifty miles south of Buenos Ayres. The giant, mushroom-shaped quartz bowlder stands upon the summit of some picturesque hills, perhaps a thousand feet in height. It weighs over seven hundred tons, and is so nicely poised that it rocks in the wind, and may be made to crack a walnut. Yet this bowlder is so firm that one of the old dictators, Rossas by name, once harnessed a thousand horses to it, and was unable to displace it. There are, of course, many such rocking-stones scattered about the world, though I know of none nearly so large."

Rock of Refuge. "In Hawaii, one of the Sandwich Islands, there is a large flat rock, called the 'Rock of Refuge.' If a criminal reaches this rock before capture, he is safe as long as he remains there. Usually his family supply him with food until he can make his escape, but he is never allowed to return to his tribe."—Killikelly's *Curious Questions.*

Rodman Gun. The name given to a cast-iron, smooth-bore cannon, invented by General Thomas J. Rodman (1815–1871), an American soldier, and widely adopted by the United States Government during the Civil War. According to Rodman's process, the cannon was cast hollow, around a core filled with water; in this way, the interior of the bore was cooled first, and the metal was thus placed in a more favorable condition to resist the shock of the discharge. Rodman succeeded by this process in casting guns greatly exceeding, in size and power, the solid ones previously constructed, and at a much lower cost.

Rodomontade. This word, meaning vain and ostentatious boasting, is derived from *Rodomont* or *Rodomonte*, a famous Moorish hero—boastful but brave—mentioned in Bojardo's *Orlando Innamorato* and Ariosto's *Orlando Furioso*. See *Gasconade*.

Roentgen Rays. The name given to a probable form of radiation discovered in December, 1895, by Professor W. C. Roentgen, while experimenting with a Crookes vacuum tube, electrically excited and enveloped in a black covering. The Roentgen rays were named X-rays by their discoverer to indicate their unknown nature, and are generally so called.

"The real nature of the x-rays is not yet known, the best authorities wavering between a radiation theory and a material one. They are transmitted through various media with varying degrees of facility, and affect silver salts. They are applicable to medical and surgical diagnosis; and silver negatives of bones, bullets, etc., which do not transmit the rays readily, in the soft tissues of the bodies, may be produced. This is called a Skotograph or Skiagraph. By interposing the substance to be examined between the Crookes' tube and a tube with a diaphragm covered with calcium tungstate, called a fluorescope, the effect is heightened, and the bullets, etc., may be readily observed."—Chandler's *Encyclopædia*.

Roe, Richard. See *Doe, John, and Richard Roe.*

Rogation Days (*Lat., rogatio, supplication*). The name given to the Monday, Tuesday, and Wednesday immediately preceding the festival of the Ascension,—so called because on those days the Roman Catholic Church enjoins that litanies be recited or sung by the clergy and people in public procession. This custom is said to have been introduced by Mamertus,

Bishop of Vienne, in the middle of the 5th century. Rogation Days were first observed in England during the 7th century; but, after the Reformation (1517), the public recitation of the litany was discontinued. See *Rogation Week.*

Rogation Week. The name given to the week in which the Rogation Days occur. It is the second week before Whitsunday, and is sometimes known as *Crop Week, Cross Week, Gang Week, Grass Week*, or *Procession Week*. See *Rogation Days.*

Roger Williams's Grave. "For the purpose of erecting a suitable monument in memory of Roger Williams, the founder of Rhode Island, his private burying-ground was searched for the graves of himself and wife. It was found that everything had passed into oblivion. The shape of the coffins could only be traced by a black line of carbonaceous matter. The rusted hinges and nails, and a round wooden knot, alone remained in one grave; while a single knot of braided hair was found in the other. Near the graves stood an apple-tree. This had sent down two main roots into the very presence of the coffined dead. The larger root, pushing its way to the precise spot occupied by the skull of Roger Williams, had made a turn as if passing around it, and followed the direction of the backbone to the hips. Here it divided into two branches, sending one along each leg to the heel, when both turned upward toward the toes. One of these roots formed a slight crook at the knee, which made the whole bear a striking resemblance to the human form. (These roots are now deposited in the museum of Brown University.) There were the graves, but their occupants had disappeared; the bones even had vanished. There stood the thief—the guilty apple-tree—caught in the very act of robbery. The spoliation was complete. The organic matter—the flesh, the bones, of Roger Williams—

had passed into an apple-tree. The elements had been absorbed by the roots, transmuted into woody fiber, which could now be burned as fuel, or carved into ornaments ; had bloomed into fragrant blossoms, which had delighted the eye of passers - by, and scattered the sweetest perfume of spring ; more than that — had been converted into luscious fruit, which, from year to year, had been gathered and eaten. How pertinent, then, is the question, ' Who ate Roger Williams ? ' "—Steele's *Popular Chemistry*.

Roi d'Yvetot. See *King of Yvetot*.

Roi Panade (*Fr., King of the Slops*). A nickname bestowed upon Louis XVIII (1814–1824), King of France, on account of his listlessness and lack of energy.

Rois Fainéants. See *Fainéants, Rois*.

Roi Soleil (*Fr., Sun King*). A nickname given to Louis XIV (1643–1715), King of France, in allusion to his custom of appearing as Apollo, the God of the Sun, at the fêtes given at court or at his nobles' palaces.

"Louis was the centre of all ; mythological or classical shows displayed his fine figure and handsome face, as a hero or a god ; he delighted to appear as an Apollo, *God of the Sun*, of culture, of the arts, dispensing vivifying smiles and warmth of life."—Kitchin's *History of France*.

Roland for an Oliver, A. This expression, meaning a retort for a retort, or the matching of one incredible lie with another, is derived from the fanciful tales told by the old chroniclers, concerning the marvellous deeds of Roland and Oliver, the two most famous of the twelve paladins of Charlemagne. These redoubtable heroes were so evenly matched that neither was able to surpass the other ; and, accordingly, to test their relative superiority, they met in single combat and fought for five successive days on an island in the Rhine, without either gaining the least advantage over the other.

Romance Languages. The name given to those modern languages that are descended, not directly from the classical Latin, but from the *Lingua Romana Rustica*, or vulgar Latin, — mixed with foreign elements. They are the Italian, Spanish, Portuguese, Provençal, French, Roumanian, and Romansch. See *Romances*.

Romance of the Rose (*Fr., Roman de la Rose*). An Old-French allegorical romance, commenced by Guillaume de Lorris in the latter part of the 13th century, and continued by Jean de Meung during the early part of the 14th. The *Romance of the Rose* treats of love in a pleasing style, and has had a remarkable influence on French literature. See *Iliad of France*.

"Although it reached the appalling length of 20,000 verses, no book was ever more popular. It was admired as a masterpiece of wit, invention, and philosophy ; the highest mysteries of theology were believed to be concealed in this poetical form, and learned commentaries were written upon its veiled meaning by preachers, who did not scruple to cite passages from it in the pulpit. But the tedious poem and its numberless imitations are nothing but rhymed prose, which it would be impossible to recognize as poetry, if the measure of the verse were taken away."—Botta's *Hand-Book of Universal Literature*.

Romances. A term originally used to denote the legendary poems and tales of the Middle Ages, so called because written in some one of the *Romance* languages,— particularly the French or Italian. The word " romance " is applied, at the present time, to any work of fiction that gives greater scope to imagination and idealization than the novel. See *Romance Languages*.

Roman Forum. See *Forum Romanum*.

Roman Law. A system of jurisprudence, more commonly known as the *Civil Law*, developed during the days of the Roman Republic and Empire. The first attempt at revision occurred in 451–450 B.C., when the *Laws of the Twelve Tables* were adopted ; but it was not until the reign of Justinian (527–565) that the entire body of Roman Law was reduced to a systematic form. This system of jurisprudence forms the basis of law in every civilized country except England and the United States, and even the English Common Law in these two countries has been greatly modified by it. The Civil (or Roman) Law prevails in Louisiana, in the form of a code based upon the *Code Napoléon* and adopted in 1825. See *Code Napoléon ; Code of Justinian ; English Law ; Twelve Tables, Laws of the*.

Romanoff, House of. The name of the present dynasty of Russia, founded by the Czar Michael Fedorovitz Romanoff, who ascended the throne in 1613. The Romanoffs are descended from one Andrew Kobyla, who came from Prussia to Moscow in 1341.

Roman Roads. The Roman Empire was intersected by roads, constructed principally between the second and fourth centuries after Christ. These highways varied in width from 8 to 15 feet, and were almost universally built in straight lines without regard to grade, probably because the use of beasts of burden as the chief means of transport made the preservation of the level an affair of minor importance. Soldiers, slaves, and criminals were employed in the construction of these highways, the durability of which is shown by the fact that, in some cases, they have sustained the traffic of 2000 years without material injury. The Roman Forum is said to have been the point of convergence of 24 roads, which, with their branches had a total length of 52,964 Roman miles. In Britain, there were four principal Roman roads, viz., *Watling Street* (from Kent to Cardigan Bay); *Iknield*, or *Ikenild*, *Street* (from St. David's to Tynemouth); *Fosse*, or *Fosse Way* (from Cornwall to Lincoln) ; and *Ermin Street* (from St. David's to Southampton). The Romans are said to have learned the art of road-building from the Carthaginians. See *Appian Way ; Flaminian Way ; Watling Street.*

Roman Walls. The generic term applied to various ramparts and fortifications erected by the ancient Romans in Britain, to protect the northern frontier of that province from the incursions of the wild Caledonian tribes. They were as follows :

(1) *The Wall of Agricola*—a chain of fortresses between the friths of Clyde and Forth—erected by Julius Agricola, the conqueror of Britain, about 81 A.D.

(2) *The Wall of Hadrian* — an earthen rampart between Solway Frith and the river Tyne—built by the Emperor Hadrian (117–138) in 121 A.D. Also called the *Picts' Wall*.

(3) *The Wall of Antoninus*—a rampart erected by Lollius Verticus about 140 A.D., during the reign of the Emperor Antoninus Pius (138–161). It is now known by the name of *Graham's Dike.*

(4) *The Wall of Severus* — a lofty and substantial wall, built in 208 A.D. by the Emperor Lucius Septimius Severus (193–211), to replace the *Wall of Hadrian*, which had proved insufficient to check the inroads of the Caledonians. See *Hadrian's Wall.*

Roof of the World. The name given by the natives to a series of broad valleys that traverse the elevated and extensive plateau-region of Pamir, in Central Asia. This lofty table-land has a mean elevation of 13,000 feet, and covers an area of about 37,000 square miles. Some of the mountain peaks attain an elevation of more than 25,000 feet above the sea-level.

Rooky Wood. This phrase, found in Shakespeare's *Macbeth*, does not, according to Brewer's *Dictionary of Phrase and Fable*, refer to a wood where rooks abound, but to a misty or dark wood. This authority asserts that the verb *to reek* (*to emit vapor*) formerly had the preterites *roke, rook,* or *roak :* hence Hamilton, in his *Wallace,* speaks of the " rooky mist."

> "Light thickens, and the crow
> Makes wing to the *rooky wood.*"
> *Macbeth*, iii, 2.

Roorback. A word used, in American political parlance, to denote any falsehood or sensational statement devoid of truth, published in the newspapers, generally before an election, for the purpose of injuring the opposite side. It is said to be derived from an absurd statement concerning James K. Polk (the Democratic candidate for the presidency) published in 1844 by the Whig newspapers, as an extract from *Baron Roorback's Tour through the Western and Southern States,* and afterwards proved to be false.

"The manufacture of *roorbacks* against Mr. Blaine, though active, is not very successful in producing a merchantable article." —*New York Tribune*, April 14, 1876.

"It was a poor day for *roorbacks* yesterday. First, Professor Lowell was going to vote for Tilden, and then he—was n't. Second, President Grant had declared that the vote of Louisiana ought to be thrown out, and then he—had n't. Third, Governor Hayes promised all sorts of strange things, and then he—did n't. These were short-legged lies, all of them; and they soon got out of breath."—*New York Tribune*, Dec., 1876.

Rope of Ocnus, Like the. This saying, meaning profitless and unavailing labor, is derived from a famous painting by Polygnotus (*fl.* 460-430 B.C.), the Greek artist, representing a poor man industriously weaving a rope of straw, while behind him stands an ass eating the completed portion. As the story goes, Ocnus was an industrious Greek, whose extravagant wife spent his money as fast as he earned it, and thus kept him continually poor. Polygnotus, hearing of the man's tribulations, painted the above-mentioned picture which, by its silent influence so wrought upon the wife of Ocnus

that she renounced her extravagant habits, and by her frugality helped to lay the foundation of her husband's subsequent prosperity.

Rosamond's Bower. A hidden labyrinth at Woodstock, England, said to have been constructed by Henry II (1154-1189) for his mistress, the " Fair Rosamond," in order that he might visit her in safety and without the knowledge of his wife, Queen Eleanor. According to Holinshed, the Queen discovered Henry's favorite by means of a silken thread which the King had drawn after him out of her chamber with his foot, and so dealt with her that she died soon after. This story of the labyrinth and the tragic fate of Rosamond is generally regarded as an invention of later times. It is known that Rosamond retired to Godstow Abbey, and died there about 1176.

Rosary.
(1) In the Roman Catholic Church, the name given *par excellence* to the series of prayers consisting of 15 decades, comprising 15 *Pater-Nosters* and *Doxologies* and 150 *Ave Marias,* divided into three parts. This is also known as the complete (or Dominican) Rosary, and the Rosary of the Blessed Virgin. Among other rosaries may be mentioned the Ordinary Rosary, the Intermediate Rosary, the Smaller Rosary, and the Angelical Rosary.
(2) The name given to the string of larger and smaller beads used by the Roman Catholics as an aid in repeating their *Pater-Nosters* and *Ave Marias.*

Roses, Wars of the. A series of sanguinary contests for the possession of the English throne, waged by the adherents of the Houses of York and Lancaster, whose badges were the white and the red rose, respectively. The struggle commenced with the battle of St. Albans (1455), and lasted until 1485,—a period of 30 years,—when Henry Tudor (of Lancaster) defeated and killed Richard III (of York) at

Bosworth Field. The two Houses were finally united in the person of Henry Tudor (afterwards Henry VII), who in 1486 married Elizabeth of York, daughter of Edward IV. It is estimated that the Wars of the Roses occasioned the deaths of twelve princes of the blood, 200 nobles, and 100,000 of the gentry and common people of England.

Rosetta Stone. A slab of black basalt—3 feet long, 2½ feet wide, and 10 inches thick — discovered in 1799, near Rosetta, Egypt, by M. Boussard, an officer of engineers, during the French occupation of that country. It was conveyed to England in 1802, and deposited in the British Museum in London. This stone bears a trilingual inscription, in honor of Ptolemy Epiphanes (205–181 B.C.), written in hieroglyphic or sacred, demotic or common, and Greek characters ; and was deciphered through the labors of Dr. Thomas Young in 1818 and those of Champollion in 1822. The Rosetta Stone furnished the clew for the decipherment of the Egyptian hieroglyphics, and is chiefly famous on that account.

Rosicrucians. A secret fraternity alleged to have been founded during the latter part of the 14th century by Christian Rosenkreuz, a German mystic, who dwelt for a time in India and Egypt, where he acquired a profound knowledge of the occult arts. The Rosicrucians, like the alchemists, pretended to transmute metals, to prolong life, and to possess knowledge of what was occurring in distant places. They first became known to the world early in the 17th century, through the publication of certain documents said to have been issued by them ; but, according to many authorities, their existence was extremely doubtful. The Rosicrucians were also called the *Brothers of the Rosy Cross*, from the notion that the name is derived from *crux* (*cross*), and *rosa* (*rose*).

Brewer, however, says that the word Rosicrucian comes from *ros* (*dew*) and *rosa* (*rose*).

" Dew was considered by the ancient chemists as the most powerful solvent of gold ; and *cross* in alchemy is the synonym of light, because any figure of a cross contains the three letters L V X (light)."— Brewer's *Dictionary of Phrase and Fable*.

Rosin Bible. A name sometimes given to the version of the Bible published at Douay, France, in 1609, in which the word *rosin* is used instead of *balm*. See *Douay Bible*.

" Is there no *rosin* in Gilead? is there no physician there ? "—*Jeremiah* viii, 22.

Roslin Chapel. An exquisite chapel, adjoining the ruins of Roslin Castle, 6½ miles south of Edinburgh. It is a gem of Gothic architecture, and was originally intended for the choir of a collegiate church. The chapel was built by William St. Clair in 1446, and was used until the time of James VI (afterwards James I of England) as the burial-place of the Barons of Roslin, who were interred in full armor beneath the structure. Sir Walter Scott refers to this fact in one of his poems. In Roslin Chapel may be seen the famous " 'Prentice Pillar," with which an interesting story is connected. It is related that the architect of the chapel, desiring to produce a column of surpassing beauty, went to Rome to acquire the necessary knowledge, but on his return found that his work had been anticipated by one of his apprentices; whereupon, in his rage, he seized a hammer and dealt his workman a death-blow.

Rossbach, Battle of. Fought at Rossbach, 22 miles southwest of Leipsic, on November 5th, 1757, between 50,000 French and Austrians, and 22,000 Prussians commanded by Frederick the Great (1740–1786). The battle resulted in a complete victory for Frederick, who lost only 540 men. The allied loss was nearly 3000 killed and wounded, 5000 prisoners,—including 5 generals and 300 officers,—and nearly 70 cannon. "The Rout of Rossbach" was long a term of reproach in the French army. Also written *Rosbach*.

Rothière, Battle of La. A battle fought at La Rothière, France, on February 1st, 1814, between the French under Napoleon I, and the Russians and Prussians commanded by Blücher. The allies were defeated.

Rothschild Family. This celebrated family of financiers takes its name from "Zum Rothen Schilde," or "Red Shield," the sign of the house in which their ancestors lived in the Jews' quarter of Frankfort-on-the-Main.

Rotten Row. This name, which is given to the fashionable equestrian road in Hyde Park, London, is said to be a corruption of the French phrase *Route du Roi (King's Road)*.

"Camden derives the word from *rotteran* (to muster); hence *rot*, a file of six soldiers. Another derivation is the Norman *Ratten Row* (roundabout way), being the way corpses were carried to avoid the public thoroughfares. Others suggest *Route du roi;* or that it is so called from the soft material with which the road is covered."—Brewer's *Dictionary of Phrase and Fable*.

Rotunda. A circular hall occupying the central part of the Capitol at Washington, D. C. It is 96 feet in diameter and 180 feet high, and is adorned with historic busts and bas-reliefs, and with eight panel pictures, by native artists, illustrating scenes in American history. At a height of 107 feet from the floor of the Rotunda is Brumidi's allegorical fresco of Washington, and above this rises the huge dome—weighing 4000 tons. See *Capitol of the United States*.

Round Churches. The name given to four English churches, so called because they have round naves, in imitation of the Church of the Holy Sepulchre at Jerusalem. They are the Temple Church, or St. Mary's, in London ; St. Sepulchre in Cambridge ; St. Sepulchre in Northampton ; and Little Maplestead.

Roundheads. A nickname given by the Royalists, during the reign of Charles I (1625-1649) to the Puritans, or Parliamentarians, because they wore their hair cut close to the head, while the Cavaliers wore theirs in long ringlets. See *Cavaliers and Roundheads*.

"The term, it is said, arose from the practice of putting a rough bowl or dish on the head and cutting the hair to the edge of the bowl."—Harper's *Book of Facts*.

"Clarendon says that when Williams, archbishop of York, was hustled by the mob, one David Hide, an officer who had been with the army in the North, drew his sword and swore that he would 'cut the throats of those Roundhead dogs,' and by this expression gave the first utterance to the name *Roundheads.*" — Brewer's *Historic Note-Book*.

Round Hill School. A celebrated private school, on a fine eminence west of Northampton, Massachusetts, established by George Bancroft and Dr. J. G. Cogswell in 1823. After Bancroft's retirement in 1830, the school was continued by Dr. Cogswell until 1836, when it ceased to exist.

"Probably no American college had at the time so large, varied, well-paid, and gifted a faculty as the *Round Hill School.* It outnumbered Harvard and Yale in the corps of its teachers, and put a complete circle about them in the comprehensiveness of its scheme of education. The first gymnasium in the country was set up in its playground, under Dr. Follen, who afterwards planted a similar one in the Delta at Cambridge. The school had a regular professor of manners, *Custos Morum*, who spent his time with the boys in their play-hours, with special purpose to correct ill-speech or violence or ungentlemanliness."—*Henry W. Bellows*.

Round Peg in a Square Hole. An expression commonly attributed to Sydney Smith (1771-1845), although probably of much earlier origin. It is found in his *Lectures Delivered at the Royal Institution* in 1824-1826.

"If you choose to represent the various parts of life by holes upon a table of different shapes, some circular, some triangular, some square, some oblong, and the persons acting these parts by bits of wood of similar shapes, we shall generally find that the triangular person has got into the square hole, the oblong into the triangular, and a square person has squeezed himself into a round hole."

Round Robin. The name given to a remonstrance or petition, signed by a number of persons, generally in a circular form, so as to avoid giving prominence to any single name. The expression is probably a corruption of the French *rond* (*round*) and *ruban* (*ribbon*), although several other derivations have been suggested with a fair degree of plausibility. This device is said to have been first used by the officials of the French Government as a means of making known their grievances. The most celebrated " round robin " in the English language is the one signed by Burke, Gibbon, Sir Joshua Reynolds, and others, and sent to Dr. Samuel Johnson, requesting him to amend the epitaph to Oliver Goldsmith in Westminster Abbey, and suggesting that it be written in English and not in Latin. Johnson accepted the " round robin " in a kindly spirit, but told Sir Joshua Reynolds, the bearer of the missive, that he would " never consent to disgrace the walls of Westminster Abbey with an English inscription."

Round Table. In Arthurian legend, a circular marble table made by the Enchanter Merlin for Uther Pendragon. It afterwards came into the possession of Leodegrance, King of Camelard, and was presented by him to Arthur, on the occasion of that prince's marriage with his daughter, Guinevere. According to tradition, it was said to have been modelled after a table made by Joseph of Arimathea, in imitation of the one used at the Last Supper, and had a seating capacity variously estimated at 13, 40, 50, 60, 100, and 150. One of the seats was always left unoccupied, because it was fatal for any person to sit in it, except the one destined to recover the Holy Grail. Malory, in his *History of Prince Arthur* (1470), says that this seat was reserved for Sir Galahad, the son of Sir Lancelot and Elaine. In the County Hall at Winchester, England, is shown a curious relic called King Arthur's Round Table, a piece of furniture of the time of King Stephen (1135–1154). It has a diameter of 18 feet, and is adorned with pictures of King Arthur and his knights. See *Knights of the Round Table; Twelve Knights of the Round Table.*

Round Towers of Ireland. The name given to certain tall, slender, circular towers of stone, found in various parts of Ireland. They are about 120 in number, and vary in height from 100 to 120 feet. They were built between the 9th and 12th centuries,— doubtless for religious purposes, since they seem to have been always in the immediate neighborhood of churches or monasteries. These Round Towers also served as places of refuge in times of danger and, after the introduction of bells, were used as bell-towers. Three similar towers are found in Scotland, — at Brechin, Abernethy, and Eglishay in Orkney.

Rowley Poems. The name given to certain literary forgeries by Thomas Chatterton (1752–1770), purporting to be the work of one Thomas Rowley, a monk of the 15th century. They consist of the tragedy of *Aella*, the *Execution of Sir Charles Bawdin*, the *Battle of Hastings*, the *Tournament*, one or two *Dialogues*, and a description of *Canynge's Feast.* According to Chatterton, the MSS. of these poems were found in the Church of St. Mary Redcliffe at Bristol.

" The celebrated Rowley controversy may be said to be practically ended, as few now contend that the so-called *Rowley Poems* had any other origin than in the brain of Thomas Chatterton."— *W. W. Skeat.*

Royal Academy. An association of artists, founded in London in 1768, under the patronage of George III (1760–1820). It maintains a free school of art for students of both sexes, and holds an annual exhibition of paintings and sculptures by modern English artists from the beginning of May to the close of July. Among the famous professors that have taught at the Royal Academy may be mentioned Johnson, Gibbon, Goldsmith, Macaulay, and Hallam. The present building of the Royal Academy (Burlington House, Piccadilly) was erected in 1868-1869. It is in the Renaissance style, and cost nearly £120,000 ($600,-000). The following is a list of the Presidents of the Royal Academy, together with the dates of their installation since its foundation :

(1) Sir Joshua Reynolds : 1768.
(2) Benjamin West : 1792.
(3) James Wyatt (election not confirmed) : 1805.
(4) Benjamin West : 1806.
(5) Sir Thomas Lawrence: 1820.
(6) Sir Martin A. Shee : 1830.
(7) Sir Charles Eastlake : 1850.
(8) Sir Edwin Landseer : 1866.
(9) Sir Francis Grant : 1866.
(10) Sir Frederick Leighton : 1878.
(11) Sir John Everett Millais : 1896.
(12) Sir Edward John Poynter : 1896.

Royal Exchange. The first Royal Exchange in London — opened by Queen Elizabeth (1558-1603) in 1579, was totally destroyed during the Great Fire of 1666. The second structure on this site was founded by Charles II (1660-1685), and completed about 1670. In 1838, it shared the fate of its predecessor, and was replaced by the present building, opened by Queen Victoria (1837-1901) in 1844, at a cost of $900,000. The Royal Exchange is the meeting-place of merchants and bankers. Lloyd's Subscription Rooms are situated in the eastern part of the building. See *Lloyd's*.

Royal George. A British man-of-war of 108 guns, lost off Spithead on August 29th, 1782. The vessel was careened to make certain repairs near the keel ; but having been heeled over too far, a sudden gust of wind washed the sea into her ports and caused her to sink with all on board. About 600 persons, including the aged Admiral Kempenfeldt, were drowned, and not more than 300 escaped.

> " A land breeze shook the shrouds,
> And she was overset ;—
> Down went the *Royal George*,
> With all her crew complete."
> *Cowper.*

Royal Institution. A scientific society in London, founded in 1799 by Benjamin Thompson (Count Rumford), Sir Joseph Banks, and others, incorporated in 1800, and reconstituted in 1810. Its chief objects are: (1) to promote scientific and literary research ; (2) to teach the principles of inductive and experimental science ; (3) to exhibit the application of these principles to the arts ; and (4) to afford opportunities for scientific study. The Institution contains extensive laboratories for physical and chemical research, a model-room, a reading-room, and a library of about 60,000 volumes. Among the famous scientists that have been connected with the Royal Institution, either as lecturers or as directors of the laboratory, may be named Thomas Young, Sir Humphry Davy, William Thomas Brande, Michael Faraday, John Tyndall, Edward Frankland, and Lord Rayleigh.

Royal Library of Berlin. Founded in 1659, and opened for public use in 1661. The present building was erected in 1774-1780. It contains more than 1,000,000 volumes and 15,000 MSS., and is entitled to receive one copy of every book published in the German Empire. About £4800 are annually expended in the purchase of new books. Among the treasures of the library may be named the MS. and first impressions of Luther's translation of the Bible ; Melanchthon's report of the Diet of Worms ; Luther's translation of the *Psalms*, Gutenberg's Bible on parchment, of 1450,—the first book printed with movable types ; the prayer-book used by Charles I of England on the scaffold ; and also the air-pump and hemispheres of Otto von Guericke, with which he made his first experiments. See *Magdeburg Hemispheres.*

Royal Library of Munich. A celebrated library at Munich, Bavaria,—the third largest collection of books in Europe. It contains upwards of 1,000,000 volumes, 30,000 MSS., 300,-000 engravings, and more than 10,000 Greek and Roman coins. Among its treasures may be named the Bible of Luther, containing the Reformer's picture and those of Melanchthon and the Elector Augustus I of Saxony.

Royal Martyr. A sobriquet conferred upon Charles I (1625–1649) of England, who was condemned to death by the High Court of Justice on January 27th, 1649, and beheaded on the 30th of the same month.

"We are at a loss to conceive how the same persons, who, on the 5th of November, thank God for wonderfully conducting his servant King William, and for making all opposition fall before him until he became our king and governor, can, on the 30th of January, contrive to be afraid that the blood of the *Royal Martyr* may be visited on themselves and their children."—*Macaulay.*

Royal Oak. A celebrated oak-tree, formerly on the borders of Staffordshire, England, in the branches of which Charles II (1660–1685) of England is said to have lain concealed for 24 hours, when fleeing from his pursuers after the battle of Worcester (1651). This tree was regarded with almost superstitious reverence by the inhabitants of the vicinity for many years ; but was finally destroyed by relic-hunters, in their eagerness to secure mementos of the King's hiding-place. It is said that an acorn from the Royal Oak, planted by Charles after the Restoration, developed into a flourishing tree, and is still standing in Hyde Park, London. See *Boscobel ; Royal Oak Day ; Worcester, Battle of.*

Royal Oak Day. " The custom of displaying a sprig of oak on Royal Oak Day (May 29th) perpetuates the manner in which the Royalists welcomed the return to England of Charles II, on his birthday, May 29, 1651, in allusion to his concealment in the oak of Boscobel, after the battle of Worcester, on the third of September previous." —Wagner's *Names and their Meaning.* See *Royal Oak.*

Royal Prerogative. A phrase used to denote the hereditary and indefeasible right of the Crown, by virtue of which certain privileges may be exercised without regard to responsibility or accountability. The term first came into general use during the struggles between the English sovereigns and their parliaments,—especially in the days of the Stuarts. Since the time of Charles I (1625–1649), the royal prerogative has been greatly curtailed.

Royal Society. A celebrated society in London, organized in 1660 for the promotion and pursuit of scientific investigation, and incorporated in 1662. It has, at the present time, a membership of about 450 Fellows and 50 Foreign Members ; and contains in its rooms, in Burlington House, a library of 50,000 volumes and a valuable collection of paintings, busts, and relics. Meetings of the Royal Society for the reading and discussion of scientific papers are held weekly on Thursday afternoons from November to June. Among its famous presidents in past years may be named Sir Isaac Newton, Sir Christopher Wren, Samuel Pepys, Sir Joseph Banks, Sir Humphry Davy, Sir Joseph Hooker, Professor Huxley, and Lord Kelvin. Among the awards of the Society are the Copley, Rumford, Davy, and Darwin Medals. The Royal Society is said to be the oldest scientific association in Europe, except the Linnæan Society in Rome.

Rozinante. The name given by Don Quixote to his famous steed. See *Don Quixote.*

"In the next place he visited his steed; and although this animal had more blemishes than the horse of Gonela, which 'tantum pellis et ossa fuit,' yet, in his eyes, neither the Bucephalus of Alexander nor the Cid's Babieca, could be compared with him. Four days was he deliberating upon what name he should give him ; for, as he said to himself, it would be very improper that a horse so excellent, appertaining to a knight so famous, should be without an appropriate name : he therefore endeavoured to find one that should express what he had been before he belonged to a knight-errant, and also what he now was : nothing could, indeed, be more reasonable than that, when the master changed his state, the horse should likewise change his name and assume one, pompous and high-sounding, as became the new order he now professed. So after having devised, altered, lengthened, curtailed, rejected, and again framed in his imagination a variety of names, he finally determined upon *Rozinante*, a name, in his opinion, lofty, sonorous, and full of meaning; importing that he had been only a *Rozin*, a drudge-horse, *before* his present condition, and that now he was before all the *Rozins* in the world." —*Don Quixote* (Jarvis's translation).

Rubicon. The ancient name of a small river that formed the boundary line between Italy and Cisalpine Gaul. It has acquired celebrity from the famous story of its passage by Julius Cæsar and his army in January, 49 B.C. See "*Die is Cast, The.*"

Ruby. This precious stone derives its name from the Latin *rubeus* (*red*).

Rudolphine Tables. A set of astronomical tables computed by Kepler on the observations of Tycho Brahe, and named in honor of Rudolph II (1576–1612), Emperor of Germany, who, after Tycho's death in 1601, assumed the cost of their publication, but failed. The "Rudolphine Tables" are the first ones based on the hypothesis that the planets revolve around the sun in elliptic orbits.

Rugby. A famous public school at Rugby, England, 83 miles northwest of London. It was founded in 1567 by Lawrence Sheriff, a London tradesman and a stanch supporter of Queen Elizabeth (1558–1603); and acquired a national reputation under Dr. Thomas Arnold, the historian, who was headmaster from 1828 until his death in 1842. The school has an attendance of about 500 students, and an income from an endowment of £5000. Among its distinguished alumni may be named Sir Ralph Abercrombie, Macready, Walter Savage Landor, Thomas Hughes, Lord Derby, Dean Stanley, Arthur H. Clough, and Matthew Arnold. An interesting account of school-life at Rugby may be found in Thomas Hughes's *Tom Brown's School Days at Rugby.*

Rumford Medal. A gold medal in the gift of the Royal Society of London, biennially awarded for discoveries in light and heat. It was instituted by Benjamin Thompson (Count Rumford) in 1797, who was himself the first recipient of that honor in 1800.

Rump Parliament. A term derisively used to denote the remnant of the Long Parliament after the forcible expulsion of the Presbyterian members by Colonel Pride, on December 6th, 1648. It contained about 80 members —all of whom were Independents— and sat until April 20th, 1653, when it was dissolved by Oliver Cromwell. The Rump Parliament appointed the commission that tried Charles I on the charge of treason. It reassembled for brief periods in 1659 and 1660. See *Long Parliament ; Pride's Purge.*

"Rum, Romanism, and Rebellion, Party of." An alliterative phrase, stigmatizing the Democratic party, used by the Rev. Dr. Samuel D. Burchard, in an address at a Republican meeting in New York City, during the presidential campaign of 1884. In the opinion of many astute politicians, this unfortunate expression alienated thousands of Roman Catholics from the Republican party in New York State, and thus caused the election of Grover Cleveland to the presidency.

Runes. The name given to the individual letters of an old alphabet called the Futhorc, from its first six letters, *f, u, th, o, r, c.* Runes are formed principally of straight lines, and are found in inscriptions on weapons, ornaments, implements, and memorial stones, in various parts of Norway, Sweden, Denmark, Germany, and to some extent in England. The runes were originally thought to have been derived from Phœnician or Latin characters, but they are now generally believed to have come from an earlier form of the Greek alphabet in use among the Milesian traders and colonists of Olbia, on the north coast of the Black Sea. The oldest runic inscriptions may possibly date from the 1st century A.D., and the latest from the 15th or 16th century. It is said that the change from the curves of the Greek characters to the straight lines of the runes was due to the necessity of carving on wood and stone.

Runnymede. A meadow on the south bank of the Thames, five miles east of Windsor, where the English barons forced King John (1199–1216) to seal the Magna Charta on June 15th, 1215. See *Magna Charta.*

Rupert of Debate. A sobriquet conferred upon Lord Stanley (1799–1869), afterwards the 14th Earl of Derby, by Bulwer, in his poem, the *New Timon*, published in 1846. See *Hotspur of Debate.*

Russian Byron. A title conferred by his countrymen upon Alexander Sergeivitch Pooshkin (1799–1837), the great national poet of Russia.

Russian Murat. A sobriquet bestowed upon Count Michael Andrievitch Miloradovitch (1770–1825), who fought with distinction against the French armies from 1799 to 1814. He attained the rank of general of infantry.

Rydal Mount. A simple, unpretentious house near the village of Rydal, in the " Lake District" of England, occupied by the poet Wordsworth (1770–1850) from 1813 until his death, a period of 37 years. It commands a superb view of Rydal Water and a part of Lake Windermere. Wordsworth is sometimes called the " Bard of Rydal Mount."

Rye House Plot. A real or, as some think, a pretended, conspiracy to assassinate Charles II (1660–1685) and his brother, the Duke of York, and place the Protestant Duke of Monmouth on the English throne (1683). It took its name from the Rye House at Broxbourne, Hertfordshire, the alleged meeting-place of the conspirators. The King and his brother were to be assassinated on their way home from Newmarket to London, but as the house in which the royal party lodged accidentally took fire, the King left Newmarket eight days earlier than was expected and the plan consequently miscarried. The Duke of Monmouth escaped to the Continent ; but Lord William Russell and Algernon Sydney were unfairly convicted of complicity in the affair and were brought to the block.

Ryswick, Peace of. A treaty of peace signed at Ryswick, a village in Holland, by France, England, Holland, the Netherlands, and Spain, on September 20th, and by Germany, on October 30th, 1697. By this treaty, France surrendered all her conquests, except Strasburg, since the Treaty of Nimeguen (1678), and Louis XIV recognized William of Orange as King of England.

S

Sabbatarians. Christians that observe the seventh day of the week (Saturday) as the true Sabbath. They are principally, if not wholly, Baptists, and are often called " Seventh-Day " Baptists. The Sabbatarians claim that the change from the seventh to the first day of the week was effected by the Emperor Constantine (306–337 A.D.), after his conversion to Christianity. In support of their peculiar belief, they assert: (1) that the seventh or last day of the week was chosen by God as a day of rest for all men ; (2) that this selection is binding on all men until the end of time ; and (3) that the Scripture nowhere requires the observance of any other day. See *Seventh-Day Baptists; Sunday.*

Sabbath-Day's Journey. A phrase used among the ancient Hebrews to denote the prescribed distance that might be lawfully traversed on the Sabbath-day. This distance seems to have been about seven furlongs (nearly a mile) from one's temporary or permanent place of abode ; beyond this a Jew could not go without violating the sanctity of the day, unless he availed himself of the appointed means for exceeding the canonical limit.

This limitation of a person's movements on the Sabbath was deduced by the Hebrew legislators from the following injunction found in *Exodus* xvi, 29, 30 :

"See, for that the Lord hath given you the sabbath, therefore he giveth you on the sixth day the bread of two days : abide ye every man in his place, let no man go out of his place on the seventh day. So the people rested on the seventh day."

"Then returned they unto Jerusalem, from the mount called Olivet, which is from Jerusalem a *sabbath day's journey.*"—*Acts* i, 12.

Sabbatical Year. The name given, among the ancient Hebrews, to every seventh year, during which they abstained from tillage of the soil, remitted all debts, and gave the spontaneous products of the fields to the poor and needy. The Sabbatical Year does not seem to have been observed prior to the Babylonian Captivity (606–536 B.C.). See *Exodus* xxiii, 10, 11 ; *Leviticus* xxv, 3-7 ; *Deuteronomy* xv, 3-11.

Sabellians. A Christian sect founded by Sabellius, a presbyter of Ptolemais, Egypt, who lived in the third century. The Sabellians denied the existence of the Trinity, and taught that the Father, Son, and Holy Ghost were simply three successive forms of manifestation of one divine substance. Sabellianism was condemned as heretical at a council at Rome in 262, and died out during the fourth century.

Sablonnière (*Fr., Sand-Pit*). A name given at one time to the site of the palace of the Tuileries in Paris, in allusion to the sand-pits that existed there. Towards the close of the 14th century, tiles were first made in these pits; but it was not until 1416 that they were called the *tuileries*, or *tile-works.* See *Tuileries, Palace of the.*

Sabreur, Beau (*Fr., Handsome Swordsman*). See *Handsome Swordsman.*

Sackville Street. A broad and handsome street in the city of Dublin, Ireland, considered by many travelers to be the finest thoroughfare in Europe. It is 120 feet broad and 700 yards long; and is adorned, midway of its length, with a splendid monument to Lord Nelson,—130 feet high.

Sacramentarians. A name originally given to the followers of Zwingli (1484–1531), who denied the doctrine of the "Real Presence." See *Real Presence.*

Sacred Heart, Feast of the. "A festival of comparatively modern institution in the Roman Catholic Church, and for a time the subject of much controversy among Roman Catholics themselves. Its origin is traced to a vision recorded of a French nun of the Order of the Visitation, named Mary Margaret Alacoque, who lived at Paray-le-Monial, in Burgundy, in the latter half of the 17th century, and whose enthusiasm led her to practice a special devotion to the heart of the Saviour. This devotion was gradually propagated in France, and at length was approved by Pope Clement XII in 1732 and 1736, and by Clement

XIII in 1765. The festival is held on the Friday after the octave of Corpus Christi."—McClintock and Strong's *Cyclopædia*.

Sacred Isle.

(1) Ireland, on account of its multitude of saints.

(2) Guernsey, one of the Channel Islands, because of its many monks.

(3) Scattery, in the estuary of the Shannon, where St. Senan or Senatus retired during the 6th century A.D., and vowed that no woman should set foot there.

(4) The peninsula of Mount Athos, which projects from Chalcidice in Macedonia into the Ægean Sea. It contains 20 large monasteries, besides hermitages and chapels, tenanted by about 6000 monks. No females, even of the lower animals, are permitted to be present or even to enter the peninsula. See *Athos, Mount*.

Sacred Wars. A term applied to several wars waged in ancient Greece for the protection of the temple and oracle at Delphi. They were as follows :

(1) *First Sacred War*. Waged in 595–586 B.C., by the Amphictyonic Council against the Cirrhæans, for robbery and outrage to the visitors to the oracle. The city of Cirrha was razed to the ground.

(2) *Second Sacred War*. Waged in 448–447 B.C., between the Phocians and Delphians for the possession of the temple ; the former, aided by the Athenians, were successful.

(3) *Third Sacred War*. Waged in 357–346 B.C., by the Amphictyonic Council, aided by Philip of Macedon, for the purpose of recovering the temple from the Phocians. The latter were conquered, and their cities devastated.

Sacro Catino (*It.*, *Sacred Basin*). An interesting relic, in the shape of a dish, in the treasury of the Cathedral of San Lorenzo at Genoa, Italy, said to have been presented by the Queen

of Sheba to Solomon, and long preserved in the temple at Jerusalem. According to another tradition, it is the dish used by Christ at the Last Supper. It was taken by the Genoese as their share of the booty, after the capture of Cæsarea in 1101, and was brought by them to Genoa, where it was held in such veneration that twelve nobles, called " Clavigeri," were appointed as its special guardians,—one for each month of the year. The *Sacro Catino* was shown once annually ; on which occasion it was held by a cord when exhibited to the people. It was deemed so valuable that the sum of 4,000,000 francs was borrowed on it within a period of 50 years. In 1476, a law was passed,— punishing with death any one that touched the *Sacro Catino*. It was taken by Napoleon I to Paris in 1809; but when restored in 1815, it was found to be broken. The fracture proved the sacred relic to be merely a specimen of antique glass.

Sadducees. An aristocratic sect among the ancient Jews, said to have been founded by one Sadoc, a rabbi, about 200 B.C. The Sadducees acknowledged only the *written* Law as binding, and totally rejected the *oral* Law and the traditions of the Pharisees. Hence, their denial of the doctrine of the resurrection of the body and of the existence of angels and spirits, on the ground that the *written* Law was silent on these points. They also believed in free will, as opposed to the predestinarianism of the Pharisees. The Sadducees were essentially a political party, and disappeared with the fall of the Jewish State. See *Pharisees*.

Sadler's Wells. The Sadler's Wells Theatre in London derives its name from the ancient holy well that once stood on the site of the present building. This well—long famous for its wonderful cures—was stopped up at the time of the Reformation (1517); but was accidentally rediscovered in 1683 by a Mr. Sadler, while digging

42

gravel in his garden. Wishing to profit by his discovery, Sadler converted his residence into a place of amusement, known as *Sadler's Musick House*, and there entertained his patrons with exhibitions of tight-rope dancing, gymnastics, conjuring, and other mild diversions,—always accompanied by music. Sixty years later, the property passed into other hands, and was converted into a theatre, although the original name was retained. The present structure dates from 1879.

Sadowa (or Königgrätz), Battle of. A desperate battle fought at Königgrätz, a town in Bohemia, on July 3rd, 1866, between 240,000 Prussians, commanded by King William I, and 220,000 Austrians under Marshal Benedek. The Austrians were signally defeated with a loss of 21,000 men killed and wounded, and 22,000 taken prisoners. The Prussian loss was about 10,000. The Prussians name the battle Königgrätz; while the Austrians call it Sadowa, from a small village nearer the centre of the battlefield.

Safa. According to tradition, a hill in Arabia where Adam and Eve met after having been separated for 200 years, during which period they had wandered homeless over the surface of the earth. See *Caaba*.

Safety Lamp. See *Davy Lamp*.

Sagas. Scandinavian myths or heroic stories—chiefly Icelandic—composed by scalds, and committed to writing about the 12th century A.D. They generally take the form of biographies, and give a faithful picture of the life and manners of the time. The most famous sagas are those of Lodbrok, Hervara, Vilkina, Völsunga, Blomsturvalla, Ynglinga, Olaf Tryggva-Sonar, Jomsvikingia, Knythinga (containing the legendary history of Iceland), and Voluspa. Many of the historical sagas are collected in the *Heimskringla* of Snorro Sturleson (1178-1241), the historian and poet. See *Eddas; Scalds*.

Sage of Chelsea. A sobriquet conferred upon Thomas Carlyle (1795-1881), the distinguished English essayist and historian, on account of his long sojourn at Cheyne Row, Chelsea, London.

Sage of Concord. A title bestowed upon Ralph Waldo Emerson (1803-1882), the famous American essayist and poet, in allusion to his place of residence at Concord, Massachusetts.

"No one who has conversed with the *Sage of Concord* can wonder at the love which his neighbors feel for him, or the reverence with which he is regarded by the scholars of England and America."—*Newspaper Biographical Sketch* (May, 1879).

Sage of Crotona. An appellation conferred upon Pythagoras [580 (?)-500 (?) B.C.], the celebrated Greek philosopher, because he established his first and chief school of philosophy at Crotona in Southern Italy, about 540 B.C. He is also called *Crotona's Sage*.

Sage of Monticello. A sobriquet bestowed upon Thomas Jefferson (1743-1826), in allusion to the wisdom displayed by him in political affairs during his residence at Monticello, Virginia, after his retirement from the presidency.

Sage of Samos. See *Samian Sage*.

Sagest of Usurpers. An epithet conferred upon Oliver Cromwell (1599-1658) by Byron in *Childe Harold*.

Sagittary. A fabulous monster, half beast and half man, introduced into the Trojan armies by Guido da Colonna, the writer. He appears as "a terrible archer, . . . who neighs like a horse, whose eyes sparkle with fire, and strike dead like lightning."

"... the dreadful *Sagittary*
Appals our numbers; haste we, Diomed,
To reinforcement, or we perish all."
Troilus and Cressida, v, 5.

"A mervayllous beste that was called *Sagittayre*, that behynde the myddes was an horse, and tofore a man. This beste was heery like an horse, and had his eyen red as a cole, and shotte well with a bowe: this beste made the Grekes sore aferde, and slewe many of them with his bowe."—Caxton's *History of Troy.*

"The *Sagittary* was the residence at the arsenal of the commanding officers of the army and navy of Venice. It is said that the figure of an archer, with his bow drawn, over the gates, still indicates the place ; and some think the Poet [Shakespeare] had himself seen it."—Hudson's *Shakespeare.*

" Lead to the *Sagittary* the rais'd search ; And there will I be with him. So, farewell."

Othello, i, 1.

Sailor King. A name popularly given to William IV (1830–1837) of England, who entered the navy as midshipman in 1779, and rose gradually by regular promotion to the rank of captain. In 1801 he was appointed admiral, and, on his retirement from active service in 1827, was made Lord High Admiral of England.

St. Andrew's. A town of Scotland, 42 miles northeast of Edinburgh, famous as the seat of the oldest university in that country. Although the schools of St. Andrew's were famous as early as 1120, the university proper was not founded until 1411. It comprises St. Salvator's College (1455), St. Leonard's College (1512), and St. Mary's College (1537). St. Salvator's and St. Leonard's were united in 1747. The average attendance is about 200. The university contains a library of 100,000 volumes, and a museum. University College at Dundee, for both sexes, is an offshoot of the university, and was opened in 1883.

St. Angelo, Castle of. See *Castle of St. Angelo.*

St. Augustine. St. Augustine, Florida, enjoys the reputation of being the oldest permanent European settlement within the limits of the United States, having been founded by the Spaniards under Pedro Menendez de Aviles in 1565, more than half a century before the landing of the Pilgrims at Plymouth (1620). With the rest of Florida, it passed into the hands of the English by treaty in 1763, was ceded to Spain in 1783, and became part of the United States in 1819.

St. Bartholomew, Massacre of. An appellation given to a dreadful slaughter of Protestants throughout France, so called because it commenced on the night of the Festival of St. Bartholomew (August 24th, 1572). This massacre was secretly ordered by Charles IX (1560–1574), at the instigation of his mother, the dowager-queen, Catherine de' Medici, and caused the deaths of 4000 persons in Paris alone. Various estimates place the number slain in the provinces at from 30,000 to 80,000. Pope Gregory III (1572–1585) ordered a *Te Deum* sung in honor of the event; and, in addition, caused a medal to be struck, and proclaimed a year of jubilee. See *Bloody Wedding; Huguenots; St. Germain l'Auxerrois.*

St. Catherine Convent. A fortress-like convent, belonging to the Greek Church, situated at the foot of one of the peaks of Mount Sinai, and said to have been founded by the Emperor Justinian in 527 A.D. It is celebrated as the place where Tischendorf discovered, in 1844 and 1859, the famous Sinaitic Codex, now in St. Petersburg. See *Sinaitic Codex.*

St. Cecilia. A famous painting by Raphael (1483–1520), now in the Academy of Fine Arts at Bologna. It was painted as an altar-piece for the Church of San Giovanni-in-Monte, near Bologna, Italy, about 1515 ; was taken to Paris by Napoleon I ; and restored in 1815. The painting represents St. Cecilia, wrapped in ecstasy, listening to the music of a celestial choir,—while at her feet the instruments of secular music lie broken and scattered. On her right are St. John and St. Paul ; on her left St. Augustine and Mary Magdalene.

" The saint is neither angelic nor ecstatic ; she is a vigorous, healthy, well-developed girl, of rich, warm blood, and gilded by the Italian sunshine with glowing and beautiful color. On her left another young girl, less robust and more youthful, has more innocence, but her purity is yet only passivity. . . . Their placid minds are not disturbed; their tranquillity is that of ignorance."— *Taine.*

St. Cloud, Palace of. A famous palace, formerly standing on an eminence on the south bank of the Seine, six miles west of Paris. It was built originally for Jerome de Gondy, a Parisian financier, in 1658, and was afterwards purchased by Louis XIV (1643-1715), and presented by him to his brother, the Duke of Orleans, who expended large sums in enlarging and embellishing it. St. Cloud was the favorite residence of Marie Antoinette, Napoleon I, and Napoleon III, and the scene of some of the most stirring events of French history. It was there that Napoleon Bonaparte dissolved the Councils of the Ancients and the Five Hundred and caused himself to be chosen First Consul, and there also that Charles X signed the ordinances that precipitated the Revolution of 1830 and lost him the throne of France. The name "St. Cloud" is derived from Cleodald, a grandson of Clovis, who, after the murder of his brothers by his uncle Clotaire, fled to this place, concealed himself in the woods, and dwelt as a hermit. After his death, he was canonized as a saint, and his name changed to St. Cloud. The palace was destroyed during the Franco-Prussian War of 1870-1871,— having been set on fire and burned by the French shells from Mont Valérien, to prevent it from falling into the hands of the Prussians. The gardens and park still exist, and are famous for their beauty.

St. Columba. An Irish missionary (521-597), who introduced Christianity into Scotland about 563. It is an interesting fact that, according to tradition, Christianity was introduced into Scotland by an Irishman [St. Columba], and into Ireland by a Scotch-

man [St. Patrick]. See *Columba's Isle; St. Patrick.*

St. Crispin. The patron-saint of shoemakers. During the reign of the Emperor Diocletian (284-305 A.D.), Crispin and his brother Crispianus— natives of Rome—accompanied St. Quentin as missionaries to Gaul, and settled at Soissons, where they preached the gospel and supported themselves by making shoes. They suffered martyrdom in 287 A.D., when, by order of the Emperor Maximianus (286-305), they were beheaded or, as some say, were cast into a cauldron of boiling lead. Crispin and Crispianus are commemorated as saints and martyrs by the Roman Catholic Church on St. Crispin's Day (October 25th). According to the legend, the benevolence of the brothers was so great that they even stole leather from the rich to make shoes for the poor. From this, deeds of charity, done at others' expense, are frequently called *Crispinades.*

Sainte-Chapelle. An ancient palace-chapel adjoining the Palais de Justice in Paris,—erected in 1245-1248 for the reception and safe-keeping of the sacred relics (now at Notre Dame) purchased by Louis IX (1226-1270) for 3,000,000 francs. The building is 115 feet long, 36 feet wide, and 112 feet high, and is considered to be one of the most perfect specimens of Gothic architecture in France. It contains two chapels, one above the other. The upper chapel was originally used by the court and the royal family, and the lower one by the domestics of the household. The former contains fifteen superb stained-glass windows, representing scenes from the Bible and the lives of the saints. See *Palais de Justice.*

Sainte Geneviève. The patron-saint of Paris, born at Nanterre about 424 A.D. She took the veil at the age of 15, and removed to Paris on the death of her parents. At the time of

Attila's invasion (451), she predicted that God would preserve the city. Later, during the Frankish invasion under Childéric, she undertook an expedition for the relief of the starving city and returned with twelve shiploads of provisions. This noble deed, together with her reputation for sanctity, raised her to a great height in the esteem of the people. She died in 512, and was buried in a church built by her over the tomb of St. Denis,—the site of which is now occupied by the Panthéon. See *Panthéon*.

St. Elmo, Castle of. A celebrated fortress at Naples, Italy, erected in 1343 A.D., and rebuilt in its present form, in the 16th century, by Pedro de Toledo. Its fortifications were at one time regarded second only to Gibraltar and Malta in impregnability, but are of little value in these days of modern warfare. They have been almost totally demolished, and the structure is now used as a military prison. A superb view of the city and bay of Naples, with Vesuvius in the distance, may be obtained from the Castle of St. Elmo.

St. Elmo's Fire. A name popularly given to a luminous appearance, sometimes seen on dark and stormy nights at the masthead and yard-arms of vessels, and also on land at the tops of church spires and trees and even on horses' manes and about human heads. It is due to the presence of electricity, generally at elevated points, where it accumulates more rapidly than it can be discharged, and is named after St. Elmo, the patron saint of sailors. A single flame is called a *Helena* or a *Corposant ;* a double flame, a *Castor and Pollux* or a *Double Corposant.*

St. Germain des Prés, Church of. One of the most ancient churches in Paris. It originally formed part of the Abbey of St. Germain, founded by Childebert in 550 A.D., in the midst of the *prés (Fr., meadows)* on the left bank of the Seine, whence the name.

" The nave is said to belong to an edifice of 1001–1014, but the style is rather that of the end of the 11th century. The choir, consecrated in 1163, was afterwards altered, particularly in the windows, which show a tendency to Gothic. During the Revolution the church was used as a saltpetre manufactory, and fell into a very dilapidated condition, but it was restored in 1824–36." —Baedeker's *Paris*.

St. Germain l'Auxerrois. A church in Paris, facing the eastern front of the Louvre, founded before the time of Charlemagne (768–814). In its present form, it dates from the 12th and 16th centuries, although portions from preceding centuries have been retained. The church is celebrated for its beautiful architecture, its superb stained-glass windows, and its magnificent frescoes. Members of the royal family were formerly baptized in the Church of St. Germain l'Auxerrois, and it was from the little bell-tower of this church that the signal for the Massacre of St. Bartholomew was given on the night of August 24th, 1572. See *St. Bartholomew, Massacre of.*

St. Giles's. A disreputable quarter of London, west of the City and northeast of Westminster. It has long been noted as a centre of poverty and vice, and was at one time the resort of the vilest and most abandoned classes of the metropolis. This region was much improved by the opening of New Oxford Street in 1849; and since that time, schools, churches, and reformatories have sprung up and have done much to improve the neighborhood. See *Seven Dials.*

St. Gotthard Tunnel. A tunnel on the line of the St. Gotthard Railway between Switzerland and Italy, piercing the Alps at an altitude of nearly 4000 feet above the sea-level. It is the longest railway-tunnel in the world,— measuring 48,651 feet (about 9¼ miles) in length, 26 feet in width, and 21 feet in height. The tunnel was begun in 1872, and completed in 1880 at an expense of over $11,000,000. The cost per lineal yard is estimated at about $700. The first passenger-train passed through the St. Gotthard Tunnel on November 1st, 1881. See *Mont Cenis Tunnel ; Simplon Tunnel.*

St. Graal. See *Grail, Holy.*

St. Grouse's Day. A nickname given in England to the 12th of August, on which day the season for grouse-shooting opens.

St. Helena. An island in the South Atlantic Ocean, 1140 miles from the west coast of Africa, discovered by the Portuguese on St. Helena's Day, May 21st, 1502. It afterwards passed into the hands of the Dutch, who held it until 1600, when they were expelled by the English,—the present owners. The island is of volcanic origin and covers an area of about 47 square miles. It is famous as the place of confinement of Napoleon Bonaparte from October 16th, 1815, until his death on May 5th, 1821. In 1840, his remains were removed to France, and were deposited in the Hôtel des Invalides in Paris. See *Tomb of Napoleon.*

St. Isaac's Church. A magnificent structure in St. Petersburg, Russia, begun in 1819 and completed in 1858, at a cost of $67,500,000. The church is in the form of a Greek cross—330 feet long by 290 feet broad—and has four principal entrances, each of which is adorned with a porch supported by polished granite monoliths, 60 feet in height and 7 feet in diameter. Over the centre of the building rises a superb dome, overlaid with gold, which, as Bayard Taylor says, "glitters over the evening horizon like a rising star." It is said that the foundation of St. Isaac's Church—built entirely upon piles, owing to the marshy nature of the ground—cost over $1,000,000. The structure is devoid of architectural beauty; but its interior is elaborately decorated, and contains paintings by leading Russian artists.

St. James's Coffee-House. A famous coffee-house in St. James's Street, London, much frequented by the members of the Whig party from the time of Queen Anne (1702–1714) until late in the reign of George III (1760–1820). It was demolished in 1806, and a large pile of buildings erected on its site. St. James's Coffee-House was a favorite resort of Swift, Garrick, Goldsmith, Dr. Samuel Johnson, Edmund Burke, and others.

St. James's Palace. A large, irregular brick building, near Pall Mall, London,—formerly a royal residence, but used at present for ceremonial purposes only. It was erected by Henry VIII (1509–1547) on the site of a hospital for lepers, dedicated to St. James; and became, after the destruction of Whitehall by fire in 1697, the chief residence of the English sovereigns from William III (1689–1702) to William IV (1830–1837). Queen Victoria, after her accession in 1837, removed the royal household to Buckingham Palace ; but, until the death of Prince Albert in 1861, she held her "levees" and "drawing-rooms" at St. James's Palace. After that event, however, the "drawing-rooms" were transferred to the larger apartments at Buckingham Palace.

Custom still recognizes the palace of St. James as the official residence of British royalty, and hence the English court is diplomatically referred to as the Court of St. James. See *Buckingham Palace.*

St. Januarius, Blood of. See *Blood of St. Januarius.*

St. John Lateran, Church of. A celebrated church in Rome, adjoining the palace of the Lateran. It outranks all the other churches of Rome in dignity—not excepting St. Peter's, —and is styled "the Mother and Head of all the Churches of the City and the

World." The original structure—dedicated to the Savior—was built by the Emperor Constantine in 324 A.D., and was presented by him to Sylvester, Bishop of Rome ; the present one—dedicated to John the Baptist — was built in 1586 by Pope Sixtus V (1585–1590). The basilica of St. John Lateran is famous as the place of coronation of newly elected popes ; it was also the scene of the five Lateran Councils —regarded as Ecumenical—the last of which took place in 1512. See *Ecumenical Councils ; Lateran, Palace of the ; Santa Scala.*

St. John the Divine, Cathedral of.

A magnificent Protestant Episcopal cathedral now in process of erection on Morningside Heights, Borough of Manhattan, New York City, the corner-stone of which was laid on St. John's Day (December 17th), 1892, by Bishop Potter of the diocese of New York. The building will have a total outside length of 520 feet and a width across the front of 192 feet. The width across the transepts will be 296 feet. The height of the two front towers will be 248 feet, and that of the main central tower (including the cross) 445 feet above the floor of the cathedral. The cost of erection is placed at more than $6,000,000, of which sum it is proposed to expend $200,000 annually until the structure is completed. The time required to build the cathedral is placed at 50 years.

St. Katherine's Docks.

A famous establishment in London on the left bank of the Thames, adjoining the London Docks, completed in 1828 at a cost of £1,700,000. It covers an area of 24 acres, and has a warehouse capacity of 110,000 tons. It is said that 1200 houses—the homes of over 11,000 inhabitants, were removed to make way for these docks. In 1863, the London Docks and the St. Katherine's Docks were united under one management. See *London Docks.*

St. Louis Bridge.

A famous steel bridge at St. Louis, Missouri, designed by Captain James B. Eads, and constructed in 1869–1874, at a cost of $10,000,000. It has a total length of 6210 feet, and is composed of three spans, each of which has an average length of 500 feet. The bridge is built in two stories,—the lower one being used for the railroad, and the upper one for vehicles and pedestrians.

St. Mark's Cathedral.

A celebrated church in Venice, Italy, dedicated to St. Mark, the patron-saint of the city. The original building was founded by the Doge Giustiniani Participazio in 829 A.D., and completed by his heirs ; it was destroyed by fire in 976, and was replaced by the present structure in 1043. St. Mark's was not converted into a cathedral until 1807,—previous to which time it was known as the Ducal Chapel. The church is in the form of a Greek cross, and has a front width of 171 feet and a height of 73 feet. The nave is 243 feet long, the transept 200 feet long, and the centre dome 92 feet high. It is in the Byzantine style of architecture, and is adorned with nearly 600 columns, brought from Greece. Over the front entrance stand the famous Bronze Horses. See *Bones of St. Mark ; Bronze Horses.*

"This singular edifice can neither be described nor forgotten. It is a strange jumble of architectural styles ; partly Christian and partly Saracenic—in form a Greek cross, crowned with the domes and minarets of a mosque. The façade is rich in mosaics, and crowded with works of sculpture and elaborately carved pillars, which have no relation to each other, and no particular adaptation to the places which they occupy. . . . The interior of St. Mark's has two obvious defects. It is too crowded and too dark. The attention is distracted by the vast mass and crowd of gilding, mosaics, and columns, of which last there are more than five hundred —all of marble and some very rare and costly ; but huddled together with tasteless profusion, and many of them, architecturally speaking, with nothing to do. There is no unity, no simplicity, and no grandeur. The general effect is poor, in spite of the wealth of materials. The first impression, which is so important in architecture, is bewildering and not imposing. Everything needs interpretation and explanation. The separate parts must be put together and a new whole formed."—Hillard's *Six Months in Italy.*

St. Mark's Column. A celebrated granite monolith in the Piazzetta at Venice, surmounted by the Winged Lion of St. Mark. It was brought—with its companion, the Column of St. Theodore—from Syria by the Doge Michiele in 1120. See *Columns of St. Mark; Lion of St. Mark; St. Theodore's Column.*

St. Michael. A famous picture by Raphael (1483–1520), in the Louvre at Paris. It was painted in 1518 by order of Pope Leo X (1513–1522) for Francis I (1515–1547) of France, and is partly the work of Giulio Romano and other pupils of Raphael. It represents the archangel triumphing over Satan, and is considered to be a work of sublime poetic character. See *Michael.*

St. Michael's Mount. An isolated, rocky eminence in Mount's Bay, Cornwall, England, connected with the mainland by a causeway, 500 yards long, which at high tide is covered by the sea. It consists of a conical granite mass—195 feet high and more than 3000 feet in circumference — surmounted by an old, picturesque castle. The place is said to have received its name from an apparition of St. Michael, which appeared to some hermits in 495 or 710 A.D. Edward the Confessor (1042–1066) founded a Benedictine priory there in 1044, which in 1088 was annexed to the Abbey of Mount St. Michael in Normandy. See *Mont St. Michel.*

St. Monday. "A holiday observed by idle workmen and many merchants." — Brewer's *Dictionary of Phrase and Fable.*

St. Nicholas. The patron-saint of Russia, and of children. He is said to have been Bishop of Myra in Lycia in the time of the Emperor Diocletian (284–305) and to have died in 326 A.D., but his personal history is almost entirely unknown. St. Nicholas's Day falls on December 6th, on which date it is still customary in Germany for some person to assume the dress and appearance of a bishop, and to distribute presents to the children—either at home or in school — as a reward of their good conduct. See *Santa Claus, or Klaus.*

St. Pancras. A parish in London, so called from the church of the same name. St. Pancras was a boy-saint who, at the age of 14, was martyred by order of the Emperor Diocletian (284–305) at Rome, in 304 A.D. He shares with St. Nicholas the honor of being the patron-saint of children. In former days he was considered the avenger of false swearing, and hence French kings confirmed their treaties in his name.

St. Partridge's Day. A nickname given in England to the 1st of September, which marks the beginning of the season for partridge-shooting.

St. Patrick. A famous Scotch missionary [372(?)–465(?) A.D.], who is said to have introduced Christianity into Ireland about 432. He is the patron-saint of Ireland, and belongs equally to history and to legend. See *St. Columba.*

St. Patrick's Cathedral.
(1) A cathedral in Dublin, Ireland, founded in 1190 by Archbishop Comyn; and restored in 1865, at a cost of £150,000, through the munificence of Sir Benjamin Lee Guinness, the famous Dublin brewer. The present building stands on the site of a church said to have been built by St. Patrick himself, and known to have been standing as late as 830,—when Gregory of Scotland worshipped there. The cathedral is adorned with numerous monuments, and contains the grave of Dean Swift and Mrs. Johnston, the

"Stella" of his poetry. Jonathan Swift (1667–1745) was appointed Dean of St. Patrick's in 1713, and retained the position until his death.

(2) A Roman Catholic cathedral on Fifth Avenue, Borough of Manhattan, New York City. The corner-stone was laid in 1858, in the presence of 100,000 persons, and the building was opened for divine service in 1879. It is built of white marble, in the decorated Gothic style that prevailed in Europe during the 13th century, and is justly considered the grandest ecclesiastical structure in America. The ground-plan is in the form of a Latin cross, and the dimensions are as follows : length, 322 feet ; breadth, including chapels, 120 feet ; breadth of nave and choir, 97 feet ; length of transepts, 172 feet ; height of nave, 100 feet ; height of aisles, 54 feet The Fifth Avenue front consists of a central gable, 156 feet in height, flanked by twin towers and spires, 330 feet high. The four altars in the cathedral cost about $100,000. The interior is lighted by 70 windows—37 of which are memorial windows. The greater number of them were made at Chartres, France, at a cost of about $100,000. The seating capacity of the cathedral is 2600, and there is space in the aisles for as many more. The total cost of the structure has been about $3,000,000.

St. Patrick's Purgatory. A cave on an islet in Lough Derg, Ireland, said to have been made by St. Patrick himself, as an entrance into Purgatory for the living sinner that might wish, while still in the flesh, to atone for his evil deeds. This legend was made the subject of a romance during the 14th century, and was dramatized by Calderon, the Spanish writer, during the 17th century.

"Who has not heard of *St. Patrick's Purgatory*, of its mysterious wonders, and of the crowds of devotees who have for ages been attracted by its reputed sanctity ?"—*Wright.*

St. Paul's Cathedral. The metropolitan church of London, built by Sir Christopher Wren in 1675–1710, at a cost of $3,700,000. It stands on the site of a Gothic church of the same name, which was destroyed in the Great Fire of 1666, and is the third largest church in Christendom,—being surpassed only by St. Peter's at Rome and Milan Cathedral. It is in the form of a Latin cross, and its principal dimensions are as follows: nave, 500 feet long and 118 feet broad ; length of transept, 250 feet ; height of interior dome above pavement, 225 feet ; height of cross, surmounting dome, above pavement, 363 feet or, as some authorities say, 404 feet. The interior is plain, and lacks the richness and warmth characteristic of Gothic churches. St. Paul's is remarkable as having been completed by one architect, one master-mason, and under one bishop. The greater part of the cost of construction was defrayed by a tax on coal.

St. Peter's Church. The metropolitan church of Rome, and the largest, most imposing, and most beautiful Christian temple ever built. It stands on the site of a church which, according to tradition, was erected by Anacletus, Bishop of Rome, in 90 A.D., over the spot where the apostle Peter was interred. In 306, Constantine I (306–337) erected a magnificent basilica on the same site, which, however, was almost totally destroyed by the Saracens. The foundation of the present cathedral was laid by Pope Julius II (1503–1513) in 1506, and the building was consecrated by Pope Urban VIII (1623–1644) in 1626. The colonnade was added in 1667, and the sacristy in 1776,—the erection of the entire structure occupying 270 years. The total cost is said to have exceeded $50,000,-000. The dimensions of St. Peter's Church are variously given. The following dimensions are taken from the *Pearl Cyclopædia* : Entire length within the walls, 613½ feet ; entire width of nave, 197¾ feet ; interior diameter of dome (designed by Michael Angelo),

139 feet ; exterior diameter of dome, 195½ feet ; height from pavement to base of lantern, 405 feet ; height from pavement to top of cross outside, 448 feet ; circumference of pillars supporting great dome, 253 feet. See *Baldacchino of St. Peter's*.

"To say that the dome of St. Peter's is sublime is a cold commonplace. In sublimity, it is so much beyond all other architectural creations that it demands epithets of its own. There is no work of man's hands that is similar or second to it. Vast as it is, it rests upon its supporting piers, in such serene tranquillity, that it seems to have been lifted and expanded by the elastic force of the air which it clasps. Under its majestic vault, the soul dilates. To act like the hero—to endure like the martyr—seems no more than the natural state of man."—Hillard's *Six Months in Italy*.

St. Peter's Statue. A bronze statue of St. Peter in St. Peter's Church at Rome,—the foot of which has been reverently kissed by many generations of devout Catholics.

"It is a story, often repeated by Protestant writers, that this identical statue is a work of antiquity ; a representation of Jupiter, baptized anew in those transition ages, 'when Pan to Moses lent his pagan horn.' But in this statement there is more of Protestant zeal than of knowledge in art ; for not only it has not that character of the head and arrangement of the hair always found in statues of Jupiter ; but its inferior workmanship, the stiffness of the attitude, and the hardness of the outline prove it to be of later date than the classical periods of art. It is probably the recast of an antique statue."—Hillard's *Six Months in Italy*.

St.-Simonism. The name given to the social and political doctrines taught by Claude Henri, Comte de Saint-Simon (1760–1825), the founder of French Socialism. He advocated the establishment of an industrial order of society, controlled by industrial chiefs, in place of the feudal and military system now in vogue; and suggested that the spiritual direction of affairs be transferred from the hands of the clergy to those of men of science. He further proposed the establishment of an international parliament, where all questions affecting Europe might be settled by arbitration. After Saint-Simon's death, his views were expanded by his followers into an elaborate system of Socialism. Auguste Comte was a disciple of Saint-Simon.

"The whole of society ought to strive towards the amelioration of the moral and physical existence of the poorest class ; society ought to organize itself in the best way adapted for attaining this end."—*Saint-Simon*.

St. Sophia. A Mohammedan mosque at Constantinople, Turkey, occupying the site of a Christian church, dedicated to St. Sophia (*Holy Wisdom*) by Constantine II (337–361 A.D.) in 360. The present structure—a fine specimen of Byzantine architecture—was founded by the Emperor Justinian (527–565) in 531 and completed in 538; but was converted into a Moslem temple by Mohammed II (1451–1481) after the fall of Constantinople in 1453. It is in the form of a Greek cross, 270 feet long by 243 feet wide, and is surmounted by a lofty dome, the centre of which is 180 feet above the pavement. The interior is lined with costly marbles and superb mosaics, and is adorned with beautiful columns of marble, granite, and porphyry. Eight of these columns were taken by the Emperor Aurelius from the Temple of the Sun at Baalbek, eight from the Temple of Diana at Ephesus, and others from the Temples of the Sun and Moon at Heliopolis, from Athens, and from the Cyclades. The gilded crescent surmounting the dome is 150 feet in diameter, and can be seen 100 miles out at sea. It is said that the gilding alone cost $50,000.

"The Latin term, *Sancta Sophia*, which translates 'αγία Σοφία, came to be taken as the name of a human person, and St. Sophia was said to have been martyred along with her three daughters, Fides, Spes, Caritas, *Faith, Hope, Charity*."—Smith's *Glossary of Terms and Phrases*.

St. Stephen's Church. The cathedral-church of Vienna, Austria, commenced in 1300 and completed in 1510. It is a superb Gothic structure

350 feet long and 220 feet broad, and is surmounted by a graceful spire, 450 feet in height. From this lofty elevation a magnificent view is obtained—not only of the battlefields of Aspern, Essling, and Wagram, but also of the city and its suburbs and the windings of the Danube. The great bell in the tower of the cathedral weighs 358 cwt., and is made of 180 pieces of cannon captured from the Turks. The interior of the church is richly decorated with stained-glass windows and is adorned with fine sculptures.

St. Swithin's Day. July 15th, so called from the legend connected with St. Swithin, Bishop of Winchester (852–862 A.D.), and tutor to King Alfred. At his request, he was buried in the churchyard of the abbey, where " passers-by might tread on his grave, and where the rain from the eaves might fall on it." After his canonization in 865, it was resolved to remove his remains to the chancel—the customary burial-place of the bishops—and July 15th was appointed for the ceremony ; but on that day and for 40 days thereafter, St. Swithin, to testify his displeasure, caused rain to fall so heavily that the monks abandoned their design as heretical and blasphemous. From this legend arose the popular superstition that if rain falls on July 15th it will continue to do so for the 40 days succeeding. Careful records kept at Greenwich Observatory for a period of 20 years show this superstition to be without foundation.

St. Tammany. A famous Indian chief, popularly canonized as a saint, —about whom many fanciful legends have gathered. He is said to have been a native of Delaware, and to have lived during the 17th century A.D. After attaining his majority, he removed to the banks of the Ohio, where he became the Grand Sachem of his tribe, and acquired a great reputation for wisdom, firmness, and moderation. According to tradition, he signed the treaty with William Penn, and was chosen by the troops of Washington as patron-saint, in place of St. George. His great maxim was : " Unite. In peace for mutual happiness ; in war for mutual defense." He is the tutelary genius of the Tammany Society, New York City ; but for what reason he is called " Saint " does not appear. See *Tammany Society.*

St. Theodore's Column. A superb granite monolith in the Piazzetta at Venice, crowned with a statue of St. Theodore reclining upon a crocodile. It was brought from Syria by the Doge Michiele in 1120. It was between the columns of St. Theodore and St. Mark that public executions formerly took place. See *Columns of St. Mark ; St. Mark's Column.*

" St. Theodore was the first patron of Venice ; but he was deposed, and St. Mark adopted, when the bones of the latter were brought from Alexandria." — Wheeler's *Familiar Allusions.*

St. Ursula, Church of. A celebrated church in Cologne, Germany, containing the bones of St. Ursula and her 11,000 virgin attendants. According to the legend, St. Ursula was the daughter of a British king, who in the 3rd or 4th century A.D. made a pilgrimage to Rome,—accompanied by 11,000 maidens,— and was received with great honors by the Pope. On reaching Cologne during the homeward journey, the entire party fell into the hands of the Huns, and were brutally murdered by them, because they refused to violate their vows of chastity. See *Eleven Thousand Virgins.*

" Early in the 12th century the citizens of Cologne in digging foundations for their new walls across the cemetery of the old Roman settlement of *Colonia Agrippina*, naturally enough found a large number of bones. These were declared by an ecstatic nun of Schönau, Elizabeth by name, to be the relics of the virgins. Unhappily many of these were soon discovered to be the bones of males, but the nun redeemed the reputation of the virgins by discovering in a series of fresh visions that a pope of the name of Cyriacus, an archbishop, several cardinals, bishops, and priests had been so charmed by the holiness of the lovely virgins as to follow them to Cologne, only to gain for themselves also the martyr's crown. But still worse, a number of young children's bones were found, and unhappily the ecstatic nun was now dead. This compromising fact, however, was explained by a vision vouchsafed to a patriotic English monk of Arnsberg to the effect that many of their married relations had accompanied the virgins on the voyage from England. But, as Schade first pointed out, Ursula is none other than a Christianised survival of old German paganism still remembered under the names of Berchta, Hulda; in Swabia, Ursel or Hörsel; and in Sweden, 'Old Urschel.' "—*Chambers's Encyclopædia.*

"This extraordinary legend is believed to have originated in the discovery of an inscription to *Ursula et Undecimilla Virgines,* the second name being read as expressive of a number, and not a person, and so converting two virgins into 11,000."—*Fairholt.*

Salamis, Battle of.

A naval battle fought, October 20th, 480 B.C., in the bay of Salamis, off the coast of Attica, between 366 Greek triremes commanded by Themistocles and others, and at least 1000 Persian vessels under Xerxes. The encounter resulted in a complete victory for the Greeks, with a loss of only 40 triremes; the Persians lost over 200 ships; and Xerxes, stricken with cowardice, retreated across the Hellespont,—leaving behind him a force of 300,000 men under Mardonius, to continue the contest.

Salem Witchcraft.

An extraordinary delusion, which broke out among the Puritans at Salem, Massachusetts, in 1692, and caused the deaths of 20 persons,—19 of whom were hanged and one pressed to death. A reaction soon after set in; and, although in January, 1693, three others were condemned, no more executions took place, and, soon after, all suspected persons were discharged from custody. The responsibility for the Salem atrocities rests mainly upon the shoulders of Cotton Mather (1663–1728), the Puritan theologian. He did much to fan the flame of fury among the New Englanders, and pursued with savage zeal all those persons supposed to be guilty of this crime. See *Witch Hill.*

Salic Law.

A law, excluding females from the throne of France, said to have been instituted by Pharamond in 421 A.D., and confirmed by Clovis I (481–511), the founder of the French monarchy, in 511. It was introduced into Spain by the Bourbons in 1700, but was formally abolished there in 1830. By virtue of the Salic Law, Hanover was separated from the English Crown on the accession of Victoria in 1837. The claim of Edward III (1327–1377) to the throne of France was barred by this law,—a circumstance which gave rise to the "Hundred Years' War" between England and France. A similar law exists, or has existed, in other European countries.

"In order to give more authority to the maxim that 'the crown should never descend to a female,' it was usual to derive it from a clause of the Salian code of the ancient Franks; but this clause, if strictly examined, carries only the appearance of favoring the principle, and does not in reality bear the sense imposed upon it."—*Putnam's World's Progress.*

"The law of the Salian Franks declared that 'no part of Salic land could fall to a woman,' as only men could render the service required of a feudal lord. It is a curious fact that, while France is the only country in Europe which forbids a woman to reign, there is no other in which women have so controlled political affairs."—Barnes's *Brief History of France.*

Salisbury Plain.

A barren, undulating tract of land in south Wiltshire, England, affording excellent pasture for sheep. It contains a remarkable group of standing stones known as Stonehenge,—supposed by many to be the remains of a temple of the Druids, although antiquaries are not agreed as to its origin or purpose See *Stonehenge.*

Sallust's House and Gardens.

A splendid mansion, surrounded by beautiful gardens, on the Quirinal Hill a

Rome, erected by Sallust (86–34 B.C.), the historian, and occupied by him until his death. After that event, the palace and grounds were purchased for the Roman Emperors, and became the residence of Nerva, Vespasian, and Aurelian. They were destroyed during the sack of Rome by Alaric in 410 A.D., and only a few ruins remain at the present day.

Salon, New. The name popularly given to the annual exhibition of modern paintings, sculptures, and other works of art of the " National Society of Fine Arts," which seceded from the " Old Salon," or " Society of French Artists," in 1890. It holds its exhibitions in the Grand Palace of the Champs Élysées. See *Salon, Old.*

Salon, Old. The name popularly given to the annual exhibition of modern paintings, sculptures, and drawings of the " Society of French Artists," formerly held in the Palais de l'Industrie, Paris, from May 1st to June 20th. It derives its appellation from the original exhibition-room in the Louvre,—known as *Le Salon*, and holds its exhibitions at present in the Grand Palace of the Champs Élysées. See *Palais de l'Industrie ; Salon, New.*

Salon Carré. A famous room in the picture-gallery of the Louvre in Paris, containing the gems of the collection. There may be seen Murillo's *Immaculate Conception ;* Paul Veronese's *Marriage-Feast at Cana ;* Raphael's *St. Michael and the Dragon, La Belle Jardinière,* and the Great *Holy Family* of Francis I ; Titian's *Entombment of Christ ;* Rembrandt's *Holy Family ;* and Leonardo da Vinci's *La Gioconda.* Correggio, Van Dyck, Guido Reni, Poussin, Philippe de Champaigne, Jordaens, Holbein the Younger, and Rubens are also represented in this collection.

Salpêtrière. A hospital and asylum for aged and insane women, in Paris, founded by Louis XIV (1643–1715).

The building, erected as an arsenal by Louis XIII (1610–1643), is called *La Salpêtrière*, because it stands on ground formerly occupied by a *saltpetre* factory. It is said that this establishment contained nearly 10,000 indigent persons in 1662.

Salt, Attic. See *Attic Salt.*

Salt in Beer. " In Scotland it was customary to throw a handful of salt on the top of the mash to keep the witches from it. Salt really has the effect of moderating the fermentation and fining the liquor."—Brewer's *Dictionary of Phrase and Fable.*

Salt in Coffin. It is still the custom in certain countries to put salt in a coffin, and for the reason, we are told, that salt is the symbol of incorruption and immortality, and is on that account peculiarly distasteful to Satan.

Salt River. An imaginary stream up which defeated politicians are supposed to be sent to oblivion.

" *Salt River*, geographically, is a tributary of the Ohio, and its course is in Kentucky. The slang political phrase 'rowed up *Salt River*,' to express the condition of a defeated candidate for office, is thus explained by Bayard Taylor : 'Formerly there were extensive salt-works on the river, a short distance from its mouth. The laborers employed in them were a set of athletic, belligerent fellows, who soon became noted far and wide for their achievements in the pugilistic line. Hence it became a common thing for the boatmen on the Ohio, when one of their number became refractory, to say to him, " We 'll row you up *Salt River*," when, of course, the burly saltmen would have the handling of him. By a natural figure of speech the expression was applied to political candidates; first, I believe, in the Presidential campaign of 1840.' But a better explanation seems to be that in the early days the river, being crooked and difficult of navigation, was a favorite stronghold for river pirates, who preyed on the commerce of the Ohio and rowed their plunder up *Salt River*. Hence it came to be said of anything that was irrevocably lost, ' It 's rowed up *Salt River*.' A third derivation makes the phrase originate in 1832, when Henry Clay, as candidate for the Presidency, had an engagement to speak in

Louisville, Kentucky, and employed a boat-man to row him up the Ohio. The boatman, who was a Jackson Democrat, pretended to miss his way, and rowed Clay up *Salt River* instead, so that he did not reach his destination until the day after the election, just in time to hear of his defeat."—Walsh's *Handy-Book of Literary Curiosities.*

Salt, Spilling of. This superstition, still current among us, is derived from the ancient Romans, who used salt in their sacrifices and regarded it as sacred to the Penates. Hence to spill it carelessly was to incur the displeasure of these household divinities. After accidentally spilling salt, the ancient Roman was wont to throw some over the left shoulder—the shoulder of ill-omen — thereby hoping to call away from his neighbor the wrath of the deity, and turn it upon himself. In the engraving of Leonardo da Vinci's *Last Supper,* the artist has represented Judas Iscariot as having overturned the salt-cellar ; but, according to good authority, the salt is not overturned in da Vinci's painting,—this being merely an interpolation made by Raphael Morghen, the original engraver of the plate.

Salt, To Sit above the. This expression, denoting superior social position, is derived from the old custom, in houses of people of rank, of placing a large silver salt-holder in the middle of a long table,—the places above which were occupied by persons of distinction, while those below were assigned to dependants and inferior guests.

" His fashion is not to take knowledge of him that is beneath him in clothes. He never drinks *below the salt.*"—*Ben Jonson.*

Salvation Army. A religious organization — quasi-military in character—founded in London in 1865, by the Rev. William Booth, a Methodist minister, under the name of the *Christian Mission.* It adopted the name "Salvation Army " in 1878. The object of the society is the evangelization of the masses, and this it seeks to accomplish by street processions — accompanied by vocal and instrumental music and banners, — by public meetings, and by house-to-house visitations. The organization consists, at the present time, of about 15,300 officers—both men and women—whose lives are entirely devoted to the work of evangelization ; it holds annually about 2,500,000 meetings both indoors and out; and extends to nearly all the countries in the world. The Salvation Army was at first treated with derision and contempt, and, at times, even subjected to violence by the masses ; but the earnestness of its members and the remarkable results achieved by them have won for the organization the respect of most of the evangelical denominations. In 1896, Commander and Mrs. Ballington Booth, formerly in command of the United States division of the Salvation Army, seceded from the parent society, and founded the " Volunteers of America," a similar organization. See *Volunteers of America.*

Samaritan Pentateuch. A version of the *Pentateuch* in use among the Samaritans, and the only portion of the *Old Testament* writings accepted by them as canonical. The existence of such a recension of the Hebrew text of the *Pentateuch* was known by the early Jewish and Christian writers ; but it was not until 1616 that a copy of it was obtained from the Samaritans at Damascus, by Pietro della Valle. In 1623, it was presented to the library of the Oratory in Paris, and in 1631 was published in the Paris *Polyglott* by J. Morinus. Widely divergent opinions exist as to the age and origin of the *Samaritan Pentateuch.* See *Samaritans.*

" There is no ground either external or internal, for assigning to the *Samaritan Pentateuch* an age earlier than the 4th century B.C., though, from its use in northern Palestine, it was formerly argued that it must have originated before the fall of the northern kingdom, or even before the revolt of Jeroboam."—*Chambers's Encyclopædia.*

Samaritans. A mixed people of ancient Palestine, composed of the remnant of the tribes of Ephraim and Manasseh, and of colonists introduced from Assyria after the " Ten Tribes " had been carried into captivity (721 B.C.). They accepted the *Pentateuch*, but rejected the rest of the sacred writings of the Hebrews. In 409 B.C., they erected a temple on Mount Gerizim,—intended as a rival to the one in Jerusalem, and thus incurred the hatred of the Jewish people ; so that for many years the " Jews had no dealings with the Samaritans." The Samaritans still have a settlement at Nablûs, consisting of about 200 persons. They observe the law, and celebrate the Passover on Mount Gerizim, with scrupulous exactness. See *Samaritan Pentateuch.*

"Then answered the Jews, and said unto him, Say we not well that thou art a *Samaritan*, and hast a devil? "—*St. John* viii, 48.

Sambo. This word, which is frequently applied to a colored person, is a corruption of *Zambo*, a native term used to denote the offspring of a negro and a mulatto.

Samian Sage. An appellation conferred upon Pythagoras [580 (?)–500 (?) B.C.,] the distinguished Greek philosopher, who, according to the generally received opinion, was born on the island of Samos. He is also called the *Sage of Samos.*

San Carlo. A famous opera-house in Naples, Italy, one of the largest and finest in Europe. It contains six rows of boxes, 32 in each row.

" I attended one performance at the theatre of *San Carlo*, a structure of immense size, containing six rows of private boxes, all glittering in blue and gold. The boxes are of large size, quite like small drawing-rooms ; and indeed they are much used by the occupants for the reception of their friends. The royal box, blazing in crimson and gold, faces the stage, and is two rows in height ; almost large enough to have a vaudeville of its own going on contemporaneously with the performance on the stage. . . . The effect of an enclosed space, of such vast extent, is very striking ; and such colossal structures present great advantages for all spectacles addressed to the eye ; but for music, vocal music at least, a smaller building is surely better adapted."—Hillard's *Six Months in Italy.*

Sancho Panza. An esquire in attendance upon Don Quixote, in Cervantes's immortal story of that name.

"In the meantime Don Quixote tampered with a labourer, a neighbour of his, and an honest man (if such an epithet can be given to one that is poor), but shallow-brained ; in short he said so much, used so many arguments, and made so many promises, that the poor fellow resolved to sally out with him, and serve him in the capacity of a Squire. Among other things, Don Quixote told him that he ought to be very glad to accompany him, for such an adventure might some time or the other occur that by one stroke an island might be won, where he might leave him Governor. With this and other promises, *Sancho Panza* (for that was the labourer's name) left his wife and children, and engaged himself as squire to his neighbour."—*Don Quixote* (Jarvis's Translation).

Sancy Diamond. A famous Indian diamond, weighing 53½ carats. It was purchased about 1570, by M. de Sancy, French ambassador at Constantinople, and was eventually sold by him to Queen Elizabeth (1558–1603) of England. James II of England, while an exile in France in 1695, sold it to Louis XIV (1643–1715) for £25,000. It was resold during the French Revolution, and later was purchased by Napoleon I. In 1825, it was bought by Prince Paul Demidoff for £80,000, and in 1865 was sold by the Demidoff family to Sir Jamsetjee Jeejeebhoy for £20,000. It was again in the market in 1889, the price asked being £20,000.

Sandie. A Scotch abbreviation of Alexander, sportively used by the English to designate a Scotchman. See *Sawney.*

Sandringham. An estate of 7000 acres in Norfolk, England, 7½ miles northeast of Lynn, belonging to the

Prince of Wales (now Edward VII), by whom it was purchased in 1862 for £220,000. The present house—a red-brick Elizabethan mansion, standing in a park of 200 acres—was erected in 1869-1871. It was the scene of the serious illness of the Prince of Wales during November and December, 1871, and of the death of his eldest son, the Duke of Clarence and Avondale on January 14th, 1892. In November, 1891, Sandringham was damaged by fire to the amount of £10,000.

Sandwich Islands. So named by Captain Cook (1728-1779), the famous navigator, in honor of Lord Sandwich, First Lord of the Admiralty.

Sangreal. See *Grail, Holy.*

Sanhedrim. The supreme national council of the Jews, traditionally supposed to have been instituted by Moses himself, but more probably founded by Ezra, after the return from the Captivity (536 B.C.). It is first mentioned by Josephus, in connection with the reign of John Hyrcanus II (76-38 B.C.). The Sanhedrim was composed of 70 or, as some say, 71 members ; was presided over by the high-priest ; and exercised administrative and judicial functions. After the destruction of Jerusalem in 70 A.D., this council led a migratory existence, and finally established itself at Babylon. It became wholly extinct in the year 425 A.D.

Sanitary Commission, United States. A commission of inquiry and advice in reference to the sanitary interests of the United States troops during the Civil War, organized June 13th, 1861, under the direction of the Secretary of War. In its efforts to supplement government deficiencies, it appealed to the people with gratifying results,—at least $25,000,000 in money and supplies being contributed during the four years of the Civil War. Fairs for the benefit of the Commission were opened in many of the principal cities

of the Union, and large sums of money were raised in this manner. It is estimated that the " Metropolitan Sanitary Fair" in New York City netted $1,184,487 ; the one in Philadelphia, $1,035,368 ; and twelve others, $425,-000. The work of the Sanitary Commission included the inspection of camps and hospitals, the furnishing of medical and other supplies, the establishment of convalescent camps, the transportation of wounded soldiers, and the maintenance of a bureau of vital statistics. See *Christian Commission, United States.*

San Paolo fuori le Mura (*It., St. Paul without the Wall*). A magnificent basilica at Rome, on the road to Ostia, 1½ miles beyond the Gate of St. Paul. It occupies the spot where the apostle Paul is believed to have been buried. Constantine first built an oratory there, and this was enlarged into a basilica in 386 and restored by Pope Leo III (795-816). In 1823, the structure was almost totally destroyed by fire, but has since been rebuilt, though in a style inferior to that of its predecessor. The present building—opened by Pope Pius IX (1846-1878) in 1854—is one of the most gorgeous Christian temples in existence.

" Its exterior is below contempt ; its interior, supported by eighty granite columns, is most striking and magnificent, but it is cold and uninteresting when compared with the ancient structure, 'rich with inestimable remains of ancient art, and venerable from a thousand associations.' "—*Hare.*

San Salvador. This name—meaning *Holy Savior*—was given by Christopher Columbus to the first land sighted by him on October 11th, 1492.

Sans - Culottes (*Fr., Without Breeches*). A name given by the aristocrats, at the beginning of the French Revolution, to the democratic party in Paris, because they gave up wearing the knee-breeches in use among the nobility, and adopted trousers, or pantaloons, instead. The term was at first applied in contempt ;

but was afterwards adopted as synonymous with "good patriots" by the popular party.

Sanskrit. The ancient classical tongue of the Hindus, and the oldest preserved form of Aryan, or Indo-European, language in existence. It ceased to be spoken about the 4th century B.C., and is preserved only in the Hindu sacred writings. Sanskrit is the parent of all the modern Aryan languages of India, and the language most closely related to the original tongue of the ancient Aryans, from which have descended the Celtic, Græco-Latin, Teutonic, Slavonic, and Persian languages. Sanskrit literature, which begins with the *Vedas*, extends back as far as 2000 or 1500 B.C.; it is extremely copious, and owes its introduction to the western world to Sir William Jones (1746–1794), the distinguished Orientalist. Sanskrit is still cultivated as a classical language by the Hindus, and remains the sacred language of the Brahmans.

"When and where it [Sanskrit] was at first a spoken dialect, is out of our power to determine; but it cannot well be regarded as of less age than the earliest Greek records; and it is probably older by centuries. It possesses a most abundant literature, in nearly every department save history; its religious and ethical poetry, its epics, its lyric flights, its dramas, its systems of philosophy and grammar, have been found worthy of high admiration and of profound study by Western scholars; they have even been ranked by some, though very unjustly, as superior to the masterpieces of the Greek and Latin literatures."—Whitney's *Language and the Study of Language.*

Sans-Souci (*Fr., Without Care*). A royal palace near Potsdam, Prussia, erected by Frederick the Great (1740–1786) in 1745–1747, as a retreat from care, and occupied by him during the last years of his life. It consists of a series of unpretentious buildings, adorned with a fine colonnade, and is interesting principally from its association with the Prussian King. There may be seen the chair in which Frederick died, his flute, and the clock

(always wound by him), which stopped at the precise moment of his death, —twenty minutes past two. The room assigned to Voltaire during his stay at Sans-Souci is also shown. See *Potsdam.*

Santa Casa (*It., Holy House*). See *Loretto.*

Santa Claus, or Klaus. The Dutch name of St. Nicholas. See *St. Nicholas.*

"The children's Christmas deity is known in the United States by this name, the Dutch form *Santa Klaas* being simply the abbreviation of Nicholas, a patron saint of unquestionable Holland ancestry."—Reddall's *Fact, Fancy, and Fable.*

Santa Croce (*It., Holy Cross*). A famous church in Florence, Italy, containing monuments erected to the memory of many of the most illustrious men of the nation, and on that account frequently styled the "Westminster Abbey of the City." It was designed by Arnolfo in 1295 and restored in the 16th century, but the present façade was not completed until 1863.

"The interior is venerable and imposing, dimly lighted by long and narrow Gothic windows of stained glass, and shrouded in the gloom which seems appropriate to a church of which the chief interest is in its tombs and monuments. Here repose the remains of Michael Angelo, Machiavelli, Galileo, Leonardo Bruno, and Alfieri; and, though partially eclipsed by these greater names, the visitor should not overlook those of Lanzi, the historian of painting, and Filicaja, the lyric poet: names not to be forgotten, so long as modest learning and poetical genius are honored among men.

'Ungrateful Florence! Dante sleeps afar.'

The people of Ravenna very properly refused to surrender to the tardy justice of the Florentines the remains of the illustrious foreigner whose last sigh they had received; and Florence could only show her sensibility to the genius of her greatest writer, by the empty honors of a cenotaph."—Hillard's *Six Months in Italy.*

Santa Croce in Gerusalemme (*It., Holy Cross in Jerusalem*). A church in Rome, Italy, said to have been founded by the Empress Helena, mother of Constantine, in 331 A.D., in commemoration of her discovery of the true cross at Jerusalem in 326. Tradition says that the plank of wood—inscribed with the words THIS IS JESUS, THE KING OF THE JEWS, and placed by Pilate on the Cross of Christ—was deposited in this church by the Empress; and it is further asserted that the soil of the foundation was mixed with earth from Jerusalem. A council met in Santa Croce in Gerusalemme as early as 433. The church was rebuilt in 1144 and modernized in 1743. See *Cross, True.*

Santa Maria. One of the three vessels with which Christopher Columbus set sail for America from Palos, Spain, on August 3rd, 1492. She was commanded by Columbus in person. See *Niña ; Pinta.*

"The *Santa Maria* was a good-sized vessel, ninety feet long, and carrying sixty-six seamen. It was decked all over, and had four masts,—two with square sails, and two with lateen-sails. The other vessels were smaller, and without decks : and they were all provisioned for a year. There were, in all, one hundred and twenty persons on this bold expedition."—Higginson's *Young Folks' History of the United States.*

Santa Saba. A noted convent in Syria, perched upon a lofty ridge overlooking the Dead Sea. It was founded in 483 A.D., by St. Saba, a native of Cappadocia and a man of extraordinary sanctity, whose triumph over the "Lion of Kidron" attracted 14,000 fellow-anchorites to share his glory and devotion. The building consists of walls, chambers, and chapels,—some constructed of masonry and some hewn from the living rock. The cave or cell in which St. Saba dwelt, although somewhat enlarged and beautified, still retains its native rudeness and simplicity. Admission to the convent is forbidden to women, under all circumstances.

Santa Scala (*It., Holy Staircase*). A flight of 28 steps of white-veined Tyrian marble in the piazza of the Church of St. John Lateran at Rome,

which, according to tradition, belonged to the house of Pilate at Jerusalem, and were made sacred by the feet of Christ as he passed to judgment. Penitents are permitted to ascend these stairs only on their knees, and so great is the number that annually makes the ascent that it has been found necessary to cover the steps with planks of wood to insure their protection. Roman Catholics assert that the Holy Staircase was carried by angels from Jerusalem to Rome ; but, according to other authorities, it was brought thither by the Empress Helena, the mother of Constantine. It was while ascending these steps that Martin Luther, then a monk, thought he heard the words, "The just shall live by faith." Mortified by the degradation to which his superstition had led him, he descended and hastened from the spot. See *St. John Lateran, Church of.*

Saragossa, Maid of. See *Maid of Saragossa.*

Saratoga, Battle of. A battle fought near Saratoga Springs, New York, on October 7th, 1777, between the British commanded by General Burgoyne and the Americans under General Gates. It was without decided result ; but Burgoyne was soon after surrounded by the Americans, and on October 17th was forced to surrender his entire army of 5791 men. An obelisk—155 feet high—erected in 1877 on a bluff above the Hudson River, commemorates this event. The surrender of Burgoyne was the greatest check sustained by the British during the War of the Revolution.

Sardinia. This word means the *Land of the Sardonion*, a Greek term used to denote a plant indigenous to that island.

Sarmatia. A name sometimes applied to the vast region of Eastern Europe, over which the ancient Sarmatians roamed. It extended from the Vistula and the Danube to the Volga and the Caucasus, and was arbitrarily divided by the ancient writers into European and Asiatic Sarmatia,—the river Don being taken as the dividing-line. The word " Sarmatia " is also used as a poetic designation of Poland.

" Yet for *Sarmatia's* tears of blood atone,
And make her arm puissant as your own !
Oh ! once again to Freedom's cause return
The patriot Tell—the Bruce of Bannockburn ! "
Campbell's *Downfall of Poland.*

Sarpedon. A son of Zeus and Laodamia, or, according to others, of Evander and Deidamia. He was a Lycian prince, who assisted Priam during the Trojan War, but was slain by Patroclus. Apollo, at the command of Zeus, placed the body of Sarpedon in charge of Sleep and Death, who transported it to Lycia and gave it honorable burial.

Sartor Resartus (*Lat., The Tailor Restitched*). A philosophic romance by Thomas Carlyle (1795–1881), which first appeared in *Frazer's Magazine* in 1833–1834. See *Teufelsdröckh, Herr.*

" The book might well have puzzled the 'book-tasters' who decide for publishers on works submitted to them in manuscript. *Sartor* professes to be a review of a German treatise on dress, and the hero, Diogenes Teufelsdröckh, is made to illustrate by his life and character the transcendental philosophy of Fichte, adopted by Mr. Carlyle, which is thus explained: 'That all things which we see or work with in this earth, especially we ourselves and all persons, are as a kind of vesture, or sensuous appearance: that under all these lies, as the essence of them, what he calls the " Divine Idea of the World "; this is the reality which lies at the bottom of all appearance. To the mass of men no such divine idea is recognizable in the world ; they live merely, says Fichte, among the superficialities, practicalities, and shows of the world, not dreaming that there is anything divine under them' (*Hero Worship*). Mr. Carlyle works out this theory—the clothes-philosophy—and finds the world false and hollow, an institution's mere worn-out rags or disguises, and that our only safety lies in flying from falsehood to truth, and becoming in harmony with the 'divine idea.' There is much fanciful, grotesque descrip-

tion in *Sartor*, but also deep thought and beautiful imagery."—*Chambers's Cyclopædia of English Literature.*

Satan. The chief of the fallen angels, who, according to the *Talmud*, was originally an archangel, but refused to do homage to Adam at the command of God, and was thereupon expelled from heaven with one-third of the angelic host. He was afterwards vanquished in battle by Michael, and cast, with all his infamous crew, into the lowest depths of hell. Satan is the most commanding and impressive character in Milton's *Paradise Lost*, and figures prominently in *Paradise Regained.*

Saturnian Days. The name given to a mythical period in the early history of Italy, when the god Saturn shared the throne with Janus, the reigning king, and by his mild, pacific, and beneficent rule, raised the people to a relatively high degree of civilization. Agriculture and the useful arts flourished throughout the land ; innocence, freedom, peace, and happiness reigned ; and sorrows were forgotten. The ancient Romans celebrated the *Saturnalia* in December of each year, in honor of Saturn. The phrase " Saturnian Days " is used, at the present time, to denote any period of peace and plenty. See *Golden Age.*

" Days came and went ; and now returned again
To Sicily the old *Saturnian reign.*"
King Robert of Sicily (Longfellow).

Saturnine. According to astrology, the character and actions of each person were supposed to be governed by the planet in the " ascendant " at the time of his birth. Hence, gloomy and morose persons were called *saturnine*, because those born under the planet Saturn were said to be thus inclined. See *Jovial ; Martial ; Mercurial.*

Satyricon. A Latin satirical romance, in mingled prose and verse, depicting the licentiousness of the upper classes in Southern Italy during the first century of the Christian era. The work is ascribed to Petronius Arbiter, a refined voluptuary at the court of Nero, who, having lost favor with the Emperor, committed suicide in 66 A.D. Fragments of the 15th and 16th books of the *Satyricon* are still extant. They are coarse in style, but contain passages of great power and beauty. See *Arbiter Elegantiæ.*

Saunders, Richard. An assumed name under which Benjamin Franklin (1706–1790) commenced the publication, in 1732, of a popular almanac, commonly known as *Poor Richard's Almanac.* See *Poor Richard's Almanac.*

Saunterer. A saunterer, according to Smith's *Glossary of Terms and Phrases*, is properly one that has performed the pilgrimage to the Holy Land (*Lat., Sancta Terra*). Webster, however, says that the word is probably derived from the French *s'aventurer* (*to adventure* [*one's self*]), through a shortened form, *s'auntrer.*

Savannah. See *First Steamship to Cross the Atlantic.*

Sawney. A name sportively used by the English to designate a Scotchman. It is a corruption of *Sandie*, which is a contracted form of *Alexander*, a popular Christian name among the Scotch. The word "sawney" also means a *simpleton.* See *Sandie.*

Saxons. The name of this ancient Teutonic people is said to be derived from the *seax*, or short crooked knife, with which they armed themselves.

Saxon Switzerland. A picturesque mountain-region in Saxony, southeast of Dresden,—much frequented by tourists. It is traversed by the river Elbe, and abounds in wild and rugged scenery, although none of its mountains rise to an elevation exceeding 2000 feet. The name " Switzerland "—as applied to this region—seems a misnomer, since the scenery of the two countries is so entirely different.

Scævola (*probably a diminutive of Lat., scæva, left-handed*). A surname given to Caius Mucius, a young Roman noble, who, according to tradition, entered the camp of King Porsenna, then besieging Rome, with the intention of killing him. Failing in the attempt, he was seized and condemned to die; whereupon he thrust his right hand into the fire and held it there until it was consumed, to show that he feared neither death nor torture. It is said that the King was so much struck by the extraordinary heroism displayed by Caius Mucius that he spared his life.

Scala Intellectus (*Lat., Steps of the Understanding*). A philosophic treatise by Lord Francis Bacon (1561–1626), constituting the fourth part of the *Instauratio Magna.* Only the opening pages were ever written. The work was so called by the author, because in it he proposed to consider the successive " steps " by which the human understanding should proceed from a study of the facts and phenomena of nature to the establishment of general laws based upon them. See *Instauratio Magna.*

Scalds. The name given to the ancient Scandinavian poets, who sang or recited verses of their own composition, commemorating the famous deeds of living heroes or of their ancestors. They were similar to the troubadours of Southern France, the minnesingers of Germany, and the bards of the Celtic tribes. Very few complete Scaldic poems are extant; but many fragments are found in the *Younger Edda* and in the *Sagas.* See *Sagas.*

Scarlet Woman. A woman described in *Revelation* xvii, and variously regarded as the personification of Papal Rome, or of worldliness in general.

Scavenger's Daughter (*more properly, Skeffington's Daughter*). An instrument of judicial torture invented by William Skeffington, a lieutenant of the Tower of London, during the reign of Henry VIII (1509–1547). It consisted of a spiked iron frame, which enclosed its victim in a deadly embrace, and so compressed the body as to start the blood from the nostrils and often from the hands.

Scheveningen. A fishing-village and fashionable seaside resort in Holland, situated on the North Sea, about two miles northwest of The Hague. It is famous as the place where Charles II (1660–1685) embarked for England, on his return to that country in 1660. A desperate naval battle was fought off Scheveningen on August 8th–10th, 1653, resulting in the defeat of the Dutch fleet and the death of its admiral, Van Tromp, at the hands of the British under Monk.

Schiehallion. A mountain in Perthshire, Scotland, famous as the place visited by Maskelyne, the astronomer-royal, in 1774, for the purpose of determining the density of the earth by means of observations made with the plumb-line. Using the facts thus obtained, James Hutton, the geologist, calculated that the density of the globe is about five times that of an equal volume of water,—an estimate which subsequent observations have proved to be substantially correct. The result of all such experiments shows the mass of the earth to be approximately 6,000,000,000,000,000,000,000 (six sextillion) tons.

Scholastics. A term frequently applied to the Schoolmen of the Middle Ages. See *Schoolmen.*

Schönberg-Cotta Family, Chronicles of the. A celebrated book by Mrs. Elizabeth R. Charles, purporting to be a record kept by the inmates of a household with which Martin Luther was on terms of close intimacy. It is so perfect in its conception, and pictures the Reformer and his friends so realistically, that the reader finds it difficult to believe that the book is not a chronicle of events that actually happened. See *Schönberg-Cotta House.*

Schönberg-Cotta House. A famous old house in the town of Eisenach, Saxe-Weimar, Germany, in which Martin Luther dwelt from 1498 to 1501, while attending school. See *Schönberg-Cotta Family, Chronicles of the.*

"Luther's schooling was completed at Magdeburg and Eisenach, and at the latter place he attracted by his singing the notice of a good lady of the name of Cotta, who provided him with a comfortable home during his stay there."—*Chambers's Encyclopædia.*

"I was at Aunt Ursula's house, which is in George Street, near the church and school. I had watched the choir of boys going from door to door through the street. No one had given them anything: they looked disappointed and hungry. At last they stopped before the window where Aunt Ursula and I were sitting with her little boy. That clear, high, ringing voice was there again. Aunt Ursula went to the door and called Martin in, and then she went herself to the kitchen, and after giving him a good meal himself, sent him away with his wallet full, and told him to come again very soon. After that, I suppose she consulted with Cousin Conrad Cotta, and the result was that Martin Luther became an inmate of their house, and has lived among us familiarly since then like one of our own cousins."—*Chronicles of the Schönberg-Cotta Family (Elsè's Story).*

Schönbrunn (*Ger., Beautiful Fountain*). An extensive palace, about two miles southwest of Vienna, erected for the Empress Maria Theresa in 1744, and used as the summer residence of the Imperial family of Austria. It was occupied by Napoleon I in 1805 and 1809, while Vienna was in the hands of the French; and there was signed the Treaty of Schönbrunn, or Vienna, between France and Austria, in October of the latter year. The palace derives its name from a beautiful fountain (*schönbrunn*) situated at the extremity of one of the avenues in the adjoining grounds. Napoleon II —afterwards the Duke of Reichstadt— died at Schönbrunn in 1832, and in the very bed that had been occupied by his father in 1809. In the courtyard of the palace, the German student Stapps made his memorable attempt to assassinate the first Napoleon in 1809, and was soon afterwards convicted and shot. See *Schönbrunn, Peace of.*

Schönbrunn, Peace of. A treaty of peace concluded between France and Austria, October 14th, 1809. By the terms of this treaty, Austria ceded to France the provinces of Carniola, Friuli, Croatia, and part of Dalmatia ; formally acknowledged the sovereigns created by Napoleon; and adopted the Continental System. Also called the Peace of Vienna. See *Continental System ; Schönbrunn.*

School-Master of the Republic. A sobriquet conferred upon Noah Webster (1758–1843), the distinguished American lexicographer, on account of the great educational influence exerted by him through the medium of his dictionaries and school-books. His spelling-book, first issued towards the close of the eighteenth century, has at the present day an annual sale of nearly one million copies.

Schoolmen. The name given to certain theological teachers of the Middle Ages, so called because they originally lectured in the cloisters, or cathedral-schools, founded by Charlemagne (768–814) and his successors, for the education of the clergy. The Schoolmen attempted the impossible task of reconciling the dogmas of faith with the dictates of reason, and indulged in metaphysical discussions of the most subtle and hair-splitting kind. Among the most famous may be mentioned Roscellinus, Abélard, Anselm, St. Bernard, Thomas Aquinas, Alexander of Hales, Duns Scotus, Albertus Magnus, William of Ockham, and Jean Gerson.

Scio's Blind Old Bard. A title conferred upon Homer (*fl.* 1000 B.C.), the Greek poet, who, according to many authorities, was born on the island of Chios (Scio). See *Blind Old Man of Scio's Rocky Isle.*

Scone, Stone of. See *Coronation Chair.*

Scotia. A former name of Scotland, but used at the present time simply as a poetic designation. It was originally applied to Ireland, which country was afterwards called *Scotia Magna,* or *Major,* to distinguish it from *Scotia Minor,* or Scotland. According to the Venerable Bede [673 (?)–735 (?) A.D.], Scotland was known as *Caledonia* until 258 A.D., when the country was invaded by the *Scoti,* an Irish tribe, and its name changed to *Scotia.* See *Caledonia.*

Scotists. A name given to the followers of Duns Scotus (1265–1308), the famous Schoolman. The Scotists were Realists. See *Angelic Doctor ; Thomists.*

Scotland Yard. A place near the Banqueting House, Whitehall, London, long famous as the headquarters of the metropolitan police. It is said to derive its name from a palace formerly standing there, in which the Kings of Scotland (from Edgar to Henry II) were lodged during their annual visits to England. In later years, Milton, Inigo Jones, Sir Christopher Wren, and other distinguished persons dwelt there. In 1890, the police headquarters were removed to the New Scotland Yard on the Thames Embankment.

"Mr. Newton, in his 'London in the Olden Time,' says, 'This property was given by the Saxon King Edgar to Kenneth III., King of Scotland, for his residence, upon his annual visit to London to do homage for his kingdom to the Crown of England.' The last of the Scottish royal family to reside here was Margaret, Queen of James IV., who took up her abode here after the death of her husband at the battle of Flodden Field."—Edwards's *Words, Facts, and Phrases.*

Scottish Hogarth. A sobriquet conferred upon David Allan (1744–1796), the noted portrait-painter.

Scottish Solomon. A title conferred by his friends and admirers upon James VI (1567–1625) of Scotland, afterwards James I (1603–1625) of England. See *Solomon of England (1)*.

" His education having been conducted by the celebrated George Buchanan, he had acquired a considerable stock of learning, but at the same time an immeasurable conceit of his own wisdom. He took every occasion to make a pedantic display of his acquirements both in conversation and in writing, for he was an author, and had published, for the use of his son, a book called *Basilikon Doron (βαϭιλικόν δῶρον)* or *Royal Gift*, besides works on demonology and other subjects."—*Student's Hume*.

Scott Monument. A graceful Gothic spire in the city of Edinburgh, Scotland, erected in memory of Sir Walter Scott (1771–1832), in 1844. It is a brown-stone structure, 200 feet high, and is adorned with statues representing several of the leading characters in the great writer's works. Under the canopy of the monument is a large marble statue of Sir Walter himself, with his favorite dog Bevis seated at his side.

Scourge of God. An epithet conferred upon Attila (434–453 A.D.), King of the Huns, who, during the fifth century after Christ, was the terror of Europe. In 452 he invaded Italy and threatened Rome itself. It was his favorite boast that where his horse had set foot grass never grew again. The expression, " Scourge of God," is first found in the *Legend of St. Loup*, composed by a priest of Troyes, during the eighth or ninth century. Genseric (406–477 A.D.), King of the Vandals, and Charles VIII (1483–1498 A.D.), King of France, received the same title.

Scouring the White Horse. See *White Horse of Berkshire*.

Scrupulous. " Scrupulous means literally having a stone in one's shoe. Those who have a stone in their shoe *halt*, and those who doubt ' halt between two opinions ' (*Lat., Scrupulus,*

gravel, small stone)."—Brewer's *Dictionary of Phrase and Fable*.

Scylla. A famous rock in the Strait of Messina, off the coast of Italy, and opposite to a whirlpool called Charybdis on the Sicilian coast. From the supposed difficulty of navigating this narrow strait in ancient times, without falling a victim to one or other of these terrors, arose the saying: *Incidit in Scyllam qui vult vitare Charybdim* (*Lat., He falls into Scylla that wishes to avoid Charybdis*). See *Charybdis*.

Sea-Girt Isle. A poetic term sometimes applied to the island of Great Britain, which is entirely surrounded by the sea.

" This precious stone set in the silver sea,
 Which serves it in the office of a wall,
 Or as a moat defensive to a house,
 Against the envy of less happy lands."
     Richard II, ii, 1.

Sea-Island Cotton. A kind of cotton grown exclusively on the islands and lowlands of South Carolina, Georgia, and Florida. It surpasses all other varieties in the fineness and length of its fibre, and doubtless owes its superiority to the saline properties of the soil and atmosphere.

Sealed Books. The name given to a number of printed copies of the *Revised Anglican Prayer-Book of 1662*, issued under the Great Seal of England, and ordered by Parliament to be preserved in certain cathedral and collegiate churches for the purpose of insuring the preservation of the text. Before their issue, they were carefully examined by commissioners appointed for the purpose, and if found to agree with the book annexed to the *Act 13 and 14 Carolus II*, were certified by them to be correct.

Seal Rocks. A series of rocks or ledges in the Pacific Ocean, near the Golden Gate, California, which at times are covered with hundreds of sea-lions basking in the sun. Some of these animals are from 12 to 15 feet in length and weigh 1000 pounds and upwards. The proximity of the Seal Rocks to the shore makes the singular bark of these animals distinctly audible above the roar of the breakers.

Sea of Marmora. This sea, lying between the Mediterranean and the Black Seas, derives its name from the small island of Marmora, or Marmara, at its western extremity, which has long been famous for its quarries of marble and alabaster. *Marmor* is the Latin for marble.

Sea of Sedge. A name given to the Red Sea, on account of the great quantities of sedge found in its waters. In the Hebrew Scriptures it is called "The Weedy or Sedgy Sea"; and Milton makes reference to it when he speaks of the fallen angels, who were as thick as

> "... scattered sedge
> Afloat, when with fierce winds Orion arm'd
> Hath vex'd the Red Sea coast, whose waves o'erthrew
> Busiris and his Memphian chivalry. . . ."
> *Paradise Lost,* i, 304–307.

Sea of Stars. A name given to the source of the Hoang-ho, or Yellow River, in Tibet, on account of the brilliant sparkle of its waters.

> "Like a *sea of stars,*
> The hundred sources of the Hoangho."
> Southey's *Thalaba the Destroyer.*

Sea-Serpents. Gigantic animals, presumably of serpentine form, popularly believed to exist, especially in the depths of the tropic seas. Scientists are divided in opinion as to the existence of these monsters, and regard the question as one of the unsolved problems of zoölogy. The sea-serpent has been frequently described by seafaring men and others. Captain McQuhae of H.M.S. *Dædalus* published in 1848 an account of a sea-serpent observed by him in the South Atlantic Ocean, not far from the coast of Africa, in the latitude of the Tropic of Capricorn. According to him, the monster measured from 12 to 15 inches in

diameter and revealed a length of at least 60 feet on the surface of the sea. Its color was a dark brown, with yellowish white about the throat. Its movement was at the rate of from 12 to 15 miles per hour.

Secesh. A slang term applied to the inhabitants of those southern States that seceded from the Union in 1860–1861, and caused the Civil War.

> "Infissiparous symbol of politic etern,
> Securing Uncle Sam what's his 'n and every State what's her 'n,
> Of strength redintegrative, of pulchritude e'er fresh,
> *Secesh* were not without thee, and without thee no *secesh!*"
> *Fugitive Poem on the Union.*

Secession-Ordinances. The following table gives the dates of the passage of the secession-ordinances by the eleven States forming the Southern Confederacy.

State.	Act of Secession.
(1) South Carolina	December 20, 1860.
(2) Mississippi	January 9, 1861.
(3) Florida	January 10, 1861.
(4) Alabama	January 11, 1861.
(5) Georgia	January 19, 1861.
(6) Louisiana	January 26, 1861.
(7) Texas	February 1, 1861.
(8) Virginia	April 17, 1861.
(9) Arkansas	May 6, 1861.
(10) North Carolina	May 21, 1861.
(11) Tennessee	June 8, 1861.

Second Charlemagne. A sobriquet conferred upon Charles V (1519–1558), Emperor of Germany.

Second Shakespeare. A title conferred upon Christopher Marlowe (1564–1593) by Edward Phillips, in his *Theatrum Poetarum.*

Second Washington. A sobriquet conferred upon Henry Clay (1777–1852), the American orator and statesman.

Sedan, Battle of. The name given to a series of desperate conflicts fought around Sedan, France, on August 29th, 30th, and 31st, and September 1st, 1870, between 250,000 Germans commanded by the King and Crown-

Prince of Prussia and 150,000 French under Marshal MacMahon. The French were totally defeated in these encounters, and on September 2nd, Napoleon III surrendered himself and his entire army of 86,000 men into the hands of the victors. It is estimated that 14,000 Frenchmen were wounded and 25,000 taken prisoners during these engagements ; 70 mitrailleuses, 400 field-pieces, and 150 fortress-guns were surrendered to the Germans. The battle of Sedan marked the downfall of the Second Empire.

Sedan-Chairs. Sedan-chairs — so called from Sedan, France, where they were originally used—were first seen in England in 1581. The Duke of Buckingham, during the reign of James I (1603–1625), used one, to the great indignation of the people, who declared that he forced men to do the work of beasts of burden. In 1634, Sir Francis Duncombe secured the exclusive privilege, for 14 years, of using and renting such chairs in England. Soon after this date they became extremely fashionable, and remained in use for 200 years.

See, the Conquering Hero Comes. A popular song found in Nathaniel Lee's play of *Alexander the Great*, and said to be an interpolation in the stage edition. It was set to music by Handel for his oratorio of *Joshua*, and was afterwards transferred by him to his *Judas Maccabæus*, an earlier production.

Seleucidæ. The name given to a dynasty of rulers that governed Syria from 312 to 65 B.C., a period of 247 years. It was founded by Seleucus, surnamed Nicator, one of the generals of Alexander the Great, who, after the death of that sovereign, became satrap of Babylonia in 321 B.C., and nine years later established himself as King of Syria or Syro-Media. The dynasty of the Seleucidæ comprised 23 kings, the last of whom was Antiochus XIII. He was deposed by Pompey in 65 B.C.,

and Syria was converted into a Roman province.

Seminary Ridge. A ridge one mile west of Gettysburg, Pennsylvania,— so called from a Lutheran Theological Seminary standing upon it. It formed part of the Confederate line during the battle of Gettysburg, and from it, under cover of a tremendous artillery fire, Lee launched his columns of attack on July 3rd, 1863, in his final attempt to break the Union line. See *Cemetery Hill.*

Seminole War. A war between the Seminole Indians of Florida and the United States Government, resulting from the refusal of the red men to remove to lands west of the Mississippi River, in accordance with a treaty made with some of their chiefs in 1832. The war broke out in 1835, and lasted seven years. The Indians signed a treaty of submission in 1839, and, after many delays, were removed to Indian Territory, where 3000 of them still live and receive an annuity of $25,000. Osceola, the Seminole leader, at whose instigation the original treaty was repudiated, was captured and cast into prison, where he died in 1837. The war cost the United States $30,000,000, and hundreds of lives.

Semiramis of the North. (1) A title conferred upon Catherine II (1762–1796), Empress of Russia, a powerful and energetic sovereign, whose private life was stained with deeds of cruelty and profligacy.

(2) An appellation bestowed upon Margaret (1380–1411), Queen of Denmark, Norway, and Sweden. She was warlike and ambitious, and possessed beauty of person and unusual charm of manner.

Semites. One of the three great families of the white, or Caucasian, race,—the two others being the Aryans and Hamites. According to a theory, now widely prevalent, the Semites migrated as nomadic tribes from Arabia into Mesopotamia not later than 4000 B.C., — overpowering the Turanian peoples found there, and spreading thence northward and westward. Their leading historical representatives are the Hebrews, Phœnicians, Assyrians, and Arabs. See *Aryans ; Hamites.*

"As to the *Semites*, there is one respect in which they have the greatest place in the story of mankind, namely, in religious development ; for the three religions that have taught men that there is but one God— namely, the Jewish, the Christian, and the Mahometan—have all come from them. But, aside from this, the Semites do not make nearly as important or as conspicuous a figure in history as do the Aryans, or Indo-Europeans." — Swinton's *Outlines of the World's History.*

Semitic Languages. The name given to an extensive family of related languages, comprising the ancient Arabic, Hebrew, Syriac, Phœnician, Chaldaic, Ethiopic, and possibly the ancient Egyptian and Coptic. The Semitic languages rank second in importance to those of the Aryan group, and are characterized by roots consisting of three consonants, and inflection by means of internal vowel change. See *Aryan Languages ; Hamitic Languages.*

Sempach, Battle of. A desperate battle fought at Sempach, Switzerland, on July 9th, 1386, between 1500 confederated Swiss and 4000 Austrians, commanded by Duke Leopold. The contest resulted in a glorious victory for the Swiss, and established the liberty of their country. According to the legend, Arnold von Winkelried, Burgher of Unterwalden, realizing the almost utter impossibility of penetrating the Austrian phalanx, grasped as many spears as he could reach, buried them in his bosom, and bore them with his weight to the earth. Through the breach thus formed, his companions rushed upon the encumbered Austrians, and slaughtered them without mercy. The victory of Sempach is still annually celebrated in Switzerland. See *Arnold von Winkelried.*

Semper Eadem (*Lat., Always the same*). A motto of Queen Elizabeth (1558–1603), afterwards adopted by Queen Mary and Queen Anne.

"Thou sun, shine on her joyously ! Ye breezes, waft her wide !
Our glorious *Semper Eadem !* the banner of our pride !"
Macaulay's *Armada.*

Senate of Women. An assembly of women in ancient Rome, established by the Emperor Elagabalus (218–222 A.D.) for the serious consideration of questions of dress and etiquette. It held its sessions in the Quirinal. The brief reign of Elagabalus — surnamed the Sardanapalus of Rome—was disgraced by cruelty, extravagance, and vice.

Sepoy Insurrection. See *Indian Mutiny.*

September Massacres. An indiscriminate slaughter of Royalists confined in the Abbaye and other prisons of Paris. It occurred on September 2nd, 3rd, 4th, and 5th, 1792, and was instigated by Marat on receipt of the news announcing the capture of Verdun by the Prussians. The number of victims is variously estimated at from 1200 to 8000 ; among them may be mentioned the beautiful Princess de Lamballe, the friend of Marie Antoinette. See *Abbaye, L' ; September-briseurs.*

"M. Taine gives the number of victims as follows : 171 at the Abbaye, 169 at La Force, 223 at the Châtelet, 328 at the Conciergerie, 73 at the Tour Saint-Bernard, 120 at the Carmelites, 79 at Saint Firmin, 170 at Bicêtre, 35 at the Salpêtrière ; among them 250 priests and the Princess de Lamballe." —*Chambers's Encyclopædia.*

Septembriseurs. A nickname given to those persons engaged in the September Massacres. These hired ruffians were 300 in number, and wore tricolored sashes about their waists. See *September Massacres.*

"Billaud-Varennes promised each of the assassins 24 louis for his work (a total of about 5000 l.), but money enough could not be raised, and the sum of 1463 livres (70 l.) is set down in the books of the Commune as still due. This surely is some blunder, for it is incredible that the government should be unable to lay hands on such a paltry sum of money."—Brewer's *Historic Note-Book*.

Septuagesima Sunday. The third Sunday before Lent, so called because it is about the seventieth (*Lat.*, *septuagesima*, *seventieth*) day before Easter.

Septuagint (*Lat.*, *septuaginta*, *seventy*). A Greek translation of the Hebrew *Old Testament*, so called because traditionally believed to have been made by 70—or, more strictly, 72 —Jews in 72 days, by order of Ptolemy Philadelphus (283–247 B.C.). Critics, however, declare it to be the work, not only of different hands, but also of different times. It probably made its appearance at Alexandria, Egypt, about 260 B.C.

"No one believes the tradition repeated by Philo, Justin, Clement of Alexandria, Epiphanius, and others : That Ptolemy, by the advice of his librarian, employed seventy-two men of learning to translate the Hebrew Scriptures into Greek. The seventy-two met in the Isle of Pharos, and in seventy-two days produced that translation. It is furthermore added that each of the seventy-two was shut up in a separate room, and when they delivered in their translations all most minutely agreed. Not a word, not a letter differed.

Richard Simon informs us that it was called the *Septuagint*, because it was approved and authorised by the Jewish Sanhedrim. The language is Greek, but many of the words are Aramaic."—Brewer's *Historic Note-Book*.

Seraglio. The ancient palace of the Sultans of Turkey, at Constantinople. It is beautifully situated on the site of ancient Byzantium, and encloses within its walls an area of nine square miles, irregularly covered with baths, mosques, kiosks, gardens, and cypress groves. The chief building is the Harem, erected as a residence for the wives of the Sultan. The outer court of the Seraglio is free to all, and is entered by the Sublime Porte. The

new palace of the Sultan of Turkey is on the Bosporus, opposite Scutari. See *Sublime Porte*.

Serapeum. A superb temple at Alexandria, Egypt, erected by Ptolemy Soter (323–283 B.C.) in honor of Jupiter Serapis. It originally contained a part of the Alexandrian Library, but after the destruction of the Museum by fire, the Serapeum became the principal depository of learning in the world. The building was destroyed by a mob of fanatic Christians, led by Archbishop Theophilus in 391 A.D., at the command of the Emperor Theodosius the Great (379–395). See *Alexandrian Library*.

Serbonian Bog. A vast marsh or bog, formerly existing in Lower Egypt, near Damietta. According to Strabo, it was a lake, 200 stadia in length by 50 in breadth. It is now nearly dry. According to Hume, whole armies have been lost in it.

" A gulf profound as that *Serbonian bog*
Betwixt Damiata and Mount Casius old,
Where armies whole have sunk : . . . "
Paradise Lost, ii, 592–594.

Serfs, Emancipation of the. In 1842, the Czar Nicholas I (1825–1855) of Russia liberated all the serfs on the Imperial domains, and in 1861, the Czar Alexander II (1855–1881) issued a decree emancipating all the serfs throughout the Empire in two years. This was accomplished on March 3rd, 1863, when 23,000,000 serfs were set at liberty.

Serpentine. A sheet of artificial water, 50 acres in extent, in Hyde Park, London, formed by order of Queen Caroline, wife of George II (1727–1760). It is used for skating in the winter season and for bathing in the summer. It is said that fully 200,000 persons (men and boys) bathe there annually.

Serpent Mound. A noted earthwork situated near Peebles, Adams County, Ohio, 71 miles east of Cincinnati. The mound has the general outline of a serpent, is 1000 feet long and 5 feet thick, and lies along a bluff that rises above a stream. The tail ends in a triple coil, while within the grasp of the extended jaws is an egg-shaped mound 160 feet long by 80 feet broad. The Serpent Mound is thought to have been constructed by the Mound-Builders, a race of men that inhabited the valley of the Mississippi and the vicinity, previous to the Indians, and was exterminated by them. See *Mound-Builders*.

Servile War. See *Gladiators' War*.

Setting the Thames on Fire. " Doing some wonderful act, or showing extraordinary power. *Thames* is thought by some to be here the word *temse* (a sieve), the rim of which might be set on fire by an active workman ; as the *Seine* also may be both the river and a fishing-net. But this seems very doubtful."—Smith's *Glossary of Terms and Phrases*.

Seven Archangels. They are Michael, Gabriel, Raphael, Uriel, Chamuel, Zophiel, and Zadkiel. The first three mentioned are the chief ones, and are frequently represented in Christian art. The last three have never been generally recognized. According to the *Koran* there are four archangels,—Gabriel, Michael, Azrael, and Azrafil. See *Azrael*.

Seven Bibles. The following list of inspired writings—seven in number —is taken from Brewer's *Historic Note-Book*. It includes most of the so-called sacred books of mankind.

(1) The Bible.
(2) The Koran.
(3) The Eddas.
(4) The Try Pitikes, or Tripitaka.
(5) The Five Kings.
(6) The Three Vedas.
(7) The Zend-Avesta.

Seven Bishops. A term applied to the seven prelates of the Anglican Church, committed to the Tower of London by Chief Justice Jeffreys, June

10th, 1688, for refusing either to read James II's *Declaration of Indulgence* or to command their clergy to do so. This declaration had for its object the removal of all disabilities from the Roman Catholics in church and state offices. The seven bishops were tried and acquitted on June 29th–30th, 1688. Their names were Archbishop Sancroft of Canterbury, and Bishops Ken of Bath and Wells, Lake of Chichester, White of Peterborough, Turner of Ely, Lloyd of St. Asaph, and Trelawney of Bristol.

Seven Bodies in Alchemy. The seven bodies recognized by the alchemists were as follows:

(1) Gold, symbolized by the Sun.
(2) Silver, symbolized by the Moon.
(3) Iron, symbolized by Mars.
(4) Quicksilver, symbolized by Mercury.
(5) Lead, symbolized by Saturn.
(6) Tin, symbolized by Jupiter.
(7) Copper, symbolized by Venus.

" The *bodies seven*, eek, lo hem heer anoon :
Sol gold is, and Luna silver we threpe,
Mars yren, Mercurie quyksilver we clepe,
Saturnus leed, and Jubitur is tyn,
And Venus coper, by my fader kyn."
Prologue to Canterbury Tales.

Seven Brothers. Alexander, Felix, Januarius, Martial, Philip, Silvanus, and Vitalis, who, with their mother, Felicitas, are said to have suffered martyrdom at Rome in 164 A.D., during the reign of Marcus Aurelius Antoninus (161–180).

" According to the legend, she [Felicitas] was a woman of high birth, who embraced Christianity and brought up her seven sons in the faith. She was denounced to Marcus Aurelius, who ordered an inquiry. The prefect ordered her to sacrifice to the gods ; she refused, as did her children. After vain efforts to break their constancy, the prefect reported the case anew to the emperor, who ordered a trial before special judges. The lady and her children were all put to death. The story is plainly of comparatively modern invention. Felicitas is commemorated in the Church of Rome Nov. 13, and her seven sons July 16. The bones of two of her sons are said to be preserved in Germany !"— McClintock and Strong's *Cyclopædia.*

Seven Champions of Christendom.
(1) St. George of England.
(2) St. Denis of France.
(3) St. James of Spain.
(4) St. Anthony of Italy.
(5) St. Andrew of Scotland.
(6) St. Patrick of Ireland.
(7) St. David of Wales.

"*The Famous Historie of the Seven Champions of Christendom* is the work of Richard Johnson, a ballad maker of some note at the end of the 16th and beginning of the 17th century."—*Child.*

Seven Chief Virtues. These, as defined by the Roman Catholic Church, are as follows :
(1) Faith.
(2) Hope.
(3) Charity.
(4) Prudence.
(5) Temperance.
(6) Justice.
(7) Fortitude.
The first three are called the holy, or theological, virtues; and the remaining four the moral, or cardinal, virtues.

Seven Churches of Asia. Seven Christian congregations of Asia Minor, to the angels (*i. e.*, ministers) of which were addressed the epistles of praise and admonition contained in the second and third chapters of the *Revelation of St. John.* They were Ephesus, Smyrna, Pergamos, Thyatira, Sardis, Philadelphia, and Laodicea.

"I was in the Spirit on the Lord's day, and heard behind me a great voice as of a trumpet, saying, I am Alpha and Omega, the first and the last: and, what thou seest, write in a book, and send it unto the *seven churches which are in Asia ;* unto Ephesus, and unto Smyrna, and unto Pergamos, and unto Thyatira, and unto Sardis, and unto Philadelphia, and unto Laodicea."—*Revelation* i, 10, 11.

Seven Cities, Island of the. See *Island of the Seven Cities.*

Seven Clerical Orders. See *Orders, Holy.*

Seven Corporal Works of Mercy.
According to the teaching of the Roman Catholic Church, these are as follows :
(1) To bury the dead.
(2) To clothe the naked.
(3) To feed the hungry.
(4) To give drink to the thirsty.
(5) To shelter the homeless.
(6) To visit those in prison.
(7) To administer unto the sick.
See *Seven Spiritual Works of Mercy.*

Seven Crosses. Brewer, in his *Historic Note-Book,* says that there are seven forms of the ecclesiastical cross. These are as follows :
(1) The Greek Cross.
(2) The Latin Cross.
(3) The Maltese Cross.
(4) The St. Andrew's Cross.
(5) The Lorrainese Cross, or Cardinal's Cross.
(6) The Tau, or Egyptian, Cross.
(7) Constantine's Cross.

Seven Days' Battles. The name given to a series of desperate conflicts during the Peninsular Campaign of the Civil War, lasting seven days (June 25th–July 1st, 1862), between the Union forces commanded by General McClellan and the Confederates under General Lee. As a result of these battles, McClellan was forced to retreat to Harrison's Landing on the James River, with a loss of 15,249 in killed, wounded, and missing. The Confederate loss was estimated at 17,583.

Seven Days' King. An appellation conferred upon Tommaso Aniello (1622-1647), an Italian fisherman, who, on July 7th, 1647, headed a successful revolt against the Viceroy of Naples, and forced him to abolish a tax on provisions. Aniello ruled the city for seven days, but during this brief period his despotic acts alienated his friends and supporters, and caused his assassination at the hands of the adherents of the Viceroy (July 16th, 1647). See *Masaniello.*

Seven Days' War. The name

given to a brief diplomatic contest between Austria and Prussia for supremacy in Germany, during the spring of 1866. As a result of these negotiations, Austria was forced to surrender the Quadrilateral to France, which, in turn, gave it to Italy. By this means, the entire Italian peninsula, with the exception of Venetia and the States of the Church, became one kingdom, under the rule of Victor Emmanuel II. See *Quadrilateral*.

Seven Deadly Sins. According to the teaching of the Roman Catholic Church, these are as follows :

(1) Pride.
(2) Anger.
(3) Envy.
(4) Sloth.
(5) Lust.
(6) Covetousness.
(7) Gluttony.
See *Mortal Sins ; Venial Sins.*

Seven Dials. A notorious region in St. Giles's, London, so called from a Doric pillar, bearing a seven-faced dial, formerly standing in the centre of a circular area where seven streets converge. This pillar was removed in 1773 ; according to some authorities, in 1777. Seven Dials was once the heart of one of the most degraded sections of London ; but in recent years some improvements have been made in the neighborhood. See *St. Giles's.*

"At night the public-houses are ablaze with light, and on Saturday evenings there is a great sound of shouting and singing through the windows, while the women stand outside and wait, hoping against hope that their husbands will come out before the week's money is all spent. Nowhere within reach of the West End of London can such a glimpse of the life of the poorer classes be obtained as on a Saturday evening at the Dials."—Dickens's *Dictionary of London.*

Seven Dolors of Mary. See *Seven Sorrows of Mary.*

Seven Gifts of the Holy Ghost. According to the teaching of the

Roman Catholic Church, these are as follows :

(1) Counsel.
(2) Fear of the Lord.
(3) Fortitude.
(4) Piety.
(5) Understanding.
(6) Wisdom.
(7) Knowledge.

Seven Great Hymns. A term collectively applied to seven Latin hymns of the Mediæval Church, famous for their sublimity, tenderness, and pathos. They are as follows :

(1) *The Celestial Country.*
(2) *Dies Iræ.*
(3) *Stabat Mater Dolorosa.*
(4) *Stabat Mater Speciosa.*
(5) *Veni, Creator Spiritus.*
(6) *Veni, Sancte Spiritus.*
(7) *Vexilla Regis.*

Seven-Hilled City. An appellation bestowed upon the city of Rome, which was originally built upon seven eminences,—the majority of which are scarcely recognizable at the present time. See *Seven Hills of Rome.*

Seven Hills of Rome. The seven hills or eminences upon which, according to the legend, the city of Rome was originally built, are as follows :

(1) The Capitoline.
(2) The Palatine.
(3) The Aventine.
(4) The Cælian.
(5) The Esquiline.
(6) The Quirinal.
(7) The Viminal.
The Janiculum, Pincian, and Vatican Hills are not reckoned among the "Seven Hills of Rome."

"Archæology has revealed the fact, however, that the oldest community upon this site was confined to a walled town on the Palatine Hill. Later the Capitoline was included, and not until Servius Tullius, who built new and more extended walls, were the five more outlying elevations included. By building and levelling, carried on during three millenniums, most of the original topographical features have been obliterated." — Walsh's *Handy-Book of Literary Curiosities.*

Seven Joys of Mary.
(1) The Annunciation.
(2) The Visitation.
(3) The Nativity.
(4) The Adoration of the Magi.
(5) The Presentation in the Temple.
(6) The Finding of Christ among the Doctors.
(7) The Assumption.
See *Seven Sorrows of Mary.*

"Strange that the 'resurrection' should be omitted. One would have supposed it would have been the joy of joys next to the nativity."—Brewer's *Historic Note-Book.*

Seven Lamps of Architecture. A celebrated work on architecture by John Ruskin (1819–1900), the art-critic. It appeared in 1849. According to the author, the seven psychical principles, or "lamps," of architecture, are as follows :
(1) The Lamp of Sacrifice.
(2) The Lamp of Truth.
(3) The Lamp of Power.
(4) The Lamp of Beauty.
(5) The Lamp of Life.
(6) The Lamp of Memory.
(7) The Lamp of Obedience.

Seven Liberal Arts. A term applied, during the Middle Ages, to the following seven branches of learning :
(1) Arithmetic.
(2) Geometry.
(3) Astronomy.
(4) Music.
(5) Logic.
(6) Rhetoric.
(7) Grammar.
The first four constitute the *quadrivium* of the Schoolmen ; and the remaining three, the *trivium.* The higher arts were first called " liberal " among the ancient Romans, because only freemen (*Lat., liberi*) were allowed to pursue them.

"Good sense, which only is the gift of Heaven,
And though no science, fairly worth the seven."
Pope.

Seven Mortal Sins. See *Seven Deadly Sins.*

Seven Planets. An expression used among the ancient astronomers to denote the seven heavenly bodies (Sun, Moon, Mercury, Venus, Mars, Jupiter, and Saturn) that had an apparent motion among the fixed stars.

Seven Rishis. In Hindu mythology, the seven " mind-born " sons of Brahma, who were said to dwell in the seven stars of the constellation known to us as the " Great Dipper."

Seven Sacraments. The Roman Catholic Church recognizes the following seven sacraments, viz.:
(1) Baptism.
(2) Confirmation.
(3) The Eucharist.
(4) Penance.
(5) Holy Orders.
(6) Matrimony.
(7) Extreme Unction.
See *Five Sacraments.*

" If any one shall say that the sacraments of the new law were not all instituted by Jesus Christ our Lord, or that they are more or less than *seven*—to wit, baptism, confirmation, the eucharist, penance, extreme unction, orders, and matrimony—or even that any one of these seven is not truly and properly a sacrament, let him be anathema."—*Council of Trent*, Session 7, Canon 1.

The Reformed Churches for the most part reject these views, and recognize two sacraments only — Baptism and the Eucharist.

"There are two Sacraments ordained of Christ our Lord in the Gospel, that is to say, Baptism, and the Supper of the Lord.

Those five commonly called Sacraments, that is to say, Confirmation, Penance, Orders, Matrimony, and Extreme Unction, are not to be counted for Sacraments of the Gospel, being such as have grown partly of the corrupt following of the Apostles, partly are states of life allowed in the Scriptures; but yet have not like nature of Sacraments with Baptism and the Lord's Supper, for that they have not any visible sign or ceremony ordained of God."—*Articles of Religion*, Article XXV.

Seven Sages. See *Seven Wise Men of Greece.*

Seven Sayings Uttered by Christ on the Cross.

(1) " Father, forgive them; for they know not what they do ! "
(2) " To-day shalt thou be with me in paradise ! "
(3) " Woman, behold thy son ! "
(4) " My God, my God, why hast thou forsaken me ? "
(5) " I thirst ! "
(6) " It is finished ! "
(7) " Father, into thy hands I commend my spirit ! "

Seven Senses.

According to very ancient teaching, man possessed seven senses, instead of five as at present reckoned. These were understanding, speech, sight, hearing, smell, taste, and touch.

"They received the use of the five operations of the Lord, and in the sixth place he imparted them *understanding*, and in the seventh *speech*, an interpreter of the cogitations thereof."—*Ecclesiasticus* xvii, 5.

" I will adore my Father,
My God, my Supporter,
Who placed throughout my head
The soul of my reason,
And made for my perception
My *seven faculties*,
Of fire, and earth, and water, and air,
And mist, and flowers,
And the southerly wind,
As it were *seven senses* of reason
For my Father to impel me :
With the first I shall be animated,
With the second I shall touch,
With the third I shall cry out,
With the fourth I shall taste,
With the fifth I shall see,
With the sixth I shall hear,
With the seventh I shall smell."
Mysterium Magnum.

Seven Sisters.

The name given to seven cannons, cast by Robert Borthwick, master of artillery, and used by the Scotch at the battle of Flodden Field (September 9th, 1513). They are mentioned in Sir Walter Scott's *Marmion*.

" And there were Borthwick's *Sisters seven*,
And culverins which France had given.
Ill-omen'd gift! the guns remain
The conqueror's spoil on Flodden's plain."
Marmion, iv, xxvii.

Seven Sleepers.

Seven noble youths of Ephesus, who, according to an early Christian legend first related by Gregory of Tours, fled from the city, during a persecution under the Emperor Decius (249–251 A.D.), and took refuge in a cave on Mount Celion. There they were discovered by their pursuers, who walled up the entrance in order to starve them to death ; but, owing to a miraculous interposition in their behalf, they were caused to fall into a deep sleep, and were thus miraculously preserved for nearly 200 years. They died soon after awakening, and their bodies were transferred to Marseilles, France, in a stone sarcophagus, which is still shown to visitors to the Church of St. Victor, in that city. According to Gregory, the names of the " Seven Sleepers" were Constantine, Dionysius, John, Maximian, Malchus, Martinian or Marcian, and Serapion. A festival in their honor is celebrated in the Roman Catholic Church on July 27th. The legend of the " Seven Sleepers " is widely current in the East. It is of Syrian origin, and occurs in the *Koran*.

" Their sleep seemed to them to have been for only a night, and they were greatly astonished, on going into the city, to see the cross exposed upon the church-tops, which but a few hours ago, as it appeared, was the object of contempt. Their wonderful story told, they were conducted in triumph into the city ; but all died at the same moment."
—McClintock and Strong's *Cyclopædia*.

Seven Sorrows of Mary.

(1) The Prediction of Simeon.
(2) The Flight into Egypt.
(3) The Loss of Jesus in Jerusalem.
(4) The Sight of Jesus Bearing His Cross.
(5) The Sight of Jesus on the Cross.
(6) The Descent from the Cross.
(7) The Entombment.

The " Festival of the Seven Sorrows of the Blessed Virgin Mary " was instituted by Pope Benedict XIII (1724–1730), in 1725. It occurs on the Friday preceding Palm Sunday. A second festival, instituted by Pope Pius VII

(1800–1823) in 1814, falls on the third Sunday in September. See *Seven Joys of Mary.*

Seven Spirits. The seven spirits that stand before the throne of God are Michael, Gabriel, Lamael, Raphael, Zachariel, Anael, and Oriphiel.

"And I saw the seven angels which stood before God ; and to them were given seven trumpets."—*Revelation* viii, 2.

Seven Spiritual Works of Mercy. According to the teaching of the Roman Catholic Church, these are as follows :

(1) To admonish the sinful.
(2) To bear wrongs patiently.
(3) To comfort the afflicted.
(4) To counsel the doubting.
(5) To forgive offenses.
(6) To instruct the ignorant.
(7) To pray for the living and the dead.

See *Seven Corporal Works of Mercy.*

Seventh-Day Baptists. A Baptist sect that observes the seventh day of the week, instead of the first, as the true Sabbath. It was founded in England in 1650, and introduced into America in 1665–1671. The original name of the denomination — Sabbatarians — was rejected by the General Conference in America in 1818, and the term, Seventh-Day Baptists, adopted instead. In 1900, they had in the United States, 114 congregations, 135 ministers, 9161 members, a publishing-house, and several colleges. See *Sabbatarians.*

Seventh Heaven. According to the Cabalistic notion, there are seven heavens, rising above one another, like the stories of a building. The seventh or highest one is the place of supreme or ecstatic bliss, where dwell God and the highest order of angels. This conception of heaven is the same as the one found in the *Koran.*

Seventy Years' Captivity. A term frequently applied to the period of 70 years (606–536 B.C.), during which the Jews were held in captivity in Babylon. See *Babylonian Captivity.*

Seven Weeks' War. A term sometimes applied to the Austro-Prussian War of 1866, which lasted from June 7th—when the Prussians entered Holstein— until July 26th, when the preliminaries of peace were signed.

Seven Wise Masters. The title of a famous collection of Eastern fables, said to have been introduced into Europe by the Crusaders during the 11th century.

"The story of the Seven Sages is of great antiquity, and in all probability of Oriental origin. There are two metrical versions of the romance in English, and also a chap-book, called *The Seven Wise Masters.* Ellis speaks of a work of Oriental origin, 'which has furnished us with an English metrical romance, named in the Cotton MS. "The Process of the Sevyn Sages," or, to use the more familiar and popular title of the prose translation, "The Seven Wise Masters." ' There are versions of the romance in Arabic, Hebrew, Greek, Latin, French, German, and other languages."—Wheeler's *Who Wrote It?*

Seven Wise Men of Greece. A designation collectively applied to seven Greek sages, whose wisdom, according to the ancients, was embodied in certain brief maxims. The following is a list of these " Wise Men," together with some of their maxims.

(1) Solon of Athens : " Know thyself."
(2) Chilo of Sparta : " Consider the end."
(3) Thales of Miletus: " Suretyship brings ruin."
(4) Bias of Priene : " Most men are bad."
(5) Cleobulus of Lindus : "Avoid extremes."
(6) Pittacus of Mitylene : " Know thine opportunity."
(7) Periander of Corinth: "Nothing is impossible to industry."

" First, Solon, who made the Athenian laws ;
While Chilo, in Sparta, was famed for his saws ;
In Miletos did Thales astronomy teach ;
Bias used in Priene his morals to preach ;

Cleobulos, of Lindos, was handsome and
  wise;
Mitylene 'gainst thraldom saw Pittacos
  rise;
Periander is said to have gained through
  his court
The title that Myson, the Chenian, ought."
                            E. C. B.

Seven Wonders of the Middle Ages.

The Seven Wonders of the Middle
Ages were as follows:

(1) The Coliseum at Rome.
(2) The Catacombs of Alexandria.
(3) The Great Wall of China.
(4) The Leaning Tower of Pisa.
(5) The Porcelain Tower of Nanking.
(6) The Mosque of St. Sophia at
Constantinople.
(7) The Ruins of Stonehenge.

Seven Wonders of the New World.
An appellation sometimes conferred
upon the following group of natural
objects in the United States of America:

(1) Niagara Falls.
(2) Yellowstone Park.
(3) Garden of the Gods.
(4) Mammoth Cave.
(5) Yosemite Valley.
(6) Giant Trees.
(7) Natural Bridge.

Seven Wonders of the World. In
ancient times, these were generally
reckoned as follows:

(1) The Pyramids of Egypt.
(2) The Hanging Gardens of Babylon.
(3) The Mausoleum at Halicarnassus.
(4) The Temple of Diana at Ephesus.
(5) The Colossus of Rhodes.
(6) The Pharos at Alexandria.
(7) The Statue of the Olympian Jove
in Elis.

Seven Years' War. The name
given to a war waged between Frederick the Great (1740–1786) of Prussia,
in alliance with England, on the one
side, and Austria, France, and Russia,
on the other. It lasted from 1756 to
1763,— a period of seven years,— but
resulted in no material advantage to
either side. Frederick, however, retained Silesia, for the possession of
which the war was fought, and raised
Prussia to the dignity of a first-class
power. It is estimated that a million
lives were sacrificed in this useless
struggle.

Seville Cathedral. A superb cathedral, of vast size, at Seville, Spain.
It was erected during the early part
of the 16th century, and measures 438
feet in length by 282 feet in breadth.
The cathedral has nine separate entrances, 93 painted windows (the most
beautiful in Spain), and a floor of
white and black marble, which cost
$125,000. It contains 37 chapels, each
one of which is a repository of wealth.
Its art-treasures also are priceless in
value. Murillo, the painter, and Fernando the son of Christopher Columbus, are buried in the cathedral.

Sèvres. A town in France, ten
miles southwest of Paris, famous for
its porcelain manufactory and museum
of ceramic art. These works were
established at Vincennes in 1745; and,
eleven years later, were transferred to
Sèvres, and made government property. They employ about 200 hands.
The *Musée Céramique*, founded in 1800
by Alexandre Brogniart, is the finest
in Europe. It is, however, chiefly
interesting to the connoisseur.

Sewers of Paris. A vast network
of drainage under the city of Paris,
having a total length of more than
1000 miles. Its construction is said
to have cost nearly $30,000,000. The
maintenance and cleansing of the
sewers of Paris cost the city about
$500,000 annually, and enlist the services of 1000 men. Water-pipes, telegraph and telephone wires, and
pneumatic tubes pass through the
sewers; but gas-pipes are excluded,
for fear of explosions. Visitors are
conveyed through the sewers by electric trains, or by boats towed by electric
traction.

Sexagesima Sunday. The second Sunday before Lent,—so called because it is about the sixtieth (*Lat.*, *sexagesima, sixtieth*) day before Easter.

Shah Diamond. A famous diamond weighing 86 carats, presented to the Czar of Russia by Prince Chosroës, younger son of the Abbas Mirza.

Shakers. A body of seceders from the "Society of Friends" or "Quakers," founded by Ann Lee ("Mother Ann") of Manchester, England, about 1757 ; and so called from the wild and violent contortions introduced by them into their form of worship. Their official title is "The United Society of Believers in Christ's Second Appearing." The sect emigrated to America in 1772, and settled near Albany in 1774. Their chief seats are at New Lebanon and Watervliet, New York. They number 15 societies in the United States, and have a membership of about 1728. The Shakers believe in spiritualism, practice celibacy and community of goods, oppose war, refrain from oaths, and denounce baptism and the Lord's Supper. They are noted for their frugality, integrity, and thrift. See *Mother Ann.*

Shakespeare-Bacon Controversy. A discussion that arose, during the nineteenth century, from an attempt, on the part of Miss Delia Bacon (1811-1859), to prove that Lord Francis Bacon is the author of the plays commonly attributed to Shakespeare. William H. Smith,—an English scholar,— Nathaniel Holmes, in his *Authorship of Shakespeare*, and Mrs. Henry Holmes have also labored in the same direction. In 1888, Ignatius Donnelly produced his work entitled *The Great Cryptogram*, wherein he endeavored to show "that Bacon's authorship is avowed under a cipher in the text of the plays in the folio of 1623." Shakespearian scholars do not accept the Baconian theory of authorship.

Shakespeare of Divines. A title conferred upon Jeremy Taylor (1613-1667), Bishop of Down, on account of his vivid imagination and fervid eloquence.

> "Old Chrysostom, best Augustine,
> And he who blent both in his line,
> The younger Golden Lips or mines,
> Taylor, the *Shakespeare of Divines.*"
> *Ralph Waldo Emerson.*

"The sermons of Jeremy Taylor are far, indeed, above any that had preceded them in the English Church. An imagination essentially poetical, and sparing none of the decorations which, by critical rules, are deemed almost peculiar to verse ; a warm tone of piety, sweetness, and charity ; an accumulation of circumstantial accessories whenever he reasons, or persuades, or describes ; an erudition pouring itself forth in quotation till his sermons become in some places almost a garland of flowers from all other writers, and especially from those of classical antiquity, never before so redundantly scattered from the pulpit, distinguish Taylor from his contemporaries by their degree, as they do from most of his successors by their kind."—Hallam's *Introduction to the Literature of Europe.*

Shakespeare's House. A house on Henley Street, Stratford-on-Avon, England, famous as the place where William Shakespeare was born on April 23rd, 1564. It was purchased by popular subscription for about £3000, on September 16th, 1847, and was carefully restored in 1858-1859. The house contains a museum, filled with relics of the poet,—among which may be mentioned a gold signet-ring, an ancient desk formerly used by him at the grammar-school, a jug from which Garrick sipped wine at the Jubilee of 1769, a specimen from the original copy of the *Merry Wives of Windsor*, a sword, and numerous portraits of the poet. The room in which Shakespeare was born has been restored, as nearly as possible, to its original state. In one of the upper apartments may be seen the famous "Stratford portrait" of the poet. See *Stratford-on-Avon.*

"The little town of Stratford-on-Avon is famous only as the birthplace of the immortal Shakespeare. Fortunately, the house in which the poet was born on the 23d of April, 1564, is now national property and is most carefully protected. Hither come every year about 14,000 visitors, most of them Americans. The building has undergone some changes since Shakespeare's time, but the old timbered framework is the same. On the first floor a little room facing the street is pointed out as the one in which the Bard of Stratford first saw the light. The walls are literally covered with inscriptions, written or carved in every tongue, and indicating thus an endless throng of pilgrims of all ranks, from prince to peasant. Elsewhere these names would be an outrage; but here, in memory of this universal genius, they seem a proof of the spontaneous, worldwide homage of mankind. Among them are the names of Byron, Sir Walter Scott, Thackeray, Dickens, Tom Moore, Washington Irving, and the Duke of Wellington."—Stoddard's *Glimpses of the World*.

Shannon. A British frigate, carrying 54 guns and 335 men, commanded by Captain Philip V. Broke. On June 1st, 1813, she captured the United States frigate *Chesapeake*, off Boston harbor, after a desperate engagement, and conveyed her to Halifax. The *Shannon* lost 26 killed and 58 wounded. See *Chesapeake*.

"As this was the only important naval capture by the British during the war, it excited great enthusiasm in England. The freedom of London and a sword were presented to Broke; he was knighted by the prince regent, and his native county, Suffolk, gave him a piece of magnificent plate. Lawrence has been charged with taking his crew into action while insubordinate and mutinous."—Harper's *Book of Facts*.

Sharp Knife. A nickname given by the North American Indians to Andrew Jackson (1767-1845), the seventh President of the United States, in allusion to his keenness of insight.

Shastras, Great. A term applied to the sacred books of the Hindus. They include the four *Vedas*, the *Vedangas*, the body of the law, and the six sacred books of philosophy.

"They are all of them written in the Sanscrit language, and believed to be of divine inspiration. They are usually reduced to four classes, which again are subdivided into eighteen heads. The first class consists of the four Vedas, which are accounted the most ancient and the most sacred compositions. The second class consists of the four *Upa-vedas*, or sub-Scriptures, and the third class of the six *Ved-angas*, or bodies of learning. The fourth class consists of the four *Up-angas*, or appended bodies of learning. The first of these embraces the eighteen Purânas, or sacred poems. Besides the Purânas, the first *Up-anga* comprises the *Ramayâna* and *Mahabhârata*. The second and third *Up-angas* consist of the principal works on logic and metaphysics. The fourth and last *Up-anga* consists of the body of the law, in eighteen books, compiled by Manu, the son of Brahma, and other sacred personages."—McClintock and Strong's *Cyclopædia*.

Shays's Rebellion. An insurrection that broke out in Massachusetts in 1786-1787, as the result of an attempt by Congress to apportion the debt of the United States among the several States of the Union. A large number of citizens, led by Daniel Shays —formerly a captain in the Continental army — took forcible possession of Worcester, and afterwards of Springfield, and endeavored to seize the arsenal there, but were speedily dispersed by the militia. The ringleaders of the movement were tried and sentenced to death, but were all eventually pardoned.

She-Bible. The name given to the corrected edition of the *Authorized Version of the Bible*, in which the word "she" was substituted for "he" in *Ruth* iii, 15. See *He-Bible*.

Shepherd Kings. The name given to a dynasty of kings — also known as the Hyksos—that ruled Egypt for five centuries (2080-1525 B.C.). They are believed to have sprung from a tribe of shepherds—possibly of Tartar origin — who invaded Lower Egypt and overthrew the native monarchy at Memphis. They were finally driven out by Ahmes, founder of the XVIIIth Dynasty. See *Hyksos*.

Sherman's March. A daring and successful march made by the army of General Sherman, during the Civil War, from Atlanta to Savannah, and thence northwards through the Carolinas to Goldsborough. The army, consisting of 60,000 infantry and artillery, and about 6000 cavalry, advanced in two columns,—subsisting almost entirely upon what could be obtained on the journey. Sherman left Atlanta on November 16th, 1864, and reached Savannah (a distance of 300 miles), about the middle of December. The city was evacuated by the Confederates on the 20th of the month, and on the following day the Union forces entered and took possession. On the 18th of January, Sherman resumed his march, and reached Goldsborough, North Carolina, on March 22nd. This exploit proved that the Confederacy had become "an empty shell,"—all the male inhabitants having been withdrawn from the interior of the country to defend its borders. See *Bummer*.

Sherwood Forest. A hilly region in Nottinghamshire, England, covering an area of about 200 square miles. It was formerly a royal forest, and was famous as the scene of the legendary exploits of the noted Robin Hood; but, at the present time, it is almost bare of trees, and is occupied by country-seats and private parks. In the neighborhood of Rotherham may still be seen portions of Sherwood Forest. See *Robin Hood*.

She-Wolf of France. A nickname conferred upon Isabella, wife of Edward II (1307–1327) of England, who, assisted by her paramour, the Earl of Mortimer, deposed her husband, and placed her son on the throne, with the title of Edward III.

Shibboleth. After the defeat of the Ephraimites by the Gileadites under Jephthah, the former fled to the Jordan, which they endeavored to cross. The Gileadites, however, took possession of the fords of the river, and whenever a fugitive attempted to pass, they commanded him to say "shibboleth," which the men of Ephraim

pronounced "sibboleth," from their inability to utter the *sh* sound. By this means the Ephraimites were detected and immediately slain. It is said that 42,000 were killed in a single day. (See *Judges* xii, 6.) The word *shibboleth* is still used to denote any criterion of opinions or manners.

"All those Hebrew names in the Old Testament which commence with the *sh* have now, through the inability of the Septuagint to render this sound in Greek, become familiar to us, through the versions that flowed from it, as beginning with the simple *s*— *e. g.*, Simon, Samaria, Solomon, Saul, etc."
—*Chambers's Encyclopædia*.

Shiites. A Mohammedan sect that recognize Ali as the first legitimate successor of Mohammed, and deny Abu-bekr, Omar, and Ohman to have been true caliphs. They reject the *Sunna*, or body of traditions, and accept only the *Koran*. The Shiites predominate in Persia, but are found also in India, Mesopotamia, and Syria. The name means *sectaries*, or *heretics*, and was given them by the Sunnites, who regard themselves as the orthodox party. See *Sunnites*.

Shilling. This word is probably derived from the Icelandic root *skilja* (*to divide*), because the coin was deeply indented with a cross to permit of its being easily broken into four parts. According to other authorities, its origin is traced to a corrupted form of the Latin *solidos*, a coin used in ancient Rome and also in the Middle Ages. The English shilling was probably coined for the first time in 1504, during the reign of Henry VII (1485–1509).

Shiloh, Battle of. A sanguinary battle fought near Pittsburg Landing, Tennessee, on April 6th–7th, 1862, during the American Civil War, between 33,000 Federals under General Grant and 40,000 Confederates under General Albert Sidney Johnston. The Federal forces were attacked and driven back on the first day of the battle; but, after receiving heavy reinforcements, they rallied on the following day and achieved a victory. The Federal losses, including killed, wounded, and prisoners, amounted to 13,573, and the Confederate losses to 10,699. The battle of Shiloh is also known as the battle of Pittsburg Landing.

Shinplaster. A slang term used in the United States to denote paper money, especially such as may have depreciated in value.

"This term is said to have arisen during the Revolutionary war. After the continental currency had become almost worthless, an old soldier who possessed a quantity of it, which he could not get rid of, very philosophically made use of it as plasters to a wounded leg. The term is now (1877) more generally used to designate notes for less than a dollar." — Bartlett's *Dictionary of Americanisms.*

Ship-Money. A tax imposed as early as 1007 A.D. by the sovereign, on the maritime towns and counties of England, for the purpose of providing and maintaining a navy for the protection of the coast. It was revived by Charles I (1625–1649) in 1634, without the consent of Parliament, and was arbitrarily levied on the whole of England. John Hampden, a squire of Buckinghamshire, resisted the payment of the tax as illegal, but was prosecuted and condemned,—four of the judges dissenting. In 1640–1641 the Long Parliament declared the levying of ship-money to be illegal, and annulled the judgment against Hampden. The imposition of this tax was one of the chief causes of the Civil War.

Shipton, Mother. See *Mother Shipton.*

Shoddy. Woolen fibre obtained from old stockings, druggets, yarns, flannels, and other refuse, and much used, during the Civil War, in the manufacture of army supplies, furnished to the United States Government by dishonest contractors. Hence the term has been colloquially applied to any vulgar assumption or display made by persons of newly acquired wealth.

"For what is the essential characteristic of *shoddy* clothing? Is it not this, that it will not *wear?* In its outside appearance it mimics good cloth, but use quickly reduces it to its elemental rags."—Whipple's *Success and its Conditions.*

Shoe at Weddings. See *Casting Shoe after Bride.*

Shopkeepers, Nation of. See *Nation of Shopkeepers.*

Shotgun Policy. A phrase used by extremists in the Northern States of the American Union to epitomize the alleged methods of violence and intimidation used in the South to control the negro vote.

Shrine of St. Thomas à Becket. A famous shrine formerly existing in Trinity Chapel, Canterbury Cathedral, England. It contained the bones of the martyr-bishop, removed thither from the crypt of the cathedral, in 1220; and remained for three centuries the object of one of the famous pilgrimages of Christendom. In 1538, Henry VIII (1509–1547) despoiled and demolished the shrine; caused Becket's name to be stricken from the Calendar; and ordered his bones to be burned and scattered to the winds. In 1500, the yearly offering to the shrine amounted to £4000; and at the time of its destruction, 26 cartloads of treasure were removed. The pavement of the chapel and the stone steps that lead up to the place where the shrine formerly stood are worn by the knees of countless pilgrims. See *Becket's Murder.*

Shrine of the Three Kings. A shrine in the Chapel of the Magi, behind the high altar of Cologne Cathedral, said to contain the bones of the three "Wise Men," who sought the infant Jesus at Bethlehem. The silver case containing these relics is ornamented with precious stones ; and is valued, with the other treasures in the chapel, at \$2,000,000. The skulls of the " Magi," adorned with diamonds and rubies, are also shown. See *Cologne, Three Kings of.*

Shrove-Tuesday. The day before Ash-Wednesday, so called because, on that day, good Christians made " shrift," or confession, and obtained absolution. It is also called *Pancake-Tuesday*, from the custom of eating pancakes on that day. Shrove-Tuesday is identical with the *Mardi-Gras* of the French. See *Mardi-Gras.*

Shyster. A term colloquially used in the United States to denote a class of men — generally lawyers of an inferior grade—who frequent the police courts of New York and other large cities, and practise in them in a tricky or unprofessional manner. The expression is also applied to any person that conducts his business in a shady way.

" When a man or woman is thrown into prison, a *shyster* leech gets access to him, and extorts from him his last cent under the pretence of obtaining his liberation."—*New York Tribune.*

Siamese Twins. The name given to two persons, *Chang* and *Eng*, of Chinese parentage, born in Siam in 1811. They were united by a fibro-cartilaginous band proceeding from the breast-bone of each,—in the centre of which was a single umbilicus. Although, physiologically, they were distinct persons, there was intercommunication between their hepatic vascular systems. The " Siamese Twins " were discovered on the banks of the Siam River, and purchased from their mother by an American, Robert Hunter, who took them to New York in 1829, and afterwards to England. Having acquired a competence by exhibiting themselves in the various countries of Europe, they returned to America, and settled in North Carolina, where they were married to two sisters and had several offspring. In 1869, they again exhibited themselves in Europe. They died on July 17th, 1874, within 2½ hours of each other.

Sibyl, Cumæan. An inspired prophetess, named Amalthea, who, according to tradition, appeared before Tarquinius Superbus, with nine books, which she offered to sell to him for 300 pieces of gold. Deeming the price exorbitant, the King declined to purchase them ; whereupon the Sibyl departed, and destroyed three of the volumes, but soon after returned with the remaining six, for which she asked the same price as for the nine. Again the King refused the offer, and again the Sibyl departed, and destroyed three more of the volumes. Not long afterward, she reappeared with the remaining three volumes, for which she still asked the original price. The curiosity of the King was now so much aroused that, after consultation with the pontiffs, he purchased the books; whereupon the Sibyl vanished. In the sixth book of Virgil's *Æneid*, Æneas consults the oracle of the Cumæan Sibyl, and is afterwards conducted by her to the lower world. See *Sibylline Books.*

Sibylline Books. A collection of oracular writings, in three volumes, said to have contained the fortunes of the ancient Roman state. According to tradition, they were purchased by Tarquinius Superbus from the Cumæan Sibyl, and deposited in the Temple of Jupiter Capitolinus at Rome,—in a stone chest, underground. They were guarded by certain officers,—at first two in number, but afterwards increased successively to ten and fifteen. The *Sibylline Books* were not open to public inspection, but were consulted only by those in charge of them, at the special command of the Senate. Whether they contained predictions, or merely directions for propitiating the gods, is difficult to determine, in consequence of the mystery that enveloped them. They were destroyed by the burning of the temple in 82 B.C.; but a fresh collection was made and deposited in the same building, when rebuilt. In 12 B.C., the *Sibylline Books* were transferred by the Emperor Augustus to the Temple of Apollo on the Palatine Hill, where they remained until publicly burned by Stilicho, between 404 and 408 A.D. See *Capitol; Sibyl, Cumæan.*

Sicilian Vespers, Massacre of the. A massacre of the French in Palermo and other parts of Sicily, so named because it commenced at the hour of *vespers* on Easter Monday (March 30th), 1282. It was occasioned by the atrocities committed under the rule of Charles of Anjou of France, who had acquired possession of the island in 1254, to the exclusion of the rightful heir; but its immediate cause was an indignity offered to a Sicilian bride by one Drochet, a Frenchman, who, under pretense of searching her for arms, handled her with great rudeness. He was instantly stabbed by a young Sicilian, and in the tumult that ensued, 200 Frenchmen were slain. In Palermo alone, 8000 French — men, women, and children—were put to the sword; while throughout the island the massacre became general, — not even the churches offering a place of refuge for the wretched fugitives. The insurrection resulted in the overthrow of the French rule, and the transfer of the island to the Spanish.

Sicily. This island derives its name from the *Siculi*, a tribe that settled there in early times.

Sick Man of the East. An appellation conferred upon the Turkish Empire which, in its present moribund state, owes its existence to the Great Powers of Europe. The phrase is derived from the words "Sick Man," applied to Turkey by the Czar Nicholas (1825–1855), in a conversation with Sir George Hamilton Seymour, British

chargé d'affaires, at St. Petersburg, on January 11th, 1854.

"We have on our hands *a sick man,*—a very sick man. It will be a great misfortune if, one of these days, he should slip away from us before the necessary arrangements have been made."—*Conversation of the Czar Nicholas, Recorded in the Blue-Book, 1854.*

Siegfried. A semifabulous personage of superior strength and beauty, who occupies a conspicuous place in various Teutonic legends, and is especially distinguished as the hero of the great German epic, the *Nibelungen-Lied.* See *Nibelungen-Lied.*

"He cannot easily be identified with any historical personage. In an old saga, he is represented as having slain a dreadful dragon, and bathed in its blood, whereby his skin became as hard as horn, except in one spot, where a leaf intervened. But he is most celebrated for having vanquished ancient fabulous royal race of the Nibelungen, and taken away their immense treasures of gold and gems. He woos, and finally wins, the beautiful Chriemhild, but is treacherously slain by the fierce and covetous Hagen, who seeks the treasures of the Nibelungen, and who skillfully draws from Chriemhild the secret of the spot where alone Siegfried is mortal, and fatally plunges a lance between his shoulders in a royal chase. Siegfried is noted for a cape which rendered its wearer invisible, and for a wonderful sword named Balmung. The former he obtained from the dwarf Alberich; the latter he is said to have forged, while yet a boy, at a traitorous smith's in the depths of a primeval forest."—Wheeler's *Dictionary of the Noted Names of Fiction.*

Siena Cathedral. A Gothic cathedral of rare beauty, at Siena, Italy, commenced in 1059, and consecrated in 1179. It occupies the site of an ancient temple of Minerva, and consists only of a transept of a much larger design, which was never completed. See *Pulpit of Siena.*

"The art treasures of the interior embrace the wonderful octagonal pulpit by Niccolo Pisano (1268), similar to the one at Pisa; the marble mosaic floor of the cathedral from designs by Buoninsegna and Beccafumi; the series of frescoes commemorative of the life of Pope Pius II., by Pinturicchio, in the Piccolomini Library, where also are preserved several choir books splendidly illuminated by Siennese artists; the celebrated font (1428) with bas-reliefs by Donatello, Della Quercia, and other sculptors, in the church of San Giovanni, situated beneath the cathedral."—*Chambers's Encyclopædia*.

Sign-Manual, Royal. A term applied, in England, to the personal signature of the monarch, which must be affixed to all writs that have to pass either the Great Seal or the Privy Seal. In general, the initial letter only of the sovereign's name is used, —followed by R, (*Lat. Rex* or *Regina*). A fac-simile of the royal signature is used when the sovereign is so ill as to be unable to write, and this is sometimes applied to deeds of minor importance.

Sîk. A chasm, or ravine, two miles in length, forming the principal means of approach to the city of Petra, in northern Arabia. It varies in width from 10 to 30 feet, and is flanked by walls of sandstone rising to a height of more than 100 feet.

"We proceed farther into the cleft, which becomes more and more narrow, and at length see an arch of a great gate, of the Roman style, which spans it. This is succeeded by niches, tablets with inscriptions, which have suffered from the atmosphere, and tombs on each side. The walls of the glen reach to such a height that the sun can scarcely penetrate. Ivy hangs down from the ridges, and fig-trees spread their branches over it. At length it is light, the glen expands, and the rosy façade of a high, magnific building hewn in the opposite rock appears, called by the people El Kasneh Faraoon, *i. e.*, the treasury of Pharaoh."— Harper's *Hand-Book to Europe and the East*.

Silent City.

(1) An appellation conferred upon Amyclæ, a town of Latium, said to have been settled by colonists from the more ancient city of the same name in Laconia. It was so called, either on account of the silence enjoined upon the inhabitants by its Lacedæmonian founders, or because of a law prohibiting anyone of its citizens to announce the approach of an enemy. This decree—enacted to prevent the spread of false rumors, ultimately caused the ruin of the city.

(2) A name given to Venice, Italy, which, owing to the absence of horses and vehicles, presents a marked contrast to the noise and din of commercial cities. See *Amyclæan Silence*.

Silhouette. The name given to the outline (generally in profile) of an object, filled in with black, such as a shadow appears to be. It derives its name from Étienne de Silhouette(1709– 1767), French minister-of-finance in 1759.

"His [Silhouette's] extreme parsimony in all matters of finance was caricatured on all sides, and any cheap mode or fashion was sarcastically called by his name. About that time these profiles were produced by projecting, by means of the light of a candle, the shadow of a face, which was traced while the sitter was in position. These, because they were cheap, were called in ridicule of the Minister, 'Silhouettes', and the name has been retained ever since."— Edwards's *Words, Facts, and Phrases*.

Silly Billy.

(1) A nickname conferred upon William IV (1830–1837) of England.

(2) An epithet bestowed upon William Frederick (1776–1834), Duke of Gloucester, nephew of George III of England, on account of his feebleness of mind.

"It is said that William, duke of Gloucester was shown one day over an asylum, and one of the inmates said, 'Why, here is *Silly Billy!*' The duke, in amazement, said to the keeper, 'The man knows me!' 'Yes,' said the keeper, 'like all lunatics, he has his lucid intervals.'"—Brewer's *Historic Note-Book*.

Silly Duke. A nickname given to John Churchill (1650–1722), Duke of Marlborough, in allusion to his peculiar habit of answering all questions that met with his disapproval with the words, "Oh, silly! silly!"

Silver Age. According to Hesiod and other Greek poets, one of the five ages into which the history of mankind was divided. It was governed by Jupiter, and was characterized by godlessness and voluptuousness. During this period the change of seasons first occurred, as well as the allotment and cultivation of the soil. The Silver Age was preceded by the Golden, and followed by the Brazen Age. See *Ages, Mythologic.*

Silver Grays. A term applied to the conservative branch of the Whig party in the State of New York. They were firm supporters of Fillmore's administration, and at a convention held at Syracuse on September 27th, 1850, they sought a vindication of the President's policy. Owing, however, to the hostility manifested against the policy of the administration, the chairman, Mr. Granger, and several others at once withdrew; and as they were men somewhat advanced in years, they received the appellation of "Silver Grays."

Silver-Tongued.

(1) Henry Smith (1550–1600), the noted preacher.

(2) Joshua Sylvester (1563–1618), translator of Du Bartas's *Divine Weeks and Works.*

(3) William Bates (1625–1699), the distinguished Puritan divine.

(4) Anthony Hammond (1668–1738), the poet.

(5) Spranger Barry (1719–1777), the "Irish Roscius."

(6) Heneage Finch, Earl of Nottingham.

Simeon Stylites. See *Pillar-Saints.*

Simon Pure. A character in Mrs. Centlivre's comedy, *A Bold Stroke for a Wife.* He is a young Pennsylvania Quaker who, while on a visit to England to attend the quarterly meeting of the sect, falls in love with Anne Lovely, a charming heiress, and, after being counterfeited by an impostor, succeeds in establishing his identity, and proving himself to be the real Simon Pure.

The expression is used colloquially to denote the "real person" or the "genuine article."

Simple Simon. A credulous, unsophisticated person,—the subject of an early tale of unknown authorship.

"We do not know whether it is necessary to seek for a Teutonic or Northern original for this once popular book." — *Quarterly Review.*

Simplon Road. A famous military road over the Simplon Pass, between Switzerland and Italy. It was built in 1800–1806, by order of Napoleon I, and cost $3,600,000. It is from 25 to 30 feet wide, and has nowhere a grade greater than one foot in thirteen. The Simplon is about 38 miles long : it is carried across more than 600 bridges, and passes through several long tunnels and over numerous galleries,—either cut out of the solid rock or built of masonry. From 30,000 to 40,000 workmen were employed on this road at one time. It has 20 stations for the shelter of travelers,—the principal one of which, near the summit, is known as the New Hospice. This was founded by Napoleon, but was not opened until 1825. See *Mont Cenis Road.*

"In the plenitude of his [Napoleon's] resources, every obstacle seemed to vanish. 'There shall be no Alps,' he said ; and he built his perfect roads, climbing by graded galleries their steepest precipices, until Italy was as open to Paris as any town in France." —Emerson's *Representative Men (Article "Napoleon").*

Simplon Tunnel. A railway tunnel now in course of construction through the Simplon,—the contract for which was signed in September, 1893. The estimated cost is placed at about $16,-000,000, and the time required is 8½ years. See *Mont Cenis Tunnel; St. Gotthard Tunnel.*

"About one thousand men are now engaged in excavating the *Simplon Tunnel* which will give France and Switzerland direct communication with Milan. The work is being pushed forward night and day, and there is every prospect of the tunnel being completed within the four and a half years still remaining on the contract. The work will differ from the Mont Cenis and St. Gotthard tunnels, as they comprise two tunnels, one for each line of track. The tunnel are fifty-eight feet apart, and are connected every 260 feet by cross-cuttings. The present contract, however, only provides for the completion of one tunnel. The excavations are now proceeding at both the Swiss and the Italian ends. The tunnel will be altogether twelve and one-half miles long, or one-fourth more than the length of the St. Gotthard, and nearly half more than the length of the Mont Cenis. The heat in the excavations is becoming somewhat troublesome."—*Engineering*.

Sinaitic Codex. A Greek uncial manuscript, containing part of the *Septuagint Version of the Old Testament* and all of the *New*,—together with portions of the Apocryphal writings—discovered by Tischendorf, the famous biblical scholar, in 1844 and 1859, in the Convent of St. Catherine, at the foot of Mount Sinai. It probably belongs to the 4th century, although many authorities assign it to the 6th. The *Sinaitic Codex* was secured for the Emperor Alexander II, as the patron of the Greek Church, and was deposited in the Imperial Public Library at St. Petersburg. See *Alexandrian Codex ; Ephraem Codex ; St. Catherine Convent ; Vatican Codex.*

Sindbad the Sailor. A merchant of Bagdad, whose marvellous adventures are related in the *Arabian Night's Entertainments*. He made seven voyages,— each filled with experiences transcending belief, — and finally settled in his native city, where he dwelt in great elegance and luxury. See *Old Man of the Sea.*

Single-Speech Hamilton. A nickname conferred upon William Gerard Hamilton (1729–1796), member of parliament, whose maiden speech, delivered on November 13th, 1755, was received with great applause, and produced an extraordinary sensation. According to Waller, " he broke out, like the Irish rebellion, threescore thousand strong, when nobody was aware, or in the least suspected it."

" It was supposed that he had exhausted himself in that one speech, and had become physically incapable of making a second;

so that afterwards, when he really did make a second, everybody was naturally disgusted, and most people dropped his acquaintance." —*De Quincey.*

Single Tax. A theory of taxation promulgated by Henry George (1839–1897), in 1887. It asserts that public revenue should be obtained by taxing land only, irrespective of the improvements upon it. According to George, this should be the only tax levied.

Sinner's Friend. A sobriquet conferred upon Father Mathew (1790–1856), the noted temperance advocate, on account of the sympathy manifested by him for the outcast and degraded. See *Apostle of Temperance.*

Sinon. A crafty Greek who, by his artful representations, induced the Trojans to admit the famous " Wooden Horse " within the walls of their city, and thus accomplished its ruin. In Dante's *Inferno*, Sinon, in company with Potiphar's wife and other choice spirits, is placed in the tenth pit, or chasm, of Malêbolgê. See *Horse, Wooden.*

Si Quis Door. A door in the north aisle of St. Paul's Church, London, so called from the ancient custom of affixing to it posters beginning with the words : " Si quis invenerit " (*Lat.,* " *If any one has found* ").

Sirens. In classic mythology, two, or sometimes three, beautiful sea-nymphs that allured voyagers by their melodious singing, and then destroyed them. Homer places them on an island near the southwestern coast of Italy ; but, according to the Roman poets, they dwelt on the Campanian coast. Ulysses escaped destruction at the hands of the Sirens by stuffing his companions' ears with wax, and tying himself to the mast of his vessel until he could no longer hear their song. When the Argonauts sailed past the abode of the Sirens, Orpheus surpassed them in singing ; whereupon, the maidens cast themselves into the sea and were transformed into rocks,—it having been decreed that they should live only until someone should prove superior to their fascinations. Their names are usually given as Parthenope, Ligia, and Leucosia.

Sirocco. See *Auster.*

Sister of Shakespeare. A title conferred upon Joanna Baillie (1762–1851), the distinguished British poet and dramatist, in allusion to the remarkable insight into human nature manifested in her plays,—several of which were acted by Kean, Kemble, and Mrs. Siddons. Among her more famous dramas may be mentioned *The Family Legend, De Montfort,* and *Basil.* Sir Walter Scott, in his introduction to the third canto of *Marmion,* pays the following tribute to her genius:

" Restore the ancient tragic line,
  And emulate the notes that rung
From the wild harp, which silent hung
By silver Avon's holy shore,
Till twice an hundred years rolled o'er ;
When she, the bold Enchantress, came,
With fearless hand and heart on flame !
From the pale willow snatched the treasure,
  And swept it with a kindred measure,
Till Avon's swans, while rung the grove
With Montfort's hate and Basil's love,
Awakening at the inspired strain
Dreamed their own Shakespeare lived again."

Sistine Chapel. A famous chapel in the palace of the Vatican at Rome, —134 feet long by 44 feet wide—erected by Pope Sixtus IV (1471–1484) in 1473, and designed for religious services during Holy Week. The ceiling is covered with frescoes by Michael Angelo and the great Florentine masters, representing scenes from the *Old Testament;* while the walls are adorned with paintings, depicting events in the lives of Moses and Christ. The wall above the altar is occupied by Angelo's sublime fresco of the *Last Judgment,* filling a space 60 feet high and 30 feet broad. This great work was designed by Michael Angelo, when in his 60th year, and required eight years for its completion. The colors, however, have been so much impaired by the dust and incense of three and a half centuries that little of the original beauty remains.

Sistine Madonna. See *Madonna di San Sisto.*

Siva. In Hindu mythology, the third god of the " Trimúrti," or Trinity, wherein he figures as the destroyer, or avenger, of the universe. As a deity, he is unknown in the *Vedic Hymns ;* but is celebrated as such in the *Purânas* and *Tantras.* He possesses five heads, and four eyes,—one of which is in his forehead and indicates his power of contemplation. Siva wears a crescent in the centre of his forehead. See *Brahma ; Vishnu.*

Six Months' War. A name sometimes given to the Franco-Prussian War of 1870–1871, which lasted from July 28th, 1870,—when Napoleon III left St. Cloud to join the army,—until January 28th, 1871,—when Paris surrendered to the Prussians.

Six Nations. A confederation of Indian tribes, formerly inhabiting the central and western part of New York State. As early as the beginning of the 17th century, the Mohawks, Oneidas, Senecas, Cayugas, and Onondagas had formed a league, known as the *Five Nations ;* but in 1712 they were joined by the Tuscaroras, a related tribe from North Carolina, and were thenceforth known as the *Six Nations.* In 1783, the Mohawks and Cayugas migrated to Canada, and the confederacy was dissolved. The total number of the " Six Nations " probably never exceeded 25,000.

Sixteen Memorable Battles. The following list of memorable battles of the world is taken from *Everybody's Pocket Cyclopædia.* Eight of the decisive battles enumerated by Professor E. S. Creasy are found in this list, which is as follows :

(1) Marathon (490 B.C.).
(2) Thermopylæ (480 B.C.).
(3) Philippi (42 B.C.).
(4) Châlons (451 A.D.).
(5) Tours (732 A.D.).
(6) Hastings (1066 A.D.).
(7) Bannockburn (1314 A.D.).
(8) Lützen (1632 A.D.).
(9) Spanish Armada (1588 A.D.).
(10) Worcester (1651 A.D.).
(11) Quebec (1759 A.D.).
(12) Saratoga (1777 A.D.).
(13) Valmy (1792 A.D.).
(14) Trafalgar (1805 A.D.).
(15) Waterloo (1815 A.D.).
(16) Sedan (1870 A.D.).

See *Fifteen Decisive Battles.*

Skinners. A name given, during the Revolutionary War, to bands of American marauders that infested the territory — known as neutral ground —extending along the east bank of the Hudson River for a distance of about 40 miles north of New York City. See *Cowboys.*

"In the zeal of service both [cowboys and *skinners*] were apt to make blunders, and confounded the property of friend and foe. Neither of them, in the heat and hurry of a foray, had time to ascertain the politics of a horse or cow which they were driving off into captivity, nor when they wrung the neck of a rooster did they trouble their heads whether he crowed for Congress or King George."—*Washington Irving.*

Skulls at Banquets. "Plutarch tells us that towards the close of an Egyptian feast a servant brought in a skeleton, and cried to the guests, ' Eat, drink, and be merry, for to-morrow you die!' "—*Brewer's Reader's Handbook.* See " *Remember Thou Art a Man!* "

"Like skulls at Memphian banquets."
Don Juan, iii, lxv.

Slave Coast. A portion of Guinea, on the west coat of Africa, famous for the slave trade, which flourished there in former times. It extends eastward from the Gold Coast to the Benin River, and is under the protection of Great Britain, France, Germany, and

Dahomey. See *Gold Coast; Ivory Coast.*

Slave Ship. A famous painting by J. M. W. Turner (1775–1851), the English artist,— now in the Boston Museum of Fine Arts.

"I believe, if I were reduced to rest Turner's immortality upon any single work, I should choose the *Slave Ship.*"—*Ruskin.*

"The following opinion, expressed by an intelligent and accomplished American artist, Mr. George Inness, is interesting for its frankness : 'Turner's "*Slave Ship*" is the most infernal piece of clap-trap ever painted. There is nothing in it. It has as much to do with human affections and thought as a ghost. It is not even a fine bouquet of color. The color is harsh, disagreeable, and discordant.' This is severe, and I think its severity is partly due to reaction against Mr. Ruskin's eloquent praises."—*Philip Gilbert Hamerton.*

Sleave-Silk. A term applied to raw, untwisted silk, as used for weaving.

"*Sleave* is unwrought silk, sometimes also called *floss* silk. It appears to be the coarse ravelled part separated by passing through the stay of the weaver's loom ; and hence called *sleaved* or *sleided* silk. In *Troilus and Cressida*, act v, sc. 1, we have,—' Thou idle immaterial skein of *sleave* silk.' And in Drayton's *Muses' Elysium :* ' Grass as soft as sleave or sarcenet ever was.'"—Hudson's *Shakespeare.*

"Sleep, that knits up the ravell'd *sleave* of care. . . ."
Macbeth, ii, 2.

Sleeping Beauty in the Wood. A French nursery-tale by Charles Perrault (1628–1703), in his *Contes des Fées.* It relates the adventures of a lovely young princess, who is shut up in an enchanted castle, where she sleeps for 100 years,—at the end of which time she is rescued by a gallant young prince, who eventually marries her. During the sleep of the princess, the castle is gradually surrounded by an impenetrable wood, but this opens of its own accord to admit the prince, on his arrival. This legend is thought to be derived from the old Norse tale of *Brynhild and Sigurd.* It has been rendered into German by Grimm, and introduced by Tennyson into his poem of the *Day Dream.* See *Klaus, Peter ; Rip Van Winkle.*

Sleepy Hollow. A charming valley, near Tarrytown, New York, through which flows the Pocantico River. It owes its fame to Washington Irving, who has celebrated its charms in his *Legend of Sleepy Hollow*, one of the tales in the *Sketch-Book.*

"Not far from this village, perhaps about three miles, there is a little valley or rather lap of land among high hills, which is one of the quietest places in the whole world. A small brook glides through it, with just murmur enough to lull one to repose ; and the occasional whistle of a quail, or tapping of a woodpecker, is almost the only sound that ever breaks in upon the uniform tranquillity. . . . If ever I should wish for a retreat whither I might steal from the world and its distractions, and dream quietly away the remnant of a troubled life, I know of none more promising than this little valley. From the listless repose of the place, and the peculiar character of its inhabitants, who are descendants of the original Dutch settlers, this sequestered glen has long been known by the name of *Sleepy Hollow*, and its rustic lads are called the Sleepy Hollow Boys throughout all the neighboring country. A drowsy, dreamy influence seems to hang over the land, and to pervade the very atmosphere." — *Legend of Sleepy Hollow* (Irving).

Slough of Despond. In Bunyan's *Pilgrim's Progress*, a miry bog into which Christian fell, while seeking to reach the Wicket Gate. Owing to the burden of sins that he bore upon his back, he was unable to get out ; but was finally extricated by Help, and set upon solid ground.

". . . This miry Slough is such a place as cannot be mended : it is the descent whither the scum and filth that attends conviction for sin doth continually run, and therefore it is called the *Slough of Despond ;* for still as the sinner is awakened about his lost condition, there arise in his soul many fears and doubts, and discouraging apprehensions, which all of them get together, and settle in this place ; and this is the reason of the badness of this ground."—*Pilgrim's Progress.*

Small Beer. Weak beer, or beer of an inferior quality. The phrase is used figuratively to denote a trifling affair or an unimportant person.

Smallest Church. An odd-looking church in the village of St. Lawrence, Isle of Wight, which, until recent years, was considered the smallest church in the world. It was 25 feet long, 11 feet broad, and about 7 feet high, and had sittings for 12 persons. Some years ago it received an addition in the form of a recess-chancel ; and can, in consequence, no longer be called the smallest church in existence. It dates back to Saxon times, and was doubtless built as a family chapel, or chantry.

" Smell of the Lamp, They." A contemptuous saying, which, according to Plutarch, was uttered by Pytheas, the Athenian orator, when referring to the orations of Demosthenes as labored productions. The allusion is to the story that Demosthenes secluded himself for months in a subterranean cavern, lighted by a single lamp, and there devoted himself unremittingly to study. The expression is used at the present day to denote productions lacking in life and spontaneity.

Smithsonian Institution. A handsome red-sandstone structure in Washington, D. C., erected in 1847–1866, at a cost of $450,000. The institution was founded in 1829, with the proceeds of a legacy of $535,000 bequeathed by an Englishman, Mr. James Smithson (1754–1829), as " an establishment for the increase and diffusion of knowledge among men." It contains a library of 150,000 volumes, and a valuable museum of natural history, besides extensive metallurgical, mineralogical, and ethnological collections. The Smithsonian fund in the United States Treasury is $703,000, the interest of which is applied to the furtherance of original scientific research. The grounds attached to the Smithsonian Institution, comprising about 52 acres, were laid out by A. J. Downing, the famous landscape-gardener.

"So far as is known, Mr. Smithson, who was distinguished as a chemist, never visited America, and had no personal relations with that country ; and his choice of Washington for the establishment of his institution is supposed to be due to his sympathy with the democratic principles represented by the Western Republic."—Baedeker's *United States*.

Smoky City. A name popularly given to the city of Pittsburg, Pennsylvania, on account of the dense pall of smoke, occasioned by the use of bituminous coal, that constantly hangs over the manufacturing portion of the town. This unfortunate state of affairs was greatly remedied by the introduction of natural gas for manufacturing purposes, in 1886 ; but the supply is gradually giving out, and the price asked (10 to 15 cents per 1000 cubic feet) is too high for the rolling-mills, which are reverting to the use of coal. See *Iron City*.

Smolensko, Battle of. A sanguinary battle, during the Russian campaign, between the French commanded by Napoleon I and the Russians under Barclay de Tolly and Prince Bagration. It was fought at Smolensko, a town on the Dnieper, 244 miles southwest of Moscow, on August 16th–17th, 1812, and terminated in favor of Napoleon. After three vain attempts and fearful loss of life, the French finally captured the city, but found it in flames,—having been set on fire by the Russians, who had retired in good order. Barclay de Tolly, the Russian commander-in-chief, by his retreat after the battle, incurred the displeasure of the Czar Alexander I, and was superseded by Kutusoff, on August 17th, 1812.

Sneezing. "The custom of saying 'God bless you' to the sneezer originated, according to Strada, among the ancients, who, through an opinion of the danger attending it, after sneezing made a short prayer to the gods, as

'Jupiter, help me.' The custom is mentioned by Homer, the Jewish rabbis, and others, and is found among savages. Polydore Vergil says it took its rise at the time of the plague, 558, when the infected fell down sneezing, though seemingly in good health."— Haydn's *Dictionary of Dates*.

"The custom of formally invoking a divine blessing on one who has just sneezed is of venerable antiquity, and is very widely spread, but its real significance is by no means so easy to determine. Rabbinical legends connect it with Jacob, but it is not possible to give any fuller answer to Pliny's question, 'Cur sternumentis salutamus?' than to say that it expresses respect to a divine intimation or to a natural sign of mortality. The most famous historical sneeze is that which was hailed as a good omen by Xenophon's ten thousand at a moment of despair."—*Chambers's Encyclopædia*.

Snow King.

(1) A nickname given in derision to Gustavus Adolphus (1611–1632), King of Sweden, by the Viennese, who declared that " he was kept together by the cold, but would melt and disappear as he approached a warmer soil."

(2) An epithet conferred upon Frederick V, Elector Palatine, who was chosen King of Bohemia by the Protestants of that country, in the autumn of 1619, but was defeated at the battle of Prague on November 8th, 1620, and deposed soon afterwards.

Snow Queen.

(1) A title conferred upon Christina (1633–1654), Queen of Sweden.

(2) An appellation bestowed upon Elizabeth of England, wife of Frederick V, Elector Palatine and King of Bohemia. See *Snow King* (2).

Soapy Sam. A nickname conferred upon Samuel Wilberforce (1805–1873), Bishop of Oxford and Winchester, which, according to Lord Houghton, originated in the following manner. The students of Cuddesdon College, desiring, on a certain occasion, to honor not only Wilberforce, but also their principal, Alfred Pott, placed on one of the pillars of the college chapel the letters S. O. (Samuel, Oxford, the bishop's see), and on another the letters A. P. The word S. O. A. P., thus formed, was at once taken up in a satiric spirit, and the combination that resulted was immediately applied to Wilberforce, and clung to him through life.

"It is said that a little girl once asked him [Wilberforce] in the presence of company, 'Why does every one call you *Soapy Sam?*' to which he replied, after a glance around the room, 'I will tell you, my darling. People call me "*Soapy Sam*" because I'm always in hot water and always come out with my hands clean.'"—Walsh's *Literary Curiosities.*

Social War. A war between Rome and her Italian allies (*Lat., socii*), caused by the struggles of the latter to obtain the rights of citizenship (from which they had been wholly excluded), as well as a share of the conquests they had helped to achieve. The contest lasted three years (91–89 B.C.), when Rome prudently terminated it by granting the privileges of citizenship to all such as should return to their allegiance. The Social War caused the destruction of 300,000 men.

Society Islands. This group of islands received its name from Captain Cook, the famous navigator, in honor of the Royal Society of England.

Socinians. The followers of Lælius Socinus (1525–1562), and Faustus (1539–1604), his nephew, whose doctrines — promulgated in 1560 — anticipated many of the theories of modern rationalism and Unitarianism. The Socinians spread rapidly through Poland, and for upwards of a century flourished there; but in 1658, by a decree of the Diet of Warsaw, they were expelled from the country. In 1661, this severe edict was reissued, and caused their complete extirpation. The Socinians denied the existence of the Trinity; the fall of man; the atonement of Christ; original sin; the resurrection of the body; the doctrine of eternal punishment; the personality of the devil; predestination; and justification by faith. These doctrines are also denied by the Unitarians of to-day. See *Unitarians.*

Sociology. A term first used by Auguste Comte (1798–1857), in his *Philosophie Positive,* to denote the science that treats of man in his social relations. See *Positivism.*

"The methods of modern *sociology* are . . . especially identified with the work of Herbert Spencer, who makes the science a series of generalisations on the correspondences and contrasts between individual organisms and communities or societies as social organisms, with their structures and functions, their periods of growth and decay. The forms of government—civil, ecclesiastical, military, industrial, ceremonial —are the structures of communities; sentiments, ideas, industrial processes, fine arts, may be regarded as functions."—*Chambers's Encyclopædia.*

Sock. A light shoe — reaching to the ankle—worn by the comic actors of ancient Greece and Rome. The word has become symbolic of comedy, and is frequently so used. See *Buskin.*

"Then to the well-trod stage anon,
If Jonson's learned *sock* be on."
Milton's *L'Allegro.*

Socratic Method. A dialectic method of reaching conclusions, by means of question and answer, adopted by Socrates in his teachings and disputations. By this device, he not only forced his disciples to think for themselves and thus to avoid error; but also, while himself professing ignorance, caused his adversaries unconsciously to make certain damaging admissions that led to a refutation of their doctrines.

Sodom, Vine of. The vine of Sodom, mentioned in *Deuteronomy* xxxii, 32, is probably a colocynth (*Lat., Citrullus colocynthis*), growing near the Dead Sea. The passage referred to is generally supposed to allude to the famous "apples of Sodom" mentioned by Strabo, Tacitus, and

Josephus. See *Apples of Sodom ; Dead-Sea Fruit.*

"It [Sodom] was of old a happy land, both in respect of its fruits and the abundance of its cities ; but now it is all burned up. Men say that, on account of the wickedness of its inhabitants, it was destroyed by lightning. At any rate, there are still to be seen remains of the divine fire and traces of fine cities ; and, moreover, ashes produced in the fruits, which indeed resemble edible fruit in color, but, on being plucked by the hand, are dissolved into smoke and ashes."—*Josephus.*

"For their vine is of the *vine of Sodom,* and of the field of Gomorrah : their grapes are grapes of gall, their clusters are bitter."—*Deuteronomy* xxxii, 32.

Soft Money. A term colloquially used in the United States of America since 1876, to denote paper money, or greenbacks, as distinguished from hard money, or gold and silver. The "Independent National" party — nick-named the "Soft Money" party—was organized in 1876. It contended for an unlimited issue of paper money, and the payment of the national debt in greenbacks instead of coin.

Softshell Baptists. A term used in the southern part of the United States to denote Baptists holding liberal views, as distinguished from Hardshell Baptists, who are rigid and narrow in theology, and oppose the formation of missionary societies, Sunday-schools, and similar institutions, as not sanctioned by Scripture. See *Hardshell Baptists.*

Softshell Democrats. The name given to the anti-slavery faction in the Democratic party in New York State from 1848 to 1854,—the pro-slavery faction being known as the "Hardshells." They were composed of the remnants of the Van Buren and Adams party of 1848. See *Hardshell Democrats.*

Soldiers' Home. An asylum for old and disabled soldiers of the regular army of the United States, situated in the environs of Washington, D. C.,

45

three miles north of the Capitol. It was founded in 1851, and its cost defrayed by a forced levy made on the inhabitants of the City of Mexico by General Scott, during his occupation of that place. The "Home" is maintained by a monthly tax of twelve cents imposed on each soldier of the regular army, for whose use it is reserved. The buildings—which are of marble, in the Norman style—shelter 600 inmates, and are surrounded by a beautiful park of 500 acres,—affording fine views. Presidents Pierce, Buchanan, and Lincoln occupied one of the smaller buildings of the "Home" during the summer months of their respective terms of office.

Soldiers' Wind. In nautical parlance, a light, favorable wind, or one that serves either way.

Solferino, Battle of. A battle fought at Solferino, a village in northern Italy, 19 miles northwest of Mantua, on June 24th, 1859, between 150,000 French and Sardinians commanded by Napoleon III and Victor Emmanuel, and about 170,000 Austrians under General Hess. The latter were defeated with a loss of 19,311 men and 630 officers ; while the allied loss amounted to 17,305 men killed and wounded, 936 officers, and 8 generals. This victory ended the war for the liberation of Italy, and was followed by preliminaries of peace, signed at Villafranca on July 12th, 1859. See *Villafranca, Peace of.*

Solid South. A phrase used to denote the unity of political action manifested by the Southern States of the American Union, in their loyal and unwavering support of the Democratic party. The expression first came into vogue in 1868; but, according to some authorities, did not make its appearance until the presidential campaign of 1876. The Republican politicians and journals point to this state of things as evidence of a continuance of the spirit of hostility to the Union that led to the Civil War. This political unity in the South has shown signs of disintegration in recent years. Of the sixteen States that constitute the Solid South, four — Kentucky, West Virginia, Maryland, and Delaware — were carried by the Republicans in 1896.

Solomon of England.

(1) A title conferred upon James I (1603–1625) of England by his friends and admiring courtiers.

"He was, indeed, made up of two men, a witty, well-read scholar, who wrote, disputed, and harangued, and a nervous, driveling idiot, who acted."—*Macaulay*.

(2) An epithet bestowed upon Henry VII (1485–1509) of England, whose pacific reign proved favorable to the industrial development of the nation. See *British Solomon ; Scottish Solomon*.

Solomon of France.

(1) An appellation conferred upon Louis IX (1226–1270) of France, who, by his earnest efforts, greatly promoted the advancement, happiness, and true greatness of his kingdom. Voltaire has said of him that " it is not given to man to carry virtue to a higher point."

(2) A title bestowed upon Charles V (1364–1380) of France, surnamed " The Wise." He was a generous and enlightened patron of letters and the arts, and may be regarded as the founder of the Bibliothèque Nationale of Paris, which, at his death, consisted of nearly 1000 volumes,—an extensive collection for that age. See *Bibliothèque Nationale*.

Solomon's Temple.

A famous temple at Jerusalem, founded by Solomon (1015–975 B.C.) in 1010 B.C., and consecrated by him in 1003 B.C. It occupied the summit of Mount Moriah, and measured 80 cubits in length, 40 cubits in width, and 30 cubits in height;—having, in addition, a porch 120 cubits high. The temple proper comprised the Holy of Holies, the Sanctuary, and the Porch, and was surrounded by spacious courts and chambers, which formed the larger part of the sacred enclosure. Within the Holy of Holies was placed the sacred Ark of the Covenant,—a chest, or coffer, in which were deposited the Tables of the Law, etc. The Sanctuary was separated from this inner apartment by an impervious veil, and contained the table of showbread, ten candlesticks of gold, and other articles of furniture. The temple was constructed entirely of white stone; while the walls and ceiling of the interior were wainscoted with cedar, and richly ornamented with gold. Solomon's Temple was repeatedly plundered by foreign invaders, and was finally burned by Nebuzaradan, Nebuchadnezzar's general, in 588 B.C. See *Herod's Temple ; Mount Moriah ; Mosque of Omar ; Tabernacle; Zerubbabel's Temple*.

Solon's Happiness.

A phrase sometimes used to signify death,—in allusion to Solon's maxim : " Count no man happy till he is dead."

" But safer triumph is this funeral pomp,
That hath aspir'd to *Solon's happiness*,
And triumphs over chance in honour's bed."
                              Titus Andronicus, i, 2.

Solon's Laws.

A code of written laws drawn up by Solon (638–558 B.C.), the Athenian lawgiver and archon, in 594 B.C., to replace those of Draco, which had become odious to the people of Athens, on account of their extreme severity. See *Draco's Laws*.

"The *laws of Solon* were inscribed on wooden rollers and triangular tablets, and were preserved first in the Acropolis, and afterwards in the Prytaneum or Town-hall. They were very numerous, and contained regulations on almost all subjects connected with the public and private life of the citizens. But they do not seem to have been arranged in any systematic manner ; and such small fragments have come down to us, that it is impossible to give any general view of them."—Smith's *History of Greece*.

Songs of the Civil War.

The following list of popular songs of the

American Civil War (1861–1865) is taken from Harper's *Book of Facts.*

(1) Battle Cry of Freedom.—*Geo. F. Root.*

"Yes, we 'll rally round the flag, boys."

(2) Battle Flag of the Republic.—*O. W. Holmes.*

"Flag of the heroes who left us their glory."

(3) Battle Hymn of the Republic.— *Julia Ward Howe.*

"Mine eyes have seen the glory of the coming of the Lord."

(4) The Blue and the Gray.—*Francis M. Finch.*

"By the flow of the inland river."

(5) Brave Boys are They.—*Henry C. Work.*

"Brave boys are they, gone at their country's call."

(6) Dixie (Southern).—*Albert Pike.*

"Southrons, hear your country call you."

(7) Dixie (Northern).—*T. M. Cooley.*

"Away down South where grows the cotton."

(8) John Brown's Body.

"John Brown's body lies a-mould'ring in the grave."

(9) Just before the Battle, Mother. —*Geo. F. Root.*

"Just before the battle, mother, I am thinking most of you."

(10) Marching through Georgia.— *Henry C. Work.*

"Bring the good old bugle, boys ; we 'll sing another song."

(11) Maryland, my Maryland (Southern).—*Jos. R. Randall.*

"The despot's heel is on thy shore, Maryland, my Maryland."

(12) O Wrap the Flag around me, Boys.—*R. Stewart Taylor.*

(13) Tramp, Tramp, Tramp.—*Geo. F. Root.*

"In the prison cell I sit."

(14) When John Comes Marching Home.—*Louis Lambert.*

(15) When this Cruel War Is over. —*Charles C. Sawyer.*

"Dearest love, do you remember?"

Son of Jupiter Ammon. A title conferred upon Alexander the Great (336–323 B.C.) by the priests of the Libyan temple of Jupiter Ammon,— the oracle of which had declared Alexander to be the son of Jove, and the destined ruler of the world.

"After marching along the coast for about two hundred miles, Alexander struck to the south-east into the desert ; when a five days' journey over pathless sands and under a scorching sun brought him to the well-watered and richly-wooded valley, containing the renowned and ancient temple of Ammon. The conqueror was received by the priests with all the honors of sacred pomp. He consulted the oracle in secret, and is said never to have disclosed the answer which he received; though that it was an answer that contented him appeared from the magnificence of the offerings which he made to the god. Some say that Ammon saluted him as the son of Jove."—*Smith's History of Greece.*

Son of Man. A title assumed by Jesus Christ, and the one by which, with few exceptions, he referred to himself. Theologians are divided as to the precise meaning of this term ; but, according to the generally accepted opinion, it denotes Christ's true humanity, or oneness with the human race.

"Jesus, on the one side, includes himself among other men—he is one of our race ; while, on the other, he thereby exalts himself above the whole race besides, as in a truly exclusive sense the Son of mankind, its genuine Offspring—the one Man towards whom the whole history of the human race was tending, in whom it found its unity, and in whom history finds its turning-point, as the close of the old and the commencement of the new æra."—*Luthardt.*

Son of the Last Man. An appellation given, during the Commonwealth, to Charles Stuart, son of Charles I (1625–1649) of England. He was thus designated in an offer of reward for his apprehension, issued by Parliament. See *Last Man.*

"Son of St. Louis, Ascend to Heaven !" These words are generally believed to have been addressed to Louis XVI (1774–1789) by his confessor, the Abbé Edgeworth, almost at the instant the knife fell that severed that ill-fated monarch's head from his body. The Abbé always denied that he was the author of this expression, and it is now known that it was invented for him by the editor of *Le Républicain Français*.

Sons of Israel. The sons of Jacob — surnamed Israel — were twelve in number. Their names were as follows: Reuben, Simeon, Levi, Judah, Dan, Naphthali, Gad, Asher, Issachar, Zebulun, Joseph, and Benjamin. See *Israel, Twelve Tribes of.*

Sons of Thunder. See *Boanerges.*

Sophists. A body of teachers in ancient Athens, during the 4th and 5th centuries B.C., who gave instruction in any or all of the higher branches of learning. Although they were not a philosophic sect, and held no doctrines in common, the Sophists were, nevertheless, skeptics, and maintained a belief in the uncertainty of all particular knowledge, and, in fact, in the impossibility of all truth. Their two leading representatives were Protagoras and Gorgias. The Sophists were charged with bringing reasoning into contempt by casting uncertainty over the most obvious truths; and, in consequence, were ridiculed and denounced by Aristophanes, Socrates, and Plato. Aristotle defined a Sophist as " a man who makes money by sham wisdom."

Sorbonne. A famous college of the mediæval University of Paris, founded in 1253 by Robert de Sorbon, chaplain and confessor of Louis IX (1226–1270), and devoted exclusively to the study of theology. As an institution of learning, it enjoyed a European reputation from the 14th to the 17th century; but, with the revival of learning, its influence gradually declined. The Sorbonne was suppressed in 1790, and its property confiscated ; but, in 1808, it was reorganized by Napoleon I (1804–1814), and became the seat of the " Académie de France ", and, subse-

quently (1816–1821), of the faculties of science, theology, and literature. In 1884–1889, new buildings were erected at a cost of $4,400,000. They contain lecture-rooms, several fine collections, and a theatre,—seating 3000 persons. The institution is attended by more than 10,000 students. In the chapel of the Sorbonne may be seen the tomb of Richelieu, designed by Lebrun, and executed by Girardon in 1694.

Sorrows of Young Werther. The title of a famous sentimental romance by Johann Wolfgang Goethe, the illustrious German poet. It appeared in 1774, and by its means the author first acquired a European reputation. Napoleon Bonaparte is said to have read the *Sorrows of Young Werther* through several times, during the Egyptian campaign of 1798–1799.

" *Werther* is but the cry of that dim-rooted pain under which all thoughtful men of a certain age were languishing : it paints the misery, it passionately utters the complaint ; and heart and voice, all over Europe, loudly and at once respond to it. True, it prescribes no remedy ; for that was a far different, far harder enterprise, to which other years and a higher culture were required ; but even this utterance of pain, even this little, for the present, is grasped at, and with eager sympathy appropriated in every bosom."—*Thomas Carlyle.*

Sou Marquée. A phrase used in the United States of America to denote anything of little or no value. It is probably derived from the French *sou marqué*, an old copper coin worth 15 deniers.

"An old copper coin known as the *sou*, crossed or marked, thereby rendering it of little or no value as currency. 'I would not give a *sou-marquée* for a thing,' means that the article in question is not worth a *marked sou;* that is, good for nothing, worthless."—Bartlett's *Dictionary of Americanisms.*

South Kensington Museum. A national collection of objects of science and art, in London, England, first opened to the public in 1857.

"The institution comprises (1) the Art Museum, (2) the India Museum, (3) various science collections. . . . The art collections comprise original works of decorative art of all periods and countries; paintings, chiefly of the English school, but including the cartoons of Raphael, the property of the crown; and reproductions in plaster, metal, etc., of sculpture, architectural decoration, and silversmiths' work. These have been acquired by purchase, gift, and loan. The cost to the nation has been about £400,000, while the value of the gifts and bequests is estimated at one million sterling. The India Museum, originally belonging to the East India Company, was handed over to the department in 1879. The science collections include machinery, naval models, etc., and apparatus for scientific teaching and research. The museum also contains art and science libraries."—*Chambers's Encyclopædia.*

South Sea Bubble. A scheme devised by Harley, Earl of Oxford, in 1711, for the purpose of restoring the national credit of England and extinguishing the floating national debt which, at that time, amounted to £10,-000,000. To accomplish this, the *South Sea Company* was organized, and agreed to assume the national debt of England and to advance the sum of £7,500,000 to the Government, in return for an annual payment of £600,000 (guaranteed for a certain period), and an exclusive monopoly of the South Sea trade. The price of the Company's stock rose steadily until 1720, when £100 shares were quoted at 1000; but the bubble soon after burst, and involved thousands in ruin. See *Mississippi Scheme.*

South Sea House. A building in Threadneedle Street, London, formerly occupied by the famous *South Sea Company,*—organized in 1711. It is now used for office purposes. See *South Sea Bubble.*

Spanish Armada. See *Armada, Invincible.*

Spanish Brutus. A sobriquet bestowed upon Alphonso Perez de Guzman (1258-1320), a famous Spanish general.

Spanish Epic Poem. An appellation sometimes conferred upon the *Chronicle of the Cid.* See *Cid, Chronicle of the.*

Spanish Grandees. The name given to the higher nobility of Spain —dating from the 13th century—who, at one time, enjoyed almost royal privileges. They held their honors by inheritance, were exempt from taxation, and could leave the kingdom and even enter the service of a foreign prince at war with Spain, without incurring the penalties of treason. In addition, they had the right to remain covered in the presence of the sovereign, and could not be summoned before any civil or criminal tribunal without a special warrant from the King. In national assemblies, the Grandees took precedence of the titled nobility. Ferdinand and Isabella greatly curtailed their peculiar privileges; and Charles V limited their number to sixteen families, and reduced them to a dependent condition. Their dignities and prerogatives were totally abolished by Joseph Bonaparte; but these were partially restored by Ferdinand VII, on his accession to the throne.

Spanish Main (*i. e., mainland*). A name popularly given by English voyagers, during the 16th and 17th centuries, to the north coast of South America, between the Orinoco River and the Isthmus of Darien, and also to the Spanish provinces of Central America bordering on the Caribbean Sea. The expression "Spanish Main" is also used to denote the Caribbean Sea itself, especially in connection with the buccaneers, who infested those waters. See *Buccaneers.*

" Formerly, that portion of the Caribbean Sea, adjacent to the northeast coast of South America, inclusive of the route traversed by Spanish merchant ships in traveling between the eastern and western hemispheres."—*Standard Dictionary.*

Spartacus's Insurrection. A term frequently applied to the revolt of Roman slaves — known also as the Gladiators', or Servile, War—because led by Spartacus, a Thracian captive and gladiator. See *Gladiators' War*.

Spartan Broth. A phrase used to denote simple fare. The allusion is to the black broth of the ancient Spartans, which formed one of their chief articles of diet.

" Meat was only eaten occasionally ; and one of the principal dishes was black broth. Of what it consisted we do not know. The tyrant Dionysius found it very unpalatable; but, as the cook told him, the broth was nothing without the seasoning of fatigue and hunger."—Smith's *History of Greece*.

Spasmodic School. A term applied to certain English poets of the 19th century, whose writings are characterized by extravagance of sentiment and expression, and abound in " spasmodic and forced conceits." Among these may be mentioned Philip James Bailey, Sydney Dobell, and Alexander Smith. They were cleverly burlesqued by Professor Aytoun, in his *Firmilian, a Spasmodic Tragedy* (1854).

Speak by the Card, To. A phrase meaning to speak precisely, or from exact knowledge. The allusion is to the " card," or chart, by which the mariner directs his course.

" And the very ports they blow,
All the quarters that they know
I' the shipman's card."
Macbeth, i, 3.

" How absolute the knave is! we must *speak by the card*, or equivocation will undo us."—*Hamlet*, v, 1.

Spectator. An English periodical, to which Joseph Addison and Sir Richard Steele were the principal contributors. It first appeared on March 1st, 1711; was discontinued in December of the same year ; and revived in 1714. In all, 635 numbers were issued,—274 of which were the work of Addison, and 240 of Steele. Addison's contributions to the *Spectator* are generally considered to be the finest specimens of essay-writing to be found in the English language, and are referred to by critics as models of style.

" The plan of the *Spectator* must be allowed to be both original and eminently happy. Every valuable essay in the series may be read with pleasure separately ; yet the five or six hundred essays form a whole, which has the interest of a novel. It must be remembered, too, that at that time no novel giving a lively and powerful picture of the common life and manners of England had appeared. Richardson was working as a compositor ; Fielding was robbing birds' nests ; Smollett was not yet born."—*Macaulay*.

Spectre of the Brocken. See *Brocken, Spectre of the*.

Spectroscope. An optical instrument used for forming and analyzing the spectra produced by the luminous vapors of bodies. It consists of a colliminating lense, a prism, and an observing telescope. The spectroscope, in its present form, was invented by the German chemists, Kirchhoff and Bunsen, about 1859.

Speed of Birds. The following interesting set of facts concerning the power and speed of birds is taken from Conklin's *Vest Pocket Argument Settler :*

" The vulture is said to fly at times at the rate of above 100 miles an hour.
The wild goose and the swallow, in their migrations, make 90 miles an hour.
The power exerted by the eagle in full flight is but a fraction of one horse power.
The common crow ordinarily lounges across country at the rate of 25 miles an hour, the speed of a railway train.
The carrier pigeon has flown long distances at rates of speed ranging from 60 up to 80 miles an hour, and for many hours together.
The power exerted by a pigeon flying is 2,200 feet per minute, 25 miles an hour nearly, at 1.20 of a horse power per pound, or 9¼ horse power for a flying machine of equally good form, weighing one ton, at 25 miles an hour, or about 50 horse power per ton weight at 50 miles.
The pelican has an expenditure of 1.11 horse power by 21 pounds of bird, and this is one horse power to 231 pounds, or about a horse power for the weight of a man, allowing ample margin for surplus power. The birds are found to have a surplus lifting power of about one-half."

Spellbinders. A term humorously applied to the Republican political orators during the presidential campaign of 1888. The expression is said to have been first used by William C. Goodloe, a member of the Republican National Committee, on observing that, in their reports to that body, the campaign speakers almost invariably spoke of having held their audiences " spellbound " with wonder and delight. The name was afterwards used by the *New York Sun* and other newspapers in referring to those Republican magnates that held a jollification at Delmonico's in the autumn of 1888, shortly after the election of Benjamin Harrison.

Spelling Reform. See *Phonetic Spelling*.

Sphinx, Great. A colossal statue —having the body of a lion and the head of a man—lying partially buried in the sand, about a quarter of a mile southeast of the Great Pyramid of Egypt. It measures 172 feet 6 inches in length by 56 feet in height, and is hewn out of the living rock, to which some masonry has been added to complete the shape. In 1816, Caviglia discovered, between the paws of the Sphinx, a small temple — formed of three hieroglyphic tablets,—dedicated to it by Thothmes III (1600 B.C.) and Rameses II (1322 B.C.). Its age has always been in doubt, but excavations made by Mariette in 1852, prove it to be older than the Great Pyramid. According to Maspero, it is older than the time of Menes, whose date, as given by Mariette, is 5004 B.C.

" I confess to strange, almost superstitious feelings as I halted before the *Sphinx*, and gazed upward on this silent and mighty monument. A huge form rising sixty feet from the ground, one hundred and forty feet long, and the head more than a hundred feet round, with mutilated but yet apparent human features, looking out toward the fertile land and the Nile. It suddenly impressed me as if it were indeed the divinity of ancient Egypt. The Arabs of the present day call it Aboolhôl, 'the Father of Terror' or immensity. An ignorant people might be easily tempted to regard it with reverence and fear."—Prime's *Travels in Europe and the East.*

Sphinx, Riddle of the. A famous riddle of antiquity propounded by the Sphinx, a fabulous monster, which appeared near Thebes in Bœotia, and destroyed every one that failed to solve the question. It ran as follows : " What being has four feet, two feet, and three feet ; only one voice ; but whose feet vary, and when it has most, is weakest ? " The oracle having asserted that the Sphinx would destroy herself as soon as the riddle was solved, —the people of Thebes, in their terror, declared that whoever should resolve this enigma and thus deliver the land from the monster, should be made king and receive Jocaste, the daughter of Menœceus, for his wife. Œdipus finally appeared, and accomplished the feat by declaring that the being in question was man, who, in infancy crawls upon all fours ; in manhood, stands erect upon two feet; and in old age, supports his tottering legs with a staff. Whereupon, the Sphinx, enraged at the solution of the riddle, threw herself headlong from the rock on which she sat, and perished.

Sphygmograph. An instrument for measuring and recording the force and extent of arterial pulsations. It was invented by Vierodt, and perfected by Marey of Paris, in 1863.

Spies of the Czar. An appellation bestowed, in recent years, upon the Cossacks of Russia, who have rendered great service to the Emperor in holding the Nihilists in check. See *Cossacks.*

Spilling Salt. See *Salt, Spilling of.*

Spinster. This name, originally applied to any unmarried woman of gentle birth, was given in accordance with the Anglo-Saxon custom, which required that every young female should herself *spin* a complete set of body-, bed-, and table-linen before entering the married state.

Spontaneous Combustion of the Human Body.

The spontaneous combustion of the human body is declared by most chemists to be an impossibility, although as many as 30 instances, resulting in death, have been recorded. Among these, the most famous are the case of Mme. Millet at Rheims in 1725, and that of a man found on fire in bed in 1847.

"Some of the alleged cases have been traced to wilful burning after murder ; some are plainly incredible ; the remainder, with the exception of the 1847 case, which remains unexplained, can all be traced to the destruction of the bodies of intoxicated brandy-drinkers, near an open fire in winter, with no one present, and no evidence forthcoming as to the time occupied in the combustion, or as to the circumstances, other than intoxication, preceding the combustion. Liebig discusses the subject in his *Letters on Chemistry*, and concludes that, while a fat, dead body charged with alcohol may perhaps burn, a living body, in which the blood is circulating, cannot take fire under any circumstances."—*Chambers's Encyclopædia*.

"The possibility of what is called *Spontaneous Combustion* has been denied since the death of Mr. Krook ; and my good friend Mr. Lewes . . . published some ingenious letters to me at the time when that event was chronicled, arguing that *Spontaneous Combustion* could not possibly be. I have no need to observe that I do not wilfully or negligently mislead my readers, and that before I wrote that description I took pains to investigate the subject. There are about thirty cases on record, of which the most famous, that of the Countess Cornelia de Bandi Cesenate, was minutely investigated and described by Giuseppe Bianchini, a prebendary of Verona, otherwise distinguished in letters, who published an account of it at Verona, in 1731, which he afterwards republished at Rome. The appearances beyond all rational doubt observed in that case, are the appearances observed in Mr. Krook's case. The next most famous instance happened at Rheims, six years earlier ; and the historian in that case is Le Cat, one of the most renowned surgeons of France. The subject was a woman, whose husband was ignorantly convicted of having murdered her ; but, on solemn appeal to a higher court, he was acquitted, because it was shown upon evidence that she had died

the death to which this name of *Spontaneous Combustion* is given."—Dickens's *Bleak House* (Preface).

Spontaneous Generation. See *Abiogenesis*.

Sporades (*Gr., σπείρω, to scatter*).

A group of *scattered* islands, about twelve in number, lying in the Ægean Sea, off the island of Crete and the west coast of Asia Minor. They were so called, in opposition to the Cyclades, which lie in a circle around the island of Delos. See *Cyclades*.

S. P. Q. R.

These letters, which were inscribed on the military standards of the Roman Empire, are the initials of the words *Senatus Populusque Romanus* (*Lat., The Roman Senate and People*).

Sprat Day.

A nickname given in England to the 9th of November, when sprats are first allowed to be sold.

Spy-Wednesday.

An old name for the Wednesday of Holy Week, so called from the treachery of Judas Iscariot who, on that day, bargained with the chief-priests for the betrayal of his Master.

Squaring the Circle.

A mathematical problem, which consists in finding a square equal in area to a circle of given radius. Its solution depends upon ascertaining the precise ratio between the diameter of a circle and its circumference, — a problem which mathematicians long ago demonstrated to be impossible of solution. The " quadrature of the circle " is one of the most famous problems of history, and has probably been the subject of more discussion than any other within the range of mathematical science.

"The area of the circle being equal to a rectangle described upon the radius and half of the circumference, it follows that the quadrature would be possible if an algebraic expression, with a finite number of terms, could be found for the length of the circumference. Hence, the problem is reduced to finding such an expression, or to finding an exact expression in algebraic terms for the ratio of the diameter to the circumference. No such expression has yet been found, and it is by no means probable that such an expression will ever be found. The problem may safely be pronounced impossible, and all attempts at the solution of the quadrature of the circle have long been abandoned by every one having the least pretension to mathematical knowledge. It is true, pretenders to the discovery of the quadrature of the circle occasionally present themselves, but they are confined to the list of what may be called mathematical quacks, and their reasoning, when intelligible, is always based upon some absurd hypothesis, or involves some mathematical absurdity easily pointed out by any one having even a smattering of geometry. Long since the learned societies of Europe have refused to examine any paper pretending to a discovery of the quadrature of the circle, classing it with the problems for the geometrical tri-section of an angle, the duplication of the cube, etc., all of which are now regarded as beyond the power of exact geometrical construction."— Davies and Peck's *Dictionary of Mathematics.*

Squatter Sovereignty. A nickname derisively applied by John C. Calhoun (1782–1850) to the doctrine of popular sovereignty in the United States. The phrase was much used by Stephen A. Douglas, who claimed to have coined it; but Charles Sumner declared that the saying was older than the Ohio statesman, and might be found in *Paradise Lost*, where the poet says that Satan was found, "*squat* like a toad, close at the ear of Eve, . . .*" See *Popular Sovereignty.*

Stabat Mater Dolorosa (*Lat., Full of Sorrow Stood the Mother*). A famous mediæval hymn, setting forth the sorrows of the Virgin Mary at the Cross. It contains ten stanzas, the first of which is as follows :

" Stabat mater dolorosa,
   Juxta crucem lacrymosa,
     Dum pendebat filius.
   Cujus animam gementem,
   Contristatam et dolentem,
     Pertransivit gladius."

The *Stabat Mater Dolorosa* is generally supposed to have been written by Jacobus de Benedictis in 1261 ; although some authorities ascribe it to Pope Innocent III (1198–1216), but without any proof. It has been set to music by Rossini, Palestrina, Astorga, Pergolese, Haydn, and others ; and is sung in the service of the Roman Catholic Church during Passion Week. The best translation of the hymn is undoubtedly that of Dr. Abraham Coles of Newark, New Jersey. Its full name is the *Stabat Mater Dolorosa ;* but it is frequently called the *Mater Dolorosa*, to distinguish it from the *Stabat Mater Speciosa,—* a hymn setting forth the joys of the Virgin Mary at the manger. The latter production is commonly ascribed to Jacobus de Benedictis — the author of the *Stabat Mater Dolorosa*, although Drs. Schaff and Coles regard it as the work of some admiring imitator. See *Dies Iræ.*

" The *Stabat Mater*, with the *Dies Iræ*, possesses the power of imparting a shadowy impression of its meaning by the melody of its verse. Its soft, sad cadence echoes the feeling of its pathetic words. In fame it ranks next to the *Dies Iræ*, yet is neither so simple nor so grand ; nor does it rise, like the Great Hymn, above sectarian faults. It has attracted the same great admiration, and been praised and repeated by the same great admirers, but always in a lesser degree. As the *Dies Iræ* has been pronounced the greatest, so the *Stabat Mater* is universally deemed the most pathetic, of hymns."—*Seven Great Hymns of the Mediæval Church.*

Stabat Mater Speciosa (*Lat., Full of Beauty Stood the Mother*). See *Stabat Mater Dolorosa.*

Stagirite. A surname conferred upon Aristotle (384–322 B.C.), the illustrious Greek philosopher, in allusion to Stagira in Thrace, the place of his birth.

"There, in a shrine, that cast a dazzling light,
Sat, fixed in thought, the mighty *Stagirite.*"
                    Pope's *Temple of Fame.*

Stalwarts. A term originally applied to those Republicans — led by Senators Conkling, Cameron, and

Logan — that opposed President Hayes's policy of conciliation towards the South ; and later (1880), given to that wing of the party that favored the nomination of General Grant for a third term. After the inauguration of Garfield in 1881, the Stalwarts in New York State — led by Conkling and Platt — bitterly opposed the administration ; and, in the quarrel that ensued, these senators resigned their seats in Congress, and sought for a vindication of their course through a re-election by the Legislature, but were unsuccessful. The death of Garfield and the succession of Arthur, a Stalwart, to the presidency, tended to heal the breach, but it was not until ex-Senator Platt obtained control of the party machinery in the State that peace was restored between the factions. See *Half-Breeds*.

Stambol. The Turkish name of Constantinople. It is specifically applied to that portion of the city—Constantinople proper — that lies south of the Golden Horn, as distinguished from Christian Constantinople, lying on the north side. Stambol occupies the site of ancient Byzantium, and contains the Mosque of St. Sophia, the Seraglio, and almost all the monuments and antiquities to be seen in the city. Christian Constantinople is preeminently a commercial quarter. Written also *Istambol*.

"The Turks call it Istambol or *Stambol*, which they pretend is a corruption of Islambol ('Islam abounding'), a name which was formerly engraved upon the coinage in lieu of Kustantîniya, the Arabic form of Constantinopolis. European writers have fancifully derived Istambol from the Greek expression εἰς τήν πόλιν, 'up to town,' but a more probable derivation makes it simply a Turkish mispronunciation of Constantinopolis."—*Chambers's Encyclopœdia*.

Standard Time. "Primarily, for the convenience of the railroads, a standard of time was established by mutual agreement in 1883, by which trains are run and local time regulated. According to this system, the United States, extending from 65° to 125° west longitude, is divided into four time sections, each of 15° of longitude, exactly equivalent to one hour, commencing with the 75th meridian. The first (eastern) section includes all territory between the Atlantic coast and an irregular line drawn from Detroit to Charleston, S. C., the latter being its most southern point. The second (central) section includes all the territory between the last-named line and an irregular line from Bismarck, N. D., to the mouth of the Rio Grande. The third (mountain) section includes all territory between the last-named line and nearly the western borders of Idaho, Utah, and Arizona. The fourth (Pacific) section covers the rest of the country to the Pacific coast. Standard time is uniform inside each of these sections, and the time of each section differs from that next to it by exactly one hour. Thus at 12 noon in New York City (eastern time), the time at Chicago (central time) is 11 o'clock A.M.; at Denver (mountain time), 10 o'clock A.M., and at San Francisco (Pacific time), 9 o'clock A.M. Standard time is 16 minutes slower at Boston than true local time, 4 minutes slower at New York, 8 minutes faster at Washington, 19 minutes faster at Charleston, 28 minutes slower at Detroit, 18 minutes faster at Kansas City, 10 minutes slower at Chicago, 1 minute faster at St. Louis, 28 minutes faster at Salt Lake City, and 10 minutes faster at San Francisco."—*World Almanac*.

Standing-Fishes Bible. A name sometimes given to a version of the Bible, printed in 1806, in allusion to a typographical error in *Ezekiel* xlvii, 10, where the word *fishers* is rendered *fishes*.

"And it shall come to pass, that the *fishes* shall stand upon it, from Engedi even unto Eneglaim ; . . . ."

Stanhope. A light two-wheeled, or sometimes four-wheeled, vehicle, without a top,—named in honor of

Lord Stanhope, for whom it was first constructed.

Stanze of Raphael. The name given to four apartments in the palace of the Vatican at Rome, adorned with frescoes by Raphael (1483 – 1520). These rooms are known, respectively, as the *Sala di Constantino ;* the *Sala d'Eliodoro ;* the *Camera della Segnatura ;* and the *Stanza of the Incendio del Borgo.*

"The frescoes here contained were the chief occupation of Raphael during the last ten or twelve years of his life. To these he dedicated the maturity of his powers and the ripened fulness of his mind. Whatever he had learned by practice, by observation, by a study of nature and the works of others, by a perception of his own defects, and by the immortal development of his genius, is here stamped in immortal lines and colors. These frescoes form the perfection of painting. It has soared to no loftier heights, and gained no more brilliant or enduring victories. The interval between the hard outlines, stiff attitudes, and somewhat languid beauty of Raphael's earliest works, and the ease, freedom, breadth, fulness, and variety of these frescoes, is amazing ; and shows that his industry and self-vigilance must have been equal to his genius."—Hillard's *Six Months in Italy.*

Star Chamber. A tribunal, consisting of a committee of the King's Privy Council, instituted, or revived, by Henry VII (1485–1509) in 1486. It had extensive powers and held itself unfettered by rules of law, dealt with civil and criminal cases by bill and information, without the intervention of a jury, and could inflict any form of punishment short of death. It was abolished by Act of Parliament in 1641, during the reign of Charles I (1625–1649). The court is said to have derived its name, either from the gilt *stars* that adorned the ceiling of the chamber in the Old Palace at Westminster, where it held its sessions; or, as is more probable, from the Jewish bonds (*starrs*), deposited there by permission of William I (1066–1087). See *Privy Council.*

"It is well known that before the banishment of the Jews under Edward I., their con-

tracts and obligations were denominated . . . starra or starrs, from a corruption of the Hebrew word shetar, a covenant. . . . The room at the exchequer where the chests containing these starrs were kept, was probably called the *starr - chamber.*"—Blackstone's *Commentaries.*

Star in the East. A miraculous star which, according to *Matthew* ii, 2-10, appeared in the East, and guided the " Wise Men " to the infant Jesus at Bethlehem.

" Some writers, following Kepler, attempt to identify the star of the Magi with a conjunction of Jupiter and Saturn, which took place three times in A. U. C. 747. This view is adopted by Ideler and Wieseler, who, however, deduce from it different conclusions as to the year of our Lord's birth. But it has recently been shown, that the appearance presented by this conjunction would by no means answer the conditions required by St. Matthew's description. The natural interpretation of the text clearly implies a supernatural appearance of a meteoric character, and not a star in the ordinary sense of the term."—*Bible Commentary.*

Star Nearest the Earth. See *Nearest Fixed Star.*

Star of India. An order of knighthood instituted in 1861, as a means of conferring honor upon eminent natives of India and also upon Englishmen that have distinguished themselves in the administration of that country. It was enlarged in 1866 and 1878 ; and consists, at the present time, of the Sovereign, a Grand Master (the reigning Viceroy), and three classes of members,— Knights Grand Commanders, Knights Commanders, and Companions.

Star of South Africa Diamond. The name originally given to the Dudley Diamond. See *Dudley Diamond.*

Star of the North. A title conferred upon Gustavus Adolphus (1611–1632) of Sweden by the Protestants of Germany, during the " Thirty Years' War." See *Lion of the North.*

" Gustavus was incontestably the first commander of his century, and the bravest soldier in the army which he had created. His eye watched over the morals of his soldiers as strictly as over their bravery."—*Schiller.*

Star of the South Diamond.

A noted diamond, discovered by a poor negress in Brazil in 1853. It originally weighed 254½ carats ; but, after being cut, its weight was reduced to 125 carats.

Star of the West.

A United States Government vessel which, on January 9th, 1861, was fired upon by the Confederates in Charleston Harbor, while attempting to convey men and supplies to Fort Sumter.

"The *Star of the West* was a steamer sent with fifty recruits and supplies to Major Anderson at Fort Sumter. It left New York on the night of January 5th, 1861, and reached Charleston Harbor on the ninth. It was fired at from sand batteries at the entrance of the harbor, and was struck once or twice, and being a merchant vessel, it was unable to return the fire. It was forced to put to sea without effecting its mission."— Gilman's *History of the American People.*

Star Routes.

A name given to those postal routes, in the United States of America, that are indicated by three asterisks (* * *) in the official publications of the Post-Office Department. They are highways on which contracts for mail-transportation are made upon bids that do not specify the mode of conveyance, but simply agree to carry the mails with care and expedition. The term "Star Routes" is often popularly used to denote those mail routes through sparsely settled regions, where the expense of the service greatly exceeds the revenue derived from it.

Stars and Bars.

A name applied to the flag of the late Southern Confederacy. It consisted of a field of three bars—red, white, and red—and a blue union with as many white stars as States. See *Stars and Stripes.*

" Our Southern boys are brave and true, and
    are joining heart and hand,
And are flocking to the *Stars and Bars*, as
    they are floating o'er our land ;

And all are standing ready with their rifles
    in their hand,
And invite the North to open graves down
    South in Dixie's land."
                    Confederate Song.

Stars and Stripes.

A name given to the flag of the United States of America, which consists of a field of thirteen stripes — alternately red and white—and a blue union containing as many white stars as States. See *Flag, United States ; Stars and Bars.*

Stars, Number of.

The number of stars is infinite. According to Flammarion, the total number visible to the naked eye—which includes the stars of the first six magnitudes — is about 7000 : excellent sight, however, distinguishes 8000, and average sight about 5700. The most powerful telescopes reveal stars of the fifteenth magnitude, which are supposed to number 56,000,000.

The following list, taken from Flammarion's *Popular Astronomy,* gives the number of *visible stars,* classified according to magnitude :

19	stars of the first				magnitude.
59	"	"	"	second	"
182	"	"	"	third	"
530	"	"	"	fourth	"
1,600	"	"	"	fifth	"
4,800	"	"	"	sixth	"
13,000	"	"	"	seventh	"
40,000	"	"	"	eighth	"
100,000	"	"	"	ninth	"
400,000	"	"	"	tenth	"
1,000,000	"	"	"	eleventh	"
3,000,000	"	"	"	twelfth	"
10,000,000	"	"	"	thirteenth	"
30,000,000	"	"	"	fourteenth	"
56,000,000	"	"	"	fifteenth	"

100,560,190

Stars of the First Magnitude.

The following list of stars of the first magnitude, in the order of their decreasing brightness, is taken from Flammarion's *Popular Astronomy.*

(1) Sirius.
(2) Canopus.
(3) Alpha Centauri.
(4) Arcturus.
(5) Vega.

(6) Rigel.
(7) Capella.
(8) Procyon.
(9) Betelguese.
(10) Beta Centauri.
(11) Achernar.
(12) Aldebaran.
(13) Antares.
(14) Alpha Crucis.
(15) Altair.
(16) Spica.
(17) Fomalhaut.
(18) Beta Crucis.
(19) Regulus.

Star-Spangled Banner. The national anthem of the United States of America,—composed by Francis Scott Key (1779–1843), while watching the unsuccessful bombardment of Fort McHenry, near Baltimore, by the British on the night of September 13th, 1814.

"The cartel-ship *Minden* was anchored in sight of fort McHenry, and from her deck Key saw, during the night of 13 Sept., 1814, the bombardment of that fortress. It was during the excitement of this attack, and while pacing the deck of the *Minden* with intense anxiety between midnight and dawn, that Key composed the song. It was first written on the back of a letter, and after his return to Baltimore copied out in full."—Harper's *Book of Facts.*

Starvation Dundas. A nickname conferred upon Henry Dundas (1740–1811), afterwards Lord Melville, in consequence of his frequent use of the word "starvation" in the course of a debate on American affairs in the British Parliament, in 1775.

State Flowers. The following are the names of the "State Flowers," chosen, in most instances, by the public school scholars of 21 States and Territories of the American Union :

(1) Alabama, *Golden Rod.*
(2) Arkansas, *Aster.*
(3) California, *California Poppy.*
(4) Colorado, *Columbine.*
(5) Delaware, *Peach Blossom.*
(6) Idaho, *Syringa.*
(7) Iowa, *Wild Rose.*
(8) Maine, *Pine Cone and Tassel.*

(9) Michigan, *Apple Blossom.*
(10) Minnesota, *Cypripedium or Moccasin-flower.*
(11) Missouri, *Golden Rod.*
(12) Montana, *Bitter Root.*
(13) Nebraska, *Golden Rod.*
(14) New Jersey, State tree, *Sugar Maple.*
(15) New York, *Rose;* State tree, *Maple.*
(16) North Dakota, *Golden Rod.*
(17) Oklahoma Territory, *Mistletoe.*
(18) Oregon, *Oregon Grape.*
(19) Rhode Island, *Violet;* State tree, *Maple.*
(20) Vermont, *Red Clover.*
(21) Washington, *Rhododendron.*

States-General.

(1) An ancient representative assembly of France, composed of the three Orders of the Kingdom,— the Nobility, the Clergy, and the Commons. It had no legislative power, and no right of redressing grievances, save by petition ; its one important function being the imposition of taxes. The States-General was first convened by Philip IV (1284–1314) in 1302, to consider certain exactions of the Pope; and again by Charles VI (1380–1422), Charles VII (1422–1461), and Louis XIII (1610–1643). It was convoked for the last time by Louis XVI (1774–1789), and assembled at Versailles on May 5th, 1789. Owing to the refusal of the Nobility and Clergy to sit with the Commons, the latter withdrew, formed the National Assembly, and proceeded to deliberate upon state affairs without reference to the other Orders. They were soon after joined by the Nobles and Clergy, at the command of the King ; but the States-General had ceased to exist.

(2) The States-General of the United Provinces of the Netherlands was a legislative body, consisting originally of five members, but subsequently increased to seven. It ceased to exist in 1795, when the French entered Holland and established the Batavian Republic. The law-making body of

the present kingdom of Holland is called the States-General. See *National Assembly of France.*

States of the Church. See *Church, States of the.*

State Rights. A doctrine based upon the theory that sovereignty ultimately resides not in the people of the United States, but in the people of the several States composing the Union. It declares that the powers exercised by the General Government are delegated to it by the States, and that all its acts must be ratified by the independent, sovereign commonwealths from which it derives its authority. It further asserts the right of any State, not only to *nullify* any act of Congress that may seem to be in excess of its authority, but even to secede from the Union. The doctrine of State Rights has played an important part in the history of the United States, and, although still a subject of controversy, it is generally considered that the right of a State to secede has been negatived by the result of the Civil War. See *Alien and Sedition Laws; Nullification Doctrine.*

Stations of the Cross. The name given in the Roman Catholic Church to a series of fourteen images, or pictures, representing the successive stages of Christ's Passion, or of his journey from the judgment-hall of Pilate to Calvary. They are usually set up in order in the nave of a church, and are successively visited, with meditation and prayer, by the faithful ; such devotion being regarded as a substitute for an actual pilgrimage to the holy places themselves, at Jerusalem.

The following are the fourteen "Stations of the Cross" :

(1) Jesus condemned to death.
(2) Jesus made to bear his cross.
(3) Jesus falling the first time under his cross.
(4) Jesus meeting his afflicted mother.

(5) Jesus assisted by the Cyrenian to bear his cross.
(6) Veronica wiping the face of Jesus.
(7) Jesus falling a second time under his cross.
(8) Jesus speaking to the women of Jerusalem.
(9) Jesus falling a third time under his cross.
(10) Jesus stripped of his garments.
(11) Jesus nailed to the cross.
(12) Jesus dying on the cross.
(13) Jesus taken down from the cross.
(14) Jesus placed in the sepulchre.

Statue of Liberty. See *Bartholdi's Statue.*

Statute of Kilkenny. A stringent enactment passed by the Irish Parliament at Kilkenny in 1367, during the reign of Edward III (1327–1377). It decreed excommunication and heavy penalties against all that should intermarry with the native Irish, or adopt any of their customs.

"It enacted among other things, 'that the alliance of the English by marriage with any Irish, the nurture of infantes, and gossipred with the Irish, be deemed high treason.' And again, 'if anie man of English race use an Irish name, Irish apparell, or anie other guize or fashion of the Irish, his lands shall be seized, and his body imprisoned, till he shall conform to English modes and customs.' Said never to have been enforced."—Haydn's *Dictionary of Dates.*

Staubbach Fall. A noted waterfall in the valley of Lauterbrunnen, Switzerland, about seven miles from Interlaken. It consists of a single fall, 980 feet high,—the water of which is shattered into dust-like spray long before it reaches the base of the cliff. The word "Staubbach" means "dust-stream." See *Giessbach Falls ; Lauterbrunnen.*

Stentor. A Grecian herald in the Trojan War, whose voice was equal to that of fifty men. He is mentioned in

Homer's *Iliad.* Stentorian tones are loud, powerful tones.

Sterling Money. A term applied to the standard money of Great Britain. It is said to be derived from *Easterling*, a name once used in England to denote a trader from the Hanse towns of the Baltic,—famous for the purity of their coinage.

"During the reign of King John the merchants of the Hansa Towns, of which the inhabitants were commonly described as *Esterlings*, because they resided in the eastern portions of Germany, having long been noted for the purity of their coinage, the king invited a number of them over to this country for the purpose of reforming and perfecting our coinage. The invitation was accepted; and ever afterwards good English money received the name of *Esterling* or *sterling* money."—Wagner's *Names and their Meaning.*

"Skeat accepts the old and often doubted etymology that the name is derived from the Hanse merchants or *Easterlings* (*i.e.*, 'man from the east'), who had many privileges in England in the 13th century, including probably that of coining money. The adjective is now used of all the money of the United Kingdom, and has long been a synonym for pure and genuine."—*Chambers's Encyclopædia.*

Stigmata. The name given to marks, corresponding to the wounds inflicted upon Jesus Christ during his Passion, believed to have been miraculously impressed upon certain individuals, as tokens of divine favor. They comprise not only the wounds in the hands and feet, and that in the side produced by the spear-thrust, but also the impressions made by the crown of thorns and by the scourging. Stigmatization is not mentioned prior to the 13th century A.D., and has been almost invariably recorded of persons within the pale of the Roman Catholic Church. The earliest and most remarkable instance is the case of Francis of Assisi (1182–1226), who, in 1224, had a remarkable vision, and, on recovering consciousness, found himself marked with the wounds of the crucifixion in his hands, feet, and right side. These mysterious impressions

are said to have remained with him until his death two years later, and to have been seen by many witnesses. As many as eighty other instances of stigmatization occur in the traditions of the Roman Catholic Church.

"Dr. Imbert Gourbeyre, in his work, *Les Stigmatisées* (1873), enumerates 145 persons, of whom but 20 were men, as having received the stigmata, and of these 80 lived before the 17th century. Apart altogether from the question of the value of the evidence offered, we may reasonably conclude that some kind of stigmatisation is a pathological condition of occasional occurrence, but from this to the assertion that it is a special sign of divine favour is a wide and an unwarrantable leap."—*Chambers's Encyclopædia.*

Stimulants. The following list of stimulants used by noted personages is taken from Brewer's *Reader's Handbook :*

(1) Bonaparte : *snuff.*
(2) Braham : *bottled porter.*
(3) Bull, Rev. William : *tobacco.*
(4) Byron : *gin-and-water.*
(5) Catley, Miss : *linseed tea and madeira.*
(6) Cooke, G. F.: *anything drinkable.*
(7) Disraeli (Beaconsfield) : *champagne jelly.*
(8) Emery : *cold brandy and water.*
(9) Erskine (Lord): *opium.*
(10) Gladstone : *sherry and egg.*
(11) Henderson : *sherry and gum arabic.*
(12) Hobbes: *cold water.*
(13) Incledon : *madeira.*
(14) Jordan, Mrs : *calf's foot jelly dissolved in warm sherry.*
(15) Kean, Edmund : *beef tea, cold brandy.*
(16) Kemble, John Philip : *opium.*
(17) Lewis: *oysters and mulled wine.*
(18) Newton : *tobacco.*
(19) Oxberry : *tea.*
(20) Pope : *coffee.*
(21) Schiller: *coffee and champagne.*
(22) Siddons, Mrs.: *porter.*
(23) Smith, William : *coffee.*
(24) Wedderburne: *blister on chest.*
(25) Wood, Mrs.: *draught porter.*

Stoa Poikile (*Gr., Painted Porch*). A famous porch, or covered colonnade, in ancient Athens, adorned with pictures, by Polygnotus, of the Trojan War, the battle of Marathon, and the Amazons. It had been at one time the resort of the poets, when wishing to recite their productions, and there Zeno established his school of philosophy in 310 B.C., and gathered about him many disciples who, from their place of meeting, became known as *Stoics*. See *Stoics*.

Stoics. A school of ancient Greek philosophers, founded in 310 B.C., by Zeno of Citium [358(?)–260(?)]. They taught that virtue is the highest good, and that it consists in the concordance of individual reason with the Divine Reason. The Stoics are also said to have originated the fourfold division of the affections : (1) desires, (2) fears, (3) pleasures, and (4) pains. They preached temperance, frugality, and abstemiousness ; and further, denied pain to be an evil,—regarding it as a mere temporary inconvenience to the body. They were rigid and austere in morals, and schooled themselves to bear with perfect equanimity any lot that destiny might appoint. For 200 years the Stoic philosophy included among its followers many of the noblest and best men of ancient Rome. See *Stoa Poikile*.

Stoke-Pogis. A village in Buckinghamshire, England, five miles from Windsor, famous for its beautiful churchyard,—the scene of Gray's immortal *Elegy*. The place has changed little since the poet's time. His grave is situated beneath the oriel window of the old church, and in the adjacent Stoke Park—once the property of the descendants of William Penn—may be seen a fine monument to the poet's memory.

Stonehenge. A rude structure of standing stones, situated on Salisbury Plain, England. It consists of two concentric circles, enclosing two ellipses, and is surrounded by an earthen rampart and ditch about 370 yards in circumference. The outer circle was originally formed of 30 pillar - stones — having an average height of 13 feet from the ground : these supported 30 others, placed horizontally upon them. Of these, 17 uprights and 6 imposts retain their original position. The inner circle— situated about 9 feet from the outer one — consisted of 40 stones of smaller size, locally known as "blue stones." Of the two ellipses within this circle, the outer one is formed of five trilithons ; and the inner one of stones varying from 6 to 8 feet high, and placed at intervals of from 5 to 6 feet. The age, origin, and purpose of this structure are unknown ; although innumerable theories have been advanced on these points, in modern days. According to Geoffrey of Monmouth, Stonehenge was erected, at the suggestion of Merlin, by Aurelianus Ambrosius, a British chieftain who lived in the fifth century, in memory of 410 nobles treacherously slain by Hengist the Saxon, about 450 A.D. Vergil Polydore says it was built as a tomb for Aurelianus ; while in the opinion of Dr. Stukely and many others, it is an ancient temple of the Druids. See *Salisbury Plain*.

"It [Stonehenge] has been attributed to the Phœnicians, the Belgae, the Druids, the Saxons, and the Danes. It has been called a temple of the sun, and of serpent worship, a shrine of Buddha, a planetarium, a gigantic gallows on which defeated British leaders were solemnly hung in honour of Woden, a Gilgal where the national army met and leaders were buried, and a calendar in stone for measurement of the solar year. The opinion of Sir John Lubbock, expressed in his *Prehistoric Times*, is that there are satisfactory reasons for assigning it to the bronze age, though apparently it was not all erected at one time, the inner circle of small inwrought 'blue stones' being probably older than the rest. By most archæologists it seems to be accepted as an exceptionable development from the ordinary type of Stone Circles, used as burial-places by the bronze-age people of Britain, though some regard its exceptional development as due rather to a religious influence than to the mere idea of the common commemoration of simple burial. But whatever may have been its origin and purpose, it is sufficiently interesting as the grandest megalithic monument in Britain." — *Chambers's Encyclopædia.*

Stones of Venice. A famous treatise on Venetian architecture by John Ruskin (1819–1900), the art-critic. This work, which appeared in 1851–1853, is exquisitely illustrated by the author from drawings made on the spot. It cost Ruskin years of patient study, and will probably be regarded by future generations as his greatest production.

Stonewall Jackson. A nickname conferred upon the Confederate general, Thomas J. Jackson (1824–1863), during the American Civil War. It is said that this sobriquet arose from a remark made by the Confederate general, Bee, while endeavoring to rally his men at the first battle of Bull Run (July 21st, 1861). "See," he exclaimed, "there is Jackson, standing like a *stone wall!*"

Stony Arabia. See *Arabia Petræa.*

Stout Harry. A nickname bestowed upon Henry VIII (1509–1547) of England, because of his rotundity of person in later life.

"He was just eighteen years of age when he came to the throne. People said he was handsome then, but I don't believe it. He was a big, burly, noisy, small-eyed, large-faced, double-chinned, swinish-looking fellow in later life (as we know from the likeness of him painted by the famous Hans Holbein), and it is not easy to believe that so bad a character can ever have been veiled under a prepossessing appearance."—Dickens's *Child's History of England.*

Strada Nuova (*It., New Street*). A celebrated street in Genoa, Italy, lined with magnificent palaces,—memorials of the ancient wealth and splendor of the city.

"The different uses to which some of these palaces are applied, all at once, is characteristic. For instance, the English Banker (my excellent and hospitable friend) has his office in a good-sized Palazzo in the *Strada Nuova.*"—Dickens's *Pictures from Italy.*

Straightout Democrats. A term applied to those Democrats that disapproved of the nomination of Horace Greeley for President by their party in 1872, and chose Charles O'Conor of New York for their candidate. Mr. O'Conor declined to run, but nevertheless polled about 30,000 votes.

Straight Street. An ancient thoroughfare in Damascus, Syria, extending east and west for about a mile. It is extremely tortuous at the present day, but is said to have been originally a broad, straight avenue. According to *Acts* ix, 11, the house of Judas, where Paul was visited by Ananias, was situated on this street.

"And the Lord said unto him [Ananias], Arise, and go into *the street which is called Straight,* and inquire in the house of Judas for one called Saul, of Tarsus : for, behold, he prayeth."—*Acts* ix, ii.

"It is not *quite* straight now, nor is its architecture peculiarly imposing, yet there cannot be a doubt of its identity. In the Roman age, and down to the time of the Mohammedan conquest, a noble street extended in a straight line from this gate westward through the city."—McClintock and Strong's *Cyclopædia.*

"*The street called Straight* is straighter than a corkscrew, but not as straight as a rainbow. St. Luke is careful not to commit himself; he does not say it is the street which *is* straight, but the 'street which is *called* Straight.' It is a fine piece of irony ; it is the only facetious remark in the Bible, I believe." — *Innocents Abroad* (Mark Twain).

Strand. This London thoroughfare, extending from Charing Cross to Temple Bar, is so called because it follows the shore-line of the Thames, which at one time was much nearer the street than at the present day.

"The *Strand*, one of the historical streets of London, was formerly the waterside road between London and Westminster. Hence its name. Between it and the river lay the palaces of the great nobles, and on the other side the green fields stretched away without

46

a break to the north. The road was bad then, and people who could afford it took boat for the City at Westminster stairs, in preference to picking their way along the ill-paved streets, with the chance of being pushed aside by the numerous lackeys and retainers into the deep holes that abounded in every direction."—Dickens's *Dictionary of London.*

Strasburg Cathedral. A superb specimen of Gothic architecture, ranking next to Cologne among the cathedrals of Germany. It was founded in 1015, on the site of a church built by Clovis (481–511) in 510, but the interior was not completed until 1275. The magnificent western façade—principally the work of Erevin von Steinbach—was commenced in 1277. The cathedral is surmounted by a lofty spire, variously estimated at from 466 to 474 feet in height. Until the completion of the spires of Cologne Cathedral (515 feet), the tower of Strasburg was generally considered to be the tallest in Europe; although that honor was disputed by the cathedrals of Rouen and Vienna. The view from the summit is grand,—comprising the Black Forest, the Vosges Mountains, and the windings of the Rhine. The interior of the church contains a famous astronomical clock, constructed by Schwilgué in 1838–1842, to replace an older one made in 1571. The cathedral was considerably injured during the siege of Strasburg by the Prussians in 1870, but has since been carefully repaired. See *Strasburg Clock.*

Strasburg Clock. A celebrated astronomical clock in the Cathedral of Strasburg, Germany, constructed in 1838–1842 by Schwilgué, a skilled mechanic of the city, to replace an older one—made in 1571—portions of which are contained in the present timepiece. It is situated in the south transept of the cathedral, and includes a planetarium and a perpetual calendar, besides automaton figures of many kinds. At noon of each day, the twelve disciples issue from a chapel-door and move in solemn procession before a

figure of Christ, which inclines its head in benediction as the figures pass by. A cock crows and flaps its wings as Peter emerges from the chapel, while Satan narrowly watches Judas as he moves along. See *Strasburg Cathedral.*

Stratford-on-Avon. A town in Warwickshire, England, famous as the birthplace of William Shakespeare (1564–1616). It contains, in addition to the house in which the poet was born, the following objects of interest :
(1) The site of the house in which Shakespeare died.
(2) The church in which he and Anne Hathaway, his wife, are buried.
(3) Edward VI's Grammar-School, where he was educated.
(4) The Shakespeare Fountain, erected in 1887 by George W. Childs of Philadelphia.
(5) The Shakespeare Memorial Theatre—holding 800 persons—built in 1877–1879, at a cost of £30,000.
At Shottery, about a mile distant from Stratford, may be seen Anne Hathaway's Cottage, purchased for the nation in 1892 for £3000. See *Anne Hathaway's Cottage; Shakespeare's House.*

Strelitzes. Originally the Imperial Guard of Russia, established by Ivan IV (1533–1584), about 1567. They increased rapidly in numbers and became a great and dangerous power in the state ; but were finally disbanded by Peter the Great (1682–1725), after their revolt in 1698. Several thousand were put to death—many of them by the Czar's own hand,—and the rest banished to Astrakhan, where they were exterminated in 1705.

Strength of Ice. " Ice one inch and a half thick will support a man ; four inches thick will support cavalry ; five inches thick will support an eighty-four-pound cannon ; ten inches thick will support a multitude eighteen inches thick will support railroad train."—*Everybody's Pocket Cyclopædia.*

Strongbow. A nickname given to Richard, son of Gilbert de Clare, Earl of Pembroke, in allusion to his great strength and skill in archery.

Stuffed Prophet. An epithet conferred upon Grover Cleveland by the *New York Sun,* during the presidential campaign of 1892, and frequently applied to him by the same newspaper during his second term of office.

Stump Orator. A phrase originally applied in the United States of America to a public speaker that made use of a tree-stump for a rostrum in open-air political meetings.

Stylites. See *Pillar-Saints.*

Styx. In classic mythology, the chief of the five rivers of the nether world,—the other four being Acheron, Cocytus, Lethe, and Phlegethon. Its waters were said to flow, " with slow and sluggish stream," seven times around the lower regions. It was across the Styx that Charon ferried the shades of the departed. The word is from the Greek, and means *hatred.*

"Abhorred *Styx,* the flood of deadly hate ";
—*Paradise Lost,* ii, 577.

Subjection of Women. A famous essay by John Stuart Mill (1806–1873), the distinguished English philosopher, —published in 1869. In this work the author takes the ground " that the principle which regulates the existing social relations between the two sexes —the legal subordination of one sex to the other—is wrong in itself, and now one of the chief hindrances to human improvement, and that it ought to be replaced by a principle of perfect equality."

" His treatise on the *Subjection of Women* is undoubtedly justified as a protest against the legal status of woman in England. But its positive side, the claims which it puts forth in behalf of woman's intellectual and artistic equality with man,

must be regarded as anything but established."—Hart's *Manual of English Literature.*

Sublime and the Beautiful, On the. The name generally given to a famous treatise by Edmund Burke (1730–1797) —published in 1756 — entitled *A Philosophical Inquiry into the Origin of our Ideas of the Sublime and the Beautiful.* It was highly esteemed for the classic purity of its style, and was regarded by Dr. Samuel Johnson as a model of philosophical criticism.

Sublime Porte. A name given by the French to the lofty gateway of the outer court of the Seraglio at Constantinople, at which justice is supposed to be administered. It is adorned with Arabic inscriptions, and guarded by 50 porters. The phrase "Sublime Porte" is frequently used to denote either the Government of the Turkish Empire, the Cabinet, or, in a diplomatic sense, the country itself. The term is applied also to a building in Constantinople containing the offices of four departments of the Turkish Government. See *Seraglio.*

Sub Rosa. " The origin of the phrase *under the rose* implies secrecy, and had its origin during the year B.C. 477, at which time Pausanias, the commander of the confederate fleet of the Spartans and Athenians, was engaged in an intrigue with Xerxes for the subjugation of Greece to the Persian rule, and for the hand of the monarch's daughter in marriage. The negotiations were carried on in a building attached to the temple of Minerva, called the Brazen House, the roof of which was a garden forming a bower of roses ; so that the plot, which was conducted with the utmost secrecy, was literally matured *under the rose.* Pausanias, however, was betrayed by one of his emissaries, who, by a preconcerted plan with the ephori (the overseers and counsellors of state, five in number), gave them a secret opportunity to hear from the lips of Pausanias himself the acknowledgment of his treason. To escape arrest, he fled to the temple of Minerva, and, as the sanctity of the place forbade intrusion for violence or harm of any kind, the people walled up the edifice with stones and left him to die of starvation. His own mother laid the first stone."

"It afterward became a custom among the Athenians to wear roses in the hair whenever they wished to communicate to another a secret which they wished to be kept inviolate. Hence the saying *sub rosa* among them, and, since, among Christian nations." —*Gleanings for the Curious* (Bombaugh).

"*Under the rose* ('sub rosa'). In strict confidence. Cupid gave Harpocrates (the god of silence) a rose, to bribe him not to betray the amours of Venus. Hence the flower became the emblem of silence. It was for this reason sculptured on the ceilings of banquet-rooms, to remind the guests that what was spoken *sub vino* was not to be uttered *sub divo*. In 1526 it was placed over confessionals. The banquet-room ceiling at Haddon Hall is decorated with roses."— Brewer's *Dictionary of Phrase and Fable*.

Sucker State. A name sometimes applied to the State of Illinois, especially by the inhabitants of the other Western States.

"The term *Sucker* as applied to an Illinoisian is attributed to a Missourian, who said to a party of Illinois men going home from the Galena mines: 'You put me in mind of suckers; up in the spring, spawn, and all return in the fall.' The old-time lead-miners always passed their winters at home, returning to Galena in the season when the sucker-fish were running plentifully. Douglas said: When George Rogers Clark's brave little army of Virginians charged into Kaskaskia, they perceived the French citizens sitting on their verandahs and imbibing mint-juleps through straws. In thunder tones the rangers shouted: 'Surrender, you suckers.'"—King's *Handbook of the United States*.

Sudarium (*Lat., handkerchief*). The napkin, or as some authorities say, the head-cloth of St. Veronica, which, according to tradition, was used by her to wipe the bloody sweat from the brow of Christ, while on his way to Calvary; and upon which the Savior imprinted his likeness, in token of his gratitude and love. See *Holy Handkerchief; Veronica.*

Suez Canal. A ship-canal, 92 miles long, piercing the Isthmus of Suez and connecting the Mediterranean and the Red Seas. It was built by a stock company, organized in 1854 by the French engineer, De Lesseps, with a capital of 200,000,000 francs (soon after increased to 300,000,000). Work was commenced in 1859 ; and on November 16th, 1869, the canal was opened, in the presence of the Emperor of Austria, the Empress of the French, the Khedive of Egypt, and others. The total cost of the undertaking is estimated at about $102,750,000. The canal is level throughout, without locks, and is 328 feet wide at the top, 72 feet at the bottom, and 28 feet deep. By means of this waterway, the distance from London to India is reduced from 11,379 miles to 7628 miles.

It is estimated that 3000 vessels pass through the Suez Canal annually,—the time required being about twenty-four hours. Since March 1st, 1887, navigation by night has been permitted to all ships provided with proper electric-lighting apparatus. In 1875, the British Government purchased the Khedive's interest in the canal for about $20,000,000, and now owns the controlling share.

"The time required to make the passage of the *Suez Canal* varies according to the amount of travel encountered, for often your steamer has to tie up for some time. My last trip was made in twenty hours, and I believe that yachts have gone through in twelve hours. The larger and heavier the vessel the slower is the necessary transit on account of the wash of the banks."—*Frank Vincent.*

Suicides. "In European cities the number of suicides per 100,000 inhabitants is as follows : Paris, 42 ; Lyons, 29 ; St. Petersburg, 7 ; Moscow, 11 ; Berlin, 36 ; Vienna, 28 ; London, 23 ; Rome, 8; Milan, 6; Madrid, 3; Genoa 31 ; Brussels, 15 ; Amsterdam, 14 Lisbon, 2; Christiania, 25; Stockholm 27 ; Constantinople, 12 ; Geneva, 11

Dresden, 51. Madrid and Lisbon show the lowest, Dresden the highest figure.

The average annual suicide rate in countries of the world per 100,000 persons living is given by Barker as follows : Saxony, 31.1 ; Denmark, 25.8 ; Schleswig - Holstein, 24.0 ; Austria, 21.2; Switzerland, 20.2; France, 15.7; German Empire, 14.3; Hanover, 14.0; Queensland, 13.5; Prussia, 13.3 ; Victoria, 11.5 ; New South Wales, 9.3 ; Bavaria, 9.1; New Zealand, 9.0; South Australia, 8.9; Sweden, 8.1; Norway, 7.5 ; Belgium, 6.9 ; England and Wales, 6.9; Tasmania, 5.3; Hungary, 5.2; Scotland, 4.0; Italy, 3.7; Netherlands, 3.6 ; United States, 3.5 ; Russia, 2.9; Ireland, 1.7; Spain, 1.4.

The causes of suicide in European countries are reported as follows : Of 100 suicides : Madness, delirium, 18 per cent.; alcoholism, 11; vice, crime, 19; different diseases, 2; moral sufferings, 6 ; family matters, 4 ; poverty, want, 4; loss of intellect, 14; consequence of crimes, 3; unknown reasons, 19.

The number of suicides in the United States, six years, 1882–87, was 8226. Insanity was the principal cause, shooting the favorite method ; 5386 acts of suicide were committed in the day, and 2419 in the night. Summer was the favorite season, June the favorite month, and the 11th the favorite day of the month. The month in which the largest number of suicides occur is July.

The number of suicides in 45 United States cities in the decade 1889–1898 was 16,409. In the principal cities the number was : New York, 3319 ; Chicago, 2937 ; Brooklyn, 1359 ; St. Louis, 1269; Philadelphia, 1165; Boston, 693. The highest rate per 100,-000 of population was St. Louis, 25.6, and the lowest Holyoke, Mass., 3.3. These figures are by Frederick L. Hoffman, in the New York *Spectator* for June 15, 1899."—*World Almanac.*

Sulky. The name given to a light two-wheeled vehicle for one person.

It was so called because, at the time of its introduction, it was asserted that none but *sulky* and selfish people would ride in a vehicle having accommodation for only one person.

Sumatra. This word is a corruption of *Trimatara* (*happy land*).

Sumptuary Laws. Laws — now generally obsolete—enacted in the supposed interest of public morals, to restrain extravagance in private expenditure,— especially in matters of food, dress, and amusements. They abounded in ancient Greece and Rome, and found great favor in the legislation of England from the time of Edward II (1307–1327) to that of the Reformation (1517). They existed in France as early as the time of Charlemagne (768–814), and continued to be enacted as late as the 17th century ; but in neither country do they appear to have been enforced to any great extent. Sumptuary laws were repealed in England in 1856.

" Most of the English *sumptuary laws* were repealed by 1 James I, chap. 25 ; but regulations of a similar kind survive in the university statutes of Oxford and Cambridge. There is a trace of the same principle in the present-day taxation of luxuries—wine and spirits, tobacco, tea, and coffee (though mainly with a view to regulating the incidence of the tax), and in the duties on male servants, armorial bearings, etc. And one reason sometimes urged for the suppression of the liquor traffic is the diminution thereby to be effected in wanton waste and pernicious luxury. In Montenegro strong laws were passed in 1883 against gloves, umbrellas, and non-national costumes." — *Chambers's Encyclopædia.*

Sunday. The first day of the week, originally dedicated to the worship of the sun,—whence its name. Being the day on which, according to the Christians, Jesus rose from the dead, it received the name of the " Lord's Day," and was kept by them, in place of Saturday, the Jewish " Sabbath," although no authority for this change is found in the *New Testament.* See *Sabbatarians.*

" A large body of Christians maintain that with the death of Christ the seventh-day Sabbath ceased for Christians, and that (apart from what Jewish Christians might have felt it their duty to do in the way of keeping the seventh day) the first day or Christian Sabbath naturally and inevitably took its place."—*Chambers's Encyclopædia.*

Sun King. See *Roi Soleil.*

Sunnites. A name given to the orthodox Mohammedans, because they accept, as of equal authority with the *Koran*, the *Sunna*, a body of traditions rejected by the Shiites. They also recognize Abu - Bekr, Omar, and Ohman as true caliphs and legitimate successors of Mohammed. The Sunnites include the greater number of the Mohammedans, and prevail in the Turkish Empire, Egypt, and Arabia; they are also found in large numbers in India and Syria. They are divided into four sects, identical in doctrine, called the *Hanbalites*, the *Shafeites*, the *Malekites*, and the *Hanefites*. See *Shiites.*

Sunnyside. A picturesque stone mansion on the Hudson River, near Irvington, New York, famous as the home of Washington Irving (1783–1859), during the later years of his life.

" The cottage stands near the river, but is hidden to the traveler by the dense growth of trees and shrubbery. It is a stone structure, made up of many gables, the eastern side being embowered in ivy, the earlier slips of which were presented to Irving by Sir Walter Scott, at Abbotsford. The original house was built by Wolfert Acker, a privy-councilor of Peter Stuyvesant, who had inscribed over the door his favorite Dutch motto, 'Lust in Rust' (pleasure in quiet) ; the house was thence called Wolfert's Rest, which the vulgar corrupted into Wolfert's Roost. It is made the subject of one of Irving's sketches in his book bearing this title."—*The Hudson River by Pen and Pencil.*

" In Irving's essay of 'Wolfert's Roost' (the old name of *Sunnyside*), he describes his home very aptly as 'made up of gable-ends, and full of angles and corners as an old cocked hat. It is said, in fact, to have been modelled after the cocked hat of Peter

the Headstrong, as the Escurial of Spain was modelled after the gridiron of the blessed St. Laurence.' The late Napoleon III was at one time a visitor at *Sunnyside ;* and here, in 1842, Daniel Webster paid Irving a visit, with appointment and credentials as Minister to Spain."—*The Hudson River by Daylight.*

Sun of Austerlitz. A name given to the sunrise of December 2nd, 1805, just before the battle of Austerlitz. It powerfully affected the imagination of Napoleon, and was hailed by him as an omen of victory.

"As the day dawned the mist which had overhung all the fateful show began slowly to ascend like a vast curtain from the broad plain. The sun rose in unclouded brilliancy, and, dissipating all remains of the vapour, disclosed to view the great Russian army commanded by Field-Marshal Kutusoff to the number of eighty thousand men, ranged in six divisions, on the opposite heights of Pratzer. The magnificence of the sunrise of this eventful morning, enhanced at the time by the previous dense mist and by the national memories ever since, has made the 'Sun of Austerlitz' proverbial with the people of France."—Horne's *History of Napoleon Bonaparte.*

Sun on Easter-Day. See *Easter-Day Sun.*

Sunset Cox. A nickname popularly conferred upon Samuel Sullivan Cox (1824–1889), the American author and legislator, whose books on foreign travel abound in eloquent descriptions of Oriental sunsets.

According, however, to Reddall's *Fact, Fancy, and Fable,* this sobriquet dates from an article by Mr. Cox in the *Ohio Statesman* of May 19th, 1853, entitled *A Great Old Sunset.*

Sun, Temple of the. See *Baalbek.*

Superb, The.

(1) A title conferred upon the city of Genoa, Italy, on account of its grand and imposing appearance, as seen from the sea.

" In due time the shores of Italy were sighted, and as we stood gazing from the decks early in the bright summer morning, the stately city of Genoa rose up out of the sea and flung back the sunlight from her hundred palaces."—*Innocents Abroad* (Mark Twain).

(2) An appellation bestowed upon General Hancock (1824–1886), in allusion to his brilliant repulse of General Longstreet's brigade at the battle of Gettysburg.

Suttee. The voluntary immolation of a Hindu widow on her husband's funeral pyre, or, in case he died at a distance, on a funeral pyre of her own. This custom which, for centuries, was practically obligatory, owing to the influence of public opinion, was abolished in British India in 1829, and in the native states under English control in 1847. The word "suttee" is also used to denote the widow so immolated.

Swamp Angel. The name given to an 8-inch, 200-pound Parrott gun, used by the Federals at the siege of Charleston, South Carolina, during the Civil War. It threw shells, weighing 150 pounds, into the city, 5½ miles distant; but burst at the 36th discharge. The *Swamp Angel* was so called because it was mounted in a morass, between Morris and James Islands, in Charleston Harbor. It was afterwards sold for old metal, and conveyed to Trenton, New Jersey ; but, on being identified, was set up on a stone pedestal in that city.

Swan of Avon, Sweet. A sobriquet bestowed upon William Shakespeare (1564–1616), by Ben Jonson, in his eulogy, entitled : *To the Memory of my beloved, the Author, Mr. William Shakspeare, and what he hath left us.* See *Bard of Avon.*

" *Sweet Swan of Avon !* what a sight it were
To see thee in our waters yet appear,
And make those flights upon the banks of Thames
That so did take Eliza and our James."

Swan of Cambray. An appellation conferred upon Fénelon (1651–1715), Archbishop of Cambray, the famous French ecclesiastic. See *Eagle of Meaux.*

Swan of Mantua. See *Mantuan Swan.*

Swan of Pesaro. A name given to Gioacchimo Rossini (1792–1868), the famous musical composer, who was born at Pesaro, Italy.

Swan-Song. The swan was called the bird of Apollo, or of Orpheus, by the ancients, and was believed by them to sing melodiously, especially at the time of its death. The origin of this notion is doubtless to be found in the Pythagorean doctrine of transmigration of souls. The phrase " swansong " is frequently used to denote the last work of an author or composer, in allusion to this ancient superstition.

Socrates refers to this belief, in the *Phædo,* as follows :

"I think men are all wrong when they say that the swans before death sing sadly, bewailing their end. They sing then most and most sweetly, exulting that they are going to their God. . . . They sing then not out of sorrow or distress, but because they are inspired of Apollo, and they sing as foreknowing the good things their God hath in store for them."

" Then, if he lose, he makes a swan-like end,
Fading in music."
Merchant of Venice, iii, 2.
" Swans sing before they die : 't were no bad thing
Did certain persons die before they sing."
Coleridge.
" Place me on Sunium's marbled steep,
Where nothing save the waves and I
May hear our mutual murmurs sweep ;
There, swan-like, let me sing and die."
Byron.

Sweating Sickness. A fatal epidemic prevalent in England and parts of the Continent during the 15th and 16th centuries. It was so called " because it did most stand in sweating from the beginning until the endying" ; and " because it first beganne in Englande it was named in other countries the Englishe sweat." The disorder was characterized by chills, high fever, pains in various parts of the body, nausea, thirst, and delirium, —accompanied by stupor and profuse perspiration. The crisis was usually passed in about twenty-four hours, although death frequently occurred within three hours from the beginning of the attack. The disease is believed to have been brought into England by the invading army of the Earl of Richmond (afterwards Henry VII), which landed at Milford Haven in 1485.

Swedenborgians. The name given to the followers of Emanuel Swedenborg (1688–1772), the famous mystic. They first met as an organized religious body in London in 1788, and assumed, in their corporate capacity, the title of " The New Church signified by the New Jerusalem in the Revelation." This organization they regard as the perfect and final Church prophesied in the *Apocalypse*. There are about 10,000 Swedenborgians in England and the United States. See *Arcana Cœlestia.*

" Their belief is that the sole deity is centred in Jesus Christ, in whom is a trinity of essentials ; that salvation is effected by faith and works combined ; that as man's soul is a spiritual body he will never resume the material body ; that the Last Judgment was effected in the spiritual world during Swedenborg's lifetime ; and that the Lord's Second Coming has taken place through the revelation of a new system of truth from the inner sense of Scripture."—Haydn's *Dictionary of Dates.*

Swedish Nightingale. A sobriquet conferred upon Madame Jenny Lind Goldschmidt (1821–1887), the celebrated Swedish vocalist.

Sweetness and Light. A phrase much affected by Matthew Arnold (1822–1888), the English poet and " apostle of culture," who borrowed it from Swift,—though not without due acknowledgment of his indebtedness. It forms the title of one of his most famous essays, from which the following passage is taken.

"The pursuit of perfection, then, is the pursuit of *sweetness and light.* He who works for sweetness and light, works to make reason and the will of God prevail. He who works for machinery, he who works

for hatred, works only for confusion. Culture looks beyond machinery, culture hates hatred ; culture has one great passion, the passion for sweetness and light. It has one even greater !—the passion for making them *prevail.* It is not satisfied till we *all* come to a perfect man ; it knows that the sweetness and light of the few must be imperfect until the raw and unkindled masses of humanity are touched with sweetness and light."

Swiss Guards. A noted regiment of Swiss mercenaries, in the service of the Kings of France, established by royal decree in 1616. They manifested great fidelity towards Louis XVI (1774–1789) during the Revolution, and were wellnigh annihilated while defending the palace of the Tuileries against the attacks of the mob on August 10th, 1792. They were reorganized in September, 1815 ; were driven from the Tuileries by the infuriated populace during the Revolution of July, 1830; and were disbanded soon afterwards. See *Lion of Lucerne; Switzers.*

Switzers. A term formerly used to denote the soldiers composing a royal body-guard, from the custom, among the Swiss, of serving European sovereigns in that capacity,—in vogue since the 15th century. See *Swiss Guards.*

" Where are my *Switzers* ? Let them guard the door."

          Hamlet, iv, 5.

Sword of Damocles. See *Damocles, Sword of.*

Sybarites. The inhabitants of the ancient city of Sybaris in Southern Italy, founded in 720 B.C., were so greatly addicted to voluptuousness and self-indulgence that their name became a byword among the peoples of antiquity. The word " Sybarite " is used, even at the present day, to denote a person devoted to luxury and pleasure.

"A tale is told by Seneca, of a Sybarite who complained that he had not rested comfortably at night ; on being asked the reason, he replied that 'he had found a rose leaf doubled under him, and it hurt him.' Byron refers to it in Don Juan :

'[Her bed] softer than the soft *Sybarite's*
    who cried
Aloud, because his feelings were too tender
To brook a ruffled rose leaf by his side.' "
            Killikelly's *Curious Questions.*

Sylva Sylvarum (*Lat., History of Nature*). A philosophic treatise by Lord Francis Bacon (1561-1626), constituting the third part of the *Instauratio Magna.* It is devoted to the facts and phenomena of natural science, and includes many observations made by Bacon himself, and collected after his death. The work was published by Dr. Rawley in 1627. See *Instauratio Magna.*

Symmes's Hole. An imaginary opening in the crust of the earth at both the north and the south poles, which, in the opinion of John Cleve Symmes (1780-1829), led to the centre. According to the theory propounded by Symmes, the earth is hollow, open at the poles, and capable of being inhabited, and contains several concentric hollow spheres. Symmes lectured and wrote in favor of his theory ; and, in 1823, formally petitioned Congress to fit out an expedition to test it. He is said to have repeatedly invited Sir Humphry Davy and Humboldt to explore this lower world. Symmes died in poverty, but his son, Americus Vespucius, revived his father's fantastic theory in 1876.

Symplegades (*Gr.,* Συμπληγάδες, *Clashing Rocks*). In classic mythology, two terrible rocks,—at the entrance to the Euxine Sea, — which rushed together with great violence and rapidity, and destroyed every vessel that attempted to pass between them. Under the protection of Athena, who held the rocks apart, the ship *Argo* made the passage in safety,—losing only a few of her stern ornaments. After this event, the Symplegades became fixed as islands. See *Argo.*

Synoptic Gospels. A term applied to the Gospels according to *St. Matthew, St. Mark,* and *St. Luke,* from their agreement in relating nearly the same events of Christ's life and ministry, in distinction from the Gospel according to *St. John,* which has its own peculiar method and point of view.

Syntaxis. A famous treatise on astronomy by Ptolemy Claudius, the Greek astronomer, who flourished at Alexandria from 130 to 150 A.D. It was written about 130, and upheld the Ptolemaic System, which was universally accepted as the true theory of the universe until set aside by the researches of Copernicus (1473-1543). See *Almagest ; Ptolemaic System.*

"This is the most ancient complete treatise on astronomy which has been preserved. Several translations and editions have been made since the invention of printing, and now every learned astronomer has it in his library. It is hardly known under its true title, for it is always called the *Almagest,* a pompous name given to it by the Arabs. In the East, the admiration for this astronomical treatise went so far that the caliphs, conquerors of the emperors of Constantinople, would only consent to make peace with the latter on the condition that they were put in possession of a manuscript copy of the *Almagest.* We have a good French translation by Halma in two volumes, of which the first, printed in 1813, has for a frontispiece a medal of the Emperor Antoninus, and the second, printed in 1816, is dedicated to King Louis XVIII."—Flammarion's *Popular Astronomy.*

Syracuse, Battle of. A naval battle fought in 413 B.C., in the Great Harbor of Syracuse, Sicily, between the Athenian fleet, composed of 110 triremes, and the Syracusan fleet, numbering 76 triremes. The Athenians were utterly routed, with a loss of 50 ships, while the Syracusan fleet was reduced to 60 ships.

T

Tabard Inn. An ancient hostelry, formerly situated in Southwark, London, famous as the place where Chaucer imagined his pilgrims to have assembled previous to their journey to Canterbury. The Tabard Inn of the poet's time was in existence as late as 1602 ; but soon after that date it was replaced by a structure in the Elizabethan style,—a portion of which remained standing down to 1875. See *Canterbury Tales*.

"A company of pilgrims, consisting of twenty-nine 'sundry folk,' meet together in fellowship at the *Tabard Inn*, Southwark, all being bent on a pilgrimage to the shrine of Thomas à Becket at Canterbury. . . . The poet himself is one of the party at the Tabard. They all sup together in the large room of the hostelry ; and after great cheer, the landlord proposes that they shall travel together to Canterbury ; and, to shorten their way, that each shall tell two tales, both in going and returning, and whoever told the best, should have a supper at the expense of the rest. The company assent, and mine host, ' Harry Bailly,'—who was both ' bold of speech, and wise and well taught,'—is appointed to be judge and reporter of the stories."—Chambers's *Cyclopædia of English Literature*.

Tabernacle. A portable tent, used by the Israelites as a place of religious worship, prior to the completion of the Temple in 1003 B.C. It accompanied them during their 40 years' wanderings in the wilderness, and was superseded by a more permanent structure set up at Shiloh by Joshua in 1444 B.C. The Tabernacle was a rectangular structure,—30 cubits long, 10 cubits wide, and 10 cubits high. It was built of shittim-wood, overlaid with thin gold plates, and was covered with curtains of fine linen and leather. The interior was divided into two unequal parts by an embroidered curtain,— known as the " veil." The larger of these, called the Sanctuary, contained the altar of incense, the table of showbread, and the golden candlestick ; while the smaller, called the Holy of Holies, contained the Ark of the Covenant and the Mercy-Seat. See *Solomon's Temple*.

Tabernacles, Feast of. One of the three great Jewish festivals,—the two others being the Passover and the Pentecost. It was instituted in 1451, in commemoration of the 40 years' wandering in the wilderness, and was observed also as a season of thanksgiving for the ingathering of the harvest. The Feast of Tabernacles was celebrated for eight days, commencing on the 15th day of the month *Tishri* (*i. e.*, 15 days after the new moon in October), during which time the people forsook their houses and dwelt in tents, or booths,—whence the name. See *Passover ; Pentecost*.

Table-Cloth. The name given to the white cloud that frequently rests upon Table Mountain, near Cape Town, Africa.

"When the wind is from the southeast a peculiar sight is witnessed upon the top and edge of this mountain, which is then fringed by a thin line of fleecy cloud. This lying flat and low on top, and gracefully falling over the edges, has happily been called the 'table-cloth.' "—Vincent's *Actual Africa*.

Table of Last Supper. A table of cedar wood in the Portico Leonino, in the Church of St. John Lateran in Rome, said to be the one on which the Last Supper was eaten.

"At St. John Lateran is preserved a table, said to be the one used by Christ at the Last Supper. Nothing is known about it, and probably very few believe it to be what it professes to be."—Brewer's *Dictionary of Miracles*.

Table of Pythagoras. The name sometimes given to the familiar arrangement of the multiplication-table, up to ten,—consisting of ten vertical columns of ten numbers each. If the numbers in the left vertical row be taken for multipliers and those in the upper horizontal row for multiplicands, then the product will be in the same horizontal row as the multiplier and in the same vertical row as the multiplicand.

Table Rock. An overhanging ledge of rock at Niagara Falls, which, at one time, jutted out from the bank of the river on the Canada side and afforded a magnificent view of the cataract. In 1850, almost the entire mass—measuring 200 feet in length and 100 feet in thickness—fell into the chasm. The name "Table Rock," still adheres to this point, although the last fragment broke off in 1862. See *Niagara Falls*.

Table-Turning. A phenomenon much discussed in England and the United States of America, in 1850, where it was also practised as a form of social diversion. Like other kindred phenomena, it is believed by many credulous persons to be due to the agency of departed spirits or to the influence of some occult psychic force ; but is, in all probability, simply the result of involuntary, unconscious, muscular action.

Tadmor. See *Palmyra, Ruins of.*

Tae-Ping Rebellion. See *Army of Women.*

Taffy. A popular designation for a Welshman. It is a corruption of *Davy*, which is a shortened form of *David* (490-544 A.D.), the patron-saint of Wales.

Tagliamento, Battle of. A battle fought in Lombardy, on March 16th, 1797, between the French, commanded by Napoleon Bonaparte, and the Austrians under the Archduke Charles. The battle resulted in a complete victory for the French.

Tâj Mahal (*Crown of Edifices*). A superb mausoleum near Agra, India, erected by the Mogul Emperor Shâh-Jehân (1627–1658 A.D.), in memory of his favorite wife, Mumtaz Mahal, who died in 1629. The building was commenced in 1630, and required for its construction the uninterrupted labor of 20,000 men for 22 years. It is built entirely of white marble, and is octagonal in shape,—the sides being 130 feet long. The roof is 70 feet from the terrace, and is surmounted by a marble dome, 70 feet in diameter and 120 feet high. The entire surface of the exterior, with the exception of the dome, is covered with arabesques and passages from the *Koran*,—the whole of which sacred volume is said to be inscribed upon the walls and corridors of the edifice. The crypt in the interior contains the sarcophagi of the Emperor and his wife, who lie buried side by side ; while the central room above is occupied by two magnificent cenotaphs of white marble, enclosed in a superb octagonal screen. The cost of the Tâj Mahal, according to a native account, is placed at somewhat more than $9,000,000 ; although some authorities say $15,000,000, and others $60,000,000.

"For grace, symmetry, material, and execution, the *Taj Mahal* surpasses the acknowledged masterpieces of architecture in all lands. It is not only the most beautiful and costly mausoleum on the face of the globe, the most faultless relic of Eastern architecture, but, taken for all in all, probably the most noble and perfect art-ideal of the kind ever embodied by man. It better deserves to be numbered among the wonders of the world than the Pyramids of Egypt, the Temple of Diana at Ephesus, or the Mausoleum erected by Artemisia. Were nothing else of interest to be seen in India, the labor and danger of a journey around the world would be amply compensated by an inspection of the stupendous miracle of art, the Palace-Tomb Taj Mahal."—Vincent's *Through and Through the Tropics.*

Talavera, Battle of. A desperate battle fought on July 27th–28th, 1809, at Talavera de la Reina, a town of Spain, 64 miles southwest of Madrid, between 19,000 English and 34,000 Spanish commanded by Sir Arthur Wellesley, and 50,000 French under Victor and Sebastiani. The French were defeated with a loss of 7000 men —killed and wounded, and retreated in the night over the Alberche. The British loss was upwards of 5000. This victory gained for Wellesley the title of Viscount Wellington of Talavera.

Tally-Ho ! A huntsman's cry to encourage his hounds, especially when the fox breaks covert. The term is also used to denote a four-in-hand coach, or drag. See *Tantivy !*

"One authority says this is a corruption of the Norman-French *tolleaux*; another derives it from *taillishors*, out of the coppice; and a third says it is the French hunting cry, *au taillis*, to the coppice, which being often repeated gives the same sound as tally-ho."
—Edwards's *Words, Facts, and Phrases.*

Talmud. The body of the civil and canonical law of the Jews, not contained in the *Pentateuch*. It is written in Aramaic, and consists of two parts, the *Mishna*, or text, and the *Gemara*, or commentary; although the name *Talmud* is sometimes restricted, especially by Jewish writers, to the *Gemara*. There are two Talmuds, (1) the *Palestinian* (commonly, but incorrectly, called the *Jerusalem*) *Talmud*, and (2) the *Babylonian Talmud*. The former was completed about the middle of the 5th century A.D., and the latter at the close of the 6th century A.D. Both contain the same *Mishna*, but different *Gemaras*. The *Babylonian Gemara* is four times as large as the *Palestinian*, and is more highly esteemed by the Jewish doctors.

"We must refrain in this place from attempting a general characterisation of the *Talmud*, a work completely *sui generis*, which is assuredly one of the most important records of humanity. Nothing can give even an approximate idea of the immensity of material, historical, geographical, philological, poetical, that lies hidden in its mounds. A contribution to the records of fanaticism may also be found in the 'exoteric' history of the *Talmud*, which was, albeit utterly unknown save by a few garbled extracts, prohibited, confiscated, burned, and generally prosecuted and inveighed against by emperors, popes, theologians, and fanatics generally, from Justinian down almost to our own day, as perhaps no other book has ever been. In our own times, however, its value begins to be recognised by great scholars, not merely as the only chief source of the knowledge of Judaism, but as the chief source—next to the gospels—even for the history of the origin and early days of Christianity; a notion long ago hinted at by eminent divines like Lightfoot and others."
—*Chambers's Encyclopædia.*

Tammany Society. A democratic political organization in New York City, named in honor of St. Tammany, a noted Indian chief. It was founded on May 12th, 1789, for benevolent and social purposes; but eventually became an important political body,—controlling the local and, to some extent, the State government, in the interests of the Democratic party. The Society was formally chartered in 1805. It erected its first "Hall" in 1811, and its present one in East Fourteenth Street in 1867–1868. See *St. Tammany.*

"This organization was formed in 1789, being the effect of a popular movement in New York, having primarily in view a counterweight to the so-called "aristocratic" Society of the Cincinnati. It was essentially anti-Federalist or democratic in its character, and its chief founder was William Mooney, an upholsterer and a native-born American of Irish extraction. It took its first title from a noted, ancient, wise and friendly chief of the Delaware tribe of Indians, named Tammany, who had, for the want of a better subject, been canonized by the soldiers of the Revolution as the American patron saint. The first meeting was held May 12, 1789. The act of incorporation was passed in 1805. The Grand Sachem and thirteen Sachems were designed to typify the President and the Governors of the thirteen original States. William Mooney was the first Grand Sachem. The Society is nominally a charitable and social organization, and is distinct from the general committee of the Tammany Democracy, which is a political organization and cannot use Tammany Hall without the consent of the Society."—*World Almanac.*

Tancred. The hero of Tasso's *Jerusalem Delivered*, and, with the exception of Rinaldo, the greatest of the Crusaders. See *Gerusalemme Liberata.*

Tantalus. In classic mythology, a son of Jupiter and the nymph Pluto, and King of Lydia, Argos, or Corinth. According to the common account, he divulged the secrets entrusted to him by Jupiter; and was, in consequence, punished in the lower world with unappeasable hunger and thirst. He was placed up to his chin in a lake, the waters of which receded whenever he attempted to drink of them; while over his head were hung clusters of luscious fruit that likewise eluded his grasp whenever he put forth his hand to reach them. In addition to these torments, Tantalus was kept in a state of constant terror lest a huge rock that was suspended above his head should fall and crush him. The verb *to tantalize*—meaning to torment by repeated disappointments in the attainment of some apparently attainable object — is derived from *Tantalus*, whose punishment was proverbial in ancient times. See *Cup of Tantalus*.

Tantivy! A hunting-cry denoting that the chase is in full swing. It is probably formed in imitation of the note of the hunting-horn, in accordance with the well-known principle of *onomatopœia*. See *Tally-Ho!*

Tàoism. One of the three religious systems of China, the other two being Confucianism, and Buddhism in its Chinese form. It was established by Lâo-tse, the famous philosopher and sage, who flourished about 500 B.C.

"Like the Brahmans of India, Lao-Tse taught the final absorption of pure and enlightened souls into the supreme eternal Spirit, and that, 'having thus become one with the supreme Reason, they will exist eternally.' He inculcated universal benevolence : we ought to show kindness not only to the sincere and virtuous, but also to the insincere and wicked. 'Those who are holy,' he says, 'will treat all men as a father treats his children.' The religion of the Tao-Sse, at the present day, seems closely allied to Boodhism ; and many of its votaries of both sexes, like the followers of Gautama, spend their lives in monasteries. The modern Tao-Sse are much addicted to superstitious observances, and deal largely in sorcery. They are very popular with the common people, and in some parts of the empire their influence rivals that of the Boodhists."—Lippincott's *Biographical Dictionary*.

Tapestries of the Vatican. A collection of tapestries in the Vatican at Rome, executed from cartoons drawn by Raphael (1483–1520) in 1515–1516, and originally intended to cover the lower unpainted portions of the walls of the Sistine Chapel. Each piece was wrought at Brussels, with great skill, in wool, silk, and gold; and cost, when completed, about £700. During the siege of Rome in 1527, these tapestries were carried off and badly damaged ; but were restored to Pope Julius III (1550–1555). In 1798, they fell into the hands of the French, and were sold by them to a Genoese Jew, from whom they were purchased by Pope Pius VII (1800–1823). They are now much faded, especially in the flesh tints. Seven of the cartoons from which these tapestries were executed are now in the South Kensington Museum, London,—having been purchased in Flanders by Charles I of England. See *Cartoons of Raphael*.

"These hang upon the walls of a gallery adjoining the Stanze. The colors are faded, and the fabric shows in many ways the injuries of time, and of the various casualties to which they have been exposed. A passing glance is the only tribute which most travellers offer them." — Hillard's *Six Months in Italy*.

Tappan Zee. A lake-like expansion of the Hudson River, extending from Dobbs Ferry to Croton Point. It is about 10 miles long and from 3 to 4 miles wide.

"In the bosom of one of those spacious coves which indent the eastern shore of the Hudson, at the broad expansion of the river denominated by the ancient Dutch navigators the *Tappaan Zee*, and where they always prudently shortened sail, and implored the protection of St. Nicholas when they crossed, there lies a small market town or rural port, which by some is called Greensburgh, but which is more generally and properly known by the name of Tarry Town."—*Legend of Sleepy Hollow* (Irving).

Tap the Admiral. A nautical phrase, meaning to tap and steal the liquor from a cask by means of a gimlet and straw. According to Hotten, the expression originated in the story that when the remains of Admiral Nelson were conveyed to England after the battle of Trafalgar (1805), they were placed in a cask, which was filled with brandy and closed. On arriving at Spithead, the cask was found to be empty, and the body of the admiral "high and dry,"—the sailors having drained off the liquor. This ridiculous and repulsive tale has no foundation whatever, in fact.

"It was not until the day after the battle that the surgeon of the *Victory* could find leisure to give a portion of his attention to the remains of the Hero. There was no lead on board to make a coffin of; a large cask called a leaguer had to serve as a shell ; the hair was cut off the head of the body, which was stripped of all clothes except the shirt; the corpse was then put into the cask, which was filled with brandy and closed. During the heavy weather that followed, Nelson's remains were placed under the charge of a sentinel on the middle deck. The cask stood on end having a closed aperture at its top and another below that the spirit might be withdrawn and renewed without disturbing the body."—*Life of Nelson* (W. Clark Russell).

Tara Hill. A small conical hill, 507 feet high, in the province of Leinster, Ireland, seven miles southeast of Navan. According to the legend, the kings of Ireland resided at Tara prior to 560 A.D., and for many centuries the Triennial Councils of Ireland held their sessions there. The famous " Coronation Stone " in Westminster Abbey is said to have been taken from Tara to Scotland. On August 15th, 1843, Daniel O'Connell held there a monster mass-meeting,—attended by 250,000 persons. See *Coronation Chair*.

" The harp that once through Tara's halls
   The soul of music shed,
Now hangs as mute on Tara's walls
   As if that soul were fled."
              Thomas Moore.

Targums. Paraphrastic translations of the Hebrew Scriptures into Chaldee,—the only language familiar to the Jews after their return from the Captivity (536 B. C.). The most famous are the *Targum on the Pentateuch*, which bears the name of *Onkelos ;* the *Targum of Jonathan Ben Uzziel on the Prophets ;* the *Targum of the Pseudo Jonathan ;* and the *Jerusalem Targum.* The *Targums* were not committed to writing until Christian times. No one of them includes the entire *Old Testament.*

"There are three *Targums* of the Pentateuch, one on the prophets, two on Esther, one on Chronicles, one on Daniel, besides those on the Psalms, Job, the Proverbs, Solomon's Song, Ruth, Lamentations, Ecclesiastes, etc."—Brewer's *Historic Note-Book.*

Tariff. This word — signifying a schedule of duties on merchandise, imported or exported — is said to be derived from *Tarifa*, a town in Southern Spain, commanding the entrance to the Mediterranean Sea, where duties were at one time levied by the Moors on all vessels passing in or out of the Straits of Gibraltar.

Tarpeian Rock. A precipice on the south side of the Capitoline Hill at Rome, from which state criminals sentenced to death were thrown headlong. It derived its name from Tarpeia, a vestal virgin and daughter of Spurius Tarpeius, the governor of the citadel, who agreed to open the gates to the Sabines — then at war with the Romans — on condition of receiving from them what they wore on their arms (meaning their bracelets). She was rewarded for her treachery by being crushed to death by the weight of the shields cast upon her by the soldiers, who shouted as they hastened by : " These are the ornaments we wear on our arms." According to the legend, Tarpeia ever sits in the heart of the rock, adorned with gold and jewels, and bound by a spell. See *Capitoline Hill.*

"The precipice from which criminals were thrown down is much diminished in height by the accumulation of rubbish beneath, but is still lofty enough to insure the death of a culprit who should be thrown from it."—Harper's *Hand-Book to Europe and the East.*

Tarshish. A famous port, or region, the location of which has never been satisfactorily determined. It is frequently mentioned in the *Old Testament*, and is generally identified with *Tartessus*, the name given by the Romans to an ancient Phœnician Colony in Southern Spain, near the mouth of the Guadalquivir. See *Andalusia*.

"For the king's ships went to *Tarshish* with the servants of Huram: every three years once came the ships of *Tarshish* bringing gold, and silver, ivory, and apes, and peacocks."—*2 Chronicles* ix, 21.

Tartar, Catch a. See *Catch a Tartar*.

Tartuffe. The leading character in Molière's comedy of the same name. He is a hypocrite and impostor, who uses religion as a cloak for his covetousness and deceit, and succeeds in ingratiating himself so thoroughly with one Orgon, a man of wealth, as to obtain from him the promise of his daughter in marriage. His true character being finally exposed, he is driven from the house and placed in jail for felony. It is said that the original of *Tartuffe* is Père Lachaise, the confessor of Louis XIV (1643–1715), whose fondness for truffles (*Fr.*, *tartuffes*) suggested the name to Molière.

Tasso and Leonora. See *Leonora d'Este*.

Tatler. A tri-weekly journal founded by Richard Steele, the noted essayist, in 1709. It was edited under the name of Isaac Bickerstaff, Esq., Astrologer, and was regularly published until 1711. Of the papers in the *Tatler*, 41 were written wholly by Addison and 34 by Addison and Steele conjointly.

Tattersall's. A celebrated horse-mart and sporting-centre in London, founded by Richard Tattersall (1724–1795) in 1766, near Hyde Park Corner, and removed in 1867 to Knightsbridge Green. The subscription-rooms at *Tattersall's* are the centre of all business relating to horse-racing and betting throughout England.

Tattooed Man. A nickname conferred upon James G. Blaine (1830–1893), as the result of a cartoon that appeared in a New York comic paper during the presidential campaign of 1884. It represented the Republican candidate—in the rôle of Phryne before her judges—tattooed with the names of the political scandals connected with his name. The picture was considered an unusually clever hit, and gained for Mr. Blaine the sobriquet that clung to him long after his defeat for the presidency.

Tearless Victory. According to Plutarch, the name given by the Spartans to the victory won by their king, Archidamus III, in 367 B.C., over the combined forces of the Arcadians and Argives, without the loss of a single man on the Spartan side. It is said that as many as 10,000 Arcadians fell in the struggle. Also called the *Tearless Battle*.

Te Deum. A famous Latin hymn of praise and supplication — so called from its first words—used in the ritual of the Roman Catholic and Anglican Churches. Its date and authorship are uncertain; but it is commonly supposed to be the joint production of St. Ambrose and St. Augustine, on the occasion of the baptism of the latter, about 390 A.D. On this account it is frequently called the "Ambrosian Hymn." It has also been ascribed to Athanasius, Bishop of Alexandria, to Nicetius, and to Hilary of Poitiers. See *Ambrosian Chant*.

"According to tradition, it was the product of a sudden inspiration of St. Ambrose on the occasion of the baptism of St. Augustine. It is thought by some to be derived from an earlier Oriental hymn, while others think it was not written till near the end of the fifth century."—*Who Wrote It?*

Teetotal. This word, as applied to total abstinence from intoxicating beverages, was first used by one Richard Turner, an artisan, who, while contending for this principle at a temperance meeting held at Preston, England, in 1833, exclaimed: "I'll hev nowt to do with this moderation-botheration pledge—I'll be reet down *tee-tee-total* for ever and ever." The word was quickly taken up, and soon after passed into general use.

"In the September of 1833, at one of the meetings of the Preston society, a working-man named Richard Turner, usually called 'Dickey Turner,' and who was a rough, humorous speaker, was insisting on the superiority of total abstinence over what was known as the 'moderation' system, and wishing to express himself very forcibly, he exclaimed, ' I 'll be reet down out-and-out *tee-tee-total* for ever and ever.' The audience cheered, and Mr. Livesey said, ' This shall be the name of our new pledge.' Dicky did not stutter, and the reduplication of the ' t ' in ' total' was simply an emphatic way of declaring his opinion."—*Chambers's Encyclopædia.*

"This is the epitaph which may be read on his tombstone at Preston, near Manchester : ' Beneath this stone are deposited the remains of Richard Turner, author of the word *Teetotal* as applied to abstinence from all intoxicating liquors, who departed this life on the 27th day of October, 1846, aged 56 years.' "—Walsh's *Literary Curiosities.*

Tel-el-Kebir, Battle of.

A desperate battle fought at Tel-el-Kebir, Egypt, on September 13th, 1882, between 13,000 British, commanded by Sir Garnet Wolseley, and 26,000 Egyptians under Arabi Pasha. The Egyptians, who occupied a strongly entrenched camp, were routed with a loss of 1500 men. The British loss was 52 killed and 380 wounded.

Telemachus, Adventures of (*Fr., Les Aventures de Télémaque*).

A famous romance by Fénelon (1651–1715), narrating the adventures of Telemachus, the son of Ulysses and Penelope, during his fruitless search for his father after the fall of Troy. The book was written to entertain the Duke of Burgundy, grandson of Louis XIV (1643–1715), whose education had been entrusted to Fénelon ; but was made public by an unfaithful servant, who was engaged to copy the manuscript and who sold it to a bookseller. Louis XIV took exception to certain passages in the work, which he declared were masked satires against his despotic rule, and endeavored to suppress it in France. It soon acquired great popularity, and was translated into the principal languages of Europe.

Telepathy.

" A word coined about 1886 from the Greek to express the supposed power of communication between one mind and another by means unknown to the ordinary sense-organs. Some members of the ' Psychical Research Society ' believe that they have established the fact that such a power does exist in the material universe, and have attempted to turn the assumption to account in the explanation of certain unexplained natural phenomena." — *Chambers's Encyclopædia.*

Telephone.

An instrument for reproducing vocal and other sounds at a distance, principally by means of electricity. J. P. Reis of Friedrichsdorf first effected the transmission of sounds by electricity in 1860–1861, and Alexander Graham Bell began his investigations on the subject in July, 1874. On February 14th, 1876, he filed a specification and drawing of the original Bell telephone, and on the same day Elisha Gray of Chicago lodged a *caveat* for a similar instrument in the Patent Office at Washington. In January, 1877, Edison's carbon loud-speaking telephone was invented. Telephonic communication between New York and Chicago (1000 miles) was opened in 1883 ; between Paris and Marseilles (563 miles) in 1888 ; and between London and Paris in 1891.

Telescope.

The first telescope is generally believed to have been made by the optician Hans Lippersheim, or Lippershey, of Middelburg, Holland, who was perhaps assisted in his work by Zacharias Jansen, also an optician, and Adriaan Metius, a noted mathematician. This instrument was presented to the States-General of Holland on October 2nd, 1608. The invention of the telescope is also ascribed to Galileo in 1609.

"This discovery, which Bacon and Porta had foreseen, was made at last almost by accident in Holland, by two spectacle-makers, Zacharias Jansen and Henry Lippershey. It is related that Jansen's children, when playing one day with two powerful magnifying glasses, happened to place them one behind the other in such a position that the weathercock of a church opposite the house seemed to them nearer and larger than usual, and their father, when he saw this, fixed the glasses on a board and gave them as a curiosity to Prince Maurice of Nassau. Whether this story be true or not, it is certain that in the year 1609, both Jansen and Lippershey made these rough telescopes as toys, though they did not know how useful they might be. But when Galileo heard of it he saw what valuable help it might afford in studying the heavens ; and he set to work immediately, and soon succeeded in making a useful instrument."—Buckley's *Short History of Natural Science.*

Tell's Chapel. A chapel on the shore of Lake Lucerne, Switzerland, erected in 1388 by the Canton of Uri, on the very spot where, according to tradition, William Tell set foot when he leaped ashore from Gessler's boat. The building was rebuilt in 1879, in strict conformity with the original design. See *William Tell.*

"Tell was bound and thrown into a boat to be taken with Gessler and his men to the Castle of Küssnacht, the residence of the tyrant. A frightful storm burst forth. Tell alone could save the party. He was unbound and pulled the boat to a rocky ledge, 'Tell's Platte' ; he there sprang on shore and disappeared. The tyrant landed, and was passing through a defile, the 'Hohle Gasse' near Küssnacht, when Tell, who lay in ambush, shot him through the heart. A rising followed, and wars with Austria, which ended in the independence of Switzerland."—*Chambers's Encyclopædia.*

Temple, The.

(1) An ancient structure formerly standing in the city of Paris. It was erected by the Knights Templars in 1212; and after the suppression of the Order in 1312, it was used as a treasury by the Kings of France. In 1792–1793, it acquired great notoriety as the place of confinement of the Royal Family. Sir Sidney Smith, Toussaint L'Overture, and Pichegru were also imprisoned there.

47

(2) A group of buildings in London, originally the headquarters of the Knights Templars. After the dissolution of the Order in 1313 the Temple became Crown-property, and in 1346 was leased to the students of the common law and converted into Inns of Court, afterwards called the Inner and Outer Temple. The Temple district, lying between Fleet Street and the Thames, is occupied almost entirely by barristers and solicitors.

Temple Bar. A famous stone gateway in London, which formerly stood at the junction of Fleet Street and the Strand, and divided the City proper from the liberty of Westminster. It was built by Sir Christopher Wren in 1669–1673, after the Great Fire of 1666, at a cost of £1398 ; and was removed in 1878–1879, and re-erected at Theobald's Park, near Chesunt, in 1888. A memorial of Temple Bar—marking the site of the old gate — was erected in 1880, at a cost of £11,500. It is adorned at the sides with statues of Queen Victoria and the Prince of Wales (now Edward VII), and is surmounted by the City griffin and arms.

" The heads of criminals used to be barbarously exhibited on iron spikes on the top of the gate. When the reigning sovereign visited the City on state occasions, he was wont, in accordance with an ancient custom, to obtain permission from the Lord Mayor to pass *Temple Bar.*"—*Baedeker's London.*

Temple Emanu-El. A superb Jewish synagogue on Fifth Avenue, Borough of Manhattan, New York City, erected in 1868, at a cost of $600,000. It is built of brown and yellow sandstone, in the Moorish style of architecture, and seats about 2000 persons. The congregation belongs to the reform-wing of the Jewish faith.

Ten Animals in Paradise. See *Animals Admitted into Heaven.*

Ten Commandments. A phrase sometimes used to denote the ten fingers ; also, the ten finger-nails, or the scratches made by them.

"Could I come near your beauty with my nails,
I 'd set my *ten commandments* in your face."
Henry VI, Part II, i, 3.

"This appears to have been a popular phrase for *the hands* or ten fingers. Thus in Selimus, Emperor of the Turks, 1594; 'I would set a tap abroach and not live in fear of my wife's *ten commandments*.' Again, in Westward Ho, 1607: 'Your harpy has set his *ten commandments* on my back.' And in Udal's version of Erasmus' Apothegms: 'When Xantippe has pulled awaye her husbandes cope from his backe, even in the open streete, and his familiar compaignons gave him a by warning to avenge suche a naughtie tricke or pranke with his *tenne commandments*."—Hudson's *Shakespeare*.

Tenedos. An island in the Ægean Sea, about five miles distant from the plain of Troy. According to Virgil's *Æneid*, the Greeks concealed their fleet behind this island, under pretense of having sailed for home, and by this stratagem induced the Trojans to receive within their walls the famous "Wooden Horse." See *Horse, Wooden*.

" Est in conspectu *Tenedos*, notissima fama
Insula, dives opum, Priami dum regna manebant,
Nunc tantum sinus et statio male fida carinis ;
Huc se provecti deserto in litore condunt."
Æneid, ii, 21–24.

Tenebræ (*Lat., Darkness*). A funereal service in the Roman Catholic Church, held on Wednesday, Thursday, and Friday of Holy Week, in commemoration of the three hours of darkness that are said to have overspread the land at the time of the Crucifixion. On this occasion, the altar is draped in black, the place of the Host is left empty, and the lights of the church are gradually extinguished one by one,—not to be relighted until Easter Eve.

Ten Great Religions. James Freeman Clarke, in his work entitled *Ten Great Religions*, gives the following as the ten leading faiths of ancient and modern times:
(1) Confucianism.
(2) Brahmanism.

(3) Buddhism.
(4) Zoroastrianism.
(5) Religion of Egypt.
(6) Religion of Greece and Rome.
(7) Teutonic and Scandinavian Religion.
(8) Judaism.
(9) Christianity.
(10) Islâm.

Ten Largest Cities in the United States. The figures given below are from the Thirteenth Census, taken in 1910:

(1) New York................. 4,766,883
(2) Chicago.................. 2,185,283
(3) Philadelphia............... 1,549,008
(4) St. Louis.................. 687,029
(5) Boston.................... 670,585
(6) Cleveland................. 560,663
(7) Baltimore................. 558,485
(8) Pittsburg................. 533,905
(9) Detroit................... 465,766
(10) Buffalo................... 423,715

Tennis-Ball of Fortune. A nickname conferred upon Helvius Pertinax, the Roman Emperor, in allusion to his checkered career. He was in turn a charcoal-dealer, a schoolteacher, a prefect, a senator, a consul, and finally an emperor. In his attempt to institute certain important reforms, he incurred the hatred of the Prætorian Guard, and was assassinated by them in 193 A.D., after a reign of three months.

Tennis-Court Oath. A solemn oath taken by the members of the National Assembly of France in 1789, to the effect " that they would continue to meet for the dispatch of business wherever circumstances might require, until the constitution of the kingdom had been established upon sound and solid foundations." The oath derived its name from the royal tennis-court at Versailles, where the Assembly met on that occasion,—admission to the hall of the " Menus Plaisirs " having been refused them by Louis XVI. See *National Assembly of France*.

Ten Persecutions. A term used somewhat arbitrarily, since the time ot St. Augustine (354–430 A.D.), to include certain persecutions of the Christians by the Roman Emperors. They are as follows :

(1) Persecution under Nero, 64 A.D.

(2) Persecution under Domitian, 95 A.D.

(3) Persecution under Trajan, 107 A.D.

(4) Persecution under Marcus Aurelius, 165 A.D.

(5) Persecution under Septimius Severus, 202 A.D.

(6) Persecution under Maximinus, 235 A.D.

(7) Persecution under Decius, 249 A.D.

(8) Persecution under Valerianus, 257 A.D.

(9) Persecution under Aurelian, 274 A.D.

(10) Persecution under Diocletian, 303 A.D.

Some authorities, in enumerating the " Ten Persecutions," omit the one under Aurelian, as small and inconsiderable ; and, insert in its stead the Persecution under Hadrian — 125 A.D. This last, however, is generally regarded as simply a continuance or revival of the Persecution of Trajan.

Ten Tables, Laws of the. See *Twelve Tables, Laws of the.*

Tenth Muse.

(1) Sappho (*fl.* 600 B.C.), the famous Greek lyric poetess.

"She is called by ancient authors the *tenth muse.*"—*Addison.*

(2) Juaña Iñez de Lacruz (1651–1695), a Mexican poetess.

"She was often called 'the Tenth Muse.'"—Lippincott's *Biographical Dictionary.*

(3) Anne Bradstreet (1613–1672), the English poetess.

(4) Margaret, (1492–1549), Queen of Navarre, author of the *Heptameron.*

(5) Hannah More (1745–1833), the distinguished English writer.

Tenth of August, Massacre of the. A term often applied to the massacre

of the Swiss Guards and others at the palace of the Tuileries, Paris, by a wild revolutionary mob, on August 10th, 1792. It is estimated that 5000 persons perished on that day. The palace was ransacked and pillaged, and the royal family were conducted to the Hall of the Feuillants, and two days later were confined in the gloomy fortress of the Temple. Marie Antoinette displayed marvellous courage on that eventful occasion ; as for Louis XVI, Alison well remarks that " he had the resignation of a martyr, not the courage of a hero."

Ten Thousand, Retreat of the. See *Retreat of the Ten Thousand.*

Ten Thousand a Year. The title of a famous novel by Samuel Warren (1807–1877). It appeared in 1841. See *Tittlebat Titmouse.*

"This novel has its faults, and grave ones ; it is too long, and, being written in the interests of the Conservative party, betrays too palpably its tendency. But with all its defects, it is a delightfully fascinating book, and some of its characters have already passed into the permanent gallery of great English creations. Tittlebat Titmouse and Oily Gammon stand on an equal footing with Oliver Twist and Uriah Heep."—Hart's *Manual of English Literature.*

"His *Ten Thousand a Year* (1841), though in some parts ridiculously exaggerated, and liable to the suspicion of being a satire upon the middle classes, is also an amusing and able novel." — Chambers's *Cyclopædia of English Literature.*

Tenth Wave. A notion prevails that the waves of the ocean increase in volume and power until they culminate in the tenth, whereupon the series begins anew. According to another theory, the series culminates in the ninth wave. There is no scientific authority for either of these beliefs.

"At length, tumbling from the Gallic coast, the victorious *tenth wave* shall ride like the boar over all the rest."—*Burke.*

"And then the two Dropt to the cove, and watch'd the great sea fall,

Wave after wave, each mightier than the last,
Till last, a *ninth one*, gathering half the deep
And full of voices, rose and plunged
Roaring, and all the wave was in a flame."
The Holy Grail (Tennyson).

Tenure-of-Office Act.

An act of Congress passed March 2nd, 1867, to prevent the President of the United States [Andrew Johnson] from removing persons from office without the consent of the Senate.

"The first Congress, in 1789, after an earnest discussion, had determined that the power of removal rested with the President alone, but the ' Tenure of Office Act,' passed March 2d, 1867, provided that there should be no removal by the President without the consent of the Senate. Mr. Johnson's chief defence in the impeachment trial, was, however, that he had merely pursued the plan adopted by Mr. Lincoln and his Cabinet."—Gilman's *History of the American People*.

"Great excitement was produced by the attempt of the President to remove Mr. Stanton in February [1868], and he was impeached of high crimes and misdemeanours by a large majority of the House of Representatives. Among the crimes charged against him was the violation of the 'Act regulating the Tenure of certain Civil Offices,' by the removal of Mr. Stanton without the consent of the Senate."—Lippincott's *Biographical Dictionary*.

Ten Virtues of the Virgin Mary.

The following are enumerated in Roman Catholic theology:
(1) Chastity.
(2) Prudence.
(3) Humility.
(4) Faith.
(5) Piety.
(6) Obedience.
(7) Poverty.
(8) Patience.
(9) Charity.
(10) Compassion.

Terpsichore.

In classic mythology, one of the nine Muses. She presided over dancing and the choral song. See *Muses*.

Terrapin Tower.

A stone observation tower formerly standing on Terrapin Rock, on the brink of the Horseshoe Fall at Niagara. It was erected in 1833, and was 45 feet high, 12 feet in diameter at the base, and 8 feet at the top. It afforded a superb view of the cataract ; but being found to be unsafe, it was removed in 1873. There is talk of rebuilding it.

"On the rocks, at the verge of the precipice, is a stone tower, erected in 1833, which is 45 feet high, with winding stairs on the inside, and an open gallery on the top, surrounded by an iron balustrade, from which, or from the end of the bridge, the effect of the Falls upon the beholder is awfully sublime."—Appleton's *Hand-Book to the United States* (1853).

Terror, Reign of.

See *Reign of Terror*.

Terror of the World.

An appellation conferred upon Attila (434-453 A.D.), King of the Huns.

Teufelsdröckh, Herr

(*Ger.*, *Devil's Dung*). An eccentric German professor, whose imaginary " life and opinions " form the subject of Carlyle's *Sartor Resartus*. See *Sartor Resartus*.

"And yet, thou brave *Teufelsdröckh*, who could tell what lurked in thee ? Under those thick locks of thine, so long and lank, overlapping roof-wise the gravest face we ever in this world saw, there dwelt a most busy brain. In thy eyes, too, deep under their shaggy brows, and looking out so still and dreamy, have we not noticed gleams of an ethereal or else a diabolic fire, and half fancied that their stillness was but the rest of infinite motion, the *sleep* of a spinning top? Thy little figure, there as in loose, ill-brushed, threadbare habiliments, thou sattest, amid litter and lumber, whole days to 'think and smoke tobacco,' held in it a mighty heart. The secrets of man's life were laid open to thee ; thou sawest into the mystery of the Universe farther than another ; thou hadst *in petto* thy remarkable Volume on Clothes."—*Sartor Resartus*, chap. iii.

Teutoberg, Battle of.

A battle fought in the Teutoberg Forest, near the waters of the Ems, where in 9 A.D. the Roman army, under Quintilius Varus, was routed with great slaughter by the Germans under Arminius. It is said that the aged Emperor Augustus, on learning of the defeat of his army, exclaimed in agony, "Varus, give me my legions." Varus and many of his officers committed suicide, —preferring death to captivity.

Teutonic Languages. A group of related languages, forming one of the branches of the Aryan, or Indo-European, family of speech. It comprises the Mœso-Gothic, Anglo-Saxon (English), Old Saxon, Friesian, Dutch, Flemish, Old High-German, Middle High-German, New High-German, Icelandic, Ferroic, Danish, Swedish, and Norwegian. See *Aryan Languages*.

Tewkesbury, Battle of. A sanguinary battle fought at Tewkesbury, England, on May 4th, 1471, between the Yorkists under Edward IV and the Lancastrians commanded by Queen Margaret, the consort of Henry VI. The latter were signally defeated,— the Queen being taken prisoner and her son slain. This battle marks the last attempt of the House of Lancaster to regain the throne.

Thalia. In classic mythology, one of the nine Muses. She presided over comedy and burlesque. See *Muses*.

Thames Embankments. See *Albert Embankment ; Victoria Embankment*.

Thames on Fire. See *Setting the Thames on Fire*.

Thames Tunnel. A brick arched passage-way under the Thames at London, commenced in 1825, under the direction of Brunel, the eminent English engineer, and completed in 1843, at a cost of £468,000. It consists of two parallel archways, each 14 feet wide, 16 feet high, and 1300 feet long. The tunnel was originally intended for carriages and pedestrians, but failed to pay expenses, and in 1865 was sold to the "East London Railway Company" for £200,000.

Thanksgiving Day. A national holiday in the United States of America, usually celebrated on the last Thursday of November. It was first observed as a harvest-festival by the Pilgrim Fathers at Plymouth, Massachusetts, in September, 1621 ; and long remained an institution peculiar to New England. Since 1863, the Presidents of the United States have appointed the last Thursday of November as a day of annual thanksgiving. The festival has been observed annually in New York State since 1817.

Thapsus, Battle of. A sanguinary battle fought at Thapsus in Northern Africa, in 46 B.C., between the army of Julius Cæsar and the forces of the Senatorial party commanded by Scipio. It resulted in a signal victory for Cæsar.

Théâtre Français. The most famous theatre in Paris, and probably in the world. It is situated in the Place du Palais Royal, and, since 1803, has been the home of the *Comédie Française*. The building was destroyed by fire on March 8th, 1900 ; but was immediately rebuilt, and opened to the public before the close of the Exposition of that year. The original structure was erected in 1782, but was much altered in later years, — the façades being modern. The Doric vestibule contained statues of Talma, M'lle Mars, and M'lle Rachel, while the foyer was adorned with busts and statues of Voltaire, Corneille, Racine, and George Sand. See *Comédie Française*.

Theatre of Marcellus. A famous ruin in Rome, commenced by Julius Cæsar (100–44 B.C.) and completed by Augustus (27 B.C.–14 A.D.), by whom it was dedicated to Marcellus in 13 B.C. It had a seating capacity of 30,000, and resembled in its exterior the Coliseum, which was probably modelled after it. The Theatre of Marcellus was several times injured and restored during the Empire, and in 1086 was converted into a fortress. In 1220 it came into the possession of the Savelli family, who retained it until their extinction in 1712, when it was purchased by the Orsini family, the present owners. Little of the original building remains, except the arcades, which are now used as shops.

Theban Legion. A Roman legion which, according to tradition, was raised in the Thebaïs of Egypt, and was composed entirely of Christians. Being commanded by the Emperor Maximian (286–305 A.D.) not only to sacrifice to the gods but also to assist in the persecution of their fellow-Christians, the soldiers refused to obey, and were all massacred about 286 A.D. Their leader, Mauritius, was canonized.

Theogony (*Gr., Origin of the Gods*). A poem commonly ascribed to Hesiod, the eminent Greek bard, who flourished about 800 B.C. It gives an account of the origin of the world, and the birth of the gods, and concludes with an account of some of the most illustrious heroes of early times.

"Bœotian tradition denied that the *Theogony* was the work of Hesiod, but Herodotus affirms it, and the internal testimony and the *Works and Days* confirm Herodotus." —*Chambers's Encyclopædia.*

"It is not probable that the *Theogony* is the production of the poet who wrote the *Works and Days*, nor was it so regarded by the ancients."—*Who Wrote It?*

Thermes, Les. Remains of Roman baths, near the Hôtel de Cluny, Paris, supposed to have been built by the Emperor Constantius Chlorus, about 300 A.D. Among the parts best preserved are the *Frigidarium*, or chamber for cold baths,—a hall 65 feet long, 37½ feet wide, and 59 feet high,—and the *Tepidarium*, or chamber for warm baths. The water necessary for these baths was brought by an aqueduct,— remains of which may still be seen in the village of Arcueil. See *Hôtel de Cluny.*

Thermometer. The invention of the thermometer is ascribed to Galileo about 1597, to Drebbel of Alcmaer in 1609, to Paulo Sarpi in 1609, and to Sanctorio in 1610. Fahrenheit's thermometer was invented about 1726, and Réaumur's and Celsius's (now called the "Centigrade") soon after. Fahrenheit's scale is in general use in England and the United States, and Réaumur's and Celsius's on the Continent. See *Barometer.*

"The thermometer was not of any great use till early in the eighteenth century, when three men, Fahrenheit, Celsius, and Réaumur, measured off the tube into degrees, so that the exact rise and fall could be known. Celsius and Réaumur took the melting point of ice as zero or 0° of their scale, but Fahrenheit took his from a mixture of snow and salt, which was the greatest cold he knew how to obtain. For this reason 32° is the freezing point of water in a Fahrenheit thermometer, and his other divisions are different from those of Celsius or Réaumur. Celsius's scale is the one now used all over the Continent, and scientific men wish to introduce it into England, because it is so much more simple than Fahrenheit's. It is called 'centigrade,' or a hundred steps, because the tube is so divided that there are exactly 100° between the freezing and the boiling point."—Buckley's *Short History of Natural Science.*

Thermopylæ, Battle of. A famous battle fought at Thermopylæ, in Northern Greece, on August 7th, 8th, and 9th, 480 B.C., between 300 Spartans and 700 Thespians, commanded by Leonidas, and the entire Persian host. For four days Leonidas and his band held the Pass of Thermopylæ against the invaders, at the end of which time Ephialtes, a Trachinian, led the Persians over the mountains by a secret path to the rear of the Greeks, who were thus placed between two hostile armies and were finally cut to pieces. One Greek only escaped, and he is said to have been loaded with reproaches for having fled.

"Go, tell the Spartans, thou that passest by,
  That here, obedient to their laws, we lie."

Theseus. A legendary hero of Attica, whose exploits rivalled those of Hercules. He (1) vanquished the Centaurs in their contest with the

Lapithæ; (2) slew the Minotaur of Crete and escaped from the Labyrinth by means of Ariadne's clew; (3) captured the Marathonian bull; (4) fought against the Amazons; (5) became King of Athens; (6) sailed on the Argonautic Expedition; (7) joined in the Calydonian hunt; (8) abducted Helen from Sparta; (9) attempted to carry off Proserpine from the lower world; and (10) rose from the dead to assist the Athenians at Marathon.

Thieves, Two. The two thieves crucified with Christ have received various names,—the penitent one being known as Demas, Desmas, Dismas, Titus, Matha, and Vicimus, and the unpenitent one as Gestas, Dumachas, Joca, and Justinus. The following lines, translated from the Latin, were repeated, during the Middle Ages, as a charm against thieves. See *Desmas*.

" Of differing merits from three trees incline,
Dismas, and Gestas, and the Power Divine;
Dismas seeks heaven, Gestas his own damnation,
The Mid-one seeks our ransom and salvation.
This charm your goods will save from spoliation."

Third Founder of Rome. A title conferred upon Caius Marius (157–86 B.C.), the Roman general, who saved the Republic from the invasion of the Teutones and Cimbri, in 102–101 B.C.

Thirteen at Table. The popular but senseless superstition that, if thirteen persons sit down to a meal at the same table, one of them will die before the close of the year, is doubtless derived from the story of the " Last Supper," when Jesus Christ sat down at meat with his twelve disciples.

Thirteenth Apostle. A sobriquet conferred upon St. John Chrysostom (347–407 A.D.), Patriarch of Constantinople, and the greatest preacher of his time.

Thirteenth Vendémiaire. See *Day of the Sections.*

Thirty-Nine Articles. The points of doctrine agreed upon by the archbishops, bishops, and clergy of the Church of England, at the convocation held in London in 1562, under Archbishop Parker. They received the royal authority and that of Parliament in 1571.

These Articles relate to the doctrine of the Trinity, the rule of faith, the doctrine concerning sin and redemption, the general theory of the Church, and the doctrine of the sacraments. The *Thirty-Nine Articles* were preceded by the *Forty-Two Articles*, prepared in 1551, and set forth in 1553. In November, 1871, the *Thirty-Nine Articles* were ordered to be removed from the curriculum of studies at Oxford University. See *Forty-Two Articles.*

Thirty Tyrants.

(1) A body of magistrates—thirty in number — chosen by Lysander, the Spartan, to rule over the Athenians in 404 B.C., at the close of the Peloponnesian War. After a rule of one year —marked by infamous cruelties—they were expelled by Thrasybulus.

(2) A set of military usurpers that aspired to the imperial purple of Rome during the reign of the Emperor Gallienus (253–268 A.D.), and by their contests imperilled the existence of the Empire. See *Tyrants.*

"The number thirty must be taken with great latitude, as only nineteen are given, and their resemblance to the thirty tyrants of Athens is extremely fanciful."—Brewer's *Dictionary of Phrase and Fable.*

Thirty Years' War. The name collectively applied to a series of wars in Germany, that lasted from 1618 to 1648, a period of 30 years. This long struggle was terminated by the Peace of Westphalia. The war had its origin in the quarrels between the Catholics and Protestants of Germany; but after 1635 it degenerated into a political struggle between Austria on the one side and France and Sweden on the other.

Thisbe. See *Pyramus and Thisbe.*

Thistle. The adoption of the thistle by the Scotch as a national emblem, is accounted for by Brewer in the following way:

"The Danes thought it cowardly to attack an enemy by night, but on one occasion deviated from their rule. On they crept, barefooted, noiselessly, and unobserved, when one of the men put his foot on a thistle, which made him cry out. The alarm was given, the Scotch fell upon the night-party, and defeated them with terrible slaughter. Ever since the thistle has been adopted as the insignia of Scotland, with the motto *Nemo me impune lacessit.*"—Brewer's *Dictionary of Phrase and Fable.*

Thomists. A name given to the followers of Thomas Aquinas (1227–1274), the noted Schoolman. The Thomists were Nominalists. See *Angelic Doctor; Scotists.*

Thousand and One Nights. See *Arabian Nights' Entertainments.*

Thrasymene, Battle of Lake. A bloody battle, fought near Lake Thrasymene in Northern Italy, in 217 B.C., between the Carthaginians, commanded by Hannibal, and the Romans under the consul Flaminius. The latter were totally routed with a loss of 15,000 killed and wounded, and 6000 taken prisoners. The Carthaginian loss was only 1500. About 10,000 Romans—covered with wounds—made their escape, leaving Flaminius dead on the field. It is recorded that an earthquake shook the neighborhood during the battle, but was totally unobserved by the combatants.

" And such the storm of battle on this day,
   And such the phrensy, whose convulsion
     blinds
 To all save carnage, that, beneath the fray,
 An earthquake reeled unheededly away !
 None felt stern Nature rocking at his feet,
 And yawning forth a grave for those who
     lay
 Upon their bucklers for a winding-sheet :
 Such is the absorbing hate when warring
     nations meet."
                    Childe Harold, iv, lxiii.

Threadneedle Street. This street in London was originally called

Threeneedle Street, and is said to have derived its name from the *three needles*, forming part of the shield of the Needle-Makers' Company's Arms. See *Old Lady of Threadneedle Street.*

" *Threadneedle Street* (London), a corruption of *Thridenal Street, i. e.*, the third street from Cheapside. (Anglo-Saxon, *thridda*, 'third')."—Brewer's *Dictionary of Phrase and Fable.*

Three Estates. See *Estates of the Realm.*

Three Gilt Balls. See *Pawnbrokers' Balls.*

Three Great Generals Never Defeated.
(1) Alexander the Great (356–323 B.C.).
(2) Julius Cæsar (100–44 B.C.).
(3) Arthur (1769–1852), Duke of Wellington.

Three Kings of Cologne. See *Cologne, Three Kings of.*

Three L's. A title collectively applied to the three great French mathematicians, Laplace, Lagrange, and Legendre.

Three-Men Wine. The name given to any wine of inferior quality, from the notion that it takes, in addition to the unwilling drinker, one man to hold him down and a second to pour the liquid down his throat.

Three R's. A phrase used to denote the fundamental elements of a primary education, which are humorously regarded as spelled *reading*, (*w*)*riting*, and (*a*)*rithmetic.*

Three Theological Virtues.
(1) Faith.
(2) Hope.
(3) Charity.

Thunderbolt of Italy. A sobriquet conferred upon Gaston de Foix (1489–1512), Duc de Nemours, in allusion to his brilliant military success, while commanding the French forces in Italy.

Thunderbolt of Painting. A title conferred upon Jacopo Robusti (1512–1594),— surnamed Il Tintoretto,— the noted Italian painter, in allusion to the vigor and rapidity of his execution. See *Tintoretto*.

Thunderer. An epithet originally conferred upon Captain Edward Sterling of the London *Times*, in consequence of an article contributed by him to that paper, beginning with the words: " We *thundered* forth the other day an article on the subject of social and political reform." The phrase is now often used to denote the newspaper itself.

"Of Edward Sterling, Captain Edward Sterling as his title was, who in the latter period of his life became well known in London political society, whom, indeed, all England, with a curious mixture of mockery and respect, and even fear, knew well as the *Thunderer* of the *Times* newspaper, there were much to be said, did the present task and its limits permit."—Carlyle's *Life of Sterling*.

Thundering Legion. A title conferred upon the twelfth legion of the Roman army, whose prayers for rain during the campaign of Marcus Aurelius against the Marcomanni in 174 A.D., were followed, according to tradition, by a violent thunder-storm which not only quenched their thirst, but, in addition, threw the enemy into confusion and secured an easy victory for the Romans.

Thunders of the Vatican. A term sometimes applied to the anathemas and denunciations of the Pope of Rome, which are issued from the palace of the Vatican. The phrase was first used by Voltaire, in 1748.

Thyestean Banquet. The name given to any banquet at which human flesh is eaten,—in allusion to Thyestes, whose two sons were served up to him at a feast given in his honor by his brother Atreus.

"In order to take revenge, Atreus, pretending to be reconciled to Thyestes, recalled him to Mycenæ, killed his two sons, and placed their flesh before their father at a banquet, who unwittingly partook of the horrid meal. Thyestes fled with horror, and the gods cursed Atreus and his house."— Smith's *Classical Dictionary*.

Tichborne Claimant. A term applied to Thomas Castro, an Australian butcher,—alias Arthur Orton of Wapping, England,—who called himself Sir Roger Charles Tichborne (lost at sea in 1854), and laid claim to the baronetcy and to large estates in Hampshire, worth about £24,000 a year. He was nonsuited, March 6th, 1872, in an effort to establish his claim; but soon after was committed for perjury, and, after a trial lasting 188 days, was found guilty and sentenced to 14 years' imprisonment with hard labor. He was released on ticket-of-leave in 1884, confessed his imposture in 1895, and died in 1898. His trial was one of the longest known in England, and cost £55,315.

Ticket-of-Leave. A written permit first granted by the English Government in 1854, whereby a penal convict was given his liberty before the expiration of his term, as a reward of good conduct while in prison. He was obliged, however, to report to the police at stated times until his sentence expired, and if a fresh crime was committed by him during that period, his ticket-of-leave was immediately recalled. It is said that 2666 convicts were thus liberated in England in 1856. In 1861–1863, the system proved to be a failure, owing to the many crimes committed by the prisoners thus set at liberty, and the practice was virtually abolished by the *Penal Servitude Act* of 1864.

Tiddy-Doll. A nickname given to Napoleon Bonaparte (1769–1821) by James Gilbray, the English caricaturist, in one of his most famous cartoons.

Tierra del Fuego (*Span., Region of Fire*). This large island—lying south of the strait that bears his name—was so called by its discoverer, Ferdinand

Magellan, on account of the numerous fires seen on it at night.

"*Terra del Fuego* was discovered by Magellan in 1520, and named 'Land of Fire,' from the fires he saw on its coasts during the night. Those fires are supposed to have been volcanic. The doubt thrown upon this opinion, by the circumstance that no volcanoes had been observed by more recent travellers, has been, in a great measure, removed by Captain Hall, who himself witnessed a volcanic eruption on one of these islands, in November, 1820."—Lippincott's *Gazetteer of the World*.

Tiers-État (*Fr., Third Estate*). The name given in France, previous to the Revolution, to the third order, or Commons, of the nation, which, together with the two privileged orders,— the Nobility and the Clergy,— composed the States-General. See *Estates of the Realm ; States-General*.

Tilbury. The name given to a kind of gig, or two-wheeled carriage, without top or cover, seating two persons. It was named in honor of its inventor, *Tilbury*, a famous London coach-builder during the early part of the 19th century.

Tilsit, Peace of. A treaty of peace between France and Russia, signed at Tilsit, a town in East Prussia, on July 7th, 1807. In accordance with its provisions, the Czar recognized the Confederation of the Rhine, and agreed to close his ports against England. Prussia was stripped of more than half of her former dominions, and her army was reduced to 42,000 men. The Emperor of Russia, in addition, recognized Napoleon's three brothers — Joseph, Louis, and Jerome, — as Kings of Naples, Holland, and Westphalia.

Tinker's Dam. " A tinker's dam is a wall of dough or of soft clay raised around a spot which a plumber, in repairing, desires to flood with solder. The material of this dam can be used only once, and is thrown away after this very temporary period of usefulness. Hence the proverb ' not worth a tinker's dam,' which either through a

perverse humor or through misunderstanding has been converted into profanity by the addition of a final *n*." —Walsh's *Literary Curiosities*. See *Dam, Don't Care a*.

Tintagel. A ruined castle on the west coast of Cornwall, famous in romance as the birthplace of King Arthur and the seat of his Court. It is also noted as the traditional residence of King Mark and Queen Isolde. Although the oldest portion of the ruins is apparently of Norman construction, it is very probable that a castle stood on the same site in Saxon times, and even earlier. Also written *Tintagil*.

" They found a naked child upon the sands
Of dark *Tintagil* by the Cornish sea,
And that was Arthur."
Tennyson's Guinevere.

Tintoretto (*It., Little Dyer*). A name assumed by Jacopo Robusti (1512–1594), the famous Venetian painter, in allusion to the occupation of his father, who was a dyer (*It., tintore*). He was surnamed *Il Furioso*, from the rapidity with which he worked. See *Furioso ; Thunderbolt of Painting*.

Tippecanoe. A nickname conferred upon General William Henry Harrison (1773–1840) during the political campaign of 1840, which resulted in his election to the presidency. The title was given to him in allusion to his victory over the Indians at the junction of the Tippecanoe and Wabash rivers in Indiana, on November 7th, 1811.

Titans. The six sons and six daughters of Uranus (Heaven) and Gæa (Earth), who, at their mother's instigation, deposed their father and liberated the Hecatoncheires and the Cyclopes from Tartarus. They afterwards waged a ten-years' war against Zeus, but were overthrown by his thunderbolts and thrust into Tartarus. During this war, Zeus and his allies were intrenched on Mount Olympus and the Titans on Mount Othrys. The name "Titans" was also given to those divine or semi-divine beings that were descended from the Titans, such as Prometheus, Hecate, Helios, and Selene. See *Briareus*.

Title on Cross. According to tradition, the wooden tablet with a superscription in Hebrew, Greek, and Latin, set up by Pilate over Christ's Cross, was discovered in Jerusalem by St. Helena, the mother of Constantine, and sent by her to Rome. It was deposited in a leaden casket above the vaulted dome of the Church of Santa Croce, and carefully bricked up,—its position being marked by an inscription in mosaic. Years after, some workmen, while engaged in repairing the church, came across the sacred relic, which, although it had been buried for more than 300 years, was found to be in a remarkably well preserved state. Pope Alexander III (1159-1181) issued a bull, commemorating this discovery and authenticating the title.

Tittlebat Titmouse. The leading character of Samuel Warren's novel, *Ten Thousand a Year*. He is an ignorant, vulgar upstart, who is suddenly raised, through the machinations of a firm of unscrupulous attorneys, to a high social position, but is eventually reduced to his proper level. See *Ten Thousand a Year*.

Toddy. The name of this beverage is derived from the Hindu *tari*, the juice of the palmyra tree, from which a spirituous liquor is obtained by fermentation.

Toledo. The principal thoroughfare of Naples, Italy, so called because laid out by Don Pedro de Toledo, in 1540. It traverses the city from north to south, for a distance of one and a half miles, and separates the ancient part of Naples from the modern part. It has been pronounced the noisiest and most densely crowded street in Europe. It is now called the *Strada di Roma* or, officially, the *Via di Roma*.

Toltecs. A people that dwelt in Mexico and Central America, prior to the Aztecs. According to tradition, they came from the north during the eighth century after Christ, and established their capital at Tulu, north of the Mexican valley. The Toltecs were a mild, peaceful people, devoted to agriculture and the arts, and especially skilled in architecture. To them is attributed the invention of the Mexican hieroglyphics and calendar. See *Aztecs*.

"All that we can gather about them with safety is that they were a sedentary Indian stock which at some remote time settled in portions of central Mexico, as, for instance, at Tula, Tullantzinco, Teotihuacan, and perhaps Cholula. Nothing certain is known of their language, and it must not be overlooked that the so-called *Toltec* names mentioned in the chronicles are in the Nahuatl idiom." — Bandelier's *An Archæological Tour in Mexico*.

Tom and Jerry. A novel by Pierce Egan, published in 1821-1822, which contains the adventures of Jerry Hawthorn, Corinthian Tom, and Bob Logic. There is also a farce with this title, written by W. T. Moncrieff, an English dramatist, produced in 1857. The name "Tom and Jerry" is sometimes used to denote a hot drink of rum and water, sweetened, spiced, and beaten up with eggs.

Tomato. The tomato is a native of South America, and was introduced into Europe by the Spaniards in 1583. In the United States, prior to 1830, it was called *love-apple*, a translation of the French name *pomme d'amour*. Some authorities say that the name *pomme d'amour* was given to the tomato on account of its supposed aphrodisiac properties ; but others assert that it is derived from the Italian name *poma dei Mori (Moor's apple),*— the tomato having been imported into Italy from Morocco. The English word *tomato* is derived from the Spanish-American *tamate*.

Tomb of Aaron. The tomb of the first Hebrew high-priest is situated upon Mount Hor, in Arabia Petræa. The present structure is a comparatively modern one, and is built of the ruins of the older tomb. The Arabs still point it out to the traveler, and tradition tends to substantiate their claim to its genuineness.

Tomb of Abélard and Héloïse. A famous tomb in the cemetery of Père-Lachaise, Paris. It consists of a sarcophagus with two recumbent figures, beneath a Gothic canopy, and is partly built of fragments from the Convent of Paraclete,—founded by Abélard,—where the tomb was originally situated. The remains of Abélard and Héloïse were removed to Paris in 1800, and in 1817 they were buried in the sepulchre where they now lie. See *Abélard and Héloïse.*

" But among the thousands and thousands of tombs in Père la Chaise, there is one that no man, no woman, no youth of either sex, ever passes by without stopping to examine. Every visitor has a sort of indistinct idea of the history of its dead, and comprehends that homage is due there, but not one in twenty thousand clearly remembers the story of that tomb and its romantic occupants. This is the grave of Abélard and Héloïse,—a grave which has been more revered, more widely known, more written and sung about and wept over, for seven hundred years, than any other in Christendom, save only that of the Saviour."—*Innocents Abroad* (Mark Twain).

Tomb of Barbarossa. Frederick I, (1152–1190) Emperor of Germany—surnamed Barbarossa,—was drowned, during the Third Crusade, while bathing in the river Calycadnus, in Asia Minor. He was buried at Antioch ; but, according to tradition, he is not dead, but sleeping,—either in the Untersberg near Salzburg, or the Kyffhaüser in Thuringia, where he sits with his six knights,—awaiting the signal to return and rescue his beloved Germany from peril. His beard has grown entirely through the stone table-slab, but it must wind itself three times around the table before

the hour of awakening comes. See *Barbarossa.*

Tomb of Cecilia Metella. A circular tower 70 feet in diameter, situated on the Appian Way, about two miles from the city of Rome. It was erected, about the time of Christ, as the burial-place of Cecilia Metella, the wife of Crassus. The outside of the structure was originally covered with the finest travertine marble, but this has been almost entirely removed to build the Fountain of Trevi. It served as a fortress in later times, and suffered much in consequence. The battlements are Middle-Age additions. The present walls are twenty-five feet thick. See *Appian Way.*

Tomb of Charlemagne. A vault in the Cathedral of Aix-la-Chapelle in Rhenish Prussia, covered with a marble slab inscribed with the words CARLO MAGNO. At his death in 814, the Emperor Charlemagne was placed therein, in a sitting posture, upon a marble throne, dressed in his imperial robes, —with his crown upon his head, his sceptre in his hand, and the Gospels lying open upon his lap. In 1001— nearly two hundred years after—the tomb was opened by order of the Emperor Otho III (996–1002), and the remains were found in a remarkable state of preservation. In 1215, by order of the Emperor Frederick II (1214–1250), the body was removed from the vault and placed in a casket of gold and silver, in which it is preserved in the treasury of the cathedral at the present day. The marble throne on which the dead Charlemagne sat for four hundred years is to be seen in the cathedral. Till 1558, it was used at the coronation of the German Emperors. The other relics found in the vault are preserved in Vienna.

Tomb of Columbus. After the death of Columbus at Valladolid, Spain, in 1506, his remains were buried in that city ; but in 1513 they were removed to Seville. In 1536, his body, together with that of his son, Diego, was taken to Santo Domingo in Hayti, and interred in the cathedral there. When, however, the Spanish part of the island of Hayti fell into the hands of the French in 1795, the Spaniards were allowed to remove the remains of the great navigator to the cathedral in Havana, where they remained until 1898 when they were transported to Spain. There is good reason, however, to believe that it was the bones of Diego, his son, and not those of Columbus himself that were removed from Hayti to Cuba ; and that the body of the discoverer of the New World still rests in the Cathedral of Santo Domingo.

Tomb of Cyrus. A remarkable ruin, in a tolerable state of preservation, at Pasargadæ in ancient Babylonia. It has been called " a house upon a pedestal," and consists of a pyramidal base constructed of huge blocks of white marble, surmounted by a house of the same material, covered with a sloping stone roof. The interior consists of a small chamber, 10 feet long, 7 feet wide, and 8 feet high, entered by a low and narrow door ; there were deposited, in a golden coffin, the remains of the great conqueror. It is supposed that a row of 24 columns (some of whose broken shafts still remain) enclosed the sacred spot. On these mutilated columns is repeatedly found the inscription (written in Persian and in the so-called Median) I AM CYRUS THE KING, THE ACHÆMENIAN.

Tomb of Dante. A small circular building at Ravenna, Italy, containing the remains of the famous poet, who was buried there with great pomp in 1321 by his friend Guido. It is said that, at some unknown period, the body of Dante was removed from the sarcophagus in which it had been originally placed, and was walled up in the Church of St. Francis, near by, in a rough box, marked *Dantis Ossa* (*Lat.*, *Bones of Dante*). This, according to

the story, was discovered by accident in 1865, and the remains, after being identified beyond any possibility of doubt, were replaced in the sarcophagus from which they had been removed.

Tomb of Mohammed. An irregularly shaped, doorless chamber in the Mosque El-Haram (*Ar.*, *the Sacred*), in Medina. See *Medina*.

"It is surmounted by a large gilt crescent above the 'Green Dome,' springing from a series of globes, and hedged in with a closely-latticed brass railing, in which are small apertures for prayer. The interior is hung with costly curtains embroidered with large gold letters, stating that behind them lie the bodies of the Prophet of God and of the first two califs—which curtains, changed whenever worn out, or when a new sultan ascends the throne, cover a square edifice of black marble, in the midst of which is Mohammed's tomb. Its exact place is indicated by a long pearly rosary—still seen in 1855—suspended from the curtain. The Prophet's body is believed to lie undecayed at full length on the right side, with the right palm supporting the right cheek, the face directed towards Mecca. Close behind him is placed in the same position, Abubekr, and behind him Omar ; and Fatimeh's house is represented by a modern erection hard by. There seems no reason to doubt that the Prophet was buried in the space (originally Ayesha's hut) now enclosed in the mosque ; nor is it likely that the grave was ever rifled. That his coffin, said to be covered with a marble slab, and cased with silver (no European has ever seen it), rests suspended in the air is of course an idle Christian fable. Of the treasures which this sanctuary once contained, little now remains."—*Chambers's Encyclopædia*.

Tomb of Napoleon. A superb mausoleum, designed by Visconti, and situated beneath the Dome of the " Invalides " in Paris. It consists of an open circular crypt, 20 feet in depth and 36 feet in diameter, in the centre of which rises a sarcophagus containing the remains of the first Napoleon. This sarcophagus — which is 13 feet long, 6½ feet wide, and 14½ feet high — consists of a single block of red granite, brought from Finland at a cost of 140,000 francs. The sides of the crypt are adorned with ten marble reliefs by Simart, and twelve colossal

Victories by Pradier. The entrance to the crypt is flanked by two sarcophagi containing the ashes of Duroc and Bertrand, the faithful friends of the Emperor. Within may be seen the marble statue of the Emperor in his imperial robes; the crown of gold voted by the town of Cherbourg; the sword he wore at Austerlitz; and the insignia used by him on state occasions. Over the bronze gateway are inscribed the words from Napoleon's will : " I desire that my ashes may repose on the banks of the Seine, in the midst of the French people whom I have loved so well." The total cost of the tomb was nearly $2,000,000. See *Hôtel des Invalides.*

Tomb of Rachel. A Mohammedan wely, or tomb, marking the burial-place of Rachel, the wife of the patriarch Jacob—situated about five miles south of Jerusalem and half a mile north of Bethlehem. Jewish, Christian, and Mohammedan tradition agree in identifying this spot with the tomb of Rachel, the wife of Jacob. See *Bethlehem.*

"And Rachel died, and was buried in the way to Ephrath, which is Beth-lehem. And Jacob set a pillar upon her grave : that is the pillar of Rachel's grave unto this day."— *Genesis* xxxv, 19, 20.

Tomb of Virgil. A Roman columbarium, or sepulchre (above the eastern entrance to the Grotto of Posilippo), near Naples, which, according to tradition, is the tomb of Virgil. It bears the following words, which are said, but without sufficient authority, to have fallen from the lips of the dying poet :

"Mantua me genuit ; Colabri rapuere ; tenet nunc
Parthenope ; cecini pascua, rura, duces."

See *Grotto of Posilippo.*

"Above the grotto are the remains of a columbarium, which time out of mind has enjoyed the honor of being called the tomb of Virgil. Nor is it by any means impossible that it is so, though it must be admitted that the weight of evidence is against the claim. But there is quite enough of interest clinging

round it from the fact that a long line of poets and scholars, beginning with Petrarch and Boccaccio, have visited the spot, more in the spirit of faith than of scepticism. There is nothing at all remarkable in the structure itself, which is of brick, shattered by time, and overgrown with myrtle, wild vines, and grass. Laurels should be there, but are not. They have frequently been planted, but the rapacity of visitors has cut them to pieces, and brought them to an untimely end. Whether Virgil were really buried here or not, it is certainly a place which a poet might well choose for his last repose. The rich life of the soil, breaking forth in a luxuriant net-work of vegetation, suggests the creative energy of genius, and breathes around an air of hope and promise."
—Hillard's *Six Months in Italy.*

Tomb of Washington. See *Mount Vernon.*

Tombs of the Judges. A series of tombs, situated at the head of the Valley of Jehoshaphat, northwest of Jerusalem.

"Though their origin is involved in mystery, they are generally supposed to have contained the remains of the members of the Jewish Sanhedrim, and the supposition is confirmed by the seventy niches within them, coinciding with the number of members composing that venerable tribunal."— Newman's *From Dan to Beersheba.*

Tombs of the Kings. A group of sepulchres, situated near Jerusalem, about half a mile to the north from the Damascus Gate.

"Though by common consent they are called the 'Tombs of the Kings,' yet there are no sepulchres beyond the walls of Jerusalem as to the origin and founder of which there is such a variety of opinions. On these points the tombs themselves are dumb, —as they contain neither device nor inscription ; and with one or two ambiguous exceptions, history is likewise silent."— Newman's *From Dan to Beersheba.*

"Howbeit they buried him in the city of David, but not in the *sepulchres of the kings.*"—*2 Chronicles,* xxi, 20.

Tombs of the Prophets. A series of sepulchres excavated from the living rock in the side of the Mount of Olives near Jerusalem. Their origin and founder are alike unknown.

Tombs of the Scaligers. A famous tomb at Verona, Italy, erected in memory of the Scaligeri, a powerful Ghibelline family, which ruled over the city during the 13th and 14th centuries.

Tombs of the Scipios. A group of ancient tombs, situated on the Appian Way, not far from Rome. They were discovered during the closing years of the eighteenth century, and are regarded by archæologists as objects of great interest. Most of the inscriptions found in these tombs have been removed to the Vatican.

"In the same room with this torso [Belvedere] is one of the most interesting objects in Rome,—the sarcophagus of gray stone found in the *tomb of the Scipios*, the shape of which is so well known by the many copies which have been spread over the world. The works of the republic are not numerous in Rome; and this venerable monument attracts us as well by its antiquity, as by its association with the illustrious family whose name it bears.'—Hillard's *Six Months in Italy.*

Tombs of the Stuarts. The last three representatives of the Stuart family—James Francis Edward (the "Old Pretender"), Charles Edward (the "Young Pretender"), and Henry Benedict (Cardinal York)—are buried in St. Peter's Church at Rome. A marble monument by Canova, bearing the names of James III, Charles III, and Henry IX, was erected over their remains in 1819.

"The crown-jewels, carried off from England by James II. 119 years before, were bequeathed by him [Cardinal York] to George IV., then Prince of Wales, who in 1819 caused Canova to erect a monument in St. Peter's that bears the names of 'James III., Charles III., and Henry IX.''—*Chambers's Encyclopædia.*

"Here repose the last of a memorable race,—a family remarkable, not for great virtues or great capacity, but for great misfortunes. Misfortunes have their dignity and their redeeming power.

Sunt lacrymæ rerum et mentem mortalia tangunt.'

No family ever underwent a more righteous retribution, or more distinctly sowed the harvest of sorrow which they reaped. But here is the end of a great historical chapter : nothing now remains but compassion. Over the dust which here reposes neither puritan nor republican would cherish the remembrance of crimes committed or wrongs endured."—Hillard's *Six Months in Italy.*

Tom, Dick, and Harry. A colloquial expression often used to denote any persons taken at random from the common run of humanity.

Tommy Atkins. A popular nickname for the British soldier.

"The term arose from a little pocketbook, or ledger, at one time served out to British soldiers, in which were to be entered the name, age, date of enlistment, length of service, wounds, medals, etc., of each individual. The War Office sent with each little ledger a form for filling it in, and the 'M or N' selected, instead of the legal 'John Doe' and Richard Roe,' was 'Tommy Atkins.' The books were instantly so named, and it was not many days before the soldier himself was dubbed 'Tommy Atkins.'"—Reddall's *Fact, Fancy, and Fable.*

Tomnoddy. The name given to a simpleton, in various parts of England.

"A puffing, fuming, stupid creature, no more like a 'Jack-a-dandy' than Bill Sikes to Sam Weller."—Brewer's *Dictionary of Phrase and Fable.*

"My Lord *Tomnoddy* got up one day,
    It was half after two,—
    He had nothing to do ;
So his lordship rang for his cabriolet."
            Barham's *The Execution.*

Tom Thumb. The professional name of Charles S. Stratton (1838–1883), a famous American dwarf, exhibited by P. T. Barnum in America and Europe, with great success. When first placed on exhibition (1842), he measured two feet in height, and weighed 16 pounds; in 1863 he had increased to 31 inches, and later to 40 inches. See *Dwarfs, Famous (8).*

"In November, 1842, I was in Albany on business, and as the Hudson River was frozen over, I returned to New York by the Housatonic Railroad, stopping one night at Bridgeport, Connecticut, with my brother, Philo F. Barnum, who at that time kept the Franklin Hotel. I had heard of a remarkably small child in Bridgeport, and, at my request, my brother brought him to the hotel. He was not two feet high; he weighed less than sixteen pounds, and was the smallest child I ever saw that could walk alone; but he was a perfectly formed, bright-eyed little fellow, with light hair and ruddy cheeks, and he enjoyed the best of health. He was exceedingly bashful, but after some coaxing he was induced to talk with me, and he told me that he was the son of Sherwood E. Stratton, and that his own name was Charles S. Stratton. After seeing him and talking with him, I at once determined to secure his services from his parents and to exhibit him in public."— *Struggles and Triumphs* (P. T. Barnum).

Tontine System. A form of life-annuity devised by Lorenzo Tonti, a Neapolitan banker, as a means of raising government loans. Tonti settled in Paris in 1650, and soon after proposed, by means of annuities, to raise the sum of 25,000,000 livres for the relief of the National Treasury. His scheme, although warmly supported by Cardinal Mazarin, was regarded with suspicion, and finally fell through. Tonti was ultimately committed to the Bastille, where he seems to have died.

Topaz. This precious stone derives its name, according to Pliny, from *Topazas*, an island in the Red Sea,— the location of which is conjectural.

Tophet. The southeast extremity of the Valley of Hinnom, near Jerusalem, where the idolatrous Israelites made their children pass through the fire to Moloch,— casting the living victims into the red-hot arms of the idol. The name "Tophet" is generally supposed to be derived from the Hebrew *toph* (*drum*), because drums were used during the sacrifices to drown the cries of the victims. This opinion, however, rests only on conjecture. See *Hinnom*.

"For *Tophet* is ordained of old; yea, for the king it is prepared; he hath made it deep and large: the pile thereof is fire and much wood; the breath of the Lord, like a stream of brimstone, doth kindle it."— *Isaiah* **xxx**, 33.

Topsy. A young slave-girl in Har-riet Beecher Stowe's novel, *Uncle Tom's Cabin*. See *Uncle Tom's Cabin*.

"She was one of the blackest of her race; and her round, shining eyes, glittering as glass beads, moved with quick and restless glances over everything in the room. Her mouth, half open with astonishment at the wonders of the new Mas'r's parlour, displayed a white and brilliant set of teeth. Her woolly hair was braided in sundry little tails, which stuck out in every direction. The expression of her face was an odd mixture of shrewdness and cunning, over which was oddly drawn, like a kind of veil, an expression of the most doleful gravity and solemnity."— *Uncle Tom's Cabin*.

To-Remain Bible. The name given to a version of the Scriptures, first published at Cambridge, England, in 1805, in allusion to a typographical error, whereby the words "to remain" were incorporated in the text. It is said that the proof-reader, being in doubt as to whether he should retain a comma, wrote concerning the matter to the editor, and received in reply the proof-sheet, with the words "to remain," written on the margin. Thinking that these words had been omitted, the proof-reader transferred them to the text, with the following result :

"But as then he that was born after the flesh persecuted him that was born after the Spirit *to remain*, even so it is now."— *Galatians* iv, 29.

Torgau, Battle of. A battle fought at Torgau, in Saxony, on November 3rd, 1760, between the Austrians commanded by Daun and the Prussians under Frederick the Great (1740–1786). The Austrians were defeated and forced to abandon the field.

Torlonia Gallery. A gallery of sculpture in the Torlonia Palace in Rome. It contains about 600 statues, a large number of which are restorations. The palace was built about 1650, and derives its present name from *Torlonia*, the Roman banker, by whom it was bought early in the nineteenth century.

Torre degli Asinelli (*It.*, *Tower of the Asinelli*). One of the two leaning towers at Bologna, Italy, so named from its builder, Gherardo degli Asinelli. It is a brick structure, 274 feet high, and has a lean of 3 feet 4 inches from the perpendicular. It is also called the *Asinella*. See *Garisenda, La.*

Torres-Vedras, Lines of. A vast series of defensive works in three lines, extending from Lisbon to Torres-Vedras — a distance of 25 miles — and encompassing an area of about 500 square miles. These fortifications were constructed by Lord Wellington (1769–1852) to resist the advance of the French into Portugal, and were occupied by him during the winter of 1810–1811.

Torricellian Vacuum. The name given to the space above the mercury in the tube of a barometer. If the instrument is rightly constructed, this space is devoid of air and aqueous vapor, and contains only vapor of mercury. It derives its name from Torricelli, the inventor of the barometer. See *Barometer.*

Torso Belvedere. A famous fragment of Greek sculpture executed, according to the inscription, by Apollonius of Athens, who probably lived in the first century B.C. It was discovered, during the sixteenth century, near the Theatre of Pompey in Rome, and is now in the Museo Pio-Clementino of the Vatican. Often called the Torso of Hercules.

"In a square vestibule at the entrance is the celebrated Torso of Hercules, known as well by the admiration of Michael Angelo as by its own merits. The great excellence of a work crowned by the commendation of so many great names must be taken on trust by those who do not see it for themselves; but as some poetry seems written exclusively for poets, so this colossal fragment addresses self to the trained eye of the artist."— Hillard's *Six Months in Italy.*

Touching for the King's Evil. See *King's Evil.*

Tour St. Jacques. A superb Gothic
48

tower in Paris, 175 feet in height, erected in 1508–1522. It was originally part of the Church of St. Jacques de la Boucherie, which was demolished in 1789. The tower was purchased by the city in 1836, and carefully restored. It now forms one of the most admired monuments of Paris. It was from the summit of the Tour St. Jacques that Pascal (1623–1662) made his first experiments in atmospheric pressure.

Tours, Battle of. A bloody battle fought near Tours, France, on October 17th, 732 A.D., between the Franks, commanded by Charles, the son of Pepin, and the Saracens under Abderrahman. The latter were utterly routed, with a loss, according to the old chroniclers, of 300,000 men. This victory saved Western Europe from Mohammedan rule, and won for Charles the title of Martel (*The Hammer*), from the vigor with which he pounded the Saracens on that memorable day. See *Martel.*

Tower-Hill. An elevated open space, northwest of the Tower of London, famous as the place of execution of state criminals and traitors. Sir Thomas More, Bishop Fisher, Henry Howard, Somerset, Lord Guildford Dudley, Algernon Sidney, Lords Kilmarnock, Balmerino, and Lovat,—all perished there. See *Tower of London.*

Tower of Babel. See *Babel, Tower of.*

Tower of David. A name frequently, but erroneously, given to the Tower of Hippicus, forming part of the ancient citadel on Mount Zion, Jerusalem. This massive structure was erected by Herod the Great (40 B.C.–1 A.D.) in memory of his brother Hippicus, who was slain in battle while fighting in his behalf.

Tower of London. The ancient citadel and state-prison of London, situated on the north bank of the

Thames, about one mile east of London Bridge. Tradition ascribes its foundation to Julius Cæsar ; but for this statement there is no evidence, although the structure may occupy the site of an old Roman fortification. The White Tower — the first part erected — was commenced in 1078 by William the Conqueror (1066–1087), and completed by his son, William Rufus (1087–1100), who, in 1098, surrounded it with walls and a moat, and built, in addition, St. Thomas's Tower and Traitors' Gate. The Tower of London has been added to by several of the sovereigns of England, and covers at the present time an area of 13 acres. It served, in mediæval times, as a palace, a fortress, and a prison ; but is used at the present day simply as an armory, and a jewel-house for the crown-regalia. See *Bloody Tower ; Crown of England ; Regalia of England ; Tower Hill ; White Tower.*

Prince :	I do not like the *Tower*, of any place.— Did Julius Cæsar build that place, my lord ?
Buckingham :	He did, my gracious lord, begin that place, Which, since, succeeding ages have reëdified.
Prince :	Is it upon record, or else reported Successively from age to age, he built it ?
Buckingham :	Upon record, my gracious lord.

Richard III, iii, 1.

Tower of Pisa. See *Leaning Tower of Pisa.*

Towers of Silence. The name given to the peculiar structures used by the Parsees for the disposal of their dead. They consist of towers—called *dakhmas*—open at the top, and covered with iron gratings upon which are placed the bodies of the dead. There the corpses remain exposed to the birds of prey and the action of the elements until the flesh has entirely disappeared and the bones have fallen into a pit beneath, whence they are

removed to a neighboring cavern. The most noted '' Towers of Silence '' are those situated in the vicinity of Bombay, India. See *Parsees.*

Towton, Battle of. A desperate and bloody battle fought at Towton, Yorkshire, on March 29th, 1461, between the Yorkists and the Lancastrians. The Yorkists won a great victory : no quarter was given, and in the battle and rout that ensued, more than 37,000 Lancastrians were slain. Henry VI (1422–1461) and his Queen, Margaret, fled to Scotland, while Edward IV (1461–1483) returned to London, and was proclaimed lawful sovereign of England.

Tractarianism. A movement in the Church of England, which originated at Oxford in 1831, and had for its object the acceptance of certain doctrines by the Anglican Communion, such as Apostolic Succession, Absolution, Regeneration by Baptism, the Real Presence, the Authority of the Church, and the Efficacy of Tradition. It derived its name from the famous *Tracts for the Times,* in which these changes of belief were earnestly advocated. The movement terminated with the secession of Newman and his followers to the Church of Rome in 1845; but its effect remained visible in the growth and development of the High Church party in Great Britain See *Puseyism ; Tracts for the Times.*

Tracts for the Times. The name given to a series of theological paper that appeared at Oxford, England during the years 1833–1841, and wer hence often called the *Oxford Tract* The principal contributors were Joh Henry Newman, Edward Bouver Pusey, John Keble, Isaac William Richard Hurrell Froude, and Arthu Perceval. See *Tractarianism.*

Trade-Winds. The trade-win are generally believed to be so calle because of their usefulness to navig tors, and hence to trade. Brew however, in his *Dictionary of Phrase and Fable*, dissents from this opinion, and says:

"It is a mistake to derive the word from *trade* (commerce), under the notion that they are 'good for trade' (Anglo-Saxon, *treddewind*, a treading wind—*i. e.*, wind of a specific 'beat' or tread ; *tredan*, to tread)."

Trafalgar, Battle of. The most famous naval battle of ancient or modern times,—fought off Cape Trafalgar, Spain, on October 21st, 1805, between the English fleet, numbering 27 ships of the line, commanded by Admiral Nelson, and the combined fleets of France and Spain, numbering 33 ships of the line, under the French admiral Villeneuve and two Spanish admirals. The allied fleet was signally defeated after a bloody contest ; their three admirals were taken, and 19 of their ships were captured, sunk, or destroyed. Nelson was mortally wounded during the action, and the chief command devolved upon Collingwood. The victory of Trafalgar crushed the naval power of France, and put an end to Napoleon's projected invasion of England. See *Trafalgar Square*.

Trafalgar Square. A fine open square in the city of London, dedicated to Lord Nelson, in commemoration of his glorious victory at the battle of Trafalgar (October 21st, 1805). In the centre of the square rises a superb granite column, 145 feet high, crowned with a statue of the admiral, 17 feet in height. Bronze reliefs, cast from cannon captured from the French, adorn the pedestal of the column, while four colossal bronze lions, modelled by Sir Edwin Landseer, couch upon pedestals at the base. The Nelson Column was erected in 1843, by voluntary contributions, at a cost of about £43,000. The Square is further adorned with two fine fountains, and with statues of George IV, Sir Henry Havelock, and Sir Charles James Napier. See *Trafalgar, Battle of*.

Tragedy. "The literal meaning of this word is ' the song of the goat.' Some suppose that the name was given because the Greek actors were dressed in goat-skins to resemble satyrs ; others that a goat was the prize for which the actors competed. The fact remains; the origin is lost."—Edwards's *Words, Facts, and Phrases*.

"A drama with a catastrophe, exhibited first at the Greek festivals of Dionysus (Bacchus), and said to be so named from the *goat* [τράγος] then offered to that god."—Smith's *Glossary of Terms and Phrases*.

Tragic Poet, House of the. See *Cave Canem, House of the*.

Traitors' Bridge. A bridge in the Tower of London, across which all persons convicted of high treason were led, on their entrance into that fortress. See *Tower of London*.

Traitors' Gate. A river-gate in the Tower of London, by which all persons convicted of high treason were formerly admitted. See *Tower of London*.

Trajan's Column. A superb marble column in Trajan's Forum at Rome, erected in 114 A.D., by the Senate and the Roman people, to commemorate the victories of the Emperor Trajan (98–117 A.D.) over the Dacians. It is 132 feet high and about 12 feet in diameter, and is constructed of 34 blocks of Carrara marble, adorned with sculptures in bas-relief. The summit—which is reached by a spiral staircase of 185 steps—was originally surmounted by a colossal gilded statue of the Emperor; but this, having fallen to the ground, was replaced by Pope Sixtus V (1585–1590) with one of St. Peter, 11 feet high. The ashes of Trajan rest beneath this column. See *Forum Romanum ; Trajan's Forum*.

Trajan's Forum. A magnificent monument of ancient Rome, built by the Emperor Trajan (98–117 A.D.) under the direction of the architect Apollodorus, and completed in about 15 years. It occupies the space between the Capitoline and Quirinal

Hills,—originally a ridge of land. This was cut away to a depth of 100 feet, and the Forum placed in the valley thus formed. It is said that the sum of $12,223,000 was paid by the Emperor to secure the land on the sides and top of the ridge. Trajan's Forum contained Trajan's Column, Trajan's Basilica, the Ulpian Basilica, and the Ulpian Library ; and was surrounded by porticoes adorned with statues and other works of art. Portions of the ruins of this Forum were excavated by Pope Paul III (1534–1550), and later by the French in 1812 ; but a large part still lies buried under the surrounding streets and buildings. See *Forum Romanum ; Trajan's Column.*

Trajan's Wall. The name given to an old Roman earthwork, 8 to 15 feet high, extending across the Dobrudja from the Danube above Czernavoda to Kustendji on the Black Sea. It was used as a rampart against the Russians in 1854.

Transfiguration. A famous painting by Raphael (1483–1520), in the Vatican at Rome, executed by order of Cardinal Giulio de Medici for the Cathedral of Narbonne, France. It remained unfinished at the time of Raphael's death, and was hung above his body as it lay in state in the Pantheon. The *Transfiguration* is, by common consent, regarded as the first painting in the world, although the combination of two scenes on one canvas has been severely criticised. The lower part was completed by Giulio Romano, one of Raphael's pupils, from designs of the master. The picture was taken to Paris in 1797, and, on its restoration to Rome, was placed in the Vatican.

"It must ever be matter of wonder that anyone could have doubted of the grand unity of such a conception as this. In the absence of the Lord, the disconsolate parents bring a possessed boy to the disciples of the Holy One. They seem to have been making attempts to cast out the Evil Spirit ; one has opened a book, to see whether by chance any spell were contained in it which might

be successful against this plague, but in vain. At this moment appears He who alone has the power, and appears transfigured in glory."—*Goethe.*

"All great actions have been simple, and all great pictures are. The *Transfiguration*, by Raphael, is an eminent example of this peculiar merit. A calm, benignant beauty shines over all this picture, and goes directly to the heart. It seems almost to call you by name. The sweet and sublime face of Jesus is beyond praise, yet how it disappoints all florid expectations ! This familiar, simple, home-speaking countenance is as if one should meet a friend."—*Emerson.*

"The picture has been criticized for its twofold action, which, it is said, makes of it, in reality, two pictures instead of one. But the subject necessarily involves two elements, the divine and the human, in order to give it completeness. The spectacle of the *transfiguration* would have been no more than a splendid vision but for the connection thus established between the Saviour's glorified state and the sufferings of humanity which were in him to find healing and relief. The contrasts afforded by such a subject—calling forth the two principles of worship and sympathy—were peculiarly suited to Raphael's genius, which was reverential, tender, and sensitive ; and it is evident that he never threw more of his own individuality into any of his works than into this, and that no one is on the whole more characteristic."—Hillard's *Six Months in Italy.*

Transpadane Republic. A republic, north of the Po, established by Napoleon Bonaparte in 1796. It included Lombardy and part of Venetia, and in the following year was united with the Cispadane Republic to form the Cisalpine Republic. See *Cisalpine Republic ; Cispadane Republic.*

Trans-Siberian Railway. "*The Siberian Railway* was commenced in 1891 to connect Vladivostock with the Russo-Siberian frontier (Ekaterinberg), a distance of about 4000 miles; Irkutsk, on the west of Lake Baikal (and about 3,830 miles from St. Petersburg), was reached in March, 1899, and the line was opened as far as Chita in December, 1899, whence it will proceed through the Trans-Baikal province (Zabaikalskaya) and the maritime province of Amur to its final destination, Peking, *via* Vladivostock. A section from Vladivostock to Khabarooka is complete, thus shortening the distance to be traversed by over 500 miles. A line is projected, but not yet officially sanctioned, from Omsk to join at Taskend with *The Trans-Caspian Railway* from Poti to Baku on the western side of the lake, and on the eastern side from Krasnovodsk, *via* Merv and Bokhara to Taskend, whence branches run to Khakand and Andijan, another branch running from Merv to Kushk, or about 80 miles east of Herat." — *Whitaker's Almanack* (1901).

Transubstantiation. A doctrine held by the Roman Catholic and Greek Churches, which asserts that the bread and wine in the Eucharist are, by consecration, miraculously converted into the actual body and blood of Christ. It was established as an article of the Roman Catholic faith by the Council of Trent (1545-1563), in the following words : " If any one shall say that, in the most holy sacrament of the Eucharist, there remains the substance of bread and wine together with the body and blood of our Lord Jesus Christ; and shall deny that wonderful and singular conversion of the whole substance of the bread into the body, and of the whole substance of the wine into the blood, the species of bread and wine alone remaining— which conversion the Roman Catholic Church most fittingly calls Transubstantiation — let him be anathema." See *Consubstantiation ; Elevation of the Host ; Real Presence.*

Transvaal. The name given to the country in South Africa, just beyond the river Vaal.

Trappists. Members of a Cistercian Order in the Roman Catholic Church, noted for the extreme austerity of its rule. It was founded in 1140, by Rotrou, Comte de Perche, in the Abbey of La Trappe, in Normandy, and was reformed in 1675 by Jean le Bouthillier de la Rancé. The Trappists now enjoin perpetual silence,— except for devotion and salutation. The members devote eleven hours of the day to prayer and meditation, and the remainder to severe manual labor. They arise at two o'clock in the morning, and retire at seven o'clock in the winter and at eight o'clock in the summer. Their thoughts are supposed to be directed solely to repentance and death, and their only speech is the responsive greeting, " Memento mori." The Trappists were suppressed during the French Revolution, but flourish at the present day in France, Italy, Germany, England, and parts of the United States.

Traveled Horses. A name frequently applied to the " Bronze Horses " of St. Mark's Cathedral, Venice, in allusion to their many migrations. For a brief account of their wanderings, see article, *Bronze Horses.*

Treacle Bible. A name sometimes given to the version of the Bible, published in 1568, in which the word *treacle* is used, instead of *balm*, in the passage : " Is there no *treacle* in Gilead ? is there no physician there ? " —*Jeremiah* viii, 22.

Treasure - Trove (*Fr.*, *Trésor Trouvé*). The name given to coin, gold or silver plate, or bullion—found hidden in the earth or other private place,—the owner being unknown. According to the Roman Law, such treasure, if found by a man on his own land, belonged to the finder ; but, if found on the land of another, was divided between the finder and the landowner. In England, treasure-trove belongs to the Crown, and concealment by the finder is an indictable offense, punishable by fine and imprisonment. If, however, the treasure is not actually covered by the earth, it belongs to the finder. In the United States, treasure-trove usually belongs to the person finding it.

Treaty Elm. An elm-tree, formerly standing in the environs of Philadelphia, under which William Penn (1644–1718) held his famous interview with the Indians, on October 14th, 1682.

"On the fourteenth of October, 1682, Penn met the Indians of the Lenni Lenape nation, under an old elm at Kensington (then Shackamaxon), to confirm a treaty which had been made with them, and so firmly was it established, and so well kept, that the savages respected its terms for sixty years, and there was no war with the Indians before the Revolution."—Gilman's *History of the American People.*

Trebia, Battle of the. A sanguinary battle fought near the mouth of the Trebia, a river of Northern Italy, in 218 B.C., between 38,000 Carthaginians, commanded by Hannibal, and 45,000 Romans under the Consul Sempronius. The Romans were totally defeated with a loss of 30,000 men,—killed, wounded, and missing. This battle was one of Hannibal's most brilliant victories, and stamped him as one of the greatest masters of the art of war.

Tree of the Knowledge of Good and Evil. A tree in the Garden of Eden, the fruit of which, according to *Genesis,* Adam and Eve were forbidden to eat, under penalty of death.

"But of the *tree of the knowledge of good and evil,* thou shalt not eat of it: for in the day that thou eatest thereof thou shalt surely die."—*Genesis* ii, 17.

" And next to life,
Our death, the *tree of knowledge,* grew fast by,
Knowledge of good bought dear by knowing ill."
Paradise Lost, iv, 220–222.

Tree of Life. A tree in the midst of the Garden of Eden, whose fruit, according to *Genesis,* if eaten by Adam and Eve, would have conferred immortality upon them.

"And the Lord God said, Behold, the man is become as one of us, to know good and evil: and now, lest he put forth his hand, and take also of the *tree of life,* and eat, and live forever:

Therefore the Lord God sent him forth from the garden of Eden, to till the ground from whence he was taken.

So he drove out the man: and he placed at the east of the garden of Eden cherubim, and a flaming sword which turned every way, to keep the way of the *tree of life.*"—*Genesis* iii, 22–24.

" In this pleasant soil
His far more pleasant garden God ordain'd;
Out of the fertile ground he caused to grow
All trees of noblest kind for sight, smell, taste;
And all amid them stood the *tree of life,*
High, eminent, blooming ambrosial fruit
Of vegetable gold."
Paradise Lost, iv, 214–220.

Trees, Largest. See *Big Trees of California.*

Trees of California. See *Big Trees of California.*

Trees of Liberty. The name given to trees, branches, or poles, set up in public places, " as symbols of growing freedom." They were frequently adorned with liberty-caps, flags, ribbons, and other devices. This custom originated in America during the War for Independence, and was adopted by the French in 1790, and by the Italians in 1848.

Tre Fontane (*It., Three Fountains*). A melancholy spot about two miles from Rome—outside the Ostian Gate, —which, according to tradition, was the scene of St. Paul's martyrdom. The name is derived from the legend of the three fountains that gushed forth at the places where the apostle's head struck the ground during the three bounds made by it after decapitation. The Church of San Paolo alle Tre Fontane stands upon the spot where the apostle is said to have been beheaded; and contains the pillars to which he is supposed to have been bound, the block of marble on which he is said to have been decapitated and the " three fountains " above mentioned.

Tremont. Trimountaine, or Tremont, is the name originally given t

Boston by the inhabitants of Charlestown, in allusion to the three summits of Beacon Hill on which the city was built. It was founded on March 17th, 1630, and on September 17th of the same year the General Court changed its name to Boston, in compliment to Mr. Isaac Johnson of Boston, England, —one of the leading men in the Massachusetts Bay Colony.

Trent Affair. On November 8th, 1861, Captain Wilkes of the United States war-steamer *San Jacinto* intercepted at sea the British mail-steamer *Trent*, and removed therefrom, on his own responsibility, James M. Mason and John Slidell, Confederate envoys accredited to Great Britain and France respectively. The prisoners were conveyed to Boston and confined in Fort Warren ; but were released on January 1st, 1862, on the formal demand of the British Government, and permitted to sail for Europe. The affair created intense excitement at the time, and threatened unpleasant relations between the two countries ; but the matter was amicably adjusted by the good sense and moderation of Secretary of State Seward and Lord Lyons, the British ambassador.

Trent, Council of. A famous council of the Roman Catholic Church, convoked at Trent, a Tyrolese city, by Pope Paul III (1534–1550) in 1545. It continued to sit, with certain interruptions, until 1563. The Council of Trent condemned the doctrines of the Reformation taught by Luther, Zwinglius, and Calvin; fixed the canon of Scripture ; declared the Church to be the interpreter of Holy Writ ; and placed tradition on a par with the Bible. The "seven sacraments," auricular confession, purgatory, original sin, indulgences, celibacy of the clergy, and transubstantiation were all made authoritative by this council. See *Seven Sacraments.*

Trenton Falls. A series of beautiful waterfalls — five in number — situated 18 miles north of Utica, New York. The descent of the stream (West Canada Creek) is through a highly romantic ravine, which for a distance of two miles has been worn by the action of the water to a depth in some places, of 200 feet below the level of the surrounding country. The total descent of the water through this gorge is estimated at 312 feet.

"It matters little when you see these Falls, whether before or after Niagara. The charm of Trenton is unique, and you will not scorn the violets and lilies because you knelt to the passion-flowers and roses. In the prime of a summer which, from the abundant rains, is singularly unworn and unwithered, a day at Trenton, because of its rare and picturesque, but harmonious, attractions, is like a feast of flowers. In some choice niche of memory you will lay it aside, not as a sublime statue nor a prophetic and solemn picture, but as a vase most delicate, symmetrical, if slight, and chased with pastoral tracery."—*Lotus-Eating* (Curtis).

Trianon, Grand. See *Grand Trianon.*

Trianon, Petit. See *Petit Trianon.*

Tricolor. A name often given to the national flag of France, which consists of red, white, and blue, in equal vertical stripes,—the blue being next to the staff. It was adopted as the national standard in 1794, and continued to be so used during the Republic and the Empire. On the return of the Bourbons in 1814, it gave place to the white flag of that dynasty ; but was restored in 1830, and has remained in use ever since.

"The French guards, when called out to disperse the mob, refused to fire. The citizens formed themselves into a National Guard, and took the blue and red colors of Paris for a cockade; La Fayette added white—the Bourbon color—saying : 'Here is a cockade that will make a tour of the world.' This was the origin of the famous *tricolor.*"—Barnes's *Brief History of France.*

"The National Assembly of France, on July 13, 1789, decided that 'the cockade should be of the colours of the city [of Paris], blue and red,' but, as these were already the colours of the house of Orleans, white, the old colour of France, was added on the proposal of M. de Lafayette."—Edwards's *Words, Facts, and Phrases*.

Tricoteuses (*Fr., Knitters*). Bands of Parisian women of the lower classes, who frequented the political meetings and executions during the French Revolution, and passed their time in knitting and watching the proceedings. See *Robespierre's Weavers*.

"The clocks are on the stroke of three, and the furrow plowed among the populace is turning round, to come on into the place of execution, and end. The ridges thrown to this side and to that, now crumble in and close behind the last plow as it passes on, for all are following to the Guillotine. In front of it, seated in chairs as in a garden of public diversion, are a number of women, busily knitting."—Dickens's *Tale of Two Cities*.

Trinity Church.

(1) A stately Gothic edifice in New York City, erected by the Trinity Corporation in 1846, at a cost of $400,000. It is built of brown sandstone, and is in the Gothic style of architecture, and is surmounted by a graceful spire,—284 feet high. The interior has a seating-capacity of about 800, and contains a fine organ, rich stained-glass windows, and a superb altar and reredos, erected as a memorial to William B. Astor by his sons. Trinity Parish is the wealthiest church corporation in the United States. It maintains, in addition to Trinity Church, eight chapels, viz.: St. Paul's, St. John's, Trinity Chapel, St. Chrysostom's, St. Agnes's, St. Augustine's, St. Cornelius's, and St. Luke's. The corporation owns property in New York City valued at $10,000,000—the annual income from which ($500,000) is expended in the care and maintenance of the parish.

"Of the large income enjoyed by Trinity not a cent is hoarded. The expenses of keeping up the estate ; the support of the chapels ; the large yearly grants to twenty-four parishes ; the payment of taxes and assessments ; and the maintenance of the several parochial schools and other parish charities exhaust the yearly income. Of the former rectors of Trinity three have been made bishops of the Church, and one was banished from the State for his royalist pro-

clivities, and became bishop of Nova Scotia."—King's *Handbook of New York*.

(2) A superb church edifice, in the Romanesque style of architecture, in Boston, Massachusetts, practically completed in 1877, at a cost of $800,-000. It is in the form of a Latin cross, and is surmounted by a massive central tower, 210 feet high, whose style was suggested by the lantern of the Cathedral of Salamanca, Spain. The interior of the church is elaborately decorated with stained-glass windows by La Farge, Burne-Jones, and William Morris. Trinity Church was for 22 years in charge of Dr. Phillips Brooks (1835–1893), who, in 1891, was chosen Bishop of Massachusetts.

Triple Alliance.

(1) An alliance concluded on January 23rd, 1668, between Great Britain, Sweden, and Holland, to protect the Spanish Netherlands against the encroachments of France.

(2) An alliance concluded in 1717, between Great Britain, France, and Holland, against Spain.

(3) An alliance concluded on September 28th, 1795, between Great Britain, Russia, and Austria, against France.

(4) An alliance concluded on March 13th, 1887, between Germany, Austria, and Italy, against France and Russia.

Tripos. An examination for honors in any one of eleven branches, especially in mathematics, held at Cambridge University, England, about June 1st of each year. The official list of the successful competitors is arranged in three grades, or classes—1st, 2nd, and 3rd,—and in the mathematical tripos these classes are known as wranglers (senior and junior), senior optimes, and junior optimes. The word "tripos" is by some authorities derived from this threefold classification, and by others from the three-legged stool on which the candidate was obliged to sit, in the 15th century.

"In the 15th cent. an 'ould bachelour,' as representative of the university, had to sit on a three-legged stool 'before Mr. Proctours' to test the abilities of the candidates for degrees by arguing some question with the 'eldest son' of them as their representative. . . . Hence the word *tripos* meant the stool and the 'ould Bachelour,' then the three classes of questionists, and lastly the examination system. . . . The word now means the classification into three classes of graduated merit adopted in the University of Cambridge, Class I. being the highest."—Brewer's *Historic Note-Book.*

Triumvirates, Roman.

(1) A league, known as the First Triumvirate, formed in 60 B.C., by Julius Cæsar, Cneius Pompey, and Marcus Licinius Crassus, for the purpose of controlling the affairs of the Roman state, in spite of the opposition of the Senate. By the terms of that compact, Julius Cæsar was chosen consul, and afterwards was appointed governor of Gaul ; Pompey received Spain and Africa, and remained in Rome ; and Crassus obtained Syria. The league was dissolved by the death of Crassus in 53 B.C., while waging war with the Parthians.

(2) A compact entered into by Octavius Cæsar, Marcus Antonius, and Marcus Æmilius Lepidus in 43 B.C., for the control of the Roman world. By the terms of the Second Triumvirate, Octavius received the West, Antony the East, and Lepidus the Province of Africa. Lepidus was soon after deposed and banished, and by the victory of Actium over Antony, in 31 B.C., Octavius was left undisputed master of the civilized world.

Triumvirate of Italian Poets.

A term collectively applied to Dante, Petrarch, and Boccaccio, the three great lights of early Italian literature. It is, however, as the "Father of Italian Prose" that Boccaccio is chiefly known.

Trocadéro.

A palace in Paris, occupying the summit of the plateau of the same name, on the right bank of the Seine, opposite the Champ de Mars. The building, which was erected in 1878, contains a grand concert-hall, capable of seating 6000 persons, and also valuable collections of plaster-casts and ethnographic curiosities. It derives its name from one of the fortresses of Cadiz, captured by the French in 1823. Napoleon I, in 1813, entertained the idea of erecting, on the plateau of the Trocadéro, a palace for his son, the King of Rome, but the reverses that soon after followed caused him to abandon the project.

Trois Frères Provençaux (*Fr., Three Brothers of Provence*).

A famous restaurant, long since closed, in the Palais Royal, Paris.

"Here we are, however, at the *Trois Frères;* and there goes my unconscious model deliberately upstairs. We 'll follow him, and double his orders ; and if we dine not well, there is no eating in France."— *N. P. Willis.*

Trojan War.

According to Homer's *Iliad*, an expedition against the city of Troy, engaged in by the combined princes of Greece, led by Agamemnon, King of Mycenæ. Paris, the son of Priam, King of Troy, having awarded the prize for superior beauty to Venus in preference to Juno and Minerva, was promised by that goddess the most beautiful woman of the age for his wife. Soon after this, he visited Menelaus, King of Sparta, and was received with great respect, but abused the hospitality shown him by inducing Helen, the wife of his host, to elope with him to Troy. The Grecian princes resolved to avenge this outrage, and sailed for Troy with an army of 100,000 men conveyed thither in 1200 open vessels. After a siege of ten years, the city was taken by stratagem, plundered, and burned to the ground (1184 B.C.). The aged king, Priam, was slain, and his family was led into captivity. Among the famous Grecian princes that distinguished themselves in the Trojan War may be named Achilles, Ajax, Menelaus, Ulysses, Nestor, and Diomedes. The Trojans were commanded by Hector, the son of Priam, and assisted by Paris, Deiphobus, Æneas, and Sarpedon.

Trossachs. A wild mountain gorge in Perthshire, Scotland, extending for about one mile from the eastern extremity of Loch Katrine. It is described in Scott's *Lady of the Lake*, and is annually visited by thousands of tourists. According to Gaelic etymologists, the word "Trossachs" is derived from *Troschen*, meaning "the rough or bristled region." Also written *Trosachs*.

"There are glens in Scotland surrounded by loftier hills, and presenting on an incomparably greater scale the characters of breadth, and depth, and wild magnificence, such as are to be witnessed in the upper defiles of Glen Nevis, amongst the gloomy recesses of Glencoe, and where Goatfell descends into the profound solitudes of Glen Sannox ; but the valley of the *Trossachs* possesses excellencies peculiarly its own, uniting grandeur and strength with a splendour and an affluence of ornament unparalleled in the scenery of Scotland."—Keddie's *The Trossachs*.

Troubadours. Poets (often of high rank) that flourished chiefly in Provence, in the south of France, during the 11th, 12th, and 13th centuries A.D., and used the *Langue d'Oc*. They produced romances, but excelled especially in lyric verse. They were usually accompanied by professional musicians, known as *joglars (Fr., jongleurs)*, who sang their masters' verses. The compositions of the troubadours may be classified under the heads of (1) *terzones*, or contests between minstrels ; (2) *chansons*, or lyrical songs ; (3) *sirventes*, or songs of war and chivalry ; (4) *serenades ;* and (5) *pastourelles*. The most famous troubadours were Raoul de Coucy, King Thibaut IV of Navarre, Adam de la Halle, and Guillaume Machault. See *Langue d'Oc ; Trouvères*.

Trouvères. Poets that flourished in the north of France during the 12th, 13th, and 14th centuries A.D., and used the *Langue d'Oil*. They excelled in romances, several of which are still extant; as the *Brut d'Angleterre*, the *Rou*, and the *Romance of the Rose*. To them are also due the *gest*, the *fabliau*, the *prose chronicle*, and the *mystery*. See *Langue d'Oil ; Troubadours*.

True Likeness of Christ. See *Christ, Likeness of*.

Trump Card. The word "trump" as here used is derived from the French *triomphe (triumph)*. The trump card is *la carte de triomphe (Fr., the triumphant card)*.

Tugendbund (*Ger., League of Virtue*). A secret society — numbering about 400—founded at Königsberg in 1808, by the Prussian minister, Stein. Although its ostensible object was the revival of patriotism and morality, its real aim was the expulsion of the French from Germany. It incurred the displeasure of Napoleon I, who demanded its suppression in 1809; but it was not dissolved until the general peace of 1815.

Tuileries, Palace of the. A famous palace in Paris, which derived its name from the tile-kilns (*Fr., tuileries*) that formerly occupied its site. It was commenced by Catherine de' Medici in 1564, continued by Henry IV (1589-1610), and completed by Louis XIV (1643-1715). The palace was sacked by the revolutionary mob in 1792, 1830, 1848, and 1870, and was almost totally burned by the Commune in 1871. Napoleon I, Louis XVIII, Charles X, Louis Philippe, and Napoleon III all resided at the Tuileries. Its union with the Louvre was accomplished by Napoleon III in 1852-1856. The Gardens of the Tuileries (west of the palace) are beautifully ornamented with trees, flowers, fountains, and statuary. The burned portion of the palace was not rebuilt.

Tulip Mania. An extraordinary craze for tulips, which prevailed in Holland in 1634-1637, during which years fabulous prices were paid for single bulbs. Owing to the ruin entailed by this form of speculation, the state put an end to the trade in these flowers.

"Beckmann ('History of Inventions') tells us that they [tulip-bulbs] were sold by weight, one root of a variety called *Admiral Leifkin*, weighing 400 perit (a weight rather less than a grain), having fetched 4400 florins. Another buyer gave twelve acres of land for a single root of *Semper Augustus*. Munting gives from the trading-books of the period a case where for a root of *Viceroy* some one agreed to deliver two lasts of wheat, four of rye, four fat oxen, three fat swine, twelve fat sheep, two hogsheads of wine, four tuns of beer, two ditto butter, 1000 lbs. of cheese, a complete bed, a suit of clothes, and a silver beaker, the total value being estimated at 2500 florins. The highest price Beckmann mentions is 7000 florins, for which sum Henry Munting in 1636 sold a tulip-root to a merchant of Alkmaar."— Edwards's *Words, Facts, and Phrases.*

Tully. A name often given by English writers to Marcus Tullius Cicero (106–43 B.C.), the famous Roman orator and statesman.

"Ye fond adorers of departed fame,
  Who warm at Scipio's worth or *Tully's* name."
          Campbell's *Pleasures of Hope.*

Tunkers (*Ger., tunken, to dip*). A sect of German-American Baptists, said to have been founded by Alexander Mack in Westphalia, in 1708. They emigrated to America in 1719, and founded a settlement at Ephrata, Lancaster Co., Pennsylvania, under the direction of Conrad Beissel (or Peysel). Subsequent settlements were made by them in Maryland, Virginia, Ohio, Indiana, and other Western States. The Tunkers are sometimes, but erroneously, called *Dunkers,* or *Dunkards.*

"Their doctrines are similar to those of the Mennonites, and in dress and manner they resemble the Friends. They use the kiss of charity, feet-washing, laying-on of hands, anointing the sick with oil ; are opposed to war, and will not engage in lawsuits. They hold love-feasts, and an annual meeting about Whitsuntide, which is attended by their bishops, teachers, and representatives chosen by the congregations. Universal redemption, though not an article of faith, is commonly held by them. Some of them are strict sabbatarians, observing Saturday as their day of rest. They oppose statistics, which they believe to savor of pride, and, therefore, trustworthy statements as to their numbers cannot be given ; they are supposed to number about 100,000. By reason of their quiet and peaceable lives they have retained a name which was given to them at first, that of 'The Harmless People.' "— McClintock and Strong's *Cyclopædia.*

Tun of Heidelberg. See *Heidelberg Tun.*

Turanian Languages. A term originally used to include all languages of Asiatic origin that are neither Aryan nor Semitic, but of late years restricted to a family of languages of the agglutinative type, in northern Europe and Asia. The term is now generally abandoned by philologists as inexact and misleading.

"The *Turanian* theory cannot . . . be taken seriously. Begot of much assumption, it vanishes before a very little criticism. Hence it is to be regretted that, while condemning it, certain authors should do the name of *Turanian* the honor of looking on it as a thing that can be no longer got rid of. It is by this very condescension that it may acquire fresh vitality, and possibly succeed in establishing itself permanently. The best means of combating it is, therefore, perhaps, to pass it over in silence. The unlucky term 'Semitic' answers at least to a well-defined collection of definite facts, and can be accepted without any reserve. But that of 'Turanian' and 'Turanian tongues' is only calculated to perpetuate serious misconceptions."—Hovelacque's *Science of Language.*

Turncoat. "The opprobrious epithet, *turncoat,* took its rise from one of the first dukes of Savoy, whose dominions lying open to the incursions of the two contending houses of Spain and France, he was obliged to temporize and fall in with that power that was most likely to distress him, according to the success of their arms against one another. So being frequently obliged to change sides, he humorously got a coat made that was *blue* on one side, and *white* on the other, and might be indifferently worn either side out. While in the *Spanish* interest, he wore the *blue* side out, and the *white* side was the badge for the *French.* Hence he was called the *Turn-coat,* by way of distinguishing him from other princes of the same name of that house."—*Gleanings for the Curious* (Bombaugh).

Turpentine State. A popular designation of the State of North Carolina, which annually produces great quantites of turpentine.

Turpin, Dick. A noted English highwayman and horse-thief, whose imaginary ride to York, on his steed "Black Bess" is graphically described by Ainsworth in his novel *Rookwood.* This episode is probably taken from a similar experience in the life of "Swift Nick Nevison," who, in 1676, is said to have robbed a sailor at Gad's Hill at 4 A.M., and to have reached York at 7.30 on the evening of the same day, —thereby establishing an *alibi.* Turpin was born at Hempstead, England, in 1705, and hanged for murder at York, on April 10th, 1739.

Turquoise. This precious stone derives its name from *Turkey,* through which country it was brought from Asia into Europe.

Tutelary Deities of London. A term applied to the giants Gog and Magog, whose effigies adorn the Great Hall of the Guildhall in London. According to tradition, they were the survivors of a race of giants that dwelt in Britain thousands of years ago, and were discovered by the Trojans when they invaded the island and founded the city of Troy-novant (London). After their capture they were chained to the gateway of a palace occupying the site of the present Guildhall, where they served as guardians until their death. See *Gog and Magog.*

Tweed. "This well-known name for a peculiar woollen cloth originated in an accident. A cloth in which the threads of the warp and the weft cross each other singly has a plain surface,

but if they cross in ones and twos alternately a diagonal effect is produced. This diagonal cloth is called '*twill*' in England, and in Scotland '*tweel.*' In an invoice of 'tweels' sent to a dealer in London the letters had been blotted, and the dealer read the name '*tweed,*' and, as the goods came from the banks of the River Tweed, the name seemed so appropriate that he adopted it. It is now universally used as the name of the cloth."—Edwards's *Words, Facts, and Phrases.*

Twelfth-Night. The eve of the festival of the Epiphany (January 6th), which occurs exactly twelve days after Christmas. It marks the close of the Christmas holiday-season, and was formerly celebrated throughout England with merrymakings of various kinds. A king and queen were chosen to preside over the revels, which lasted until midnight ; the Christmas holly and mistletoe were burned; and harmless pranks, appropriate to the occasion, were indulged in.

Twelve Apostles of Ireland. The name given to twelve Irish prelates of the 6th century A.D., disciples of St. Tinnian of Clonard. Their names are as follows:

(1) Ciaran, or Keiran, Bishop and Abbot of Saighir (now Seir-Keiran, County King's).

(2) Ciaran, or Keiran, Abbot of Clomnacnois.

(3) Colum-cille (or St. Columba) of Hy (now Iona).

(4) Brendan, Bishop and Abbot of Clomfert.

(5) Brendan, Bishop and Abbot of Birr (now Parson's-town, County King's).

(6) Columba, Abbot of Tirdaglas.

(7) Molaise, or Laisre, Abbot of Damhiris (now Devenish Island, in Lough Erne).

(8) Cainnech, Abbot of Aichadhbo, County Queen's.

(9) Ruadan, or Rodan, Abbot of Lorrha, County Tipperary.

(10) Mobi Clairenech, or the Flat-faced, Abbot of Glasnooidhan (now Glasnevin, near Dublin).

(11) Senell, Abbot of Cluain-inis, in Lough Erne.

(12) Nannuth, or Nennith, Bishop and Abbot of Inismuige-Samh (now Inismac-Saint, in Lough Erne).

Twelve Articles of the Symbol.
According to tradition, the twelve apostles met in a grotto on the Mount of Olives before their final separation, and formulated the confession of faith known as the *Apostles' Creed.* The names of the twelve apostles and the portion of the creed contributed by each one of them are given below :

(1) *Peter.* I believe in God the Father Almighty, Maker of Heaven and Earth.

(2) *John.* [And] in Jesus Christ, His only Son, our Lord.

(3) *James the Greater.* Who was conceived of the Holy Ghost, born of the Virgin Mary.

(4) *Andrew.* Suffered under Pontius Pilate; was crucified, dead, and buried.

(5) *Philip.* He descended into Hell.

(6) *Thomas.* The third day He rose again from the dead.

(7) *James the Less.* He ascended into Heaven, and sitteth on the right hand of God the Father Almighty.

(8) *Matthew.* From thence He shall come to judge the quick and the dead.

(9) *Bartholomew.* I believe in the Holy Ghost.

(10) *Simon.* The Holy Catholic Church; the communion of saints.

(11) *Matthias.* The forgiveness of sins.

(12) *Jude.* The resurrection of the body, and the life everlasting.

See *Apostles' Creed.*

Twelve Fruits of the Holy Ghost. These are as follows:

(1) Love.
(2) Joy.
(3) Peace.
(4) Longsuffering.
(5) Gentleness.

(6) Goodness.
(7) Faith.
(8) Meekness.
(9) Temperance.
(10) Chastity.
(11) Modesty.
(12) Patience.

The first nine of these are mentioned in *Galatians* v, 22, 23.

Twelve Knights of the Round Table.

(1) Lancelot.
(2) Tristram.
(3) Lamoracke.
(4) Tor.
(5) Galahad.
(6) Gawain.
(7) Gareth.
(8) Palornides.
(9) Kay.
(10) Mark.
(11) Mordred.
(12) One of the following: Acolon, Ballamore, Beleobus, Belvoure, Bersunt, Bors, Ector de Maris, Ewain, Floll, Gaheris, Galohalt, Grislet, Lionell, Marhaus, Paginet, Pelleas, Percival, Sagris, Superabilis, and Turquine.

See *Knights of the Round Table ; Round Table.*

Twelve Labors of Hercules. See *Hercules, Twelve Labors of.*

Twelve Paladins of Charlemagne. Twelve famous warriors of the court of Charlemagne, — sometimes called the " Twelve Peers," from the equality that existed among them. Their names are generally given as follows :

(1) Astolpho.
(2) Ferumbras, or Fierabras.
(3) Florismart.
(4) Ganelon.
(5) Maugris, or Malagigi.
(6) Namo, or Nayme de Bavière.
(7) Ogier, the Dane.
(8) Oliver.
(9) Otuel.
(10) Rinaldo.
(11) Roland.
(12) One of the following: Basin de

Genevois, Geoffrey de Frises, Guérin, duc de Lorraine, Guillaume de l'Estoc, Guy de Bourgogne, Hoël, comte de Nantes, Lambert, prince de Bruxelles, Richard, duc de Normandie, Riol de Mans, Samson, duc de Bourgogne, and Thiery.

Twelve Peers of France. The term "Peers of France" signified those that held directly from the Crown. Their number was not limited during the feudal system ; but under Philip Augustus (1180–1223) it was confined to six lay peers and six clerical peers. The lay peers were the Dukes of Normandy, Burgundy, and Aquitaine, the Counts of Flanders, Champagne, and Toulouse. The clerical peers were the Archbishop of Rheims, the Bishops of Laon, Noyon, Beauvais, Châlons, and Langres. It was before this body—called the Court of Peers—that King John of England was summoned to appear, to clear himself of the charge of having murdered his nephew Arthur. Failing to comply, he was found guilty of "murder by treachery, the most aggravated form of homicide," and was adjudged to have forfeited his fiefs.

Twelve Tables, Laws of the. A famous code of Roman laws, drawn up by the Decemvirs to protect the Plebeians against the oppressions of the Patricians. The first ten tables were enacted in 451 B.C., and the two remaining ones were added by a second decemvirate in 450. These last contained regulations obnoxious to the common people, and were styled by Cicero "the two tables of unjust laws." The *Laws of the Twelve Tables* were engraved on bronze plates (some say on blocks of wood or ivory), and set up in the Comitium. They constituted the basis of the written law of Rome, and, as late as the time of Cicero, were committed to memory by every schoolboy. The original tablets are said to have been destroyed during the sack of Rome under Brennus, in 390 B.C.

Twelve Tribes of Israel. See *Israel, Twelve Tribes of.*

Twenty-Ninth Bulletin. A famous bulletin issued by Napoleon I at Malodeczno, Russia, on December 3rd, 1812,—announcing the disasters that had befallen the Grand Army during the Russian campaign. It reached Paris on December 17th—a few hours before the return of the Emperor,—and filled the city with mourning.

"On the 3d of December, the emperor issued his twenty-ninth and last bulletin, which made France and the world comprehend, in some degree, how the invasion of Russia had ended. For the first time he then spoke of his retreat ; he avowed such part of his misfortunes as he could not wholly deny ; he attributed his calamities to the severity of the weather."—Knight's *Popular History of England.*

Two Foscari. See *Foscari, Two.*

Two Services. The Church of the Holy Ghost at Heidelberg, Germany, is divided into two equal parts by a partition - wall extending the entire length of the building. One of these halves forms a Roman Catholic and the other a Protestant church; and, as a result, there is often witnessed the strange spectacle of two services performed at the same time, under one roof. It is said that in 1719, the Elector Palatine tried to deprive the Protestants of their portion; but the attempt raised such an outcry that he was forced to remove his Court to Mannheim.

Two Sicilies. The name given to the Kingdom of Naples and Sicily, founded by Roger II about 1130 A.D., and overthrown by Garibaldi in 1860. It was annexed to the Kingdom of Sardinia during the same year.

Tyburn. The chief place of execution in London from 1196 until 1783. The real site of Tyburn is a matter of dispute, but it is supposed to have been situated near the lower corner of Edgeware Road. On January 30th, 1661, the bodies of Oliver Cromwell,

Ireton, and Bradshaw were exposed at Tyburn. It derived its name from *Twaburne* (*two rivulets*), and was so named from two small streams that met in that locality and flowed into the Thames. The first execution in front of Newgate Prison took place on December 9th, 1783. See *Newgate ; Tyburn-Tree.*

Tyburnia. A fashionable quarter of London, north of Hyde Park. It includes Portman and Grosvenor Squares, and is referred to by Thackeray as "the elegant, the prosperous, the polite Tyburnia, the most respectable district of the habitable globe."

Tyburn-Tree. The name popularly applied to the gallows that stood at Tyburn. It is said to have been so called because malefactors were at one time hanged on the elm-trees that grew on the banks of the *Twaburne* (*two rivulets*), in the vicinity. See *Tyburn.*

Tyler - Davidson Fountain. A superb bronze fountain at Cincinnati, Ohio, erected in 1871, at a cost of nearly $200,000. It was designed by August von Kreling, and cast at the Royal Bronze Foundry in Munich.

"It stands on a freestone esplanade, 400 feet long and 60 feet wide. In the center of a porphyry-rimmed basin 40 ft. in diameter is the quatrefoil Saxon porphyry base supporting the bronze-work, whose base is 12 ft. square and 6 ft. high, with infant figures at each corner representing the delights of children in water. Bas-relief figures around the base represent the various uses of water to mankind. From the upper part of the bronze base extend 4 great basins, and from the center rises a column, up whose sides vines ascend and branch at the top in palm-like frondage. Around this column are groups of statuary ; and on its summit stands a gigantic female figure, with outstretched arms, the water raining down in fine spray from her fingers."—Appleton's *Guide to the United States.*

Tyler's Insurrection. An uprising of the English peasantry in 1381, led by Wat, the Tyler (a tiler of roofs). According to tradition, the insurrection was occasioned by an insult offered to Wat's daughter by a tax-gatherer ; but the real cause was the imposition of a poll-tax of three groats to defray the expenses of a war with France. On the 12th of June, 1381, the insurgents, to the number of 100,000 men, assembled at Blackheath, and, on the 14th, murdered the Archbishop of Canterbury and the Royal Treasurer. At an interview with Richard II, held in Smithfield on the 15th, Wat Tyler addressed the King in a menacing manner, and was at once dispatched by William Walworth, Lord Mayor of London ; whereupon the King ordered the rioters to retire,— promising them a redress of their grievances. Soon after their departure from the city, the insurrectionists were attacked by Sir R. Knollys and a band of knights, and dispersed with great slaughter. It is estimated that 7000 of their number perished in prison and on the scaffold.

Tyndale's Bible. The name given to an English translation of the *New Testament* by William Tyndale (1484– 1536), the reformer and martyr, published at Worms in 1525. He published later editions in 1534-1535, and also translated the *Pentateuch* and other books of the *Old Testament* in 1530–1536. His works have great merit, and form the basis of all the English translations of the *New Testament* that have appeared since his day. See *Cranmer's Bible.*

"The merits of Tyndale must ever be recognised and honored by all who enjoy the English Bible—for their authorized version of the New Testament has his for its basis. He made good his early boast that ploughboys should have the Word of God." —McClintock and Strong's *Cyclopædia.*

Tyrants. A term used in ancient Greece to denote those persons that exercised supreme power without legal warrant. They were not necessarily arbitrary or oppressive rulers, but simply individuals that had usurped the sovereignty. Solon objected to this use of the word, and chose in preference that of *archons* (*rulers*). Among the wise and enlightened "tyrants" of Greece may be named Pisistratus, Orthagorus, Hiero, and Polycrates. See *Thirty Tyrants*.

"It was of the essence of a '*tyrant*' that he had attained supreme dominion through a violation of the laws and liberties of the State; having done which, whatever the moderation of his after-rule, he would not escape the name."—*On the Study of Words* (Trench).

Tyrian Dye. A violet-purple dye-stuff discovered by the inhabitants of Tyre, about 1500 B.C. It was obtained from various species of mollusks,— especially from the *Murex trunculus* and the *Murex brandaris*. The art is said to have been lost about 1000 A.D.

"It is said that Hercules Tyrius, having observed his dog's lips to be stained after eating a shell-fish named *murex* or *purpura*, was thereby led to invent the dye." — Haydn's *Dictionary of Dates*.

U

Uffizi Palace. A famous edifice in Florence, Italy, containing, with the exception of the Royal Gallery (El Museo) at Madrid, the richest and most varied collection of art-treasures in the world. The building was erected by Cosmo de' Medici (1389–1464). It is connected, by means of a covered passageway, with the Pitti Palace on the opposite side of the Arno. See *Museo; Pitti Palace; Ponte Vecchio*.

"Here, for the first time, the traveller from the North is made to feel the full power of art, for though Paris, Dresden, Munich, Vienna, Venice, and Bologna are rich in pictures, yet in sculpture there is comparatively little till we come to Florence. In the galleries and corridors of the *Uffizi*, we understand, as never before, what is meant by the antique, and see the Greek and Roman mind as it expressed itself in bronze and marble."— Hillard's *Six Months in Italy*.

Ultima Thule (*Lat., Farthest Thule*). An expression used by the ancient Romans to denote the most northerly part of the world known to them. Pliny says that it was an island in the northern ocean, discovered in the 4th century B.C., by the navigator Pytheas of Massilia, who reached it after a six days' voyage from Orcades. This region has been variously identified by modern writers with Norway, Iceland, Denmark, the Orkney Islands, and especially with the Shetland Islands. "Ultima Thule" is often used as a synonym for a remote, unknown region, or for an unattainable goal.

Ultramontanists (*Lat., ultra montes, beyond the mountains*). A term originally used in France to denote the party in the Roman Catholic Church that advocated the concentration of all power in the hands of the Pope, in opposition to the Gallican faction, which favored a more independent development of the national churches. Since 1870, the name has been given to those persons that maintain the infallibility of the Pope, as established by the Vatican Council. The doctrine of papal supremacy was held principally by the theologians of Italy, and hence the name *Ultramontanists* (*beyond the mountains*, i. e., *the Alps*) was applied to them and to all others holding similar views.

Umbrellas. The origin of umbrellas is unknown, although they frequently appear in the sculptures of Egypt, Nineveh, and Persepolis. They were used by the women of ancient Greece and Rome, and this custom was probably continued in Italy from early times. It was not, however, until the 17th century A.D., that they were introduced into England, and for a long time their use was limited to the fair sex.

"There is a very general belief that umbrellas were invented and first used by Jonas Hanway, the celebrated philanthropist of the last century. This is an error. Hanway was perhaps the first *man* who walked London streets with an umbrella over his head to keep off the rain, and we are told that 'after continuing to use one for thirty years he saw them come into general use.' He died in 1786, so that the date when he introduced them must have been between 1750 and 1760. The earliest use of umbrellas, however, dates back two or three thousand years before this. On one of the ancient bas-reliefs brought from Nineveh by Layard, and now in the British Museum, there is a representation of a slave holding an umbrella over the head of the king as he rides in his chariot. And in Bohn's edition of ' Aristophanes,' vol. i., p. 413, the following stage direction occurs, ' Enter Prometheus, muffled up and covered with an umbrella.' "—Edwards's *Words, Facts, and Phrases*.

Una. In Spenser's *Faerie Queene*, a lovely maiden, who is the personification of Truth. She is called Una (*Lat., One*), either because of the singleness of purpose that characterizes Truth, or on account of her unique beauty of character. She visits the court of Gloriana, and begs the Faerie Queene to assign to one of her knights the task of slaying the dragon that devastates her father's kingdom and keeps him prisoner. The Red Cross Knight is appointed the lady's champion, and together they set out on their adventures. After various thrilling experiences the dragon is slain, and Una and the knight are united in marriage. See *Faerie Queene*.

Uncial Letters. Large letters of nearly uniform size, found in manuscripts from the 4th to the 8th century A.D. These letters resemble capital letters, but have a greater roundness. The word "uncial" is derived from the Latin *uncia* (*inch*).

"The present distinction of large letters (capitals) and small did not come into use before the ninth century. In conformity with ancient usage, the manuscripts executed before this period are written in large disconnected letters (the so-called *uncial*), without any marks of interpunction, or even division of words."—Barrows's *Companion to the Bible*.

Uncle Sam. A cant or vulgar name for the United States Government. See *Brother Jonathan*.

"Immediately after the last declaration of war with England, Elbert Anderson, of New York, then a contractor, visited Troy

49

on the Hudson, where was concentrated, and where he purchased, a large quantity of provisions, beef, pork, &c. The inspectors of these articles at that place were Messrs. Ebenezer and Samuel Wilson. The latter gentleman (invariably known as ' *Uncle Sam,*') generally superintended in person a large number of workmen, who, on this occasion, were employed in overhauling the provisions purchased by the contractor for the army. The casks were marked ' E. A. —U. S.' This work fell to the lot of a facetious fellow in the employ of the Messrs. Wilson, who, on being asked by some of his fellow-workmen the meaning of the mark (for the letters U. S., for United States, were then almost entirely new to them), said, ' he did not know, unless it meant *Elbert Anderson* and *Uncle Sam,*'—alluding exclusively, then, to the said ' *Uncle Sam* ' Wilson. The joke took among the workmen, and passed currently ; and ' *Uncle Sam* ' himself, being present, was occasionally rallied by them on the increasing extent of his possessions. . . .

Mr. Wilson died in Troy, New York, in August, 1854, at the age of eighty-four years ; and the 'Albany Argus,' in noticing his death, referred to the circumstance above stated as the origin of the popular sobriquet of *Uncle Sam*."—Frost's *Naval History of the United States*.

Uncle Tom's Cabin. A famous American novel by Harriet Beecher Stowe (1811–1896), setting forth the enormities of negro slavery. It was published in 1852, and greatly contributed to the emancipation of the negroes in the United States of America. Uncle Tom, the chief character, is said to have been drawn from Josiah Henson, a Maryland slave, who escaped to Canada after 42 years' bondage. He was subsequently ordained, visited England in 1877, and was presented to Queen Victoria at Buckingham Palace. He died at Dresden, Ontario, on May 5th, 1883, aged 93 years. See *Topsy*.

"*Uncle Tom's Cabin* was published in 1852. Its success was unprecedented in the annals of literature. In less than nine months, the sale had exceeded a million of copies ; the author and the publishers had made fortunes out of it ; more than thirty rival editions of it had been published in London alone, besides numerous other editions in different parts of Scotland and Ireland ; it was translated into every living language that possessed a popular literature ; and Harriet Beecher Stowe, before comparatively unknown, even in her own country, became as familiar a name, in every part of the civilized world, as Shakespeare or Homer." —Hart's *Manual of American Literature.*

Unconditional Surrender Grant. A nickname given to General Ulysses S. Grant (1822–1885), eighteenth President of the United States.

Unction, Extreme. See *Extreme Unction.*

Underground Railroad. A term popularly used in the United States of America, before the abolition of slavery, to denote the numberless ways in which fugitive slaves from the Southern States were assisted to a place of safety either in Canada or the North. It was often humorously contracted to U. G. R. R.

"Secret movement which began with Pennsylvania Quakers, became organized 1838, and till the Civil War aided the escape of fugitive slaves. There were various routes from the Northern slave States to Canada ; on each of these were stations one day's journey apart, where the runaways were fed and cared for. The reputed president, Levi Coffin, 1798–1877, is said to have helped about 100 slaves annually to freedom."— *Chandler's Encyclopædia.*

Undine. The title of a celebrated romance by De la Motte Fouqué (1777–1843), which appeared in 1811. It is founded on a tale by Theophrastus Paracelsus, in his *Treatise on Elemental Sprites.* According to the Paracelsists, Undines are water-sprites, that readily intermarry with human beings, and, on bearing children, receive a soul. Their husbands must not venture on the water with them, or, at least, must not vex them while there, else they will at once return to their native element.

Undulatory Theory of Light. A theory to explain the phenomena of light, propounded by Hooke and Huyghens about 1672, and confirmed by Thomas Young in 1801. It asserts that the form of energy called light is propagated through the ether by a wave-motion imparted to it by the vibrations of the molecules of the radiant body. This theory is now universally accepted. See *Corpuscular Theory of Light.*

Unigenitus (*Lat., Only-Begotten*). A famous bull (so called because it begins with this word) issued by Pope Clement XI (1700–1721), in 1713, and confirmed by Pope Benedict XIII (1724–1730) in 1725. It was directed against a French translation of the *New Testament,* with notes, published by Quesnel, a noted Jansenist. The bull was obtained through the efforts of Louis XIV (1643–1715) and the Jesuits, and produced intense excitement throughout France. See *Jansenists ; Jesuits.*

Unitarians. A name given to those Christians that reject the doctrine of the Trinity. They have existed in the Christian Church, under various names, from the earliest days ; but did not receive the title "Unitarians" until the 16th century. They appeared in England about 1700, and were joined by many Presbyterian bodies in 1730. The Unitarian movement in the United States commenced in 1812, and was a schism from Trinitarian Congregationalism in New England. The Unitarians have in the United States about 437 congregations and 68,250 members. See *Socinians.*

"Unitarianism has been held by individuals, and by many non-orthodox bodies of Christians, as in the present day by the Hicksite Friends, and in Great Britain by a small body that has separated from the Presbyterians, but the name is specifically applied in the United States to the doctrines of those New England Congregational churches that became Unitarian under the leadership of Channing and others early in the 19th century, and to their present representatives. The more conservative of these accept the Bible and the divinity (as distinguished from deity) of Christ, while the more radical are rationalistic, and some hold merely a form of deism."—*Standard Dictionary.*

United Provinces. The seven northern provinces of the Netherlands —Holland, Zealand, Utrecht, Friesland, Groningen, Overyssel, and Guelderland, which, by the Treaty of Utrecht (January 23rd, 1579), formed a union for mutual protection. They declared their independence of Spain in 1581, but this was not acknowledged until 1609.

United States Bank. See *Bank of the United States.*

United States Military Academy. A national institution for the education of officers for the United States Army, at West Point, New York, founded by Congress in 1802, and greatly extended in scope in 1812. The total number of cadets authorized is 481,— each Congressional district, each Territory, and the District of Columbia being entitled to one appointment, and the President of the United States to twelve. The age of admission is between 17 and 22 years, and the course of study lasts four years. Each cadet is required to take an oath of allegiance, and to bind himself to serve the United States for eight years from the time of his admission. He receives $540 annual pay, and is graduated as second lieutenant in the United States Army. On July 28th, 1817, Brevet-Major Sylvanus Thayer assumed control of the Academy as superintendent, and "from this period," says Captain Edward C. Boynton, in his *History of West Point*, "the commencement of whatever success as an educational institution and whatever reputation the academy may possess throughout the country and abroad for its strict, impartial, salutary, elevating, and disciplinary government must be dated."

The number of cadets at the Academy is usually about 550; while the total number of graduates from 1802 to 1912, inclusive, has been 5112. The military and academic staff consists of 128 persons. See *United States Naval Academy; West Point.*

United States Naval Academy. A national institution for the education of officers for the United States Navy, at Annapolis, Maryland, founded in 1845 by George Bancroft, Secretary of the Navy during the administration of President Polk (1845–1849). In May, 1861, the Academy was removed to Newport, Rhode Island, on account of the Civil War ; but was re-established at Annapolis in 1865. Each Congressional district, each Territory, and the District of Columbia is entitled to one appointment, while to the President of the United States is granted the privilege of naming ten cadets at large. The age of admission is between 15 and 20 years, and the course of study lasts four years and is followed by two years at sea, after which the final examinations are taken. Each cadet binds himself to serve the United States for eight years from the time of his admission to the Academy. He receives $500 a year from the date of his entrance. See *United States Military Academy.*

Universal Doctor. A sobriquet conferred upon Alain de Lille (1114–1203), the noted French Schoolman and theologian.

Universal Genius. An appellation bestowed upon Sir William Petty (1623 – 1687), the English political economist.

Universalists. A body of Christians whose distinctive article of faith is the ultimate salvation of all rational creatures. The sect was founded in England by James Relly in 1750, and in America by John Murray in 1770. It has prospered in the United States, especially in New England, but has made little progress in Great Britain. Universalism is avowed in the *Talmud*, and is ascribed to Origen also. It was taught by certain of the early Church Fathers, but was opposed by St. Augustine and condemned by the Fifth

General Council at Constantinople in 553 A.D.

Universal Language. See *Volapük*.

Universal Spider. A sobriquet conferred upon Louis XI (1461-1483), King of France, in allusion to his cruel and crafty nature.

Universities Founded. The following dates are taken from *Chandler's Encyclopædia:*

(1) PARIS	1109	A.D.
(2) SALAMANCA	1209	"
(3) BOLOGNA	1116	"
(4) PADUA	1222	"
(5) NAPLES	1224	"
(6) ROME	1303	"
(7) PERUGIA	1306	"
(8) FLORENCE	1320	"
(9) PAVIA	1361	"
(10) FERRARA	1391	"
(11) OXFORD	1133	"
(12) CAMBRIDGE	1257	"
(13) ST. ANDREW'S	1411	"
(14) GLASGOW	1453	"
(15) EDINBURGH	1582	"
(16) DUBLIN	1592	"
(17) PRAGUE	1348	"
(18) CRACOW	1364	"
(19) VIENNA	1365	"
(20) HEIDELBERG	1385	"
(21) COLOGNE	1388	"
(22) LEIPZIG	1409	"
(23) BASEL	1460	"
(24) TÜBINGEN	1477	"
(25) GÖTTINGEN	1737	"
(26) BERLIN	1809	"
(27) BONN	1818	"
(28) UPSALA	1477	"
(29) COPENHAGEN	1475	"
(30) LEYDEN	1575	"
(31) DORPAT	1622	"
(32) MOSCOW	1755	"
(33) ST. PETERSBURG	1819	"

University Extension. An educational movement for extending to the masses the advantages of university instruction by means of systematic courses of lectures and classes, at various important centres of population. The scheme originated at the University of Cambridge, England, in 1872, and was introduced into the United States by Provost William Pepper of the University of Pennsylvania, in 1890.

"From Philadelphia the movement has extended to many States. In Rhode Island Brown University has organized many centres. In New York the University of the State, through its [former] Secretary, Melvil Dewey, has arranged for Extension lectures in many important towns and cities. Rutgers College, as the agricultural college of New Jersey, has offered scientific courses especially for the farmers of the State. The Universities of Wisconsin, Indiana, Kansas, and California have done much for their respective States. Chicago University has provided a special University Extension Division, with three departments: (1) Lecture-study; (2) Class-work; (3) Correspondence. Conferences held from time to time in Philadelphia have been an important feature of the movement. The Society publishes valuable syllabi, giving a careful outline of the lectures, together with lists of recommended books and questions for essays in connection with the lecture courses."—*World Almanac.*

University of Chicago. An institution of learning at Chicago, Illinois, incorporated in 1890, and opened in 1892 with 600 students. Its endowment amounts to $12,500,000—of which $7,500,000 has been given by John D. Rockefeller. The university grounds cover an area of 24 acres. The plan provides for 40 buildings, about 15 of which have been already erected. The University comprises the four faculties of Philosophy, Sciences, Arts, and Commerce and Politics. There are at present about 300 instructors, 4550 students, and over 300,000 books in the library. The famous Yerkes Observatory forms part of the University of Chicago. See *Yerkes Observatory.*

University Settlements. Homes established in the poorer sections of cities, where cultivated persons may dwell and strive to elevate the lives of those around them. For this purpose, lectures, studies, and devices of all kinds are resorted to. The movement originated in England in 1867, and later was fostered by the University of Cambridge; in 1887, it made its appearance in New York as a "Neighborhood Guild," and by 1896 it had spread to the chief cities of the United

States. Among the most noted "settlements" in America may be named the College Settlement in New York, the College Settlement in Philadelphia, the Hull House in Chicago, and the Denison and Andover Houses in Boston.

Unknown, Great. See *Great Unknown*.

Unser Fritz (*Ger., Our Fritz*). A title popularly conferred by the Prussian soldiers upon Frederick William (1831–1888), the Crown Prince, afterwards Frederick III, Emperor of Germany. See *Frederick the Noble*.

Unspeakable Turk. A phrase that came into prominence in England during the Bulgarian insurrection of 1876. It originated with Thomas Carlyle, and made its appearance in a published letter of his, in which occurred the following sentence :

"The *unspeakable Turk* should be immediately struck out of the question, and the country left to honest European guidance."

Untamed Heifer. So Elizabeth (1558–1603), Queen of England, is called in the *Martin Marprelate Tracts*.

Unter den Linden (*Ger., Under the Lindens*). A famous street in Berlin, Prussia, extending from the Brandenburg Gate to the Royal Palace, and deriving its name from the avenues of lime-trees (interspersed with chestnuts) with which it is planted. It resembles the boulevards of Paris, although inferior in length, and is flanked with handsome palaces, spacious hotels, and attractive shops, between which the long vistas of a number of side streets are visible at intervals. The length of the street, from the Brandenburg Gate to the equestrian statue of Frederick the Great, is about two-thirds of a mile,— to the palace-gate, about one mile. See *Brandenburg Gate*.

Upas-Tree. A tall Javanese tree (*Antiaris toxicaria*), whose juice contains a virulent poison.

"According to the story told by a Dutch surgeon, Foersch, about the close of the 18th century, its exhalations were fatal to both animal and vegetable life, so that birds flying over it fell dead, and a desert surrounded each tree. Specimens have been cultivated in British hothouses and botanic gardens since 1844 with no ill effects, and this story is now known to be false. It may have had its origin in the fact that the tree sometimes grows in low valleys in Java where the escape of carbonic-acid gas from crevices in the ground is so abundant as to be fatal to animals."—*Standard Dictionary*.

"Up, Guards, and at them !" A famous saying commonly believed to have been uttered by the Duke of Wellington (1769–1852), at a critical moment during the battle of Waterloo. The expression was disclaimed by Wellington, who wrote as follows in reply to an inquiry from J. W. Croker:

"What I might have said, and possibly did say, was, 'Stand up, Guards!' and then gave the commanding officers the order to attack. My common practice in a defensive position was to attack the enemy at the very moment at which he was about to attack our troops."

Upholsterer of Notre Dame. An appellation bestowed upon the Duc de Luxembourg (1628–1695), in allusion to the number of flags captured at the battle of Fleurus (1690), and sent by him to decorate the cathedral of Notre Dame, in Paris.

Upper Ten Thousand. A phrase meaning the upper circles of society. It was coined by N. P. Willis (1806–1867), the American author, and was originally applied by him to the fashionables of New York City, who, in his opinion, numbered about 10,000. Also written *Upper Ten*. See *Four Hundred*.

Urania. In classic mythology, one of the nine Muses. She presided over astronomy. See *Muses*.

Uriel. According to Christian and Jewish tradition, one of the seven archangels that stand around the throne of God,—the other six being Gabriel, Michael, Raphael, Chamuel,

Zophiel, and Zadkiel. He is mentioned in the Second Book of *Esdras;* and is described as "the angel of thunder and lightning" in the Book of *Enoch.* Milton calls him "the sharpest sighted Spirit of all in Heav'n."

"Th' Arch-Angel *Uriel,* one of the seven
Who in God's presence, nearest his throne,
Stand ready at command ; . . ."
         Paradise Lost, iii, 648-650.

Urim and Thummim. Objects mentioned in the *Old Testament* in connection with the Jewish high-priest's breastplate. They were apparently a pair of decorations used as an oracle on critical occasions, although their nature has been the subject of many conjectures.

"Professor Plumptre supposes the *Urim* to have been a clear and colorless stone set in the breastplate of the high priest as a symbol of light, answering to the mystic scarab in the pectoral plate of the ancient Egyptian priests, and that the *Thummim* was an image corresponding to that worn by the priestly judges of Egypt as a symbol of truth and purity of motive. By gazing steadfastly on these, he may have been thrown into a mysterious, half ecstatic state, akin to hypnotism, in which he lost all personal consciousness, and received a spiritual illumination and insight."—Webster's *International Dictionary.*

"Thou shalt put in the breastplate of judgment the *Urim* and the *Thummim.*"—*Exodus* xxviii, 30.

Ursa Major (*Lat., Greater Bear*). See *Bear, Great.*

Ursa Minor (*Lat., Lesser Bear*). See *Bear, Little.*

Ushant. An island off the northwest coast of France, near Brest, in the vicinity of which were fought two naval battles between the French and the English. The first contest, fought on July 27th, 1778, was indecisive ; but the second, which took place on June 1st, 1794, resulted in a signal victory for the English. In this engagement, Lord Howe, the British admiral, with 25 ships, defeated the French fleet of 26 vessels, under Villaret - Joyeuse, — capturing seven and dismasting ten.

Utilitarianism. An ethical theory that finds in utility the sole standard of morality, and accordingly determines the rectitude of an action by its usefulness. It is also termed "the greatest happiness theory," or the theory that makes the greatest happiness of the greatest number the test and criterion of right. Among the most famous advocates of the Utilitarian Theory may be named Jeremy Bentham, John Stuart Mill, Cumberland, and Hume. The word was first used by Bentham about 1802, although Mill believed that he was the first to use it in philosophy, in 1823,—having found it in Galt's *Annals of the Parish.*

"I did not invent the word, but found it in one of Galt's novels, the 'Annals of the Parish,' in which the Scotch clergyman, of whom the book is a supposed autobiography, is represented as warning his parishioners not to leave the Gospel and become *utilitarians.* With a boy's fondness for a name and a banner I seized on the word, and for some years called myself and others by it as a sectarian appellation ; and it came to be occasionally used by some others holding the opinions which it was intended to designate. As those opinions attracted more notice, the term was repeated by strangers and opponents, and got into rather common use just about the time when those who had originally assumed it laid it down that along with other sectarian characteristics." — John Stuart Mill's *Autobiography.*

Utopia (*Gr., Nowhere*). An imaginary island described in Sir Thomas More's famous political romance, entitled *De Optimo Reipublicæ Statu, deque Nova Insula Utopia,* originally published in Latin in 1516 and translated into English in 1551. It is the seat of an ideally perfect commonwealth, the inhabitants of which enjoy the benefits of just laws and enlightened institutions. The reputed discoverer of the island of Utopia was Raphael Hythloday, a companion of Amerigo Vespucci.

"The intention of Sir Thomas More is to set forth his idea of those social arrangements whereby the happiness and improvement of the people may be secured to the utmost extent of which human nature is susceptible ; though, probably, he has pictured more than he really conceived it possible to effect. Experience proves that many of his suggestions are indeed Utopian. In his imaginary island, for instance, all are contented with the necessaries of life ; all are employed in useful labour ; no man desires, in clothing, any other quality besides durability ; and since wants are few, and every individual engages in labour, there is no need for working more than six hours a day. Neither laziness nor avarice finds a place in this happy region ; for why should the people be indolent when they have so little toil, or greedy when they know that there is abundance for each ? All this, it is evident, is incompatible with qualities inherent in human nature : man requires the stimulus of self-interest to render him industrious and persevering ; he loves not utility merely, but ornament ; he possesses a spirit of emulation which makes him endeavour to outstrip his fellows, and a desire to accumulate property even for its own sake."—Chambers's *Cyclopædia of English Literature*.

V

Vaccination. The name given to the process of inoculating with vaccine (the virus of cow-pox), with the view of protecting the patient against an attack of smallpox. It was introduced into England by Dr. Jenner in 1796–1798, and, despite the fierce opposition both of the medical profession and of the public, spread rapidly over Europe, and became a universal practice before 1816. Vaccination was made compulsory in England in 1853, and in Scotland and Ireland in 1863. Additional compulsory acts were passed in England in 1867, 1871, and 1874 ; and it is estimated that 95 per cent. of the inhabitants of that country are vaccinated. A society for the abolition of compulsory vaccination was founded in England in 1870, and a great demonstration in opposition to the practice was held at Leicester in 1885. Dr. Jenner (1749–1823) was the recipient of many honors during his lifetime. He received £10,000 from the Parliament of Great Britain

in 1802, and £20,000 additional in 1807. Napoleon I held him in high esteem, and liberated, at his request, seven persons who, as prisoners of war, were detained in France. See *Inoculation*.

Val d'Arno (*It., Vale of the Arno*). The valley of the river Arno, in Tuscany, in which Florence is situated. It is noted for its beauty and its historic associations.

"Through this smiling region the Arno steals to the sea, a slender, thread-like stream, which has but little influence upon the landscape."—Hillard's *Six Months in Italy*.

"... Whose orb
Through optic glass the Tuscan artist views
At evening from the top of Fesolé,
Or in *Valdarno*. . . ."
Paradise Lost, i, 287–290.

Valentia. A name given by the ancient Romans to the southern part of Scotland, in honor of the Emperor Valentinian (364–375).

Valentine's Day. "The 14th of February, on which, in England and Scotland in former times, each young bachelor and maid received by lot one of the opposite sex as ' valentine ' for the year. It was a kind of mock betrothal, and was marked by the giving of presents. From Pepys's *Diary* we see that married as well as single people could be chosen. The usage no doubt grew out of the old notion, alluded to by Chaucer and Shakespeare, that on this day birds first choose their mates. The observance of St. Valentine's day degenerated into the usage of youths and maidens sending each other by post prints of a sentimental kind, such as Cupids, transfixed hearts, and the like. Another and less pardonable form is the sending of ludicrous caricatures, often vulgar enough; but such boorish witticisms are fast dying out. Several saints of this name (one of them a martyr at Rome under Claudius) were venerated on February 14 ; but the observances seem to be connected rather with the spring-time than with the career or character of the saints whose name is thus taken in vain."— *Chambers's Encyclopædia.*

Vale of Cashmere. An elevated valley in the Himalayas, north of the Punjab, through which flows the river Jhelum. It is about 120 miles long, with a mean breadth of 75 miles, and is famed for the beauty of its scenery and the charm of its climate. The level portion of the valley is about 80 miles long by 20 broad, and varies from 5000 to 7000 feet in elevation above the sea-level. Owing to its altitude and consequent coolness, it is visited by thousands of Europeans during the hot months of the year. It is said that the natives of the Vale of Cashmere derive the peculiar pattern that marks all India shawls from the graceful curves of the river Jhelum as it meanders through the valley.

Vale of Enna. A valley near the ancient city of Enna (now Castro Giovanni) in Sicily, where, according to tradition, Proserpine (Persephone) was carried off by Pluto, while gathering flowers.

　　　　　" She moved
Like Proserpine in *Enna*, gathering flowers."
　　　　　Tennyson's *Edwin Morris.*

" The Golden Horn is my fish-preserve; my flocks of golden fleece are pastured on the plain of Marathon, and the honey of Hymettus is distilled from the flowers that grow in the *vale of Enna*—all in my Spanish domains."—Curtis's *Prue and I.*

Vale of Tempe. A romantic mountain-gorge in the north of Thessaly, between Mounts Olympus and Ossa, through which the river Peneus flows on its way to the sea. It is about six miles long, and varies in width from 100 to 2000 paces. The Vale of Tempe was highly praised by the ancient Greek poets for its surpassing beauty, and is still greatly admired for the grandeur of its scenery. It was of great strategic importance in warfare,—being the only pass through which an army could invade Thessaly

from the north. According to Greek tradition, Neptune opened this cleft in the rock with a blow of his trident, and thus released the waters from their imprisonment in Thessaly. From this circumstance in the ravine received the name of Tempe (*Gr.*, τέμνω, *to cut*). It was one of the favorite haunts of Apollo.

" They would have thought, who heard the strain,
They saw in *Tempe's vale* her native maids,
Amidst the festal-sounding shades
To some unwearied minstrel dancing."
　　　　　Collins's *Ode to the Passions.*

Valhalla.

(1) In Scandinavian mythology, the palace of immortality at Asgard, whither the souls of heroes slain in battle are conveyed by the valkyries, at the command of Odin, and where they pass their days in feasting.

(2) A Temple of Fame, on the Danube near Ratisbon, erected in 1830–1842 by King Ludwig (1825–1848) of Bavaria, in memory of the illustrious men of Germany. It is adorned with statues of deceased military heroes, statesmen, poets, and philosophers, from earliest times until the present day. It is a superb marble structure, and cost over $3,000,000. Written also *Walhalla.*

Valjean, Jean. The hero of Victor Hugo's famous novel *Les Misérables*, which appeared in 1862.

Valley Forge. A village situated about 20 miles northwest of Philadelphia, famous as the scene of Washington's encampment during the winter of 1777-1778. There his army—reduced to 11,000 men—suffered every conceivable hardship with Spartan heroism. See *Brandywine, Battle of the.*

" At *Valley Forge* the soldiers slept without blankets; and many had to sit up all night by their fires. At one time there were more than a thousand without shoes; and you might track them in the snow by their bleeding feet. Even the sick often had to lie on the ground for want of straw. They had scarcely any horses; and the soldiers made little carts to draw their wood and provisions to their huts. Officers on parade sometimes wore old blankets or faded bedquilts to cover them. The troops were hardly ever paid; and the money in which they were paid had almost lost its value. Food was scarce; and the gloomy saying was, 'No bread, no soldier!'"—Higginson's *Young Folks' History of the United States.*

Valley of Jehoshaphat. The name given, in modern times, to the deep ravine east of Mount Moriah, Jerusalem. It extends from north to south, for a distance of half a mile, from the Garden of Gethsemane to the village of Siloam, and separates the city from the Mount of Olives. The valley is traversed by the brook Kedron, and is filled with tombs. The Jews believe that the Last Judgment is to take place there, in accordance with the prophecy uttered by *Joel* iii, 12:—" Let the heathen be wakened, and come up to the *valley of Jehoshaphat:* for there will I sit to judge all the heathen round about."

Vallombrosa (*It., Shady Valley*). A Benedictine abbey, 15 miles east of Florence, founded about 1038 A.D. by John Gualbert. These magnificent conventual buildings—erected in 1673—are situated in a secluded valley of the Apennines, and are surrounded by forests of fir, beech, and chestnut trees. The abbey was suppressed in 1869, and converted into a school of forestry. Vallombrosa was visited by Dante, and is mentioned by Ariosto in the *Orlando Furioso*, and by Milton in the *Paradise Lost*. It is much resorted to by artists and tourists; but owes its chief celebrity to the allusions made to it in literature.

" Thick as autumnal leaves that strew the
　　brooks
　In *Vallombrosa*, where the Etrurian
　　shades
　High over-arch'd imbow'r."
　　　　Paradise Lost, i, 302-304.

Valmy, Battle of. A battle fought at Valmy in northeastern France, on September 20th, 1792, between the French under Kellermann and the Prussians commanded by the Duke of Brunswick. The former were victorious. The battle of Valmy is famous as the first success of the Republic of France, and the beginning of that series of remarkable victories that led the French in triumph to the gates of Moscow. Kellermann was created Duke of Valmy by Napoleon I, in 1808.

Vandals. A Teutonic race, whose frightful ravages were among the chief causes of the downfall of the Roman Empire. In 406 A.D. they crossed the Rhine and entered Gaul, and three years later (409) they made their appearance in Spain, and founded an empire there in 411. After 20 years' warfare with the Romans and their fellow-barbarians, the Goths and the Suevi, the Vandals passed over into Africa, under the dreaded Genseric; subdued the Roman territory; and captured Carthage in 439. In 455, Genseric, in command of a powerful fleet, sailed for Italy and captured Rome, which was given over to pillage. The Vandal kingdom in Spain was overthrown by the Moors, and the one in Africa by Belisarius, the general of the Emperor Justinian, in 534. See *Andalusia.*

Vanity Fair.

(1) In Bunyan's allegory, the *Pilgrim's Progress*, the name of a fair, held in the town of Vanity. It was established almost 5000 years ago by Beelzebub, Apollyon, and Legion, who perceived that all pilgrims, on their journey to the Celestial City must needs pass through this town. The fair lasted all the year round, and was devoted to the sale of " houses, lands, trades, places, honours, preferments, titles, countries, kingdoms, lusts, pleasures, and delights of all sorts; as whores, bawds, wives, husbands, children, masters, servants, lives, blood, bodies, souls, silver, gold, pearls, precious stones, and what not." Christian and Faithful on their way

through *Vanity Fair*, were denounced, arrested, beaten, and finally placed in an iron cage. Faithful was burned at the stake ; but Christian escaped and proceeded on his journey.

"Then I saw in my dream, that when they were got out of the Wilderness, they presently saw a Town before them, and the name of that Town is *Vanity;* and at the Town there is a Fair kept, called *Vanity Fair:* it is kept all the year long; it beareth the name of Vanity Fair, because the Town where it is kept is lighter than Vanity ; and also because all that is there sold, or that cometh thither, is vanity : as is the saying of the wise, ' All that cometh is vanity ! ' "— *Pilgrim's Progress.*

(2) The title of a famous novel by William Makepeace Thackeray (1811–1863).

Vassar College. An institution for the higher education of women, at Poughkeepsie, New York, founded in 1861 by Matthew Vassar (1792–1868), a wealthy brewer of that city, and opened in 1865 with a complete corps of instructors and 350 students. It has an endowment fund of over $1,-100,000, together with buildings and collections of great value. Vassar College was the first institution in the world established to give women a complete collegiate education. It has, at present, 110 instructors, 1043 students, and a library of 76,156 volumes.

Vatican. The largest and most magnificent palace in the world, situated on the ancient Mons Vaticanus, a hill of Rome, on the right bank of the Tiber. Its foundation is ascribed to Constantine, Liberius, and Symmachus, and also to Pope Eugenius III (1145–1153) in 1146. It was rebuilt in 1280, and was made the permanent residence of the Pope on his return from Avignon, in 1378. The Vatican contains 11,000 apartments (some authorities say 7000) of various sizes, 20 courts, 8 grand staircases, and 200 smaller ones. Its collections of paintings, statuary, bronzes, gems, marbles, books, and MSS. are the

most famous in the world. See *Vatican Hill ; Vatican Library.*

" The palace of the *Vatican* bears the same relation to other palaces that St. Peter's does to other churches. It is, indeed, not a palace, but a congress of palaces. One of the stories with which the traveller in Rome is amused, is, that the Vatican with its gardens, and St. Peter's, occupy as much space as the city of Turin ; and, as it has never been contradicted, it is probably true. The Vatican comprises a papal palace, a library, and a museum ; and is said to contain between four and five thousand apartments. As a museum of art, it is the first in the world. In sculpture, it not only surpasses any other collection, but all other collections put together. The whole of Europe could furnish nothing to rival the Vatican. It also comprises the highest triumphs of painting, in the frescoes of Raphael and Michael Angelo. He who has seen the Vatican has seen the utmost point reached by the human mind and hand in these two arts. The world is no more likely to witness any thing beyond what is here visible than to have a nobler epic than the Iliad, or a greater dramatist than Shakespeare."—Hillard's *Six Months in Italy.*

Vatican Codex. A Greek uncial manuscript, in the Vatican Library at Rome, containing the greater part of the *Septuagint Version of the Old Testament,* and the *New Testament,* as far as *Hebrews* ix, 14. It probably belongs to the 4th century ; and, in Tischendorf's opinion, is one of the thirty copies of the Scriptures prepared by Eusebius, at the command of Constantine, in 330. Cardinal Mai's edition appeared in 1857, and a revision of it in 1859. The *Vatican Codex* is of the highest authority ; but, owing to the jealous care with which it is guarded, it is practically inaccessible to biblical scholars. See *Alexandrian Codex ; Ephraem Codex ; Sinaitic Codex.*

Vatican Hill. A famous hill in the city of Rome, crowned by the palace of the Vatican. It is situated on the right bank of the Tiber, but is not one of the " Seven Hills of Rome." See *Seven Hills of Rome ; Vatican.*

Vatican Library. A famous library, in the palace of the Vatican at Rome, founded by Pope Nicholas V (1447–1455) in 1448. It contains about 24,000 MSS., and upwards of 50,000 printed books. Among its treasures may be mentioned the *Vatican Codex ;* the famous MS. of *Virgil,* dating from the fifth century ; the MS. of *Terence,* of the ninth century ; the MS. of *Dante,* in the handwriting of Boccaccio and annotated by Petrarch ; and the *Cicero de Republica,* considered the oldest Latin MS. in existence. The Grand Hall of the Library is 240 feet long and 52 feet broad. It is elaborately frescoed, and is adorned with vases of porphyry, urns of malachite, gold crosses, and solid silver candelabra, — presents to various popes by royal admirers. See *Vatican.*

" In entering this, the oldest and the most celebrated library in Europe, every one who has the slightest tinge of literary enthusiasm must be conscious of a peculiar feeling of reverence. But this first emotion is soon displaced by blank astonishment, from the fact that no books are anywhere to be seen. The visitor is conducted into a noble hall of splendid architectural proportions and embellishments, surrounded by an immense double gallery,— the whole adorned with frescoes, busts, statues, and columns, but the books and manuscripts are shut up in cabinets of painted wood, and hidden from vulgar gaze, like the beauties of an eastern harem."
—Hillard's *Six Months in Italy.*

Vauxhall Gardens. A popular place of amusement in London, opened in 1660, and closed in 1859, after an existence of nearly 200 years. It was situated in Lambeth, opposite Millbank, near the manor of Vauxhall, Falkeshall, Fox-hall, or Faukeshall, from which it derived its name. Pepys mentions Vauxhall Gardens in his *Diary,* under date of May 28th, 1667, and refers to the entertainment as " mighty devertising "; while Thackeray gives a graphic description of the place in his novel *Vanity Fair.* During the season of 1823, 133,279 persons visited Vauxhall, and the receipts amounted to £29,590. On the supposed last night (September 5th, 1839), 1089 persons were present.

Vedas. Sacred writings of the Hindus—comprising hymns, prayers, and liturgies—said, according to tradition, to have been compiled by Vyása, about 1200 B.C. They are written in Sanskrit, and are divided into four parts, viz., the *Rig-Veda,* the *Sama-Veda,* the *Yajur-Veda,* and the *Atharva-Veda.* Professor Max-Müller's edition (prepared under the patronage of the East India Company) appeared in 1849–1874. Four volumes of H. H. Wilson's edition were published in 1850–1867, and the two remaining volumes (completing the work) in 1889. See *Puránas.*

" *Veda* means originally knowing or knowledge, and this name is given by the Brahmans not to one work, but to the whole body of their most ancient sacred literature. . . . The name of *Veda* is commonly given to four collections of hymns, which are respectively known by the names of ' Rig-Veda,' ' Yagur-Veda,' ' Sâma-Veda,' and ' Atharva-Veda.' " — Max - Müller's *Chips from a German Workshop.*

"The term *Veda,* literally 'knowledge,' originally designates the whole immense mass of the earlier religious literature, metrical and prosaic, of India, representing several distinct and diverse periods of belief and culture. . . . It is perhaps not worth while to attempt fixing the Vedic period more nearly than by saying that general considerations seem to refer it, with much probability, to the earlier half of the second thousand years preceding the Christian era (B.C. 2000–1500). The time which the hymns themselves cover cannot be measured by less than centuries ; and how much later, where, and under whose direction, their collection may have taken place, it is not now possible to determine."— *William Dwight Whitney.*

Vendée, Rising of La. An uprising of the inhabitants of La Vendée, (a maritime province of western France), in favor of the Bourbons, in 1793. The insurrection was crushed by General Hoche in 1796, and the Vendeans were subjected to merciless cruelty. It is said that this civil war caused the death of 100,000 Frenchmen. Georges Cadoudal, the last Vendean chief, was convicted of participation in the royalist plot to murder

Napoleon Bonaparte, then First Consul ; and was executed in 1804.

"This country, bounded by the Loire and the sea, and crossed by few roads, had retained its ancient feudal customs. The nobles habitually lived on their estates, keeping up a kind intercourse with their simple and sturdy tenants, who, in turn, were devotedly attached to their landlords, their religion, and the old monarchical government."—Barnes's *Brief History of France*.

Vendôme Column. See *Column of Vendôme*.

Venerable. A title conferred upon Bede, the English monk and ecclesiastical writer of the eighth century A.D.; upon Guillaume de Champeaux, the scholastic philosopher of the twelfth century ; and upon Peter, Abbot of Cluny. The title " Venerable " is bestowed at the present day in the Anglican Church upon archdeacons ; and is given in the Roman Catholic Church to persons that have attained the first degree of sanctity, but have not yet been canonized.

Venial Sins. A term applied, in the Roman Catholic Church, to slight, pardonable transgressions, — such as may render the transgressor liable to purgatory, but not to hell. As distinguished from " mortal sins," they are " those of ignorance and negligence, and such as are considered small in their nature." Protestants do not recognize this distinction between " mortal sins " and " venial sins." See *Mortal Sins ; Seven Deadly Sins*.

Venice Academy of Fine Arts. A gallery of art in Venice, Italy, occupying the building formerly used for the convent of La Carita. It contains a fine collection of paintings, chief among which is Titian's *Assumption of the Virgin*. See *Assumption of the Virgin*.

Veni, Creator Spiritus (*Lat.*, *Come, Creator Spirit*). One of the " Seven Great Hymns " of the Mediæval Church. It is popularly ascribed to

Charlemagne (768–814), but the evidence in favor of its composition by Pope Gregory the Great (590–604) is much more convincing.

"Anciently it was sung not only at Whitsuntide, but, as still in the Roman Catholic Church, on the most solemn occasions—at the election of a pope and of bishops, at the coronation of kings, at synods, and at the elevation and translation of the relics of saints. Its ' more than ordinary worth and dignity ' have been recognized by the Church of England, ' when, dismissing every other hymn, she has yet retained this in the offices for the ordaining of priests and the consecrating of bishops.' It is certainly one of the most magnificent compositions, mingling prayer with praise—grand, full-chorded, rich in tone and melody, and at the same time soft, sweet, and touching. In a simple manner it unites the doctrinal with the practical —the full-rounded statement of scriptural truth with conscious need and joyous utterance."— McClintock and Strong's *Cyclopædia*.

Veni, Sancte Spiritus (*Lat.*, *Come, Holy Spirit*). One of the "Seven Great Hymns " of the Mediæval Church. It is generally ascribed to Robert the Pious (996–1031), King of France, and is called the most beautiful of all Latin hymns.

"The ability of Robert II. to have composed the hymn which ranks next to the *Dies Iræ* and *Stabat Mater*, is not improbable, for, according to the chronicle of Saint Bertin, he was a saint, a poet, and a musician."— *Seven Great Hymns of the Mediæval Church*.

" Veni, Vidi, Vici " (*Lat.*, "*I came, I saw, I conquered*"). A famous despatch sent by Julius Cæsar (100–44 B.C.) to the Roman Senate, announcing his victory over Pharnaces, King of Pontus, son of Mithridates, at the battle of Zela (47 B.C.). This is perhaps the most laconic despatch ever penned. According to Plutarch, Cæsar used these words in announcing his victory to his friend Amintius. See *Zela, Battle of*.

"In the account he [Cæsar] gave Amintius, one of his friends in Rome, of the rapidity and dispatch with which he gained his victory, he made use only of three words, ' I came, I saw, I conquered.' Their having all the same form and termination in the Roman language adds grace to their conciseness."—Langhorne's *Plutarch*.

Venus. See *Aphrodite*.

Venus Anadyomene (*Venus Rising from the Sea*). A famous statue of Venus in the palace of the Vatican at Rome. It represents the goddess in a crouching attitude, with both hands elevated. The figure is draped below the hips, and the drapery is gathered into a knot in the centre. It is below life-size, and is of Roman workmanship. See *Phryne*.

Venus Borghese. A celebrated statue by Antonio Canova (1757–1822), in the Villa Borghese at Rome. It was modelled after Pauline Bonaparte, sister of Napoleon I, and represents the goddess reclining upon a couch, with the right hand supporting the head and the left holding an apple. The statue is draped from the hips, and is, without doubt, the most famous Venus of modern times. It is also called the *Venus Victrix*.

"In another room of the upper suite is Canova's celebrated statue of the Princess Pauline Borghese, . . . which enjoys a certain factitious interest from its supposed history, beyond that which its intrinsic merits, as a work of art, can claim. The statue is in a recumbent posture, reclining on a couch, which is also sculptured out of marble, and the upper part of the person is supported by marble cushions. The costume, with the exception of a very light scarf, is that of Eve before the fall; and there is a consciousness of nakedness in the air and expression which obtrudes the fact offensively upon the attention. Its merits appeared to me to consist rather in the satin-like softness and polish given to the surface of the marble, than in the grace or proportions of the figure. The subject, too, was of a kind calculated to bring out rather the shadows than the lights of Canova's genius."—Hillard's *Six Months in Italy.*

Venus Callipyge. A famous statue of Venus, found among the ruins of Nero's Golden House at Rome, and now in the National Museum in Naples. It is generally attributed to Praxiteles. The head, right arm, and one of the legs are restorations.

"The *Venus Callipygis*, apparently a boudoir ornament, reminding one of the pretty license of our eighteenth century."—*Taine.*

Venus de' Medici. A noted statue of Venus in the Tribune of the Uffizi Gallery in Florence, supposed to be the production of Cleomenes, the Athenian sculptor, who flourished about 250 B.C. It was discovered at Hadrian's Villa, near Tivoli, about 1680, and was brought to Florence in 1695 by Cosmo de' Medici III, from which circumstance it derives its name. The statue, when found, was in 13 pieces, with the arms missing, but was restored by Bernini. It is only 4 feet 11 inches in height, but is generally considered the ideal of female beauty.

"The statue is but four feet eleven inches in height, which gives a sort of doll-like character to the whole figure. The hands—a modern restoration—are unnecessarily bad: the head is small in proportion to the body ; and there is a sort of vacant simper upon the face. There is certainly wonderful beauty in the undulating outline of the whole form. The lines flow into each other as softly and delicately as if the winds of summer had moulded the frame. But this seems hardly enough to call forth the raptures into which so many intellectual men have fallen over her. Admirable as is the workmanship, the expression has in it more of earth than of heaven. She is not a goddess, unconscious alike of her beauty and nakedness,—into whose bosom no ray of human passion or human weakness has ever darted,—but a lovely woman who knows her power and enjoys her triumphs."—Hillard's *Six Months in Italy.*

Venus of Canova. A famous statue of Venus by Antonio Canova (1757–1822), in the gallery of the Pitti Palace in Florence. Its attitude is somewhat similar to that of the Venus de' Medici.

"Although undoubtedly a figure of great beauty, it by no means struck me as possessing that exquisite and classic perfection which has been ascribed to it."—*Bayard Taylor.*

"It seemed to me that the artist had tried to produce something that should be more beautiful than beauty ; as if a painter should try to paint a picture which should be bluer than blue, or redder than red. The true line of grace is thus overstepped, and prettiness and affectation are the result."—Hillard's *Six Months in Italy*.

Venus of Capua. A well-known statue of Venus, found at Capua, Italy, and now in the National Museum in Naples. The arms, Cupid, and base are restorations.

"The supple and soft limbs, the beauty of the attitude, and the elegant harmony of the whole composition so far impose upon the imagination as to make us think we are looking on some living form, standing motionless on a pedestal. She tramples under foot Minerva's helmet, and bears on her forehead Juno's diadem."—*Handbook to National Museum*.

Venus of Cnidus.

(1) A celebrated statue of Venus by Praxiteles, the Greek sculptor, who flourished about 350 B.C. It was purchased by the inhabitants of Cnidus in Asia Minor, and was placed in the temple of the goddess in that city, from which circumstance it derived its name. So great was its fame that travelers from all parts of the civilized world made voyages to Cnidus to behold it. Nicomedes, King of Bithynia, offered to pay off the entire debt of the city in return for this statue, but so great was the love of the Cnidians for the image of the goddess that they preferred to suffer any privation rather than part with it. It was subsequently taken to Constantinople, where it was destroyed by fire in 475 A.D.

(2) A noted statue of Venus in the Vatican at Rome, said to be the most perfect copy of the Venus of Praxiteles in existence.

(3) A famous statue of Venus in the Glyptothek at Munich, considered by some to be of Roman workmanship, and by others to be the work of Praxiteles himself. See *Phryne*.

Venus of Milo. A world-renowned statue of Venus in the gallery of the Louvre in Paris. It was discovered in 1820 by a peasant in the island of Melos (or Milo), at the entrance to the Greek Archipelago, and was purchased by the French Government for 6000 francs. Its age is unknown ; but it is assigned to the 4th century before Christ,—the golden period of Greek art.

"This is the only statue of Aphrodite handed down to us which represents her not merely as a beautiful woman, but as a goddess. The form is powerful and majestic, and yet instinct with an indescribable charm of youth and beauty, while the pure and noble expression of the head denotes the goddess's independence of all human requirements and the calm self-sufficiency of her divine character. The fact that this beautiful work, notwithstanding its great excellence, is not one of those which have been specially extolled by ancient authors, affords us an approximate idea of the beauty of those lost masterpieces which formed the great marvel of antiquity."—*Lübke*.

Venus of the Capitol. A superb statue of Venus in the Museum of the Capitol in Rome. It was discovered about the middle of the 18th century in the Suburra on the Viminal Hill, in an almost perfect state of preservation. It is perhaps the loveliest of all the statues of the goddess, and belongs to the best period of Greek art.

"The truthfulness and beauty with which nature is reproduced in the *Venus of the Capitol* made this statue a subject of scandal to the austerity of the early Christians. Without doubt, the desire to protect it from their mutilation caused it to be carefully buried ; hence its entire preservation. Thus its danger became its salvation."—*Ampère*.

Venus, Pauline. A name sometimes given to the *Venus Borghese*, because modelled after Pauline Bonaparte, the sister of Napoleon I. See *Venus Borghese*.

Venus Victrix. See *Venus Borghese*.

Vernon Gallery. A collection of paintings of the English School—162 in number — presented to the British Government by Mr. Robert Vernon (1774–1849) in 1847, and now in the South Kensington Museum, London. It contains many masterpieces of Gainsborough, Eastlake, Landseer, and Turner.

Verona, Arena of. A famous ruin, situated at Verona, Italy, remarkable for its almost perfect state of preservation. It is 513 feet in length, 410 feet in breadth, and 98 feet in height. It is three stories high, 1500 feet in circumference, and has seats for 24,000 spectators. The amphitheatre dates from 90 A.D., and is still used for theatrical purposes.

Veronica (*True Image*). The likeness of Christ, said to have been miraculously imprinted on the sudarium with which he wiped the bloody sweat from his brow, while on his way to Calvary. This sacred relic is preserved in St. Peter's Church in Rome, although Milan and several other places also claim to possess the original. The name " Veronica " is also given, in Catholic legend, to the woman that offered her veil to the Savior. Tradition identifies her with Berenice, the daughter of the Canaanitish woman healed by Jesus. See *Holy Handkerchief ; Sudarium.*

"In St. Peter's at Rome, one of the chapels under the dome is dedicated to *St. Veronica*. An ancient image of our Saviour, painted on linen, and styled the Vera Icon (whence it is supposed that the name of *Veronica* is derived), is regarded by the people as the veritable napkin of St. Veronica, and is exhibited among the relics of the Church."—*Mrs. Jameson.*

Versailles, Palace of. A magnificent palace at Versailles, France, eleven miles southwest of Paris, founded by Louis XIII (1610–1643), and greatly extended and embellished by Louis XIV (1643–1715) at a cost of over $200,000,000. It became the royal residence in 1682, and was successively occupied by Louis XIV, Louis XV, and Louis XVI. During the Revolution, it narrowly escaped being sold, and in the time of the Empire was neglected, owing to the great expense that its repair would have entailed. Versailles became the residence of Louis Philippe (1830–1848) in 1830, and was converted by him into a National Museum in 1837,—a use to which it is still devoted. In 1870, the palace became the headquarters of the German army ; and there King William of Prussia was proclaimed Emperor of Germany on January 18th, 1871. After the conclusion of peace, it was the seat of the French Government until 1879, after which date the Chambers transferred their sittings to Paris.

"I used to abuse Louis XIV for spending two hundred millions of dollars in creating this marvelous park, when bread was so scarce with some of his subjects ; but I have forgiven him now. He took a tract of land sixty miles in circumference, and set to work to make this park and build this palace, and a road to it from Paris. He kept 36,000 men employed daily on it, and the labor was so unhealthy that they used to die and be hauled off by cart-loads every night. The wife of a nobleman of the time speaks of this as an '*inconvenience*,' but naively remarks that it does not seem worthy of attention in the happy state of tranquillity we now enjoy."—*Innocents Abroad* (Mark Twain).

Vesta, Temple of. A small, circular building, situated on the bank of the Tiber at Rome, near the Cloaca Maxima. It is surrounded by a peristyle of marble columns—originally twenty in number—nineteen of which still remain. The entablature of the temple is gone, and the roof—composed of red tiles—rests directly upon the capitals of the columns.

"It is a pretty toy of a building ; too small —to borrow an expression of Horace Walpole's—to live in, and too large to hang at one's watch-chain. The form and features are multiplied in an immense progeny of bronze models and inkstands to which it has given birth."—Hillard's *Six Months in Italy.*

Vestiges of the Natural History of Creation. A famous work, which upholds the Lamarckian theory of organic development. It was published anonymously in 1844, but is confidently believed to have been written by Robert Chambers (1802–1871). It excited great interest, and was regarded, until the publication of Darwin's *Origin of Species* in 1859, as the chief authority in England on the question of Natural Selection in plants and animals.

"In my own opinion it [the *Vestiges*] has done excellent service in this country in calling attention to the subject, in removing prejudice, and in thus preparing the ground for the reception of analogous views."— *Charles Darwin*.

Vexilla Regis. A Latin hymn composed by Venantius Fortunatus (530–609 A.D.). It takes its name from the first words *Vexilla Regis Prodeunt* (*Lat., The Kingly Banners Forward Go*). This hymn was originally sung in procession on Good Friday, before the Mass of the Presanctified ; but was afterwards adapted for use in the Western Church during Passion-tide. An English version of the hymn is now in general use in the Church of England.

Via Appia (*Lat., Appian Way*). See *Appian Way*.

Via de' Bardi. A famous old street in Florence, Italy, which originally extended from the Ponte Vecchio to the Piazza de' Mozzi, at the head of the Ponte alle Grazie. A considerable portion of it has disappeared, in consequence of public improvements made within recent years. In George Eliot's *Romola*, the *Via de' Bardi* was the street in which the blind scholar, Bardo de' Bardi, and his daughter dwelt.

"The house in which Bardo lived was situated on the side of the street nearest the hill, and was one of those large sombre masses of stone buildings pierced by comparatively small windows, and surmounted by what may be called a roofed terrace or loggia, of which there are many examples still to be seen in the venerable city."— *Romola* (George Eliot).

Via Dolorosa (*Lat., Sorrowful Way*). A name popularly given, since the Christian era, to a narrow, crooked street in Jerusalem, extending from St. Stephen's Gate to the Church of the Holy Sepulchre. According to tradition, it was over this road that Jesus Christ passed on his way from the prison of Antonia to Calvary,— the place of the crucifixion.

"Along this dreary walk, amid its shadows and solemn memories, a wounded spirit finds companionship. As the industrious shrine-makers of this and of other ages, the monks have consecrated eight stations in this narrow street, commemorative of as many events in our Lord's journey from the dungeons of Antonia to the site of Calvary. In the northern wall of the Temple area are the two arches, now walled up, where stood Pilate's staircase, down which our Lord descended after his sentence was pronounced, and directly opposite is the Church of the Flagellation, marking the place where he was scourged. Not many paces to the west is the *Ecce Homo* arch, where Pilate exclaimed to the infuriated mob, 'Behold the man !' At the bottom of a gentle descent the lane turns to the left, and then to the right. Beyond this angle is shown a deep impression in the solid stone wall, made by the shoulders of Jesus when he leaned against it at the time he fainted. Near it is the house of St. Veronica, the illustrious woman who presented the Savior with a handkerchief to wipe his bleeding brow. From her residence to the terminus of the street the gloom and silence are painful ; and at well-apportioned intervals are indicated, by broken columns, the places where Simon was compelled to bear the Redeemer's cross, where Jesus addressed the weeping daughters of Jerusalem, and where his tragical death occurred."—Newman's *From Dan to Beersheba*.

Via Flaminia (*Lat., Flaminian Way*). See *Flaminian Way*.

Via Sacra (*Lat., Sacred Way*). A winding street in ancient Rome, traversing the Roman Forum and extending from the Arch of Fabius to the Arch of Titus. It was the route taken by triumphal processions on their way from the Campus Martius to the Capitol. The great blocks of lava with which this roadway was paved still remain, for the most part, *in situ*.

Viaticum (*Lat., Provision for a Journey*). A term used in the early Christian Church to designate the sacraments of Baptism and the Eucharist which were regarded as necessary to sustain Christians in their journey through this life to the other world. The word is, however, used mo specifically at the present day to denote the sacrament of the Eucharist as administered to a person at the point of death. In some cases, the sacred elements were placed in the coffin of the deceased person. According to the 13th canon of the Nicene Council no one is to " be deprived of his perfect and most necessary *viaticum* when he departs out of this life."

Vicar of Bray. A clergyman of the Church of England, who managed, by skilfully adjusting his religious opinions to the requirements of the times, to retain his preferments during the reigns of Henry VIII, Edward VI, Mary, and Elizabeth. Other authorities, however, make him a subject of Charles II, James II, William and Mary, Anne, and George I. His name is variously given as Symon Symonds, Simon Alleyn or Allen, and Pendleton. The phrase " Vicar of Bray " is commonly applied to one that renounces allegiance to his party whenever he finds his safety or his interests imperilled.

Vicar of Wakefield. A famous tale by Oliver Goldsmith (1728-1774). It appeared in March, 1766, and immediately established the author's reputation as a novelist. The book was published through the influence of Dr. Samuel Johnson, who obtained from the publisher the sum of £60 for the MS.

" It is not to be described, the effect which Goldsmith's *Vicar* had upon me just at the critical moment of mental development. That lofty and benevolent irony, that fair and indulgent view of all infirmities and faults, that meekness under all calamities, and the whole train of kindred virtues, whatever names they bear, proved my best education."—*Goethe*.

Victoria. A low, four-wheeled, open carriage—seating two persons—with a calash-top and an elevated seat for the driver. It was introduced in 1838, the year of the coronation of Queen Victoria, and was named in her honor.

50

Victoria Bridge. A famous tubular railway bridge across the St. Lawrence River at Montreal, Canada. It was built in 1854-1859, under the superintendence of Robert Stephenson, and was formally opened by the Prince of Wales in August, 1860. The structure is 9144 feet in length, and is composed of 25 spans,—the central one measuring 330 feet, and the others 242 feet each. The distance between the summer level of the river and the under surface of the central tube is 60 feet. It is estimated that there are 9044 tons of iron in the tubes, and that the entire painted surface equals 32 acres in area. The total cost of the bridge was £1,700,000. It was seriously damaged by floating ice in January, 1855 ; but the stone piers escaped injury.

Victoria Embankment. A superb granite embankment extending along the north bank of the Thames at London, from Westminster Bridge to Blackfriars Bridge,— a distance of more than a mile. It has a roadway 64 feet in width, and is protected on the river side by a granite wall, 8 feet thick. The Embankment is planted with rows of trees, and communicates with the river at intervals by means of stone steps, leading to floating steamboat wharves. Part of the land reclaimed from the Thames has been converted into gardens, adorned with statues of William Tyndale, Robert Burns, John Stuart Mill, Brunel, and others. One of the chief embellishments is Cleopatra's Needle, erected on its present site on September 12th, 1878. The Victoria Embankment was constructed in 1864-1870, at a cost of nearly £2,000,000. See *Albert Embankment ; Cleopatra's Needles ; Obelisk in London.*

Victoria Nyanza, Lake. A freshwater lake in eastern equatorial Africa, discovered by Captain John H. Speke in 1858, and afterwards explored by him and Captain J. A. Grant, in 1862. It has an area of about 27,000 square miles, and lies about 3900 feet above sea-level. The native name of the lake is Ukerewe. See *Albert Nyanza, Lake.*

Victoria Regia. A species of water-lily, named in honor of Queen Victoria of England. It is a native of Brazil and Guiana, and has circular leaves six feet in diameter and pink-white flowers a foot in diameter. A superb lily of this species was brought from Guiana to England by Sir Robert Schomburgk in 1838. The *Victoria Regia* was successfully grown in the open air in 1855.

Victory. The flag-ship of Admiral Nelson (1758–1805) at the battle of Trafalgar. The vessel is anchored in the harbor of Portsmouth, England, and is kept in a fine state of preservation. It was on her quarter-deck that Nelson received his fatal wound.

> "At the head of the line goes the *Victory*,
> With Nelson on the deck,
> And on his breast the orders shine
> Like the stars on a shattered wreck."
> *Lord Lytton.*

Victory of Samothrace. A superb fragment of ancient sculpture in the Louvre at Paris. It consists of a colossal winged statue, without head or arms, carved in commemoration of the naval victory of Demetrius Poliorcetes, 305 B.C. This figure, which is represented as alighting on the prow of a galley, is remarkable for its noble proportions and grand vitality,—making it one of the masterpieces of the majestic style.

Vienna, Congress of. A meeting of the allied powers of Europe at Vienna, to settle the affairs of the Continent of Europe after the fall of the first Napoleon. The Congress met for the first time on September 20th, 1814, and continued its sessions until June 10th, 1815. England was represented by Castlereagh, and afterwards by Wellington ; Russia by Alexander I and Nesselrode ; Austria by Metternich ; Prussia by Hardenberg ; and

France by Talleyrand. All the leading powers received important accessions of territory.

"It was arranged to give to England the Cape of Good Hope, the Mauritius, Malta, and Corfu ; to Russia were assigned Finland and Poland ; to Austria were assigned Lombardy and the Venetian States ; to Prussia were allotted Saxony, Franconia, and Swedish Pomerania ; to the Archduke Ferdinand was allotted Tuscany ; to the King of Sardinia was allotted Genoa ; to Marie Louise, wife of Napoleon, were assigned Parma and Placentia ; to Sweden was assigned Norway; and to Ferdinand IV of the Bourbon line were allotted the Two Sicilies."—Brewer's *Historic Note-Book.*

Vienna, Peace of. See *Schönbrunn, Peace of.*

Vienna Gallery of Fine Arts. An academy of art at Vienna, Austria, founded by Leopold I (1658–1705), Emperor of Germany, in 1692. It occupies a Renaissance edifice erected in 1872–1876, and contains a gallery of paintings,— representing almost every school of art,— a library, and a collection of 17,000 drawings and water-colors, 61,000 engravings and woodcuts, and 5000 photographs. The chief treasures of the gallery are the Dutch masters of the seventeenth century.

Villa Borghese. A country-seat, in the outskirts of Rome, near the Porta del Popolo, belonging to the Borghese family. The principal building, or casino, was originally a summer residence, but is now used as a museum of statuary. It contains Canova's *Venus Borghese*, the *Dancing Faun*, and the statues of *Anacreon* and *Alcæus*. The grounds, which are very extensive and beautifully laid out, are a favorite place of resort for the citizens of Rome during the spring months. See *Borghese Palace.*

"The entrance to the *Villa Borghese* is just beyond the Porta del Popolo. The grounds, which are three miles in circuit, are thrown open to the public as freely as if they belonged to it. At all times, numerous parties will be found availing themselves of this generous privilege, some in carriages some on horseback, but mostly on foot; for, as a place of resort, it is more popular with persons of modest condition among the Romans than with the favored classes."—Hillard's *Six Months in Italy*.

Villa d'Este. A ruined villa near Tivoli, Italy, built in 1549 by Pirro Ligorio, for Cardinal Ippolito d'Este, son of Alfonso II, Duke of Ferrara. It belongs at the present time to the Duke of Modena, the direct descendant of its founder. The building, which is stately and imposing, is surrounded by wild and impressive gardens, whose ruined terraces command superb views of the Campagna.

"In the after part of the day, we paid a visit to the *Villa d'Este*, a building which, from its formal and elaborate magnificence, might stand as a representative of its whole class. Vast sums of money were lavished upon its waterworks, its terraces, its stiff plantations, and its broad flights of steps. It is now uninhabited and falling to decay; but the garden—with its pines, cypresses, and avenues of box, left by their unpruned growth to form an 'obsolete prolixity of shade'—still retains a melancholy charm; and from the casino a wide and lovely landscape is commanded." — Hillard's *Six Months in Italy*.

". . . I am a suitor of Vittoria Colonna; I walk with Tasso along the terraced garden of the *Villa d'Este*, and look to see Beatrice smiling down the rich gloom of the cypress shade."—Curtis's *Prue and I.*

Villafranca, Peace of. The name given to the preliminaries of peace signed by the Emperors of France and Austria at Villafranca, Italy, on July 12th, 1859, after the battle of Solferino. These preliminaries formed the basis of the Treaty of Zurich (signed November 10th, 1859), whereby Lombardy was ceded by Austria to Sardinia, and an Italian Confederation —under the presidency of the Pope— was determined upon. In addition, the rights of the ex-sovereigns of Modena, Parma, and Tuscany were reserved. See *Solferino, Battle of.*

Villa Reale. A fashionable pleasure-ground and promenade in the street called the *Chiaja*, in Naples, Italy. It is about a mile in length and 200 feet in width, and borders upon the bay, from which it is separated by a substantial stone wall. The grounds are beautifully laid out in the Italian style, and are adorned with fountains and statues. The *Villa Reale* is now called the *Villa Nazionale*.

"It is nearly a mile long; shaded with orange-trees, myrtles, and acacias; sparkling with fountains, and adorned with marble statues and vases gleaming through the foliage. On one side is a row of tall, showy houses; on the other, the broad mirror of the bay, from which the light is thrown and multiplied in dazzling gleams. . . . Here is everything that can restore the weary or amuse the idle,—a prospect of indescribable beauty; the breezes and voices of the sea; the rich foliage of the south; the gay faces of men and women, and children sporting round the fountains."—Hillard's *Six Months in Italy*.

Ville de Havre. A steamship of the *Compagnie Générale Transatlantique* (5100 tons burden), which, on November 22nd, 1873,—during her voyage from New York to Havre,—was struck by the Scotch sailing-vessel *Lochearn*, and sank within twelve minutes. Out of 313 persons on board, 226 perished. The *Lochearn* was abandoned by her crew, who were rescued and taken to Plymouth, England. The officers of the *Lochearn*, after a judicial examination, were exonerated in England, but were censured in France.

Villenage. A system of land-tenure introduced into England after the Norman Conquest (1066 A.D.), whereby the occupants of the soil were kept in a condition of servitude, and were permitted to hold land only on condition of performing menial services for their lord and superior. Such persons were called *villeins* (of or pertaining to the *vill*), whence is derived the common English word *villain*. Villenage, although never formally abolished in England, ceased to exist during the 16th century. Also written *villanage*, *villeinage*.

Vinegar Bible. The name popularly given to an edition of the Bible, published in Oxford, England, in 1717. It is so called from a typographical error in the heading of *Luke* xx, where the phrase " The Parable of the Vineyard " is made to read " The Parable of the Vinegar."

Violet Crowned City. See *City of the Violet Crown.*

Virginia. The name given to the first permanent English settlement in North America,—made at Jamestown in May, 1607. The territory was discovered by John Cabot in 1497, and was taken possession of by Sir Walter Raleigh (1552–1618) on July 13th, 1584, from whom it received the name of Virginia in honor of Elizabeth, the Virgin Queen.

Virginia Bible. The name given to a version of the Bible translated into the native language of the North American Indians of Virginia. The first edition appeared in 1661–1663.

Virgin of Guadalupe. The patron-saint of Mexico, and more especially of the Mexican Indians. According to the legend, the Virgin Mary appeared to a converted Indian, named Juan Diego, in 1531, on the hill of Tepeyacac, near the City of Mexico, and, addressing him in his own language, told him that she wished a temple built to her on that very spot. At the foot of the hill is the Church of Nuestra Señora de Guadalupe, completed in 1709. It contains an exquisite picture of the Virgin, said to have been miraculously imprinted by her on the surface of Diego's blanket. Guadalupe Hidalgo, with the sanctuary of the Virgin of Guadalupe, is situated about two miles north of the City of Mexico.

Virginius. A schooner sailing under the American flag, suspected of conveying men and munitions of war to the Cuban insurgents. The vessel left New York for the West Indies on October 4th, 1873, but was captured by the Spanish gunboat *Tornado*, and taken to Havana on October 31st. Captain Fry, the commander of the *Virginius*, and 44 others — being accused of complicity with the insurgents — were shot without a trial. The affair caused intense excitement in the United States, and threatened to embroil that country in a war with Spain; but peace was finally restored by the return of the *Virginius* and her survivors to the United States authorities.

Virgin Queen. A title popularly conferred upon Elizabeth (1558–1603), Queen of England, although its aptness has been questioned by many historians. See *Maiden Queen.*

Virgins, Eleven Thousand. See *St. Ursula, Church of.*

Viri Romæ (*Lat., Heroes of Rome*). The title of an elementary Latin text-book by Charles François L'Homond (1727–1794). It contains brief accounts of the lives of the leading men of Rome, arranged as exercises for translation. The book enjoyed great popularity during the first half of the nineteenth century.

Vishnu. In Hindu mythology, the second god of the " Trimúrti," or Trinity, in which he figures as the preserver of the universe. His friendship for man was manifested in his *avatars*, or incarnations, which, according to some authorities, numbered ten, and according to others twenty-two. Of these *avatars* the two principal ones were the seventh, as Ráma, the hero of the *Rámáyana*, and the eighth, as Krishna, the hero of the *Mahábhárata*. Vishnu is generally represented as a dark-blue man, having four arms; and is worshipped chiefly by the middle classes. He originally figured as a sun-god in the oldest *Vedas*, but gradually increased in importance until in the later *Purána* he became the supreme deity. See *Brahma ; Siva.*

Visible Speech. The name given to a system of symbols designed to represent all the articulate sounds possible of production by the human voice. It was invented by Alexander Melville Bell, and first published by him in 1867. According to Bell, fifty of these symbols are sufficient to represent the sounds of all languages. The alphabetic characters composing Bell's System — thirty of which are called radical — are, to a certain extent, pictorial representations of the organs that produce the sounds. Curves are used to represent consonants, and straight lines are made the basis of vowel representation ; and by this means a complete alphabet has been constructed.

Visigoths. A term applied to the Western Goths, as opposed to the Ostrogoths, or *Eastern* Goths. This distinction arose about 330 A.D. See *Goths ; Ostrogoths.*

Vision of Mirza. A famous allegory by Joseph Addison (1672–1719), forming *Paper No. 159* in the *Spectator.*

" Vales, soft, Elysian,
Like those in the *vision*
Of *Mirza*, when, dreaming,
He saw the long hollow dell,
Touched by the prophet's spell,
Into an ocean swell,
With its isles teeming."
Whittier.

Vision of Piers Plowman. A satirical allegory, written in alliterative verse, and generally ascribed to Robert, or William, Langland. It should be carefully distinguished from *Piers Plowman's Creed* and the *Plowman's Tale,*—both of which, although by the same hand, are of unknown authorship.

Vital Force. The name given to that form of energy which, according to certain biologists, is the cause of all the vital phenomena manifested in plants and animals, as distinguished from the physical and chemical forces. Humboldt defined vital force as " an

unknown cause preventing the elements from obeying primitive affinities " ; but this theory is rejected by many biologists, who attribute all plant and animal life to the action of physical and chemical forces alone.

" The *vital forces*, according to Cope, are nerve force (*neurism*), growth force (*bathmism*), and thought force (*phrenism*), all under the direction and control of the vital principle. Apart from the phenomena of consciousness, vital actions no longer need to be considered as of a mysterious and unfathomable character, nor vital force as anything other than a form of physical energy derived from, and convertible into, other well-known forces of nature."—Webster's *International Dictionary.*

Vita Nuova (*It., New Life*). The title of a famous work by Dante Alighieri (1265–1321), wherein he relates with exquisite pathos how he first saw " the glorious lady of his heart, Beatrice." It is doubtless his earliest production.

" The *Vita Nuova* is the earliest of Dante's writings, and the most autobiographic of them in form and intention. . . . Literally *The New Life*, it has been questioned whether this phrase meant simply early life, or life made new by the first experience and lasting influence of love. . . To him it was the record of that life which the presence of Beatrice had made new."—*Charles Eliot Norton.*

Vittoria, Battle of. A famous battle fought near Vittoria, Spain, on June 21st, 1813, between the French, commanded by King Joseph Bonaparte and Marshal Jourdan, and the English and Spanish under Wellington. The French were totally defeated, with the loss of all their artillery, baggage, and treasure, and as a result of this battle, they were eventually obliged to retire from Spain.

Vivien. A shameless and wily wanton at the Court of King Arthur, about 450 A.D. She became the mistress of Merlin the Enchanter, and having, by her importunities, wrung from him the secret of his charm, she enclosed him in a hollow oak, where he lay, " lost to life, and use, and name, and fame.'' Her adventures form the subject of the poem *Merlin and Vivien*, in Tennyson's *Idylls of the King*. See *Lady of the Lake (1); Merlin*.

Vocal Memnon. See *Memnon*.

Volapük (*World-Speech*). A universal language invented by Johann M. Schleyer at Constance, about 1879, and taught by him in Paris in 1886. The roots are principally borrowed from the Latin, German, and English languages, and the orthography is strictly phonetic. Volapük was adopted, to a limited extent, in commercial correspondence ; but is now almost a thing of the past. Its use in diplomacy and science was warmly recommended by the " London Philological Society," in 1887. According to Harper's *Book of Facts*, the following are the leading peculiarities of Volapük :

(1) Alphabet consists of 27 letters, 8 vowels and 19 consonants.

(2) Each letter has but one sound.

(3) Consonants are sounded as in English, except *c* and *j ; g* is always hard, and *h* is an aspirate.

(4) Accent invariably on the last syllable.

(5) One conjugation and no irregular verbs.

(6) All word-forms and inflections are regular.

(7) Adjectives, verbs, and adverbs regularly formed from substantives.

(8) *W* becomes *v*, and *l* is substituted for *r*.

(9) Words are as far as possible reduced to one syllable.

(10) Nouns have one declension and four cases.

(11) Adjectives are formed by adding *ik* to the substantive, and adverbs by adding *o* to the adjective, as *fam* (*glory*), *famik* (*glorious*), and *famiko* (*gloriously*).

Voltaic Pile. The name given to an electric battery invented in 1804 by Alessandro Volta (1745–1827), profes-

sor of physics at the University of Pavia. It consists of an alternating series of copper and zinc disks, separated by pieces of cloth moistened with salt water, or water acidulated with nitric acid. The " Voltaic Pile" was afterwards superseded by Volta's "Crown of Cups," and this in turn was followed by Grove's nitric acid battery and Bunsen's carbon battery.

Volunteers of America. A philanthropic and religious organization established in March, 1896, by Commander and Mrs. Ballington Booth. It is similar to the " Salvation Army," from which it is an offshoot, and is organized in military style,—after the model of the United States army. It aims to reach with the gospel the millions of the lower and middle classes, whom other religious organizations have thus far failed to attract. See *Salvation Army*.

Voodooism. A degraded form of religion prevalent among the negroes of Hayti and the Southern States of the American Union. It is supposed by many to be a relic of the fetichistic religion of equatorial Africa, and to include human sacrifices and cannibalism among its rites; but belief in the existence of such practices has been shown to be unsupported by any trustworthy evidence. Moreover, such deeds, if they occur at all, are the work of a few superstitious fanatics. The word " Voodoo " is probably derived from *vaudoux* (*negro sorcerer*), a Creole form of the French *Vaudois* (*Waldenses*), who were represented by their enemies as addicted to the practice of sorcery and necromancy.

Vulcan. In classic mythology, the god of fire, the patron of blacksmiths and workers in metals, and the armorer of the gods. He was the son of Jupiter and Juno, or, according to some accounts, of Juno alone. Owing to his weakness and lameness, he incurred the displeasure of his mother, and was cast by her from Olympus.

After dwelling for nine years with Thetis and Eurynome in a grotto beneath Oceanus, Vulcan returned to Olympus, but was cast out a second time for presuming to side with his mother in a quarrel between her and Jupiter. He lighted on the island of Lemnos, and there set up his forges; but afterwards removed them to the volcanic islands of Lipari, near Sicily, where he forged the thunderbolts of Jupiter, and other marvellous implements. Vulcan was sometimes called Mulciber and Lemnius.

" Nor was his name unheard or unadored
In ancient Greece ; and in Ausonian land
Men called him *Mulciber ;* and how he fell
From heaven they fabled, thrown by angry
    Jove
Sheer o'er the crystal battlements : from
    morn
To noon he fell, from noon to dewy eve,
A summer's day ; and with the setting sun
Dropped from the zenith like a falling star
On Lemnos, the Ægean isle."
                Paradise Lost, i, 738–746.

Vulgate. The name given to the Latin Version of the Bible in use in the Roman Catholic Church. It is attributed to St. Jerome, about 384 A.D., and was authorized by the Council of Trent in 1546. The *Vulgate* displaced an earlier edition, called the *Italic,* which is said to have been made at the beginning of the second century. A critical edition of the *Vulgate,* printed by command of Pope Sixtus V (1585–1590) in 1590, was superseded by that of Pope Clement VIII (1592–1605) in 1592. This last is known as the *Clementine Bible,* and is the official edition of the *Vulgate* now in use in the Roman Catholic Church. The first *printed* edition was the work of Gutenberg and Faust, and probably appeared about 1455. The word " Vulgate " is derived from the Latin *vulgata, sc. editio (an edition for common use).*

W

Wacht am Rhein (*Ger., Watch on the Rhine*). A German national song, written by Max Schneckenburger, in 1840. It has been set to music several times, but the air with which it is generally associated was written by Carl Wilhelm, formerly Capellmeister at Crefeld, in Rhenish Prussia. The song was extremely popular during the Franco-Prussian War of 1870–1871.

Wagon Boy. A sobriquet popularly conferred upon Thomas Corwin (1794–1865), the American statesman, who, when a lad, conveyed a wagon-load of provisions to General William Henry Harrison (1773–1841), then engaged in war with the Indians on the northern frontier. Young Corwin remained with the army until the close of the campaign, and proved himself " a good whip and an excellent reinsman."

Wagram, Battle of. A sanguinary battle fought at Wagram, a village near Vienna, on July 5th and 6th, 1809, between the French, commanded by Napoleon I, and the Austrians under the Archduke Charles. The latter were defeated with a loss of 25,000 men killed and wounded and 20,000 taken prisoners, but retired into Moravia in good order. The battle of Wagram was followed by the armistice of Znaim and the Treaty of Vienna, whereby Austria ceded all of her seacoast to France; paid a large money indemnity; agreed to enforce the Continental System; and recognized Joseph Bonaparte as King of Spain.

Wahabees. A puritanical sect of Mohammedans, which arose about 1750, and established its rule in Arabia under Abd-el-Wahab. They claim to be the true followers of the Prophet, and protest strongly against the corruptions of Islâm,— denouncing the use of spirituous liquors and tobacco, usury, and card-playing, and inveighing against extravagance in dress or display of any kind. The Wahabees endeavored to propagate their doctrines with the sword, and were for a time eminently successful — capturing Mecca and Medina, — but were finally defeated and scattered by Mehemet Ali and Ibrahim Pasha, his son. The survivors fled to the deserts of Arabia, whence they emerged in large numbers in 1828, and again in 1863, on which latter occasion they extended their dominion as far as the Persian Gulf. They number about 4,000,000 at the present day.

Walcheren Expedition. The name given to an attempt made by the English in 1809 to capture Antwerp and destroy the French fleet in the river Scheldt. The effort resulted in a disastrous failure, and caused the loss of 7000 men by death, and the permanent disablement of about 15,000. The expedition—consisting of 37 men-of-war, 23 frigates, and at least 200 smaller vessels, carrying about 40,000 men— succeeded in capturing Flushing and the island of Walcheren, but failed utterly to reduce Antwerp. Flushing was evacuated on December 23rd, 1809, and the British forces, sadly reduced by fever, returned to England.

Walden Pond. A beautiful lake, near Concord, Massachusetts, famous as the spot where Henry D. Thoreau (1817–1862), the distinguished author, lived in studious retirement for nearly two years. *Walden ; or, Life in the Woods*, published by Thoreau in 1854, contains an account of this period of his life.

"In 1845 Thoreau borrowed Mr. Alcott's axe, and went and built himself a shanty in the woods by *Walden Pond* on land owned by Mr. Emerson. He went there, he said, for seclusion and solitude that he might the better study nature and become acquainted with himself. . . . While here he demonstrated to himself that a man can support himself on less than $100 per year and have two thirds of his time to himself. He spent nearly two years at Walden. He says: ' I left the woods for as good a reason as I went there.' "—*Chambers's Encyclopædia.*

Waldenses. A numerous sect, dwelling chiefly in northern Italy, founded in 1170 A.D., by Peter Wal-

dus, or Waldo, a wealthy merchant of Lyons, France, who sold his goods and gave the proceeds to the poor, and afterwards devoted his life to preaching the gospel of Christ. The Waldenses opposed the corruptions of the Church, were excommunicated for disobedience in 1184, and were finally condemned by the Lateran Council in 1215. They were cruelly persecuted in 1655, and again in 1686, in consequence of the revocation of the Edict of Nantes. In 1848, the Waldenses finally secured equal rights with the Roman Catholics ; since which time they have steadily increased and number at the present day 25,000 in Piedmont alone. They have schools and churches in various parts of Italy, Sicily. and Sardinia, and colonies in America. See *Albigenses.*

" Two theories have been broached to account for the origin of the name—the one that it is derived from Peter Waldo, the Lyonnese reformer ; and the other that it is derived from ' vallis,' a valley, the *Valdenses* or *Waldenses* being inhabitants of the valleys of Piedmont. Waddington, in his *History of the Church*, has given the authorities for both these theories."—McClintock and Strong's *Cyclopædia.*

Wales, Prince of. See *Prince of Wales.*

Walhalla. See *Valhalla.*

Walking Stewart. A sobriquet conferred upon John Stewart, the famous English traveler, who journeyed on foot through India, Persia, Arabia, Abyssinia, Nubia, parts of Europe, and the United States. He died in 1822.

" A most interesting man, whom personally I knew ; eloquent in conversation ; contemplative, if *that* is possible, in excess ; crazy beyond all reach of hellebore (three Anticyræ would not have cured him), yet sublime and divinely benignant in his visionariness ; the man who, as a pedestrian traveller, had seen more of the earth's surface, and communicated more extensively with the children of the earth, than any man before or since ; the writer, also, who published more books (all intelligible by fits and starts) than any Englishman, except, perhaps Richard Baxter, who is said to have published three hundred and sixty-five *plus* one, the extra one being probably meant for leap-year."—*De Quincey.*

"It does not appear that Stewart had any special purpose in these incessant perigrinations, further than to gratify the love of seeing in all parts of the habitable globe. He made no notes of his tours, left no reflections; the only conclusion of a general import which he seems to have arrived at was that the time would come when *ladies* would cease to bear children, leaving travail entirely to poor people."—Walsh's *Handy-Book of Literary Curiosities.*

Wallace of Switzerland. A title conferred upon Andreas Hofer (1767–1810), the Tyrolese patriot, who attempted to free his country from the French and Bavarian yoke, but was betrayed, tried, and executed.

Wallenstein. The title of a famous drama by Johann Christoph Friedrich Schiller (1759–1805), written in 1798–1799. Carlyle declared it to be "the greatest dramatic work of which the 18th century can boast." The play consists of three parts: *Wallenstein's Lager* (*Wallenstein's Camp*), *Die Piccolomini* (*The Piccolomini*), and *Wallenstein's Tod* (*Wallenstein's Death*).

Wall of China. See *China, Great Wall of.*

Walloons. The inhabitants of the southeastern part of Belgium, occupying the tract from Dunkirk to Malmedy. They are of mixed Celtic and Romanic stock, and are descended from the ancient Belgæ, who maintained their existence among the Ardennes Mountains when the rest of Gaul was overrun by the conquering Germans. The Walloons number nearly 3,000,000, and are characterized by darker hair and complexion, and greater activity, than their Flemish neighbors. Owing to their cruel persecution by the Duke of Alva, many of the Walloons took refuge in England, where they were kindly received by Queen Elizabeth. The Walloon language is now simply a provincial *patois,*— French having been substituted for it.

Wall Street. A street in the Borough of Manhattan, New York City, which extends in a curved line from Broadway to the East River—a distance of about half a mile. It is the principal financial centre of the United States, and derives its name from the old wall that extended along it during the old Dutch days, and marked the northern boundary of the town of New Amsterdam.

Walpurgis Night. The eve of May 1st, the day of the canonization of St. Walpurga, who came from England to Germany, was made abbess of Heidenheim, and died about 779 A.D. On this night the witches are said to hold high revelry with their master, the Devil, on the summit of the Brocken, in the Harz Mountains,—riding thither on broomsticks and he-goats.

Walter Scott of the Middle Ages. A title conferred upon Jean Froissart (1337–1410), whose *Chronicles* present a brilliant and vivid picture of the manners and customs of the 14th century.

Waltz. A popular round dance in ¾ time. It originated in Germany during the latter part of the 18th century, but did not become fashionable until 1800. It was introduced into England by Baron Neuman and others in 1813.

Wandering Jew. A legendary personage condemned to wander over the earth until the second coming of Christ, for reviling the Savior while on his way to Calvary. According to Matthew Paris and Roger Wendover, he was a porter in the service of Pontius Pilate, named Cartaphilus; but others identify him with Ahasuerus, a cobbler, on whose doorstep Christ attempted to rest, when overcome with the weight of his cross. Ahasuerus drove the Savior from his door with curses, whereupon Jesus calmly replied: "I truly am going; but thou shalt wander over the earth until I return!" Southey's *Curse of Kehama*, Croly's *Salathiel*, and Sue's *Le Juif Errant* make use of this legend, although not in its original form. See *Cartaphilus*.

Ward, Artemus. A pseudonym adopted by Charles Farrar Brown (1834–1867), the famous American humorist.

War of Liberation. The name given to the war waged by Germany in 1813–1814, to free itself from the oppressive rule of the first Napoleon. It ended with the treaty of Kiel, January 14th, 1814.

"The French yoke was thrown off everywhere. The Confederation of the Rhine was dissolved. The garrisons left in Germany surrendered. The kingdom of Westphalia ceased to exist. Hanover reverted to England."—Barnes's *Brief History of France*.

Wars of the Roses. See *Roses, Wars of the.*

War Started by Water. The "War of the Spanish Succession" (1701–1713) is said to have been caused by the spilling of a glass of water. According to the story, one Mrs. Mashaur, while carrying a glass of water, became involved in a quarrel with the Marquis de Torey. In some unaccountable way the water was spilt, which so incensed the nobleman that he stirred up enmity between the courts of England and France, and thus precipitated the "War of the Spanish Succession." This tale, which is probably without foundation, may have originated from the French play, *Un Verre d'Eau.*

Wartburg, Castle of. A castle near Eisenach, Germany, famous as the place to which Martin Luther was conveyed for safety by his friend, the Elector of Saxony, after the Diet of Worms, and where he translated the Bible into German. The great Reformer dwelt at Wartburg from May, 1521, to March, 1522, and there may be seen the chapel in which he preached and the room in which he dwelt, with the famous ink-stain still visible upon the wall. The castle was built in 1069–1072, and restored about 1851–1860. It was famous also as the meeting-place of the Minnesingers, during the poetic contest known as the "War of the Wartburg," about 1207. St. Elizabeth dwelt there during the years 1511–1527.

Warwick Castle. A stately castle in Warwickshire, England, overlooking the river Avon. It is the residence of the Earl of Warwick, and one of the finest homes of the English nobility. The present castle covers three acres of ground, and was commenced during the reign of Edward III (1327–1377). Cæsar's Tower (147 feet high) is the oldest portion of the structure, while Guy's Tower (128 feet high) was built in 1394. These towers are considered by many to be the most beautiful in existence. Warwick Castle was unsuccessfully besieged during the Civil War. In 1759 it passed into the possession of Lord Brooke — created Earl of Warwick — who expended at least £20,000 upon it. It contains a valuable collection of paintings by Van Dyck, Rubens, Holbein, and others, besides curios and relics of Warwick, the "King-Maker," and Oliver Cromwell.

Warwick Vase. A celebrated antique marble vase, discovered in Hadrian's Villa at Tivoli, Italy. It is seven feet in diameter, and has a capacity of 168 gallons. It is now in the greenhouse at Warwick Castle, Warwickshire, England. See *Warwick Castle.*

"On a pedestal, surrounded by all manner of flowering shrubs, stands this celebrated antique. . . . It is beautifully sculptured with grape-leaves, and the skins and claws of the panther—these latter certainly not an inappropriate emblem of the god of wine, beautiful but dangerous."—*Harriet Beecher Stowe.*

Washington City. " The government of the Federal City (as President Washington called it until the commissioners gave it his name in 1791) has been since 1874 vested in a commission of three officers, appointed by the President and Senate. They have charge of all municipal and administrative affairs, police, street-improvements, schools, etc., while Congress is the sole legislature of the city and District, the citizens having no suffrage. As the Government owns nearly half the property in the District, and the city exists largely for the benefit of its officers,—legislative, executive, and judicial,— it has been settled by act of Congress that the Government pays half the annual expenses of the city government, the other moiety being taxed upon the property of the citizens. This government by commission has on the whole worked well in practice."—*Chambers's Encyclopædia.*

Washington Crossing the Delaware.

(1) A famous historical painting by Emanuel Leutze (1816–1868), a German-American artist. It was formerly owned by the late Marshall O. Roberts, a New York merchant, but is now in the possession of the Metropolitan Museum of Art in that city.

(2) A well-known historical painting by Thomas Sully (1783–1872), in the Boston Museum of Fine Arts.

Washington Elm. A famous elm-tree in Cambridge, Massachusetts, once the site of Indian councils, and of town-meetings in colonial days. Under its branches, General George Washington assumed command of the American army on July 3rd, 1775. An iron railing encloses the tree, and a granite tablet commemorates the event. The Washington Elm is said to be at least 300 years old.

" Nearer the colleges stands the branching elm—twin heir with the Charter Oak of patriotic story—under which Washington took command of the revolutionary army."

—George William Curtis's *Address on Lowell.*

Washington, Houdon's. A celebrated marble statue of George Washington, in the Central Hall of the Capitol in Richmond, Virginia. It was executed by Jean Antoine Houdon (1741–1828), who visited this country for that purpose in 1785, on the invitation of Dr. Benjamin Franklin.

"Methinks I see his venerable form now before me, as presented in the glorious statue by Houdon, now in the capital of Virginia. He is dignified and grave ; but the concern and anxiety seem to soften the lineaments of his countenance."—*Daniel Webster.*

Washington Monument.

(1) A white marble obelisk in the City of Washington, D. C., erected as a national memorial to the " Father of His Country." It is 555 feet high, and is the tallest structure on the globe, with the exception of the Eiffel Tower. The base is 55 feet square, with walls 15 feet thick, and the total weight of the structure is 90,854 net tons. The top—which is pyramidal in shape—terminates in a metallic tip, constructed of the largest piece of aluminium ever fashioned. The interior of the monument is lighted by electricity, and contains a stairway composed of 800 steps, and an elevator that reaches the top in seven minutes. The corner-stone of the Washington Monument was laid on July 4th, 1848, in accordance with Masonic rites. The work progressed slowly until 1854, when it was discontinued for lack of funds ; but in 1880 it was resumed by the Government, and in 1884 the monument was completed at a cost of $1,200,000. It was dedicated with appropriate ceremonies on February 22nd, 1885.

(2) An imposing monument in Baltimore, Maryland, erected in 1815–1829, to the memory of George Washington. It consists of a marble column, 130 feet high, resting on a pedestal, 35 feet high, surmounted by a colossal statue of the patriot and hero. The

summit, which is reached by a spiral staircase, commands a superb view of the city and vicinity.

Washington of South America. A title conferred upon Simon Bolivar (1783–1830), the liberator of South America from the dominion of Spain. He was the first president of the Republic of Colombia, formed by the union of the Provinces of New Granada and Venezuela.

Washington of the West. A sobriquet conferred upon General William Henry Harrison (1773–1841), in allusion to his successful campaign against the British forces in Canada, during the War of 1812.

Waterloo, Battle of. A famous battle fought at Waterloo, Belgium, on June 18th, 1815, between the French army of 72,000 men and 246 guns, commanded by Napoleon I, and the allied forces, consisting of 67,500 men and 156 guns, under the Duke of Wellington, assisted by the Prussians under Field-Marshal von Blücher. The French were utterly defeated with a loss of 30,000 men ; while the loss of the allies was about 23,000. The battle of Waterloo resulted in the second abdication of Napoleon, and his subsequent deportation to St. Helena. The French named the battle from Mont St. Jean, the key of the British position, and the Prussians from La Belle Alliance, the French centre. See *Belle Alliance.*

Waterloo Hero. A nickname bestowed upon the Viscount Rowland Hill (1772–1842), the English general, who served with marked distinction at the battle of Waterloo. Although five times wounded during the contest, he led his troops in the triumphant charge at the close of the day.

Watling Street. An ancient Roman military road in Britain, extending across the island in a westerly direction. Commencing at Richborough or Dover, it ran through Canterbury and Rochester to London, and thence across the island to Chester and York. Portions of the road still exist as an important highway, and the part that extends through London retains its name to the present day. Watling Street, in the days of the Britons, was a mere track through the forest, but was converted into a military highway by the Roman general, Vitellianus, whose name was corrupted into *Watelain*, and this, later, into *Watling*. The term " Watling Street " was frequently used in England, during the Middle Ages, to denote the Milky Way. See *Roman Roads.*

Wayside Inn. An old colonial tavern, still standing in the town of Sudbury, Massachusetts. It was made famous by Longfellow's *Tales of a Wayside Inn.*

" The old Howe Tavern in Sudbury, Mass., has been made memorable by Longfellow's beautiful poem, ' Tales of a Wayside Inn,' and an added interest is given to the poem when we know that this gathering of ' friends ' was not a mere poetical fancy, but a fact, and that among the *dramatis personæ* are many well-known characters."— Killikelly's *Curious Questions.*

Wealth of Nations. A famous treatise on economics by Adam Smith (1723–1790), which, according to Buckle, is " probably the most important book which has ever been written, whether we consider the amount of original thought it contains or its practical influence." It appeared in 1776, under the title—*An Inquiry into the Nature and Causes of the Wealth of Nations.*

Weather Bureau. The United States Weather Bureau was established by act of Congress on February 9th, 1870, as a department of the United States Signal Service, under the War Department; but on June 30th, 1891, it was transferred to the Department of Agriculture. The present system of weather forecasts originated with

Prof. Cleveland Abbé, of Cincinnati, Ohio, who, on September 1st, 1869, commenced the publication of the Weather Bulletin of the Cincinnati Observatory, for the benefit of the Cincinnati Chamber of Commerce. The great success of these forecasts resulted in the presentation to Congress of a memorial signed by all the Boards of Trade and Chambers of Commerce in the country, calling for a national system of weather-predictions,—a memorial, which resulted in the Congressional act of 1870.

"The great value of the service lies in *simultaneous* weather observations throughout the U. S., transmitted twice daily by telegraph to Washington, from which are made synoptic weather maps and press reports telegraphed to all points. Cautionary storm signals are displayed for the shipping at all seaport and lake stations. For the benefit of agriculture, special *Farmers' Bulletins* are issued from the Washington office at 1 A.M., and distributed by the 'Railway Weather Bulletin Service,' so that, in the remotest sections, the farmer may know at an early hour the probabilities for the day. The title 'Old Probabilities,' familiarly applied to the head of the Weather Bureau, was first given in 1869 to Prof. Abbé, and he was chosen in 1870 by Gen. Myer to prepare 'probabilities' or storm-warnings." —Harper's *Book of Facts.*

W. C. T. U. The Woman's Christian Temperance Union (W. C. T. U.) was organized in Cleveland, Ohio, in 1874, as an outgrowth of the famous "Woman's Crusade" against the saloons in 1873-1874. It is now regularly organized in the 45 States and in every Territory of the Union, and has a membership, including the children's societies, of about 500,000. The headquarters are at Chicago, Illinois, where are located the Woman's National Temperance Hospital, the Woman's Temperance Temple (costing over $1,000,000), and the Woman's Temperance Publishing House. This last-named establishment has 7 editors and 110 employés, and issues 110,000,000 pages of printed matter annually. The World's W. C. T. U., founded in 1883, has auxiliary societies in more than 40 countries and provinces. **See** *Whiskey Insurrection.*

Wedding Anniversaries.
(1) First Anniversary, Cotton Wedding.
(2) Second Anniversary, Paper Wedding.
(3) Third Anniversary, Leather Wedding.
(4) Fifth Anniversary, Wooden Wedding.
(5) Seventh Anniversary, Woollen Wedding.
(6) Tenth Anniversary, Tin Wedding.
(7) Twelfth Anniversary, Silk and Fine Linen Wedding.
(8) Fifteenth Anniversary, Crystal Wedding.
(9) Twentieth Anniversary, China Wedding.
(10) Twenty-fifth Anniversary, Silver Wedding.
(11) Thirtieth Anniversary, Pearl Wedding.
(12) Fortieth Anniversary, Ruby Wedding.
(13) Fiftieth Anniversary, Golden Wedding.
(14) Seventy-fifth Anniversary, Diamond Wedding.

Wedding-Ring. The custom of placing a wedding-ring upon the third finger of the left hand of the bride originated with the ancients, who believed that the nerve of that finger connected with the heart. According to Pliny, wedding-rings were made of iron ; in Tertullian's time, of gold.

Wedgwood Ware. A kind of fine earthenware, produced by Josiah Wedgwood (1730-1793), the famous Staffordshire potter. One of the most remarkable varieties is the jasper-ware, consisting of white cameo-reliefs on a blue ground.

Weeping Philosopher. A sobriquet conferred upon Heraclitus of Ephesus (*fl.* 500 B.C.), the Greek philosopher, who is said to have grieved over the follies and weaknesses of mankind. See *Laughing Philosopher*.

" The name of Democ'ritus, the laughing philosopher, being often coupled with that ot Heracli'tus, the *weeping philosopher*, many speakers are apt to accent the latter, incorrectly, on the second syllable."— Wheeler's *Dictionary of the Noted Names of Fiction*.

Weird Sisters. The name given to the three witches, in Shakespeare's tragedy of *Macbeth*.

" I dreamt last night of the three *weird sisters:*
To you they have show'd some truth."
Macbeth, ii, 1.

Welsh Rabbit. This expression— meaning a dish of toasted bread and cheese, variously prepared — is by many authorities supposed to be a cor-ruption of " Welsh rarebit "; others, however, consider it as merely a humorous designation.

" This name [*Welsh rabbit*] for toasted bread and cheese is properly ' Welsh rare-bit.' " — Edwards's *Words, Facts, and Phrases*.

" One of the most curious and curiously successful feats of the amateur etymologist is that which has changed *Welsh rabbit*, which is right, into Welsh rarebit, which is wrong, and has forced the wrongful change upon the English-speaking world. It has ever been a common habit with the A. E., when the meaning of a word does not seem obvious to him, to remedy the difficulty by a slight change that makes it apparently reasonable. Coming across the word *Welsh rabbit*, he gazed through solemn spectacles at this mare's nest, and decided that a bit of toasted cheese could not by any stretch of the imagination be considered a game ani-mal, but it might well be a rare bit. So he jumped at the conclusion that time, and the corruptions which time effects must have done their work on this word, and decided to restore the original beauty and signifi-cance. Hence we have Welsh rarebits on all our *menus*. . . . Now this is all wrong. *Welsh rabbit* is a genuine slang term, be-longing to a large class of similar terms de-scribing in a humorous manner the special dish, product, or peculiarity of a particular district."—Walsh's *Handy-Book of Literary Curiosities*.

Wenonah. The mother of Hia-watha, in Longfellow's poem of the same name. Her lover, Mudjekeewis, the West Wind, having proved false to her, Wenonah died of a broken heart.

Western Church. A name some-times given to the Roman Catholic Church to distinguish it from the Eastern, or Greek, Church, from which it separated in 1054 A.D. See *Greek Church*.

Western Empire. The Western Empire, like the Eastern, was founded by Theodosius the Great who, at his death in 395 A.D., divided the Roman Empire into two parts,—his son Arca-dius receiving the eastern portion, and his son Honorius the western. The latter had Rome for its capital, and comprised Italy, Gaul, Spain, Britain, western Illyricum, and Africa. After an existence of nearly 100 years, the Western Empire succumbed to Odoa-cer, chief of the Heruli, who, in 476 A.D., deposed Romulus Augustulus, and assumed the title of King of Italy. See *Eastern Empire*.

Western Reserve. The name for-merly given to a tract of land on Lake Erie, reserved by the State of Connect-icut at the time of the cession, to the Federal Government, of the Northwest Territory by the States of New York, Pennsylvania, Virginia, Massachu-setts, and Connecticut. It comprised nearly 4,000,000 acres, and was finally disposed of by Connecticut in small lots to traders,—thus creating a splen-did school-fund for the State. In May, 1880, Connecticut, through Governor Trumbull, relinquished to the United States Government its jurisdiction over the " Western Reserve," which after-wards became part of the State of Ohio. It was largely settled by New Englanders. See *New Connecticut ; Northwest Territory*.

Westminster Abbey. A noted abbey-church in London, England, the early history of which is involved in obscurity. Portions of the struc-ture belong to the time of Edward the

Confessor (1042–1066); but the abbey, as it now exists, was mainly built during the reign of Henry III (1216–1272), in honor of the royal saint. It is in the form of a Latin cross, and measures (including Henry VII's Chapel) 513 feet in length ; the length of the transept from north to south being 200 feet. The Abbey contains twelve chapels, and is the burial-place of thirteen kings of England and five queens in their own right, as well as many queens-consort. Nearly all the kings and queens of England have been crowned there ; and, since the reign of Edward I (1272–1307), have used the famous Coronation Chair. Westminster Abbey contains a long series of monuments to distinguished men, and is regarded by the English as the national Valhalla, or Temple of Fame. The 800th anniversary of its foundation was celebrated on December 28th, 1865. See *Coronation Chair ; Poets' Corner.*

"The spaciousness and gloom of this vast edifice produce a profound and mysterious awe. We step cautiously and softly about as if fearful of disturbing the hallowed silence of the tomb; while every footfall whispers along the walls, and chatters among the sepulchres, making us more sensible of the quiet we have interrupted. It seems as if the awful nature of the place presses down upon the soul, and hushes the beholder into noiseless reverence. We feel that we are surrounded by the congregated bones of the great men of past times, who have filled history with their deeds, and the earth with their renown." —*Washington Irving.*

Westminster Assembly. An assembly appointed by the Long Parliament to formulate a creed and determine upon a form of worship and government for the Church of England. It met at Westminster Abbey in 1643–1649, and was composed of 121 divines (Presbyterians and Independents) and 30 laymen (10 of whom were lords and 20 commoners), together with 4 clerical and 2 lay commissioners from the Church of Scotland. Among the results of its deliberations may be mentioned the *Directory of Public Worship* (1644) ; the *Confes-*

sion of Faith (1646) ; the *Larger Catechism* (1647) ; and the *Shorter Catechism* (1647). The proceedings of the Westminster Assembly were annulled at the Restoration (1660) ; but the several formularies above mentioned remain to this day the authorized Presbyterian standards of faith and practice. See *Westminster Catechisms ; Westminster Confession of Faith.*

Westminster Catechisms. The name given to the two catechisms prepared by the Westminster Assembly of Divines. The *Larger Catechism* — designed for use in public worship — was completed on October 22nd, 1647; and the *Shorter Catechism* —for the instruction of the young—on November 25th of the same year. The *Shorter Catechism* is merely an abridgment of the *Larger.* See *Westminster Assembly ; Westminster Confession of Faith.*

Westminster Confession of Faith. A confession of faith and summary of doctrine, in 33 articles, set forth by the Westminster Assembly in 1646. It was adopted by the General Assembly of the Church of Scotland on August 27th, 1647, and still remains the standard of faith among Anglo-Saxon Calvinists. See *Westminster Assembly ; Westminster Catechisms.*

"Out of these walls [Westminster Abbey] came the Directory, the Longer and Shorter Catechisms, and that famous *Confession of Faith* which, alone within these Islands, was imposed by law on the whole kingdom ; and which, alone of all Protestant Confessions, still, in spite of its sternness and narrowness, retains a hold on the minds of its adherents to which its fervour and its logical coherence in some measure entitle it."—*Dean Stanley.*

Westminster Hall. A venerable hall, forming part of the ancient palace of Westminster, London, founded by the Anglo-Saxon kings and occupied by their successors as late as the reign of Henry VIII (1509–1547). It is 290 feet long, 68 feet wide, and 92 feet high, and is said to be the largest room in Europe having a wooden ceiling unsupported by columns. Westminster Hall serves at the present day as a vestibule to the Houses of Parliament, and is rich in historic associations. Within its walls were held the trials of Charles I, the Earl of Strafford, and Warren Hastings, as well as coronation feasts, and festivals without number. King John (1199–1216) established the courts of law at Westminster Hall, where they remained until 1883, when they were removed to the new buildings on the Strand. The roof and windows of Westminster Hall were seriously injured by an explosion of dynamite on January 24th, 1885 ; but all traces of that outrage have since been removed.

Westminster Palace. The name frequently applied to the vast structure in London containing the Houses of Parliament. It occupies the site of the old palace of Westminster, which served as the residence of the sovereigns of England from Edward the Confessor (1042–1066) to Henry VIII (1509–1547). See *Houses of Parliament*.

Westmoreland. This word originally denoted the land occupied by the *Westmorings*, or people of the Western moors.

West Point. A spot of great natural beauty on the west bank of the Hudson River, about 50 miles from New York City. It was a point of great strategic importance during the Revolutionary War, and was held by the Americans during the entire period of their struggle for independence, although nearly lost to them in 1780, through the treason of Benedict Arnold. West Point is the site of the United States Military Academy, founded in 1802. Washington's headquarters were located there in 1779. See *United States Military Academy*.

What Cheer Rock. A rock on the Seekonk River, Providence, Rhode Island, famous as the first landing-place of Roger Williams (1607–1683), the founder of the colony, who had been banished from Massachusetts for his religious opinions. According to tradition, when Williams first set foot on this rock he was hailed by the Indians with the words: " What cheare, Netop (Friend) ? "

" It is amusing to see to what objects this word *Whatcheer* is applied in Rhode Island, no one of which has the least connection with it."—Bartlett's *Dictionary of Americanisms*.

Wheel, Breaking on the. A barbarous mode of capital punishment formerly in use in various countries of Europe. It was practised in Scotland as late as 1604, in France until 1789, and in Germany until 1827. In this mode of punishment, the victim was bound to a wheel, with his arms and legs extended along the spokes, and while the wheel was rapidly revolved his limbs were fractured by successive blows from an iron bar in the hands of the executioner. The French word *roué* is derived from this form of punishment.

Whirlpool Rapids. The name given to the rapids in the Niagara River, below the Falls, in the vicinity of the whirlpool. Owing to the narrowness of the channel (300 feet) and the rapid descent of the river at this point, the vast volume of water is forced to assume a convex shape,—the centre of the stream being twenty feet higher than the edges.

"The surges did not look like the gigantic ripples on a river's course, as they were, but like a procession of ocean billows ; they rose far aloft in vast bulks of clear green, and broke heavily into foam at the crest."—*William Dean Howells.*

Whiskey. This word is probably derived from the Irish *usquebaugh* (*water of life*).

Whiskey Insurrection.
(1) An outbreak in western Pennsylvania in 1794, resulting from an attempt, on the part of the United

States Government, to enforce the excise law (imposing taxes on distilled liquors) enacted by Congress in 1791. Two proclamations from President Washington having failed to quell the disturbance, it was suppressed by an armed force under General Henry Lee, Governor of Virginia.

(2) An attempt made in 1873-1874 by the women of southern Ohio and New York to prevent the sale of liquor by singing and praying in front of saloons and public-houses. The "Woman's Christian Temperance Union" (1874) and the "Blue Ribbon Organization" (1878) are outgrowths of this movement. See *W. C. T. U.*

Whiskey Van. A nickname given to Martin Van Buren (1782-1862), the eighth President of the United States, by his political opponents.

Whispering Gallery. A gallery in the cupola of St. Paul's Cathedral, London, famous for a curious echo, similar to that in the Conservatoire des Arts et Métiers at Paris. If a slight whisper be uttered near the wall, on one side of this gallery, it will be distinctly audible to a person near the wall on the opposite side,—a distance, in a straight line, of 108 feet, or of 162 feet, if measured around the semicircle.

Whist. A game at cards, supposed to be of English origin. It is thought to be a development, either of the game of Trump (*triumph*)—played in the time of Henry VIII (1509-1547)—or of Rough and Honors. Whist (*whisk*) is mentioned by Taylor, the Water-Poet, in 1621, and by Butler in his *Hudibras*, published in 1663; and is described in Charles Cotton's *Compleat Gamester* (1674). The game became general at the close of the 17th century.

Whitechapel. A parish in the eastern part of London, inhabited by artisans. Whitechapel Road traverses the region, and is continued by Mile-

End Road, leading to Bow and Strafford. Much excitement was caused in this district, during the year 1888, by the murder and brutal mutilation of fallen women. These outrages were known as the "Whitechapel Murders."

White Cross Society. A society to encourage personal purity among men, organized in England in 1883 by Miss Ellice Hopkins. It received the support of the Bishops of Durham and Lichfield and other Anglican prelates, and has had marked success in Liverpool, Oxford, and Edinburgh. The same work was taken up in New York City in 1883-1884, and has spread throughout the United States and Canada.

"The principal purposes of this organization are:
(1) To urge upon men the obligation of personal purity.
(2) To raise the tone of public opinion upon the subject of morality.
(3) To secure proper legislation in connection with morality—one law only for men and women."— *World Almanac.*

White Elephant. A variety of Asiatic elephant in which the coloring-matter of the skin is deficient. The white elephant is really of a pink or pale yellow color, and is highly prized on account of its rarity. It is revered as an incarnation of Buddha, and bears the title of "Lord." Among the titles of the King of Siam, the proudest is that of the "Lord of the White Elephant."

"Is the *white elephant* white, or only so by a figure of speech? To this question it is impossible to answer yes or no. The Siamese never speak of a white elephant, but of a *chang pouk* or strange colored elephant. The hue varies from a pale yellowish or reddish brown to a rose. Buffon gives it as ash-gray. Judging from the specimens which I have seen both at Mandalay and Bangkok, I should say it was generally a light gray, with spots or splashes of pink."— *White Elephants* (Vincent).

Whitehall. A famous royal palace, formerly situated in Whitehall, London, of which the banqueting-hall—

built by James I (1603–1625) — is all that remains at the present day. Whitehall was originally the residence of the Archbishops of York, but was confiscated by Henry VIII (1509–1547) after the fall of Wolsey, and made a royal residence. It was there that Henry VIII met Anne Boleyn, and there also that he died. Elizabeth was taken thence as a prisoner, but returned Queen of England. Charles I, Oliver Cromwell, and Charles II dwelt at Whitehall, and it was through an opening made in the wall of the banqueting-hall that Charles I was led forth to the scaffold in the street in front. After the destruction of the palace by fire in 1697, the royal residence was transferred to St. James's Palace, and the banqueting-hall became a royal chapel.

"Little did James think that he was raising a pile from which his son was to step from the throne to the scaffold."—*Pennant.*

White Horse of Berkshire.

The name given to the colossal figure of a galloping horse, on a hillside at Uffington, Berkshire, England, formed by removing the turf and revealing the chalk-formation underneath. This effigy, which measures 355 feet from nose to tail, is traditionally said to commemorate the victory of Ethelred and his brother Alfred (afterwards Alfred the Great) over the Danes at Ashdown, in 871 A.D. The White Horse of Berkshire may be seen at a distance of 16 miles, in clear weather. It is periodically cleaned by the inhabitants of the neighboring country, and this ceremony of preserving the outline of the gigantic steed is popularly known as the "Scouring of the White Horse." A graphic description of one of these gatherings, which occurred in 1857, may be found in Thomas Hughes's book, entitled *The Scouring of the White Horse* (1859). These "scourings" occurred fifteen times between the years 1755 and 1884. Among other "White Horses" in England may be named those at Westbury, Cherhill, Marlborough, Pewsey, Broad Hinton, and Wootton Bassett.

White House.

A popular designation of the Executive Mansion at Washington, D. C., which is a freestone structure, painted white. The White House was founded in 1792 ; first occupied by President Adams in 1800 ; burned by the British in 1814 ; and rebuilt in 1819. It is an imposing building — two stories in height — and is said to have been modelled after the palace of the Duke of Leinster.

White House of the Confederacy.

A mansion in Richmond, Virginia, occupied during part of the Civil War (1861–1865) by Jefferson Davis (1808–1889) as President of the Confederate States of America. The house is now a museum of Confederate relics.

White Lady.

A mysterious female personage, said to haunt the palaces and castles belonging to the King of Prussia. According to the legend, she appears only to forebode the death of some member of the royal family. Her last appearance, it is said, was in 1879, just prior to the death of the Prince Waldemar. She is always dressed in snow-white garments and carries a bunch of keys at her side.

"There are two white ladies, in fact—one the countess Agnes of Orlamunde, and the other the princess Bertha von Rosenberg, who lived in the fifteenth century. The former was buried alive in a vault in the palace. She was the mistress of a margrave of Brandenburgh, by whom she had two sons. When the prince became a widower, Agnes thought he would marry her, but he made the sons an objection, and she poisoned them, for which crime she was buried alive. Another version is that she fell in love with the prince of Parma, and made away with her two daughters, who were an obstacle to her marriage, for which crime she was doomed to 'walk the earth' as an apparition.

The princess Bertha is troubled because an annual gift, which she left to the poor, has been discontinued. She appears dressed in white, and carrying at her side a bunch of keys."—Brewer's *Reader's Handbook.*

White League. A military organization formed at New Orleans, Louisiana, in 1874 to resist the aggressions of the recently enfranchised negroes and their friends, the "Carpet-Baggers." On September 14th of the same year, the White League attempted to take possession of a shipload of arms consigned to them from New York City, but were resisted by the State authorities. This action precipitated a riot in which more than 100 persons were killed. See *Carpet-Baggers*.

White Prince. A title conferred upon Belisarius (505–565 A.D.), the famous general in the service of Justinian, during the war against the Vandals in Africa in 534. The word "Belisarius" is derived from the Slavonic *Beli-tzar* (*white prince*).

White Quakers. An appellation conferred upon those Quakers that seceded from the main body about 1840. They were so called in allusion to their white garments.

White Queen. A title conferred by the French upon Mary, Queen of Scots, because she wore white mourning for her husband, Lord Darnley.

White's. A famous club-house on St. James's Street, London. It was established in 1698 as White's Chocolate House, and in former days was noted for its high play. It has occupied the present site since 1755. The bow-window of "White's" has figured in many novels. See *Brooks's*.

"*White's* was from the beginning principally a gaming club. The play was mostly at hazard and faro; no member was to hold a faro bank. Whist was comparatively harmless. Professional gamblers, who lived by dice and cards, provided they were free from the imputation of cheating, procured admission to *White's*. It was a great supper-house, and there was play before and after supper, carried on to a late hour and heavy amounts."—Timbs's *Clubs and Club-Life in London*.

White Sea. This arm of the Arctic Ocean, extending into the northern part of Russia, derives its name from its proximity to regions of snow and ice. The surface is usually frozen from the beginning of September until the end of May, and during the rest of the year the sea is filled with floating ice.

White Surrey. The horse ridden by Richard III (1483–1485) at the battle of Bosworth Field. See *Bosworth Field, Battle of*.

"Saddle *White Surrey* for the field to-morrow."—*Richard III*, v, 3.

White Terror. A term applied to the reactionary period following the second restoration of the French Bourbons in 1815, when many atrocious acts were committed, particularly by the Jesuits.

White Tower. The name given to the central and oldest part of the Tower of London, so called on account of the white stone used in its construction. The structure is 116 feet long, 96 feet broad, and 92 feet high, and has walls 13 to 15 feet thick, surmounted with battlements at the angles. The White Tower contains the Chapel of St. John—one of the best specimens of Norman architecture in England; the apartments in which Sir Walter Raleigh was confined, and in which he wrote his *History of the World;* the staircase under which the bones of the two unfortunate princes, murdered by their uncle, Richard III, were found; the Council-Chamber, where Richard II abdicated the crown; and the Horse-Armory. See *Tower of London*.

White Trash. A term applied by the negroes of the South to the poor white people. These were also known as "Mean whites," and "Poor white folks."

Whitsunday. A festival in the Christian Church, introduced to commemorate the descent of the Holy Ghost upon the apostles on the Jewish day of Pentecost. It is a movable feast, and occurs on the seventh Sunday (or the fiftieth day) after Easter. Whitsunday is a corruption of White-Sunday, and is derived from the *white* robes in which the newly baptized were required to attend mass on that day. See *Pentecost*.

Whittington Stone. A stone at Highgate, London, near the Whittington Almshouses, where, according to tradition, Sir Richard Whittington [1358 (?)-1413] stopped to rest, after leaving London in despair. While seated there, his attention was arrested by a merry peal from Bow-Bells, which seemed to his disordered mind to repeat the words, " Turn again, Whittington, thrice Lord Mayor of London." Acting upon this suggestion, he retraced his steps, and in later years succeeded in fulfilling the prophecy. The identity of this stone, which is now part of a lamp-post, is more than doubtful. See *Bow-Bells*.

Wicked Bible. The name given to an edition of the Scriptures, printed in London in 1631, in which the word *not* was accidentally omitted from *Exodus* xx, 14, causing the verse to read, " Thou shalt commit adultery." It is said that, owing to the zeal of Dr. Usher, the printers — Robert Barker and Martin Lucas — were fined £2000 or £3000 for this typographical error. The *Pearl Bible*—printed in 1653—was also called the *Wicked Bible*, because of the following errata :

" Neither yield ye your members as instruments of righteousness [*for* unrighteousness] unto sin."—*Romans* vi, 13.

" Know ye not that the unrighteous shall inherit [*for* shall not inherit] the kingdom of God."—*1 Corinthians* vi, 9.

Wickliffites. The followers of John Wickliffe (1324-1384), the pioneer of the English Reformation. The Wickliffites denied the doctrine of transubstantiation and opposed papal authority, the celibacy of the clergy, and the priestly power of absolution. They were cruelly persecuted in England, but their doctrines spread into

Bohemia, and bore fruit in the teaching of John Huss (1369-1415) and his followers. Thirty years after Wickliffe's death, the Council of Constance condemned as heretical 45 articles taken from his writings, and ordered his remains to be exhumed and burned. This sentence was executed 13 years later. See *Lollards*.

Wide-Awakes. The name given to certain campaign clubs organized by the Republican party during the presidential election of 1860. The first step in their formation was made at Hartford, Connecticut, in 1859, when Cassius M. Clay addressed the Republicans of that city ; but it was not until the following year that the movement became general. The " Wide-Awakes " paraded at night, wearing black oilskin hats and capes and carrying swinging torches. It is estimated that 500,000 were enrolled in these organizations during the campaign of 1860.

Wife - Hater Bible. The name given to an edition of the Bible printed in 1810, in which occurs the following *erratum :*

"If any man come to me, and hate not his father, and mother, and wife, and children, and brethren, and sisters, yea and his own wife [*for* life] also, he cannot be my disciple."—*Luke* xiv, 26.

Wild Boy. See *Peter, the Wild Boy*.

Wild-Cat. A term applied to worthless paper - money before the Civil War, in allusion, it is said, to the notes of an insolvent bank in Michigan,—which notes were adorned with the vignette of a panther, an animal popularly known in that State as a wild cat.

" We had to sell some of our land to pay taxes on the rest,—and then took our pay in *Wild-cat* money that turned to waste paper before we could get it off our hands."—Clavers's *Forest Life*.

Wilhelm Meister. See *Meister, Wilhelm*.

Wilhelmshöhe.   A palace near Cassel, Germany, famous as the place of detention of Napoleon III (1852–1870), after his defeat at Sedan, in September, 1870. It is sometimes called the German Versailles, and is situated in the midst of a lovely park adorned with beautiful fountains and cascades. On a neighboring hill is the "Giant's Castle," a structure surmounted by a colossal statue of Hercules (a copy of the "Farnese"), 31 feet in height, —in the hollow of whose club eight persons can stand at one time. See *Farnese Hercules.*

Willey House.   A modest dwelling-house in the Crawford Notch, New Hampshire, famous as the scene of a terrible disaster on the night of August 28th, 1826, which caused the death of all the members of the Willey family—seven in number—together with two hired men. Warned by the roar of an approaching landslide, the inmates of the house rushed out to escape destruction, but were overwhelmed and crushed, while the house remained unharmed, owing to the presence, in the rear, of a huge rock that sheltered it by parting the avalanche. The Willey House remained standing until the autumn of 1899, when it was destroyed by fire.

"The first traveller who afterwards forced his way through the chaotic ruin in the Notch found the Willey House deserted, with the doors unclosed and the Bible lying open on the table. He gave the alarm in Conway, and the people who came up found the bodies of Mr. and Mrs. Willey, two of their children, and two hired men, buried in the slide and sadly mutilated. The bodies of the other three children were never recovered. It is supposed that the family left the house in apprehension of the rising floods of the Saco, and retreated to a point farther up on the mountain, where they were overtaken by the avalanche and swept away to a fearful and united death. Had they remained in the house, they would have been safe, for it was not moved by the water, and the slide parted at a great rock behind it and reunited below, leaving the house intact. A theory has been advanced to the effect that the fatal slide was caused, not by a heavy rain-storm, but by the break-

ing of massive clouds on the ridges of Mt. Willey."—Sweetser's *White Mountains.*

William Rufus.   William II (1087–1100) of England was surnamed Rufus (*Lat., ruddy*) from his florid complexion, or, as some say, from the color of his beard.

William Tell.   "Scientific historians have established beyond the shadow of a doubt that the Swiss Confederation was not founded by William Tell, as the chroniclers would have us believe. His name cannot be found in the archives of any of the cantons. The story of his famous shot is full of discrepancies, especially as regards the bailiff Gessler, and, what is now considered conclusive proof of his legendary character, at least six similar episodes have been discovered in the mythical histories or ballads of Teutonic nations. Denmark, Iceland, Holstein, England, the Rhine country, and Norway, as well as Switzerland, have their William Tell, under another name, and surrounded by different geographical features, to be sure, but nevertheless in every case possessing the same essential points of resemblance. The traditional archer has, therefore, been abandoned by all serious historians as the founder of the Swiss Confederation."— Walsh's *Handy-Book of Literary Curiosities.* See *Tell's Chapel.*

William the Conqueror.   William I (1066–1087) of England was surnamed the "Conqueror," from his victory over the Saxons at the battle of Hastings (October 14th, 1066).

William the Silent.   A title conferred upon William of Nassau (1533–1584), Prince of Orange, on account of his sparing use of speech.

Wilmot Proviso.   The name popularly given in the United States of America to an amendment to a bill authorizing President Polk to purchase territory while negotiating peace with Mexico. It was offered by David

Wilmot, a Democratic representative from Pennsylvania, on August 8th, 1846, and provided that slavery should be forever excluded from the territory thus acquired. The amendment passed the House of Representatives, but was rejected by the Senate. The following are the terms of the *Wilmot Proviso :*

"Provided, that, as an express and fundamental condition to the acquisition of any territory from the Republic of Mexico by the United States, by virtue of any treaty which may be negotiated between them, and to the use by the executive of the moneys herein appropriated, neither slavery nor involuntary servitude shall ever exist in any part of said territory, except for crime, whereof the party shall first be duly convicted."

Wimbledon. An open heath, seven miles southwest of London, famous as the annual meeting-place of the "National Rifle Association" from 1860 to 1889. Since 1889, the meetings have been held at Bisley Common, near Woking. See *Creedmoor.*

Winchester School. A famous public school at Winchester, England, founded by William of Wykeham, in 1387. It has ranked for centuries among the leading public schools of England, and is attended by about 450 boys. Among the famous men that have been educated at Winchester may be named Sir Thomas Browne, the poets Collins and Young, Lemprière, Dr. Thomas Arnold, and Sydney Smith.

Windsor Castle. The principal residence of the British sovereigns, situated in the town of Windsor, on the river Thames, about 22 miles southwest of London. The castle was founded by William the Conqueror (1066–1087) and greatly enlarged by Henry I (1100–1135) and Henry II (1154–1189) ; but it was Edward III (1327–1377) who caused the removal of the old structure and the erection of the present one on the same site, under the direction of William of Wykeham. Since that time, Windsor Castle has been repeatedly enlarged.

During the reign of George IV (1820–1830) restorations were commenced, and these were completed in the reign of Victoria (1837–1901) at a cost of £900,000. Among the objects of interest in the Castle may be mentioned St. George's Chapel, or the Chapel of the Knights of the Order of the Garter; Albert Chapel — a magnificent memorial of the Prince Consort ; the State Apartments; St. George's Banqueting Hall ; the Guard Chamber; and the Round Tower. Windsor Forest, in the immediate vicinity, contains 59,600 acres.

Wingless Victory, Temple of. See *Nike-Apteros, Temple of.*

Winter Palace. A huge structure in St. Petersburg, Russia, used by the Emperor and his Court during the winter season. It occupies the site of a former palace, erected in 1754 and destroyed by fire in 1837. The present vast and imposing pile of buildings, erected in 1837–1839, measures 455 feet in length and 350 feet in breadth. Some idea of its immensity may be formed from the statement that during the winter it is occupied by more than 6000 persons belonging to the Czar's household. Among the finest apartments in the Winter Palace may be named the Hall of St. George, or Audience Chamber; the Throne-Room of Peter the Great ; the Gallery of the Field-Marshals ; the Alexander Gallery ; the Empress's Drawing-Room ; and the Salle Blanche, — a beautiful room in white and gold. This is the scene of the court fêtes, which are noted throughout Europe for their magnificence. The picture-gallery of the Winter Palace contains one of the finest collections in the world.

Wise Men of the East. A term collectively applied to the three "magi," who came from the East to salute and adore the infant Jesus at Bethlehem, in Judea. According to the commonly accepted tradition, their names were Balthazar, Gaspar, and

Melchior. See *Balthazar ; City of the Three Kings ; Cologne, Three Kings of ; Gaspar ; Magi ; Melchior.*

"Other names are given to the three wise men : as (1) Apellius, Amerus, and Damascus ; (2) Magalath, Galgagath, and Sarasin; (3) Alor, Sator, and Peratoras. Others say they were Shem, Ham, and Japheth, who had fallen asleep, and woke at the Nativity. St. John Chrysostom tells us that St. Thomas baptized the three kings or wise men which came to Bethlehem to adore the infant Jesus, after which he went to India to preach the gospel."—Brewer's *Dictionary of Miracles.*

"Klopstock, in *The Messiah*, v, says there were six 'Wise Men of the East,' who, guided by the star, brought their gifts to Jesus, the 'heavenly babe,' viz., Hadad, Selima, Zimri, Mirja, Beled, and Sunith."— Brewer's *Reader's Handbook.*

Wisest Fool in Christendom. An epithet generally supposed to have been bestowed upon James I (1603– 1625) of England by the Duke of Sully, minister of Henry IV of France. What Sully really called him was "the most learned fool in Christendom."

Wisest Man of Greece. A title conferred upon Socrates (469–399 B.C.), the famous Greek philosopher, by the Delphic oracle.

"'T is because I alone of all the Greeks know that I know nothing" was the sage's modest comment, on hearing the declaration of the oracle.

Wit, Attic. See *Attic Wit.*

Witchfinder-General. A title assumed by Matthew Hopkins (1600– 1647), a cruel fanatic, who traveled through the eastern counties of England in search of witches, and succeeded in one year (1644) in bringing 60 poor wretches to the stake. Being finally accused of witchcraft, Hopkins was subjected to his own favorite test of swimming, and, happening to float, was declared to be a wizard and put to death. See *Witchfinders.*

Witchfinders. The name given to a set of cruel fiends that traveled through England about the middle of the 17th century, seeking out persons accused of witchcraft, and forcing them to confess by means of examinations and tortures. See *Witchfinder-General.*

Witch Hill. A rocky eminence near Salem, Massachusetts, famous as the spot where 19 persons were hanged as witches and one was pressed to death, during the witchcraft delusion in 1692. Also called *Gallows Hill.* See *Salem Witchcraft.*

Witch of Endor. A famous sorceress consulted by Saul (1095–1055 B.C.), King of Israel, on the night before his defeat and death in battle with the Philistines on Mount Gilboa. At the King's request, the Witch of Endor called up Samuel, who foretold the fate of Saul. According to a tradition preserved by Jerome, the Witch of Endor was the mother of Abner, the commander-in-chief of the royal forces and the cousin of the King. On this account, she had escaped from the wholesale destruction of witches made by order of Saul.

"Then said Saul unto his servants, Seek me a woman that hath a familiar spirit, that I may go to her, and enquire of her. And his servants said to him, Behold, there is a woman that hath a familiar spirit at En-dor. And Saul disguised himself, and put on other raiment, and he went, and two men with him, and they came to the woman by night : and he said, I pray thee, divine unto me by the familiar spirit, and bring me him up, whom I shall name unto thee."— *1 Samuel* xxviii, 7–8.

Witenagemót (*Anglo-Saxon, Meeting of the Counsellors*). A form of parliament in England in Anglo-Saxon times, convened by the King at stated periods, to deliberate upon affairs of state. Previous to the formation of the Heptarchy in 827 A.D., each state had its own Witenagemót, but after that date there was one general assembly for the entire country. The Witenagemót was composed of ecclesiastics, aldermen, and large landowners, and met annually on Christmas,

Easter, and Whitsuntide. It deliberated upon all new laws, regulated the kingly succession, levied taxes, negotiated treaties, appointed bishops, and constituted a supreme court of justice.

Without the Pale. See *Pale.*

Wives of Literary Men. According to Brewer's *Reader's Handbook,* Addison, Byron, Dickens, Dryden, Albert Dürer, Hooker, Ben Jonson, W. Lilly (second wife), Milton, Molière, More, Sadi, Scaliger, Schlegel (both wives), Shakespeare, Shelley (first wife), Socrates, and Wycherley (first wife) were unhappy in the married state; while Thomas Moore, Walter Scott, and Wordsworth had no occasion to repent of their choice.

Wizard. A sobriquet conferred upon John Sobieski (1674–1696), King of Poland, by the Turks, in consequence of his marvellous victories over them.

Wizard of the North. A sobriquet conferred upon Sir Walter Scott (1771–1832), the famous Scottish poet and novelist, " in allusion to the magical influence of his works, which on their first appearance fascinated their readers even more, perhaps, than they do now."

Wolf of the Capitol. A famous bronze figure of a she-wolf nursing two infants, in the Capitol at Rome. It is of unknown age, and is supposed by some authorities to be identical with the bronze wolf mentioned by Dionysius as standing near the Temple of Romulus, under the Palatine Hill; others, however, consider it to be the wolf referred to by Cicero and commemorated by Virgil.

"In this palace is one of the most interesting objects in Rome,—the celebrated *Bronze Wolf of the Capitol,*—generally believed to be the very group alluded to by Cicero in one of his harangues against Catiline, and commemorated by Virgil in his well-known lines. In such controversies, the wish is father to the faith ; and we cannot listen to the arguments in an impartial spirit. The sceptic has as ungracious an office as the devil's attorney who is heard against the claims of a saint proposed to be canonized. The wolf is a gaunt and grim image, of antique workmanship, and with none of the amenities of Greek art. The infants seem disproportionately small."—Hillard's *Six Months in Italy.*

Wolverine State. A title popularly bestowed upon the State of Michigan, in allusion to the great numbers of wolverines with which it was formerly infested.

Woman as Holy Ghost. The following account of Wilhelmina, a princess of Bohemia, who appeared at Milan during the 13th century, and declared herself to be the incarnation of the Holy Ghost, is taken from Killikelly's *Curious Questions :*

" She appeared in Milan, and announced her gospel, a profane and fantastic parody, centring upon herself the great tenet of the Fraticelli, the reign of the Holy Ghost. In her, the daughter, she averred, of Constance, Queen of Bohemia, the Holy Ghost was incarnate. Her birth had its annunciation, but the angel Raphael took the place of the angel Gabriel. She was very God and very woman. She came to save Jews, Saracens, false Christians, as the Saviour the true Christians. Her human nature was to die as that of Christ had died. She was to rise again, and ascend into heaven. As Christ had left his vicar upon earth, so Wilhelmina left the holy nun Mayfreda. Mayfreda was to celebrate the mass at her sepulchre, to preach her gospel in the great church at Milan, afterwards at St. Peter's at Rome. She was to be a female pope, with full papal power to baptize Jews, Saracens, unbelievers. The four gospels were replaced by four Wilhelminian evangelists.

She was to be seen by her disciples, as Christ after his resurrection. Plenary indulgence was to be granted to all who visited the convent of Chiaravalle, as to those who visited the tomb of our Lord : it was to become the great centre of pilgrimage. Her apostles were to have their Judas, to be delivered by him to the Inquisition. But the most strange of all was, that Wilhelmina, whether her doctrines were kept secret to the initiate, lived unpersecuted, and died in peace and in the odor of sanctity. She was buried first in the Church of St. Peter in Orto : her body was afterwards carried to the convent of Chiaravalle. Monks preached her funeral sermon ; the saint wrought miracles lamps and wax candles burned in profuse splendor at her altar ; she had three annual festivals ; her Pope Mayfreda celebrated mass.

It was not till twenty years after, that the orthodox of the Milanese clergy awoke in dismay and horror ; the wonder-working bones of St. Wilhelmina were dug up and burned ; Mayfreda, and one Andrea Saramita, expiated at the stake the long unregarded blasphemies of their mistress.''

Wonder, Eighth. See *Eighth Wonder of the World.*

Wondrous Maid. An appellation conferred upon Joan of Arc (1411–1431), whose marvellous deeds were attributed by the French to divine intervention, and by the English to collusion with the Evil One.

Wondrous Three. A phrase collectively applied to the English statesmen, Fox, Pitt, and Burke, by Lord Byron in his *Monody on the Death of Sheridan.*

Wooden Horse. See *Horse, Wooden.*

Wooden Walls. At the time of the second Persian invasion of Greece (480 B.C.), the Athenians consulted the oracle at Delphi, and were counselled to place reliance in their '' wooden walls,''—meaning their fleet. In the naval battle of Salamis, which ensued, the Persians were ignominiously routed and the city of Athens saved.

'' Pallas hath urged, and Zeus, the sire of all,
  Hath safety promised in a *wooden wall ;*
Seed-time and harvest, sires shall, weeping, tell
  How thousands fought at Salamis and fell.''   *E. C. B.*

Woodman, Spare that Tree ! A popular song by George P. Morris (1802 – 1864), the American author, beginning with the words:

'' *Woodman, spare that tree !*
  Touch not a single bough !
In youth it sheltered me,
  And I 'll protect it now.''

Wood of the Cross. According to an ancient legend, three trees sprang from Adam's body, buried at Hebron, and were transplanted by David to Jerusalem, where they grew into one tree. Solomon, it is said, attempted to use this triple tree for the principal support of the Temple; but, finding it too short, set it aside. It was afterwards used for the Cross of Christ; and, after that event, was buried and lay undisturbed for nearly 300 years, when it was discovered in 326 by St. Helena, the mother of Constantine. See *Cross, True.*

Woolly-Heads. A term derisively applied to that branch of the Whig party that favored negro emancipation and sympathized with the views of William Lloyd Garrison and Wendell Phillips.

'' The law, it seems, it did n't work exactly
      as it ought,
  Though Greeley kept a-sayin' so, and so
      his readers thought.
They 're mighty bright, them *woolly-heads ;* they think they find a prize,
  If they can only pull their wool o'er other
      people's eyes.''

Woolsack. The name given to a large square sack of wool covered with red cloth, without back or arms, which forms the seat of the Lord Chancellor of England in the House of Lords. It is said that woolsacks were placed in the House of Lords, during the reign of Edward III (1327–1377), to remind the peers of the importance of that staple commodity. The Lord Chancellor occupies the '' Woolsack'' as Speaker to the House, but not in his judicial capacity.

Worcester, Battle of. A battle fought at Worcester, England, on September 3rd, 1651, between the Scottish army, commanded by Charles II, and the Parliamentary forces under Oliver Cromwell. It resulted in the total defeat of the Royalists, with a loss of 4000 killed and 7000 taken prisoners,—most of whom were sent to bond-service in the American colonies. Charles, after experiencing great hardships, escaped to France. Cromwell always referred to the battle of Worcester as his '' crowning mercy.''

Words in the English Language, Number of. The number of words in the English language has never been accurately estimated. It is said that the *Standard Dictionary* contains over 300,000 words, and the *Century Dictionary* 225,000. Not more than 30,000 of these are in practical use. Shakespeare, in all of his productions, makes use of about 15,000 words, and Milton of about half as many. Persons of superior culture are familiar with at least 5000 words ; ordinary persons, with about 2000 or 3000 words; while the more illiterate classes find 300 words sufficient to express their limited stock of ideas.

Works and Days. The title of a celebrated didactic poem by Hesiod (*fl.* 800 B.C.), the Greek poet. It abounds in maxims and rules written in a simple style, and presents an invaluable picture of the village community as it existed in Greece in early times. The ancients regarded the *Works and Days* as the only genuine production of Hesiod.

"The *Works and Days* is generally considered to consist of two originally distinct poems, one containing the good advice to his brother, preaching up honest labour and denouncing corrupt and unjust judges ; the other, the real *Works and Days*, containing advice as to the days lucky or unlucky, proper or improper, for the farmer's work."—*Chambers's Encyclopædia.*

World, History of the. The title of a work composed by Sir Walter Raleigh (1552–1618), during his imprisonment in the Tower of London. The first and only volume, published in 1614, brought the narrative down to 170 B.C. (the epoch of the second war of Rome against Macedon). The sale of the book was suppressed in 1615, as "too saucy in censuring the acts of kings." Oliver Cromwell was a great admirer of the work, and commended it to his son Richard, in 1650, in the following words : " Recreate yourself with Sir Walter Raleigh's *History ;* it is a body of history, and will add much more to your understanding than fragments of story." Raleigh's *History of the World* was written for Henry, Prince of Wales, the eldest son of James I; but his untimely death in 1612 caused the author to lose all interest in the completion of the work.

World's Columbian Exposition. See *Columbian Exposition.*

World's Oldest Book. " Max Müller says that the oldest book in the world is the *Rig Veda*, which was in existence, complete as we have it now, 1500 years before Christ, and not the so-called *Book of the Dead* from Egypt, consisting of disjointed fragments collected from many sources, the earliest of which may possibly be dated as early as 6000 B.C."—Conklin's *Vest-Pocket Argument Settler.* See *Book of the Dead ; Vedas.*

World's Wonder. A sobriquet conferred upon Elizabeth (1558–1603), Queen of England.

" Worse than a Crime." The famous saying, " It is worse than a crime,—it is a blunder" (*Fr.,* "*C'est plus qu'un crime,—c'est une faute*"), said to have been uttered concerning the execution of the Duc d'Enghien, is generally attributed to Talleyrand. Fouché, however, in his *Mémoires*, claims the expression for himself, but in the slightly altered form, " It is more than a crime,—it is a political fault."

Wörth, Battle of. A battle fought at Wörth, a village of Alsace, on August 6th, 1870, between the Prussians, commanded by the Crown Prince, and the French under Marshal MacMahon. The French were totally defeated with a loss of 5000 killed wounded, and missing, and 5000 taken prisoners. The Prussian loss was estimated at about 8000.

Wranglers. The name given to those persons that have attained the first class in the public examination for mathematical honors at the Universit of Cambridge, England,—the one standing the highest being termed the Senior Wrangler. See *Tripos*.

Wyoming, Massacre of. The name given to a frightful massacre committed in the Valley of Wyoming, Pennsylvania, on July 3rd–5th, 1778, during the Revolutionary War. On June 30th of that year, 400 British soldiers and 700 Seneca Indians invaded the valley and were opposed by only 300 men,—the greater portion of the able-bodied male inhabitants being on duty under General Washington. The Americans were defeated in battle on July 3rd, and took refuge in Forty Fort ; but surrendered two days after, on promise of protection. The British, however, were unable to restrain the savage instincts of their Indian allies, who attacked the settlers with renewed vigor on the evening of July 5th, set fire to their dwellings, and murdered many of the inmates. Campbell, the Scottish poet, has commemorated this tragic event in his *Gertrude of Wyoming*.

X

X, XX, and XXX. These letters are placed on barrels of beer and ale to denote the quality and strength of the liquor. The single X originally represented the excise tax of 10 shillings paid on beer of a certain quality, and thus became a sign for that quality. Later XX, XXX, and even XXXX were added to represent beer and ale of double, triple, and quadruple the strength of the X brand.

Xerxes's Invasion of Greece. Xerxes I (485–465 B.C.), King of Persia, invaded Greece in 480 B.C., with an army—including women, eunuchs, and servants— of 5,285,220 souls. According to Herodotus, however, the expedition numbered 2,641,610 fighting-men, 1207 ships of war, and 3000 smaller vessels. This mighty host crossed the Hellespont by a bridge,

consisting of a double line of boats, and consumed seven days and nights in its passage. After forcing the Pass of Thermopylæ, where he was held at bay with his entire army, for three days, by 300 Spartans, under Leonidas, Xerxes advanced to Athens and burned the city ; but was checked in his onward march at Salamis, where the naval power of Persia was crushed by the Greeks under Themistocles Xerxes hastened back to Persia in mortification and despair, leaving the command of the expedition to Mardonius ; but that able general was defeated and slain by Pausanias at the battle of Platæa (479 B.C.), and with his death perished all hopes of the conquest of Greece.

Xenophon's Retreat of the Ten Thousand. See *Retreat of the Ten Thousand*.

X Rays. See *Roentgen Rays*.

Y

Yale University. Chartered as the Collegiate School of Connecticut by an act of the General Court of the Colony, on October 9th, 1701. The college was first established at Saybrook, " as the most convenient place at present " ; but was removed to New Haven in 1717. It was named in honor of Elihu Yale of London — a native of New Haven — who amassed a large fortune in India, and donated the sum of about $2000 to the institution. In 1913, Yale University had 431 instructors, 3263 students, and 893,937 volumes in the library.

" Never was human distinction so cheaply purchased as that which perpetuates the otherwise almost unknown names of John Harvard and *Elihu Yale*."—Johnston's *Connecticut*.

Yankee. This word is said to be a corruption of *English* or *Anglais*, pronounced *Yenghies, Yanghies, Yankees*, by the Massachusetts Indians, and bestowed by them upon the New England colonists. It was derisively applied by the British soldiers to the New Englanders, during the Revolutionary War (1775–1782), and later by the Confederates to the Federals, during the Civil War (1861–1865). The word is often indiscriminately used in Great Britain, at the present day, to denote the entire population of the United States.

"It was in use in Boston about 1765, but is claimed to have circulated in Cambridge slang as early as 1713, with the sense of 'excellent.' If so, it is the same word we meet in Scotch *yankin*, 'active,' *yank*, 'a sharp stroke.' "—*Chambers's Encyclopædia*.

Yankee Doodle. An American national air, the origin of which is involved in obscurity. It is generally thought to be an English tune, introduced into America by the British troops about 1775, — the words of which were written by Dr. Schuckburgh, or Schnekburgh, a surgeon in the army of Lord Amherst during the French and Indian War (1755–1763). The air has been popular in the United States since its introduction, and was first printed in Arnold's opera, *Two to One*, in 1784.

"There has been much discussion as to the origin of the term *Yankee Doodle*, and of the well-known tune which bears this name, without coming as yet to any satisfactory conclusion. In England, the air has been traced back to the time of Charles I.; and it appears that the doggerel verses that are sung to it can claim nearly as respectable an antiquity. This, however, is not all. The song is said to be identical with one sung by the agricultural laborers in the Netherlands. Kossuth and his fellow Hungarians, when in this country, are said to have recognized it as one of the old national airs of their native land. And recently Mr. Buckingham Smith, our then Secretary of Legation at Madrid, has asserted that it is the ancient Sword Dance of the Biscayans."—Bartlett's *Dictionary of Americanisms*.

"You may talk about your 'Dixie's Land,'
   And sing it like a noodle;
The good old tune for North and South
   Is famous *Yankee Doodle*."
          Song from the Rebellion Record.

Year of Corbie. During the "Thirty Years' War" (1618–1648), the Imperialists, taking advantage of the absence of the French army, penetrated into France in 1636, and reached Corbie, about 50 miles from Paris. They might easily have captured the city, but preferred to retire and enjoy the rich booty already secured. So great was the terror of the Parisians, and so vivid their memory of it, that they long styled that crisis the "Year of Corbie." See *Thirty Years' War*.

Yellow=Book. A name popularly given to a volume containing the reports and other proceedings published by the French Government, because usually bound in yellow paper wrappers. See *Blue-Books ; Red-Book*.

Yellow Jack. A nickname for yellow fever, in common use among seamen. The phrase probably originated in the use of the yellow jack, or flag, by naval hospitals and vessels in quarantine, to indicate the presence of contagious disease.

Yellow Sea. This inlet of the Pacific Ocean, washing the eastern coast of China, derives its name from the color of the alluvial soil borne down into it by the rivers Hoang-ho and Yang-tsze.

Yellowstone National Park. A national pleasure-ground — occupying the extreme northwestern corner of Wyoming, as well as small portions of Montana and Idaho — set apart by act of Congress in 1872, for the benefit and enjoyment of the people of the United States. The original tract covered an area of 357 square miles ; but to this has been added in recent years a forest reservation of 2000 square miles on the south and east, — making a total area considerably greater than that of the State of Connecticut. The central portion of the Yellowstone National Park is a volcanic plateau, having an average elevation of 8000 feet above the sea, surrounded by snow-clad mountains rising from 2000 to 4000 feet above the general level. This entire region—

containing some of the most magnificent scenery in the world—has been the scene of remarkable volcanic activity within recent geologic times, and abounds in geysers, boiling-springs, waterfalls, lakes, rivers, terrace- and crater-formations, deep cañons, obsidian cliffs, petrified trees, and sulphur hills. An attempt has been made to make the Park a vast game-preserve, and great numbers of wild animals—including bisons, elk, deer, antelopes, big-horn sheep, and bears—are sheltered within its precincts. Shooting is forbidden at all times, but fishing is freely allowed. The Yellowstone National Park is under the exclusive control of the Secretary of the Interior, and two companies of United States cavalry are stationed there to protect the forests and natural curiosities. See *Cañon of the Yellowstone*.

Yerkes Observatory. A famous astronomical observatory — belonging to the University of Chicago—situated at Lake Geneva, Wisconsin. It was founded by C. T. Yerkes in 1897 and completed at a cost of $500,000, and contains the largest and most powerful refracting telescope in existence, with the exception of the one in Paris now in course of construction. This instrument has an object-glass 40 inches in diameter (made by Alvan Clark & Company of Cambridge, Mass., at a cost of $100,000), and a tube 62½ feet in length. See *Lick Observatory; University of Chicago*.

Yggdrasil. In Scandinavian mythology, a famous ash-tree—known also as the *Tree of Existence*, the *Tree of Life and Knowledge*, the *Tree of Grief and Fate*, and the *Tree of Time and Space*—under which the Norse gods meet in council. It has three roots,—one of which (*Urdar*) centres in heaven, the second (*Mimir*) in earth, and the third (*Hoergelmir*) in hell; while its branches tower up above the heavens and spread over the entire earth. In the tree abide an eagle, a squirrel, and four stags; and at its root lies the dragon Nidhug, gnawing it away. The squirrel, Ratatosk, runs up and down the tree, seeking to stir up strife between the eagle and the dragon.

Y. M. C. A. The first "Young Men's Christian Association" was founded in London by Mr. George Williams in 1844 ; and since that time thousands of similar societies have been established in Great Britain, Germany, and the United States of America. These number, at present, 8612 throughout the world,—2192 of which are in North America.

" The total membership of these American associations is 563,479; they occupy 756 buildings of their own, valued at $60,454,336, and have a total net property of $19,341,272, including 570 libraries, containing 474,685 volumes. They employ 3633 general secretaries and other paid officials, and expended last year (1912) for current expenses—local, state, and international — $11,302,547." — *World Almanac.*

York Minster. A magnificent cathedral at York, England, in many respects the most remarkable of all English churches. The present structure was commenced prior to the year 1100, and was completed in 1472. It is 514 feet long and 250 feet wide at the transepts, and has a central tower, 216 feet high, with two western towers —flanking the façade—each 202 feet high. The west front is one of the most ornate façades ever erected, and contains a window, 54 x 30 feet, which still retains the original glass. The great East Window, 76 x 32 feet, is the largest window in England still containing the original glass, and is by many considered to be the most beautiful window in the world. The Chapter-House, an octagonal structure decorated with geometric tracery, is unsurpassed in England.

Yosemite Valley. A gorge, or cañon, on the west slope of the Sierra Nevada, about 140 miles east of San Francisco, California, noted for the beauty and sublimity of its scenery.

It is about eight miles long and from half a mile to nearly two miles broad, and is traversed by the Merced River. This famous valley is about 4000 feet above sea-level, and is enclosed by massive walls towering from 3000 to 5000 feet higher. Among the most striking objects of interest may be named the world-renowned " El Capitan," the "Three Brothers," the "Yosemite Falls," "Yosemite Point," the " Royal Arches," the " South or Half Dome," " Sentinel Dome," " Glacier Point," " Sentinel Rock," " Cathedral Rock," " Bridal Veil Fall," and " Mirror Lake." Yosemite Valley is the property of California, having been presented to the State by act of Congress in 1864. See *Bridal Veil.*

Young Chevalier. A title popularly bestowed upon Charles Edward Stuart (1720–1788), grandson of James II of England, and claimant for the throne. He is also known as the " Young Pretender " and the " Young Cavalier." See *Pretenders.*

Young Cub. A nickname given to Charles James Fox (1749–1806), the English statesman.

Young England. The name given to a party of young Tory aristocrats, founded in England during the Corn-Law agitation (1839–1846). They earnestly opposed the repeal of the *Corn Laws,* and aimed at a revival of the manners and customs of mediæval times, which, in their opinion, had been sadly altered by the rise and development of commercialism among the upper classes. Lord John Manners, C. Baillie, G. Smythe, and Benjamin Disraeli were among the leaders of the movement. Disraeli favored the " Young England " party in his novel, *Coningsby,* published in 1844.

Young Germany. The name given to a school of letters, organized in Germany after the emancipation of that country from the despotic rule of the first Napoleon. It endeavored to reflect the tendencies of modern thought and to embody the political hopes and aspirations resulting from the spread of liberal ideas throughout Europe. The failure of the Revolution of 1848 caused the dismemberment of the organization. Among the chief exponents of " Young Germany " may be mentioned Heinrich Heine, Karl Gutzkow, Heinrich Laube, Robert Heller, and Gustav Kühne.

Young Ireland. The name given to a political party in Ireland in 1848, organized to unite both Catholics and Protestants in a supreme effort to separate Ireland from the British Crown. Its leader was William Smith O'Brien. It differed from the " Old Ireland " party, which was organized on a sectarian basis and sought the aid of the Catholics alone in the repeal of the union between Great Britain and Ireland.

Young Italy. A political association formed at Marseilles, France, in 1831, by Giuseppe Mazzini (1805–1872), the Italian agitator and patriot. It aimed to create a free, independent, and united Italy, under a republican form of government. Independent and unified Italy became an accomplished fact in 1870 ; free Italy is yet to come. See *Carbonari.*

Yule-Log. The burning of the Yule-log at Christmastide, in parts of England and the Continent, is a survival from an ancient festival annually held among the northern nations to celebrate the return of the sun after the winter solstice (December 21st). The Yule-log is thought to bring good fortune, and frequently part of it is saved to light the new one in the following year. The Italians regard the charred Yule log as a preventive against lightning. " Yule " is an old word for Christmas, and is still so used provincially.

Z

Zadkiel. According to Christian and Jewish tradition, one of the seven archangels that stand around the throne of God,—the other six being Gabriel, Michael, Raphael, Chamuei, Uriel, and Zophiel. The Jews called Zadkiel the angel of the planet Jupiter.

Zama, Battle of. A battle fought at Zama, near ancient Carthage, in 202 B.C., between the Romans, commanded by Scipio, and the Carthaginians under Hannibal. The latter were routed with great slaughter,—losing more than 40,000 killed and taken prisoners. The Roman loss was estimated at about 2000 killed and wounded. The battle of Zama ended the Second Punic War, and left Carthage at the mercy of Rome.

Zela, Battle of. A desperate battle fought at Zela, Pontus, in 47 B.C., between the forces of Julius Cæsar and those of Pharnaces, King of Pontus and son of Mithridates. It was after his victory over Pharnaces that Cæsar penned his laconic despatch to the Roman Senate in these famous words, "*Veni, vidi, vici*" (*Lat., "I came, I saw, I conquered"*). See "*Veni, Vidi, Vici.*"

Zend-Avesta. See *Avesta.*

Zerubbabel's Temple. The second temple at Jerusalem, erected on the site of the Temple of Solomon, after the return of the Jews from the Babylonian Captivity. The foundation was laid by Zerubbabel in 536 B.C., and the structure was completed and dedicated in 515 B.C.,—twenty-one years after. The dimensions of this temple exceeded those of Solomon's, being 70 cubits long, 60 cubits broad, and 60 cubits high, but the interior furniture was inferior in splendor, the Ark of the Covenant was wanting, and only one golden candlestick remained. Zerubbabel's Temple was plundered and profaned by Antiochus Epiphanes (175–164 B.C.) in 168; but three years later it was restored by Judas Maccabæus and dedicated anew to the worship of Jehovah. The building was demolished in 19 B.C., and Herod's Temple was erected on the site. See *Herod's Temple ; Mosque of Omar ; Mount Moriah ; Solomon's Temple.*

Zodiac. An imaginary belt extending around the celestial sphere, within which lie the orbits of the sun, moon, and planets. It extends eight degrees on each side of the ecliptic, or apparent path of the sun, and is divided into twelve equal parts, each one of which is marked by a constellation. The names of these are as follows : *Aries* (the *Ram*), *Taurus* (the *Bull*), *Gemini* (the *Twins*), *Cancer* (the *Crab*), *Leo* (the *Lion*), *Virgo* (the *Virgin*), *Libra* (the *Balance*), *Scorpio* (the *Scorpion*), *Sagittarius* (the *Archer*), *Capricornus* (the *Goat*), *Aquarius* (the *Water-Bearer*), and *Pisces* (the *Fishes*).

Zodiacal Light. The name given to a singular phenomenon, consisting of a faint beam of light lying near the ecliptic, on both sides of the sun. It has a flat, lenticular shape, and is visible only in the evening after twilight or in the morning before dawn. The Zodiacal Light is supposed to be due to the reflection of the sun's rays from meteoric matter revolving about that luminary nearly in the plane of the ecliptic. It was carefully observed by Tycho Brahe, Descartes, and others, but especially by Cassini, who in 1683 gave it its present name.

Zollverein (*Ger., Customs-Union*). A union of the German states formed, under the leadership of Prussia, for the purpose of establishing a uniform system of tariffs and a common custom-house frontier. The first step in that direction was taken in 1818, but it was not until some years later that the movement became at all general. In 1834, eighteen states had joined the Zollverein ; in 1835–1838, five more were added; and in 1842–1852, five additional ones. After the Austro-Prussian War of 1866, a new Customs-Union was formed between the North German Confederation and the states of Bavaria, Würtemberg, Baden, and Hesse, and this remained in operation until the establishment of the Empire in 1871.

Zoölogical Gardens. A triangular enclosure, north of Regent's Park, London, belonging to the Zoölogical Society, and containing a superb collection of animals. The gardens, which cover an area of about 21 acres, were first opened to the public in 1828.

Zophiel. According to Christian and Jewish tradition, one of the seven archangels that stand around the throne of God,—the other six being Gabriel, Michael, Raphael, Chamuel, Uriel, and Zadkiel. Zophiel is introduced by Milton into *Paradise Lost*, where he figures as a scout, who announces to the heavenly host the return of Satan's forces to renew the attack. The word " Zophiel " means " the spy of God."

" Back with speediest sail
Zophiel, of Cherubim the swiftest wing,
Came flying, and in mid-air aloud thus cry'd:
Arm, warriors, arm for fight ; the foe at hand,
Whom fled we thought, will save us long pursuit
This day."

Paradise Lost, vi, 534–539.

Zounds. A corruption of the phrase " God's wounds," formerly used as an oath, or as an expression of anger. Similarly, *'Sdeath*, *'Slid*, *'Sblood*, are corruptions of *God's death, God's lid, God's blood*.

Zutphen, Battle of. The name given to a skirmish that took place between the Spanish and the Dutch forces at Zutphen, Holland, on October 2nd, 1586. It was in this engagement that the amiable and accomplished Sir Philip Sidney received his death-wound.

Zu-Zu. A name familiarly applied to the zouaves in the Union army during the Civil War (1861–1865).

" My love is a *Zu-zu* so gallant and bold ;
He 's rough, and he 's handsome, scarce nineteen years old."

Comic Song.